Architectural
Engineering
Design:

Mechanical Systems

ARCHITECTURAL ENGINEERING DESIGN:
MECHANICAL SYSTEMS

Includes one diskette

Robert Brown Butler

McGraw-Hill

New York San Francisco Washington, D.C. Auckland Bogota
Caracas Lisbon London Madrid Mexico City Milan Montreal
New Delhi San Juan Singapore Sydney Tokyo Toronto

McGraw-Hill

*A Division of The **McGraw·Hill** Companies*

1 2 3 4 5 6 7 8 9 0 DOC/DOC 0 9 8 7 6 5 4 3 2

PN 138547-9
Part of ISBN 0-07-138546-0

This book's sponsoring editors were Wendy Lochner and Larry Hager, its editing supervisor was Steven Melvin, and its production supervisor was Sherri Souffrance. The text was set in BuQuet, BuHB, and other fonts created by Robert Brown Butler; and the volume was printed and bound by R. R. Donnelley & Sons Company.

McGraw-Hill books are available at special quantity discounts to use as premiums and sales promotions, or for use in corporate training programs. For more information write to the Director of Special Sales, McGraw-Hill, Two Penn Plaza, New York, NY 10121-2298. Or contact your local bookstore.

This book is printed on acid-free paper.

This book is dedicated to Robert Sterman and Michael Geoghaean, one of whom was killed and the other electrocuted in accidents caused by architectural engineering errors. May they not have fallen in vain.

You have to have a grammar in order to have a language. And then you can use it for normal purposes and you speak in prose, and if you are good you speak a wonderful prose, and if you are really good you can be a poet. I think that is the same in architecture. Then if you have to construct something you can make a garage out of it or you can make a cathedral.

Mies van der Rohe

When the creative architect knows how to play upon the stupendous keyboard of mechanization, we need not feel troubled about the future of architecture.

Siegfried Gideon

CONTENTS

3 CLIMATE CONTROL

4 PLUMBING

5 ELECTRICAL

6 ILLUMINATION

7 **ACOUSTICS**

A **APPENDIX**

TABLES

PREFACE

An irrefutable fact about society today is that the vast majority of its citizens could not function economically or domestically but for buildings. Indeed, virtually every one of us today has spent most of our lives in buildings, from the obstetric suite to the roof that shelters the lamp that brightens the page you are now reading; and only a few hours of each day, on the average, do we venture out of these interiors onto the ground around them, even though the area of the latter is far greater. And every one of the buildings we occupy is made safe and comfortable by architectural engineering. Without this science, every building we have ever entered, ever walked in, ever slept in, ever gazed at from the window of another would be a pile of rubble. This is why Æ (architectural engineering) design is one of the most vitally important professions in the world today.

Only a small percentage of our citizenry is entrusted with making all these buildings safe and comfortable for all others. And these chosen few deserve to have the very best information available —the latest, most thorough, most truthful, most ethical— that would enable them to do their jobs perfectly well. Unfortunately, every so often something comes along that renders obsolete the accumulation of knowledge and routines that seemed so perfectly satisfactory only a few years or decades ago. Of course, that 'something' today is desktop computers. Remember how we used to love our slide rules? Then our calculators? Now desktop computers offer Æ designers a quicker and more accurate way to solve equations. Now one can look at a computer display window of an algebraic formula with its equation listed at the top, its unknowns in a short column below, a data entry pane beside each unknown, and a COMPUTE button at the bottom, then utilize these graphics in a manner that removes all the cumbersome number-crunching and anxiety-inducing error-making previously associated with this labor.

However, computers have further allowed the very way that algebraic formulas have been presented for a century to change for the better. Dating back to the late 1800s, the principle way of presenting a mathematical formula has been to derive it from a theory; and a formula rarely wandered far from the theory to which it was tethered because it was often difficult to use and one always needed its basis near in case the answer didn't seem right or someone disputed the result. But now that even lengthy formulas filled with many unknowns festooned with exponents and logarithms and trig functions take hardly more than a double-click to solve, *their users can now relate less to the theories from which each is derived and more to the purpose for which each is intended.* Thus with the advent of desktop computers, algebraic formulas can be tailored to size each functional component in a building so they all appear less as applications of theory and more as recipes in a cookbook. And that is exactly what this publication is: a collection of *recipes* for sizing nearly every functional component in any kind of building in the world.

The importance of this new format that shifts a formula's emphasis from origin to result can be explained more clearly by analogy. Suppose you want to bake a cake. According to the 'theory' approach, you would analyze the cake-baking process somewhat as follows: "Now I will need yeast to make the cake dough rise; and if I want a cake of a certain cylindrical volume I will use the chemical reaction for the conversion of yeast to gas to find the amount of yeast required to produce the volume of gas I need to make my cake rise the proper amount; then I will perform similar analyses for the other ingredients to find the amounts of each I will need to bake my cake." But the recipe approach, as expostulated herein, simply involves finding a 'cookbook' that contains 'recipes' for baking every kind of cake you could think of, then using the selected recipe's specified amounts of each ingredient to bake the cake you want. Lest you think this idea is new, architecture abounds with algebraic recipes. For example, the Pythagorean theorem is a formulaic 'recipe' that Pythagoras devised centuries ago to replace the ponderous theorizing one previously undertook to find the third side of a right triangle given its first two sides.

Thus this recipe approach as promulgated herein replaces much theoretical pondering for sizing almost any functional component in a building with easy-to-use formulas that almost any schoolboy can employ. Sure, you have to be a little careful in the way you measure things; but is this any different than before? And is accuracy sacrificed with this new method? No: it is more assured. And have the theories that underlay such analysis been negated in any way? No —no more than putting a sign in front of a window makes everything behind it vanish. Thus this recipe approach is easier to grasp intellectually and easier to implement physically while sacrificing nothing but drudgery and error. This approach is such an obvious outgrowth of the influence of desktop computers that if this author hadn't thought of it first, someone else would have surely done so soon afterward; for as Frank Lloyd Wright once said of one of his innovations: "I am here writing no more than the too specific outline of a practical ideal perceiving Change as already upon us."

Of course a volume that employs such a new approach should have an Appendix that describes how each newly-developed formula is derived from the theories upon which it is based. This book has this also.

This recipe approach has also created some computer-active fallout that further simplifies Æ design. For example, an Æ designer must often utilize a tedious multi-step routine to size every small part of a complex structural or mechanical component in a way that takes much time but saves little money. An example is the design of the stiffeners in a built-up beam or plate girder. In the past, this labor involved a detailed analysis of each pair of end stiffeners, first-end stiffeners, point-load stiffeners, and intermediate stiffeners; and if this work was going to take a couple hours anyway, why not try to pare every piece down to its leanest shape? But if such work now takes only ten minutes, the question is reversed. Not only does such laborious paring make no sense —for why should an owner spend $100 more in consultation fees to save $50 in building costs?— the formulas themselves can often be simplified at the expense of creating a slightly larger subcomponent; which makes the slightly larger part safer as well as lowering the designer's consultation fee more than the cost of the part is increased. The recipe approach also simplifies the tedious trial-and-error process that prevails in much of Æ design; because this approach enables one to see how a final result may vary not by re-solving the whole equation but often by simply varying a number in a data entry pane. The recipe approach also helps Æ designers deal with the fact that many formula unknowns used today are merely probability posing as perfection. For example, take the nameplate rating of an electric motor or appliance such as your computer: This machine consumes its nameplate power about as often as a 300 HP car flies down a freeway at 90 miles an hour; so such a formula is rarely precise. Since the recipe approach places more emphasis on the unique nature of each unknown, it makes it easier to understand each's range of probability more than the expounding of the overall formula's underlying theory ever would. It also helps one understand why, as Einstein once said: "Every field equation should include a cosmological term." [†]

This cosmological aspect also reveals that nothing is as simple as we have been taught to believe. Indeed, Einstein's theory of relativity tells us that light does not travel in a straight line as we may have learned in physics, but takes a path that bends, however slight. And our world is not really a system of Cartesian coordinates in which every point of reality is felicitously positioned in a rigid matrix of parallel rows extending in the three orthogonal directions —that instead, the real world is a maze of Gaussian coordinates in which every graph line bends. So nothing is straight: everything bends. What subtle implications this has for architecture! And only because it is impossible to utilize all these incredibly varied details in their truest form do we distill them into 'simple' concepts of

---

[†] *Relativity, The Special and General Theory*, Albert Einstein (Crown Publishers,

geometry and physics and algebra —an anemic act which this thick and thorough volume and its mate guiltily and sheepishly promote.

We need no further proof than this to know that one's vision must ever exceed one's grasp.

A word about this publication's graphics and typography. The author designed the book's page layouts and the following fonts used in its text: *BuQuet,* a text font of technically efficient letters and appropriate symbols; *BuHB,* a typeface that resembles the author's architectural hand lettering; and three keycap fonts, *BuKeycap, BuOpenkeycap,* and *BuKOkeycap,* which enable the equations' computer-access codes to resemble keyboard keys. Such design is certainly appropriate for a book of this kind, for typography is indeed the architecture of semantics.

The author will be exceedingly grateful to anyone who brings to his attention any errors of commission or omission in this volume and its accompanying disk, or who may have suggestions as to how either may be improved; as it rarely happens that such a pioneering work as this is free from all error. As this volume and other related texts prepared by this author are intended to become the definitive references for architectural engineering design, for this very reason the greatest accuracy is sought. Thus, by offering your keen and clarifying aid, you will perform a valuable service to members of the Æ community, and ultimately the public.

Finally, the author takes extreme pleasure in acknowledging those who assisted him in preparing this sizable volume and its accompanying disk. Acknowledgees at McGraw-Hill are Wendy Lochner, this volume's initial sponsoring editor; Larry Hager, the volume's final sponsoring editor; Stephen Melvin, the book's Senior Editing Supervisor; Scott Grillo, Publisher of McGraw-Hill's Technical Books; Sherri Soufrance, the volume's Production Supervisor; Dagmar Burdette, Editorial Assistant; and Margaret Webster-Shapiro, Associate Director of Creative Art. Acknowledgees who reside closer to the author's refuge are Harry Wirtz, authority on all aspects of computer technology and graphics; Duane Degutis, computer technician who kept the author's computers running for the duration of this lengthy project; Peter DiBart, computer graphic artist; Elaine Ramsey and Robert Costanzo, computer programmers who wrote most of the code for the book's computerized disk of formulas; and the author's wife, Janis Y. Butler.

Robert Brown Butler
Box 513, Somers, NY 10589

IN MEMORIAM

As this book was about to go to press, two commercial jet liners crashed into the World Trade Center Towers and destroyed them.

Aside from the horrific nature of this tragedy, the most apparent fact regarding Æ science is that a new phrase has been added to its vocabulary: *downward domino collapse* —the progressive failure of each floor of a tall building upon the one just below due to the accumulating gravity load of the failed floors above, all initiated in each of these two towers by an incredible explosion that shattered four-hour-rated cladding that enclosed each building's columnar supports and allowed its exposed steel members, no longer protected by a sprinkler system that was also shattered, to heat quickly to a temperature of 1,200—1,500° F at which all semblance of strength was lost.

However, why did these buildings fail below the level of the lowest undamaged floor? Obviously the floors that were immolated in exploded fuel would have collapsed once their steel columns and beams became so hot that they lost their strength; and just as obviously the floors above them would have fallen. But how about the floors below? The first completely undamaged floor below the destroyed ones carried no more weight than before the plane's explosion occurred. Indeed, it carried *less* weight due to all the load that had been converted to smoke above. So why did it fail? The answer? *Impact load.* When the uppermost floors suddenly slumped downward when the destroyed floors failed, they formed a massive impact load of some 150,000 tons —which landed on the first undamaged floor below with such a terrific thud that no structure could have withstood it. So, each floor broke one by one. The lesson? Unlike what most structural texts say, impact loads can *not* be considered to be twice normally applied loads —that instead, their *downward velocity* combined with their mass must be known to quantify them well. Certainly such knowledge of impact loads would not have saved the World Trade Center; but such knowledge will lead to the safer design of all structure in all future buildings there and elsewhere.

What other lessons can Æ designers learn from this disaster?

▸ Don't make buildings so tall. Indeed, the global race to build the world's tallest building is now over.

▸ Leave more area around tall buildings so that if they *do* collapse, there will be less chance of their damaging adjacent edifices. Certainly no structure could resist a 200-ton missile carrying 20,000 gallons of gasoline; but crowding several other buildings around the Towers' bases was a bit inexcusable. Also, such buildings can fail in another way besides downward domino collapse: a terrific explosion on the side of one's base can make it topple over to one side —and this can lead to a more conven-

tional lateral domino collapse of any number of buildings located close to each other horizontally.

▶ Make fire stairs wider. In the sickening equation that describes
how many people can escape quickly from them in a disaster, one
fact is irrefutable: the wider the stairs, the more who can escape.
The World Trade Tower's 56 in. wide exit staircases were wide
enough for everyone in both buildings to have escaped before
they collapsed —but safe can always be made safer, especially
where tens of thousands of innocent people are concerned.

▶ Pay close attention to air filtration in a building's climate control
system, no matter what the building's size. Due to the World
Trade Towers' collapse, a cloud of thick dust was raised that
entered air intake louvers in buildings for miles around. The
more efficient a building's HVAC system air filters are, and the
more quickly they can be accessed and replaced, the more habitable the building will remain after disaster strikes.

▶ Provide buildings with more intercommunications. More public
address intercoms. More sensors and notifiers. More videoconferencing. More space for conductor enclosures and chases.
More effective grounding pathways into the substrate below the
foundations. Any electronics that promote increased security
and freer communication at the same time, not only inside a
building but between anyone inside and anyone outside.

Finally, *question authority*. The most far-reaching foundation of
this book and its companion volume and their computerized disks of formulas is that their author questioned every aspect of Æ design; and he
was frankly surprised at the errors —regarding not only impact load but
staircases, horizontal shear, electronic equipment grounding, the ratio
of men's to women's toilets in public rest rooms, and others — that he
found. Such questioning led him to develop hundreds of new formulas
and procedures for selecting and sizing today's building's functional
components. No, he did not heed the man with the bullhorn who said:
"Stay where you are and you will be safe." No; because his thoughts were
based on a more inquiring concern regarding the exigencies at hand,
which led him to safer methods of designing the same realities he had
been familiar with for so many years before. And you should do the same.
Question what you read in here. For you, your clients, and ultimately for
the many who will use each building you may help design. For Æ science,
as fully advanced as it may seem at any one moment, is barely a century
old now —an intellectual child in a Homeric world— and it must grow still
more if, Atlas-like, it is to carry a civilized world on its shoulders in our
darkest hours.

INTRODUCTION

1.A. GENERAL

This publication includes two Æ (architectural engineering) handbooks, this one dealing with the design of mechanical systems and related components, the other doing the same with structural systems. Each volume also contains an interactive CD-ROM of its algebraic formulas that enables each equation to be solved quickly and accurately by computer.

These handbooks and their accompanying disks contain architectural engineering information and algebraic equations for conceptualizing, selecting, and sizing virtually every functional component in any kind of building, from shed to skyscraper, anywhere in the world. With these references, an Æ designer can quickly determine whether a functional component is large enough to be safe for its intended purpose, yet not so large that money is wasted. Certainly these volume-cum-disks are thorough compilations of technical knowledge acquired from academic study, official research, and established office practice. But they also contain countless practical, insightful, and even a few horrifying anecdotes gleaned from construction experiences, water-cooler dissertations, trade magazine edifications, and numerous other in-the-field events as they relate to our species' ongoing need for safe and comfortable shelter.

These publications also emphasize the latest computerized controls being incorporated into every functional aspect of today's buildings. Today's Æ designers cannot claim to be up with the times if they do not understand TBM systems. This includes the incredible production and energy savings they can bring, the problems they create, and the solutions today's engineers are evolving to eliminate the latter.

These volumes also stress that a vital aspect of any functional component's design involves adequate access for maintaining it after construction; because it can be said that no matter how good any part is, it always fails eventually. Architects may think, and rightfully so, that maintenance is not their problem; but *accessing* maintenance is no one else's problem. More than ever before, occupants of modern buildings are prisoners of maintenance; and today's Æ designers should be an ally to these often-overlooked confinements and not an adversary.

These volumes also emphasize environmentally appropriate architecture whenever possible. They expostulate the view that not only should every building inflict minimum damage to its site and environs, but every material in them should inflict minimum environmental damage, undergo minimum processing, create minimum packaging waste, and consume minimum energy on its journey from its home in the earth to its grave on the site. Indeed, the hallmarks of environmental design —more than economizing energy use and minimizing toxic waste— are creating maximum comfort in minimum volume and assembling natural materials simply. There is a vital reason for this: the *wilderness ratio*, which states that

> Every urban square mile requires about fifty square miles of wilderness to purify its air, recycle its water, absorb its wastes, modify its climate, and provide a substantial portion of its food and fiber needs without economic cost or human management. [†]

In architecture this is the ultimate catchment. The wilderness ratio indicates that we all must do everything we can to preserve nature as much as possible —not so our children may enjoy its serene majesty someday, but simply so they may *breathe*. This is especially important with buildings, for their construction and operation is a conspicuously consumptive use of natural resources; thus this publication promotes every possible energy-conserving measure involved in erecting and occupying built environments. Such concern certainly includes conservation of electricity; as in the United States an estimated 35 percent of all CO_2 (a greenhouse gas), 65 percent of all SO_2 (a leading contributor of acid rain), and 36 percent of all NO_x (a major ingredient of smog) are produced by the generation of electricity. [‡] But such concern also involves advocating thicker envelope insulation, structure with maximum strength-to-weight ratios, efficient lighting and climate control systems, occupancy sensors that turn lights and heating off when a space is unoccupied, daylight harvesters that dim artificial lights when sunlight enters interior spaces, plumbing fixtures with no-touch controls that reduce water consumption, TBM systems that lead to lower energy use, and any other means of producing the greatest effect with the smallest mass or means. Each comprises environmental design so far as architecture is concerned, as a way of providing greater opportunity to do the same in the near and far future.

Also let it never be said that these two volumes, in their preoccupation with a building's solid parts, imply that they are more important than the spaces they enclose. On the contrary! Obviously the Essence of Architecture is creating habitable and comfortable interior spaces —for without the voids, you have no solids. But just as obviously, you cannot have the spaces without their defining solids, a fact that Laotze poetically described twenty-five centuries ago when he said:

[†] *The Ecological House*, Robert Brown Butler (Morgan & Morgan, Dobbs Ferry,

Thirty spokes converge in the hub of a wheel;
But use of the cart depends on the part
   Of the hub that is void.

A clay bowl is molded by its base and walls;
But use of the bowl depends on the hole
   That forms its central void.

Floor, walls, and roof form the shape of a house;
But use of the place depends on the space
   Within that is void.

   Thus advantage is had from whatever there is;
   While use derives from whatever is not.

In this endless architectural interplay, the essence of habitable space underlines the need for its physical imperatives —and these books, by their preoccupation with the latter, hope to ennoble the nature of the former.

Finally, these volumes' methods of selecting and sizing virtually every functional component in a building —of paring each down to its elemental nature and nothing more— promote all that is beautiful in architecture. For the truest beauty results from doing what is supremely appropriate and the subtraction of all else. For example, take the caryatids of the Erechtheion in Athens, perhaps the loveliest columns ever devised: only when each slender feminine waist was given the slimmest section that would support the mass above could these graceful forms transcend the bland loyalty of posts to become a beauty so supreme that they hardly seem like structural supports at all. Such functional modeling is all a building needs to be beautiful. No excess. No frills. No confections masquerading as purpose. No appliqués as are so often borrowed from the almsbasket of historically worn architectural motifs whose perpetrators typically have no more concept of their meaning than did Titania of the donkey she caressed.

Indeed, regarding architectural beauty, an Æ designer needs no more inspiration than a simple flower. From what does its beauty derive? Not from perpetrators of vanity lurking within that blossom's corm, yearning to conjure a titillating aspect upon an innocent eye. And not from any external molders who aver to do the same. No, its beauty derives from nothing more than the stern utilitarian arrangement of each tiny part, wherein each element has the most utilitarian size, each has the most utilitarian shape, each connects to each other in the most utilitarian way, and each interfunctions with the others in the most utilitarian manner, wherein each molecule in each part is located for a purpose —in which even the dabs of garish color on the frilly petals are, at least to a bee's eye, no more than applications of stern utility.

So be it with buildings.

NY, 1981)   ‡ from p. 2: *Occupancy Sensor and Lighting Controls,* a product   ▌▌

1.A.1. Terms & Symbols

The architectural symbols and abbreviations used throughout this text are listed below. Familiar quantities have the usual letters (e.g. d for the depth of a beam), but most are symbolized by the letter that best typifies them in each problem. Thus one letter may denote different values in different formulas. In this book, formulas contain no fractions unless unavoidable (e.g. $A = B/_C$ is written as $A\ C = B$ or $B = A\ C$), partial integers appear as decimals instead of fractions (e.g. ½ appears as 0.5), feet-and-inch dimensions usually appear as decimals to the nearest hundredth of a foot (thus 2'-4⅝" is written as 2.39 ft), and degree-minute-second angle measures are expressed in degrees to four significant figures (thus 31°-43'-03" becomes 31.7175°); as in each instance such notation is cleaner and takes up less space. Also, numerical values are usually taken to three significant figures in exact-value equations ($A = B$) and to two significant figures in estimate-value equations ($A \approx B$); and most weight and measure abbreviations are not followed by a period (e.g. ft, lb, sec). However, *inch* is abbreviated as *in.* to differentiate it from the word *in*; but even this measure may have no period after it if its meaning is obvious, as in in/LF.

Throughout this text, take care to use the same units of measure as listed in each equation's menu of unknowns. For example, if a quantity is in feet and your data are in inches, be sure to convert your data to feet before solving the equation.

1.A.1.a. Mathematical Symbols

Symbol	Meaning
=	Left side of equation equals right side.
≈	Left side of equation approximately equals right side.
≠	Left side of equation does not equal right side.
≥	Left side of equation equals or is greater than right side.
≤	Left side of equation equals or is less than right side.
⊥	Two straight lines or flat plane are perpendicular to each other.
‖	Two straight lines or flat surfaces are parallel to each other.
$A^{0.5}$	Square root of A; A to the 0.5 power. This book's exponential expressions are not written with square root signs.
$\lvert A \rvert$	Use only the integer portion of value A. E.g. $\lvert 2.39 \rvert = 2$.
$\lvert A \blacktriangleright \rvert$	Use next highest integer above value A. E.g. $\lvert 2.39 \blacktriangleright \rvert = 3$.
$\lvert A \blacktriangleright \rvert_{0.5}$	Use the next highest multiple of 0.5 above A. E.g. $\lvert 2.39 \blacktriangleright \rvert_{0.5} = 2.50$. Similarly, $\lvert A \blacktriangleright \rvert_{2.0}$ means to use the next highest multiple

brochure for Leviton Mfg. Co. (Little Neck, NY, 1996), p. 3.

of 2 above A; e.g. $|2.39 \rightarrow|_{2.0} = 4.00$.

sin A Sine of angle A. In a right triangle, sin A = opposite side/hypotenuse, cos A = adjacent side/hypotenuse, and tan A = opposite side/adjacent side.

$\sin^{-1} A$ Arcsin A, or sine of the angle whose value is A. If sin A = B, then $\sin^{-1} B$ = A; also true for $\cos^{-1} A$ and $\tan^{-1} A$. This book does not use the terms asin, acos, and atan.

π Pi, equal to 3.1416.

5'-11"   Five ft eleven in, or 5.92 ft.

31° 43' 03"   31 degrees, 43 minutes, 3 seconds; or 31.7175°. 1° = 1.0000°, 01' = 0.0167°, and 01" = 0.000278°. In this book, angle measures are never in radians.

➕   (1) The most desirable of several values under consideration. (2) Desirable characteristics of a building component.

➖   Undesirable characteristics of a building component.

1.A.1.b. Abbreviations and Terms in the Text

Symbol   *Meaning*

A   Amp, amps, ampere, amperes.

Æ   Acronym for architectural engineering.

α Sabin(s): a measure of sound absorption

ac   Acre(s). 1 ac = 43,560 ft^2. A square acre = 208.71 ft on each side. 640 ac = 1 sq mi.

ach   Air changes per hour.

apsi   Atmospheric pressure based on 0 psi at a complete vacuum. 14.7 apsi = 0.0 spsi.

ASL   Above sea level; e.g. 5,280 ft ASL.

ß   Total ray or beam concentration factor: a light fixture's ratio of spherical-to-axial output.

Btu   British Thermal Unit(s): amount of heat required to raise the temperature of 1 lb of water 1° F. 1 Btu = 0.293 watts.

C   Celsius, a unit of temperature measure based on the Kelvin scale; also Centigrade. Water freezes at 0° C and boils at 100° C. 1° C = 1.8° F. 0° C = 273 K = 32° F.

C   Cooling load: a term used in climate control system design.

cd   Candela: the basic metric unit of luminous intensity. 1.00 candelas = 12.6 footcandles.

CDCP   Centerbeam candlepower, measured in candelas; light output along the axis of a lamp with a specified beamspread.

¢   Centerline. Center-to-center is ¢-¢, and ¢ of gravity refers to a shape's enter of gravity.

¢ Unit cost in cents.

℞ Circuitry load: capacity of an electrical circuit or component in amps, volts, or watts.

cf Cubic feet. cfm = cubic feet per minute.

cmil Circular mil, (also *CM*), a unit of size for electric wire. 1 cmil = area of a circle 1 mil (0.001 in.) in diameter. C-S area of a 1 in. diameter wire = 1,000,000 cmil.

℧ Room Coefficient of Utilization: the ratio of useful light to actual light in an architectural space.

Ɒ Amount of daylighting arriving at an interior space or visual task, measured in footcandles (fc).

ₛ Decibel, or decibels: a measure of sound intensity.

Δ difference or change of a quantity such as temperature, pressure drop, operating costs, etc.

δ (1) diameter of a circle; (2) depreciation of illumination due to factors such as voltage fluctuation, dirt accumulation, temperature increase, maintenance cycles, and rated lamp life.

$ Unit or total cost in dollars.

ε Efficiency of a mechanical or electrical component or system, usually measured in percent.

ε Total electrical load of a conductor or system.

F Fahrenheit: a unit of temperature based on the Rankine scale. Water freezes at 32° F and boils at 212° F. 1° F = 0.556° C. 32° F = 0° C = 273 K = 492° R.

fc Footcandle(s): a unit of light intensity arriving from a natural or artificial light source; also illuminance. 1.0 fc = amount of light incident on a ⊥ surface 1.0 ft from a candle.

ft Foot, or feet. ft^2 = square foot, ft^3 = cubic foot. 1 ft^3 of water = 7.48 gal = 62.4 lb.

ft^2/min Square feet per minute.

fall/ft Fall per linear foot: e.g. 0.5 in/ft = ½ in. downward for each horizontal foot outward. Also known as slope, incline, or pitch. All these terms are denoted by the symbol Δ.

fpm Feet per minute. fps = feet per second.

f.u. Fixture unit: a unit for estimating waterflow into or out of a plumbing fixture. 1 f.u. ≈ 2 gpm of fluid flow.

gal Gallon(s). gpm = gallons per minute.

gr Grain: a unit of weight. 7,000 gr = 1 lb.

H Heating load: a term used in climate control system design.

℉P Horsepower. 1 ℉P = 746 watts = 33,000 ft-lb.

hr Hour(s). 8,760 hr = 1 yr. 720 hr ≈ 1 month.

Hz Hertz, or cycles per second: (1) a unit of frequency for alternating electrical current, usually 60 Hz.; (2) the vibration frequency of a sound, usually between 20 and 8,000 Hz.

Φ   Illuminance: the amount of illumination, measured in footcandles (fc), arriving at a visual task from a light source.

IIC   Impact isolation class: a unit for measuring solid-borne sound absorbed by a type of building construction; also I_{IC}.

in.   Inch(es). in^2 = square inch. in^3 = cubic inch.

in. wc   inches water column: a measure of air pressure; also in. wg (inches water gauge). 407.4 in. wc = 33.95 ft wc = 14.7 psi = 30.0 in. Hg (mercury) = 1.00 atmosphere at 62° F.

κ   A term used to denote a constant or coefficient.

k unit of thermal conductivity for an insulation or type of construction. $k = U$ per in. thickness of insulation.

K   Kelvin: a unit of absolute temperature on the Celsius scale. 1 K = 1° C. 0° K = absolute zero = 273° C.

kWh   Kilowatt-hour: a unit of electrical power equal to 1,000 watts of electricity consumed per hour.

λ   (1) unit light source length or width factor: the effective distance between a light source and its task plane based on a ratio of the light source's face length or width and the distance between it and the task plane; (2) wavelength of a sound, measured in cycles per second (Hz).

lb   Pound(s). 13.8 cf of dry air at room temperature weighs 1 lb.

lb/ft^2 Pounds per square foot; also psf. Lb/in^2 = psi = pounds per square inch; lb/in^3 = pounds per cubic inch; lb/lf = plf = pounds per linear foot.

◇   Output of an artificial light source, measured in lumens (lm).

LF   Linear foot or feet.

lm   Lumen: a unit of light energy emitted from a natural or artificial light source. One candle emits 12.6 lm of light.

log   Logarithm. In this volume all logarithms are to the base 10.

Ł   Loudness limit: difference between the emitted and received sounds of two adjacent spaces, measured in dB.

max.   Maximum.

min.   (1) minimum; (2) minute.

mi   Mile(s); mi^2 = square mile(s). mph = miles per hour or mi/hr.

mo   Month.

η   Unit near-field length or width factor: the effective amount of light emitted from a natural or artificial light source based on a ratio of the light source's face length or width and the distance between it and the task plane.

Ŋ   Light source near-field factor: the effective amount of light arriving at a task plane based on the light source's lamp and near-field factors λ_L, λ_W, η_L, and η_W.

NG   No good: the value being considered is not acceptable.

N2G	Not too good: the value being considered may be acceptable but is not very satisfactory.
η	Number or quantity of a building material, component, or similar entity; usually an unknown factor.
Θ	Occupancy factor: the number of feasible or actual occupants occupying a floor area in a building.
o.c.	On center: refers to a dimension from the center lines of two materials or assemblies; also *center-to-center* or ¢-¢.
OK	Okay: the value being considered is acceptable.
?	A quantity or term whose value is presently unknown.
ø	Phase factor (e.g. single or three phase) for electric wiring.
Þ	Pipe flow: volume of liquid or gas flowing through a plumbing pipe, conduit, or system.
pLF	Pounds per linear foot.
ppd	Pipe pressure drop: the amount of pressure loss experienced by a liquid or gas flowing through a length of pipe due to friction; also known as ΔP.
ppm	Parts per million.
psf	Pounds per square foot.
psi	Pounds per square inch.
Q	Airflow velocity: speed of supply or return air through a duct, measured in fps, mph, or cfm.
Ω	Rated power (wattage) of a generator, motor, pump, or other component that either produces or consumes electricity.
R	(1) Rankine, a unit of absolute temperature on the Fahrenheit scale. $1° R = 1° F$. $0° R =$ absolute zero $= -460° F$. (2) thermal resistance of an insulation or construction assembly; also known as *R-factor*. $R = {}^1/_U$.
ρ	Ray concentration factor. A light fixture's spherical rays may be concentrated due to an enclosure factor ρ_e, a geometric contour factor ρ_c, and a reflector finish factor ρ_f.
r.h.	Relative humidity: amount of moisture in the air relative to its saturation at a given temperature.
⊿	Slope, incline, or pitch of a linear direction or surface.
sec	Second(s). 60 sec = 1 min.
Φ	Solar heat gain: a measure of solar heat energy entering an interior space during cold weather; also *insolation* or *incident clear-day insolation*.
σ	Specific gravity: the unit weight of a solid or liquid compared to that of water (σ of water = 1.00), or the unit weight of a gas compared to that of air (σ of air = 1.00).
sf	Square foot (feet). 100 sf = 1 square.
spsi	Standard pressure based on 0 psi at atmospheric pressure. 0.0 spsi = 14.7 apsi.

STC   Sound Transmission Class: a unit for measuring sound absorbed by a type of building construction; also S_{TC}.

ton   (1) a measure of weight that equals 2,000 lb; (2) a measure of heating or cooling capacity that equals 12,000 Btu. 1 ton is also the approximate weight of 32 ft^3 of water.

τ Transmittance: portion of light passing through glazing or other transparent or translucent material.

U A unit of thermal conductivity for an insulation or type of building construction, usually part of a building envelope; also known as *U-factor.* $U = {}^1/_R = k \times$ thickness of insulation (in).

u.o.n.   Unless otherwise noted: a popular abbreviation in architectural working drawings.

υ Kinematic viscosity of a contained liquid, usually measured in ft^2/sec.

v Velocity, usually measured in fps or mph.

V   Volt(s): unit of electromotive force in an electrical circuit.

VG   Very good: the value being considered is desirable.

W   Watts: a unit of power in an electrical circuit, appliance, or electrical component. 1 watt = 1 amp $\times$ 1 volt; or W = A V.

yd   Yard(s). Yd^2 = square yard(s). yd^3=cubic yard(s).

yr   Year(s): a unit of time. A *mean solar year* is 365 days, 5 hours, 48 minutes, and 49.7 seconds long.

1.A.1.c. Unusual Terms in the Text

aspect ratio   Ratio of a long side to a short side of a rectangular duct.

azimuth   The sun's orientation from true north, degrees; e.g. 136° E of N describes an angle with one side aimed at due north and the other side aimed 136° east (clockwise) of due north.

belvedere   A box-like ventilator with louvers on each side located on the peak of a gable roof; it utilizes the prevailing windflow to draw warm air from interior spaces below.

berm   A usually long, narrow, several-foot-high rise in terrain that is often artificially made to shield a building from climatic forces, block unwanted sight lines, direct water runoff, introduce sloping contours, protect utility conveyances in the ground below, and the like.

bus   A rigid copper or aluminum bar, tube, or rod that conducts electricity; also *bus bar* or *busbar.*

busway   A rigid metal conduit that encloses and protects a bus or busbar; also *bus duct* or *busduct.*

cobrahead   A roadway luminaire mounted on a tall post whose top extends outward several feet and whose end has a hooded reflector resembling a serpent's head.

dryvit A stucco-like material used as an exterior finish.

endbell The usually convex end of an electric motor.

EMF Abbreviation for electromotive force, a type of electronic interference on electric wiring.

efficacy A light source's output divided by its total power input.

enthalpy The quantity of heat contained in air as a function of its temperature and relative humidity, measured in Btu/lb. Air at 78° F and 50% r.h. (standard room temperature during warm weather) has an enthalpy of approximately 30 Btu/lb, a value which is considered as the optimal enthalpy value for comfortable warm weather.

envelope The outermost surface of a building (lowest floor, outer walls, and roof) which usually contains thermal insulation.

eutectic a thermodynamic term pertaining to the nature of heat transfer between two media at the heat of solidification (freezing) temperature of one medium.

insolation Sunlight entering a solar collector or interior space through glazing facing the sun.

leader A primarily vertical duct for carrying rainwater from the gutter to the ground. Also *downspout*.

ohmic An electrical conductor whose voltage/amperage ratio remains constant. A conductor in which this ratio is not constant is *non-ohmic*.

orientation The siting of a building, landmark, or architectural detail according to a direction of the compass.

perc Abbreviation for *percolation*: seepage of water through a porous material, usually soil. A *perc test* is a method of testing a soil's porosity.

poke-through A floor-mounted electrical outlet with a stem through which wiring extends from a conduit or plenum in the floor below.

square A unit of roof area measure equal to 100 ft^2.

swale A usually marshy depression in an area of fairly level land.

therm A quantity of heat equal to 100,000 Btu that is used to measure amounts of natural gas.

throw The horizontal or vertical axial distance an airstream travels after leaving an airduct grille to where its velocity is reduced to a specific value. Also called *blow*.

tympan (1) a usually small surface in a folded plate structure that braces similar surfaces through their edges-in-common and is also braced by them; (2) a thin surface that receives sound waves on one side and magnifies them to usually annoying levels on the other side.

1.A.1.d. Metrication

In 1994 the U. S. Government mandated that all future federal projects be constructed according to the International System of Units, commonly known as the *metric* or *SI system.* Thus has begun our society's official, if dilatory, march toward conversion from the traditional inch-pound
(IP) system to the more worldly SI. In order to foster and facilitate the use
of the SI system, this book includes in its Appendix of Useful Formulas a
full page of common IP-to-SI conversions, each of which is accompanied by
a DesignDisk access code number that enables its mathematics to be performed automatically, either from IP to SI or vise versa, by computer.

The SI system of measures has six basic units as listed below:

Unit	IP std.	SI std.	Conversion
Length	foot	meter	3.28 ft = 1 m
Mass	ounce	gram	1 oz = 28.35 gm
Time	second	second	same
Temperature	°F	°C	1.8°F = 1°C, 32°F = 0°C
Electric current	ampere	ampere	same
Luminous intensity	lumen	candela	12.6 lm = 1 cd

SI quantities are further defined by the following prefixes :

pico- (p)	=	1/1,000,000,000,000 or 10^{-12}
nano- (n)	=	1/1,000,000,000 or 10^{-9}
micro- (μ)	=	1/1,000,000 or 10^{-6}
milli- (m)	=	1/1,000 or 10^{-3}
centi- (c)	=	1/100 or 10^{-2}
deci- (d)	=	1/10 or 10^{-1}
deka- (da)	=	10 or 10^{1}
hecto- (h)	=	100 or 10^{2}
kilo- (k)	=	1,000 or 10^{3}
mega- (M)	=	1,000,000 or 10^{6}
giga- (G)	=	1,000,000,000 or 10^{9}
tera- (T)	=	1,000,000,000,000 or 10^{12}

SI units are also combined to create numerous *derived units*, an example
being 1,000 grams × 1 meter/sec^2 = 1 Newton (an inertial quantity).

The U. S. government recognizes three levels of conversion from IP
to SI: *rounded-soft, soft*, and *hard.* Rounded-soft conversions involve
rounding an IP unit to an approximate SI unit (e.g. 12 in. ≈ 300 mm); soft
conversions equate an SI unit to its exact IP equivalent (e.g. 12 in. = 304.8
mm); and hard conversions involve retooling of manufacturing processes
to make products with SI dimensions (e.g. retooling a former 12.0 in. dimension to become 300 mm). In architecture the biggest SI changes usually
involve plan dimension scales. Several SI scales commonly used in
European architectural plan measures are fairly easily adapted to
American plan measures, as described below:

SI scale	Replaces IP scale of	Size difference
1:1	actual size	same
1:5	3" = 1'-0" (1:4)	20% smaller
1:10	1½" = 1'-0" (1:8)	20% larger
	1" = 1'-0" (1:12)	20% smaller
1:20	½" = 1'-0" (1:24)	20% larger
1:50	¼" = 1'-0" (1:48)	4% smaller
1:100	⅛" = 1'-0" (1:96)	4% smaller
1:200	1/16" = 1'-0" (1:192)	4% smaller
1:500	1" = 32' (1:384)	23.2% larger
1:1000	1" = 64' (1:768)	23.3% larger
	1" = 100' (1:1200)	20% smaller

At some future time each architect may convert to SI measures on a particular project. This is usually done as follows: (1) agree with the owner and contractor in advance on how completely the project will be measured in SI; (2) decide at what stage along a continuum of plans, working drawings, shop drawings, product specifications, and operation manuals all parties will begin using the new measures and discarding the old; (3) prepare a complete list of exact conversions and their abbreviations to be used by all parties; and (4) before performing calculations convert all base data to SI; don't start with one system and try to end up with the other. In this work do not use double-unit notation, e.g. 12 in. (300 mm).

In this volume, all numerical values are in IP measurements. However, an SI edition of this volume is being prepared for those users who may prefer it to the IP edition.

1.A.2. Jurisdictional Constraints

Before initiating a building's design, the architect or engineer must thoroughly review all official codes and ordinances in the jurisdiction in which the building will be erected. This process typically involves determining which codes and ordinances govern each part of a particular design, contacting the appropriate authorities, then working with them to determine the specificity and extent of all applicable regulations. Such analysis generally proceeds from MACRO to MICRO as follows:

Zoning ordinances. These are general requirements regarding a building's relation to its property and surrounding areas that often influence permitted uses, construction types, installation of life safety measures, and even character of design. They include:

▸ Environmental considerations (selection of wilderness areas, preservation of endangered species, elimination of toxics, etc.).
▸ Designation of historical and archaeological landmarks.

Much of the data in the section on metrication was obtained from *Plumbing En-*

▸ Determination of adequate open spaces, recreation, and other public amenities.
▸ Classification of land uses and building occupancies.
▸ Developmental regulations for residential subdivisions, office parks, industrial complexes, and the like.
▸ Public transportation requirements (vehicular traffic flow, access, onsite parking, pedestrian flow, etc.).
▸ Site development limitations (excavation, tree removal, erosion prevention, grading, etc.).
▸ Lot and yard requirements (area, frontage, width, length, etc.).
▸ Building setbacks (front, side, rear, number of floors, maximum heights, etc.).
▸ Property locations (access to outdoor spaces, projection limits beyond exterior walls, party wall requirements between multiple occupancies, minimum spatial dimensions outside openings, specifications for courtyards and connecting arcades, etc.).
▸ Signage requirements and restrictions.
▸ Special requirements for commercial, industrial, and institutional occupancies.

Deed restrictions. These include easements, mineral rights, water rights, grazing rights, other agricultural regulations, environmental restrictions, and the like. They are usually described in the owner's deed or subdivision regulations.

Code regulations. These are construction requirements that are meant to ensure safe structure and adequate fire protection. The architect should also incorporate into design specifications all relevant NFPA (National Fire Protection Association) bulletins, especially the Life Safety Code NFPA 101), then proceed to any other applicable documents referenced therein. Other building code requirements involve:

▸ Specification standards for building materials including wood, steel, concrete, masonry, gypsum, glass, plastics, and adhesives.
▸ Proper installation of electricity, gas, and other local utility services, including power generating systems.
▸ Provision of adequate water supply and sanitary drainage.
▸ Interior space requirements (room sizes, ceiling heights, window areas, doorway widths, stair dimensions, etc.).
▸ Provisions of adequate light and fresh air for occupied spaces.
▸ ADA (Americans with Disabilities Act) accessibility and use.
▸ OSHA (Occupational Safety & Health Administration) regulations.
▸ Special requirements for mixed occupancies.
▸ Methods of emergency evacuation and exit.
▸ Proper construction and operation of elevators, dumbwaiters, escalators, and moving walks.

- ▸ Proper construction and operation of mechanical systems (heaters, coolers, humidifiers, dehumidifiers, blowers, exhausts, etc.).
- ▸ Energy conservation standards.
- ▸ Construction inspection schedules, including issuing of building permits and certificates of occupancy.
- ▸ Protection of buildings from degradation and destruction by weather, water, adverse subsoil conditions, corrosion, decay, lack of aeration, and other damage that could occur over time.

An Æ designer should make every effort to comply with all codes and ordinances that may apply to a building's design and construction; for, if anything, the Code is a minimum requirement, which is often less than recommended, which is often less than optimal. However, if the designer or owner believes a certain exception to a code ordinance would not violate the spirit for which it was intended, he or she may be granted a *variance* for said exception by jurisdictional authorities. Indeed, although official building codes are often considered to have a timeless aura, each is revised every few years to remain current with changes indicated by ongoing natural disaster research, shifting sociological priorities, and improved energy conservation measures.

1.A.3. Preparation of Drawings

While the clarity of all working and mechanical drawings associated with a building's design is the responsibility of the architect, the task of assigning responsibility for the specific design of engineered components is often not so clear. For example, if a contractor hires a steel fabricator to prepare shop drawings that facilitate construction work and the drawings are okayed by the architect, then the connection fails, who is liable? In most cases this responsibility reverts to the architect, because all aspects of design —essentially those parts of the building that do not exist before construction and do remain after construction— are the architect's domain, and because he or she is expected to snoop, pry, and prod regarding the fulfillment of said obligations. Accordingly, usually the only way that anyone other than the architect may be held liable for any part of a building's design is for all five of the following to occur:

1. The architect must obtain in writing the services of the authority to whom he or she will delegate part of the original design obligation.
2. The delegated authority performing the services must be a licensed professional, not a proprietary detailer; then the onus of implied warranty typically falls on the authority whose field of

expertise is of a more specialized nature.

3. The delegated authority must be hired by the architect, not by the contractor or owner or any of their assigns.

4. The delegated authority must sign his or her drawings in writing.

5. During construction the architect should receive from the delegated authority a written report that the latter has inspected the work and found it to be in compliance with the Plans.

Note that if the architect's request is not in writing (i.e. is not a bona fide effort to delegate responsibility), or the specialist is not licensed (i.e. does not have official status as a professional in the eyes of the law), or the specialist is hired by the contractor or the owner (i.e. is someone whose project responsibility lies outside the domain of design), or the architect does not receive the engineer's drawings and inspection reports in writing (i.e. the delegation of responsibility is not fully consummated), then the architect is not considered to have really surrendered that portion of the domain of design to another party —in which case any delegation on the architect's part may be considered as merely *de gratia*, even spurious. This concept of "eminent domain" as the controlling factor in matters of architectural liability goes far toward enabling an architect to pick his or her way successfully through today's litigation minefields.

1.A.4. Computerization

Inside this volume's back cover is the DesignDISK, a CD-ROM that is a computerized version of all the book's formulas which enables them to be solved quickly and accurately. However, despite these extremely useful features, the disk cannot be used effectively without the text; because much related Æ information, not to mention drawings, is often required to select the proper formula to solve, which is best presented where it won't take up the screen space needed to use the formula windows; and due to electronic limitations the data for each unknown in the DesignDISK's no-math menus is limited to one line while the data needed to fully understand many unknowns often takes several lines to describe. Examples are constants or coefficients whose value is selected from several numbers which are easily listed in two or more lines in the text's no-math menu, or a bar graph a few lines away, or in a nearby graph or drawing or the text itself; and unknowns that require minor math operations to determine its numerical value, whose full descriptions can be presented only in the text. So, while the disk is quick and accurate, the book is more accessible, dependable, and thorough. Thus, as marvelous as the DesignDISK is, you simply cannot fully utilize its advantages with the book opened next to you.

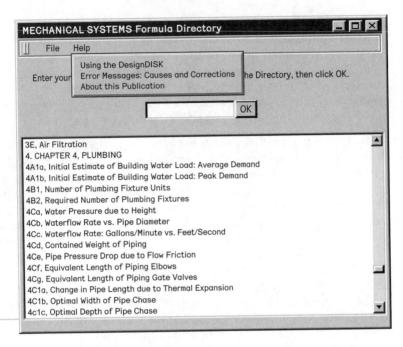

Fig, 1-1. The DesignDisk's Formula Directory window.

Related to this is the text that describes how to use computer software, which is typically accessed from its Help pulldown menus, as is shown in this disk's Formula Directory in Fig. 1-1. In this publication this text is duplicated below, where it will not take up any screen space, and where it can be accessed when the computer is malfunctioning or not running.

USING THE DesignDISK

The DesignDISK that accompanies this book is a computerized version of the volume's algebraic formulas. This software enables you to solve any unknown in the book's equations quickly and error-free without using any other mathematical method, device, or operation.

Use of this disk begins by installing it properly on your computer. Then, open the disk by clicking on its icon. First a proprietary JAVA.exe splashscreen (the 'black box') appears on your monitor, then a few seconds later the DesignDisk's Formula Directory appears on the screen [Fig. 1-1]. The Formula Directory is a dialog box that has beneath its title bar a small data entry pane with an OK button on its right, and below this pane is a much larger window that displays a long list of all the book's formulas. In the Directory, each line lists the title of one of the book's formulas, or the title of a multi-step design sequence that may contain several formulas;

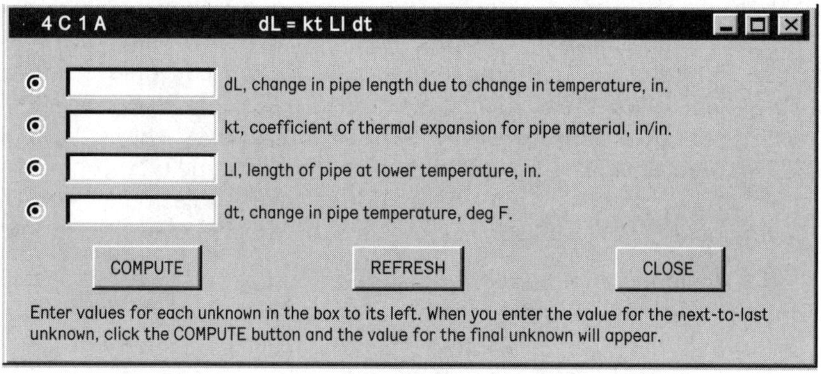

Fig. 1-2. A formula window of the DesignDisk.

and beside each title is an alphanumeric access code, such as 2C2a1, that also appears as miniature typewriter keys beside the same formula or design sequence in the book. Thus, after noting the alphanumeric access code of the formula you want to solve in the book, find the same code number in the Directory by moving the scroll bar on the directory window's right, then click anywhere on the formula's access code or title: the access code immediately appears in the data entry pane above. Then click the pane's OK button, and the formula's dialog box quickly appears on the monitor. You can also "direct dial" the desired formula by typing its access code directly in the data entry pane then clicking OK. Also, instead of scrolling through the entire list of formulas to find the one you want, you can go directly to the head of any chapter in the Formula Directory by simply typing its chapter number in the data entry pane.

Each formula has a dialog box that has a header that displays the formula, below which extends a vertical row of data entry panes in which each pane represents a formula unknown [Fig. 1-2]. To the left of each pane is a radio button, to each pane's right is one of the equation's unknowns with a one-line description further to the right; and below these items are three rectangular buttons named **COMPUTE, REFRESH,** and **CLOSE.** To solve any unknown in a formula, do the following:

1. Click the radio button beside the data entry pane for the unknown you want to solve: the button fills with a big black dot.
2. Enter numerical values in all the other panes.
3. Click **COMPUTE**: your answer quickly appears in the pane beside the black dot.

If your answer is unsatisfactory, enter new values in one or more of the entry panes whose radio buttons are blank; or click **REFRESH** to clear all values from the panes. If you want to solve another unknown, click the radio button beside its pane and repeat steps 2 and 3 above. When you are finished with a formula, click **CLOSE,** and the formula window will disappear and you will return to the Formula Directory. You can also operate a Formula Window from the keyboard by (1) pressing the **TAB** key to cycle the cursor down through the entry panes and across the **COMPUTE, REFRESH,** and **CLOSE** buttons then back to the top pane (you can reverse this cycle by by pressing TAB + SHIFT), then by (2) pressing Ⓒ to COMPUTE an answer, Ⓡ to REFRESH the panes, or Ⓧ to CLOSE the window.

If a design example requires a series of steps to solve, the Formula Window first displays the equation for Step 1. Then when you press COMPUTE to finish this step, the Window for the next step appears —until all the example's steps that contain equations appear in a nearly vertical cascade with only their title bars and part of their data entry panes visible. You need to return to a step? Click on its title bar, and its Window moves to the front of the cascade. You can even go directly from the Formula Directory to any step in any design sequence by typing in the Directory's data entry pane the formula's access code, then 's' (for step), then the step's number. For example, if you want to use Step 4 in Example 3E3a, type 3E3as4.

USING THE TRANSFER FORMULAS

A number of equations in the volume, *Structural Systems,* have a black keyboard key with a white letter and number in it. These keys indicate the use of transfer formulas, which are the beam load formulas that appear in that volume's Table 2-2, Allowable Live Loads, and the geometric section formulas that appear in Table 2-6, Properties of Geometric Sections. These formulas may be used to find values that are subsequently used in their parent formulas as follows:

1. When an equation in the book has a black keyboard key in it [e.g. **A?**], note the white letter in the key: it may be a **V** (for a beam's maximum shear load), **U** (other beam shear load), **M** (a beam's maximum bending moment), **N** (other beam bending moment), **D** (maximum beam deflection), **A** (a geometric shape's section area), **S** (a shape's section modulus), or **I** (a shape's moment of inertia).
2. Knowing the particular beam load or geometric condition for which the parent equation is being used to solve, go to Table 2-2 or 2-6 in the *Structural Systems* volume and find the formula that best describes the condition under consideration. Beside each formula is a black key with a white letter and number in it: this is the parent equation's transfer formula.
3. Enter the appropriate transfer formula's access number in the Directory's data entry pane, then click OK. When the transfer formula's window appears, reposition its window and the parent for-

mula's window so each are adjacently visible on the monitor.

4.   Solve for the value in the transfer formula that appears in the parent formula, enter this value into the proper entry pane of the parent formula, then solve the parent formula.

TIPS YOU'LL BE GLAD WE TOLD YOU ABOUT

You can tile or overlap any number of windows so only part of their entry panes are visible, enabling you to work on several equations at once.

Before working with any formula dialog box, you may find it less distracting to minimize the proprietary JAVA.exe window that opened before the Formula Directory appeared.

In the equations, exponents to the 2nd power are displayed as A≤, exponents to the 3rd power appear as A≥, and all other exponents except 1.00 are described by a carat followed by the exponent, as in Â0.75.

This software can display only alphanumeric characters (the 26 upper and lower case letters and 10 numbers). Thus some of the unique symbols that appear in many of the two books' equations are replaced by an appropriate alphabet letter.

When typing an access code into the data entry pane of the Formula Directory, you can use either upper or lower case letters regardless of how they appear in the Directory. For example, you can enter 2B1 as 2b1.

When entering the values of a variable, do not insert commas in long numbers. Enter 1800000, not 1,800,000, and 0.0000098, not 0.000,009,8.

Numbers longer than 6 significant figures on either side of a decimal are displayed in exponential form (e.g. 8 significant figures to the left of the decimal reads as 1.44e+008, and 8 significant figures to the right of the decimal reads as 1.44e-008)

In multi-step examples, the formula window for each subsequent step appears only if you activate the radio button beside the top data entry pane in the open window before clicking COMPUTE. If you have solved an unknown other than the top variable, you must click the radio button beside the top pane to access the next step.

In a multi-step sequence, any steps without equations have no formula windows. Thus if a seven-step sequence has equations only in Steps 1, 4, and 6, it has only four formula windows whose step sequence is 1, 4, and 6 (not 1, 2, 3, 4, 5, 6).

A COMPUTING TOOL WITH NEAR-UNIVERSAL APPLICATIONS

The DesignDISK can be used for much more than solving the equations found in its parent volumes. For example, do you need to use the Pythagorean theorem? Or the quadratic equation? Or do you want the value of three numbers multiplied together? From the Formula Directory you can access a formula that contains the exact algebra you seek, then use it to quickly find your answer. A few such No-Math possibilities are listed below.

Desired Equation	Formula Access Code
Pythagorean theorem ($A = [B^2+C^2]^{0.5}$)	*MS* or *SS* A35a
Quadratic equation	*MS* or *SS* A11
Value of two multiplied numbers ($A = B + C$)	*MS* 2C1, *SS* 2B5a
Value of three multiplied numbers ($A = B\ C\ D$)	*MS* 3D1, *SS* 8B1
Value of four multiplied numbers ($A = B\ C\ D\ E$)	*MS* 3D2, *SS* 8F4
Value of up to 7 multiplied numbers ($A = B\ C\ D\ E\ F\ G\ H$)	*MS* 6A1d
Value of one number divided by another number ($A = B/C$) ...	*MS* 2C25
Value of two added numbers ($A = B + C$)	*MS* 2E8b, *SS* 5C1s5
Value of up to nine added numbers ($A = B + C + D$, etc.)	*MS* 4B1, *SS* 8F3
Value of one number minus another number ($A = B - C$)	*MS* 2Ba
Value of two numbers minus a third number ($A = B + C - D$) ...	*MS* 3B1a
Comparative costs of 2 similar products (lamps, motors, etc. ..	*MS* 6B4

Each volume, *Structural Systems* (SS above) and *Mechanical Systems* (MS above), also contains a lengthy Appendix of Useful Formulas —more than 300 in all, which may used to solve many algebra, geometry, or physics equations and perform many metric or nonmetric conversions that may appear in many architectural engineering design scenarios.

ERROR MESSAGES: CAUSES AND CORRECTIONS

While using the Formula Directory and the dialog boxes for each formula, you may occasionally make an error which will cause one of the following messages to appear:

ERROR MESSAGE 1. Your formula access number is invalid. Please re-enter a different formula access number.
Cause: You entered an invalid formula access number in the Formula Directory's data entry pane.
Correction: Choose a valid number from the Directory or the DesignDISK's accompanying volume.

ERROR MESSAGE 2: Your variable input is invalid. Please enter a valid number.
Cause: You entered a non-numeral in a formula window data entry pane.
Correction: Enter a valid number in the pane.

ERROR MESSAGE 3: You cannot divide by zero or take the root of a negative number. Please re-enter your values.
Cause: A variable functioning as a divisor has been given a value of zero; or a log, trig, or exponential function is not structured properly.

Correction: Check all your variable input values for the formula being used and re-enter the variable(s) causing the error.

ERROR MESSAGE 4: You cannot solve for this variable in this equation. Please choose a different unknown for which this equation should be solved.

Cause: A very few equations have variables that appear twice and have different exponents that make
them quadratically unsolvable.

Correction: Do not try to solve the equation for these variables (do not turn their radio buttons ON).

1.A.5. Designer's Responsibility

Although the information presented in this volume is based on sound engineering principles, test data, and field experience of respected authorities over a period of several decades as well as the author's forty years' experience in architectural design and construction, no part of the information herein should be utilized for any architectural engineering application unless the design is thoroughly reviewed by a licensed architect or professional engineer who is competent in the particular application under consideration. Moreover, said authority shall accept legal responsibility for all applications of said information.

The author, by making the information in this professional handbook and its accompanying disk, publicly available cannot be considered as rendering any professional service; nor does he assume any responsibility whatsoever regarding the use of any of said information by any other individual or organization whether they are licensed or otherwise.

Furthermore, neither the author nor the publisher make any representation or warranty regarding the accuracy or conceptual propriety of any information contained in this handbook or its disk. Neither shall the author or the publisher be liable for any demand, claim, loss, expense, liability, or personal injury of any kind arising directly, indirectly, or remotely from the use or omission of any information contained in this handbook or its accompanying disk. Any party using said information assumes full liability arising from such use.

These legal precepts are explained here once and for all so that they need not be described repeatedly throughout this lengthy text.

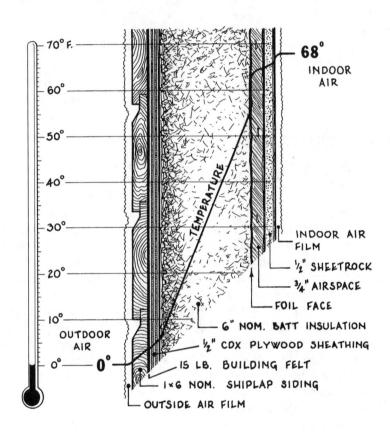

70° F.

68°
INDOOR
AIR

60°

50°

40°

30°

TEMPERATURE

INDOOR AIR
FILM

20°

½" SHEETROCK

¾" AIRSPACE

FOIL FACE

10°

6" NOM. BATT INSULATION

OUTDOOR
AIR

½" CDX PLYWOOD SHEATHING

0°   0°

15 LB. BUILDING FELT

1×6 NOM. SHIPLAP SIDING

OUTSIDE AIR FILM

Heat flow through a typical wall section

CLIMATIC FORCES

2.A. GENERAL

Sun, rain, wind, heat, and cold shape architecture in many ways. The forces these elements rail against a building vary from subtle to stupendous, from intermittent to unceasing, from tranquil absence to several occurring at the same time. Designing a building to resist them also has its subtle and dominant elements, which may be distilled to three aspects:

1. Designing a building's exterior to resist the forces of climate. This is covered in this volume's Sec. 2.A. to 2.D.
2. Quantifying a building's thermal loads and optimizing the possibility of utilizing solar energy based on local climate patterns and extremes. This is covered in Sec. 2. E.
3. Maintaining constant comfort inside a building by properly selecting and sizing its climate control system. This is covered in Chapter 3.

2.A.1. Microclimate Factors

Frank Lloyd Wright said: "I think it far better to go WITH the natural climate than try to fix a special artificial climate of your own." Indeed, a little weatherwise jujitsu —of tricking the natural features and forces around a building into working for you instead of against you— can be worth an inch or two of extra insulation in its facades as well as a substantial portion of its ongoing energy expenses.

Design for climate begins with analyzing the building's surrounds for at least 200 ft in every direction if it is two stories tall or less, regardless of the location of its property lines. If the building is taller, as good a general rule as any is to analyze its surroundings in every direction for a distance of 150 ft plus twice its height.

2.A.1.a. Breezes [†]

In the continental United States, winds generally blow from west to east. Warm breezes born in the Pacific or Gulf of Mexico usually arrive from the southwest, while cold fronts originating in the Arctic and northern Canada arrive from the northwest. In temperate and cool climates (average annual temperature is less than about 65°), a building should generally be exposed to the southwest and sheltered from the northwest, and where temperatures are warmer the opposite should be done.

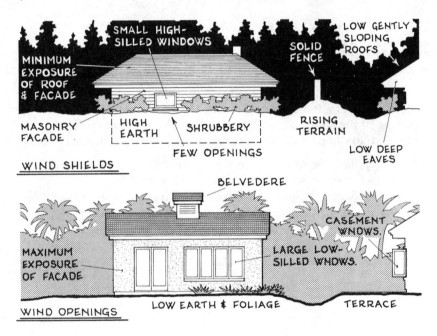

Fig. 2-1. Wind shields and openings.

As prevailing winds glide over trees, roofs, and prominences in terrain, eddies of swirling or stagnant air fill yards, streets, and other open areas below. When these currents sluice though narrow openings or slide down the sides of hills, bluffs, and long buildings, they increase in speed. Where such breezes are desirable insofar as nearby architecture is concerned, the building should open to them with broad lawns, other low ground covers, porches, terraces, exposed facades with large openable windows, and casement windows whose opened sashes can scoop passing breezes indoors. Where such breezes are undesirable, the building should shield itself from them with berms, solid fences, shrubs, low eaves, masonry walls with small windows, and added insulation.

[†] Much of the information in Sections 2.A.1.a., 2.A.1.b., and 2.A.1.c. were taken

2.A.1.b. Foliage

A building shrouded in foliage will experience gentler breezes, more equable temperatures, and more humid air than one in a clearing nearby. This is desirable in some regions and undesirable in others. In temperate and cool climates, high-branched deciduous trees should rise around the building's southern half and low-branched evergreens around the north. In warmer climates, high-canopied evergreens (e.g. palm trees) are desirable.

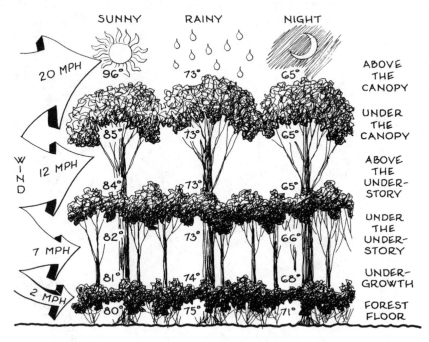

Fig. 2-2. How foliage affects microclimate.

Foliage is beneficial in other ways. Dense arrays muffle sounds from neighboring areas and are excellent at maintaining privacy. Masses of foliage, by generating oxygen, also freshen the breezes flowing above them; and their leaves absorb carbon dioxide, sulphur dioxide, chlorine, nitric oxide, and other noxious gases as well as collect airborne particulate pollutants. Indeed, almost 200 years ago Washington Irving described the biomechanical advantages of foliage well when he said:

> As the leaves of trees are said to absorb all noxious qualities of the air, and breathe forth a purer atmosphere, so it seems as if they drew from us all sordid and angry passions, and breathed forth peace and philanthropy. There is a serene and settled majesty in woodland scenery that enters into the soul, and dilates and elevates it, and fills it with noble inclinations.

from the *Ecological House*, Robert B. Butler (Morgan & Morgan, Dobbs Ferry,

2.A.1.c. Terrain

Wind blows over a landscape much as water flows over the bed of a stream. Where the ground is smooth, currents flow evenly; where it is rough, air flows fast over the high spots and slowly over the low. Over depressions, stagnant 'air ponds' tend to form which are cooler and clammier than air only a few yards away. Where the ground slopes, during warm sunny weather air typically flows uphill until midafternoon, then downhill till dawn, to offer free ventilation to any building in its path. Also, *concave terrain* (a slight depression of usually soft wet soil) is typically a bad place to build, while *convex terrain* (a slight rise of usually hard dry soil) is typically a good place to build. Ground surfaces also affect the temperature of

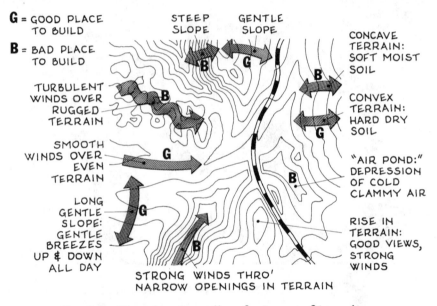

Fig. 2-3. Warming & cooling features of terrain.

the air above. On a sunny day when the thermometer reads 80°, nearby air may be 73° above a pond, 78° above a lawn, 83° over a wood deck, 87° above bare earth, and 103° above asphalt. The more heat the ground absorbs during the day, the warmer the air above it is at night. Light surfaces are cooler and more reflective than dark. Also, an area cast in sunlight will be about 12° warmer than a shaded area a few feet away. All these factors can add up to a big difference in a building's seasonal heating and cooling loads.

What is the density of air if its temperature is 82° F, its elevation above sea level is 4,250 ft, and the barometric air pressure is 29.92 in?

New York, 1981), pp. 12–21.

2|A|1|c|a) **Air pressure is in. Hg:** $D(459.7 + F) = 1.325\,\kappa_e\,B$
      b) **Air pressure is psi:** $D(459.7 + F) = 2.697\,P$

D = density of air, ? pcf. Air at sea level at room temperature (68°) and normal atmospheric pressure has a density of 0.073 pcf.
F = temperature of air, 82° F
κ_e = elevation coefficient, based on elevation above sea level, from the bar graph below. At an elevation of 4,250 ft ASL, $\kappa_e \approx 0.85$.

Elevation above sea level

1.00   0.962 0.925 0.890 0.856   0.824   0.793 0.763 0.734 0.705 0.677

0   1,000 2,000 3,000 4,000 5,000 6,000 7,000 8,000 9,000 10,000

κ_e = elevation coefficient

B = effective barometric pressure, in. Hg. This is typically an air pressure adjusted for a local elevation that is used to forecast the weather. If B is the air's actual pressure in in. mercury (Hg.), disregard the air's elevation above sea level, in which case κ_E in formula a = 1.00. Here B = 29.92 in. Hg.
P = Actual air pressure, psi. Not applicable.

$$D(459.7 + 82) = 1.325 \times 0.85 \times 29.92 \quad ... D = 0.062 \text{ pcf}$$

2.B. SUN

The angle and intensity at which the sun's rays strike the ground are a function of the site's local latitude as well as the time of day and time of year. The formulas in Example 3 below are used to find the sun's altitude and azimuth for any northern latitude at any time of year. By setting the sun's altitude at zero, the sunrise and sunset time for any date can be found; and by setting the sun's azimuth at zero (due south), its altitude at noon on any date can be found. Using these formulas with a computer allows one to plot solar trajectories across the sky quickly and accurately. The formulas do not consider daylight savings time.

To determine the amount of solar energy, or *solar heat gain*, that a building may utilize to heat its interior spaces, see Sec. 2.E.5.

Example 1. On February 21 what is the sun's maximum altitude above level terrain that is located at N 41°-23' latitude?

2|B|a) $\angle = \kappa_a - L$

$\angle$ = solar altitude: vertical angle of sun above horizon at noon due south on Feb. 21, **?** °. Interpolate for intermediate values between the 21st days of consecutive months.

κ_a = solar altitude coefficient. From Table 2-1, κ_a for Feb. = 78.5°.

L = local latitude; round off to nearest half degree. 41°-23' ➡ 41.5°

$$\angle = 78.5 - 41.5 = 37°$$

Example 2. What is the length of a shadow on level terrain from the peak of a 66 ft tall church in Concord, New Hampshire if the sun is 48° above the horizon?

---

2)B)b)
$$H = S \tan \angle$$

H = height of object casting the sun's shadow, ft. H = 37 ft.

S = length of cast shadow, horizontal projection, **?** ft

$\angle$ = solar altitude: vertical angle of sun above horizon, °. $\angle$ = 48°.

$$37 = L \tan 48° \quad ... L = 33.3 \text{ ft}$$

Note: To determine the length of a shadow on nonlevel or uneven terrain, cut a vertical section through the apex of the building in the direction of the solar azimuth, then measure the shadow's length on the ground.

Example 3. What is the sun's altitude at noon, Dec. 21, on a site in Ashland, Oregon? On this date what is the sun's azimuth at 9:15 AM?

---

2)B)c) **Altitude:**

$$\sin \angle_v = \sin L \sin [23.5 \sin 0.98 (D - 81)] - \cos L \cos (15 T) \cos [23.5 \sin 0.98 (D - 81)]$$

2)B)d) **Azimuth:**

$$\tan \angle_h = \frac{\sin (15\ T) \cos [23.5 \sin 0.98 (D - 81)]}{[23.5 \sin 0.98 (D - 81)] + \sin L \cos (15\ T) \cos [23.5 \sin 0.98 (D - 81)]}$$

TABLE 2-1: SOLAR ALTITUDE ANGLES

MONTH & DATE	ALTITUDE,° at noon due south
Jan. 21 ..... 69.5° – local latitude	July 21 ..... 110.5° – local latitude
Feb. 21 ..... 78.5° – local latitude	Aug. 21 .... 101.5° – local latitude
Mar. 21 ..... 90.0° – local latitude	Sep 21 ...... 90.0° – local latitude
Apr. 21 .... 101.5° – local latitude	Oct. 21 ..... 78.5° – local latitude
May 21 ..... 110.5° – local latitude	Nov. 21 ..... 69.5° – local latitude
June 21 .... 113.5° – local latitude	Dec. 21 ..... 66.5° – local latitude

$\angle_v$ = solar altitude: vertical angle of sun above horizon, **?** °. At sunrise or sunset, $\angle_v = 0°$. Round off $\angle_v$ and $\angle_h$ to nearest half degree.

$\angle_h$ = solar azimuth: horizontal angle of sun from due south, **?** °. Minus values indicate $\angle_h$ is east of south; plus values indicate $\angle_h$ is west of south. At noon due south, $\angle_h = 0°$.

L = latitude of site, °. From atlas, Ashland, OR, is at 42.2° N. latitude.

D = day of year: number of day in year, as in schedule below:

Jan. 1 = 1	Apr. 1 = 91	Jul. 1 = 182	Oct. 1 = 274
Feb. 1 = 32	May 1 = 121	Aug. 1 = 213	Nov. 1 = 305
Mar. 1 = 60	Jun. 1 = 152	Sep. 1 = 244	Dec. 1 = 335

Dec. 21 = 335 + 21 = day 356

T = time of day, decimal hr. At noon, $T = 12.0$. At 9:15 AM, $T = 9.25$.

Substituting in the above equations:

Altitude: $\angle_v = 14°$ above horizon

Azimuth: $\angle_h = -38.5° = 38.5°$ east of south

Note: To find sunrise and sunset azimuths, in formula 2)B)c) set $\angle_v = 0$ and solve for T. Then, knowing L, D, and T, in 2)B)d) solve for $\angle_h$.

2.B.1. Angle of Incidence

The formula below allows one to compute the angle formed between the sun and a planar surface no matter where the sun is in the sky or in what horizontal or vertical direction the plane is facing.

When the altitude of the sun is 50° above the horizon and its azimuth is 45° west of south, what angle does it make with a roof facing south-southeast that slopes 60°?

2)B)1)a)

$$\sin \angle_A = \sin \angle_H \cos \angle_S + \cos \angle_H \sin \angle_S \cos (\angle_D + \angle_F)$$

$\angle_A$ = angle of difference between incident sunrays and surface, **?** °

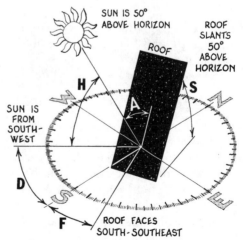

Fig. 2-4. Sun angle on sloping roof.

$\angle_H$ = solar altitude: vertical angle of sun above horizon, 50°
$\angle_S$ = slope of planar surface to horizontal, 60°
$\angle_D$ = solar azimuth: at southwest, horiz. angle of sun from due south = 45°
$\angle_F$ = orientation of planar surface from due south, 22.5°

$$\sin \angle_A = \sin 50° \cos 60° + \cos 50° \sin 60° \cos (45° + 22.5°)$$
$$\angle_A = 36.5°$$

2.B.2. Overhangs

A roof eave or other projection above a predominantly south-facing window, and even east- and west-facing windows, can shield the glazing below from high-angle summer sunrays while letting low-angle winter rays enter indoors. But in the spring and fall this technique is only partly successful, because then the sun's trajectories are alike the same number of days before and after the winter solstice while the weather is usually not. For example, in southern New York, on September 10 the average daily temperature is 64°, while on April 1, when the sun's path through the sky is the same, the average daily temperature is only 41°. Thus in this area in early September an occupant most likely wouldn't want the sun shining through his or her window, while on April 1 he could use all the free heat he could get. Similar conditions exist in most of this nation's central latitudes. Obviously certain heating and cooling savings can be realized by carefully placing permanent overhangs over such openings, but maximum savings can be realized only with overhangs that move or can be adjusted.

Example 1. If a roof extends 48 in. from a vertical facade oriented due south and the sun's angle above the horizon at noon is 35°, how much of the facade is cast in shade?

2)B)2)a) $H \cos \angle_a = L \tan \angle_v$

H = height of shadow on facade, measured down from lowest tip of overhang, **?** in.
$\angle_a$ = angular difference between facade orientation and solar azimuth.
    Here $\angle_a = 0° ➡ \cos 0° = 1.00$.
L = horizontal length of overhang, 48 in.
$\angle_v$ = solar altitude: vertical angle of sun above horizon, 35°.

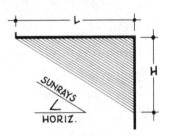

Fig. 2-5. Shaded overhang.

$$H = 48 \tan 35° = 33.6 \text{ in.}$$

> **Example 2.** A roof extends 30 in. beyond a vertical facade oriented south-southeast, and when the sun's azimuth is south-southwest its altitude is 52°. At this time how much of the facade is cast in shade?

2)B)2)a) $H \cos \angle_a = L \tan \angle_v$

H = height of shadow on facade, **?** in.
$\angle_a$ = angular difference between facade orientation and solar azimuth. If facade faces SSE (22.5° east of south) and sun's azimuth is SSW (22.5° west of south), $\angle_a = 22.5 + 22.5 = 45°$.
L = horizontal length of overhang, 30 in.
$\angle_v$ = solar altitude: vertical angle of sun above horizon, 52°

$$30 \tan 52° = H \cos 45°   \ldots H = 54.3 \text{ in.}$$

2.C. WATER

In a building, about the only place where water belongs is inside refrigerators and plumbing systems. Anywhere else, and the building's life is in mortal danger. The most immediate strategy, obvious to all engaged in architectural design and construction, is to thwart and divert the approaching liquid at every outer surface of the building. This includes watertight roofing and flashing, networks of gutters and downspouts from eave to finished grade, watertight foundation walls, and accurately-laid networks of perforated drains below grade.

If waterproofing were only this simple, designers of buildings would enjoy more pleasant nights of sleep. Unfortunately, water has an insidious way of materializing out of thin air via the laws of condensation, a contradictory way of flowing uphill via the laws of osmosis, and a downright diabolical way of converting seemingly well-thought-out assemblies of barrier walls, weep holes, flashing, and sealants into conduits that actually send the water indoors —to become a welcome mat for rotting, spalling, rust staining, and colonies of carpenter ants and termites.

Regarding potential water damage to buildings, an excellent preventive technique is to insert a layer of 90 lb rolled roofing —*not* tarpaper— between every contiguous surface of wood-to-metal, wood-to-masonry, or metal-to-masonry, as well as between any two metals that are far apart in the galvanic series. Perhaps the only exception to this is flashing imbedded in masonry. A layer of this material absolutely prevents moisture penetration that would otherwise occur due to water condensation and temperature differentials between the surfaces-in-common. This lamina is also a far superior vapor barrier than polyethylene; because its granular texture contains tiny airspaces which retain minuscule collections of moisture, whereas polyethylene's slick surface actually collects moisture and within a few years it usually becomes brittle and cracks — then it will promote what it was meant to prevent. A layer of 90 lb rolled roofing is also thick, strong, and insulating, and is impregnated with asphalt, which in addition to being water-repellent is impervious to all kinds of acids, alkalis, and electrolytes that commonly leach out of woods, cements, bricks, rocks, and metals. Thus insertion of 90 lb rolled roofing —or pieces of asphalt shingles, which is the same material— between every seam of wood-to-metal, wood-to-masonry, and metal-to-masonry should be a Code-mandated axiom in building construction.

Another important moisture preventive is venting, particularly in roofs between insulation and sheathing. In warm humid regions, this space may need to be 8 in. deep and accompanied by wide continuous screened vents at every eave and peak in a building's roof.

2.C.1. Hydrostatic Head

The force of water in the earth below an area's local water table can turn a building's basement into an empty boat and pop it out of the ground —a phenomenon well-known to swimming pool contractors. Where moist subsoil conditions could rise above a basement's floor level during any part of the year, the basement should have foundation drains laid no more than 16 ft apart beneath its floors as well as around them, and each drain should slope down at least $1/16$ in/LF to an outfall well away from the building.

> A 20 × 40 ft concrete basement floor in a residence lies below the surrounding water table during part of the year. What is the total pressure potential beneath this floor if no sub-slab drains are laid?

2)C)1) $P = A H$

P = total pressure against underside of construction, ? lb
A = area of underside of construction, sf. A of basement floor, 24 × 40 = 960 sf.
H = hydrostatic head, psf. Water-saturated soil tends to act as a static fluid in which an immersed object obeys the lays of buoyancy; thus such soil can exert an upward force that equals its unit weight which may be as much as 140 pcf, or 140 psf against a surface.

$$P \approx 960 \times 140 \approx 134,000 \text{ lb} \quad \text{... 67 tons!}$$

2.C.2. Precipitation [†]

Precipitation is the descent from the sky of several kinds of moisture, particularly rain and snow, and its deposit on buildings and terrain. If the moisture falls on a building, its upward surfaces shed the water or snowmelt by gravity, usually to nearby terrain; if the moisture falls on terrain, its vegetation absorbs the moisture and its topography drains it to lower levels. Whether shed by a building or topography, the water often flows through an open channel known as a *gutter* or a *storm drain*. Even if the channel is covered, as are storm drains, the drainage is still open; because the waterflow, even if it completely fills the channel, moves by gravity and not pressure as it does in plumbing supply systems.

Every open channel that carries water has a *wetted perimeter* (the portion of the channel's perimeter that is submerged by the waterflow) and a *hydraulic radius* (the section area of the channel's waterflow divided by its wetted perimeter). Thus the formula for a channel's hydraulic radius is

$$R_h = A_{sec}/P_w$$

Formulas for obtaining the hydraulic radius of certain circular pipes, box channels, and half-hexagonal channels are given below.

2│C│2│1│ **Pipe flowing half full:**
$$R_h = 0.5\ \pi\ r^2/0.5 \times 2\ \pi\ r = 0.5\ r$$

2│C│2│2│ **Pipe flowing full:**
$$R_h = \pi\ r^2/2\ \pi\ r = 0.5\ r$$

2│C│2│3│ **Box channel flowing full:**
$$R_h = b\ d/(b + 2\ d)$$

2│C│2│4│ **Half-hex channel flowing full:**
$$R_h = 0.5\ r \times 0.866\ r \times 3/3r = 0.43\ r$$

The half-hex channel section above is also known as a *semi-hexagonal* or *regular trapezoidal* open channel. It is generally the most efficient noncircular channel section.

> What is the hydraulic radius of a circle that flows one-third full?

2│C│2│5│ $$R_h = A/P_w$$

Solution: Finding A in the above formula is easy ($A = 0.33\ \pi r^2$), but finding P_w is often tedious. It is done as follows:

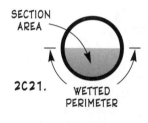

SECTION AREA

2C21.   WETTED PERIMETER

2C22.

2C23.

2C24.

Fig. 2-6. Open channel geometry 1.

[†] Much of the information regarding the open channel formulas in this section

Referring to the sketch at right, the shaded area S is a spherical segment whose area is

$$A = \pi \{0.5 \, [h \, (r - h)]^{0.5} + h^2\}$$

Thus A for any fractional or decimal portion of a circle when the portion is a spherical segment may be written as below, wherein F equals the fractional or decimal portion of the circle:

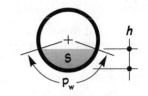

$$A = F \pi r^2 = \pi \{0.5 \, [h \, (r - h)]^{0.5} + h^2\}$$
$$\therefore F = \pi \{0.5 \, [h \, (r - h)]^{0.5} + h^2\}/r^2$$

Solve for h. Then, knowing h and r, find $r - h$ as sketched to the right.

From $\cos \Theta = (r - h)/r$, find Θ

Then from $r \Theta = 57.3 \, P_w$, find P_w

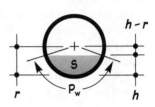

Fig. 2-7. Open channel geometry 2.

Due to the above complicated mathematics, R_h is generally solved only for the simplest circular relationships or where an open channel's section dimensions are known. Thus one usually begins by knowing a channel flow's section area A (or its flow in cfm) and its wetted perimeter P_w, then uses these values to find the section's hydraulic radius R_h, whose value is then used to size almost any channel of gravity-induced waterflow, from a custom gutters to an irrigation canals. However, these formulas are accurate only if the waterflow is smooth-flowing, which usually occurs if its slope is below about 11° (0.19 or 2.33:12 pitch). For steeper slopes and turbulent waterflows, the formulas may still be useful for general estimating.

The formulas that follow for sizing gutters, leaders, footing drains, and storm drains are simplified variations of the above mathematics. Also, it is a good idea to size channels at 0.8 capacity, to leave room for extreme situations. A round pipe's hydraulic radius at 0.8 capacity = 2.26 r.

A general formula for finding the maximum waterflow in any open channel of any cross-section is

2)C)2)6 $508 \, \kappa_R \, Q = \varDelta^{0.5} \left[\dfrac{\text{section area of waterflow in channel (in.)}^{1.67}}{\text{wetted perimeter } "\quad"\quad"\quad"\quad \text{(in.)}^{0.67}} \right]$

κ_R = roughness coefficient of channel's inner surface, from Table 2-3.
Q = volume of waterflow, cfm
$\varDelta$ = average slope of channel from inlet to outlet, ft/ft. This equals (upper elevation – lower elevation) ÷ horizontal distance between upper and lower elevations.

This formula may also be used to estimate the highest flood stage level of a stream or river valley.

was obtained from *Introduction to Fluid Mechanics*, William Haberman & James

2.C.2.a. Gutters †

A gutter collects rainwater draining from a roof, then leads it away from the building it falls on. These long narrow channels may be made of aluminum, copper, galvanized steel, plastic, and wood; and their sections may be the common ogee profile, semicircular, rectangular, any other shape, or simply a trough of flashing installed near the bottom of a roof, as were the gutters of Frank Lloyd Wright's Robie House (see Fig 2-7A). Such elegance is testimony to this man's genius, as it shows how he often created beauty out of simple utility —an outstanding ability of his that has gone largely unnoticed down through the decades.

Today the most common gutter section nationwide for residences and small commercial buildings of almost any size, economic situation, and climatic exposure is one with a rectangular back and an ogee front known as K-style. This section is shown in Fig. 2-8B.

Gutters must be designed precisely if they are to maximize the longevity of the parent architecture; yet, unfortunately, designing gutters will never be an exact science. This is primarily due to the vagaries of rainfall, whose intensity in any area can only be estimated. For this and numerous other reasons, an Æ designer must be especially alert when selecting and sizing this component. Thus he or she should know the subject well, never hesitate to oversize this relatively low-costing component, and always insist that the installer meticulously adhere to construction specifications. Beyond this, long-lasting gutters are designed as follows:

▶ A gutter can be any width, but this usually varies from 4–8 in. A gutter is usually at least 4 in. wide so one's hand can clean it. Narrower gutters are often installed below very small roofs.

▶ A gutter's depth should be 0.5–0.75 its width and its top should be slightly wider than its bottom. Half-round gutters drain better than do other sections and less water generally remains in one's curved bottom. For this reason flat-bottomed gutters should pitch more steeply than half-round ones to keep stagnant water from remaining in them which can breed mosquitoes.

▶ Every gutter should pitch at least $\frac{1}{16}$ in/LF to facilitate drainage. Do not for aesthetic reasons run a gutter level for appearance; because the only reason for a gutter is functional —and if this is violated, much damage can occur to the parent building.

▶ A gutter exceeding 50 ft in length requires an expansion joint, which must be at a pitch peak because water cannot flow over an expansion joint; thus such a gutter requires a downspout on each side. Downspouts are usually located at a gutter's ends or quarter-lengths; thus in the latter position a properly-pitched gutter would have a very slight "W" elevation profile.

▶ A gutter's top front edge should be (1) at least $\frac{1}{2}$ in. below the

John (Prentice-Hall, Englewood Cliffs, NJ, 1971); pp. 224–31.   † A primary

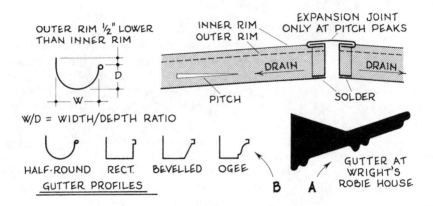

Fig. 2-8. Gutter details.

plane of the roof's pitch above to prevent sliding branches, clumps of leaves, and snow from tearing the gutter from the building; (2) no more than $\frac{3}{4}$ in. below the roof's pitch plane to keep descending roof rainwater from shooting over its top; and (3) at least 1 in. lower than the gutter's back edge so if it fills it will overflow away from the building. Remember that the steeper the roof, the greater is the rainwaterflow's velocity at its base.

▸ The sheeting for aluminum gutters (the most popular kind) is usually .028 or .032 in. thick. The thicker sheeting is only slightly more expensive but is considerably more durable. Copper gutters, especially custom-made ones, should be thicker.

▸ Where a roof valley drains into a gutter, during heavy rains the intersecting roof planes may concentrate the collected waterflow so much that it can overshoot the gutter at its corner or tear the gutter from the building. This is especially a problem if the roof is large and steep. Then an L-shaped sheet metal baffle may be installed in the valley above the gutter.

▸ Copper gutters develop an attractive verdigris patina after a few years, but water dripping from them can form green stains on surfaces below, and cedar-shingle roof runoff corrodes copper.

▸ A gutter is usually attached to the building by one of several kinds of hangers. The best hangers do not extend over the top of the gutter but cradle it from underneath, as then the gutter is easier to clean from below.

▸ Large flat roofs may have interior rain-leader traps located at slight depressions toward which the surrounding roof slopes at least $\frac{1}{4}$ in/LF. Such roofs typically have at least 4 in. high cant strips around their perimeters.

source for the information in this and the following two sections was Andy Engel's

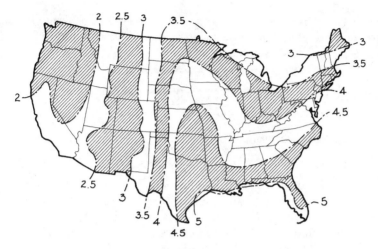

Fig. 2-9. Rainfall intensity map.

Unfortunately, there is probably not a single standardized gutter sold in the nation's building supply stores today that does a perfect job of satisfying all the criteria above. For example, a semicircular gutter's front is rarely 1 in. lower than its back, the most widely-sold gutter has a mosquito-breeding flat bottom, the vast majority of gutter hangers extend over the gutter's top, and valley baffles are rarely found in any lumberyard. Even costly custom-made gutters are typically formed by machines with standard dies, which do not satisfy all the above criteria. Thus if you want to design the perfect gutter for a client, today you almost have to teach someone how to do it. This must be one reason why Frank Lloyd Wright turned his office into a school or 'Fellowship', where his employees were often 'students' who went to the site to construct the Plans.

The primary determinants of a gutter's size are the maximum local rainfall intensity and the roof's watershed area. The rainfall intensity is generally the most intense 5-minute rate of rainfall to be expected in the region, which is taken to be 1.5 its maximum hourly rainfall intensity. A gutter's watershed area is not the surface area of the roof that drains into the gutter, or even its horizontally projected area, but its horizontally projected area plus half its vertically projected area; because rain rarely falls vertically. Thus a 4-in-12 pitch rectangular roof that is 12 ft wide and 4 ft high has a watershed area of $(12 + \frac{1}{2} \times 4) \times$ the roof's length. Such algebra also leads to proper gutter sizing if a large facade rises above the roof that drains into the gutter; as then any rainfall intercepted by the facade is accounted for. If the seam of two pitched roofs at right angles to each other forms a valley, the waterflow from both roof planes drains into a continuous L-shaped gutter; then the roof's watershed length = 0.5 (roof eave length + roof peak length).

"All About Rain Gutters", *Fine Homebuilding* magazine (Taunton Press, New-

Example 1. If a residence near Tampa, FL, has a 54 × 32 ft gable roof with a 6/12 pitch and semicircular gutters, how wide should the gutter along each eave be if it has a downspout at each end?

2)C)2)a)1) Ogee section: $W R = 800\,\eta\,\kappa_\varDelta\,w^{2.67}$

2) Half-round section: $W R = 390\,\eta\,\kappa_\varDelta\,\delta^{2.67}$ ... ➕

3) Rect. section: $W R = 2{,}500\,\eta\,\kappa_\varDelta\,(w\,d)^{1.67}\,(w + 2\,d)^{-0.67}$

4) Any section: $W R = 2{,}500\,\eta\,\kappa_\varDelta\,(A)^{1.67}\,(P_w)^{-0.67}$

W = watershed area of roof drained by each gutter, sf. W = area of horizontal projection + 0.5 area of vertical projection if roof slopes + 0.5 area of any facade above roof that drains into gutter. Assume gabled roof drains to gutters on each side ➡ 2 gutters. At 6/12 pitch, $W = 54 \times 32/2 + 0.5 \times 54 \times 6/12 \times 16 = 1{,}080$ sf.

R = maximum rainfall intensity, based on 50-year-frequency storm, in/hr. From Fig. 2-9, R for northern Florida ≈ 5 in/hr.

η = number of leaders each gutter drains into. Here assume at least 1 leader at each end ➡ $\eta = 2$. If δ computed below is undesirably large, consider adding a third leader near the gutter's center.

$\kappa_\varDelta$ = gutter slope coefficient based on its pitch, from bar graph below. The more visible the gutter, usually the shallower its pitch. Here gutter is prominently visible ➡ use $1/16$ in/LF pitch ➡ $\kappa_\varDelta = 0.072$.

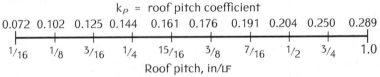

k_P = roof pitch coefficient

| 0.072 | 0.102 | 0.125 | 0.144 | 0.161 | 0.176 | 0.191 | 0.204 | 0.250 | 0.289 |

| $1/16$ | $1/8$ | $3/16$ | $1/4$ | $15/16$ | $3/8$ | $7/16$ | $1/2$ | $3/4$ | 1.0 |

Roof pitch, in/LF

Fig. 2-10. Roof pitch coefficient bar graph.

w = min. top width of gutter if it is an ogee or rectangular section, in.
δ = minimum diameter of gutter if it is a half-round section, in.
d = minimum depth of gutter if it is a rectangular section, in.
A = section area of gutter if it is any section, in².
P_w = wetted perimeter of gutter if it is any section, in.

$1{,}080 \times 5 = 390 \times 2\;0.072 \times \delta^{2.67}$ ... $\delta = 5.5$ ➡ 6 in. dia.

Example 2. A restored turn-of-the-century bank in Cripple Creek, CO, has a flat roof with a cornice on the front and party walls on each side. If the roof is 62 ft deep and 46 ft wide and a rectangular gutter along the back has a downspout at each end, size the gutter.

town, CT); Aug/Sep 1999, pp. 96–103.

2)C)2)a)3) **Rect. section:** $W R = 2,500\,\eta\,\kappa_{\varDelta}\,(w\,d)^{1.67}\,(w + 2\,d)^{-0.67}$

W = watershed area of roof drained by each gutter, sf. As roof is flat or nearly so and drains on only 1 side ➡ 1 gutter. ∴ $W = 62 \times 46 = 2,850$ sf.

R = maximum rainfall intensity, based on 50-year-frequency storm. From Fig. 2-9, R for central Colorado ≈ 3 in/hr.

η = number of leaders gutter drains into. Assume 1 leader at each end ➡ $\eta = 2$.

$\kappa_{\varDelta}$ = gutter slope coefficient depending on its pitch, from bar graph on previous page. Here the gutter is at rear of building where attractiveness matters little ➡ use maximum pitch of $\frac{1}{2}$ in/LF ➡ $\kappa_{\varDelta} = 0.204$.

w = minimum top width of gutter if it is an ogee or rectangular section, in. Here try $w = 4$ in. and solve for d.

d = min. depth of gutter if it is a rectangular section, ? in. $d \geq 3\frac{1}{2}$ in.

$2,850 \times 3 = 2,500 \times 2 \times 0.204 \times (4\,d)^{1.67}\,(3\,d)^{-0.67}$ ... $\delta = 1.73$ ➡ $3\frac{1}{2}$ in.

Example 3. A 12-story apartment in Dubuque, IA, has a 16 × 24 ft flat entrance canopy near the base of its front facade. If half-round gutters on each side of the canopy drain into downspouts at their back ends and the facade rises 135 ft above the canopy, size the gutters.

---

2)C)2)a)2) **Half-round section:** $W R = 390\,\eta\,\kappa_{\varDelta}\,\delta^{2.67}$

W = watershed area of roof drained by each gutter, sf. W = area of horizontal projection + 0.5 area of vertical projection if roof slopes + 0.5 vertical area of any facade above roof that drains into gutter. Roof is flat and drains on 2 sides ➡ 2 gutters. $W_{hor} = 16 \times 24/2 = 192$ sf. W_{ver} of wall above each roof gutter = $24/2 \times 135 = 1,620$ ft. ∴ $W = 192 + 0.5 \times 1,620 = 1,000$ sf.

R = maximum rainfall intensity, based on 50-year-frequency storm. From Fig. 2-9, R for eastern Iowa ≈ 4 in/hr.

$\kappa_{\varDelta}$ = gutter slope coefficient depending on its pitch, from bar graph on previous page. Here gutters are at side of canopy where attractiveness is neither a plus or minus; but the steeper the pitch, the smaller the gutter ➡ try maximum pitch of $\frac{1}{2}$ in/LF ➡ $\kappa_{\varDelta} = 0.204$.

η = number of leaders each gutter drains into. 1 leader at the gutter's back end ➡ $\eta = 2$.

δ = minimum width of semicircular gutter, ? in.

$1,000 \times 4 = 390 \times 2 \times 0.204 \times \delta^{2.67}$ ... $\delta = 3.34$ ➡ 4 in.

Note: Since an ogee section's width w is usually 4.5 in, formula 2)C)2)a)1) is commonly used to determine this section's number of leaders.

2.C.2.b. Leaders

Also called downspouts, leaders generally have round or rectangular sections with plain or corrugated profiles. The latter are more resistant to damage from freezing. Every gutter should have at least two leaders in case one is clogged, each should have a minimum section area of 7 in² for the first 100 sf of horizontal roof area and 1 in² for each added 100 sf, and leaders should not be more than 50 ft apart on any gutter. Any leader that is not vertical or nearly so should have its section area enlarged according to Formula 2.C.2.b.3. below. Other guidelines:

▶ Wide downspouts clog less easily than narrow ones.

▶ If a gutter is connected to its downspouts with sheet metal screws, flowing debris can catch on them; but if blind rivets are used they must be drilled out if the assembly ever needs to be taken apart for cleaning or painting. Instead, rivet the leader to the bottom art of the gutter's inlet flange, and screw the inlet flange's upper part to the gutter's bottom so the screw tips protrude from the gutter's underside. Use short screws and paint their tips if they will be unsightly.

▶ Use as few elbows as possible, have a long vertical run above each, and avoid slanting leaders if possible.

▶ Secure each leader to the building with a U-shaped holddown at its top, bottom, and at each floor level.

▶ Install basket strainers at the top of every downspout; especially if it empties into any subsurface piping below it.

Regarding interior downspouts: the inlet of each should be fitted with a strainer, the downspout diameter should be 1 in. larger than the gutter outlet diameter, and no wood or masonry or metal should touch the downspout's outer surface other than at structural supports. Both inlets and downspouts should be wrapped in double vapor barrier or equal and enclosed with 4 in. batt insulation to keep surface condensation and any subfreezing temperatures from damaging adjacent construction.

Roof runoff management doesn't end at the bottom of the leaders but only when the runoff is well away from the building. Under the base of leaders that drain small roof areas locate a metal or concrete splash pan. If this is unsightly or impractical, lay subsurface drain piping that conveys the water to an outfall at least 20 ft from the building. This piping should be large enough, steep enough, and smooth enough (flexible corrugated piping is a poor choice here as it collects silt) to keep silt and leafy debris from potentially clogging it. The outfall should empty into a pebbled or cobbled retainage area, its opening should be covered with mesh or porous cap that bars entry by vermin and is easily removable for cleaning, and the outfall should be accessible for servicing in deep snow.

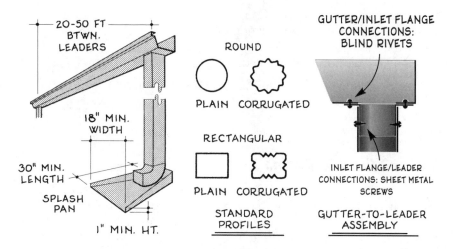

Fig. 2-11. Gutter leader details.

Example 1. A bank in Cripple Creek, CO, has a 62 × 46 ft flat roof that drains into a gutter with a round downspout at each end. What is the downspouts' diameter?

⌐2⌐C⌐2⌐b⌐1⌐ **Round sections:** $W R \approx 304\, \delta^{2.67}$ ... ⊕

   ⌐2⌐ **Rectangular sections:** $W R \approx 420\, (w\, d)^{1.33}$

W = watershed area of roof drained by each leader, sf. W = area of horizontal projection + 0.5 area of vertical projection if roof slopes + 0.5 vertical area of any surface above roof that drains onto it. Roof is drained by 2 leaders ➡ W = 62 × 46/2 = 1,430 sf.

R = maximum rainfall intensity, based on 50-year-frequency storm. From Fig. 2-9, R for central Colorado ≈ 3 in/hr.

δ = minimum diameter of round leader section, ? in. $d \geq 2.5$ in.

w = width of rectangular section, in. $b \geq 2$ in. Not applicable.

b = depth of rectangular section, in. $b \geq 2$ in. Not applicable.

$$1,430 \approx 28.5 \times 3 \times \delta^{2.67} \quad ... \delta = 2.88 \Rightarrow 3 \text{ in.}$$

Example 2. If part of the downspout in the above example slopes at a 6-in-12 pitch over a shed roof behind the bank's first floor, what is the downspout's minimum diameter above this area?

⌐2⌐C⌐2⌐b⌐3⌐ $A_p \approx A_v (1 + \cos^2 \angle)$

A_p = required section area of nonvertical leader, **?** in^2. $A_p \leq 2A_v$.
A_v = section area of vertical leader, in^2. From Step 1, d = 2.61 in.
∴ $A_v = 0.785\ d^2 = 0.785 \times 2.61^2 = 5.35$ in^2.
∠ = angle from horizontal of leader, °. ∠ = $\tan^{-1} {}^6/_{12}$ pitch = 26.6°.

$$A_p \geq 5.35\ (1 + \cos^2 26.6°) \geq 9.62 \text{ in}^2 \rightarrow 3.5 \text{ in. dia.}$$

2.C.2.c. Footing Drains

Every foundation wall below grade should be as waterproof as the hull of a boat. This is done by covering the wall's outer surface below grade with a layer of thick gooey asphalt laid on with a trowel —*not* the liquid kind that is painted on with a brush— down to the wall's base, over the top of the footing protruding below, and down the side of the footing down to its bottom edge. Then a minimum 4 in. diameter perforated drain should be laid completely around the building with its crown 4 in. below the floor inside the wall. The drain should slope at least $^1/_{16}$ in/ft both ways from its crown to a dry well or surface outfall some distance from the building, it should be covered with gravel 1 ft deep, and a wide strip of resin paper should be laid over the gravel to retard siltation around the drain. Failure to heed these strict guidelines is the chief cause of leaky basements. For these reasons, one of the most important occasions for an Æ designer to make a periodic inspection of the construction site is just before the foundation is backfilled. Otherwise, *caveat emptor.*

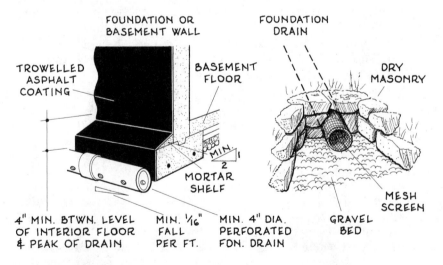

Fig. 2-12. Footing drain & outfall design details.

Several springs outside a shopping center basement wall have a water discharge rate of 70 gpm. If a PVC drain installed outside the footing slopes 1/8 in. fall/ft, what is the drain's minimum diameter?

2)C)2)c)1) $5.6 \, n \, Q = \kappa_{\varDelta} \, \delta^{2.67}$

n = roughness coefficient of footing drain. From Table 2-3, n for PVC piping = 0.010.

Q = water discharge rate into footing drain, 70 gpm

$\kappa_{\varDelta}$ = footing drain slope coefficient, depending on pitch, from Fig. 2-10 on page 38. At $^1/_8$ in/LF, $\kappa_{\varDelta}$ = 0.102.

δ = minimum diameter of footing drain, ? in. $\delta \geq 4$ in. dia.

$5.6 \times 0.010 \times 70 = 0.102 \times \delta^{2.67}$ ... $\delta \geq 8.2$ in. ➡ use 9 in.

2.C.2.d. Storm Drains

Waterflow collected by storm drains may include direct rainfall, water-flow from paved surfaces that arrived from other areas, overflow from ponds and other bodies of water, snowmelt from roofs, melting snow from spring thaws, subsoil waterflow from springs and seeps, foundation drainwater, pump or ejector drainage, and clearwater waste from industrial operations. These waterflows are quantified in three ways:

Runoff. Surface drainage of excess rainfall or snowmelt from a roof or area of terrain. Usually around 60–70 percent of a region's rainfall becomes runoff; but its flow may vary greatly according to the amount of rain-fall, type of ground cover, saturation and permeability of the underlying soil, slope of terrain, and horizontal area of drainage.

Discharge. Waterflow from such non-rainfall sources as under-ground springs, excavation seeps, dehumidifier and air-conditioner con-densate, pump and ejector drainage, and industrial operation wastes. Once the discharge's source is found, its flow is usually easy to measure.

Fixture unit waste. Drainage from spigots and other plumbing out-lets that do not empty into sewage or septic systems. Such flow may empty into turnaround drains, street gutters, storm drains, terrain depressions, and the like. One fixture unit ≈ 2 gpm ≈ 48 sf of horizontal area receiving 4.0 in/hr of rainfall.

After these flows have been quantified for a particular drainage area, an open or closed channel is usually sized to carry the flow to safe discharge areas such as stormwater retention basins and terrain depressions. If the largest flow is storm drainage, the chief measure of one's design is a severe 'superstorm' that is expected to occur at a certain interval based on empirical data: e.g. a 6 in/hr rainfall for 30 minutes every 50 years. But it is difficult to predict such storm drainage accurately because (1) the rainfall itself can't be predicted accurately; (2) it is difficult to determine the porosity of the soil hidden beneath the drainage area; (3) the water absorption of any foliage growing on the drainage area varies depending on its biology, season of year, and density of growth; (4) in northern latitudes the drainage may include snowmelt during spring thaws; and (5) normally porous soil may be fully saturated after recent rains. Indeed, analysis of all the great floods indicates that each resulted from prolonged rains that had thoroughly saturated normally porous soils until they were as impermeable as pavement. Thus, it is prudent to assign a porosity value of 1.0 for the subsoil of any drainage area whose overflow could endanger human welfare —but then, the channel might be so large that its initial cost would be unaffordable.

Regarding such conflicts, what are the optimal solutions? As a way of answering this question, the author describes an event that occurred on his property during the incredible rainfall of Hurricane Floyd in September 1999. Twenty-five years earlier, he had installed under his driveway a 36 in. diameter culvert that received the drainage from a 54 acre watershed of mature woodland forest, an environment that had the maximum water retentivity it could have. A few years later he converted a topographic depression beside his driveway into a one-third-acre pond whose outflow was over a small dam in front of the culvert. During this work the local Department of Environmental Conservation paid the site a visit, and after inspecting the premises ordered him to build a concrete channel spillway from another part the pond's edge; because, they said, if the pond ever overflowed, it could flood a neighborhood of houses downstream. At this time the author hadn't had the vaguest thought of building a spillway. But then he got to thinking: if any rainfall was so heavy that it would make the pond overflow, its erosive power could wash away a spillway too, especially if it was small. So, instead of building the recommended concrete spillway, he graded a nearly flat 50 ft-

TABLE 2-2: RUNOFF COEFFICIENTS FOR GROUND SURFACES [†]

GROUND SURFACE	Runoff coefficient, κ_R
Forests ..... 0.05–0.15; Saplings, orchards, chaparral	0.10–0.20
Gardens, lawns, meadows, ground cover	0.10–0.25
Gravel roads & walks	0.25–0.60
Loose block pavements with uncemented joints	0.40–0.50
Stone & brick pavements with uncemented joints	0.50–0.70
with tightly cemented joints	0.75–0.85
Asphaltic & concrete pavements in good condition	0.85–0.90
Watertight roof surfaces	0.95–1.00

[†] This table's values were abstracted from the *Standard Handbook of Engineering*

wide area extending from one side of the pond, covered the whole area with a 6 in. layer of softball-sized rocks, covered the rocks with 4 in. topsoil, then planted the topsoil with a ground cover of hardy grass —to create a meadow-like *soft-path spillway* that would spread the erosive power of any potential outflow gently over a 50 ft wide area. Subsequently, the biggest storm his pond ever experienced was a summer afternoon "50 year superstorm" of three severe thunderstorms in a row that filled the 36 in. culvert to within 6 in. of its top. That experience instilled in the author a smug sureness that he had designed his system well.

Then came "Flood Floyd" in September 1999. At this storm's intensity, not only was the 36 in. culvert was filled with thundering outflow, the pond spillway was under a 7 in. sheet of water that was 75 ft wide! Counting the filled culvert and the 7 in. × 75 ft section area of the spillway overflow, the system's overflow was *more than seven times its designed capacity for a 50 year superstorm!* The author's design had failed! Or had it? The next morning he surveyed the scene. The grassy spillway was lushly combed with leafy debris from the 54 acre forested watershed upstream. Amid the litter lay a 13 in. fish that a day before had dwelled in the quiet depths of the pond. Otherwise the grass and its environs were completely undamaged.

What lessons can be learned here? First, the worst storm an area may ever experience will likely be not just a little worse than the second-worst storm, but *much worse*! Thus wise design includes not only ample safety factors, but an orchestration of several soft-path methods that would minimize any damage that could conceivably result if failure did occur. Second, think of the Department of Environmental Conservation here: how many times when a government authority orders an owner or designer to do something, they whiningly resist, or piously apply for a variance, or fudge the drawings, or hide a Code violation in construction that can't be inspected, or otherwise devise a minimal design? But here the designer allowed the authority's order to give power to his imagination —to create a design that worked even better than they could have imagined. Third, think of the larger picture for a moment. What if this design scenario was not just a little pond in a little neighborhood, but a wide river sluicing with millions of cfm of waterflow that drained thousands of square miles of watershed, one with hundreds of thousands of people living along its banks? What then?

Below are several added guidelines for designing storm drains:

▶   Storm drain design requires analysis of watershed areas, discharge paths, recharge basins, erosion potential, ground cover regeneration, and limnological factors, for which topographic and foliage data of the drainage area are absolutely necessary.
▶   Soil retainability may be increased with landscaping, porous pavements, onsite infiltration, strips of ground cover alternating with areas of paving, etc.

- Storm and sanitary sewers should be designed for 0.8 full capacity. A pipe's hydraulic radius at 0.8 capacity = 2.26 r.
- A storm drain should slope steeply enough to remove deposits that may accumulate during periods of low flow.
- The minimum flow velocity in sanitary sewers is 2.0 fps, but 2.5 fps is better; this keeps solids from settling out of the fluid. The minimum flow in storm sewers 2.5 fps but 3.0 is better, because in them sand and grit usually enter the flow.
- The maximum flow in storm and sanitary sewers is 8 fps.
- Every storm drain should have a flared end section at the inflow end to guide runoff into it and one at the outflow end to minimize undercut erosion.
- Intersecting drains of different diameters should be laid crown-to-crown with the larger diameter on the downstream side.

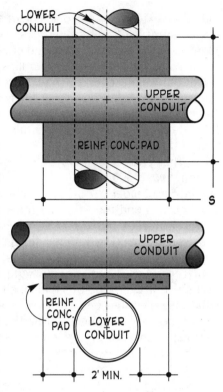

Fig. 2-13. Concrete pad between crossing storm drains.

A serious problem with storm drains occurs when they cross over or under water supply mains or any other plumbing waste piping, sanitary sewer, or storm drain. When such crossings cannot be avoided, a square concrete pad must be laid between the two conduits that is at least 8 in. deep, is centered over the vertical intersections of the pipes' centerlines, has sides that are at least 4 ft longer than the pipes' maximum diameters, and contains #4 rebars spaced 1'-0" o.c. each way. Technically the pad must be designed either to support the load of the upper conduit when full or to bridge the void of the lower conduit when empty; but the above specifications are adequate for all but very large conduits in soft soil.

Another perennial problem with storm drains is the groundwater that may enter its seams. If the conduit is below the surrounding soil's water table, such leaks are almost impossible to repair unless the conduit is large enough for a worker with a wheelbarrow to walk into. Even worse, any hole through which adjacent groundwater can leak into the conduit is a hole that its flow can leak out of —sometimes with calamitously erosive effect to the enveloping terrain. Even a minor defect in a storm drain's joinery can fail years later and create a sudden major problem in the community where the conduit is laid. Thus, ideally, after every multisectioned storm drain is laid, it should be given a compression test as is done with common household plumbing after it is installed. But we live in a practical world; so here the best we can usually do is to see that every joint is perfectly aligned and perfectly sealed —with cement if the pipe is masonry, with mastic if it is vitreous or plastic, with lead and oakum if it is cast iron; then loads of impermeable soil should be packed around every seam. Such installations are often so vital to public welfare that it is wise to have a certified inspector onsite at all times. Certainly one's salary would be minor compared to the money spent in laying the conduit or repairing any subsequent damage. Another reason for such careful joinery is that a storm drain often experiences so much thermal expansion due to the temperature differential between its flow and the enveloping subsoil that even perfect joinery will loosen after a few decades. Then all that can be said of "perfect work" is that it extends the life of the installation from the near to the far future.

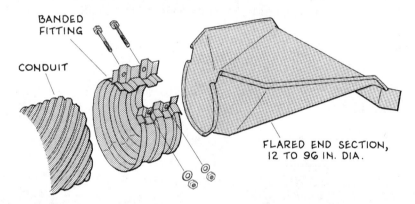

Fig. 2-14. Flared end section for storm drains.

Storm drain design generally proceeds as follows:

1. Draw longitudinal section profiles through the general ground area where the conduits will be installed.
2. Compile and analyze extensive subgrade data of surrounding soils, groundwater characteristics, local soil surface conditions, any nearby building foundations, and all underground utility services in the vicinity of the conduits that will be laid.
3. Draw a plan of the storm drainage system showing all inlets, mains, branches, and outlets with accompanying topographic references.
4. Size the system, link by link, from the inlets downstream to the outlet; then check that all flow rates are within acceptable limits.

Example 1. The 54 × 128 ft flat roof of an office near Atlanta, GA, is drained by four vitrified clay pipe leaders which empty beneath the building into a similar main carrying 82 fixture units of graywater waste. What diameters are required for the branches and the main?

2)C)2)d)1) $n(RW + 3.9\,F) = 11.7\,\kappa_\Delta\,\delta^{2.67}$

n = roughness coefficient of inner surface of conduit.
From Table 2-3, n for vitrified clay sewer pipe = 0.013.

R = maximum rainfall intensity, based on 50-year-frequency storm, in/hr.
From Fig. 2-9, R for Atlanta ≈ 4.5 in/hr.

W = watershed area drained by roof parking area, or other surface, horizontal sf. Roof area drained by each branch = 54 × 128/4 = 1,728 sf; area drained by the main = 54 × 128 = 6,912 sf.

F = number of fixture units, if any, emptying into conduit. 0 units empty into the branches and 62 units empty into the main.

κ_Δ = conduit slope coefficient depending on its pitch, from Fig. 2-10. As steep pitches may not be feasible beneath the building, use 0.125 in. ➡ κ_Δ = 0.102.

δ = minimum diameter of conduit, ? in.

Branch: $0.013\,(4.5 × 1,728 + 0) \approx 11.7 × 0.102 × 0.125^{0.5}$
$$\delta = 5.26 \text{ in.} \blacktriangleright 6 \text{ in.}$$

Main: $0.013\,(4.5 × 6,912 + 3.9 × 82) \approx 11.7 × 0.102 × 0.125^{0.5}$
$$\delta \approx 8.86 \text{ in.} \blacktriangleright 9 \text{ in.}$$

TABLE 2-3: ROUGHNESS COEFFICIENTS FOR CONDUITS [†]

PIPE OR CHANNEL SURFACE	Roughness coefficient, κ_R
Sheet steel, aluminum, or galvanized metal piping or ducting	0.009
Copper or steel pipe, neat cement, PVC other smooth plastic piping	0.010
Finished concrete, planed wood, cast iron	0.012
Vitrified sewer pipe, riveted steel pipe, unplaned wood	0.013
Unfinished concrete	0.014
Poorly jointed concrete pipe	0.015
Smooth brick	0.016
Rough brick, tuberculated iron pipe, smooth stone	0.017
Smooth earth, firm gravel	0.020
Rough earth, rubble	0.025
Laid untamped gravel	0.028
Muddy ditches & riverbeds with some stones & weeds	0.030
Earth with loose stones or weeds	0.035
Ditches & riverbeds with rough bottoms & thick vegetation	0.040

[†] This table's values were abstracted from the *Standard Handbook of Engineering*

Example 2. A grassy swale about 480 × 55 ft in size beside a 3.6 acre parking lot near Chicago requires culvert drainage under an entrance drive. If half the parking lot drains into the swale, which drains into an annular metal culvert that slopes at 1 in. fall/ft, size the culvert.

2)C)2)d)2) $n(R\,W_1\,\kappa_{P1} + R\,W_2\,\kappa_{P2} + \cdots + R\,W_z\,\kappa_{Pz} + 3.9\,F) = 11.7\,\kappa_\varDelta\,\delta^{2.67}$

n = roughness coefficient of inner surface of conduit. From Table 2-3, n for metal pipe with annular corrugations = 0.024.

R = maximum rainfall intensity. From Fig. 2-9, R for Chicago ≈ 4 in/hr.

W = watershed area drained by each kind of terrain or surface, sf. W_1 = area drained by parking lot = 0.5 × 3.6 × 43,560 = 78,400 sf. W_2 = area drained by swale = 480 × 55 = 26,400 sf.

κ_P = permeability factor for each terrain or surface drained, from Table 2-2. κ_{P1} for paved parking lot ≈ 0.90; κ_{P2} for grassy swale ≈ 0.25.

F = number of fixture units, if any, draining into conduit, 0 units.

$\kappa_\varDelta$ = conduit slope coefficient depending on its slope, from Fig. 2-10. Minimum slope = $\frac{1}{4}$ in/LF. Slope = 1 in/LF ➡ $\kappa_\varDelta$ = 0.289.

δ = minimum diameter of conduit, ? in.

$$4 \times 0.024 \times (0 + 78,400 \times 0.90 + 26,400 \times 0.25) \approx 11.7 \times 0.289 \times \delta^{2.67}$$
$$d \geq 17.8 \text{ ➡ } 18 \text{ in. dia.}$$

2.C.2.e. Drywells

A drywell is a covered pit with walls of open bricks or concrete blocks laid on their sides through which flows water discharged from roofs, basements, turnarounds, and the like. If the wall is brick, each horizontal pair has a 2–3 in. space between them and the areas of contact between vertical bricks is mortared. If the wall is concrete block, three-celled blocks should be used, and the blocks' inner corners should be mortared to rigidify the wall. After the wall is built, the space between it and the exposed excavated earth is filled with clean coarse gravel or crushed stone.

A drywell's effective absorption area is the cylindrical area of the edge of excavated earth between the top and bottom plane of the well's wall plus the floor area inside the wall; but the floor is usually omitted to simplify calculations and create a slight safety factor. Drywells should be at least 10 ft from septic tanks and lot lines, 20 ft from buildings, and 100 ft from water supply sources. Their bases must lie above the highest annual level of the local water table; they cannot accept toilet wastes; and they cannot be built in rock, hardpan, dense clay, or other soil whose permeability is less than 1 min/in. If soils of two or more permeabilities lie within the well's

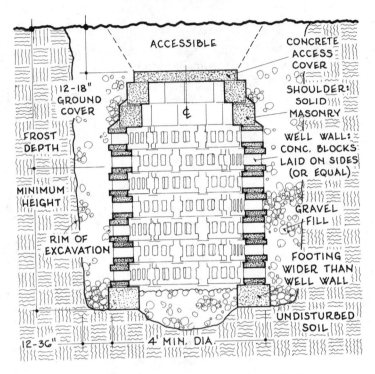

Fig. 2-15. Drywell construction details.

Labels in figure:
ACCESSIBLE
CONCRETE ACCESS COVER
12-18" GROUND COVER
SHOULDER: SOLID MASONRY
₵
FROST DEPTH
WELL WALL: CONC. BLOCKS LAID ON SIDES (OR EQUAL)
MINIMUM HEIGHT
GRAVEL FILL
RIM OF EXCAVATION
FOOTING WIDER THAN WELL WALL
UNDISTURBED SOIL
12-36"
4' MIN. DIA.

depth, their average permeability is found from

$$1/p_{aver} = A_1/p_1 + \dots + A_z/p_z$$

A six-unit apartment near St. Louis has four leaders draining from a 2,600 ft² roof into a drywell located near a rear corner of the building. If the property perc tests are 4 min/in. drop, what is the drywell's optimal size?

2)C)2)e) $W R \approx 188\, \delta\, h\, P$

W = roof or watershed area (1.0 horizontal + 0.5 vertical projection) drained by drywell, sf. Use roof area = 2,600 sf.

R = maximum rainfall intensity. in/hr. From Fig. 2-9, R for St. Louis ≈ 4.5 in/hr.

δ = diameter of drywell, measured at inner face of wall, ft. A good initial diameter to try is 5 ft.

h = minimum height of drywell, from local frost depth to base, ? in.

P = perc test result of surrounding soil, 4 min/in. drop.

$$2{,}600 \times 4.5 \ = \ 188 \times 5 \times h \times 4 \qquad ... \ h = 3.1 \ \text{ft}$$
Base of drywell = 3.1 ft + 2.5 ft local frost depth = 5.6 ft below grade

2.C.3. Flood Force

The damage that can be caused by even a small stream that has risen to flood stage is staggering. This is primarily because the erosive power of water relates to the fifth power of its speed. Thus if a stream's speed doubles, its erosive force is $2^5 = 32$ times greater; and if its speed quadruples, its erosive force is more than a thousand times greater. For example, take a peaceful woodland creek averaging 12 ft wide and 1 ft deep that flows at a barely perceptible one-half mile an hour. If very heavy rainfall —and perhaps some heedless site clearing upstream— turns this waterway into a floody torrent that is 60 ft wide and 12 ft deep and flows at 10 miles an hour, its erosive power is increased nearly 100,000,000 times. This is enough to tear centuries-old oaks from their deep-pile foundations along the banks and convert them into battering rams whose impact force depending on the water's sluice velocity may exceed the lateral resistance of vehicular bridge abutments.

When siting a building near a lake or stream, examine the land beyond the water's edge. If it slopes gently for a few yards from shore, then rises steeply a few feet, then becomes fairly level again, these contours may indicate the flood level of once-a-century superstorms. Then no building should be placed below the crest of the rise.

2.D. TEMPERATURE

Owing to changes in temperature, no part of a building is ever still. Such expansion and contraction not only creates problems in long exterior walls and large roofs, it can also cause trouble in large interior spaces if vacancies, blackouts, or acts of terrorism shut down a building's climate control system during very hot or cold weather.

To avoid damage to a building due to thermal movement, expansion joints are installed in any dimension exceeding about 100 ft. Although each such joint is designed primarily to accommodate thermal stress in a single direction, each must accommodate thermal movement, lateral shear, impact, and vibration loads from every direction. Each joint must also be able to move freely, must allow its elastic seal to expand when fully compressed, must not separate when fully extended, should never be painted, its surfaces sliding against each other must have low coefficients of friction, and its horizontal joints must not have slots that could fill with dirt or debris. An expansion joint must also be strong, watertight, sound-retarding, and resistant to decomposition by sunlight, ozone, winter maintenance chlorides, and abrasives. And every expansion joint should be field-adjusted for exact temperature when it is installed.

All this is a tall order for a thin piece of material. Fortunately, many expansion joints listed in Sweet's Catalogue do all the above jobs well. Some expand and contract as much as 6 in, and they have a wide variety of cross-sections such as elastomeric pads, accordion glands, fluted slip-plates, tongue-and-groove fittings, and steel springs.

When designing an expansion joint for a given temperature range, it is wise design to add 10° to the maximum temperature differential.

A 320 ft brick wall between two buildings has a maximum temperature of 140° F when exposed to summer sunlight and a minimum temperature of –30° F on a cold winter night. If the wall's expansion joints are 1 in. wide, how many should the wall have?

TABLE 2-4: THERMAL EXPANSION COEFFICIENTS

MATERIAL	Rate of exp., in/in ° F.	MATERIAL	Rate of exp., in/in ° F.
Brick	0.000,0035	Cement, Portland	0.000,0070
Concrete	0.000,0065	Glass	0.000,0047
Granite, slate	0.000,0040	Limestone	0.000,0038
Marble	0.000,0056	Plaster	0.000,0092
Sandstone	0.000,0044	Tile, structural clay	0.000,0033
Aluminum	0.000,0128	Copper	0.000,0098
Iron, cast	0.000,0059	Iron, wrought	0.000,0067
Lead	0.000,0157	Steel, structural	0.000,0067
Zinc, rolled	0.000,0173	Fiberglass	0.000,0098
Acrylics	0.000,0450	Polycarbonates	0.000,0375
Polyvinyl chloride (PVC)	0.000,0300	Chlorinated PVC	0.000,0340
Polyethylene	0.000,0900	ABS	0.000,0600
Polybutylene (PB)	0.000,0720		

WOODS expansion ‖ grain, in/in ° F.		WOODS expansion ⊥ grain, in/in ° F.	
Fir	0.000,0021	Fir	0.000,0320
Maple	0.000,0036	Maple	0.000,0270
Oak	0.000,0027	Oak	0.000,0300
Pine	0.000,0030	Pine	0.000,0190
Plywood	0.000,0034	Plywood	0.000,0034

Step 1. Compute the length of construction required for each joint.

2)D

$$\Delta_e = 12\,\kappa_t\,E\,(\Delta t + 8)$$

Δ_e = maximum length of increase in expansion joint, 1.00 in.
κ_t = coefficient of thermal expansion for construction between two
    expansion joints. From Table 2-4, κ for brick = 0.000,0035 in/in.
E = maximum length of construction between expansion joints, ? ft
Δt = temperature differential of construction, °F. 140° – (–30°) = 170° F.

$$1.00 = 12 \times L \times 0.000,0035 \times (170 + 8) \quad \ldots \quad L = 130 \text{ ft max.}$$

Step 2. Find the number of expansion joints required.

$$\eta = |(L/E) + \kappa_e + 1|$$

η = total number of expansion joints required in construction, ? units
L = total length of construction, 320 ft
E = maximum length of construction between expansion joints, from
    Step 1, 130 ft
κ_e = end factor. $\kappa_e = 0$ if the construction containing expansion joints
    abuts no construction at either end, 1 if it abuts construction at
    one end, and 2 if it abuts construction at both ends.
    As this wall exists between two buildings, $\kappa_e = 2$.

$$\eta = |(320/130) + 2 + 1| = |5.46| = 5 \text{ joints}$$

Note: To promote uniform thermal expansion throughout the construction, the joints should be placed at fairly even intervals. Thus in the wall above, a joint could be placed at each end and the remaining three joints spaced at, say, 320/3 ±10 percent = 96–118 ft intervals in the wall.

2.E. HEAT FLOW†

A comfortable indoor environment has a year-round temperature between about 67° F in winter and 77° F in summer. When outdoor temperatures range higher or lower, heat migrates through the building's envelope
(its outer surface formed by its lowest floor, exterior walls, and roof) from
the warmer area to the cooler. The greater the temperature difference
between the indoor and outdoor areas, the faster the heat flow; the thicker the thermal barrier between the two areas, the slower the heat flow. The
amount of heat flowing outdoors during the average coldest part of winter
—the *winter design temperature*— determines heating loads, while the
amount of heat flowing indoors during the average warmest part of summer

† The author's knowledge on the subject of this section was obtained largely

—the *summer design temperature*— determines cooling loads. These loads must be computed for a building's every interior area where human comfort is a priority before the building's heating and cooling systems can be sized: in large buildings, this may involve hundreds of calculations. As they are highly interrelated, this section's problems comprise a sequence that is generally followed from beginning to end to determine a building's total thermal loads. Then the resulting loads may be used to select and size the building's climate control systems as described in Chapter 3.

As heat flows through any portion of a building envelope, so does water vapor. Unfortunately, the moisture carries most of the heat. Even worse, as the moisture passes through the envelope's insulation from its warm side to its cold side, the moisture's temperature steadily lowers, until it often falls below the air's dewpoint whereupon its precipitates out of the air and condenses in the insulation, where it instantly reduces its ability to insulate and eventually can degrade this thermal barrier and the construction around it. Thus this moisture migration must be minimized, especially in warm humid regions. A common way to do this to install aluminum foil facing, polyethylene sheeting, or other water vapor barrier on the warm side of the insulation. Obviously in cold climates the warm side is on the interior side, and in cold climates it is on the exterior side. But what about temperate climates, where the average annual temperature is near 65° F? Then where does the barrier go? Whether inside or outside, it seems moisture will collect in the insulation during a good part of the year. The answers to this dilemma are few but finite: (1) in temperate climates use insulations that are least affected by water: styrofoam boards instead of batts if possible; (2) install imperfect vapor barriers so most of the moisture is kept out of the insulation while usually enough air travels through in the opposite direction soon afterward to remove what little moisture is there (this usually works well with foil-faced fiberglass insulation because each batt has a thin seam between each side and the adjacent wood framing that allows the batt to breathe a little); and (3) superinsulate whenever possible, as thicker insulation means less airflow means less waterflow means less condensation in the insulation.

There are four kinds of heat flow that affect a building's interior spaces, as described below:

Conduction of heat through the building envelope. This is heat migrating through the envelope construction and insulation. It is quantified by cataloguing the nature and thickness of every material that comprises every surface area of the envelope. It is reduced by installing thicker insulation, using smaller windows fitted with double glazing, surrounding facades with foliage, installing multizone controls in large floor areas and behind different facade orientations, and the like.

Convection of heat via air infiltration through seams and openings in the building envelope. Infiltration airflow is one of the most poorly understood aspects of architectural physics; thus its thermodynamics are explained here. The theory behind infiltration loss is that according to Boyle's Law, a gas's pressure × volume ÷ absolute temperature remains constant $(PV/T = \kappa)$. Thus as air temperature goes down, either its pressure or volume must go down; and because a region's air pressure varies only within a narrow barometric range, it is its volume that goes down. Thus cold air is denser than warm, because the same molecular mass has shrunk. Thus, normally, if the temperature inside a building is 70° F while the temperature outside is 0° F, the outdoor air is 13 percent denser than the indoor air; and this causes the outdoor air to press against every seam and crack and pore in the building's envelope in an effort to equalize the pressure of the indoor air. Thus, according to Boyle's Law, *infiltration airflow varies directly according to the temperature differential between indoors and outdoors.* So if it is a nice spring day and the temperature on both sides of a building envelope is 68°, the infiltration airflow through the envelope is not "0.5 airchanges per hour of the building's interior volume" —as one 'authoritative' text on this subject has stated— but zero! Because if you have no ΔT you have no infiltration airflow. Similarly, if it is –20° F outside the building and a snuggly 70° inside, again the infiltration airflow is not "0.5 airchanges per hour of the building's interior volume" but probably twice this amount. Thus, according to Boyle's Law, a building's infiltration heat loss *must be a function of a specific temperature to be meaningful.* Accordingly, the building air infiltration losses listed in this text's Table 2-6 are based on an outdoor design temperature of 20° F. Then if a building's infiltration heat loss is computed at an indoor temperature of 65° and the outdoor design temperature is other than 20°, the building's actual number of air changes per hour of infiltration airflow = $(65 - T_o)/(65 - 20)$ × no. AC/hr from Table 2-6. This algebra accurately estimates the infiltration heat loss for a building in any climatic region.

A building's infiltration air loss is also difficult to quantify due to the following additional variables:

▸   The amount of heat conveyed in infiltration airflow varies according to the relative humidity at the moment of airflow.
▸   The velocity of any wind blowing around a building greatly affects its infiltration airflow heat losses. Winds create a positive net pressure against a building's windward facade, a negative net pressure against its lee facade, and a slightly negative net pressure on any facades perpendicular to the windflow due to the aerosol effect; and these values change with every frequent shift in the wind's speed and direction.
▸   Since hot air rises (due to its lighter density as described above), even a one-story building will experience more infiltra-

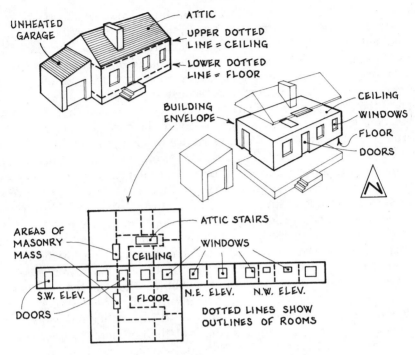

Fig. 2-16. Residential envelope spreadsheet.

tion airflow at its top than its base.
▶ The introduction of fresh air into the HVAC system of a commercial building unravels any effort to equate the above-listed variables. This is also true of any industrial processes that draw in or release outdoor air during its operation.
▶ In an occupancy that has a fireplace or furnace flue, warm air flowing up the flue during winter also unravels any efforts to equate the variables listed above.

Altogether, the above aberrations render almost meaningless any effort to quantify infiltration heat losses in a building. Still, a formula that is only slightly accurate —especially if its vagaries are known—is better than one that is less so. Beyond this, infiltration heat flow through a building envelope is reduced by sealing all envelope seams, using nonporous construction materials (e.g. plaster instead of drywall), installing buffered entries, and the like. The colder the climate, the more cost-effective these measures are.

Auxiliary heat gain radiated within the building envelope via occupants' metabolism and Btus emitted from lights and machines. The amount of this internally generated heat is often considerable, and thus

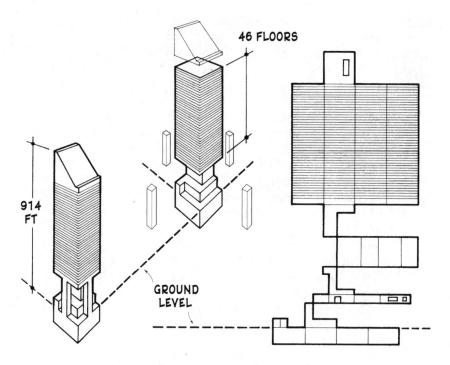

Fig. 2-17. Office envelope spreadsheet.

should be included in any thermal heat flow calculation. It is obviously desirable in cold weather and undesirable in warm. In warm weather it may be reduced by installing efficient lighting and machinery, using occupancy sensors that turn off heating and lighting when a space is vacant, isolating and reducing the output of heat-producing industrial processes, installing exhaust fans that remove heat from its source before it spreads to adjacent areas, incorporating total management systems that administrate energy flow in a building, and the like.

Solar heat gain arriving through areas of glazing in the building envelope. This heat flow is also desirable in cold weather and undesirable in warm. It is controlled by installing movable insulation inside any glazing exposed to the sun, constructing overhangs and other sunshields outside such glazing, giving floorplans efficient configurations and optimal orientations, surrounding the building with deciduous foliage, and the like.

Heat flow calculations may be *design temperature* or *energy audit*. The first are used to size heating and cooling systems, and the second are used to estimate the energy cost of a proposed system or compare two or more such systems. Performing either calculation requires local climatic data. If this is unavailable, the U.S. Department of Commerce offers monthly degree-day data for nearly 300 U.S. cities in its publication, *Comparative Climatic Data*, which may be purchased from the National Climatic Data Center, 151 Patton Ave, Asheville, NC 28801; (704) 271-4800. Even if local climatic data is available, microclimatic conditions for a particular building site may differ from reported data, as the latter is often obtained at a local airport, not down at the lakeshore or near a hilltop.

An organized way to perform thermal calculations is to begin with a *building envelope spreadsheet*. This involves mentally peeling away all architectural appendages —chimneys, cornices, attics, entrance canopies, crawlspaces, garages, and the like— down to the building's outer skin of occupied spaces, then arranging the skin as a foldout drawing that is used to enter thermal data related to each surface. Figs. 2-16 and 2-17 show how such a spreadsheet may be prepared for a small residence and a large commercial building.

Perhaps "average" rarely has less meaning than when it comes to computing a building's heating and cooling loads, because most of the unknowns vary so greatly. Thus, often the more detailed this work becomes, the more *in*accurate may be the results. Therefore, as one uses the detailed guidelines of this section to track every Btu migrating through a building envelope, be ever mindful that a conceptually simpler approach may lead to equally accurate results and be quicker besides.

2.E.1. Insulation

Since any undesired heat loss or gain through a building envelope is an economic loss, architectural materials that impede heat flow are commonly installed in building envelopes. These materials' selection is based on relative values such as C (thermal conductivity), K (thermal conductance), U (heat flow coefficient), and R (thermal resistance). The first three terms describe the speed at which heat migrates through a given material, while R, being the reciprocal of these terms, describes a material's ability to *resist* heat flow. Thus, because it is resistance that you want, a material's "R value" is generally the most conceptually appropriate term to use in thermal calculations. Also, a material's R-value increases linearly as its thickness or insulation ability increases, while the other terms have a high-low relation that can be confusing.

Other thermodynamic considerations influence the choice of insulation and its supporting construction, as described below:

▶ **Perimeter Heat Flow.** When many small pieces of insulation are fitted into a network of construction (as within the studs and plates of a wood stud wall), the pieces of construction forms a "thermal grille," much like the fins on a motorcycle motor, through which heat migrates more swiftly than it does through the insulated areas. If such construction is excessive, the insulation's effectiveness is largely negated.

▶ **Surface air film.** A thin film of insulating air covers the inner and outer exposed surfaces of the building envelope. The rougher the surfaces and the less exposed they are to prevailing winds, the thicker the airfilm and the slower the heat flow through the envelope.

▶ **Moisture.** Whenever moisture collects within the building envelope, it must be removed or it will degrade the construction. Thus a little air infiltrating through the envelope is usually desirable. Indeed, it is often wiser to omit the vapor barrier and compensate for its absence with thicker insulation.

2.E.1.a. Types of Insulation

Insulation is generally made as *batts*, *boards*, and *fills*. Each is described below. Standard insulation R values are listed in Table 2-5.

Batts

These are fluffy masses of spun glass that are usually fitted snugly into the voids of wood frame construction. The batts are $14\frac{1}{2}$ in. wide for members spaced at 16 in. o.c. and $22\frac{1}{2}$ in. wide for members 24 in. o.c. Batts resist heatflow most efficiently if compressed slightly and no air voids remain along their sides or corners.

➕ Economical, effective. Small pieces may be stuffed into any size void. Effective as acoustic insulation.

➖ Loses its R value if saturated with moisture. Must be completely enclosed as its fibers are a particulate air pollutant.

Boards

These are plywood-like sheets of rigid foam or fiber attached to walls or roofs or laid under concrete floor slabs. A few popular foams in ascending order of R value (usually at increasing price) are beadboard, styrofoam, urethane, and isocyanurate. A thin layer of styrofoam is often installed behind aluminum siding. Two fiberboards are Celotex® and corkboard; their R values are lower than foams.

● Won't decompose when placed in contact with earth; thus they are excellent below-grade insulations. Styrofoam, urethane, and iso-cyanurate have high R values and are surprisingly strong; each will support a surface load of 3,000 psf, thus they are acceptable insu-lation under some interior loadbearing walls.

● Most foam insulations emit volumes of poisonous gasses when exposed to fire; thus they should not be installed indoors.

Fills

These are usually granules poured into small construction voids such as cells in concrete blocks, but they may also be foams placed in uninsulated wall cavities in old buildings by inserting a nozzle through a hole in a fin-ished surface, then patching the hole afterward.

● Often the economical choice in unusually shaped or highly inac-cessible locations.

● Any obstructions within the construction cavity create a void in the insulation, an unknown and unremediable situation.

Regarding the most eco-nomical thickness of insulation, a common misconception cur-rently exists as exemplified by the graph shown in Fig. 2-18, which actually appeared in a respected engineering journal.[†] The caption under the graph said, "The most economical thickness of insulation for a given project is based on the cost of the insulation and the cost of energy." This graph indi-cates that by adding the Y-axis values of insulation and local energy costs anywhere along the X-axis, one may obtain the insu-lation's life-cycle cost for any thickness; then by plotting these

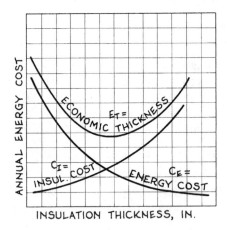

Fig. 2-18. Economic thickness of insulation: Part 1.

values for a number of thicknesses one may obtain the insulation's trough-shaped "economic thickness" profile, whose optimal thickness (e.g. 6 in. for a residence's exterior walls) as indicated by the bottom of the trough is the most economical, and that any greater or lesser thickness will have diminishing returns during the life of the construction.

However, this graph has three flaws. (1) As the unit cost of insulation usually decreases as its thickness increases (e.g. if 4 in. batts cost $1.00 per sf of area then 10 in. batts will cost somewhat less than $2.50 per sf of area), the *insulation cost* line should not sag downward as in Fig. 2-18 but should bulge upward as shown in the second graph shown in Fig. 2-19. This alone would flatten the *economic thickness* curve slightly and push its trough further to the right, thus indicating a greater optimal thickness. (2) Insulation cost is a *present cost* while energy cost is a *future cost*, and if the latter rises considerably during the life of the construction, the total cost of energy flowing through the insulation will be correspondingly greater than the insulation's initial cost; then the *energy cost* line would slope more steeply. (3) It is not the *annual energy cost* that is relevant here but the *total energy cost* during the life of the construction; thus the total energy savings realized by thicker insulation during this period would be still greater than its initial cost even if the latter remained stable over time.

Thus the graph's *energy cost* line should be positioned higher still, as appears in the second graph in Fig. 2-19. This would cause this graph's *economic thickness* line to have an entirely different profile, as indicated by its 'revised E_T' line. This final line indicates that the insulation's optimal thickness is much more than what was originally thought —that especially in cold regions you can't put enough insulation in a building's roof and outer walls; that in reality long-term economy depends on other factors, chiefly any increased cost of construction that may be required to house the thicker insulation.

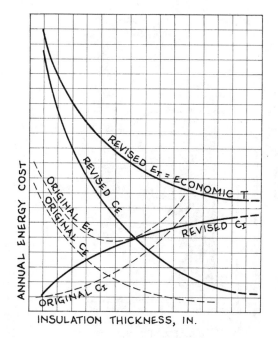

Fig. 2-19. Economic thickness of insulation: Part 2.

Engineer magazine (Cahners Publishing Co., Des Plaines, IL); Jan. 1995, p. 104.

2.E.1.b. Superinsulation

As a result of the Energy Crisis of the late 1970s, architects found that by increasing the thickness of insulation in a building's walls from the then-standard 4 inches to 10 inches or more, the building's life-cycle energy costs would be significantly reduced. Unfortunately, no cost-effective method of actually building such superinsulated walls ever gained popularity in this country. However, during that time the author developed the *Insulation Cage*, a superinsulated wall that is simple to build, economical, requires no new tools or techniques, and is even an improvement on contemporary construction methods in several ways. It is described below.

The Insulation Cage is a wood frame construction that includes an outer 2×4 bearing wall, an inner 2×3 nonbearing wall, and a 3½ in. air-space between. Thus the Cage's actual thickness = 3½ in. outer wall + 3½

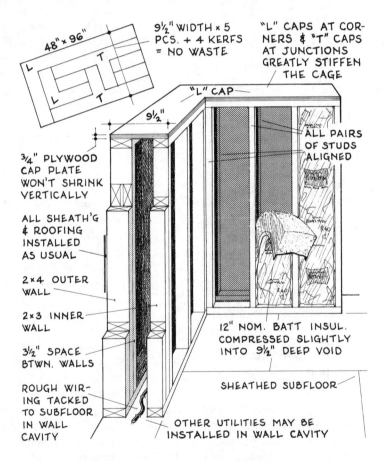

Fig. 2-20. The Insulation Cage.

in. airspace + 2½ in. inner wall = 9½ in. This construction has three advantages over other superinsulation wood framing. (1) The Cage can be built with the same tools and skills used for wood framing. (2) Its outer and inner walls can be built separately and, as each is light, can be raised quickly. (3) The 2×10s normally used as cap plates on a 10 in. nom. wall are replaced by 9½ in. wide strips of ¾ in. plywood, which alone has ten advantages: (1) the ¾ in. plywood top plate is lighter and easier to handle than the 2×10; (2) the plywood's laminated ¾ in. thickness is actually stronger across its width than a 2×10; (3) five 9½ in. wide pieces of plywood can be cut from one 48 in. wide sheet at absolutely no waste counting the four ⅛ in. saw kerfs in each 48 in. width; (4) L-shaped and T-shaped cap plates can be cut easily and fitted perfectly onto the framing's L and T corners, which automatically aligns and strengthens these structural intersections; (5) the flat plywood caps won't shrink vertically over time; (6) after the cap plates are nailed down all sheathing and roofing proceed exactly as normal; (7) when the electricians arrive they can lay their wiring directly on the floor in the 3½ in. wide space between the Cage's outer and inner walls instead of drilling holes in every stud (which weakens them), then laboriously pulling the wiring through each one; (8) the 3½ in. void between the walls facilitates other utility installations in the Cage; (9) since each pair of 16 in. o.c. studs in the two walls are aligned to create a series of neat rectangular voids between the studs, 12 in. batts of insulation can be tucked snugly into these 9½ in. deep voids (batts are more thermally efficient if compressed slightly); and (10) all interior finishes are applied to the insides of the 2×3 studs exactly as with normal 2×4 framing.

Thus the Insulation Cage contains 12-in-10 in. of superinsulation and the 3½ in. airspace between the two walls breaks perimeter heat flow. Indeed, this wall is so thermally superior that the usual poly vapor barrier may be omitted —more labor eliminated— which further extends the wall's life by letting it breathe better. And the Cage is stronger and more rigid than that of any 2×6 framing at little extra cost.

2.E.2. Conduction & Infiltration Heat Flow

Conduction is heat gained or lost through the building envelope's solid surfaces while infiltration is heat gained or lost through any openings such as pores, cracks, flues, and vents. Since both heat flows are functions of the building's indoor/outdoor temperature differential, their calculations may be combined. Design heating or cooling loads that are computed to size climate control systems are *design temperature* calculations, while design heating or cooling loads computed for a period of time, usually a month or a heating or cooling season, are *energy auditing* calculations. Winter and summer design temperatures are considered to occur at 7:00 A.M. on Jan. 21 and 3:00 P.M. on July 21. A little-known fact about these dates is that, on the average for most U.S. localities, around Jan. 21 is when half the winter degree-days are usually experienced during each winter season and around July 21 is when half the summer degree-days are usually experienced during each summer season. Thus these dates can be said to represent the statistical halfway mark for each winter and summer season: i.e. winter is "half over" on about Jan. 21, and summer is "half over" on about July 21.

Below is a rudimentary heat flow equation that may be used for quickly estimating the conduction heat loss or gain through a building envelope for purposes of preliminary design. Surprisingly it can be nearly as accurate as far more detailed and time-consuming analysis.

$$\Sigma H \text{ or } \Sigma C = (T_i - T_o) \left(\frac{\text{Surface area of building envelope}}{\text{Average } R \text{ value of building envelope}} \right)$$

2.E.2.a. Design Heating Load

A 24 × 40 ft two-story residence near Albany, NY, is nestled into an evergreen-forested hill rising to the northwest, the direction of prevailing winds. Its thermopane windows and exterior doors are weatherstripped, its outer walls and upper ceiling have a vapor barrier between the framing and interior sheetrock finish, all utility penetrations are sealed, and light fixtures are not recessed. The roof is asphalt shingle on plywood sheathing on Warren trusses 24 in. o.c., with 10 in. nom. batt insulation above the ceiling, and attic access is by a pulldown ceiling staircase. If the rooms are standard height, what is the design conduction-infiltration heating load through the second floor ceiling?

2)E)2)a) **Step 1.** Find the thermal resistance of each surface area of the building envelope depending on its construction, as follows:

    a. **Envelope has one construction type and no unheated voids:**

$$R = R_c + R_i t$$

    b. **Envelope has more than one construction type:**

$$A R = A_1 (R_{c1} + R_{i1} t_1) + \dots + A_Z (R_{cZ} + R_{iZ} t_Z)$$

    c. **An unheated void (attic, garage, etc.) is between the indoors and outdoors:**

TABLE 2-5: INSULATING VALUES OF BUILDING MATERIALS [†]

R-VALUES OF BUILDING MATERIALS

MATERIAL   Thermal resistance, R per in. thickness

Fiberglass batts	3.5	Mineral wool loose fill	3.3
Styrofoam boards	5.0	Urethane or isocyanate boards ..	6.5
Vermiculite loose fill	2.1	Tripolymer foam	4.5
Roof deck slabs	2.6	Sawdust or shavings	2.2

Reflective surface on batts or boards (exposd to min. $\frac{1}{2}$ in. airspace) +2.0
Mineral fiberboard, core or roof insulation, acoustic tile, perlite 2.7
Oak, maple, other hardwoods 0.9   Plywood, fir, pine, other softwoods 1.3
Granite, marble, other hard stones 0.06
Soft stones, sand, clay tile, concrete block, face brick 0.11
Gypsum, plaster, stucco, cement, common brick, hollow clay tile 0.20
Roofing: asphalt, roll roofing, or built-up roofing on plywd sheathing 1.5
$\frac{1}{2}$ in. slate only .... 0.05;   Sheet metal only ...... negl
Siding, shingles, $7\frac{1}{2}$ in. exposure .... 0.9;   w/ insulated backing .. +0.5
Glazing: single pane 2 .... 1.7/unit;   plus storm windw ... 2.8/unit
Glazing: thermopane, $\frac{3}{16}$ in. airspace 1.3; $\frac{1}{2}$ in. airspace 1.5
   Above w/ low -E coating: $E_{0.60}$ .... +0.2; $E_{0.20}$ .... +0.7
   Above w/ insect screens over openable windows .... +1.5
Doors: wood solid-core, 1 in. thick .... 1.6; $1\frac{1}{4}$ in. thick 1.8
   $1\frac{1}{2}$ in. thick .... 2.0;   2 in. thick 2.3
   $1\frac{3}{4}$ in. steel w/ mineral fiber core ... 1.7;   w/ urethane core 2.5
      Above w/ metal storm door .... + 1.1;   w/ wood storm door .... +1.7
Flooring: $\frac{1}{8}$ in. asphalt or linol. tile 0.05; $\frac{1}{8}$ in. cork tile 0.3
   1 in. ceramic tile or terrazzo ..... 0.08; $\frac{3}{4}$ in. hardwood 0.7
   Concrete, 4 in. on 4 in. gravel, no insulation below 0.6
Carpet: synthetic, $\frac{1}{4}$ in. thick .... 1.0;   Each added $\frac{1}{4}$ in. T .... +0.4
   Above w/ $\frac{1}{4}$ in. mat, foam, or rubber waffle under ... +0.7; $\frac{1}{2}$ in. .. +1.5
   Above if wool .... multiply above values × 1.5
   Above w/ 2 in. styrofoam below ...... 11;   w/ 4 in. styrofoam below 21
Airspaces, $\frac{3}{4}$–4 in.: vert. or hor. heat flow up, 0.8; hor. heat flow down 1.1

PERIMETER HEAT FLOW FRACTIONS

CONSTRUCTION P per envelope surface

Concrete floor slab, rigid insulation under & around edges 0.93
Masonry wall, rigid insulation inside, outside, or between withes 0.95
Concrete block wall, cavities filled w/ loose insulation 0.68
Curtain walls: glazing .... 1.20;   spandrels 0.77
Wood stud wall, batts in cavities ... 0.77;   w/ rigid insul. outside 0.83
Metal stud wall, batts in cavities ... 0.80;   w/ rigid insul. outside 0.87
Stud wall w/ much glass or doors ... 0.30;   w/ rigid insul. outside 0.50
Wood or metal stud wall, cavities empty, rigid insulation on outside .. 0.93
Wood or metal frame roof, batts in cavities, 0.86; rigid insul. on top . 0.89
Concrete roof w/ rigid insulation on top 0.93
Roof or ceiling insulation w/ large skylight, flue, or hatch area 0.42
Wood frame floor above crawlspace or unfin. basement w/ stair entry ... 0.83
   Large windows ... 1.10;   Large doors (garage doors, etc.) 1.05
Wood frame construction w/ no insulation 1.00

[†] The primary source for this table's values was *Time-Saver Standards for*

$$R = R_c + R_i t + R_o \qquad \dots \oplus$$

R = total thermal resistance of building envelope, ? units

$R_{c\,1,\,c2,\,c3\dots cZ}$ = unit R-value of each uninsulated envelope const.: $R_u \approx 3$ if roof, wall, or wood floor; 2 if conc. floor; 1 if glazing. Here $R_u \approx 3$.

$R_{i\,1,\,i2,\,i3\dots iZ}$ = unit R-value of each envelope insulation, if any, per in. thickness. From Table 2-5, R of batts/in. thickness = 3.5.

$t_{1,\,2,\,3\dots Z}$ = thickness of each envelope insulation, in. 10 in. nom. = 9.5 in.

A = surface area of total envelope construction, sf. Not applicable.

$A_{1,\,2,\,3\dots Z}$ = surface area of each type of envelope construction if more than one, sf. Not applicable.

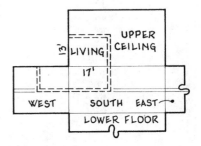

Fig. 2-21. Partial envelope spreadsheet of building.

R_o = R-value of second part of envelope if unheated void is between indoors and outdoors. R of outer roof ≈ 3.

$$R \approx 3 + 3.5 \times 9.5 + 3 \approx 39.3$$

Step 2. Find the temperature at the outer surface of the envelope:

a. Envelope is above fin. grade (if grade is sloping, use average height of exposure):

$$T_o \approx 65 - \kappa_w (65 - T_d) \qquad \dots \oplus$$

b. Envelope is a wall below finished grade down to 20 ft:

$$T_o \approx T_a - \kappa_d (T_a - T_d)$$

c. Envelope is a floor area within 20 ft of finished grade, measured down wall and in under floor from ground level:

$$T_o \approx T_a - \kappa_{ad} (T_a - T_d)$$

d. Envelope is a wall or floor area more than 20 ft below finished grade, measured down and in from ground level:

$$T_o \approx T_a$$

e. Envelope is floor area above unfinished basement or crawlspace:

$$T_o \approx T_i + 9 - \kappa_w (T_i - T_d)$$

T_o = effective air temperature at outer surface of envelope, ? °F

Architectural Design Data; John Callender, Editor (McGraw-Hill, New York, 1974);

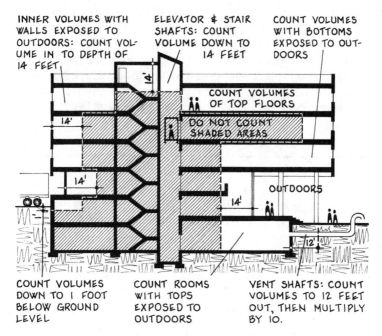

INNER VOLUMES WITH
WALLS EXPOSED TO
OUTDOORS: COUNT VOL-
UME IN TO DEPTH OF
14 FEET

ELEVATOR & STAIR
SHAFTS: COUNT
VOLUME DOWN TO
14 FEET

COUNT VOLUMES
WITH BOTTOMS
EXPOSED TO OUT-
DOORS

COUNT VOLUMES
OF TOP FLOORS

DO NOT COUNT
SHADED AREAS

OUTDOORS

COUNT VOLUMES
DOWN TO 1 FOOT
BELOW GROUND
LEVEL

COUNT ROOMS
WITH TOPS
EXPOSED TO
OUTDOORS

VENT SHAFTS: COUNT
VOLUMES TO 12 FEET
OUT, THEN MULTIPLY
BY 10.

Fig. 2-22. Building interior air changes per hour.

TABLE 2-6: BUILDING INTERIOR AIR CHANGES PER HOUR [1]

TYPE OF SPACE	Single glass, no weatherstrip	Storm sash or weatherstrip
No windows or exterior doors	0.7	——
One room surface exposed to outdoors	1.2	0.8
2 room surfaces " " " 1.6, 1.1; 3 room surfaces " " "		1.9, 1.3
Entrance halls	2.0	1.4
Small rooms w/ large openings	multiply above amount × 1.2	
Ceilings & outer walls w/ plaster (not sheetrock) interior finish, stucco exterior finish, or vapor barrier	multiply above amount × 0.4	
Rooms having exterior walls w/ all seams and utility penetrations sealed and/or top floor ceilings w/ insulation on top of interior walls and/or no recessed illumination.	multiply above amount × 0.7	
Unopenable glass	multiply above amount × 0.7	
Awning or casement windows	multiply above amount × 0.9	
Rooms w/ HVAC ducts outside bldg. envelope	add 0.3 to above amounts	
Fireplace: loose damper	add 2,500 ft³/V to above total	
Tight damper or glass doors	add 1,000 ft³/V to above total	
Woodstove: non-airtight envelope	add 1,500 ft³/V to above total	
Airtight envelope	add 300 ft³/V to above total	

1. When using this table, do not count shaded interior volumes in Fig. 2-22.

κ_w = windchill exposure factor. Building is on evergreen-forested hill-side rising to NW, envelope is well-shielded from winds ➡ from Table 2-7, κ_w for roof = 1.03.

T_d = winter design temperature, °F. From Fig. 2-24, T_d for Albany = -3° F.

T_a = average annual temp. for region, from Fig. 2-23. Not applicable.

κ_d = depth coefficient, based on maximum depth of soil d (ft) at bottom of envelope surface, according to the bar graph below:

Maximum depth of soil at bottom of envelope, ft

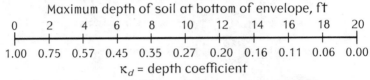

κ_d = depth coefficient

κ_{ad} = depth coefficient, based on average depth of soil d (ft) at bottom edge of envelope. Find maximum depth of soil d (ft) at bottom of envelope surface, then enter 0.5 d in bar graph above to find κ_{ad}.

T_i = ambient indoor temperature, deg F.

$$T_o \approx 65 - 1.03 [65 - (-3)] = -5° F$$

Step 3. Compute the design heating load through the envelope.

$$\mathbf{H}_{ci} = (A/R\, P + 0.018\ V\eta)\ (T_i - T_o)$$

$\mathbf{H}_{ci}$ = design heating load due to conduction-infiltration through area of envelope construction during cold weather, **?** Btu/hr

A = surface area of envelope construction, sf.
  Area of upper story ceiling = 40 × 24 = 960 sf.

R = thermal resistance of building envelope. From Step 1, R = 39.3.

P = perimeter heat flow fraction, a heat flow adjustment for const. types. From Table 2-5, P for frame roof w/ batt insulation = 0.86.

V = volume of room(s) behind envelope, cf. From Fig. 2-22, count volumes of top floors. $V \approx 40 \times 24 \times 8 \approx 7,700$ cf.

η = no. airchanges/hr for room behind envelope. η = 0.022 $(T_i - T_o)$ × no. airchanges/hr from Table 2-6. Since building is small, most 2nd floor rooms have a side wall + end wall + ceiling (3 surfaces) exposed to outdoors. ∴ from Table 2-6, weather-stripped openings:

Rooms w/ 3 surfaces exposed to outdoors 1.3
Ceilings & outer walls w/ plaster interior finish, stucco exterior finish, poly vapor barrier, or Tyvek® wrapping ...... multiply above amount × 0.4
Rooms having exterior walls with all seams & utility penetrations sealed & top floor ceilings w/ insulation on interior walls & recessed illumination .... multiply above amount × 0.7

$$\eta = 0.022 [65 - (-5)] \times 1.3 \times 0.4 \times 0.7 = 0.55$$

T_i = ambient indoor air temperature, usually the thermostat setting, °F. For general comfort occupancies (homes, hotels, offices, etc.) T_i =

65–75°; for retail (stores, supermarkets, banks, beauty shops, etc.) T_i = 63–73°; for assembly (auditoriums, restaurant, churches, bars, etc.) T_i = 68–75°; for industrial (assembly lines, fabrication areas, machinery areas, and mechanical equipment rooms for any occupancy) T_i = 60–70°. Use lower values where energy efficiency is a priority. Here assume $T_i \approx 65°$.

T_o = effective air temperature at outer surface of envelope construction, °F. From Step 2, T_o = -5° F.

$$\mathbf{H}_{ci} \approx (960/39.3 \times 0.86 + 0.018 \times 7{,}700 \times 0.55)[65 - (-5)]$$
$$\mathbf{H}_{ci} \approx 7{,}300 \text{ Btu/hr}$$

The next few pages show several tables and graphs that are used for estimating heating and cooling loads.

The Windchill Factor Table at right measures the influence of windspeeds on effective temperatures just outside a building's facades and roof. The more exposed these surfaces are to local winds, the lower the effective temperature just outside.

The *Average Annual Temperature (AAT) map* of Fig. 2-23 is useful in several ways. First, the ground temperature 20 ft below grade is about the same as the local AAT all year round; thus summer and winter temperatures just outside any below-grade portion of a building will orient toward this thermal norm more than above-ground temperatures; so the deeper a building is nestled in the ground, the more the temperature of its

TABLE 2-7: WINDCHILL FACTORS

CONDITION	Exposure factors [1]
ENVELOPE IS: Well-shielded: solid wind screen around whole surface	1.03 / 1.0
Mostly shielded: few openings in surrounding wind screen	1.10 / 1.05
Partly shielded: ± 50% gaps in surrounding windscreen	1.15 / 1.10
Mostly exposed: little protection from direct or diagonal winds	1.3 / 1.15
Highly exposed: Facade or roof on exposed hill; or upper part of tall building	1.6 / 1.3

1. Numbers beside buildings are for walls, numbers above them are for roofs.

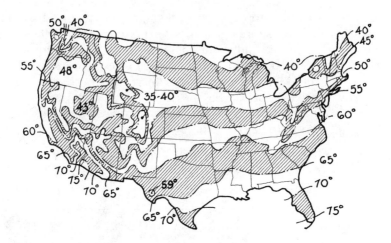

Fig. 2-23. Average annual temperature map. [†]

lowest rooms will approach the local AAT. In cooler regions, the earth surrounding such interiors may insulate them in winter and keep them cool in summer; but in regions with perennially high humidity, the cooler walls and floors below grade may cause the moisture in the air to condense on their surfaces and grow mildew if the moisture isn't removed by dehumidifiers or air conditioning. In warm regions where the AAT is above 65°, the ground beneath a building has little cooling power in summer, but during cold winter weather the surrounding earth can help keep the spaces above warm. This heat flow is promoted by making the bottom floor a concrete slab on grade with 4 in. styrofoam insulation laid beneath it several ft in from its

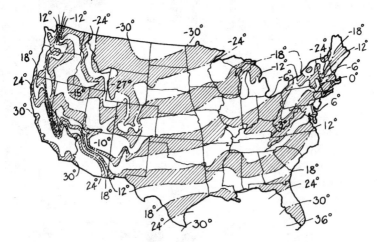

Fig. 2-24. Winter design temperature map.

[†] This map graph first appeared in the *Ecological House*, Robert B. Butler (Mor-

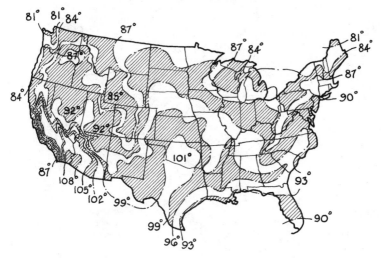

Fig. 2-25. Summer design temperature map.

perimeter with no styrofoam in the center, which creates a heat reservoir below the floor's central area that sends heat into the rooms above as it escapes through the room's envelopes. Finally, as a region's ground water temperature is usually the same as its AAT, Fig. 2-23 may be used to determine a building's water heating or cooling loads.

The *Winter Design Temperature Map* of Fig. 2-24 shows the average lowest temperature a region experiences during 95 percent of its winter heating season; and the *Summer Design Temperature* and *Summer Design Humidity Maps* of Fig. 2-25 and 2-26 show the average highest temperature and humidity a region experiences during 95 percent of its summer cooling

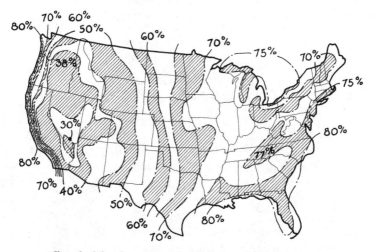

Fig. 2-26. Summer design humidity map.

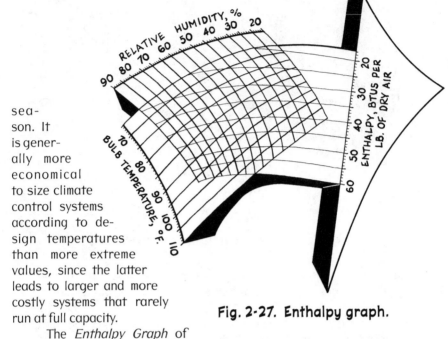

Fig. 2-27. Enthalpy graph.

sea-
son. It
is gener-
ally more
economical
to size climate
control systems
according to de-
sign temperatures
than more extreme
values, since the latter
leads to larger and more
costly systems that rarely
run at full capacity.

The *Enthalpy Graph* of
Fig. 2-27 is used to size a cooling system given the local summer design temperature and humidity, as enthalpy is a thermodynamic measure of the air's
heat content, which is a function of its temperature and humidity. For example, an enthalpy of 30 Btu/lb of dry air is considered the optimal comfort
level of interior air, a condition that occurs at temperature/humidity levels
of 67°/90 percent, 72°/70 percent, 77°/50 percent, and 88°/30 percent. Thus
88° in Aspen may be delightful while 88° in Miami is unbearable.

2.E.2.b. Design Cooling Load

The 72 × 98 ft west facade of a building in Dallas, TX, has offices that
are 12'-0" high (floor-to-floor), 12'-0" wide, and 16'-0" deep; and each
floor has a thermopane ribbon window with caulked frames (R = 2.7,
weight = 10 psf). Each window has louvers behind it that are closed
about two-thirds of the time due to warm sunny weather, its sill and
head heights are 2'-6" and 6'-6", and the horizontal panels between
them are light brown insulated wall panels (R = 16, wt = 17 psf). What
is the design cooling load through the facade?

2)E)2)b) **Step 1.** Find the average total thermal resistance of each part of the envelope construction, as follows:

a. Envelope has one construction type and no unheated voids:

$$R = R_c + R_i t$$

b. Envelope has more than one construction type:

$$A R = A_1 (R_{c\,1} + R_1\, t_1) + \ldots + A_z (R_{cz} + R_z\, t_z) \quad \ldots \oplus$$

c. An unheated void (attic, garage, etc.) is between the indoors and outdoors:

$$R = R_c + R_i t + R_o$$

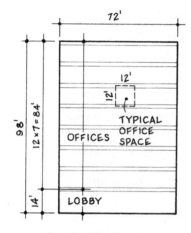

R = total thermal resistance of envelope construction, **?**

$R_{c1, c2, c3\ldots cz}$ = unit R-value of each uninsulated envelope const. : ≈ 3 if roof, wall, or wood floor; 2 if concrete floor; 1 if glazing. R_{c1} of const. 1 (glazing) is given as 2.7. R_{c2} of construction 2 (insulated wall panels) is given as 16.

$R_{i1, i2, i3\ldots iz}$ = unit R-value of each envelope insulation if any. Here the R for each insulation is included in the R-values for each construction in the envelope.

$t_{1, 2, 3\ldots z}$ = thickness of each envelope insulation if any, in. These are also included in the R-values for each const. in the envelope.

Fig. 2-28. Envelope spreadsheet of building.

A = surface area of total envelope construction, sf. Ignore areas more than 1 ft below finished grade. From Fig. 2-22, if offices begin 14 ft above ground level, $A = (98 - 14) \times 72 = 6{,}050$ sf.

$A_{1, 2, 3\ldots z}$ = surface area of each type of envelope construction, sf. As all office units in facade are uniform in area, portion of facade glazing = portion of glazing in each office. $\therefore A_1 = 6\text{-}6" - 2\text{-}6")/12\text{-}0" \times 6{,}050 = 2{,}000$ sf and A_2 = area of facade – area of wall panels = $6{,}050 - 2{,}000 = 4{,}050$ sf.

R_o = R-value of outer part of envelope construction if an unheated void is between indoors and outdoors: $R_o \approx 3$ if roof, wall, or wood floor; 2 if concrete floor; 1 if glazing). Not applicable.

$$6{,}050\, R = 2{,}000 \times 2.7 + 4{,}050 \times 16 \quad \ldots R = 11.6$$

Step 2. Find the temperature at the outer surface of the envelope:

a. Envelope surface is above grade and exposed to direct sunlight at least 2 hours daily (if grade is sloping, use average height of exposure):

$$T_o \approx T_d - \kappa_{lo} + \kappa_u \, \kappa_i \, \kappa_c \, [^{1,200}/(6 \, R + \omega)] \quad \dots \ \oplus$$

b. Envelope surface is above grade and receives little sunlight daily (if grade is sloping, use average height of exposure):

$$T_o \approx T_d$$

c. Envelope surface is a wall below finished grade down to 20 ft below grade:

$$T_o \approx T_a + \kappa_d \, (T_d - T_a)$$

d. Envelope surface is a floor area within 20 ft of finished grade, measured down the wall and in under the floor from ground level:

$$T_o \approx T_a + \kappa_{ad} \, (T_d - T_a)$$

e. Envelope surface is a wall or floor area more than 20 ft below finished grade, measured down and in from ground level:

$$T_o \approx T_a$$

f. Envelope surface is a floor area above an unfinished basement or crawlspace:

$$T_o \approx T_i - 9 + {}^{(T_d - T_i)}/_{\kappa_w}$$

T_o = effective air temperature at outer surface of envelope construction, ? °F

T_d = summer design temperature, °F. Use local data when available. From Fig. 2-25, T_d for Dallas area = 99° F.

κ_{lo} = latitude-orientation factor: adjustment for latitude and orientation of envelope construction according to degree deviations below. Interpolate for intermediate values.

LAT, °N.	S	SE/SW	E/W	NE/NW	N	Horiz.
24	-6	3	0	2	1	1
32	3	1	0	1	1	1
40	1	0	0	2	1	1
48	4	3	1	0	0	0

For 32° N. lat., κ_{lo} for Dallas area = 0.

κ_u = umbra fraction: portion of envelope that is unshaded during day. κ_u = 1.0 if unshaded all day and 0 if shaded all day. Interpolate for intermediate values. As adjustable louvers shade interiors about $2/3$ day during warm sunny weather, interiors are unshaded 0.33 day ➡ $\kappa_u = 0.33$.

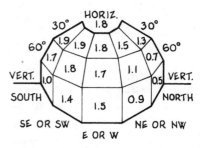

Fig. 2-29. Incidence factors.

κ_i = incidence factor, if envelope faces other than vertical or due south. From Fig. 2-29, κ_i for vertical facade facing west = 1.5.

κ_c = color coefficient. $\kappa_c = 1.0$ if envelope exterior is black or very dark, 0.8 if medium grey, 0.5 if light or white, and 0.7 if glass. Interpolate for intermediate values. At 0.7 for glazing and 0.55 for light brown, average $\kappa_c \approx 0.7 \times$ 0.33 facade for glazing + 0.55 × 0.67 facade for panels ≈ 0.60.

R = R-value of envelope construction. From Step 1, R = 11.6.

ω = unit weight of envelope const., psf of surface area. If ω of ribbon windows = 10 psf and ω of wall panels = 17 psf, $\omega \approx 0 \times 0.33$ facade area for glazing + 17 × 0.67 facade area for wall panels = 14.7 psf.

T_a = average annual temp. for region, from Fig. 2-23. Not applicable.

κ_d = depth coefficient, based on maximum depth of soil d (ft) at bottom of envelope surface, according to the bar graph below:

Maximum depth of soil at bottom of envelope, ft

0	2	4	6	8	10	12	14	16	18	20
1.00	0.75	0.57	0.45	0.35	0.27	0.20	0.16	0.11	0.06	0.00

κ_d = depth coefficient

κ_{ad}= depth coefficient, based on average depth of soil d (ft) at bottom edge of envelope. Find maximum depth of soil d (ft) at bottom of envelope surface, then enter 0.5 d in bar graph above to find κ_{ad}.

T_i = ambient indoor indoor temperature, °. Not applicable.

κ_w = windchill exposure factor, from Table 2-7. Not applicable.

$$T_o \approx 99 - 0 + 0.33 \times 1.5 \times 0.60 \left[1{,}200/(6 \times 11.6 + 14.7)\right] \approx 103° \text{F.}$$

Step 3. Compute the design cooling load through the envelope.

$$\mathbf{C}_{ci} = 0.074 \, V \eta \, (H_o + H_i) + A \, \kappa_f \, (T_o - T_i)/R \, P$$

$\mathbf{C}_{ci}$ = design cooling load due to conduction-infiltration through one area of envelope construction during warm weather, ? Btu/hr

V = volume of room(s) behind envelope, cf. From Fig. 2-22, count volumes to depth of 14 ft. V = 14 × 86 × 72 = 87,000 cf.

η = number of airchanges/hr for room(s) behind envelope. $\eta = 0.022 \, (T_o - T_i) \times$ no. airchanges/hr from Table 2-6. From Table 2-6, η for weatherstripped openings:

One surface exposed to outdoors 0.8
Small rooms w/ large openings .... multiply above amount × 1.2
Unopenable glass .... multiply above amount × 0.7

$$\eta = 0.022 (103 - 77) \times 0.8 \times 1.2 \times 0.7 = 0.38$$

H_o = enthalpy of outdoor air during warm weather, Btu/lb, from summer design temperature and relative humidity, as below:

From Fig. 2-25, summer design temperature for Dallas area .... 99°
From Fig. 2-26, summer design humidity for Dallas area 65%

From Fig. 2-27, enthalpy at 99° & 65% r.h. = 53 Btu/lb

H_i = enthalpy of indoor air during warm weather, Btu/lb. At 77° F. and 50% r.h. (summer indoor conditions), $H \approx 30$ Btu/lb.

A = surface area of envelope, sf. From Step 1, $A = 6,050$ sf.

κ_f = fan factor. If a ventilation fan is within envelope (as between a roof and suspended ceiling or in attic), $\kappa_f = 0.75$; otherwise $\kappa_f = 1.0$. Here $\kappa_f = 1.0$.

T_o = air temp. at envelope's outer surface, ° F. From Step 2, $T_o = 103°$ F.

T_i = ambient indoor air temperature, usually the thermostat setting, ° F. For general comfort and assembly occupancies, $T_i = 74-78°$; for retail, $T_i = 76-80°$; for industrial, $T_i = 77-82°$. Use the lower values where energy efficiency is a priority. Here $T_i \approx 77°$. T_i is generally considered to occur at 50% relative humidity.

R = average thermal resistance of envelope. From Step 1, $R = 11.6$.

P = perimeter heat flow fraction. From Table 2-5, P for curtain wall glazing = 1.2 and for curtain wall spandrels = 0.77. ∴ average $P = 1.2 \times 0.33$ facade area for glazing + 0.77×0.67 facade area for wall panels = 0.91.

$$\mathbf{C}_{ci} = 0.074 \times 87,000 \times 0.38 (53 - 30) + 6,050 \times 1.0 \,^{(103 - 77)}/(11.6 \times 0.91)$$
$$\mathbf{C}_{ci} = 71,000 \text{ Btu/hr}$$

2.E.2.c. Energy Auditing

Example 1. A residence near Albany, NY, has a design heating load of 24,900 Btu/hr and a winter design temperature of -2° F. If the area normally experiences 1,349 heating degree-days in January, how much energy is needed to heat the house during this month?

2)E)2)c)1) Heating Load: $24 \, d_d \, \mathbf{H}_{ci} = \text{\EUR} (65 - T_d)$

d_d = number of heating degree-days during period of energy audit.

d_d for January in Albany, NY = 1,349 heating degree-days.

$\mathbf{H}_{ci}$ = design heating load (conduction-infiltration) through building envelope during period of energy auditing, 24,900 Btu/hr

€ = total heating energy used by building during period of energy audit. € for Jan., ? Btu.

T_d = design temperature at design heating load, from Fig. 2-25 or local data. T_d = – 2° F.

$$24 \times 1,349 \times 24,900 = € [65 - (-2)] \quad \ldots € = 12,000,000 \text{ Btu}$$

Example 2. An office building in Dallas, TX, has a design cooling load of 387,000 Btu/hr and a summer design temperature of 104° F. If the normal cooling degree-days for Dallas in July is 614, how much energy is required to cool the building during this month?

---

2)E)2)c)2) Cooling load: $24\ d_d\ \mathbf{H}_{ci} = € (T_d - 77)$

d_d = number of cooling degree-days during period of energy audit. d_d for July in Dallas area = 614 cooling degree-days.

$\mathbf{H}_{ci}$ = design cooling load (conduction-infiltration) through building envelope during period of energy auditing, 387,000 Btu/hr

€ = total cooling energy used by building during period of energy auditing. € for July, ? Btu.

T_d = design temperature at design cooling load, from Fig. 2-25 or local data. T_d = 104° F.

$$24 \times 614 \times 387,000 = € (104 - 77) \quad \ldots € = 211,000,000 \text{ Btu}$$

2.E.3. Auxiliary Heat Gain

This is the heat added to interiors by occupants, lighting, appliances, and other internal heat sources. In warm weather these gains are usually maximum around the warmest time of day (mid-afternoon), and thus are added to conduction-infiltration cooling loads. During cold weather they are usually minimal during the coldest time of day (before sunrise); thus only the gains occurring at this time are added to heating loads.

Although auxiliary heat gain can comprise a significant portion of a building's heating or cooling load, it is difficult to estimate accurately because (1) human metabolic rates vary according to one's weight and activity, (2) where lighting and machines add heat to indoor spaces, their amounts often vary widely due to their specific nature, (3) the nameplate ratings of most electric motor-driven appliances overstate the actual power consumption by a factor of 2 to 4 because such equipment rarely runs at full speed, (4) the shedded heat may be radiant or convective, and radiant heat generally moves outward radially from the source and does not become a heating load until it strikes a distant surface, while convection heat is a warm air current that becomes an interior heating load immediately on leaving the source, and (5) these thermal migrations can be highly eccentric in unusually-shaped spaces and where sunlight or daylight enters an occupied area. Still, it is wise design to include whatever values that are obtainable for the heating loads in the equations below.

Conduction, infiltration, and auxiliary heat gain are often all that is needed to compute a building's total heating and cooling loads.

2.E.3.a. Heating and Cooling Loads

Example 1. What is the design auxiliary heat gain in winter for a residence for a family of four near Albany, NY?

2)E)3)a)1) Design heating load: $H_a = M + H + 3.42\,W\,Q$ ... ➕

H_a = auxiliary heat gain added to interior spaces at time of design heating load (usually 7 A.M.), ? Btu/hr

M = metabolism of occupants at time of design heating load, Btu/hr. At 7 A.M. in winter occupants are probably sleeping. From Table 2-8, M = 250 for sleeping man, 210 for sleeping woman, and 190 for sleeping child. ∴ M = 250 + 210 + 2 × 190 = 840 Btu/hr.

H = average heat gain from appliances and motors in use at time of design heat load. Use Table 2-8 as a guide for determining H for each occupancy and time. Here $H \approx 0$.

W = average wattage of lighting in use at time of design heating load. At 7 A.M., W is probably near zero. Here assume 30 watts.

Q = portion of lighting wattage emitted as heat at time of design heating load. Q = 0.88 for incandescent, 0.85 for quartz, 0.66 for fluorescent, 0.63 for mercury or metal-halide, 0.59 for sodium. Here assume Q is half incandescent and half fluorescent = (0.66 + 0.88)/2 = 0.77.

$$H_a \approx 840 + 0 + 3.42 \times 30 \times 0.77 \approx 920 \text{ Btu/hr}$$

Example 2. What is the summer auxiliary heat gain in a 12 × 16 ft office in Dallas, TX, if the space is typically used by one person and is illuminated by four ceiling-mounted 4 × 40 watt fluorescent fixtures?

2)E)3)a)2) Design cooling load: $C_a = M + H + 3.42 \, W Q$ ... ⊕

C_a = design auxiliary heat gain added to interior spaces at time of design cooling load (usually 3 P.M.), ? Btu/hr

M = average metabolism of occupants at time of design cooling load, Btu/hr. Assume half men and half women. From Table 2-8, M for seated, writing, or light work = 480 for men and 410 for women. ∴ M = 0.5 (480 + 410) = 445 Btu/hr.

H = average heat gain from appliances and motors in use at time of design cooling load. Use Table 2-8 as a guide for determining H for each occupancy and time. From Table 2-8, H for general office space = 2.5 Btu/hr-sf. ∴ total H ≈ 12 × 16 × 2.5 ≈ 480 Btu/hr.

W = average wattage of illumination in use at design cooling load, watts. If 4 fluorescent fixtures w/ 4 lamps each at 40 watts/lamp are on at 3 P.M., W = 4 × 4 × 40 = 640 watts.

Q = portion of illumination wattage emitted as heat at time of design cooling load. Q = 0.88 for incandescent, 0.85 for quartz, 0.66 for fluorescent, 0.63 for mercury or metal-halide, 0.59 for sodium. Here Q = 0.66.

$$C_a = 445 + 480 + 3.42 \times 640 \times 0.66 = 2,200 \text{ Btu/hr}$$

TABLE 2-8: METABOLISM OF HUMAN ACTIVITIES

ACTIVITY OF OCCUPANT	METABOLISM, Btu/hr		
	Man	Woman	Child
Sleeping	250	210	190
Seated: quiet, as in theater	360	300	270
Writing or light work	480	410	360
Eating (includes heat emitted by food)	520	450	400
Typing or clerical	640	540	480
Standing: slow walking	800	680	600
Light machine work	1,000	850	600
Heavy work, lifting	1,600	1,300	1,100
Walking, 3 miles per hr.	1,000	850	750
Jogging, gym athletics	2,000	1,700	1,500

Example 3. What is the maximum heat loss through the walls of a 28 ft long 4 in. diameter uninsulated type K copper pipe that conveys hot water whose maximum temperature is 140° through an unheated crawl space that is as cold as 35° in winter?

2)E)3)a)3) $H [R_c \, t_c + R_i \, t_i + (0.53 - 0.0014 \, \Delta T)] = A \, \kappa_o \, \Delta T$

H = total heat loss through wall of duct or pipe through which heat flows, ? Btu/hr

R_c = unit R-value of duct or pipe material, R/in. thickness. $R = 0.034$ for steel, 0.029 for copper, 0.057 for aluminum, 0.91 for wood, and 0.115 for concrete. R_c for copper = 0.029.

t_c = thickness of duct or pipe material, in. From p. 260, thickness of 4 in. dia. type K copper pipe = 0.134 in. Metal must be ≤ $\frac{3}{8}$ in. thick for this formula to be valid.

R_i = unit R-value of any insulation around duct or pipe, R/in. thickness. Here $R_i = 0$.

t_i = thickness of any insulation around duct or pipe, in. $t_i = 0$.

ΔT = temperature difference between inside and outside of duct or pipe, ° F. $\Delta T = 140 - 35 = 105°$ F.

A = surface area of duct or pipe, sf. A of pipe or circular duct = 0.26 $L_{ft} \, \delta_{in}$. ∴ $A = 0.26 \times 28$ ft × 4.125 actual in. dia. = 30.0 sf.

κ_o = orientation coefficient for each duct or pipe surface based on if it faces up, down, or to the side. κ_o for surfaces of metal pipes and ducts w/ circular or rectangular sections = 1.00. Otherwise κ_o = 1.00 for sides of any material, 1.03 and 0.94 for wood tops & bottoms, and 1.08 & 0.93 for concrete tops and bottoms. Here κ_o = 1.00 for total surface.

$$H [0.029 \times 0.134 + 0 + (0.53 - 0.0014 \times 105)] = 30.0 \times 1 \times 105$$
$$H = 8{,}140 \text{ Btu/hr}$$

Example 4. How much heat is lost through the above pipe if it is wrapped in 1 in. molded mineral wool insulation whose R-value = 3.33?

2)E)3)a)3) $H [R_c \, t_c + R_i \, t_i + (0.53 - 0.0014 \, \Delta T)] = A \, \kappa_o \, \Delta T$

R_i = unit R-value of insulation around duct or pipe, 3.33.
t_i = thickness of insulation around duct or pipe, in. $t_i = 1.0$.
     All other values are as defined in previous example.

$$H [0.029 \times 0.125 + 3.33 \times 1.0 + (0.53 - 0.0014 \times 105)] = 30.0 \times 1 \times 105$$
$$H = 726 \text{ Btu/hr}$$

Example 5. How much heat is lost through the walls of a 24 × 42 in. rectangular HVAC duct made of 22 ga. galvanized sheet steel if the duct is 46 ft long and it carries air at 140° F above the suspended ceiling of the office area below whose temperature is typically 70°?

2]E]3]a]3] $H [R_c\, t_c + R_i\, t_i + (0.53 - 0.0014\, \Delta T)] = A\, \kappa_o\, \Delta T$

H = total heat loss through walls of duct or pipe through which heat flows, **?** Btu/hr

R_c = unit R-value of duct or pipe material, R/in. thickness. R = 0.034 for steel, 0.029 for copper, 0.057 for aluminum, 0.91 for wood, and 0.115 for concrete. R_c for galv. sheet steel = 0.034.

t_c = thickness of duct or pipe, in. From outside reference, thickness of 22 ga. sheet metal = 0.0313 in. Metal must ≤ $^3/_8$ in. thick for this formula to be valid.

R_i = unit R-value of any insulation around duct or pipe, R/in. thickness. Here R_i = 0.

t_i = thickness of any insulation around duct or pipe, in. t_i = 0.

ΔT = temperature difference between inside and outside of duct or pipe, ° F. ΔT = 140 – 70 = 70° F.

A = surface area of duct or pipe, sf. A = (2 sides × $^{24}/_{12}$ + 2 sides × $^{42}/_{12}$) × 46 = 506 sf.

κ_o = orientation coefficient for each duct or pipe surface based on if it faces up, down, or to the side. κ_o for all metal surfaces of pipes and ducts w/ circular or rectangular sections = 1.00. Otherwise κ_o = 1.00 for sides of any material, 1.03 and 0.94 for wood tops & bottoms, and 1.08 & 0.93 for concrete tops and bottoms. Here κ_o = 1.00 for total surface.

$$H [0.034 \times 0.0313 + 0 + (0.53 - 0.0014 \times 70)] = 506 \times 1 \times 70$$
$$H = 72,400 \text{ Btu/hr}$$

Example 6. How much heat is lost through the walls of the above duct if it is wrapped in 6 in. nom. batt insulation?

2]E]3]a]3] $H [R_c\, t_c + R_i\, t_i + (0.53 - 0.0014\, \Delta T)] = A\, \kappa_o\, \Delta T$

R_i = unit R-value of insulation enveloping container material, R/in. thickness. From Table 2-5, R_i for batt insulation = 3.5.

t_i = thickness of insulation enveloping container material, 6 in. All other values are as defined in previous example.

$$H [0.034 \times 0.0313 + 3.5 \times 6 + (0.53 - 0.0014 \times 70)] = 506 \times 1 \times 70$$
$$H = 1,460 \text{ Btu/hr}$$

Example 7. What is the energy payback span of the duct insulation in Example 6 if it costs $520 in materials and labor to install, the #2 fuel oil that heats the airflow costs $1.96 per gallon, and during the winter the parent HVAC system runs an average 6 hr/day?

2)E)3)a)4)　　　　　$\$_i \, E_f = t_o \, \$_o \, t \, (Q_u - Q_i)$

$\$_i$　=　initial cost of energy-saving insulation, $520

E_f　=　energy content of fuel consumed, Btu/unit of energy. From Table 4-5, energy content of #2 fuel oil = 147,000 Btu/gal.

t_o　=　operating time of system that consumes the fuel, hr/unit of time. Here t_o = average 6 hr/day.

$\$_o$　=　operating cost of system that consumes the fuel, $/unit of time. Here $\$_o$ = unit cost of fuel consumed in operating system = 1.96/gal. However, it is wise design to double this amount to include maintenance operation costs. ∴ $\$_o \approx 1.96 \times 2 \approx \$3.92$/gal.

t　=　timespan of energy payback span, days, months, years, etc. Here T = unit of time used for ϕ above = ? days.

Q_u　=　energy lost when ducting or piping is uninsulated, Btu/hr. From Example 3 above, H_u = 72,400 Btu/hr.

Q_i　=　energy lost when ducting or piping is insulated, Btu/hr. From Example 4 above, H_u = 1,460 Btu/hr.

　　$520 \times 147,000 = 6 \times 3.92 \times T \, (72,400 - 1,460)$　　　... T = 46 days!

Note: Although this energy payback span is extremely desirable, in reality the system's operating costs should also include the energy required to run the HVAC system's supply and return air fans, chiller, and cooling tower plus all maintenance costs associated with the system's operation. Still, the payback for this installation is probably less than $1\frac{1}{2}$ years.

2.E.3.b. Energy Auditing

　　Seasonal auxiliary heat gains may vary widely according to building type, occupancy patterns, and time of year. They may be estimated by averaging their unknowns for the months of January and July. If these two amounts differ, interpolate for the intervening months.

Example 1. What is the total auxiliary heat gain for January in a 2,000 ft^2 residence for a family of four near Albany, NY?

2)E)3)b)1) Heating season: $H_a = t(M + H + 3.42\ W\ Q)$ ... ✚

H_a = auxiliary heat gain added to interior spaces in Jan., **?** Btu/hr
t = period of heat flow, days. t for Jan. = 31 days.
M = average daily metabolism of occupants, Btu/day. Assume average
      400 Btu/hr × 4 occupants × average 0.5 occupancy × 24 hr/day =
      400 × 4 × 0.5 × 24 = 19,200 Btu/day.
H = average heat gain from appliances and motors, Btu/day.
      From Table 2-9, H for residences ≈ 1 Btu/hr-sf.
      ∴ total H ≈ 2,000 × 24 ≈ 48,000 BtU/day.
W = average wattage of illumination used per day, watts/day. If 8
      incandescent lamps averaging 75 watts/lamp are on 6 hours/day,
      W = 8 × 75 × 6 = 3,600 watts/day.
Q = portion of lamp wattage emitted as heat. Q = 0.88 for incandes-
      cent, 0.85 for quartz, 0.66 for fluorescent, 0.63 for mercury or
      metal-halide, 0.59 for sodium. Here Q = 0.88.

  H_a ≈ 31 (19,200 + 48,000 + 3.42 × 3,600 × 0.88) ≈ 2,420,000 Btu

---

Example 2. What is the total auxiliary heat gain for July in the Dallas,
TX, office described in Example 2.E.2.b. above?

---

2)E)3)b)2) Cooling season: $C_a = t(M + H + 3.42\ W\ Q)$ ... ✚

C_a = design auxiliary heat gain added to interior spaces at time of de-
      sign cooling load (usually 3 p.m.), **?** Btu/hr
t = period of heat flow, days. t for July = 31 days
M = average daily metabolism of occupants, Btu/day. For 1 occupant at
      445 Btu/hr × $^2/_3$ of 8 hr workday, 445 × 0.67 × 8 = 2,400 Btu/day.
H = average heat gain from appliances and motors, Btu/day. From
      Table 2-9, H for offices, general = 2.5 Btu/sf. If office is used 8
      hr/workday, H = 12 × 16 × 2.5 × 8 = 3,840 Btu/day.

TABLE 2-9: AUXILIARY HEAT GAINS FOR MACHINERY

TYPE OF SPACE	Heat gain, Btu/hr-ft^2
Single family residences......... 1	Apartments, condominiums 1.5
Restaurants: eating areas 3	Commercial kitchen areas ... 30–50
Hospitals 2	Laboratories 5–50
Offices: general 2.5;	computer display areas 4
Purchasing and accounting departments 6–7
Manufacturing: assembly, stamping, etc. .... 15–20, but varies widely
Plating, forming, curing, etc. .... 50–200, but varies widely

W = average wattage of illumination used per day, watts/day. If 4 fluorescent fixtures containing 4 lamps each at 40 watts/lamp are on 9 hr/day, $W = 4 \times 4 \times 40 \times 9 = 5{,}760$ watts/day.

Q = portion of lamp wattage emitted as heat. $Q = 0.88$ for incandescent, 0.85 for quartz, 0.66 for fluorescent, 0.63 for mercury or metal-halide, 0.59 for sodium. Here $Q = 0.66$.

$$\mathbf{C}_a = 31 (2{,}400 + 3{,}840 + 3.42 \times 5{,}760 \times 0.66) = 596{,}000 \text{ Btu}$$

2.E.4. Pickup Heating Load

When interior spaces are unheated for an extended time during cold weather, heat drains out of the solid masses within the spaces —furniture, interior construction, and other indoor objects— as the enveloping indoor air temperature becomes lower; then when the heat turns back on, a portion of the Btus in the warming air flow back into the solids. In an occasionally heated building, this effective heat loss can considerably influence the heating system's size. Thus pickup heating load is usually a *design* calculation. Since these loads vary according to the masses and surface areas of the solids within the building envelope, computation is rarely precise; still, it aids in determining the building's actual energy demands. During warm weather, the above-described heat massing occurs in reverse; thus if the temperature in an uncooled room rises appreciably, some of the air heat migrates into the room's solid masses; then when the air temperature cools, the heat stored in the solids flows back into the surrounding air. This could be called a pickup cooling load. However, these loads are usually much less than pickup heating loads because the temperature differentials are less, and the excess indoor heat is often largely removed by ventilating. Thus pickup cooling loads are rarely computed.

Although the above-described pickup heating load occurs only in occasionally heated interior spaces, a second kind occurs in nearly every heating or cooling system every time it is turned on. This is because the usually metallic machinery and ducting of most heating systems weigh a lot and have a high specific heat. Therefore, if a system turns on after it hasn't run for a while (i.e. is cold), part of the produced heat is absorbed by the system's machinery and ducting. This occurs in the solid parts of an electric baseboard heater, in the boiler and floor loops of a radiant floor heating system, in the burner box and metal tube of a radiant ceiling heater, and in the compressor and radiator of a heat pump every time these units turn on and off. The absorbed Btus can even be computed by knowing the weight of the machinery and ducting, its specific heat, and its temperature when cold and warm. This quantity could be called *mass heating load,* and it also occurs in reverse in the solid parts of every cooling system when it turns on and off (although then the Btus are usually absorbed by nearby interior spaces). Theoretically this heat should be added to a system's design heating load to determine the full effective load the system requires to operate as desired; but in reality such computation isn't necessary because in continually heated spaces the system rarely cools down completely, and the system rarely needs to deliver the full amount of its design heating load the moment it turns on. Another example of mass heating load occurs every time a plumbing hot water faucet is turned on or off. If the faucet has been off for a while, the standing hot water in the pipe between the hot water heater and the faucet has cooled; then when the faucet is turned on, the cold water flows out before the hot water arrives. Thus with each on/off cycle the water heater heats an added volume of water equal to the displaced cold water.

A small church in Dubois, WY, is used for services every Sunday. If the heat is turned on two hours before morning services in winter and the assembly area's design heating load is 216,000 Btu/hr, what is the building's estimated pickup heating load?

2)E)4) $\qquad$ $H_p \approx P H_{ci}$

H_p = design pickup heating load for interior space(s) during cold weather, ? Btu/hr

P = pickup heating load fraction: portion of heat load absorbed by interior masses based on frequency of heat flow as described below. Interpolate for intermediate values.

Type of heat flow	Pickup heating load fraction P
Heat off for 6 hr or nightly setback of 10° F	0.1
Heat off for 12 hr or nightly setback of 20° F	0.2
Heat off for 18 hr or nightly setback of 10° F	0.3
Heat off for 30 hr or more	0.4

P for heat turned off for 30 or more hours = 0.4.

H_{ci} = design heating load of interior space(s) due to conduction-infiltration during cold weather, 216,000 Btu/hr

$$H_p \approx 0.4 \, (216,000) \approx 86,000 \text{ Btu/hr}$$

2.E.5. Solar Heat Gain

Solar heat gain is the amount of the sun's energy that enters indoors through glazing in the southerly surfaces of a building envelope during cold weather. Although this heating load is conceptually simple, it has numerous variables. First, the sun's energy fluctuates according to sunspots and other hyperactivity occurring on its surface. Second, the amount of solar energy that enters the earth's atmosphere varies from about 445 Btu/sf·hr on Dec. 21 when the sun is closest to the earth to about 415 Btu/sf·hr on Jun. 21 when it is farthest away. Third, as this energy enters the earth's troposphere, some is scattered by the air's molecules and some is absorbed by the molecules depending on the air's temperature, chemical composition, and moisture content. Fourth, as a site's elevation above sea level increases, the sun's energy increases (at mile-high Denver it is about 7 percent greater than at sea level). Fifth, as the sun descends from directly overhead tow near the horizon, the air its rays travel through becomes thicker, which decreases their intensity. However, even when the sun is only 15° above the horizon, its intensity is still 95 percent of what it is when it is directly overhead. Thus, for all practical purposes, the sun's average intensity as it reaches the earth's surface at sea level at noon on a clear day when it is at least 15° above the horizon is normally taken to be about 300 Btu/sf·hr on a surface perpendicular to the arriving rays. However, when the sun descends below 15°, its intensity decreases so rapidly that for all practical purposes its heating value is nil. This is just as well, because on most building sites low obstacles such as surrounding foliage, nearby rooftops, and rises in terrain often block the incoming rays. Finally, during cloudy weather, the sun's incoming energy is diffused so greatly that the little amount that reaches the earth is also unusable. Thus an important aspect of solar heat gain is a given day's average percentage of sunshine due to cloudy weather based on local climate data. †

From all the above, the following facts can be gleaned. (1) On almost every building site in the United States, the sun's intensity is about 300 Btu/sf·hr. (2) This energy is available from about 9:00 A.M. to 3:30 P.M. even in late December almost everywhere in the country (Alaska excepted). (3) Most regions in this country experience at least 50 percent clear weather all winter long. (4) Most buildings in America have large surface areas that are exposed to the sun almost all day long.

The conclusion from these four facts is irrefutable: a *huge* amount of free solar energy is potentially available for heating interior spaces in buildings all over America. Indeed, during the energy crisis of around 1980, numerous methods of utilizing this energy were devised. During this time, no solar energy device received more media support than did the solar flat plate collector. This was typically a plywood-sized sheet of glazing laid over a similarly sized box only a few inches deep whose inside was

† The facts in this paragraph were obtained from *Direct Use of the Sun's Energy,*

painted black so the shallow container would retain a maximum amount of the solar radiance that passed through the glass; then the retained heat was conveyed via piping or ducting to the building's interior spaces. By arranging many of these wafer-like boxes all over a building's roof or south facade, a large part of the occupants' fossil fuel heating bills could conceivably be eliminated. But when word got out that these devices were abysmally inefficient, their sales plummeted to nearly nothing, all within a few months in 1981. Sadly, not only did the public lose confidence in bad solar energy concepts, but in good ones also.

Specifically, why *did* solar flat plate collectors fail? (1) They were too shallow. Imagine trying to collect enough energy in a container a few inches deep to heat a container that is 30 *feet* deep? (2) Too little insulation (usually 1 or 2 in.) was added to the collectors' sides and backs while the parent container —the building— was wrapped in 6 in. or more. Storing heat in such a porous thermal barrier was like using a sieve to hold the gasoline that runs your car. (3) The collected energy was usually transferred several times between the collector and the indoor spaces as follows: the collected radiance (itself a media transfer) was usually absorbed by water circulating in pipes (media transfer 2) which carried the energy to the building's basement where it was emptied into a room-sized "rock storage unit" (media transfer 3); then at night air passing through the storage unit rocks ducted the energy indoors (media transfer 4). Forgetting the fact that some of the energy escaped from the pipes and ducts as it was conveyed, such flow ignored a basic principle of physics: *whenever energy is transferred from one medium to another, some is irretrievably lost.*

From all the above, how could one create an efficient collector of solar energy? One way to begin would be to do the opposite of what was mistakenly done before: i.e. (1) make the containers deep, maybe as deep as the building itself; (2) add much insulation to the collector's sides and back, maybe as much as is fitted into the building's envelope; (3) keep the energy media transfers to a minimum. If the sunrays passing through the glazing entered directly into interior spaces, there would be only *one* media transfer. And if the glazing were nearly as high and wide as the building itself... Aah, but that would be too simple!

Indeed, a skeptic might ask: "This big solar collector the size of a house you're making that's so deep and thickly insulated and simple: what about the side with all the glass in it?"

"What about it?"

"How're you going to keep all the energy you've collected during the day from flowing back out through the glass at night?"

"Cover the glass with movable insulation."

"But how? Those areas of glass are *big.*"

"True."

"So where are you going to find any insulation that's big enough to cover all that glass and move out of the way when it should?"

"How about garage doors? They're big, and they move. When closed they could cover the glass, and when open they could lay against the ceiling above."

"But garage doors aren't insulated."

"Then we'd insulate them."

"But how?"

"An overhead garage door is just a few horizontal panels that are hinged together; so if you built thick insulated panels the same size as the garage door panels then bolted them together with the same hardware, you'd have an insulated overhead garage door."

"... But it would be *heavy*, wouldn't it?"

"Sure. But in Sweet's Catalog there's an overhead garage door built for a shipyard that's 40 feet high and 150 feet long. I'm sure that door is heavy, but I'm sure it works too. In fact, the firehouse here in town has garage doors that are 26 feet wide and 13 feet high, and they're made of the same panels and hardware as any other garage door, and it goes up and down pretty easy. I know, 'cause I tried it."

"But if these doors are really big and filled with insulation, when they're closed the rooms behind them are gonna be dark."

"Then use translucent insulation."

"Aw, come on."

"No, really... you ever heard of bubblepak?"

"... Sure."

"Well, bubblepak is just a thin sheet with a lot of little airspaces which light can pass through. In a way it's no different than fiberglass insulation, which is nothing but glass, which as a solid is actually a bad insulator. So if you stacked a dozen sheets of bubblepak together, you'd have thick translucent insulation."

"... Hmm!"

"Not only that, but you know that thin transparent film that's mounted between the panes of certain kinds of thermopane windows to increase their R-value? Heat Mirror® it's called. A company out in California will sell it to you by the roll. And if you sandwiched a sheet of Heat Mirror® between the layers of bubblepak, you'd have a high-R-value insulation. One that was translucent too. And it'd be so light that you could easily make it go up and down."

"I guess you could...."

Someday, solar energy will be a *very* practical and economical means of keeping a building's interior spaces warm in winter in nearly every part of this country. But when that time has come, the incoming rays will likely not reduce the overall size of the building's mechanical heating system; because the system's maximum heating load usually occurs just before dawn when no incoming radiance is available to reduce it. But solar energy could greatly reduce the amount of fossil fuels the building's heating system may consume during a 24 hour period. Thus solar heat gain is typically an *Energy Audit* calculation.

An important consideration for any solar collector is the angle its glazing makes with the ground, because the angle the sunrays make with the glazing affects the amount of energy that enters indoors. The glazing can be vertical, which is usually the easiest to construct; but if you want to collect the most energy, the glazing should tilt at an angle equal to the site's latitude plus 20°. This is because the day on which half of a region's winter degree-days have occurred is, on the average, around Jan. 20, which statistically is also around the coldest part of the year; and on this date the sun's angle at noon due south is 70° minus the local latitude anywhere in the country; and the angle perpendicular to this is the local latitude plus 20°. Thus Table 2-10 lists two insolation values: the clear-day insolation that strikes vertical glazing, and the clear-day insolation that strikes glazing tilting at an angle from horizontal equal to local latitude plus 20°.

A 24 × 40 ft solar house near Albany, NY, has a two-story south wall of Andersen window units mounted in front of an innovative arrangement of counter-balanced panels of thick translucent insulation (see Fig. 2-30) that is activated by a computerized thermostat, which opens the panels when the sun is shining, then closes them when a cloud passes in front of the sun, when sunrays are weak (i.e. early morning and late afternoon) and at night . The solar glass is vertical, faces south-southeast, and is shaded during the summer by three large maple trees whose trunks are 40 ft away; and in front of the facade is a level lawn that is snow-covered an average 25 days in January. What is the solar heat gain from this system in January?

Step 1. Compute the incident clear-day insolation on a vertical surface based on the site's latitude and period of the energy audit.

2 E 5 $\Phi_c \approx \Phi_g - 0.125\,(\Phi_g - \Phi_s)\,(L - L_g)$

Φ_c = incident clear-day insolation (solar heat gain) for latitude of site and period of audit, from Table 2-10, **?** Btu/day-sf.
From atlas, latitude of Albany area = 42°-40'.

Φ_g = greatest incident insolation value below site latitude; select from 24, 32, 40, or 48°, Btu/day-sf. Greatest Φ_g below 42°-40' is 40°.
∴ as period of audit is for month of Jan., from Table 2-10, Φ_g for Jan. at 40° lat. = 1,500 Btu/day-sf.

Φ_s = smallest incident insolation value above site latitude; select from 24, 32, 40, or 48°, Btu/day-sf. Smallest Φ_s above 42°-40' is 48°.
From Table 2-10, Φ_s for Jan. at 48° lat. = 1,310 Btu/day-sf.

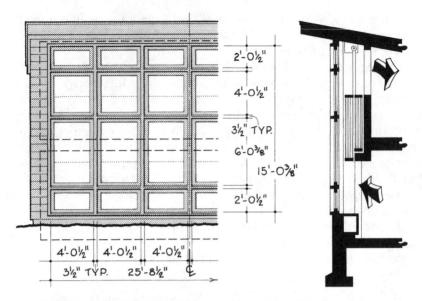

Fig. 2-30. South elevation and section of solar house.

L = latitude of site, decimal degrees. 42°-40' = 42.7°.

L_g = greatest latitude value below site latitude; select from 24, 32, 40, or 48°. Greatest latitude value below 42°-40' is 40°.

$$\Phi_c \approx 1{,}500 - 0.125 \, (1{,}500 - 1{,}310) \, (42.7 - 40) \approx 1{,}440 \text{ Btu/day-sf}$$

Step 2. If additional sunshine reflects from the ground in front of the solar glazing, compute the glazing's ground reflection factor.

TABLE 2-10: INSOLATION, BTUS/CLEAR DAY, SF

LATITUDE, °	INSOLATION ON GLAZING THAT IS VERTICAL				
	Nov. 21	Dec. 21	Jan. 21	Feb. 21	Mar. 21
24°	1,350	1,445	1,385	1,075	610
32°	1,450	1,515	1,490	1,310	900
40°	1,460	1,470	1,500	1,500	1,185
48°	1,280	1,095	1,310	1,540	1,395

INSOL. ON GLAZING THAT TILTS AT ∠ FROM HORIZ. = LOCAL LAT. + 20°					
LATITUDE, °	Nov. 21	Dec. 21	Jan. 21	Feb. 21	Mar. 21
24°	1,950	1,965	1,995	1,835	1,380
32°	1,855	1,915	1,890	1,885	1,570
40°	1,695	1,720	1,735	1,865	1,690
48°	1,385	1,395	1,415	1,775	1,725

† This table's values are based on data obtained from *Direct Use of the Sun's*

$$\kappa_g \approx \kappa_s \left[\kappa_c + S\,(0.7 - \kappa_c)\right]$$

κ_g = ground reflectance factor: portion of sun reflected onto solar glazing from ground in front. Use only if glazing is vertical or nearly so, glazing is at or near ground, and ground is fairly level in front of glazing; otherwise κ_g = 0. Here κ_g = ?

κ_s = ground smoothness factor. κ_s = 1.0 if ground is fairly smooth, 0.5 if varied or slightly rocky. Interpolate for intermediate values. As lawns are usually smooth, κ_s = 1.0.

κ_c = ground color factor. The darker the ground, the lower its κ_c. From Table 2-11, κ_c for vegetation, medium-dark green (most lawns) = 0.17.

S = snow cover reflectance. From Table 2-11, S for snow cover for average 25 days/month in Jan. = 0.5.

$$\kappa_g \approx 1.0\ [0.17 + 0.5\ (0.7 - 0.17)] \approx 0.44$$

Step 3. Compute the solar heat gain through the solar glazing.

$$\Phi_a \approx 0.010\ \Phi_c\ t\ P\ A\ \tau\ \kappa_u\ \kappa_i\ \kappa_a\ (1 + \kappa_g)\ (1 + 0.000014\ E)$$

Φ_a = average solar heat gain through solar glazing during period of energy audit, ? Btu

Φ_c = incident clear-day insolation based on latitude of site and month of audit, from Step 1, 1,440 Btu/day-sf

t = period of energy audit, days. For January audit, t = 31 days.

P = average percentage of local sunshine during period of audit. From *Comparative Climatic Data*, © U.S. Department. of Commerce, average percent of possible sunshine for Albany, NY, in Jan. = 46%.

A = surface area of glazing, sf. From Andersen Window Catalog, glazing area of windows shown in Fig. 2-30:

TABLE 2-11: GROUND REFLECTANCE FACTORS

NATURE OF GROUND just outside collector surface	Reflectance factor
Ground color: new asphalt, slate, other very dark surfaces	0.05
Dark dirt surface: dark brown, dark grey, deep red, etc.	0.10
Medium dark surface: red brick, weathered wood deck, etc.	0.13
Vegetation, medium to dark green (most lawns)	0.17
Concrete, yellow vegetation, light gravel, light dirt, light sand	0.25
Sand, white or near-white	0.50
White smooth surface	0.70
Snow cover reflectance: less than 3 days per month	0.00
Average 5 days/month 0.10 Average 10 days/month	0.20
Average 15 days/month 0.30 Average 20 days/month	0.40
Average 25 days/month 0.50 Average all month long	0.60

Energy, Farrington Daniels (Ballantine Books, New York, 1964), pp. 18–34.

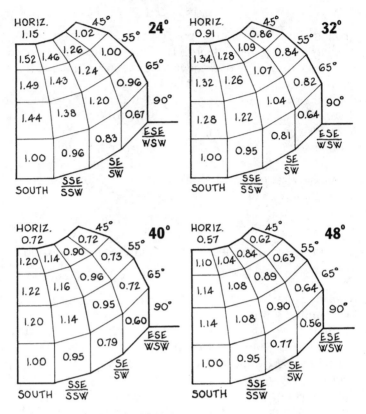

Fig. 2-31. Collector inclination/orientation incidence factors.

Glazing areas *A* & *D* (unit A41): 2 × 6 × 433/16" × 19³⁄₄" ... 71.1 sf
Glazing areas *B* (unit A42): 6 × 433/16" × 43⁵⁄₈" .... 78.5 sf
Glazing areas *C* (unit A43): 6 × 433/16" × 67½" .... 121.0 sf

Total surface area of glazing .... 271.0 sf

τ = transmittance fraction: portion of solar energy passing through glazing. From Table 6-10, τ for clear standard thermopane = 0.78.

κ_u = umbra fraction: portion of collector area exposed to daily sun. κ_u = 1.0 if area is exposed to sun all day, 0 if area is in shade all day. Interpolate for intermediate values. Typical κ_u for sunrays passing through deciduous tree branches in winter ≈ 0.8.

κ_i = incidence factor: portion of sunlight absorbed by collector if its surface varies from vertical due south. From Fig. 2-31, κ_i at 40° latitude for vertical surface facing south-southeast = 0.95.

κ_a = local clarity fraction: clearness of local atmosphere depending on location, smog, and other environmental factors as described below:

Region or Condition	Clarity fraction during winter months (κ_a)
Deep South	0.90
Florida, Gulf Coast, mid-south, West Coast	0.95
Northern plains, Rocky Mountains, near Canadian border	1.05
All other areas in conterminous 48 states	1.00
Continuous light smog or local haze	subtract 0.1 from above values
Continuous heavy industrial smog	subtract 0.2 from above values

From atlas, Albany is in 'All other areas' zone. $\therefore \kappa_a = 1.0$.

κ_g = ground reflectance factor. From Step 2, $\kappa_g = 0.44$.
E = elevation above sea level, ft. Albany is near sea level ➡ $E \approx 0$.

$$\Phi_a \approx 0.010 \times 1,440 \times 31 \times 46 \times 271 \times 0.78 \times 0.8 \times 0.95 \times 1.0 \ (1 + 0.44)$$
$$\Phi_a \approx 4,750,000 \ \text{Btu for January}$$

2.E.6. Thermal Massing

For many, the concept of thermal massing evolves from the architecture of the pueblos in the Southwest, whose thick south-facing adobe walls absorb sunrays during the day and radiate the stored Btus into interior spaces at night to reduce these buildings' heating loads. However, the efficacy of this method of utilizing solar energy depends on several local climatic factors that exist in few other areas. They are:

High ratio of sunshine-to-cloudiness. In the Four Corners region of the Southwest, the sun in January shines 80 percent of the day, compared to about 50 percent in New York City, 40 percent in Chicago, and less than 30 percent in Seattle. But even more important than percentage of sunshine is the ratio of sunny-to-cloudy sky, because during sunshine the solar radiance is driven into the thermal massing while during cloudy weather it 'shifts into reverse' and backs out. Thus 80 percent sunshine has an 'in/out ratio' of 80/20 ≈ 4 while this ratio for 50 percent sunshine ≈ only 1; thus the theoretical net gain of thermal massing at 80 percent sunshine is actually *four times greater* than it is at 50 percent sunshine.

Large daily temperature range. In the high desert of the Southwest, the difference between daily high and low temperatures is often 35° —nearly twice that in most other areas of the country, which causes greater amounts of midday heat to be driven more deeply into the masonry than would occur in areas of lower daily temperature differences.

High elevations. At six thousand feet above sea level, the air is thinner and sunrays are 10–15 percent stronger than at lower elevations.

Highly reflective terrain. The Southwest's smooth, mostly bare light-orange rocky earths reflect much more radiance onto nearby south-facing facades than do more earthen terrains covered with foliage.

Cooler indoor temperatures. 55° indoor temperatures are quite comfortable for pueblo dwellers while anything less than 65° is considered uncomfortable in so-called modern buildings. Cooler indoor temperatures increase the amount of effective heat that flows indoors.

These factors combine to drive great amounts of radiance deep into the exposed pueblo masonry where after sunset it migrates readily to interior spaces. But in other regions where these factors are absent, thermal massing must be carefully located well indoors, have maximum surface-to-volume exposure to interior spaces, be enclosed by a superinsulated building envelope, have windows covered with thick movable insulation to keep the collected heat indoors when the sun isn't shining, and be constructed economically.

Otherwise, the result won't be worth the effort.

If thermal massing is built as described above, it works as follows: When the sun's rays become strong enough near mid-morning, the panels of movable insulation covering the solar glass open, then the sun shines through the glass and heats the indoor air and adjacent thermal massing, until by early afternoon the temperature of both is, say, 75° (if the massing is exposed to direct sunlight its temperature may be 8–10° higher). As the sun weakens in late afternoon, the movable insulation closes over the solar glass; then during the night as indoor air heat flows slowly through the superinsulated envelope, heat flows equally slowly from the thermal massing back into interior spaces; so the indoor air cools more slowly than if the massing weren't there. If indoor temperatures fall to, say, 65° by sunrise the next morning, the massing has released (75 − 65 = 10)° Btus per unit mass × its capacity to hold heat. Most masonry holds heat effectively only to depths of 4–6 in. Liquid massing often works better, because it can disperse heat within its mass via convection as well as conduction.

Although concrete or masonry floor slabs usually form the bottom of a building, they thermomass rather well because the Δt between the air above and the earth below is usually low, and, since heat rises, the massed heat will not tend to migrate downward. A good floor under a wall of thermal massing is 6 in. concrete on 4 in. styrofoam insulation. Styrofoam is surprisingly strong, as it has a compressive strength of 20 psi ≈ 3,000 psf; thus it will support an 8 ft high grouted 8 in. concrete block wall if rebars are laid in the concrete beneath the wall as shown in Fig. 2-32.

Another approach to thermal massing is *electric thermal storage (ETS) units*. These are cabinet-sized electric heaters (typical dimensions are $24\frac{1}{2}$ in. high, $10\frac{1}{2}$ in. deep, and 30–58 in. long) that contain a number of high-density ceramic bricks that can store much heat for extended periods of time. During off-peak hours each unit stores electrically produced heat in the bricks which are stacked in an insulated chamber, then when the heat is needed during on-peak hours when energy rates are higher, a small

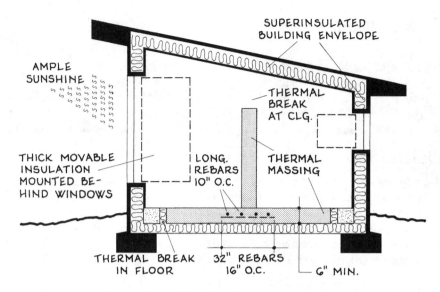

Fig. 2-32. Effective thermal massing.

blower circulates interior air slowly and quietly through the bricks. The units are intended for residential and small commercial occupancies, each requires a 240 V outlet, and a humidifier can be added. Thus, instead of thermomassing the sun's energy, this appliance does the same with electricity. Its bricks are removable, which suggests a host of apparently yet-unexplored applications for them. For example, the manufacturer uses the bricks in a heat pump booster and a furnace it makes, but would they also work if exposed to sunlight? And could they be used to build the walls of a fireplace? ETS units are made by the Steffe Corp. of Dickinson, ND.

TABLE 2-12: CAPACITANCE OF BUILDING MATERIALS [†]		
MATERIAL	Capacitance, Btu/cf · °F.	Latent Heat of Fusion, °F.
Red brick	24.6	—
Fire brick	43.6	—
Sand	18.1	—
Gypsum	20.3	—
Fresh Water	62.4	—
Concrete, granite	31–32	—
Growing soil	13.9	—
Still air	0.018	—
Paraffin	38.4	3,570 at 115°
Glauber's salt	—	7,760 at 73°
Sodium Sulphate	—	6,600–9,000 at 65–89°

[†] the primary source for this table's values was *The Solar Home Book*, Bruce

2.E.6.a. Heating Load

A two-story solar residence in Albany, NY, has a 24 ft long, 8 ft high, 4 in. thick red brick wall running down the center of the lower floor. If indoor temperatures rise to 76° on a clear day and nightly temperatures fall to 65°, how much heat does the wall store?

2)E)6)a)
$$H_{tm} = C V (T_a - T_e)$$

H_{tm} = design latent heat stored by thermal massing, **?** Btu/day
C = capacitance of thermal massing: capacity to store thermal energy, Btu/cf·°F. From Table 2-12, C of brick = 24.6 Btu/cf·°F.
V = volume of thermal massing, cf. 24 × 8 × 4 in/12 ft = 64 cf.
T_a = temperature of thermal massing at maximum heat absorption, 76°F
T_e = temperature of thermal massing at maximum heat depletion, 65°F

$$H_{tm} = 24.6 \times 64 \times (76 - 65) = 17,000 \text{ Btu/day}$$

2.E.6.b. Energy Auditing

In the previous example, how much heat does the thermal massing store during the month of January?

2)E)6)b)
$$H_{tm} \approx 0.010 \, t \, C \, V \, P \, (T_a - T_e)$$

H_{tm} = latent heat stored by thermal massing for period of energy audit, **?** Btu. Formula is valid only if envelope is superinsulated and insulation covers glazing at night.
t = period of energy audit, days. For January audit, t = 31 days.
C = capacitance of thermal massing, Btu/cf·°F. From previous example, C = 24.6 Btu/cf·°F.
V = volume of thermal massing, from previous example, 64 cf
P = average percentage of local sunshine during period of energy audit. From *Comparative Climatic Data*, © U.S. Department. of Commerce, P for Albany, NY, area in Jan. = 46%.
T_a = temperature of massing at maximum heat absorption, 76°F
T_e = temperature of massing at maximum heat depletion, 65°F

$$H_{tm} = 0.010 \times 31 \times 24.6 \times 64 \times 46 (76 - 65) = 247,000 \text{ Btu}$$

Anderson (Cheshire books, Harrisville, NH, 1976).

2.E.7. Total Solar Energy Savings

To determine a solar heating system's cost-effectiveness, one must compute the energy savings of the parent building as below:

> If the backup heating system in a superinsulated solar house near Albany, NY, is electric baseboard and the electricity costs 11¢ per kWh, what is the building's estimated January heating bill? Its design heating loads for this month are conduction/infiltration = 12,000,000 Btu, auxiliary heat gain = 2,420,000 Btu, solar heat gain = 5,050,000 Btu, and thermal massing = 200,000 Btu.

Step 1. Find the solar heating system's Solar Load Ratio for the period of the energy audit.

2)E)7) $$\kappa_{slr} = \Phi_a/(H_{ci} + H_p + H_{tm} - H_{ah})$$

κ_{slr} = Solar Load Ratio: ratio of solar heat gain to design heat loss through the building envelope, **?**

Φ_a = average solar heat gain through solar glazing during period of energy audit, Btu. Φ_a for Jan. = 4,690,000 Btu.

H_{ci} = design heating load due to conduction-infiltration through building envelope during period of energy audit, Btu. H_{ci} for Jan. = 12,000,000 Btu.

H_p = design pickup heating load for interior spaces during cold weather during period of energy audit, 0 Btu

H_{tm} = average latent heat stored due to thermal massing during period of energy audit, Btu. H_{tm} for Jan. = 200,000 Btu.

H_{ah} = design auxiliary heat gain added to interior spaces during period of energy audit, Btu. H_{ah} for Jan. = 2,420,000 Btu.

$$\kappa_{slr} = 4,690/(12,000 + 0 + 200 - 2,420) = 0.48$$

Step 2. Find the building's Heating Load Fraction. In the bar graph of Fig. 2-33, if the Solar Load Ratio = 0.48, Heating Load Fraction = 0.52.

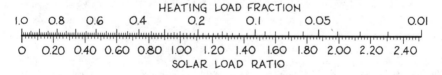

Fig. 2-33. Solar Load Ratio vs. Heating Load Fraction.

Step 3. Compute the cost of heating the solar architecture for the period of the energy audit.

$$\$_h \, \kappa_e \, \varepsilon \; = \; 100 \; \kappa_{hlf} \, \$_u \, (H_{ci} + H_p + H_{tm} - H_{ah})$$

$\$_h$ = cost of heating the solar architecture during period of energy audit, **?** dollars for Jan.

κ_e = energy conversion factor. From Table 3-1, 1 kWh = 3,413 Btu.

ε = efficiency of backup heating system, %.
From Table 2-13, ε for electric baseboard heaters $\approx$ 90 %.

$\$_u$ = unit cost of energy, dollars. From local data, ¢ = $0.08/kWh.

κ_{hlf}, H_{ci}, H_p, H_{tm}, and H_{ah} are as previously defined

$$\$ \times 3{,}413 \times 0.9 \; \approx \; 0.52 \times 0.08 \, (12{,}000{,}000 + 200{,}000 + 0 - 2{,}420{,}000)$$
$$\$ \; \approx \; \$133$$

Note: The building's heating cost is very low because (1) its heat losses are low due to its superinsulated envelope, (2) much of the remaining loss is replenished by solar energy, and (3) further heat is conserved with thermal massing.

2.E.8. Summary of Loads

2.E.8.a. Total Heating Load

> **Example 1.** What is the total design heating load of a solar house near Albany, NY, if its design conduction/infiltration heating load is 24,900 Btu/hr, auxiliary heat gain is 930 Btu/hr, thermal massing load for January is 200,000 Btu, and the average solar heat gain for January is 5,050,000 Btu?

2)E)8)a) $\qquad$ $H = \Phi_h + H_{ci} + H_p + H_{tm} - H_{ah}$

H = total heating load at design temperature, **?** Btu/hr

TABLE 2-13: EFFICIENCY OF HEATING SYSTEMS

TYPE OF HEATING SYSTEM	Approximate efficiency, %
Electric baseboards, infrared electric units, kerosene space heaters .	90
Gas-fired furnaces w/ makeup air, gas-fire radiant ceiling units	80
Oil-fired furnaces w/ air ducts, hot water boiler w/ water baseboards ..	70
Wood or coal stoves (non-airtight), Rumford fireplaces	40
Above stoves, airtight	60
Fireplaces w/ conventional open hearths	20
Above w/ glass doors	40

Φ_h = solar heat gain, Btu/hr. As solar heat gains typically have little effect on design heating load around sunrise in Jan., Φ = 0.

H_{ci} = design heating load due to conduction-infiltration through building envelope during cold weather, 24,900 Btu/hr

H_p = design pickup heating load for interior spaces during cold weather in Jan., 0 Btu/hr

H_{tm} = design latent heat stored by thermal massing, Btu/hr. As thermal massing typically has little effect on design heating load around sunrise in Jan., H_{tm} = 0.

H_{ah} = design auxiliary heat gain added to interior spaces at heating load design temperature, 930 Btu/hr

$$H = 0 + 24,900 + 0 + 0 - 930 = 24,000 \text{ Btu/hr}$$

Example 2. What is the total design heating load of a small church in Dubois, WY, if its conduction-infiltration heating load is 216,000 Btu/hr and its pickup heating load is 86,000 Btu/hr?

---

2)E)8)a) $$H = \Phi_h + H_{ci} + H_p + H_{tm} - H_{ah}$$

H = total heating load at design temperature, **?** Btu/hr

Φ_h = solar heat gain, Btu/hr. Assume 0.

H_{ci} = design heating load due to conduction-infiltration through building envelope during cold weather, 216,000 Btu/hr

H_p = design pickup heating load for interior spaces during cold weather, 86,000 Btu/hr

H_{tm} = design latent heat stored by thermal massing, Btu/hr. Assume 0.

H_{ah} = design auxiliary heat gain added to interior spaces at heating load design temperature, 0 Btu/hr

$$H = 0 + 216,000 + 86,000 + 0 - 0 = 302,000 \text{ Btu/hr}$$

2.E.8.b. Total Cooling Load

What is the total design cooling load of an office unit in a building in Dallas, TX, if its design conduction-infiltration cooling load is 2,800 Btu/hr and its auxiliary heat gain is 2,560 Btu/hr?

---

2)E)8)b) $$C = C_{ci} + C_{ah}$$

C = total cooling load at design temperature, **?** Btu/hr

C_{ci} = design cooling load due to conduction-infiltration through building envelope during warm weather, 2,800 Btu/hr

C_{ah} = design auxiliary heat gain added to interior spaces at cooling load design temperature, 2,560 Btu/hr

$$\text{C} = 2,800 + 2,560 = 5,360 \text{ Btu/hr}$$

2.E.8.c. Total Energy Auditing

As the length of heating and cooling seasons varies greatly in different regions of the country, an easy way to perform a building's energy auditing calculations is on a monthly basis. If local monthly degree-day data for heating and cooling seasons is not available, this information may be obtained from the U.S. Department. of Commerce publication, *Comparative Climatic Data*; then energy auditing involves filling in the schedule below. This schedule may be enlarged on a photocopier. In many regions, spring and fall months often have heating and cooling loads.

ENERGY AUDITING SCHEDULE

Month	H_{ci}	C_{ci}	H_{ah}	H_p	Φ_h	Δ_{tm}	H	C
JAN	——	——	——	——	——	——	——	——
FEB	——	——	——	——	——	——	——	——
MAR	——	——	——	——	——	——	——	——
APR	——	——	——	——	——	——	——	——
MAY	——	——	——	——	——	——	——	——
JUN	——	——	——	——	——	——	——	——
JUL	——	——	——	——	——	——	——	——
AUG	——	——	——	——	——	——	——	——
SEP	——	——	——	——	——	——	——	——
OCT	——	——	——	——	——	——	——	——
NOV	——	——	——	——	——	——	——	——
DEC	——	——	——	——	——	——	——	——
ANNUAL	——	——	——	——	——	——	——	——

PROJECT DESIGN WEATHER DATA

Data	Amount	
LOCAL LATITUDE.........................	_____	°
MAXIMUM RAINFALL INTENSITY...........	_____	in/hr
MAXIMUM WIND PRESSURE...............	_____	psf
EARTHQUAKE ZONE......................	_____	
AVERAGE ANNUAL TEMPERATURE.........	_____	°
WINTER DESIGN TEMPERATURE...........	_____	°
SUMMER DESIGN TEMPERATURE.........	_____	°
AVERAGE RELATIVE HUMIDITY............	_____	%
SUMMER DESIGN ENTHALPY..............	_____	Btu/lb
LOCAL CLARITY FRACTION...............	_____	
SUN ANGLE DUE SOUTH, NOON JUN 21...	_____	° alt.
SUN ANGLE DUE SOUTH, NOON DEC 21...	_____	° alt.

INSOLATION DATA, BUT/FT^2 PER DAY:

NOV. 21	DEC. 21	JAN. 21	FEB. 21	MAR. 21	APR. 21
_____	_____	_____	_____	_____	_____

SPECIAL CONSIDERATIONS:

(This databox may be duplicated and
affixed to drawings or specifications)

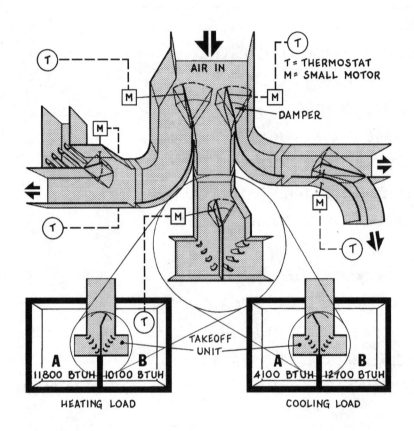

AIR IN

T = THERMOSTAT
M = SMALL MOTOR

DAMPER

TAKEOFF UNIT

A 11800 BTUH | **B** 10100 BTUH

A 4100 BTUH | **B** 12100 BTUH

HEATING LOAD

COOLING LOAD

DUCTING TAKEOFFS

CLIMATE CONTROL

3.A. GENERAL

During periods of thermal imbalance between indoors and outdoors, a building's climate control system creates the opposite effect of the weather outside to keep its interior spaces continually comfortable. In addition to maintaining ideal temperatures such systems optimize humidity, freshen the air, remove airborne contaminants, and eliminate odors. The result is what HVAC engineers call IAQ: *indoor air quality.*

Modern climate control system design is complex due to a number of factors, as summarized below:

Interchanging componentry. Today's interior environments can be made comfortable with a number of different systems whose componentry can be combined in many ways.

Complex requirements. Many modern buildings have continually changing occupancies that impose constantly changing comfort demands on existing climate control systems.

Computerization. The computerized controls that operate many buildings today are often difficult to learn, not yet fully developed, and have high initial costs which often obscure their long-term economies.

Systems integration. Many climate control systems contain plumbing, wiring, and other componentry which may introduce integration problems with other mechanical systems.

Public utility options. As some electric utilities have found it more economical to promote energy efficiency than build more power plants, they may offer energy-saving perquisites that can reorder an architect's priorities for designing cost-effective buildings.

The Energy Policy Act of 1992. As a way of making our nation's future more secure and emphasizing the importance of energy conservation as an investment, the government has mandated more stringent energy efficiency standards for a number of climate control systems and related componentry. This may create fundamental changes in the selection of some of these components in the future.

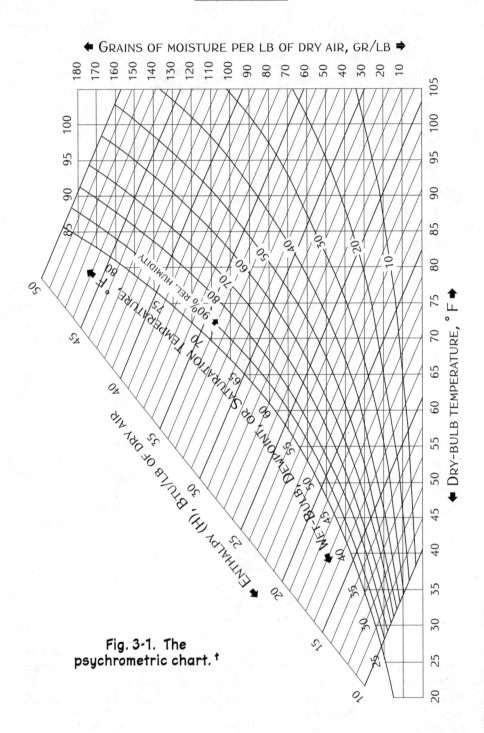

Fig. 3-1. The psychrometric chart. †

3.A.1. Psychrometry

The psychrometric chart is a cleverly constructed nomogram that describes several properties of atmospheric air. Although the arrangement of crisscrossing lines is based on semi-empirical research and its parameters are essentially arbitrary, this graph has evolved into a highly authoritarian 'air atlas' that possesses the highest credibility in our engineering culture. Like what the periodic chart does for the elements and quantum physics does for the atom, the psychrometric chart makes supreme sense and order of something we cannot see.

The psychrometric chart shown in Fig. 3-1 contains four different graph coordinates. They are

1. **Dry-bulb temperature** (in ° F)... ||||| lines; the thermometer temperature. The scale for these lines extends along the bottom of the graph.
2. **Wet-bulb temperature** (° F) ... ＼＼＼ lines, as measured by a thermometer whose bulb is covered by a wetted wick and exposed to rapidly moving air. Wet-bulb temperature is always lower than dry-bulb temperature except at 100 percent humidity; then the wet-bulb temperature becomes the *dew-point temperature*; then if the temperature falls any lower, water falls out of the air —i.e. becomes dew or collects in tiny droplets on surfaces exposed to the air. The scale for these lines extends along the prominent upper-left curve and then the top of the graph. Related to wet-bulb temperature is *enthalpy*, measured in Btu/lb of dry air. Enthalpy (H) is the amount of moisture that air holds at a given temperature: it is the true "effective temperature" of warm air; as such it is a function of dry-bulb temperature and relative humidity. The enthalpy scale is the inclined straight-line scale beyond the upper left of the graph.
3. **Air moisture** (grains/lb of dry air) ... ☰ lines. Also known as *humidity ratio*, this is the weight of water (lb or gr) per lb of dry air. The scale for these lines is along the right of the graph.
4. **Relative humidity** (percent)... ⟋⟋ lines. This is the percent ratio of actual water vapor in the air to the saturated water vapor in the air at a given temperature. Typical percentages for a particular region are often given in published climatic data. The scale for these lines extends in a downward curve through the central part of the graph.

Regarding the above scales, the dry-bulb temperature and relative humidity scales describe what we feel every day. Equally important for Æ design is enthalpy and air moisture, because these values define the adiabatic processes that underlie the selecting and sizing of climate control

System Design, prepared by the Carrier Corp. (McGraw-Hill, New York, 1965);   ⫼

systems. Another commonly used term is *atmospheric* or *barometric pressure* (in. Hg). This is the pressure of the air or atmosphere as measured by the height of a column of mercury whose norm at standard conditions of temperature (0° C. or 32° F.) and gravity (sea level) is 760 mm (29.91 in. or 1,013 millibars). In other words, at sea level the atmosphere's pressure is normally 29.91 in, which may vary from about 27.3 to 31.1 in. depending on the weather. Atmospheric pressure also decreases as the elevation above sea level increases. However, at any elevation above sea level, the barometers of local meteorologists are usually adjusted to provide readings that relate to sea-level norms. Atmospheric pressure is commonly recorded by an aneroid barometer, an instrument that contains no liquid, operates independently of gravity, and is portable so it can be used under conditions that are prohibitive for mercury barometers.

The effect of increasing altitude on the various scales of the psychrometric chart is as follows: the dry-bulb temperature lines are unchanged, the wet-bulb temperature lines move farther part, the air moisture lines move upward, the relative humidity curves move farther apart, and the specific volume lines move upward to the right.

The many different kinds of climate control systems installed in today's buildings use several different kinds of fuel. Thus it is helpful to have the energy conversion table below. Its heat content values are approximate: e.g. that of oak varies slightly according to subspecies, density, and local growing conditions. Even the heat content of oil and gas vary slightly from one region to another.

TABLE 3-1: ENERGY CONVERSION FACTORS

FUEL	COAL (lb)	OIL (gal)	PROPANE (therm)	ELECTRIC (kWh)	OAK (lb)	SOLAR (square)
COAL (lb)	14,600 BTU	0.160	0.195	4.28	3.73	0.487
OIL (gal)	6.23	91,000 BTU	1.213	26.67	23.27	3.033
PROPANE (therm)	5.137	0.824	75,000 BTU	21.97	19.18	2.500
ELECTRIC (kWh) .	0.234	0.038	0.046	3,413 BTU	0.87	0.114
OAK (lb)	0.268	0.043	0.052	1.15	3,910 BTU	0.130
SOLAR (square) .	2.055	0.330	0.400	8.79	7.67	30,000 BTU

pp. 115–117.

Example 1. What is the enthalpy of indoor air whose temperature is 68° F and relative humidity is 50 percent?

From the psychrometric chart of Fig. 3-1, at a dry-bulb temperature of 68° and relative humidity of 50 percent, enthalpy = 24.5 Btu/lb of dry air.

Note: An enthalpy of about 25 Btu/lb of dry air is considered to be the most comfortable temperature and humidity during cold weather.

Example 2. What is the dew point of the air in Example 1?

The dew point of air at a certain temperature and humidity is found from the psychrometric chart of Fig. 3-1 as follows: After locating the point of 68 ° F and 50 percent r.h. on the chart, proceed horizontally to the left to the upper leftmost curve of the graph, then read the scale ➡ dew point = 49°.

Example 3. What's the volume of 1 lb of air whose enthalpy = 25 Btu/lb?

From Fig. 3-1, at H = 25 Btu/lb, 1 lb of air has a volume of 13.4 cf.

Example 4. What is the enthalpy of indoor air whose temperature is 78° F and relative humidity is 50 percent?

From Fig. 3-1, at a dry-bulb temperature of 78° and relative humidity of 50%, enthalpy = 30.1 Btu/lb of dry air.

Example 5. What is the dew point of the above air?

After locating the point of 87° and 50 percent r.h. in Fig. 3-1, proceed horizontally to the left to the upper leftmost curve of the graph, then read the scale ➡ dew point = 58°.

Example 6. What's the volume of 1 lb of air whose enthalpy = 30 Btu/lb?

From Fig. 3-1, at H = 30 Btu/lb, 1 lb of air has a volume of 13.8 cf.

3.B. SYSTEM COMPONENTS

Climate control systems have numerous components-in-common which are described in detail in the following sections. Typical IAQ parameters for these systems are:

Temperature: 67–78° year-round. A room's temperature should not vary more than 5° F between 4 in. and 67 in. above its floor.

Humidity: 40–60 percent all year round.

Airflow: 10–50 fpm.

CO_2: should not exceed 800 parts per million.

Static air pressure: positive for spaces that generate clean air, negative for spaces that generate dirty or foul air.

Pollution: low levels of dusts, molds, odors, noxious gases, VOXs (volatile organic compounds), microbes, chemicals, etc.

Adequate illumination: at least 50 fc in all areas related to monitoring and maintaining climate control system componentry.

Since a climate control system's operating costs during its expected life usually far exceed its initial cost, the unit cost of the energy a particular system consumes may often determine which system is most feasible for a given installation. Thus the following four heat content equations may be used to determine whether electricity, fuel oil, propane, or natural gas is the most economical energy for a given installation. But even these equations cannot inform a designer or client how much the energy costs in a given locality may vary in the future.

3)B)1)	Electric resistance heat:	E_{MBtu} = ____ ¢/kWh × 293
2)	No. 2 fuel oil:	E_{MBtu} = ____ \$/gal × 7.14
3)	Propane:	E_{MBtu} = ____ \$/gal [100 psi] × 422
4)	Natural gas:	E_{MBtu} = ____ ¢/therm × 10.0

E_{MBtu} = million Btus of energy consumed by the energy used

3.B.1. Sensors [†]

A good guide for providing sensors in today's climate control systems is: if you can't measure it, you can't manage it. Thus today's computerized climate control systems often have extensive networks of "slave" sensors that detect a single indoor air quality —temperature, humidity, CO_2, etc.— then emit an electronic impulse that informs "master" sensors how to operate the system's motors, dampers, and other controls. The most common master sensor is the thermostat. One often has HI and LO tempera-

---

[†] Much of the information for indoor air quality sensors in general and CO_2 sen-

ture settings, START and STOP time settings, SETBACK and SETFORWARD temperature settings, and other IAQ monitoring controls. A thermostat should be visible anywhere in the space it serves, and should be located away from heating and cooling units, supply registers, windows, major doorways, motors, and other hot or cold spots. Several kinds of slave sensors are described below.

Temperature. These usually dime-size detectors measure temperature levels in a duct or near a piece of equipment. They are inexpensive, respond quickly to temperature changes, have excellent long-term stability, are virtually unaffected by wiring distances, and are highly accurate over short temperature ranges. Some can even perform self-tests and notify host controls if they need recalibrating and can perform other diagnostic sensing that ensures system integrity.

Humidity. These sensors measure the relative humidity in outdoor, supply, or interior air. When combined with temperature sensors they become enthalpy sensors, which are the surest means of maintaining comfortable indoor air. During warm weather, air is considered to be optimally comfortable at an enthalpy of about 30 Btu/lb of dry air, which occurs at a temperature of 77° and relative humidity of 50 percent. Enthalpy also equals 30 Btu/lb when the air's temperature and humidity is 65° at 100 percent, 67° at 90 percent, 70° at 76 percent, 75° at 58 percent, 80° at 44 percent, 85° at 33 percent, and even 90° at 24 percent. At all these temperatures and humidities air usually feels comfortable.

Dew point. These are enthalpy sensors that tell when a cold airflow is about to become saturated with water vapor. This is often necessary in air conditioning systems, particularly in humid regions where such sensing keeps moisture from condensing in ducting by informing precoolers or dehumidifiers to remove additional moisture from preconditioned air.

Smoke. These sensors range from isolated ceiling-mounted detectors containing a battery and buzzer to extensive networks in which each sensor is connected by a double-jacketed wire run through fire-resistant steel conduit to central controls. Maximum unit coverage is usually 900 sf and pairs should be placed no more than 41 ft apart. In extensive systems, sensing of fire or smoke typically causes the affected area's floor-level return air ducts to close, ceiling-level return air ducts to open, all supply ducts to close, and all exhaust air to be directed outdoors. When smoke sensors and static air pressure (s.a.p.) sensors are combined, controls can activate emergency ventilators that pull combustion gases from fire exit zones and toward dead-end areas, thus moving the smoke away from the direction occupants are fleeing. Thus fire exit routes should be designed as positive static air pressure zones and each should have return air grilles in its ceiling or high in its walls. Beyond these logistics, effective location of smoke sensors is difficult, because air micromovement in the vicinity of a fire is unpredictable since some smokes are lighter than air while others are heavier; thus different smokes can stratify within a small area or move in layers and not activate sensors only inches away. Smoke sensors should also be activated automatically and not manually, because when a fire breaks out, occupants often flee to a safe area before thinking of sending an alarm; then their notification from safe refuges could send inaccurate locational data to controls, which could cause smoke to flow toward safe areas instead of from them.

Static air pressure. Also known as *s.a.p. sensors*, these detect air pressure in an interior space. A positive (+) s.a.p. indicates a clean area from where fresh air may flow into adjacent areas, while a negative (−) s.a.p. indicates a dirty or foul area (kitchen, rest room, industrial operation, etc.) into which cleaner air should flow. Thus these detectors can induce air to flow from any one space to another. For example, odors may be removed from a public restroom by locating a positive s.a.p. sensor near a supply air grille above the entrance door and a negative s.a.p. sensor near a return air grille above the toilets. The greater the pressure differential between two such sensors, the faster the airflow between them. S.a.p. sensors can be calibrated to accuracies of 0.001 in. wg. The general formulas for computing static air pressure losses in HVAC systems are

3)B)1)a) $\Delta P_T = \Delta P_i + \Delta P_d - \Delta P_r$

ΔP_T = total static air pressure (s.a.p.) loss from beginning to end of any continuous length of HVAC ducting, in. wg.

ΔP_i = initial s.a.p. loss at the beginning of duct, in. wg. This loss is usually due to the operating pressure of the discharge fan, and it is a function of the velocity of the duct airflow as follows:

3)B)1)b) $\Delta P_i = (v_i/4005)^2$

3)B)1)c) $\Delta P_i = (Q_i/4005\ A_i)^2$

v_i = initial velocity of airflow in duct, fpm
Q_i = initial volume of airflow in duct, cfm
A_i = initial section area of ducting, sf

ΔP_d = unit s.a.p. loss due to duct friction. As air flows through a duct it experiences a continual loss in pressure depending on the airflow velocity, the duct's section area, the duct's length, and the roughness of the duct's inner surface as follows:

3)B)1)d) $10{,}700{,}000\ \Delta P_d\ s^{1.22} = \kappa_r\ L\ v_i^{1.82}$ wherein

s = width of one side of duct if it is square, in. If duct is rectangular, $s = 0.5\ b\ d$; if duct is round, $s = 0.785\ \delta$.

κ_r = inner wall surface roughness coefficient. $\kappa_r = 0.009$ for galvanized sheet steel. This value may be used for almost any duct metal or smooth duct lining.

Dilemma", *Engineering Systems* magazine (Business News Publishing Co., Troy, MI)

L = length of ducting run, ft. L may be the duct's total length or it may be taken as 1.0 ft so that a unit ΔP_d throughout the ducting system is obtained.

v_i = initial velocity of ducting airflow, cfm.

ΔP_r = s.a.p. regain at duct outlet, in. wg. As a duct's airflow nears its outlet, the impeding mass of air immediately in front of it becomes absent and thus the airflow velocity increases slightly (thus its pressure decreases slightly) as it leaves the outlet. This pressure regain depends on the airflow's initial velocity at the face of the discharge fan (v_f) and its theoretical outlet velocity (v_o) as follows:

$\boxed{3}\boxed{B}\boxed{1}\boxed{e}$ If $v_f > v_o$: $\Delta P_r = 0.75\,[(v_i/4005)^2 - (v_o/4005)^2]$

$\boxed{3}\boxed{B}\boxed{1}\boxed{f}$ If $v_f < v_o$: $\Delta P_r = -1.1\,[(v_o/4005)^2 - (v_i/4005)^2]$

v_o = velocity of airflow at duct outlet, cfm

CO_2. When humans exhale, their breath contains about 3.8 percent or 38,000 ppm of CO_2. This amount normally dissipates into the surrounding air, which if outdoors has a concentration of about 0.04 percent or 400 ppm in rural areas and about 550 ppm in urban areas. If several people are in an indoor space with unopenable windows, as they breathe they slowly deplete the room's supply of oxygen and increase its level of CO_2 by the same amount. However, while a room's oxygen may be depleted from a normal 21 percent to about 16 percent before its occupants feel uncomfortable, if the CO_2 level increases from 0.04 percent to about 0.15 percent —1/50th the depletion of oxygen— occupants begin to feel uncomfortable. Thus CO_2 is a far more accurate indicator of indoor fresh air than oxygen. CO_2 levels are also more easily equated with occupancy loads and activities (e.g. sedentary, dancing, athletic); they are generated by humans at fairly predictable rates, their concentrations are easily measured, they degrade slowly, and CO_2 does not react readily with other gases. Average O_2 depletion/CO_2 production levels for various human activities are sleeping ≈ 0.5 cf/hr, office work ≈ 0.85 cf/hr, walking at $2\frac{1}{2}$ mph ≈ 1.2 cf/hr, and heavy exercise ≈ 2.5 cf/hr.

The OSHA-proposed maximum CO_2 level for human occupancies is 800 ppm, a level that is considered as optimal for indoor human occupancy. Also, never confuse carbon dioxide (CO_2) with carbon monoxide (CO). Notice the extra oxygen molecule that carbon dioxide has. Carbon monoxide has a craving for it —which makes this gas deadly to humans.

In an HVAC system CO_2 sensors may be installed as follows. Each HVAC zone has a CO_2 sensor just inside its supply air grille and another just inside its return air grille (or as part of a wall thermostat located away from doors, openable windows, vents, etc.), then the whole building has a CO_2 sensor inside its outdoor air intake which monitors the level of outdoor air. When the return air sensor in any zone detects a CO_2 level above,

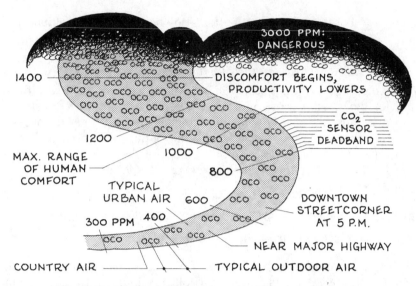

Fig. 3-2. Typical CO₂ concentration levels in air.

say, 1,000 ppm, it notifies host controls, which command the splitter damper between the outdoor air intake and the zone's supply air grill to open wider, then the zone's air becomes diluted with outdoor air whose CO_2 level is typically about 400 ppm. This "ΔC" of 1,000 – 400 = 600 ppm represents a fresh airflow of about 18 cfm per sedentary occupant in the zone. After fresher air arrives, the CO_2 level steadily lowers; then when it falls below, say, 550 ppm, host controls readjust the splitter damper. In well-tuned systems, the damper cycles on and off less frequently if the system is programmed to continually deliver fresh air (as opposed to cycling on and off according to a prescribed timespan). This continuous-airflow strategy is known as *demand-controlled ventilation* (DCV), or CO_2-based DCV, and it allows spaces to be ventilated not in terms of their design occupancy (i.e. fully occupied) but by actual occupancy, which conserves energy during periods of low occupancy or vacancy. A related strategy is *trend measurement*, in which a CO_2 sensor records periodic readings for an intermittent and predictable occupancy (e.g. classrooms, cafeterias, auditoriums), then host controls mix the required fresh air just before the space is to be occupied.

CO_2 sensors typically have a range from 0–0.5 percent (0–5,000 ppm) and are accurate to ±0.002 percent (±20 ppm). Each should be easily accessible, as they usually need to be recalibrated annually.

Example 1. A cafeteria in an office building with landscaped grounds typically seats 220 people plus a staff of 15 during lunch. Based on CO_2 levels, what is the optimal ventilation load for this space?

<u>3</u> <u>B</u> <u>1</u> <u>g</u> $500\ Q\ =\ \Theta\ \eta\ (C_i - C_o)$

Q = optimal ventilation load based on CO_2 concentration, **?** cfm
Θ = fresh air requirement per occupant, based on activity, cfm/occ.
    From Table 3-7, Θ for cafeteria = 20 cfm/occupant
η = number of occupants in zone. 220 + 15 = 235 occupants.
C_i = indoor CO_2 setpoint, use 1,000 ppm unless otherwise noted.
C_o = outdoor CO_2 level, ppm. As building surrounds are landscaped,
    assume normal outdoor CO_2 level of 400 ppm. In highly polluted
    urban areas, C_o may equal 600–700 ppm.

$$500\ Q\ =\ 20 \times 235\ (1,000 - 400)$$
$$Q\ =\ 5,640\ \text{cfm during lunch}$$

Example 2. In the above example, between 1:30 and 2:55 the cafeteria typically contains only 20 people and 8 staff members. What is its optimal ventilation load during this time?

$$500\ Q\ =\ \Theta\ \eta\ (C_i - C_o)$$

Q = optimal ventilation load based on CO_2 concentration, **?** cfm
Θ = fresh air requirement per occupant, based on activity, cfm/occ.
    From Table 3-7, θ for cafeteria = 20 cfm/occ.
η = number of occupants in zone. 20 + 8 = 28 occupants.
C_i = indoor CO_2 setpoint, 1,000 ppm
C_o = outdoor CO_2 level, 400 ppm

$$500\ Q\ =\ 20 \times 28\ (1,000 - 400) \qquad \dots Q\ =\ 672\ \text{cfm}$$

VOC. When these sensors are exposed to certain volatile organic compounds —aerosols, hydrocarbons, carbon monoxide, other odorless gases, products of combustion, and other noxious aromatics— they emit an electronic pulse that activates an alarm or increases fresh airflow that dilutes a zone's undesired air to acceptable levels. Rather than being calibrated to known measures, these sensors are basically ON/OFF switches whose factory-made setpoints are programmed to say "yes" or "no" to the presence of a certain quantity of pollutant in the air. Their setpoints can be precisely tailored to detect almost any compound at any temperature, humidity, or concentration.

These sensitive probes are best installed where quick and dangerous changes in indoor air quality could be caused by airborne chemicals whose presence is difficult to detect by smell. A prime example is the possibility of deadly carbon monoxide near generators, furnaces, water heaters, and other fuel-operated appliances. Such machines should be separated from habitable spaces by solid construction and be vented to the outdoors. VOC sensors are also desirable in chemical, industrial, and other environments that may endanger occupant welfare, and they also double as occupancy sensors —for after all, people are volatile organic compounds. Each probe is usually installed as a wall-mounted unit that may emit audible or visual alarms, provide a readout of detected concentrations, or interoperate with programmed controls that activate ventilation systems. Each unit should be accessible for maintenance and have reset capabilities.

Drawbacks of VOC sensors are that they cannot measure CO_2 levels, they react differently to different contaminants, and they cannot distinguish between harmful and harmless volatile compounds (e.g. benzene vs. perfume).

3.B.2. Ducts and Fittings [†]

A common method of conveying conditioned air is through tubes of sheet aluminum or steel that have square, rectangular, round, or oval sections and which are connected with several kinds of joints as shown in Fig. 3-3. Ducts whose diameters or short-side dimensions are 6 in. or less are usually made in multiples of 1 in, while larger ducts are made in multiples of 2 in. Ordinary work consists of slip-in ducts with screwed fittings, good work has machine-formed bolted ducts with cleaned and degreased interior surfaces, and best work has flanged and gasketed connections. A special high-speed variable-air-volume (VAV) duct known as *rigid spiral tubing* has machine-formed round or oval lengths with spiral-lock seams and welded joints.

The most frequently used material for air ducting is hot-dip galvanized sheet steel, the familiar metal with a spangle finish. Its zinc coating is classified from G01 to G360, the G indicating galvanized and the number indicating the amount of zinc per sf of sheet. Thus the bigger the number the thicker the galvanizing. Common grades are G60 for dry indoor ducts and G90 for wet indoor installations or outdoor exposures. The yield strength of the underlying steel is typically 30,000 psi at a temperature limit of 650° F. A similar material is electrogalvanized cold-rolled steel: this has a dull grey matte finish minus the spangle. This finish may seem more attractive to some eyes, but it is not as durable. The underlying steel may also be coated with aluminum (used where ducting is subjected to temperatures as high as 1,000° F) or polyvinyl chloride (used for below-grade and fume exhaust ducts). Ducting may also be stainless steel (used for kitchen and laboratory fume exhausts), aluminum (used for indoor swimming pool exhausts), or copper (used as decorative ducting in restaurants, etc.). Due to aluminum's low modulus of elasticity, it must be 44 percent thicker to

[†] The information in this and the following two sections was obtained largely from

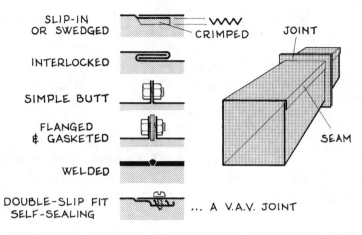

Fig. 3-3. Types of duct joints.

equal the deflection of steel. If two pieces of ducting or their supports, accessories, or connectors are different metals such as aluminum, steel, and copper, they should never be installed next to each other without an isolating medium placed between them, the most common such media being zinc chromate primer and gasketing.

Ducting should generally run as straight and clear of obstructions as possible, contain no corners or crannies that could collect dust and dirt, and have access portals that allow inspection and cleaning of every LF of length. Horizontal runs should pitch at least $1/8$ in/LF to prevent moisture collection. Minimum metal gauge thicknesses for ducting are:

Rectangular ducts: max. dimension, in.	Round ducts: max. dia., in.	Minimum t, U. S. metal gauge
up to 30	8	24
up to 60	24	22
up to 90	48	20
more than 90	72	18

A serious airflow problem in ducting is *stratification*. This is the forming of different horizontal or vertical layers of temperature, humidity, or other air property in the airflow within a section area of ducting. This causes airflow properties to be other than their computed or expected values; which can lead to discomforting air delivery, excessive cycling and breakdown of subcomponents, and wasted energy. Stratification typically occurs where two different kinds of air —e.g. supply and return air— are mixed. The best way to eliminate it is to introduce a little turbulence into the airflow immediately downstream of the mixing area, usually by introducing vanes or other minor obstructions into the airflow. Filters also help here, as they diffuse the airflow. For this reason ducting should not zealously promote laminar airflow.

Ducts may be wrapped with sound-absorbing materials or thermal insulation on the outside, or they may be lined with the same on the inside. Inner surfaces should always be inert, impermeable, non-outgassing, noncombustible, non-shedding, and easy to clean. Lined ducts are slightly more resistant to airflow (thus they require more powerful fans which increase energy costs) but they attenuate sound more effectively. The best liners have sleek surfaces that foster smooth airflow up to 6,000 cfm and temperatures to 250° F. Duct insulation is usually 1 or 2 in. fiberglass batts wrapped with vapor barriers and taped at seams and support penetrations. These thermal barriers eliminate condensation and corrosion on cooling ducts and they typically reduce heat flow through the metal by about 1 Btu/hr-sf-Δf° F, which may allow slightly smaller ducts and central units to be installed.

Ducting requires many kinds of fittings that connect them at intersections and obstructions, where runs are not straight, and where controls are installed. The most common fittings are described below:

Elbows. The most common of many kinds are shown in Fig. 3-4. Generally the higher the air velocity through the elbow, the larger should be its radius. Long-radius elbows should be used wherever possible. Square-vaned elbows are generally used where limited space prevents the use of round elbows.

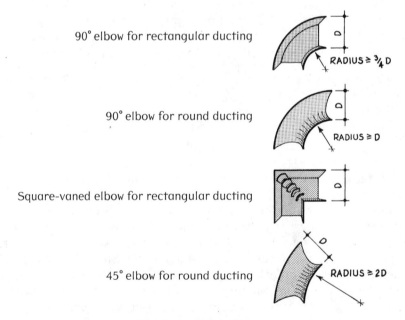

90° elbow for rectangular ducting

RADIUS ≥ ¾ D

90° elbow for round ducting

RADIUS ≥ D

Square-vaned elbow for rectangular ducting

45° elbow for round ducting

RADIUS ≥ 2D

Fig. 3-4. Duct elbows.

Corp. (McGraw-Hill, New York, 1965), chapters 2 and 6.

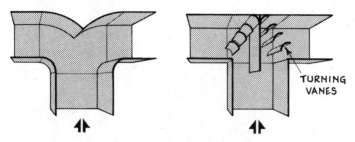

Fig. 3-5. 90° Tees used for rectangular ducting.

Tees. These may be round or rectangular, one's stem may form an angle of 45 to 90° with its top, and the three intersecting ducts may have different sizes. Round tees rarely have redirecting vanes in them, and 90° tees are usually installed only where air velocities are low.

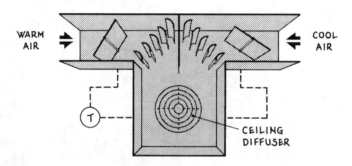

Fig. 3-6. Duct mixing box.

Mixing Boxes. These are used for mixing proper proportions of hot and cold air to create the desired temperature in a space. They usually contain a thermostatically operated movable damper and vanes to redirect the airstream in a confined volume.

Takeoffs. Also known as splitter dampers, these duct intersections contain a thermostat-controlled damper that divides the air for two spaces with different heating and cooling loads. This chapter's frontispiece figure on page 102 shows three takeoffs in which a typical heating/cooling load of one of them is described as follows: in winter, space *A* has a slightly higher heating load than space *B*; but in summer, space *B* has a much higher cooling load than space *A* (this could happen if the building is in a warm region and space *B* has an exterior wall with a large area of glass facing southwest). The takeoff continually divides the incoming air according to the variable loads required in each space.

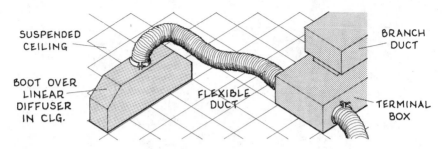

Fig. 3-7. Flexible ducts.

Flexible Ducts. These are usually 3 or 4 in. diameter flexible conduits that carry small amounts of incoming air from the end of branch ducts to registers in small spaces. Since friction loss is higher than in round ducts, they are best used only for short runs. They may be used in high-velocity as well as low-velocity systems.

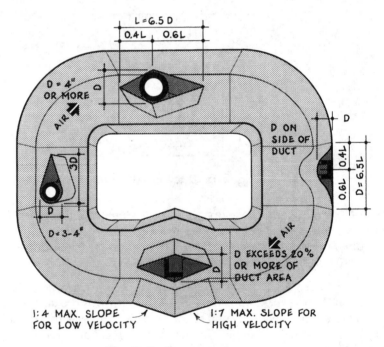

Fig. 3-8. Easements.

Easements. These are installed inside a duct to streamline any hangers, circular obstructions more than 4 in. diameter, stays, or other shapes more than 3 in. wide. If the easement exceeds 20 percent of the duct area, the duct openings on each side should be designed separately.

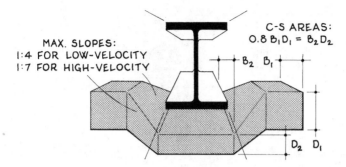

Fig. 3-9. Transformation.

Transformations. These are used to change the shape of a duct that passes obstructions or to increase or decrease a duct area. They may be round, rectangular, or round-to-rectangular.

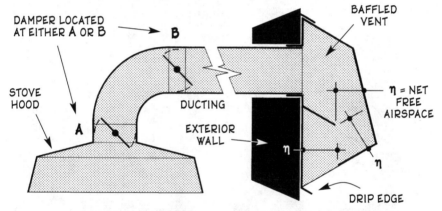

Fig. 3-10. Baffled stove hood exhaust vent.

Exhaust Vents. When stale or foul air is removed from a building, it usually exits through one or more exhaust vents on the roof or high on an exterior wall. Such vents usually face downward; but if the wall is tall, during windy rainy weather strong updrafts can flow up the building's side and send rain into such vents. This common occurrence has a simple solution: install baffles inside the vent that keep rain-laden updrafts from entering it as sketched in Fig. 3-10. A baffled vent can be as small as a residential kitchen stove hood vent or as large as an office tower HVAC exhaust air vent. The baffles inside should *not* be horizontal —as then they collect water and make ideal perches for the nests of pigeons and other birds. When one thinks of how bats and cliff swallows build their homes, even vents with slanted baffles should be located where they can be periodically inspected and cleaned if necessary.

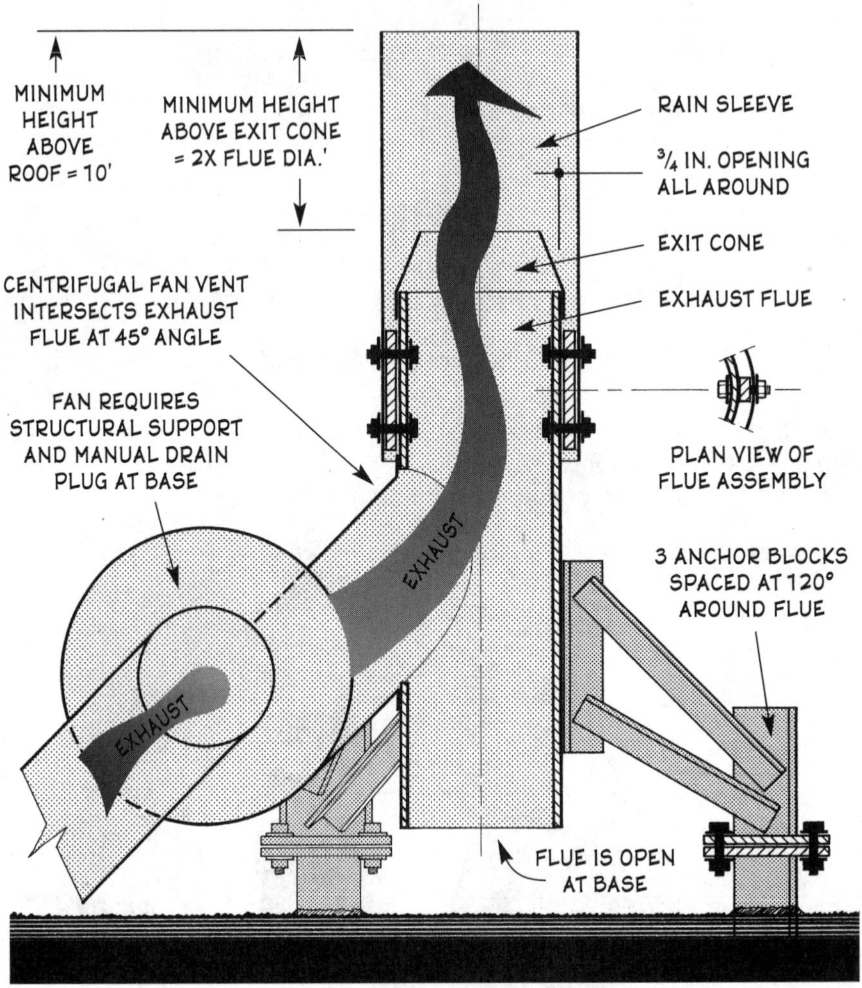

DRIP EDGE

MINIMUM HEIGHT ABOVE ROOF = 10'

MINIMUM HEIGHT ABOVE EXIT CONE = 2X FLUE DIA.'

RAIN SLEEVE

¾ IN. OPENING ALL AROUND

EXIT CONE

EXHAUST FLUE

CENTRIFUGAL FAN VENT INTERSECTS EXHAUST FLUE AT 45° ANGLE

FAN REQUIRES STRUCTURAL SUPPORT AND MANUAL DRAIN PLUG AT BASE

EXHAUST

EXHAUST

PLAN VIEW OF FLUE ASSEMBLY

3 ANCHOR BLOCKS SPACED AT 120° AROUND FLUE

FLUE IS OPEN AT BASE

Fig. 3-11. Roof-mounted HVAC return air vent. †

Another exhaust vent problem has to do with HVAC return air vents on the top of large buildings. Such openings often handle great volumes of air which is best ejected straight upward; but then rain could easily enter the ducting. This problem is solved as sketched in Fig. 3-11: mount a slightly larger-diameter vertical duct sleeve above the vertically oriented return air vent so the rain striking its inside surfaces flows outside the circumference of the return air vent. This technique utilizes the fact that rain rarely falls straight downward. Still, the sleeve's length should be at least 4 times its diameter, and the lower part of the return air vent should have a 45° elbow in which the airflow enters from the side and any rain that enters the vent drains out the bottom.

† The primary source for this figure was Amanda McKew, "HVACR Designer Tips:

Probably the exhaust vent that causes the most trouble for its size is the little residential clothes dryer vent. Indeed, 14,000 fires per year are caused by faulty dryer venting, and this doesn't count the vastly larger number of such vents that disintegrate due to corrosion. Through these usually 4 in-diameter openings flow much moisture- and lint-laden hot air; and this mixture of water, contaminant, and heat can destroy all but perfectly designed exhaust vents, especially ones that may empty where similar conditions exist outdoors, as often occurs in automotive and industrial urban environments. Thus this vent's ducting should not be too large (as then the force of the airflow is diminished which allows lint to fall out and remain in the ducting, which creates a fire hazard), or too small (as then the airflow is restricted and lint again collects inside), or too long (25 ft is maximum, minus 5 ft for each elbow). The ducting to each vent should also be rigid (as the ridges inside the length of a flexible duct catch lint, which creates a fire hazard), the duct lengths should not be connected with hose clamps or tape and not screws or rivets (as these project inside the duct and snag lint, which creates a fire hazard), and the vent opening should not be screened (as this collects lint, which creates a fire hazard) but should have a back-draft damper (a spring- or gravity-controlled flap that remains shut until the airflow pushes it open).

Another duct that causes a lot of trouble is the common commercial kitchen stove hood. One's exhaust is usually hotter than most duct airflows and is laden with grease which drops out of the airflow as it cools. If the grease has had an unsupervised opportunity to build up through the duct's length, a stove-top fire can send torch-like flames into the hood which ignite the grease buildup —then even if the duct contains fire suppressant activators the incipient fire can quickly overwhelm the suppressant and roar like a giant Roman candle through the length of the ducting. This is the cause of 7 percent of all commercial building fires. The Code-mandated fireproofing for this ducting is multiple layers of $5/8$ in. gypsum; but when gypsum is subjected to temperatures exceeding 212° — which happens routinely here— it experiences calcination (loss of its hydrated moisture content), which reduces its fire-protective power. Thus have evolved special design and construction parameters for commercial kitchen stove hoods. The prime purpose of each is to prevent flame penetration into the exhaust ducting, with secondary requirements being to keep duct temperatures below 200°, remove any particles in the airflow, and be easily cleaned. A stove hood duct is a complexly integrated system that has several distinct parts. First is the hood; each has an architectural and fire-rated classification. Architectural classes are *low wall* (a low canopy that is installed where ceiling height is limited; it may also have a back shelf), *wall* (a tall canopy mounted against a wall; it usually has a cornice on three sides), and *island* (a tall canopy suspended from the ceiling; it has a cornice all around). Fire-rated classes are *Type I* (the unit collects and removes grease and smoke) or *Type II* (the unit removes only steam, vapors, heat, and odors). A Type II hood is usually just a canopy that contains a thin removable filter; but a Type I hood requires a high-velocity airflow and a UL-certified grease filter or extractor, which may be one of three kinds: *water-wash extractor* (the airstream flows through a series of baffles which extract the grease by centrifugal force then the grease is cleaned from removable gutters by a daily wash cycle), *baffle filter* (same as above, except the extracted grease collects in removable filters), or *removable extractor* (the grease is extracted from the airstream by a removable filter or cartridge). Then there's the ducting. This should run as straight as possible from the hood to the exhaust fan at the duct's end, each length should pitch at least ¼ in/LF toward the hood or grease reservoir (this pitch should be 1 in/LF if the duct is more than 75 ft long), the duct's top or sides should have gasketed cleanout doors no more than 12 LF apart through

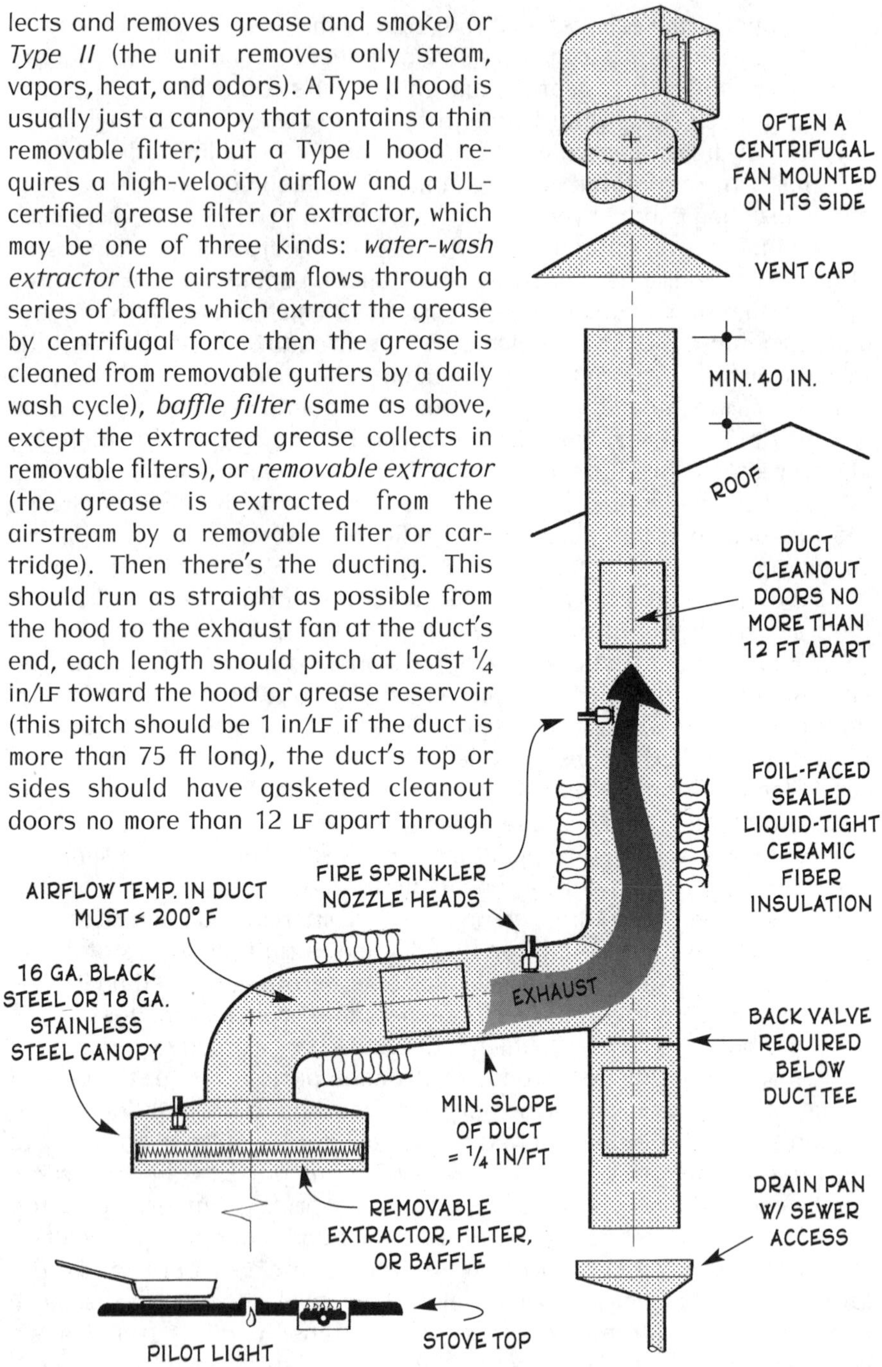

OFTEN A CENTRIFUGAL FAN MOUNTED ON ITS SIDE

VENT CAP

MIN. 40 IN.

ROOF

DUCT CLEANOUT DOORS NO MORE THAN 12 FT APART

FOIL-FACED SEALED LIQUID-TIGHT CERAMIC FIBER INSULATION

BACK VALVE REQUIRED BELOW DUCT TEE

DRAIN PAN W/ SEWER ACCESS

EXHAUST

FIRE SPRINKLER NOZZLE HEADS

AIRFLOW TEMP. IN DUCT MUST ≤ 200° F

16 GA. BLACK STEEL OR 18 GA. STAINLESS STEEL CANOPY

MIN. SLOPE OF DUCT = ¼ IN/FT

REMOVABLE EXTRACTOR, FILTER, OR BAFFLE

PILOT LIGHT

STOVE TOP

Fig. 3-12. Commercial kitchen stove hood design. [†]

Troy, MI); Sep 1998, p. 44. † A primary source for this figure and related text was

which can enter a power washer with revolving brushes, and this cleanability requires every duct length to pitch to low points with sewer drain access (this is done easily by orienting most of the duct vertically and locating a 45° tee at its base). The duct should also be insulated for its whole length, preferably by a recently developed foil-faced, sealed, liquid-tight, ceramic fiber insulation that requires no chase. Then there's the exhaust fan at the duct's end. This is usually an upblast power roof ventilator or a centrifugal fan with backward-inclined blades. It must be at least 10 LF upstream of the hood and any other supply air intakes, at least 40 in. above the roof line, and its weight requires structural support. Finally there's a variety of mechanical and electric controls, which regulate not only the hood/ducting airflow and required fire sensing and suppression devices, but often the kitchen area airflow and its makeup air.

Kitchen stove hood design typically involves determining the nature and volume of the cooling exhaust effluent, selecting the filters, designing a high-velocity duct stack, selecting and sizing the fan on top, and incorporating the controls. Also it is usually not wise design to base the kitchen area's cooling requirements on the same room temperature as that of adjacent spaces (the dining area for example); instead, create adequate spot cooling and ventilation for the kitchen occupants without creating drafts above the stove area that could blow out gas pilot lights. Airflow requirements for commercial stove hoods are listed below.

Low wall canopy, w/ or w/o backshelf .... cfm = 300 × hood or shelf length
Wall canopy .... cfm = 100 × hood area
Island .... cfm = 150 × hood area
Ranges, ovens, non-grease-producing units .... 150 cfm
Fryers, griddles (for high-capacity units add 50 fpm) .... 250 fpm
Charbroilers, woks, high-heat producers fueled by gas .... 300 fpm
Charbroilers fueled by wood, charcoal, or mesquite .... 500 fpm
Food preparation area air req. .... 12–15 AC/hr (minimum 1,500 fpm)
Food preparation area makeup air .... 10–15% of above

3.B.3. Registers

Also known as grilles, supply and return air registers for heating and cooling systems should be as far apart as possible in each space (ideally in opposite walls, opposite corners, with one near the ceiling and one near the floor); and grilles should be located where occupants or furnishings will not block them. Supply grilles should direct incoming air across wall and floor surfaces without creating drafts, and their vanes should spread the air evenly into the space. A register's total outer dimension is usually $1\frac{1}{2}$ in. longer and wider than its duct.

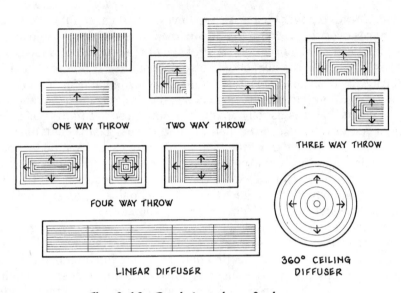

Fig. 3-13. Register sizes & shapes.

An important property of a register is its *throw*. This is a function of its vane configuration and the velocity of airflow in the duct behind it. A wall register's throw should be about $\frac{3}{4}$ the distance between its grille and the other side of the room if no registers are there. Ideal throw is an initial velocity of 50 fpm at 6.5 ft above the floor, decreasing to 25 fpm at the end of throw. Above 50 fpm papers blow off a desk, while below 15 fpm air feels stagnant. Excessive air at supply grilles may also create a plume of negative air pressure that can pull air in from adjoining spaces when the opposite is desired. This is a problem in access floor plenums beneath computer areas, where hot air may be drawn in from above as cool air enters the plenum. A register's throw is typically controlled by the angle of its vanes, three of which are sketched in Fig. 3-14.

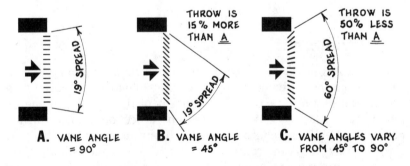

Fig. 3-14. Register throws.

Business Information, Des Plaines, IL); Jan. 2000, p. 57–8.

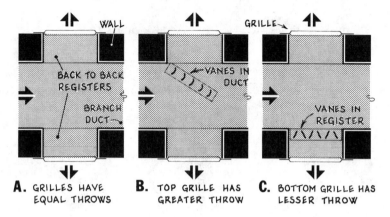

A. GRILLES HAVE EQUAL THROWS   **B.** TOP GRILLE HAS GREATER THROW   **C.** BOTTOM GRILLE HAS LESSER THROW

Fig. 3-15. Back-to-back grilles in ducting.

When two grilles are mounted back-to-back, either both throws must be equal or vanes must be mounted behind them to control the airflow (Fig. 3-15). Register throw ranges are usually listed in product catalogs.

3.B.4. Fans

In air-media climate control systems, fans are what move the airflow. They may be *axial* or *centrifugal*, as described below. Both may move supply or exhaust air, and their motor drives may be direct or by belt or chain.

Axial fans. In these units the airstream moves parallel to the axis of fan rotation. Axial fans are economical and take up little extra space, but the duct that contains them is usually larger and they are less efficient because part the airflow is deflected outward. They are preferred for low-pressure nonducted airflow, and because they are relatively noisy they are often used in recreational and industrial settings. Where they are exposed

TABLE 3-2: OPTIMAL DUCT REGISTER VELOCITIES	
OCCUPANCY	Terminal velocity, fpm
Broadcast studios, dormitories, hospital rooms	300–500
Residences, apartments, hotel & motel bedrooms, classrooms, laboratories, private offices, assembly & worship areas	500–750
Movie theaters, restaurants, bars, dance halls, barber shops	1,000
General offices, hotel entrance lobbies, small retail areas ...	1,000–1,250
Recreation, sports assembly, large retail areas, shipping areas	2,000

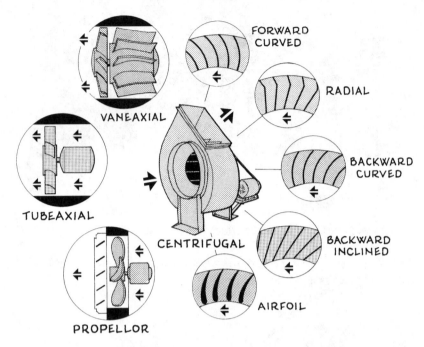

Fig. 3-16. Types of fans in climate control systems.

to dirty airstreams, they should have belt drives that keep the motor out of the airflow. There are three types: *tubeaxial, vaneaxial,* and *propeller.* The first two are mounted in ducting, while propeller fans are typically mounted in walls, roofs, and unitary forced-air systems. Propeller fans with variable-pitch vanes are often used to satisfy inflow requirements with long periods of reduced capacity operation and/or s.a.p. sensors.

Centrifugal fans. In these units the exiting airstream moves perpendicular to the axis of fan rotation. Centrifugal fans can operate at low speeds, can be adjusted more accurately for specific airflow requirements, and are more efficient where air volumes are large and under high pressure. They are better where the fan is installed inside ducting, the ducting changes direction, inflow/outflow duct diameters are different, hooded exhausts are installed, and quiet operation is a priority. But centrifugal fans require more space, are harder to clean, and are more expensive. There are five kinds, based on blade orientation: *forward-curved, radial, backward-curved, backward-inclined,* and *airfoil.* Straight blades are the most economical, but airfoil blades are the most efficient, and they are normally used in high-capacity and high-pressure scenarios where energy savings outweigh high initial costs. As forward blades are more pressure-inducing, they are installed in systems with high pressure requirements or high air friction losses, while backward blades are best where volumes are

high and ducts are short. Radial blades are rarely used, as their advantages lie between forward and backward curves and thus they have no
optimal features. Centrifugal fans have a variety of drive arrangements,
motor mounts, and discharge orientations.

In addition to primary air fans there are *booster fans* (they increase
s.a.p. in a particular zone), *recirculating fans* (they increase supply air
without increasing primary air), and *return air fans* (they mix return air
and outdoor air in large systems with high air friction losses).

Fan design involves (1) finding the unit's airflow delivery rate; (2)
determining air friction losses in any ducting; (3) determining the airflow's
total air pressure differential for its zone; (4) computing the fan horsepower; and (5) selecting the fan based on required horsepower, desirable
sound levels, allowable space, practical drive arrangements, and feasible
discharge orientations. As these calculations are lengthy for a component
that normally has little impact on other architectural components aside
from choice logistics, they are not included here. Also, optimal capacities
of many fans are created onsite by giving them adjustable vanes, variable-
volume controls, variable-speed motors, or dampers that regulate incoming or outgoing air. Variable-speed motors are the most efficient, though
they cost more, but they are usually more economical over time.

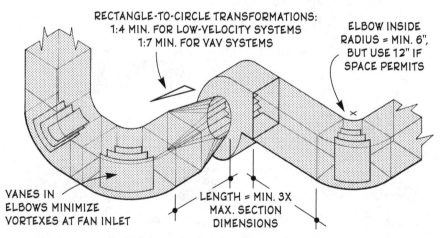

RECTANGLE-TO-CIRCLE TRANSFORMATIONS:
1:4 MIN. FOR LOW-VELOCITY SYSTEMS
1:7 MIN. FOR VAV SYSTEMS

ELBOW INSIDE
RADIUS = MIN. 6",
BUT USE 12" IF
SPACE PERMITS

VANES IN
ELBOWS MINIMIZE
VORTEXES AT FAN INLET

LENGTH = MIN. 3X
MAX. SECTION
DIMENSIONS

Fig. 3-17. Proper inlet and outlet ducting for fans.

An important aspect of an HVAC fan is the nature of its entering and
exiting airflow. If either is turbulent, the fan's effective airflow can be
reduced by 45 percent. Turbulence is caused chiefly by bends in the ducting just before and after the fan. To promote laminar airflow in these areas,
the fan's ducting should be straight for at least 10 diameters on each side.
If this is unachievable due to spatial constraints, the elbow should be

vaned and given as large a radius as possible. The incoming and outgoing ducts should be concentric with the corresponding fan face, and any branch ducts intersecting the main ducts near the fan should also have their axes coincide, or else capacity-robbing vortexes will develop outside the fan openings. Another promoter of smooth airflow is a splitter located inside the entering duct; this increases the airflow's straight length-to-width ratio, which is the essential strategy behind installing straight runs, turning vanes, and large-radius elbows as mentioned above. Good and bad examples of a fan's connecting ducting are sketched in Fig. 3-17.

Two important fan accessories are *vibration isolators* that reduce noise transmission and *drain pans* that collect water condensation. All parts of every fan should be accessible for servicing.

3.B.5. Thermal Energy Storage

Many public utilities offer reduced rates for off-peak electrical use. Thus it often pays to convert off-peak electricity into thermal energy that can be stored for later use during on-peak hours. There are two kinds of such storage: *heat* and *cold*, and there are several kinds of each. Thus the following is a conceptual encapsulation of this energy storage.

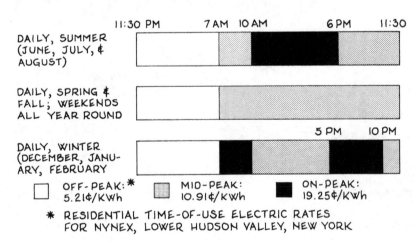

Fig. 3-18. Typical electric meter rate schedule.

Each system contains a large thickly insulated tank usually filled with water, brine, or glycol-water solution into which two serpentine networks of pipes, coils, or electric cables are immersed, one near the bottom of the solution, the other near the top. In heat storage units, during off-

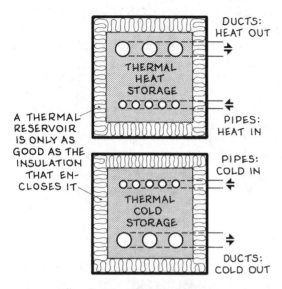

DUCTS:
HEAT OUT

THERMAL HEAT STORAGE

PIPES:
HEAT IN

A THERMAL RESERVOIR IS ONLY AS GOOD AS THE INSULATION THAT EN- CLOSES IT

PIPES:
COLD IN

THERMAL COLD STORAGE

DUCTS:
COLD OUT

Fig. 3-19. Thermal energy storage schematic.

peak hours a liquid or gas which has absorbed heat from cheap electricity flows through the bottom pipes and empties its excess Btus into the tank; then during on-peak hours a cold medium flows through the top pipes and removes the heat and delivers it to indoor spaces in cold weather during the day when electrical rates are high. In cold storage units the process is reversed. In both systems the warmer ducts are on the top, and the 'energy in' ducts are typically smaller than the 'energy out' ducts.

There are two basic kinds of thermal cold storage: *chilled water* and *ice*. The thermal energy transferred for each equals Δt + latent heat of fusion (144 Btu/lb of H_2O). For example, a perfectly efficient chilled water reservoir at 35° F whose temperature rises to 55° during its useful work theoretically contains 55 – 35 = 20 useful Btu/lb of stored water, while a reservoir of ice at 29° under the same conditions contains 55 – 29 + 144 = 170 useful Btu/lb of stored water. Thus ice storage systems produce the same chilling capacity in a smaller space due to the 144 Btu/lb heat of fusion capacity of water. But if the ice buildup in ice systems becomes more than $1\frac{1}{4}$ in. thick, it imposes a eutectic penalty on the system; thus at least most of the ice that forms each day should melt before the next day. Typical piping is thin-walled copper tubing for chilled water systems and S40 black pipe or galvanized steel pipe for ice systems.

Thermal energy storage systems work best in areas with large daily and yearly temperature swings, high electric rates, and large cost differences between on- and off-peak rates. System design typically involves quantifying on- and off-peak heating or cooling loads, sizing the reservoir and piping to handle the off-peak load, then sizing the circulation system to handle the on-peak load. Overall efficiency must exceed about 1.2 × the ratio of off-peak/on-peak electric rates. For example, if the ratio of off-peak/on-peak rates is 0.27 (as it is in the author's locale), system efficiency must exceed 0.27 about 1.2 × 0.27 ≈ 0.33. With each system it is important to note the following performance specifications: maximum latent heat storage and net sensible heat storage in ton-hr, charge/dis-charge cycle flow rates, container dimensions ($L \times W \times H$), container oper-ating weight when full, required floorspace, and maximum operating tem-perature and pressure.

At Stanford University is one of the world's largest ice thermal stor-age facilities. In this system a $160 \times 160 \times 24$ ft deep tank filled with water contains four huge banks of 1 in. galvanized steel pipe through which flow a 26 percent solution of Dowtherm SR-1 ethylene-glycol-based fluid whose freezing point is $10°$ F. The system's ice-build mode usually begins at 7 P.M.; then the SR-1 fluid is cooled to $18°$ F by three screw chillers housed in a nearby building then pumped at up to 28,000 gpm through the pipes in the storage tank, which freezes the water enveloping the coils. Full ice-build usually takes 8–14 hours depending on the day's weather and the next day's projected cooling load. Around noon the next day the system switch-es to ice-burn mode; then the SR-1 fluid loops continuously through the pipes in the water storage tank and several heat exchangers in the nearby building that interface with water arriving from 70 academic and research buildings on campus. In the heat exchangers the SR-1 fluid's temperature rises from 34 to $53°$ while the water temperature falls from 58 to $41°$; then the chilled water flows through 13 miles of insulated underground piping to cool the buildings on campus. [†]

> How much floor area is required for a thermal heat storage facility in a high-rise apartment building near Chicago if the building's design heating load is 600,000 Btu/hr?

Step 1. Draw a daily load profile of the building's hourly heating loads based on design heating loads and local climate data. From local climate data, the design temperature for Chicago is $-10°$ and the diurnal tempera-ture range in January is $16°$; thus on the coldest day of the year the tem-perature may fluctuate as shown in Fig. 3-20. Then compute the hourly heating loads as shown in the small table below.

Hr.	Temp. at hr, °F	Δt at hr, °F	Hourly heating load = design htg. load $\times \Delta t_{hr}/\Delta t_{max}$ Btu/hr
7 A.M.	−10	70 − (− 10) = 80°	600,000 × 80/80 = 600,000
8 A.M.	−8	70 − (− 8) = 78°	600,000 × 78/80 = 585,000
9 A.M.	−5	70 − (− 5) = 75°	600,000 × 75/80 = 563,000
10 A.M.	−2	70 − (− 2) = 72°	600,000 × 72/80 = 540,000
Etc.			

Step 2. Size the thermal heat reservoir. Completing the above table and blocking the on-peak and mid-peak heating loads in the daily load pro-file indicates that the reservoir's required capacity is 8,800,000 Btu/hr.

[†] "Case in Point", *Engineered Systems* magazine (Business news Publishing Co.,

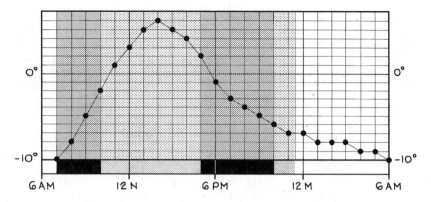

Fig. 3-20. Daily load profile of building heating load.

3)B)5) $H \approx 62.5 \, V \Delta t$

H = total on-peak and off-peak heating load, 8,800,000 Btu/hr.
V = volume of thermal heat reservoir, **?** cf of water
Δt = temperature differential of reservoir, $^\circ$ F. If system heats water to
      160° for conditioned air at 120°, Δt = 160 − 120 = 40° F.

$$8,800,000 \approx 62.5 \times 40 \times V \quad ... \; V \approx 3,500 \text{ cf}$$
If reservoir is 8 ft high: floor area ≈ 3,500/8 ≈ 440 sf
If floor area is square: $440^{0.5} \approx 21 \times 21$ ft

Step 3. Estimate the unit's required floor area for the thermal heat storage unit. By adding 1 ft perimeter insulation/construction and a 3 ft access aisle all around, the required area is

$$(21 + 1 + 3)\,(21 + 1 + 3) \approx 625 \text{ sf}$$

3.B.6. Heat Recovery

In almost every building, a certain portion of the energy consumed to keep occupants comfortable escapes from the building, usually up the chimney as hot flue gases, through outlet vents as stale air, or down the drain as warm waste water. Recapturing this wasted energy and reharnessing its Btus to further enhance the occupants' comfort offers tantalizing opportunities for economically-minded and environmentally conscious owners and Æ designers. Such opportunities lurk whenever the cost of recovery is usually less than about 70 percent of the market value of the original energy consumed. However, quantifying such operations accurately is usually quite difficult because each equation unknown usually has a wide range of foreseeable values. Thus the following formula is highly conceptual. Still, it may serve as a guide toward turning inefficiency to advantage in almost any building, whether it be a home, small business, large corporation, or industrial campus.

3)B)6) $$H_L\,\varepsilon \approx \varepsilon\,\$\,T$$

H_L = heat lost due to conventional operation, Btus/hr
ε = overall efficiency of heat recovery operation
ε = unit energy savings of recovery operation, Btu/hr
$\$$ = hourly value of recovered energy, dollars
T = timespan of recovery operation

3.C. TYPES OF SYSTEMS

A climate control system may be likened to a tree with *roots* (service entries, furnaces, air handling units, etc.), a *trunk* (main ducts, pipes, conductors), *branches* (lateral ducts, pipes, wires), and *buds* (thermostats, humidistats, and sensors). Total building climate control systems have also been categorized as one "giant tree" or an "orchard of small trees." The primary criteria for choosing any climate control system are the advantages versus drawbacks of each system and the owner's goals. The latter may be low initial cost, low operating cost, adequate level of performance that matches the competition, or ultimate in performance no matter what the cost. A few other criteria are size, weight, noise level of operation, reliability, and serviceability.

The advantages and drawbacks of the most common climate control systems are listed below.

Electric Heating

➕ Units are compact, noiseless, odorless, and easily installed. They require no fuel storage, flues, ducts, or furnace or extra floor space. Electric cables have many small applications.

➖ Units do not humidify, filter, or ventilate air. Operating costs are high in areas with high electrical rates. Areas around units must be kept clear of furniture, drapes, etc.

Radiant Floor Heating

➕ May be electric cable or copper tubing embedded in concrete slab.

Eliminates cold drafts, doesn't circulate dust and other airborne contaminants. Efficient where winters are mild.

⊖ High initial cost, requires precise construction. Settling problems can crack concrete, resulting in broken wires or leaky tubes that are expensive to repair. Water systems are **NG** if the water contains chemicals that leave deposits in pipes.

Radiant Ceiling Heating

⊕ Either electric cables or gas-fired tubes. Gas-fired units are economical, available in a variety of sizes and shapes, effective in spaces with high ceilings, and easily relocated as occupancy requirements change. They also do not produce or disperse airborne pollutants. Ceiling-mounted electric cables are quiet, and may be useful where spaces requiring heating are above.

⊖ Gas-fired units are mostly an industrial system for poorly insulated buildings. Correct location is critical. **NG** for occupancies w/ cooling operations (ice skating rinks, supermarkets with open freezers, etc.). Electric cable units are inefficient.

Electric Heating and Cooling

⊕ Small through-the-wall units are easy to install and usually require only an electrical outlet to run. Some models humidify, filter, and freshen air year-round. Useful in architecture with many small rooms requiring individual climate control; economical in areas with low electric rates.

⊖ **NG** in large spaces. Operating costs are high in areas with high electric rates.

Hot Water Heating

⊕ Works well in residences and small buildings with high heating and low cooling loads. A volume of water can transfer almost 3,500 times more heat than the same volume of air ➡ much less space is required to run plumbing instead of ducting to the heating units.

⊖ Does not humidify, filter, or ventilate air. Central heating system takes up considerable space. Plumbing must be protected from freezing in winter and condensation in summer.

Steam Heating

⊕ Usually smaller than other systems of comparable capacity.

Leftover steam from industrial or other large operations may be used for cooking, sterilizing, running small industrial processes, and driving generators.

➖ Complicated; heavy, can be noisy, pipes are very hot, high steam pressures can cause cause componentry to explode, extensive safety componentry and controls are required. Usually practical only for large buildings or groups of buildings where economies of scale are more advantageous for large-volume systems.

Air Heating

➕ Can ventilate, humidify, and filter incoming air. Practical in homes and other small buildings in cold regions.

➖ Bulky furnace, ducting, and chimneys take up space and are costly. Natural convection currents carry the heat upward if registers are not well located. Drafts stir up dust, excessive air movement has a cooling effect on the body.

Air Cooling

➕ Compact packages are easily installed in walls or roofs and thus are good for one-story buildings. Can humidify, filter, and freshen air. Capacities vary from $1/3$ to 50 or more tons. Some units have small capacity for heating. Efficient in warm climates.

➖ Impractical in regions with mild summers.

Air Heating and Cooling

➕ Versatile centralized system, most effective in regions with variable climates. **VG** in buildings with large interior volumes, multiple zones requiring constant temperature/humidity control, and/or large steady loads having modest ventilation requirements.

➖ Expensive, usually must be custom-assembled onsite. Requires considerable component balancing to operate smoothly. **N2G** for spaces with large ventilation requirements.

Air-Water Heating and Cooling

➕ Versatile, centralized system. Can satisfy a wide variety of heating and cooling loads, including reversible heat flow requirements (where heating is required in one area and cooling in an adjoining area) for a large number of spaces at relatively lower cost. Small componentry requires less space for installation, making it desir-

able in tall buildings and other structures with minimum spatial requirements for mechanical equipment. Individual zones are virtually
self-balancing.

⊖ Complicated, costly. Usually unfeasible unless smaller volume of
componentry can lower architectural costs.

Heat Pump

⊕ Good where winter temperatures remain above 35° F for prolonged
periods, outside air requirements are low, ratio of heating to cooling loads ≤ 0.6, and where electric rates are low. Operates more
quietly than most other systems and less floorspace is required for
mechanical equipment. Water-source heat pumps are feasible where
water media are available, then they work well in colder climates.
Because no fuel is burned the unit requires no venting.

⊖ High initial cost, impractical in large multi-zoned buildings. Part of
machinery must be located outdoors. Compressor noise may affect
site planning. Air-to-air systems require backup heating at temperatures below 35°.

Humidification

⊕ Installed either as part of HVAC system controls in large buildings
or as portable stand-alone units in small areas. Good for cooling
interiors with gentle airflow in hot dry weather. Can be used to add
moisture to spaces in cold dry weather or where industrial operations remove excess moisture from interior air.

⊖ NG in humid weather, where interior air is not dry, or where interior
airflow is fast. Installations in hermetically sealed interior spaces
require careful design; overdesign in any space can create condensation problems.

Dehumidification

⊕ Installed either as part of HVAC system controls or as portable
stand-alone units in small areas. Effectively cools interiors in warm
humid weather; works best in hermetically sealed spaces or where
occupancies produce moisture (cooking, swimming, industrial operations, etc.) that can't be quickly vented outdoors.

⊖ NG in dry climates. Undesirable where interiors create dust or
other airborne particulates that must be removed by large volumes
of circulating air.

Today, each of the above climate control systems is capable of being operated by advanced computer technology whose initially higher unit cost is usually offset by improved efficiency, smaller systems, and longer life. These systems can continually monitor and maintain required outdoor air volumes and air pressures for each space, track the energy consumed by the operation of any combination of terminals, document the testing of smoke controls and other life safety systems, and trend facility operations for purposes of cuing maintenance personnel to inspect and service componentry at optimal run times.

However, much can go wrong with modern climate control systems. In fact, as many as 30 percent of America's 4.5 million sealed-window offices and public buildings may be suffering from 'HVAC havoc' or 'Sick Building Syndrome.'[†] A well-publicized situation gone awry was the Imperial Polk County Courthouse in Bartow, Florida. This "Showcase Courthouse," a ten-story building with two three-story wings, had all the most modern design features associated with halls of justice: separate elevator banks for police, public, and prisoners; secured linkage of prisoner elevators and holding cells via an underground tunnel; and secured corridors for the public, police, and judges. The building's roof, rising above its prominent cornice at a gentle 3-in-12 pitch, was attractive clay tile laid on a roll roofing cap sheet over a composite decking of waferboard/rigid insulation/cement fiberboard. The building's facades were a sandwich construction of elegant brick veneer backed by asphalt waterproofing on concrete block infill, rigid foam insulation, and metal furring finished with gypsum board, with PVC flashing installed at every brick relieving angle and around every window. Inside, all lobby and corridor walls were clad in the finest marble veneer, all courtrooms and judges' chambers were paneled with custom millwork, and most other interiors were finished with vinyl wallcovering and broadloom carpeting. The highly efficient variable-air-volume HVAC system included 67 chilled-water air-handling units that were oversized to accommodate any cooling demand in the hot humid climate of central Florida and were governed by an advanced ddc system that provided environmental controls for every individual office and courtroom via a central computer console. One would think that nothing could possibly go wrong with such masterly design, advanced technology, and familiar construction details whose durability had been proven over time— all of which was completed in 1987 at a total cost of $37 million.

Soon after the building was occupied, it was found that rainwater didn't drain properly off the roof —because a 3-in-12 pitch is too shallow for clay tile. Water remaining on the roof in this locale of high rainfall began to leak through numerous holes in the improperly installed cap sheets under the clay tile, began to delaminate the decking, started draining into ceilings and exterior walls, became trapped behind facades of brick veneer with clogged or missing weepholes, migrated through concrete block infills incom-

[†] Mark Skaer, "Editor's Page", *Engineering Systems* magazine (Business News

pletely coated with waterproofing and now laced with cracks due to a lack of control joints, and entered through gaps in the through-the-wall flashing. More water entered around windows whose flashing did not extend to the brick facing or lacked turned-up edges at sills. Soon moisture had saturated ceiling tiles, gypsum wallboard, and broadloom carpeting —a flow that was increased not only by high vapor pressures from the warm humid climate outdoors and low vapor pressures from the cool dry air inside, but also by negative indoor air pressures caused by an unbalanced HVAC system that exhausted more air than it drew in through its outside air intakes. Because the outside intakes were protected by insect screens rather than bird screens with larger mesh openings, the screens soon became clogged with dust and debris, decreasing the outside airflow and increasing interior negative pressures even more. The oversized HVAC air handlers also did not contain reheat coils —thus they satisfied dry-bulb temperatures quickly and cycled off before dehumidification was complete. Humidity levels rose constantly above 80 percent. Occupants complained.

The HVAC system was retrofitted with reheat coils and thermostatic controls that automatically adjusted chilled water temperatures. Still the system failed to dehumidify interior spaces adequately, which prevented thorough redrying of interior finishes and underlying construction. Mold began to grow in the gypsum backing behind the marble facing in the lobbies and corridors. Interior air circulated into the cavities behind the facing —because the seams in the marble facing had not been adequately sealed— allowing the mold in the gypsum to migrate into interior spaces. Similar colonies of mold flourished behind the vinyl wallcovering and millwork paneling throughout the building. Occupants experienced stinging eyes, runny noses, wheezing, coughing, shortness of breath, chest tightness, headaches, drowsiness, asthma, allergies, and other symptoms of Sick Building Syndrome.

Investigations followed. The vinyl wallcovering —which was found to have acted as a vapor barrier between the facade construction and interior spaces— was removed from the inside of every exterior wall, then the damaged gypsum board behind was sanded and painted.

Still, complaints increased. Consultants were called in. They found massive blooms of *Aspergillus versicolor* and *Stachybotrys atra* throughout the building. Physicians conducted an extensive study of the occupants. Finally in July, 1992, the local health department condemned the courthouse as a threat to human health and ordered it closed.

Soon massive remediation began. All contaminated materials were removed by methods similar to asbestos remediation, which required every piece of construction removed from the building to be HEPA-vacuumed, double-sealed, and placed in secured dumpsters by workers wearing full-face respirators, white gloves, and Tyvek® suits. Much of the marble and millwork finish was removed to reach the contaminated materials behind them, 500,000 sf of ceiling tile were removed and shredded onsite, six miles of flexible ductwork were removed and discarded, every article of furniture was HEPA-vacuumed prior to temporary storage offsite, and every file and document in the whole building was cleaned one page at a time on specially constructed vacuum tables. All interior surfaces, light fixtures, piping, and remaining ducting inside and out were also thoroughly recleaned by hand. On the roof, all the clay tile and underlying cap sheets were removed, each piece of delaminated decking was repaired or replaced, then a batten-seam copper roof was laid over a rubberized asphalt membrane. Every square foot of the building's ten-story brick facades was scaffolded; then 800,000 bricks were removed, all improperly built concrete block infills were removed and replaced, all cracks in the remaining walls were filled with mortar, all infills were thoroughly covered with thick asphalt waterproofing, new copper flashing was installed, then new brick facades were built with proper control joints, anchors, and ties. Every window was also removed, cleaned, and remounted on new subframing and proper flashing. Then all 67 of the HVAC system's chilled-water air handlers were removed and replaced with new units that forced longer cooling cycles and boosted dehumidification. Reheat capability was again added, existing electrostatic air filters were supplemented with high-efficiency air filters, every condensate line was pitched and bottom-tapped to ensure complete drainage, and controls were extensively modified to monitor return air for precise levels of relative humidity, CO_2, and temperature.

In early 1996 the building was reoccupied, eight years after it had opened. What was the remedial expense of this calamity of faulty design, poor workmanship, and inadequate supervision that occurred in this 37 million dollar building? Another 37 million dollars! The citizens of Polk County collected $13 million from the architect, engineers, contractor, and subcontractors plus $25.8 million from the builder's insurance carrier.[†]

In any building large or small, Æ designers must have at least a conceptual knowledge of today's climate control systems, be eager to learn new methods of solving old problems, be quick to obtain the services of specialists whenever necessary, and have a sternly objective snoop, pry, and prod attitude regarding construction supervision.

One new approach to designing modern climate control systems, especially large ones, is *multiple module redundant design* (MMRD). This involves installing several smaller units of the same total capacity as one large, then adding one more small unit so any one may be serviced on the fly if necessary without affecting total system operation. For example, if a building's computed heating load is 1,000,000 Btus, instead of installing one large unit of this capacity you might install five 200,000 Btu multiple module units then add a sixth for redundant design. Then, since a heating system's greatest demand usually occurs during a very short period in winter, during most of the season when loads are less, a number of smaller units can satisfy any momentary heating demand at considerably less cost (this process is known as *step-firing*). Each of the smaller units will also cycle on and off less, which means longer life expectancy and less maintenance. An MMRD system is also more economical because the smaller a unit, the less its mass and thus the less heat it will absorb while operating (this is important because all the heat stored in a unit's mass is eventually shed as rejected heat according to the principle of mass heating load as described in Sec. 2.E.4.). MMRD systems also require less headroom and can be arranged more flexibly (e.g. in L-shaped plan configurations) than 'one-clunker' systems. Such control strategies allow more efficient operation for setbacks (nights, weekends, etc.), setforwards (e.g. 1 hour before work begins), multi-zone occupancies, zones with wide load swings, and other programmable use patterns. MMRD systems can also be programmed to rotate the on-off cycling of its units —a process known as *alternate-lead firing*— so that each unit operates an approximately equal amount of time over the long haul. Finally, no matter how many units a system has, it should include *staging logic* that operates its mixing valves to minimize thermal shock in any boiler when it refires after a lengthy shutdown. All these logistics apply to cooling systems as well.

General considerations for designing climate control systems are:

▶ Compare the problem's magnitude with the cost of the solution.
▶ Examine local climate conditions and utility costs before making any conclusions regarding the cost-effectiveness of any system.
▶ Think of what the system provides instead of the system itself; because occupants want comfort and production, not fancy equipment.
▶ Heat or cool the occupants, not the building.
▶ Design for the maximum but remember the minimum.
▶ Be aware of life-cycle costs.
▶ Consider possible escalation of load demands due to future tenancy changes or extensive upgrading.
▶ Isolate unique requirements that demand individual solutions.
▶ Know the spatial requirements and weight of each system component. All units should have ample service access area (generally a 3 ft spatial envelope around and above each unit).
▶ Design large heating/cooling networks to have multiple panel boxes, circuit breakers, and feeder cables. Then any circuitry overload won't knock out the whole system and any hot spot has a better chance of activating only its own circuit breaker.
▶ Provide maintenance access to all parts of systems. This includes items requiring periodic cleaning (louvers, grilles, filters, duct interiors, air-handling equipment, etc.) plus items that need

periodic recalibrating, adjusting, or replacement (sensors, actuators, valves, lamps, fan belts, etc.). Remember that all equipment, regardless of quality, fails eventually .

▶ Design systems to operate quietly, especially near offices, classrooms, and sleeping areas.

Following is an outline for designing climate control systems:

1. Determine design parameters and prioritize conservation measures. Determine winter and summer design temperatures, design relative humidity, average annual temperature, ventilation requirements, pollution problems, lighting levels, machinery loads, and occupancy loads.
2. Divide the architecture into zones according to spatial functions, envelope exposures, and orientations-in-common. Identify exposure criteria such as R-values, floor areas, use loads, solar incidence, etc., for each zone.
3. Compute thermal loads for each zone: design heating and cooling loads, and energy auditing for heating and cooling seasons.

   (Generally all the above was described in Sec. 2.E.)

4. Select climate control systems and identify components and locations. Lay out mechanical rooms (location and size), distribution trees, and outlets (location and type). Determine if any conflicts exist with structural, fire safety, and other utility systems; integrate with these systems whenever possible. Where thermostats are installed, locate each so it is visible from anywhere in the zone it serves.
5. Check thermal calculations with system layouts, integrate climate control systems with design, prepare mechanical drawings.

3.C.1. Electric Heating

Electric heating units contain a thick wire-like heating element whose resistance converts electric current into heat that radiates or is fan-driven into nearby spaces. The units usually operate on 120, 208, or 240 volts. Some units include a thermostat, while others are connected to a thermostat mounted in the heated zone. There are several kinds of these units:

Baseboards. Long thin units mounted at the base of walls. Units may be connected to create any length. Simple, easy to install, unobtrusive.

Floor inserts. Thin units fitted into floors so the grille on top aligns with the floor. Good for locations under floor-length glass.

Spot. Small units for spaces with little wall or baseboard area.

Surface-mounted. A variety of units that can be mounted onto a wall. Good on masonry and other hard surfaces.

Semi-recessed. Units that fit partly into walls or ceilings. Good for soft-hard construction such as drywall on masonry walls.

Recessed. Units that fit into walls or ceilings with the grille on or near the surface. Good for fitting into stud walls.

Fan-driven. Heating units equipped with a fan that pushes the heat in a desired direction. Not silent, but they circulate heat well. Good for ceiling-mounted units in garages and industrial areas.

Radiant cables. Also known as *heat tracing*, these are electric wires that are installed on eaves, entrance aprons, and the like to melt snow and ice from these areas. Similar cables keep plumbing, moisture-filled air lines, refrigeration drain lines, and interior downspouts from freezing. Still others maintain desirable temperatures in commercial dishwashers in restaurants and dialysis water systems in hospitals. They are unacceptable as freeze deterrents in fire sprinkler piping.

Electric heating units cost little to install, take up little space, require no central units that occupy more space, and need little servicing or maintenance. Although they waste little energy *per se*, the more a unit is recessed, the more its produced heat is absorbed by the surrounding construction. For example, when a baseboard unit is mounted against an exterior stud wall, an estimated 20 percent of its produced heat exits through the back of the unit into the framing just behind. A more cost-effective arrangement may be to superinsulate the occupancy's exterior walls and mount the baseboard heaters against interior walls. Drawbacks of electric heating units are that the heating elements fatigue with constant use, typical efficiency losses being 10 percent after 10 years, and they are uneconomical where electricity costs significantly more than oil or gas.

Electric heating cables used to melt snow outdoors generally cost more to operate than do similar water heating piping; but the cables are smaller, more flexible, won't break if they freeze, and if they do break for any other reason no flooding will occur. The operating costs of both electrical and water-based methods of melting snow should also be balanced against the cost of salting or shoveling otherwise-present snow, the cost of cleaning entrance areas of tracked-in salt and snow, and the fact that pavements last longer when not subjected to frost.

Example 1. The conference room in a real estate office has a 12 ft electric baseboard heater, but in very cold weather the room remains chilly. If the design heating load of the room is 10,200 Btu/hr, how much extra baseboard heating should the space have?

3)C)1)a) $H \leq 3\, L\, H_{cap}$

H   = design heating load of
      space, 10,200 Btu/hr
L   = req. length of electric
      baseboard heating, ? ft
H_{cap} = heating capacity of
      selected unit, watts/LF.
      Wattage is usually listed
      in product catalogs or
      on heater package; it ≈
      175 watts/LF.

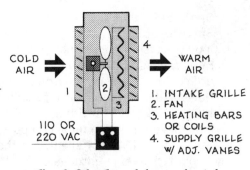

COLD AIR

WARM AIR

110 OR 220 VAC

1. INTAKE GRILLE
2. FAN
3. HEATING BARS
   OR COILS
4. SUPPLY GRILLE
   W/ ADJ. VANES

Fig. 3-21. Fan-driven electric heating unit operation.

$$10{,}200 \leq 3 \times L \times 175$$
$$L \leq 19.4 \rightarrow 20 \text{ ft} \quad \dots \text{ Required extra length: } 20 - 12 \geq 8 \text{ ft}$$

Example 2. The owner of a bus terminal wants to install an electric spot heater in the wall of a men's room that has a design heat loss of 3,900 Btu/hr. What capacity should the unit have?

3)C)1)b) $H \leq 3\, H_{cap}$

H   = design heating load of space, 3,900 Btu/hr
H_{cap} = heating capacity of selected unit (wattage of any electric unit is
      listed on its package), ? watts

$$3{,}900 \leq 3\, H_{cap} \quad \dots H_{cap} \geq 1{,}300 \text{ watts}$$

Example 3. A 10 ft length of 3 in. diameter supply main is exposed to the air in the unheated basement of a 3 story apartment complex near Mobile, AL. If the lowest temperature ever recorded in the area is 8° F, what is the required wattage of an electric heat tracing cable wrapped around this piping?

3)C)1)c) $\Omega = 0.17\, d^2\, L\, (177 - T_o)$

Ω = required output of electric heat tracing cable, ? watts
d   = diameter of pipe to be heated, 3 in.
L   = length of pipe to be heated, 10 ft
T_o = lowest likely local subfreezing temperature, ° F.
      Use 5° below area's lowest recorded temperature. $T_o = 8 - 5 = 3° F$.

$$\Omega = 0.17 \times 3^2 \times 10\, (177 - 3) = 2{,}660 \text{ watts}$$

The cable and piping should be wrapped in nonflammable insulation

Example 4. The concrete entrance apron of a synagogue near St. Louis requires radiant heating to keep ice from forming on it in winter. If the design temperature is 10° F and it rarely snows more than two in/hr there, how much radiant heating should be installed?

Solution: In the radiant slab output data below, find the area's specified design snowfall in the leftmost column, which here is 1–2 in/hr; then move to the right to the radiant slab output under the specified design temperature of 10°... the answer is 64 W/sf. Interpolate for intermediate values.

Design snowfall, in/hr	Radiant slab output, W/sf at design temp.			
	30° F	20° F	10° F	0° F
0–1	25	35	43	51
1–2	46	55	64	74
2–3	68	79	90	98

Note: Electric heating cable for concrete slabs is typically made in capacities of 10, 20, 40, and 60 W/sf. Even in severely cold climates, 60 watt cable is usually satisfactory. Otherwise an elaborate system of piping containing heated antifreeze is usually devised. Radiant slab surfaces must be pitched slightly for drainage, and the slabs may contain probe thermostats that activate electric heating systems when the slab is below 32° F and moisture sensors that activate when the surface becomes wet.

3.C.2. Radiant Floor Heating

By embedding electric cables or loops of piping containing hot water in concrete floors at least 5 in. thick poured on 4 in. rigid insulation, the floor will radiate a comfortable uniform heat into the spaces above.

In electric systems, the cable is prefabricated as imbeddable panels or field-cut to length, then installed and connected as electricians do with wiring. As every linear foot of a cable's length gives off the same amount of heat, equal spacing between cables creates uniform heat.

In water systems, copper, steel, or plastic piping extends from a central heating unit, then loops beneath the heated area. Supply mains are typically $\frac{3}{4}$ or 1 in. diameter rigid copper pipe, and heating coils or loops are $\frac{1}{2}$ in. diameter flexible copper or plastic tubing. Flexible plastic tubing is currently gaining popularity because it is light, costs less, can easily be bent, and will not corrode. Water heating loops may be arranged continuously, in grids (usually better in larger areas), or in combinations, as sketched in Fig. 3-22. Layouts should have as few joints as possible, circuit loops should be placed in parallel rows, bend radii should be as large

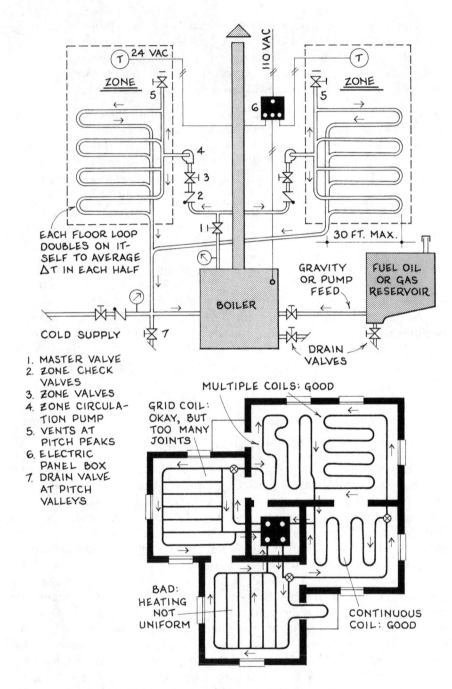

Fig. 3-22. Radiant floor heating systems.

1. MASTER VALVE
2. ZONE CHECK VALVES
3. ZONE VALVES
4. ZONE CIRCULATION PUMP
5. VENTS AT PITCH PEAKS
6. ELECTRIC PANEL BOX
7. DRAIN VALVE AT PITCH VALLEYS

24 VAC
110 VAC

ZONE

EACH FLOOR LOOP DOUBLES ON IT-SELF TO AVERAGE ΔT IN EACH HALF

30 FT. MAX.

GRAVITY OR PUMP FEED

FUEL OIL OR GAS RESERVOIR

BOILER

COLD SUPPLY

DRAIN VALVES

MULTIPLE COILS: GOOD

GRID COIL: OKAY, BUT TOO MANY JOINTS

BAD: HEATING NOT UNIFORM

CONTINUOUS COIL: GOOD

as possible, and all metal joints should be soldered and not threaded. Waterflow should be routed from the perimeters of floor areas toward their centers, and, as the piping in each circuit cools slightly from start to end, each succeeding length of parallel piping should be placed slightly closer (say $\frac{1}{8}$ in.) to the upstream length to foster uniform heating. Good water temperatures are 100–110° at the boiler through the supply mains down to 90–100° at the control valves where the circuits begin, then down to 80° through the loops. If incoming water temperatures are higher, the floor may feel hot to the touch, which is **NG** for children. All control valves must be easily accessible as they may require periodic readjusting.

Radiant floor heating is feasible in one-floor buildings with slab-on-grade construction, especially if they have large interior spaces, high ceilings, or large exterior doors that may be opened and closed frequently. As this heating requires much lower temperatures than other water heating systems, it has lower fuel costs (which makes it more advantageous in areas with high energy costs), inherently higher efficiency, less scale buildup in boilers, and several lesser advantages than other water systems. Traditionally the biggest drawbacks of radiant floor heating systems have been high initial cost, the need for meticulous onsite construction, and operation failures due to cracked concrete slabs and cracked and corroded piping; but these drawbacks have been reduced by the recent introduction of flexible plastic piping.

Regarding waste emitted or rejected by radiant floor heating systems: perhaps only 15 percent of the heat radiated from the cables or pipes migrates downward if the slab is well insulated below and around its edges. Electric systems also lose a few percentage points of efficiency due to resistance in the cables, and in piping systems the water should not contain any minerals or other impurities that could leave deposits in the piping. As the maximum capacity of these systems is rather small compared to other systems, they are usually feasible only in climates not exceeding about 4,000 winter degree-days or in superinsulated buildings.

Water-based radiant floor heating systems can also melt snow from outdoor areas in winter. Known as hydronic snow-melting systems, each is typically a dedicated loop of copper or plastic piping that runs through a heat exchanger, then loops back and forth beneath a concrete slab area that receives the snow. The heat exchanger is critical because without it the hot water ($\approx$ 140–180°) from the central heating unit would likely cause serious cracks in the slab ($\approx$ 0–32°) that receives the snow. Thus the exchanger's heat-source side may operate at 140° while the slab-side piping is filled with glycol solution whose flow is regulated by a circulating pump and temperature sensors that keep its solution from rising much above freezing. Embedded in the slab should be one or more snow/ice detectors that initiate pipeflow upon a simultaneous sensing of slab temperatures below, say, 34° and moisture on the slab. The detectors must be located not only in areas that receive snowfall but also where wind-blown snow could accumulate well under roof areas that block direct snowfall. Every part of the slab surface must slope enough to shed the melted snow; otherwise the system could operate long after the snow has fallen if temperatures remain below the detector sensor setpoint.

Although hydronic snow-melting systems are a viable method of removing snow from outdoor areas, their multiple subcomponentry is costly, every subcomponent requires careful design, and they are usually economical only where electric rates are high. These systems typically require an output of 100–150 Btus/sf, and they can be sized according to the formula below, which includes typical losses incurred in the heat exchanger:

3)C)2)a)
$$A \approx 2.45 \, Q \, (T_i - T_o)$$

A = floor area of surface receiving snowfall, sf
Q = required waterflow to melt snow from area, gpm
T_i = highest temperature of liquid in piping, °. This is usually 35–40°.
T_o = lowest temperature of liquid in piping, °. This is usually the region's winter design temperature.

An interesting application of hydronic snow melting is at the Wiggins Airway airport hangar in Manchester, NH. The hangar doors, which are large enough for two Lear jets to enter and leave the building at the same time, ride on metal tracks recessed into the concrete floor, and during the area's very cold and snowy winters the tracks tend to clog with thick layers of ice which makes it difficult to operate the doors. Thus a single radiant floor heating loop was installed alongside the track's entire length to keep ice from building up at the base of the doors. [†]

A day-care center near Jacksonville, FL, has a concrete floor on which children play and take naps on padded mats. If the 24 × 42 ft floor has a radiant floor water heating system and the building's design heating load is 14,000 Btu/hr, size the system's supply main, return main, and circuits if they are plastic pipe and the water's initial temperature is 110° F. What is the system's required waterflow?

Step 1. Size the system's piping, as described below:

Mains: As this a fairly small floorplan, use ³⁄₄ in. piping. Otherwise size the mains according to Sec. 4.C.

Circuits: These are parallel runs of typically ½ in. flexible copper or plastic tubing in which the optimal spacing between runs is determined by the formula below.

3)C)2)b)
$$\mathbf{H} \, S = 17 \, \kappa_h \, A \, (T_s - T_r)$$

[†] The author regrets that he has lost the reference that describes this installa-

H = design heating load of interior spaces above radiant floor water heating system, 14,000 Btu/hr

S = optimal spacing of parallel runs in system piping, ? in. If $S \leq 6$ in, a floor water radiant heating system is not strong enough to satisfy load ➡ select another heating system or supplement floor heating with other systems. If $S \geq 18$ in, select a lower average water temperature.

κ_h = comparative heating value of water if it contains glycol. If water contains no glycol, $\kappa_h = 1.0$; if 30% glycol, $\kappa_h = 0.976$; if 50% glycol, $\kappa_h = 0.904$. Here $\kappa_h = 1.0$. Interpolate for intermediate values.

A = floor area of system, sf. Subtract 1 ft from perimeter of heating area all around. $A = (24 - 1)(42 - 1) = 943$ sf.

T_s = supply or initial water temperature of system, 110° F. Feasible T_i usually $\approx 95{-}120°$ F.

T_r = return water temperature of system, 85° F.

$$14{,}000 \times S = 17 \times 943 \times (110 - 85) \quad ... \; S = 28.6 \text{ in.}$$

28.6 in. spacing is too wide ➡ use a lower initial temperature
Recomputing T_s at $S = 18$ in. ➡ $T_s = 99°$

Step 2. Determine the system's pipe flow requirements.

$$H = 490 \; \kappa_h \; Þ \; (T_s - T_r)$$

H = design heating load of floor area above system, 14,000 Btu/hr

Þ = required pipe flow of system, ? gpm

T_s = supply or initial water temperature of system, from Step 1, 99° F.
κ_h and T_r are as previously defined.

$$14{,}000 \leq 490 \times 1.0 \times Þ \times (99 - 85) \quad ... \; Þ \geq 2.0 \text{ gpm}$$

3.C.3. Radiant Ceiling Heating [†]

Radiant ceiling heating is performed by a variety of ceiling-mounted units that contain tubes of hot gases, infrared heating elements, or quartz lamps. The emitted radiance typically heats spaces from the bottom up by warming floors, occupants, and furnishings first, then the air above is heated via convection.

In a typical gas-fired unit, a sealed fireproof box contains a burner activated by a spark ignitor or glow-bar (the latter is unaffected by chemicals, moisture, and dust and thus is better in harsh environments), then a blower sends outdoor air across the burner into a thin metal tube on the other side. The tube may have an I, L, T, and Z configuration up to 40 ft long,

tion; it appeared in an engineering magazine.   [†] Much of the information in

which may be mounted at up to 45° inclines (always with the burner at the lower end), and it typically has a 180° U-bend at half its length so the return half doubles on itself to average heat losses along its length, then a half-cylindrical polished aluminum reflector is mounted above the tube to direct the radiance downward. The units run cleanly and quietly, capacities range from 80,000–200,000 Btu/hr, thermostatic controls offer low and high firing modes, and close-area fittings allow mounting near walls, over doorways, and in corners. The best units have factory-assembled burner boxes, which if enamel-coated are more attractive and longer-lasting. There are also more efficient direct-fired units that release heat directly into indoor spaces, but they introduce water vapor into the air. In some occupancies this may be desirable, while in others resulting condensation can degrade insulation, invite rot, and lead to other problems.

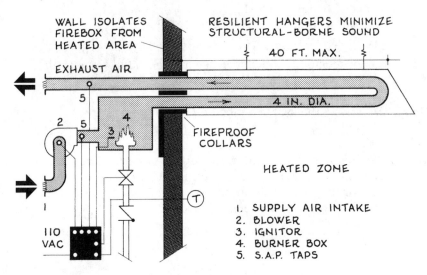

Fig. 3-23. Gas-fired ceiling heating componentry.

Gas-fired heaters work best where ceilings are high, floors are concrete, large exterior doors are frequently opened, occupants engage in mild physical activity, and the presence of airborne dust particles makes air heating systems undesirable. Optimal mounting heights are 4–6 ft above occupant activities, and simple chain hangers allow units to be relocated easily to satisfy changing occupancies. The units should be placed at least 3 ft from all light fixtures, utility conveyances, and structural members; and they are NG above areas containing flammable substances or where volatile gases could contact the tubing.

Infrared ceiling-mounted heaters are usually small individual units made in a variety of sizes (including portable units), wattages from 2–50 kW, and voltages of 120, 208, 277, and 480 V. They are installed like fluorescent light fixtures; their heating elements when turned on provides low-level lighting; and they have no ducts, vents, blowers, or moving parts. They are suitable for small industrial spaces and outdoor areas in cold regions where they can also melt snow and ice from walks, building entries, railroad waiting platforms, ATM aprons, and similar pedestrian areas.

Quartz lamp heaters have one or two tubular quartz infrared lamps up to 40 in. long mounted in cylindrical reflectors. They utilize the large amounts of heat wasted by these lamps and illuminate the spaces below. They are an excellent heat source in small spaces that need constant illumination at night, but in summer they are **N2G** unless the space they are in is well ventilated and the units are connected to occupancy sensors.

Example 1. A cabinetmaking shop in Reno, NV, desires a gas-fired overhead radiant heating system since air heating creates airborne dust in woodworking areas. If the 40 × 120 ft floor area has a design heating load during work hours of 275,000 Btu/hr, what is the system's optimal number of units, length, and spacing?

3)C)3)a) Gas-Fired Units: $H \approx L\, H_{cap}$

H = design heating load of interior space(s), 275,000 Btu/hr
L = required linear footage of selected unit, **?** ft
H_{cap}= heating capacity of selected unit, Btu/LF. Typical capacity for
      high-firing mode ≈ 3,000 Btu/LF. Use more specific figures from
      manufacturers' catalogs when available. Here use 3,000 Btu/LF.

    275,000 ≈ 3,000 L ... L ≈ 92 ft ➡ try 3 units at 30 LF each
    If area is 40 × 120 ft, arrange units as shown in Fig. 3-24

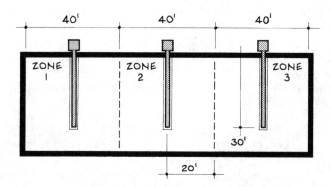

Fig. 3-24. Ceiling plan of radiant ceiling heaters.

> **Example 2.** A taxi waiting area inside the entrance of an airport in Springfield, IL, needs to be heated to 60° F when it is 0° outside. If the space is 12 ft wide, 22 ft long, and 11 ft high, what size ceiling-mounted infrared heater should the space have?

3)C)3)b) Infrared Units: $190\,H \approx V\eta\,(T_i - T_o)$

H = design heating load of interior space(s), **?** watts
V = volume of space to be heated, cf. $12 \times 22 \times 11 = 2,900$ cf.
η = number of air changes per hour (ach). For areas near building entries, assume 6 ach unless otherwise noted.
T_i = design indoor temperature, 60° F
T_o = design outdoor temperature, 0° F

$$190\,H \approx 2,900 \times 6\,(60 - 0) \qquad ...\Delta \geq 5,500\ \text{watts}$$

3.C.4. Electric Heating/Cooling

An electrical heating and cooling system is typically a small unit mounted under a window if the sill is high enough, or in a wall where its grillage can disperse conditioned air into the heart of the room. Each unit is thermostatically controlled and it heats, cools, filters, and ventilates the air in its zone. Some units have high-ventilation fans and grilles with adjustable vanes. Capacities range from about 6,500 to 30,000 Btu/hr for cooling and to 35,000 Btu/hr for heating, and power is usually 120 or 240 volt single phase. When these units produce cooling air, they usually produce a condensate which must be drained. In small units this usually drips onto the ground just outside the wall the unit is mounted in, and in large units it falls into a pan that empties into a sanitary or storm drain. Condensate pans require periodic cleaning, which requires service access; or else any standing water can become an incubator of mosquitoes, Legionnaire's disease, and other microbial proliferations.

System design involves determining the capacity and number of units required and locating the units.

> The drafting room of a local tool and die company has four large windows with 40 in. sills in its two exterior walls. If the room has a design heating load of 57,000 Btu/hr, design cooling load of 44,500 Btu/hr, and low ventilation requirements, what size heating-cooling units should the room have?

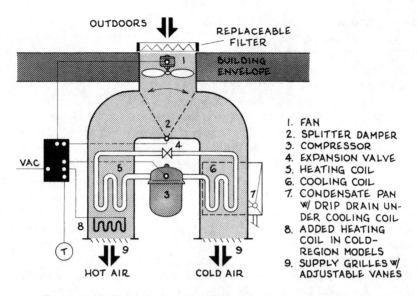

Fig. 3-25. Electric heating/cooling unit componentry.

1. FAN
2. SPLITTER DAMPER
3. COMPRESSOR
4. EXPANSION VALVE
5. HEATING COIL
6. COOLING COIL
7. CONDENSATE PAN W/ DRIP DRAIN UNDER COOLING COIL
8. ADDED HEATING COIL IN COLD-REGION MODELS
9. SUPPLY GRILLES W/ ADJUSTABLE VANES

Solution: Find the units heating and cooling capacity from the formulas below. The larger load determines the minimum wattage of each unit.

3)C)4)a)   Heating load: $H \leq 4 \, \eta \, H_{cap}$

   b)   Cooling load: $C \leq 3 \, \eta \, C_{cap}$

H = design heating load of interior space(s), 57,000 Btu/hr
C = design cooling load of interior space(s), 44,500 Btu/hr
η = number of units required to condition space. The best arrangement is one unit under each window ➡ 4 units.
H_{cap} = heating capacity of selected heating unit, ? watts
C_{cap} = cooling capacity of selected cooling unit, ? watts

   Heating: $57,000 \leq 4 \times 4 \, H_{cap}$ ... $H_{cap} \geq 3,560$ watts
   Cooling: $44,500 \leq 3 \times 4 \, C_{cap}$ ... $C_{cap} \geq 3,710$ watts   ... ➕
   From product catalogs select a unit whose capacity $\geq 3,710$ watts

3.C.5. Hot Water Heating

Hot water heating systems include a boiler and piping loops to several heating circuits or zones, each of which includes a number of baseboard convection heating units or fin tube convectors usually located under windows. These versatile systems are also used to heat domestic hot water, swimming pools, hot tubs, radiant floor heating loops, and outdoor snow melting aprons as well as heating coils inserted into forced-air heating units. The piping can also extend from heat pumps and can even be used for cooling; for chilled water can run through them in summer as well as hot water in winter. Thus a creative Æ designer can leverage the strengths of several climate control systems to achieve what none can do alone.

In the boiler, the water flows through a cast iron or steel heat exchanger suspended above an oil or gas burner and is heated to temperatures of anywhere from 140 to 200°. The heat exchanger may be *water tube* (water flows through tubes around which the combustion gases flow) or *fire tube* (hot combustion gases flow through tubes around which the water flows); and the fuel may be gas, oil, or even wood products such as scrap lumber, sawdust pellets, recycled paper, and crop residues. Combustibility of wood product fuels is greatly affected by their moisture content; thus each must be dried first. If the design heating load exceeds 200 MBtu/hr, a multiple-module boiler system is usually installed. Then during mildly cold weather the smaller boilers can operate one at a time; so the overall efficiency of these systems increases as the number of boilers increase. Multiple boilers also allow one boiler at a time to be serviced without interrupting the system's operation, and smaller lighter boilers require narrower doorways and fewer people to install. Efficient boiler operation also includes clean-burning fuels, low excess-air firing, low-NOX burners, and flue-gas recirculation. Heating efficiencies range from about 50–75 percent depending on age, duty cycle, fineness of adjustment, and cleanliness of heat exchange surfaces. One drawback to these systems, multiple-boiler systems in particular, is that each separate boiler requires adequate airflow intake and a flue.

Several piping layouts are used in these systems, depending on the size and arrangement of the spaces served. If a zone has more than three units, its piping should be two-pipe reverse-return. Sophisticated controls enable each loop to have different temperature gradients and water circulating rates if necessary. Straight runs should not exceed 30 ft due to thermal expansion, all runs should slope at least $\frac{1}{8}$ in. fall/ft, pitch peaks should have vents so any air trapped in the system can be bled, pitch valleys should have spigots so the system can be drained, and the piping main to each zone should be valved so it can be drained without shutting down the whole system. A mixing valve should also connect the supply and return lines just outside the boiler, and thermal sensors should be installed on each line, as these controls minimize thermal shock in the boiler when it refires after a lengthy shutdown. Supply water design temperatures are usually 170, 180, 190, or 200° F., with a 20° drop assumed through zones, and water velocities are 1–4 gpm (higher velocities create noise while lower velocities require larger and more costly piping).

If the piping could freeze, an antifreeze such as ethylene or propylene glycol may be added to the water. Both these fluids are stable over a

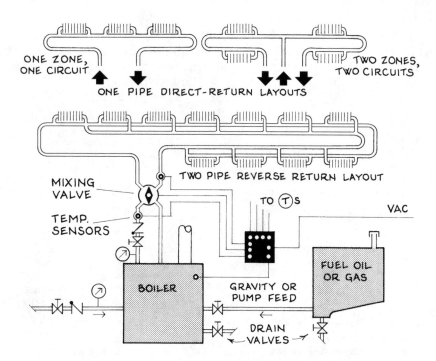

ONE ZONE, ONE CIRCUIT

TWO ZONES, TWO CIRCUITS

ONE PIPE DIRECT-RETURN LAYOUTS

TWO PIPE REVERSE RETURN LAYOUT

MIXING VALVE

TEMP. SENSORS

TO (T)S

VAC

FUEL OIL OR GAS

BOILER

GRAVITY OR PUMP FEED

DRAIN VALVES

Fig. 3-26. Hot water heating componentry.

wide range of temperatures and when used with an inhibitor are noncorrosive; but glycol solutions require 20 percent larger air expansion tanks, cannot be run through galvanized piping, and need a strainer or other means of sediment removal in the piping. As ethylene glycol transfers heat better and is less viscous, it requires a less powerful pump for a given design. Solution design involves determining the system's minimum temperature, then computing the proper percentage of glycol. Avoid overconcentrated systems, as they are more costly and reduce system efficiency.

Although hot water heating is strongly associated with baseboard units, the end-use piping can be configured into any kind of radiant heating panel: horizontal, vertical, inclined, large, small, square, bizarre shapes, seat warmers, bed warmers, you name it. Some manufacturers' catalogs offer everything from towel racks to imitations of old steam radiators, with many products available in no-polish brass and enameled cast iron finishes, as well as many colors available to match any decor. This is big business. The opportunities for custom-fabricating are even greater. Think of the shapes that flexible copper tubing can be bent into. Or how about arranging a few short lengths of thin copper pipe and a dozen 90° elbows into a row of towel racks whose continuous hot-water piping weaves in and out of a bathroom wall? The author saw such a row of hot-water copper pipe towel rack warmers in a house near Monterey, CA, in 1971.

Hot water heating system wastes are primarily heat losses through the piping and hot gases up the boiler flue. The first is minimized by insulating all piping and fittings, the second by efficient boiler operation. The thermal plume in the flue also offers opportunities for heat reclamation.

Specifications for three boilers made by one company are below:

Input, Btu	500,000	750,000	1,000,000
Output, Btu	420,000	630,000	840,000
H × W × L, in.	49×26×27	56×27×27	66×30×27
Footprint, sf	4.75	4.85	5.5
Flue connection, in. diameter	6	8	9
Hot water piping (in & out), in. dia. ...	2	2	$2\frac{1}{2}$
Gas piping connection, in.	1	1	$1\frac{1}{4}$
Combustion air inlet, in. dia.	5	5	6
Electric power, volts/amps	115/6	115/7	115/8
Shipping weight, lb	550	580	610

Example 1: Pipe Size. If the hot water heating system for a 2,800 ft^2 residence near Hartford, CT, has a design heating load of 52,000 Btu/hr, what are the optimal pipe diameters for its supply circuit, baseboard heaters, and return circuit?

Solution: Pipe sizing for hot water heating systems is as follows:

1. Organize the interior spaces to be heated into zones.
2. Determine the piping length for each zone. This is roughly the perimeter of each zone plus twice the distance (horizontal plus vertical) from boiler to zone.
3. Compute the number of fixture units for each zone by dividing the total piping length by 10.
4. Knowing the initial pressure, head, pipe length, and minimum fixture pressure, estimate the pipe pressure friction loss from Sec. 4.C.
5. Knowing the number of fixture units and pipe pressure loss, find the supply circuit pipe diameter from Fig. 4-7, page 267.

For most residential and small commercial buildings with one- or two-pipe reverse return systems, the above procedure boils down to 1 in. diameter pipe for supply circuits (maybe $1\frac{1}{4}$ in. for larger first-class jobs), and $\frac{3}{4}$ in. pipe for zones and return circuits.

Example 2: Boiler Capacity. If the design heating load for an industrial building near Chicago is 270,000 Btu/hr, size the boiler for its hot water heating system.

3)C)5)a) $\qquad H_{cap} \geq \mathbf{H}\,(1.25 + 0.000{,}034\,E)$

H_{cap} = heating capacity of selected boiler, **?** Btu/hr
H = design heating load of space, 270,000 Btu/hr
E = elevation above sea level, ft. If less than 1,000 ft, use $E = 0$.

$$H_{cap} \geq 270{,}000\,(1.25 + 0) \geq 338{,}000 \text{ Btu/hr}$$

Example 3: Boiler Access Floor Area. What floor area is needed for a water boiler with a 32 × 34 in. base?

---

3)C)5)b) $\qquad A \approx (L + 5)\,(W + 5)$

A = approximate floor area for boiler and perimeter access, **?** sf
L = length of boiler base, ft. 34 in. = 2.83 ft.
W = width of boiler base, ft. 32 in. = 2.67 ft.

$$A \approx (2.83 + 5)\,(2.67 + 5) \approx 60 \text{ sf}$$

Area should be nearly square and doesn't include base of chimney

Note: The above formula may be used to estimate the floor area required for almost any floor-mounted climate control system unit.

Example 4: Baseboard Heater Unit Length. A manager's office has a design heating load of 5,500 Btu/hr and three windows. If the water baseboard heaters under each window are rated at 640 Btu/hr-LF at 190° F and 20° drop, what are their lengths?

---

3)C)5)c) $\qquad \mathbf{H} \leq L\,H_{cap}$

H = design heating load of space, 5,500 Btu/hr
L = total length of heating units installed in space, **?** ft
H_{cap} = heating capacity of selected unit (rating as listed in product catalog), 640 Btu/hr-LF

$$5{,}500 \leq 640\,L \quad \dots\, L \geq 8.60 \text{ ft total length} \rightarrow 3 \text{ ft each}$$

Example 5: Flue Size and Height. What is the optimal chimney size and height for an H.B. Smith G300-7W boiler?

Solution: In the H. B. Smith product catalog find the *Dimensions and Ratings* page. Beside *G300-7* and under *Chimney size* are the numbers 8 × 12 × 20 → the flue should be at least 8 in. wide, 12 in. deep, and 20 ft tall.

3.C.6. Steam Heating [†]

Superficially, steam heating is similar to hot water heating, except the water is heated to above-boiling temperatures which delivers more energy in a smaller volume to the radiators in the occupied spaces, which theoretically allows the system's componentry to take up less space and cost less. However, the nature of steam requires additional componentry that raises system costs to levels that often make its economic benefits questionable.

In a steam heating system, water is heated in a boiler to above its boiling point, which changes it to steam. At normal atmospheric pressure, each pound of water, whose volume is about 27 cubic inches, absorbs 970 Btus of energy and expands until its volume is 27 cubic *feet*. Due to the great heat and pressure involved, the boiler is usually cast iron, the pipes through which the steam flows up are steel, and the radiators in the heated spaces are usually cast iron. Inside each radiator the steam is exposed to a large surface area of thin metal, whose near-room temperature on the outside lowers the steam's temperature back to below its boiling point, which reduces the steam's volume and releases its 970 Btu/lb of heat to the radiator metal, which conducts the Btus to the interior air. The steam is now water, which flows back down to the boiler where the cycle starts anew. Obviously these systems must be airtight; yet each must have valves or vents that allow the steam to expand and contract safely; and the valves must maintain an even pressure throughout the system.

Another difficulty with steam heating is that just after the steam has formed immediately above the turgidly boiling water, it contains much moisture —a condition known as *wet*— most of which must be removed. Thus the airspace above the water can't be too small (then the steam propagation space is reduced and its pressure becomes dangerously high) or too large (then the steam pressure won't be enough to propel it upward to all the radiators). Also, the outlets in the boiler's top must be just the right number to minimize the entrained moisture that rises from the boiler, the vertical outlets must connect to a horizontal *header* that must be the right diameter and length to collect all the steam from the outlets while keeping any entrained moisture from rising further, and the riser extending from the header must be the right diameter to make the steam flow at the proper velocity (too slow and the steam will not have enough momentum to reach all the radiators; too fast and the steam will be noisy and its pressure will be dangerously high). Essentially all this anatomy converts the initially wet steam to dry steam, the definition of *dry* being less than 2 percent of entrained moisture. In today's systems, the crucial zone above the boiler's water level is usually outfitted with digital controls that maintain optimal pressure/moisture conditions throughout the system.

Another crucial aspect of a steam heating system is its operating pressure. Whether measured in psi, psia, psig, in. Hg, or oz/in^2, it is a major

---

[†] The primary source for this section was *Simplified Design of HVAC Systems,*

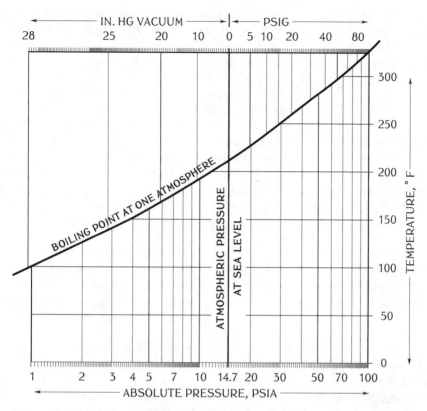

Fig. 3-27. Thermodynamic relation between water and steam. [†]

system design parameter. These terms are interrelated as follows. Psia is simply psi in terms of the atmospheric pressure (e.g. 0 psi = 14.7 psia); psig is the same as psi when it is *above* normal atmospheric pressure (e.g. 5 psig = 5 psi above normal pressure); in. Hg is the amount that psi is *below* normal atmospheric pressure, measured in inches mercury (e.g. 1 in. Hg = –0.491 psi below normal pressure); and oz/in² is merely another way of describing psi (e.g. 8 oz/in² = 0.5 psi). Most systems operate at the lowest pressure required to drive the steam to the remote radiator, as then they are safer and less costly to manage. The steamflow may also be enclosed in a vacuum, as then the boiling point is lower. For example, in a system operating at a vacuum pressure of 20 in. Hg (– 9.82 psi), the water converts to steam at a safer 161°. A system's pressure can also be made to vary from well below to well above normal, then the system can more efficiently convert water to steam at well below 212° in mild weather and well above 212° in very cold weather. These are known as *variable vacuum systems*. They are highly efficient; but if one develops the slightest leak, its efficiency

William Bobenhausen (Wiley, New York, 1994); pp. 227–48. [†] This graph was plummets. Thus variable vacuum systems usually have an expensive high-horsepower backup vacuum pump. These systems are rarely used today.

A steam heating system boiler may be *fire-tube* or *water-tube*, and its piping may be *one-pipe* or *two pipe*. In a fire-tube boiler, a plurality of tubes carry hot gases that heat the enveloping water; while in a water-tube boiler the tubes carry water that is heated by enveloping hot gases. In a one-pipe system, one pipe carries the steam up to the radiators and carries the water condensate back down. These systems are simpler and less expensive, but are less efficient because the steam and water flow against each other in the same pipe. One-pipe systems are usually found today only in old buildings. In a two-pipe system, the steam flows up one pipe to the radiators and the water flows back down a second pipe. All piping should be thickly insulated to minimize heat loss, to keep condensation from forming on their surfaces, and to protect anyone who might touch them, as they are very hot. As for the radiators, they may be cabinet convectors, shielded fin-tube units, loops of radiant floor piping, or a number of unit section assemblies that are fitted together to produce the required output. The heat outputs of factory-made units are typically listed in manufacturers' catalogs, so all a designer needs to do is select one or more units of adequate output. The radiators are usually activated by the same kind of thermostats that activate other heating systems.

Steam systems have a few drawbacks. When water converts to steam, its greatly expanding volume can cause any part of its highly pressurized container to explode. The high pressure also causes the steam to move through the pipes at speeds of 100–200 feet per second —so if the piping springs a leak, the hot steam jets out at dangerously high velocities. Thus all steam containers —boilers, pipes, radiators— must be made of thick cast iron or double extra-heavy steel, and all connections must be threaded and sealed. Steam heating systems can also be noisy if the piping isn't sized accurately. Also, due to the high operating temperatures, the boilers can be corroded on the inside by water impurities and on the outside by water vapor that forms as a byproduct of the combustion fuels. Thus the supply water should be softened, filtered, and treated until it is reasonably pure; the boiler should have one or more blowdown taps; and the combustion gases must not leave the boiler too quickly (then their temperature remains well above boiling and excess heat is lost up the flue) or too slowly (then the temperature drops below boiling and water vapor forms). Also, the system designer must always be aware that the pipes could freeze.

A steam heating system is best designed by envisioning its water as a medium that experiences a cycle with an *absorption* side and a *radiation* side. On the absorption side, the water enters the boiler at a temperature of, say 50°, then is heated to an above-boiling temperature of, say, 240° (this amount should be at least 20° above boiling to account for the steam's temperature drop as it flows from the boiler to the radiators). In this case,

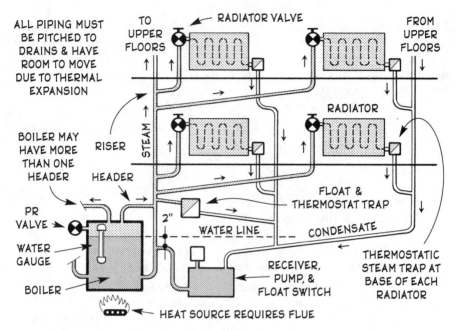

ALL PIPING MUST BE PITCHED TO DRAINS & HAVE ROOM TO MOVE DUE TO THERMAL EXPANSION

TO UPPER FLOORS

RADIATOR VALVE

FROM UPPER FLOORS

RADIATOR

BOILER MAY HAVE MORE THAN ONE HEADER

RISER

STEAM

HEADER

FLOAT & THERMOSTAT TRAP

PR VALVE

2"

WATER LINE

CONDENSATE

WATER GAUGE

RECEIVER, PUMP, & FLOAT SWITCH

THERMOSTATIC STEAM TRAP AT BASE OF EACH RADIATOR

BOILER

HEAT SOURCE REQUIRES FLUE

Fig. 3-28. Two-pipe steam heating system.

assuming the heating occurs at normal atmospheric pressure, the heat that each lb of water absorbs is

(boiling pt. - T_{min}) + heat of vaporization + (T_{max} - boiling pt.)

Typical numbers for this scenario would be

(212 - 50) + 970 + (240 - 212) = 1,160 Btu absorbed per lb of H_2O

On the cycle's radiation side, the amount of heat that each lb of steam releases inside the radiators is

(T_{enter} - boiling pt.) + heat of condensation + (boiling pt. - T_{exit})

Assuming that the steam's temperature drops from 240° to 220° in the supply piping and the water condensate exits the radiators at a below-boiling point temperature of, say, 170°, the numbers for this scenario would be

(220 - 212) + 970 + (212 - 170) = 1,020 Btu released per lb of H_2O

Thus, if a space requires 10,000 Btu/hr to remain warm in winter based on its design heating load, it requires 10,000 ÷ 1,020 = 9.8 lb of steam; then the amount of energy required to send the steam to the radiators would be 9.8 × 1,160 = 11,400 Btu/hr. However, to this amount must be added a pickup heating load due to the amount of heat that is absorbed by the system's heavy masses of boilers, piping, radiators, and other componentry plus a few other inefficiencies here and there. This inefficiency factor is usually taken to be 1.6. Thus the approximate amount of energy required to heat the space would be 11,400 × 1.6 ≈ 18,000 Btu/hr. In similar fashion, the designer finds the weight of the steam flowing through each pipe in the system, then sizes the pipe. These mathematics are all formalized below.

A steam heating system is designed as follows.

Step 1. Knowing the building's total design heating load, find the design heating capacity of the steam heating system from

3)C)6) $H_{cap} = 1.6\,\mathbf{H}\,(T_{max} + Q - T_{min})/(T_{enter} + Q - T_{exit})$

H_{cap} = heating capacity of selected unit, Btu/LF.
$\mathbf{H}$ = design heating load of interior space(s) or building, Btu/hr
Q = heat of vaporization/condensation of H_2O; this = 970 Btu/lb of H_2O if the system operates at normal atmospheric pressure. If otherwise, find Q from the bar graph below.

Air pressure, in. Hg or psig

| ← in. Hg vacuum →|← psig pressure → |
20	10	4	2	0	1	2	3	4	5	10	15	50
161	192	205	209	212	216	218	222	225	227	240	250	281

Heat of vaporization/condensation, Btu/lb of H_2O

T_{max} = maximum temperature of steam in boiler, ° F. This is usually at least 20–25° above the boiling point of water.
T_{min} = temperature of incoming water, ° F. This is initially the temperature of the building's cold water supply, but after initial cycling it is more likely to be 150–170 ° F.
T_{enter} = temperature of steam as it enters the radiators, ° F. This should be a few degrees above the water's boiling point.
T_{exit} = temperature of water as it exits the radiators, ° F. This should be below the water's boiling point, but the cooler the water is while it is still in the radiator, the more heat it imparts to the adjacent interior space. Optimal T_{exit} = 150–170°.

Step 2. Determine the unit pressure drop per 100 LF of the system's piping (Δp below). This is usually 1–8 oz/in² depending on the system's total heating capacity and the length of its supply piping. Generally the larger the system, the greater the pipe pressure drop between the boiler and the remote radiator; and the steam's total pressure drop (ΔP below) must always exceed this amount (otherwise the steam won't reach the remote radiator). In most small systems (H_{cap} ≤ 250,000 Btu/hr), Δp ≈ 2 oz/in². Once Δp is determined, find the system's total pressure drop from

$$\Delta P \geq 0.02\,\Delta p\,L$$

ΔP = total pressure of steamflow in system, oz/in^2 or psig
Δp = unit pressure drop of steamflow per 100 LF of pipe, oz/in^2
L = maximum length of piping in system: length of piping from boiler to remote radiator, ft

Step 3. Determine the amount of the building's total heating load that flows through each pipe in the system, then size each pipe according to

$$C\,\sigma_{vs} \geq 19.6\ Q\,v\,\delta^2$$

C = portion of system's design heating capacity that flows through each pipe section, Btu/hr

σ_{vs} = specific volume of steam at system pressure, cf/lb. This is found by entering the system's total pressure of steamflow (psig) which was found in Step 2 in the bar graph below:

Air pressure, in. Hg or psig

←— in. Hg vacuum —|←——— psig pressure ———→

20	10	4	2	0	1	2	3	4	5	10	15	50
75	39	31	29	27	25	24	22	21	20	16	14	8

Specific volume of steam, cf/lb

Q = heat of vaporization/condensation of H_2O; this = 970 Btu/lb of H_2O if the system operates at normal atmospheric pressure. If otherwise, find Q from the bar graph in Step 1.

v = velocity of steamflow through piping, normally 100–140 fps. Velocities to 200 fps are OK in industrial and other settings where pipe noise in not a major concern. Normally this is set at about 125 fps, then the formula is solved for δ below; then after δ is sized the formula is rerun to solve for v to see if its value is acceptable.

δ = diameter of pipe through which steam flows (interior dimension), in. Solve for this value, then increase to nearest standard diameter.

Note: The above is a general formula for sizing steam piping. Several more specific formulas for sizing this piping in low-pressure systems are below.

3|C|6|a] One-pipe systems, supply risers, upfeeds[a] $C = 11\ Q\ \delta^{2.55}$
      b] Radiator valves, vertical connections[b].. $C = 7\ Q\ \delta^{2.58}$
      c] Radiator & rise runouts .... $C = 7\ Q\ \delta^{2.37}$
      d] Branch vertical piping[c] .... $C = 14\ Q\ \delta^{2.70}$
      e] Branch horizontal piping .... $C = 14\ Q\ \delta^{2.57}$
      f] Two-pipe systems (1–6 psig boiler press.) $C = 76\ \Delta p^{0.54}\ \delta^{2.60}$

a. If $\Delta p \geq 0.063$ psi/100LF, use formula 6.
b. Pipe diameter must ≤ 2 in.
c. If $\Delta p \geq 0.042$ psi/100LF, use formula 6.

Step 4. Lay out the piping system. Make sure enough space exists around every part, especially at the ends of long runs, because steam piping experiences much more thermal expansion than other piping due to the higher temperatures involved. Supply pipes should pitch upward in the direction of flow at least $\frac{1}{4}$ in/10 LF (this is the *minimum* pitch that is allowed where a sag might occur; thus $\frac{1}{8}$ in/LF is wiser design), and, similarly, return piping should pitch downward in the direction of flow at least $\frac{1}{2}$ in/10 LF. Finally, as scale and corrosion occur in steam piping more than almost any other kind, every LF of length must be drainable by drain or blowoff valves installed at the lowest elevations of each run.

3.C.7. Air Heating

An air heating system includes a furnace in which an ignited fuel warms fan-driven air to 120–145° F, which flows through ducts to registers in the occupied spaces. Higher temperatures lead to high duct airflow velocities that create resonant noise, while lower temperatures lead to low duct airflow velocities that require larger and more costly ducting. The maximum run from furnace to farthest register should ≤ 80 ft, and the ducting is most efficient if round or nearly square. All ducts should be wrapped in insulation, especially where they pass through unheated voids, and flexible connections are often installed between the furnace and main ducts to reduce sound transmission from the furnace. If return air ducts are installed, computerized controls may include setbacks, setforwards, occupancy sensors, and sensors for static air pressure, VOCs, and CO_2. The thermal plume of waste heat in the furnace flue also offers heat reclamation opportunities for hot water heating and heat pump cycling.

A furnace must have fresh air to ensure full combustion of its fuel. In southerly climes and where the furnace is not confined, combustion airflow is never a problem. But in northerly regions where the furnace is usually completely indoors, often within airtight construction, a sized conduit should run as straight as possible from the outdoors to within 24 in. of the furnace's air intake; otherwise the unit's operation may be dangerously inefficient. Both ends of the conduit should be screened with at least $\frac{1}{4}$ in. mesh, the outside opening should face downward, and the area around it should be clear of any possibly accumulating snow and growing foliage. In large systems this conduit often connects directly to the furnace, which has a motorized damper that turns on when the igniter needs fresh air.

As good a rule as any for sizing the air intake conduit is 2 in^2 of conduit section area per 1,000 Btu/hr of fuel consumed. Never obtain the fresh airflow from nearby occupied spaces. Thus, where these conduits are

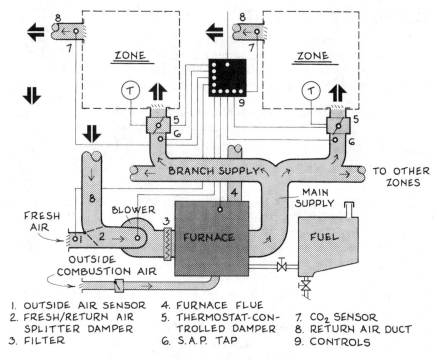

1. OUTSIDE AIR SENSOR
2. FRESH/RETURN AIR
   SPLITTER DAMPER
3. FILTER
4. FURNACE FLUE
5. THERMOSTAT-CON-
   TROLLED DAMPER
6. S.A.P. TAP
7. CO_2 SENSOR
8. RETURN AIR DUCT
9. CONTROLS

Fig. 3-29. Air heating system componentry.

installed, the furnace area should be partitioned from adjacent spaces and the intervening door weatherstripped. Also, since the conduit will carry cold air during extremely cold weather, clad it in insulation and keep it well away from any water pipes, floor drains, and other water-filled equipment. A few other variables regarding the conduit's optimal size are the temperature of its intake air and the ratio of its section area vs. the net free area of its intake screen. Here it is impossible to quantify all the variables involved, that the finest solutions require adroit conceptualizing.

In air heating systems, wall-mounted registers should be close to floors and under windows, floor-mounted registers should be near exterior walls and also under windows, and grilles should direct airflow across nearby wall or floor surfaces or in directions that avoid drafts. For details on register design, see Sec. 3.B.3.

Example 1: Furnace Capacity. A residence in Denver, CO, has a design heating load of 62,000 Btu/hr. If the house has an air heating system, size the furnace.

<u>3</u><u>C</u><u>7</u><u>a</u> $H_{cap} \geq H\,(1.15 + 0.000,034\ E)$

H_{cap}= heating capacity of selected furnace, **?** Btu/hr.
     Use net ratings as listed in product catalogs.
H   = design heating load of space, 62,000 Btu/hr
E = elevation above sea level, ft. E for Denver = 5,280 ft.

    $H_{cap} \geq$ 62,000 (1.15 + 0.000,034 × 5,280) $\geq$ 82,400 Btu/hr
      Select furnace whose capacity $\geq$ 82,400 Btu/hr

Note: The catalog or specifications from which the furnace is selected should also give the unit's minimum flue section area and height.

Example 2: Duct Size. What is the optimal size for two main ducts of equal capacity for the above furnace?

<u>3</u><u>C</u><u>7</u><u>b</u> $H \leq 0.65\ A\ \kappa_d\,(T_h - T_i)$

H = design heating load of space or heating capacity of selected furnace, 89,000 Btu/hr
A = minimum section area of duct (not including insulation), **?** in^2
κ_d = duct velocity factor. From Table 3-3, κ_d for main duct in res. = 8.
T_h = temperature of heated air, 130° F
T_i = temperature of indoor air, assume 68° F unless otherwise noted

    89,000 $\leq$ 0.65 × A × 8 (130 – 68)   ... $A \geq$ 276 in^2 for both ducts
  One duct $\geq$ 276/2 $\geq$ 138 in^2 ➡ 12 × 12", 10 × 14", 14" diameter, etc.

Note: If the duct is more than 40 ft long or its width-to-depth ratio exceeds 2.5, its size should be increased according to its air friction losses and/or aspect ratio as described in Sec. 3.C.i.1.

TABLE 3-3: DUCT VELOCITY FACTORS

BUILDING TYPE	DUCTS		
	Main	Branch	Outlet
Residences	6.5	5	3.5
Theaters, assembly areas	8	6	4
Apartments, hotel & hospital bedrooms	10	7	4
Private offices, conf. rooms, libraries, schools ...	12	8	6
General offices, banks, fine restaurants, stores ..	15	9.5	7
Average retail, cafeterias	18	12	9
Industrial, recreation, service, rest rooms	22	18	12

1. These duct velocity factors are for low-velocity systems.

3.C.8. Air Cooling

Generally known as air conditioning, air conditioners, or AC units, air cooling systems are compact units usually installed in windows, exterior walls, or on flat roofs. The incoming air may be cooled in an air-to-air heat exchanger or by refrigerating coils, then in smaller models the cooled air flows directly indoors through the machine's supply air grilles while in larger units the air may pass through a small network of ducts into several spaces. The best units have environmental controls, can handle up to 50 percent outside air, are fitted with air filters, operate quietly, and are usually easily maintained via hinged access panels, accessible fan motors, and easy pull-out filters. The newest models also have computerized controls, which enable them to be incorporated into total building management systems. Some systems also have return air ducting, and many include a small heating coil to satisfy moderate heating loads in winter, a feature that makes these units popular in the southern half of the United States. Typical cooling capacities run about 400 cfm of cooling air per ton of refrigeration, and sizes range from 0.5–20 tons. The mechanics of these systems have changed little since the 1950s.

If an air cooling system humidifies air, it should not be oversized, as then the system will tend to overcool the space, which (1) induces its humidity to rise rapidly to levels that turn the system back on, which results in frequent cycling and increased wear and tear; and (2) causes the humidity to rise above the dew point which makes moisture precipitate out of the air, which can lead to massive buildups of mildew that can practically destroy the building —as it did to the Imperial Polk County Courthouse in Barstow, FL, as described in Sec. 3.C.

An air cooling system's registers should be located in ceilings or at least 6'-6" high on walls. Ceiling registers should be round or square and near the center of the zone, and wall registers should be no farther than 10 ft apart to prevent dead air spots. Grilles should prevent drafts from forming in the lower 6 ft of the zone, which is best done by directing air across nearby wall or ceiling surfaces. For detailed information on register design, see Sec. 3.B.3.

When an air cooling unit removes water from air, the water collects on its cooling coils, and then must be drained. In small wall-mounted AC units, the condensate often simply drips onto the ground just outside the wall the unit is mounted in; but in large systems, it usually empties into a condensate pan that must be carefully designed in terms of local summer design temperature, total system capacity, cooling coil size, pan pitch, drain diameter, U-trap height, and even coordination of static air pressures. Since condensate pans are notorious collectors of particulate debris, each should have an oversize-diameter drain with a removable filter screen and U-trap, and each must be accessible for periodic cleaning.

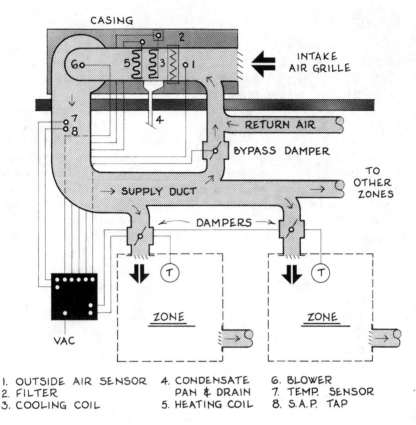

CASING

INTAKE AIR GRILLE

← RETURN AIR

BYPASS DAMPER

→ SUPPLY DUCT

TO OTHER ZONES

← DAMPERS →

ZONE

ZONE

VAC

1. OUTSIDE AIR SENSOR
2. FILTER
3. COOLING COIL
4. CONDENSATE PAN & DRAIN
5. HEATING COIL
6. BLOWER
7. TEMP. SENSOR
8. S.A.P. TAP

Fig. 3-30. Rooftop AC unit componentry.

Air cooling system wastes are primarily cooling losses through the surfaces of the ducting. This is minimized by wrapping the ducts in insulation, which should always be done with ducts located in unconditioned voids.

> **Example 1: Unit Capacity.** If the design cooling load of the living-den-dining area in a house near Dallas is 51,000 Btu/hr, what is the capacity of a unit air conditioner serving this zone?

3 C 8 a] Cooling, Btu/hr: $12,000\ C_{cap} \geq \mathbf{C}_{btu}\,(1.15 + 0.000{,}034\ E)$

b] Cooling, tons: $C_{cap} \geq \mathbf{C}_{ton}\,(1.15 + 0.000{,}034\ E)$

C_{cap} = cooling capacity of selected AC unit, ? tons
$\mathbf{C}_{btu}$ = design cooling load, Btu/hr. Not applicable.
$\mathbf{C}_{ton}$ = design cooling load, tons. $\mathbf{C}$ = 51,000 Btu/hr/12,000 = 4.25 tons.

E = elevation above sea level, ft. From atlas, E of Dallas ≈ 500 ft.
      If E ≤ 2,000 ft, use $E = 0$.

$$C_{cap} ≥ 4.25 (1.15 + 0)   ... C ≥ 4.89 \text{ tons}$$
Install two 2.5 ton units in two windows in the area

Example 2: System Capacity. A large one-floor auto dealership near Atlanta is to be air-conditioned with roof-mounted AC units. If the building plan and design cooling loads for each space are as shown in Fig. 3-31, how many AC units are required, what are the cooling capacities of each, and how should each space be cooled?

Space	Cooling load, tons
A. Showroom	10.30
B. Owner's office	0.53
C. Sales & secretarial	1.09
D. Service manager's office	0.39
E. Garage	14.50
F. Parts department	1.41

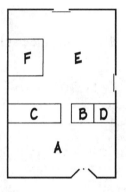

Fig. 3-31. Floor plan and cooling loads of spaces.

Solution: Select by trial and error a unit whose tonnage supplies all of a larger space (showroom or garage) and one or more smaller spaces.

Step 1. Due to the shape of showroom **A**, two rooftop units will cool this space, so try a unit size based on two units. Cooling load/2 units = 10.3/2 = 5.15 tons/unit ➡ two 5 ton units w/ no cooling remaining for other spaces.

Step 2. Assume that parts department **F** will be cooled by the units installed for garage **E**, then investigate the loads for these areas. Load **E** + Load **F** = 14.5 + 1.41 = 15.9 tons ➡ four 5 ton units, with possibly enough cooling left for spaces **B**, **C**, and **D**. Leftover load from E and F = 4 × 5 − 15.9 = 4.1 tons.

Step 3. Add the cooling loads for spaces **B**, **C**, and **D** and compare the sum with the leftover load from spaces **E** and **F**.

$$\text{Loads } B + C + D = 0.53 + 1.09 + 0.39 = 2.01 ≤ 4.1$$
∴ four 4 ton units are **OK** for spaces **B–F**

Note: Two 5 ton units and two 4 ton units will also work for spaces **B-F**. Either way, locate the units over the spaces as shown in Fig. 3-32*A*.

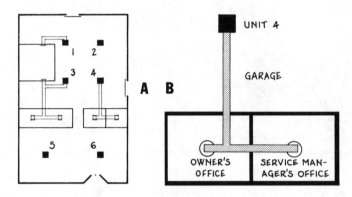

Fig. 3-32. Floor plan with ducts and grilles located on it.

Example 3: Duct Size. Part of the one-floor auto dealership above is cooled by a roof-mounted 5-ton AC unit as shown in Fig. 3-32*B*. If most of the cooling from this unit flows into the garage and the rest flows into two offices whose loads are 0.39 and 0.53 tons, what is the size of the main duct from the AC unit into the offices?

3)C)8)c) Cooling, Btu/hr: $\quad C_{btu} \geq 15 \, \kappa_d \, A$

    d) Cooling, tons: $\quad 800 \, C_{ton} \geq \kappa_d \, A \quad \ldots$ ✚

C_{btu} = cooling capacity of selected unit, Btu/hr. Not applicable.

C_{ton} = cooling capacity of selected unit, tons. $\nabla = 0.39 + 0.53 = 0.92$ tons.

κ_d = duct velocity factor. From Table 3-3, $\kappa_d = 22$ for main duct in industrial area (garage) and 12 for main duct in office. Use smaller value of 12.

A = minimum section area of duct (not including insulation), ? in^2

$$800 \times 0.92 \geq 12 \, A$$
$$A \geq 61.6 \text{ in}^2 \text{ ➡ } 8 \times 8 \text{ in, } 6 \times 12 \text{ in, } 9 \text{ in. dia., etc.}$$

Note: If the duct exceeds 40 ft in length or its width-to-depth ratio exceeds 2.5, its size should be increased according to air friction losses and/or the duct's aspect ratio as described in Sec. 3.C.9.a, Example 2, Step 8.

3.C.9. Air Heating/Cooling

An air heating and cooling system may be as small as a refrigerator-sized unit that heats, cools, humidifies, and filters but does not ventilate air; or as vast as a heating, ventilation, and air conditioning (HVAC) system whose air handling unit alone is the size of a mobile home, whose main duct may be as large as a hallway, and whose tentacles of ducting snake hundreds of feet into every corner of the building. Regarding small systems, one company makes an attractive 33 × 33 × 94 in. standup unit that has a capacity of 3 or 5 tons, has frontal access to all components (allowing it to fit into a corner or snugly between other furnishings), and contains microcontrols that intelligently determine air requirements and maintain efficient operation. The unit can discharge conditioned air upward (good for normal spaces) or downward (good for cooling under raised floors), and "has everything in one cabinet from one supplier" except a plumbing connection to a remote condenser or chiller.

In large HVAC systems, a central air handling unit drives conditioned air through an extensive distribution network of ducting, often called a *supply tree*, to all interior spaces, then a similar *return tree* draws stale air back to the central unit for reconditioning. Each system typically maintains desirable temperatures and humidities, keeps air fresh, and removes odors and particulates everywhere in the building; thus they are especially appropriate in large hermetically sealed 'air aquarium' occupancies. Many such systems today also have computerized fire-control overrides, which in case of fire switch supply plenums to 100 percent outdoor air, activate dampers to remove accumulating gases from areas of incipient fires, and draw undesirable air from affected areas after the fire is out. In such systems sensor location is strategically important.

The most important components of large HVAC systems are the *air handling unit, ducting*, and *cooling tower*. These are described below.

An air handling unit is a little factory that makes clean air. Raw outside air and previously-used stale air enter one end of this production line; then impurities are removed, additives are added, and the air is further refined until it is continually comfortable to the occupants. Each unit typically has two fans that keep the air moving through it (one fan pulls stale air in from the return ducts while the other pushes fresh air out into the supply ducts), and each has two or more dampers that during hot or humid weather mix return air with outdoor air to meet fresh air demands, as it is often more economical to recondition part of the return air rather than continually use 100 percent outdoor air as supply. In large buildings whose occupants, lighting, machinery, and other internal heat sources generate so much heat that even during cold weather interior spaces require cooling rather than heating, an *outside air economizer* may use chilly outdoor air to cool interior spaces instead of doing the same with fossil fuels, which saves energy and allows system componentry to be simpler and smaller. An air handling unit's primary subcomponents are further described below. [†]

Intake louver. This is a usually rectangular opening that is sized to receive the building's required intake airflow, its design parameters being a minimum 4 × 4 ft face area and 1 sf opening area/400 cfm of required air. As this opening must minimize the entry of rain, snow, paper, trash, birds, roof dust, and any particulate exhausts from nearby buildings, it is usually hooded, fitted with a louver of horizontal vanes, and contains one or two $\frac{1}{2}$ in. wire mesh screens before the louver. Also a pair of center-opening doors are often installed outside the opening to protect the area just inside during hurricanes, blizzards, and other extreme weather. Thus the opening must be accessible by maintenance personnel for periodic cleaning and removal of collected debris. The opening's sill should be at least 2.5 ft above the area in front (higher if local snowfall may be deeper) and it should be 6–12 ft back from the edge of a fairly flat roof because (1) if placed farther back, during hot weather the intake air will flow over a long hot roof area and be heated before entering the air handling unit, which increases cooling loads, (2) if placed closer, during rainy weather possible updrafts against the side of the building will send water into the air handling unit, and (3) the 6–12 ft flat width provides comfortable access for maintenance personnel. An HVAC intake louver should never be near motor vehicle activity, trash dumpsters, or discharge air from cooling towers.

Air heating/cooling systems often require exhaust air louvers through which may flow much of the system's stale air. These openings are designed similarly as intake louvers with the air flowing in reverse. Parameters for sizing them are minimum 3 × 3.5 ft face area and 1 sf opening area/500 cfm of required air.

Primary damper. Located just behind the air intake louver, this is a second louver with rotatable horizontal vanes that regulate the incoming airflow based on momentary system loads and the amount of return air entering the system. The blades may be up to 12 in. wide and are usually made of 16 ga. galvanized steel. A similar relief damper is usually placed on return air openings as an exhaust system check valve and to relieve the building of excess air pressure. The floor below each such damper should have a floor drain with a 4 in. curb beyond.

Air intake filter. Behind the intake damper is usually an air filter, after which the air that enters the handling unit is essentially clean. The pressure drop through this semi-barrier must be included when totalling the static air pressure against the operating fan.

Heating coils. During cold weather this mechanism adds heat to the intake/return airflow. Each coil is typically a panel of finned steam pipes that warms the airflow to desired temperatures. Preheater coils may also

---

[†] The primary source for air handling componetry was the *Handbbook of Air Con-*

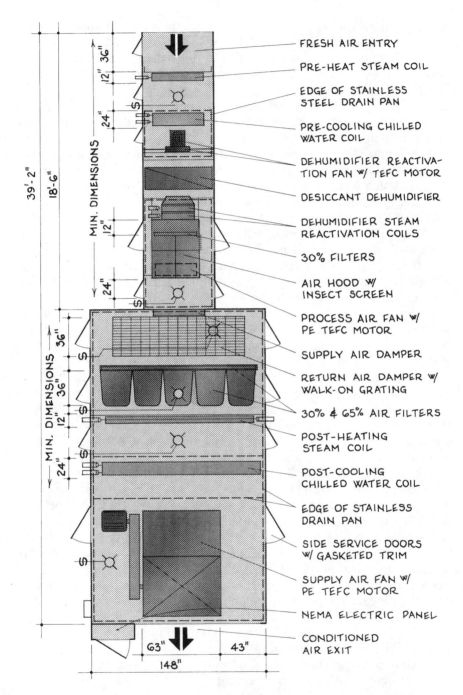

Fig. 3-33. Air handling unit, large HVAC system. †

be installed before and after any return air intake, and, if winter temperatures are well below freezing, just inside the primary damper to eliminate any ice buildup further inside. The number of rows and fin spacing in each panel of coils is usually determined by the manufacturer based on the required temperature rise at each panel. An additional floor drain with curbs all around is installed under each panel, and a drain valve is installed on the lowest pipe in each coil so it can be drained in case the system fails during subfreezing weather.

Cooling coils. During warm weather this mechanism subtracts heat from the intake/return airflow. Each coil is a panel of looped piping through which flows chilled water from the HVAC system's refrigeration unit, or *chiller*. Since HVAC systems usually do more cooling than heating, these units can be quite large. The pipe diameter, pipe spacing, and overall design of each coil is usually done by the manufacturer based on the system's total cooling load and the required temperature drop at each coil. As with heating coils, each coil requires a floor drain below it with curbs all around plus a drain valve on the lowest pipe to protect the coil if the system fails during subfreezing weather. ∠

Sprayers. These are additional panels of piping that humidify or wash the airflow at various stages of conditioning. Each is usually followed by an eliminator that prevents entrained water in the airflow from entering the ducting beyond the air handling unit.

Filters. These are usually porous panels fitted across the airflow's full section area where they strain particles from it. There are several kinds, as described in Sec. 3.D.1. As no one filter removes every pollutant, an air handling unit often has more than one kind which together maintain clean indoor air. Since most filters slow the airflow, a correspondingly stronger fan and motor is needed to maintain required airflow. All filters must have access area for inspection, cleaning and replacement.

Supply fan. This whirling bladed or vaned device drives the conditioned airflow into the main supply duct and ultimately through every outlet grille in the building. Thus this fan must be powerful, which means it is large, heavy, and noisy. The fan and its motor are typically sized by the manufacturer based on their operating loads; then the two machines are mounted on vibration isolators sized according to the fan's blade frequency, the fan's inflow and outflow openings are fitted with flexible connections between the air handling unit and the discharge ducting, and its electric wiring is suspended from acoustic hangers. After this componentry is designed, the weight of the fan, motor, mount, and all accessories is added to the building's structural loads.

Unit casing. This is the shell that encloses the air handling unit componentry. It alone is an important system component, and in large HVAC systems it may be the size of a mobile home. It must be shaped to enhance linear airflow, which minimizes air stratification and irregular flow

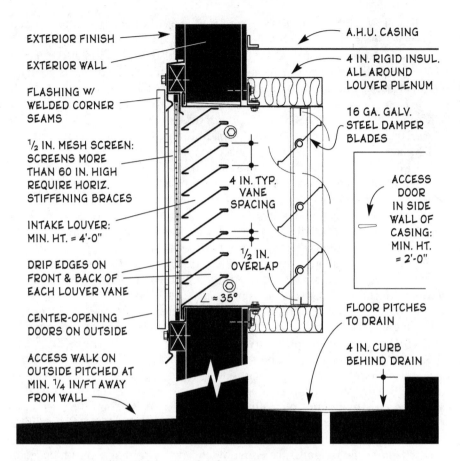

EXTERIOR FINISH

EXTERIOR WALL

FLASHING W/
WELDED CORNER
SEAMS

½ IN. MESH SCREEN:
SCREENS MORE
THAN 60 IN. HIGH
REQUIRE HORIZ.
STIFFENING BRACES

INTAKE LOUVER:
MIN. HT. = 4'-0"

DRIP EDGES ON
FRONT & BACK OF
EACH LOUVER VANE

CENTER-OPENING
DOORS ON OUTSIDE

ACCESS WALK ON
OUTSIDE PITCHED AT
MIN. ¼ IN/FT AWAY
FROM WALL

4 IN. TYP.
VANE
SPACING

½ IN.
OVERLAP

∠ ≈ 35°

A.H.U. CASING

4 IN. RIGID INSUL.
ALL AROUND
LOUVER PLENUM

16 GA. GALV.
STEEL DAMPER
BLADES

ACCESS
DOOR
IN SIDE
WALL OF
CASING:
MIN. HT.
= 2'-0"

FLOOR PITCHES
TO DRAIN

4 IN. CURB
BEHIND DRAIN

Fig. 3-34. Intake louver componentry.

patterns; and its subcomponents should be centrally aligned, which increases operation efficiency and minimizes plenum air pressure losses. The casing is usually sheathed with sheet steel that is thick and strong enough to support itself and withstand the inner pressures and vibrations created by the moving airflow. Every seam and edge of the sheathing's walls and ceilings are screwed to edge supports and diagonal bracing, both of which are usually 1½ × 1½ in. steel angles whose thicknesses are based on the structural loads of each piece. The base of the walls are typically anchored with small expansion bolts placed 12–16 in. o.c. in concrete curbs that are at least 3 in. high × 4 in. wide. Every few linear yards of the casing's length should have a hose inlet to facilitate cleaning of the numerous areas served by the floor drains under each damper, coil, and sprayer; and the airflow inlet and outlet connections at each end must be structurally strong, acoustically absorbent, and vibration-resistant. If the unit is so large that each section is a small room that one can walk in, each such section needs a ceiling light activated by a wall switch outside and a sheet steel access door faced with $\frac{1}{2}$ in. sound-absorbing insulation and rimmed with felt gasketing. As every air handling unit casing is usually lined with access doors or smaller access portals on both sides, each requires an access aisle on each side whose width equals half the casing's width: i.e. if the casing is 8 ft wide, each access aisle must be $\frac{1}{2} \times 8 = 4$ ft wide. This width is necessary so that maintenance personnel can pull the coils and filters out and service them when necessary.

Part of an air handling unit's design involves knowing how its componentry will be installed. It does not promote good contracting politics to have to tear down recently-built walls to maneuver an AHU's modules into place, or —as happened in Kansas City recently— cut a particular unit into 28 pieces so it can be taken up an elevator. Here a little design foresight can lead to lower budgets and happier coffee breaks later on.

The second major component of large HVAC systems is the cooling tower. In large HVAC systems all of the cooling load —heat transmission, lighting, occupants, outside air, fans, pumps, etc.— is usually conveyed via warmed water to one or more of these units where the excess heat is rejected into the atmosphere. There are two basic cooling towers: *absorption* and *chiller*. Absorption units are usually older, about 60 percent larger than electric chiller towers, and require more energy to run. One's primary size determinant, aside from its cooling load, is the local wet-bulb temperature. 78° is representative of most temperate areas in the U.S., but this may be as low as 61° in dry regions such as central Arizona (where a correspondingly smaller tower is required) and as high as 82° in a place like New Orleans (where a larger tower is required). In cooling tower operation the dew-point air temperature is usually detected by a sensor, which modulates the chilled water supply valve plus outdoor and return air dampers. Other cooling tower design parameters are:

Flow: typically 2.5 to 3.0 gpm/ton of chiller.

Range: the design Δt of condenser water cooling is usually from 95° entering temperature to 85° exiting temperature.

Approach: the Δt between the water's exiting temperature and the system's wet-bulb temperature. Trying to reduce the approach below about 7° greatly increases the tower's required size.

Cooling towers should be located well away from any air intake or windows of the parent or adjacent buildings, and plenty of space must exist around each unit to allow smooth airflow into its fans. As the incoming air mixes turgidly with the water as its heat is removed, the water becomes highly oxygenated, which fosters corrosion, scaling, and growth of microorganisms. Thus cooling towers are usually made of noncorrosive materials (stainless steel, fiberglass, reinforced polyester, etc.), which typically cost 20–40

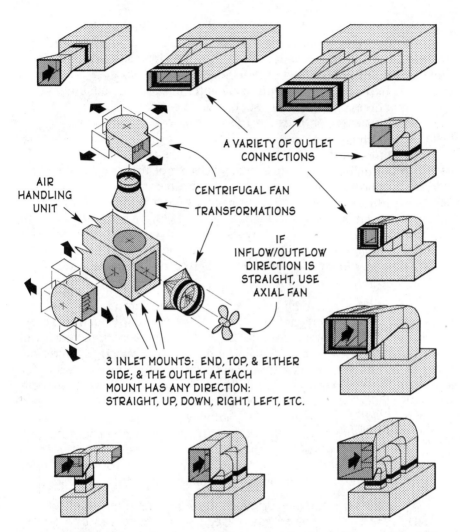

Fig. 3-35. Inlet and outlet fan connections for air handling units.

percent more; but this is almost always recouped after a few years of operating life, and stainless steel is strong and rigid —important properties for a container that may hold tons of water and be exposed to high winds.

Although the thermodynamics of cooling towers are conceptually simple, they require extensive understanding of many details that are typically the province of mechanical engineers. Important specifications are:

Capacity: tons.
Dimensions: footprint, height.
Weight: total weight as well as psf of the unit's footprint.

Volume and prevailing **Direction** of entering/exiting airflow.

Enclosure: how the surrounding architecture will affect tower performance. This also includes any nearby buildings or landmarks that could appreciably affect entering and exiting airflow.

Freeze protection of piping: the interiors of large buildings often require air conditioning in subfreezing weather.

Service access: routes, portals, and emergency exits from inside the tower.

Installation: placing a cooling tower in the center of a roof usually requires a heavier crane than placement of the tower near a side, and the crane's staging area must be located in advance and designed to be structurally adequate; unless the tower is delivered by helicopter, which is sometimes done. Other installation problems are interruption of traffic, hauling permits, time restrictions, police and fire escorts, etc. Although these are primarily the concern of the contractor, designer input can often shrink these problems considerably.

The third major component of large HVAC systems is the ducting that extends from the air handling unit to every interior area in the building. Each may be a low-velocity or high-velocity system. In low-velocity systems, maximum airflow is normally 1,200–2,200 fpm but in certain industrial applications it may exceed 2,500 fpm, while in high-velocity systems the maximum airflow may be as high as 5,000 fpm. The primary criterion for choosing one system or the other is that high duct velocities require considerably smaller ducts, which means lower duct installation costs and possibly lower floor-to-floor heights; but they also require larger fans and motors, which means higher operating costs, more sound generated, and more extensive soundproofing. The choice is essentially low initial costs vs. low operating costs; but the larger the system, the more the balance generally leans toward lower initial costs and a high-volume system.

A problem with all HVAC component piping is that it tends to clog and corrode over time. A clever method of cleaning it is the *brush-and-basket system.* This involves interference-fitting into each pipe a cylindrical nylon or steel brush whose diameter is slightly larger than that of the pipe and which has a polypropylene nose cone on each end to provide a piston seal, installing a catch basket at each end of the pipe, then turning water alternately on and off from each side of the brush which pushes it back and forth inside the pipe. The result: automatic in-line scouring of inner pipe walls that greatly reduces fouling, pitting, leaking, and shutdowns.

HVAC system design includes establishing fresh air requirements, sizing the unit, sizing supply and return ducting, selecting desirable duct layouts and fittings, and designing and locating the outlet grilles. Typical HVAC system operating temperatures are:

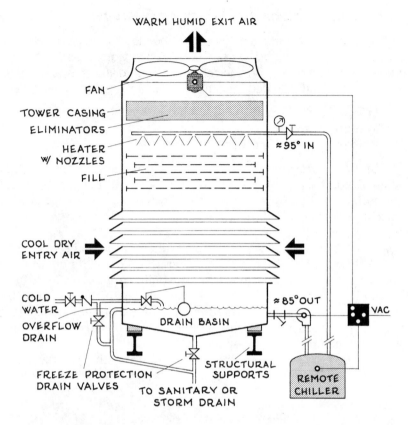

Fig. 3-36. cooling tower componentry.

Heating air .... 120–145° F
Heating indoor temperature .... 68° F at 50% r.h.
Cooling air .... 50–60° F
Cooling indoor temperature .... 77° F at 50% r.h.

The whole system should be designed before the building's structure is designed, because the weight of every component and any size constraints should be known first. However, an Æ designer may be confronted with a Catch-22 dilemma because he or she may need to know the structure size before sizing the AHU and may need to know the AHU size before sizing the structure. Two solutions to this dilemma are estimates by experienced designers and extensive collaboration between specialists.

Every part of a large HVAC system should be accessible for monitoring and maintenance.

3.C.9.a. Low-Velocity Air Ducting Systems [†]

Also known as conventional ducting, low-velocity air ducting in HVAC systems is usually defined by the static airflow pressure differential between one's discharge fan and remote outlet. For these systems this differential is typically divided into three static air pressure classes:

Low pressure: s.a.p. 2.50–3.75 in. wg.
Medium pressure: s.a.p. of 3.75–6.75 in. wg.
High pressure: s.a.p. of 6.75–12.75 in. wg.

Static air pressure is the key to successful system design, because once all the ducts' theoretical airflows are known, the s.a.p. differentials at each outlet can be adjusted so the airflow in occupied spaces between adjacent outlets can be directed as desired. The design method for sizing low-velocity HVAC ducting that follows is known as the *equal friction method*. It is generally superior to another method, the *static-regain method*, for most low-volume HVAC systems. A fact of life about any low-velocity ducting is airflow leakage. It usually varies from 5–30 percent depending mostly on quality of workmanship. Anything less than 10 percent is usually acceptable. This quantity is usually not added to duct design calculations because the leakage is usually conditioned air that enters the building's interior spaces.

The formula in Example 1 below is useful for estimating the size of an HVAC air handling unit at the preliminary stages of a building's design.

> **Example 1: Preliminary Design.** For preliminary design, estimate the size of an air handling unit for a 3 story rectangular building that is 64 × 90 (north facade) ft. Basis is 72° wet-bulb temperature, 55° discharge air, and 15 percent outside air.

Step 1. Estimate the building's required air supply.

3)C)9)a) $Q \approx \eta [12 L_n + 12 L_e + 21 L_s + 24 L_w + (L_n - 24)(L_e - 24)]$

Q = estimated required building supply air, **?** cfm
η = number of floors in building (perimeters aligned), 3 floors
L_n = length of north facade, 90 ft. $L_n \geq 48$ ft.
L_e = length of east facade, 64 ft. $L_e \geq 48$ ft.
L_s = length of south facade, 90 ft. $L_s \geq 48$ ft.
L_w = length of west facade, 64 ft. $L_w \geq 48$ ft.

$$Q \approx 3 [12 \times 90 + 12 \times 64 + 21 \times 90 + 24 \times 64 + (90 - 24)(64 - 24)]$$
$$Q \approx 24,000 \text{ cfm}$$

Step 2. Estimate the air handling unit's cooling capacity.

[†] The primary source for this and the following section was the *Handbook of Air*

$$1,200 \ C \ \approx \ Q \ (3 + 4 \ S_a)$$

C = capacity of air handling unit, **?** tons
Q = required building supply air, from Step 1, 24,000 cfm
S_a = portion of outside air used as supply air. 15% = 0.15

$$1,200 \ C \ \approx \ 24,000 \ (3 + 4 \times 0.15) \quad \ldots C \ \approx \ 72 \text{ tons}$$

Step 3. Estimate the air handling unit's height and width. This is based on the surface area of the unit's chilled-water coil.

$$Q \ \approx \ 400 \ A$$

Q = required building supply air, from Step 1, 24,000 cfm
A = required surface area of a.h. unit's chilled-water coil, **?** sf

$$24,000 \ \approx \ 400 \ A \quad \ldots A \ \approx \ 60 \text{ sf}$$

Unit height: $h \approx 4$ ft if $A \leq 30$ sf, 6 ft if $A \leq 72$ sf, 9 ft if $A \leq 108$ sf, and 12 ft if $A \leq 144$ sf. If $A \geq 144$ sf, install more than one unit. Here $A = 60$ sf ➡ $h \approx 6$ ft. Add minimum 3 ft clearance above unit.
Unit width: $A = h \ w$. If $A = 60$ sf and $h = 6$ ft, then $60 \approx 6 \ w$ ➡ $w \approx 10$ ft. Add 3.5 ft access aisles on each side.
Unit length: Rough out the HVAC system, determine the unit's required components and estimate their depths as shown in Fig. 3-37, then add them to obtain the unit's estimated length.

Example 2. An eight-story corporate office building near Cleveland, OH, has a total heating load of 2,560,000 Btu/hr and a total cooling load of 1,414,000 Btu/hr. If the building has a conventional or low-velocity HVAC system and the most feasible ducting layout for each floor is shown in Fig. 3-37, size the system's ducting.

Design strategy: This system has several initial considerations and con-clusions derived therefrom that are customarily made before any calcula-tions are performed, as follows:

    Consideration 1. The HVAC system's three most important nonduct-ing components (air handling unit, chiller, and cooling tower) should be located as near each other as is practical to minimize initial and operating costs. If any one component is so large that it would be more economical to have two or more smaller units, it is often more practical to divide the whole system into a corresponding number of smaller systems and locate them strategically throughout the building.
    Conclusion 1. An experienced designer of these systems would like-ly conclude that the above-described building is so large that it is hard to

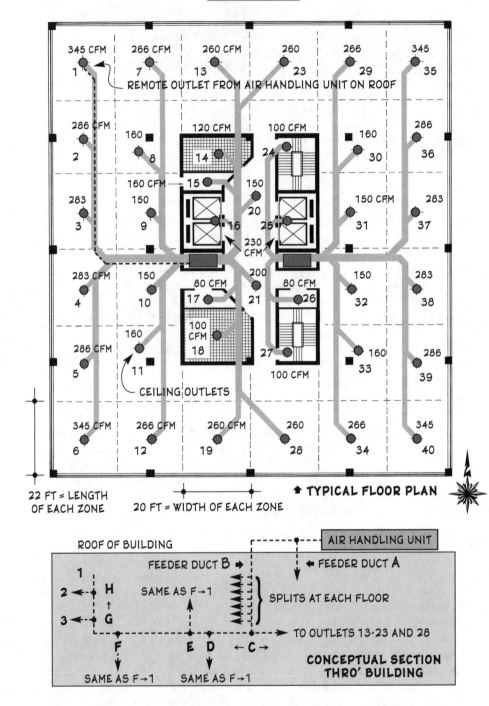

Fig. 3-37. Plan of low-velocity air ducting system.

tell whether a low-velocity or high-velocity HVAC system would be more economical overall. Since low-velocity systems are usually impractical in buildings that are more than 120 ft tall and this eight-story building is certainly lower than that, the designer may well say, "Let's go with a low-V system first and see what happens."

Consideration 2. The system's air handling unit should be located where its sound propagation can be most tolerated: e.g. away from any conference, sleeping, and assembly areas. As sound typically travels horizontally through a building's occupied spaces more easily than vertically, usually the best location for the air handling unit is on the building's top or its bottom. If the unit is on top, sound propagation is even less of a problem, but then the unit's considerable weight must be added to the building's structural loads for the height of the building. But a top location has other advantages: (1) fresh intake air is usually more available, especially in urban environments, (2) foul air is exhausted more easily, and (3) slightly less power is required to drive the airflow through the ducting, because a column of air has a 'head' as surely as does a column of water. For example, if a building is only 270 ft tall, the air at its top is 1 percent thinner than the air at its base (the air at the top of the Empire State Building is 5 percent thinner than the air at its base); so when an AHU discharge fan must drive the ducting airflow upward, it has to 'pump' a tiny bit harder than when it sends the air downward. Although the difference in power consumption is very slight, when it is summed for the length of a building's rated life, its total amount may be less than the building's initial increased structural costs due to the unit's top location.

Conclusion 2. Locate the air handling unit, chiller, and cooling tower on the building's roof. Then the system is a *central station system* or a *unitary equipment installation*. From Table 3-3 the recommended maximum velocity of the ducting's airflow can now be determined: for general offices, main ducts, duct velocity factor = 15; v_{max} = 15 × 100 = 1,500 fpm.

Consideration 3. A large HVAC system is usually packaged and shipped with all major components completely built so that they only need to be assembled after being positioned onsite. But getting them to their proper positions requires logistical planning.

Conclusion 3. The componentry of this large rooftop package will probably be lifted into place by a crane. At this time visualize how a crane of the proper height and tonnage capacity will load, lift, and unload the system's componentry to the building's roof. A ground-level staging area must be provided that is large enough and has adequate bearing strength to support the crane's operation. This is also a good reason to locate the componentry not near the center of the roof but near one side, as then the horizontal vector of the crane's load path will be less.

Consideration 4. Wherever the air handler is located, consider its size and shape. A unit for an HVAC system this size will likely be 30–40 ft long. The unit's dehumidifier or air-handling section usually dictates the unit's overall height and width, which is important in basement installations; but on rooftops the unit's weight is a more serious matter.

Conclusion 4. Align the air handling unit's ₵ with the ₵ of a girder spanning two of the building's columns below: this is the most efficient location for this structural load. Avoid center-of-bay locations as they greatly increase maximum deflections in this roof area.

Consideration 5. Knowing that the system's air handling unit is on the building's roof, that one or two main feeder ducts will extend from the AHU down through the building's full height, and that on each floor a network of branch ducts will fan out from the feeder ducts to every outlet grille on the floor, map out the longest duct run from FAN to remote outlet. This is the duct path that creates the highest resistance to the ducting airflow and for which the ducting should be designed.

Conclusion 5. This longest duct run is sketched in Fig. 3-37. Regarding further design, the equal-section segments of this duct path are denoted as follows: $FAN ➡ B ➡ C ➡ D ➡ E ➡ F ➡ G ➡$ outlet 1.

Now the ducting may be designed as follows:

Step 1. Locate the air duct grilles or outlets in their most feasible positions on each floor. In a general office area this is usually done by arranging them in a grid pattern, then determining the most feasible and efficient route of branch ducting to each outlet on the floor. This has been done in Fig. 3-37. Note that each ceiling outlet in the general office area serves a specific floor area, or outlet bay area, of approximately $22 \times 20 \approx 440$ sf. Also note that each rest room, elevator shaft, stairwell, and electrical closet (E) has an outlet (each may be mounted in the ceiling or high on a wall).

Step 2. Determine the portion of the building's heating load that must be delivered to each outlet on each floor in the building. To the extent that each floor has the same plan, this work may need to be done for only one or two floors. This labor is also made easier by analyzing the building's envelope spreadsheet or whatever tabulations were made to determine the building's total heating and cooling loads.

A crucial consideration: although each duct outlet generally serves an equal floor area or zone, *the heating and cooling loads of each zone may vary widely*, because any floor areas bordered by exterior walls usually require different loads. For example, in Fig. 3-37 compare outlets 1, 2, and 9. Although each outlet serves the same floor area, zone 1 is bordered by 42 LF of exterior wall, zone 2 by 20 LF, and zone 9 by zero LF. Thus the three outlets should have different supply air delivery rates to satisfy their different heating and cooling loads. If the outlets' primary intent is to satisfy ventilation requirements, that's a different story; but two of the most widely-used texts on this subject wrongly describe the sizing of such duct outlets only in proportion to their floor areas served —and this may be why many HVAC systems require so much balancing and tinkering after they are installed and still they cause a lot of Sick Building Syndrome. Since the top story's ceiling and the bottom story's floor are part of the building's envelope, these two stories also have different heating and cooling loads than the interior floors, and thus they too have correspondingly different supply air delivery rates. A third load imbalance occurs because during certain times of year the zones behind one facade may require heating while similarly occupied zones behind another facade may require cooling. For example, on a sunny mid-May morning in Cleveland, the perimeter office areas behind the building's shaded west facade will likely require heating while the areas behind the building's sunlit east facade will likely require cooling. If the HVAC system supplies only warm or cool air, both comfort requirements cannot be satisfied at the same time. Three solutions to this are (1) install adjustable louvers behind the building's facades, (2) design the HVAC system primarily to satisfy cooling loads then install in each zone's branch duct a splitter damper that contains reheat coils, or (3) install an air-water heating/cooling system as described in Sec. 3.C.10. Usually the most common solution employed is (2). Also, for simplicity's sake only, the heating and cooling loads for all eight floors of this building are considered as equal in the calculations that follow.

Step 3. Knowing the building's total heating and cooling loads and v_{max}, and tentatively assuming that the primary feeder duct at the face of the discharge fan is square, size this duct from the two formulas below. The larger size governs.

3)C)9)b) a. Heating load: $s \geq 12.4 \, [^{H}/v_{max} \, (T_h - T_i)]^{0.5}$

b. Cooling load: $s \geq 2.58 \, (^{C}/v_{max})^2$

s = width of one side of duct section if it is square, ? in. This is the section's clear width from one inner face to the opposite inner face. This dimension does not include any lining inside or outside the duct wall.

H = design heating load of HVAC system, 2,560,000 Btu/hr

C = design cooling load of HVAC system, 1,414,000 Btu/hr

v_{max} = maximum recommended velocity of ducting airflow, 1,500 fpm

T_h = temperature of heated air, assume 140° F unless otherwise noted

T_i = optimal temp. of indoor air, ° F. Assume 68° F for heating load.

Heating load: $s = \left[165 \times 2{,}560{,}000/1{,}500 \, (140 - 68) \right]^{0.5} = 62.5$ in.

Cooling load: $s = \left[7.13 \times 1{,}414{,}000/1{,}500 \right]^{0.5} = 83.1$ in.   ... ➕

Step 4. Knowing s and v_{max}, find the ducting's unit s.a.p. loss due to duct friction from

$$10,700,000 \, \Delta P \, s^{0.122} = \kappa_r \, L \, v_{max}^{1.82}$$

ΔP = unit s.a.p. loss due to duct friction, ? in. wg/LF of ducting.
Here solve for ΔP at length of duct = 1.00 ft, then use ΔP as a reference value in subsequent calculations.

κ_r = inner wall surface roughness coefficient of duct.
κ_r for galvanized sheet steel = 0.009.

L = length of duct, ft. From above, unit L = 1.00 ft.
s and v_{max} are as previously defined

$$10,700,000 \times 83.1^{0.122} \, \Delta P = 0.9 \times 1.00 \times 1,500^{1.82}$$
$$\Delta P = 0.000231 \text{ in. wg/LF of duct}$$

Step 5. Make a schedule of the duct lengths that comprise the system's longest ducting run from discharge fan to remote outlet. This is the duct path that was described in Consideration 5 above as *Fan* ➡ *AB* ➡ *C* ➡ *D* ➡ *E* ➡ *F* ➡ *G* ➡ outlet 1. From examination of Figs. 3-37, the duct segment *Fan* ➡ *B* extends from the air handling unit's discharge fan on the building's

DUCT PATH SIZING SCHEDULE

1	2	Duct airflow vols at each split, cfm		5	6	7	8	9	10
	Length of duct segment in col. 1, ft			% airflow in ducts		% section area in each branch duct		Section area of each duct, in²	
DUCT SEGMENT		Airflow into longest run	Airflow away fr longest run	Into long'st run	From long'st run	Long'st run	Other run	Long'st run	Other run
Fan ➡ A	7	70,000	—	100	—	100	—	6,910	—
A ➡ B₈	10 + 2e	42,800	29,190	59.5	40.5	67.0	48.5	4,630	3,350
B₈ ➡ B₇	12	37,460	5,350	87.5	12.5	89.5	19.0	4,410	880
B₇ ➡ B₆	12	32,100	5,350	85.7	14.3	88.5	21.0	3,900	930
B₆ ➡ B₅	12	26,760	5,350	83.3	16.7	87.0	23.5	3,400	920
B₅ ➡ B₄	12	21,404	5,350	80.0	20.0	84.5	27.0	2,880	920
B₄ ➡ B₃	12	16,050	5,350	75.0	25.0	80.5	32.5	2,320	940
B₃ ➡ B₂	12	10,700	5,350	66.7	33.3	73.5	41.0	1,710	950
B₂ ➡ C	12	5,350	5,350	50.0	50.0	58.0	58.0	990	990
C ➡ D	15 + 2e	2,980	2,370	55.7	44.3	63.5	52.5	630	520
D ➡ E	4	2,410	571	80.8	19.2	85.5	26.0	540	170
E ➡ F	18	1,830	580	75.9	24.1	81.0	31.5	440	170
F ➡ G	16 + 2e	914	914	50.0	50.0	58.0	58.0	260	260
G ➡ H	20	631	283	69.0	31.0	75.5	37.5	200	100
H ➡ 1	24 + 1e	345	286	54.7	44.3	62.5	52.5	125	—

Fig. 3-38. Duct path sizing schedule.

roof to junction A where it branches into two feeder ducts A and B, of which the segment to pt. B is the longer; then duct segment $B \rightarrow C$ extends down from the roof to the first floor where it splits into branch ducts at each floor level and into a final branch at pt. C on the first floor; then duct seg-ment $C \rightarrow D$ extends horizontally above the first floor's finished ceiling where it branches at junction D, then duct segments $D \rightarrow E$, $E \rightarrow F$, $F \rightarrow G$, and $G \rightarrow 1$ extend and branch similarly to remote outlet 1.

In column 1 of the schedule that comprises the longest duct run of Fig. 3-38, enter the name of each duct segment in the run.

In column 2, assume that the lengths of each duct segment are obtained from other parts of the Plans, then enter their lengths in this col-umn. The letter e denotes the number of elbows in each duct segment.

Regarding columns 3 and 4 of the schedule: first determine the re-quired cooling load to be delivered to each outlet on each floor (here assume the outlet lengths on all eight floors are identical). Remember the loads are not all the same because their floor areas are the same. Next, find the airflow required to meet each cooling load from the formula

> **a.** $\mathbf{C}_o = 20.2\ Q$ wherein

$\mathbf{C}_o$ = cooling load of each outlet, Btu/hr. If the system's heating load governed the sizing of the primary duct's side s in Step 3, then each outlet's required airflow is found from

> **b.** $\mathbf{H}_o = 0.87\ Q\ (T_h - T_i)$

Q = volume of airflow required to satisfy each outlet's cooling load, cfm

Then, knowing the required cooling or heating airflow for each outlet, sum the airflows that branch from each duct split on the floor. To obtain these amounts, work upstream from the outermost ducts toward the central feed-er ducts B and A, then up through each floor to the discharge fan. Finally, enter the two airflow rates that stem from each split in the ducting in columns 3 and 4 of the schedule. For example, if the design airflow rates for outlets 1, 2, and 3 are 345, 286, and 183 cfm, in columns 3 and 4 the entries for duct segment $H \rightarrow 1$ are 345 and 286 cfm, the entries for duct segment $G \rightarrow H$ are 345 + 286 = 631 cfm and 286 cfm, and the entries for duct segment $F \rightarrow G$ are 631 + 283 = 914 cfm and (because duct segment $F \rightarrow 4 \rightarrow 5 \rightarrow 6$ = duct segment $F \rightarrow G \rightarrow H \rightarrow 1$) also 914 cfm.

After filling in columns 3 and 4, to fill in columns 5 and 6 simply make a ratio of the numbers in columns 3 and 4 to determine the percent airflows at each duct split that flow into the longer run (col. 5) and the shorter run (col. 6). For example, in line $H \rightarrow 1$, at duct split H, 345 cfm from col. 3 flows into the longest duct while 286 cfm from col. 4 flows into the other duct. Thus in col. 5 enter the percent that flows into duct $H \rightarrow 1 = 100(345/_{345 + 286})$ 54.7 percent, then in col. 6 enter the remainder (45.3 percent).

Step 6. Determine the percentage section area of each branch duct compared to its stem duct area at each duct split. These are the equivalent section areas of each branch duct if it is square that will maintain equal duct friction in each duct after each split. The equivalent areas for each pair of branch ducts will be entered in columns 7 and 8 of the schedule, then later these effective square areas will be used to redimension each duct segment if it is round or rectangular. This time, start at the beginning of the ducting (e.g. the section area of the primary duct at the face of the discharge fan) and work downstream toward the outlets. The percent areas of the two branching ducts is found from the bar graph below as follows: if the airflow in the longer branch duct is 59.5 percent, enter the bar graph's lowest scale at its left, move to the right to 59.5, then read the number just above: it is 67 percent of the stem duct's area. The shorter branch duct's section area is found by subtracting 59.5 from 100 = 40.5 percent, then entering the same graph scale and proceeding to 40.5 and reading the number just above: it is 49 percent of the stem duct's area. Note that the branch duct area is 67 + 49 = 116 percent of the stem duct area; the area increase compensates for the friction loss incurred at the duct split and ensures that the branch airflows have approximately the same unit pressure drop per LF of run as does the stem airflow. The bar graph has been used to obtain the entries in columns 7 and 8 of the schedule.

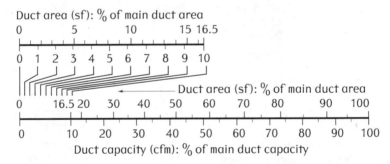

Fig. 3-39. Duct sizing bar graph.

Step 7. Find each duct's section area. Again start at the fan face and work downstream toward the outlets as follows. From Step 3, if the primary duct's side = 83.1 in, its effective section area = 83.1^2 = 6,910 in^2; so enter this number in Line *FAN* ➡ *A*, col. 9 of the schedule. Then in the next line down, which is line A ➡ $B_{8th\,fl}$, if col. 7 says the area of feeder duct B is 67.0% of the stem duct's area, this duct's effective section area = 0.67 × 6,910 = 4,630 in^2, and similarly the area of feeder duct A is 0.49 × 6,910 = 3,360 in^2. Thus on line A ➡ $B_{8th\,fl}$ in col. 8 enter 4,630 in^2 and in col. 10 enter 3,360 in^2. In like manner find the effective section areas of each branch duct and enter their values in columns 9 and 10 of the schedule.

Step 8. Determine the most feasible sections for each length of ducting. Until now every duct section has been considered as square; but in some places, such as where little headroom exists between a suspended ceiling and the structure above where a horizontal duct must be installed, rectangular sections are the rule and not the exception; and in other places, especially where small ducts run, they are often more efficient and less expensive if round; and when the ducting is really small, 3 or 4 in. diameter flexible conduit may be the best choice. Here this sizing will be done only for a few of the duct segments in the schedule.

Referring to the first line of column 9 of the schedule: the section area of the primary duct that runs from the discharge fan to the A–B split at pt. A is 6,910 in^2. Depending on available space, nearby structural obstructions, etc., this and all other duct sections are sized as follows:

Step 8a. **If section is square:** $A_\square = s^2$

Wherein s = length of one side. Solve for s, then:
If $s < 48$ in, select the next largest multiple of 2 in.
If $s \geq 48$ in, select the next largest multiple of 4 in.

Step 8b. **If section is round:** $A_\bigcirc = 0.933\ \delta^2$

Wherein δ = section's diameter. Solve for δ, then:
If $\delta < 48$ in, select the next largest multiple of 2 in.
If $\delta \geq 48$ in, select the next largest multiple of 4 in.

Step 8c. **If the section is rectangular:** $A_\square = a\,b$

Wherein a and b are the rectangle's sides, $a > b$,
and $b \geq 6$ in. Select a reasonable value for a,
then find b from $b = A_\square \div a$, then
If a or $b < 48$ in, select the next largest multiple of 2 in.
If a or $b \geq 48$ in, select the next largest multiple of 4 in.

An important consideration for any rectangular section is its *aspect ratio*: the ratio of the rectangle's long side to its short side, or a/b. If the section's aspect ratio ≥ 2.0, its section area must be increased according to

Step 8d. $a_{new}\,b_{old} = A_{old}\,\{1 + 0.072\,[(A_{old}/b^2) - 1\} = A_{new}$
Knowing b and A_{old}, solve for a or A_{new}.

For example, say the chase through which vertical duct $B \rightarrow B_8 \rightarrow B_7 \rightarrow B_6 \rightarrow B_5 \rightarrow B_4 \rightarrow B_3 \rightarrow B_2 \rightarrow C$ extends down from the roof to the first floor can be only 44 in. wide. Then this duct's width could be 44 in. for its whole 84 ft length while its long side becomes progressively shorter at each floor, as sketched in Fig. 3-40. Then at the duct's top just above the 8th floor it would be sized as follows:

$A_{B8} = 4,630$ in^2 $= a\,b$ wherein shorter side $b = 44$ in.
$\therefore\ a = 4,630/44 = 105.2$ in.

Check aspect ratio ≤ 2.0: 105.2/44 = 2.39 ➡ **NG**
∴ $a \times 44 = 4{,}630 \{1 + 0.072 [(^{4{,}630}/_{44^2}) - 1\}$
$a = 115.7$ in.

As $a < 48$ in, select next largest multiple of 2 in:
44 ➡ 44 in.
As $b \geq 48$ in, select next largest multiple of 4 in:
115.7 ➡ 116 in.
Size of duct at top of run: 44 × 116 in.

At the duct's bottom just above the first floor, it is sized as follows:

$A_C = 990$ in^2 $= a\,b$ where longer side $a = 44$ in.
∴ $b = 990/44 = 22.5$ in.
Check aspect ratio ≤ 2.0: 44/22.5 = 1.96 ➡ **OK**

As $a < 48$ in, select next largest multiple of 2 in:
44 ➡ 44 in.
As $b < 48$ in, select next largest multiple of 2 in:
22.5 ➡ 24 in.
Size of duct at bottom of run: 44 × 24 in.

Thus duct $B ➡ B_8 ➡ B_7 ➡ B_6 ➡ B_5 ➡ B_4 ➡ B_3 ➡ B_2 ➡ C$, or duct $B–C$ for short, should be similarly sized at each junction where its stem divides into two branches at each floor, as sketched at right. Due to this page's limitations of space, the vertical length of this duct between each split is significantly reduced.

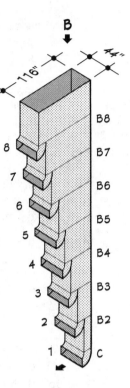

**Fig. 3-40.
Duct section 1.**

Now let's examine the bottom of duct B-C where it splits into the two horizontal ducts $C ➡ D ➡ E ➡ F$ and $I ➡ J ➡ K$, etc. Here duct segment $C–F$ is the larger, and from the schedule of *Step 5* its section area at junction $C = 630$ in^2; then its area becomes progressively smaller toward its far end, as sketched below. Say the available vertical space between the suspend-

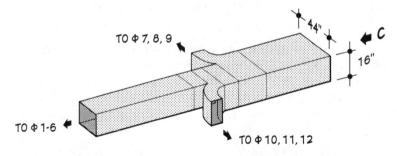

Fig. 3-41. Duct section 2.

ed ceiling below this duct and the building's structure above is only 17 in. Then b = 16 in. (the next lowest multiple of 2 in.) and a is found from

$$A_C = 630 \text{ in}^2 = a \quad \text{wherein shorter side } b = 16 \text{ in.}$$
$$\therefore a = 630/16 = 39.4 \text{ in.}$$
Check aspect ratio ≤ 2.0:   39.4/16 = 2.46 ➤ **NG**
$$\therefore a \times 16 = 630 \{1 + 0.072 [(^{630}/_{16}{}^2) - 1\}$$
$$a = 43.5 \text{ in.}$$
As a < 48 in, select next largest multiple of 2 in: 43.5 ➤ 44 in.
Size of duct $C \blacktriangleright D \blacktriangleright E \blacktriangleright F$ at start of run: 16 × 44 in.

Every segment of this duct may now be designed with a uniform depth of 16 in. from junction C to junction F. For example, at junction F,

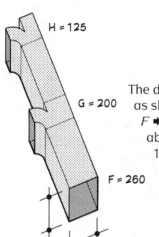

H = 125

G = 200

F = 260

16"

$$A_{FG} = 260 \text{ in}^2 = a\,b = 16\,b$$
$$\therefore b = 260/16 = 16.3 \text{ in.}$$
Here a width of 16 in. is **OK**
Size of duct at junction FG: 16 × 16 in.

The duct segment $F \blacktriangleright G \blacktriangleright H \blacktriangleright$ can now be designed as sketched at left. The section dimensions of duct $F \blacktriangleright G$ is 16 × 16 in; then, similarly as computed above, the section dimensions of duct $G \blacktriangleright H$ are 16 × 14 in, and the dimensions at junction H are 16 × 8 in. However, the remaining duct segment $H \blacktriangleright 1$ may be more efficiently designed if its section is round. Therefore, check

$$A_\bigcirc = 0.933\,\delta^2$$
$$125 = 0.933\,\delta^2$$
$$\delta = 11.6 \blacktriangleright 12 \text{ in.}$$

Fig. 3-42.
Duct section 3

As 12 in. is less than the maximum allowable headroom, duct segment $H \blacktriangleright 1$ can have a 12 in. diameter as sketched below.

If a final duct segment is less than 12 ft long and its airflow is 25–175 cfm, it may be sized as a 3 or 4 in. diameter flexible conduit. Then, knowing the duct's airflow, find its effective pressure drop from the graph in fig. 3-44.

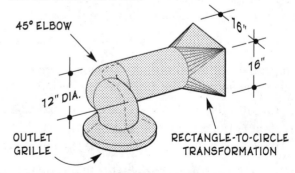

45° ELBOW

16"

16"

12" DIA.

OUTLET GRILLE

RECTANGLE-TO-CIRCLE TRANSFORMATION

Fig. 3-43. Duct section 4.

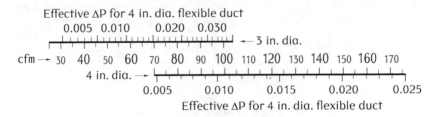

Fig. 3-44. Bar graph for sizing flexible conduits.

Note: If the interior of any duct is fitted with acoustic liners, its section dimensions as computed above must be the minimum clear width between the inner faces of the inserted liner.

The ducting system is now essentially designed. Subsequent steps deal with refinements.

Step 9. Find the effective length of each duct segment. Here this will be done only with the system's longest duct run as outlined in the schedule of Step 5. Usually the effective length of every tee, elbow, contraction, transformation, obstruction, etc. is found either by extensive tables or formulae; then all the fittings' effective lengths are added to each duct segment's actual length to obtain its effective length L_e. But in most cases, a much simpler and reasonably accurate method of finding L_e is to borrow a page from plumbing design: include a safety factor for a normal number of fittings. Then its effective length may be found from

$$L_e \approx 1.2\,L$$

L_e = equivalent length of ducting: this includes the length of the duct plus a safety factor for a normal number of fittings, ? ft
L = actual length of ducting, ft. From col. 2 of schedule of Step 5, L = 198 ft.
v_i = initial duct airflow velocity at face of discharge fan, fpm. From initial conclusion 2, v_i = 0.9.

$$L_e = 1.2 \times 198 = 238 \text{ ft}$$

Step 10. Determine the duct's unit s.a.p. drop due to duct friction depending on the shape of the duct's section as described below:

a. Circular duct: $\Delta P_d = 0.00137\,(1 - 0.000034\ E)\ \kappa_r\,L_e\,Q^{1.82}/\delta^{4.86}$
b. Square duct: $\Delta P_d = 0.00076\,(1 - 0.000034\ E)\ \kappa_r\,L_e\,Q^{1.82}/s^{4.86}$
c. Rectang. duct: $\Delta P_d = 0.00076\,(1 - 0.000034\ E)\ \kappa_r\,L_e\,Q^{1.82}/(a\,b)^{2.43}$

ΔP_d = unit s.a.p. drop in duct due to airflow friction loss, in. wg/LF

E = elevation of building site above sea level, ft. Any estimate of E within-
in a few hundred ft is **OK**. From atlas, E for Cleveland = 600 ft.
L_e = equivalent length of ducting, from Step 9, 238 ft
Q_i = initial airflow rate in duct at face of discharge fan, cfm.
From col. 3 of schedule of Step 5, Q_i = 70,000 cfm.
κ_r, δ, s, a, and b are as previously defined.

Tentatively assuming the duct is square:

$$\Delta P_d = 0.00076\,(1 - 0.000034 \times 600)\,0.9 \times 238 \times 70{,}000^{1.82}/84^{4.86}$$
$$\Delta P_i = 0.047 \text{ in. wg/LF}$$

Step 11. Find the duct's initial static air pressure loss due to its initial velocity from

$$\Delta P_i = 0.0013\,(1.0 - 0.000034\ E)\,(Q_i/A_i)^2$$

ΔP_i = initial s.a.p. loss due to operation of discharge fan, in. wg/LF
A_i = section area of duct at face of discharge fan, in².
A_i of square duct whose side = 84 in. is 84 × 84 = 7,056 in².
All other values are as previously defined.

$$\Delta P_i = (1.0 - 0.000034 \times 600)\,(70{,}000/27.8 \times 7{,}056)^2 = 0.125 \text{ in. wg}$$

Step 12. For each outlet in the ducting find the static pressure regain at the outlet. Static pressure regain could be called the 'gush effect', because as air flows through most of the ducting it has a 'plug' of air in front of it that slows it down slightly; but as the air nears an outlet, the plug dissipates, which creates a 'loss of normal pressure loss' —i.e. a pressure regain. Although static pressure regain is usually low in low-velocity ducting, it can be significant in high-velocity systems.

Before each duct's static pressure regain can be found, the airflow's velocity at the beginning and end of the duct must be known. Here this calculation will be performed only for the ducting's remote outlet 1.

    a. **Inlet velocity:** $v_i = 144\ Q_i/A_i$
    b. **Outlet velocity:** $v_o = 144\ Q_o/A_o$

Q_i = initial volume of airflow rate in duct at inlet, cfm.
From col. 3 of schedule of Step 5, Q_i = 70,000 cfm.
A_i = section area of duct at inlet, in². From Step 10, A_i = 7,056 in².
Q_o = final volume of airflow in duct at outlet, cfm.
From col. 3 of schedule of Step 5, Q_o = 345 cfm.
A_o = section area of duct at outlet, in². From Step 8, final duct segment
$H \rightarrow 1$ has 12 in. dia. ∴ $A_o = 0.785\ \delta^2 = 0.785 \times 12^2 = 113$ in².

    a. **Initial velocity:** $v_i = 144 \times 70{,}000/7{,}056 = 1{,}430$ fpm
    b. **Final velocity:** $v_\emptyset = 144 \times 345/113 = 439$ fpm

Then, knowing the outlet airflow's initial velocity v_i and final velocity $v_ø$, find the outlet's static pressure regain from formula **c** or **d** below:

  c. If $v_i \geq v_o$ **(the usual situation):**

  $$\Delta P_r = 0.75 \ (1 - 0.000034 \ E) \ [(v_i/4,005)^2 - (v_o/4,005)^2] \quad \dots \ \bm{+}$$

  d. If $v_i < v_o$:

  $$\Delta P_r = 1.10 \ (1 - 0.000034 \ E) \ [(v_i/4,005)^2 - (v_o/4,005)^2]$$

ΔP_r = static pressure regain at outlet, in. wg
        All other values are as previously defined.

$$\Delta P_r = 0.75 \ (1 - 0.000034 \times 600) \ [(1,430/4,005)^2 - (345/4,005)^2]$$
$$\Delta P_r = 0.088 \text{ in. wg}$$

Step 13. Find the total static air pressure loss at each outlet. Here this calculation is performed only for remote outlet 1.

$$\Delta P_t = L_e \Delta P_d + \Delta P_i - \Delta P_r$$

ΔP_t = total static air pressure loss at outlet, **?** in. wg/LF
L_e = equivalent length of duct, from Step 9, 238 ft
ΔP_d = unit static air pressure drop in ducting due to airflow friction loss, from Step 10, 0.047 in. wg/LF
ΔP_i = initial static air pressure loss due to operating pressure of discharge fan, from Step 11, 0.125 in. wg/LF
ΔP_r = static air pressure regain at outlet, from Step 12, 0.088 in. wg/LF
        All other values have been previously defined.

$$\Delta P_t = 238 \times 0.047 + 0.125 - 0.088 = 11.2 \text{ in. wg.}$$
This is a fairly large total pressure loss;
it suggests there may be a better way to design this system

Step 14. Design the grille for each outlet. This is done by (1) determining the outlet's optimal throw by analyzing the space its airflow is entering, (2) estimating the outlet grille's throw from the formulas below, (3) comparing the optimal throw with the actual throw, and (4) making any adjustments if necessary. Here this is done only for remote outlet 1.

(1) Analyze the space the outlet airflow is entering. From the duct layout on each floor as sketched in Fig. 3-37, assume a ceiling outlet, then draw a section through the space as sketched in Fig. 3-45. Assume the spatial dimensions that are shown. This analysis indicates that the outlet's average throw is about 8.5 ft.

(2) Knowing the outlet's airflow velocity, estimate the outlet's average throw from the formulas below:

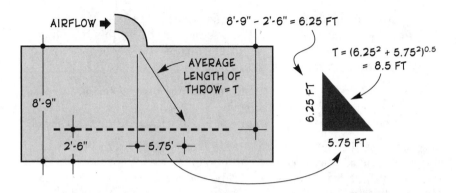

Fig. 3-45. Section through space served by outlet 1.

a. Straight throw (outlet vanes arranged as |||||||||||):
$$T = 0.0015 \, v^{1.5}$$

b. Spread throw (outlet vanes arranged as \\\\\\||/////):
$$T = 0.0028 \, v^{1.5}$$

T = throw of vaned outlet, **?** ft
v = outlet airflow velocity, fpm

In this space, a spread throw is recommended because the levels of the office desktops (a good average working height for this occupancy) are wide compared to their distance from the outlet. As $v = Q$ [outlet airflow volume, fpm] ÷ A [section area of outlet, sf], and as Q can be obtained from col. 3 in schedule of Step 5 and A was found in Step 8, the outlet's airflow velocity can be found from

c. $Q = v A$
       $345 = v \times 0.785 \times 12^2/144$ ... $v = 440$ fpm
For spread throw, $T = 0.0028 \times 440^{1.5} = 13.8$ ft

(3) Compare the outlet's optimal throw with its actual throw:

$$T_{optimal} \overset{?}{=} T_{actual}$$
8.5 not ≈ 13.8 ➡ NG

(4) Make any adjustments if necessary. If T_{actual} is too long, consider one or more of the four remedies below. If T_{actual} is too short, consider the opposite of the remedies below.

Remedy 1. Use a wider throw. This could be done here by installing a grille with ultra-spread vanes.
Remedy 2. Move the grille farther from the task plane.
Remedy 3. Aim the airflow obliquely across the task plane, or

install a grille with ultra-spread vanes.

Remedy **4.** Increase the outlet's section area. Try this by using $Q = \mathcal{V}/A$ to decrease the outlet's airflow velocity by increasing the outlet's section area as below:

If $T_{optimal} \approx 8.5$ ft, then for an optimal spread throw,
$$8.5 \approx 0.0028\,v^{1.5} \quad \dots v = 210 \text{ fpm}$$
Then $345 = 210/A \quad \dots A = 345/210 = 1.64$ sf or 237 in^2

Thus increase the outlet's section area from 125 in^2 to 237 in^2 to create the grille's optimal throw. However, this section area is not the grille's total area but its *net free area*, which is the section area of the open spaces between whatever vanes or lattices the grille's face may have. To find the grille's full area, use the formula below:

d. $$A_{tot}\,\kappa_{nfa} = A_{nfa}$$

A_{tot} = required total face area of grille, ? in^2

κ_{nfa} = net free area factor of grille. Say the selected grille's open spaces occupy 60% of its face area; then $\kappa_{nfa} = 0.60$. This data is often listed in manufacturers' catalogs. If not, the grille's face area may have to be measured manually; such labor would be worth the few minutes it would take if many such grilles were to be installed throughout the building.

A_{nfa} = net free area of grille, in^2. This equals outlet's originally req. section area, or 237 in^2.

$$A_{tot} \times 0.60 = 237$$
$$A_{tot} = 395 \text{ in}^2$$

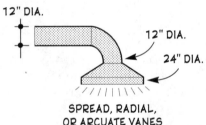

12" DIA.

12" DIA.

24" DIA.

SPREAD, RADIAL,
OR ARCUATE VANES

Tentatively assuming that this grille is circular, the outlet duct behind it can be now be resized as follows:

$$A_o = 395 = 0.785\,\delta^2$$
$$\delta = 22.4 \text{ in}^2 \quad \dots \text{ use 24 in. dia.}$$

Fig. 3-46. Section through duct outlet and grille.

Step 15. Design the return grilles for each outlet. Here only the return grille for the floor area served by outlet 1 will be designed. First, find the return air grille's net free area from

a. $A_{nfa-r} = 0.8\,A_{nfa-s} = 0.8 \times 237 \quad \dots A_{nfa-r} = 190$ in^2

Then find the return grille's required total face area from below. Again say the selected grille's open spaces occupy 60 percent of its face area.

b. $A_{tot}\,\kappa_{nfa} = A_{nfa-r}$
$$A_{tot} \times 0.60 = 190 \quad \dots A_{tot} = 317 \text{ in}^2$$

If the grille is circular:

$$A_o = 317 = 0.785\ \delta^2 \quad \ldots \delta = 21.7\ in^2 \Rightarrow use\ 22\ in.\ dia.$$

The return air grill should be located where it will promote maximum air circulation throughout the space between it and the supply air grilles. Sometimes it is wise design to have two return air grilles instead of one.

Example 2. After the HVAC ducting was designed throughout the building of the previous example, it was found that the static air pressure drop to outlet 15 in the men's room is 11.9 in. wg, while the s.a.p. drop to outlet 19 in a public hallway just outside the men's room is 11.7 in. wg; thus the higher air pressure in the men's room induces foul air to flow from that room into the hall. If the diameter of duct outlet 15 is 10 in. and that of duct outlet 19 is 8 in, how can the foul airflow be reversed so that air flows from the hall into the men's room?

Solution: If a duct outlet's diameter is decreased its airflow velocity increases, which increases the s.a.p. drop at the outlet. Thus the foul airflow may be reversed either by decreasing the diameter of duct outlet 15 or by increasing the diameter of outlet 19. Usually it is better to do a little of both. Thus try decreasing the diameter of duct outlet 15 from 10 to 8 in. and increasing the diameter of duct outlet from 8 to 12 in. The minimum s.a.p. differential required to move air between two spaces is usually 0.03 in. wg, average is 0.05 in. wg, and maximum is 0.15 in. wg. Recomputing the pressure drop to this outlet according to Steps 12–14 above:

Revised s.a.p. drop to outlet 15:   11.9 ➧ 11.7 in. wg at 8 in. dia.
Revised s.a.p. drop to outlet 19:   11.7 ➧ 11.8 in. wg at 12 in. dia.

Example 3. What is the weight of a primary duct assembly that is constructed of galvanized sheet steel and dimensioned as sketched in Fig. 3-47 below?

Step 1. Examine the duct assembly's drawings, then measure and tabulate the area of every surface.

From said measuring, the assembly's top, bottom, side, and end surfaces together are found to have a total area of 172,000 in^2, or about 2,000 sf.

Step 2. Determine the thickness of the duct metal's surfaces from Table 3-4. This table indicates what a duct's minimum gauge thickness should be based on the minimum dimension of its largest surface. Since the assem-

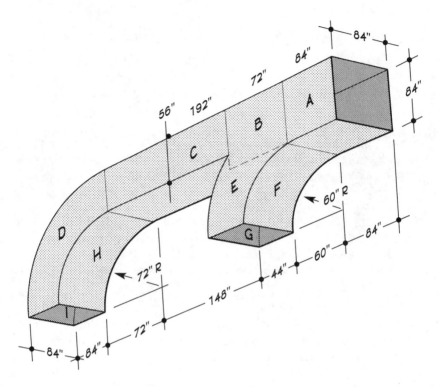

Fig. 3-47. Primary duct assembly.

TABLE 3-4: SHEET METAL WEIGHTS & THICKNESSES

TYPE OF METAL	UNIT WEIGHT, PSF, AT EACH GAUGE THICKNESS						
	26	24	22	20	18	16	14
Hot rolled steel	0.750	1.000	1.250	1.500	2.000	2.500	3.125
Galvanized steel	0.906	1.156	1.406	1.656	2.156	2.656	3.281
Stainless steel	0.790	1.050	1.310	1.580	2.100	2.630	3.280
Aluminum	0.015	0.288	0.355	0.456	0.575	0.724	0.914
Copper	0.737	0.932	1.178	1.484	1.869	2.355	2.972

TYPE OF METAL	THICKNESS, IN, AT EACH GAUGE THICKNESS						
	26	24	22	20	18	16	14
Hot rolled steel	0.018	0.024	0.030	0.036	0.048	0.060	0.075
Galvanized steel	0.022	0.028	0.034	0.040	0.052	0.064	0.080
Stainless steel	0.019	0.025	0.031	0.038	0.050	0.063	0.078
Aluminum	0.015	0.020	0.025	0.032	0.040	0.051	0.064
Copper	0.016	0.020	0.025	0.032	0.040	0.051	0.064

bly's various panels are fairly similar in area, it is best to make all the panels the same thickness. Do not consider curved surfaces unless they are at least twice as large as the largest flat surface.

From examination of Fig. 3-47, the surface with the largest least dimension is panel *A*, whose least dimension is 84 in. If the ducting is galvanized sheet steel, from Table 3-4 the minimum gauge thickness for sheet steel whose least dimension is 84 in. is 20 gauge.

Step 3. Find the unit weight of the metal used in making the total duct assembly. From Table 3-4, the unit weight of 20 ga. galvanized steel = 1.656 psf. Thus the total weight of the ducting's surfaces is

$$2,000 \text{ sf} \times 1.656 \text{ psf} = 3,312 \approx 3,300 \text{ lb}$$

Step 4. Add to the above amount the weight of the other materials the ducting is made of: shells, vanes, fire dampers, seam strips, girth reinforcing, corner reinforcing, diagonal bracing, stay bracing, support bracing, access door framing, acoustic mounts, probably two buckets of screws and bolts, probably insulation on the outside, and possibly acoustic lining on the inside. In lieu of more articulate data, assume that all these materials weigh 2.2 × the sheet metal's estimated weight. Thus the assembly's total estimated weight is

$$3,300 \ (1 + 2.2) = 10,600 \text{ lb}$$

3.C.9.b. High-Velocity Air Ducting Systems [†]

Also known as VAV ducting or VAV systems, this ducting is smaller and lighter than low-velocity ducting, which may lead to lower buildings and less structure. Balanced against this is the need for more powerful fans and motors, which means higher operating costs. But slightly lower buildings may also mean slightly less elevator operation, slightly less maintenance, and a number of other minuscule advantages relating to economies of scale. So the decision is usually based on depthful circumspection + adroit conceptualizing + extensive experience.

High-velocity ducting can handle airflows as high as 6,000 fpm, and duct diameters may range from 3–60 in. Thus these systems can handle volumes of airflow exceeding 100,000 cfm. The ducting is almost always round, as circular surfaces are more inherently rigid than square or rectangular ones, and the ducts are typically made of a spirally braced tubing aptly named SpiriPipe. Elbows, tees, and other fittings are carefully selected in terms of efficiency more than expense; they are usually located uniformly apart from each other to promote smooth airflow; and all seams are sealed,

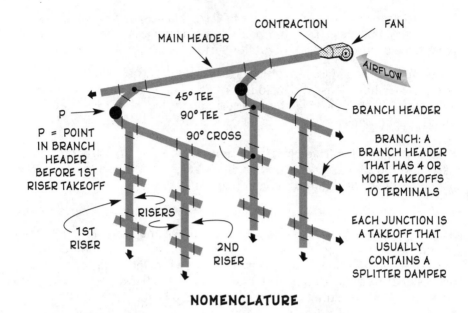

NOMENCLATURE

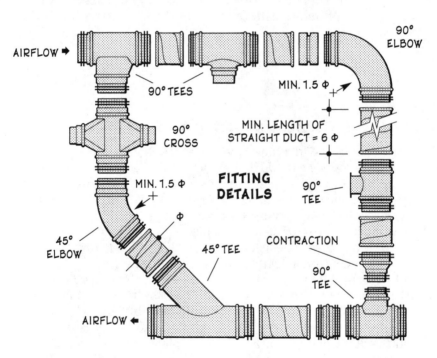

Fig. 3-48. High-velocity air ducting details.

with the overall goal being to avoid excessive pressure drops and minimize noise. Thus the air is truly pumped through the network of ducting, where-as, comparatively speaking, the air in low-velocity ducting is merely encouraged. However, return air in high-velocity systems is usually via more conventional low-velocity ducting.

An important trait of VAV systems is that they usually only cool, because the heating of each interior space is often produced by its occu-pants, machinery, and lighting and the space's perimeter surfaces often have no temperature differentials on the other side through which the accumulating heat can escape. However, in the large interior volumes typ-ically served by these systems, the spaces next to exterior walls often need heating during cold weather while more interior spaces still require cool-ing. Thus this system has VAV or control boxes, which not only can add heat to a duct's airflow via a small reheat coil mounted inside the box, but it can add fresh air to a space that has become stuffy (this typically happens when an occupied space requires little or no heating or cooling, which causes its supply duct spitter damper to close) by again activating the box's reheat coil, which notifies the box's controls that the space needs cooling which opens the damper to introduce the required ventilation air-flow. Thus a VAV box provides final control of the airflow to the spaces it serves (thus it may often cure a few design errors that might have occurred upstream). For these reasons, buildings with high-velocity air ducting may have as many as 1 VAV box per 500 sf of floor area. These boxes usually require little design, aside from determining one's maximum reheat capa-bility, specifying its digital controls and tethered thermostat, and making sure it has enough room in an already-cluttered suspended ceiling plenum.

Example 1: Unit Capacity. A hospital near St. Louis, MO, has a design heating load of 1,190,000 Btu/hr and a cooling load of 640,000 Btu/hr. If the building has a variable air volume heating system, what are its design heating and cooling capacities?

---

3)C)9)b)1)a) **Heating load:** $H_{cap} \geq$ **H** $(1.15 + 0.000034\ E)$

      b) **Cooling load:** $C_{cap} \geq$ **C** $(1.15 + 0.000034\ E)$

H_{cap} = design heating capacity of selected system, ? Btu/hr
C_{cap} = design cooling capacity of selected system, ? Btu/hr
H = design heating load of architecture, 1,190,000 Btu/hr
E = elevation of site above sea level, ft. If $E \leq 1,000$ ft, use $E = 0$
C = design cooling load of architecture, 640,000 Btu/hr

$$H_{cap} \geq 1,190,000\ (1.15 + 0) \geq 1,370,000 \text{ Btu/hr}$$
$$C_{cap} \geq 640,000\ (1.15 + 0) \geq 736,000 \text{ Btu/hr}$$

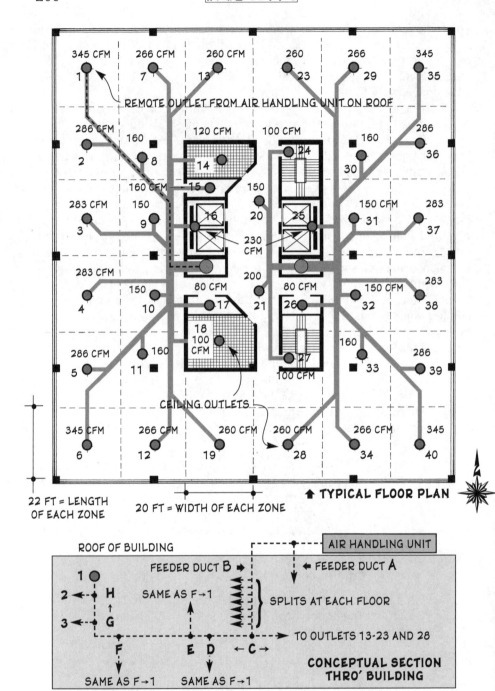

Fig. 3-49. High-velocity air ducting layout.

Example 2: Duct Sizing. The developers of the 8-story office building near Cleveland, Ohio, that was designed in Example 1 of the previous section have decided that, due to excess space and added weight requirements, the building's HVAC system should have smaller and lighter high-velocity ducting. Using the same site and building data presented in the previous section, size the system?

Initial considerations. The following logistical guidelines are important for designing efficient high-velocity HVAC ducting:

▸ Network symmetry greatly improves balanced airflow distribution throughout the ducting. It also reduces design and layout time, construction costs, and onsite balancing of system componentry.

▸ The ducting's initial velocity at the air handling unit's discharge fan face usually depends on whether the system is a 12-hr or a 24-hr operation. 12-hr operations are primarily daytime occupancies (e.g. offices), while 24-hr operations are typically hospitals, high-rise apartments, and other occupancies with overnight sleeping areas. Thus since higher airflow velocities generally create more noise, 24-hr operations usually have slower airflows.

▸ The design friction loss from the discharge fan to a point in each branch header that is immediately before the first riser takeoff should be as nearly equal as possible.

▸ The longest run should have the highest airflow velocities.

▸ The length-to-diameter ratio of each ducting run should be approximately the same throughout the system.

▸ A good design velocity for all terminal runs is 2,000 fpm.

Step 1. As the ducting layout for the low-velocity system described in the previous section is not symmetrical (the airflow volumes in feeder ducts *A* and *B* were 61 percent and 39 percent), this layout is replaced by the more symmetrical ducting plan drawn in Fig. 3-49. Note that branch headers *A* and *B* have almost equal loads, as do the risers that branch from pt. *C* and the two pair of branches that branch from points *D* and *E*.

Step 2. Knowing the building's design heating and cooling loads and the nature of its occupancy, determine the ducting airflow's initial or maximum velocity, which occurs at the face of the air handling unit's discharge fan. The recommended initial velocity for 12-hr operations is 3,000–5,000 fpm and for 24-hr operations is 2,000–3,000 fpm, but maximum velocities may be as high as 6,000 rpm. For this generic 12-hr occupancy, tentatively select a maximum velocity of 5,000, then choose the larger duct diameter as computed by the two equations below:

3)C)9)b)2) **a. Heating load:** $\delta = \left[\dfrac{196\ H}{\mathcal{V}_{max}\ (T_h - T_i)}\right]^{0.5}$

b. Cooling load: $\delta = \left[\dfrac{8.50\ C}{\mathcal{V}_{max}}\right]^{0.5}$

δ = diameter of round duct at face of discharge fan, ? in.
H = design heating load of building, 2,560,000 Btu/hr
C = design cooling load of building, 1,414,000 Btu/hr
$\mathcal{V}_{max}$ = maximum velocity of airflow in ducting, 5,000 fpm
T_h = temperature of heating load airflow, $\approx 140°$ F.
T_i = ambient indoor temperature of occupancy during winter heating season, usually 68° F.

$\quad$ **a. Heating load:** $\delta = \left[\dfrac{196 \times 2,560,000}{5,000\ (140 - 68)}\right]^{0.5} = 37$ in.

$\quad$ **b. Cooling load:** $\delta = \left[\dfrac{8.50 \times 1,414,000}{5,000}\right]^{0.5} = 49$ in. $\quad$ ... $\oplus$

Round off duct diameter to next highest integer up to 12 in,
$\quad$ then next highest multiple of 2 up to 28 in,
$\quad$ then next highest multiple of 4 up to 40 in,
$\quad$ and next highest multiple of 5 up to 60 in.
$\quad$ Here $\delta = 49$ in. $\rightarrow$ 50 in.

Step 3. Knowing δ and $\mathcal{V}_{max}$, find the duct's equivalent friction loss per LF from

$$9,577,000\ \Delta P\ \delta^{1.22} = \kappa_r\ L\ \mathcal{V}_{max}^{1.82}$$

ΔP = unit duct friction loss due to airflow, in. wg/LF
δ = diameter of round duct at face of discharge fan, 50 in.
κ_r = roughness coeff. of inner surface of ducting.
L = length of ducting, ft. Here solve equation for ΔP at $L = 1.00$ ft, then use ΔP as a reference value in subsequent calculations.
$\mathcal{V}_{max}$ = maximum velocity of airflow in ducting, 5,000 fpm

$$9,577,000 \times \Delta P \times 50^{1.22} = 0.9 \times 1.0 \times 5,000^{1.82}$$
$$\Delta P = 0.0043 \text{ in. wg/LF}$$

Step 4. Make a schedule of the duct lengths for the HVAC system's longest ducting from its discharge fan to its remote outlet. Here, since the ducting network is highly symmetrical, all of the peripheral outlets have nearly the same run, but because the corner outlets have the greatest cooling loads one should be the remote outlet.

$\quad$ The remainder of this system design will be brief, as it is similar to that performed for low-velocity ducting and because high-velocity ducting usually requires fewer calculations due to its usually greater symmetry. For the sake of brevity, the following analysis utilizes airflow quantities from the duct layout shown in Fig. 3-49.

Step 4 a. Duct diameter of remote outlet 1:
$$Q_1 = v A$$
$$345 \text{ cfm} = 2{,}000 \text{ fpm} \times A \quad \dots A = 0.173 \text{ sf} = 24.9 \text{ in}^2$$
$$\text{If duct is round, } A = 0.785 \, \delta^2 = 24.9 \text{ in}^2$$
$$\delta = 5.6 \text{ in.} \; \rightarrow \text{use 6 in. dia. duct}$$

Step 4 b. Duct diameter of segment $G \rightarrow H$: From the bar graph in Sec. 3.C.i.1, Example 2, Step 6, on page 186, when a duct divides in half (symmetry), each branch duct's section area = 58 percent of the stem duct's section area. Thus at each symmetrical split a good shorthand method is to multiply each outflow area by 58/50 = 1.16.
$$1.16 \, Q_{GH} = v A$$
$$Q_{GH} = 345 + 286 = 630 \text{ cfm, and } A = 0.785 \, \delta^2$$
$$1.16 \times 630 = 2{,}000 \text{ fpm} \times 0.785 \, \delta^2$$
$$\dots \delta = 0.68 \text{ sf} = 8.19 \text{ in}^2$$

Here select a slightly *smaller* diameter, as this slightly increases the incoming velocity. If this is done upstream to the discharge fan, the airflow velocity will ideally increase gradually until it is about 5,000 fpm.

$$\therefore 8.19 \text{ in.} \; \rightarrow \text{use 7 in. dia. duct}$$

Step 4 c. Recompute v and use its value in the next upstream calculation:
$$Q = 0.785 \, v \, \delta^2$$
$$631 = 0.785 \times v \times (7 \text{ in}/12 \text{ in/LF})^2 \quad \dots v = 2{,}360 \text{ fpm}$$

Duct diameter of segment $D \rightarrow G$:
$$1.16 \, Q_{DG} = v A$$
$$Q = 345 + 286 + 160 + 283 + 150 = 1{,}220 \text{ cfm, and } A = 0.785 \, \delta^2$$
$$1.16 \times 1{,}220 = 2{,}360 \times 0.785 \, \delta^2$$
$$\delta = 0.87 \text{ ft} = 10.5 \text{ in.} \; \rightarrow \text{use 9 in. dia. duct}$$
$$\text{Recompute } v \; \rightarrow Q = 0.785 \, v \, \delta^2$$
$$1{,}220 = 0.785 \times v \times (9 \text{ in}/12 \text{ in/LF})^2 \quad \dots v = 2{,}760 \text{ fpm}$$

Duct diameter of segment $C \rightarrow D$:
$$1.16 \, Q = v A$$
$$Q = 1224 + 230 + 160 + 150 + 120 + 266 + 260 = 2{,}400 \text{ cfm}$$
$$1.16 \times 2{,}400 = 2{,}760 \times 0.785 \, \delta^2$$
$$\delta = 1.13 \text{ ft} = 13.6 \text{ in.} \; \rightarrow \text{use 12 in. dia. duct}$$
$$\text{Recompute } v \; \rightarrow Q = 0.785 \, v \, \delta^2$$
$$2{,}400 = 0.785 \times v \times (12 \text{ in}/12 \text{ in/LF})^2 \quad \dots v = 3{,}060 \text{ fpm}$$

Duct diameter of segment $B \rightarrow C$:

$$1.16 \, Q = v \, A$$
$$Q \approx 2{,}400 \times 2 = 4{,}800 \text{ cfm}$$
$$1.16 \times 4{,}800 = 3{,}060 \times 0.785 \, \delta^2$$
$$\delta = 1.52 \text{ ft} = 18.3 \text{ in.} \rightarrow \text{use 16 in. dia. duct}$$
$$\text{Recompute } v \rightarrow Q = 0.785 \, v \, \delta^2$$
$$4{,}800 = 0.785 \times v \times (16 \text{ in}/12 \text{ in/LF})^2 \quad \dots \, v = 3{,}440 \text{ fpm}$$

And so on, up through the riser to the primary duct, then to the face of the discharge fan. The final calculation should resemble the following:

Duct diameter of primary duct *FAN* ➔ *Z*:
$$Q = v \, A$$
(Here the 1.16 is removed for the initial duct of the run).
$Q \approx 70{,}000$ cfm, and v should be at or near 5,000 fpm.
Solve for δ and compare with δ_1 found in Step 2 above.
If they are the same or nearly so, use δ_1 and system design is **OK**.

If the two diameters are not nearly the same, a serious problem exists if δ is less than δ_1; as then the initial duct airflow velocity is substantially greater than the system's maximum design velocity. In this case go back to duct segment *G* ➔ *H* and increase the duct diameters slightly upstream until $\delta \approx \delta_1$. If δ is considerably larger than δ_1, three choices are available: (1) use the larger diameter δ and all the downstream duct diameters designed thereto, (2) go back to duct segment *G* ➔ *H* and *decrease* the duct diameters slightly upstream until $\delta \approx \delta_1$, (3) do an interpolative combination of (1) and (2).

Example 3: Return Duct Size. What is the minimum return duct size for a 30 × 66 in. supply duct?

3)C)9)b)3) $A_r \geq 0.80 \, a \, b$

A_r = minimum section area of return duct, ? in^2
a = wider dimension of duct, 66 in.
b = narrower dimension of duct, 30 in.

$$A_r \geq 0.80 \times 66 \times 30 \geq 1{,}590 \text{ in}^2$$
$$\text{Use 24} \times \text{66 in, 30} \times \text{52 in, etc.}$$

Note: In an enclosed centralized air system, return airflow should ≈ 80 percent of supply airflow in every space. Thus the section area of each return outlet, branch duct, and main duct should $\approx 0.8 \times$ supply section area. For sizing ducts with special ventilation requirements, see Sec. 3.D.

3.C.10. Air-Water Heating/Cooling

In these complex systems, a large air handling unit conveys fresh air at high speeds through extensive VAV (variable-air-volume) ducting to all spaces while heated and chilled water flows to the same areas; then in each space an air duct and two water pipes converge in small fan-coil units that portion the required conditioning to the occupants. Thus the system's ducting is designed similarly as are high-velocity air ducting systems. As for this system's other components, some are of too great a variety to possibly be described fully here, while others are described elsewhere in this lengthy chapter. Thus this section describes their basic operation as it pertains to this system, then concludes with an example of the conceptual decisions that are typically involved in selecting these systems.

Primary air apparatus. Also known as an *air handling unit*, this is a long rectangular tube containing much subcomponentry that was described in Sec. 3.C.9.a. Outdoor air is pulled through its intake louver by a large primary fan at a face velocity of 500–800 fpm, then the air passes through inlet guide vanes or dampers that control its volume, preheaters that prevent freezing air from entering the dehumidifier in winter, high-efficiency filters that remove dirt particles and entrained dust, sprays that add humidity in winter, dehumidifiers that remove water vapor in summer, reheaters that warm the air to about 85° F, and finally the primary fan, which drives the air through the supply ducting. The primary air apparatus is sized according to the building's fresh air requirements, usually in cfm.

Chiller. This is a large refrigerator that makes cold water for the fan-coil units in the occupied spaces and the dehumidifier coils in the primary air apparatus. The evaporator usually cools the water to 35–48° F, and the heat buildup in the condenser is piped out as hot water to the cooling tower. More than one chiller is often installed as an application of the "MMRD" approach described in Sec. 3.C. on page 139. Two units each sized at 60 percent of the total load is a minimum, 3 × 40 percent is better, and 4 × 30 percent is better still. Before freon was banned, unit choices were usually limited to either a monolithic R-11 centrifugal or R-22 reciprocating model; but now an Æ designer can choose between a number of refrigerants, compressors, drivers, fuel streams, and other subcomponentry to custom-design the most appropriate package for a given application. The variety of viable choices is mind-boggling: absorption, electric, variable-speed electric, gas-fired, gasoline-driven, steam turbine, centrifugal, reciprocal, rotary, single-stage absorbers, dual-effect absorbers, series-flow or parallel-flow piping, hybrid systems, multiple-fuel operation, asymmetric partitioning, chiller/genset packages, chiller/ice-storage systems, etc. Some chillers require combustion air, flues, and acoustic isolation, and almost every one requires thick insulation between its outer surfaces and the surrounding air; this includes the piping, which should always be as simple as

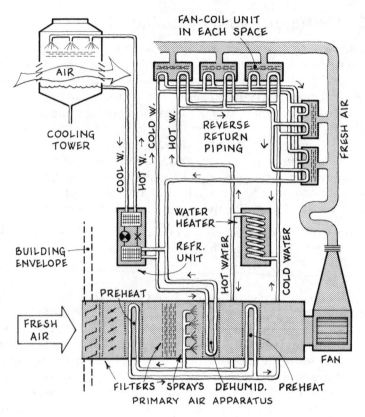

Fig. 3-50. Air-water heating & cooling system.

possible. A chiller's refrigeration load is typically determined by the sum of the maximum individual room peak loads, not the system's design peak load.

Cooling Tower. This dissipates the heat carried by the water from the chiller condenser. The warm water discharges through nozzles at the tower's top, falls as spray, is cooled by air flowing through the tower's sides, collects in a basin at the bottom, then flows back to the chiller. The tower should be placed where it is exposed to prevailing winds, should rise at least 100 ft from chimneys or other sources of heat or contaminated air, its airflow should enter and leave rapidly, and it should have a hose bibb. In subfreezing weather its operation can create ice buildup in its basin, nozzles, and louvers; thus these parts may require heating. The cooling tower is sized by the chiller's condenser temperature and the wet-bulb design temperature. Higher condenser temperatures mean smaller towers.

Water Heater. This heats the water pumped to the fan-coil units and often supplies the heat for the preheater and reheater in the primary air apparatus. The heater's exiting water temperature usually equals the fan-

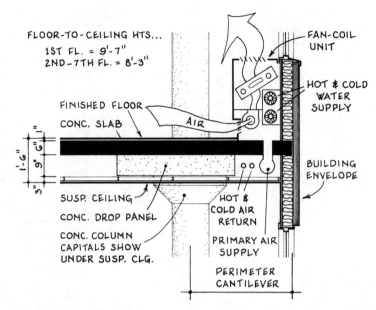

Fig. 3-51. Section through air-water HVAC system fan-coil unit.

coil units' highest required temperature plus 15–20°. The water heater is sized to handle the design heating load × 1.2 plus any water heat needed to raise the temperature of the primary air.

Fan-coil Units. These box-like units are located in each occupied space, usually under windows. In each, supply air mixed with room air passes through a small radiator containing either hot or cold water depending on the room's air temperature. Unit size depends on the total heating or cooling load of the floorspace served.

Ducting. Due to the system's high air velocities (usually 2,500 to 3,000 fpm in the risers and 1,500–2,000 fpm in the headers), rigid spiral tubing is used instead of sheet metal ducting and all fitting seams are welded to eliminate leakage. VAV ducts also require precise air-volume control with *control boxes* or VAV boxes, three of which are shown in this chapter's frontispiece figure. Each contains an air guide vane and throttle controls. Also, duct air friction losses usually ≈ 0.25 in. wg. per 100 LF. Air ducting is sized according to the required volume of primary air and the air's velocity.

Piping. This plumbing carries hot and cold water from the heaters and refrigerating units to the fan-coil units in each space. Each plumbing circuit requires a pump and its layout should be reverse return. Allowances for thermal expansion must be made in all piping, and the total system requires an open expansion tank to permit air venting and water expansion caused by changes in temperature. All supply water piping should be wrapped in minimum 1 in. insulation.

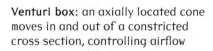
Venturi box: an axially located cone moves in and out of a constricted cross section, controlling airflow

Damper box: a square or rectangular damper in a cube-like box controls airflow.

Pitot tube: a U-shaped tubular probe experiences a pressure differential, then an interpretive sensor operates the damper.

DDC controls: a thermostat ⓣ or air-flow sensor Ⓢ activates direct digital controls that activate an air damper, fan, and valves to produce the re-quired air at the desired temperature.

S = AIRFLOW SENSOR	
D = DAMPER	H = HEATING COILS
F = FAN	RV = REHEAT VALVE
MV = MANUAL VALVE	BV = BALANCE VALVE
YS = Y-STRAINER	FC = FLEXIBLE DUCT CONNECTION
AB = AIR BLEED	DDC = DIRECT DIGITAL CONTROLS

Fig. 3-52. VAV duct damper control strategies.

In an air-water HVAC system, the cooling tower is usually on the roof, the fan-coil units and related pipes and ducts are on the perimeter of each floor, and the other components are in the basement. The cooling tower typically requires about 1 sf of roof area per 400 sf of gross building area, is 15–40 ft high, and when full weighs 125–200 psf. The system's perimeter components and enclosing construction usually require 2–3 percent of the gross floor area, the interior bundling of piping and ducting requires about 2 percent more, and electrical and plumbing shafts need another 1 percent. The basement is usually 3–5 percent of the gross building area and 13–18 ft tall. Static air pressure and CO_2 sensors are typically installed throughout the ducting system and interior spaces, as optimal system operation is often created by careful tuning of these detectors throughout the building.

A developer plans to build an office building on a downtown lot in a medium-sized city. The Local Building Code describes setbacks and 72 ft envelope height limits for the property as shown in Fig. 3-52. The developer needs at least 8½ ft clear floor-to-ceiling heights on each floor; but as conventional steel frame construction requires about 12 ft from floor to floor with ceiling-to-floor heights being 30-36 in., the developer can fit only six floors of this construction into the 72 ft envelope height limit. However, she wonders if there may be a way to squeeze seven floors into the envelope, with each level measuring slightly more than 10 ft from floor to floor and 18–20 in. from finished ceiling to finished floor above. What kind of structural/HVAC system would work well in this situation?

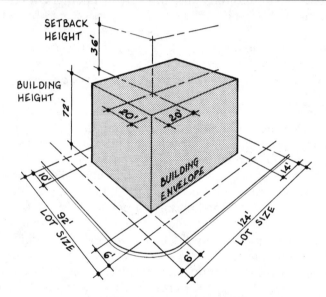

Fig. 3-53. Building envelope perspective.

One solution: If the floor system is reinforced concrete flat plate with 6 in. floor slabs, and 8 in. drop panels, the building's finished ceiling-to-finished floor heights would measure about 18 in. and thus its floor-to-ceiling heights would be about 8'-9". Adding a short cantilever around the perimeter of each floor slab would create enough clearance beneath the floor for primary ducts and pipes of an air-water HVAC system and create enough space above the floor for water supply and return pipes, supply air headers, and fan-coil housings. A section through this construction appears in Fig. 3-53.

3.C.11. Heat Pumps [†]

In a heat pump, heat is treated as a compressive quantity that exists independently of ambient temperature gradients. Then, after a certain quantity is compressed, it can be moved from a lower to a higher temperature more efficiently than by producing the same amount by exothermic reaction. As usual, the heat must exist in a medium of some kind, which in the case of heat pumps is a refrigerant that can be compressed and expanded. Thus a heat pump's operation is basically a four-step cycle in which a refrigerant at room temperature (1) is supercooled by expansion to temperatures that may be well below 0° F, (2) absorbs heat via a network of coils (the absorber) that are immersed in a medium whose temperature is usually 35–45° F, (3) is compressed, which raises its temperature to well above 100°, then (4) radiates its heat through a network of coils (the radiator) that are immersed in a medium that is warmed until the refrigerant is again at room temperature. The process can be reversed, and its cycling is governed by a thermostat that activates the compressor when heat needs to be removed from the absorber or added to the radiator.

The nature of the absorber (also known as *cold end*) and radiator (also known as *hot end*) usually defines the heat pump's operation. The enveloping medium for either may be air, water, nonwater liquid, or even a solid. For example, in an *air-to-air heat pump* the absorber coils are mounted where currents of chilly air pass through them and its radiator coils are placed where currents of air requiring warming pass through them; in a *water-to-air heat pump* the absorber coils are immersed in a pond, stream, swimming pool, or well; and in a *ground-coupled heat pump* the absorber coils are buried about 6 ft below grade. Since the temperature around the absorber should remain above 32°, water-source and ground-source installations make heat pumps more feasible in northerly climates. The absorber coils may also be mounted in a chimney, graywater holding tank, or solar collector; then if the radiator coils are immersed in circulating water, an occupancy's rejected flue heat, warm waste water, or solar energy can be used to produce hot water. By mounting the absorber in an insulated container and locating the radiator just outside, the heat pump cycle becomes the familiar refrigerator, which may be as small as an under-counter unit in an efficiency apartment or as large as a multistory cold-storage facility in a meat-packing plant. A heat pump's cycle may be reversed simply by reversing the refrigerant flow with a rotating valve, which allows air conditioners to double as heaters in cold weather. Add to these possibilities all kinds of heat-rejecting and heat-hungry industrial processes, and heat pump operation is one of the most useful energy-saving mechanisms in architecture.

In small heat pump systems, the absorber and radiator may be housed in a box-like unit that straddles the building envelope. In larger

[†] A primary source for this section was *Modern Refrigeration and Air Condition-*

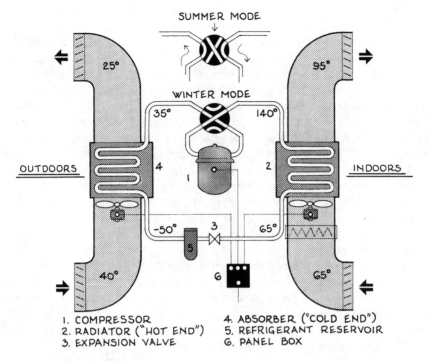

SUMMER MODE

WINTER MODE

25° 95°

35° 140°

OUTDOORS 4 2 INDOORS

-50° 3 65°

40° 6 65°

1. COMPRESSOR
2. RADIATOR ("HOT END")
3. EXPANSION VALVE

4. ABSORBER ("COLD END")
5. REFRIGERANT RESERVOIR
6. PANEL BOX

Fig. 3-54. Heat pump componentry.

systems the absorber is often placed outdoors, preferably behind foliage or other visual obscuration, and the radiator is located indoors, usually where its ducting will be short. Above about 1,800 sf of floor area per unit, duct expense and less flexible climate control become limiting factors. Capabilities range from about 15,000–50,000 Btu/hr for heating and cooling loads. Sophisticated controls involving multiple thermostats, motorized dampers, and variable-speed blowers and compressors also allow zoned heating and cooling with one unit.

The initial cost of a heat pump installation may be considerably reduced if its absorber coils are laid below grade while a related part of the building is being constructed. If the building's plumbing system drains into a leaching field, its drain tile trenches can be dug deeper and an absorber coil network of ¾ in. polyethylene piping laid 2 ft beneath the drain tile. If a swimming pool is near the building, a similar network of absorber coils can be laid in the bottom of the pool's excavation before its concrete floor is poured. Conceivably the absorber coils could be laid beside the footing drains extending around a building's perimeter before the footing area is backfilled. If a pond at least 8 ft deep is on the property, grids of ¾ in. polyethylene piping whose lengths are spaced 2 ft apart may be lowered into the water (here part of the water's edge must be excavated so the emerging coils are in the ground below local frost level). On sites that have a drilled well with a large waterflow rate, the whole wellhead volume can be used as an absorber coil; and even if the well's waterflow rate is inadequate a second well can often be drilled at the same time at less unit expense. Another approach was taken by the Southeast Elementary School near Des Moines, Iowa, where no less than 120 vertical wells were drilled 175 ft deep in wet clay soil within a 60 × 750 ft outdoor area for the sole purpose of housing the absorber coils for a 130-ton heat pump system. Then 10 miles of polyethylene piping were laid from the immersed coils to 42 water-source heat pumps inside the school. The system consumes 54 percent less energy than a similarly sized hydronic system at a sister school. In each of the above situations, the absorber coil should be sturdily made and must be pressure-tested before being buried. [†]

Heat pump design for climate control systems involves selecting the capacity and number of units, locating the components, sizing the piping or ducting, locating the outlets, and selecting the registers. The absorber and radiator coils must be accessible for periodic cleaning, and refrigerant runs between the four basic processes should be short and insulated when possible. Also, beware of contaminants in any cold media that could degrade the absorber coils, such as salty air in coastal installations, corrosive gases in industrial environments, and chemically impure water.

A vital part of any heat pump or refrigeration system is the refrigerant that carries the Btus between the absorber and radiator. Such a fluid must have a high coefficient of heat transfer and should be noncorrosive, nontoxic (especially when the cold end is buried below grade), nonflammable (especially if the warm end is located indoors), and remain stable for long periods of operation. Since the banning of ozone-depleting Freon, numerous refrigerants have been used that are more environmentally acceptable than methane- and glycol-based alternatives. An old standby is ammonia. Sometimes referred to as R-717, this natural compound is energy-efficient, occupies little volume, is easily available, and its technology is simple, proven, and well-known worldwide. Another advantage of ammonia is that it is "self-alarming" —a polite way of saying its potent smelling-salts odor offers quick notification of any leak in the system. But any occupancy containing ammonia must be isolated from other areas, surrounded by firewall construction, well-vented, and directly accessible to the outdoors; and all piping containing ammonia must be sensor-wired for leaks and connected to alarms and automatic shutdown devices. On the plus side, sensor-wiring allows ammonia operations to be coordinated with microprocessor controls and programmed for remote offsite monitoring via modem and phone linkage. Added advantages and drawbacks of ammonia refrigerant are: described below.

land, IL, 1975); Chapter 23, esp. Fig. 23-65, p. 827.   [†] Robert Beverly, "A Ground-

➕ Ammonia costs less than $1 per lb compared to about $3 for R22 and $18 for R-502. Its light weight allows compressors to run more economically, which means less horsepower, smaller compressors, and less dead load. It is highly soluble in water and ecologically safe: it creates no side effects due to global warming or depletion of the ozone layer. Oil separates easily from it, which may simplify any recovery and recycling efforts.

➖ Ammonia cannot be exposed to copper in any part of a refrigeration system; thus other metals (usually steel) are used, which transfer heat less well and cost more. Ammonia's expansion/evaporation machinery also generates much heat; thus it must be stronger and heavier and requires more cooling.

A special heat transfer problem occurs with walk-in freezers. If one's floor is placed on the ground, the subfreezing air above can cause moisture in the subsoil directly below to freeze and expand —which has been known to raise a freezer locker floor a full foot above its intended level. For large floor areas thick insulation will not eliminate the problem, because a uniform thermal gradient will soon establish itself through the floor. The solution? Heavily insulate the floor, install a plenum between the insulation and the ground, then ventilate the plenum with near-room-temperature air. Another possibility: install a radiant heating concrete floor slab under the insulation.

Example 1: Unit Capacity. A 2,600 ft² residence near Nashville, TN, is to be heated and cooled by heat pumps. If the dwelling's design heating and cooling loads are 57,000 Btu/hr and 73,000 Btu/hr, what is the system's design heating/cooling capacity?

---

3)C)1)1)a)   a. Heating load: H_{cap} ≥ 1.15 **H**
              b. Cooling load: C_{cap} ≥ 1.15 **C**

H_{cap} = heating capacity of selected unit, **?** Btu/hr
C_{cap} = cooling capacity of selected unit, **?** Btu/hr
H   = design heating load of interior spaces, 57,000 Btu/hr
C   = design cooling load of interior spaces, 73,000 Btu/hr

   Heating: H_{cap} ≥ 1.15 × 57,000 ≥ 66,000 Btu/hr
   Cooling: C_{cap} ≥ 1.15 × 73,000 ≥ 84,000 Btu/hr   ... ➕

Note: Registers for heat pump ducting are the same as those for other air heating or cooling systems.

breaking Approach", *Engineered Systems* magazine (Business News Publishing

> **Example 2: Number of Units.** How many heat pumps should the house in the above example have?

<u>3</u><u>C</u><u>1</u><u>1</u><u>b</u>) $|P_{cap}/50{,}000| + 1 \geq \eta \geq |P_{cap}/15{,}000| + 1$

P_{cap} = design heating/cooling capacity of heat pump, Btu/hr.
   Use larger number from previous example ➜ $M_{cap} \geq 84{,}000$ Btu/hr.
η = number of units required, **?** units. Optimal size ≈ 35,000 Btu/hr.

$$|84{,}000/50{,}000| + 1 \geq \eta \geq |84{,}000/15{,}000| + 1$$
   2 ≥ η ≥ 6 ➜ optimal range of units is 2 to 6   ... try 2 or 3 units
   2 units: 84,000/2 ≥ 42,000 Btu/hr
   3 units: 84,000/3 ≥ 28,000 Btu/hr

The house may have two heat pumps ≥ 42,000 Btu/hr cooling capacity each or three units ≥ 28,000 Btu/hr cooling capacity each. With two units the system cost is less, but the ducts are longer and their enclosing construction cost is greater. The deciding factor is usually the length of ducts.

> **Example 3: Duct size.** If the design heating capacity of a residential heat pump is 42,000 Btu/hr and the unit heats the supply air to 95° F, the air flows through one main duct, and the indoor temperature is 68° F, size the supply and exhaust ducts.

Solution: If both heating and cooling capacities are given, size the units according to the higher load capacity.

<u>3</u><u>C</u><u>1</u><u>1</u><u>c</u>)   a. **Heating load, Btu/hr: $\mathbf{H}_{btu}$** ≤ $0.65 \, \kappa_d \, A \, (T_h - T_i)$ ... ➕
          b. **Cooling load, Btu/hr: $\mathbf{C}_{btu}$** ≤ $15 \, \kappa_d \, A$
          c. **Cooling load, tons:** $800 \, \mathbf{C}_{ton}$ ≤ $\kappa_d \, A$

$\mathbf{H}_{btu}$ = heating capacity of selected unit, 42,000 Btu/hr
$\mathbf{C}_{btu}$ = cooling capacity of selected unit, Btu/hr. Not applicable.
$\mathbf{C}_{ton}$ = cooling capacity of selected unit, tons. Not applicable.
κ_d = duct velocity factor. From Table 3-3, κ_d for main duct
       in residence = 8.
A = minimum section area of duct (not including insulation), **?** in^2
T_h = temperature of heated air, 95° F
T_i = temperature of indoor air, 68° F

$$42{,}000 \leq 0.65 \, A \times 8 \, (95 - 68)$$
$$A \leq 299 \; in^2 \;➜\; 12 \times 25 \; in., \; 15 \times 20 \; in., \; 20 \; in. \; dia., \; etc.$$

Note: If the duct ≥ 40 ft long or its width-to-depth ratio ≥ 2.5, its size

Co., Troy, MI); Mar 1999, pp. 86–89.

should be increased according to its air friction losses and aspect ratio as described in Sec. 3.C.i.1., Example 2, on page 187. Also, since heat pump supply and return air volumes are usually equal, all supply and exhaust duct sizes as well as register sizes are similar. The formula for duct sizing depends on if the system is designed primarily for heating or cooling and whether the cooling load is in tons or Btu/hr. 1 ton = 12,000 Btu/hr.

3.C.12. Water Cooling [†]

In semi-arid regions that are more than about 4,000 feet above sea level (this includes one-third of the conterminous United States) an economical method of cooling interior spaces in warm weather is with naturally chilled water. This seemingly contradictory technology utilizes the fact that during the summer semiarid regions often experience clear night skies that are 30–50° cooler than mid-afternoon temperatures. Thus by midnight even in summer, the top of a building's roof can become quite cold. Then if

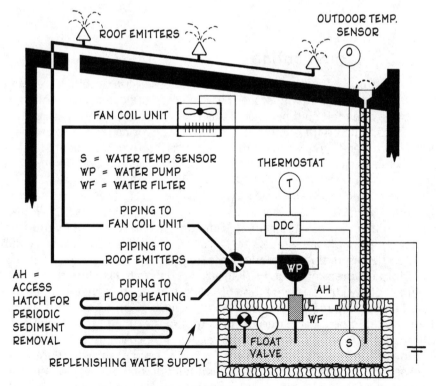

Fig. 3-55. Night roof spray cooling system.

[†] The primary source for this section was Richard Bourne, "Night Moves"

water is sprayed or trickled onto the roof from midnight till sunrise, it becomes chilled; then the following day when temperatures are warm, the chilled water circulates through cooling coils in the building's indoor spaces. Each system includes an array of roof-mounted emitters, roof drains, a water reservoir, a small electric motor-driven pump with a filter and controls, and cooling coils, the latter of which typically take the form of a fan-coil unit, subfloor tubing, or even water baseboard units. Thus it is possible that the cost of the cooling coil hardware can be allotted to the building's heating system.

This method of cooling, known as a *night roof spray cooling system*, is simple and affordable, is easily designed and constructed, requires little from the parent building other than a nearly flat roof of metal or other smooth material, has been proven to be economical by detailed monitoring, and little water is lost during its operation. The system also keeps roofs clean and protects the building from fire. Indeed, its only drawbacks seem to be lack of familiarity and industry inertia. An experienced manufacturer of these cooling systems is Integrated Comfort, Inc. of Davis, CA.

3.C.13. Humidification

Most likely the first humidifier used in American architecture was a pan of water on a Franklin stove. Even in colonial days it was known that wintry air often felt cold because it was dry —that one way to "warm it up a little" was to boil a little water vapor into it. This principle works as well in winter weather today, whether the steam arrives from a dedicated vessel hardly the size of a teapot that is activated by a manual on-off switch or a unitary boiler in a vast HVAC system operated by digital controls.

Humidification is also performed in a number of other ways. One could be called *pluming*. This is done by spraying water against a spinning disk, discharging compressed air into a thin waterstream to create an atomized mist, forcing high-pressure water through nozzles fitted with pins that shatter the impacting nozzleflow into fog, or immersing high-frequency vibrators in water which forces mist-sized droplets to rise into the air. The result is always the same: a plume of water droplets tiny enough to evaporate in an expanding airstream within a prescribed carrying distance, with humidification being maximum at the outlet, diminishing steadily down the plume and outward from its axis, and ending with complete evaporation of the introduced moisture and no condensation on any surface. Pure water is essential, as it minimizes nozzle-head buildup and suspension of impurities in the humidified air. Another common method of humidification is to enter moisture into duct airstreams with wetted wicks, steam jets, revolving

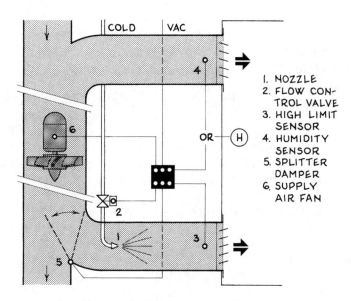

1. NOZZLE
2. FLOW CON-
   TROL VALVE
3. HIGH LIMIT
   SENSOR
4. HUMIDITY
   SENSOR
5. SPLITTER
   DAMPER
6. SUPPLY
   AIR FAN

Fig. 3-56. Humidifier operation.

wetted screens, open trays, and water pans or vaporizers inside furnaces and gas-fired heaters. A third method is well-known as *evaporative cooling*. This involves adding cool moisture to dry hot air, then the water droplets suck Btus from the air to lower its temperature. Anyone who has draped a wet towel over his or her head while under a hot sun has created a portable evaporative cooler. On a larger scale this thermodynamic process is enhanced by air movement —either natural air currents or fan-induced airflow— wherein optimal airflow is usually about 500 fpm (about 12 mph). In these systems the wetted components are made of noncorrosive materials, the wetted media is located in dark areas well inside the unit to discourage the growth of algae, and any water-collecting surfaces are sloped for draining. The makeup water should be supplied by a drinkable water source, and every part of the unit or system should be accessible for maintenance. Evaporative cooling systems have also been integrated into mechanical cooling systems where they typically act as precoolers to reduce the mechanical system's refrigeration load. In desert environments, evaporative coolers are often accompanied by concrete block screens, louvered doors, transoms, and other perforated construction that promotes natural air circulation while preserving privacy.

A humidifier can be quite small: one under-the-counter unit measures only 9.5 × 8.7 × 7.7 in, yet it has four 1¼ in. diameter flexible distribution hoses that can deliver 4 lb/hr of water vapor to computer cabinets, museum exhibit cases, and other small enclosures. A medium-sized system typically serves a few hundred square feet of floorspace. One's outlets are typically sized for airflows of 500–600 fpm and should be at least 18 in. below ceilings and 8 ft from any seated occupants, and the occupancy's optimal humidity level is usually 40–60 percent, as below this level physical irritations occur while above this level condensation may form on glazing and other interior surfaces. A large system typically includes (1) a small atomizing spray or mist nozzle mounted inside each air supply duct near the center of the duct's airstream and 10–12 ft before any turns, obstructions, or grilles; (2) a high-limit sensor placed several feet downstream of each nozzle to detect oversaturation; (3) a humidity sensor just inside each return air grille; and (4) controls that interconnect the nozzles and sensors to duct dampers and humidistats. Large humidification systems often maintain optimal hygroscopic conditions in textile mills, printing plants, tobacco processors, and other large industrial environments. In any system, if local water is not pure enough, the system may have a bottled water or distilled water supply, stainless steel or PFA plastic piping, and water-quality probes.

Designing any kind or size of humidification system usually involves little more than finding the required lb/hr of moisture to be added to occupied spaces, which is easily determined once design outdoor and indoor temperature and humidity levels are obtained. Outdoor levels are usually based on regional design temperatures at 40 percent relative humidity. In any system the nozzles or aerosols through which the water vapor enters the air should be easily removable for cleaning. The supply piping or tubing should also have a strainer just upstream of the nozzles, because whenever water circulates through a pump, particles constantly wear off the enclosing metal and rubber surfaces and enter the waterflow.

Since humidification is often an intermittent, variable, and unpredictable phenomenon, an essential component of all but the smallest systems is a humidistat. Each should be strategically located in the conditioned area, preferably as far from the system's nozzles as possible, about midway between the top and bottom of the zone, and if possible on the prevailing windward wall of the conditioned area. A humidistat may be electrically or hygroscopically operated (the latter is installed where electrical operation could be a fire hazard). Equally as important as the humidistat is a method of circulating the air in the conditioning area. For this reason many humidifiers, even small ones, are equipped with circulating fans.

An innovative system of evaporative cooling has been installed in a factory in Greenville, SC. On the building's 250,000 sf flat roof was laid a network of piping with many small water-emitting sprayheads which create an expansive misting system that considerably lowers the ambient temperature above the roof envelope. The piping is divided into 60 zones, each controlled by a 24 VAC solenoid valve whose temperature is monitored by a local thermal sensor that sends its data to a central controller, which decides when a sprayhead should activate and for how long, thus minimiz-

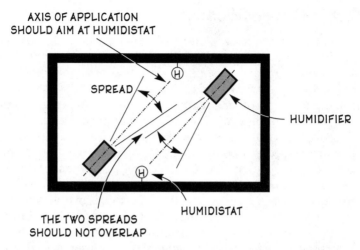

AXIS OF APPLICATION
SHOULD AIM AT HUMIDISTAT

SPREAD

HUMIDIFIER

HUMIDISTAT

THE TWO SPREADS
SHOULD NOT OVERLAP

Fig. 3-57. Optimal arrangement for a two-humidifier installation.

ing water waste and runoff. The piping is also mounted a few inches above the roof on supports that accommodate expansion and contraction caused by year-round temperature fluctuations. Thus this system reduces the Δt through the roof, which decreases this large low building's cooling load in this region of long hot summers by a cool $13,000 a year. An additional $66,000 in roof insulation was eliminated by having the system installed. [†]

> What is the maximum winter humidification requirement for a typical office of 28 people in Cleveland, OH?

$\underline{3}\underline{C}\underline{1}\underline{3}$ $12,000 \, H = \eta \, Q \, (h_i \, c_i - h_o \, c_o)$

H = design humidification load for occupied space(s), **?** lb/hr
η = number of occupants in space, 28
Q = required airflow for occupied space, cfm. From Table 3-7, Q for office areas = 20 cfm.
h_i = optimal indoor relative humidity, usually 50%
c_i = water content of saturated indoor air at optimal indoor temperature (usually 70°), gr/cf. From Table 3-5, c_i for 70° F = 8.10 gr/cf.
h_o = design outdoor relative humidity for site, usually 40%
c_o = water content of saturated outdoor air, usually at winter design temperature, gr/cf. From Fig. 2-24, winter design temperature for Cleveland, OH = -6°; from Table 3-5, c_i for -6° F = 0.34 gr/cf.

$12,000 \, H = 28 \times 20 \, (50 \times 8.10 - 40 \times 0.34) \quad ...H = 18.3 \, \text{lb/hr}$

[†] "Case in Point", *Engineering Systems* magazine (Business News Publishing

3.C.14. Dehumidification

Dehumidifiers remove water from warm humid air to make it feel cooler, eliminate hazards such as slippery floors, and minimize mildew growth on interior fabrics, rotting of wood, and rusting of metals. Such systems are economical in supermarkets, food preparation areas, schools, libraries, swimming pools, and other occupancies that may generate unwanted moisture or require its removal. There are two kinds of dehumidifiers: *chillers* and *absorbers*. Chillers use mechanical refrigeration to cool supply air below a prescribed dew point, causing the water to fall out of the air; then the drier air is reheated to a specified temperature and humidity. Chillers can be combined with numerous other mechanical devices —precoolers, reheating coils, evaporative cooling, energy-recovery systems, etc.— to maintain any indoor air temperature and humidity desired; but they can be complex and costly. Absorbers draw water from the air with hygroscopic chemicals which, when saturated, have the moisture removed from them.

A highly efficient absorber of water is the *desiccant dryer*. In this machine a water-absorbing chemical known as a desiccant is thinly spread on a large porous wheel that slowly rotates, then half the wheel's area is exposed to a stationary duct through which flows humid air while the wheel's other half is exposed to a second hot or dry airstream that removes the collected water. The amount of moisture removed depends primarily on the temperature of the regenerating air, and also on the temperature and humidity of the supply air, velocity of each airstream, type of desiccant, depth and diameter of the wheel, and the wheel's rotation speed. If the regenerating airstream is hot, the system is known as *active*; if it is dry the system is *passive*. Active desiccant systems dry the supply air continuously in any kind of weather, but their operating costs are higher due to the energy required to heat the regenerating airstream.

Desiccant dehumidification is a superb method of maintaining con-

TABLE 3-5: WATER CONTENT IN SATURATED AIR

t_o, °F	c_o, gr	t_o, °F	c_o, gr	t_o, °F	c_o, gr	t_o, °F	c_o, gr	t_o, °F	c_o, gr
10	0.29	34	2.29	54	4.72	74	9.15	94	16.9
5	0.35	36	2.47	56	5.06	76	9.75	96	17.8
0	0.48	38	2.66	58	5.41	78	10.4	98	18.9
5	0.61	40	2.86	60	5.80	80	11.0	100	20.0
10	0.78	42	3.08	62	6.20	82	11.8	102	21.1
15	0.99	44	3.32	64	6.62	84	12.5	104	22.3
20	1.24	46	3.56	66	7.07	86	13.3	106	23.6
25	1.56	48	3.83	68	7.57	88	14.1	108	24.9
30	1.95	50	4.11	70	8.10	90	14.9	110	26.3
32	2.13	52	4.41	72	8.59	92	15.8	112	27.8

Co., Troy, MI); Jun 1995, p. 20.

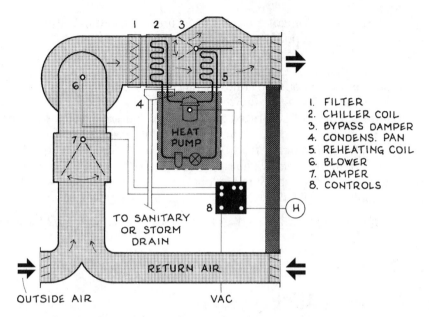

1. FILTER
2. CHILLER COIL
3. BYPASS DAMPER
4. CONDENS. PAN
5. REHEATING COIL
6. BLOWER
7. DAMPER
8. CONTROLS

TO SANITARY
OR STORM
DRAIN

RETURN AIR

OUTSIDE AIR   VAC

Fig. 3-58. Dehumidifier operation in chiller unit.

stant air temperature and humidity levels in indoor spaces, which is often important in industrial operations. However, these machines vary the supply air volume by 10–15 percent because adding or subtracting moisture from air has an accordion effect on its volume; so they are **N2G** in hermetically sealed 'air aquariums'. During cold weather a desiccant dryer's operation can be reversed by sending the warmed regenerating air into indoor spaces and the cooled water-removed air outdoors.

An outstanding example of desiccant dehumidification is the Borden facility in Northbrook, IL, which produces 1,000,000 boxes of Cracker Jacks each day. As the product's corn pops, it liberates moisture, which if not removed quickly from the air is reabsorbed by the popped corn and hygroscopic caramel, which would form a gooey brick inside the package —not the "surprise in every box" one would want. But by passing large volumes of desiccant-dried cold air over the popping corn until it is sealed in cartons, as much as 2,200 lb of water —more than a ton— is removed from the assembly lines every hour. [†]

What is the maximum summer dehumidification requirement for a typical office of 28 people in Cleveland, OH?

3]C]1]4] $12,000 \, D = \eta \, Q \, (h_o \, c_o - h_i \, c_i)$

[†] "Issues & Events", *Engineering Systems* magazine (Business News Publishing

D = design dehumidification load for occupied space(s), **?** lb/hr
η = number of occupants in space, 28
Q = required airflow for occupied space, cfm.
From Table 3-7, Q for office areas = 20 cfm.
h_o = summer design outdoor relative humidity for site, %.
From Fig. 3-26, h_o for Cleveland area = 75%.
c_o = water content of saturated outdoor air at summer design temperature, gr/cf. From Fig. 3-25, summer design temperature for
Cleveland area = 90°; from Table 3-5, c_o for 90° F = 14.94 gr/cf.
h_i = optimal indoor relative humidity, usually 50%
c_i = water content of saturated indoor air at optimal indoor temperature
(usually 75°), gr/cf. From Table 3-5, c_i for 75° F = 9.45 gr/cf.

$$12{,}000\ D\ =\ 20 \times 28\ (75 \times 14.94 - 50 \times 9.45) \quad \ldots D\ =\ 30.2\ \text{lb/hr}$$

3.D. VENTILATION

By far the best ventilating unit is an open window. Its cost is low, it is 100 percent efficient, its "hands-on" technology is simple, it is made in many sizes, and is widely available. It is easily the most common ventilator world-wide. Its airflow is also refreshing, is suggestive of freedom and independence, and tends to keep us in touch with Nature. A window's advantages can be improved by doing the following:

▶ Make floorplans no more than 36–40 ft wide.
▶ Locate thermal massing indoors to smooth out daily temperature swings.
▶ Locate summer-sun-blocking overhangs or sunscreeens above the windows.
▶ Install manually operable thermostatic controls.
▶ In buildings two or more stories high do not locate ground-level pedestrian areas directly below the windows. Instead fill these environs with attractive shrubbery, ground covers, and other unwalkable vegetation —which also emphasize the natural ambi-ence enhanced by the ventilation.

Another good natural ventilating unit is the rooftop ventilator. These units are typically located near the center of a large-roomed building, usu-ally at the peak of the roof where exposure to the prevailing winds above is greatest and interior convection currents below are maximum. The units' tops intercept the prevailing winds, which create a gentle atomizer effect in them, which draws upward uncomfortably warm indoor air that has risen to the highest part of the ceiling just below; then as the bad air is drawn upward

Co., Troy, MI); Sep 1994, p. 12.

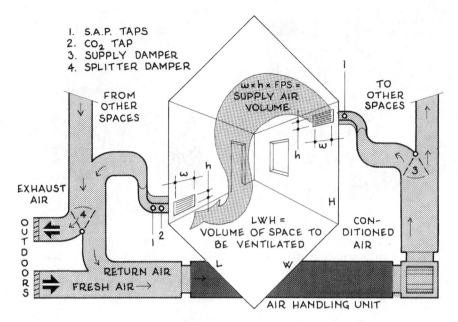

1. S.A.P. TAPS
2. CO_2 TAP
3. SUPPLY DAMPER
4. SPLITTER DAMPER

Fig. 3-59. Typical ventilation pathways.

fresh air is induced to flow through open windows located around the lower outer edge of the building. Three common rooftop ventilating units are the *ridge ventilator, circular ventilator,* and *turbine ventilator.* Each is described in Figs. 3-60, 61, and 62. Circular and turbine units can be installed in roofs that slope as much as 6 in 12, but they are much less effective there, especially if the roof plane is on the lee side of prevailing winds and the unit's top is below the roof's peak. These ventilators also work better if the roof is not closely surrounded by hilly terrain or tall foliage.

The three natural air ventilators above are sized as follows. Knowing the local prevailing windspeed and the design temperature difference between the indoors and outdoors, determine the building's ventilation requirements, then select one or more units from Table 3-6 below. Interpolate for intermediate values.

At times it is necessary to use more mechanical means of supplying fresh air to modern interior spaces. A chief method today is the large HVAC systems that serve hermetically sealed 'air aquariums.' In such buildings, outdoor fresh air enters a supply air louver, is impelled by a fan through filters and conditioners, flows into an occupied space, exits as stale air, then flows through a return air duct to where a splitter damper sends part of the stale air outdoors and the rest back into the supply duct where it mixes with more fresh air. If stale air sensors (usually CO_2 sensors) notify controls that interior spaces need more fresh air, the splitter damper sends a greater por-

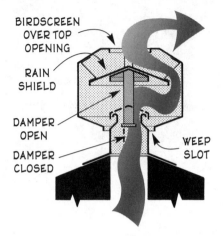

BIRDSCREEN OVER TOP OPENING

RAIN SHIELD

DAMPER OPEN

DAMPER CLOSED

WEEP SLOT

This galvanized steel ridge vent has a slot in its base and a lift damper inside that is opened by a chain from below; then convection air flows through slots in the unit's top.

Fig. 3-60. Ridge ventilator. [†]

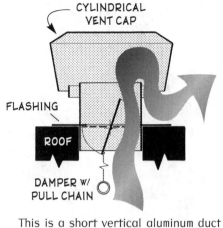

CYLINDRICAL VENT CAP

FLASHING

ROOF

DAMPER w/ PULL CHAIN

This is a short vertical aluminum duct with a cylindrical vent cap on top and a chain-operated disc damper near its base. Opening the damper allows warm air to flow upward and outside.

Fig. 3-61. Circular ventilator.

TABLE 3-6: ROOFTOP VENTILATOR CAPACITIES

Airflow volumes are in cfm
RIDGE VENTILATORS w/ 4 IN × 10'-0" OPENING

PREVAILING WINDSPEED	← Δ temperature between indoors & outdoors →						
	0°	5°	10°	15°	20°	25°	30°
4 mph	205	270	330	380	425	470	510
6 mph	470	340	415	480	540	595	640
8 mph	315	415	500	580	655	720	775
10 mph	370	485	590	680	770	845	910
12 mph	425	560	675	780	880	970	1,050

GLOBE AND CIRCULAR VENTILATORS [1]

PREVAILING WINDSPEED	← Δ temperature between indoors & outdoors →						
	0°	5°	10°	15°	20°	25°	30°
4 mph	100	110	120	130	140	155	170
6 mph	125	135	150	165	180	195	215
8 mph	150	165	180	200	220	240	260
10 mph	175	195	215	235	255	280	305
12 mph	200	220	245	270	295	320	350

1. For 8 in. dia. turbine ventilators, multiply above airflow volumes × 1.00.
   For 12 in. dia. turbine ventilators, multiply above airflow volumes × 2.27.
   For 12 in. dia. circular ventilators, multiply above airflow volumes × 1.94.

[†] The author regrets that he has lost the source for the rooftop ventilators in

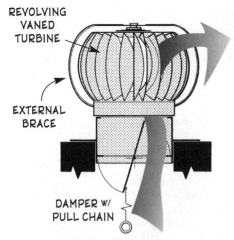

REVOLVING
VANED
TURBINE

EXTERNAL
BRACE

DAMPER w/
PULL CHAIN

Also a *globe ventilator,* this is a short vertical duct with a vaned turbine on top. When prevailing winds make the turbine rotate, it sucks air from below.

Fig. 3-62. Turbine ventilator.

tion of the stale air outdoors, a dedicated exhaust fan draws more stale air out, or supply fans pull more outdoor air into the ducting. In such systems fresh-air supply louvers cannot be near return air outlets, cooling tower exhausts, exhaust airstreams from other buildings, service areas, parking areas (not even illegal parking zones where a driver might wait for a passenger), chimney tops or plumbing vents, within 8 ft of the ground, or near areas of standing water (such as just above flat roofs). Each louver also must be protected from entry or obstruction by insects, birds and nests, rodents, debris, updrafting rain, and swirling snow. Exhaust louvers also cannot be near building entrances, operable windows, or intake vents.

Other mechanical ventilation design guides are:

▸ The amount of incoming air in a duct depends on the pressure differential at the end of the duct and its net open area.
▸ Poor mixing of airstreams of different densities (e.g. different temperatures or humidities) can create mixed air temperatures that are different from what calculations indicate.
▸ Supply air should not be delivered into a space as much as it should be delivered to where its occupants are located.
▸ Too little ventilation results in lower IAQ; too much ventilation results in wasted energy.
▸ Using large volumes of outdoor air to dilute indoor contaminants usually costs more than recirculating and filtering part of the air.
▸ Where waste-emitting equipment or processes are located, install exhaust fans that send bad air directly outdoors.
▸ Installing CO_2 sensors in densely occupied spaces saves energy.

There are three general kinds of mechanical ventilation, usually depending on the kind of space to be ventilated:

Flow tracking. Fresh air requirements are based on similar amounts required by similarly occupied spaces: e.g. floorplans with numerous similar-sized occupancies such as offices, hotel rooms, and classrooms.

Figs. 3-60, 3-61, and 3-62 and the related ventilator capacities in Table 3-6;

Demand controlled. Fresh air requirements are determined by specific needs of certain areas or equipment. Examples are public restrooms, commercial cooking areas, and laboratory fume hoods.

Air pressure management. Fresh air requirements are based on pressure differentials between s.a.p. sensors located in adjacent spaces. Examples are large open areas, interpenetrating spaces, public circulation areas, and rooms with irregular perimeters. Air flows from the lower s.a.p. to the higher, and the greater the s.a.p. differential between two areas the faster the airflow between them.

Computing a zone's ventilation requirements usually depends on if its unit fresh airflow requirements are in cf per occupant, cf per floor area, cf per spatial unit (e.g. a toilet stall), or a zone's number of air changes per hour. Every mechanical ventilation system also requires one or more return air vents for exhausting the building's stale or foul air. The most efficient ones face straight up and use the exhaust flow's velocity to send it as high into the outside air as possible. One such vent is sketched in Fig. 3-11.

Example 1. A bedroom window in a hillside residence a south of Carmel, CA, overlooks the Pacific Ocean 400 ft to the west. If the double-hung window is 32 in. wide × 48 in. high, the room's floor area is 12 × 14 ft, an open doorway on the wall opposite the window allows incoming air to flow freely through the room, and prevailing winds blowing off the Pacific Ocean are rarely less than 12 mph, how high must the window's lower sash be above its sill to satisfy the bedroom's fresh air requirements?

Step 1. Determine the window's volume of incoming airflow.

3)D)1) $$Q \approx v A \varepsilon$$

Q = volume of incoming airflow, **?** cfm
v = velocity of airflow, fpm. 1 mph = 88 fpm. As prevailing windspeed usually ≈ 0.6 ambient breeze speed, $v = 12 \times 88 \times 0.6 \approx 630$ fpm.
A = maximum free area of open window, sf. From catalog or manual measurement, maximum lower sash opening of 32 × 48 in. double-hung window is about 28 in. wide × 21 in. high ≈ 588 in². Converting in. to ft, 588 ÷ 144 = 4.1 sf.
ε = efficacy of opening. ε = 0.90 if opening is in a wall or roof surface that faces prevailing winds, 0.55 if surface is perpendicular to prevailing winds, and 0.15 if surface faces away from prevailing winds. Interpolate for intermediate values. Here $\varepsilon \approx 0.90$.

$$Q \approx 630 \times 4.1 \times 0.90 \approx 2,390 \text{ cfm}$$

the source was a product catalog.

Step 2. Determine the room's fresh air requirements. Assuming the bedroom is normally occupied by two people engaged in passive to light activity, from Table 3-7, fresh air requirement for light activity ≈ 20 cfm·occupant. At two occupants, the fresh air requirement ≈ 2 × 20 × 40 cfm.

Step 3. Determine the height of the sash opening that is required to satisfy the room's fresh air requirements.

$$\frac{H_{req}: \text{Required ht. of opng}}{H_{max}: \text{Maximum ht. of opng}} = \frac{Q_{req}: \text{Required fresh airflow of opng}}{Q_{max}: \text{Maximum fresh airflow of opng}}$$

$$^h/_{21} = {^{40}}/_{2,300} \quad ... \; h = 0.37 \text{ in.} \; \rightarrow \text{about } \tfrac{3}{8} \text{ in.}$$

Example 2. The same hillside residence overlooking the Pacific as described in the previous example has casement windows on the house's north and south facades; thus when the windows are half open they scoop the prevailing wind blowing alongside the house indoors. If the windows are 32 in. wide × 48 in. high, during average prevailing windflow how much fresh air does each of these manually operated scoop ventilators redirect indoors?

---

3)D)2) $Q \le v \, w \, h \, \mathcal{E}$

Q = volume of incoming airflow, **?** cfm

v = velocity of airflow, fpm. 1 mph = 88 fpm. As prevailing windspeed usually ≈ 0.6 ambient breeze speed,
v = 12 × 88 × 0.6 ≈ 630 fpm.

Fig. 3-63. Plan of casement window ventilator.

w = width of wind scoop area when window is half open, ft. Half open ≈ 45°. ∴ w = sash width × sin 45° = 28 × 0.707 = 19.8 in. From catalog or manual measurement, sash width of 32 in. casement window is about 28 in; but the horizontal distance from the sash's frame inset to the outer surface of the building's finish must be subtracted from w. Say this ≈ 3 in. Then w = 19.8 – 3 ≈ 16.8 in. Converting to ft: 16.8/12 = 1.4 ft.

h = height of wind scoop, ft. This is the height of the sash. From manufacturer's catalog or manual measurement, h for 48 in. high casement window = 44 in. Converting to ft: 44/12 = 3.67 ft.

ε = efficacy of opening. ε = 0.90 if opening is in a wall or roof surface that faces prevailing winds, 0.55 if surface is perpendicular to prevailing winds, and 0.10 if surface faces away from prevailing winds. Interpolate for intermediate values. Here the window's opened sash faces prevailing winds. ∴ ε ≈ 0.90.

$$Q \approx 630 \times 1.4 \times 3.67 \times 0.90 \approx 2,900 \text{ cfm}$$

Example 3. The same hillside residence overlooking the Pacific Ocean as described in the previous two examples has a belvedere mounted at the peak of a cathedral ceiling over the living area as drawn below. Given the data in the drawing, how much air is drawn upward through the house by this method of natural ventilation?

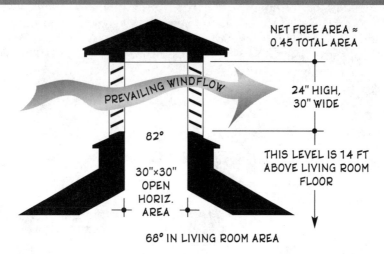

Fig. 3-64. Section through belvedere ventilator.

Strategy: The belvedere as sketched above induces natural airflow in two ways: the *aerosol effect* and the *stack effect*. Each is described below:

a. Aerosol effect: This is a suction created by the prevailing winds blowing through the belvedere's slatted horizontal openings which are located above the columnar opening just below. Its airflow is quantified as

3 D 3 a $\qquad$ $Q_a \approx 44\, A\, \varepsilon$

Q_a = volume of exiting airflow due to aerosol effect, **?** cfm
A = area of opening, sf. Here A = smaller of two openings between top of room and outdoors; opening 1 is the columnar airspace below the belvedere, and opening 2 is the net free area between the slats

in one of the belvedere's walls. From the sketch, opening area 1 = 30 × 30 = 900 sf, and opening area 2 = 0.45 × 24 × 30 = 324 in². Use smaller area and convert to ft: A = 324/12 = 22.25 sf.

ε = efficacy of opening. ε = 0.90 if opening is in a wall or roof surface that faces prevailing winds, 0.55 if surface is perpendicular to prevailing winds, and 0.10 if surface faces away from prevailing winds. Interpolate for intermediate values. Here $\varepsilon \approx 0.90$.

$$Q_a \approx 44 \times 2.25 \; 0.90 \approx 89 \text{ cfm}$$

b. Stack effect: This is the amount of air that is drawn upward due to the temperature difference between the room's lowest and highest levels; because warmer air is less dense and thus rises which pulls up the air below. These thermodynamics are quantified by

3)D)3)b) $Q_s \approx 70 + 3.7 \, (h \, \Delta T)^{0.62}$

Q_s = volume of exiting airflow due to stack effect, **?** cfm
h = height of temperature differential, ft. From the sketch, the upper temperature of 82° is 14 ft above the living room floor. If assumed lower temperature of 68° is 3 ft above the floor, h = 14 – 3 = 11 ft.
ΔT = temperature differential between lower and higher level, ° F.
ΔT = 82 – 68 = 14° F.

$$Q_s \approx 70 + 3.7 \, (11 \times 14)^{0.62} \approx 154 \text{ cfm}$$

c. Total ventilation airflow:
3)D)3)c) $Q_T \approx Q_a + Q_s$
$$Q_T \approx 89 + 154 \approx 243 \text{ cfm}$$

Note: The stack effect occurs not only in large airspaces that are many feet tall: it may also occur in an uninsulated stud wall in the voids between the wall's interior and exterior finishes, and it may occur between the panes of glass in a thermopane window. In both cases the air rises against the warm surface, turns at the top, descends against the cold surface, then turns at the bottom to create a convection loop that can drain much warm air horizontally through the construction. The remedy? Fill the voids between the studs with insulation, and place the two glass panes close enough together so the loop cannot form.

Example 4. The house next door to the residence overlooking the Pacific Ocean as described in the previous three examples has a solar chimney constructed at the peak of its roof as drawn in Fig. 3-65. Given the data in this drawing, what is the natural ventilation airflow induced by this architecture on a hot sunny day?

Strategy: The solar chimney sketched at right induces natural airflow via the *stack effect*, which is quantified from

<u>3|D|4</u>　$Q_s \approx 70 + 3.7\,(h\,\Delta T)^{0.62}$

Q_s = volume of exiting airflow due to stack effect, **?** cfm

h = height of temperature differential, ft. From the sketch, the upper temperature of 82° is 18 ft above the living room floor. If assumed lower temperature of 68° is 3 ft above the floor, h = 18 − 3 = 15 ft.

ΔT = temperature differential between lower and higher level, ° F. Here ΔT at higher level = 135°. Assume temperature at lower level is an uncomfortable 88°. ∴ 135 − 88 = 47° F.

$$Q_s \approx 70 + 3.7\,(15 \times 47)^{0.62}$$
$$Q_s \approx 286 \text{ cfm}$$

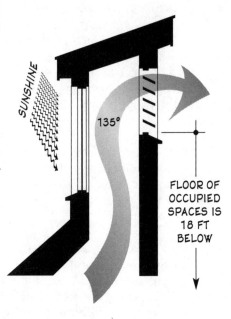

135°

SUNSHINE

FLOOR OF OCCUPIED SPACES IS 18 FT BELOW

Fig. 3-65. Section through solar chimney.

A question for designers: Could a conventional masonry or metal chimney be converted into a solar chimney by mounting a pane of Pyrex glass in its south side between the roof and the top of the chimney? Then in summer the natural airflow could be controlled by the fireplace damper below.

Example 5: Fresh Air Requirement. What are the ventilation requirements for an office conference room that seats 24 people?

<u>3|D|5</u>　**Required air per occupant:**　$Q \geq F_o\,\eta$　　... ➕
　<u>6</u>　**Required air per floor area:**　$Q \geq F_a\,A$
　<u>7</u>　**Required air per spatial unit:**　$Q \geq 1.15\,F_u\,\eta$
　<u>8</u>　**Required air per air changes:**　$Q \geq 0.02\,F_{ac}\,V$

Q = required airflow delivery rate, (fresh or exhaust air), **?** cfm.
F_o = unit fresh air requirement per occupant, cfm.
　　From Table 3-7, F_o for conference room = 50 cfm.
η = number of occupants in space, 24 people
F_a = unit fresh air requirement of floor area, cfm. Not applicable.

A = total floor area, sf. Not applicable.
F_u = required fresh air for spatial unit (toilet, urinal, stove hood, etc.), cfm. Not applicable.
N = number of spatial units served. Not applicable.
F_{ac} = unit fresh air requirement, number of air changes/hr. Multiply by safety factor of 2.5 unless specific data is given. Not applicable.
V = volume of ventilated space: L × W × H, cf. Not applicable.

$$Q \geq 24 \times 50 \geq 1{,}200 \text{ cfm}$$

Example 6: Exhaust Fan Size. If the painting room in an auto body repair shop is 28 ft long, 16 ft wide, and 10 ft high, size the exhaust fan.

---

3)D)5)   Required air per occupant: $Q \geq F_o \eta$
   6)   Required air per floor area: $Q \geq F_a A$
   7)   Required air per spatial unit: $Q \geq 1.15 F_u \eta$
   8)   Required air per air changes: $Q \geq 0.02 F_{ac} V$ ... ➕

Q = required airflow delivery rate, (fresh or exhaust air), **?** cfm
F_o = unit fresh air requirement per occupant, cfm. Not applicable.
η = number of occupants in space. Not applicable.
F_a = unit fresh air requirement of floor area, cfm. Not applicable.
T = total floor area, sf. Not applicable.
F_u = required fresh air for spatial unit (toilet, urinal, stove hood, etc.), cfm. Not applicable.
η = number of spatial units served. Not applicable.
F_{ac} = unit fresh air requirement, number of air changes/hr. Multiply by safety factor of 2.5 unless specific information is given. From Table 3-7, F_h of localized bad air ≥ 6 × 2.5 safety factor.
V = volume of ventilated space, 28 × 16 × 10 ft = 4,480 cf

$$Q \geq 0.02 \times 6 \times 2.5 \times 4{,}480 \geq 1{,}340 \text{ cfm}$$

Example 7: Exhaust Fan Size. What is the optimal size for an exhaust fan in a men's room with seven toilets and five urinals?

---

3)D)5)   Required air per occupant: $Q \geq F_o \eta$
   6)   Required air per floor area: $Q \geq F_a A$
   7)   Required air per spatial unit: $Q \geq 1.15 F_u \eta$ ... ➕
   8)   Required air per air changes: $Q \geq 0.02 F_{ac} V$

Q = required airflow delivery rate, (fresh or exhaust air), **?** cfm

F_o = unit fresh air requirement per occupant, cfm.
From Table 3-7, F_o for conference room = 50 cfm.

N = number of occupants in space, 24 people.

F_a = unit fresh air requirement of floor area, cfm. Not applicable.

T = total floor area, sf. Not applicable.

F_u = required fresh air for spatial unit (toilet, urinal, etc.), cfm.
From Table 3-7, F_u for each toilet or urinal = 50 cfm.

η = number of spatial units served. 7 toilets + 5 urinals = 12 units.

F_{ac} = unit fresh air requirement, number of air changes/hr. Multiply by
safety factor of 2.5 unless specific data is given. Not applicable.

V = volume of ventilated space: L × W × H, cf. Not applicable.

$$Q \geq 1.15 \times 12 \times 50 \geq 690 \text{ cfm}$$

Example 8: Supply Duct Size. If the conference room in a fish hatchery requires 880 ft^3 of fresh outdoor air when fully occupied and the supply air duct is 22 ft long from the outdoor air grille to the conference room supply grille, size the duct.

---

3)D)9)
$$Q \leq A\,\kappa_d$$

Q = required airflow delivery rate, (fresh or exhaust air), 880 cfm

A = minimum section area of duct (not including insulation), **?** in^2

κ_d = duct velocity factor. From Table 3-7, κ_d for main duct to a conference room area = 12.

$$880 \leq 12\,A \quad \ldots A \geq 75 \text{ in}^2 \Rightarrow 8 \times 10 \text{ in, 10 in. dia., etc.}$$

Note: If the duct length $\geq$ 40 ft or its width-to-depth ratio $\geq$ 2.5, its size should be increased according to air friction losses and aspect ratio as described in Sec. 3.C.i.1, Example 2, on page 187.

Example 9: Exhaust Fan Size. A 24-seat conference room requires 1,200 ft^3/min of fresh air when fully occupied. If the HVAC system supplies 240 ft^3 of fresh air into the room and an exhaust fan removes excess smoky air when required, size the exhaust fan.

---

3)D)10)
$$Q_{exi} + Q_{add} \geq Q_{tot}$$

Q_{exi} = ventilation rate of existing exhaust system, 240 cfm

Q_{add} = additional ventilation required, **?** cfm

Q_{tot} = total ventilation required of exhaust system, 1,200 cfm

$$240 + Q_{add} \geq 1,200 \quad \ldots Q_{add} \geq 960 \text{ cfm}$$

Example 10: Exhaust Duct Size. A ventilation fan in the ceiling of a men's room is rated at 720 ft³/min. If the exhaust air passes through 24 ft of ducting to a louver in the exterior wall, size the duct.

3)D)1)1) $Q \leq 0.8 \, A \, \kappa_d$

TABLE 3-7: FRESH AIR REQUIREMENTS

OCCUPANCY   Minimum airflow, F_o = cfm/occupant [1]

Inactivity: reclining, sleeping, bedrooms, dorms, hotel/motel rooms	10
Passive activity: auditoriums, churches, theaters, classrooms, libraries, museums, lounges, rest rooms, apartments	15
Light activity: food prep & eating areas, lobbies, offices, retail areas, music rooms, school labs, sports assembly	20
Moderate activity: lobbies w/o seating, hallways, bars, locker rooms, beauty parlors, light recreation, cold food service areas, hospital wards, private offices w/ smoking, walking activities	25
Active work: shipping rooms, dance halls, kitchens, hot food service areas, recreation, machine work	30
Strenuous activity: gymnasiums, conference rooms w/ smoking	50
Smoking lounges, other indoor smoking areas	60

FLOOR AREA   Minimum airflow, F_a = cfm/floor area

Corridor	0.33 ft³/min/ft² floor area
Garages	1.5 ft³/min/ft² floor area
Commercial kitchens	4.0 ft³/min/ft² floor area

SPATIAL UNIT   Minimum airflow, F_u = cfm/ spatial unit

Ladies' rooms	35 ft³/min per toilet
Men's rooms	50 ft³/min per toilet or urinal
Canopy or fume hoods	60 ft³/min/ft² per hood face area

AIR CHANGES/HR   Minimum airflow, F_h = no. air changes/hr

Localized bad air	6-60 air changes/hr
Factory operations	obtain specific data for each analysis
Smoke exhaust systems	6 ac/hr outside air to interiors affected by fire

1. Recommended airflow for any occupancy ≈ 1.5 ft³/min-occupant.

Q = required airflow delivery rate, (fresh or exhaust air), 720 cfm
A = minimum section area of duct (not including insulation), **?** in^2
κ_d = duct velocity factor. From Table 3-7, κ_d for outlet duct from a service area = 12.

$$720 \le 0.8 \times 12\,A \quad ... A \ge 73\ \text{in}^2 \blacktriangleright 8 \times 10", 10"\ \text{diameter, etc.}$$

Note: If the duct length exceeds 40 ft or its width-to-depth ratio exceeds 2.5, its size should be increased according to air friction losses and aspect ratio as described in Sec. 3.C.i.1., Example 2, on page 187.

Example 11. An enclosed parking garage in downtown Chicago requires ventilation to keep vehicular exhaust emissions at safe levels. If the 12,400 sf garage has 42 parking spaces, its floor-to-ceiling height is 9'-1", the vehicles are standard-size automobiles parked by attendants, and most vehicles remain in the garage from 8 A.M. to 5 P.M., size the ventilation system.

---

3)D)1)2) $A\,h\,C_o\,Q \approx 486\,\eta\,\kappa_v\,\epsilon\,t$

A = floor area of enclosed parking area, 12,400 sf
h = clear floor-to-ceiling height of enclosed parking area, ft.
 9'-1" = 9.08 ft.
C_o = maximum acceptable level of carbon monoxide in enclosed parking area, ppm. This should never exceed 25 ppm.
Q = required airflow of ventilation system, **?** air changes/hr [ACH]
ϵ = emission rate per vehicle, gr/min. ϵ varies significantly according to size of vehicle engine, whether engine is hot or cold, ambient air temperature at time of engine startup (e.g. season of year), and age of vehicle (older vehicles generally have higher emission rates). Typical CO emissions of auto engines are listed on the next page:

Type of engine/starting/season	Emissions, grams/min
Cold-engine starting in summer (90° F)	3.7 gm/min
Hot-engine starting in summer	1.9 gm/min
Cold-engine starting in winter (32° F)	18.9 gm/min
Hot-engine starting in winter	3.4 gm/min

The above values are intended to exemplify the design scenario more than articulate the reality involved. For a design scenario as serious as this, always obtain articulate data relating to the specific circumstances involved. Here the worst condition is starting a car after it has been parked for several hours in winter ➡ cold-engine starting in winter = 18.9 gr/min.

η = number of parking spaces in enclosed parking area, 100
κ_v = fraction of vehicles operating at one time. If the cars are parked by attendants, assume that no more than 8 are driven at one time during rush hour dropoff and pickup. $\therefore \kappa_v$ = 8/100 = .08.
t = operating time for each car from dropoff to parking or from parking to pickup, sec. Assume this activity has been measured and found to be 2 min and 12 sec ➡ t = 132 sec

$$12,400 \times 9.08 \times 25 \times Q \approx 486 \times 18.9 \times 100 \times 0.08 \times 132$$
$$... \, Q \approx 3.5 \text{ ACH}$$

Note: The design parameters for enclosed parking garage ventilation systems are different from those for normally occupied spaces, primarily due to the rate at which vehicular engines produce carbon monoxide and the much lower pollutant concentration levels that are acceptable for this poisonous gas in enclosed indoor spaces.

3.E. AIR FILTRATION [†]

A human breathes about 1,000 times an hour, and every breath should be comfortable. Unfortunately, when we are indoors our lungs are often exposed to a veritable mist of *particulates* (minute solids drifting in air currents: dust, dander, pollen, lint, smoke, soot, etc.), *microbes* (bacteria, viruses, spores, molds, fungi, etc.), *gases* or *odors* (aromas from foods, hair sprays, insect sprays, electrical operations, machinery, chemicals, new furniture and drapes, etc.), and a great variety of occasionally encountered toxic chemicals. A chief method of removing these floating, swirling, settling nebulae of noxious elements is to run a climate control system's conditioned airflow through filters. This not only creates healthier interiors, it improves occupants' productivity and morale and reduces system maintenance and life-cycle costs.

Filters are typically rated in terms of *arrestance* (ability to strain hair, lint, dandruff, dust and other particles out of the airstream), *efficiency* (ability to remove sub-visible particles such as carbon black, fly ash, and pollutants), *airflow resistance* (the degree to which the filtering slows the airflow, thus requiring a correspondingly stronger fan and motor to maintain the required airflow), *airstream velocity* (typically 125–150 fpm for high-efficiency filters, to 500 fpm for medium-efficiency ones, and to 625 fpm for low-efficiency units), and *lifespan*. High arrestance and high efficiency generally indicate greater dust-holding capacity, lower face velocity, higher airflow resistance, and shorter life. Since no one filter completely removes every pollutant, they are frequently combined to remove an acceptably high percentage of every kind from indoor air as well

---

[†] An important source for this section was Ronald Fink, "Cleaning the Air 101",

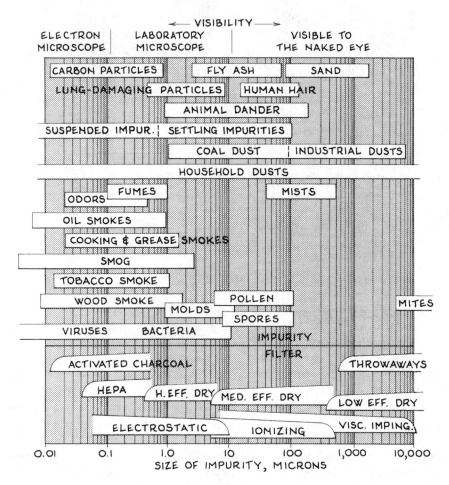

Fig. 3-66. Air cleaner efficiency chart. †

as outdoor supply air entering a climate control system. When a filter is no longer useful, it is usually cleaned in place, removed and cleaned, or thrown away and replaced.

The most common air filter today is the *porous-media filter*. This is a porous material that is fitted across a duct's full section area where it strains particles out of the airflow. A newly installed porous-media filter slows the duct's airflow somewhat due to its thickness, density, and material, which requires the climate control system's fan and motor to be enlarged to maintain the required airflow; but increasing filter efficiency also reduces supply air requirements and thus the size of ducts, fans, louvers, boilers, chillers, and other system components. A drawback to porous-media filters is that its pores become increasingly clogged over

Engineered Systems magazine (Business News Publishing Co., Troy, MI); Jul 1998, time. But, since the duct's airflow usually decreases only slightly until the filter reaches a certain saturation at which time its airflow rapidly declines, computerized s.a.p. sensors can be placed before and after the filter that notify maintenance personnel when its initial ΔP has increased by a pre-scribed amount; then the filter is efficiently replaced.

A few other kinds of filters send electrical or chemical charges across the duct in various ways that 'zap' the particles out of the airflow; these methods continually maintain the duct's full section area. Some filters are also impregnated with antimicrobial agents that minimize propagation of microbes that could flow downstream in concentrated form.

The most common filters used today are described below.

Dry Media

This filter is a typically 2–6 in. deep frame that contains a dry throwaway mat of cellulose, glass fibers, treated paper, cotton batting, or porous medi-um. When the filter becomes clogged it is discarded. Optimal airflow ≈ 350–500 fpm. They are 5–30 percent efficient.

➕ Good for low dust loads, prefiltering in large systems, and remov-ing microscopic particles of light concentration; often installed with viscous impingement filters. Easily replaceable, low unit cost.

➖ Inefficient, small holding capacity, high service cost, short life. They do not filter microbes, gases, and odors. Unecological in that they are a throwaway item.

Cleanable Media

These are similar to dry media filters except that when they become clogged they are removed, easily cleaned or re-oiled, then reused. They are used for airflows of about 300 fpm and are 65–80 percent efficient.

➕ Ecologically viable, requires no replacing.

➖ Requires maintenance staff and cleaning space.

Aluminum Mesh

This is a panel of aluminum that contains baffled meshes of different den-sities. It is strong and thus is used in ducts with large section areas, is washable in detergents and chemicals, and is highly durable. It is an excel-lent collector of grease and messy industrial substances that with most fil-ters are difficult to trap and clean. Although aluminum mesh filters do not directly collect tiny particles, microbes, and odors, these contaminants often adhere to the greasy or sticky substances that one does collect. Its metal is also good for filtering hot airflows; thus this is the best filter for restaurant stove hood ducting. It can be used for high airflows and is 30–70 percent efficient.

➕ Strong, nonflammable, durable, low resistance, good for high-velocity airflows, ideal for trapping grease, prevents radio-frequency interference from entering the ducting. Good for large areas, reusable.

➖ High initial cost, heavy, requires maintenance. Generally won't filter small particles, microbes, odors, or gases.

Viscous Impingement

This is a fairly coarse and durable filter that is periodically covered with oil or grease. Optimal airflow ≈ 200–800 fpm; efficiency varies.

➕ VG for removing pollens, dusts, ashes, mists, oil smokes, and visible particles of high concentration. Great capacity, long-lasting, needs little service. A good pre-filter for other types.

➖ Won't filter lints, viruses, bacteria, tobacco smoke, or toxins.

High-efficiency Particulate (HEPA)

This filter has a pleated arrangement of blankets or mats whose surfaces have tiny pores that can remove very small particulates. Optimal airflow ≈ 10–125 fpm, and removal efficiency is up to 99.97 percent for 0.3 μ particles.

➕ Able to remove fine particles including some bacteria and odors. Used in small pharmaceutical and other chemical environments.

➖ Filter membranes can become a breeding ground for microbes; is also a poor remover of many odors, gases, and microbes. They greatly reduce airflows at normal and higher velocities and thus require powerful blowers to be effective (thus they are N2G for interiors with large airflow requirements). They do not last long and thus require frequent changing.

Activated Charcoal

Also known as carbon media filters, these are replaceable cartridges or panels that have a foam or fabric medium filled with granulated carbon or activated charcoal. The carbon acts not only as a physical filter but absorbs numerous odors and heavy gases. Optimal airflows are low, but they are highly efficient at removing specific odors and toxins.

Cleaner Efficiency Chart, back cover of an advertising brochure prepared by Five

➕ Good for removing particles of all sizes including smokes, certain microbes, most odors, and specific chemical toxins. Can be installed in central systems or individual rooms.

➖ Greatly reduces airflow, requires frequent changing, acts as a breeding ground for microbes. Carbon has a certain capacity for absorption beyond which it becomes inert and ceases functioning.

Roll-type Disposable

This is a moving filter roll that passes through the airstream that rewinds on a takeup spool as it becomes clogged. It is used for medium airflows and is 20–50 percent efficient.

➕ Long-lasting, constantly clean with constant airflow resistance, is an economical prefilter.

➖ Rather low efficiency, requires parasitic electricity to operate.

Automatic

This is an arrangement of overlapping filter panels that are attached to a chain which moves the panels across the airstream then through an oil bath. Optimal airflow ≈ 500 fpm, and they are 80–90 percent efficient.

➕ Airflow resistance is fairly constant, filter is constantly clean.

➖ Costly, bulky, requires parasitic electricity to operate.

Ionic or Ionizing

In this system electrically generated negative ions are introduced into the airflow where they attract airborne particles and make them stick to each other until they are so heavy that they fall out of the air. Their optimal effect depends on lengthy exposure to large volumes of slowly circulating air. Thus they work best in rooms filled with a pollutant such as cigaret smoke or industrially produced inhalant.

➕ Effective in removing low concentrations of smoke and similar small particulates from large volumes of interior air. The ions travel freely through the air and can improve the air far away.

➖ N2G when applied inside ducting or HVAC componentry, requires extra equipment and parasitic energy to operate. As the particles fall out of the air, the treated interior's floors, tables, and counters need periodic cleaning.

Seasons Corp., 1995; and (2) *Handbook of Air Conditioning Design*, prepared ‖

Electrostatic

In these filters the airstream passes through an electrostatic field between two metal plates charged with up to 12,000 volts which impart an electric charge to the particles that makes them adhere to the plates. The removed particles then fall into a collector tray or are removed by rotating the plates through an oil bath. They typically consume about 8 watts per 1,000 cfm of airflow, are used for airflows of 250–500 fpm, and are 75–90 percent efficient (usually the slower the airflow, the greater the efficiency).

➕ Good for low-velocity and high-volume airflows that contain a large amount of very small particles. They remove microscopic particles efficiently, create low resistance to airflow, and induce low pressure drops within the airstream. Suitable where equipment is relatively inaccessible or where service is infrequent. This filter has been used in industry smokestacks for many years to remove particulate emissions.

➖ High initial and operating costs, requires extra space for transformer and rectifier. Air exceeding 70 percent humidity may adversely affect operation, **NG** in linty atmospheres and white rooms unless after-filters are used. After-filters may also be required to catch large particles that flake off the plates.

Ultraviolet

This method uses ultraviolet light to destroy any bacteria, molds, or fungi that pass through its rays. Its efficiency depends on the light's intensity and the airflow's length of exposure. Thus the lower the airflow's volume and velocity, the more effective the exposure.

➕ Does not reduce ducting airflow, requires no intermittent cleaning. UV rays are often used as a sanitizing agent by medical facilities.

➖ Has no effect on particulates, requires extra equipment and parasitic energy to operate. Humans and any other desirable animals must be shielded from exposure to UV light.

Ozone

This method introduces ozone into the ducting airflow where the chemical's extra atom of oxygen attaches to microbes and organic gases, which neutralizes them and produces free oxygen. This action is not limited to the ozone's point of entry into the airstream but continues as this oxidizer circulates in occupied spaces. Thus its effectiveness does not depend on optimal duct airflow or random-selection efficiency as much as ducting con-

by the Carrier Corp. (McGraw-Hill, New York, 1965), p. 5-62.

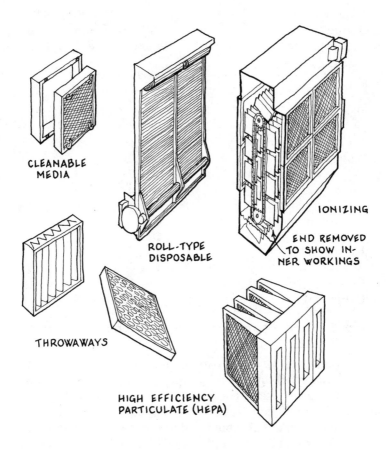

CLEANABLE MEDIA

ROLL-TYPE DISPOSABLE

IONIZING

END REMOVED TO SHOW IN- NER WORKINGS

THROWAWAYS

HIGH EFFICIENCY PARTICULATE (HEPA)

Fig. 3-67. A few HVAC filters.

figurations, air grille designs, and room circulation patterns that mix the ozone thoroughly with the airflow. This method has one big drawback: in-haled ozone can damage one's lungs. Thus this method requires exact quantifying of the pollutant and its remover. Ozone is also slowly-reacting, so it takes long airflows to be fully effective.

➕ Does not reduce ducting airflow, can be installed in central ducting or individual rooms, requires no intermittent cleaning. Good when the unwanted microbes or organic gases can be quantified, and where considerable but not complete removal of the specified pollu-tant is satisfactory.

➖ Has no effect on particulates, requires extra equipment and extra energy to operate. Reacts slowly and nonreacting molecules are dangerous to human health.

The chart below indicates a filter's ability to remove pollutants from interior air. The dot's size indicates the filter's effectiveness at removing a particular pollutant: the larger the dot, the greater the effectiveness.

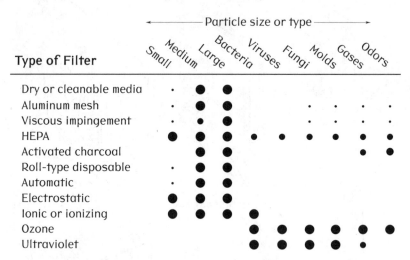

Fig. 3-68. Ability of filters to remove pollutants from air.

Air filters are typically installed in a rack or bank located just after the supply air fan in furnaces, heat pumps, and air handling units. Most small and medium-sized air conditioners use porous-media panel filters of about 30 percent efficiency to protect the equipment and reduce maintenance as well as benefit occupants. All filters require plenty of access area for inspection, cleaning and replacement. In small systems they should be no more than 8 ft above the floor, and they shouldn't be located above plumbing fixtures, large furniture, delicate equipment, or other hard-to-reach areas. In large systems each filter should have inspection/service access immediately before and after it. Air filters are typically selected as follows:

▶ Determine the size, concentration, and character of contaminants in the supply and return air. This may be done by general data, experience, or laboratory analysis.
▶ Determine the size of the particles that should be removed and the optimal efficiency of removal.
▶ Select a unit that combines the desired efficiency and economy of operation.

The following formula is used to find the effective airflow of a duct that is fitted with a filter of a particular resistance.

3)E) $Q_e = 100 \, Q_d/(100 - F)$

Q_e = effective filtered airflow in duct, fpm
Q_d = initial design airflow in duct, fpm
F = filter airflow resistance, or pore-to-solid ratio, in duct, %

> If a supply duct's established airflow requirement of 100 ft³/min requires a 40 percent efficient filter, how much should the duct's airflow be increased to maintain adequate airflow requirements?

Solution: In the Equivalent Filter Airflow Resistance Graph in Fig. 3-69, locate the intersection of the horizontal *filter adsorption efficiency* line of 40 percent with the vertical *supply air ventilation rate* line of 100 cfm, then read the increased airflow from the diagonal *revised air requirement* lines ➡ airflow increase ≈ 38 cfm. For electronic, ionizing, or charged media filters, reduce this value by 80 percent (i.e. multiply it by 0.20).

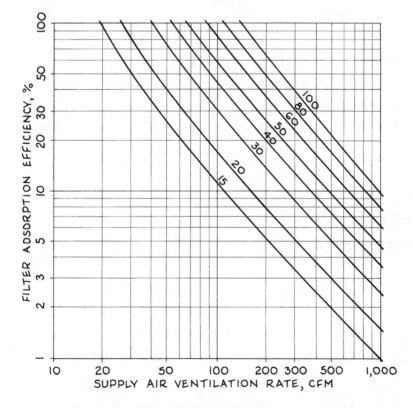

Fig. 3-69. Filter airflow resistance graph. †

† Forrest Fenci, "Managing School IAQ", *Engineered Systems* magazine (Busi-

CLIMATE CONTROL SYSTEM DESIGN DATA

Criteria	Amount

BUILDING, ROOM, OR SPACE _____

TEMPERATURE . . . .   _____ °F

RELATIVE HUMIDITY . . . .   _____ %

STATIC AIR PRESSURE   __ + __ - __ = _____ in. wg

AIR EFFICIENCY: PREFILTERED . . . .   _____ %

      FILTERED . . . .   _____ %

OUTSIDE AIR VENTILATION . . . .   _____ cfm

RECIRCULATION W/in ROOM OR SPACE?

    Yes _____ No _____ . . . .   _____ cfm or %

EXHAUST ALL AIR OUTDOORS?

    _____Yes _____ No _____ . . . .   _____ cfm or %

MINIMUM AIR CHANGE . . . .   _____ /hr

MAX. CO_2 LEVEL . . . .   _____ ppm

VOC SENSORS? TYPE, MIN. LEVEL . . .   _____ ppm

AUXILIARY HEAT GAIN: LIGHTS . . . .   _____ watts/sf

      OCCUPANTS . . . .   _____ Btu/hr

      EQUIPMENT . . . .   _____ Btu/hr

OCCUPANCY . . . _____ HR/DAY . . .   _____ days/wk

NOISE LEVEL . . . .   _____ dB

SPECIAL CONSIDERATIONS:

(This databox may be duplicated and
attached to drawings or

ness News Publishing co., Troy, MI); Feb 1995, p. 32.

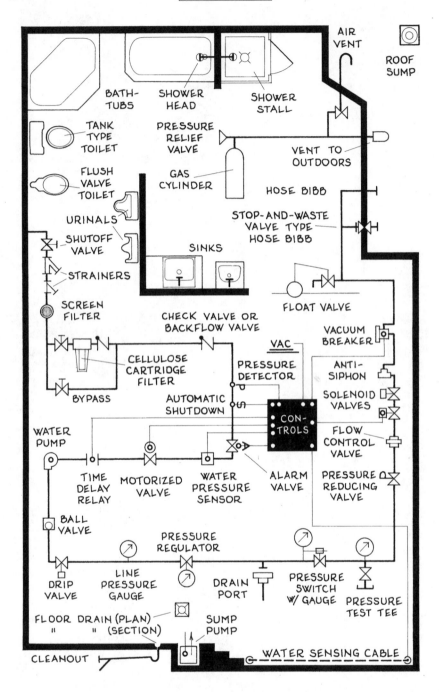

Plumbing symbols

PLUMBING

4.A. GENERAL

In today's buildings, all occupancies must be provided with a supply of drinkable water that has enough volume and pressure to make it easily available. This refers to all plumbing components needed to supply the water safely, and all required to carry it safely away.

Plumbing systems are chiefly *gravity-septic, well-septic,* or *meter-sewage.* In gravity-septic systems, the supply water arrives from a stream or other surface source located at an elevation above the building and acquires its pressure from gravity, then its waste discharges into a septic/leaching field at least 100 ft downstream from the surface source. In well-septic systems, the supply water arrives from a dug or drilled well and acquires its pressure from a pump, then the waste discharges into the same kind of septic/leaching network as does a gravity system. In meter-sewage systems the supply water enters from a pressurized public main, then the waste drains into a public sewer system. Gravity-sewage, well-sewage, and meter-septic systems are also possible, but uncommon.

A building's plumbing system has three parts: *supply* (the piping that brings the water to its points of use), *fixtures* (point-of-use receptacles that receive the supply water and discharge the waterborne wastes), and *waste* (the piping and venting that convey the wastes and any associated gases from its points of use to outside the building). The essential component is the fixtures: without them there is no need for the others. The chief criteria for designing a plumbing system are its number of fixtures, number of fixture units, supply main flow rate, and water pressure at the highest fixture. Initial cost is typically only a portion of projected life-cycle costs. For example, in commercial buildings a fixture's cost is usually no more than the cost to maintain it for a few months; thus any features that reduce maintenance costs usually pay for themselves quickly. When renovating existing buildings, all old piping should be cleaned or replaced.

The major plumbing authorities (BOCA, ICBO, SBCCI, and IAPMO) are planning a combined plumbing code, which hopefully will eliminate the alphabet soup of regulations regarding plumbing systems in buildings.

4.A.1. Initial Estimate

An initial estimate of a proposed building's water demands is often required at its earliest stages of design. There are four general kinds of water demand: *occupancy, climate control, fire protection,* and *special loads.* The water required for fire protection is computed separately from the others; because when it is needed, occupants are rarely imposing other demands on the water supply.

> What are the estimated average and peak water demands for a proposed 500 bed hospital near Atlanta, GA?

4)A)1)a) **Average demand:** $B_{awd} \cong \eta \, \theta_{awd} [1 + 0.00077 \, (T_d - 65)] + S$

    b) **Peak demand:** $\quad B_{pwd} \cong \eta \, \theta_{pwd} [1 + 0.00115 \, (T_d - 65)] + S$

B_{awd} = average water demand of building, ? gal/day
B_{pwd} = peak water demand of building, ? gpm
η = number of occupants in building, 500 units
θ_{awd} = average water demand per occupant, gal/day.
     From Table 4-1, θ_a for hospitals = 175 gal/day.
θ_{pwd} = peak water demand per occupant, gpm.
     From Table 4-1, θ_p for hospitals = 0.50 gpm.
T_d = summer design temperature for building location, °F.
     From Fig. 2-25, T_d for Atlanta area = 93°.
S = average or peak water demand of any special loads. None given.

$$B_{awd} \approx 500 \times 175 [1 + 0.00077 \, (93 - 65)] \approx 90{,}000 \text{ gal/day}$$
$$\theta_{pwd} \approx 500 \times 0.50 [1 + 0.00115 \, (93 - 65)] \approx 258 \text{ gpm}$$

TABLE 4-1: ESTIMATED WATER SUPPLY DEMANDS

OCCUPANCY	Average demand, gal/day-occ.	Peak demand, gal/min-occ.
Assembly, theaters, lecture halls, etc...	5 per seat + employees	0.17
Churches, mosques, synagogues	5 (add 5 for food service)	0.12
Factories, no showers	15	0.12
w/ showers	25	0.50
Hospitals	175	0.50
Hotels, motels	75	0.43
Offices, stores, airports, bus terminals	10 (add 5 for food service)	0.09
Residences: homes, apartments	100	0.33
Restaurants, dinner only	20	0.15
Two meals per day	35 (50 for 3 meals/day)	0.13
Schools, w/ food service	25	0.12
w/ gym & showers	30	0.40

4.B. FIXTURES

A plumbing fixture typically includes an *inlet* where the building's water supply arrives , a *receptacle* that temporarily contains the water for a specific purpose, and a *drain* where the portion of water that is unused but rendered impure plus any matter added to the water exits. Each fixture must also have a smooth nonabsorbent surface, have a small vent 1 in. below its rim that allows it to drain if its outlet becomes clogged (the vent's level is the fixture's *flood rim*), include a 1 in. air gap between the bottom of the inlet and the top of both the drain and flood rim, be adequately supported when filled, be well illuminated and ventilated, be free of concealed fouling surfaces, and have adequate space all around for cleaning. ADA Design Guidelines for plumbing fixtures are given in Volume 1, Sec. 8.L.

Lavatories: Small sinks that may be set in counters, hung from walls, or mounted on legs. Wall-hung models are the easiest to clean but the easiest to damage. Spouts waterflow should be laminar, quiet, and splash-free. Flat-bottomed models drain more slowly than ones with bowl-shapes, but they usually contain more volume below the rim and are more likely to preserve the trap seal. Each should have a 14–22 in. wide vanity on each side and a 24–30 in. deep aisle in front. Any exposed undersink plumbing of public lavatories should have thermally resistant coverings that prevent harm to wheelchair users. In trough and multiple-wash sinks, each 18 in. of outer rim equals one lavatory unit. Waste outlets require stoppage. Typical rim-to-floor heights: nursery school and kindergarten children = 26 in; grade school children = 28 in; all others: 32 in.

Sinks: These are larger lavatories for janitorial, kitchen, and laundry use as well as work sinks in schools and many industrial settings. The drain of each should have a basket strainer. Public buildings should have one janitorial sink per 100 occupants on each floor. Janitorial sink outlets require strainers and stoppage. Island sinks are usually vented by extending the drain below floor level (where its trap must be accessible from the space below) and pitching the vent $\frac{1}{4}$ in/ft upward under the floor to a vent stack in a nearby wall. Typical rim-to-floor heights: kindergarten children = 24 in; grade school children = 27 in; others = 32 in.

Bathtubs: Minimum size = 30 × 60 in, with at least 18 in. clearance on one side and at open ends. Waste outlets require stoppage. Any wall abutting a bathtub rim should be nonabsorbent to at least 6'-8" above the floor, have seamless corners, and contain a large molded shelf that can also function as a handle.

Showers: Minimum size = 30 × 34 in. with 30 in. clearance in front. Pan rims must be at least 2 in. above the stall floor if masonry (not counting rounding) and 6 in. above if steel. Average shower temperature ≈ 105°. Hot shower temperature ≈ 110°.

Toilets: These may be floor-mounted or wall-hung. The former is

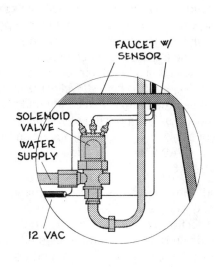

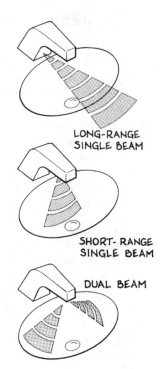

FAUCET w/ SENSOR

SOLENOID VALVE

WATER SUPPLY

12 VAC

LONG-RANGE SINGLE BEAM

SHORT-RANGE SINGLE BEAM

DUAL BEAM

Fig. 4-1. No-touch controls for plumbing fixtures.

more difficult to clean. Each requires at least 18 in. ¢-to-side clearance and 24 in. in front of its front edge. Elongated models with open-fronted seats are best for public use. The water closet compartment requires an openable window or mechanical exhaust ventilation, its walls must be impervious to water and easily cleanable, and its floor should be as large as space permits. For temporary locations at construction sites, carnivals, and other outdoor activities served by porto-potties, provide one unit per 30 occupants. Typical rim-to-floor heights: nursery school and kindergarten children = 12 in; grade school children = 14 in; others = 15 in.

Urinals: These may be stall, pedestal, or wall-mounted. Each requires 15 in. ¢-to-side clearance and 30 in. in front, nonabsorbent wall surfaces must extend 24 in. to each side and 4'-0" above the floor, and partitions are usually installed between them. Trough urinals are prohibited in permanent facilities. A new waterless urinal contains liquid whose specific gravity is less than the water in the bowl so the urine passes through the lighter liquid without requiring flushing while the latter maintains the fixture's trap seal, then the waste urine overflows into a concealed open drain.[†] Typical lip-to-floor heights: nursery school and kindergarten children = 14 in; grade school children = 18-20 in; all others = 22–24 in.

Drinking fountains: Generally one on each occupied floor in pub-

---

† Dave Barista, "The Need to know on Low-Flow", *Building Design & Construction*

lic facilities, located in circulation areas but not rest rooms. The bubbler must be above the basin's rim and hooded to deter saliva contamination. Where food is consumed indoors, water stations may be substituted for drinking fountains. Typical rim-to-floor height: pre- school children = 24 in; grade school children = 28 in; others = 40 in.

Dishwashers: Each requires a separate trap. Required hot water temperature for commercial dishwashers = 160–180°.

Other: Any water receptacle (fountain, pool, aquarium, baptistery, bidet, floor drain, etc.) that receives supply water or empties into waste systems is a plumbing fixture. In each case its unit supply or drainage flow rate (i.e. fixture unit value) must be specified.

One fixture unit has a theoretical peak liquid flow of 0.5 gpm (0.067 cfm) into or out of the fixture and a periodic flow rate of approximately 14 gal/day. Thus a standard plumbing fixture runs a theoretical 28 minutes per day. There are four kinds of fixture unit flows:

Cold water/flush valve toilets. Flush valve toilets consume more water than flush tank models. As systems increase in size, this difference lessens, which indicates a diversity factor for larger systems.

Cold water/flush tank toilets.

Hot water. This does not include water to toilets, hoses, and other cold-water-only fixtures.

Waste water. This is only water that flows down the drain, not water that evaporates, is drunk, is used for cooking, or is consumed by other activities. Waste waterflow normally equals 95 percent of supply waterflow.

Important design considerations for plumbing fixtures are:

Transient vs. static occupancies. Transient occupants typically use a fixture once and they're gone (e.g. restaurants, stores, hotels, and public assemblies), while static occupants use the same fixture frequently and are more familiar with them (e.g. residences, schools, offices, and other businesses). Fixtures for transient occupants should be simpler, more functional, and in compliance with ADA guidelines; while ones in static occupancies offer greater opportunity for stylish or decorative fixtures that satisfy individual desires.

Public vs. private occupancies. Public fixtures experience much more touching and banging than private ones; thus they should have stubbier handles and spouts, rounded corners, concealed supply and waste lines, and shutoff valves accessible to service personnel but not the public.

Wipedown vs. washdown cleaning requirements. *Wipedown* methods involve contacting the fixture with a rag or other handheld item, while *washdown* methods involve hoses or other remote devices. Rooms in which the latter is performed require floor drains.

An important new plumbing fixture development is *no-touch controls*, in which an infrared sensor turns the water on when a user nears the spout. These "smart handles" not only gratify a desire for water almost on neural impulse, they conserve water, reduce fixture wear and tear, are sanitary, reduce maintenance, and facilitate barrier-free access. Their operation may include a timer that delays shutoff several seconds after one's hands are removed (so the valve won't recycle on and off as one's hands move in and out of the zone) and a vandal-deterrent timer that activates shutoff if an obstruction remains in the zone. As the timers are susceptible to calibration drift due to fluctuating water pressures and debris buildups in the valve openings, they must be accessible by maintenance personnel. The actual no-touch controls may be:

Long-range single beam: this creates a long narrow detection zone that activates flow when one stands in front of the fixture. It is versatile but will activate waterflow if someone walks past the fixture.

Short-range single beam: this creates a fairly small detection zone under the spout within the lavatory bowl.

Short-range dual beam: small sensors on each side of the spout aim into the bowl; they detect a wider area and are more reliable.

The best no-touch controls have waterproof electronic components, vandal-proof assemblies, water-conserving flow restricters in the valves or spouts, and automatic shutoffs. Design should also consider the possibility of sunlight and mirror reflections activating any sensors, and of dark skin tones and dirty hands not reflecting infrared beams (some sensors have adjusters that allow settings at effective reception levels). Control circuitry may be 12 VAC or small batteries mounted in the spout or under the counter. No-touch controls have been installed in sinks, toilets, urinals, showerheads, fountains, even soap dispensers (one model squirts 2 cc of liquid soap with each activation of the faucet), and self-sensing dryers that are more sanitary and consume less electricity than push-button units. Another increasingly popular control is *thermostatic valves*: faucet handles with temperature scales that allow one to dial the desired water temperature before turning on the water. Their anti-scald upper limits (120° is common) make them especially desirable for small children, the disabled, and the elderly. Some models even have temperature settings and digital clock settings that can lower temperatures during sleeping hours or raise them during periods of maximum use.

An adventurous example of no-touch controls is in the Madonna Inn in San Luis Obispo, California. Here "caveman" urinals built of large rocks contain no-touch controls that send waterfalls cascading down the rocks when the fixture is used. How recently were these advanced activators installed? In 1960 when the Inn opened. [†]

Table 4-2 lists typical plumbing fixture requirements for common occupancies. However, in some occupancies user needs may vary consider-

---

[†] Tina Kelley, "Behind Smart Bathroom Fixtures: No Genie, Just Technology"; The

TABLE 4-2: PLUMBING FIXTURE REQUIREMENTS

NO. OF OCCUPANTS	LAVATORIES M	F	WATER CLOSETS M	F	URINALS M	FOUNTAINS

ASSEMBLY: theaters, auditoriums, lecture halls, concert halls, courtrooms, stadiums, gymnasiums, arenas, etc.:

To 100	1	2	1	2	1	1/75 occ.
To 200	2	3	1	4	1	"
To 500	3	5	2	8	2	"
500+	1/175	1/100	1/250	1/65	1/250	"

DORMITORIES: school or labor, per floor:

To 20	2	2	1	2	1	1/75 occ.
20+	1/20	1/15	1/40	1/20	1/60	"

Bathtubs or showers, M or F: 1/8–150 occ., 1/20 above 150 occ.

EATING PLACES: restaurants, cafeterias, cafes, dining halls, etc.:

To 50	1	1	1	2	1	1/75 occ.
To 100	1	2	1	3	1	"
100+	1/125	1/80	1/200	1/50	1/200	"

Each kitchen must have its own rest room with lavatory and toilet

HOSPITALS: ward rooms, per floor:

Per patient	1/10	1/10	1/8	1/8	0	1/75 pat.

INDUSTRIAL: warehouses, shops, factories, foundries, etc., per floor:

To 50	1	2	1	2	1	1/75 occ.
To 100	2	3	1	4	1	"
To 250	3	5	2	8	2	"
250+	1/60	1/50	1/100	1/30	1/100	"

INSTITUTIONAL: other than hospital or penal: residents, per floor:

	1/10	1/10	1/25	1/25	1/50	1/75 occ.

Patients' bathtubs or showers, M or F: 1/8 occ. on each occupied floor
Staff: same as office or public buildings

NIGHT CLUBS: discotheques, lounges, bars, casinos, amusement parks, etc.

	1/150	1/100	1/150	1/75	1/150	1/75 occ.

OFFICE OR PUBLIC BUILDINGS: public & employees, per floor:

To 50	1	2	1	2	1	1/75 occ.
To 125	2	3	1	4	1	"
To 300	3	5	2	8	2	"
300+	1/75	1/65	1/150	1/40	1/150	"

PENAL INSTITUTIONS: employee use, per floor:

	1/30	1/30	same as office		1/50	1/75 occ.

Prisoners: 1 lavatory & toilet/cell, 1 drinking ftn/cell block floor

RELIGIOUS: churches, synagogues, mosques, kingdom halls, etc.

	1/150	1/100	1/150	1/75	1/150	1/75 occ.

SCHOOLS: nursery, elementary, child care centers, per floor:

	1/50	1/50	1/100	1/35	1/40	1/75 occ.

Middle school, high school, college, trade, adult education:

	1/60	1/50	1/100	1/45	1/60	1/75 occ.

New York Times; date unknown [late 2000]. [†]This table was originally adapted

ably. For example, "Schools" may be kindergarten (which should have a lavatory next to each classroom), elementary (which require low and high toilets, sinks, and mirrors), or high school (which need vandal-resistant fixtures and showers). Recent research also indicates that women, due to anatomical differences, more restrictive clothing, and childcare activities, spend more than twice as much time in rest rooms per visit than men, and 90 percent of women wash their hands after relieving themselves compared to 30 percent for men. Thus if men and women visit public rest rooms equally, a modular 'potty parity' public rest room should have two toilets, two urinals, and three lavatories for men and eight toilets and five lavatories for women. Thus the traditional 'butterfly' bathroom plan —of equal 'wings' on each side of a chase 'spine'— is woefully inequitable. Accordingly, the fixture requirements in Table 4-2 are a revision of standard Code data.

When a plumbing fixture is served by both hot and cold water, its fixture load is often considered to be 0.75 the values listed in Table 4-2 for the hot and cold water supply loads at each outlet.

Example 1. How many fixture units are in the plan in Fig. 4-2?

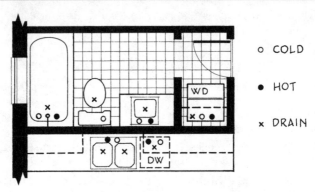

COLD

HOT

DRAIN

Fig. 4-2. Partial houseplan showing plumbing fixtures.

4)B)1)
$$F_T = F_1 + F_2 + ... + F_z$$

F_T = total number of fixture units in plan, ? f.u.
F_1 = number of fixture units for each plumbing fixture, f.u.
   From Table 4-3, F_1 for flush tank bathroom unit = 6 f.u.
F_2 = number of fixture units for clothes washer, from Table 4-3, 2 f.u.
F_3 = number of fixture units for kitchen sink, from Table 4-3, 2 f.u.

$$F_T = 6 + 2 + 2 + 2 = 12 \text{ f.u.}$$

Step 1. Find the occupancy load per floor. If occupancies vary from floor to floor, proceed to Step 2 for each floor.

Example 2. How many plumbing fixtures are required in a two-story office building with 75 men and 57 women employees if an approximately equal number of employees are on each floor?

4)B)2) $\Theta = F\eta$

Θ = total occupancy load of building, 75 men and 57 women
F = occupancy load per floor, **?** occupants
η = number of floors in building, 2 floors

    Men: 75 = $F \times 2$ ... F = 38 occupants
    Women: 57 = $F \times 2$ ... F = 29 occupants

Step 2. Find the required number of fixtures for each floor from Table 4-2. Enter the graph at OFFICE OR PUBLIC BUILDINGS, public & employees per floor, then proceed to the line "To 50 [employees]" ➡ the answer is one lavatory and one water closet and one urinal for 38 men, two lavatories and two water closets for 29 women, and one fountain per floor.

Note: Standard fixture unit values notwithstanding, a typical shower runs for about 10 minutes at 5 gpm ≈ 50 gal of water consumed, while a typical tub contains about 30 gal of water consumed.

═══ TABLE 4-3: PLUMBING FIXTURE UNIT VALUES ═══

FIXTURE	FIXTURE UNITS, priv.	pub.	Minimum pressure, psf
Urinal: flush tank, pedestal, siphon jet, blowout	2	4	15
Flush valve, stall, wall lip, or washout	2	8	15
Toilet: flush tank	3	4	8
Flush valve	6	8	15
Lavatory or wash sink	1	2	8
Dental lavatory, resid. kitchen waste grinder	1	1	8
Self-closing faucet	1	1	12
Bathtub: no shower	2	4	8
With shower	2	4	12
Stall shower	2	2	12
Bidet	3	–	8
Bathroom (wc, lav, tub): flush tank wc = 6; flush valve wc in priv. bath			8
Kitchen or service sink, DW, clothes washer	2	3	8
Bar sink	1	3	8
Drinking fountain	–	1	15
Water cooler	–	1	8
Hose bibb	2	4	30
Fire hose	0	0	30
Lawn sprinkler ... Coverage area × ½ in. depth of water/hr. (0.3 gal/hr-ft²)			

New York, 1987), p. 7-21; then this table was revised based on Gregg Lieder-

4.C. SUPPLY PLUMBING

Supply plumbing includes all piping and related components from the water source to the fixtures. The componentry running from source to building must be laid below the local frost line. The water supply piping is often exposed to the following additional subsoil conditions which could cause it to leak or rupture:

▸ Seasonal expansion/contraction due to temperature changes in the surrounding earth. You have to go about 21 ft down before temperatures become uniform year-round.

▸ Earth settling, either due to intermittent shifting caused by saturation by heavy rains or to vibrations from heavy vehicular traffic, nearby railways, etc.

▸ Corrosion of metal piping in moist subsoils due to galvanic reaction with buried metals, woods, cinders, de-icing salts percolating into the soil, high- or low-pH groundwater, fertilizers, or large roots of dead trees. Even lumps of clay backfill in sandy soil will corrode metal pipes at points of clay contact.

▸ Electrical discharges from nearby ground rods. These should be buried at least 10 ft from any below-grade piping.

Thus water supply piping should be installed below grade as follows:

▸ Make the burial trench at least 12 in. wide on each side.
▸ Shovel-backfill with clean sand 6 in. above and below each pipe.
▸ Cover the piping with resin paper or strips of 90 lb roofing felt on top of the sand backfill.
▸ In meter-sewage systems, place the main above and to one side of the sewer (see Fig. 4-3). Never locate the sewer above the main, one above the other, or side-by-side.

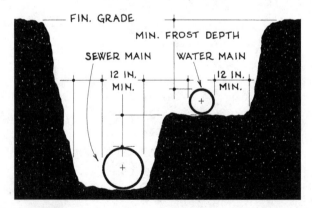

Fig. 4-3. Location of plumbing mains & sewers in a trench.

▸ Sleeve the piping where driveways cross over it with conduit of at least 4 in. larger diameter; and do not pass piping under footings but sleeve it through the foundation wall above.
▸ Know that the only sure data-gathering is onsite inspection.
▸ Retain plan records of exact dimensions where piping is laid.

A supply water main typically requires just inside the building (1) a service valve, (2) an accessible strainer that removes any grit or other particles from the inflowing water, (3) an easily visible meter that measures the waterflow, (4) a backflow preventer that keeps any water in the building from flowing backward and contaminating the public water supply, (5) a shut-off valve with a drain port for emptying the plumbing system if necessary, and (6) a protective air gap between the drain port and a nearby floor drain. If these components are below grade, the floor should slope at least $\frac{1}{8}$ in/LF from enclosing walls toward a central drain that empties into a sump pump connected to emergency power, and the walls should have continuous water sensing cable 1 in. above the floor that is connected to a 24-hour-a-day monitor/alarm upstairs. If all service componentry is above grade, its drain port may flow via gravity to a spill tap and splash block just outdoors.

W = WATER SERVICE FROM PUBLIC MAIN	8. UTILITY ROOM FLOOR DRAIN
1. WATER SERVICE VALVE	9. PRESSURE TEST TEE
2. STRAINER	10. THRUST BLOCKS AS REQ.
3. METER	11. DRAINAGE BACKFLOW VALVES
4. BACKFLOW VALVE	12. SUMP PUMP W/ EMERGENCY POWER
5. SHUTOFF VALVE	13. WATER SENSING CABLE
6. DRAIN PORT W/ FIXED AIR GAP	14. WATER SENSING CABLE LEAD TO MONITOR/ALARM STATION
7. FLOOR DRAIN W/ STANDPIPE	

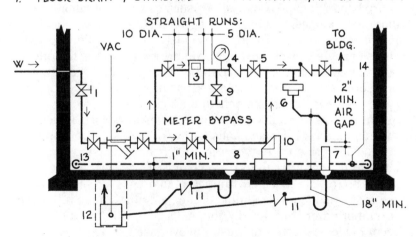

Fig. 4-4. Typical plumbing service components for commercial buildings. [†]

In meter/sewage systems (and a few well/septic systems), the water supply may be *upfeed* (water is pumped up from the lowest floor by initial pressure from the supply main or holding tank) or *downfeed* (water is pumped to a tank on or near the roof then flows by gravity down to the fixtures). The lowest floors fed have the highest pressures. Supply main pressure is typically 50–70 psi, and this must deliver at least 15 psi and no more than 60 psi to every fixture in the building. Technically a sink or tub or shower may have an inlet pressure as low as 8 psi, but one's plumbing is usually connected to a nearby toilet whose minimum inlet pressure is always 15 psi.

A water main's initial pressure must be great enough to overcome all reductions due to pipe length, wall irregularities, number of fittings, and net vertical distance traveled while still delivering the required pressure at the remote outlet. However, piping design is a highly inexact science due to the following:

▸ The fundamental piping design parameter, *fixture unit flow*, is a rough estimate based on continuous vs. intermittent water demands in a great variety of occupancies, which is then used to estimate supply delivery rates, pipe diameters, and component capacities. Thus using this value is a bit like rounding off your own weight to the nearest hundred pounds.

▸ Another important design variable, *pipe flow friction loss*, varies widely because it is too tedious to sum all the tiny increments of flow friction loss caused by each valve, tee, elbow, and other fitting in every system; thus instead an average loss is usually taken, based on "normal pressure drop and normal number of fittings." Flow friction losses also increase unpredictably at sharp bends, in pipe constrictions such as valve thresholds and diameter changes, and in runs exceeding 80 ft.

▸ Initial water pressure often varies widely. Municipal water pressures are often several psi higher in the morning than the afternoon and are often higher in October than July; and the initial pressure of any water tank varies considerably as its pump cycles between cutoff and activation modes.

▸ As water flows through a pipe, a viscous shear occurs between the fluid and its enclosing walls that varies considerably with changes in temperature (water at 40° F is twice as viscous as water at 90° and four times as much at 170°).

▸ In this era of increased environmental awareness, rising water use costs, and legal mandating of efficient plumbing fixtures, the amount of water traditionally equated with one fixture unit is becoming less, which could result in oversized system components and sluggish waterflow that could cause more stoppages.

▸ Our technological age is seeing a proliferation of piping design

p. 37.   † From p. 257: Joseph Pietro, "A Practical Approach to Backflow Prevention",

software that lulls the user into believing that all the above variables are nonexistent —that the perfect diameter for any pipe lies only a double-click away. On the contrary! Not only does a successful designer need to be keenly aware of all the above variations every LF of the way, he or she must have a perceptive understanding of how all the subtle plumbing puzzle pieces fit together into complete and coherent systems.

From the above it is easy to see why supply piping design is highly inexact, why approximations are acceptable, and why all solutions should include a slight safety factor. Due to the vagaries involved, it usually pays to organize all initial data into an accurately scaled building schematic that shows floor-to-floor heights, piping dimensions, initial pressure ranges, remote pressure requirements, fixture unit values at every outlet, and conversion of any nonfixture demands to equivalent flow. Every LF of piping should also (1) be heated above 32°, (2) be pitched slightly, (3) have taps that allow drainage from peaks to valleys, (4) have enough chase and riser space to allow movement due to thermal expansion, (5) be supported closely enough to prevent pipe sags between supports, (6) have its contained weight added to structural calculations, and (7) be accessible for maintenance and future upgrading. Hot and cold pipes should also be spaced at least 6 in. apart or have insulation placed between them to prevent heat interchange; and in top-quality work both pipes should be insulated, hot water to minimize heat loss and cold water to prevent surface condensation.

Below is a brief description of common kinds of supply piping.

Copper [†]

This piping is available in soft and hard tempers and several weights. Soft-tempered copper, also known as annealed copper or flexible copper tubing, is usually sold in $\frac{1}{2}$ and $\frac{3}{4}$ in. diameters and rolls to 100 ft long; it is typically installed in short lengths that cause little pipe friction, where flexible fixture leads are desired, where the pipe must be bent around obstacles or in confined areas where soldered fittings are impractical, and where slightly greater resistance to freezing is desired. Hard-tempered copper, also known as *drawn tubing*, is sold in straight lengths up to 20 ft and in four common weights: *K* (the heaviest, it may be used for all underground and interior service), *L* (used for above-ground service only), *M* (used only for above-ground supply, waste, and vents), and *DWV* (the lightest; used only for above-ground drain, waste, and vents). Types *K, L,* and *M* are color-coded (the ID printing on type *K* is green, on *L* is blue, and on *M* is red). Type *K* tubing usually costs about 25 percent more than type *L*, which generally costs about 25 percent more than type *M*. Connections are usually soldered but may be threaded. Nominal diameters are $\frac{1}{2}$, $\frac{3}{4}$, 1, $1\frac{1}{4}$, $1\frac{1}{2}$, 2, $2\frac{1}{2}$, 3, 4, 6, 8, 10, and 12 in. Outer diameters are $\frac{1}{8}$ in. greater than nominal sizes, and wall thicknesses vary as exemplified by the few pipe sizes and types listed below:

Nom. dia., in.	$\frac{1}{2}$	$\frac{3}{4}$	1	$1\frac{1}{2}$	2	3	4	6
Type K	.049	.065	.065	.072	.083	.109	.134	.192
Type L	.040	.045	.050	.060	.070	.090	.110	.140
Type M	.028	.032	.035	.049	.058	.072	.095	.122

➕ Lightweight, easy to install, versatile, resists rust, is highly resistant to air and salt water.

➖ Cannot be used to transport steam or any liquids or gases > 300° F, pressures >150 psi, or velocities > 8.0 fps. Only type K pipe can be used for fire sprinkler systems. Cannot carry highly acidic or alkaline wastes or be exposed to aggressive soil conditions.

Plastic

The most common kinds of plastic piping are:

ABS (acrylonitrile-butadiene-styrene): a rigid black pipe that is fairly strong and economical. Typical diameters are $1\frac{1}{4}$, $1\frac{1}{2}$, 2, $2\frac{1}{2}$, 3, 4, and 6 in; maximum pressure = 40 psi at 100°. The most common plastic piping for drains and vents.

PVC (polyvinyl chloride): a rigid white pipe that is strong and economical. It resists most acids and alkalis but not chlorinated hydrocarbons and certain solvents. Typical diameters are $1\frac{1}{4}$, $1\frac{1}{2}$, 2, $2\frac{1}{2}$, 3, 4, and 6 in; maximum pressure = 40 psi at 100°; maximum temperature for nonpressure use = 180°. Used for cold water supply, drain, waste, vent, and some process piping.

CPVC (chlorinated polyvinyl chloride): a cream-colored rigid pipe that is very strong and has a chemical resistance similar to PVC. Common diameters are $\frac{1}{2}$ and $\frac{3}{4}$ in; maximum pressure = 100 psi at 180°. Used for hot and cold water supply as well as process piping.

PE (polyethylene): a flexible tubing that can be snaked through walls and around corners, can bend without breaking when buried in settling soil, and is highly resistant to unusual soil conditions. Typical diameters are $\frac{3}{4}$, 1, $1\frac{1}{2}$, and 2 in; maximum pressure = 40 psi at 100°; maximum temperature for nonpressure use = 180°. Used for low-pressure cold water underground services.

PB (polybutane): a flexible tubing that can also be snaked through walls and around corners. Connections are usually compression type; it cannot be solvent-welded. Typical diameters are $\frac{3}{4}$, 1, $1\frac{1}{2}$, and 2 in; maxi-

---

pp 37–40. † From p. 259: Much of the information on copper piping was obtained

mum pressure = 40 psi at 180°; maximum temperature for nonpressure use = 200°. Used for low-pressure hot and cold water supply. Since chlorinated water conveyed by PB piping has caused its acetyl fittings to leak, manufacturers have discontinued this piping, even though the acetyl fittings can be replaced by metal ones.

Common connections for the above plastic pipes are solvent cemented, threaded, and clamped/inserted fittings.

PEX (crosslinked polyethylene): [†] a recently developed flexible tubing that is strong, light (a 300 ft coil of $\frac{1}{2}$ in. tubing weighs only 16 lb), nontoxic, and resistant to high temperatures, pressures, and corrosion. The tubing's flexibility also allows it to be snaked through small openings, enables small pipes and bends to be installed in small and hard-to-reach areas, and reduces the likelihood of bursting due to freezing. After being heated its molecular structure returns to its original size, shape, and strength; thus watertight connections are easily made onsite. Typical diameters are $\frac{3}{8}$, $\frac{1}{2}$, $\frac{3}{4}$, and 1 in; maximum pressure = 160 psi at 73°, 100 psi at 180°, 80 psi at 200°; and an assortment of copper/PEX fittings are available. Minimum bend radii = 3 in @ $\frac{3}{8}$ in. diameter, $3\frac{3}{4}$ in @ $\frac{1}{2}$ in, $5\frac{1}{4}$ in @ $\frac{3}{4}$ in, and $6\frac{3}{4}$ in @ 1 in. It is used for hot and cold water supply, radiant and baseboard heating, snow melting, irrigation. **NG** for natural gas.

➕ Lowest cost, lightest weight, simplest assembly. Resistant to normal groundwater acids and alkalis. Best for irrigation of lawns, gardens, athletic fields, golf courses, and other unsleeved low-pressure underground installations.

➖ Is more easily cracked or crushed than copper or steel, has high coefficient of expansion, is brittle at low temperatures, loses strength above 180° F, and cannot withstand pressures above 100 psi. Pipes flex when water is turned off, making them prone to fatigue-cracking over time, thus they require frequent support. Usually not allowed for commercial plumbing.

Steel

Steel piping is available in galvanized or black types in standard (the most common), extra heavy, and double extra heavy weights. Galvanized pipe resists rust better, but black is the finest piping if it is to be exposed to fire or high temperatures. Connections are threaded. Common diameters are $\frac{1}{4}$, $\frac{3}{8}$, $\frac{1}{2}$, $\frac{3}{4}$, 1, $1\frac{1}{4}$, $1\frac{1}{2}$, 2, $2\frac{1}{2}$, 3, 4, 5, 6, 8, 10, and 12 in.

➕ Best for high temperatures, pressures, and velocities. Lowest coefficient of expansion. The strongest piping; thus its lengths require the least support.

➖ Expensive, heavy, brittle in very cold temperatures.

Cast Iron

This piping is available in standard, ductile iron (stronger and more corrosion-resistant), and high-silica (acid-resistant); it is used for sanitary waste, vent, storm drain, and other non-pressure applications. Modern connections are hub-and-spigot with neoprene gaskets (best for most underground assemblies), and no-hub with stainless steel worm-gear clamps (more economical, usually best above grade). Unit lengths are usually 3–4 ft; common diameters are 2, 3, 4, and 6 in.

➕ Low material cost, easy to assemble, unaffected by fire, resistant to subsurface corrosion.

➖ Heavy, high labor costs, can't be used for pressure situations. Bell and hub types are **NG** for water supply.

Sometimes two pipes of different metals must be connected together. This often occurs in renovations where copper piping must attach to old galvanized steel piping. In such situations the two dissimilar metals must never touch each other; otherwise galvanic corrosion will destroy one of them. This is avoided by installing (1) a *dielectric union*, a threaded connection that holds a rubber washer and plastic collar between the two dissimilar metals; (2) a *dielectric coupling*, a threaded steel sleeve with a plastic inner liner that separates the two metals; or (3) an *alternative dielectric fitting*, a nipple with a brass coupling on each side which, when threaded with the two pipes, forms a nonreactive metal connection between them. These three connections are sketched in fig. 4-5.

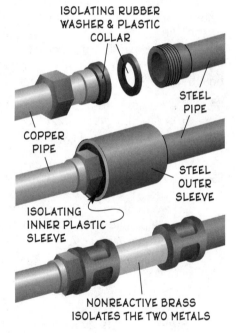

Fig. 4-5. Dielectric unions for pipes of dissimilar metals.

As important as the pipe is the water. What is its mineral, particulate, and air content? Is it acidic, alkaline, neutral, hard, soft? A water sample should always be tested by a laboratory prior to plumbing system design, because this may influence the selection of piping, fittings, filters, softeners, and other components.

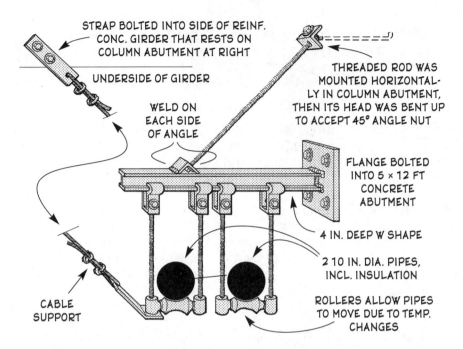

Fig. 4-6. Innovative piping support in Grand Central Station.

Another important, and often overlooked, aspect of supply plumbing is the piping's filled weight. Especially with large-diameter plumbing, each intermittent support must be carefully designed to carry sometimes a ton of load as the filled pipe snakes through plenums, cavities, and other utilitarian voids in the construction and possibly experiences constant changes in temperature. Such supports often require a design ingenuity that far exceeds what would seem appropriate for such subservient utilitarian conveyances —until one considers the result of its absence. Such an ingeniously designed support is shown in Fig. 4-6.

A good rule of thumb for estimating unusual water supply demands is to multiply the average hourly load by 2.0 to 2.5.

> **Example 1.** What is the pressure at the bottom of a vertical water-filled pipe that is 72 ft tall?

4)C)a)
$$\Delta P = 0.433 \, \Delta h$$

ΔP = pipe pressure drop due to increased height, **?** psi
Δh = change in height that induces pressure drop, 72 ft

$$\Delta P = 0.433 \times 72 = 31.2 \text{ psi E}$$

the information on PEX plastic piping was obtained from the *AQUAPEX Install-*

> **Example 2.** Considering the formula in Example 1, what is the maximum height of a plumbing pipe if the water pressure at the top must be 15 psi and the water supply pressure at the bottom cannot exceed 60 psi?

4)C)a)
$$\Delta P = 0.433 \, \Delta h$$

ΔP = pipe pressure drop due to increased height, psi. Here ΔP = pressure at the bottom - pressure at the top = 60 - 15 = 45 psi.
Δh = change in height that induces pressure drop, **?** ft

$$45 = 0.433 \times \Delta h \quad \dots \Delta h = 104 \text{ ft}$$

Note: This is an important dimension for plumbing system design in tall buildings. This is because each plumbing fixture must have a pressure between 15 psi and 60 psi; thus the source of these pressures can be no more than 104 vertical ft above or below the remote fixture. Thus in tall buildings, unitary plumbing systems of no more than this height are usually piggybacked on top of each other for the height of the building.

> **Example 3.** If water flows through a short length of Schedule 40 steel pipe at 80 gal/min, what is the pipe's optimal diameter?

4)C)b)
$$Þ = 15 \, d^2$$

$Þ$ = waterflow rate in pipe at normal temperature and pressure, 80 gpm.
d = optimal inside diameter of copper, steel, or plastic pipe, **?** in.

$$80 = 15 \, d^2 \quad \dots d = 2.31 \rightarrow 2\tfrac{1}{2} \text{ in.}$$

> **Example 4.** In the pipe above, what is the waterflow rate in ft/sec?

4)C)c)
$$Þ_{gpm} = 2.45 \, Þ_{fps} \, d^2$$

$Þ_{gpm}$ = volume of waterflow in pipe, from Example 3, 80 gpm
$Þ_{fps}$ = velocity or waterflow in pipe, **?** fps
d = nominal inner pipe diameter, from Example 3, 2.5 in.

$$80 = 2.45 \, Þ_{fps} \times 2.5^2 \quad \dots Þ_{fps} = 5.22 \text{ fps}$$

> **Example 5.** What is the contained weight of the pipe in Example 4?

4)C)d)
$$\omega_t = \omega_p + 0.34 \, d^2$$

ation Handbook, 5th edition, © 1996 Wirsbro Inc., Apple Valley, MN.

ω_t = total unit weight of pipe and contained water, **?** plf
ω_p = unit weight of pipe, plf. From Table 4-4, unit weight for $2\frac{1}{2}$ in.
       diameter Schedule 40 steel pipe = 5.79 plf.
d = inner pipe diameter, in. From Table 4-4, inner dia. of $2\frac{1}{2}$ in. nom.
       Schedule 40 steel pipe = 2.47 in.

$$\omega_t = 5.79 + 0.34 \times 2.47^2 = 7.86 \text{ plf}$$

Example 6. An eight-unit apartment is served by a submersible well pump and pressure tank system whose maximum pressure is 60 psi. If each apartment has 14 fixture units, the toilets are flush tank, maximum length of piping is 68 ft, head is 23 ft, and required pressure at the highest fixture is 12 lb/in, size the service main.

Step 1. Estimate the pipe pressure drop due to coldwater flow friction.

4)C)e) $L \Delta P \approx 57\, P_i - 67\, P_h - 29\, H$

L = effective length of pipe (includes safety factors for normal meter
       pressure drop and normal number of fittings), 68 ft
Δ_P = estimated pipe pressure drop for length of run, **?** psi
P_i = initial or minimum water pressure, 60 psi
P_h = required pressure at highest or farthest fixture outlet, 12 psi
H = height of flow, or head, 23 ft

$$68\, \Delta P \approx 57 \times 60 - 67 \times 12 - 29 \times 23 \quad \ldots \Delta P \approx 28.7 \text{ psi}$$

TABLE 4-4: FILLED WEIGHTS OF COMMON PIPING

PIPE DIA. nom. in.	STEEL Sch. 40	STEEL Sch. 80	COPPER Type K	COPPER Type L	COPPER Type M	ABS	PVC	CPVC
$\frac{3}{8}$	0.65	0.80	0.32	0.26	0.21	0.16	0.20	0.23
$\frac{1}{2}$	0.98	1.19	0.44	0.39	0.31	0.25	0.32	0.36
$\frac{3}{4}$	1.36	1.66	0.83	0.66	0.55	0.38	0.50	0.56
1	2.05	2.48	1.18	1.01	0.84	0.60	0.78	0.88
$1\frac{1}{4}$	2.92	3.55	1.57	1.44	1.25	0.95	1.23	1.40
$1\frac{1}{2}$	3.21	4.39	2.11	1.91	1.73	1.25	1.62	1.83
2	5.10	6.30	3.36	3.09	2.83	1.94	2.51	2.84
$2\frac{1}{2}$	7.86	9.49	4.94	4.55	4.15	2.85	3.68	4.17
3	10.77	13.11	6.87	6.31	5.70	4.22	5.45	6.17
4	16.30	19.96	11.56	10.56	9.92	6.96	9.00	10.17
5	23.28	28.65	17.47	15.70	14.84	10.62	13.73	15.53
6	31.48	39.86	25.07	21.81	20.66	15.01	19.39	21.95

Values are in lb/LF

Step 2. Convert any nonfixture unit flow to equivalent fixture unit flow.

$$Þ_e \approx \kappa_f (F_c + 0.071 \, F_n)$$

$Þ_e$ = total equivalent fixture unit flow through pipe, ? f.u.
κ_f = pipe friction factor. $\kappa_p = 2.0$ if pipe is cast iron, wrought iron, galvanized iron, or steel; 1.0 if copper or brass. Here $f_p = 1.0$.
F_c = coldwater fixture unit flow, f.u.
    $F_c = 14$ fixture units per apt. × 8 apartments = 112 f.u.
F_n = equivalent nonfixture unit flow, if any, gal/day. Here $F_n = 0$.

$$Þ_e \approx 1.00 \times 1.0 \, (112 + 0.08 \times 0) \approx 112 \text{ f.u.}$$

Step 3. From Fig. 4-7 find the minimum pipe diameter from the intersection of the vertical *fixture unit line* with the horizontal *pressure drop line*; at this point also note the water velocity in fps. At 112 fixture units (flush tank) and a pressure drop of 28.7 psi, minimum pipe diameter ➡ 3 in. type *M* copper and water velocity ≈ 25 fps.

Step 4. If the water velocity ≥ 8 fps, resize the pipe as below. In most systems a reasonable upper limit for water velocity is 6 fps.

$$d_r \geq 0.0156 \, d \, v^{0.5}$$

d_r = resized pipe diameter, if necessary, ? in.
d = previous pipe diameter, from Step 3, 3 in.
v = flow velocity through pipe, fps. From Step 3,
    $v \approx 25$ fps. ➡ ≥ 8 fps, ∴ pipe requires resizing.

$$d_r \geq 0.0156 \times 3 \times 25^{0.5} \geq 5.3 \quad ➡ \quad 5 \text{ in. dia. } \textbf{OK}$$

Example 7. A four-story office building requires a copper water supply main from the city main which has a street pressure of 50 psi. If the building has 176 flush valve fixture units, the piping from main to farthest fixture is 260 ft long, the head from the main to a roof cooling tower spigot is 46 ft, and this spigot requires the system's maximum flow pressure of 30 psf, size the supply main.

Step 1. Compute the pipe pressure drop due to coldwater flow friction.

$$L \Delta P \approx 57 \, P_i - 67 \, P_m - 29 \, H$$

L = length of pipe, 260 ft
ΔP = estimated pipe pressure drop for maximum length of run, ? psi
P_i = minimum initial water pressure, 50 psi
P_m = required fixture pressure at highest or farthest outlet, 30 psi

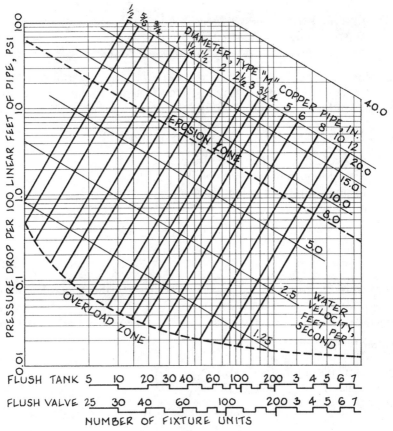

EROSION ZONE: AT VELOCITIES ABOVE UPPER DOTTED
LINE, PIPE EROSION MAY OCCUR; CHOOSE LARGER DIA-
METER PIPE.

OVERLOAD ZONE: AT VELOCITIES BELOW LOWER DOTTED
LINE, PLUMBING SYSTEM LOAD IS TOO GREAT OR INCOM-
ING PRESSURE IS TOO LOW; REDESIGN SYSTEM.

Fig. 4-7. Pipe diameter sizing graph. [†]

H = height of flow, or head, 46 ft

$$260\ P \approx 57 \times 50 - 67 \times 30 - 29 \times 46 - 18 \times 10 \qquad ... \Delta P \approx -2.75\ \text{psi}$$

Note: When ΔP is either minus or so low that it falls in the overload zone
in Fig. 4-7, the initial water pressure is not enough to overcome the pressure drop created by the pipe's length, head, and flow pressure demands.
Then the system must be redesigned, either by increasing the initial pipe
pressure and/or decreasing the pressure drop by dividing the piping into
smaller systems.

[†] This graph was adapted from the *Building Construction Handbook, 3rd Edi-*

> **Example 8.** What is the equivalent length of a 60 ft long 2 in. diameter pipe that has 24 elbows in it?

Solution: As the pipe's length has a greater-than-normal number of fittings, its equivalent length may be found from the formula below. This formula is valid if each elbow's radius ≈ 3 × pipe diameter.

4]C]f]
$$L_e \approx L + 1.33\,\eta\,\delta$$

L_e = equivalent length of pipe with elbows, ? ft
L = actual length of pipe with elbows, 60 ft
η = number of elbows in length of pipe, 24
δ = diameter of piping, 2 in.

$$L_e \approx 60 + 1.33 \times 24 \times 2 \approx 124 \text{ ft}$$

> **Example 9.** What is the equivalent length of a fully open 3 in. diameter gate valve?

4]C]g]
$$L_e \approx 6\,\delta$$

L_e = equivalent length of gate valve, ? ft
δ = diameter of gate valve, 3 in.

$$L_e \approx 6 \times 3 \approx 18 \text{ ft}$$

4.C.1. Thermal Expansion

When a pipe experiences temperature changes, whether due to the water in it or the air around it, the pipe can shorten or lengthen. This is true not only for water supply piping but also waste piping. Fig. 4-8 shows the approximate deformations of certain installed piping configurations.

Thus all piping must be free to move due to thermal expansion; but at the same time all such piping must be firmly supported. The way to do both is to (1) install snug fasteners that hold each pipe firmly in place laterally but let it move longitudinally, (2) do not install fasteners within 16 diameters of any tee or elbow, (3) in any straight run exceeding about 10 ft for hot water pipes and 20 ft for cold water pipes install a bend, gooseneck, or other configuration that allows the ends to move longitudinally, (4) leave at least 2 in. space beyond the end of every length of piping, on the other side

tion; Frederick Merritt (McGraw-Hill, New York, 1975); p. 21-26.

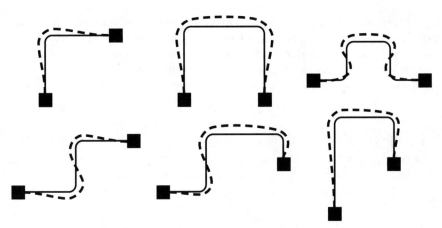

Fig. 4-8. Deformations of pipe shapes subjected to thermal expansion.

of every tee stem, and on both inside directions of each elbow. Such fasteners not only firmly support the pipe and allow it move thermally, they will further protect it from building settling, vibrations, and any movement of surrounding soil. A good expansion joint for large commercial piping is a *swing joint*, shown in Fig. 4-9. This forgiving joinery is also excellent protection against earthquakes.

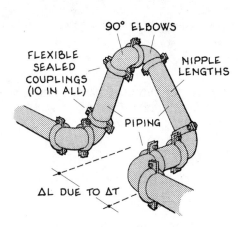

Fig. 4-9. Swing joint.

Another kind of piping thermal expansion occurs when the water expands much more rapidly than the pipe containing it. This doesn't happen very often, but when it does the result can be disastrous. For example, if the temperature in a large hot water heater for an industrial facility increases by 80° F after a shift change in which many employees take a shower, the resulting quick depletion and immediate reheating of the hot water supply can create a large pressure increase in the pipes leading into and out of the heater tank. If these lines have a supply-side check valve (which they usually do) and the waterflow to downstream outlets is cut off (as it is when the faucets are turned off), the resulting pressure buildup can crack the hot water heater lining, collapse its flue which can cause a backup of deadly carbon monoxide, rupture pump seals, damage the solenoid valve, and even cause porcelain fixtures to explode. All this is easily avoided by installing a small expansion tank on the source-side of the water heater after the check valve. Such water heaters should also be sized in terms of the water volume in the tank and their confining piping as well as the Δt between the system's cold and hot water.

Example 1. If a 40 ft copper pipe is warmed from 40° to 180° F during periods of hot water flow, how much does the pipe lengthen?

---

4)C)1)a) $\Delta L = \kappa_t L_L \Delta t$

ΔL = change in pipe length due to change in temperature, ? in.
κ_t = coefficient of thermal expansion for pipe material, in/in.
From Table 4-5, κ_t for copper = 0.000,009,8 in/in.
L_L = length of pipe at lower temperature, in. L_L = 40 ft × 12 = 480 in.
Δt = change in pipe temperature, ° F. Δt = 180° – 40° = 140° F.
Δt may occur in supply or waste runs.

$$\Delta L = 480 \times 0.000,0098 \times 140 = 0.659 \text{ in.}$$

Example 2. What size chase should a $1\frac{1}{2}$ in. hot water pipe have?

---

4)C)1)b) $W \geq \kappa_w (\delta + \kappa_f)$
        c) $D \geq \kappa_d (\delta + \kappa_f)$

W = optimal width of chase section, ? in. Round off to next 0.5 in.
D = optimal depth of chase section, ? in. Round off to next 0.5 in.
κ_w = chase width factor. κ_w = 1.6 for supply, 1.4 for waste, and 1.2 for vent piping. Here κ_w = 1.6.
κ_d = chase depth factor. κ_d = 1.3 for supply, 1.2 for waste, and 1.1 for vent piping. Here κ_d = 1.3.
δ = pipe diameter, in. $1\frac{1}{2}$ in. = 1.50 in.
κ_f = pipe function factor. κ_f = 2.0 if pipe is supply, 1.4 if waste or vent. As pipe is supply, κ_f = 2.0.

$$W \geq 1.6 (1.50 + 2.0) \geq 5.6 \blacktriangleright 6.0 \text{ in.}$$
$$D \geq 1.3 (1.50 + 2.0) \geq 4.55 \blacktriangleright 4.5 \text{ in. } \textbf{OK}$$

Note: If a hot and cold supply pipe are in one chase, add 2 × (d_{hot} + d_{cold}) in. to the required chase width (or depth if one pipe is above the other) for the pipes. If two waste or vent pipes are in one chase, subtract 2 in. from the required width for both pipes.

4.C.2. Water Hammer ·

During the time that a faucet, a pump, or valve is off, behind the piping closure awaits a long cylindrical mass of water. When the valve is opened, the liquid cylinder lurches forward and is replaced by more liquid —then when the valve is turned off the moving incompressible cylinder behind the valve slams into its face like a battering ram, then its energy rebounds as a hydraulic pressure wave that may travel back through the piping at nearly 3,000 miles an hour, straining every elbow and fitting as it goes, rebounding continually from one end to the other until its energy finally dissipates. The greater the pressure, the larger the diameter, and the longer the straight run of pipe before the valve, the more severe the shock. If you've ever wondered why a plumbing connection suddenly springs a leak after years of perfect service or a water pump suddenly starts rattling on its mount, the answer is probably a straw-that-broke-the-camel's-back failure due to hydraulic shock. This is the biggest reason why plastic piping is a poor choice for all but small low-pressure systems, why steel is best for large-diameter piping, and why *all* piping should be securely installed to its supports at regularly short intervals.

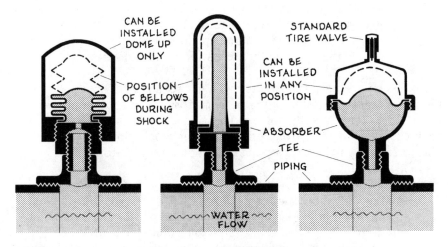

Fig. 4-10. Three kinds of water hammer arresters.

A traditional method of eliminating water hammer has been to install on each fixture lead an air chamber. But these have been found to be useless in relieving this considerable force because they quickly fill with water. Instead the piping should be fitted with water hammer arresters. These cylindrical devices contain a double chamber (one filled with water and the other with a cushion of compressible air, with an elastic membrane in between) that is mounted on a stem whose diameter is $\frac{1}{2}$–2 in. The units are best located a few feet before bends and diameter reductions at the ends of straight runs, each must have its air-volume capacity listed on it, and the required number depends on the units' volumes, type of base connection, and the plumbing system's total fixture load. Since water hammers tend to lose their volume over time, each must be accessible for periodic testing (the air chambers typically have a standard tire valve which allows them to be easily recharged).

> If the waterflow in a $1\frac{1}{2}$ in. copper pipe has a maximum velocity of 7 ft/sec and the pipe has a meter-to-constriction length of 68 ft, how many water hammer arresters, if any, does this pipe require?

4)C)2)a)   **Threaded base connection:** $C \approx F^{0.67}$

      b)   **Soldered base connection:** $C \approx F^{0.74}$

C = required air volume of water hammer arresters with threaded or soldered bases in plumbing system, **?** in^2. Assume threaded bases.

F = number of fixture units in plumbing system, 36

$$C \approx 36^{0.67} = 11.0 \ in^2$$

Any number of arresters whose total air volume $\geq 11.0 \ in^2$ is **OK**
If more than 1 arrester is selected,
space them on main branches throughout the system

Since water hammer arresters are not required by most codes, many plumbing systems today do not have them, primarily due to initial costs and chase limitations. Then the following formula may be used to find the feasible pressure, and thus the diameter, of a water supply pipe with no arresters. This formula is particularly important for hot water plastic piping.

4)C)2)c) $v \, L = 14.3 \, t \, (P_i + \Delta P)$

v = maximum velocity of waterflow, fps

L = length of water supply piping, ft. Count only length from outlet upstream to next-to-last reduction of pipe diameter: e.g. if pipe reduces from 1 to $\frac{3}{4}$ in. diameter 30 ft upstream of outlet and reduces from $1\frac{1}{4}$ to 1 in. 26 ft further upstream, $L = 30 + 26 = 56$ ft.

t = cycle time for opening or closing valve, sec. Most occupants take about 1.5 sec to close a conventional hot or cold water plumbing fixture valve. Larger-diameter commercial valves operated by service personnel take longer. A rational rule of thumb for design: $t \approx$ pipe diameter $\times$ 1.4.

P_i = water pressure at valve when fully open, psi

ΔP = water pressure increase at valve due to pressure surge caused by shutoff, psi. $P_i + \Delta P$ must $\leq$ piping's maximum safe pressure.

4.C.3. Pipe Insulation

Plumbing piping should be insulated if:

▶ It is exposed to subfreezing temperatures. This includes the possibility of power outage coinciding with very cold weather.
▶ It contains hot water. The cost of insulation is usually quickly returned by savings accruing from reduced heat loss.
▶ It is exposed to humid air. Otherwise, condensation collecting on the pipes, especially if they carry cold water, can eventually rot or corrode adjacent wood or metal construction.
▶ It is part of an interior roof drainage system.
▶ It is wrapped with electric heat tracing cable.
▶ It conveys air or gas from a central compressor or cylindrical gas supply. When such gases flow through the regulator they expand greatly, which causes them to cool so much that adjacent air moisture often condenses on the pipes.
▶ The piping conveys a hot gas from a combustion process, such as a boiler, furnace, or internal combustion generator.

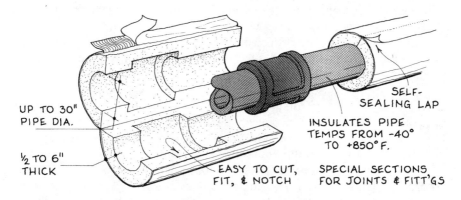

UP TO 30"
PIPE DIA.

½ TO 6"
THICK

EASY TO CUT,
FIT, & NOTCH

SELF-
SEALING LAP

INSULATES PIPE
TEMPS FROM -40°
TO +850° F.

SPECIAL SECTIONS
FOR JOINTS & FITT'GS

Fig. 4-11. Molded slip-on pipe insulation.

Pipes and fittings are typically insulated with wrapped flexible batts or lightweight molded slip-on sections. All should have a sealed vapor barrier on the outside and have all seams taped; and all must accommodate pipe movement due to thermal expansion, which is done by slightly compressing the batts and not exceeding 20 ft for continuous runs of taping. As insulated pipes have much greater diameters, they require correspondingly larger chases and risers. Pipe insulation becomes more cost-effective as pipe diameter increases due to the greater volume of heat in the pipe and the greater surface area through which it can escape.

4.C.4. Supply Components

Aside from piping, elbows, and tees, water supply plumbing requires several other important fittings if it is to operate as required. These include meters, filters, service valves, pumps and their motors, softeners, heaters, and a variety of water reservoirs, all as described below.

4.C.4.a. Water Meters

Water meters are installed in buildings where water use is measured. There are four general kinds:

Disc meters. Also known as *displacement, rotary piston,* or *plunger duplex piston meters,* these meters have diameters to 6 in. and operating capacities to 1,000 gpm. In each unit the water enters a small chamber where its volume is continually measured. They are highly accurate and can handle large flows; but at high water velocities meter pressure losses may approach 20 percent and continuous fast flow damages the mechanisms (thus they are used only in low-velocity water systems), and they typically experience high pressure drops (thus they are used only where such drops are acceptable and where absolute accuracy is required, such as measuring waterflow into boilers).

Current meters. Also known as *velocity, torrent, Venturi,* or *turbine meters,* their diameters range from 2–20 in. and usually contain a turbine or spindle whose rotation measures the waterflow's velocity and volume. As they can handle large volumes of water at fast flows while imposing minimum pressure losses on the flow, they are used mostly in large buildings.

Proportional meters. These deflect part of the waterflow past a recorder which measures the total flow. They are used in industrial complexes, municipal pumping stations, and other large-volume scenarios.

Compound meters. These are a combination of displacement and current meters and have diameters from 3–12 in. One kind contains a disc that measures small flows and a turbine that measures large flows. They are good for fire protection systems and large facilities with widely varying water demands.

Each water meter should be within 3 ft of the building wall at the main's point of entry (or it can be outdoors under shelter protected from freezing). It should have the same diameter as the parent piping, be level, have straight runs at least 10 × pipe diameter before the meter and half this length after the meter, be firmly supported at least 3 ft above the floor, have dials that are readable by a person standing beside them, and be visible from the center of the mechanical equipment area.

4.C.4.b. Pumps

Also called *circulators*, each of these mechanical devices produces a volume of fluid flow at a certain pressure. The fluid may be water, petroleum, compressed or vacuum air, medical gas, fuel gas, or any other liquid or gas. The pump may be *centrifugal* (generates pressure by the force of its impeller rotating at high speed), *rotary* (generates pressure either by an off-center rotor pressing against the walls of a cylindrical chamber or a rotating axial screw), or *reciprocal* (a piston or diaphragm action drives the fluid forward). Each has a *suction pipe* (where the fluid enters the pump) and a *discharge pipe* (where the fluid leaves the pump). The suction pipe requires a backflow prevention valve, the discharge pipe should have a pressure regulating valve and extend straight from the pump for 24 pipe diameters to ensure maximum initial flow, and both pipes require flexible connections at the pump plus resilient hangers to 30 ft away. Since a pump is always driven by an external power source, usually an electric motor or internal combustion engine, the two components must have a common shaft with a flexible coupling and possibly a gearbox with a drive train. All this machinery must be mounted on an absolutely rigid base, which, depending on the machinery's size, may include a concrete inertia block, vibration isolator pads, resilient mounts, and a raised housekeeping pad to facilitate cleaning. Each assembly also requires access space all around for inspection and servicing.

A pump's most vital dimensions are its *suction head* (vertical distance between the suction pipe intake and the pump impeller) and *discharge head* (vertical distance between the pump impeller and the discharge pipe outflow). Since water cannot be sucked upward more than 33.95 ft but can be pumped upward to almost any height (the same relation is true for other fluids depending on their specific gravities, a pump is usually located near the level of its suction pipe intake. The suction and discharge pipe lengths as well as their materials, fittings, valves, and entrance conditions also influence the pump's design. If the fluid is a gas whose specific gravity is nearly that of air, its suction and discharge heads have only a slight effect on the pump's design. Multiple pumps can also be connected in series (then their head pressures are additive and their total discharge rate equals that of the weakest pump) or in parallel (then their discharge rates are additive and their total head pressure equals that of the lowest head).

The horsepower required to turn a pump under load is its *brake horsepower*. This is a function of the pump's flow requirements, net suction intake-to-discharge outflow head, head friction losses, pump efficiency, and viscosity of the fluid being pumped. As a fluid's viscosity generally varies according to its temperature, if this varies significantly it is impossible to size the pump exactly; then the fluid's average or 'eye' viscosity is normally used. Today's pump motors may also have *variable-speed drives* (VFDs)

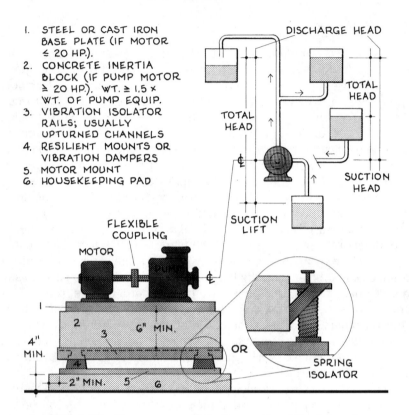

1. STEEL OR CAST IRON BASE PLATE (IF MOTOR ≤ 20 HP.).
2. CONCRETE INERTIA BLOCK (IF PUMP MOTOR ≥ 20 HP.). WT. ≥ 1.5 × WT. OF PUMP EQUIP.
3. VIBRATION ISOLATOR RAILS; USUALLY UPTURNED CHANNELS
4. RESILIENT MOUNTS OR VIBRATION DAMPERS
5. MOTOR MOUNT
6. HOUSEKEEPING PAD

DISCHARGE HEAD

TOTAL HEAD

TOTAL HEAD

SUCTION HEAD

SUCTION LIFT

FLEXIBLE COUPLING

MOTOR

PUMP

4" MIN.

2" MIN.

6" MIN.

OR

SPRING ISOLATOR

Fig. 4-12. Pump assembly, base, & critical levels.

that increase efficiency and thus energy consumption and operating life if the pump's flow requirements change constantly, as occurs in most climate control systems. Even if the pumped fluid's speed remains constant, a VFD enables the motor to vary its speed to compensate for slight inaccuracies in calculations, which eliminates the need for large safety factors. Numerous kinds of software are also available which enable a pump to be sized quickly, but one should be familiar with one's input parameters before using it. Otherwise, an effective procedure for pump design is as follows:

1. Sketch an elevation of the system based on its original design criteria that shows the level of the liquid before pumping, the level of the pump axis, and the level of the liquid after pumping.
2. Determine the pump's capacity unit (e.g. fps, fpm, gpm, gal/hr, acre·ft/day). In most situations the unit is obvious or determined by the pump's manufacturer.
3. Find the pump's effective head (ft of water). If the pumped liquid is not water, its effective head = specific gravity (σ) × actual head.

4. Consider the properties of the liquid being pumped, particularly
    its temperature, specific gravity, and viscosity; which are related.
    Viscosity is especially important if the fluid is a gel, slurry, crude
    oil, or paper stock.

5. Select the class and type of pump. The three mechanical classes
    of pumps and their attributes are:

    Centrifugal: Best for moving large volumes of water at low-to-
    medium pressures; good for steady flows, low-to-high discharge
    pressures, and dirty, abrasive, or partly solid liquids.

    Rotary: Best for moving viscous or high-pressure liquids; good
    for steady flows, medium discharge pressures, and small-to-medi-
    um capacities. **NG** for abrasive liquids.

    Reciprocating: Good for high discharge pressures and small
    capacities, clean and clear liquids, and pulsing flows. **NG** where
    pulsing flows are undesirable.

6. Determine whether the pump should be horizontal or vertical.
    Horizontal pumps usually occupy less floor space and are more
    flexibly useful, while vertical pumps require less headroom, expe-
    rience less corrosion and abrasion, and are easier to maintain.

7. Determine whether the pump should be single-suction or double-
    suction. Single-suction pumps are good for up to 50 gpm capaci-
    ties and 50 ft heads, while double-suction pumps are good for
    capacities up to 1,000 gpm and 300 ft heads.

8. Compute the pump's required horsepower, then select a unit of
    adequate horsepower or equivalent wattage.

9. Noting the pump's dimensions and weight, add this data to the
    Plans.

10. Depending on the occupancy and other design criteria, isolate
    the machinery's vibration and noise with acoustic attenuation
    devices as described in Sec. 7.C.4.a.

11. Design the general pump area to maintain sanitary conditions.

12. Verify the pump's performance after installation.

The following formula could be called the *basic head pump formula*. It
is used to find the net actual head that is typically used in computing pump
horsepower.

4)C)4)b)1) $H \approx H_a - H_f + H_s - H_v$

H = net actual head or height of waterflow of pump, ft

H_a = local atmospheric head: the atmospheric head at standard atmos-
    pheric conditions (sea level at 30.00 mm barometric pressure). At
    sea level, H_a usually equals 33.95 ft. At other elevations above sea
    level H_a may be adjusted according to (1 − 0.000034 E). If the

pump's net discharge head is required, $H_a = 0$.

H_f = pipe friction head: the energy loss of the liquid flowing through the suction pipe due to wall resistance of the pipe, fittings, valves, and entrance conditions. In small systems this typically ≈ only 2-3 ft.

H_s = static suction lift head: the vertical distance between the horizontal ¢ of the pump impeller and the reservoir's free surface, ft. If reservoir's free surface is below the impeller, H_s is +; if above the impeller, H_s is − and is known as the *static suction head*.

H_v = vapor pressure head: vapor pressure of water in air at standard atmospheric conditions (14.7 psi at 70° F), which causes the local atmospheric head to be slightly less; this could be called the "water vapor friction loss", as it is analogous to the engine friction loss that makes an engine less efficient. H_v typically = 0.84 ft.

> If a dining hall and bathhouse facility for a Girl Scout camp near Lake Placid, NY, has a design fixture unit flow of 128 gal/min and is located 54 ft above its water supply reservoir, what size pump should its water system have?

4)C)4)b)2)

$$40 \text{ ℙ } Ɛ ≈ σ Þ κ_v H$$

ℙ = required pump horsepower, **?** hp

Ɛ = pump efficiency, %. Use 65% unless specific data is available.

σ = specific gravity of liquid being pumped. σ of water = 1.0.

Þ = pump capacity or flow, 128 gpm

$κ_v$ = water viscosity factor, according to the bar graph below:

Normal water temperature

32°	50°	75°	100°	125°	150°	175°	200°	212°
2.00	1.41	1.00	0.75	0.59	0.49	0.40	0.35	0.33

$κ_v$ = water viscosity factor

As groundwater temperature ≈ local AAT, from Fig. 2-23, AAT for Lake Placid region ≈ 40° ➔ κ ≈ 1.70. If liquid is not water, let $κ_v$ = 1.0 in lieu of more definitive data, especially if pipe flow is at or near room temperature.

H = total discharge height (head) or vertical distance between pump and level of pumped liquid, ft. Here each fixture requires at least 15 psi pressure. As 1 ft of head = 0.433 psi, equivalent head for 15 psi = 15/0.433 = 34.6 ft. ∴ H = 54 + 34.6 = 89 ft.

$$40 \text{ H} \times 65 ≥ 128 \times 1.70 \times 89 \quad ... \text{ H } ≥ 7.4 \text{ hp}$$

4.C.4.c. Filters

Even drinkable water may contain particles which can damage piping and equipment; or it may not be not pure enough for certain medical, scientific, or industrial applications. The usual remedy is to filter the water after it enters the building and before it passes through any plumbing component, including pumps and meters.

The three basic filters are described below.

Gravity beds. These are pressurized or nonpressurized cylinders that contain beds of sand, gravel, or diatomaceous earth which strain particles out of the percolating water. The beds are usually $2\frac{1}{2}$–3 ft deep and at least 3 ft in diameter (but this can be much larger), and the water is 3–5 ft deeper above. Filtration ranges from 3–20 gpm per ft^2 of bed area, sand uniformity must be 1.75 or less, water velocity in underdrains should not exceed 2 fps, required cleansing frequency is 2–12 times per year, and at least two units are needed to permit alternate cleaning. When the medium becomes saturated, it is usually cleansed by backwashing, which can be performed by computerized controls that initiate each cycle by opening valves at a prescribed pressure drop, then reverse the cycle after a programmed period of regeneration. Sand has a typical settling factor of 1.16 (0.86 × initial volume, pcf).

➕ Good for removing fine particles, large bacteria, scale, grit, and rust from constant waterflows. Used for swimming pools, fountains, bathing, and toilet flushing. Diatomaceous earth beds create clearer and purer water than sand beds.

➖ Bulky; cannot remove chemicals, coliform bacteria, and toxins. N2G for intermittent waterflows.

Strainers. This is typically a circular bronze or stainless steel screen mounted in the supply piping to catch any particles in the waterflow. Each should have a cover with a small clear polycarbonate window that allows visual inspection of the screen. These filters are best installed in pairs to permit alternate cleaning. Two arrangements are shown in Fig. 4-13. A valve is located just downstream of each filter to prevent backflow while the unit is being serviced. Layout *A* creates slightly less friction loss due to linear flow, provides double straining, and fits better in long narrow spaces; but layout *B* is simpler, more economical, and takes up less area.

➕ Economical, takes up little space, good for filtering normally pure water that may occasionally contain particulate matter. Used in systems with pumps and in rural installations where creek water supply must be filtered after storms.

➖ Collected particles can greatly reduce pressure drop if filter is not frequently serviced. Cannot filter very small particles or chemicals.

Cellulose cartridges.
These fuzzy white cylinders are fitted into clear polycarbonate containers through which the coldwater supply flows and can be inspected. There are two common sizes: about 3 in. diameter × 10 in. high, and about 7 in. diameter × 13 in. high. They are often installed beneath counters before kitchen sink faucets where most drinking water is drawn, as there they filter less water and need to be replaced less often. They are common in small buildings where the water arrives from drilled wells and contains iron and other smelly or discoloring minerals. They remove particles down to 5 microns including chlorine, many chemicals, giardia, and some bacteria.

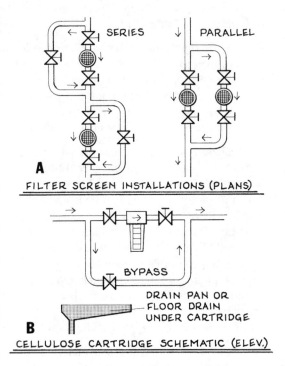

Fig. 4-13. Two filter installations.

➕   Removes the great majority of pollutants commonly found in suburban and rural water supplies. Compact, serviceable by untrained personnel.

➖   Must be protected from freezing; **NG** for filtering water above 100° F. Tap water should be run 10–15 sec to remove any fines suspended in the container, especially if the water is used for drinking.

Water filtering may also be associated with other forms of purification in water treatment facilities. These include *softening* (this is described in Sec. 4.C.4.h.), *chlorination* (adding small amounts of chlorine to kill any bacteria that may be in the water, then adding 0.25 ppm of ammonia to remove the chlorine odor), *aeration* (entraining air into the water to remove H_2S and other groundwater odors), and *carbon activation* (filtering the water through beds of activated charcoal to remove undesirable tastes, odors, and colors; this normally requires 10–20 lb of activated charcoal/million gallons of water but may require as much as 50–100 lb). Although these specifications are for municipalities, they may be useful for large-occupancy buildings.

4.C.4.d. Valves [t]

Valves regulate flow through piping and isolate plumbing components, systems, or operations when they need servicing or repair. Thus the inlet and outlet pipes of all plumbing components should be valved. Each should be easily accessible, and the floor below should be waterproof and drainable. A valve is usually turned on and off by a handle, the most common being *handwheel* (a round handle that is rotated several times from off to fully on), *fin* (a blade-like handle that fully opens or closes the valve with a quarter turn), and *nut* (a small square or hex head that is turned with a wrench). If a valve's closure is perpendicular to flow, it causes little friction loss when open; if parallel to flow it may cause considerable flow friction loss when open, especially at high velocities.

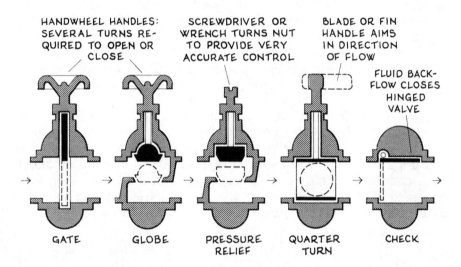

HANDWHEEL HANDLES: SEVERAL TURNS RE-QUIRED TO OPEN OR CLOSE

SCREWDRIVER OR WRENCH TURNS NUT TO PROVIDE VERY ACCURATE CONTROL

BLADE OR FIN HANDLE AIMS IN DIRECTION OF FLOW

FLUID BACK-FLOW CLOSES HINGED VALVE

GATE   GLOBE   PRESSURE RELIEF   QUARTER TURN   CHECK

Fig. 4-14. The five basic valves.

The five basic plumbing valves are described below.

Globe valves. This is the common outdoor hose bibb or spigot valve; it has a handwheel handle and parallel-to-flow closure. It increases flow friction losses but offers precise regulation of flow and is good for starting and stopping flow. They are best for isolating low-pressure components or zones requiring frequent maintenance. An important globe valve is the *frostproof sill cock*. This valve has a 8 or 12 in. long shaft with a rod inside that has its handle on one end and its valve port on the other, so when the shaft is located in an insulated exterior wall the handle is outdoors while the valve port is indoors where it won't freeze in cold weather.

Gate valves. These have handwheel handles and perpendicular-to-flow closures. They increase flow friction losses little, should remain fully open or closed, and are NG for regulating flow. They are used for isolating plumbing zones or components that need infrequent servicing or repair.

Pressure relief valves. Also known as PRV valves, these typically have a nut handle that allows precise pressure reduction with a wrench which also offers security from unauthorized operation. If gauges are installed just before and after the valve, the exact pressure difference caused by turning the nut is immediately known. This is the most effective and economical method of limiting high-pressure flow to acceptable levels. Also, where ΔPs are great, a destructive collapse called *cavitation* may occur; then two PRV valves may be installed in series. Parallel hookups are used where flow rates vary widely, as then one valve cannot reduce the pressure precisely for minimum and maximum flows; then one valve is typically sized to carry 80 percent of the flow. PRV valves are often slightly smaller than the lines in which they are installed.

Quarter-turn valves. Also known as *ball, plug,* or *butterfly,* these valves typically have fin handles whose directions indicate whether the valve is open or closed. They are quick-operating, are excellent for starting and stopping flow, and increase pressure losses only slightly. They are used primarily for full-open/full-close regulation of flow.

Check valves. Also known as *swing, lift, backflow, double-disc,* or *tilting disc,* these valves have a hinged disc, often with a rubber seating ring, that lays against the valve inlet port so that it allows full forward flow but clamps shut when flow reverses. Perpendicular-to-flow types affect flow friction losses little but they usually are not as durable, while with parallel-to-flow types the reverse is true. Check valves are used primarily to eliminate inconvenience or damage that could result from backflow.

If the inlet and outlet pressures for a PRV valve are 180 and 40 psi, is there a danger that cavitation will occur? If so, what is the remedy?

---

4)C)4)d)
$$\kappa_c (P_i - P_o) \approx 2 (P_o + 14.7)$$

κ_c = cavitation constant, **?** If $\kappa_c \le 1.0$, cavitation will likely occur and more than one PRV valve should be installed in series.
P_i = valve inlet pressure, 180 psi
P_o = valve outlet pressure, 40 psi

$\kappa_c (180 - 40) \approx 2 (40 + 14.7)$ ... κ_c = 0.78 ➡ 2 PRV valves required
Set κ_c = 1.0, then find minimum P_o for PRV valve 1 ➡ $P_o \approx 50.2$ psi
By setting P_i = 50 psi and recomputing κ_c,
determine if a third PRV valve is required.
If P_i = 50, κ_c = 5.06 ➡ 2 PRV valves **OK**

Edition, Alfred Steele (Construction Industry Press, Elmhurst, IL, 1982), Chap. 22.

4.C.4.e. Water Supply Delivery Rate

Every drilled well should be protected from surface-water inflow by the installation of a concrete or steel casing (or equal) that extends at least 15 ft deep below the groundline immediately around the wellhead.

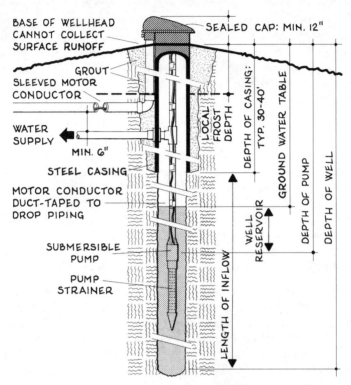

Fig. 4-15. Anatomy of drilled well with submersible pump.

A rural motel obtains its water supply from a drilled well with a submersible pump. If the building contains 132 fixture units, what is the minimum water flow rate that should be struck in the well?

4)C)4)e)   Þ ≈ 0.2 (F + 0.071 F_n)

Þ = supply water delivery rate, ? gpm
F = number of fixture units served, 132 units
F_n = nonfixture unit hot water required for commercial or industrial processes, if any, gpm. None given.

Þ ≈ 0.2 (132 + 0) ≈ 26 gpm

4.C.4.f. Small Water Supply Tanks

In rural residences and other small buildings, several kinds of sealed tanks are often used to maintain desired water supply pressures. Such reservoirs are usually an integral part of well-septic systems; but they are also installed in meter systems where the water main pressure is inadequate or where temporary dips in pressure during periods of peak demand might inconvenience occupants. Each such tank requires a pressure relief valve near its top, a check valve on its outlet pipe, and a nearby electrical outlet that usually connects to a pump. The tank must be in an enclosed but accessible area that is protected from freezing temperatures, and its floor should be waterproof and slope to a drain. There are three general tank sizes:

Petite: cylindrical 'hydrocell' units about 8 in. dia. × 24 in. high and other point-of-use models that fit into an under-vanity cabinet or small space along a water supply line. They are installed near Jacuzzi hot tubs, commercial dishwashers, and other fixtures that require higher-than-normal pressures or are more than 40 ft from larger central units.

Small: upright cylinders that are common in residences and small-to-medium commercial buildings.

Large: usually room-sized cylindrical or rectangular shapes for large buildings. These are described in the section that follows.

There are several common methods of sizing pressurized water supply tanks in small buildings: (1) capacity ≈ 10 × peak water delivery rate (gpm), (2) 25 gallons per occupant in residences, and (3) 15 minutes of storage per commercial occupant at peak water demand plus a fire protection reserve. Since water is densest at 39° F and expands by 1/23 its volume from 40–212° F, every water tank requires a 10 percent expansion airspace at its top.

An often-overlooked fact about plumbing systems is that every water supply pipe is a reservoir, one with a cylindrical volume that equals its section area × its length. Thus the cylindrical wellhead of a drilled well serves as a water reservoir for its submerged pump. This fact has numerous other applications in plumbing system design.

> **Example 1.** How many gallons of water are contained in an 8 in. diameter drilled wellhead that is 400 ft deep?

4]C]4]f]1) $2,200 \, V = L \, \delta^2$

V = volume of water tank, cf. 1 cf of liquid contains 7.49 gal.
L = height of tank or length of pipe, in. 400 ft = 4,800 in.
δ = clear inner diameter of tank or pipe, in. Here δ = 8 in.

$$2,200 \ V = 4,800 \times 8^2 \quad ... \ V \approx 139.6 \text{ cf}$$
$$\text{Number of gal} = 139.6 \times 7.49 = 1,046 \text{ gal}$$

Note: This formula can be used to obtain the volume of fluid contained in any length of pipe.

Example 2. If a motel built on country property has 132 fixture units, what is the optimal size of its plumbing system's water pressure tank?

4│C│4│f│2│ $C \approx .5 \ (F + 0.071 \ F_n)$

C = capacity of water pressure tank, **?** gal
F = number of fixture units served, 132 units
F_n = nonfixture unit hot water required for commercial or industrial processes, if any, gpm. None given.

$$C \approx 5 \ (132 + 0) \approx 660 \text{ gal}$$

4.C.4.g. Large Water Supply Tanks [†]

A large building is a container that uses a lot of water. The only way to satisfy the many fixture demands by all the occupants and operations at any one moment in large buildings, some of which may be hundreds of feet tall, is to have a meticulously thought-out linkage of pipes, pumps, and tanks all operating within proper pressure parameters, all existing in an overall matrix of well-defined zones. In large buildings this plumbing *linkage logistic* usually needs to be thought out first, even before structure. And these logistics are best penetrated through an understanding of water tanks. To this network must be added water requirements for fire protection and climate control, whose amounts are typically supplied by separate plumbing systems.

There are four kinds of large water tanks in buildings: *gravity, suction, surge,* and *booster pumps* (the last is essentially the absence of tanks). Although each has several small advantages, each has one major disadvantage, which often is the clue to selecting the most suitable kind. Following is a description of the four kinds of water tanks for large buildings, in which the major disadvantage of each is underlined.

Gravity tanks

These are nonpressurized reservoirs of water located above the plumbing systems (usually on the building's roof or a tower nearby) which

---

[†] The primary source for this section was *Advance Plumbing Technology*, Alfred

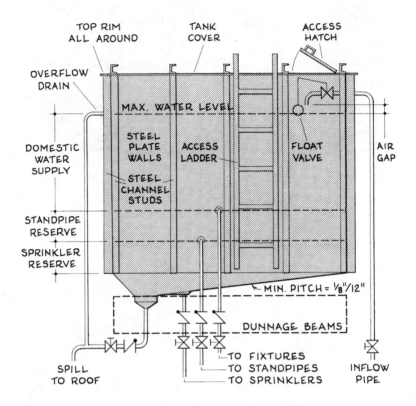

Fig. 4-16. Gravity tank details.

satisfy fixture pressure requirements by downfeeding or gravity. Although a pump is required to fill the tank, no mechanical means are necessary to ensure a continuous water supply. The downward range of a gravity tank may also be increased by pressure regulating valves, which reduce excessive pressures at otherwise excessive depths.

⊕ Simple, reliable, economical. Fewer regulating valves and controls than other tanks. Operates during power outages.

⊖ Cannot satisfy minimum pressure requirements of any fixtures within $20/0.433 = 46$ vertical ft below the tank. For this reason, 12 psi faucets and 8 psi toilets are often specified for the upper stories of gravity tank-fed systems. <u>Gravity tanks are very heavy.</u> This includes not only the weight of the water but also the substantial construction required to contain it and the weight of related facilities. Thus all supporting structural members must be larger. It takes only about 32 cf of water (≈ 240 gal) to weigh 1 ton.

Steele (Construction Industry Press, Elmhurst, IL, 1984), chapter 7.

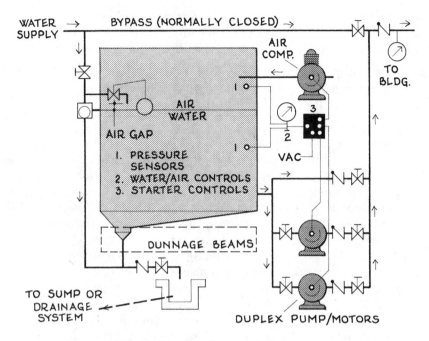

Fig. 4-17. Suction tank details.

Suction tanks

This is a reservoir of hermetically sealed water accompanied by one or more pumps that continually supply water of adequate pressure to all fixtures in its zone. Although such a tank is usually located at the bottom of its zone, it is sometimes better located at or near the top. For example, a suction tank at the base of a 50 ft tall building must produce 20 + 50 × 0.433 = 42 psi of pressure to satisfy all fixture requirements; but the same tank at the building's top would require only 20 psi (actually slightly less due to the head between the tank's underside and the highest fixtures below) to satisfy all fixture requirements. A suction tank can be considerably smaller than a gravity tank, and it can supply all fixtures during brief power outages. Suction and gravity tanks can also be combined creatively. For example, a large gravity tank on a building's roof can have a small 'sidearm' suction tank (much as water baseboard system boilers have sidearm water heaters) that supplies water of adequate pressure to the fixtures immediately below.

One problem with suction tanks is that, as one's pressurized water level lowers, the air above expands which lowers the water pressure, while at the same time the lower water level correspondingly increases the head and thus the water pressure at the fixtures above. Sometimes these differences balance each other out, and sometimes they don't; thus a suction tank's maximum and minimum design scenarios must always be investigated. This tiny fact can 'make or break' the effectiveness of this system.

➕ Fairly compact. Comparatively little power is required to satisfy pump demands. Tank may be located anywhere in the building, including underground areas outdoors.

➖ Protection from physical damage and corrosion is absolutely necessary, because a tiny leak in the tank will render the whole system inoperable. <u>Only a small portion of the pressurized water is usable</u>; this is because it takes only a small drawdown of water to lower the tank's pressure to where it can no longer satisfy the minimum pressure demands of the fixtures served. For example, if a suction tank containing 120 cf of water (about 900 gal) also contains 10 cf of air at a design pressure of 60 psi (note that the tank is almost full and its water pressure is very high), it would take only a 20 cf drawdown to reduce the air pressure to 20 psi; then the remaining water —83 percent of its original volume— becomes unusable. Thus a suction tank must contain a considerable amount of air at the maximum system pressure or its pump must cycle on and off frequently (which consumes more energy and wears it out faster). Thus with suction tanks the optimal air/water ratio at maximum pressure is a critical design factor.

Surge tanks

This is a gravity or suction reserve that is used to smooth out jagged peak demands or compensate for erratic pressure variations in the water supply. For example, when water is supplied by a public main, sudden demands by neighboring buildings can create a pressure dip analogous to an electrical brownout that temporarily lowers water pressure to unacceptable levels. In such cases a surge tank maintains adequate flow and pressure until the public main pressure returns to normal.

➕ Simple, safe. A plumbing system application of the principle of redundant design.

➖ A surge tank is <u>an additional reservoir that is theoretically unnecessary if the parent system is designed correctly</u>. Unfortunately, 'correctly' may involve adhering to design parameters that are unrealistic or unattainable.

Suction tanks and surge tanks are also known as *pneumatic* and *hydropneumatic storage tanks*. One's capacity in gallons usually ≈ 10 × its

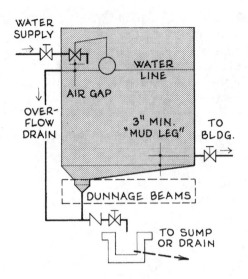

Fig. 4-18. Surge tank details.

pump's capacity in gpm. These reservoirs usually have controls that maintain a minimum reserve of 10–20 percent of the tank's volume to keep the tank from running dry and damaging the pump. Such tanks also should not experience more than six cycles per hr; thus one's withdrawal rate (no. gal withdrawn per cycle) depends on the tank's air volume at its lowest and highest pressures as well as more basic criteria relating to occupancy loads. Thus, after these tanks are sized, the following formula should be run to verify or revise the tank's size:

4)C)4)9)1)

$$W = V_L - V_L P_L/P_H$$

W = withdrawal rate of suction or surge tank per operating cycle, gal. This amount × 6 should ≤ hourly demand on the system.

V_L = air volume in tank at its lowest pressure, cf

P_L = lowest air pressure in tank, psi

P_H = highest air pressure in tank, psi

Booster pumps

These are continuously running pumps with variable-speed drives that maintain near-constant water supply pressures.

➕ Eliminates the need for bulky gravity and suction tanks, which reduces building spatial and structural requirements. The most common method of maintaining water pressure in today's tall buildings which contain commercially leased floor-space.

➖ A second water reservoir is always required. Booster pumps must run constantly to maintain uniform water pressure, and thus they are energy-wasteful. Today this disadvantage can be reduced considerably by installing 'MMRD' type systems that include several step-firing pumps with variable-speed drives, pressure-regulating valves, and computerized controls.

Example 1. A commercial building near Salt Lake City has a plumbing system with an estimated peak water supply demand of 880 gal/min (after use-factor adjustments) that requires a suction tank. If the tank has a triplex pump/motor, the maximum pump cycle is six per hr, the highest fixture is 54 ft above the tank, and the tank's withdrawal capacity is 30 percent, what is the tank's total capacity?

Step 1. Find the volume required to hold the suction tank's water.

4︶C︶4︶9︶2︶ $\qquad$ $400\ D_p \approx \eta\ C\ V_w\ H$

D_p = peak demand of water supply, 880 gpm
η = number of pumps in system. A triplex assembly has 3 pumps.
C = number of pump cycles per hour, 6
V_w = water volume of suction tank, **?** cf. 1 cf = 7.49 gal; 1 gal = 0.134 cf.
H = total water discharge height or head, 54 ft

$$400 \times 880 \approx 3 \times 6 \times V_w \times 54 \quad \dots V_w \approx 362\ cf$$

Step 2. Find the suction tank's total air-water volume.

$$P_{min}(V_t - V_w) = 0.01\ V_w\ W_c\ P_{max}$$

P_{min} = minimum pressure of water supply, assume 20 psi
V_t = total air-water volume of suction tank, **?** cf
V_w = water volume of suction tank, from Step 1, 652 cf
W_c = water withdrawal capacity of suction tank, 30%
P_{max}= maximum pressure of water supply, assume 60 psi

$$20\ (V_t - 652) = 0.01 \times 652 \times 30 \times 60 \quad \dots V_t = 688\ cf$$
One possible size: 7 × 10 × 10 ft

Example 2. What size pumps should the above suction tank have?

4︶C︶4︶9︶3︶ $\qquad$ $D_p \approx C\eta$

D_p = peak demand of water supply, from Example 1, 880 gpm
C = required pump capacity for suction tank, **?** gpm
η = optimal number of pumps in system. From Example 1, η = 3 units.

$$880 \approx C \times 3 \quad \dots C \approx 293\ gpm$$

Example 3. What is the above pump's required horsepower?

4⟧C⟧4⟧9⟧4⟧ $\qquad$ $92 \text{ ℍP } \varepsilon \approx C P_{max}$

ℍP = required horsepower of pump, **?** hp
ε = pump efficiency, %. Use 65% if specific data is unavailable.
C = capacity or maximum waterflow of pump, from Example 2, 293 gpm
P_{max} = maximum pressure of water supply, from Example 1, 60 psi

$$92 \times \text{ℍP} \times 60 \approx 293 \times 60 \quad \ldots \text{ℍP} \approx 2.93 \rightarrow 3 \text{ hp}$$

Example 4. If the above reservoir is a gravity tank, what is its size?

4⟧C⟧4⟧9⟧5⟧ $\qquad$ $V_w \approx 4.25 \, D_p$

V_w = total volume of water reservoir, **?** cf
D_p = peak demand of water supply, 880 gpm.

$$V_w \approx 4.25 \times 880 = 3{,}740 \text{ cf}$$

Example 5. If the above gravity tank has a duplex pump system, what is the required capacity of each pump?

4⟧C⟧4⟧9⟧6⟧ $\qquad$ $D_p = C \, \eta$

D_p = peak demand of water supply, from Example 4, 880 gpm
C = required pump capacity for gravity tank, **?** gpm
η = optimal number of pumps in system. Duplex system = 2 units

$$880 = Þ \times 2 \quad \ldots Þ = 440 \text{ gpm}$$

Example 6. After considerable analysis, a booster pump is to be installed in a building near Salt Lake City with a peak water supply demand of 880 gpm after use factor adjustments. If a multi-pump assembly with control sequencing is installed, size the system.

Step 1. Determine the booster pump's required horsepower.

4⟧C⟧4⟧9⟧7⟧ $\qquad$ $325{,}000 \text{ ℍP} \approx C \varepsilon W_p$

ℍP = required horsepower of booster pump, **?** hp
C = capacity or maximum waterflow of pump, gpm. Booster pump capacity should ≥ momentary peak water demand ➡ make C = 880 gpm.
ε = pump efficiency, %. Use 65% unless otherwise noted.
W_p = maximum pressure of water supply, use 60 psi u.o.n.

$$325{,}000 \; \text{HP} \; \geq \; 880 \times 65 \times 60 \qquad \dots \text{HP} \; \geq \; 10.6 \; \text{hp}$$

Step 2. For multi-pump systems, select the optimal number of pumps according to the MMRD feasibility schedule below. The smallest pump should ≈ 10–25 percent of total load, $\eta - 1$ pumps should ≈ 80 percent of total load, and the total pump capacity should ≥ 110 percent of total load.

If 3 pumps: % load for each pump is 25 + 55 + 55
If 4 pumps: % load for each pump is 15 + 35 + 35 + 35
If 5 pumps: % load for each pump is 15 + 25 + 25 + 25 + 25
If 6 pumps: % load for each pump is 12 + 20 + 20 + 20 + 20 + 20

At 10.6 hp, consider only three or four pumps, then select lowest total horsepower that satisfies required amount.
@ 3 pumps the most feasible HP is: 3 + 5 + 5 = 13
@ 4 pumps the most feasible HP is: 2 + 3 + 3 + 3 = 11   ... ✚

Example 7. If a building's peak waterflow from the public main is 500 gal/min and its peak demand is 720 gal/min, what is the optimal size of its emergency water reservoir?

4)C4)9)8) $$V_r = 2.9 \, (D_p - Þ)$$

V_r = optimal volume of surge tank or emergency reserve, **?** cf
D_p = peak demand of water supply, 720 gpm
Þ = water supply delivery rate, 500 gpm

$$V_r = 2.9 \, (720 - 500) = 640 \; \text{cf}$$

4.C.4.h. Water Softeners

When a building's water supply contains calcium or magnesium salts at concentrations exceeding 5 gr/gal, the salts form a whitish scale in pipes, tanks, water heaters, and even cookware, and they reduce the quality of washed and laundered articles. The salts are removed by water softening, a process in which a sodium-ion resin in a pressurized filter replaces the incoming calcium and magnesium ions, then a second tank filled with brine periodically replenishes the resin when its sodium nears depletion. Although a system's capacity is theoretically the water supply demand × water hardness × cycle time, the systems are often 'sized' by a time-and-error adjustment of the cycle. For example, if a residence has a 24,000 grain capacity unit installed, the owner may set the cycle time clock day dial

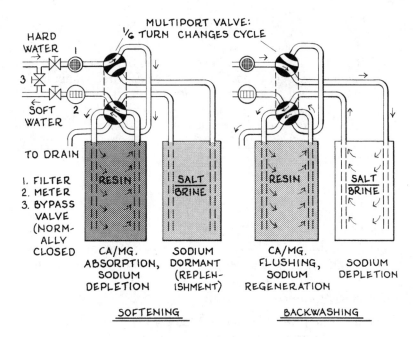

MULTIPORT VALVE:
⅙ TURN CHANGES CYCLE

HARD WATER →

3

← SOFT WATER 2

TO DRAIN

1. FILTER
2. METER
3. BYPASS VALVE (NORMALLY CLOSED

CA/MG. ABSORPTION, SODIUM DEPLETION

SODIUM DORMANT (REPLENISHMENT)

CA/MG. FLUSHING, SODIUM REGENERATION

SODIUM DEPLETION

SOFTENING

BACKWASHING

Fig. 4-19. Water softener operation.

at anywhere up to 6 days (taking care to set the time clock dial in the early A.M. or other time when the usually 1–2 hr regeneration cycle will occur while no water is being used), then if the water begins to taste funny within 6 days, the owner resets the day dial to a lower number of days.

Residential and small commercial water softeners are available in capacities to 128,000 grains for treating hardnesses up to 100 gr/gal, and most units also remove iron and manganese salts up to 5 ppm. Such units typically require a 110 VAC electrical outlet, operate at pressures of 25–100 psi, and should be located on strong waterproof floors that slope at least ⅛ in. fall/ft to a drain. If larger capacities are required, units may be installed in series or have large custom resin-filled tanks. If occupants require a salt-free diet, the water-softener chemistry can be altered to satisfy this need. After a unit is selected, its contained weight should be added to structural loads, and 30 in. should be added to three sides of its footprint to determine the unit's required floorspace.

The water for a commercial building near Salt Lake City has a hardness of 33 grains/gal. If the building's average water supply demand is 880 gal/day and feasible softener cycle times range from 2 to 6 days, size the softener system.

4)C)4)h) $\qquad\qquad C = D_a\,t\,(H-4.0)$

C = regeneration capacity of water softener system, ? grains. Solve for this value, then from the specifications below select the unit with the next largest capacity above the computed value. If C exceeds the largest capacity, use more than one unit.

CAPACITY, grains	Max. raw water hardness gr/gal	Max. iron/ manganese content, ppm	Approx. unit size, in. D × W × H	Approx. weight when full, lb
16,000	40	2	18 × 25 × 42	430
24,000	50	3	18 × 26 × 51	480
32,000	75	5	18 × 27 × 55	510
64,000	100	5	18 × 36 × 55	590
96,000	100	5	18 × 38 × 61	690
128,000	100	5	18 × 42 × 55	800

D_a = average water supply demand of occupancy, 880 gal/day
t = water softener cycle time, days. Solve for lower and upper limits at $t_L = 2$ days and $t_U = 6$ days.
H = hardness of water, 33 grains/gal

> Lower cycle time: $C = 880 \times 2\,(33 - 4.0) = 51,000$ grains
> Upper cycle time: $C = 880 \times 6\,(33 - 4.0) = 153,000$ grains
> Considering the softener unit choices in the above data, further analysis indicates the following:

Cycle   Cycle regeneration capacity – Min. unit size = Excess

2 days	51,000 - 64,000 = 13,000 gr
3 days	77,000 - 96,000 = 19,000 gr
4 days	102,000 - 128,000 = 26,000 gr
5 days	128,000 - 128,000 = 0 gr ... ➕
6 days	153,000 - (128,000 + 32,000) = 7,000 gr

Use 128,000 grain unit @ 5 day cycle

4.C.4.i. Water Heaters

A water heater is a sealed reservoir with an energy source that produces hot water for use by the occupants. The reservoir may be a cylindrical tank with a burner at its base, sidearm unit on a furnace, coils in a steam boiler, exhaust jacket on an internal combustion engine, heat exchanger in an exothermic industrial process, even piping loops immersed in a thermal hot spring. The heater's storage capacity is a function of the fixture units it serves and the water temperature it produces, and each is generally classed as a residential or commercial unit depending on the occupancy it serves. Residential unit capacities typically range from 5–125 gal, while commercial capacities range from 40–500 gal or more. The energy source may be electricity, gas, or fuel oil; and each has in addition to its storage capacity a *draw capacity* (maximum gal/hr of hot water the unit can produce during its peak hour of daily use), *recovery capacity* (maximum gal/hr at which the unit can replenish its hot water supply), and an *input rating* (maximum energy the unit's heat source can consume in 1 hr, measured in Btus for gas and oil heaters and kW for electric heaters). The maximum water pressure a unit can deliver is 160 psig, each unit requires controls that limit its water temperature to 210° F at near-sea-level elevations and lower temperatures at higher elevations, each unit must have a pressure relief valve and a tap for flushing and cleaning, the unit's floor should be waterproof and slope at least $1/8$ in/ft to a drain, the unit's weight should be added to structural loads (total load = shipping weight × gallon capacity × 8.33 lb/gal), and each unit should be installed in a well-ventilated area. In any water heating system, three temperatures must be known before it can be properly designed:

Entering temperature: the temperature of the cold water entering the tank. This is usually the groundwater temperature (the local AAT), which usually ranges from 35°–90°. The colder the entering water, the more heat that is required to raise it to the exiting temperature.

Ambient temperature: the temperature of the air around the tank. During winter this may be much lower than indoor temperatures if the unit is in a basement. The colder the ambient temperature, the faster the contained water cools and the more the unit must operate to maintain the exiting temperature. This variable does not affect unit capacity.

Exiting temperature: the temperature of the heated water as it leaves the tank; this is also known as the *preset hot water temperature* or the hot water plumbing's *tap temperature*. This varies according to use requirements and energy conservation measures. Typical exiting temperatures ≤ 120° F for residential general use, 140° for residential dishwashing, and ≥ 170° F for commercial use. The higher the exiting temperature, the smaller the unit, the less it weighs, the less floorspace it takes up, and the less it costs; but its unit operating costs are higher due to the greater heat loss of standing water. Lower exiting temperatures also greatly reduce tank corrosion and scale accumulation.

In addition to making hot water for the occupants, today's commercial water heaters have a second function: to kill *Legionella* bacilli. These deadly germs enter humans via inhalation of aerosolized water droplets and particles containing the bacilli (no infection via ingestion of contaminated water or from other persons is known), and are more common than one might think: Random water samples from more than 100 New York City commercial buildings in the mid-1990s found *Legionella* bacilli in nearly 20 percent of them. *Legionella* bacilli cannot grow below 68° F (but they can remain dormant at lower temperatures); they propagate between 68–122° F (ideal growth range is 95–115°); and they die within 6 hours at 131°, within 32 minutes at 140°, within 2 minutes at 151°, and instantly at 158° (disinfection range is 158–176°). In addition to high temperatures these bacteria can be killed by desiccation, UV radiation, and a few minutes' exposure to air. Thus the upper limit of ΔT calculations for commercial hot water systems is usually taken at 170°, as the extra 12° considers typical thermostat cycling to ensure a continuous hot water tank temperature of 158°. For this reason commercial reservoirs are often sized to hold only a day's supply of water. *Legionella* bacilli also require some kind of sediment to grow in; this can be a layer of mineral particles settling out of the water supply, scale buildup in a tiny recess of a fitting or the bottom of a water heater, or even a slimy biofilm of algae or other biota anywhere in the hot water supply. These stable habitats for *Legionella* bacilli can be eliminated by bleeding and flushing all water heaters and cooling towers twice a year. The threat of infection is also reduced if the system's piping is not oversized, has a minimum of elbows and other fittings, has straight runs after valves and other constrictions, and contains no air chambers, stems for future expansion, or other unused sections of piping. †

A perennial dilemma with hot water delivery is that when a hot water faucet is turned on after it has been off for awhile, the pipe's standing water between the faucet and the HWH has become cold and must flow out before hot water arrives, which forces the HWH to heat an added volume of water equal to the displaced cold water. In poorly designed systems, this wasted mass heating load can be as much as 5 gallons. This problem is minimized by placing hot-water fixtures near water heating sources, insulating the intervening piping, and installing small electrically operated point-of-use water heating units near the faucet. The latter method is the only practical solution for remote fixtures that use little hot water.

The general formula for sizing a domestic water heater is

HW ≈ no. occupants × 5 + dishwashing (5 if by hand, 10 if by
   machine) + no. clothes washers × 20 + no. full baths × 12

Then, assuming possession of a manufacturer's catalog of unit storage capacities, select a unit whose gallon capacity ≥ HW.

A procedure for designing a commercial water heating system is:

1. Find the capacity of each hot-water plumbing fixture, count them up, then apply a diversity factor. This is the format that underlies formulas 4C4i1 and 2 on the next page.
2. After determining the unit's optimal capacity, adjust this amount based on the unit's entering, ambient, and exiting temperatures.

---

† The primary sources for the data on *Legionella* were (1) Matthew Freije's "Legion-

3.   Consider the unit's energy source. Gas, oil, electric? Which is
       cheapest and most convenient? Gas and oil units require a flue
       and outdoor fresh air, but electric units have a slower recovery
       rate which usually requires installing a unit with 15–20 gal
       greater storage capacity, which costs more to operate; which may
       be **OK** if local electric rates are significantly lower.
4.   Make sure the mechanical room door is wide enough to get the
       unit inside. Don't use the door's catalog width, but know its
       actual clear opening between the jamb side trim and the hinge
       side edge that projects furthest when the door is fully open.

       Every hot water heater is usually more thermally efficient if it is de-
signed to maintain 80 percent combustion efficiency, is equipped with
intermittent ignition, has fan-assisted combustion or a flue damper (commercial units only), and is encased in minimum R-12.5 insulation.

> If a gas hot water heater serving a four-unit apartment containing 51
> fixture units heats water to 130° F, what is its minimum capacity?

Step 1. Find the theoretical capacity of the water heater.

4)C)4)i)1) **Gas heaters:** $220 (F + 2 F_n) \approx C_g (T_h - T_c)$
       2) **Electric heaters:** $245 (F + 2 F_n) \approx C_e (T_h - T_c)$

F = number of hot water fixture units served, 51 units
F_n = amount of nonfixture unit hot water required, gpm. This is some-
       times relevant for industrial applications. Here F_n = 0.
C_g = capacity of gas hot water heater, ? gal
C_e = capacity of electric hot water heater, ? gal. Not applicable.
T_h = temperature of heated water, 130° F
T_c = temperature of cold water, ° F. Use T_c = 55° or local AAT unless
       more definitive data is available. Here T_c = 55°.

       $220 (51 + 2 \times 0) \approx C_{gas} (130 - 55)$ ... C = 150 gal

Step 2. Find the water heater's effective capacity from the fixture unit
diversity bar graph below. At a theoretical capacity of 150 gal ➡ effective
capacity ≥ 89 gal.
                        Theoretical capacity

21 30   50   100   2   3   5   1,000   2   3   5   10,000   2
├┬┬┬┴┬┬┬┴┬┬┬┬┴┬┬┬┬┬┬┬┴┬┬┴┬┬┴┬┬┴┬┬┬┬┴┬┬┬┬┬┬┬┴┬┬┴┬┬┴┬┬┴┬┬┬┬┴┬┬┬┬┤
21   30   50   100   2   3   5   1,000   2
                 Diverse or effective capacity

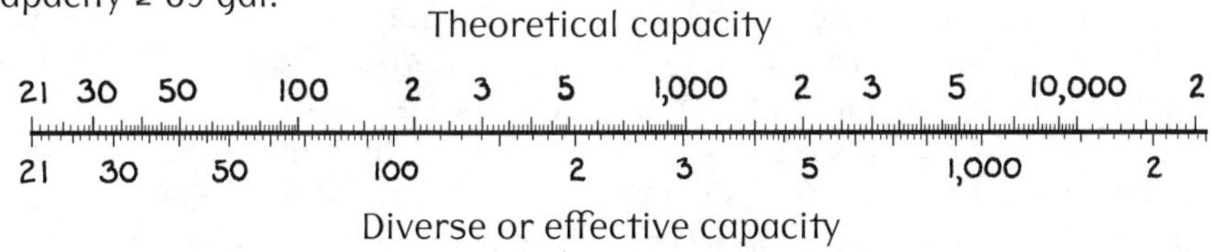

Fig. 4-20. Diversity bar graph.

4.C.5. Water Heat Reclamation

Wherever wasted heat occurs in or near a building, its energy can be recaptured by exposing the escaping Btus to a thin container of circulating water that absorbs the heat, then carries it to a more useful location in the building. A few heat sources that lend themselves well to these exchanges are flue gases, warm graywater, light fixtures, electric motors, refrigerators, and internal combustion engines. Removing such heat can also improve the source's performance: e.g. lights operate more efficiently and last longer if they are cool, and air conditioning is more efficient the more its machinery runs cool. Thus such thermal hitch-hiking often has a double energy value.

An excellent method of retrieving wasted energy is with a heat pump. The pump's cold end is immersed in the rejected heatflow, whether it be air or liquid, then the retrieved Btus are carried to the pump's hot end, which is immersed in the fluid that needs heating. The technology behind such thermal transfer is the same as that of the decades-old refrigeration industry. Such systems usually require considerable cleverness to actuate —thus they are a good example of substituting imagination for money.

4.C.6. Solar Water Heating

An ecological —and often economical— method of heating water for architectural use is to expose it to the sun. In many regions of the world this is a common way of producing hot water for small buildings, and was even popular in many southern regions of this country as late as the 1930s. Since there are a great variety of solar water heating devices worldwide, the following is a conceptual account of available components.

The surface that exposes the water to the sun is typically a planar network of small piping oriented toward the south so it receives the greatest amount of solar radiance year-round. The piping usually has a pane of glazing just in front and a layer of insulation immediately behind and around its sides, all of which form a thin panel or collector with a large surface area. In the Northern Hemisphere the panel's optimal horizontal angle, or azimuth, is due south (although 30° east or west of south will still collect 87° of the optimum), and its optimal tilt above horizontal for year-round collecting is about 20° + the local latitude.

The best piping for solar water heating is thin-walled small-diameter flexible copper tuning: it conducts heat well, is economical, won't rust, and can be easily bent. This tubing is more efficient if flattened slightly; and it is more energy-absorbent if coated with a *selective surface* or *low-E coating*, a paint or electroplating that absorbs much incident shortwave energy while

(Business News Publishing Co., Des Plaines, IL), Nov 1997, pp. 28–30; and (2) Jack

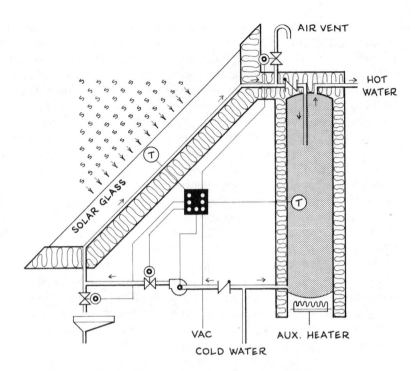

Fig. 4-21. Making hot water from sunshine.

radiating little of the converted longwave energy. Steel pipe is **N2G** for solar water heating because it is rigid and doesn't conduct heat as well as copper, and plastic pipe and Solaroll® (a black plastic multi-tubing that was popular in the 1970s) are **NG** for producing drinkable hot water because at high temperatures these materials leach their molecules into the circulating fluid. The best glazing is tempered glass: it is highly resistant to breakage from falling branches, its coefficient of thermal expansion is one-sixth that of plexiglass, and it doesn't turn brittle after a few years' exposure to sunlight. The insulation on the panel's back and sides should be thick —6 in. or more— because trying to trap the sun's energy with poorly insulated collectors is like using a sieve to hold the gasoline that runs your car. If the sides of two panels abut each other, the seam needs no insulating. The best insulation is usually Styrofoam: it is thermally and physically strong, requires little perimeter-heat-losing structural support to hold it in place, and is water-repellent. Fiberglass batts are not a wise choice because they are structurally weak and lose their insulating value if they are wet, which is apt to happen in installations exposed to the sky.

The water that flows through the sun-exposed piping, entering it cold and leaving it warm, is pushed through the piping by a small pump or by a natural phenomenon called *thermosiphoning*, which is the upward movement of the water due to its being heated which makes it expand slightly and become lighter than the cooler water below. After leaving the piping the water enters a holding tank, which should be near the collectors and also be thickly insulated, as should the piping between it and the collector area. If the water is circulated through the piping via thermosiphoning, the tank should be located near the top of the collectors. For an average-sized residence the tank should hold 60–80 gallons, and it should have an auxiliary heat source to maintain its optimal temperature during cloudy weather.

A controversy regarding solar water heaters is whether its circulating fluid should be the water used or a water/glycol solution. Water alone doesn't require an energy-robbing heat exchanger (a component in which a 3–4° F temperature loss typically occurs between the inlet and outlet surfaces of the metal interface that transfers the heat), but water can freeze while water/glycol won't. Thus, during the solar heydays of the late 1970s, nearly all but this country's most southerly solar collectors heated water/glycol then ran this solution through a heat exchanger to warm the actual water used; but unfortunately, this double-plumbing heat transfer added just enough extra cost and inefficiency to make these systems uneconomical. Another drawback in the late 1970s was the unavailability of computerized controls. But today, a few strategically located thermal sensors can notify a computer chip to drain a collector's plumbing when the temperature falls below, say, a safe 38°, then refill it when the temperature rises enough to reheat the circulating water. With these components now widely available, it may be time to revive this venerable technology.

The following performance criteria are typical of well-designed solar water heating systems:

▶ Optimal system flow rates are usually 0.03-0.04 gpm·sf of collector area, and pipe diameters maintain fluid flows of 2–6 fps. However, above 4 fps efficiency lowers.
▶ If the collector piping has an expansion tank (good in any region with hot summers and cold winters), the tank volume should ≈ 12 percent of the collector fluid loop volume.
▶ The storage tank insulation should ≥ R-30. Maximum thicknesses lead to minimum heat losses —for tanks, pipes, and any other component that holds the heated water. Remember that insulation is a one-time cost that reduces a lifetime cost.
▶ The sun has little radiance when it is less than 15° above the horizon. This significantly reduces its net useful hours in northern latitudes, especially if much cloudy weather occurs in winter.

An effective solar water heater can be built onsite by a carpenter out of lumberyard material, except for the selective surface, which may require electroplating.

Publishing Co., Troy, MI), Jan 2000, pp. 80–88.

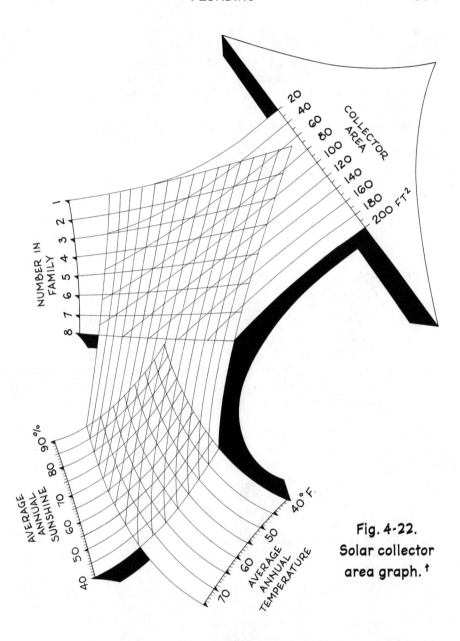

Fig. 4-22.
Solar collector
area graph. †

A family of four living near Amarillo, TX, plans to obtain hot water from solar collectors. If the local annual temperature averages 57° and the skies are clear 73 percent of the year, size the system.

† this figure was taken from *The Ecological House*, Robert B. Butler (Morgan

Step 1. Determine the system's optimal collector area from the Solar Collector Area Graph of Fig. 4-22. Find where the *AAT line* for 57° meets the *Annual Sunshine line* for 73 percent, then follow the line from this point first to the *Number in Family line* for four people, then to the *Collector Area* scale ➡ 74 sf. This is for energy-conservative household use of hot water.

Step 2. Size the system's solar hot water reservoir as follows:

4)C)6)a) **Capacity, gallons:** $C \approx 2\,A$

b) **Capacity, cubic ft:** $C = 0.27\,A$

C = storage capacity of solar hot water reservoir, gal or cf
A = optimal area of solar collector glazing, sf

4.C.7. Irrigation [†]

Any planted environment —lawn, shrubs, or trees— requires water. If rainfall is inadequate during the growing season, below-grade plumbing with sprinkler heads protruding above the soil may be installed. Such systems give a brighter healthier look to athletic fields, broad lawns around residences and country clubs, golf club greens and fairways, and crops that might otherwise wilt and die during hot weather.

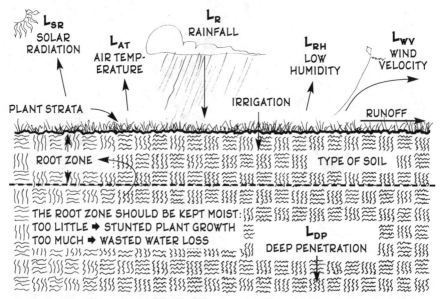

Fig. 4-23. Ecological factors affecting plant irrigation.

& Morgan, Dobbs Ferry, NY, 1981), p. 87.   [†] The primary source for this section

When rainfall or sprinkler water enters the soil, its molecules form a film around the soil particles via a static-electric attraction known as *adhesion*. As more water enters the soil, the liquid molecules' attraction to each other fills the pores between the soil's particles via *cohesion*. As still more water enters, its added weight on the water below pushes the lower water deeper into the soil via *gravitation*. As more water enters and the soil saturation deepens, friction between the adhesive nature of the soil particles and the cohesive nature of the water sets in and slows the effect of gravitation via *resistance*. Finally, when so much water has entered the soil that the force of resistance equals the pull of gravitation, any added water cannot enter the soil and becomes *runoff*. This five-step process is greatly influenced by the soil's permeability: the less permeable the soil, the slower the above processes. The amount of irrigation water a planted environment requires also relates to the nature of plant strata's root zone, type of supporting soil, and other factors as sketched in Fig. 4-23. All the above factors are combined in the general formula

$$A\,(C + I) \;=\; L_r + L_{sr} + L_{at} + (100 - L_{rh}) + L_{wr} + L_{dp}$$

A = area of plant strata to be irrigated
C = capacity of subsoil to retain water
I = irrigation cycle time
    All other values are defined in Fig. 4-23.

Theoretically all the above values must be quantified, but in reality most cannot be except in the most exacting circumstances; then the values usually become maxima or minima. Then the above formula distills to

4)C)7) $9,500\,\mathcal{E}\,Q \;=\; A\,D\,C\,W$

$\mathcal{E}$ = biotic efficiency of rainfall application or irrigation event, depending on local climatic condition as follows: low desert = 0.60; high desert = 0.65; hot dry = 0.70; temperate = 0.75; cool = 0.80. If irrigation events are necessary, $\mathcal{E}$ will likely be hot dry or less ≤ 0.70.
Q = required irrigation waterflow, gpm. This equation is typically solved for this value, which then is used to size the irrigation's required piping according to Example 4)C)5).
A = area of plant strata to be irrigated, sf
D = depth of roots in plant strata, ft. 1.3 ft is a general value. $D \approx$ 1.0 ft for short plant strata (e.g. close-cropped lawns) in dry soil.
C = capacity of subsoil to retain water, in/ft depth. Typical values are coarse gravelly soil = 0.5, fine sand = 1.0, sandy loam = 1.5, loam = 2.0, clayey loam = 2.2, and fine topsoil = 3.0 in/ft depth.
W = portion of water depletion that maintains non-wilting plant strata, %. Typical values are 50% for medium-value turf and 75% for low-value turf. Use more articulate data when available.

was *The Site Calculations Pocket Reference*, Ed Hannon (Wiley, NY, 1999); pp.   ▯

4.C.8. Swimming pools †

A swimming pool is a complicated occupancy. One's purpose may range from athletics to zoology, its shape may range from rectangular to a bizarre array of arcs, its function may be public or private, it may be used day and night or only to look at, and each may have related occupancies such as decking, sexually separate dressing and showering facilities, snack bars, kitchens, meeting areas, lifeguard offices, medical facilities, parking, and never enough area for storage. But no matter how complex this occupancy is, a thin thread of simplicity always runs through its core. For example, every swimming pool has water, of a certain area, volume, and temperature. From these simple parameters evolves a container of clean clear liquid rimmed with the right number of rightly sized and placed inlets and outlets plus a rightly sized pump, filter bed, backwash pump, chlorinator, water heater, strainers, related piping and controls, and all the maintenance access that this combination of components requires.

All the spatial design criteria leading to a pool's optimal area and depth is usually distilled to an optimal volume, which then is used to size the aqueous occupancy's every plumbing subcomponent. However, the first act in designing a swimming pool is to consider its purpose. Recreation? Competition? Health? Luxury? Such initial considerations plus the nature of the site usually suggest the pool's shape. Then envision the enhancements the pool should have: broad terraces, elaborate entrances, lavish foliage, sinuous rims assembled of exquisite tiles, mosaiced bottoms, fountains, sculptures, rock gardens, sliding boards, Jacuzzis, cabanas, gazebos —everything but mermaids. Finally, never forget that these occupancies are dangerous. *People can get killed in them*, and in a surprising number of ways. A designer's imagination must be infused with this vital fact so a lacquer of safety is applied over every surface of the pool's design: nonskid trim on every step, life preservers within easy reach on every side, grounded electrical wiring, and so much more. Even the most seemingly innocuous shallow pool can be a death trap. For example, in 1999 a friend of the author's family was in an amusement park when he spied a child laying face down in a small pool of foot-deep water. He immediately jumped in to rescue the child —and was electrocuted. The cause? Faulty groundwiring in the little pump that fed the shallow pool.

The mechanical design of an outdoor swimming pool is surprisingly simple. But indoor pools have an added mechanical dimension: excess humidity. This can coat every surface with a slimy sheen of condensation, obscure vision through any enclosing glazing, and penetrate beyond interior surfaces to foster mold, rot, and corrosion in the building's structure. These problems are avoided by (1) fitting the occupancy with a powerful dehumidification system, and (2) installing a 6-mil vapor barrier behind every interior finish in which every seam is overlapped and taped. These

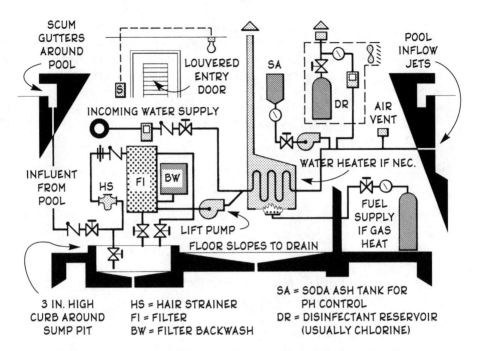

Fig. 4-24. A swimming pool's mechanical componentry.

two solutions allow the installation of such materials as gypsum wallboard (OK if it is rated MR for moisture-resistant) and woodwork (leave it unpainted so it can breathe). But the best finishes in these spaces are moisture-resistant tile, brick, stone, and stucco. But these surfaces spawn another problem: echoes. Here the designer has an elegant solution: plants. Tall broad-leaved plants spilling out of every corner, long rows of foliage in front of glazing, large potted plants scattered everywhere else. What could be more compatible with water?

    If an indoor swimming pool has large areas of glazing in its ceiling and walls, condensation can be a serious problem. But here is where the powerful dehumidification system comes in. Take the enclosed swimming pool and 1,800 gallon hot tub at the Pocmont Resort & Conference Center in Bushkill, PA. Here even in zero-degree weather the glass is clear, and when a bather steps across the patio, the watery footprints vanish in seconds; because the pool has a 53 lb/hr moisture-removing capacity system that maintains a constant 50 percent relative humidity above the water. In this cleverly designed system, part of the fresh air supply enters through ceiling-mounted fabric ducts that do not collect condensation, whose grilles are positioned to bathe each pane of roof glazing with thin streams of warm dry air. This ducting is so light that it arrived in a few UPS packages and took only 5 hours of unskilled labor to install. In the floor along the glass windows are PVC-coated steel ducts whose grilles bathe the wall-mounted panes with more warm dry air. Every aluminum mullion between the greenhouse array of glazing in the roof and walls has a rubber gasket between its interior and exterior; and beneath the patio's ceramic tile floor is a radiant heating system that keeps the floor toasty warm —a delight when a bather may gaze at two feet of snow outside.[†]

After a swimming pool is designed, its mechanical components may be selected and sized as follows:

Step 1. Knowing the pool's shape, compute its surface area. If the area requirements depend on the pool's occupancy load, it may be sized from

4)C)8) $$A = 25 B$$

A = minimum area of pool based on its occupancy load, sf
B = maximum number of bathers planned to use the pool

Step 2. Knowing the pool's surface area, determine the depth of every part of its area from the following criteria:

Wading areas for children .... 12–24 in. deep
General shallow areas .... min. 3'-6" deep
Areas where diving is permitted from pool edge .. min. 9'-0" deep
Plummet depths beneath diving boards:
    Beneath 1 meter boards .... min. 11'-0" deep and 20' wide
    Beneath 3 & 5 meter boards ... min. 12'-0" deep and 24' wide
    Beneath 10 meter towers .... min. 15'-0" deep and 28' wide
If tank's floor-to-side seams are round ..... vertical radii ≤ 2'-0"
Floor inclines .... max. 1:12 down to 4'-6" deep
    From 4'-6" deep .... max. 1:3 down to pool's max. depth

Step 3. Knowing the pool's depth in every area, find its volume, possibly by using the excavation volume formulas given in Volume 1, Sec. 8.D. For

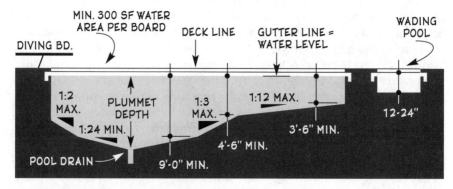

Fig. 4-25. Recommended swimming pool dimensions.

(McGraw-Hill, New York, 1995); pp. 2-58 to 2-61. [†] "Case in Point", *Engineered*

subsequent calculations, assume the pool's capacity = 100,000 gal.

Step 4. Knowing the pool's volume, determine the capacity of its circulation pump. The pool's volume requires at least three turnovers per day to keep its water properly treated and fresh.

$$V_p = 480 \ C_p$$

V_p = volume of swimming pool, 100,000 gal
C_p = capacity of circulating pump, gpm. This is usually a double-suction centrifugal pump, as reciprocating pumps produce pulsations in the filters and single-suction pumps generally wear out faster. In public pools two pumps of the required capacity are usually installed, then continuous operation is ensured if one pump needs servicing.

$$100,000 = 480 \ C_p \qquad \ldots C_p = 208 \ \text{gpm}$$

Step 5. Determine the circulating pump's full discharge head. The pump must deliver at least 15 psi pressure to each pool inlet after overcoming friction losses due to piping, fittings, filters, and possible heating.

  a. Head in ft: $H_{ft} \geq 1.1 \ (35 + L_{pf} + L_f + L_h)$
  b. Head in psi: $H_{psi} \geq 0.48 \ (35 + L_{pf} + L_f + L_h)$

H_{ft} = total discharge head of pump, ft. 1 $H_{ft} \times 0.433 \ H_{psi}$.
H_{psi} = total discharge head of pump, psi.
L_{pf} = pump head loss due to system piping and fittings, ft. This is rarely more than 10 ft.
L_f = equivalent pump head loss due to filtration, ft. This usually ≈ 50 ft for sand or permanent media filters and 90 ft for diatomaceous filters. Here assume 50 ft.
L_h = equivalent pump head loss due to heating, ft. If no heating is required, $L_h = 0$; otherwise L_h rarely exceeds 10 ft.

$$H \geq 1.1 \ (35 + 10 + 50 + 10) = 116 \ \text{ft or 50 psi}$$

Step 6. Determine the pool's amount of makeup water flow. When a swimmer enters the pool, a volume of water equal to the swimmer's weight is displaced which flows into outlets at the pool's edge; then when each swimmer leaves the pool the displaced water is replenished from a local water source or by recirculating the outlet waterflow after purification. Assuming that a swimmer weighs 160 lb, a pool's makeup waterflow is found from

$$Q_m = 0.32 \ B$$

Q_m = pool's rate of makeup waterflow, gpm
B = maximum number of bathers planned to use the pool.
     Here assume that $B = 100$ bathers.

Systems magazine (Business News Publishing Co., Troy, MI); May 2000, pp. 20-22.

$$Q_m = 0.32 \times 100 = 32 \text{ gpm}$$

Step 7. Knowing the capacity of the pool's circulating pump, compute the effective bed area of the filtration system. Whether the system is permanent media or diatomaceous earth, its optimal filtration rate is usually about 2.5 gpm·sf.

$$C_p = 2.5 \, A_f$$

C_p = capacity of pool's circulating pump, from Step 3, 208 gpm
A_f = effective bed area of filtration system, sf

$$208 = 2.5 \, A_f \quad \dots A_f = 83 \text{ sf}$$

In some pools two identical filters of similar capacity are installed, so one can backwash its filtering media or be serviced while the other continues to operate. If only one filter is installed, it usually backwashes late at night when the pool isn't being used. There are also two general kinds of filtration systems, whose selection is based on the following criteria:

> **Sand or permanent media:** Waterflow rates can be as high as 20 gpm/sf of bed area, they have a high dirt-holding capacity, and their backwash rates are high. Rugged, dependable, simple to operate, economical: The "Chevrolet" system.

> **Diatomaceous earth:** Produces a brilliantly clear water, and the open tank allows thorough visual inspection and quick access to filter componentry at all times. Pump horsepowers are smaller; but the system is more complicated, costs more to run, and is 2–3 times larger per 1,000 gal of water filtered: The "Cadillac" system.

Permanent media filters are usually cylindrical while diatomaceous earth filters are usually rectangular. A multiple bar graph showing approximate filter dimensions versus pool water volume appears in Fig. 4-26 below.

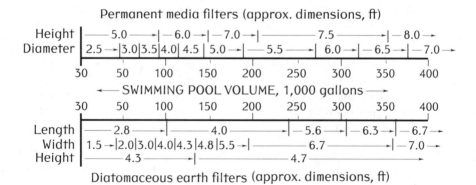

Fig. 4-26. Swimming pool volume versus filter dimensions.

Step 8. Size the pool's backwash sump pump and sump tank. Common sump pump capacities used for backwashing swimming pool filters are 12.5 and 15 gal. The slower pump takes longer to cleanse the filter bed but requires a smaller sump tank.

$$V_s \geq 0.133 \, A_f \, C_s$$

V_s = required volume of sump tank, cf
A_f = effective bed area of filtration system, from Step 7, 83 sf
C_s = capacity of sump pump used for backwashing filter system, usually 12.5 or 15 gpm. Here assume 12.5 gpm.

$$V_s \geq 0.133 \times 83 \times 12.5 = 138 \text{ sf} \Rightarrow \text{one size} = 4 \times 5 \times 7 \text{ ft}$$

Step 9. Determine the pool's optimal number of inlets from

$$C_p \geq \eta \, C_i$$

C_p = capacity of pool water circulating pump, from Step 4, 208 gpm
η = optimal number of inlets around pool's perimeter
C_i = optimal discharge capacity of each inlet, gpm. Each inlet should discharge 10–20 gpm, and they should be located equidistantly no more than 30 ft apart around the pool perimeter. This calculation cannot be performed until the pool perimeter is known.

Note: Each outlet is customarily a single drain located at the bottommost level of the pool's floor and is usually sized to drain the pool between 4 and 12 hr. However, the pool cannot drain faster than the capacity of the sewer the water drains into, and its rate of drainage is a function of not only the drain's diameter but also the solid-to-opening ratio of its cover plate. Thus a pool's drain cannot be correctly sized unless the solid-to-opening ratio or net free area of its cover plate is known.

Step 10. Size the pool's disinfecting system. Chlorine is the most common swimming pool disinfectant, but bromine and ozone are used also. If chlorine, the system continually drips the chemical into the pool's inlet water-flow to maintain a constant 0.5 ppm of chlorine in the pool water. Thus

$$1,920,000 \, Q_d = \eta \, V_p$$

Q_d = amount of disinfectant required to disinfect pool water, lb/day
η = number of hours per day pool is open, hr. If pool is open from 9 A.M. to 6 P.M. every day, η = 9 hr.
V_p = volume of swimming pool, from Step 3, 100,000 gal

$$1,920,000 \, Q_d = 9 \times 100,000 + 480 \times 9 \times 32 \quad \ldots \; Q_d = 0.54 \text{ lb/day}$$

Step 11. Size the pool's water heater if one is necessary. Unless the pool is an outdoor pool that is open only during the summer, its incoming water supply is probably heated to the pool water's desired temperature.

$$t\,H_p = 48,000,000\ C_p\,(T_i - T_o) + H_m$$

t = time required to heat total volume of pool water, hr. 48 hr is generally allowed to heat commercial swimming pools; then $t = 48$.

H_p = amount of energy required to heat the pool water, **?** Btu/hr

C_p = capacity of pool water circulating pump, from Step 4, 208 gpm

T_i = desired temperature of pool water, ° F. Typical indoor pool water
temperatures are 75–85° for pleasure swimming, 77-80° for competitive swimming, and 97–104° for whirlpools and spas. 80° is a good
average for pools used for pleasure and competitive swimming.

T_o = temperature of local water supply that is heated to pool water's
desired temperature, ° F.

H_m = heat migration losses through the building envelope while pool is
filling, Btu/hr. During the many hours it takes to heat the pool
water to the desired temperature, some of the heat migrates
through the pool's floor and sides as well as into the air above the
water then through the walls and roof that enclose the air. This
escaping heat should be quantified and its hourly loss included in
the above formula as H_m. This amount may be determined by using
this volume's heat flow calculations in Sec. 2.E.

Climate control system guidelines for indoor swimming pools are:

▸ Optimal indoor pool air temperatures are 75–85° for pleasure swimming, 77–85° for competitive swimming, and 80–85° for whirlpools
and spas. 82° is a good average for multiple occupancies.

▸ Fresh air requirements = 0.5 cfm/sf of pool and deck area. This is
primarily to remove pool odors, and it must ≥ 25 cfm required for
each occupant engaged in moderate activity.

▸ Supply air circulation volume = 4–8 AC/hr. If other parameters
permit, this can be lower because highly humid air is rarely uncomfortable to swimming pool occupants.

▸ Air velocity above deck and diving areas ≤ 25 fpm. Higher velocities make bathers feel chilly.

▸ Air velocity above pool water ≤ 10 fpm. Higher velocities increase
evaporation ➡ increases room humidity ➡ increases energy consumed to reduce humidity.

▸ Air supply outlets should aim toward the coldest envelope surfaces above the pool water to prevent condensation from forming
on these surfaces. The largest such surfaces are usually wall and
ceiling glazing. Direct supply air across them in thin planes beginning at one edge. Avoid pocketed skylights.

▸ Return air grilles for removing warm moist air should be located
near the top of the room.

▶ If the natatorium has a spectator area, its occupants should not experience the same moist air that is above the pool. This is achieved by locating air supply grilles low behind the spectators and return air grilles high on the water's other side.

Wiring and electrical outlet requirements for swimming pools are:

▶ All metal within 5 ft of pool water must be bonded and grounded with 8 AWG copper wiring. This includes light shells, wall switches, steel reinforcing, drains, inlets, ladders and handrails, motor bases, metal conduits, etc.

▶ Around outdoor pools any wall switches must be at least 5 ft above the water level and 10 ft from the water's edge. Around indoor pools these dimensions increase to 7.5 ft and 10 ft and the fixtures must be enclosed.

▶ Any junction box must be at least 4 ft from the water's edge.

▶ Any GFCI outlet must be at least 10 ft from the water's edge.

▶ Any underwater pool lighting must $\geq$ 18 in. below the water level.

▶ Pool pumps, panel boxes, transformers, and any related componentry must be at least 5 ft from the water's edge, and any related wiring must run through metal conduit.

▶ Any outdoor overhead wiring must be at least 22 ft above pool water and 14 ft above diving boards.

▶ Some local building codes prohibit electrical power wiring directly above the water in indoor swimming pools. If this is the case and illumination is desired directly above the water, light pipes may be installed whose guides extend over the water if their endfeeders are at least 6 ft behind the vertical projection of the water's edge. An example of such an installation is the Municipal Swimming Pool in Las Vegas, which has 12 pairs of sulphur lamp-illuminated light pipes, each 66 ft long, above its 75 × 165 ft swimming area.

4.D. NONWATER PLUMBING

Plumbing systems often convey liquids and gases other than drinkable water. For example, every house with a gas stove has nonwater plumbing, hospitals often have eight separate gas plumbing systems, nonpure water plumbing is standard in waste treatment plants, and nonwater plumbing is common in oil refineries and many industrial facilities. Moreover, the technology of such plumbing is vintage 19th century, since it was used to convey fuels to the gaslights of that era. Nonwater plumbing also includes pure water plumbing, whose design requires special components.

4.D.1. Process Piping †

This piping is used for conveying liquids other than water. It is designed much as water supply plumbing except that pipe pressure drop is a function of the conveyed fluid's specific gravity and viscosity as compared to water. When this piping carries petroleums, chemicals, toxic wastes, and other environmentally damaging fluids it requires *containment piping*, an enclosure of significantly larger-diameter piping that protects the carrier conduit from damage and prevents leaks from escaping into surrounding media. Process piping may be metal, thermoplastic, or flexible double-wall hose. Thermoplastics are economical, they include split systems that can be easily installed around existing plumbing to allow easy replacing of damaged or contaminated pipes, and clear thermoplastic piping is unsurpassed for visual display. For each system the designer researches the chemical compatibility of each piping with the conveyed liquid, selects the materials, then lays out the system, taking care that the lengths and fittings of the carrier and containment piping are configured the same and their axes coincide, that sleeving and thermal expansion joints align, and that the outer piping's inner dimensions are always larger than the inner piping's outer dimensions. A few carrier/containment piping pairings are 2/4, 3/6, 4/8, 6/10, 8/12, 12/18, and 30/42 in. Large-diameter systems often have access chases that are big enough to walk in and manholes at every elbow. Containment piping usually requires double-walled holding tanks and leak detection systems. The latter may include continuous tracer wire under the outer piping, graphic annunciators that provide visual readouts of the network, automated monitors, sampling ports (small glass windows in the piping), and alarms.

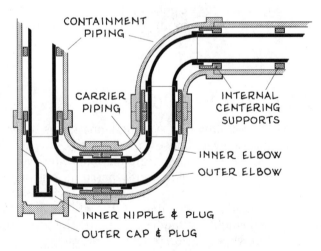

Fig. 4-27. Containment piping details.

---

† This section's information on containment piping was taken from Christopher

A gasoline pipe in an aircraft factory runs from a holding tank well outside the building to the engine-testing section inside. If the line is 172 ft long, has few bends, a head of 8 ft, an initial flow of 80 gpm at 60 psi, and requires 24 psi pressure at the outlet valve, size the piping.

Step 1. Estimate the pipe pressure drop due to flow friction.

4)D)1) $\qquad L\,\Delta P \approx 57\,P_i - 67\,P_m - 29\,H$

L = effective length of pipe (includes normal number of fittings), 172 ft
ΔP = estimated pipe pressure drop due to flow friction, ? psi
P_i = initial water pressure, 60 psi
P_m = minimum fixture pressure at highest or farthest outlet, 24 psi
H = head or height of flow, 8 ft

$$172\,\Delta P \approx 57 \times 60 - 67 \times 24 - 29 \times 8 \quad \dots \Delta P \approx 13.6 \text{ psi}$$

Step 2. Convert the nonwaterflow to equivalent water fixture unit flow.

$$Þ_{fu} \approx 49,000\ Þ_{gpm}\,\sigma\,\upsilon$$

$Þ_{fu}$ = total equivalent fixture unit flow through pipe, ? f.u.
$Þ_{gpm}$ = nonfixture unit flow, if any, through pipe, gpm. $Þ_{gpm}$ = 80 gpm
ß = specific gravity of liquid flowing in pipe. σ for gasoline = 0.91.
υ = kinematic viscosity of liquid flowing in pipe. From fluid mechanics book, υ for gasoline at room temperature ($\approx 70°$) = 4.8×10^{-6}.

$$Þ_{fu} \approx 49,000 \times 80 \times 0.91 \times (4.8 \times 10^{-6}) \approx 17 \text{ f.u.}$$

Step 3. Find the minimum pipe diameter from Fig. 4-7. As this graph's pressure drop scale is for 100 LF of pipe and the gas line is 172 ft long, use ΔP = 13.6 psi × 100/172 ft = 7.91 psi at 17 fixture units (flush tank) ➜ minimum pipe diameter = $1\frac{1}{4}$ in.

Step 4. Convert the liquid's pipe flow from gpm to fps.

$$Þ_{gpm} = 2.45\ Þ_{fps}\,d^2$$

$Þ_{gpm}$ = volume of liquid or gas flow through pipe, 80 gpm
$Þ_{fps}$ = velocity of liquid or gas flow through pipe, ? fps
d = clear inside diameter of pipe, in. $1\frac{1}{4}$ in. = 1.25 in.

$$80 = 2.45\ Þ_{fps} \times 1.25^2 \quad \dots Þ_{fps} = 20.9 \text{ fps}$$

Step 5. If the liquid velocity exceeds 8 fps, resize the pipe as below.

$$d_r = 0.353\ d_i\ Þ_{fps}^{\,0.5}$$

d_r = resized pipe diameter, if necessary, ? in.

d_i = initial pipe diameter, 1.25 in.
P_{fps} = theoretical pipe flow velocity, from Step 4, 20.9 fps.
As $P_{fps} \geq$ 8 fps, pipe needs resizing as below:

$$d_r = 0.353 \times 1.25 \ (20.9)^{0.5} \quad \ldots \ d_r = 2.02 \text{ in.} \blacktriangleright 2 \text{ in. } \textbf{OK}$$

4.D.1.a. Pure Water Plumbing [†]

Pure water plumbing is a specialized assembly of piping, fittings, pumps, tanks, and other componentry that satisfies a demand for absolutely pure water, usually for a medical or industrial application. However, there are numerous kinds of 'pure water'. One may be 100 percent free of minerals and particulates, while another may have a complete absence of organic matter. Although pure water plumbing systems can vary greatly, their design is typically a function of inlet quality versus required outlet quality, with minor criteria being the usual water pressure, water temperature, and chemical tolerances. The best piping is usually stainless steel but some is plastic, joints should be minimized by using long straight runs, support spans must be short enough to eliminate all sags, systems must be fully drainable with no dead ends allowed, and all lengths must be accessible. Although these systems are designed and installed by water treatment specialists or chemical and plumbing engineers, a generalist designer should have a conversant knowledge of them.

Related to pure water plumbing is *distilling*.[‡] This involves separating water from nonvolatile contaminants by boiling it, condensing the steam by cooling, then collecting the condensate in a reservoir. The boiler must have a removable top so any scale buildup inside may be removed, a drain for flushing residual contaminants, and its outlet located above its inlet. A purity monitor is usually installed between the boiler and the tank; and automated valves may be installed that keep the boiler full, open its drain at programmed intervals to flush the contaminants, and reroute any detected substandard water to a drain. All inner surfaces of any pipes and fittings that contact the distillate must be coated with pure tin; as aluminum, steel, and even Pyrex glass will impart trace impurities into the liquid. Storage tank capacities are usually about 10 × the rate of distillation, and systems are generally rated in terms of the number of gallons distilled per hr. Under perfect conditions 1 boiler hp will evaporate 4.14 gal/hr of water at 212° F. The more the boiler is insulated, the more efficient its operation and the less heat that enters surrounding areas. Distillers are heavy, so one's contained weight should be added to structural loads.

magazine (TMB Publishing Co., Northbrook, IL); Nov/Dec 1994, p. 36. [†] The infor-

4.D.2. Gas Plumbing Systems

There are two general kinds of gases conveyed by plumbing: *medical* and *fuel*. Although medgases are noncombustible, some, such as O_2 and compressed air, vigorously support combustion; thus all fire safety measures for the latter apply to the former. In both medical and fuel gas systems, the gas is driven via pressure from a public supply main, pressurized cylinders, or pumps. System sizing usually begins at the remote outlet and proceeds upstream through the stems, branches, risers, and mains to the service components. Warning devices are always required; they may include pressure sensors, supply monitors, reservoir gauges, reserve lines, automatic shutoff valves, notifiers to central controls, and audible or visual alarms that activate if pressures rise or fall outside normal ranges. As most sensors and gauges need to be periodically recalibrated, they must be accessible. Other requirements are:

▶ Gas meters should not be near heat-producing devices, under windows or steps, or where they could be damaged.
▶ In multiple occupancies a separate meter must be installed for each occupancy. No downstream interconnection of gas lines between meters is allowed.
▶ All pipe lengths must be plainly marked.
▶ Horizontal piping runs should pitch at least $\frac{1}{16}$ in/ft up in the direction of flow, and accessible drip valves with drainage pans should be installed at all low points.
▶ Supply cannot proceed from a smaller to a larger diameter pipe.
▶ Risers should be centrally located so that gasflow to the branches on each side is fairly even. In large systems, more than one riser enhances even flow and offers redundancy in case one fails. Every riser requires a shutoff valve at its base.
▶ All pipe fasteners must prevent longitudinal movement without denting the pipe, and lengths between fasteners should be short enough to prevent pipe sag.
▶ Every stem requires a shutoff valve just before its outlet.

In multiple occupancies, required flow capacities are often reduced by diversity factors that allow smaller pipe diameters, which is economical and minimizes the possibility that oversized systems will experience moisture problems. But diversity factors should always be investigated, because some appliances, e.g. gas stoves in apartment buildings, may occasionally all be used at the same time. Also beware of diversity factors listed in step form, such as 100 percent for 1–7 units, 75 percent for 8–20 units, etc. According to these numbers (which recently appeared in an engineering magazine), the required gasflow for 8 units is actually 14 percent *less* than for 7 units. Better is a bar graph as appears in Fig. 4-29.

mation on pure water plumbing was obtained primarily from Henry Razouk's "Pure ▐

> What is the velocity of a gas through a 2 in. pipe if its volume of flow is 7 fpm?

4)D)2)

$$3.06 \, Þ_{cfm} = Þ_{fps} \, d^2$$

$Þ_{cfm}$ = volume of liquid or gas flow through pipe, 7 cfm
$Þ_{fps}$ = velocity of liquid or gas flow through pipe, ? fps
d = inside diameter of piping, 2 in.

$$3.06 \times 7 = Þ_{fps} \times 2^2 \quad \ldots Þ_{fps} = 5.36 \text{ fps}$$

4.D.2.a. Medical Gases [†]

Also known as *medgases*, these are used in hospitals, dentists' offices, medical clinics, and numerous industrial and scientific applications that do not involve combustion or heat production. Their piping is type *IPS* threaded brass pipe or type *TB* or *K* copper tubing, and each is sized according to the gas's required outlet volume (liters/min or cfm). Each supply main must have a pressure relief valve set at 1.50 normal line pressure that extends outdoors at least 12 ft above grade, all valves must be 300 psi-rated brass or bronze ball valves, and each outlet requires a shutoff valve and a quick-coupler located 4–5 ft above the floor. Each medgas system usually has narrow operating temperature parameters that require visual and audible alarms that activate when pressure rises or falls 20 percent above or below normal, and system notifiers must be located in telephone switchboards, maintenance areas, and security offices. Spans between supports for $\frac{1}{2}$ in. diameter piping ≤ 6 ft, for $\frac{3}{4}$–1 in. ≤ 8 ft, and for $1\frac{1}{4}$ in. ≤ 10 ft. Requirements for common medgases are described below.

Oxygen (O_2). This gas is stored as a liquid in cylinders either inside the building or in large hermetic reservoirs at least 50 ft outdoors. When released it becomes a gas (1 gal liquid O_2 ≈ 115 cf gas). Systems are designed at initial pressures of 55 psi, ppd (permissible pressure drop) of 5 psi from supply head to remote outlet, and outlet pressures ≥ 50 psi at required flow (e.g. 200 liters/min for surgery and 10 liters/min for nasal tubes). Two O_2 outlets are customarily installed at each hospital bedside in case one fails.

Nitrogen (N_2). In hospitals this gas usually has supply pressures of 50 psi for cleaning, 160 psi for nonorthopedic tool use (ppd to remote outlet ≤ 20 psi), and 250 psi for orthopedic tool use (ppd ≤ 50 psi).

Nitrous oxide (N_2O). In hospitals this gas typically has a flow of 20 liters/min and a remote outlet pressure of 50 psi. In dental offices its sup-

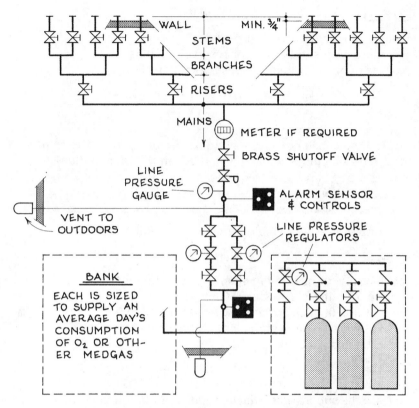

Fig. 4-28. Medical gas piping system componentry.

ply pressure is 80–100 psi and chair outlet pressure is 50 psi.

Ethylene (C_2H_4). As an anesthetic this gas has virtually no ill effects on bodily functions, and during post-surgery it fosters rapid recovery. When mixed with oxygen it is explosive and highly flammable.

Cyclopropane (C_3H_6). This is a nonmetabolized anesthetic which when inhaled produces a reversible nontoxic depression of tissue excitability. Other commonly used inhalation anesthetics are halothane, methoxyfluorane, and diethyl ether.

Carbon dioxide (CO_2). This nonflammable gas is used in anesthesia with oxygen to control respiration and circulation. In post-surgery its use hastens the elimination of anesthesia gases.

Helium (H_2). A light, chemically inert, noncombustible anesthesia.

Example 1. If a gas is stored at 600 psi in a cylinder whose volume is 1.76 ft³, what is the gas's outlet volume?

4)D)2)a)1) $\qquad$ $14.7\ V_g = P\ V_c$

V_g = volume of gas at normal atmospheric pressure, **?** cf
P = pressure of gas in cylinder or reservoir, 600 psi
V_c = volume of gas in cylinder or reservoir, 1.76 cf

$$14.7\ V_g = 600 \times 1.76 \quad \ldots V_g = 71.8 \text{ cf}$$

Example 2. A 36 bed hospital requires an oxygen outlet by each bed. If the system's piping is type K copper, length to remote outlet is 182 ft, ppd is 5 psi, and outlet requirements are 8 liters/min, what size shutoff valve should be installed at the oxygen supply reservoir?

Step 1. Compute the peak volume of flow in the piping.

4)D)2)a)2) $\qquad$ $Þ = \eta\ F\kappa_d$

$Þ$ = peak volume of gas flow in pipe, **?** cfm. 28.3 liters = 1 cf.
η = number of outlets in system, 36 units
F = rate of flow at each outlet, cfm. $F = 8$ L/min ÷ 28.3 L/cf = 0.283 cfm.
κ_d = diversity factor for systems with multiple outlets, from Fig. 4-29.
      At 36 units, $\kappa_d = 0.40$.

$$Þ = 36 \times 0.283 \times 0.40 = 4.07 \text{ cfm}$$

Step 2. Size the supply main (which includes its shutoff valve diameter).

$$L\ \kappa_m\ \sigma^{0.5}\ Þ^2 = 120,000\ \Delta P\ d^5$$

L = length of pipe (includes allowance for normal no. of fittings), 182 ft
κ_m = pipe material coefficient. $\kappa_m = 2.0$ for iron or steel, 1.0 for copper
      or brass. Here $\kappa_m = 1.0$.
σ = specific gravity of gas in pipe. From Table 4-5, σ for oxygen = 1.11.
$Þ$ = peak volume of gas flow in pipe, from Step 1, 4.07 cfm
ΔP = permissible pressure drop (ppd) in piping, 5.0 psi.
      If ΔP is in inches mercury (in. Hg), 1 psi = 2.04 in. Hg.
d = minimum pipe diameter, inside dimension, **?** in. Minimum d = 0.5 in.

$$182 \times 1.0 \times 1.11^{0.5} \times 4.07^2 \approx 120,000 \times 5.0\ d^5 \quad \ldots d = 0.35 \ \text{➡}\ \tfrac{1}{2} \text{ in.}$$

Units

1	2	3	4	5	6	7	8	9	10	11	12+
1.00	0.98	0.93	0.86	0.78	0.70	0.62	0.55	0.49	0.45	0.42	0.40

Diversity

Fig. 4-29. Diversity factor bar graph.

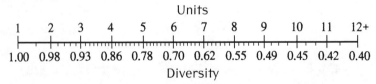

was obtained from *Advanced Plumbing Technology*, Alfred Steele (Construction

4.D.2.b. Compressed Air [†]

Compressed air is ambient air that has been squeezed into a smaller volume and stored in a hermetically sealed container; then when a valve on a pipe extending from the container is opened the high-pressure air rushes out. Later a pump returns the contained air to its original compression. Compressed air is used in hospitals, numerous industries, and in nearly every motor vehicle service facility to operate a variety of air-driven power tools and perform cleaning operations. Similar plumbing is employed in large CO_2 fire suppression systems.

The heart of every compressed air system is a pump. As described in Sec. 5.C.4.b. there are three kinds: *centrifugal, rotary,* and *reciprocating.* Centrifugal pump-driven compressors are generally used to produce large volumes of compressed air at relatively low pressures, liquid-sealed rotary pumps are used to produce small volumes at high pressures, and reciprocating pumps are used to produce large volumes at high pressures. Centrifugal compressors take up less space, use more power per unit output, and need less filtration than rotary compressors, while reciprocating compressors are usually more powerful and more efficient but are large. The pump is usually belt-driven by a squirrel-cage induction electric motor, but synchronous motors may be used when power-factor correction is desired. As the pumps are usually noisy, they are typically mounted on vibration isolators, their inlet and outlet stems have flexible connections, and their exhausts are fitted with mufflers.

A compressed air system may be *unit* (several small compressors supply a few nearby outlets) or *central* (one central compressor supplies all outlets). Unit systems generally satisfy small compressed air requirements in scattered areas while central systems satisfy large requirements in concentrated areas. A compressed air system may be further categorized as single-stage, two-stage, air-cooled, or water-cooled, usually depending on its power and pressure parameters as sketched in Fig. 4-30. In addition to a pump, most systems have an *intake filter* (to protect the com-

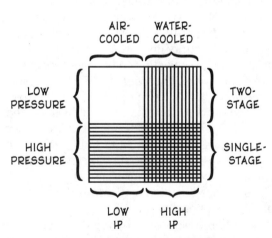

Fig. 4-30. Compressed air system parameters.

Industry Press, Elmhurst, IL, 1984), pp. 70–75.   [†] From p. 316: the primary

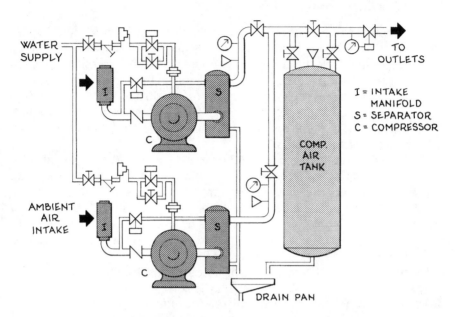

Fig. 4-31. Duplex compressed air system componentry.

pressor from particulate damage), *afterfilters* (to protect the regulators and lines from oils and impurities imparted to the air by machinery wear during operation), possibly a *dehumidifier* (to remove moisture in the line), an *air receiver tank* (to dampen pump oscillations and collect moisture condensate), an *automatic tap* at the bottom of the air receiver (to drain the condensate), a *drain pan* below the tap (to empty the condensate into waste plumbing), *visual* and *audible alarms* (to notify authorities when pressures rise above or fall below accepted norms), connection to an *emergency generator* (in case power fails during operation), and *controls*. Each system is typically rated in terms of its *free air capacity* (the air pressure at the compressor intake); and its compressed air requirements are usually specified in *acfm* (air volume based on actual pressure and temperature) and not *scfm* (air volume based on sea level pressure of 14.7 psi at 60° F). Large systems are often designed as MMRD systems with multiple pumps and computerized controls, in which the capacity of η - 1 compressors ≥ the peak load. The components of any system are usually housed in a small utility area. The usual life of a compressor is about 20 years.

Compressed air systems are often complicated by the fact that when air is compressed it heats up, and this thermal buildup not only imposes an additional work load on the pump, it increases the air's pressure which makes it difficult to maintain uniform operating pressures. Thus in large

sources for this section were (1) *Advanced Plumbing Technology*, Alfred Steele

systems the pump cylinder head may be jacketed with circulating water, the supply main may be run through a water heat exchanger, refrigeration may cool the pump cylinders or the intake air, or the system may be divided into multistage compressors with intercoolers between each stage. In small systems the added heat is usually removed simply by exposing all piping and container surfaces to ambient air or plenty of ventilation.

Compressed air piping is usually designed at manifold pressures up to 200 psi, remote outlet pressures to 50 psi, and velocities ranging from 3.5–4,000 fpm. The piping requires regulators, pressure relief valves, test points, and automatic purge drains. After each system is installed its piping should be subjected to an air pressure test.

As standard outdoor air at 68° F weighs 0.075 lb/cf, the unit weight of compressed air = 0.075 × number of atmospheres of compression. In large systems the compressed air's weight is added to structural loads. Sea-level air pressure is 0 psi acfm and 14.7 psi scfm. A compressed air system is usually designed as follows:

Step 1. List all the devices and the number of each that will use the compressed air, locate a convenient air outlet for each device, and list the free compressed air requirement at each outlet in cfm. After laying out the system in plan and elevation, tabulate the length of piping from each compressor to each outlet it serves. This table will later list the size of each length of piping plus the airflow rate and air pressure at each outlet.

Step 2. Determine the system load diversity factor for all outlets or devices that will use the compressed air at any one time. This is usually estimated by carefully thinking out how the devices will use the compressed air, particularly the frequency, length of time, criticality of use, and portion of maximum possible workload of each device. For example, if three hospital surgical suites require compressed air outlets, all three might be used at the same time and thus a critical situation would arise if one was inoperative; thus the load factor for this scenario is $3/3$ = 1.00. Another example: if a truck assembly line has 24 workstations that require compressed air outlets and motion studies indicate that each worker uses compressed-air-driven power tools an average 0.93 hours a day, one could say this occupancy's load diversity factor is $9.93/8$ × a 2.5 "coincidence factor" = 0.29.

Step 3. When selecting the compressor unit, consider its *discharge pressure* and required *capacity*. The discharge pressure should be at least 10 psi greater than the required pressure at any outlet for small systems and as much as 25 psi greater for large systems with long compressor-to-outlet runs. Typical air pressure for compressed air tools = 90 psi.

Step 4. Compute the system's peak demand flow.

(Construction Industry Press, Elmhurst, IL, 1984); Chapter 19; (2) Jerry Van

4)D)2)b)1) $D_p = 1.1 \kappa_d F (1 - 0.000034 E)$

D_p = peak demand of compressed air system, ? cfm.

κ_d = diversity factor, based on feasible ratio of maximum number of outlets used at any one time to total number of outlets.

F = actual fixture flow, fpm. Peak airflow rate ≤ 4,000 fpm.

E = elevation of occupancy above sea level, ft

Step 5. Size each length of piping.

$$L \kappa_m \sigma^{0.5} Þ^2 = 120,000 \, \Delta P \, d^5$$

L = length of piping (includes allowance for normal no. of fittings), ft

κ_m = pipe material coefficient.

κ_m = 2.0 for iron or steel piping, 1.0 for copper or brass.

σ = specific gravity of gas flowing in pipe, spsi.

If air pressure is in actual psi or apsi, $\sigma_{spsi} = (\sigma_{apsi} + 14.7)/14.7$.

Þ = peak volume of gas flow in pipe, fpm

ΔP = permissible pressure drop in piping (also ppd), psi. If ΔP is in in. mercury (in. Hg), 1 psi = 2.04 in. Hg. ΔP should not ≥ 5.0 psi.

d = minimum pipe diameter, inside dimension, in. Minimum d = 0.5 in.

Step 6. Size the compressor.

$$67 \, \text{HP} = Þ \, P_i \left\{ [(P_i - 14.7)/_{14.7}]^{0.29} - 1 \right\}$$

HP = required horsepower of compressor, hp

Þ = peak volume of gas pipe flow in pipe, fpm

P_i = initial pressure in piping, psi. This should ≥ 50 psi + ΔP above.

Example 1. If a volume of air has a pressure of 100 psi at actual capacity (acfm), what is its pressure at standard capacity (scfm)?

---

4)D)2)b)2)   **Pressure, psi:** $P_{acfm-psi} + 14.7 = P_{scfm-psi}$ ... ➕

3)   **Pressure, in. Hg:** $P_{cfm} + 29.92 = P_{cfm}$

$P_{acfm-psi}$ = actual pressure of air volume (acfm = cubic feet per minute at actual conditions of pressure), 100 psi acfm

$P_{scfm-psi}$ = standard pressure of air volume (scfm = cubic feet per minute at specified standard conditions of pressure), ? psi scfm

$P_{acfm-Hg}$ = actual pressure of air volume, in. Hg

$P_{scfm-Hg}$ = standard pressure of air volume, in. Hg

$$100 + 14.7 = S_{cfm} \quad \dots \, S_{cfm} = 114.7 \, \text{psi}$$

4.D.2.c. Vacuum Air

For architectural considerations, a vacuum is a negative air pressure below a standard barometric air pressure of 29.92 in. This 'minus air pressure' may be stated in terms of *atmospheres, vacuum pressure, actual pressure,* or *standard pressure.* For example, a 40 percent vacuum = 0.60 atmospheres = a vacuum pressure of 12.0 in. Hg = an actual pressure of –12.0 in. Hg = a standard pressure of 29.92 – 12.0 = 17.92 in. Hg.

Vacuum air is stored in hermetically sealed containers. When a valve on a pipe extending from the container is opened a suction occurs which draws air into the system, then a pump later returns the contained vacuum to its original pressure. Vacuum air is used in hospitals to clean instruments, remove fluids from surgical incisions, perform post-operative drainage, suck spent flammable heavier-than-air anesthesia gases from operating room floors, and other tasks. Vacuum air systems also have many applications in laboratories and industries, and they are installed as cleaning systems in homes, apartments, and hotels.

A unitary vacuum air system typically includes a galvanized or stainless steel tank, air inlets, a pump, exhaust outlets, a means of trapping collected liquids and solids, piping, and controls. The pump is similar to that used for compressed air except the inlets and outlets are reversed. Each pump is rated in actual volume capacity (acfm) at the lead pump cut-in (usually 16 in. Hg), off-the-shelf models are available up to 200 cfm, and custom units have been made for capacities up to 9,000 cfm. As the pumps are usually noisy, they are typically mounted on vibration isolators, their inlets and outlets have flexible connections, and exhaust outlets are fitted with mufflers. Each system may have a number of pump configurations: simple single-stage pumps, two- or multi-stage reciprocating pumps, roughing-down pump plus a mechanical reducer, etc. High-vacuum systems are dangerous due to their strong suctionability.

Unlike in compressed air systems, air pressure changes rarely create problems in vacuum air systems, because in them ΔP never varies by more than one atmosphere while in compressed air systems ΔP may vary by many atmospheres. However, vacuum air systems often leak, often as much as the total volume handled by the pump. This is because air pressure tests are harder to perform on vacuum systems because the usual method of painting each fitting seam with soapsuds doesn't form an expanding bubble at each possible leak, and compressor vibration can cause tiny leaks to form after the system is installed and tested. The first problem is eliminated by modifying each pump so its cycle can be reversed, and the second problem is minimized by mounting the pump on acoustic vibrators and fitting its inlet and outlet with vibration arresters. For sanitary reasons each vacuum system must be easily dismantled and the inner surface of each component including all piping and fittings should be washable; and after each

Engineer magazine (TMB Publishing Co., Northbrook, IL); Jul/Aug 1994, p. 36;

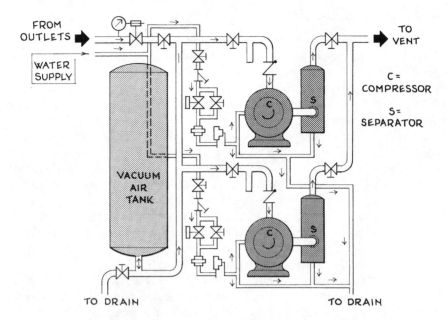

FROM OUTLETS

WATER SUPPLY

TO VENT

C = COMPRESSOR

S = SEPARATOR

VACUUM AIR TANK

TO DRAIN   TO DRAIN

Fig. 4-32. Vacuum air system componentry.

cleaning the reassembled system should be retested. Still the design of each system should incorporate a leakage factor. This should be about 1.2 in new systems that have short runs, few fittings, vibration arresters at each compressor inlet and outlet, and reversible cycles; and correspondingly higher where the opposite conditions occur.

Another potential problem with vacuum systems is that creating the vacuum air can significantly reduce its temperature, which can change its volume; then the system could have trouble maintaining uniform operating pressures. In small systems this temperature decrease is usually negated by the small amount of heat released by the operating machinery; but in large systems, each pump and its outlet may need to be shrouded with refrigerated condensers and traps.

Vacuum air systems are commonly designed with an outlet rating of 12 in. Hg, hose diameter of $1\frac{1}{2}$ in, and an air velocity of 3,000–4,500 fpm. The piping must be corrosion-resistant and is usually sized to maintain a vacuum pressure of 10–15 in. Hg at any outlet, which usually requires an operating range of 15–19 in. Hg at the vacuum receiver. Minimum pipe diameter is $\frac{1}{2}$ in, but $\frac{1}{4}$ and $\frac{3}{8}$ in. diameters are OK for outlet stems in small systems. Two or more pumps are usually installed in each system, in which the capacity of each $\approx (\eta - 1)$ pumps ≥ 1.1 peak load. Hospital vacuum systems require audible and visual alarms that activate when the vacuum falls below a preset level, usually 10 or 12 in. Hg. Each system also requires exhaust air outlets, which should be placed where the escaping air won't come into contact with flammables, won't be objectionable, and where its noise isn't annoying. A usually safe place to empty nonliquid nonsolid vacuum exhaust is into HVAC return ducting.

With some vacuum systems, pump-down time is an important criterion for sizing the compressor(s). Pump-down time may be computed as follows:

4) D) 2) c) 1) $tD = V\kappa_p$

t = vacuum system pump-down time, min
D = pump displacement, cfm
V = volume of vacuum air system including all piping and fittings out to all outlet valves, cf
κ_p = pump-down factor, for single- or multi-stage pumps based on required vacuum pressure of in. Hg from bar graph below:

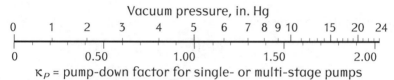

Vacuum pressure, in. Hg

| 0 | 1 | 2 | 3 | 4 | 5 | 6 | 7 8 9 10 | 15 | 20 24 |

| 0 | | 0.50 | | 1.00 | | | 1.50 | | 2.00 |

κ_p = pump-down factor for single- or multi-stage pumps

Fig. 4-33. Pump-down factor bar graph.

A seven-floor vacuum cleaning system in a hotel near San Juan, Puerto Rico, has 372 outlets. If 35 cfm of vacuum air at 3.0 in. Hg is required at each 1½ in. outlet, the length of run from receiver to remote outlet is 392 ft, maximum pressure differential between the outlets and receiver is 12.0 in. Hg, all lines are schedule 40 steel pipe, and typical system operation involves two chambermaids cleaning the rooms on each floor from early morning until all rooms are cleaned, size the supply main and compressor.

Step 1. Compute the system's peak demand airflow.

4) D) 2) c) 2) $Þ = \kappa_d F$

$Þ$ = peak volume of vacuum airflow in system, ? cfm
κ_d = diversity factor for systems with multiple outlets. Typical system operation involves two maids cleaning rooms on each floor ➜ no more than two hoses are connected into any one branch at any time. ∴ $\kappa_d = 2 \times 7 =$ maximum 14 outlets in use at one time.
F = required vacuum airflow at each outlet, given as 35 cfm

$$Þ = 35 \times 14 = 490 \text{ cfm}$$

Step 2. Size the piping.

$$L \, \kappa_m \, \sigma^{0.5} \, Þ^2 \; = \; 120{,}000 \; \Delta P \, d^5$$

L = effective length of pipe (including normal number of fittings), 392 ft
κ_m = pipe material coefficient. κ_m = 2.0 for iron or steel piping, 1.0 for copper or brass. κ_m for schedule 40 steel piping = 2.0.
σ = specific gravity of gas. If vacuum pressure = 3.0 in. Hg, σ = (29.92 − 3.0)/29.92 = 0.90.
$Þ$ = peak volume of vacuum airflow in pipe, from Step 1, 490 cfm
ΔP = permissible pressure drop in pipe, psi. As 2.04 in. Hg = 1 psi, ΔP = 12.0 in. Hg = 12/2.04 = 5.88 psi.
d = minimum pipe diameter, inside dimension, **?** in. Minimum d = 0.5 in.

$$392 \times 2.0 \times 0.90^{0.5} \times 490^2 \; = \; 120{,}000 \times 5.88 \; d^5$$
$$d \; = \; 3.12 \; \blacktriangleright \; 3 \text{ in. probably } \mathbf{OK}$$

Step 3. Size the compressor.

$$Þ \, (14.7 - P_v) \; = \; 3.22 \; Þ \left\{ [^{14.7}\!/_{(14.7 - P_v)}]^{0.29} - 1 \right\}$$

$Þ$ = required horsepower of vacuum air compressor, **?** hp
$Þ$ = peak volume of vacuum air flow in pipe, from Step 1, 490 cfm.
P_v = maximum vacuum air pressure in pipe, psi. From Step 2,
  $P_v = \Delta P$ = 5.88 psi.

$$Þ \, (14.7 - 5.88) \; \geq \; 3.22 \times 490 \left\{ [14.7/(14.7 - 5.88)]^{0.29} - 1 \right\}$$
$$Þ \; \geq \; 28.6 \text{ hp}$$

4.D.2.d. Fuel Gases

Propane, butane, and other flammable gases are used to heat interior spaces as well as run stoves and hot water heaters in homes, low-rise apartments, and small commercial buildings. A typical installation is a large cylinder at 80–120 psi capped with a gauge, regulator, and shutoff valve located just outside the building with a line of flexible copper tubing running indoors. The cylinder should be well-ventilated and accessible by truck, the gas line should be at least 10 ft from any windows and stairways, typical pressure drop from regulator to remote outlet is 0.2–0.5 in. wg (1 psi = 27.7 in. wg), and iron or steel piping cannot be used because they can create sparks when struck. In multi-outlet systems, minimum pipe diameter is ¾ in. type L copper for mains and risers; otherwise the piping is usually sized according to the gas's heating value and Btu ratings of the appliances served. Fuel gas heating values often vary slightly from the values given in Table 4-5 due to impurity of source, method of processing, and local mixing standards.

A serious problem with fuel gases is that they may contain a small amount of moisture, which if it condenses in a sag in the line where it passes through a cold space, the collected water could freeze and split the pipe and an explosion could occur. This danger is eliminated by slightly pitching each horizontal run and installing at its low point a drip valve, which may be a tee whose stem aims down and is fitted with a short extension and spigot valve. A drip valve must also be installed at the base of every riser, where the usual elbow can be replaced by a tee whose stem connects to the supply pipe and whose lower opening is fitted with a spigot valve. Drip valves also act as sediment traps that keep particles in the gas from clogging valve seats, burner orifices, and other small passageways; as such impurities may arrive in the gas or enter the piping as dust, insect debris, or other matter during storage before construction or assembly onsite. Every drip valve must be accessible —then a quick opening and closing of its handwheel blows out any collected moisture or debris.

Below every drip valve should be a drain pan, which must be carefully designed. Its basin should be strong (16 ga stainless steel is good), the basin should be covered to keep out birds and rodents, it should have a 4 in. curb all around (higher if nearby induced vortexes or blowing air could be a problem), it should slope at least $\frac{1}{2}$ in/LF toward a screened drain, the drain's diameter should be at least $1\frac{1}{4}$ in. and at least the exit diameter of the fluid's source, the drain should be as short and straight and vertical as possible, and indoor drain pans require traps. The pan area should be small; as the smaller it is, the less material that is used and the smaller the basin area for mosquito breeding, debris collecting, and bacteria growing.

Every part of a fuel gas system must be accessible for inspection and maintenance; not just its major components and safety devices, but every linear foot of line and every fitting no matter how small. *There should be no exceptions to this.* This fact was borne out during a tragedy near the author's home a few years ago. The scene was a popular restaurant whose dining room was built over an abandoned swimming pool which had not been filled in. Just outside the building stood a large propane tank, whose line extended through a low crawlspace alongside the empty swimming pool to the restaurant's kitchen. As businesses go, this was a small commercial occupancy. Who would have guessed that two lives would be lost in a scenario as innocuous as this?

The gas line had a slight sag between two of its supports.

The crawlspace was too low to allow access for inspection of every linear foot of the line.

The crawlspace was unheated.

A tiny amount of moisture got into the line.

During a period of zero weather the moisture in the line froze.

A crack appeared in the line.

Gas leaked slowly out of the line. Being slightly heavier than air and concealed from dispersing winds, the gas settled in the empty pool.

For several months the gas rose in the pool, inch by inch.

One day the next summer, the restaurant's staff arrived about three o'clock on a sunny Saturday afternoon to get the place ready for business that night. As the floor in the dining area was still dirty from the night before, one of the staff rolled in a cannister vacuum cleaner, inserted its plug into a nearby wall outlet, then leaned down to turn on the vacuum cleaner's switch a few inches above the floor—

BOOOM! The whole restaurant was blown into the sky by a swimming pool filled with ignited propane. Two hearses soon arrived on the scene, accompanied by five ambulances. [†]

Never say that because the building you are designing is small, *access to every linear foot* of its mechanical componentry doesn't matter.

Fuel gas plumbing may also convey fuel from supply tanks to gasoline and diesel generators. Conceptually each installation is as simple as the line running from an automobile gas tank to its engine; but in large

TABLE 4-5: PROPERTIES OF COMMON GASES

Values at 60° F. at sea level

GAS	SPECIFIC GRAVITY	HEATING VALUE
Atmosphere at sea level	1.00	... supports combustion
Compressed air .... 1.00 × no. atmos. pressure		... supports combustion
Vacuum .... 1.00 × no. atmos. pressure		... supports combustion
Oxygen (O_2)	1.11	... supports combustion
Nitrogen (N_2)	0.97	0
Nitrous oxide (N_2O)	1.52	... supports combustion
Carbon dioxide (CO_2)	1.53	0
Carbon monoxide (CO)	0.97	0
Hydrogen (H_2)	0.07	275 Btu/ft^3
Helium (He_2)	0.14	0
Argon (Ar_2)	1.65	0
Neon (Ne_2)	0.67	0
Ammonia (NH_3)	0.60	0
Propane (C_3H_8)	1.52	2,370 Btu/ft^3
Butane (C_4H_{10})	2.01	2,977 Btu/ft^3
Methane (CH_4)	0.55	995 Btu/ft^3
Acetylene (C_2H_2)	0.91	1,455 Btu/ft^3
Coal gas	≈ 0.55	≈ 450 Btu/ft^3
Natural gas (mostly methane + others)	≈ 0.63	≈ 1,000 Btu/ft^3
Fuel oil, light industrial (no. 1)		144,000 Btu/gal
Medium industrial (no. 2)		147,000 Btu/gal
Heavy industrial (no. 1)		150,000 Btu/gal
Gasoline, kerosene		132,000 Btu/gal

buildings, these systems require a dizzying array of subcomponents from each main tank to the small day tanks beside the generators. To begin with, each line requires containment piping for its whole length, hydrocarbon sensor cable under all containment piping and around the edges and undersides of the main tanks, filters and oil/water separators to remove any impurities and moisture, and circulators to keep the fuel flowing slowly through the filters and separators so it will be fresh and pure at all times. Then each oil/water separator requires a reclamation tank for any collected fuel, a sanitary sewer for any collected water, and two pumps in case one fails. Then every subcomponent in the whole system requires alarm wiring that notifies central controls of any malfunction, and the day tanks require programmed tank-level switches (these work much like the float balls in toilet tanks). Finally all the above must be duplicated in case one main tank ever fails or runs dry.

If a fuel gas system has a meter, it should be clearly visible as one enters the room in which it is installed, and it cannot be located under a window or steps, near a doorway, close to a boiler or other heat source, or in any other area where it could be easily damaged.

Typical natural gas use rates of certain domestic appliances are

```
Water heater, side-arm or circulating type ........  25,000 Btu/hr
Water heater, automatic instantaneous ...........  37,500 Btu/hr
Gas stoves: each top burner, household stove ...   12,500 Btu/hr
        Professional stove ....................  15,000–16,000 Btu/hr
        Each oven burner ............................  20,000 Btu/hr
```

Regarding commercial stoves, professional chefs almost always prefer gas burners over electric ones because gas heat is instant the moment it is turned on, the immediate high heat sears food better, the heat is easily varied and can be controlled by sight, and the heat disappears the instant the burner is turned off. But chefs usually prefer electric ovens because their even heat is better for baking. Gas burners are usually ring- or star-shaped: ring burners cost less and are less likely to clog, but star burners are usually more powerful and distribute the heat more evenly.

When a lighter-than-air gas flows up a pipe, its pressure increases as the gas rises according to the formula below. This formula may also be used to compute pressure changes of heavier-than-air gases, but it does not consider pipe pressure losses due to pipe length.

4)D)2)d)1) $\Delta P = 0.0147\, h\, (1.00 - \sigma)$

ΔP = pressure increase or decrease of lighter-than-air or heavier-than-air gas, psi. If σ of gas > 1.00, ΔP is minus.

h = height of travel of lighter-than-air or heavier-than-air gas, ft

σ = specific gravity of lighter-than-air or heavier-than-air gas

Plains, IL); Feb 1995, p. 40.   † From p. 319: The primary source for this and the ▌

An 8 unit apartment building has a piping layout for propane-operated appliances as shown in Fig. 4-33. If the reservoir is two 500 gallon tandem-mounted cylinders and all piping is type *K* copper tubing with brass fittings, size the system.

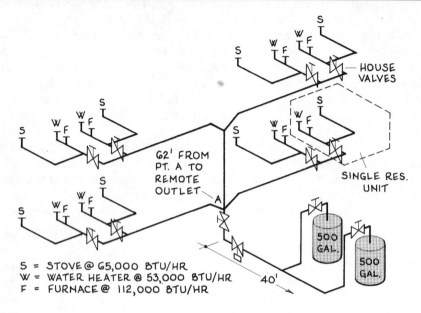

S = STOVE @ 65,000 BTU/HR
W = WATER HEATER @ 53,000 BTU/HR
F = FURNACE @ 112,000 BTU/HR

Fig. 4-34. Fuel gas system layout details.

Solution: Branches may be $^3/_8$ in. flexible copper tubing for runs to about 80 ft for propane or butane and 50 ft for natural gas. As the maximum branch run here is 62 ft and the gas is propane, $^3/_8$ in. flexible copper tubing is **OK** for all stems and branches upstream to the risers. The minimum riser diameter is $^3/_4$ in, which is certainly adequate here, which leaves only the 40 ft main to be sized as below.

Step 1. Compute the piping's peak volume of flow.

4)D)2)d)2) $Є = 60 Þ Q$

$Є$ = rated energy use of appliances served by piping, Btu/hr.
   From Fig. 4-34, $Є = 8 (65,000 + 55,000 + 112,000) = 1,860,000$ Btu/hr.
$Þ$ = peak volume of gas flow in piping, **?** cfm
Q = typical heating value of commercial gas, Btu/cf.
   From Table 4-5, Q for propane = 2,370 Btu/cf.

$$1,860,000 = 60 \, Þ × 2,370 \quad \ldots Þ = 13.1 \text{ cfm}$$

following section was *Advanced Plumbing Technology*, Alfred Steele (Construction

Note: Here it is unwise to apply a diversity factor for the 24 outlets; as all stoves, water heaters, and furnaces in the apartment building could be operating at the same time just before dinner on a winter evening.

Step 2. Size the piping.

$$L \, \kappa_m \, \sigma \, 0.5 \, Þ^2 \; = \; 120{,}000 \, \Delta P \, d^5$$

L = effective length of pipe (including normal number of fittings), 48 ft

κ_m = pipe material coefficient. κ_m = 2.0 for iron or steel piping, 1.0 for copper or brass. Here κ_m = 1.0.

σ = specific gravity of gas in pipe. From Table 4-5, σ for propane = 1.52.

$Þ$ = volume of gas flow in pipe, from Step 1, 13.1 cfm

ΔP = permissible pressure drop of gas flow in pipe, 0.5 in. wg.
If 1 psi = 27.7 in. wg, 0.5 in. wg = 0.5/27.7 = 0.018 psi.

δ = minimum pipe diameter, inside dimension, **?** in. Minimum δ = 0.5 in.

$$48 \times 1.0 \times 1.52^{0.5} \times 13.1^2 \; = \; 120{,}000 \times 0.018 \, \delta^5$$
$$\delta \; = \; 1.36 \; \blacktriangleright \; 1\tfrac{1}{2} \text{ in. dia.}$$

4.E. WASTE PLUMBING

Also known as DWV (drain-waste-vent) systems, waste plumbing carries waste liquids and solids from fixtures to sewers or septic systems in a manner that prevents depositing, clogging, and fouling of residues. Each such system has three networks: *sanitary drains* that descend from the water-seal traps required just below each fixture, *septic* or *sewage drains* that carry the wasteflow, and *air vents* that enable any gases in the wasteflow to escape outdoors through openings in the top of the building. Piping for these networks is usually copper or plastic. Pipe diameters cannot decrease in the direction of flow, all sanitary drains require cleanouts that allow every LF of piping to be cleared in case it becomes clogged, and any trapped runs (waste runs that must go uphill) require mechanical pumping systems. Waste plumbing is usually sized downstream, from fixture traps to the sewage or septic system. Sewage flow is usually considered as 95 percent of supply water flow.

If any plumbing waste is detrimental to public sewage systems or ground water supplies, special treatment is required in which official authorities must be informed of (1) the nature of the use that generates the waste; (2) the composition, concentration, and quantity of waste; and (3) the nature, water demands, and byproducts of the treatment process. Since storm sewers cannot receive plumbing fixture wasteflow and their size is a function of rainfall and/or ground runoff, storm sewer sizing is covered in Sec. 2.C.2.d.

Industry Press, Elmhurst, IL, 1984), Chapters 22 an 24.   † From p. 328: This

4.E.1. Sanitary Drains

Sanitary waste drain systems include piping, fittings, food grinders, grease interceptors, sumps, ejectors, and any other components involved in collecting or conveying sanitary wastes from fixtures to septic tanks or public sewers.

Sanitary wastes are categorized as follows:

Clearwater: storm water, condensates, and other clear wastes requiring some filtration and purification to become drinkable.

Graywater: wastewater from sinks, showers, bathtubs, dishwashers, clothes washers, etc., which can be filtered and chemically treated to be reusable at least for flushing toilets.

Brownwater: effluent from toilets and urinals.

Blackwater: greases, chemicals, and toxic liquids draining from commercial or industrial operations. These usually require specific analysis and treatment overseen by jurisdictional authorities.

Well-designed sanitary drainage systems include the following:

▶ Ideal pipe pitch is $\frac{1}{4}$ in/LF for nongreasy wastes and $\frac{3}{8}$ in/LF for greasy wastes. At lesser pitches too many things can go wrong, and pitches exceeding $\frac{1}{2}$ in/LF are apt to clog because the liquids flow too fast and leave the solids behind. Pitches greater than about 7 in/LF are OK, as then the solids drain by gravity.

▶ Straight runs do not exceed 100 ft for metal piping or 30 ft for plastic piping, all turns have ample chase space, and hangers allow for slight lateral movement of suspended piping.

TABLE 4-6: SANITARY DRAIN, TRAP, AND VENT DIAMETERS

PLUMBING FIXTURE	Minimum diameter, in.
Lavatory, drinking fountain, bidet, dental cuspidor	$1\frac{1}{4}$
Bathtub w/ or w/o shower, multiple lavatory, domestic dishwasher, domestic kitchen sink w/ or w/o either food waste grinder or dishwasher, laundry sink w/ or w/o tray, commercial lavatory (beauty parlor, barber shop, etc.), surgeon's or laboratory sink	$1\frac{1}{2}$
Domestic kitchen sink w/ food waste grinder & dishwasher, comm'l kitchen sink w/ or w/o food waste grinder, comm'l food waste grinder, service sink, shower stall, urinal, floor drain	2
Domestic kitchen sink w/ tray & waste food grinder	$2\frac{1}{2}$
Sink w/ flushing rim, flush valve water closet [1]	3
Flush tank water closet [1]	4

1. Vent diameters from single units may be 2 in.

account is based on the author's familiarity with the premises of the disaster and

▶ Cleanouts are required at every direction change exceeding 45°, at the upper terminus of horizontal branches, before and after each length that has three 45° bends, at maximum 50 ft intervals in up-to-4 in. diameter piping, at maximum 100 ft intervals in larger piping, at the base of all stacks, and within 10 ft of the junction of the building drain and the sewer (this is known as the *house* or *building trap*). Each cleanout must have the same diameter as the pipe it serves up to 4 in. diameter, 3 ft clear access all around, adequate headroom, and 8 ft clear access in front for coiling cleanout snakes, placing motorized equipment, and depositing removed wastes. Where nearby construction prevents any of the above, the cleanout stub must extend to an access area beyond.

▶ Piping does not pass above any electrical equipment or a 2 ft area around such equipment. Where this is unavoidable the invasive piping is encased in secondary containment piping over the electrical zone and the containment piping's lower end is fitted with a basin and drain line.

▶ Piping receiving refrigeration and chiller condensates, roof drainage in cold weather, and other low-temperature wastes is vapor-barriered and insulated.

▶ Any stubs installed for future drain outlets do not exceed 24 in.

▶ Consider using energy reclamation heat exchangers for any wastes from hot water fixtures. For example, a residential bathtub of hot water contains enough heat to keep the bathroom and an adjacent bedroom warm for a day of 20° weather.

Convincing clients of the importance of effective sanitary waste systems is often difficult because they often cost what seems to many clients a disproportionate sum of money, it is quite natural for clients not to think of the realities involved, and the consequences that can erupt due to lack of attention to small details can be extremely discomforting to occupants.

Another problem is that due to today's increased environmental awareness and legal mandating of more efficient plumbing fixtures, the waterflow traditionally equated with a fixture unit may soon be less, which could result in oversize piping, slower waterflows that do not always wash away solid deposits on pipe walls, and more frequent stoppage. Although water conservation is a matter of ever-increasing importance, zeal exceeding knowledge can make conditions worse instead of better.

An office park contains six buildings whose sanitary drains (excluding storm drainage) empty into one main that drains into a city sewer. If the buildings have 624 fixture units and the main pitches $\frac{1}{2}$ in. fall/ft to the city sewer, what is the main's diameter?

Step 1. If the drain's pitch is not given, determine its optimal pitch by analyzing the plans. Minimum fall = $\frac{3}{8}$ in/ft for $1\frac{1}{2}$ or 2 in. diameter drains and $\frac{1}{4}$ in/LF for larger drains. Here a fall of $\frac{1}{2}$ in/LF is given.

Step 2. Find the drain's diameter.

4E1 $\qquad\qquad F + 0.08\ W\ =\ 10\ d^{2.67}\ \Delta^{0.5}$

F = number of fixture units of wasteflow that empties into drain, 624 units

W = wasteflow rate from nonfixture unit sources only, if any, gal/day. None given.

d = minimum pipe diameter, inside dimension, ? in.

Δ = slope or pitch of waste drain, in/ft. $\frac{1}{2}$ in. fall/ft = 0.5 in/ft.

$\qquad 624 + 0\ =\ 10 \times d^{2.67} \times 0.5^{0.5}$ $\qquad ... \ d\ =\ 5.34$ in. ➡ **6 in. dia.**

4.E.1.a. Waste Grinders [†]

Solid plumbing wastes often require grinding before they drain into a sewer or septic system. This may occur wherever food is processed, displayed, served, or disposed. Grinders for other solid wastes are also installed in hospitals, dental offices, and many industrial occupancies. Their mulchy discharges cannot pass through grease interceptors or recovery units. Each unit is usually operable by an ON/OFF switch, and the best have the following features:

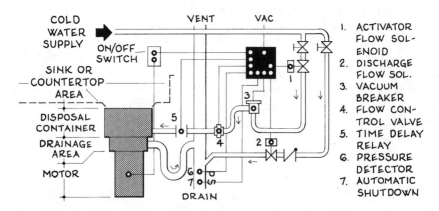

Fig. 4-35. Commercial food waste grinder details.

[†] The primary source for this section was Ron George's "Designer's Guide: Piping

- A reversible motor that improves operation efficiency.
- Two solenoid valves, one that lets water enter the grinder after it turns on and another on a second water line that enters just below the grinder to help flush the slurry down the drain.
- A vacuum breaker that prevents water from rising back into the sink in case the removal of disposal is sluggish.
- A flow control valve that eliminates excess water consumption.
- A time delay relay that allows water to run a short while after the grinder shuts off to clean the disposal container.
- A pressure detector that shuts off the motor if waterflow cannot wash the slurry down the drain.
- Automatic shutdown when the drain is clear.

Waste grinder design typically involves selection from a catalog based on desired specifications, or for industrial applications a company engineer usually determines the size. Units are usually installed under kitchen sinks in residences and under prewash scrap sinks in restaurants. Typical power requirements are up to 10 hp or 220 V on 40–50 amp circuits.

4.E.1.b. Floor Drains

Floor drains are a surprisingly common plumbing component, as they are installed in basements, garages, parking facilities, gas stations, food processing areas, commercial kitchens, supermarkets, dairies, locker rooms, gang showers, HVAC condensate basins, waste cleaning areas, and many industrial facilities. Each floor drain requires a removable *inlet grate* at or slightly below the finished floor, a *sediment bucket* just below which collects solids without impeding drainage flow (this may contain pans, separators, interceptors, or collectors), a *check valve* where backflow could occur, a *tailpiece* that empties into a metal trap with a minimum 3 in. vertical seal, a *vent*, and a *drain*. The depth of all these parts often approaches 24 in. This, plus the pitch of the outlet pipe and the fact that the drain may be in the lowest part of a building, often influences the design of the whole building as well as the drain itself. The drain's required vent, which must pitch slightly upward before becoming vertical, may also affect architectural design if it is long. Other requirements are:

- The floor area being drained must pitch at least $\frac{1}{8}$ in/ft down in all directions toward the drain's inlet grate, and the floor area should be rimmed by an integral baseboard at least 4 in. high.
- Floor drains cannot convey heavy greases or particulates, fecal or organic wastes, or large liquid flows.

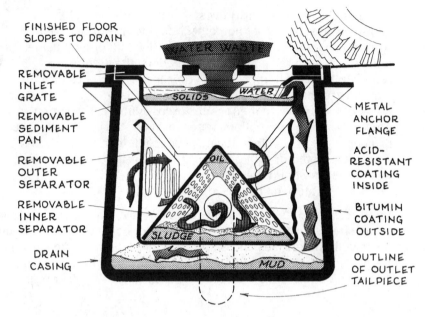

FINISHED FLOOR
SLOPES TO DRAIN

REMOVABLE
INLET
GRATE

REMOVABLE
SEDIMENT
PAN

REMOVABLE
OUTER
SEPARATOR

REMOVABLE
INNER
SEPARATOR

DRAIN
CASING

WATER WASTE

SOLIDS   WATER

OIL

SLUDGE

MUD

METAL
ANCHOR
FLANGE

ACID-
RESISTANT
COATING
INSIDE

BITUMIN
COATING
OUTSIDE

OUTLINE
OF OUTLET
TAILPIECE

Fig. 4-36. Floor drain/separator details and operation.

▸ The inlet grate must be rust-proof and able to withstand truck traffic. Good materials are cast iron and rustproof steel.

▸ The section area of the sediment bucket must be at least 1.5 times the open area of the inlet grate above.

▸ The drain must be 2 pipe sizes larger than the tailpiece diameter (select from $1\frac{1}{4}$, $1\frac{1}{2}$, 2, $2\frac{1}{2}$, 3, 4, 6, 8, and 10 in.) so that air remains in the top half of the drain at all times.

▸ The drain must pitch from $\frac{1}{4}$ in/LF ($\frac{1}{2}$ in. is better) to 6 in/LF down.

▸ Each drain should have a primary vent from the basin, a relief vent from just below the trap, and relief vents at maximum 100 ft spacing along long runs, with the section area of each vent being at least 0.5 the section area of the parent piping.

Where a large food prep or slop sink drains into the outlet of a floor drain nearby, a sinkful of water going down the sink drain can create a miniature Old Faithful in the floor drain. The solution? Connect the sink drain to the floor drain well *below* its tailpiece and install a backflow valve just above. If the sink drainage includes considerable grease or particulate matter, its drain must be entirely separate from the floor drainage.

On parapeted flat roofs, roof drains must be installed, each in a slight depression, and each should be capped with a nonrusting domed strainer with debris guard slots, or with a half-dome corner strainer if the drain is at the edge of a parapet. Clear opening areas should ≤ 1.5 × inlet pipe area below. The piping tailpiece and surrounding construction must be protected against condensation and thermal expansion.

> What size floor drain is required for a commercial kitchen whose area is 280 ft^2?

4)E)1)b) $\delta = 0.134\,A^{0.5}$

δ = minimum diameter of floor drain tailpiece, **?** in.
A = area of floorspace to be drained, 280 sf. If this exceeds 500 sf, more than one drain should be installed.

$$\delta = 0.018\,A^{0.5} = 2.24 \rightarrow 2\tfrac{1}{2} \text{ in. dia.}$$

Drain pipe diameter must be two pipe sizes larger than drain diameter: From list of copper piping diameters on p. 260, $2\tfrac{1}{2}, 3, 4 \rightarrow 4$ in.

4.E.1.c. Grease Separators [†]

Also known as separators, grease traps, grease collectors, interceptors, manual grease interceptors, automatic grease removers, and sludge pits, these tank-like units collect and retain greases, food solids, detergents, chemicals, and other plumbing wastes before they flow out of the building. Each tank may be of reinforced concrete, stainless steel, or fiberglass, and it usually has a deep-seal trap, double venting, acid-resistant finish on the inside, bitumen or equal coating on the outside, and a manhole on top with plenty of area around it. The tank collects fats, oils, and greases (FOGs), prevents onsite blockages in plumbing waste drains, and minimizes downstream accumulations of waste.

In a grease separator, the plumbing wasteflow typically empties into one end of a tank filled with previous effluent at about mid-height where a baffle or tubular Tee reduces its velocity and provides a surface area for its particles to adhere to. After the wasteflow has become still or static, if its temperature is about 70° the FOG globules typically rise about 3 in/min to form a layer of scum on the top and the heavier-than-water particles typically descend at similar speeds to form a layer of sludge on the bottom. Then as wasteflow continually enters one end of the tank, the level of the already-present effluent slowly rises inside a second tubular Tee at the other end of the tank through which the excess effluent flows into a sewer. While all of the above occurs, any fumes arriving with the wasteflow exit through a vent in the tank's top. Periodically the floating wastes are skimmed off the top and the settled solids are pumped off the bottom.

[†] The primary sources for this section were (1) Robert Tolar's "Grease Sepa-

From the above, the tank's volume and depth obviously are crucial design parameters; as they must allow the just-entered wasteflow to become static without overly agitating the already-present effluent, then retain the wasteflow long enough to allow its particles to fully rise or sink before being disturbed by the next entry of wasteflow. Although the above physics could be distilled to a concise design formula, it would be fairly useless due to the following variables:

▶ Variability of the wasteflow's volume. If the volume is too great or the tank is too small, some of the already-present effluent will flow out of the tank before its particles have had time to fully rise or settle. For this reason a unit's peak flow rate is usually more important than its daily volume.

▶ Variability of the wasteflow's content. The wasteflow may have a very high volume of FOGs and solids one moment (such as just after a chef has cleaned a few fish) and virtually none the next moment; and a few commercial kitchens have potato peelers, fruit pulpers, tilt kettles, bakery sinks, and other fixtures that sporadically send large masses of food down the drain.

▶ Variability of the wasteflow's temperature. The wasteflow may be as hot as dishwashing water or as cold as discarded icewater.

▶ Variability of the FOGs: some may cling strongly to food particles then remain perpetually suspended in the static effluent.

▶ The buildup of scum and sludge layers steadily diminishes the tank's effective volume unless the unit is pumped out frequently.

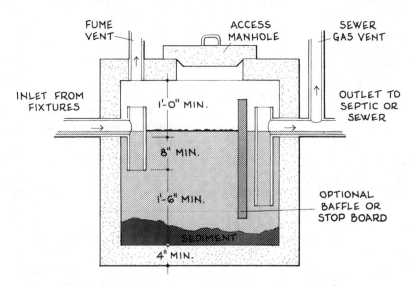

Fig. 4-37. Grease or waste separator details.

Optimal periodicity is every 24 hr, but such a strict timeframe is rarely adhered to or enforced.

▶ A host of "social" factors, such as unreliable manufacturer's claims and ratings, varying code standards, lax pumping schedules, shortage of enforcement personnel, out-of-sight/out-of-mind mentality of owners, and, yes, pass-the-buck attitudes of designers. Even worse, many codes *require* that food grinder and dishwasher waste bypass grease collectors and discharge directly into sewers, and the EPA refuses to differentiate between FOGs and petroleum-based oils, which can greatly overload some systems while greatly underloading others.

However, an understanding of the above variables indicates the following general design parameters for this cantankerous component:

▶ Make the effluent reservoir large and shallow. An optimal volume would be length ≈ 2.3 width and width ≈ depth ≥ 3.5 ft. Also OK are compartmentalized units that considerably reduce turbulence of the existing effluent caused by the entering wasteflow.

▶ Locate the tank's inlet baffles so they contort the entering wasteflow while being easily removable and easily cleaned.

▶ Promote uniform temperature of the effluent by placing the tank indoors where the space above remains at room temperature.

▶ Install a manhole on top that is big enough for a person to climb into and remove the baffles and clean the interior with a hose. Today's best units have a round gasketed steel plate clampdown cover with a non-skid top surface that is suited for pedestrian traffic. The manhole cover should be round, as then it can't fall through the opening if it slides over it.

▶ Have plenty of floor area around the manhole for a pump truck to park nearby and personnel to administer pumping apparatus. The floor should be easily cleanable; so it should have a drain, and the wall nearby should have a hose bibb and rack.

▶ In commercial occupancies with food prep facilities, design dishwasher operation so at least its pre-rinse cycle discharges into the separator; then it is more environmentally acceptable for the cleaning cycle effluent to discharge directly into a sewer.

Each separator must be designed so it is not a health hazard, its contents cannot damage the lowest levels of the building, and all maintenance can be easily performed. The unit should also be designed so if it is not serviced adequately the in-house situation will worsen, as opposed to local waste treatment facilities being overburdened or the environment being polluted beyond the property. The easiest way to do this is *not* to oversize the unit.

More utopian design measures for grease separators are:

(Business News Publishing Co., Troy, MI); Jun 1998, pp. 38–41; (2) Robert Tol-

- ▶ Motivate manufacturers to make and rate units accurately according to the above-defined parameters.
- ▶ Provide methods of introducing biochemical disassemblers into the effluent. Since oils, FOGs, and food particles are mostly hydrocarbons, recent research indicates that certain bacteria and enzymes can disassemble these components until most C, H, and O atoms are released as carbon dioxide and water.
- ▶ Encourage jurisdictional authorities to enact stricter waste discharge standards (150 mg/liter is becoming a widely accepted limit), introduce mandatory pumping schedules, enforce codes strictly, and levy heavy fines for violations.

Grease separators for many kinds of eating occupancies can be sized according to the formulas below:

4)E)1)c)1) Restaurants, luncheonettes, fast food services, and other occupancies that serve nonscheduled meals to a nonspecific number of occupants:

$$C_g = 0.09\, \kappa_A\, \eta\; H\; G\; S$$

4)E)1)c)2) Hospitals, nursing homes, schools, and other occupancies that serve scheduled meals to a specific number of occupants:

$$C_g = 0.14\, M\, G\, S$$

C_g = minimum interior capacity of grease separator, cf. $V \geq 100$ cf. Once C_g is known, it is used to determine the grease trap's $L\, W\, H$ if rectangular or its diameter and depth if cylindrical.

κ_A = facility access coefficient, depending on principal customer access to the facility. $\kappa_L = 1.25$ for freeways and expressways, 1.0 for recreation areas, 0.8 for main highways, 0.5 for lesser roads. This amount can vary considerably depending on the popularity of the occupancy. For example, a four-star restaurant on a rural country road could have a κ_L of 0.7 while an out-of-favor restaurant on a main highway could have a κ_L of 0.2.

η = number of seats in dining area. If the occupancy is rarely full, a fractional value for η is appropriate. For example, if a cafe has 30 seats and is rarely more than $^2/_3$ full, $\eta \approx ^2/_3 \times 30 = 20$.

H = number of hours per day occupancy is open, hr.

M = number of scheduled meals served per day, 1, 2, or 3.

G = wasteflow rate per seat per hr per meal served, gal. A general value for $G \approx 4.5$ gal. Use more articulate data if available.

S = sewage capacity factor, depending on whether grease trap outflow drains into public sewer or onsite leaching field. If public disposal, $S = 1.7$; if onsite disposal, $S = 2.5$.

ar's "Wastewater Woes"; *PM Engineer* magazine; Aug. 1999, pp. 32–35; and (3) Max

> If a tannery near Lander, WY, produces a heavily grease-laden efflu-
> ent of 360 gal/day, what size grease separator should its plumbing
> system have?

Step 1. Find the capacity of the separator's reservoir.

4)E)1)c)3) $C = 0.19 (14 F + W)$

C = rated static holding capacity of grease separator, cf
F = fixture unit flow, if any, emptying into separator. None given ➜ 0.
W = peak volume of wasteflow draining into separator, gal/day.
   Here Q = 360 gal/day.

$$C = 14 \times 0 + 360 = 360 \text{ cf} \geq 60 \text{ cf} ➜ \textbf{OK}$$

Step 2. Size the reservoir. The equation below assumes optimal reservoir
dimensions of depth ≈ width ≈ 2.3 length.

$$C \approx 2.3 \ d^3$$

C = rated static holding capacity of grease separator, 362 cf
d = optimal depth of separator, ft

$$362 = 2.3 \ d^3 \quad ... \ d = 5.4 \text{ ft}$$
Optimal depth ≈ 5.4 ft, width ≈ 5.4 ft, length = 12.4 ft

4.E.1.d. Sump Tanks & Ejectors

When sanitary drainage occurs below the level of a building's sanitary waste main or the public sewer, power-operated equipment must be
installed to pump the waste upward so it can flow out of the building. If the
waste is clearwater or light graywater, a *nonairtight sump* may be used,
then the unit's intake orifice is located in a pit that sucks up the drainage.
As sump pumps are often installed to remove flat roof drainage or basement leakage due to severe storms, such units should be connected to
emergency power, as they may be needed when local power has failed.

If the waste contains sewage or other smelly or dangerous substances, a *pneumatic ejector* with an airtight receiver must be installed
below the lowest level of the building's pitched sanitary waste main. Thus an
ejector is often the deepest plumbing component in the building. As such it
may affect the design of the building's lowest spaces and related construction. Also, wherever an ejector is installed, all plumbing fixtures situated
above the building's sanitary waste main should gravity-drain directly into

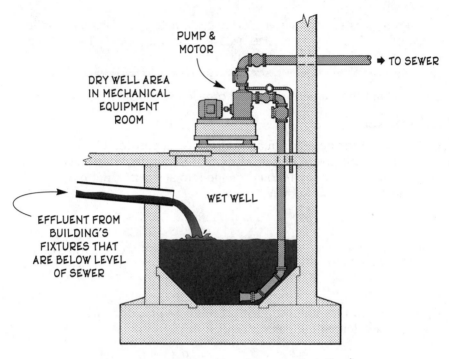

PUMP &
MOTOR

DRY WELL AREA
IN MECHANICAL
EQUIPMENT
ROOM

→ TO SEWER

WET WELL

EFFLUENT FROM
BUILDING'S
FIXTURES THAT
ARE BELOW LEVEL
OF SEWER

Fig. 4-38. Wastewater ejector details. †

the main (then if the ejector fails any mess will be minimal), and every fixture located below the sewer main must be fitted with a backflow valve to minimize possible flooding in its area. Dual-pump ejectors are best, because they offer redundant operation in case one pump fails; and the discharge pipe, whose diameter is usually 3 in, should be as short and as devoid of bends and fittings as possible. Ejectors are common in downtown commercial buildings having two or three basement levels below the sidewalk or street outside.

Sizing a pneumatic ejector is a chancy proposition, due to the many variables involved, both present and future. Indeed, one engineer in charge of designing a pneumatic ejector facility for an expanding Massachusetts biotechnology company said that "no matter how meticulously each drop is accounted for using standard design criteria, reality behaves differently." So this engineer, instead of estimating the company's daily and peak wasteflows by algebraic formulas as a basis for selecting and sizing a newer and larger system, performed what he called "a sophisticated bucket test:" he simply timed how long the building's occupants took to fill the existing sump basin during normal working hours, how long it took the system's ejector to empty the basin, and how long it took after the ejector had switched off until it reactivated after the basin had refilled. Then, armed with computer tech-

†This figure was based on *Consulting-Specifying Engineer* magazine (Cahners

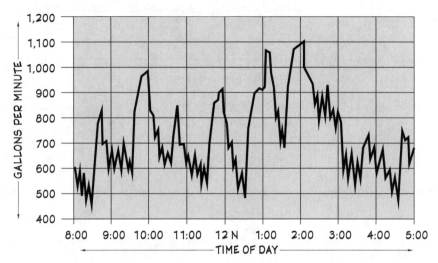

Fig. 4-39. Simulated sewage ejector inflow graph.

nology, he plotted a computerized graph, shown above, of this on/off cycling for a full workday. Notice how this graph indicates greatly increased waste-flows at 10 o'clock, noon, and 2 o'clock —times when company employees take their coffee and lunch breaks. After using programmable-logic controllers to trace the wasteflows from the company's every plumbing fixture, the engineer used a subroutine algorithm to construct a computer model that simulated minute-by-minute flow rates, sump basin levels, and pump start/stop frequencies for the entire plumbing waste system. Then he imposed projected future waste loads onto the existing load profile to forecast 1-, 5-, 10-, and 20-year increments in the company's wasteflows. From here it was "easy" to determine how large the newer system should be, and in what future year the system should likely be upgraded. Thus an innovative engineer applied computer technology to a complex design scenario to create an invaluable forecasting/design tool that enabled everyone involved to see the results of the company's expansion well in advance. [†]

Notwithstanding the obvious merits of the above approach, a few algebraic formulas for estimating the size of a pneumatic ejection system based on standard design criteria are offered below.

In a 16 story building in downtown Denver, CO, the lowest 140 fixture units lie below the level of the public sewer main out front. If an ejector is installed just inside the front facade and the bottom of its basin lies approximately 31 ft below the sewer main, size the unit and the area in which it is installed.

Step 1. Add up the fixture units located below the sewer main that will discharge into the ejector. This is given as 140 fixture units.

Step 2. Compute the ejector's unit capacity.

4)E)1)d) $V = 0.53 (F_u + 0.07 \ W)$

V = required interior volume of ejector, **?** cf
F_u = fixture unit wasteflow draining into ejector, 140 f.u.
W = nonfixture unit wasteflow draining into ejector, gal/day. None given.

$$V \geq 0.53 (140 + 0) \geq 74.2 \text{ cf}$$

Step 3. Estimate the ejector's height.

$$h \approx 0.08 \ V + 3.75$$

h = estimated total height of ejector, including depth of basin and subdrain invert, **?** ft
V = required interior volume of ejector, from Step 2, 74.2 cf

$$h \approx 0.08 \times 74.2 + 3.75 \approx 9.69 \text{ ft}$$

Step 4. Determine the ejector's required access floor area.

$$A \approx (d + 6)^2$$

A = required access floor area for ejector, **?** sf
d = diameter of ejector, ft. Standard diameter of most duplex pump ejectors = 3 ft. Use more definitive data when available.

$$A \approx (3 + 6)^2 \geq 81 \text{ cf}$$

4.E.2. Vents

A plumbing vent is a vertical (or nearly so) pipe of air, open at the top, whose base preserves the seal of each plumbing fixture trap it rises from by collecting gases in the waste plumbing system and sending them upward until they are outdoors. Where temperatures fall below -30°, a vent may require frost closure protection by (1) extending the vent only 1–2 in. above the roof, (2) increasing its diameter just below the roof, (3) installing flashing with an airspace between the vent and the building, or (4) circling the vent at roof level with hot tubing or heat tracing cable.

A plumbing vent's top may open through a side wall as well as the roof. However, a side vent cannot penetrate beyond the wall's face but must be recessed in an open box whose bottom surface must not be flat or shelf-like; as then birds will roost there and rainwater, winter snow, and ice will collect there. Ideally the box's bottom surface should slope 45° down from its back. A vent should also never open into an attic or any other unoccupiable indoor space, even if the area is louvered, because plumbing waste gases usually have a foul odor and can be poisonous.

> What is the optimal diameter of a 51 ft vent stack that rises from a 4 in. sewer main whose drainage flow is 104 fixture units?

TABLE 4-7: REQUIRED VENT SIZES AND LENGTHS

Soil or waste stack dia, in.	Min. fixture unit flow	← MINIMUM DIAMETER OF REQUIRED VENT, IN. →								
		1¼	1½	2	2½	3	4	5	6	8
		Maximum length of vent, ft ↓								
1¼	2	30								
1½	8	50	150							
1½	10	30	100							
2	12	30	75	200						
2	20	26	50	150						
2½	42			30	100	200				
3	10			30	100	200	600			
3	30				60	200	500			
3	60				50	80	400			
4	100				35	100	260	1,000		
4	200				30	90	250	900		
4	500				20	70	180	700		
5	200					35	80	350	1,000	
5	500					30	70	300	900	
5	1,100					20	50	200	700	
6	300					25	50	200	400	1,300
6	620					15	30	125	300	1,100
6	960						24	100	250	1,000
8	600							50	150	500	1,300
8	1,400							40	100	400	1,200
8	2,200							30	80	350	1,100
10	1,000							75	125	1,000
10	2,500							50	100	500
10	3,800							30	80	350

This table is adapted from the National Plumbing Code.

Step 1. Find the total equivalent fixture unit waste flowing in the drainage system served by the vent.

$$4)E)2)$$ $$W_t \approx F + 0.071\ W$$

W_t = total equivalent fixture unit waste served by vent, ? f.u.
F = fixture unit waste served by vent, 104 f.u.
W = nonfixture unit waste served by vent, gpm. $W = 0$.

$$W_T \approx 104 + 0 \approx 104\ \text{f.u.}$$

Step 2. Knowing the sewer main diameter, fixture unit load, and vent length, find the vent diameter from Table 4-7. At 4 in. waste stack diameter, 104 fixture unit flow, and 51 ft length, $d = 2\frac{1}{2}$ in.

4.E.3. Septic Tanks

A septic tank is an underground container that receives sewage from a building and after a few days' retention discharges a clarified effluent into a leaching field. Both tank and field are best located in grassy open areas, but not under parking areas or where heavy loads could compact the soil above.

> A well-known wildlife artist has purchased a three bedroom farmhouse with a barn. She plans to live in the house with her family and convert the barn into a studio that will contain eight plumbing fixture units and other water-consuming activities that will produce an effluent of an estimated 50 gal/day. As the farm's cesspool is no longer functional, a new septic system will receive the effluent from the house and barn. Size the septic tank for this system.

$$4)E)3)$$ $$C \approx 100 + 33\ (B - 2) + 2.5\ F + 0.2\ W$$

C = interior capacity of septic tank, ? cf
B = number of bedrooms, if any, in building whose household fixture units drain into septic tank, 3 units. $B \geq 2$.
F = number of plumbing fixture units, if any, draining into tank, 8 f.u.
W = amount of nonfixture unit waste, if any, draining into tank, 50 gal/day

$$C = 100 + 33\ (3 - 2) + 2.5 \times 8 + 0.2 \times 50 = 163\ \text{cf}$$
If length = 9 ft, $w\ d = 173/9 = 19.2$ sf
If width = 4 ft, $d = 19.2/4 = 4.8$ ft → 5 ft
One size: 9 ft long × 4 ft wide × 5 ft deep

Vincent Manas, Editor (McGraw-Hill, New York, 1987); p. 12-49, Table 12.21.5.

4.E.4. Leaching Fields

A leaching field is a network of porous drains that receives effluent from a septic tank, then discharges it via seepage into the surrounding soil. The drains must be 4 in. in diameter, slope at $\frac{1}{16}$ to $\frac{3}{8}$ in. fall/ft, and be at least 8 ft from buildings, 5 ft from property lines, and 100 ft from wells, streams, ponds, and lakes. Minimum area = 750 sf unless otherwise specified by local code. One fixture unit ≈ 14 gal sewage/day.

A leaching field's drains must lay below the region's deepest penetration of frost in winter. If this is impossible due to underlying rock strata, the leaching field must be built aboveground as follows: (1) Spread a bed of sand or small gravel over the rocks for the full leaching field area until the bed's top is 3 ft above the rocks; (2) spread a 6 in. deep layer of 1 in. diameter gravel on the sand; (3) place 4 in. diameter leaching drains at least 4 ft apart on the gravel; (4) cover the drains with a 6 in. deep layer of 1 in. diameter gravel measured from the drains' tops; (5) add soil above the gravel until the depth from ground level to the drains' tops equals the local frost depth; then (6) plant the leaching field area with hardy ground cover. Even though these layers are several feet deep, the final ground level still must not slope toward the building from where the sewage originates. Where this is impossible, either the building must be relocated at a higher elevation or a sewage pump system must be installed.

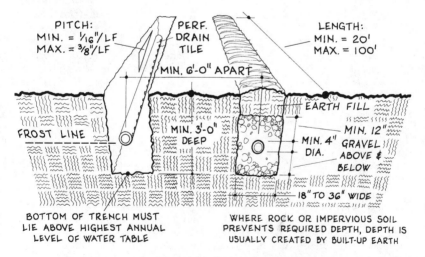

Fig. 4-40. Leaching field drain tile details.

Size the leaching field for the septic tank in the previous example if the perc test result is 5 minutes per in. drop.

Step 1. Find the length of the leaching tiles.

4]E]4] $\qquad$ $L \approx 0.57\,w\,(92\ B + 7\ F + 0.6\ W)\ P^{0.39}$

L = minimum length of leaching field drainage tile, **?** LF
w = minimum width of each leaching field trench, ft. Use 3 ft u.o.n.

TABLE 4-8: ESTIMATED SEWAGE FLOW RATES [†]

OCCUPANCY	gal/day·occupant or other unit
Airports	15/employee + 4/passenger
Apartments	1 BR = 125, 2 BR = 250, 3 BR = 325
Luxury	multiply above × 1.3
Assembly: lecture halls ...... 2/seat; theaters, auditoriums	3/seat
Bowling alleys	75/lane
Campgrounds: Flush toilets, no showers	25/site
Day, no meals served ... 15/camper; overnight, full facility	100/site
Recreational vehicle areas w/ hookup	100/vehicle
Carwashes: tunnel .... 80/car; handwash .... 20/5 min cycle	
Country clubs, health clubs, gymnasiums	25/locker
Churches .... 4/seat; w/ kitchens	7/seat
Dance halls	5/occupant
Day camps	15/camper & staff
Dental offices	750/chair·day
Factories .... 25/person·shift not including industrial wastes	
+ showers .... +10/employee; + cafeteria .... +5/employee	
Hospitals	150/bed
Hotels: no kitchen .... 60/bed; w/ kitchen	70/bed
Laundromats .... 50/wash cycle or 400/machine/day	
Nursing or rest homes	125/bed
Motels .... 50/bed; w/ kitchen	60/bed
Offices .... 15/employee or 0.1/sf floor area	
Picnic areas w/ flush toilet	50/car
Parks: mobile home	250/space
Residences .. 1 BR = 150; 2 BR = 300; 3 BR = 400; 4 BR = 475; 5 BR = 550	
Luxury	multiply above × 1.2
Restaurants, cafeterias 15/occ/meal; + cocktail lounge .... +3/occupant	
If on freeway ...... 70/occupant; curb service .... 50/car space	
Rooming houses	40/guest
Schools: elementary .... 15/student; intermediate & high ... 20/student	
+ gym & showers ... +15/locker; + cafeteria .... +3/student;	
Administrative staff & office	20/employee
Service station .... 900 for 1st bay; additional bays ..... add 500/bay	
Shopping malls .... 15/employee; moviegoers 3/occupant	
Stores .... 20/employee; w/ public toilets .. 1/10 ft² sales area	
Swimming pools: private or public w/ bath houses ...... 10/swimmer & staff	
Taverns & cocktail lounges	20/occupant
Trailer parks, tourist camps: w/ central bathhouse 35; w/ built-in baths 50	

[†] Much of this table was abstracted from *Rural Water Supply* (New York State Dept.

B = number of bedrooms, if any, whose household fixture units drain into leaching field, 3 units.

F = number of commercial plumbing fixture units of wasteflow, if any, that drain into leaching field, 8 f.u.

W = volume of nonfixture wasteflow, if any, that drains into leaching field, 100 gal/day

P = perc test result, 5 min/in drop

$$L = 0.57 \times 3 \times (92 \times 3 + 7 \times 8 + 0.6 \times 100) \times 5^{0.39} = 1{,}260 \text{ LF}$$

Step 2. Find the area of the leaching field.

$$A \geq 6\,L$$

A = minimum area of leaching field, **?** sf
L = minimum length of drainage tile, from Step 1, 1,260 ft

$$A \geq 6 \times 1{,}260 = 7{,}560 \text{ sf}$$

4.E.5. Water Reclamation

Aldo Leopold said that water does not flow from upstream to downstream but in a circle —a Round River— meaning that whatever you use will come back to you. This is why well-septic systems are ecologically better than meter-sewage systems; as each is a Round River that returns the used water to nearly where it was drawn, transforming the cubic acre the incoming and outgoing systems share into a giant filter that keeps the water perpetually pure. Thus a well-septic system doesn't consume water at all, but is a natural way of borrowing. And any foliage above the leaching effluent is made more luxuriant: a completion of another of Nature's cycles.

Regarding meter-sewage systems, a project conducted by the Institute of Land and Water Research at Penn State University in the 1960s indicated that if the effluent of a typical city of 100,000 were treated in a manmade lake (a feasible method of purification by water treatment plants then) the lake would require 1,290 acres of area to purify the water. But if the same effluent emptied into a forest where it filtered through the foliage and topsoil then flowed out of its streams, only 129 acres would be needed to make it pure. [†] This is Round River technology at its best.

In the old days, many a rural home had a Round River of sorts: its roof's gutters and leaders collected rainfall runoff and emptied it into a *cistern*, a usually room-sized reservoir built of concrete and hidden below grade, usually near a corner of the house where the leaders were shortest. This tank had a large screen filter that strained the leader runoff as it

of Health, Albany, NY, 1992); p. 17, Table 2.   † *The Ecological House*, Robert ‖

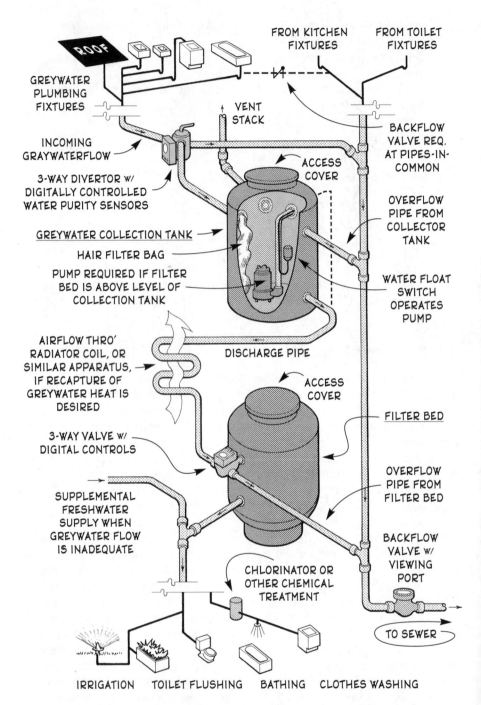

ROOF

GREYWATER
PLUMBING
FIXTURES

FROM KITCHEN
FIXTURES

FROM TOILET
FIXTURES

VENT
STACK

INCOMING
GRAYWATERFLOW

3-WAY DIVERTOR w/
DIGITALLY CONTROLLED
WATER PURITY SENSORS

ACCESS
COVER

GREYWATER COLLECTION TANK

HAIR FILTER BAG

PUMP REQUIRED IF FILTER
BED IS ABOVE LEVEL OF
COLLECTION TANK

BACKFLOW
VALVE REQ.
AT PIPES-IN-
COMMON

OVERFLOW
PIPE FROM
COLLECTOR
TANK

WATER FLOAT
SWITCH
OPERATES
PUMP

AIRFLOW THRO'
RADIATOR COIL, OR
SIMILAR APPARATUS,
IF RECAPTURE OF
GREYWATER HEAT IS
DESIRED

DISCHARGE PIPE

ACCESS
COVER

3-WAY VALVE w/
DIGITAL CONTROLS

FILTER BED

SUPPLEMENTAL
FRESHWATER
SUPPLY WHEN
GREYWATER FLOW
IS INADEQUATE

OVERFLOW
PIPE FROM
FILTER BED

CHLORINATOR OR
OTHER CHEMICAL
TREATMENT

BACKFLOW
VALVE w/
VIEWING
PORT

TO SEWER

IRRIGATION   TOILET FLUSHING   BATHING   CLOTHES WASHING

Fig. 4-41. Anatomy of a graywater recycling system. [†]

B. Butler (Morgan & Morgan, Dobbs Ferry, NY, 1981); p. 88.   [†] Much of the infor-

entered, drainage piping that allowed the tank to be emptied for periodic cleaning, and a manhole-like access cover that penetrated above the ground through which a person could climb down a ladder inside to clean its floor and walls of collected debris. The cistern's retained water was used for irrigation, toilet flushing, clothes washing, and even bathing. This was high technology in the days before the Rural Electrification Act.

But then electricity came, and spawned the submersible well pump. Then in an era of plentiful watts and water, the cistern became a figment of history.

But then computers came, and spawned digital controls. Then in an era of scanty watts and water, the cistern returned. At least this may be said a few decades hence, by a future historian who assesses the then-most recent proliferations in water reuse technology. This is because recently a system methodology based on computerized controls has been developed that enables water draining from certain plumbing fixtures, roofs, and outdoor pavements to be recycled after minor treatment for operating fire sprinklers, flushing toilets, irrigating plants, and running industrial operations in today's buildings —and such digital manipulations may very quickly become very popular due to the kind of water and electricity shortages that are beginning to plague California today, with more than a few other localities inevitably following close on their heels. Such water reuse has acquired the name of *greywater retainage* or *greywater recycling*. These systems allow the reuse of water that is already onsite and has been paid for, and they can retain warmer-than-indoor-temperature greywater until its excess Btus have entered indoor spaces instead of flowing out the building. Greywater recycling is also highly efficient —in most applications nearly 100 percent— and its energy savings may be especially achievable in residences, which often have the optimal combination of plumbing fixtures that can produce and reuse greywater. Its economies are also feasible in any commercial occupancy that has a large roof, parking areas, a swimming pool, a lot of greywater producers such as bathtubs, showers, or drinking fountains (e.g. hotels and gymnasiums), or a lot of greywater reusers such as toilets, fire sprinklers, and plants needing watering. Thanks to digital controls, such systems are now viable for almost every building in America: not only in Western states where water is scarce, but also in the rainfall-rich Northeast (remember New York's three-year drought in the Mid-1960s?), throughout the South where average annual rainfall approaches 50 in. but where droughts occur with maddening frequency, and even in the Pacific Northwest where a region may receive 90 in. of rain a year but often none during the summer and early fall. Indeed, the cost-benefits of graywater recycling can only increase in the future, as burgeoning populations impose ever-increasing demands on the nation's water and energy resources.

A graywater recycling system's design begins with defining exactly what graywater is. In most occupancies it is discharge from plumbing fixtures that hasn't mixed with kitchen, toilet, or urinal waste and is virtually odorless. In residences, drainage from bathtubs, showers, and clothes washers typically comprises 95 percent of all graywaterflow. Thus the first conceptual move in creating a GW recycling system in any occupancy is to disconnect the contributing fixtures' waste drains from kitchen and toilet drains. Two added considerations are (1) has the graywater been treated with a chemical (e.g. chlorine or ozone) or does it contain any chemicals such as nonbiogradable laundry detergent that would make it less desirable for recycling?; and (2) should the retained graywater be treated with any chemical to render it more desirable for recycling? Thus in every design scenario the plumbing componentry and typical occupancy behavior must be meticulously analyzed. A good design flow rate for graywater production in residences, as recently prescribed by the U.S Department of Reclamation for conservation funding purposes, is 40 gal/occ per day.

The componentry of a modern graywater recycling system is sketched in Fig. 4-42. Here the graywaterflow from the building's contributing fixtures drains into a single pipe that flows through an accessible bag filter that collects hair and other large particles, then into a small cistern, which can also serve as a settling tank. This reservoir should should have an intake baffle that minimizes turbulence of the incoming waterflow, a vent, an overflow drain to the building's sewer, easy service entry for cleaning the bag filter and removing settled matter from its bottom, plenty of room around the service entry, and a means of flushing its interior by a source of fresh water. Every fixture draining into the cistern must have a backflow valve between the fixtures' drain and any downstream kitchen or toilet waste drain, each backflow valve should ideally have a water purity sensor that activates a diverter valve which empties its wasteflow into the sewer if it detects contamination, and all drainpipe pitches must $\geq 1/4$ in/LF. All this may sound complicated, but it is no more so than the on-off float switch in every toilet tank today which took a few decades to figure out and which now is commonplace. Indeed, for many applications a properly-sized grease separator will satisfy most of the above requirements.

After the cistern is a pump that moves the retained graywater either through a filtering bed or to its recyling destination. The pump may be inside the tank and activated by a common float switch, or be just outside the tank and activated by digital controls. If the graywater is warm, the pump may push the liquid through a network of small-diameter piping that acts as a heat exchanger through which either air flows to absorb the excess Btus and deliver them to indoor spaces, or through which cold water flows to be preheated before entering a hot water heater. The pump could be run by electricity; but another tantalizing possibility, one that has been little exploited but would be easy to do, would be to power it with an exercycle accompanied by a storage battery. Bicycle technology is widespread

and highly efficient, would improve the health of the operator, could supply power to other electrical outlets in the occupancy as well, and lends
itself wonderfully to small ecologically-oriented applications.

If the graywater must be filtered, this can be done with the kind of
off-the-shelf sand filter commonly used with swimming pools, which typically removes solids down to about 115 microns and is backwashed periodically with fresh water. If the graywater is used to irrigate plants, both its
reservoiring and filtering can be achieved with a subsoil construction
known as a *mini-leaching field* or *subsurface drip irrigation system*: this
is simply a miniatured version of the 'Forest Filter' described earlier in this
section. A mini-leaching field can be as petite as a 2 × 6 ft indoor planter
or as expansive as all the foliage around a large building; and each can
either absorb all the graywater it receives or filter it for purer applications
downstream. If the planter is indoors, it should be an open tank whose
basin pitches $\frac{1}{8}$ in/LF toward a screened drain; then each is filled with a
bed of 9–12 in. topsoil spread upon one or more rows of drip irrigation
emitters placed 14 in. apart and laid on a 4 in. bed of $\frac{1}{2}$–$\frac{3}{4}$ in. gravel. This
construction provides the plants above with optimal root coverage of irri-
gation waterflow. Regarding the planters' optimal bed area, this is estimated from

4)E)5) $A = 3\,\kappa_g\,\eta\,P^{0.39}$ wherein

A = bed area of planters, sf
κ_g = coefficient of graywaterflow per occupant, gal/day. In residential
        occupancies κ_g usually ≈ 40 gal/day; but this amount should be ana-
        lyzed carefully for each application.
η = number of occupants who generate the graywaterflow
P = perc test result of planter bed topsoil, min/in drop

In modern graywater recycling systems as described above, the introduction of just one digitally activated sensor can turn a system that
was previously unthinkable into one that is highly practical. This is a noble
beauty of digital technology. Unfortunately, in some localities these infant
developments are ahead of their time, because some Codes today actually
prohibit graywater recycling systems on the grounds that they are unsafe
for children to play in —as if these sealed systems cannot be made any
more childproof than a common aspirin bottle! But gentle pressure from
enlightened owners and well-informed designers always has a way of bringing well-meaning but misinformed authorities around —eventually. Another difficulty with graywater recycling systems is that they do not lend themselves well to many retrofitting possibilities. Even when a retrofit is feasible, meticulous analysis and much imagination is often required for successful implementation.

A graywater recycling system is designed as follows:

IL); Jul/Aug 1998, pp. 30–33.

1. Determine the system's *design flow capacity*: the amount of graywater produced by the occupancy. Isolate the graywater-producing fixtures, then either add up their projected waste-flows or assign an overall unit value per occupant served.

2. Estimate the system's *recycling capacity*: the amount of graywater that can be feasibly reused by the occupancy. Isolate the graywater-reusing fixtures or applications, then sum their required or projected flow rates. Foliage areas can often be sized to utilize the system's full design flow capacity.

3. Determine the methods of graywater collection and dispersal.

4. Determine the required water delivery pressure and how the pressure will be generated. Ideally the required pressure will be low and can be gravity-generated.

5. Select the methods of filtration (hair, porous baffles, sand, etc.) and how each will be periodically cleaned or maintained.

6. Draw a plot plan of the GW recycling system if part of it is to be outside the building. This resembles a site plan for a conventional leaching field system: it should show the system's property lines, the building's well location or supply water entry, graywater discharges, piping layouts, topography, slopes, soil types, perc test results, paved areas, etc.

7. Describe the system's method of construction: the proverbial Working Drawings and Specifications.

4.F. FIRE SUPPRESSION

Firefighters have said: "The first five minutes of a fire are more important than the next five hours."[†] Thus fire suppression systems must ensure prompt discovery of incipient fires, quick notification to occupants and firefighters, ready control everywhere in the building, and safe evacuation of occupants. The best systems usually cost more, but they often result in lower building insurance premiums that return the extra outlay in a few years. Comprehensive design includes:

Identifying the hazards. Every occupancy should be examined for every potential source of fire: this includes obvious sources such as hot spots and open flames as well as appliances, light fixtures, radiant heating, smoking, sparks, static, frictional heat, sources of spontaneous combustion, lightning, etc. Then consider the materials around each source: those that burn, those that support combustion, those that produce toxic gases, and the surface area and thickness of each. If flammable liquids are involved, find the specific gravity of each. From these investigations an

[†] Alvin Vener, "Smoke and Fire control"; *Engineered Systems* magazine (Business

accurate map of an area's fire hazard areas can be drawn.

Determining appropriate response. This involves conceptualizing layouts (firefighter access, siamese connections, vertical reach of firetruck ladders, etc.) in consideration of possible fire hazards and nature of the architecture. Some fire eruption scenarios may require tight enclosure while others need much ventilation, and some equipment may require specific response controls: e.g. some electrical equipment requires that its power be shut off before its fire-suppression agent activates.

Designing the system. This includes planning the installation and activation of all system components and controls as well as determining the amount of storage, chase, and access space required for each. In varying interior environments and especially where different machinery is present, optimal methods may differ fundamentally in small areas: e.g. one area may require an effective water-spray delivery pattern while an area only a few yards away can be protected only by a foam. Thus flexibility is often vitally important. One way to promote this is to design small-scale fire-suppression systems that can be as easily moved as the operations they serve. System design also includes such architectural considerations as enabling occupants and firefighters to reach extinguishers and hose racks, installing eyebrows over atriums and open spaces, fitting facades with fire-resistive spandrels, and interrupting shafts and risers every fifth floor.

Protecting the occupants. This includes determining the maximum number of occupants in a space, compartmentalizing each floor into at least two zones separated by a 2 hr fire barrier, designing exit routes, and providing the number of exits required.

Protecting the building. This includes providing dikes and drains for water applications, recovery depressions for certain gases, cleanability of areas afterward, and the like.

Common fire suppression systems are described briefly below. Before using this section you may want to read Sec. 5.C.5.b. Fire Signal Wiring, and Volume 1, Sec. 8.K. Fire Protection.

Standpipes

This system is a network of firehose racks, at least one on each floor, that is connected to a water supply. It is a ready means of controlling fire by both firefighters and untrained personnel.

➕ VG for suppressing fires quenchable by water and where fires may occur during periods of occupancy. Required in buildings whose upper floors can't be reached by ground-level firefighting equipment.

➖ NG for electrical or flammable fluid fires. High-velocity streams of water can damage furnishings. Required water reservoir is heavy which poses structural problems if placed on roof.

Sprinklers

This system has heat-sensitive heads that open when nearby air reaches a specified temperature. The system has an onsite water reservoir, and design includes drainage of piping and inundated floor areas.

➕ Good in large open areas near or on ground level (usually required in areas of 1,500 sf or more), where occupants are few, or fires are likely to occur during off-hours.

➖ NG for electrical or flammable oil fires or where contents are valuable. Systems require adequate water supply, pressure or power for pumping water, and floor drainage.

Portable Extinguishers

These are chemically filled cylinders that are mounted in accessible locations near fire hazards. Upon discovering a fire, an occupant dismounts the unit and discharges its contents.

➕ A versatile method of suppressing small incipient fires by untrained personnel. Units are easily mounted, relocated, and refilled. Installation requires little building expense.

➖ Good for only small fires. Each extinguisher must contain the proper chemical for the type of fire likely to occur.

CO_2

In this system carbon dioxide is stored under pressure; then when activated the heavier-than-air gas is discharged through nozzles and smothers the fire. Installation size may range from a portable extinguisher to a network of spray heads connected to an onsite reservoir.

➕ Used in confined and unoccupied areas (chases, display cases, voids above suspended ceilings, etc.), and where flammable liquids, electrical hazards, or valuable contents prohibit the use of water. Has no residual effects on food or equipment, does not conduct electricity, leaves no residue.

➖ Good for small surface fires only. NG for chemicals with bonded O_2 molecules, reactive metals, or metal hydrides. Since a 9 percent CO_2 concentration causes loss of consciousness, this gas is potentially lethal to occupants, animals, and firefighters. The heavier-than-air gas stratifies at floor levels where it can be dangerous to occupants in adjacent spaces or lower levels.

Foams

In this system a detergent concentrate is stored under pressure; then when activated the detergent mixes with water and the sudsy solution is driven by a large blower through a nylon net that creates an avalanche of foam. As the foam advances across burning surfaces it seals all oxygen entry and prevents reignition of already-extinguished areas.

➕ **VG** for liquid fires in industrial areas, airports, and other confined spaces containing flammable oils and open structures. Systems are lightweight, fast-operating, and won't damage most delicate machinery. As the foam is life-supporting it will not harm anyone trapped in the building or putting out the fire.

➖ **NG** outdoors or in areas with windy or turbulent air. Foam must be rinsed away afterward, or it can cause maintenance and moisture damage problems.

Halon Alternatives

In this system a gas that is usually colorless, odorless, and a non-conductor of electricity is stored at high pressure in a cool area; then when activated the gas discharges through nozzles as a slightly heavier-than-air mist that smothers and cools the fire. The mist may be a streaming agent (it remains as a liquid for a while after application) or a total flooding agent (it quickly vaporizes on application).

➕ Lightweight, fairly nontoxic, creates little environmental impact, requires little or no cleaning afterward. **VG** for putting out electrical fires in small spaces containing valuable contents. Good where water or space for bulkier systems is unavailable.

➖ Good for small surface fires only. Most agents will not extinguish burning metals or self-oxidizing materials. High concentrations can cause dizziness and impaired breathing. Present halon alternatives are denser and have lower fire-quenching capacities, requiring redesign of former halon systems.

4.F.1. Standpipe Systems

This method of fire suppression is required in any building more than 90 ft tall, but it is worth the reduced insurance premiums in almost any commercial occupancy. Each system includes a siamese at ground level, standpipe zones in the building, hose racks on each floor, and either a gravity-feed water reservoir on the roof or a suction tank/upfeed pump near ground level. Due to water pressure limitations a standpipe zone cannot exceed 275 ft in height: if the building is taller, each upper zone is piggy-backed onto the zone below with the 'rooftop reservoir' of the zone below becoming the 'ground-level suction tank' of the zone above. In any zone the maximum pressure at the bottom hose is 80 psi and minimum pressure at the top hose is 12 psi (25 psi is better). Every area of each floor should be within 130 ft of a standpipe. Typical hose valve diameter = $2\frac{1}{2}$ in.

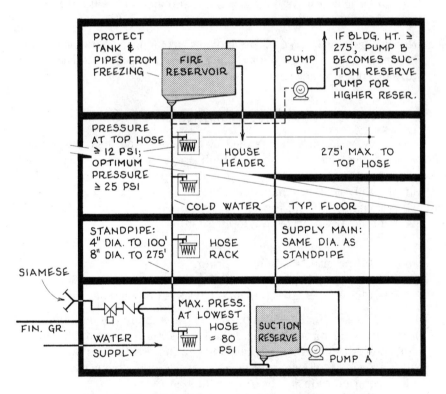

Fig. 4-42. Standpipe sprinkler system details.

A special kind of siamese connection is a fire hydrant. Usually these are public street appurtenances and thus are not considered as a building plumbing fixture; but many large buildings set in landscaped environments may need a fire hydrant. Then each is located alongside a road, it typically has two or three outlets, its supply of usually nondrinkable water typically arrives in a 2½ in. diameter main, and the water discharges at a rate of 250 gpm through a 1⅛ in. diameter nozzle.

Each standpipe firehose is a 1½ or 2½ in. diameter flexible canvas hose 50–100 ft long that is stored in a *firehose rack*, a wall-mounted cabinet with a clear glass door at eye level. Enough cabinets are located on each floor so one hose can reach any floor area, the best locations usually being by exit doors of enclosed stairways. As this is a good place for portable fire extinguishers, they are often installed beside firehose racks.

Space requirements for standpipe system components are:

Standpipe chases: Section width ≈ 2 ft; section depth ≈ 2 ft + 1 ft/standpipe. Ample space for installation, inspection, and maintenance must exist around any expansion loops.

Firehose racks or cabinets: Typical height = 2'-5" to 3'-7", width = 1'-9" to 2'-11", depth = 8" to 9".

Roof reservoirs and suction tank/upfeed pumps: 3 ft aisle around required floor areas for each reservoir.

Example 1: Water Pressure. What is the water pressure at the bottom of an 8 in. dia. standpipe system express riser that is 240 ft tall?

4)F)1)a) $\qquad$ $P = 0.433\,H$

P = water pressure at bottom of pipe, **?** psi
H = head or height of waterflow, 240 ft

$$P = 0.433 \times 240 = 104 \text{ psi}$$

Example 2: Standpipe Diameter. If the firehose system of a 360 ft tall office building has two firehose racks on each floor, what are the diameters of its standpipes?

Step 1. Find the building's required number of standpipe zones.

4)F)1)b) $\qquad$ $Z = |0.00364\,H|$

Z = required number of standpipe zones, **?** zones
H = height of building, 360 ft

$$Z = |0.00364 \times 360| = |1.31| \rightarrow 2 \text{ zones required}$$

Step 2. Find the required standpipe diameter(s). If $Z \geq 1$, system is multizone, then use 8 in. diameter express riser in all but top zone. If fraction of Z = 0.00–0.36, pipe diameter in top zone = 4 in; if fraction of Z = 0.37–0.54, pipe diameter in top zone = 6 in; if fraction of Z = 0.00–0.36, pipe diameter in top zone = 8 in.

$Z \geq 1$ ➡ use 8 in. dia. express riser in all but top zone
Fraction of Z = 0.31 ➡ standpipe dia. in top zone = 4 in.

Example 3: Standpipe Weight. What does an 8 in. diameter water-filled extra strong steel express riser standpipe weigh per floor if the floor-to-floor height is 12'-0"?

4)F)1)c)
$$W = H(w + 2 + 0.34\ d^2)$$

W = contained weight of pipe per floor, **?** lb
H = height or length of pipe per floor, ft. 12'-0" = 12.0 ft
w = unit weight of pipe, plf. From Table 4-4, w of 8 in. diameter extra strong steel pipe = 43.4 plf. Thin-walled pipe cannot be used for standpipe plumbing.
d = pipe diameter, 8 in.

$$W = 12.0\ (43.4 + 2 + 0.34 \times 82) \approx 806\ \text{lb per floor}$$

Example 4: Expansion Loops. If an express riser of 8 in. copper pipe in an office building in Richmond, VA, requires a thermal expansion loop every 70 ft along its 282 ft height, how wide should be the loop and how much chase should it have?

Step 1. Find the lateral length of the expansion loop.

4)F)1)d)
$$Ł \approx 430\ \kappa_t\ L\ (\Delta t + 5)\ d^{0.5}$$

$Ł$ = lateral length of expansion loop if configured as in Fig. 4-43A, **?** in.
κ_t = coefficient of thermal expansion of pipe material, in/in. From Table 2-4, κ_t for copper = 0.000,009,8 in/in.
L = length of piping between expansion loops, ft. Maximum length for straight runs of large-diameter piping = 70 ft ➡ L = 70 ft.
Δt = safe temperature range of riser, °F. For cold water piping, Δt = indoor temperature – lowest annual outdoor temperature. ∴ if room temperature = 70° and from climatic data lowest annual outdoor temperature for Richmond, VA = – 12°, Δt = 70 – (–12) = 82°.
d = inside diameter of piping, in. d = 8 in.

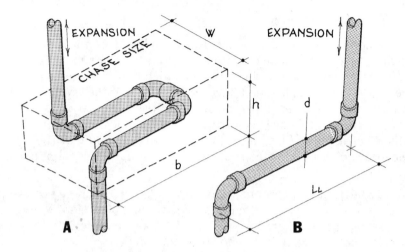

Fig. 4-43. Riser expansion loop details.

Ł ≈ 430 × 70 × 0.000,009,8 × (82 + 5) × 8^{0.5} ≈ 73 in.

Note: If the expansion loop is configured as in Fig. 4-43*B*, its lateral length (ft) ≈ 0.6 L d (in) above. This formula may be used to compute the required length or offset for any piping due to thermal expansion.

Step 2. Size the chase required for the expansion loop.

a. **Length:** $b ≈ Ł + 1.5 (d + 2)$
b. **Height:** $h ≈ 144 \, \kappa_f L \, (\Delta t + 5) + 1.5 (d + 2)$
c. **Width:** $w ≈ 1.2 (5.5 \, d + 2)$

b = minimum length or breadth of chase, as shown in Fig. 4-43, **?** in.
h = minimum height of chase, as shown in Fig. 4-43, **?** in.
w = minimum width of chase, as shown in Fig. 4-43, **?** in.
   If loop is configured as in Fig. 4-43*B*, $w = 1.2 (d + 2)$.
Ł = lateral length of expansion loop, from Step 1, 73 in.
d = inside diameter of piping, in. From Step 1, $d = 8$ in.
κ_f = coefficient of thermal expansion of pipe material, in/in.
   From Step 1, $\kappa_f = 0.000,0098$ in/in.
L = length of piping between expansion loops, from Step 1, 70 ft
Δt = safe temperature range of riser, °F. From Step 1, $\Delta t = 82°$.

Length: $b ≈ 73 + 1.5 (8 + 2) ≈ 88$ in.
Height: $h ≈ 144 × 70 × 0.000,0098 (82 + 10) + 1.5 (8 + 2) ≈ 24$ in.
Width: $w ≈ 1.2 (5.5 × 8 + 2) ≈ 55$ in.

4.F.1.a. Reservoirs

Whether the fire water supply is gravity-feed from the roof or upfeed from the basement, it should contain a 30 minute water supply for use until firefighters arrive, have a float control switch that activates a refill pump when the water draws low, and have a drain tap. In either system a few toilets are usually connected to the stored water to keep it fresh. Although roof reservoirs are heavy, they are more dependable because they operate if the electric power fails, which often happens during fires. The formulas below may be used for sizing roof reservoirs or upfeed suction tanks.

> **Example 1.** If a suction tank system requires a 30 minute water supply reservoir for firefighting in a 3-story building (height to highest hose = 34 ft) and there are 2 firehose racks on each floor, what is the supply delivery rate for the hoses on the top floor?

4)F)1)a)1) $Þ = 119 \, η \, (25 + 0.433 \, H)^{0.5}$

Þ = rate of hose waterflow at remote outlet, **?** gpm
η = number of hoses in use on each floor, 2 units
H = head or height from reservoir base up to highest hose outlet, 34 ft

$$Þ = 119 × 2 (25 + 0.433 × 34)^{0.5} = 1,500 \text{ gpm}$$

> **Example 2.** If a standpipe system in a 130 ft tall building has a rooftop reservoir for firefighting that contains a $\frac{1}{2}$ hour water supply, size the reservoir. What does it weigh when full?

Step 1. Find the delivery rate of the firehose with the greatest pressure.

4)F)1)a)1) $Þ = 119 \, η \, (25 + 0.433 \, H)^{0.5}$

Þ = rate of hose waterflow at remote outlet, **?** gpm
η = number of hoses in use on each floor, assume 1 hose u.o.n.
H = head or height from reservoir base down to lowest hose outlet, 130 ft

$$Þ = 119 × 1 (25 + 0.433 × 130)^{0.5} = 1,070 \text{ gpm}$$

Step 2. Find the volume of water required for the reservoir.

$$V = 4.0 \, Þ$$

V = volume of water required for reservoir, **?** cf
Þ = maximum rate of hose waterflow, from Step 1, 1,070 gpm

$$V ≥ 4.0 × 1,070 ≥ 4,280 \text{ cf}$$

Step 3. Size the reservoir.

$$V \approx L\,W\,H$$

V = required volume of water for reservoir, from Step 2, 4,280 cf
L = optimal length of reservoir, **?** ft
W = optimal width of reservoir, **?** ft
H = optimal height of reservoir, **?** ft

$$4,280 \approx L\,W\,H$$
Try L = 40 ft ➡ $W\,H$ = 4,280/40 = 107 sf
Try W = 12 ft ➡ H = 107/12 = 8.9 ft
One solution: $L\,W\,H$ = 40 × 12 × 9 ft

Step 4. Estimate the reservoir's weight when full.

$$w \approx 62.4\,L\,W\,H$$

w = estimated weight of reservoir (water only) when full, **?** lb
L = optimal length of reservoir, from Step 3, 40 ft
W = optimal width of reservoir, from Step 3, 20 ft
H = optimal height of reservoir, from Step 3, 9 ft

$$W \approx 62.4 \times 40 \times 12 \times 9 \approx 270,000 \text{ lb} \qquad \dots 135 \text{ tons}$$

4.F.2. Sprinkler Systems

When a fire breaks out indoors, hot gases rise to the ceiling then billow outward, superheating the ceiling structure, causing it to lose strength until it may fail under its own weight. Research indicates that sprinkler systems will suppress 95 percent of such fires.

A sprinkler system includes a number of orifices or heads that contain thermal fuses which, on melting at a specified temperature, allow water to discharge. The water flows to the heads via a system of mains and risers that contain sensor-activated valves which trigger an alarm when the standing water begins to flow. Each system requires at least one siamese in each building front, electrical hookups to manually activated fire alarm systems, fire-control overrides in HVAC ducting, firewalls between sprinklered and nonsprinklered areas, waterproof floors sloping to drains or scuppers, and quick shutdown capability once a fire is out to minimize water damage (a recently developed type known as *flow control heads* close automatically once temperatures have cooled). Control valves should be easily accessible to firefighters and service personnel yet protected from vandals. If the system has a pipe-in-common with the building or city water supply, the pipe should contain a check valve because standing water in

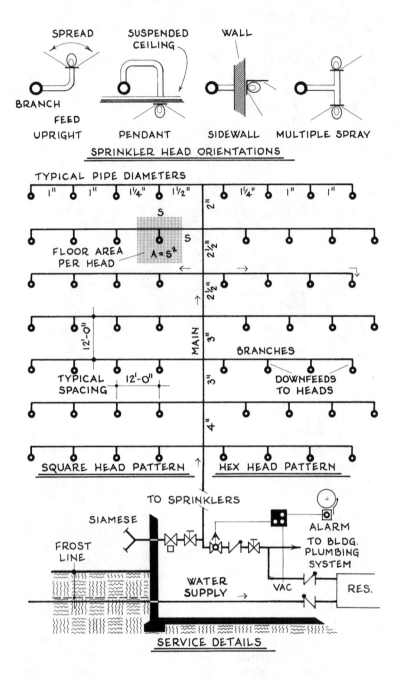

SPREAD   SUSPENDED   WALL
              CEILING

BRANCH
FEED
UPRIGHT   PENDANT   SIDEWALL   MULTIPLE SPRAY

SPRINKLER HEAD ORIENTATIONS

TYPICAL PIPE DIAMETERS

1"   1"   1¼"   1½"   2"   1¼"   1"   1"

S

FLOOR AREA   2½"
PER HEAD   A = S²   S

2½"

12'-0"   3"   MAIN   BRANCHES

TYPICAL   12'-0"   3"   DOWNFEEDS
SPACING   TO HEADS

4"

SQUARE HEAD PATTERN   HEX HEAD PATTERN

TO SPRINKLERS

SIAMESE   ALARM

FROST   TO BLDG.
LINE   PLUMBING
SYSTEM

WATER   VAC   RES.
SUPPLY

SERVICE DETAILS

Fig. 4-44. Sprinkler system layout details.

sprinkler piping can become stagnant over time and thus should not enter freshwater piping. A fire sprinkler system also requires a reservoir, whose location influences the layout of mains, branches, and feeds to sprinkler heads. In most fires only a few heads open, and after a head has opened its thermal fuse is replaced. As the heads must also be periodically cleaned and inspected, each must be accessible by service personnel.

Sprinkler systems are installed in all kinds of commercial, institutional, and industrial buildings. The heads are typically mounted near ceilings in rooms of any size as well as in atriums and fire refuge areas, under and above staircase landings, near fire exits, by openable windows, and in exhaust air ducts. Such systems should be dry pipe and have pressurized reservoirs so they will operate if the power fails. A little-explored possibility to date is placing sprinkler heads on the roofs of buildings in areas threatened by forest fires.

Sprinkler system design typically proceeds upstream from the heads, branches, mains, and risers to sizing the reservoir. The heads and piping may be arranged as shown in Figs. 4-43 and 4-44. All runs must be braced in both directions, drainable (but not into sewers), and protected from freezing and corrosion. Since thermal expansion is a serious consideration due to hot fire temperatures, one end of each run should be free, each turn should have ample space around it, and hangers should allow the piping to move laterally. System design includes the weight of pipes when full and these dead loads should be added to structural loads.

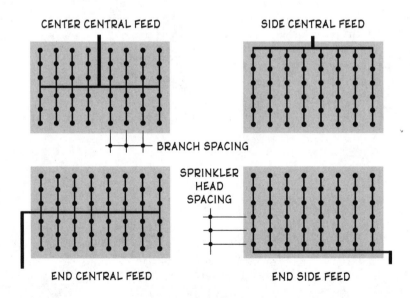

Fig. 4-45. Types of sprinkler system layouts.

4.F.2.a. Sprinkler Heads

Each sprinkler head, in addition to having the proper coverage area and adequate waterflow, must aim an unobstructed spray in the proper direction. Any object more than 4 in. wide and less than 24 in. from any head, or any "shadow" that subtends an angle greater than 9.5° behind which no spray can reach, constitutes an obstruction: this includes beams, truss struts, soffits, ducts, pipes, light fixtures, columns, signs, curtains, etc. Thus proper sprinkler design requires 3-D visualization of the surrounds of each head. Where an obstruction exists, either remove it, relocate the head, or install an extra head to cover the obstructed area.

Sprinkler heads must also be arranged so the spray from one will not cool the thermal fuse of another, they must be away from unit heaters and smoke exhaust outlets, and they must never be field-painted. The spread of each head is determined largely by its deflector design: flat deflectors create conical spreads, small diameters send the water more vertically, large diameters send it more horizontally, slotted edges divide the water into droplets or mist based on the slot size (these reduce temperatures more than quench fires), and sidewall heads (L-shaped deflectors) direct the water horizontally.

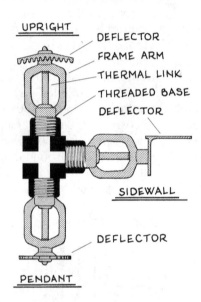

UPRIGHT

DEFLECTOR
FRAME ARM
THERMAL LINK
THREADED BASE
DEFLECTOR

SIDEWALL

DEFLECTOR

PENDANT

Fig. 4-46. Sprinkler heads.

4.F.2.b. Types of Installation

The 96 × 140 ft floor area of a furniture factory in High Point, NC, needs a fire sprinkler system. If the furniture is wooden tables and chairs, the ceiling is exposed, and the owner's cousin works for a steel company, what system is best for this facility?

Step 1. Determine the occupancy's Hazard Class from below. Where specific conditions merit a more hazardous rating, use it.

Class I, Light Hazard: Schools, offices, most public buildings, museums, theaters including stages, restaurant seating, libraries except large stack areas, nursing homes, residences, and the like.

Class II, Ordinary Hazard: Retail areas, auto parking garages, bakeries, laundries, machine shops, paper mills, restaurant kitchens, wood assembly, piers and wharves, warehouses, and the like.

Class III, Extra Hazard: Airplane hangars, factories of combustibles (lumber, textiles, etc.), areas of great heat (metal extruding, die casting, etc.) or flammable fluids (paints, oils, etc.), and the like.

Class HS, High-Piled Storage: Warehouses containing combustible items that are stored more than 15 ft high.

The occupation most resembling the furniture factory is
'wood assembly' ➡ Class II, Ordinary Hazard

Step 2. Select the type of sprinkler head from below:

Small orifice: Orifice diameters are $1/4-7/16$ in; these are used only in certain hydraulically designed wet systems in light hazard occupancies of small area. Orifices smaller than $3/8$ in. require supply-side strainers.

Spray: The standard head, widely available at low cost. Orifice diameter is usually $1/2$ or $17/32$ in. and head pressure is 15–60 psi.

Large drop (LD): A large-orifice head used where storage is 15–30 ft high. They produce higher flow rates and use more water; thus piping may be larger but the heads cost less. Orifice diameter is $5/8$ or $3/4$ in, head pressure is 25–95 psi, and maximum number of heads is 20 per rack.

Early suppression fast response (ESFR): An extra-large-orifice head that is used in warehouses whose storage is up to 35 ft high. These high-flow heads can protect all hazards, but they require a nearly flat roof ($\leq$ 1/12 pitch) and no obstructions. Their extreme water demands also require larger piping and use of a fire pump, and their heads are expensive. Orifice diameter is $3/4$ in, head pressure is 50–175 psi, and maximum number of heads is 12 per rack.

Water mist: A recently developed sprinkler head that is described in Sec. 4.F.6. Halon Alternatives.

The building is not a warehouse and/or
little potential exists for high-hazard fires to spread fast and
release much heat in a short time ➡ spray heads

Step 3. Select the sprinkler head's orientation, from below:

Upright: Heads rise above the pipes and cast spray over horizontal area. Good above suspended ceilings and where hot gases may be more dangerous than flames.

Pendant: Heads hang down from pipes and cast spray over horizontal area. Good for quenching flames from ordinary combustibles in large open areas, especially ones without suspended ceilings.

Sidewall: Heads aim sideways and spray vertical areas.

Multiple spray: Sprinklers spray up and down at the same time. Good where fire hazards exist above and below ceilings, but expensive.

Large open area and no suspended ceiling ➡ pendant orientation

Step 4. Select the type of sprinkler system from below:

Wet-pipe: Water is present in all piping; thus an opened sprinkler head discharges water immediately. The simplest, most economical, most dependable, and fastest-operating system, it requires little maintenance. NG in areas subject to freezing, where water damage is a concern, or where hazards mandate a more effective system.

Antifreeze: A wet-pipe system whose water supply contains antifreeze to prevent freezing. This is generally limited to small systems, and the supply must be periodically drained, tested, and refilled.

Dry-pipe: Pipes contain a gas which escapes when heads open, then the water follows. Good in areas subject to freezing such as unheated buildings and service docks. Because they respond more slowly than wet-pipe systems, their coverage is limited, but dry-pipe racks can branch from wet-pipe mains. Dry-pipe systems require air compressors, heated main controls, and pitched piping that allows drainage after use.

Preaction: A wet-pipe system that is activated by heat or smoke sensors instead of sprinkler heads. It responds faster than dry-pipe systems, but is expensive and requires more maintenance. These systems may be single interlock (requires only one alarm to activate) or double interlock (requires two alarms, each a fail-safe for the other, to activate).

Deluge: A dry pipe system with open heads; thus when any one sprinkler is activated the whole system area is covered. Used in high-hazard areas and where the potential for rapidly spreading fires (e.g. oil slicks) is possible, but it requires a large water supply. Some buildings have dry pipe preaction deluge systems.

Foam water: A concentrate is mixed with water to produce a foam that discharges through the heads onto a fire. Good for flammable liquid storage areas, aircraft hangers, and other high-hazard areas where water application is inadequate; but it is expensive, creates removal problems afterward, and its piping has high static pressures which could cause leaks and other damage.

Flexible stainless steel hose stem: Single feeds made of flexible stainless steel. Good for mounting in exhaust air ducts and other small spaces where rigid piping is unfeasible or difficult to install. Also good where upgrading or tenancy changes require a small number of new heads.

> Building is heated (i.e. temperature is above freezing) and fire
> is not likely to spread rapidly ➡ wet-pipe sprinkler system

Step 5. Select the type of piping from below:

Steel: Stronger, but may degrade in areas of high humidity, salty air, or where harmful gases are present. Thin-walled steel piping should not be used for sprinkler systems.

Copper: Lighter, but more susceptible to damage by high temperatures. All connections must be threaded.

> In lieu of more definitive data, assume the owner can buy
> steel piping at a discount from his cousin at the steel company

Step 6. Select the type of water supply system from below:

Gravity-feed: Water flows down from a roof reservoir. To maintain 25 psi discharge pressure at the sprinkler heads, the reservoir must be mounted on a tower whose lowest level is at least 58 ft above the sprinkler heads. On some sites this is a good idea.

Upfeed: Sprinkler head water is pushed upward by a pump.

> Roof structure is light steel and occupants are at ground level
> where they can escape easily ➡ upfeed system

4.F.2.c. System Design

Fig. 4-47 on the next page shows a design flow chart for fire sprinkler systems that streamlines a normally exasperating process. The method described is known as *pipe schedule design*, as opposed to *hydraulic design*, which is a scientifically meticulous and more detailed but more laborious method. In nearly all cases pipe schedule design is adequate.

> If the pendant spray heads for the fire sprinkler system in the above 96 × 140 ft furniture factory are located just below an open ceiling of longspan steel joists, the building's structural bays are 24 × 28 ft, and the plumbing supply main pressure is 60 psi, design the fire sprinkler system. This includes head coverage areas and spacings, pipe sizes, and waterflow requirements.

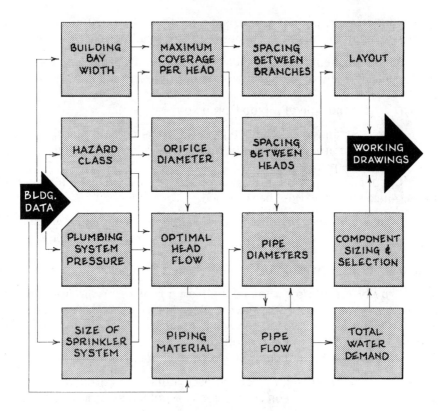

Fig. 4-47. Sprinkler system design flow chart.

Step 1. Determine the sprinkler head spacing requirements from Table 4-9. First find the maximum coverage per head based on the building's construction and occupation Hazard Class ➡ for *spray heads, below ceiling, unobstructed noncombustible construction, Hazard Class II*, maximum coverage per head is 225 sf. Then determine the most feasible spacing between the heads based on the maximum coverage per head and the building's structural bay dimensions. As 225 sf = 15 × 15 and the structural bays are 24 × 28 ft, a good sprinkler head module is 12 × 14 ft. This is within the required 8–15 ft min-max spacing for spray heads as listed in Table 4-9.

Step 2. Determine the spacing between the heads on each branch. At maximum 225 sf coverage and 15 ft spacing between heads, use 14 ft to create a sprinkler head plan module that aligns with the 28 ft wide bay dimensions. Then the actual coverage per head = 14 × 14 = 196 sf. The system's ceiling plan may now be drawn. At this point the system's number of sprinkler heads should be determined, either by adding them up or by area of floor coverage ÷ area of coverage per head.

TABLE 4-9: SPRINKLER HEAD DESIGN DATA [†]

SPACING REQUIREMENTS

SPRINKLER HEAD TYPE	Hazard Class ➡	I	II	III	S
Spray heads, below ceiling, unobstructed or obstructed noncombustible construction		225	130	100	100
Above ceiling, pipe schedule design		200	150	105	—
Above ceiling, hydraulic design		225	175	120	—
Large drop (LD) heads		—	—	—	130
Early suppression fast response (ESFR) heads.		—	—	—	100
Space between heads, ft min/max: spray heads ..		8/15	8/15	6/12	6/12
LD heads		—	—	—	8/12
ESFR heads		—	—	—	8/10
Distance below ceiling or roof, ft.					
Spray heads (min. clear to storage = 18 in)		1-12 ft for all classes			
LD heads (min. clear to storage = 36 in)		6-8 ft for all classes			
ESFR heads (min. clear to storage = 36 in)		6-14 ft for all classes			

ORIFICE DIAMETERS

Hazard Class	Orifice diameters, in.
I, hydraulic design in small spaces w/ low water req.	$\frac{1}{4}$ $\frac{5}{16}$ $\frac{3}{8}$ $\frac{7}{16}$
All other I, II, III	$\frac{1}{2}$ $\frac{17}{32}$
III w/ high water req. in case of fire, large drop (LD) heads	$\frac{5}{16}$ $\frac{3}{4}$
Early suppression fast response (ESFR) heads	$\frac{3}{4}$

OPTIMAL WATERFLOW RANGE PER HEAD [1]

Orifice dia, in.	Haz. Class	Pressure psi	Flow/head gpm	Orifice dia, in.	Haz. Class	Pressure psi	Flow/head gpm
$\frac{1}{4}$	I	7–15–60	4–6–12	$\frac{17}{32}$	I	15–25–95	29–41–80
$\frac{5}{16}$	I	7–15–60	5–8–15	$\frac{17}{32}$	II	20–30–95	33–45–80
$\frac{3}{8}$	I	7–15–60	7–11–22	$\frac{17}{32}$	III	25–35–95	37–49–80
$\frac{7}{16}$	I	7–15–60	11–17–34	$\frac{5}{8}$	III	25–50–95	55–80–150
$\frac{1}{2}$	I	15–25–95	21–29–57	$\frac{5}{8}$	LD	25–75–95	55–100–150
$\frac{1}{2}$	II	20–30–95	24–32–57	$\frac{3}{4}$	ESFR	50–75–95	95–125–190
$\frac{1}{2}$	III	25–35–95	27–34–57				

1. Max. allow. floor area for one sprinkler system riser is 52,000 ft^2 for Hazard Class I or II, 25,000 ft^2 for Hazard Class III (pipe schedule design), and 40,000 ft^2 for Hazard Class III (hydraulic design) or High-piled Storage.

Step 3. Determine the sprinkler heads' orifice diameter based on the occupancy's Hazard Class from Table 4-9. The choices for Hazard Class II are $\frac{1}{2}$ or $\frac{17}{32}$ in. Due to the factory's large amount of wood raw materials and manufactured tables and chairs, select $\frac{17}{32}$ in.

[†] Most of the data in Tables 4-9 and 4-10 was obtained from *NFPA 13, Standard*

Step 4. Knowing the occupation Hazard Class, head orifice diameter, initial pressure of the building's plumbing system, and overall size of the sprinkler system, determine its optimal waterflow range per head from Table 4-9. At *Hazard Class II, orifice diameter of $^{17}/_{32}$ in, initial pressure of 60 psi, and plan dimensions = 96 × 140* = 13,440 sf (note the maximum floor area protection for one sprinkler system riser as listed at bottom of Table 4-9), the minimum-optimal-maximum waterflow range is 33–45–80 gpm. Here the actual flow may be computed according to Sec. 5.C.1, given the system's initial pressure, length of pipe, head pressure, and maximum fixture pressure range of 20–95 psi. Considerable leeway exists here. Say this system's optimal waterflow per head is found to be 42 gpm.

Step 5. From Table 4-10 find the diameter of each length of piping in the system, based on whether it is copper or steel. The diameter for each length of pipe is based on the number of heads it feeds, and they are sized from the outermost upstream head through the branches back to the main. Here, for steel piping for a Hazard Class II occupancy, the selected diameters are 1 in. to the outermost two heads, 1¼ in. to the nextmost three heads, 1½ in. to the nextmost five heads, etc.

Step 6. Compute the total water demand for the system.

TABLE 4-10: SPRINKLER PIPING CAPACITIES

Pipe Dia., in.	STEEL: SCHEDULE 80(X) Weight, pLF Empty	Full	Max. no. heads[1] Hazard Class I	II	III	COPPER: TYPE "K" HARD Weight, pLF Empty	Full	Max. no. heads Hazard Class I	II	III
1	2.17	2.48	2	2	1	0.84	1.18	2	2	1
1¼	3.00	3.55	3	3	2	1.04	1.57	3	3	2
1½	3.63	4.13	5	5	5	1.36	2.11	5	5	5
2	5.02	6.30	10	10	8	2.06	3.36	12	12	8
2½	7.66	9.49	30	20	15	2.92	4.94	40	25	15
3 ...	10.3	13.1	60	40	27	4.00	6.87	65	45	27
3½ ...	12.5	16.4	100	65	40	5.12	9.01	115	75	40
4 ...	15.0	20.0	—	100	55	6.51	11.6	—	115	55
5 ...	20.8	28.7	—	160	90	9.67	17.5	—	180	90
6 ...	28.6	40.0	—	275	150	13.9	25.1	—	300	150
8 ...	43.4	63.2 (for express risers use 8 in. diameter steel only)								

1. Steel or copper pipe diameters for LD heads are 1 in. to outermost head, 1¼ in. to nextmost 2 heads, 1½ in. to nextmost 3 heads, 2 in. to nextmost 6 heads, and 2½ in. to max. 20 heads in each rack. Corresponding diameters for ESFR heads are 1¼ in. to outermost head, 1½ in. to nextmost 2 heads, 2 in. to nextmost 4 heads, and 2½ in. to max. 20 heads in each rack.

4)F)2)c)   Þ $C = QA$

Þ = required waterflow for fire sprinkler system riser, ? gpm
C = area of coverage per sprinkler head, from Step 2, 196 sf
Q = optimal waterflow per sprinkler head, from Step 4, 42 gpm
A = total floor area covered by fire sprinkler system riser, from Step 4,
     13,440 sf

$$Þ \times 196 = 42 \times 13,440 \qquad ... Þ = 2,880 \text{ gpm}$$
This amount may be used to size all system supply components

Step 7. Lay out in plan the sprinkler water supply system. Each sprinkler requires a primary and secondary method of water supply. The primary supply is automatically activated by the building's electric system, must be of sufficient capacity and pressure to operate the system, and is usually a part of the building's general plumbing system. The secondary supply operates if the building's electric system fails and renders the general plumbing system inoperable; then an onsite generator activates the secondary system controls. Each system connects to an onsite reservoir with a half-hour supply, an electric motor-driven pump that utilizes the reservoir water and/or draws the water from a municipal main, and a siamese connection at the building edge for use by fire trucks.

Here also consider any outdoor sprinklers that may need to be installed to protect roofs, cornices, facades, window areas, and even landscaping. If any piping could be exposed to subfreezing temperatures, it should be part of an antifreeze, dry-pipe, or deluge type system.

Step 8. Size the secondary water supply reservoir.

   a. Gravity-feed: Þ $t = 30 V$
   b. Upfeed pump: Þ $t = 77 C$ ... ✚

Þ = required waterflow of fire sprinkler system, 2,880 gpm
t = time duration of water reservoir supply, min. $t = 30$ min. for Hazard
     Class I, 60 min. for Hazard Class II, and 90 min. for Hazard Class
     III. Here $t = 60$ min.
V = required capacity of gravity-feed reservoir, cf. If system has fewer
     than 40 heads, V = water demand of four heads. Not applicable.
C = required capacity of upfeed pump reservoir, ? cf. If system has
     fewer than sprinkler 16 heads, C = total water demand of four heads.

$$2,880 \times 60 = 77 C \qquad ... C = 2,240 \text{ cf}$$
If $h = 10$ ft, $w\,b = 2,240/10 = 224$ sf
If $w = 12$ ft, $b = 224/12 = 18.7$ ft
One size: 10 ft high × 12 ft wide × 18 ft long

4.F.2.d. Floor Drains

Sprinklered areas require waterproof floors rimmed by integral 4–6 in. high baseboards and the floors should pitch ¼ in. fall/ft toward drains and/or scuppers to facilitate water removal. Each scupper should have a screened hood to prevent entry of rodents, birds, and bugs.

> In the above furniture factory in North Carolina, size the sprinkler system floor drain diameters if each structural bay is 24 × 28 ft.

Step 1. Determine the number of floor drains required per structural bay.

$$4\boxed{F}\boxed{2}\boxed{d} \qquad \eta = |0.002\, A|$$

η = no. of floor drains required in bay or other floor area

A = floor area per bay, should be 250–500 sf. 24 × 28 = 672 sf.

$$\eta = |0.002 \times 672|$$
$$\eta = |1.34| \Rightarrow 2 \text{ drains/bay}$$
Divide each bay as in Fig. 4-48

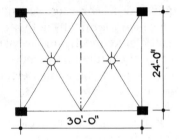

Fig. 4-48. Bay floor drain area.

Step 2. Find the minimum diameter of each floor drain.

$$\delta = 1.13\,(A\,\kappa_a)^{0.5}$$

δ = minimum diameter of each floor drain, ? in.

A = area of floor drained by each drain outlet. A = 24 × 28/2 = 336 sf.

κ_a = drain area factor, 0.050 for Hazard Class I, 0.057 for Hazard Class II, 0.076 for Hazard Class III. Add 0.013 for nonwatertight floor and 0.013 for contents subject to water damage. Here κ_a = 0.057.

$$\delta \geq 1.13\,(336 \times 0.0567)^{0.5} \geq 4.95 \Rightarrow 5 \text{ in. dia.}$$

4.F.3. Portable Extinguishers

These cylindrical units typically weigh 10–40 lb, are 20–30 in. high, have a discharge range of 30–50 ft, and discharge for 12–30 seconds. Each should be mounted conspicuously near eye level along fire exit routes, should be removable and usable by an inexperienced female operator, and should not weigh more 20 lb unless intended to be used by firefighters. Their contents are classed as described below:

A Contains water-based agents for use on wood, paper, and textile fires. Numerals before the letter indicate extinguishing potential: e.g. 40A will extinguish 20 times as much as 2A.

B Contains smothering or flame-interrupting chemicals for use on flammable liquids. Numerals before the letter indicate the area of liquid fire that an untrained operator can be expected to extinguish: e.g. 40B will extinguish about 40 sf of deep-liquid fire.

C Contains electrically nonconducting chemicals for use on fires on or near electric motors, switches, appliances, computers, and telecommunication equipment. Will operate at –40° F.

ABC Contains primarily ammonium phosphate for use on ordinary combustibles, flammable oils, and electrical wiring. **N2G** for electrical fires because it leaves a harmful residue.

D Contains dry chemical powders designed for use on specific combustible metals as listed on the extinguisher's nameplate.

4.F.4. CO$_2$ Systems

Here the plumbing may be as simple as a short pipe between a gravity tank and a nozzle aimed at a piece of equipment, or as complex as a network of piping between a large pneumatic reservoir and many spray heads. A CO$_2$ system may also include detectors, motorized dampers, smoke exhaust fans, and other controls. The areas served should allow occupants to escape quickly and keep the heavier-than-air gas from draining into adjacent lower floor areas. CO$_2$ system piping is usually small-diameter and its controls are generally designed by engineering specialists, while the Æ designer provides adequate access space for the piping, reservoir, and controls.

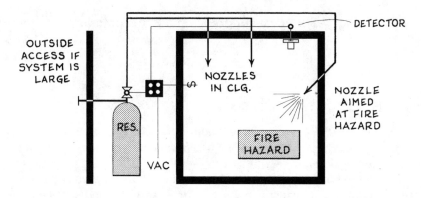

Fig. 4-49. CO$_2$ fire suppression system details.

4.F.5. Foam Systems

In these systems the foam concentrate extinguishes fires involving gasoline, oils, and other flammable liquids. They are often installed in large open industrial interiors such as aircraft hangars and manufacturing facilities. As the foam is 99 percent air, occupants and firefighters may advance through it safely, and later the foam is easily rinsed away. The piping is connected to circuitry that activates evacuation sirens and opens large vents in roofs or upper walls in case of fire. Foam systems are usually designed by engineering specialists, but the architect or general engineer should have a conversant understanding of them.

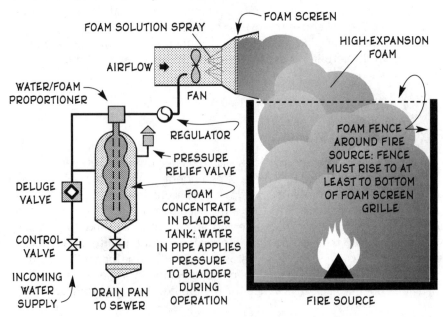

Fig. 4-50. Foam suppression system details

4.F.6. Halon Alternatives

On Jan. 1, 1996, the U.S. Government banned all domestic production and importing of Halon 1301. The EPA has released a preliminary list of acceptable Halon alternatives; but at present, as all are denser and have lower fire-quenching capacities, their incorporation requires redesign of existing Halon-based systems. In particular, reservoirs and supply piping usually must be larger to offer the same required coverage.

Three general kinds of Halon-alternative fire suppressants are presently acceptable, as described below:

Streaming agents. These nonwater suppressants usually discharge from a hand-held fire extinguisher nozzle that produces a spray, mist, fog, or jet that covers the fire. They generally protect a particular process or piece of equipment and work best when the fire is small.

Total flooding agents. When these nonwater suppressants are discharged they vaporize into a gas whose temperature drops greatly. They are best for deep-seated fires such as overheated circuits in computer equipment and beneath access floors, in which the gas invades every cranny to smother and cool the fire. These suppressants are stored under pressure in a reservoir connected to process piping that usually terminates at ceiling-mounted nozzles; thus they are pre-engineered systems.

Water mist. This is a metricated pre-engineered deluge sprinkler system whose atomizing nozzles produce a fine mist of water that is used to extinguish flammable liquids whose metal storage tanks do not exceed 500 gallons. The mist cools the flame and absorbs radiant heat around it, which turns the water droplets into steam, which expands greatly and displaces the air that feeds the fire. The system works rapidly, is highly effective, and uses less water than standard sprinklers; but its coverage is limited, as follows:

Maximum nozzle coverage = 4.0 m^2 (43 sf).
Maximum nozzle distance from walls = 1.0 m (39.4 in)
Maximum nozzle spacing = 2.0 m (78.7 × 78.7 in)
Maximum ceiling height of coverage area = 5.0 m (16.4 ft)
Maximum volume of coverage area = 500 m^3 (17,657 sf)
Minimum water reserve = 30 min.

Water mist systems have the following drawbacks: (1) breezes and ventilation drafts can disperse the mist, (2) they work only on small incipient fires when the nozzles are aimed directly at the fire's base (which may be hard to arrange in advance of a fire and requires a sensitive and swiftly acting alarm), (3) their high operating pressures (175–250 psi) usually require air compressors with separate piping, (4) the nozzles' tiny orifices require fine strainers, and (5) the systems are expensive. In summary, water mists may be used to protect valuable or irreplacable equipment where standard sprinkler and gaseous systems are unacceptable.

For any Halon-alternative fire suppressant to be effective, the fire hazard area must contain the suppressant for a considerable time. Thus enclosing walls and ceilings should have few or no openings, every entry door should automatically close after being opened, and the area must be fully ventilatable after the fire is out.

ABBREVIATIONS

A	ANTENNA	S	SWITCH, SINGLE POLE
B	BELL OR GONG	S_2	SWITCH, DOUBLE POLE
BAT	BATTERY	S_3	SWITCH, 3 WAY
C	CABINET	S_D	SWITCH, AUTOMATIC DOOR
CB	CIRCUIT BREAKER		
CH	CHIME	S_K	SWITCH, KEY OPERATED
D	DIMMER	S_{RC}	SWITCH, REMOTE CONTROLLED
EM	EMERGENCY		
F	FAN	S_T	SWITCH, TIME DELAY
FA	FIRE ALARM	T	THERMOSTAT
FS	FUSED SWITCH	T_C	TELEPHONE CLOSET
G	GROUND	TEL	TELEPHONE
GFCI	GROUND FAULT CIRCUIT INTERRUPTER	TV	TELEVISION
		U	UTILITY
I, IA	INTRUSION DETECTOR OR ALARM	UG	UNDERGROUND
		UON	UNLESS OTHERWISE NOTED
IC	INTERCOM		
J	JUNCTION BOX	WM	ELECTRIC WATT-HOUR METER
L, LTG	LIGHTING		
LV	LOW VOLTAGE	WP	WEATHERPROOF
M	MOTOR	X, EX	EXIT LIGHT
OS	OCCUPANCY SENSOR		
P	PANEL BOX		
R	RANGE		

WIRING SYMBOLS

Electrical abbreviations and plan symbols
(More electrical symbols are at the end of this chapter)

ELECTRICAL

5.A. GENERAL †

Since the late 1970s, the subminiaturization of electric circuits de-signed for specific logic functions has led to increasingly powerful and versa-tile computers, computer-activated sensors, and the organization of these units into vast electronic networks that are imparting to the buildings in which they are installed the character of human nervous systems. As a result, today's building electrical systems are undergoing a veritable revolution in design, construction, and operation.

But these advances have a darker side. For these vast computerized networks are often plagued with mysterious losses of power, voltage swells and sags, overheating, humming, lost data, and nuisance tripping of circuit breakers. Obviously there are two revolutions in building systems going on here: one positive, one negative.

The basis for the negative side is twofold: (1) the larger that a build-ing electric system containing computerized components is, the greater the size difference between its largest feeder conductor (the cable or busway leading from the service switchgear to the first laterals) and the smallest conductors in the computerized units (the microscopic filaments in the micro-processor chips); and (2) the filaments in the microchips are not true con-ductors but metalloid *semiconductors* (usually silicon) whose electron flow does not obey the normal ohmic laws of conductivity. These two facts and their deleterious effect on modern electrical systems are explained below.

Every wire has a usually cylindrical volume, equal to its section area times its length , which contains a reservoir of electrons. Obviously a long thick wire, such as a feeder main, has a far greater capacity to store elec-trons than a microprocessor filament; and a larger wire often contains a far denser concentration of electrons due to its higher voltage and amperage. Now when the circuitry between a massive feeder main and a tiny micropro-cessor filament is opened, the far greater number of electrons in the larg-er conductor surges forward in a huge wave; this flow becomes increas-ingly turbulent as it enters each narrower conductor, until by the time the electrons squeeze through each microprocessor filament their sinusoidal

380

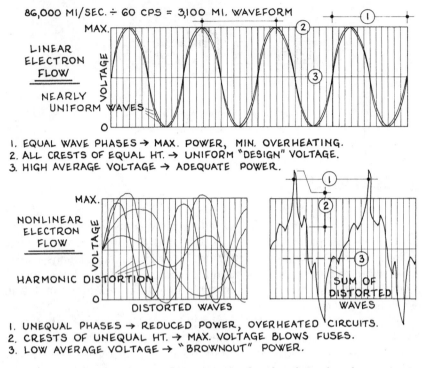

86,000 MI/SEC. ÷ 60 CPS = 3,100 MI. WAVEFORM

LINEAR ELECTRON FLOW
NEARLY UNIFORM WAVES

1. EQUAL WAVE PHASES → MAX. POWER, MIN. OVERHEATING.
2. ALL CRESTS OF EQUAL HT. → UNIFORM "DESIGN" VOLTAGE.
3. HIGH AVERAGE VOLTAGE → ADEQUATE POWER.

NONLINEAR ELECTRON FLOW
HARMONIC DISTORTION
DISTORTED WAVES
SUM OF DISTORTED WAVES

1. UNEQUAL PHASES → REDUCED POWER, OVERHEATED CIRCUITS.
2. CRESTS OF UNEQUAL HT. → MAX. VOLTAGE BLOWS FUSES.
3. LOW AVERAGE VOLTAGE → "BROWNOUT" POWER.

Fig. 5-1. Sinusoidal wave action in electric wire.

waves have become so misshapened that their highest crests (effective amperage) often trip circuit breakers while their average crest heights (effective power) are so much lower that the electrons haven't enough inertia to perform their intended function. All this creates less power and lower efficiency at a greater expenditure of energy, which also heats up circuitry and equipment which shortens their lives. These electromagnetic aberrations are described visually in Fig. 5-1.

Due to these disturbances, building engineers have developed power conditioning devices such as harmonic filters, correction capacitors, power conditioners, surge suppressors, isolated transformers, and synchronous motors to clean up the turbulent waveforms and return them to near-linear flow. Even more important for Æ designers, all these electronic developments —the revolutionary advances, the unforeseen drawbacks, the devised remedies— are having a major impact on the way space is allotted in buildings. Old methods of wiring buildings via random bundling in leftover cavities after the ducting and plumbing is in place are being replaced by independent wire management systems that require systematically arranged chases and other voids. And the old rob-Peter-to-pay-Paul method of tucking an extra

(Intertec Publishing Co., Overland Park, KS) from 1994 to 1997.

fuse box into a corner of a janitor closet or garage is being replaced by whole rooms connected by corridors big enough to walk in that are all filled with stepdown transformers, closet-sized breaker boxes, long shelves, and thick tubes filled with numerous conductors of different voltages which must be well apart from each other, and other componentry needed to regulate the miles of added circuitry. Even in residences, the usual stapling of Romex cables to joists and running them through holes in stud walls is slowly being replaced by laying conductors in metal trays located in easily accessible chases or shafts, which require articulately defined space. Concepts of electrical usage are also changing from day-one needs to planning for all kinds of future tenancies and constant upgrading. Thus modern electrical systems now require large amounts of space that must be sized as surely as lobbies and hallways between occupied areas are sized, that must have access portals to every area as surely as rooms along hallways need entrance doors, that must be ventilated and cooled as surely as public spaces are ventilated and cooled. Thus, wise is today's architect who, having knowledge of these dynamics, adds 15 or 20 percent to his or her habitable interior volumes for the installation of whatever electric conductors, enclosures, cavities, and accompanying access areas that may be required to make comfortable those volumes that are the reason for the building's being.

Also due to this revolution, Æ designers need, for the first time, a design vocabulary for those utilitarian spaces that exist solely to accommodate the installation, maintenance, and upgrading of electrical systems. Fortunately, in building engineering circles these volumes have already evolved a nomenclature of their own, as follows:

Entrance facility. A usually large area that houses service and antenna entrances, transformers, switchgear, onsite generators, and related equipment. This area requires two emergency exits, including one to the outdoors. All large electrical components require 3.5 ft front and side access, 2.5 ft rear access, and 3.0 ft ceiling clearance for installation, diagnosis, and maintenance.

Backbone. A horizontal chase that carries feeders and laterals from entrance facilities to electrical closets. In large buildings this space is often big enough to hold several trays of thick wiring on both sides plus enough space in between for two workers pushing a four-wheeled cart loaded with tools and equipment.

Riser. A vertical chase that carries feeders and laterals from entrance facilities to electrical closets. Its section area is also often large enough to accommodate numerous wire management systems and a worker. Backbones and risers are usually located near elevators, stairways, hallways, and storerooms and away from occupied spaces.

Manhole. A room located at an elbow or tee intersection in a backbone. Each manhole should be wider than the intersecting chases and large enough to satisfy the pulling requirements of the cables installed. Its access portal is usually a standard door; but manholes located outdoors between large buildings are often entered through the traditional ceiling-mounted circular cast iron hatch cover.

Power closet. An electrical closet that houses only power wiring and related components, terminations, and connections. In today's office buildings these spaces may be 200 sf in area, and one is typically required for every 7,500–10,000 sf of floor area.

Telecom closet. An electrical closet that houses only telecommunication signal wiring, components, and connections. High-voltage wiring should not be nearby. In occupancies with extensive electronic equipment, telecom closets may be larger than power closets. Large buildings should have at least one power closet and telecom closet on each floor, and horizontal lengths between each kind cannot exceed 295 ft.

Equipment room. A space that houses large electrical componentry such as elevator motors and switchgear, mainframe computers, and telecommunication systems. This enclosure is typically located along a backbone or beside a riser, and all large components in it require at least 3.5 ft frontal access, 2.5 ft side and rear access, and 2.0 ft ceiling clearance.

Pathway. A horizontal chase or plenum that carries power and signal wiring from electrical closets to end-use areas. It is usually located above suspended ceilings or below access floors.

Workstation. An occupied end-use area where power and signal wiring terminate at an array of computerized equipment and where a number of faceplates and patch panels may be mounted in floor outlets, above-counter raceways, and built-in furniture as well as walls.

5.A.1. Elements of Electricity [†]

Electricity is the flow of electrons through a material that has a propensity to carry them. For example, a cubic inch of copper contains 1.31 × 10^{29} free electrons that are just waiting to move this energy. This movement is induced by locating a surplus of the electrons at one end of the material —its **+** or positive terminal— and a deficit at the material's other end —its **−** or negative terminal. The difference of electrons between the surplus and the deficit is the conductor's *voltage*, and their density or number is its *amperage*. To elucidate this, imagine that the conductor is a tall diving tower with several people at the top who want to dive into the water at the tower's base: the tower's height is its voltage, and the number of divers at the top is its amperage. Thus the total power of the divers to make

---

[†] Much of this section's information was abstracted from "The Encyclopedia of

a big splash in the water is their height × their weight —or *watts*. Thus we have the fundamental electrical formula

volts × amps = watts

Now when a diver jumps from the top of the tower, as he or she sails through the air, the air tries to resist his movement —and the same is true of any medium through which electrons flow. Even if the voltage and amperage are low and the medium is thick and contains a lot of free electrons (i.e. is a good conductor), the electrons will still incur a certain amount of resistance, however infinitesimally small. In electrical terms, the conductor's ability to resist the flow of electrons is aptly known as *resistance*. This lost energy always manifests itself as heat generated in the conductor. Thus resistance does two things: it reduces electric power, and it produces heat. Resistance is not always undesirable. Indeed, some conductors are purposely designed to generate a lot of heat-producing resistance when electrons pass through them, an example being the little wires inside a toaster that glow hotly when its lever is pressed down.

Thus a conductor's electrons have an *arriving power* at one end, suffer a *power loss* due to the conductor's resistance as they flow through its length, and have a slightly lower *delivered power* at the conductor's other end. This relation can be described by the sketch and the formula below:

ARRIVING POWER   DELIVERED POWER

|◄———————— RESISTANCE ————————►|

Fig. 5-2. Relation between arriving and delivered power in a wire.

Arriving power - Resistance = Delivered power

Although electrical power is described by the formula, volts × amps = watts, the electrical industry now refers to electricity's arriving power as V A (or kVA, which = 1,000 VA) and its delivered power as W (or kW, which = 1,000 W). Thus these terms may be described by the formulaic ratio:

$$\frac{kW}{kVA} = \frac{\text{delivered power}}{\text{arriving power}} < 1.0$$

Now suppose for a moment that everything is perfect and a conductor offers no resistance to its flowing electrons and thus kW = kVA; then the above ratio would equal 1.0. Now in trigonometry, 1.0 can be represented by the term cos 0°, as this equals 1.0. Thus the above ratio can be rewritten as

$$\frac{kW}{kVA} = \cos \emptyset$$

This notation allows the above relation to be described geometrically. Thus, if a conductor's arriving and delivered power are known, the terms' relationship can be described as sketched below:

Fig. 5-3. Geometric relation 1 of electric power terms.

Now anyone who knows a little physics will recognize that this triangle is a vector diagram, in which the electricity's arriving energy is the Pythagorean component of the triangle's horizontal and vertical legs. Now look at the vertical leg in the above triangle for a moment... this little vector is what causes all the trouble in today's electrical systems —because it represents the *reactive power* generated in a conductor by its resistance to electron flow; and, by virtue of the above geometry, this troublesome energy can be quantified. Thus the ratio delivered power/arriving power is known as *power factor*, an important term in the design of electric motors; because these machines contain a lot of wiring which generates resistance, which creates a sizable vertical vector of this impeding power. But today this is combatted by installing in the motor an electronic subcomponent that diverts part of its arriving electron flow into a quantity of *leading power* that equals the produced reactive power, and thus creates a stable electron flow. Thus in such motors the above vector diagram may be redrawn as

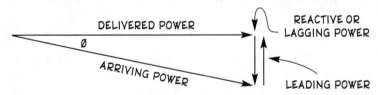

Fig. 5-4. Geometric relation 2 of electric power terms.

Reactive power is produced not only by electric motors. Every electronic component produces it, as does every lamp except incandescent and quartz lamps. However, each of these users of electricity has a means of negating this reactive power: in electronic equipment they are known as *capacitors*, and in lamps they are called *ballasts*. In each device, part of its power is sent through these leading-power producers to negate the reactive power generated by the rest of the electron flow. That is, if all goes well.

1999, pp. 25–30.

5.A.2. Measuring Electric Power

Today's computers can do a lot more than measure the kilowatts consumed in a building. They can provide readings of workday/nonworkday use, electric use at 30-minute time intervals, weekly and seasonal breakdowns, indoor temperatures and humidities every hour of the year, comparisons of present-to-past energy use, electrical use by every mechanical/electrical system component down to the smallest branch duct damper, and anything else a programmer asks them to provide.

Example 1. How much electrical power is in an electrical service entrance of 240 volts single phase at 100 amps?

---

5)A)2)1) $W = \Phi A V$

W = total electric load of circuit or system, **?** kWh. 1,000 watts = 1 kWh.
Φ = phase factor, 1.0 for single phase, 1.73 for 3 phase. Here Φ = 1.00.
A = rate of flow of electric current, 100 amps
V = potential difference of electric current, 240 volts

$$W = 1.00 \times 100 \times 240 = 24,000 \text{ watts or } 24 \text{ kWh}$$

Example 2. What is the total electric load of an conductor that delivers 220 volt three-phase power at 50 amps?

---

5)A)2)1) $W = \Phi A V$

W = total electric load of circuit or system, **?** kwh. 1,000 w = 1 kWh.
Φ = phase factor, 1.0 for single phase, 1.73 for 3 phase. Here Φ = 1.73.
A = rate of flow of electric current, 50 amps
V = potential difference of electric current, 220 volts

$$W = 1.73 \times 50 \times 220 = 19,000 \text{ watts or } 19.0 \text{ kWh}$$

5.A.3. Types of Electrical Systems

A building's electrical system has three parts: *service* (where the electricity enters and is regulated), *distribution* (the conductors that carry the current to all parts of the building), and *circuits* (where the current is utilized); and each may be classed as *small*, *medium*, or *large*, as described in the sections that follow.

5.A.3.a. Small Electrical Systems

These systems typically have a service of 120/240 volts at 60–200 amps and one panel box of circuit breakers or fuses, with possibly an adjacent panel for electric heating.

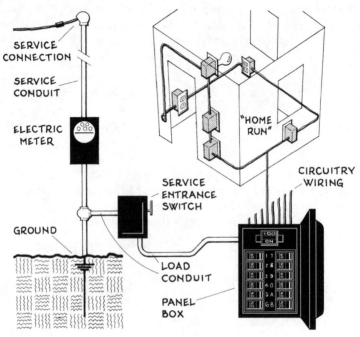

Fig. 5-5. Small electrical system.

A small electric system rarely has any large motors, three-phase wiring, or extensive distribution networks; and convenience outlets and lighting fixtures in each space are usually on the same circuit. Such systems are typically found in residences and small commercial buildings.

5.A.3.b. Medium Electrical Systems

These systems are typically regulated by a main switchboard near the service entry and several smaller panel boxes elsewhere in the building. The service, which may be as high as 600 volts and 800 amps, may include three-phase wiring, large feeder conductors located in fireproof enclosures, convenience outlets and lighting fixtures on separate circuits, and a large motor or two having its own circuit. Some systems may have remote electrical closets with stepdown transformers and telecom switchboards.

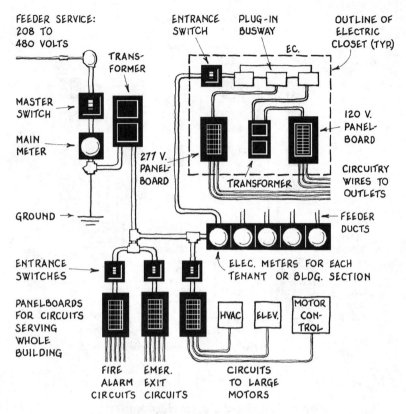

Fig. 5-6. Medium electrical system.

Medium electrical systems are found in apartment complexes, motels, recreation centers, and small- to medium-sized commercial buildings.

5.A.3.c. Large Electrical Systems

These systems may serve acres of floor area. The primary service is usually 2,400, 4,160, 7,200, or 13,200 V, and it typically passes through a large stepdown transformer before entering extensive regulating equipment housed in a large mechanical room. Distribution systems include long feeders, extensive laterals, and large electrical closets containing small stepdown transformers and panelboards throughout the architecture; and large motors operate elevators, central HVAC equipment, and heavy business or industrial machinery. Circuitry wiring is typically laid above suspended ceilings, under access floor panels, or in wall-mounted raceways.

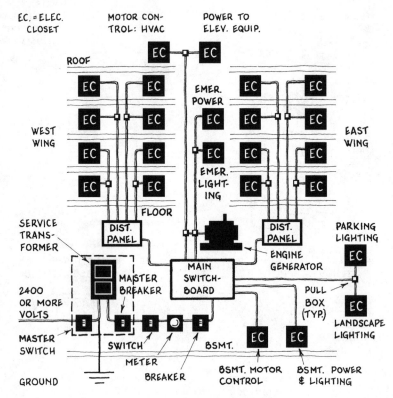

Fig. 5-7. Large electrical system.

In large electrical systems, feeder and branch conductors are placed in protective enclosures that require ample chase space for full-length maintenance, heat removal, and future upgrading. Today's large systems also require extensive grounding and power conditioning devices to maximize clean electron flow in every conductor.

5.A.4. Design of Systems

When designing electrical systems, always remember that electricity is dangerous. It can kill people, and it can burn buildings down. All National Electric Code (NEC) requirements which may govern specific design should be interpreted liberally on the side of safety.

Electrical system design generally proceeds opposite the flow of electrons, from the outlets upstream through the laterals and feeders back to the service entry. Following is a detailed design checklist.

1. Prepare with the client a list of all planned electric usage in and around the architecture. This data should include convenience and lighting requirements, nameplate wattage of electrical equipment, and service requirements. Sum the total wattage, then add a 20 percent 'future factor.' Often this list cannot be completed at the pre-design stage due to the nature of flexible-use tenancies and other unknown factors. Following is a conceptual checklist:

   a. **Exterior:** garage door opener, front and back entry lights, walkway, parking, landscaping, floods for outdoor activities, signage, ground fault interruption (GFI) outlets front and back, time-controlled sprinklers.

   b. **Entry:** doorbells, addressor devices, occupancy sensors, security systems, video surveillance, time clocks, fire detection/alarms, emergency exit lights, elevators.

   c. **Lighting:** switches (1, 2, 3 way), fixtures, energy-saving lighting, programmed dimmers, occupancy sensors, timers, automatic storeroom switches, emergency lighting.

   d. **Communication:** closed circuit TV, modems, voice/teledata networks, coaxial cables, fiber optics, telephones, intercoms.

   e. **Environmental controls:** thermostats, humidistats, supply and exhaust ventilation, static air sensors, CO_2, VOC, and airborne particulate sensors.

   f. **Electrical/mechanical equipment:** service panel, heating and cooling, humidifiers, dehumidifiers, dampers, hot water heater, central vacuum system, well pump, sump pump, fans, thermostat-controlled vents, onsite electrical generators.

   g. **Occupant-operated equipment:** computers, printers, disk drives, copiers, motors, industrial equipment, microprocessor controls for machine tools and industrial applications.

   h. **Baths:** fans, heat lamp w/ timer switch, Jacuzzi, exerciser.

   i. **Kitchen:** stove, hood fan, refrigerator, dishwasher, garbage disposal, microwave, special appliances, dumbwaiters.

   j. **Laundry:** washer, dryer, ironing.

   k. **Grounding devices/systems:** lightning, equipment.

   l. **TBM systems:** tailor to specific needs.

2. Make an initial estimate of the architecture's total electric load, either by adding the total wattage in the detailed list above or by estimating the total load (Sec. 6.B).

3. Organize the building's electrical loads into convenience, lighting, appliance, motor, and signal circuits (Sec. 6.C). Include switching, dimming, controls, dimensions, mounts, and weights.

4. Prepare schematics for all building management systems, including data regarding installation, connecting, testing, diagnosis, etc.

5. Prepare a panel schedule of all power and signal circuit loads with voltage, amperage, and areas or equipment served by each.

6. Select and size the conductors for each circuit based on voltage drops, occupancies, and other locational factors (Sec. 6.D).

7. Select and size the distribution branches and feeders. This includes conductor and conduit types as well as line diagrams for all structured distribution systems (wireways, raceways, cable trays, etc.) with listed loads, branch and feeder sections and connectors, and system identification codes (Sec. 6.D).

8. Size any risers, backbones, shafts, chases, manholes, electrical closets, and other cavities required to enclose the conductors and distribution systems; and design access openings for installation, diagnosis, and upgrading (Sec. 6.E).

9. Select and size the service components, and determine spatial requirements for each. This includes entrance conductors, overcurrent protection devices, switchgear, panelboards, transformers (capacities and stepdown ratios), onsite generators and controls, and related equipment. List sizes, types, styles, catalog numbers, and other pertinent information. (Sec. 6.F).

10. Determine with the local utility all source-side installation requirements such as power poles (location, insulators, guy wires), weatherheads, any outdoor transformers, electric meter, type of service entry, and nature of other service components as indicated by the architecture and its total electric load.

11. Check all calculations with licensed authorities, then verify or adjust initial estimates.

5.B. INITIAL ESTIMATE

A building's total electric load should be estimated in advance of detailed design to determine its likely service ampacity and voltage, if for no other reason than to notify the public utility. Table 5-1 lists electric use and service load factors for common building types. The use loads, which do not include climate control systems, may also vary because (1) cooking and other kitchen operations may run on gas or steam; (2) in elevatored buildings the elevator motor energy use per unit floor area increases as buildings become taller; (3) industrial facilities or special equipment may run on a number of other energies. Due to these variables, all initial electric energy estimates should be verified after the building and its electric system is designed.

Standard base ampacities for building electric systems are 60, 100, 200, 400, 600, 800, 1,000, 1,200, 1,600, 2,000, and 2,500 amps.

> What is the estimated electrical service load of an elementary school whose gross floor area is 28,450 ft^2?

Step 1. Estimate the building's required total electric load.

5]B] $\qquad\qquad \epsilon \approx \kappa_U A$

ϵ = estimated electric service load of building, **?** watts
κ_U = load use factor. From Table 5-1, κ_U for grammar schools = 8 W/sf.
A = gross floor area of building, 28,500 sf

$$\epsilon \approx 28,450 \times 8 \approx 228,000 \text{ watts or } 228 \text{ kWh}$$

Step 2. Knowing the building service load's total wattage, select its voltage from Table 5-1. At 228 kWh, the service's voltage is 208V.

Step 3. Find the building's base ampacity.

═══ TABLE 5-1: ELECTRIC SERVICE LOADS [1] ═══

SERVICE LOAD, kWh or kVA	Type of building	Service voltage
To 12	Small residences, outbuildings	120
12-96	Typical residential, small commercial	240
96-900	Typical commercial	208
400-2,000	Large or specialized commercial-industrial	480
2,000 + ...	Skyscrapers, corporate offices, other large structures 2,400, 4,160, 7,200, 13,200, 34,500	

LOAD USAGE	Type of building	Estimated watts/ft^2
Very low	Parking garages, unmechanized barns, buildings whose use requires little electricity	1-2
Low	Residences, apartments, hotels, motels	4
Low-medium	Grammar schools, athletic facilities, supermarkets, retail, museums, churches, movie theaters	6
Medium	Senior high schools, universities, offices, taverns, restaurants, opera houses, bus terminals	8
Medium-high ...	Night clubs, luncheonettes, hospitals, spaces w/ round-the-clock use of electricity	10
High	Factories, industrial laboratories, buildings w/ constantly-used large machinery	12–15
Very high	Semiconductor fabrication plants	30–50
Extremely high ..	Data processing & telecommunication centers ...	100

1. These loads do not include heating and cooling of occupied spaces.

$$\epsilon = 1.73 \, A \, V$$

ϵ = total electric service load of building, watts.
From Step 1, ϵ = 228,000 watts.
A = base ampacity of electric load, ? amps
V = voltage of electrical service, 208 volts

$$228,000 = 1.73 \, A \times 208 \qquad ... A = 639 \text{ amps}$$

Step 4. Find the service ampacity by selecting the smallest number above the base ampacities listed in the text of Sec. 6.B. ➡ the smallest number above 639 is 800. Thus the estimated service load is 208 V at 800 A.

5.C. ELECTRICAL CIRCUITS

An electrical circuit is a continuous path of conductors and outlets through which flows a stream of electrons. Each begins with a *fuse* or *circuit breaker*, continues via a *live leg* (black, red, or blue wire) through each outlet to the remote outlet, then returns via a *neutral leg* (white wire) through each outlet which terminates through the circuit breaker. The live and neutral legs are accompanied by a green *ground wire* that also runs through every outlet, where it gathers stray electrons then carries them safely into the ground under the building. Even though a circuit's individually insulated wires run inside a second larger jacket of insulation, many of the electrons tunneling through this double layer of insulation still migrate through it to create a cylindrical field of reactive energy around the conductor. And it is the incredible number of these errant forces, known as *electromagnetic interference* or *EMI*, that in recent years has changed conductors —those thinnest and most easily concealed of a building's functional components— from something architects rarely needed to think about into something they must think about every time they design a space. This is because when two conductors lay side by side, the electrons migrating from one often return to the other —a phenomenon known as *mutual impedance*, which causes the two fields to oppose each other in ways that reduce their power. In the days of 60-amp panel boxes and little wiring, these clashing forces rarely caused any trouble. But nowadays, when dozens of such wires may be laid in a narrow trench duct, trillions of swarming electrons can disrupt the operation of electrical devices up to several feet away. Thus Æ designers must now imagine a huge cylinder of electromagnetic interference the size of a 6 ft diameter steel culvert centered around every spaghetti-like array of wires installed in any space in order to protect nearby occupants and equipment. At pres-

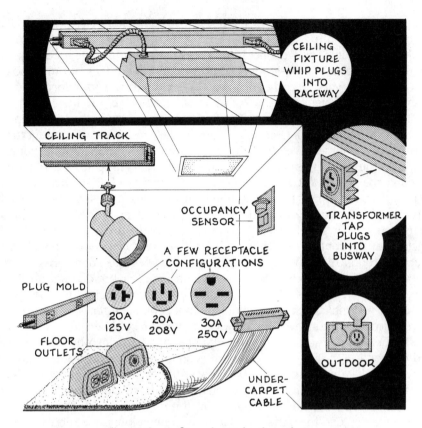

Fig. 5-8. A few electrical outlets.

ent, three strategies have evolved to provide this protection: *grounding*, *distancing*, and *shielding*. Each is described below:

Grounding: removing the disturbing electrons from reactive areas by running one or two ground wires from each piece of electronic equipment to nearby steel or reinforced concrete structure or underfloor signal reference grids.

Distancing: locating electronic devices and occupants at least four ft from all wiring runs and separating circuits of different voltage.

Shielding: placing barriers between reactive areas and occupants, examples being shielded twisted-pair cables in metal conduits, and sheets of insect screen or lead-lined drywall behind all finished surfaces that enclose large electronic equipment.

Aside from the above strategies, circuitry design still involves determining the nature and number of electric outlets in each space, combining them in convenient groups of voltage and amperage, then selecting proper conductors, switches, and outlet boxes for each circuit. If possible this work utilizes furniture layout plans and lists of equipment to be installed. Although switches and connections rarely affect interior space requirements or the size of functional components, this is not true of outlet boxes because they vary greatly in size. For example, the standard one-receptacle wallbox measures $2 \times 2\frac{1}{2} \times 3$ in, while a floor box in the exhibit hall of the Los Angeles Convention Center is 30 in. square and 20 in. deep.

A note about connections. In each, the only means of conductance from wire to terminal is through the mutual points of surface contact between the two metals plus a microscopically small 'jump' area immediately around the points of contact. Indeed, even when two flat surfaces contact each other, the two surfaces may touch only at their peaks, or *asperites*, to create an actual area of contact that may be much smaller than the apparent area,, which significantly increases the conductor's resistance in the vicinity of the connection. Thus the worst kind of connection is a solid wire curled around a threaded stud. Almost as bad is two solid wires twisted together inside a wire nut. Better is two stranded or braided wires twisted together. Better still is a braided copper wire securely bolted to a holed lug or a flat terminal block—a mechanical connection. Better yet is a braided wire crimped to the sleeve of a lug. Even better is a soldered connection that fuses the two conductors together. And best of all is an exothermically welded connection that not only fuses the conductors together but eliminates any bimetallic interface that would exist if the two conductors were dissimilar metals —which occurs when ground grid conductors are bonded to structural steel columns. In any connection the adjoining surfaces should be clean and dry, and the bolts of mechanical connections should be accurately torqued. These are the things that owl-like architects specify in their drawings and proddingly look for during periodic visits to the site.

There are five general kinds of circuits: *convenience*, *appliance*, *lighting*, *motor*, and *signal*. They should be separate from each other, except in small buildings where lighting and convenience outlets in one space may be combined. Each of these circuits is described below.

5.C.1. Convenience Circuits

Convenience circuits carry electricity to portable luminaires and small appliances, usually via a series of recessed wallboxes or surface-mounted plug strips. Each 120 V outlet is generally rated at 2.5 A in residences and 4 A in commercial occupancies, and circuit loads are 12 A maximum on 15 A circuits and 16 A maximum on 20 A circuits. In general-use areas up to 16 ft wide, no wall surface can be more than 6 horizontal ft from an electrical outlet; this dimension wraps around corners, extends under counters and bookshelves and windows, and includes any wall area more than 2 ft wide but does not include doorways and fireplaces. Other Code requirements and design guidelines are listed below:

▶   A room's required number of outlets should be spaced as equally apart from each other as is practical.
▶   Walls more than 16 ft apart require at least one floor outlet per 100 sf of mid-floor area (measured 8 ft in from perimeter walls).
▶   Unfinished rooms require at least one outlet per 20 LF of wall area plus two per 1,000 sf of floor area.
▶   Hallway outlets require at least one outlet per 10 LF on one wall and one 20 amp outlet per 50 LF of hallway length.
▶   Kitchen wall counters require at least one outlet per 6 LF within 18 in. above the countertop, and island or peninsula counters require one outlet per 4 LF within 12 in. below the countertop.
▶   All kitchen counter, bathroom, and outdoor outlets in every occupancy require GFI protection.
▶   The smallest wire for any 120 V conductor is 14 AWG copper.

Example 1. How many convenience outlets are required for a 21 × 40 ft drafting room? What is the room's convenience circuitry load?

$\underline{5}\underline{)C}\underline{)1}\underline{)1}$ **Outlets for finished areas:** $\eta \; = \; 0.083 \, P + 0.01 \, A$ ...
   $\underline{2}$ **Outlets for unfinished areas:** $\eta \; = \; 0.05 \, P$

η = required number of convenience outlets in area, **?** units
P = perimeter of area served by outlets, ft. 2 (21 + 40) = 122 ft.
A = area of any part of room more than 8 ft in from perimeter, sf.
   $A = (l - 16) \, (w - 16) \; = \; (21 - 16) \, (40 - 16) = 120 \text{ sf.}$

$$\eta \; \geq \; 0.083 \times 122 + 0.01 \times 120 \; \geq \; 11.3 \; \Rightarrow \; 12 \text{ outlets}$$

$\underline{5}\underline{)C}\underline{)1}\underline{)3}$ **Convenience circuit load:** $\diamond = \eta \, A$

$\diamond$ = electric circuitry load, **?** amps
η = required number of outlets. From Step 1, η = 12 units.
A = rated amperes per outlet, 4 amps in commercial spaces

$$\diamond \; = \; 12 \times 4 \; = \; 48 \text{ amps at 120 volts}$$

Example 2. How many convenience outlets should a 12 × 18 ft living room have? What is the room's convenience circuitry load?

<u>5</u><u>C</u><u>1</u><u>1</u> **Outlets for finished areas:** $\eta = 0.083\,P + 0.01\,A$ ... ✚
   <u>2</u> **Outlets for unfin. areas:** $\eta = 0.05\,P$

η = required number of convenience outlets in area, **?** units
P = perimeter of area, ft. $P = 2\,(l + w) = 2\,(12 + 18) = 60$ ft.
A = area of any part of room more than 8 ft from walls, sf. $A = 0$.

$$\eta = 0.083 \times 60 = 4.98 \rightarrow 5 \text{ outlets}$$

<u>5</u><u>C</u><u>1</u><u>3</u> **Convenience circuit load:**   ◇ $= \eta\,A$

◇ = circuitry load, **?** amps
η = required number of outlets, 5 units
A = rated amperes per outlet; use recommended 2.5 amps
      in residential spaces (Code minimum = 1.5 amps)

$$◇ = 5 \times 2.5 = 12.5 \text{ amps at 120 volts}$$

5.C.2. Appliance Circuits

These are circuits for areas of heavy electrical use such as kitchens, workshops, school laboratories, theater projection booths, and most industrial operations. In apartments and residences at least two 20 amp appliance circuits with no more than three outlets per circuit should be installed in kitchens, pantries, dining rooms, and family areas. In commercial occupancies appliance circuits are sized as specifically required.

Electric ranges and other large appliances require a minimum two-pole (240 V) circuit with an 8 kWh load. Gas ranges require a 120 V outlet for clocks, lights, and minor appliance use related to cooking. In case a future tenant may want to convert to electric range cooking, it is wise to install a two-pole outlet behind every stove.

Any fire pumps in commercial buildings must be on separate emergency circuits, and their transformers must be dedicated (serve only the fire pump motor and associated controls).

5.C.3. Lighting Circuits

Lighting outlets are usually located in a ceiling or at least 6'-8" high on a wall. One is required in every general occupancy area, every unfinished area used for storage or that contains equipment requiring servicing, and every 200 sf of general unfinished areas. Multiple luminaires in

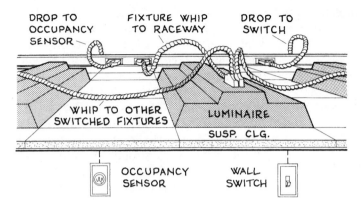

Fig. 5-9. Luminaire circuitry.

each space should be on at least two circuits in case one fails. No light fixture may be within 3 horizontal ft or 8 vertical ft of a bathtub or showerstall. In closets and small storage areas, every fixture should be enclosed, at least 12 in. from any stored or stationary object, at least 6 in. out from the edge of any shelving or cabinetry, and preferably mounted directly above the inside header of the entry door. Porcelain light sockets and breaker panels in storage areas are **NG**. Wherever lighting wiring crosses an expansion joint, the wiring must be flexible. Fixture whips for commercial luminaires cannot pass through ceilings, floors, walls, doors, windows, or other openings; nor can they be concealed behind finishes other than where removable panels provide access to the whips' total length.

Lighting outlet loads are based on the type of lighting used. Design load per outlet is 240 W or 2.0 A at 120 V. Outlet loads for fixtures of higher wattage and ones with ballasts or transformers are based on actual wattage or ampere rating of the total fixture. Loads for continuous lighting (3 hours or more: e.g. office lighting, storewindow displays, etc.) cannot exceed 80 percent of branch circuit rating.

Light switches may be snap, slide, rotary, touch, or interior/remote control. Manually operated switches may be located at the light source (e.g. pull chains and socket-mounted ON/OFF switches), in the same room as the light (e.g. wall switches), or remotely located (e.g. outdoor security lighting switches mounted in a control room). An increasing number of remotely operable switches today are wireless. An *illuminated switch* contains a tiny light that turns on when the switch is off to make it visible in the dark. A *pilot switch* contains a tiny light that turns on when the switch is on. A *press switch* is a small rocker that allows no-hands operation by one carrying a large object. A *tether switch* is a dimmer-operated switch on a short cord that can be placed within easy reach of an occupant: this is an excellent switch for task lighting as it enables an occupant to adjust distant light sources while remaining at work. Some tether switches today are wireless and thus can be carried around. Ambient and public circulation lighting should have an illuminated switch (so they can be found in the dark) located at chest height within 2 ft of the striker side of each entry. All circulation lighting, and any floor area of ambient lighting with more than one entry, should have two-way switches installed by each entry so the lighting can be turned on at one doorway and turned off at another: if this is done in every space, two-way switch linkage will exist along every room-to-room pathway, then occupants can continually turn switches on in front of them and off behind them as they step through the spaces. Where several switches are mounted together, consider ganging them vertically instead of horizontally: they'll fit into the framing better.

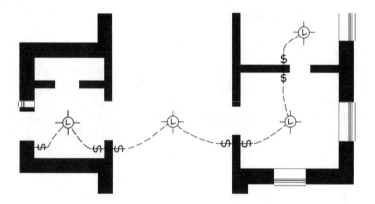

Fig. 5-10. Linking light switches.

TABLE 5-2: OCCUPANCY LIGHTING LOADS

OCCUPANCY	Estimated unit load, Watts/ft^2
Warehouses, storage areas, mechanical equipment areas	0.2
Halls, lobbies, stairways, library stacks, commercial garages	0.5
Armories, assembly, churches, recreational, service areas	1.0
Clubs, court rooms, hospitals, hotels, industrial areas, restaurants, other spaces whose ambient lighting levels exceed 35 fc	1.5
Barber shops, beauty parlors, residences, schools, stores, other spaces whose ambient lighting levels exceed 60 fc	2.0
Banks, offices, retail outlets, industrial areas, other spaces whose ambient lighting levels exceed 90 fc	2.5
Offices and industrial areas requiring exact work, other spaces whose ambient lighting levels exceed 150 fc	3.0

1. This table may be used to estimate an occupancy's number of circuits and wire sizes but not task illumination levels. Use more definitive data when available.

Example 1. What is the estimated lighting circuitry load of a 12 × 18 ft residential living room? How many lighting outlets are required?

⑤Ⓒ③① Lighting circuitry load: $\diamond_L\, V \approx \kappa_L\, A$

$\diamond_L$ = estimated lighting circuitry load, **?** amps
V = voltage of lighting system, usually 120 volts
κ_L = lighting load factor. From Table 5-2, κ_L for residence = 3 W/sf.
A = net floor area of illuminated space, sf. A = 12 × 18 = 216 sf.

$$\diamond_L \times 120 \; \approx \; 3 \times 216 \qquad \ldots \diamond_L \; = \; 5.4 \text{ amps at 120 volts}$$

⑤Ⓒ③② Lighting outlets: $\diamond_L = \eta\, A$

$\diamond_L$ = estimated lighting circuitry load, amps. From above, $\diamond$ = 5.4 amps.
η = required number of outlets for lighting, **?** units
A = rated lighting outlet load, 2.0 amps unless otherwise noted

$$5.4 \leq \eta \times 2.0 \qquad \ldots \eta \geq 2.7 \Rightarrow 3 \text{ outlets}$$

Example 2. What is the lighting load for an office with 18 ceiling-mounted fixtures containing four F40T12CW lamps each?

⑤Ⓒ③③ $\diamond_L\, V \approx \kappa_b\, \eta\, \epsilon$

$\diamond_L$ = estimated lighting circuitry load of room, space, or zone, **?** amps
V = voltage of lighting system, usually 120 volts
κ_b = ballast factor. $\kappa_b \approx 1.0$ if lamp is incand. or quartz, 1.15 if fluorescent or metal-halide, 1.11 if mercury, 1.18 if sodium. $\kappa_b \approx 1.15$.
η = number of lamps in space. 18 fixtures × 4 lamps/unit = 72 lamps.
ϵ = rated electric output of each lamp or fixture. ϵ of F40T12CW = 40 w.

$$\diamond_L \times 120 \; \approx \; 1.15 \times 72 \times 40 \qquad \ldots \diamond_L \approx 28 \text{ amps}$$

5.C.4. Motor Circuits [†]

More than 60 percent of all electricity consumed in America is used to operate motors. Even in residences the percentage is high, since refrigerators, dishwashers, clothes washers, dryers, CD players, vacuum cleaners, computers, and printers all have motors. The most important criterion for selecting an electric motor is its required *horsepower* (1–200 or more). Other important criteria are described on the next page.

[†] Primary sources for this section were several issues of EC&M magazine

NEMA designation: A for high peak loads, B for general-purpose use, C for rapidly accelerating loads, D for heavy starting loads, E or PE for high-efficiency motors.

Speed: A motor's speed varies according to the number of poles (always a multiple of 2) in its stator according to the formula

motor rpm × no. of poles = 120 × voltage frequency (Hz)

Thus at a standard voltage frequency of 60 Hz, a 2-pole motor runs at 3,600 rpm, 4-pole at 1,800, 6-pole at 1,200, 8-pole at 900, 10-pole at 720, 12-pole at 600, and 14-pole at 541 rpm.

Efficiency: a motor may be *standard efficiency* (SE) or *premium efficiency* (PE). A motor's efficiency represents the portion of its electrical input that is converted to rotational energy while the remaining input (100 percent - efficiency percent) is converted to heat. Recently developed PE motors run so much more efficiently than SE motors that they often pay for themselves in a few months' time; but they draw about twice as much inrush current when they start (a PE motor typically draws 12 × its full load current when starting while an SE motor typically draws only 6 × its full load current). High inertial loads can multiply these amounts by 1.5; thus such motors may need ramp-starting or larger circuitry. Table 5-3 lists common horsepowers and typical efficiencies of SE and PE motors.

Duty cycle: Certain operating patterns require different motor designs to maximize efficiency and minimize temperature buildups and maintenance as follows: *continuous duty* motors operate fairly constant loads for indefinitely long periods; *varying duty* motors operate variable loads for variable periods; *short-time duty* motors operate constant loads for short specified periods; *periodic duty* motors operate constant loads for on/off periods; *intermittent duty* motors operate on/off according to load/no load conditions, load/rest conditions, or load/no load/rest conditions; and *reversing duty* motors operate at forward and reverse speeds.

Torque: Depending on the motor's use it must have sufficient torque of three kinds: *breakaway* or *starting torque* to overcome the initial inertia of the machinery the motor operates, *pull-up* or *rated-load torque* to accelerate the motor to the required speed, and *breakdown torque* to overcome peak loads without stalling.

Environmental condition (corrosive, hazardous, hot, dusty, outdoor, etc.): several kinds of motors are available depending on the environment they operate in, as follows:

Induction motors: Also known as squirrel-cage, SE, or standard efficiency, this is your stock electric motor.

Totally enclosed fan-cooled (TEFC) motors: These run well in moist and poorly ventilated areas.

Explosion-proof motors: These are made for hazardous environments in which explosive vapors may be present.

(Intertec Publishing Co., Overland PArk, KS) published 1994–1997.

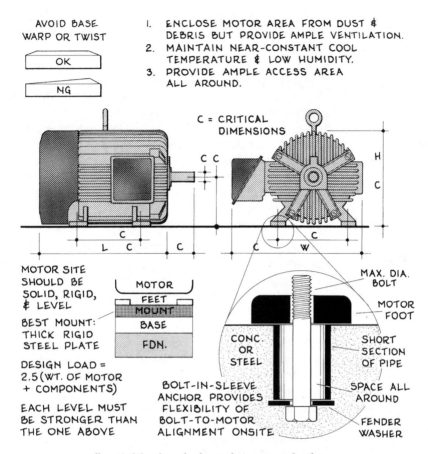

AVOID BASE
WARP OR TWIST

1. ENCLOSE MOTOR AREA FROM DUST &
   DEBRIS BUT PROVIDE AMPLE VENTILATION.
2. MAINTAIN NEAR-CONSTANT COOL
   TEMPERATURE & LOW HUMIDITY.
3. PROVIDE AMPLE ACCESS AREA
   ALL AROUND.

OK

NG

C = CRITICAL
DIMENSIONS

C C

H

C

C

L C   C   C   W

MOTOR SITE
SHOULD BE
SOLID, RIGID,
& LEVEL

MOTOR

FEET

MOUNT

BEST MOUNT:
THICK RIGID
STEEL PLATE

BASE

FDN.

DESIGN LOAD =
2.5(WT. OF MOTOR
+ COMPONENTS)

EACH LEVEL MUST
BE STRONGER THAN
THE ONE ABOVE

CONC.
OR
STEEL

BOLT-IN-SLEEVE
ANCHOR PROVIDES
FLEXIBILITY OF
BOLT-TO-MOTOR
ALIGNMENT ONSITE

MAX. DIA.
BOLT

MOTOR
FOOT

SHORT
SECTION
OF PIPE

SPACE ALL
AROUND

FENDER
WASHER

Fig. 5-11. Good electric motor design.

Chemical service motors: These have corrosion-resistant parts and one-way condensation drains in the endbells and are finished with a chemically inert enamel. They are highly resistant to heat and corrosion.

Premium efficiency (PE) motors: These are highly efficient motors that produce less heat, vibrate less, require less maintenance, and last longer. But they have high-torque starting requirements (typical of pumps and elevators) which can cause nuisance tripping of motor circuits. This may be remedied with variable-speed drives, electronic time delays, and automatic clutches. Oversized circuit breakers for electric motors are NG, because then they might not open as intended for normal-load faults.

Synchronous motors: These maintain clean electron flow for continuous steady-speed loads such as fans, pumps, and compressors where the electrical system contains considerable reactive power. They operate much like generators whose input energy is electricity, and some generators are indeed known as synchronous generators. These motors require an automatic governor or constant operator; otherwise they can actually export reactive current and self-destruct.

Motor accessories include longer cords, rodent screens, lint-proof fan covers, drip covers that prevent moisture entry in carwashes and other wet installations, anti-condensation heating units inside the stator housings, internal thermostats that cut power when the motor overheats, weatherproofing for outdoor installations, fungus-proofing for tropical installations, tachometer mounts, and numerous shaft modifications. Line accessories include voltage regulators, surge suppressors, ramp starters that reduce excess inrush currents and motor wear, and variable frequency drives that enable variable-load-operating motors to reduce power at low loads and conserve energy.

An electric motor is typically designed as follows:

1. Consider the motor's use and select its NEMA designation, speed, efficiency, and duty cycle.

2. If the motor runs a pump, vaneaxial fan, or other variable-speed device, consider using a motor with a variable frequency drive. A VFD reduces the motor's voltage frequency (Hz), which makes the motor run at less than its rated speed when its load decreases; thus the motor consumes less power when the power is not needed.

3. Determine the motor operation's starting torque, rate-load torque, and breakdown torque (lb·ft), then select a motor whose three torques meet or exceed these requirements.

4. Knowing the motor's rpm and torque, find its horsepower from 5,250 HP × motor efficiency (percent/100) = motor torque × rpm.

5. Knowing the motor's horsepower, determine its voltage and amperage from HP = 0.746 kW = 0.746 kVA, then size its circuit. A motor circuit should be sized at 1.25 × nameplate wattage for low-torque starting and continuous-duty loads (e.g. fan operation), and at 1.40 × nameplate wattage for high-torque starting and intermittent loads (e.g. elevator operation). If the circuit is oversized, during normal-load operation the extra power is wasted, while during partial-load operation the motor generates more heat and produces less power (at 75 percent full load a motor has only 56 percent full power).

6. Knowing the motor's horsepower, determine its footprint, either from Table 5-3 or a manufacturer's catalog.

7. Consider the machinery the motor will drive. Note the length and diameter of the shafts-in-common, the nature of any couplings and gears, the type of mount required, etc. Then design a mount that is large and strong enough to support the motor/machinery assembly, rigid enough (Δ_{max} ≤ 1/480 span) to keep the motor shaft

and drive train aligned, inertially heavy enough to resist starting torque and operating vibrations, and perfectly level. The best mount is thick steel plate on a thick concrete inertia block. Then determine the design load of the total assembly plus its mount: this ≈ 2.5 × (weight of motor + componentry + mount structure). This load must be carried down through the mount and floor structure to the building foundation. Finally, locate every motor exceeding 7.5 hp on the building plans, locate its outlet conveniently nearby, and add a 2–4 ft service aisle all around.

8. Determine the motor's cooling load requirements. This is done by finding the selected motor's heating load from Table 5-3, then providing an equal amount of cooling to the motor area.

9. Determine the motor's ventilation requirements. As a motor's temperature rating (usually 40° C or 104° F) is the maximum ambient temperature at which it should operate, the heat it continually produces must not be allowed to raise the motor's ambient operating temperature above its temperature rating; otherwise the motor will rapidly degrade. In cold and temperate weather this is easily done with outdoor ventilation; but in warm weather and where the motor is enclosed indoors, a means of cooling the surrounding air must be installed. Here the design indoor temperature is not at or just below the motor's temperature rating but is near normal room temperature, because (1) if the motor area's ambient temperature is substantially above that of any adjacent spaces the intervening walls must be thermally reinforced with insulation, and (2) an electric motor should be easily accessible by service and maintenance personnel, and 104° is *not* an accessible temperature to work in. Thus the air around an electric motor, especially if it is large, should be thermostatized to keep the air at a workable temperature, say 80°.

10. Consider the noise the motor assembly makes and how much it can be tolerated in adjacent spaces, then design acoustic measures.

Example 1. A city in Florida uses 200 hp electric pumps to maintain its municipal water supply, in which two pumps are always operating while the third acts as standby in case of malfunction or required maintenance. Since the pump motors need rewinding, authorities believe this would be a good time to switch from SE to PE motors. If a new SE motor costs $5,214, a PE motor costs $6,205, and the local utility rate is $0.075/kWh, what is the payback span for the PE motors?

Step 1. Compute the annual operating cost savings due to the more efficient units.

5)C)4)1) $\Delta_{ac} = 0.009 \text{ ¢ } \eta \, \kappa_c \in t \, (100/\varepsilon_o - 100/\varepsilon_n)$

Δ_{ac} = difference in annual operating costs of compared units, ? $/yr.

¢ = unit cost of electricity, ¢/kWh. Local utility rate = 7.5 ¢/kWh.

η = number of compared units. No. of SE or PE motors, 3 units.

κ_c = power conversion factor. κ_c = 0.746 if rated power of compared units is hp, 1.00 if kVA, 0.001 if watts. Here κ_c = 0.746.

$\in$ = rated electrical power of each unit, hp or watts. $\in$ = 200 HP.

t = operating time of the compared units run, hr. If each motor runs $2/3$ of year, t = 0.67 × 24 × 365 = 5,870 hr.

ε_o = operational efficiency of old unit(s) being compared, %. From Table 5-3, ε_o of 200 hp SE motor = 93.6 percent. For lamps use efficacy.

ε_n = operational efficiency of new unit(s) being compared, %. From Table 5-3, ε_n of 200 hp PE motor = 95.0%. For lamps use efficacy.

$$\Delta_{ac} = 0.009 \times 7.5 \times 0.746 \times 3 \times 200 \times 5,870 \, (100/93.6 - 100/95.0)$$
$$\Delta_{ac} = \$2,790$$

TABLE 5-3: ELECTRIC MOTOR SPECIFICATIONS [†]

	SE (STD. EFFICIENCY) MOTORS				PE (PREM. EFFICIENCY) MOTORS			
HP [2]	Efficiency %	Size L × W × H	Wt. lb	Htg. load Btus	Efficiency %	Size L × W × H	Wt. lb	Htg. load Btus
1 ..	72.1	11×9×7	38	3,400	... 82.5	11×9×7	31	2,200
2 ..	76.1	13×11×9	58	6,400	... 84.0	12×9×7	37	4,600
3 ..	78.5	14×11×9	73	9,400	... 86.5	13×11×9	51	5,900
5 ..	80.3	15×11×9	82	15,500	... 87.5	15×11×9	93	9,500
7.5 ..	83.3	17×14×11	160	23,000	... 88.5	18×14×11	160	15,800
10 ..	84.7	18×14×11	200	30,000	... 89.5	20×14×11	200	20,00
15 ..	86.6	21×18×13	280	44,000	... 91.0	21×18×13	280	28,000
20 ..	87.8	23×18×13	324	59,000	... 91.0	23×18×13	324	41,000
25 ..	88.8	24×20×15	356	72,000	... 91.7	24×20×15	404	48,000
30 ..	89.4	25×20×15	376	86,000	... 92.4	25×20×15	456	62,500
40 ..	90.4	26×22×16	490	114,000	... 93.0	26×22×16	560	72,500
50 ..	91.1	28×22×16	531	143,000	... 93.0	28×22×16	614	91,000
60 ..	91.6	28×25×18	733	172,000	... 93.6	28×25×18	716	94,000
75 ..	92.2	30×25×18	790	212,000	... 94.1	30×25×18	766	127,000
100 ..	92.8	33×25×20	957	283,000	... 94.1	45×33×22	1,850	145,000
125 ..	93.2	35×25×20	1,063	353,000	... 94.5	45×33×22	1,850	180,000
150 ..	93.4	38×33×23	1,200	420,000	... 95.0	48×33×22	1,850	233,000
200 ..	93.6	40×33×23	1,420	570,000	... 95.0	48×33×22	2,250	317,000

1. The data in this table are average estimates for common 1,800 rpm open motors. Corresponding data for specific models may vary slightly.
2. The most commonly-used motor horsepowers are in boldface.

† Much of this table's data was taken from the *Leeson Motors Stock Catalog* (Lee-

Step 2. Compute the energy payback span for the compared units. If this ≤ 7 years, the PE motors are economically feasible.

$$E_p \Delta_{ac} \approx \eta \,(\$_{in} - \$_{io})$$

E_p = feasible energy payback span for compared units, ? yr
Δ_{ac} = difference in annual operating costs of compared units, from Step 1, \$2,790/yr
η = number of compared units, from Step 1, 3 units
$\$_{in}$ = initial cost of new unit(s). Each PE motor costs \$6,205.
$\$_{io}$ = initial cost of old unit(s). Each SE motor costs \$5,214.

$Y \times 2{,}790 \approx 3\,(6{,}205 - 5{,}214)$ ... $Y \approx 1.06$ yr ... about 13 months!

Note: This formula may be used to compare the annual energy savings for any new versus old component (lamps, heaters, added insulation, etc.).

Example 2. If the initial torque load of a continuous-duty PE motor in a cardboard recycling plant in York, PA, is 60 ft-lb at 1,750 rpm and the electric power is 230 V, 60 Hz, 3 phase, what is the motor's minimum horsepower? What size circuit breaker should it have?

Step 1. Find the motor's horsepower based on its initial torque load.

5)C)4)2) $T \, \upsilon \;=\; 47 \; \text{HP} \; \mathcal{E}$

T = initial torque load of motor, 60 ft-lb
υ = rotational velocity or shaft speed of motor, 1,750 rpm
HP = required horsepower of motor, ? hp. Solve for this value, then select next largest number in "HP" column in Table 5-3. Rated HPs in boldface are slightly more economical.
$\mathcal{E}$ = operational efficiency of motor, %. Use a trial efficiency selected from listed motor efficiencies in Table 5-3 to compute HP, then adjust $\mathcal{E}$ or HP if necessary. Try $\mathcal{E}$ = 90 %.

$60 \times 1{,}750 \;=\; 47 \; \text{HP} \times 90$ ... HP = 24.8 ➜ 25 hp
Efficiency check: from Table 5-3, $\mathcal{E}$ of 25 hp PE motor = 91.7 percent
$60 \times 1{,}750 \;\le\; 47 \; \text{HP} \times 91.7$ ... HP = 24.4 ≤ 24.8 ➜ 25 hp **OK**

Note: The required horsepower for a centrifugal pump based on the specific gravity, viscosity, and height of discharge of the liquid being pumped may be determined by the formula in Sec. 5.C.4.b.

Step 2. Size the circuit breaker required for the motor.

◇ $\mathcal{E} \, V \;=\; 43{,}100 \; \kappa_d \, \Phi \; \text{HP}$

◇ = minimum circuit breaker size, **?** amps at selected voltage
ε = operational efficiency of motor served by circuit breaker, %.
From Step 1, ε = 91.7 %.
V = selected peak line voltage of electrical circuit, 230 volts
κ_d = motor duty factor. κ_d = 1.25 for continuous duty, 1.40 for intermittent duty. As motor operates continuously, κ_d = 1.25.
Φ = phase factor, 1.00 if single phase, 1.73 if 3 phase. Φ = 1.73.
ℍℙ = required horsepower of motor, from Step 1, 25 hp

$$◇ \times 91.7 \times 230 \ge 43,100 \times 1.25 \times 1.73 \times 25$$
$$◇ \ge 110 \text{ amps at 230 volts}$$

Example 3. A 24 in. diameter attic fan in a residence in Denver, CO, has a design capacity of 8,600 cfm. If the motor's shaft speed is 1,500 rpm, its operational efficiency is 65 percent, and the power is 120V, 60 Hz, single phase, size the fan's circuit breaker.

Step 1. Compute the motor's required horsepower.

⑤ⓒ④③ $75 \, ℍℙ \, ε \, (1 - 0.000034 \, E) = f \rho \, (0.00057 \, v)^2$

ℍℙ = required horsepower of motor, **?** hp. Solve for this value, then
select next largest number in the ℍℙ column in Table 5-3.
Rated ℍℙs in boldface are slightly more economical.
ε = operational efficiency of motor, 65 %
E = site elevation above sea level, ft. If elevation is below 3,000 ft, use
$E = 0$. Here E for Denver = 5,280 ft.
f = fan airflow capacity, actual or required, cfm. f = 8,600 cfm.
ρ = static resistance of airflow, in. wg (in. water gauge). Ventilation
fans installed in exterior walls or ceilings or fans with short ducting (i.e. inner air pressure is near outer air pressure) operate
against little static resistance; then use $\rho \approx 1.15$. Any filters in
airstream increase static resistance to fan operation. If static
resistance is in psi, $\rho_{iwg} = 0.068 \, \rho_{psi}$.
v = rotational velocity or shaft speed of fan, rpm. v = 1,500 rpm.

$$75 \, ℍℙ \times 65 \, (1 - 0.000034 \times 5,280) \ge 8,600 \times 1.15 \, (0.00057 \times 1,500)^2$$
$$ℍℙ \ge 1.81 \text{ hp} \rightarrow 2 \text{ hp}$$

Step 2. Size the circuit breaker required for the fan motor.

$$◇ \, ε \, V = 43,100 \, \kappa_d \, Φ \, ℍℙ$$

◇ = minimum circuit breaker size, **?** amps at selected voltage
ε = efficiency of motor served by circuit breaker, from Step 1, 65%.

V = selected peak line voltage, 120 volts

κ_d = motor duty factor. κ_d = 1.25 for continuous duty, 1.40 for intermittent duty. As motor operates continuously, κ_d = 1.25.

Φ = phase factor, 1.00 if single phase, 1.73 if 3 phase. Φ = 1.00.

ⱵP = required horsepower of motor, from Step 1, 2 hp

$$\diamond \times 65 \times 120 \geq 43,100 \times 1.25 \times 1.00 \times 2$$
$$\diamond \geq 13.8 \text{ amps at } 120 \text{ volts}$$

This motor can be protected by a standard 15A circuit breaker

---

Example 4. How much cool air is required to maintain a comfortable
working environment around a 100 ⱵP synchronous electric motor
whose rated temperature is 40° C if the motor and its drive train have
an overall efficiency of 87 percent?

Step 1. Determine the amount of heat produced by the operating motor.

5⦘C⦘4⦘4⦘ $H \, \varepsilon$ = 2,545 ⱵP (100 - ε)

H = heat produced by continually operating electric motor, ? Btu/hr

ε = operational efficiency of motor, 87%

ⱵP = rated horsepower of electric motor, 100 ⱵP

$$H \times 87 = 2,500 \times 100 \, (100 - 87)$$
$$H = 38,100 \text{ Btu/hr}$$

Step 2. Compute the cooling airflow required to remove the heat produced
by the motor.

$$C = 108 \, Q \, (t_m - t_i)$$

C = cooling load required to remove heat produced by continuously
operating motor, Btu/hr. This equals H from Step 1 ➡ 38,100
Btu/hr.

Q = incoming cooling airflow required to remove unwanted heat, ? cfm

t_m = rated temperature of motor, ° F. 40° C = 104° F.

t_i = desired temperature of air around motor, ° F.
A safe working temperature = 80° F.

$$38,100 = 1.08 \, Q \, (104 - 80) \qquad ... \, Q = 1,470 \text{ cfm at } 80° \text{ F}$$

5.C.5. Signal Circuits

These are specialized low-voltage circuits that include everything from doorbells to total building management (TBM) systems. Each has three components: a *transmitter* (the unit that sends the electromagnetic signal), *conductor* (the wiring between the transmitter and receiver), and *receiver* (the unit that receives the incoming electromagnetic signal and converts it to perceptible form). The primary function of signal circuits is to ensure proper building operation, and in today's computerized world their applications are rapidly increasing. To mention only one example: a control strategy for hotels and motels involves having the occupancy sensor in each room notify the front desk when the room is occupied, notify security personnel if anyone but registered guests or the maid is in the room, notify a fire control panel so that in case of fire firefighters would need to search only occupied rooms, and activate climate control system setbacks when the room is vacant.

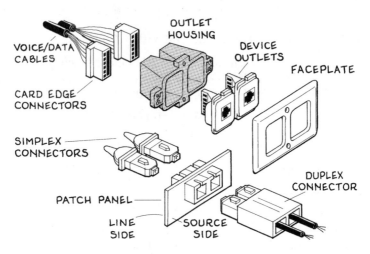

Fig. 5-12. Signal circuit outlets.

In small buildings, all signal circuitry is typically installed on one low-voltage (usually 24 VAC) control panel. But in large buildings a great number of signal circuits may require structurally independent wire management systems, separate electric closets, and NASA-style control centers whose walls are filled with pilot lights, dials, control switches, and TV monitors. As signal wiring is fragile, it should have no tight bends (3 in. diameter is minimum, 6 in. is better), be protected from any mechanical or physical contact such as pedestrian or vehicular traffic, be shielded from rodents, and should not be exposed to harsh, hazardous, dirty, or corrosive environments. The best enclosures are usually wireways, because (1) their hinged tops or sides eliminate pulling and allow easy removal and lay-in of conductors during installation and upgrading, (2) they eliminate the need to staple wires to framing members, which may damage them, and (3) they are superior to cable trays insofar as their full enclosures minimize electromagnetic shielding from adjacent circuitry. All enclosures should be fully sleeved, firestopped at wall and floor penetrations, and located away from all heat-producing equipment, ducts, and grilles.

5.C.5.a. Workstation Wiring

Perhaps the most familiar signal circuitry that has evolved in today's buildings is the computer workstation, in which a well-trained employee commands an array of computers, printers, modems, telephone handsets, dedicated FAX lines, LANs, ethernets, token rings, and related telecommunication media. Such stations may be located in the center of a floor area, next to a wall, or in a cubicle surrounded by shoulder-high walls that offer privacy for the occupant when seated yet allow surveillance of large areas when the occupant stands. In large offices, these stations may be interconnected to form vast electronic networks involving hundreds of workers.

Each of these areas requires extensive electrical support componentry to function properly. This typically includes several duplex power outlets and telecom outlets, related adapters and connectors, and ample space for a spaghetti array of cords and conductors on both sides of the receptacles. All source-side power and signal wiring should be laid in separate enclosures, usually below raised floors or above suspended ceilings. Access to this wiring for servicing and upgrading must be easy, should involve minimum disturbance to nearby workers, and requires ample sizing of all chases and plenums. In fact, some full-access floor plenums under computer areas are as deep as 24 in, and in large buildings the electrical closets they branch from may be 200 sf each for power and signal componentry.

As computer workstations typically generate up to five times more heat per sf than normal office spaces, they require demanding climate controls. Optimal temperatures are 70–75° F, relative humidity is 50 percent ±6 percent (below this level static occurs, while above this level circuitry corrosion increases), airflow should be 500–600 cfm per ton of cooling capacity (high cfms reduce air stratification and hot spots), aiming of airflow is important, and filtration should be 85 percent. Because computers and their componentry typically generate three to five times more heat than the metabolism of occupants, and because computer operators have been known to work at all hours, cooling in these areas should be operable every hour of the year, including weekends.

5.C.5.b. Fire Signal Wiring

When a fire breaks out, usually either fire signal circuit sensors detect it or an occupant sets off an alarm. Either way, an electric impulse notifies central controls; which activate alarms throughout the building, turn on fire suppression systems and fire controls, indicate escape routes for occupants, and notify local police and fire departments.

For a building's total fire control program to work effectively, every transmitter and receiver in its circuitry must be carefully selected and located. This especially includes audio devices (sirens, bells, loudspeakers, intercoms, etc.) and visual devices (exit signs, lights) that notify occupants of fire and indicate paths of escape. Typical Code requirements for visual notification devices are:

▸ They should be mounted in all public circulation areas and common use areas.
▸ Each should be mounted more than 80 in. above the floor or 6 in. below the ceiling, whichever is lower.
▸ Each should contain a minimum 75 fc (measured at the floor) white xenon strobe lamp that emits 1–3 flashes/sec.
▸ No floor area shall be more than 50 ft from such a device, except in large spaces more than 100 ft across; then the devices should be no more than 100 ft apart on the perimeter walls.

Although advocates for the hearing-impaired believe that brighter and faster strobe lights are more satisfactory, advocates for epileptics point out that strobe lights can induce seizures in certain people afflicted with this disorder, thus they urge that these lights be dimmer and slower. This proves that it is impossible for even the best systems to be satisfactory to all parties involved.

5.C.5.c. TBM Systems

The most evolved signal circuitry today is the assembling of virtually every technical and operative aspect of a building into TBM systems that conserve energy and increase productivity. The creation of such "intelligent architecture" recognizes the fact that energy is the lifeblood of modern commerce: its optimal use increases profits, improves worker morale, and even enhances our nation's future welfare. Although the incorporation of TBM systems in America's buildings is still in its toddler stages, its basic components are already well established, as described below.

Command center. An area of floor space at a central location in the building, accompanied by considerable wall area plus 3 ft wide access aisles behind the walls to facilitate mounting, reactive power diagnosis, and upgrading of components. These areas should have redundant HVAC operation in case one unit shuts down.

Decoder module. This serves as a bridge between any old electromechanical and new microprocessor systems and allows replacements, conversions, and ongoing upgrading of facilities.

Logic elements. Solid-state circuitry with multiple contacts that allow operations within certain parameters. An example is *if/then* functions: e.g. (1) *if* the bedroom light turns on, and (2) *if* it is a weekday, and (3) *if* it is between 7 and 8 A.M., *then* turn on the coffeemaker in the kitchen. A near-infinite array of such functions can be custom-made by today's source-code writers of computer programs, even when the software is onsite and the operator is hundreds of miles away.

Detectors. Today there are hundreds of kinds: heat and motion sensors, gas and odor detectors, visible and IF light sensors, sound detectors and regulators, photoelectric eyes, limit switches, proximity switches, centrifugal switches for measuring speed or flow of industrial operations, and the like that provide information to control-circuit logic chips: these are the "five senses" of any successful TBM system.

Controls. Pushbuttons, joysticks, selector switches, dial and clock settings, capacitors that store electrons, thermocouples that change heat energy into electrical impulses, transistors that regulate electric signals, choke coils that impede or amplify a current or change its phase, and other means of activating circuits, motors, systems, and other operations.

Monitoring devices. Lights, meters, clocks, timers, gauges, digital readouts, phones, mikes, computer screens with keyboards, other audio and visual communication devices.

Signaling devices. Pilot lights, warning lights, bells, alarms, LED displays, and other devices that alert occupants to specified conditions.

Solenoids. A solenoid is an electromagnetic coil which, when energized, pulls an iron plunger into its core and thus changes electrical energy into reciprocating energy. They are used to operate valves, handles, and other mechanical switches.

Graphic annunciator. Usually a custom floorplan display that provides the viewer with easy identification, location, and status of all on-premises events and system components.

Phone transponder. A transmitter/receiver that enables a user to operate remote system circuitry (such as turning on the lights outside a service entrance), either by entering the proper alphanumeric signal on the telephone keypad or by voice command. One can also be activated by reception of predetermined signals.

Battery packs. Emergency electricity storage units that ensure system operation in case the power fails.

Archives. Computerized storage of all data pertaining to system operation for historical analysis, trend logging, and future printouts. Point-and-click programming makes the system user-friendly.

Together these components not only can manage nearly every aspect of a building's operation, they actually thrive on monolithicity and complexity. The key that opens the door to their broad range of applications is *direct digital controls*. DDC electronics have greater capabilities than analog systems, and they cost no more while providing communication to and standardization in any number of distant outlets. Such controls constantly monitor environmental conditions and operations within a building: gathering data, continually adjusting building control components to meet predetermined setpoints, modifying and remeasuring when additional parameters are necessary, ensuring that all pre-established requirements are constantly satisfied, portraying all operations in detailed multicolor graphic form, and downloading all data for later analysis. This is not simply energy management, but high-speed peer-to-peer information management within a multi-tasking 'Windows' environment. Possible control strategies approach the infinite, as indicated below:

Climate control. High/low temperature and humidity limits, airflow via static air pressure sensors, dedicated exhaust air fan operation, outside/recirculation air proportioning, splitter and bypass damper modulation, enthalpy modulation (using outdoor air to reduce cooling loads when total heat content of outdoor air is less than that of indoor return air), CO_2 or VOC presence, presence of any other airborne particulate (if it has an odor or chemical formula, a sensor can usually be made to detect it), differential-pressure notification of dirty filters, temperature setbacks and setforwards with scheduled time settings, etc.

Lighting control. Zonal on/off scheduling, daylight harvesting, occupancy sensing, landscape lighting at night (including scheduling for holidays and daylight savings time), manual override circuits, etc.

Fire control. Smoke or heat detection, alarms, prerecorded evacuation instructions, activation of sprinkler systems, notification of fire department, illumination of exit routes, opening of exit doors, activation of smoke dampers and roof hatches, elevator capturing, etc. Circuits may include redundant wiring that ensures overall operability in case one part is destroyed.

Simulated alarm modes. Circuitry that tests building alarms as a way of reducing extensive physical testing such as fire drills.

Security control. Codified access portals (entrance door locks opened by key, card, or password), clock and program timers that activate operations and record personnel entry and exit, sensors mounted at doors and windows, surveillance TV cameras and monitors, intrusion alarms (such as activation of sirens and floodlights when an infrared sensor detects a

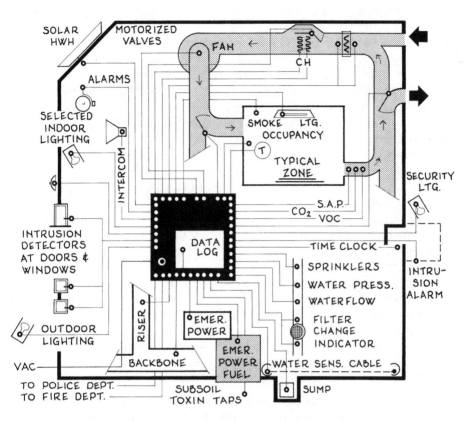

Fig. 5-13. TBM system schematic.

person climbing over a fence around a service area at night), notification of police department, etc.

Intercom systems. Microphones and other transmitters for announcing, music, paging, etc., as well as loudspeakers, telephone hookups, and other outlets for notification.

Energy management. Circuitry that records excess heat emitted by light fixtures, climate control units, industrial operations, etc., and activates remedial measures.

Equipment operation scheduling. Scheduled on/off operation of equipment, industrial processes, etc., including duty cycling (shutdown of motors, fans, pumps, etc. during periods of no-load operation), malfunction diagnosis, shutdown of defective equipment, etc.

Multiple module boiler optimization. Continuous alternate-lead step-firing of multiple boilers based on momentary heating loads. Also entering and exiting water temperatures at each boiler.

Multiple module chiller optimization. The same with cooling system chillers as with heating system boilers.

Off-peak boiler and chiller temperature resetting. Conserves energy by resetting water temperatures during off-peak hours.

Hot water temperature resetting. Reduction of hot water heater (HWH) temperatures as climate control system heating loads decrease: this reduces heat loss from equipment and piping.

Strain gauges. Sensors that measure expansion/contraction of a material or construction upon exposure to a certain thermal or material load stress.

Toxic waste detection. Hydrocarbon and other chemical sensors installed in containment piping or buried in the ground to detect/record leaks and spills.

Proprietary applications. Custom computerized sensing, operating, or recording of commercial or industrial operations.

Monitoring. Supervision circuitry that indicates when a certain signal component is malfunctioning.

Archiving. Computerized record-keeping of all signal circuitry activity, recording sensor data for historical analysis, trend logging, etc., including readouts of all data and energy consumption

Standby power sourcing. Activates standby generation of electricity or batteries in case of power failure, regulates power during surges and brownouts, detects and remedies any harmonic distortion or other frequency excursions in any circuit, etc.

Not only can total building management systems be designed to operate virtually every electromechanical aspect of a building, they can operate many different buildings. A sterling example of this is the central energy management system installed by Builders Square in more than 100 of their home improvement centers throughout the United States and Puerto Rico. From one central office, a single operator can open on a computer monitor a graphic-display map of the U.S. and Puerto Rico; then after double-clicking on a state this geographic area appears showing the location of each store in a map of Interstate highways and any time-zone lines. A second double-click on a store name calls up that outlet's building control system, then all its operating data is scrolled onto the screen. From this point on the operator has full control of every sensor in the building. Some sensors notify the operator when something is wrong, and often exactly what is wrong, while others allow him or her to reset certain controls (such as adjust the outside-air intake damper of a rooftop HVAC unit for improved energy-efficient operation). Still others activate certain building operations according to preprogrammed schedules (e.g. controls that turn on the store's lights in stages from when its employees arrive until the store opens, then stages them off after closing). Once a week, each store downloads its logged data to the central office, which stores it on disks for filing and reviewing. The operator often tries various energy-saving scenarios for a particular store, then analyzes the saved data logs to see what works best. The operator also analyzes the operations of stores with unusually high utility bills, then tries to reduce their energy costs. All this from a seat in front of a computer monitor, by making only a few strokes on the keyboard or double-clicks with a mouse. [†]

The possibilities for multi-location total building management systems go far beyond retail store chains and industrial operations. For example, a commercial property owner could manage hundreds of tenancies over a widespread area. Or the proprietors in a commercial area could form an 'on-line combine' that could manage every individual building. Or a public utility could energy-manage whole suburban areas involving hundreds of residences. But such systems are only as advanced as the facility manager's knowledge of the installation and its advantages. At present, other obstacles to widespread use are (1) high initial cost, (2) inability of central management to understand exactly how the requirements of their building operations may be economized by these systems, and (3) big-brother paranoia and other forms of industry inertia.

In many buildings today, TBM systems are being designed not by architects or engineers but by system manufacturers. They'll analyze a building's needs, integrate controls and equipment for maximum efficiency and comfort, map the wiring layouts, program the logic controller, install everything including the sensors and wiring, check unit inputs and outputs at startup, debug the system, complete final documentation, and even train operation and maintenance personnel. All the Æ designer really needs to do is allow enough space for the components and enough access area for maintenance. The latter area is important, because in these systems every component, no matter how small, typically requires constant monitoring, frequent diagnosis, and occasional repair. Regarding design, there are two kinds of systems: *owner/operator-programmed* and *manufacturer-programmed*. If the building plans are prepared on computer-aided design and manufacturing (CAD/CAM) software, the relevant drawings can be easily initialized to a compatible computerized TBM program.

TBM systems have developed to where several manufacturers have a component that works particularly well, but they are not yet interchangeable. Thus a typical buyer of these systems is currently confronted with a choice of either having to put up with a less-than-optimal installation, or having its managers make Herculean efforts to understand the language of more than one system —a dilemma akin to the language barriers existing among trading nations.

Fortunately, this dilemma has given birth to two new data communication protocols, called *BACnet* and *LonMark*, each of which allows a Tower of Babel of sensors, controllers, and panels made by a variety of manufacturers to be easily defined, developed, and made interoperable without the installation of interpretative gateways, the latter of which introduce much complexity into such systems and require much learning by operating personnel. Such systems even allow one to access each building component while protecting the proprietary nature of its own internal design. The implications of this well-conceived and much-needed communication technology go far beyond the potential advantages to TBM systems; for not only do such systems act as diplomats who can expedite 'trade agreements' between 'negotiating' partners, this very act transforms provincially oriented networks into a global village of user-intimacy in which nearly every imaginable use can be satisfied in a manner that is practically risk-free to everyone involved, from manufacturer to occupant. Indeed, its relatively painless applicability may soon expand beyond TBM technology to create opportunities in all kinds of factory automation, process control, distribution networking, and service provision.

Moreover, the influence of BACnet and LonMark could be sociological, because the extensibility of this revolution-within-a-revolution de-emphasizes the role of the technical specialist and exalts the role of the creative generalist. Thus those employees who take home tomorrow's fattest paychecks may be those who, instead of having an in-depth knowledge of one or more specialized disciplines, are capable of seeing beyond the detail level of such systems and perceiving application potentials from consumers' points of view. [†]

5.C.6. Circuit Summary

When all electric loads are computed, they are organized into circuits as follows:

▸ Convenience and lighting outlets are divided into 15, 20, and (often in commercial architecture) 25 and 30 amp circuits.
▸ Appliance circuits are arranged in the 20, 25, or 30 amp units for which they were designed.
▸ Signal systems have their own circuits, usually 12 or 24 V.
▸ An accounting of circuits is made with the voltages, amperages, and areas served by each. This becomes the Panel Schedule. It is one of the most important documents of the working drawings.
▸ The Panel Schedule is used to size the panel or circuit breaker boxes, in which 20–30 percent vacant breaker space is usually added for future expansion.
▸ The total load is determined and compared with initial estimates.
▸ Each large machine is given a separate circuit. If the machine is

a heater or air conditioner or includes a motor, its conductor and circuit breaker are sized as follows:

Heaters: *Minimum circuit breaker size:* Nameplate amperage × 1.25. This is the unit's full-load amperage (FLA).
Minimum conductor size: $C V = 200 \, \Phi \, \Omega \, A \, L$ (see Sec. 6.D.1).

Air conditioners: *Minimum circuit breaker size:* Given unit's tonnage, find its FLA from Table 5-4, then choose next-highest circuit breaker size above unit's FLA. Given unit's kW rating, find its FLA from kW × 1.25, then in Table 5-4 choose next-highest circuit breaker size above unit's FLA.
Minimum conductor size: Use same formula as for heaters.

Motors: Use unit's nameplate voltage and amperage to find its FLA from Table 5-4; then,
Minimum circuit breaker size: Multiply FLA × 2.5, then select next-highest standard fuse size above this amount.
Minimum fuse or time-delay fuse size: Multiply FLA × 1.75, then in Table 5-4 select next-highest circuit breaker size above this amount.
Minimum conductor size: Use the same formula as for heaters.

After all the circuit loads are designed, it is fairly easy to sort out their voltages and sum their amperages. Then, working upstream from

TABLE 5-4: FULL-LOAD AMPERAGES FOR MACHINES [†]

AIR-CONDITIONING UNITS		SINGLE-PHASE ELECTRIC MOTORS			
Unit size, tons or kW	Full-load Amps	Unit size, HP	←— Full-load amperage —→		
			115 volts	208 volts	230 volts
1½ HP	13	⅙	4.4	2.4	2.2
1¾ HP	15	¼	5.8	3.2	2.9
2 HP	18	⅓	7.2	4.0	3.6
2½ HP	21	½	9.8	5.4	4.9
3 HP	25	¾	13.8	7.6	6.9
3½ HP	28	1	16	8.8	8.0
4 HP	31	1½	20	11	10
5 HP	37	2	24	13.2	12
5 kW	23.4	3	34	18.7	17
6 kW	27.6	5	56	30.8	28
7 kW	31.8	7½	80	44	40
8 kW	36	10	100	55	50
10 kW	45	15	135	75	68
12 kW	54	20	170	94	85
15 kW	66	25	205	113	103

[†] From p. 416: Information on BACnet and related systems was obtained pri-

remote circuit breaker panels to the service entrance, determine the power requirement of every lateral, feeder, and primary conductor in the building. The circuit summary is also used to indicate the number of circuit conductors, the routes each will take from its panel box to each outlet, and even the number of bends in each route and the angle of each bend for purposes of designing and locating any required pull boxes.

5.C.7. Grounding

A ground is an uninterrupted low-impedance pathway that gathers excessive voltage in or around a building and carries it into the earth below. There are four grounding systems: *grounded conductor networks*, *ground fault circuit interruption (GFCI) circuitry*, *lightning rods*, and *information technology equipment (ITE) sites*. Each is described below:

Grounded conductor network. This includes a third wire known as a *groundwire*, *neutral*, or *greenwire* that accompanies the hardwiring in every circuit in a building. These required conductors interconnect every receptacle in a circuit then extend upstream, conjoining at every intersection into a single conductor, until a primary groundwire passes through the main panel box and connects to a grounding rod just outside the building's service entrance. Many domestic environments with computers and other electronic equipment now include surge protectors as added security for their grounded conductor networks.

GFCI circuitry. This is a network of wiring in residences and small commercial buildings that interconnects all electrical outlets in wet areas (e.g. kitchens, baths, basements, garages, outdoors, etc.) as well as any electrically heated floor systems in kitchens, bathrooms, hot tub areas, or other wet areas to one or more ground rods buried outside the service entrance. Grounding rods are further described on page 424.

Lightning rods are pointed air terminals that are located on the highest parts of a building and have conductors that carry any lightning charge usually down the building's outer surface into the ground.

ITE sites are sub-floor networks of conductors that collect fault current from anywhere inside the building.

Large buildings should have at least two grounding systems, and all three systems should be separate; otherwise disasters from crossover currents, particularly lightning, can result. However, complete isolation of all grounding pathways is electronically impossible.

marily from (1) Mark Skaer's 'ASHRAE's baby takes a bow"; *Engineered Systems*

5.C.7.a. Lightning Rods †

Lightning is the completion of an electric circuit from earth to sky. As this powerful force —up to 6 trillion watts— searches blindly for a terminal, prominent elevations and metals offer the best opportunities for discharge —the worst for architecture. Thus the design of lightning rods depends on a building's profile plus the resistivity of the earth below.

The essential componentry of a lightning arrestor system includes *air terminals*, *conductors*, and *ground terminals*, as described below.

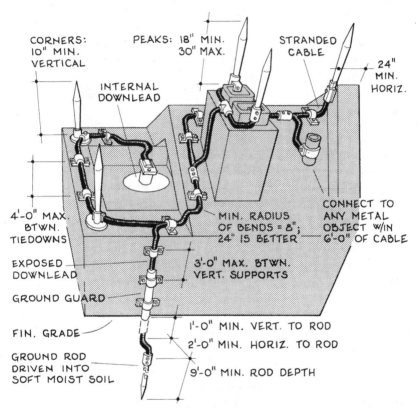

Fig. 5-14. Lightning rod details.

Air terminals. These are solid copper or aluminum rods with pointed tips that are installed on peaks, ridges, chimneytops, parapets, soil stacks, cornices, and other building prominences. Minimum rod diameters are $\frac{1}{2}$ in. for copper and $\frac{5}{8}$ in. for aluminum, the tips must rise 18–30 in. above their base connections, they should be spaced no more than 20 ft apart, and at least two terminals should be placed as far apart as possible on the roof. The more prominent terminals should also form a 30° cone of protection down from its tip; if any part of the building appears between two such projected cones, another terminal should be placed there.

Conductors. These are stranded or braided copper or aluminum cables that connect every air terminal and metal object on the roof (vents, antennae, gutters, etc.) to form continuous loops that extend down the building's sides well into the ground. Ideally these conductors should be oversized and heavily insulated (some electric utilities overinsulate them by a factor of as much as 10 to minimize flashover to adjacent conductive sources). Each layout should be simple and direct and have at least two downleads located as vertically and as far apart as possible. All connections should be crimped or welded and not bolted, minimum bend radius of any conductor is 8 in. (24 in. is much better), and downleads should be anchored to the building's side at no greater than 3 ft intervals. If the building is less than 75 ft tall, all cables should be at least 17 ga. (59,500 cmil) if copper and at least 14 ga. (98,500 cmil) if aluminum; if above 75 ft they should be at least 15 ga. (119,000 cmil) if copper and at least 13 ga. (197,000 cmil) if aluminum. In tall buildings, intermediate floor ground loops should be located about every 20 floors.

Ground terminals. These are $\frac{1}{2}$ in. copper or $\frac{5}{8}$ in. lead-covered aluminum rods (copper is more desirable) whose pointed bottoms are driven at least 10 ft into the ground, preferably in perennially moist soil. Where bedrock or other obstructions limit depth, a greater number of shallower rods are required. If onsite electrode potential tests indicate highly resistive soil, a trench may be dug and filled with rock salt, $CuSO_4$, $MgSO_4$, or other electrolyte to ionize the soil. Drilled well casings make excellent grounds, but they usually exact the price of a functioning water pump when they act as lightning rods. Downlead-to-terminal connections must be protected from aerial corrosion (one of the worst is exhaust from nearby clothes dryer vents) as well as settling, stormwater erosion, and galvanic reaction due to runoff from metal gutters.

Sometimes a building contains such hazardous material or delicate electronics that an extensive *dissipation array lightning avoidance system* is installed. [†] This is one or more metal spires, each resembling the frame of a very large umbrella, whose bases are well rooted in the ground under the building and whose tops rise well above the building's peak so the earth's electric charge can effectively rise to a level above the building: then when the sky above becomes charged, the electrons gathering in the spires keep the differential between sky and earth below what is required to form a bolt of lightning. These systems still require lightning arresters and surge protectors to keep any transient waves from entering through the building's power and telecom conductors.

In residences and small commercial buildings, all kinds of metal stove pipes, cast iron vent stacks, TV aerials, and metal roofs are often uti-

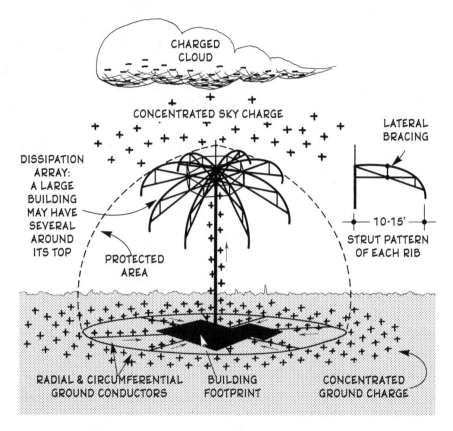

Fig. 5-15. Dissipation array lightning avoidance system.

lized as lightning rods, but with dubious effect. For example, any metal flue acting as a lightning rod should have a #2 or larger copper wire extending from its very top down to well into the ground; but then the flue is not really a lightning rod at all but merely a support for one —a metal structure that can add a dangerously dispersive character to the conductor itself. The same holds for TV aerials and plumbing vent stacks. As for metal roofs, in regions of low thunderstorm intensity they may be ungrounded; then the owners accept the very low risk that the building will never be struck by lightning. But in Florida, the Midwest, and other regions that experience a great number of thunderstorms a year, grounded metal roofs minimize the chance of electromagnetic forces entering through the roof (usually via plumbing vents) and forming damaging voltage spikes indoors. A metal water supply or waste main may be used as a grounding electrode, but it should never be the only such ground, and it should always be bonded to the building's primary grounding electrode system. An underground gas pipe should never be used as a grounding electrode, but it too should be bonded to the building's primary grounding electrode system. If a tall tree rises near a small building, the edifice may be reasonably shielded from lightning by strapping a #2 copper wire to the tree's trunk, extending the wire well above the tree's apex, and inserting the wire's bottom 10 ft into a 2 in. diameter hole bored through the roots at the tree's base.

> A country club near Grosse Point, MI, requires an interior lightning rod. How should it be installed?

Solution: If the lightning rod conductors must be located indoors, each should be housed in 4 in. minimum diameter (6 in. is better) heavy-duty plastic conduit and run continually behind face masonry or structural steel into the ground. Concrete reinforcing may be used as a secondary conductor, if all rebar overlaps are welded and not tied. Avoid any metals of poorer conductivity within 6 ft of the rod, as they may form high-impedance flashover paths with destructive results.

5.C.7.b. ITE Sites

A recent "white paper" by the Computer and Business Equipment Manufacturers Association (CBEMA) states that "75 percent of the problems with perceived power quality are actually grounding problems."[†] The kind of grounding that today's computerized interior environments require to isolate any internal fault currents is known as an *information technology equipment* grounding structure —or ITE site. Its componentry includes *grounding return paths*, a *signal reference grid* on each floor, and a *ground electrode system* beneath the building, as described below:

Grounding return paths. These are typically 6/0 AWG copper wires that connect each potential source of fault current on each floor. They should bond every circuit (convenience, motor, etc.), every metallic network in the building (conduits, piping, ducting, raceways, alarm systems, panelboxes, etc.), every ITE load (sensitive equipment plus dedicated outlet boxes), every length of BX cable at both ends, and every computer workstation, electrical closet, and switchgear to a larger grounding network that carries the fault current into the earth beneath the building. Since high-frequency currents associated with surge events travel on a conductor's outer surface, this circuitry should be stranded or braided cable as they have a much greater surface area than solid wires. Each

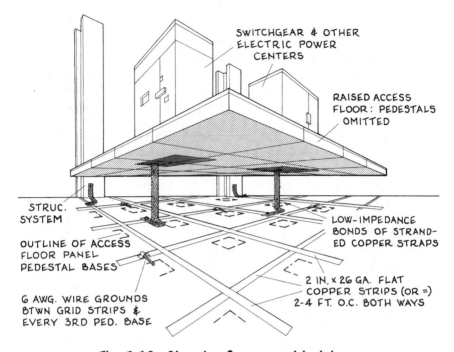

Fig. 5-16. Signal reference grid wiring.

return should be no longer than necessary, have a minimum number of bends (these should be less than 90° if possible), have no coils or sharp bends, never run upward, and not be bonded to perimeter grid conductors (those located nearest exterior walls) because these should be reserved for absorbing lightning and other outdoor electromotive loads. One grounding network must not connect to or even come near another —as then a surge current could jump from one network to another and possibly enter a nearby circuit with devastating results. In fact, there have been cases in overgrounded systems where harmonic interference has jumped from one grounding network through a nearby network of busducts and lighting circuits to a ground at some distant location and caused all sorts of power disruptions along the way. Thus grounding system design is meticulous work that must not be under- or overdone.

Signal reference grid. This is usually either a standard 2 × 2 ft raised access floor whose mains and laterals are bolted rigidly together at every intersection, or a 2 × 2 ft grid of bare 4/0 AWG stranded copper cable or 2 in × 26 gauge copper straps located just below each floor in the building. Each intersection of conductors in this grid is bonded together, and in multistory buildings the grid is usually bonded to every steel and reinforced concrete column which in turn carries any collected fault current down into the ground. All transformers and major service components are usually bonded to this grid. The best connection to column steel is an exothermic weld, as it offers maximum contact and has no galvanic-reaction interface between the usually dissimilar metals. Exothermic welds are especially important for rebar connections, because a bolted or mechanical connection usually contacts the rebar at only two or three lug projections; unless the lugs are ground off, which is labor-intensive. The only valid reason for not using exothermic weld ground connections on steel and reinforced concrete columns is if the connection may possibly be moved in the future. Before making any such connection, thoroughly clean all paint, primer, scale, etc. from the metal surface to be bonded.

Ground electrode system. In an application of the adage that a chain is only as strong as its weakest link, a vital part of any ITE site is the earth in which the ground wiring terminates. If this material is too dry, or too hard, or too chemically inert, it must somehow be made more conductive: otherwise the thwarted current can actually jump back into the building —often with devastating results. In such systems the ground fault current usually enters through a solid copper ground rod buried deeply in the soil; then the electrical charge flows outward through the rod's surface and then radially into the surrounding earth until the charge is dissipated to safe levels at a certain distance from the rod. Thus the charge experiences the greatest soil resistance immediately on leaving the rod, before it has expanded and dissipated in a sizable bulb of earth around the rod. For example, if the rod is $\frac{3}{4}$ in. diameter copper buried 10 ft in solid clay soil, the charge must pass through a copper-to-soil surface area of about 280 in^2; and if the copper's resistivity is typically 4.4×10^{-6} ohms·in. while the enveloping soil's resistivity is either 0.8 ohm·in. if clay, 7.6 ohm·in. if silty sand, or 20 ohm·in. if gravelly sand, then the electric charge must suddenly transfer from one medium to another that may be a million times more resistant. Then it becomes prudent to greatly reduce the soil's resistivity depending on the amount of the charge that may potentially enter it. Thus the first step in designing a ground electrode system is to conduct an *onsite electrode potential test* to determine the local soil's water table and its resistivity. Then one or more of the following solutions may be devised:

1. If the soil is copper-corrosive, the ground rod must be a material other than copper, usually zinc-coated or stainless steel. But these are considerably less conductive.
2. If the soil is dry, extend the rod down to the soil's permanent water table. This increases the rod's surface area and decreases the resistivity of part of the soil that envelops it. If the rod is hammered into the soil, it must not be bent or otherwise damaged by such installation. Stronger steel rods clad in

copper are not recommended here, because if a hammered steel rod incurs a scratch that cuts to the core metal during its installation, the resulting galvanic reaction will first corrode the copper, then allow moisture in the surrounding soil to rust the steel until it disappears. For these reasons ITE site ground rods are usually installed in holes as described below.

3.   Drill a 1 ft diameter hole in the soil (2 ft diameter is better in highly resistive soils), then immerse the rod in the hole and backfill the void between it and the soil with rock salt, bentonite, $CuSO_4$, $MgSO_4$, or other ground-enhancing compound that ionizes the soil. Poured concrete is also a fairly good conductor here.

4.   Increase the rod's surface area by increasing its diameter, increasing its depth in the soil, or using copper pipe which offers a larger surface area with less copper. In fact, a large-diameter copper pipe is one of the best grounds possible — provided this is its only function. If such a pipe is immersed in a 2 ft diameter hole, its hollow interior and the void around it is filled with a ground-enhancing compound, and 1 in. diameter holes are drilled along the pipe's length to increase the contact between the compound on each side, this is the best possible ground short of solution 5 below.

5.   Where the soil is rock, limestone, or other highly resistive medium a few feet down, dig a 2 ft wide trench at least $2\frac{1}{2}$ ft deep around the building just outside its foundation, lay in the trench an *uninterrupted ground ring* of $\frac{3}{4}$ in. braided wire, install at each column coordinate a bonding jumper that extends beyond the building foundation to intersect the ground ring, then fill the trench with 12 in. of copper sulfate or other ground-enhancing compound. This creates a grid-to-ring grounding network beneath the whole building. Every wire in this network should be bare and at least 2/0 AWG solid copper, each wire intersection should be bonded together, and the base of every column should be bonded to this grid. If the columns are more than 32 ft apart, approximately every 1,000 sf of the building's footprint should be enclosed by additional electrode grid wires.

For most ITE sites, usually all that is necessary is a perimeter network of $\frac{3}{4}$ in. diameter copper rods installed in 16 in. diameter holes filled with poured concrete at a specified interval around the building. The bulb of soil allotted to each rod should normally have a diameter ≈ 2.2 × the rod's depth; so if the rods are 10 ft deep they should be about 22 ft apart. The ground that connects the top of each rod should be welded and not clamped, as the former creates more intersurface area, eliminates galvanic reaction, and never needs periodic tightening.

A well-designed ITE site is a low-impedance, highly redundant, three-dimensional, equal-potential network of conductors that drains all fault current directly (i.e. past other nearby equipment and occupants where sideflash could occur) to an effective ground, as opposed to allowing any stray electrons to find such pathways in a random manner. It is the essential foundation upon which all successful operation of sensitive electronic equipment in a building rests. Although ITE sites are fairly easy to incorporate into new buildings, they are generally a problem for retrofits for occupancies that may contain considerable electronic equipment.

5.D. CONDUCTORS

Conductors carry electricity from a building's service entrance to its outlets. They may be copper or aluminum, but the latter is only 61 percent as conductive and requires more skillful installation. A conductor may be a *wire* (single filament of drawn metal), *stranded cable* (several filaments wound together), *strip* (thin wide piece of metal), or *busbar* (a rigid bar). Stranded cables are more flexible than wires and conduct electricity more efficiently. Both are sized in American Wire Gauge (AWG) units or circular mils (cmil or CM). AWG sizes range from 36 (0.0050 in. dia.) to 4/0 (0.460 in. dia.); each size is 1.123 times larger than the next smaller size. One cmil is the area of a circle of 0.001 in. diameter; so a wire that has a 1 in. diameter = 1,000,000 cmils or 1,000 kcmil. Only 4/0 AWG and larger wires are sized in cmils. A conductor should be no more than slightly oversized or it may not provide normal overload protection.

Every conductor has a field of electromagnetic interference (EMI) around it which cannot be fully confined even by thick insulation. As EMI is directly proportional to a wire's voltage and inversely proportional to the distance cubed from its axis, conductors of different voltage must be placed at least several inches apart or laid in separate enclosures. EMI is also why outdoor transformers should be at least 20 ft from buildings and pedestrian areas, why occupants should not remain near large electric motors or mainframe computers for long periods, and why high-voltage feeders and laterals should be located away from spaces occupied for long periods and are better placed near hallways, storerooms, stairways, and elevators.

Since electricity generates heat, all feeders and laterals in commercial buildings must be installed in nonflammable enclosures in well-ventilated airspaces. Otherwise the conductor's efficiency is reduced, its insulation deteriorates, and the surrounding construction may catch fire. Thus every conductor has a *conductor size* (capacity of the wire, cable, strip, or busbar based

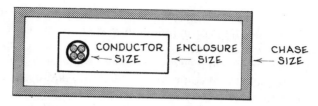

Fig. 5-17. Relation between conductor, enclosure, and chase.

on its voltage, amperage, phase, and insulation), an *enclosure size* (size of the conduit, wireway, raceway, or cable tray that carries the conductor), and a *chase size* (size of the shaft, riser, backbone, or manhole that houses the enclosure). In this era of proliferating electronics, chases must also allow wider spacing between conductors due to EMI plus access for installation, diagnosis, servicing, and upgrading. Thus in the following sections on conductors and enclosures, special attention is given to the sizing of chases.

5.D.1. Flexible Cable

This is an easily bendable copper or aluminum wire sheathed with rubber, plastic, nylon, or spiral steel. Although it is sold in every AWG wire size, the most popular sizes are thinly jacketed 14 AWG and 12 AWG conductors that are easily fitted into small cavities and threaded through small holes in stud walls. Flexible cable is made in several different kinds as follows:

NM (nonmetallic). This cable has two solid copper conductors jacketed in PVC plus a third copper ground wire wrapped in kraft paper, which are all sheathed in a second jacket of PVC. In addition to being inexpensive, lightweight, and easily bent, this wire is easily cut and stripped with common hand tools which makes it the most easily installable conductor for individual circuits containing a multiplicity of outlets, receptacles, and switches. However, the wiring can be easily pierced by nails and cut by other tools after it is installed, it should not be exposed to sunlight, it cannot be installed in wet locations because the ground wire's kraft paper wrapper tends to disintegrate when it gets wet, and it cannot be used in buildings that are more than three stories high. This conductor is commonly known as Romex cable, a name derived from its 1922 invention in Rome, NY, as an "experimental wire". The experiment was obviously a success, because the company now sells 10 million pounds a month. †

BX cable. This also has two PVC-jacketed solid copper conductors plus a third kraft-papered copper ground wire, but they are wrapped in a spiral metal jacket which makes the cable heavier and less flexible but less susceptible to being damaged after it is installed. BX cable also cannot be installed in wet locations or in buildings more than three stories high.

UF (underground feeder). In this cable two solid copper conductors are jacketed in PVC, then they and the unwrapped ground wire are encased in a solid PVC jacket that contains UV-inhibiting additives. Thus this cable can installed anywhere: on the roof, in the air, underwater, in the ground, etc. Two subtypes are *SE (service entrance)* and *USE (underground service entrance)* type cable. When any of these are installed underground, each should be enclosed by metal underground cable whose joints are water-sealed, the enclosure must be at least 24 in. below grade or below local frost depth, whichever is greater, the enclosure must slope at least $\frac{1}{4}$ in./LF down and away from the building, and under paved areas the enclosure must run through minimum 4 in. diameter PVC conduit. All underground conductors must be separated horizontally and vertically from any other conductor enclosures by at least 4 in. concrete or 12 in. earth, separated at least 6 in. vertically and 12 in. horizontally from any water, gas, or oil piping, and located at least 5 ft below the tops of railroad tracks.

Other common flexible cables are *flexible metal cable* (a small-diameter whip that extends from junction boxes to nearby recessed light fixtures), *plenum-rated fire alarm/control cable* (a fire-resistant cable that connects fire detection/alarm components and is laid in or near return air ducts), *signal circuitry cable* (small multi-stranded wiring used for computer and communication systems), and numerous conductors that have almost any core wrap or metal shielding required for special installations.

Flexible cable conductor sizes for common circuits less than 100 ft long are 14 AWG wire for 15 A at 120 V, 12 AWG wire for 20 A at 120 V, and 10 AWG wire for 30 A at 120 V. Maximum voltage drops are 1 percent in secondary conductors (e.g. wiring from remote lamp ballasts to luminaires) and transformer wiring to low-voltage fixtures, 3 percent in the maximum length of one feeder or one branch circuit to its farthest outlet, and 5 percent in the total length of any feeder/circuit run to the remote outlet. Since sharp curves increase impedance, minimum bend radii for most wiring is 15 diameters, but 30 diameters is better (some high-flex cables with extra-fine strands may be bent to radii as little as 5 diameters if they carry low currents). Thus large wiring requires large chase spaces at bends and terminals.

When a flexible cable is enclosed in a conduit, if it has a noncircular section (such as 12-2 AWG Type NM cable which is 0.48 in. wide × 0.20 in. thick), its effective section area is based on a circle whose diameter equals its largest radial dimension. Thus the effective area of 12-2 NM cable is not $\pi \times 0.20 \times 0.48/4 = 0.075$ in^2, but $\pi \times 0.48^2/4 = 0.180$ in^2. Also, minimum pull box dimensions for flexible cable enclosed in rigid conduits are 8 × the conduit diameter: e.g. where a $2\frac{1}{2}$ in. rigid conduit enters and leaves a pull box, its ends must be 8 × $2\frac{1}{2}$ = 20 in. apart.

(Intertec Publishing Co., Overland Park, KS), Jun 2000, pp. 35–38. [†] From p. 422:

➕ The standard wiring for small wood or metal frame construction. Its footage and fittings require no predesign or rigid dimensioning, it is easily fitted into exposed framing, requires little chase or cavity space, can be easily routed around obstructions, and allows flexible positioning of outlets.

➖ When used as feeder cables it must be encased in rigid metal shielding which requires considerable chase or shaft space. Not cost-effective in renovations where new electric loads necessitate tearing open existing walls and ceilings.

Example 1. What size conductor is required for a copper feeder cable carrying 480 V at 200 A single phase whose run from switchgear to electrical closet is 185 ft?

Solution: Try different wire sizes in the formula below until one is found that has a voltage drop of less than 5 percent. Trial 1: try no. 2 AWG copper wire at 480 volts and 200 amps:

5)D)1)1) **Amperage is given:** $C\,V\,\Delta V \;=\; 200\,\Omega\,\Phi\,A\,L$ ... ➕

2) **Wattage is given:** $C\,V^2\,\Delta V \;=\; 200\,\Omega\,\Phi\,\omega\,L$

C = section area of conductor, circular mils. From Table 5-5, C for no. 2 AWG wire = 66,360 cmil.
V = voltage of circuit, 480 volts
ΔV = voltage drop through length of conductor, (maximum = 5%), ? %
Ω = resistance of conductor material, ohms/cmil-ft.
  Ω = 10.7 for copper, 17.7 for aluminum. Here Ω = 10.7.
Φ = phase factor, 1.00 for single phase, 1.73 for 3 phase. Φ = 1.00.
A = ampacity of circuit, if given, amps. 200 amps.
ω = wattage of circuit, if given, watts. Not given.
L = length of conductor, ft. L of cable from switchboard to electrical closet = 185 ft.

$$66{,}360 \times 480 \times \Delta V \;=\; 200 \times 1.00 \times 10.7 \times 200 \times 185$$
$$\Delta V \;=\; 2.49\% \;\blacktriangleright\; \text{OK}$$

Example 2. A farmer in Florida has a machine repair shop 800 ft behind his house which has 120/240 V electrical service, and he wants to replace the shop's old gasoline generator with overhead electrical wiring. If he needs 12 kWh to run an arc welder and power tools and to light the place at night, what size copper wire should he run?

TABLE 5-5: FLEXIBLE CABLE DATA †

CABLE TYPE	Group No. ↓	↓ Max. Oper. Temp, °F.	Applications
A	_	392	Leads in heating appliances
AC ("BX")	_	167	Small buildings to 3 floors tall
MC (incl. CS & ALS)	_	185	All above-ground except corrosive
MI	_	185	All except highly corrosive
NM, NMC ("Romex")	_	167	Small buildings to 3 floors tall
SIS, TA, TBS	_	194	Switchboard wiring only
USE	_	167	Underground service entry
UF	_	167	Submersible water pumps
RH	1	167	Dry locations only
RHH	1	194	Dry locations only
RHW	1	167	Dry and wet locations
T	2	140	Dry locations only
THW	2	167	Dry and wet locations
TW, RUW	2	140	Dry and wet locations
RUH	2	167	Dry locations only
THHN	3	194	Dry locations only
THWN	3	167	Dry and wet locations
FEP, PFA	4	194	Dry locations only
FEPB	4	392	Dry locations: special heat applications
Z	4	194	Dry locations only
XHHW	5	194	Dry locations only
ZW	5	167	Wet locations

WIRE SIZE	Section area of conductor only, cmil	Section area including insulation, in² according to GROUP NO. above				
		1	2	3	4	5
16 AWG	2,580	0.020	0.011	0.008	0.007	—
14 AWG	4,109	0.023	0.014	0.009	0.009	—
12 AWG	6,530	0.028	0.017	0.012	0.012	—
10 AWG	10,380	0.046	0.022	0.018	0.016	—
8 AWG	16,510	0.085	0.047	0.037	0.027	0.046
6 AWG	26,240	0.124	0.082	0.052	0.072	0.062
4 AWG	41,740	0.161	0.109	0.085	0.096	0.085
2 AWG	66,360	0.207	0.147	0.118	0.132	0.118
1 AWG	83,690	0.272	0.203	0.159	—	0.159
1/0 AWG	105,600	0.311	0.237	0.189	—	0.189
2/0 AWG	133,100	0.358	0.278	0.227	—	0.227
3/0 AWG	167,800	0.415	0.329	0.272	0.246	0.272
4/0 AWG	211,600	0.484	0.390	0.328	—	0.328
250 kcmil	250,000	0.592	0.488	0.403	—	0.403
300 kcmil	300,000	0.684	0.558	0.467	—	0.470
350 kcmil	350,000	0.762	0.629	0.531	—	0.531
400 kcmil	400,000	0.837	0.697	0.593	—	0.593
500 kcmil	500,000	0.983	0.832	0.716	—	0.716
600 kcmil	600,000	1.194	1.026	0.879	—	0.904
700 kcmil	700,000	1.336	1.158	1.001	—	1.030

Trial 1: try no. 4 wire at 120 volts:

5)D)1)1) **Amperage is given:** $C V \Delta V = 200 \, \Phi \Omega \, A \, L$
 2) **Wattage is given:** $C V^2 \Delta V = 200 \, \Phi \Omega \, \omega \, L$ ... ➕

C = section area of wire, circular mils.
   From Table 5-5, C for no. 4 AWG wire = 41,740 cmil.
V = voltage of circuit. Assume 120 volts
ΔV = voltage drop thro' line, (maximum is 5%), **?** %
Φ = phase factor, 1.00 for single phase, 1.73 for 3 phase. Φ = 1.00.
Ω = resistance of conductor material, ohms/cmil-ft.
   Ω = 10.7 for copper, 17.7 for aluminum. Here Ω = 10.7.
A = ampacity of circuit, if given, amps. Not given.
ω = wattage of circuit, if given, watts. 12 kWh = 12,000 watts.
L = length of run, ft. L from house to shop = 800 ft.

   $41{,}740 \times 1{,}202 \times \Delta V = 200 \times 1.00 \times 10.7 \times 800 \times 12{,}000$
   $\Delta V = 34.2\%$ ➡ way too high ➡ **NG**
Try no. 1 wire at 240 volts ... recomputing, $\Delta V = 4.26\%$ ➡ **OK**

5.D.1.a. Supported Wiring

   A suspended conductor must obviously be able to support itself between its supports at each end. However, it also must be able to support any ice that may build up on it in winter, resist any wind that may blow against it when its lateral area is greatly thickened by such ice, and resist the increased tension at its supports caused by low temperatures that slightly shorten its length. In icy windy weather, these forces can increase a wire's effective weight by ten times its still dry weight. Then, if the conductor is long and thick, it may be necessary to attach it at uniform intervals to a stronger steel cable that can support them both. Such linear structural support is known as *messenger-supported wiring*. Unfortunately, the forces involved are very difficult to quantify accurately; thus the formula below is a simplified estimate. Typical analysis involves finding the maximum self-supported length of the copper conductor; then, if this is less than the cable's actual span between its supports, finding the minimum diameter of the steel cable required to carry them both.

5)D)1)a) $1.39 \, \kappa_L \, \omega \, L^2 = f_t \, \delta^3$

κ_L = excess load factor that considers ice deposits, wind load, and increased cable tension during cold weather. κ_L = 11 for AWG 4 wire, 7.6 for AWG 2, 6.3 for AWG 1, 5.2 for AWG 0, 4.4 for AWG 2-0, 3.7 for AWG 3-0, 3.2 for AWG 4-0 wire, and 8 for steel cable.

Overland, KS), Feb 1996, p. 33. Another important source for this section was ▍

ω = unit weight of copper conductor or steel carrier cable, lb/LF. Data for several copper conductors is below. Steel weighs 449 lb/cf.

AWG size	4	3	2	1	0	2-0	3-0	4-0
dia., in.	0.232	0.260	0.290	0.328	0.369	0.413	0.463	0.518
wt, lb/LF	0.039	0.050	0.062	0.079	0.099	0.124	0.155	0.194

L = length of copper conductor or steel cable, ft. If the two ends are at different elevations, L = direct distance between them.

f_{tc} = tensile strength of copper conductor or steel cable, ksi. Typical $f_{t\text{-}copper}$ = 20 ksi and typical $f_{t\text{-}steel}$ = 36 ksi.

δ = diameter of copper conductor or steel cable, in. If the wire's AWG size is known, its diameter can be found from the above bar graph. Wires smaller than AWG 6 should not be used for overhead cable.

5.D.1.b. Junction Boxes

Junction boxes are the terminating enclosures for the conductors that extend from the circuit breaker boxes. Each is a small metal or plastic box in which its wires connect to plug or switch receptacles. Although each box is sized according to the size and number of conductors it contains, one's size as dictated by most building codes is dangerously small. For example, most codes say each 14 AWG and 12 AWG wire requires at least 2.00 in³ and 2.25 in³ of space in any box; but if an electrician sizes a box according to these capacities, there is usually so little room left between the receptacles and the box's sides that the electrician has to cram the wires in with thrusts of a pointed instrument —which can cut the wires' insulation, loosen them from their terminals, and leave no space to visually check the connection before the box is closed. And, if the conductor is aluminum, one bend can break it. The situation is worse if the box contains three-phase connections or screw twist nuts, if the twist nuts' bases are taped, if any aluminum-to-copper connections inside require splices or oxidation-deterrent pastes, if the box contains internal cable clamps, if the receptacle has projections through which screws are inserted to secure it to its support, or if the box contains any bonding jumper or groundwire connection (which it should have). Sometimes many of these items are in one box!

A far safer guide for sizing a junction box is to consider that a standard two-outlet household junction box has a volume of 12.0 in³, into which two 12 AWG conductors will fit comfortably. This is 6.0 in³ per conductor — 2.7 times the usual Code requirement. Thus this text advises the following minimum unit conductor volumes for sizing any junction box:

AWG wire size	14	12	10	8	6
Minimum volume per wire, in³	5.0	6.0	7.0	8.0	10.0

For such a little container that can cause so much trouble if something goes wrong, this is a prudent design measure. Also, any conductor that passes through the box on its way to a further termination should be counted as ½ conductor; as should each receptacle yoke or strap, any aluminum-to-copper splice, any other splice, and each ground connection inside.

5.D.2. Rigid Multi-Outlet Assemblies

These are long thin rigid shapes of uniform cross-section into which small wires or strips are fitted. They are variously known as lighting tracks, plug molds, wiremolds, type FC cables, and surface raceways. Their lengths are easily cut and mounted against walls or ceilings, and an array of el-bows, tees, crosses, couplings, and extensions allow flexibility of installa-tion. Various receptacles, fixture stems, and extension cords may be

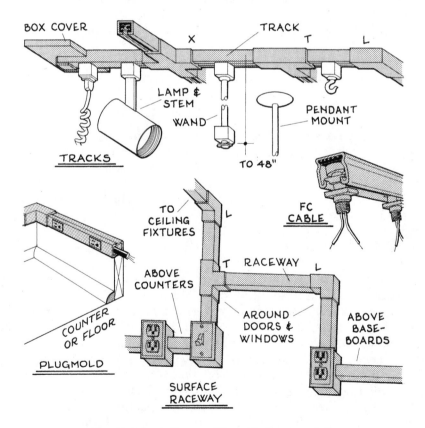

Fig. 5-18. A few multi-outlet assemblies.

2000, pp. 38-44. † From p. 427: *Fine Homebuilding* magazine (Taunton Press,

plugged into them at almost any interval, and some units may be installed outdoors. Capacities of tracks and plug molds are typically the same as those of flexible cable (e.g. 15A at 120V for 14 AWG wire or equal), while type FC cable contains 10 AWG copper wire only with maximum taps per circuit totaling 15 A at 300 V, and surface raceway cross-sections may be as large as $3\frac{1}{2} \times 4\frac{3}{4}$ in. and hold up to 30 separate conductors.

When designing rigid multi-outlet assemblies, the architect usually draws the system on the interior elevations and/or ceiling plans, then the architect or engineer sizes the circuits.

➕   Suitable where the architecture permits no recessing, where outlets are required at frequent intervals, and in renovated areas where changing electric requirements would otherwise necessitate tearing open existing walls and ceilings.

➖   Units cannot extend through walls, floors, and similar barriers. They cannot be subjected to severe physical damage, installed in hazardous locations, or exposed to corrosive vapors. Where used for different circuits, each conductor must run in a separate unit identified by a contrasting interior color finish.

5.D.3. Busways [†]

Also called *busducts*, these conductors contain several copper or aluminum bars with spaces between them that enable their ends to interlock to form continuous lengths. After their housings are fastened together, electric outlets called *tap boxes* are plugged into the bars' sides, allowing connection to laterals, transformers, switchgear, motors, and other equipment. Busways may be short feeders with taps only at the ends and centers, plug-in buses with continuous taps that allow convenient plugging every few inches along their lengths, outdoor buses with weatherproof enclosures and no taps at all, and trolley buses that move on tracks. Feeder buses are typically made in 1 in. increments from 16–120 in, while plug-in and outdoor buses usually come in lengths of 48, 72, 96, and 120 in. All can be assembled quickly and are easy to refigure; circuit breakers are easily installed between the taps and conductors; and a variety of tees, elbows, crosses, reducers, and end closures allow these systems to be run horizontally or vertically anywhere in a building. The bars themselves may be *spaced* (small insulators are placed at intervals between the bars) or *sandwiched* (thin continuous strips of insulation are laid between the bars). Sandwiched constructions are lighter, simpler, stronger, more rigid, more compact, incur less inductive reactance between the bars, and have lower ventilation requirements.

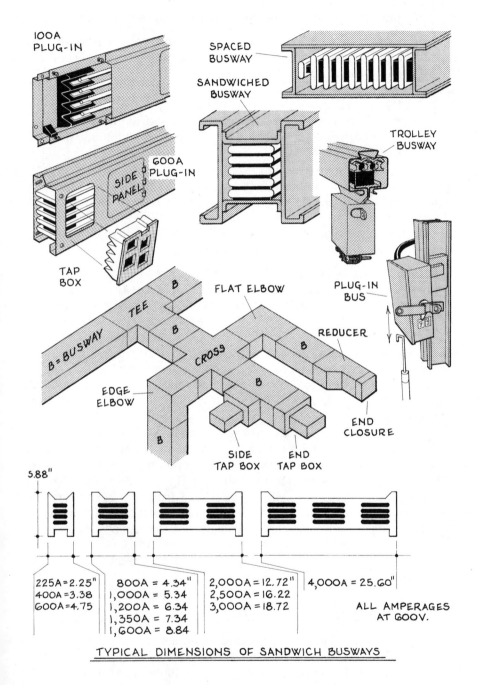

Fig. 5-19. Busway details.

Busways have several important components, as described below.

Hangers: the mounts that support the runs. Maximum spans between them are 5 ft for outdoor runs, 10 ft for indoor horizontal runs, and 16 ft for indoor vertical runs.

Expansion fittings: short feeders with built-in expansion joints (limit = ±1.5 in) that relieve any strain caused by thermal movements in busses that cross expansion joints or have long straight runs that are fixed at one or both ends. Any straight runs more than 60 ft long and sections crossing building expansion joints require expansion fittings.

Heaters: actually ventilators, these are installed in weatherproof busses to remove accumulating heat from around the bars. One heater is required per 7 LF of run and each heater requires a thermostat, but up to 20 heaters may be governed by one thermostat.

Weather seal: also called a gasket, one is required at every busway penetration through the building envelope.

Busways are usually the most economical system in industrial settings with high voltages and amperages, and they can be easily reassembled to accommodate changing conditions. Their section areas are up to 70 percent less than those of multiple-conduit runs of equal ampacity, and since each essentially carries the same electric load in one large conductor instead of several separate ones as in conduits, a diversity factor can lower power requirements and unit sizes by as much as 40 percent, which leads to smaller service loads, switchgear, chases, and floor spaces with correspondingly lower costs. However, busways require well-ventilated chases or shafts, and extensions through walls and floors must be in unbroken lengths.

Busways are designed as follows. (1) The Æ designer determines the size, material, and type (feeder, plug-in, lighting, etc.) of each section given its voltage, amperage, phase, number of poles, and use. An example is 600 V 400 A 3Φ 4 pole copper plug-in busway. (2) The Æ designer prepares a detailed layout of all runs showing all dimensions from ¢s of busses, wall and floor penetrations and thicknesses, fittings, and options. (3) The manufacturer builds the busway in section and labels them in sequence according to the Drawings. Thus this is a predesigned and prefabricated system, which means there is no room for flexibility on the site, yet there are fewer surprises during construction.

➕ Flexible, versatile, compact, light, energy-efficient, low first cost, low labor costs. Easy to install future taps anywhere along lines.

➖ Bulky, delicate, must be connected to solid structure. Cannot be installed in hoistways or in moist, corrosive, or hazardous areas. Less efficient than cables, which leads to higher operating costs, greater power losses, and greater heating loads. If the heat can be used to advantage, this drawback is negated.

Schram, Editor (National Fire Protection Association, Quincy, MA, 1983), pp. 450–

Size the chase for two 600 V 400 A 3Φ 4 pole copper plug-in busways.

5)D)3) $A \approx 0.007 \, \eta \, [(w_b + 10)(d_b + 6)]^{1.1}$

A = section area of busway chase or shaft, ? sf
η = number of busways in chase, 2
w_b = width of each busway, in. From Fig. 5-19, w_b for 600 A busway =
   4.75 in. Minimum chase width = w_b + 10 in.
d_b = depth or height of each busway, in. From Fig. 5-16, d_b for 600 A
   busway = 5.88 in. Minimum shaft depth = d_b + 12 in.

$$A \approx 0.007 \times 2 \, [(4.75 + 10)(5.88 + 6)]^{1.1} \approx 4.1 \, sf$$

Note: One side of each chase or shaft must be accessible by removal of panels for its total length except at passages through walls.

5.D.4. Flat Conductor Cable

   Also known as *undercarpet wiring* or *NEC type FCC cable*, this branch circuitry conductor has several flat copper ribbons encased in a tough polyvinyl insulator that is barely $\frac{1}{32}$ in. thick and up to several inches wide. The cable is taped or glued to the subfloor and covered with a grounded polyester or metal plate which is essentially undetectable beneath carpeting, especially if it is deep-pile. Cable ends are sealed against liquid spillage and components include connectors, adapters, receptacles, and converters to other wiring. Voltage ≤ 300 V, and current

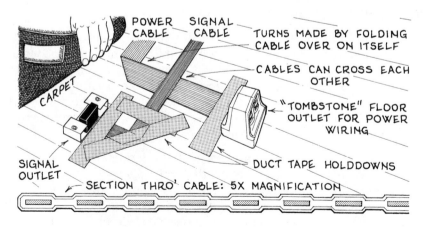

Fig. 5-20. Flat conductor cable details.

≤ 20 A for convenience/appliance circuits and 30 A for individual circuits.

When specifying flat conductor cable, the architect notes the selection on the plans, then usually provides the contractor with a furniture layout plan showing floor outlet locations with required power, equipment, and signal loads.

➕ Accessible, flexible, has virtually no construction impact. Allows easy reworking of wiring systems in old buildings. Carpet squares may be readily removed and the wiring underneath changed with minimum disruption to surrounding activities.

➖ Not permitted in residences, schools, hospitals (not even in office areas of these buildings), wet locations, hazardous areas, or outdoors. May be installed only on hard smooth continuous subfloors under carpeting. Carpets may experience excessive wear at cable locations ➡ N2G for thin carpets.

5.E. ENCLOSURES

In residences, flexible cable is routinely threaded through and stapled to framing members from panelboards to outlet boxes. But in most commercial structures, all conductors must be placed in articulately sized fireproof enclosures. Such enclosures are described below.

5.E.1. Rigid Conduit

Also known as raceway or metal conduit, this is a fireproof metal tubing that contains one or more flexible cables; then the tubes are connected with couplings, T's, L's, boxes, drains, and expansion joints to form a completely enclosed raceway system. Since each cable must be threaded through each section and fitting, lengths cannot exceed 100 ft or have more than two bends; otherwise pull boxes must be installed to facilitate installation. Common rigid conduits are listed below.

Steel. Either *electric metal tubing* (EMT), *intermediate metal conduit* (IMT), or *rigid steel* (RS). EMT has the thinnest walls and RS the thickest. Steel conduits are used primarily where the enclosure requires structural support. They cannot be placed in contact with earth or other metals, and they should not be installed in moist or corrosive environments (an exception being galvanized metal conduit in concrete) or where vibration or noise

Fig. 5-19 was the *Electrical Distribution and Control Products Digest* (Square D

transmission are a problem. Diameters range from $\frac{1}{2}$–4 in.

Aluminum. Compared to steel this conduit is lighter, more workable, nonmagnetic, nonsparking, and noncorrosive in air; but it is weaker, more thermally expansive, and corrosive in earth or concrete unless sleeved. Diameters range from $\frac{1}{2}$–$3\frac{1}{2}$ in.

Flexible metal. A flexible tubing of spirally wound metal sleeved in a liquid-tight sun-resistant jacket. It is used to connect recessed lighting fixtures, cross expansion joints, circumvent obstructions, and connect motors requiring vibration or noise isolation. It may be buried in earth, used outdoors, and placed in moist and corrosive environments. Diameters are $\frac{1}{2}$ and $\frac{3}{4}$ in, maximum lengths are 6 ft, and each conduit can hold only one wire.

Rigid nonmetallic conduit. This is typically PVC or high-density polyethylene that may be buried underground, encased in concrete, or exposed to corrosive situations if ambient temperatures remain below 122° F. Since it emits a toxic gas when ignited, it cannot be used for interior wiring. Diameters range from $\frac{1}{2}$–6 in.

➕ Rigid conduit is economical, versatile, easily field-assembled, and feasible in one- or two-story buildings with simple runs.

➖ Installation is labor-intensive, pull boxes require extra floor space. N2G for thinly insulated wires, long runs, runs with numerous bends. Conduits and fittings are difficult to disassemble and wires cannot be repulled ➡ N2G where renovation possibility exists. Any electrical fire in a conduit can send smoke to ends of runs that are far from the source of combustion.

NEC guidelines for designing rigid conduits are given below. If these guidelines are not followed, the usual onsite labor of pulling the conductors through the conduits could break small cables, scrape the insulation off large cables which could cause short-circuits deep inside the conduit, and distend the length of any cable which would increase its resistance to electron flow (which reduces its delivered power and heats it up more). This labor can also be very strenuous, especially if a cable has a kink in it; and all it takes to put a kink in a cable is for an inexperienced laborer to unwind it improperly from its reel —which happens all the time when such labor is unsupervised. Thus it is often wise design, not to mention good construction politics, to make rigid conduits one size larger than is required, especially if they are large.

▸ A rigid conduit cannot exceed 100 ft, it can include no more than 360° of bends in its length between pull points (otherwise more pull boxes must be installed along its length), and the pull force required to install its cables must ≤ 100 lb for power conductors or FO cables and ≤ 25 lb for datacom cables.

▸ The number of conductors that can fill a rigid conduit is a function of each conductor's section area as measured from the outer surface of its insulation. If a conductor is noncircular, its design section area for fill purposes equals the square of its maximum diameter $\times$ $\pi/4$, or 0.785 δ^2.

▶ Conductors of different diameters can be installed in one conduit, but datacom cables cannot be enclosed with power cables. FO cables can be enclosed with power or datacom cables.

▶ If one conductor is housed in a rigid conduit, the conductor's section area cannot exceed 53 percent of the section area circumscribed by the conduit's inner diameter. If three or more conductors are housed in the conduit, the sums of their section areas cannot exceed 40 percent of the conduit's section area.

> How many 3 in. diameter rigid metal conduits are required to carry 18 type RHH 1/0 AWG and 26 type RHH 4 AWG flexible cables? What size chase is needed for these enclosures?

5)E)1)a) **Conduit size:** $0.31 \, \eta \, \delta^2 \geq \eta_1 A_1 + \dots + \eta_z A_z$

η = minimum number of conduits required, **?** units
d = diameter of conduits, 3 in.
η_1 = number of first type of cables to be carried, 18 units
A_1 = section area of first type of cable to be carried, in^2.
   From Table 5-5, A for type RHH 1/0 AWG cable = 0.311 in^2.
η_2 = number of second type of cables to be carried, 26 units
A_2 = section area of second type of cable to be carried, in^2.
   From Table 5-5, A for type RHH 4 AWG cable = 0.161 in^2.

$$0.31 \, \eta \times 3^2 \geq 18 \times 0.311 + 26 \times 0.161$$
$$\eta \geq 3.51 \;\blacktriangleright\; 4 \text{ conduits}$$

5)E)1)b) **Chase width:** $w \approx \eta_w (d + 1) + 15$
     c) **Chase height:** $h \approx \eta_h (d + 3) + 13$

w = estimated width of chase, **?** in. Minimum w = 16 in.
η_w = number of conduits arranged across width of chase, 4 units
h = estimated height of chase, **?** in. Minimum h = 16 in.
η_h = number of conduits arranged through height of chase, assume one row. If diameters vary, use maximum diameter in row.
d = diameter of conduits, 3 in.

$$w \approx 4 \, (3 + 1) + 15 \approx 31 \text{ in.}$$
$$h \approx 1 \, (3 + 3) + 13 \approx 19 \text{ in.}$$

tion's information was obtained from the *National Electric Code Handbook, 1984*

5.E.1.a. Pull Boxes [t]

A pull box is a usually rectangular metal box with a removable cover that is installed along a rigid conduit to facilitate the installation of its conductors. Each such box needs to be sized as surely as the conduits and cables extending between them; and each is designed in terms of the way its conductors enter and exit through its sides, as follows:

Straight pull boxes: conductors exit box through side opposite the one they entered.

5)E)1)a)1) $L \geq 8\,\delta_{max}$
    2) $W \geq 6\,\delta_{max}$

U-pull boxes: conductors exit box through same side they entered.

5)E)1)a)3) $L \geq 9\,\delta_{max}$
    4) $W \geq 6\,\delta_{max}$

Angle pull boxes: conductors exit box through a side adjacent to the one they entered.

5)E)1)a)5) $L \geq 6\,\delta_{max} + S$
    6) $W \geq 6\,\delta_{max} + S$
    7) $A \geq 6\,\delta_{max}$

Depth of any pull box: Minimum 2 × diameter of largest conduit entering or exiting the box.

5)E)1)a)8) $D \geq 2\,\delta_{max}$

δ_{max} = diameter of largest conduit entering box, in.
L = min. interior clear length of longer side of box, in.
W = min. interior clear width of shorter side of box, in.
A = min. diagonal distance between conduits entering in adjacent walls of box, in.
S = sum of all less-than-maximum-diameter conduits entering the box, in.

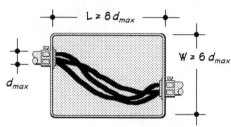

Fig. 5-21. Straight pull box.

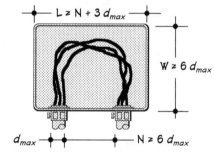

Fig. 5-22. U-pull box.

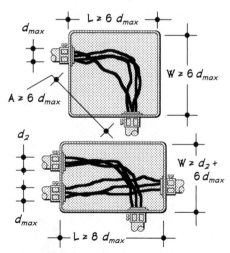

Fig. 5-23. Angle pull boxes.

Edition; Peter Schram, Editor (NPFA, Quincy, MA, 1983); Art. 328, p. 316.

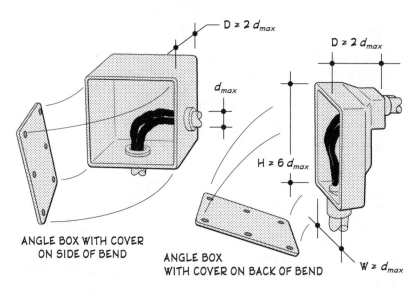

Fig. 5-24. Location of cover plates on angle pull boxes.

Angle pull boxes may also have the removable cover on a side or a back of a bend as sketched in Fig. 5-24. Minimum box dimensions are as shown, and all box dimensions shown are from inner faces of enclosures. If any box contains more than one entering and exiting conductor, the conduits should be arranged to facilitate the easiest pulling and simplest fitting of conductors into the enclosure.

5.E.2. Wireways [†]

These sheet-metal troughs with hinged tops or sides allow easy lay-in of up to 30 conductors; and they may be sealed, gasketed, and enameled to protect the enclosed wires from oil, water, dirt, dust and physical damage. They are made as square ducts, shallow trenches for horizontal runs, and thin-wall ducts for vertical runs. Square ducts may be $2\frac{1}{2}$, 4, 6, 8, and 12 in. square and typical lengths are 12, 24, 36, 48, 60, and 120 in. Common fittings are elbows, tees, crosses, couplings, closing plates, poke-throughs, and converters to other systems. Spans between supports ≤ 10 ft for horizontal runs and 15 ft for vertical runs. Wireways often require pullboxes where their conductors make radical changes in direction, but such enclosures aren't subject to as stringent requirements as are pullboxes for rigid conduit. A new wireway resembling a 6 or 7 in. wood or vinyl baseboard contains two to four channels for power, data, voice, and other wiring. It is easily mounted above work counters, then faceplates or patch panels can

---

[†] From p. 441: Much of this section was taken from Mike Holt's "Sizing Pull and

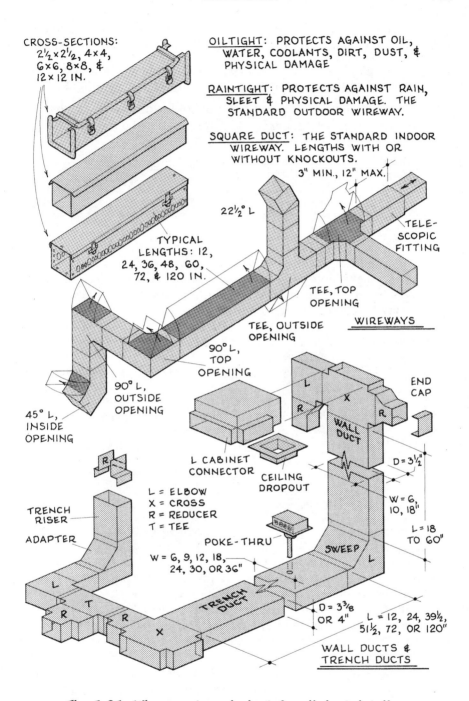

CROSS-SECTIONS:
2½ x 2½, 4 x 4,
6 x 6, 8 x 8, &
12 x 12 IN.

OILTIGHT: PROTECTS AGAINST OIL,
WATER, COOLANTS, DIRT, DUST, &
PHYSICAL DAMAGE

RAINTIGHT: PROTECTS AGAINST RAIN,
SLEET & PHYSICAL DAMAGE. THE
STANDARD OUTDOOR WIREWAY.

SQUARE DUCT: THE STANDARD INDOOR
WIREWAY. LENGTHS WITH OR
WITHOUT KNOCKOUTS.

3" MIN., 12" MAX.

22½° L

TYPICAL
LENGTHS: 12,
24, 36, 48, 60,
72, & 120 IN.

TELE-
SCOPIC
FITTING

TEE, TOP
OPENING

TEE, OUTSIDE
OPENING

90° L,
TOP
OPENING

WIREWAYS

90° L,
OUTSIDE
OPENING

45° L,
INSIDE
OPENING

END
CAP

L

X

R

R

WALL
DUCT

D = 3½"

L CABINET
CONNECTOR

CEILING
DROPOUT

W = 6,
10, 18"

L = ELBOW
X = CROSS
R = REDUCER
T = TEE

L = 18
TO 60"

TRENCH
RISER

ADAPTER

POKE-THRU

SWEEP

L

W = 6, 9, 12, 18,
24, 30, OR 36"

L

T

R

R

TRENCH
DUCT

X

D = 3⅜"
OR 4"

L = 12, 24, 39½,
51½, 72, OR 120"

WALL DUCTS &
TRENCH DUCTS

Fig. 5-25. Wireway, trench duct, & wall duct details.

be installed anywhere along its surface. It has a clean look, eliminates cluttered above-counter cords, and is easy to reconfigure as needs change.

➕ Versatile, compact. Easy to install, splice, tap, and upgrade. Economical for many commercial and industrial applications.

➖ Permitted only for exposed work. Cannot be installed in corrosive or hazardous environments. Most systems must be designed in advance and assembled onsite according to plans.

> What size wireway is required to carry 8 THW 4 AWG conductors and 3 THW 2/0 conductors?

5)E)2) $\qquad 0.20\, A_t \geq \eta_1 A_1 + \ldots + \eta_z A_z$

A_t = total minimum section area of wireway, **?** in². Solve for A_t, then choose next-largest-size section from $2\frac{1}{2} \times 2\frac{1}{2}$ in. = 6.25 in², 4 × 4 = 16 in², 6 × 6 = 36 in², 8 × 8 = 64 in², or 12 × 12 = 144 in².

η_1 = number of 1st cable 1 to be carried, 8 units

A_1 = section area of 1st cable to be carried, in². From Table 5-5, A for type THW 4 AWG flexible cable = 0.109 in².

η_2 = number of 2nd cable to be conveyed, 3 units

A_2 = section area of 2nd cable to be carried, in². From Table 5-5, A for type THW 2/0 AWG flexible cable = 0.278 in².

$$0.20 \times A \geq 8 \times 0.109 + 3 \times 0.278$$
$$A \geq 8.53\ \text{in}^2 \blacktriangleright 4 \times 4\ \text{in.}$$

5.E.3. Cable Trays †

Also known as *ladder racks*, these enclosures are a rigid system of troughs, racks, or trays that are typically 3–36 in. wide and 4–12 in. high, have grilles or other openings on their undersides that allow quick dissipation of heat, and have open or easily removable tops that allow easy lay-in and upgrading of conductors anywhere along the trays. Peaked covers can be fitted over the trays where debris or corrosive vapors could settle on the cables, a variety of fittings enable the trays to run horizontally or vertically and extend through walls and floors, and other systems may feed into or branch from them. The trays are typically made of low-carbon or stainless steel, aluminum, fiberglass, and plastic. Steel is best for large deep trays that contain many conductors, aluminum is easier to install and its nonmagnetic nature reduces power losses from high-voltage conductors, and nonmetallic trays are usually more economical for small systems.

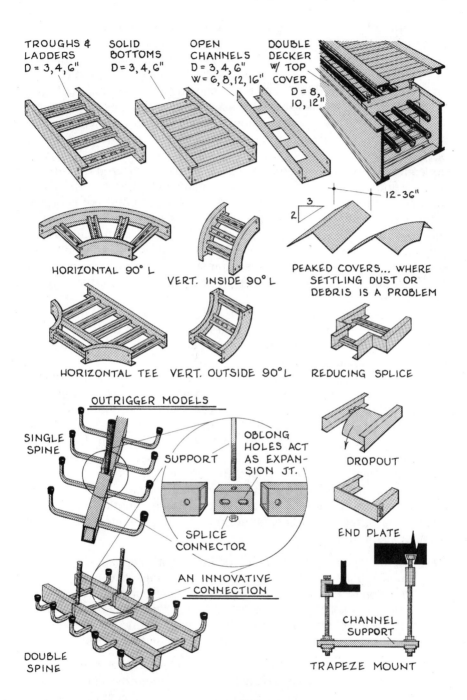

TROUGHS & LADDERS D = 3, 4, 6"

SOLID BOTTOMS D = 3, 4, 6"

OPEN CHANNELS D = 3, 4, 6" W = 6, 8, 12, 16"

DOUBLE DECKER W/ TOP COVER D = 8, 10, 12"

12-36"

HORIZONTAL 90° L

VERT. INSIDE 90° L

PEAKED COVERS... WHERE SETTLING DUST OR DEBRIS IS A PROBLEM

HORIZONTAL TEE

VERT. OUTSIDE 90° L

REDUCING SPLICE

OUTRIGGER MODELS

SINGLE SPINE

SUPPORT

OBLONG HOLES ACT AS EXPANSION JT.

DROPOUT

SPLICE CONNECTOR

END PLATE

AN INNOVATIVE CONNECTION

CHANNEL SUPPORT

DOUBLE SPINE

TRAPEZE MOUNT

Fig. 5-26. Cable trays, fittings, & accessories.

Each material is resistant to certain kinds of corrosion and highly susceptible to others; so design involves a matching of material with the installation's environment. The trays should run continuously for the length of the installation (but they can be discontinuous at elevation changes), and cables of widely differing voltages should not be laid together (barrier strips and RF-shielded trays are used for control and signal wiring).

Cable trays are installed under ceilings, in utility trenches and tunnels, and below raised access floors. Aerial installations are typically supported by pipe racks, shelf brackets, and trapeze mounts. The trays cannot convey single conductors, vertical runs must be covered to at least six ft above floors, they require lateral bracing (usually short lengths of tubular steel flattened at the ends and bolted to tray mounts) both perpendicular and parallel to their lengths, and they cannot be used to support raceways and other utility conveyances. Also it was found after the Los Angeles earthquake of January 1994, that long straight runs of cable trays sometimes acted as battering rams against the walls at each end. A *cablebus* is similar to a cable tray, except it has a smaller frame that is grilled on its bottom.

An innovative and economical tray for small-to-medium installations has a single spine on one side that eliminates half the required supports and allows easier lay-in since the installed cables don't need to be threaded between double hanger supports. It is made from 6–36 in. wide, supports up to 100 plf, and has a clever telescoping fitting that simultaneously joins two sections, connects them to a support, and acts as an expansion joint. Another economical tray for small installations is sheet metal joists or wide studs laid on the flat.

Cable tray design involves (1) selecting the type of tray based on the cables to be conveyed and the installation environment, (2) determining the method of support and their spans (the heavier and deeper the tray the longer the span, up to 20 ft), and (3) sizing the trays based on the number of cables it will carry. Since there are at least 16 combinations of tray constructions, voltage levels, conductor criteria, and use factors, the formulas below are estimates.

➕ Low initial cost, easy to install and maintain, low power losses. Good in buildings that may require renovating because easy lay-in of conductors eliminates cutting old cables, abandoning them in place, or resplicing them. Water cannot collect in the trays, smoke cannot travel through them as it can through conduits, and they require fewer span supports than wireways and raceways.

➖ Most trays are bulky and require large chases. They cannot be installed in hoistways, corrosive or hazardous environments, or areas subject to physical damage. They usually must be assembled onsite according to detailed plans.

> What size cable tray is required to carry 18 4/0 AWG type XHHW conductors? What size chase does the tray require?

5]E]3]a] **Tray width:** $W \approx 5 (\eta_1 A_1 + ... + \eta_z A_z)$
          Tray height: $H \approx 6$ in. unless otherwise specified

W = minimum width of tray, **?** in. Std. widths = 6, 12, 18, 24, 30, 36 in.
η_1 = number of first type of conductor in tray, 18 units
A_1 = section area of first type of conductor in tray. From Table 5-5, A for 4/0 AWG type XHHW cable = 0.484 in^2. Similarly sized cables if smaller than 1/0 AWG may be laid in 2 or 3 layers.

   $w \geq 5 (18 \times 0.484) \geq 43.6$ in. → try 2 trays each 24 in. wide

5]E]3]b] **Chase width:** $W \approx 22 + w$
      c] **Chase height:** $H \approx 18 + h + 18 (S - 1)$

W = estimated width of chase or shaft, **?** in.
w = width of tray, in. From Step 1, w = 24 in.
H = estimated height of chase or shaft, **?** in^2. 12 in. clear must exist between trays and underside of lowest part of ceiling.
h = height of each tray, in. From Step 1, h = 6 in.
S = number of stacked trays in system. S = 2.

   $W \approx 22 + 24 \approx 46$ in. $H \approx 18 + 6 + 18 (2 - 1) \approx 42$ in.

5.E.4. Raised Access Floors

This flexible system of adjustable pedestals, grid supports, and finished floor panels is assembled above a structural subfloor to create a full-access plenum beneath the occupied spaces. Pedestal heights range from 4–24 in. (usually 6–8 in. for general wiring and 24 in. under computer systems), the floor panels are 18–36 in. square (24 × 24 in. is common), and the underfloor area may serve as a return plenum for conditioned air (then grilles are cut into the floor panels). All wiring must be laid in trenches or trays, the floor must be high enough to allow sufficient plenum airflow, and the pedestals must be laterally braced both ways (usually by diagonal guy wires and turnbuckles). The underfloor wiring usually runs from large electrical closets (typical area ≈ 120 sf), and just inside the closet's access door is usually a small landing and short staircase down to the subfloor on which the cables are laid. The system is desirable in large open areas with a high density of electrical operations that may frequently change.

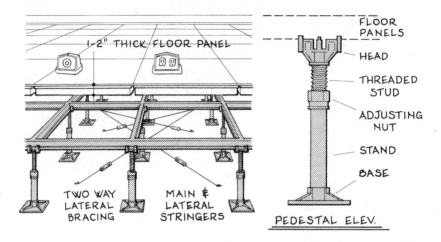

Fig. 5-27. Raised access floor details.

➕ Maximum access and flexibility, low first cost, low maintenance cost. They allow simple subfloors, and no occupancy layouts are required before construction.

➖ Increases heights of new buildings, decreases floor-to-ceiling heights in renovations. Will not support heavy floor loads.

5.E.5. Underfloor Raceways [†]

These are networks of small ducts located in or below concrete slabs in which are installed conductors that carry power, telecom, and signal wiring to outlets anywhere in the floor. If future requirements change, new inserts may be tapped to any duct in the slab and new outlets installed. These enclosures offer large conductor capacity, versatility, and flexibility in large open areas where wall outlets are not available. As the $2\frac{1}{2}$–5 in. poured concrete slab is a heavy dead load, these enclosures are usually integrated with structural floor systems, and the type that is selected generally depends on the floor system used. For example, *underfloor raceways* work best in poured concrete slabs in large one-story buildings, *cellular floor raceways* are compatible with structural steel, and *cellular concrete floor raceways* are appropriate for precast concrete slabs. With concrete raceways the ducting runs parallel to the structure, while in the other two systems ducting and structure are independent of each other. Underfloor raceways are further defined as *single-level* and *two-level*. In single-level

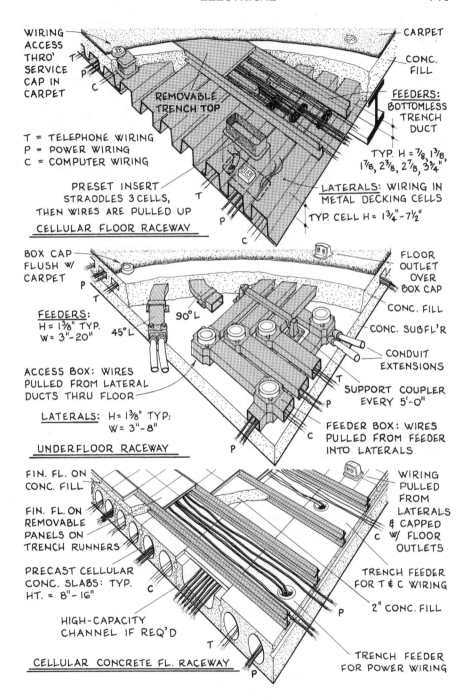

WIRING ACCESS THRO' SERVICE CAP IN CARPET

CARPET

CONC. FILL

FEEDERS: BOTTOMLESS TRENCH DUCT

REMOVABLE TRENCH TOP

T = TELEPHONE WIRING
P = POWER WIRING
C = COMPUTER WIRING

TYP. H = 7/8, 1 3/8, 1 7/8, 2 3/8, 2 7/8, 3 3/4"

PRESET INSERT STRADDLES 3 CELLS, THEN WIRES ARE PULLED UP

LATERALS: WIRING IN METAL DECKING CELLS

TYP. CELL H = 1 3/4" - 7 1/2"

CELLULAR FLOOR RACEWAY

BOX CAP FLUSH W/ CARPET

FLOOR OUTLET OVER BOX CAP

FEEDERS:
H = 1 3/8" TYP.
W = 3" - 20"

90° L

45° L

CONC. FILL

CONC. SUBFL'R

CONDUIT EXTENSIONS

ACCESS BOX: WIRES PULLED FROM LATERAL DUCTS THRU FLOOR

LATERALS: H = 1 3/8" TYP:
W = 3" - 8"

SUPPORT COUPLER EVERY 5'-0"

FEEDER BOX: WIRES PULLED FROM FEEDER INTO LATERALS

UNDERFLOOR RACEWAY

FIN. FL. ON CONC. FILL

FIN. FL. ON REMOVABLE PANELS ON TRENCH RUNNERS

WIRING PULLED FROM LATERALS & CAPPED W/ FLOOR OUTLETS

PRECAST CELLULAR CONC. SLABS: TYP. HT. = 8" - 16"

TRENCH FEEDER FOR T & C WIRING

2" CONC. FILL

HIGH-CAPACITY CHANNEL IF REQ'D

CELLULAR CONCRETE FL. RACEWAY

TRENCH FEEDER FOR POWER WIRING

Fig. 5-28. Underfloor raceways.

raceways the feeders and laterals are all on one level, a typical layout having shallow header trenches located under main hallways with the laterals branching into occupied spaces on each side. In two-level systems, feeders and laterals run 90° to each other on different levels and their crossings are junction boxes where the feeders subdivide.

Underfloor raceways are used in offices, museums, merchandising areas, and industrial facilities where large open floor areas have high-density power requirements that may change frequently. They offer more wiring and easier subdividing and are best for random furniture arrangements, but they require deeper concrete toppings and create heavier floors. In these systems location of electrical closets is critical.

➕ Large capacity, high versatility, little interference with other utility conveyances, allows flexible wall and furniture layouts, simplifies floor finishing. Wiring may be installed without waiting for erection of walls and installation of equipment and built-in furniture, which leads to shorter construction times. Good where occupancies require a high density of electric outlets in large floor areas and where furniture layouts change frequently.

➖ Expensive, often underutilized, usually low cost-effectiveness. Cannot be installed where corrosive vapors exist or in Hazard II and III occupancies.

5.E.6. Overhead Raceways

These enclosures are similar to raised access floors except the wiring arrives from above the ceiling instead of beneath the floor. The wiring is usually laid in wireways or cable trays, from which whips extend to ceiling light fixtures and downleads enter wall partitions below to switches, phones, computers, and convenience outlets. The wireways and cable trays must hang from the structure above rather than bear on the suspended ceiling below. Any part of the system is accessed by lifting the suspended ceiling's lay-in panels.

➕ Good where alterations involve extensive lighting changes and in large floor areas with many movable wall partitions. Good in renovated rooms with high ceilings.

➖ Ceiling-to-floor voids add to building heights. Impractical where most electrical outlets are floor-based.

Edition; McGuiness, Reynolds, & Stein (Wiley, New York, 1986); pp. 764-67.

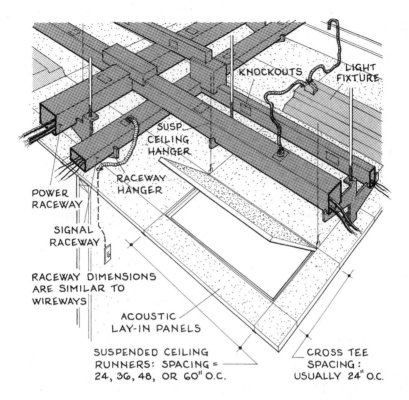

Fig. 5-29. Overhead raceways & suspended ceilings.†

Regarding the suspended ceilings beneath overhead raceways: these are constructed of inverted T-shaped *runners* that are tied to wires suspended from the structural ceiling, then slightly smaller *cross tees* are fitted between the runners and lightweight *acoustical panels* are laid upon the small shelves formed by the edges of the runners and tees. The runners are usually 10 or 12 ft long and are spaced 24, 36, 48, or 60 in. apart, and the usual cross tee spacing is 24 in. The runners may have end couplings that allow assemblies of long runs, grid adapters for direction changes in hallways and similar spaces, fittings for inclined and vertical installations, and thermal expansion couplings to keep them from elongating during fires. The panels have a variety of collars and trims for sprinkler heads, lighting fixtures, duct grilles, and other penetrations. Suspended ceilings may be installed only indoors and they have three structural classes: *light* (5–12 psf), *intermediate* (12–16 psf), and *heavy* (16 or more psf). They require lateral bracing and runner end abutments against enclosing construction in any dimension exceeding 24 ft.

† The information in this figure and related text was taken from the *Sweet's*

5.E.7. Manholes

In the old days, when most buildings were designed for specific occu-pancies and they contained no computers and much less wiring, the only manholes anyone knew of were the ones out in the middle of the street. But now that many commercial occupancies seem to change almost annually and each requires an ever-changing, ever-increasing amount of electric power, these round access holes and the chambers below often can be found at nearly every interior bend and intersection of large subterranean hall-ways lined with racks and trays and bundles of conduits. These enclosures have become so important that the NEC has begun to outline Code require-ments for their construction, and OSHA now classes them as underground confined spaces —which opens the door to a host of regulations in case their nature violates the spirit of wise design.

A manhole is essentially a very large pull box. Thus the principles that govern the design of a pull box govern the design of a manhole. Specifically, the chamber below each cover should have plenty of room inside for the end of a thick bundle of conductors to enter through a large conduit in one wall, turn as much as 180°, then exit through a large conduit in another wall. Thus each chamber should have a 2 ft wide entry/exit bor-der for the conductors plus space enough in the center for 2 workers, their toolboxes opened on the floor, an inspector, and space for coiling, bend-ing, pulling, and pushing each possibly wrist-thick bundle of power cables that customarily fill these rooms. Given the above specifications, it is hard to imagine a well-designed manhole being less than about 8 × 10 ft in size plus the thickness of its loadbearing walls. These spaces also require lighting, heating, cooling, and ventilation —which means lampholders, switches, grilles, and thermostats within easy reach and easy view. If the chamber is entered from above, the manhole cover cannot be directly above any conduits or equipment, and it must have a corrosion-resistant ladder whose rungs and rails do not obstruct the vertical projection of the manhole cover opening. If the chamber's access is through a wall-mounted door, this entry should be installed with panic hardware and swing out-ward. If the room contains any large equipment such as a transformer or switchgear, the doors must be wide enough to accommodate the unit's installation and removal. The ceilings may need to support vehicular traf-fic, the walls filled with conduit cavities must support the ceilings, the floors must support 120 psf of live load, and the clear height to the lowest ceiling projection including conduit supports should be 6'-8".

As for the old-fashioned manhole cover, modern technology has not improved on its design. Each should be at least 26 in. in diameter and round, as then if it slides it cannot fall through the access hole. (If the manhole is rectangular it must be at least 22 × 26 in. in size and have a restraining mechanism). A manhole cover typically weighs more than 100 lb,

its top surface is usually textured to be walked or driven on, and for security reasons it usually requires a proprietary tool to open.

> What is the minimum length and width of a rectangular manhole that
> houses 22 conduits whose largest diameter is 3 in. if all 22 conduits
> enter through one wall of the manhole, 12 of them exit through a sec-
> ond wall, and the other 10 exit through a third wall?

Solution: Sketch an interior elevation of the bank of conduits in each
wall, then note the number of columns and rows in each bank. Here the
bank of 22 entering conduits would likely have 4 columns and 6 rows, the
bank of 12 exiting conduits would likely have 3 columns and 4 rows, and the
bank of 10 exiting conduits would likely have 3 columns and 4 rows.

5JEJ7Ja]   **Length of manhole:** $L \geq \delta\,(\eta_{tot} + \eta_{out}) + \delta\,(c_e + c_x + r_e + r_x)$

    b]   **Width of manhole:** $W \geq \delta\,(\eta_{in} + \eta_{out}) + \delta\,(c_e + r_e)$

L = minimum length of rectangular manhole, in. $L \geq 96$ in.
W = minimum width of rectangular manhole, in. $W \geq 90$ in.
δ = largest diameter of all conduits in manhole, 3 in.
η_{tot} = total number of conduits entering manhole, 22
η_{out} = largest number of conduits exiting one wall of manhole. 12 con-
    duits exit thro' one wall and 10 thro' another wall ➡ $\eta_{out} = 12$.
η_{in} = largest number of conduits entering one wall of manhole. $\eta_{in} = 22$.
c_e = number of columns in largest bank of entering conduits, 4
c_x = number of columns in largest bank of exiting conduits, 3
r_e = number of rows in largest bank of entering conduits, 6
r_x = number of rows in largest bank of exiting conduits, 4

    Length of manhole: $L \geq 3\,(22 + 12) + 3\,(4 + 3 + 6 + 4) = 153$ in.
    Width of manhole: $W \geq 3\,(22 + 12) + 3\,(4 + 6) = 132$ in.

Note. The above dimensions may be adjusted slightly as long as their sums
$\geq$ the above total. For example, 160 × 128 in. is satisfactory; and these
numbers are also multiples of 16 in. and thus may facilitate construction.

5.F. SERVICE

Electrical service components include the entrance, meter, master
switch, circuit breakers, transformers, panel boards, onsite generators,
service heads to enclosures, conductor grounding, and related components. In small buildings most of these units are mounted on a small wall

Guide (Chicago Metallic Corp., Chicago, IL).

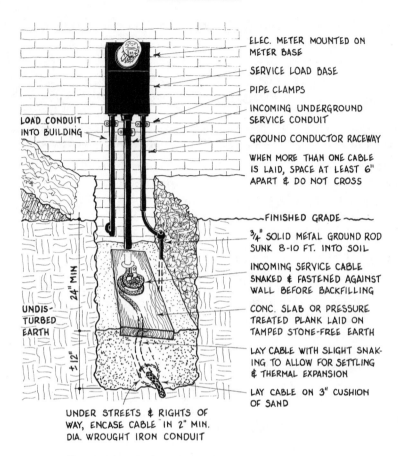

ELEC. METER MOUNTED ON METER BASE

SERVICE LOAD BASE

PIPE CLAMPS

INCOMING UNDERGROUND SERVICE CONDUIT

GROUND CONDUCTOR RACEWAY

WHEN MORE THAN ONE CABLE IS LAID, SPACE AT LEAST 6" APART & DO NOT CROSS

FINISHED GRADE

¾" SOLID METAL GROUND ROD SUNK 8-10 FT. INTO SOIL

INCOMING SERVICE CABLE SNAKED & FASTENED AGAINST WALL BEFORE BACKFILLING

CONC. SLAB OR PRESSURE TREATED PLANK LAID ON TAMPED STONE-FREE EARTH

LAY CABLE WITH SLIGHT SNAKING TO ALLOW FOR SETTLING & THERMAL EXPANSION

LAY CABLE ON 3" CUSHION OF SAND

LOAD CONDUIT INTO BUILDING

UNDIS-TURBED EARTH

24" MIN

± 12"

UNDER STREETS & RIGHTS OF WAY, ENCASE CABLE IN 2" MIN. DIA. WROUGHT IRON CONDUIT

Fig. 5-30. Underground service entries.

panel with an access aisle in front, just inside where the electric service conduit perforates the building envelope. In large buildings the same elements may require a large room comprising 2-3 percent of the building's total floor area, with ceilings 12–15 ft high and two or more exit doors. Whatever the extent of this equipment, it must be protected from excess humidity, dirt, dust, corrosion, and moisture during rainy weather; and the area just outside the electric service entrance should not be near sidewalks, driveways, garbage storage, chutes, awnings, shutters, gutter splash basins, water runoff from any area, or corrosive reagents. Indeed, such a seemingly innocuous arrangement as a clothes dryer vent emptying into smoggy urban air just above a patch of acidic soil can dissolve a nearby service entrance ground rod connection in a few months.

Typical underground and overhead service entries are shown in Figs. 5-30 and 5-31.

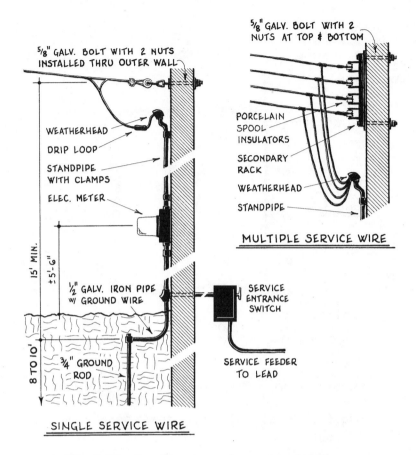

Fig. 5-31. Overhead service entry details.

6.F.1. Switchgear [†]

Also known as switchboards, load centers, panelboards, panel boxes, and fuse boxes, these enclosures receive power from utility grids or onsite generators, pass it through an entrance switch or main circuit breaker, then divide it into smaller blocks of power that are routed through easily accessible circuit breakers or other 'amptraps' before it is utilized on the premises. This componentry may be as small as a residential 'medicine cabinet' fuse box, or as large as several refrigerator-sized units placed side-by-side. In large commercial buildings, a primary load center is located just inside the service entrance, then satellite centers containing stepdown transformers are installed in electrical closets throughout the building. In apartments, shopping malls, and other multiple tenancies, a primary load center is placed after the main meter at the service

[†] Most of the information on uninterrupted power sources in this section was

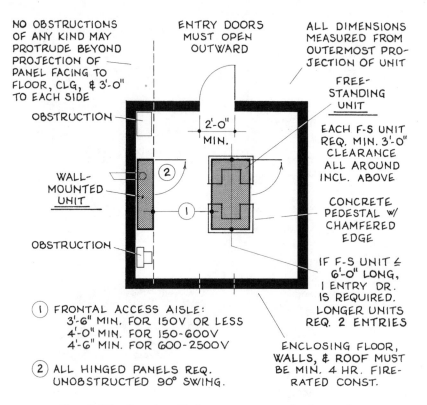

NO OBSTRUCTIONS OF ANY KIND MAY PROTRUDE BEYOND PROJECTION OF PANEL FACING TO FLOOR, CLG, & 3'-0" TO EACH SIDE

OBSTRUCTION

WALL-MOUNTED UNIT

OBSTRUCTION

ENTRY DOORS MUST OPEN OUTWARD

2'-0" MIN.

ALL DIMENSIONS MEASURED FROM OUTERMOST PRO-JECTION OF UNIT

FREE-STANDING UNIT

EACH F-S UNIT REQ. MIN. 3'-0" CLEARANCE ALL AROUND INCL. ABOVE

CONCRETE PEDESTAL W/ CHAMFERED EDGE

IF F-S UNIT ≤ 6'-0" LONG, 1 ENTRY DR. IS REQUIRED. LONGER UNITS REQ. 2 ENTRIES

① FRONTAL ACCESS AISLE:
   3'-6" MIN. FOR 150V OR LESS
   4'-0" MIN. FOR 150-600V
   4'-6" MIN. FOR 600-2500V

② ALL HINGED PANELS REQ. UNOBSTRUCTED 90° SWING.

ENCLOSING FLOOR, WALLS, & ROOF MUST BE MIN. 4 HR. FIRE-RATED CONST.

Fig. 5-32. Good switchgear access design: plan.

entrance, then satellite panelboards are mounted after the meters for each tenant. Also qualifying as switchgear are ground fault monitors, shunt filters that block harmonic distortions, and harmonic filters that keep distortions from re-entering the electron grid. Each unit should be dust-tight and leakproof, have welded seams and sealed surfaces that resist humidity and corrosion, contain audible or visual alarms that notify authorized personnel when a malfunction occurs, and have tightly fitting doors.

Wherever switchgear is located, no piping, ducting, or other mechanical equipment that is unrelated to the electrical unit's operation can be located within 6 ft above said electrical unit; unless the unit is protected from leakage, condensation, or breaks in said foreign equipment by intervening drain pans that extend the length and width of the electrical unit and empty into a plumbing waste drain.

Due to the vagaries of modern computerized technology, a particular switchgear accessory has evolved to maintain clean electron flow in a building's wiring: the *uninterrupted power source*, or UPS. Its dazzling array of functions is described below.

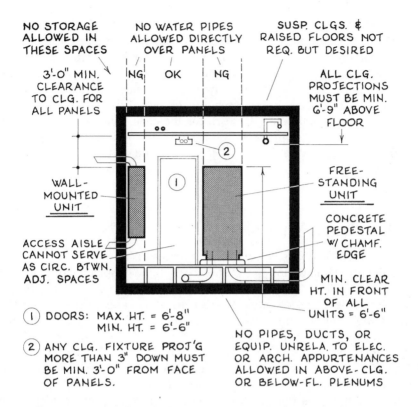

NO STORAGE ALLOWED IN THESE SPACES

NO WATER PIPES ALLOWED DIRECTLY OVER PANELS

SUSP. CLGS. & RAISED FLOORS NOT REQ. BUT DESIRED

3'-0" MIN. CLEARANCE TO CLG. FOR ALL PANELS

NG | OK | NG

ALL CLG. PROJECTIONS MUST BE MIN. 6'-9" ABOVE FLOOR

WALL-MOUNTED UNIT

FREE-STANDING UNIT

CONCRETE PEDESTAL W/ CHAMF. EDGE

ACCESS AISLE CANNOT SERVE AS CIRC. BTWN. ADJ. SPACES

MIN. CLEAR HT. IN FRONT OF ALL UNITS = 6'-6"

① DOORS: MAX. HT. = 6'-8"
   MIN. HT. = 6'-6"

② ANY CLG. FIXTURE PROJ'G MORE THAN 3" DOWN MUST BE MIN. 3'-0" FROM FACE OF PANELS.

NO PIPES, DUCTS, OR EQUIP. UNRELA. TO ELEC. OR ARCH. APPURTENANCES ALLOWED IN ABOVE-CLG. OR BELOW-FL. PLENUMS

Fig. 5-33. Good switchgear access design: section.

▶ It minimizes spikes, surges, dips, and brownouts in the power supply as well as isolates ground faults and lightning strikes.
▶ It allows maintenance on a single circuit or component without interrupting power to other circuits or equipment.
▶ Units typically have battery-packs that maintain power during short blackouts, then the batteries recharge when the power comes back on. Some have trend monitors that predict battery failure and LED displays that indicate remaining run time.
▶ Added control software can map displays of circuits, monitor performance of electric components, produce readouts of output waveforms in any conductor, activate audio and visual alarms when any malfunction occurs, download operational data for record-keeping and later analysis, and allow password-protected monitoring and operation from remote locations.

Uninterrupted power sources are efficient, quiet, and are made in attractive cabinets with space-saving footprints. Some cabinets provide frontal access to all interior components for servicing, which allows the unit to be tucked into a corner or squeezed between other equipment, while others are mounted on swivel casters that allow easy installation, servicing, relocation, and upgrading. Proper sizing is important, because each unit must be large enough to regulate the circuitry it monitors, but, since the units are expensive, overdesign wastes money. UPS systems are usually sized by a process known as balanced power design by highly specialized engineers who generally work for the companies that make the units. Typical capacities range from 10–1,250 kVA; and a large model may weigh 300–400 lb, have a footprint of 30 × 30 in, and be 60 in. high.

5.F.2. Transformers [t]

A transformer is a ferromagnetic core with a primary and secondary winding fitted into a tank-like casing in which the coupled windings, based on the ratio of their sizes, convert AC power from one voltage to another. In most buildings, *service transformers* are installed near the service entrance where they step the utility voltage down usually to 480 or 600 V; then *distribution transformers* in electrical closets step this down further to 120, 208, 240, or 277 V. Each unit has a nameplate rating based on its wattage capacity, which normally ranges from 5–500 kVA. Transformers whose capacities exceed about 750 kVA are usually found only in tall buildings, extensive industrial facilities, and electric utility substations. Single residences rarely contain transformers, as their voltage is usually stepped down by utility-owned bucket transformers mounted on neighborhood utility poles.

In large buildings the main transformer is generally the most vulnerable and costly component in the electrical system and the heaviest and most difficult to replace. The primary criterion for selecting one is the required input/output voltage and ampacity (anticipated load + small overload + potential load growth during next 20 years). Beyond this, selecting the proper unit for a given application usually involves a bewildering array of choices and tradeoffs, with a lot of bias thrown in by manufacturers and product literature. The following describes the essential design choices.

There are two types of transformers: *dry type* and *liquid type*. In dry type units, the core and windings are fitted into a metal casing which may be air-sealed, have louvers that allow natural ventilation, or include ducts through which flows cooling air driven by thermostatically activated fans. In liquid type units, the core and windings are fitted into a sealed metal casing filled with a dielectric liquid that insulates and cools the windings as well as protects them from moisture and corrosive air. A liquid type unit looks different than a dry type because its exterior has in addition to its input/output terminals a liquid level indicator, pressure gauge, relief valve, tem-

APC Product Brochure 996-0436 (American Power Conversion Corp., 1995).

perature gauges for each winding, drain tap, and a containment pan beneath the casing for catching any fluid leaks. Liquid type units cost more and must be enclosed by fire-resistive construction, but they run more efficiently, are quieter, cool better, and last longer. Although dry type units are generally about 95 percent efficient while liquid types approach 98 percent efficiency, with transformers a little efficiency goes a long way because they operate constantly and handle large loads; thus dry type units can build up a lot more heat in a small area, which can degrade wires and insulation and appreciably shorten the unit's life. Thus liquid type trannies are usually installed where constant-use loads more nearly match maximum loads and local utility rates are high. All transformer areas require thermostatically controlled air conditioning and ample ventilation; and where these loads are large, liquid type units are even more desirable. However, dry type units are the usual choice for installations of 500 kVA or less.

The next step in selecting a transformer is usually easy: copper or aluminum windings? Aluminum windings cost less and weigh less, but their lighter weight makes them bulkier, which has led numerous manufacturers to install copper and aluminum windings of equal capacity in the same casing; thus trannies of equal kVA capacity generally have the same footprint. This is normally all the selecting that is required for most commercial, institutional, and light industrial applications, aside from a few preferential details like finishes, shape aesthetics, and selection of controls.

The next step in selecting a transformer regards the possibility of its being exposed to any of the following conditions.

Harsh environments. This includes vapors, fumes, moisture, humidity, salt spray, airborne dust, and the like. The best transformers for such conditions are cast coil units whose cores and windings are cast in a protective layer of epoxy or polyester resin, which keeps the windings cooler and tends to hold them still during severe power jolts. Economical solutions for mildly corrosive environments are dry type units with sealed stainless steel casings. In harsh environments, all transformer leads and accessories must also be protected.

Excessively high temperatures. Ambient temperatures in transformer areas should remain between 0–100° F and not exceed 85° on a daily basis. Otherwise the best transformer is either a liquid type unit whose usual mineral oil fill is replaced by a heavy hydrocarbon, silicone fluid, or other high-heat-transfer liquid; or a dry type whose windings have class F (185° C) or class H (220° C) insulation. Standard winding insulation is Class B, which withstands ambient temperatures up to 150° C.

Excessive EMI in the building's electron grid. If the EMI is *transverse mode* (line-to-line), consider installing surge suppressors and harmonic filters before the transformer's inlet terminals. If the EMI is *common mode* (line-to-ground), place metal shielding between the two windings. If the common-mode EMI is severe, consider an *isolation transformer*, a unit whose primary winding is further separated from its secondary, or a *κ-factor rated transformer*, a unit that withstands the heating effects of EMI-infected current. In all cases, try to minimize the EMI before it ever arrives at the trannie with proper grounding and load-side power conditioners at all related electronic equipment.

Heavy initial loads. If initial loads such as surges from large motor startups or jolts from deep-welding operations are likely, the transformer should be securely mounted to inertia blocks and/or have epoxy windings that withstand the surge jolts.

Heavy use loads. If a transformer carries very heavy loads, its stepdown losses may be reduced by up to two-thirds if its standard silicon steel core is replaced with an amorphous metal core. However, these cores are cost-effective only for large liquid type units.

Highly variable loads. Transformers are most economical when they run at 80–100 percent of full load most of the time. Below this they operate less efficiently (then the next smaller unit should probably be installed); while above this they burn out faster (then the transformer area should either have air conditioning that keeps the windings cool or a low-temperature-rise unit whose windings are of larger wiring).

Other transformer concerns are:

Danger of fire. Because transformers can explode, they require fire alarms, mounted fire extinguishers nearby, and well-marked exits from the area. Indoor units must be enclosed by three hr fire-rated construction including doors, unless the area is protected by sprinklers, CO_2, or other approved fire suppressant; then the construction's fire rating may be 1 hr. All entry doors should have locks, be fitted with panic bars or pressure plates, and swing outward. Water fire suppression systems are acceptable for most transformers because their materials are mostly nonflammable and in a fire event the circuit breakers cut the power.

Voltage regulation. Where voltages vary and the transformer is large, it may require an *automatic tap changer*, a regulator that operates only when a voltage surge or sag occurs. If the voltage varies frequently and the trannie's load requires constant voltage, or where variable-speed, variable-lighting, or variable-heat control is required, a *variable voltage transformer*, a unit with a rotatable toroid winding that allows its primary/secondary ratio to fluctuate, may be installed.

Circuit breakers. Every transformer requires a source-side and a line-side circuit breaker to protect primary and secondary windings from overheating and degrading.

Single-phase wiring for three-phase units. Useful here is a *transformer disconnect*, which is a single-phase power electric outlet.

Location. Transformers are best located near their largest loads to

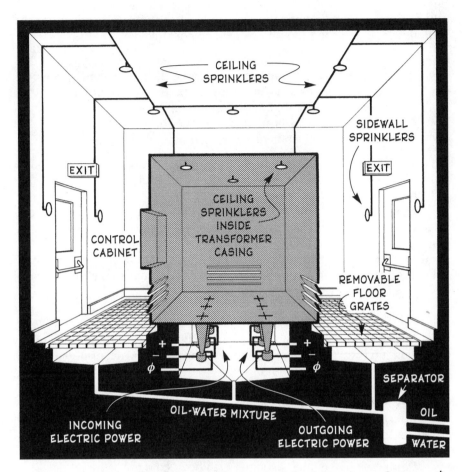

Fig. 5-34. Water fire suppression system for large transformers.[†]

reduce cable costs and line load losses. Units may be indoors or outdoors, on roofs, and against walls as well as on floors. When indoors, the floor area must pitch to a drain, and the main entry door should be wide enough for the unit to pass through if it needs to be replaced (it is wise to add 4–8 in. in case the unit is upgraded by a larger model). Since transformers have high centers of gravity, in seismic zones they require triple-strength anchorage and possibly diagonal bracing. Each unit should have a 3 ft access aisle on at least three sides, its weight should be added to its supports, and it should be located on the Plans. Outdoor units are typically placed in vaults surrounded by foliage, where they cost less, take up no building space, reduce noise indoors, and are easier to service.

Sound transmission. Most operating transformers emit a constant hum, which may annoy occupants. If a transformer is to be located near other occupied spaces, the loudness limits of the affected spaces should be determined and the following remedies undertaken:

▶ Select a transformer whose rated sound level according to Table 5-6 is 6 dB lower than the loudness limits of the adjacent spaces.
▶ Mount the transformer on isolation pads that minimize solid-borne sound transmitted to distant areas.
▶ Enclose the transformer in sound-attenuating construction.
▶ Select a unit whose coils are immersed in liquid or epoxy resin.

Rated lifespan. A transformer's normal lifespan is 20–40 years. Careful attention to load-matching profiles and vault area thermodynamics can make them last twice as long.

Energy conservation. Special energy-saving transformers are made whose coils are larger and more efficient. They are heavy, but have lower energy losses, minimum operating costs, and longer lives.

Ventilation. Transformers require about 100 cfm of air per kWh of net energy loss, and free net areas of inlet and outlet vents should generally be 1 sf per 100 kVA of rated capacity.

Common transformer accessories are:

▶ Lifting holes or hooks on unit that facilitate installation, relocation, and replacement if necessary. These may be accompanied by overhead trolley hoists.
▶ Internal lightning arresters.
▶ Key locks for casing openings.
▶ Internal thermostats that activate overheating alarms.
▶ Heaters that prevent condensation in the windings of units installed in humid areas or which may experience long shutdowns.
▶ Double-shell casings through which flows cold air.
▶ Rodent guards for open casings.

TABLE 5-6: TRANSFORMER SOUND LEVELS †

TRANSFORMER CAPACITY, kVA	Oil-immersed	Dry type, general purpose	Dry type, self-cooled ventilated	Dry type, self-cooled sealed
0–9	55	40	58	57
10–50	55	45	58	57
51–150	55	50	58	57
151–300	55	55	58	57
301–500	56	60	60	59
501–700	57	—	62	61
701–1,000	58	—	64	63

SOUND LEVEL, dB

May 1996, p. 34. † From p. 461: The source for this figure was Consulting-Speci-

▶ Special legs and bases for a variety of mounting situations.

Example 1. What is the optimal capacity for a transformer whose estimated building service load is 208 volts at 800 amps?

5) F) 2) 1) $833 \, \epsilon = V A$

ϵ = optimal power capacity or nameplate rating of transformer, **?** kVA. Solve for this value, then select from Table 5-7 the next highest transformer capacity.
V = voltage of transformer service load, 208 volts
A = amperage of transformer service load, 800 amps

$$833 \, \epsilon = 208 \times 800 \quad ... \, \epsilon = 200 \text{ kVA} \Rightarrow 225 \text{ kVA}$$

Example 2. What are the primary and secondary amperages of a 225 kVA 600 V delta/208 wye/120 V liquid-filled transformer?

Step 1. Find the transformer's primary amperage.

5) F) 2) 2) $1{,}000 \, \epsilon = \Phi \, V_p A_p$

ϵ = power capacity or nameplate rating of transformer, 225 kVA
Φ = phase factor, 1.00 if single phase, 1.73 if three phase. Nameplate notation contains a wye, delta, Δ, or $3\Phi \Rightarrow \Phi = 1.73$.
V_p = primary voltage of transformer, 600 volts
A_p = primary amperage of transformer, **?** amps

$$1{,}000 \times 225 = 1.73 \times 600 \times A_p \quad ... \, A_p = 217 \text{ amps}$$

Step 2. Find the transformer's secondary amperage.

$$971 \, \epsilon = \Phi \, V_s A_s$$

ϵ = power capacity or nameplate rating of transformer, 225 kVA
Φ = phase factor, from Step 1, 1.73
V_s = secondary voltage of transformer, 120 volts
A_s = secondary amperage of transformer, **?** amps

$$971 \times 225 = 1.73 \times 120 \times A_s \quad ... \, A_s = 1{,}050 \text{ amps}$$

Example 3. What floor area is required for the transformer in the example above if it is wall-mounted?

464

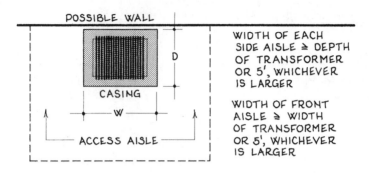

Fig. 5-35. Access aisles for wall-mounted transformer.

⑤Ⓕ②③ $A \geq (w + 5)(d + 3.5) \geq 30 \text{ sf}$

A = required floor area for wall-mounted transformer, ? sf

w = width of transformer, ft. From Table 5-7, w of a 225 kVA liquid-filled transformer = 3.33 ft.

d = front-to-back depth of transformer, ft. From Table 5-7, d of a 225 kVA liquid-filled transformer = 2.67 ft. Add 1.5 ft for floor-mounted units.

$$A \geq (3.33 + 5)(2.67 + 3.5) = 51 \text{ sf} \quad \ldots \oplus$$

TABLE 5-7: TRANSFORMER SPECIFICATIONS [1]

TRANSFORMER CAPACITY, kVA	Approximate size $h \times w \times d$, ft.	Approximate weight			
		Type 1	Type 2	Type 3	Type 4
10	1.25 × 0.83 × 1.00	165	180	200	230
15	2.25 × 1.67 × 1.33	220	240	260	300
25	2.50 × 1.67 × 1.67	245	280	310	400
50	3.00 × 1.67 × 1.67	350	400	450	600
75	3.50 × 2.50 × 2.00	475	600	700	900
100	4.00 × 2.67 × 2.50	650	720	1,000	1,200
150	4.00 × 3.00 × 2.50	800	1,100	1,100	1,500
225	4.20 × 3.33 × 2.67	1,030	1,300	1,450	2,100
300	4.67 × 4.00 × 3.00	1,450	1,800	2,000	3,000
500	5.00 × 4.67 × 3.00	2,100	2,550	3,100	4,400

Type 1. Dry type ventilated transformers, aluminum windings.
Type 2. Dry type ventilated transformers, copper windings.
Type 3. Energy-saving, nonlinear, control power, or shielded isolated trans.
Type 4. Non-ventilated, liquid-filled, or cast coil transformers.
   1. Dimensions & weights in this table are averages and do not apply to variable-voltage transformers. Consult mfrs. for more specific data.

and page unknown. † From p. 462: This table's data was abstracted from the

5.F.3. Onsite Generation

In many buildings, an on-premise method of generating electricity is required to satisfy the need for continuous power during any number of failure scenarios. The usual way to do this is to connect an internal combustion engine to a dynamo, then add a fuel tank and a means of exhaust. Such units are usually classed as small or large. Small units, commonly known as *portable standby generators*, are described in Sec. 5.F.3.a. Large units, often called *gensets*, are typically installed in hospitals and other occupancies where lives could be lost if the grid electrical system failed, and in hermetically sealed commercial buildings where a nonoperating HVAC system could cause the building's telecommunications equipment to fail within a short time. Since gensets are costly, one's electric load is usually only the portion of a building's load that is needed to maintain its critical operations if utility power is lost. Thus initial design involves anatomizing the building's most important electric loads as a way of determining which should be satisfied by each system, as outlined below:

Critical loads. These are loads which if not powered would compromise life safety, seriously damage process equipment, or cause great economic loss. These include emergency and exit lighting, fire and security system alarms, fire pumps, public communication, panic control, hospital life-support systems such as iron lungs and surgery anæsthesia applications, computer command centers, and orderly shutdown of other systems. These loads also include such 24/7 activities as industrial process equipment, "911" emergency centers, banking systems, global financial centers, telecommunication networks, and overnight delivery operations. For these loads generation must activate within 10 seconds after power is lost.

Essential or standby loads. These include systems or equipment whose operation is important to the occupants' welfare but not life-threatening. These include a building's general lighting where task lighting is lost, any refrigeration, most HVAC operation, water pumping/pressure maintenance, smoke removal, sewage disposal, and certain industrial processes. For these loads standby generation normally activates within 60 seconds after power is lost.

Nonessential loads. These include systems or equipment whose operation may seriously affect comfort but not production, such as general lighting where task lighting is on, storage and eating/coffee area lighting, entrance and reception area lighting, climate control of these spaces, and nonessential production operations.

Continuous production-related loads. These are loads that often draw steady power for more than three hours: e.g. HVAC operation, lighting, and continuous process operations.

Noncontinuous production-related loads. These are loads that vary according to periodic-duty cycles (presses, conveyors, grinders, etc.), intermittent-duty cycles (pumps, fans, etc.), short-duty cycles (overhead doors, elevators, etc.), and varying-duty cycles (welding operations, photo-copying, vacuuming, etc.).

Noncoincident production-related loads. These are dissimilar loads from a common outlet that are unlikely to be energized at the same time, which allows the lesser load to be ignored in system capacity calculations.

Large electric loads. When a large electric motor turns on, its high initial inrush current can cause a genset's starter contacts to chatter and its engine to stall due to insufficient acceleration torque. Such electric motors often require three times their normally rated power to keep their initial spikes from disrupting genset operation; thus if such a motor is a critical load, it may require a ramp-starting mode that greatly reduces its initial power surge.

After a generator's load is determined, in large buildings at least three units are usually installed: two to satisfy required load conditions at any time plus a standby unit in case of malfunction or maintenance. In any system the generated electricity must be separated from the utility power supply by parallel conductors, enclosures, and controls up to the hot-tie breaker; then the downstream power requires protective relays, bypasses, and synchronizing equipment to protect systems and personnel. The best systems also have autostarters, separate metering, output circuit break-ers, voltage regulators, and manual overrides that enable an operator to transfer utility power to generator power if he or she foresees a problem, such as anticipated repairs or the approach of a severe thunderstorm.

Almost as important as the nature of a genset's loads is the nature of the fuel one consumes. The three most common fuels a genset runs on are gasoline, diesel, and propane. Each is detailed below:

▶ **Gasoline.** This fuel is economical and easily available, its engines start better in cold weather, and the generators can be small; but gasoline storage for large systems is complex. First the fuel for each system must be stored in at least two tanks, each tank must large enough to satisfy the emergency demands of the total sys-tem, and each tank and its related components must be protected from ignition and impact loads. Each gasoline and diesel fuel tank must also have the following: a backup circulation pump in case the first pump fails, two trickle-circulation pumps for each tank to keep the fuel fresh when the generators aren't running (gasoline and diesel fuel grow stale after about a year's storage), a filter and water separator for each circulation pump, and a small water waste reservoir with a return fuel line to the main tank for each water separator. All gasoline and diesel fuel piping below grade must also be sleeved in containment conduit that drains into a reclamation reservoir, and this double plumbing must have hydro-

tor (McGraw-Hill, New York, 1995); p. 4.26.   † From p. 468: This figure was adapt-

carbon sensor wiring beneath it which extends beneath every tank to notify authorities of any leaks or spills.

▶ **Diesel.** This fuel is the least volatile of the three fuels, doesn't grow stale as fast as gasoline, and is cheaper than gasoline. Thus it is commonly used in large systems that are likely to run steadily. But diesel fuel has the same storage/circulation problems as gasoline and requires special starting below about 45° F. Thus it is **N2G** for outdoor installations in cold climates.

▶ **Propane.** Also known as LPG, this fuel is economical, burns clean, requires less engine maintenance, has no below-grade environmental liabilities, and since it is a pressurized gas it requires no pumps. But propane fuel tanks must be outdoors preferably well away from the building, the tanks require surer protection from impact damage than do gasoline reservoirs, their usually long fuel lines must be sized to minimize pipe friction losses as in any other plumbing, the fuel lines must also be sleeved in protective conduits (but they do not require reclamation reservoirs), the tanks and lines also require filters and water separators for removing contaminants and condensation from them, and any exposed components must be protected from inclement weather, corrosion, high heat, and vandals. Since propane leaks around the engine can cause its heavier-than-air vapors to cover the surrounding floor, the engine's floor must slope to vents that drain to lower levels outdoors or vacuum pumps must be installed, each entry door threshold should be at least two steps above the engine room floor, and the floors outside the entry doors cannot be at lower levels. Propane is also unreliable where earthquakes and other disasters could simultaneously interrupt electric and gas lines; thus in such areas propane cannot be stored onsite for large systems.

Occasionally an electric generator may be driven by a *gas turbine engine*. These are small and light and create minimum vibration; but they are slow-starting (which negates an often-important requirement of onsite generation), their operation emits a high-pitched whine, and their hotter and greater-in-volume exhaust requires larger and longer exhaust piping than do other systems. Two combinatory power sources are also feasible for certain occupancies: *cogeneration* and *synchronous generation*. Cogeneration involves jacketing the engine's cylinders and exhaust with a water or air circulating system that reuses the generator's usually 60–70 percent of its engine's fuel energy that is rejected as heat. Synchronous generation includes a sophisticated assembly of tandem generation, interactive governors, corrective condensers, and kvar regulators that produces clean power for circuits that may produce much reactive current.

from *Sweet's Catalog, 1981 Edition* (McGraw-Hill, New York); Sec. 16.3/Cat,

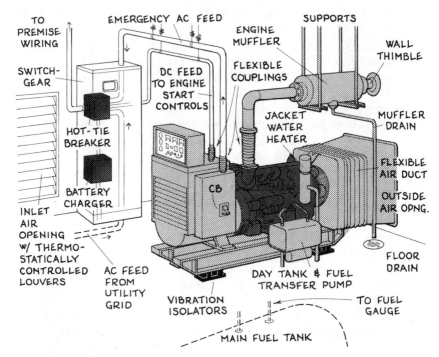

Fig. 5-36. Good onsite generator design. [†]

A few other important design considerations of on-site generators of electricity, whether they are large or small, permanently anchored or portable, are:

▸ **Access.** Each genset should have a 3–5 ft access aisle all around and be located near the incoming service and primary switchgear. At least one entry door should have vehicular access and be wide enough to replace the unit if necessary; or the engine room could have a knockout wall.

▸ **Vibration isolation.** This is essential under genset bases and at all incoming and outgoing lines, pipes, and ducts.

▸ **Air quality.** Adequate cooling and ventilation should flow through the entire engine room and around the genset and exit without recirculating. Heaters or dehumidifiers should be installed where moisture could collect in the generator windings.

▸ **Exhaust system.** As this can be noisy, hot, and deadly, each should contain no leaks, have floating supports that do not bear on the genset, enter the outdoors through a fireproof thimble, and never connect to another exhaust. Since sounds are magnified in the direction the outlet is aimed, the outlet should not

p. 11, prep. by Caterpillar Tractor Co.   [†] From p. 469: This figure was adapted

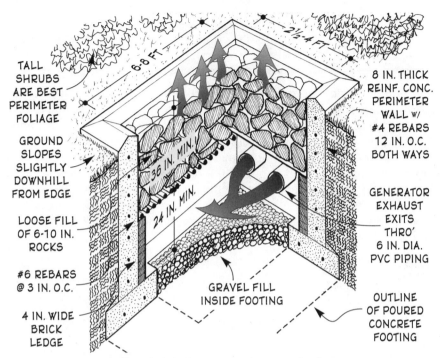

Fig. 5-37. Genset exhaust pit. [†]

face pedestrian areas or nearby windows or doors. Upward aim is **OK** if rainfall is kept out of the opening; and downward aim is **VG**, especially if it ends 1–2 ft above a drip drain concealed by foliage. In large buildings a genset exhaust outlet is usually a large reinforced concrete pit that muffles noise, safely disperses the exhaust fumes, and eliminates costly vertical piping to rooftops. One possible design is sketched in Fig. 5-37.

After the January 1994 earthquake in Los Angeles, an investigation was made of emergency generation performance in numerous local buildings. Why did some systems work and some fail?

Why they worked: Proper design and installation, adequate fuel supply, clean fuel, regular servicing and exercising under load, outdoor installation, oversized vibration isolator mounts, a protective steel canopy above the genset whose top sloped 30–45° toward one end.

Why they failed: Improper installation, lack of exercising, dead batteries, empty fuel tanks, old fuel, fuel contaminated with water or dirt, lines severed, pumps broken, filters clogged, hose and belt breakage, inadequate vibration isolators, equipment crushed or shaken apart, natural gas power supplied by local utility conduits. [‡]

from *Consulting-Specifying* magazine (Cahners Business Information, Des

470

Example 1. How much fresh airflow does a 50 kVA internal-combustion engine genset in a building in Dallas, TX, require for safe and efficient operation?

Solution: The engine requires air for carburetion and for cooling its radiator. The equation below combines both kinds. The cooling air is typically drawn through the radiator by a large engine-driven fan located behind the radiator; thus the engine's radiator end must be exposed to the incoming airflow, and after the air has flowed over the engine it must be induced to flow continually until it is out of the room. The engine's combustion air also must be piped safely out of the building via a sealed exhaust system.

Step 1. Determine the internal-combustion engine's carburetion and radiator airflow requirements.

5)F)3)a) $\qquad A \approx 156\ \Omega$

A = internal combustion engine's airflow requirements, **?** cfm
Ω = generating capacity of genset, kw or kVA. Ω = 50 kVA.

$$A \approx 156 \times 50 \approx 7{,}800\ \text{cfm}$$

Step 2. Determine the engine room's maximum cooling load from

$$\mathbf{C} \approx A\,(t_o - t_i) + 2{,}400\ \Omega$$

$\mathbf{C}$ = maximum cooling load of room in which genset is operating, **?** Btu/hr
A = airflow requirements of engine, from Step 1, 7,800 cfm
t_o = summer design temperature for location of occupancy, °F. From Fig. 2-25, summer design temperature for Dallas, TX = 100°.
t_i = desired indoor temperature of occupancy, °F. In an engine room during the summer, 82° is an acceptable temperature.
Ω = generating capacity of genset, kW or kVA. Ω = 50 kVA.

$$\mathbf{C} \approx 7{,}800\,(100 - 82) + 2{,}400 \times 50 = 260{,}000\ \text{Btu/hr}$$

Example 2. What size fuel tank should a 50 kW internal-combustion engine genset have? What size day tank should it have?

Step 1. Determine the capacity of the engine's fuel tank.

5)F)3)b) $\qquad C \approx 48\ \eta\ \kappa_{HP}\,\kappa_F\,\kappa_E\ \Omega$

C = optimal capacity of fuel tank for internal combustion engine, **?** gal
η = number of days between fuel delivery. Say the local fuel company's delivery schedule is every 7 days; then η = 7 days.

Plaines, IL); May 1998, p. 72. ‡ From p. 469: Robert Lawrie, "Generator Power

κ_{IP} = kilowatt-to-horsepower conversion factor. 1 HP = 0.746 kW.

κ_F = fuel consumption factor. Internal-combustion engines typically use about 0.047 gal/hr for each HP of engine.

κ_E = engine load factor. As internal-combustion engines are typically governed to run at about 85% of full capacity, κ_E = 0.85.

Ω = generating capacity of genset, kw or kVA. Ω = 50 kVA.

$$C \approx 48 \times 7 \times 0.746 \times 0.047 \times 0.85 \times 50 = 500 \text{ gal}$$

Step 2. Determine the capacity of the engine's day tank. This tank is usually located in the engine room near the engine and typically holds enough fuel to operate the engine for 4–8 hr at full load.

$$C_d \approx \eta \, \kappa_{IP} \, \kappa_F \, \Omega$$

C_d = optimal capacity of day tank for internal-combustion engine, ? gal

η = number of hours of engine operation supplied by day tank, hr.
Here let η = 6 hr.

κ_{IP}, κ_F, and Ω are as previously defined.

$$C_d \approx 6 \times 0.746 \times 0.047 \times 50 = 10.5 \text{ gal} \rightarrow 10 \text{ gal is OK}$$

5.F.3.a. Portable Generators [†]

These usually small generators are typically powered by an internal combustion engine and are used to produce electricity for residences and small commercial buildings during utility power outages. Each unit typically includes a small dashboard of controls and several 120 V and 240 V plug outlets, it can usually be carried by two or three people, and it is often mounted on wheels or skids to increase its portability.

Although a 1,500 watt generator can run one or two appliances at a time, serious installations begin at about 4,500 watts because it usually takes 3,500 watts to start a $\frac{3}{4}$ HP submersible water pump. Indeed, a 6 kW unit can usually power a water pump, refrigerator, microwave oven, a few lights, TV, and a computer; and a 10 kW unit can usually add to these loads a freezer, small hot water heater, and a few household circuits. Each unit must be connected to a panel box that has a *double-pole double-throw switch* (an ON-OFF-ON failsafe switch whose manual activation simultaneously cuts off the utility power grid as it opens the generator's circuitry); otherwise the generated electricity can rerout into the utility grid and possibly electrocute utility line workers. Each unit is usually electric-started by a small battery, the unit should be grounded to a $\frac{3}{4}$ in. copper rod buried at least 6 ft in the earth nearby, and all circuits served should be grounded through the generator to this rod. Each installation should have a wiring plan drawn that shows its componentry and the appliances it serves, and it should be installed by a licensed electrician.

Standby generators are not all independent luxury to a rural habitat. They can kill in two ways —by electrocution and by carbon monoxide poisoning; thus they must be carefully placed in dry well-ventilated areas. Never locate one in a basement or garage, no matter how open to the outdoors the installation may seem to be. One homeowner was killed by a garage-installed unit when, after he had carefully left the garage door open one night for ventilation, a strong wind blowing through the open garage door blew the kitchen-to-garage door wide open and the resulting draft carried the deadly fumes indoors. Thus these generators must not be placed near any exterior door, window, or vent. The noisy motor should also be placed on acoustic mounts in an acoustically sealed compartment and its noisy exhaust muffled. An economical acoustic mount can be made by cutting an old tire in half through its tread, then laying the two halves tread down on the floor beneath the generator. Another idea: mount near the generator a utility-powered light socket with a green light bulb that can be seen from indoors; then when the local power comes back on, the occupants will know even if the generator isn't running.

By the way, internal combustion engines are considerably less powerful at high elevations than they are at sea level; because the thin air is less able to drive the pistons inside the cylinders. One's power decreases to about 78 percent at 7,000 ft above sea level, 74.5 percent at 8,000 ft, 71 per cent at 9,000 ft, 68 percent at 10,000, and 61 percent at 12,000 ft.

5.G. NATURAL ENERGY

When it is uneconomical or unecological to obtain electricity from a public utility, the desired electrons may be generated onsite by wind, water, sunshine, or other locally available power. Such systems may be the result of the latest technical research, a fashioning of Third-World-style village technology, or simply a homemade contraption.

However, harnessing natural energy is not as easy as turning on a switch and settling into the old routines. First, all end-use applications should be highly efficient; because it doesn't make much sense to go to the trouble of setting up these systems if they must produce more-than-necessary energy to be useful. So natural energy use begins with building thickly insulated envelopes, using energy-efficient refrigerators and compact fluorescent light bulbs, and incorporating other energy-efficient measures and appliances into the occupants' patterns of electrical use. If the natural energy will be used to heat or cool interior spaces, the spaces them-

land Park, KS); Sep 1994, p. 75.   † from p. 417: Much of this section's information

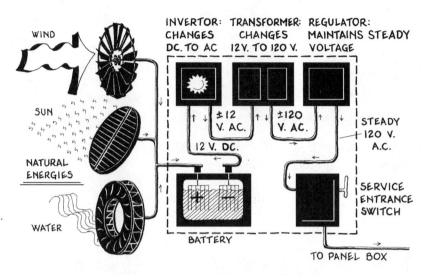

Fig. 5-38. Onsite generation of electricity.

selves must be efficiently designed —for in architecture the biggest ener-
gy-saver by far is maximum comfort in minimum volume. Second, home-made
kilowatts do not tend to arrive as continually and predictably as utility-
made ones. Of course, if the occupants have a backup, the only sign that
they might have run out of natural energy may be a click or flickering of the
lights as the circuitry transfers from one load to the other.

At a more detailed level, harnessing natural energy begins with (1) an
objective analysis of the site's feasible power potential (i.e. the energy's
ranges, patterns, maximums and minimums), (2) a list of every electrical
device the occupants plan to operate (this includes nameplate wattages and
expected hours-per-day each device will be used), and (3) matching the
site's feasible power potential with the occupants' energy use loads. If the
first item falls short of the second, a more practical energy use pattern can
be mapped out. One good strategy: design each system to satisfy a combination of *critical* (e.g. refrigerators and lamps), *convenience* (e.g. TV), and
intermittent (e.g. coffee maker) loads; then if possible or practical, use the
local utility grid as a backup. Since the naturally generated electricity is
first stored in batteries, this 'electron warehouse' must also be sized —
which not only involves determining the proper number of batteries but sizing the *inverters* that change the battery current from DC to AC, sizing the
transformers that produce the desired voltage, sizing the *regulators* that
maintain steady voltage under varying loads, arranging all this equipment
efficiently, and providing adequate access space around it. Finally, natural
energy systems are invariably plagued by a host of onsite problems such as
ice, dust, lightning, vibration, and even bullets —so a near-clairvoyant

thinking out in advance is often the most essential design skill that leads to a system's successful operation.

> **Average Daily Electric Load.** If the monthly utility bills of a family of four average $67.43 and the local cost of electricity is 7.25¢ per kWh, what is the household's total average daily electric load?

5]G]a]

$$\$ \approx 0.30 \, ¢ \, \epsilon_a$$

$\$$ = dollar amount of monthly electric bill, $67.43

¢ = local unit cost of electricity, cents/kWh. ¢ = 7.25.

ϵ_a = average daily electric load of occupancy, **?** kWh/day

$$67.43 = 0.30 \times 7.25 \times \epsilon \quad ... \, \epsilon_a = 31.0 \text{ kWh/day}$$

> **Critical Daily Electric Load.** What is a good ballpark estimate of the critical daily electric load for the household in the problem above?

5]G]b]

$$\epsilon_c \approx 1.5 \, \eta + 2$$

ϵ_c = critical daily electric load of occupancy: energy required to operate refrigerators, a few lamps, and essential electric appliances run by onsite generation systems, **?** kWh

η = number of occupants using the generated electricity, 4

$$\epsilon_c \approx 1.5 \times 4 + 2 \approx 8 \text{ kWh/day}$$

Note: This equation may be used to estimate the optimal size of a small generator for use in homes and small businesses during power outages.

5.G.1. Wind Power [†]

There are many ways to use a gust of wind to make a light bulb glow. In fact, a 1980 issue of *Wind Power Digest* analyzed nearly 50 different wind generators in that year alone. Little wonder, because wind power is a never-ending nonpolluting source of energy all over the world. On the minus side, the finest-made wind propeller can be at most only 59 percent efficient; because when the wind strikes the propeller blades, at least 41 percent of the energy is deflected outward as the blades are pushed around. These system's efficiencies are further lowered by similar imperfections in every other mechanical and electrical subcomponent. However, low machine efficiencies never stopped Henry Ford, whose automobile engines even today

Dec 1999/Jan 2000, pp. 97–101. [†] Much of this section's information was obtained

do not exceed efficiencies greater than about 30 percent.

Since a horizontal-axis-bladed wind generator mounted on a mast or tower is generally the most efficient and reliable method today, only it will be discussed further. One's components are described below.

Prop. This includes two or three long slender blades mounted on a horizontal axle to create a vertical disk area that intercepts the wind. Three blades are better, as they rotate faster in lower winds and run more smoothly in choppy or shifting windstreams. The blades should also have a feathering mechanism that changes their angles at high windspeeds (this lowers rpms and keeps the prop from self-destructing); and the prop requires a large tail vane to keep its disk area facing into the windstream as well as a 360° rotatable base.

Motor. This includes a gearbox that steps up the prop speed and an alternator —not a generator— that transforms the prop's shaft energy into useful electrons. Alternators are used because they require no brushes that must be periodically replaced and they operate at lower and variable rpms. For small systems a common car alternator works well, and its regulator can be used to maintain uniform voltage to the batteries. The motor should also have a load monitor that keeps the batteries from overcharging when too much power is produced and activates backup systems when too little power is produced.

Tower. This should rise at least 15 ft above any trees, rooftops, and other obstructions within a 300 ft radius. This tall narrow structure must support the full weight of the prop/motor assembly plus a 120–150 mph lateral load against the prop disk area, it must be climbable (and someone onsite must be able to climb it), its foundation must be at least 5 ft deep, and it should not be mounted on top of the building that houses the occupants' use of the generated energy.

Six mph is the minimum average windspeed for feasible generation of a wind prop, and 15–25 mph is optimal. If a wind generator operates only one-fourth of the time, it will still run more than 2,000 hr/yr; thus it requires lubricating and other frequent maintenance —usually at the top of the tower— if it is to provide long-lived high performance. Each prop/motor assembly should be easily shut off, have blade clearance from maintenance areas, and have no exposed shafts or other hazards.

A family has found their electrical energy use load to be 23 kWh/day average and 6 kWh/day critical. Near their residence is a hill which tests reveal has an average windspeed of 15 mph 40 ft above its crest. If the largest-diameter propeller that can be installed at this location is 16 ft, will these conditions allow the installation of a system that will satisfy the family's critical electric load?

from the *Energy Primer* (Portola Institute, Menlo Park, CA, 1974), p. 77-101.

Step 1. Compute the generating system's electric power potential. The formula below is for a wind generator whose mechanical and electrical subcomponentry is 70 percent efficient.

5)G)1)　　　　　　　　　　$5,900\,\Omega \approx \delta^2 v^3$

Ω = electric power potential of prop-driven wind generator, ? watts
δ = propeller diameter, ft. Use maximum feasible diameter of 16 ft.
v = average onsite wind velocity, 15 mph

$$5,900\,\Omega \geq 16^2 \times 15^3 \quad \dots \Omega \geq 146 \text{ watts}$$

Step 2. Compare the system's power potential with the occupancy's critical daily electric load.

$$\Omega \approx 42\,\varepsilon_c$$

Ω = electric power potential of wind generator, from Step 1, 146 watts
ε_c = critical daily electric load of occupancy, kWh/day. Solve for ε_c, then compare with given critical electric load = 6 kWh/day.

$$146 \approx 42 \times \varepsilon_c \quad \dots \varepsilon_c \approx 3.5 \geq 6 \Rightarrow \text{not enough}$$

Step 3. Estimate the cost of installing the wind generator, its tower, and battery storage system, then compare this total cost with the system's potential energy savings according to the payback span formula below:

$$\$ \approx S\,E_p$$

$\$$ = total cost of installation, ? dollars
S = annual energy savings due to installation, ? dollars
E_p = estimated energy payback span, years. If $E_p \geq 7$, system is feasible.

(No calculations due to lack of data)

5.G.2. Water Power [†]

A mass of water at an elevation above a given occupancy is one of the simplest and steadiest forms of potential energy. The central element of this conversion is a waterwheel or turbine, but several other components are just as important. Each is described below.

Dam. This is a barrier at least several feet high that is built across a stream to raise the height of its water level and direct its flow to a penstock, or outflow conduit, near the dam's upstream side. Its best plan shape is a horizontal arch whose crown faces upstream, as then the impounded water's pressure pushes the dam's usually earthen or concrete mass

---

[†] Much of this section's information was obtained from the *Energy Primer* (Portola

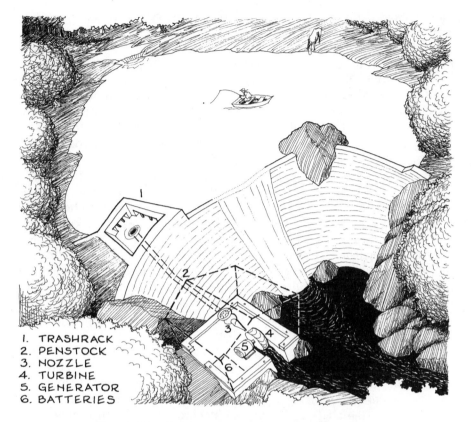

1. TRASHRACK
2. PENSTOCK
3. NOZZLE
4. TURBINE
5. GENERATOR
6. BATTERIES

Fig. 5-39. Water power generating system.

together, which imparts to these strong-in-compression materials a rational structural integrity and reduces the chance of leakage through them. The dam's crest should be much thinner than its base, its two ends should meet the banks on each side at an elevation above the stream's highest flood stage level, from one part of the crest should descend an outflow raceway (this carries the streamflow that normally doesn't enter the penstock), from another part of the crest should descend an overflow spillway (this carries infrequent floodwater flow safely over the dam), and both the outlet raceway and overflow spillway must be erosion-proof. Most important, the dam's mass must be heavy enough to remain firmly in place when the water behind it is at its highest level during the region's severest storms and floods. This mass must resist the impounded water by gravity and not lateral resistance, which requires that it be designed algebraically as described on page 481. A well-designed dam also has a gently sloping uphill face so any uprooted trees floating downstream during storms or floods will tend to slide over it instead of ram into it, and its base should have a large-

Institute, Menlo Park, CA, 1974), p. 52–76.

diameter pipe with a gate valve for draining the reservoir. Earthen dams must contain absolutely no organic matter and no boulders unless each one is separately pounded into the soil (otherwise a space will likely remain around where the boulder's usually round underside rests on the soil below and this is where leaks will likely occur). Clay usually forms good dams, but sand is terrible because it is porous. The impounded water's shoreline should be mapped and staked in advance with a surveyor's transit and all foliage and topsoil removed from the area within before it fills; and a settling pool should be located between the pond and its inlet with room alongside for a backhoe and dump truck to enter and periodically remove accumulated sediment. Dam design is described in greater detail on pp. 480-2.

Aside from generating electricity, the impounded reservoir can supply water to the occupants, reduce the effects of downstream flooding and erosion, and be used for swimming, boating, fishing, fire protection, irrigation, and watering livestock. Drawbacks of dams are their usually high cost, initial environmental destruction on and around them, inlet siltation, and tendency to raise the water table around the shoreline, which may be desirable. Since dam building is a serious matter, the environmental impact of each on its site and surrounding environs must be thoroughly assessed in advance. This includes investigating any riparian and appropriative rights as well as all local water use regulations.

Penstock. This is the pipe that carries the water from the top of the dam to the bottom of the turbine: this is what transforms the site's potential energy into kinetic energy. Its upper end is usually a screened trashrack that keeps debris out of its opening, and its bottom is fitted with a nozzle that squeezes the power of the aqueous energy into a much smaller area, thus magnifying the impact load that strikes the turbine blades. The penstock should be as short and as vertical as possible (if more than 50 ft long its diameter should be sized in terms of flow friction losses), it should have a valve along its length, and any bends should have large radii. Where prolonged freezing temperatures are likely, the conduit must be insulated, heated, or buried underground. Its opening should be located below the deepest level of ice formation in winter, which, depending on the water moving around it, is usually about one-third the local frost depth.

Instead of a penstock, some water power systems have an open channel or millrace that conveys the aqueous energy to a large wheel, like the old millwheels. This componentry is desirable for large streams with low heads. Waterwheels cost more, but they pack a lot of inertial energy. They are usually about 65 percent efficient, and there are three kinds: *undershot* (best for waterflows with little head), *breast* (good for 3–10 ft heads), and *overshot* (good for 10–30 ft heads).

Turbine. This is a small-diameter wheel with cylindrically arranged fins or blades that receives the water from the nozzle and converts its vertical head pressure into rotational energy. Thus the horizontal axis of the water's contact against the blades marks the lowest level of the water's head. Each turbine should be encased in a housing because its high turning speeds (often 1,000 rpm) can be dangerous. The most efficient turbine is usually a Pelton wheel; at heads of 50 ft or more, no other turbine is as effective. A turbine can be made by a local welder, but this precisely-made component is usually purchased from a manufacturer.

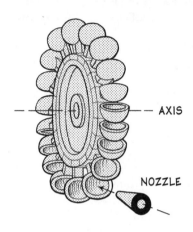

Fig. 5-40. Pelton wheel.

After the power water strikes the turbine blades, its tailwater should flow quickly and freely downstream. The more the water lingers around the blades, the more it is apt to slow them down. The turbine should also be mounted as low as possible to maximize the system's head yet its blades' tips must clear the tailwater's highest annual level. A good design: install 'double-spoon' blades that deflect the nozzleflow to the sides, provide ample room on each side of the whirling blades for the tailwater to flow away, and have the dam's outflow pass alongside the turbine to help pull the tailwater quickly downstream.

Generator. This is a wired armature and stator that converts the turbine's rotational energy into electricity. One's design usually involves determining the turbine's speed, then selecting a gearbox that speeds up the turbine to 3,600 rpm or 1,800 rpm if the electricity is 60 Hz. 1,200 rpm, 900 rpm, and even 600 rpm generators are available, but they usually cost more per kilowatt generated. As the generator rarely turns uniformly at its design speed, it usually has a regulator that maintains uniform voltage.

A water turbine can generate much electricity from little waterflow, especially if the flow is steep. In fact, a waterflow of only 1 cfs can often generate more than what one household needs. Such generation is virtually pollution-free, produces virtually no waste, and 80–90 percent of the nozzleflow can be converted to rotational energy at the turbine shaft. Such production is most feasible in hilly country with mild wet climates, and is least feasible in flat dry country with long cold winters. Chief design strategies are (1) maximize the head, (2) minimize the cost of the dam and length of the penstock, and (3) minimize ecological disruption around the installation. As the waterflow of many streams vary greatly after storms and from season to season, the designer should know the site's lowest and highest waterflows and water levels. Also, an acre-ft of water will provide a steady-state waterflow of 1 cfm for 30 days not counting water loss due to evaporation.

A family of five in western North Carolina plans to install a water turbine on a swiftly flowing stream near their house. They have found
their daily electricity usage to be 47 kWh average and 9.5 kWh critical, and have determined that they can create a 46 ft head by building
a small dam at the top of a steep fall and piping the water to a generator at the bottom. If the stream's rate of flow during late summer, usually the time of lowest water, is only 2 ft³/sec, will this be enough to
satisfy their electrical demands?

Step 1. Compute the generating system's electric power potential.

5)G)2) $660\ \Omega \approx H\mathcal{E}V$

Ω = electric power potential of water generator, **?** kWh
H = head or vertical distance of waterflow between its crest and striking of turbine, 46 ft
$\mathcal{E}$ = efficiency of generating system, equals efficiency of each separate
component of system multiplied together, %. In lieu of more definitive data, 45% is a good initial working number.
V = volume of waterflow that strikes turbine, 2 cfs

$$660\ \Omega \approx 46 \times 45 \times 2 \quad ... \Omega \approx 6.3\ \text{kWh}$$

Step 2. Compare the occupancy's daily critical electric load with the system's electric power potential.

$$\mathcal{E}_c \leq 24\ \Omega$$

$\mathcal{E}_c$ = critical daily electric load of occupancy, kWh/day. Solve for $\mathcal{E}_c$, then
compare with given daily critical electric load = 9.5 kWh/day.
Ω = electric power potential of water generator, from Step 1, 6.3 kWh

$$\mathcal{E}_c \leq 24 \times 6.3 = 151\ \text{kWh/day} \geq 9.5 \rightarrow \text{way OK}$$
... much more than daily needs

Step 3. The family should compare the system's total cost to its potential
energy savings according to the energy payback formula described in Sec.
5.G.1. before proceeding with construction.

After the water-powered generating system has been sized, the dam
must be designed. The prime consideration is that the gravity load of the
dam's weight must be at least 1.5 times the lateral load of the impounded
water. The dam is usually designed by drawing a tentatively assumed section through the dam's deepest part, then proceeding as described below.

Step 1. Find the area of a section through the dam as shown in Fig. 5-41.

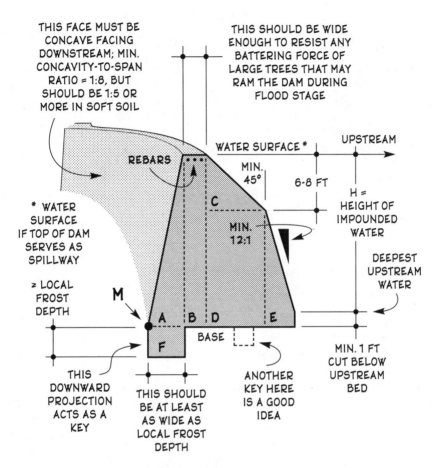

THIS FACE MUST BE
CONCAVE FACING
DOWNSTREAM; MIN.
CONCAVITY-TO-SPAN
RATIO = 1:8, BUT
SHOULD BE 1:5 OR
MORE IN SOFT SOIL

THIS SHOULD BE WIDE
ENOUGH TO RESIST ANY
BATTERING FORCE OF
LARGE TREES THAT MAY
RAM THE DAM DURING
FLOOD STAGE

WATER SURFACE *

UPSTREAM

REBARS

MIN.
45°   6-8 FT

H =
HEIGHT OF
IMPOUNDED
WATER

* WATER
SURFACE
IF TOP OF DAM
SERVES AS
SPILLWAY

C

MIN.
12:1

DEEPEST
UPSTREAM
WATER

≥ LOCAL
FROST
DEPTH

M

A B D   E

BASE

MIN. 1 FT
CUT BELOW
UPSTREAM
BED

THIS
DOWNWARD
PROJECTION
ACTS AS A
KEY

F

THIS SHOULD
BE AT LEAST
AS WIDE AS
LOCAL FROST
DEPTH

ANOTHER
KEY HERE
IS A GOOD
IDEA

Fig. 5-41. Section through dam showing design criteria.

Step 2. Find the center of gravity of the dam's section.

Step 3. Find the hydrostatic pressure of the impounded water against the dam's upstream side according to

5)G)2)a) $P_w \leq 0.5\ w\,h^2$

P_w = total pressure of impounded water against full height of dam, lb
w = unit weight of water, 62.4 lb/cf for fresh water
h = height of dam, ft

Step 4. Since the dam's total weight should be at least 1.5 the total hydrostatic pressure of the impounded water against the dam's upstream face, investigate the dam's weight/pressure resistance ratio by taking moments about point M in Fig. 5-41 as follows:

$$\Sigma M_{dam} \geq 1.5 \, \Sigma M_{water}$$

ΣM_{dam} = sum of moments of dam: unit weight of dam × area of maximum section × length of section's moment arm. This formula is usually solved for the dam's area of maximum section; then the area's longitudinal dimension is lengthened if the formula is not satisfied.

ΣM_{water}= sum of moments of water: total pressure of water against dam [P_w from Step 3] × length of water's moment arm

Step 5. Find the minimum soil pressure beneath the dam that is required to support it according to

$$f_b \leq W/A + M/S$$

f_b = actual unit bearing load of dam upon underlying soil, psf. This must ≤ safe unit bearing strength of underlying soil. If not, the dam's base must be enlarged.

W = total weight of 1 ft wide strip of dam at its thickest part: this equals area of maximum section thro' dam × unit weight of dam's mass, lb

A = area of 1 ft wide strip of dam at its thickest part: this equals length (ft) of dam's maximum section as described in Fig. 5-41 that contacts the underlying soil, sf

M = net moment of 1 ft wide strip of dam at its thickest part as described in "W" above (this moment is taken at point N in Fig. 5-41 and is the weight of the maximum section × its moment arm + weight of water pressing against the section's upstream face × its moment arm), ft·lb

S = horizontal section modulus of 1 ft wide strip of dam at its thickest part as described in "W" above (the section's axis of moments passes thro' its base at point N in Fig. 5-41), ft³

Note: This minimum pressure occurs at point M, but since the actual pressure prism of the soil beneath the dam is trapezoidal, the allowable soil pressure gradually becomes slightly less toward N. But here it is a good idea to use the prism's "maximum minimum soil pressure" as the design pressure for all the soil beneath the dam as an added safety factor.

5.G.3. Photovoltaics [†]

Imagine having sheets of windowglass which when exposed to the sun produce electricity. Due to recent developments in photovoltaic technology, this is now available. One kind is a thermopane-like glazing that contains

---

[†] Much of the information for this and the following section was abstracted from

grids of hair-like wires between its two panes and has electrical contacts at two opposite corners that allow the wire grids to be connected together, then shallow mullion caps fit over the adjoining panes' seams and contain the wires extending along the panes' edges. This glazing, which looks like deeply tinted glass, also allows the passage of daylighting, which makes it a superb skylighting. Although the panes can't be cut onsite, they can be manufactured in any size; thus they can be made to fit the shape of the architecture instead of the other way around. Similar technology has spawned solar-absorbing spandrel glazings and sheet metal panels that can be installed as curtain walls, roofs, awnings, sunscreens, and other envelope constructions. Companies have also begun plastering silicon cells on all kinds of roofing materials —tab shingles, roof tiles, selvedge edge-like strips, and standing seam metal roofing. Hundreds of these "sunslates" wired together have actually started to eliminate a few homeowners' electric bills. Another innovation is 2 × 5 ft silicon-cell sunscreens mounted above windows, where they collect the sun's energy and keep heat out of indoor spaces. All these magnetic wave pumps can work on any building surface, horizontal or vertical. Some are assembled in small groups with easily pluggable connectors, like Christmas tree lights, while others are wired together one unit at a time; and some systems perform better in heat while others work better in cold. In most installations the current flows to sub-array collector boxes and then to telecom closet-like PV equipment rooms. Altogether these products are a fine way to use sunlight to freeze meat.

A few public utilities are also trying to make silicon cells affordable to homeowners and small business operations. For example, Arizona Public Service will equip homeowners in off-grid areas with a ground-based array of photovoltaic or PV panels that will produce enough power for most domestic uses, a generator that runs when the sun won't shine, and a propane tank that fuels the generator.[†] Someday such systems may run everything in a house *and* produce enough energy to run an electric car battery.

Unfortunately, this wondrous technology has its drawbacks. One is that it usually takes someone with the combined talents of a roofer, glazier, and electrician to install these systems. Another is that PV cells take a lot of energy to make —often more than they can collect in 50 years of operation, which is reflected in their high pricetags. Another is that even the best silicon-cell technology available today is still only about 15 percent efficient. Even the systems leased by Arizona Public Service end up costing their users about a dollar per kilowatt-hour produced. Thus while PV technology holds great promise, it is a movement that is in need of a breakthrough. Until then their most cost-beneficial applications are limited to off-the-grid installations such as billboards, railroad signals, vehicle traffic counters, highway lighting, and bus stop shelter lighting. Now if someone will only find a way to make electricity from chlorophyll ....

Another problem with photovoltaic cells is that their ratings are

(1) John Wiles' "Photovoltaics: Electrical Power from Sunlight": *EC&M* maga-

often misleading. Many have a generic watts-per-day rating, e.g. 14 W/sf·day; but a PV array with such a rating would produce nowhere near as much electricity per day in Alaska as it would in Arizona. Thus a PV cell should be rated in terms of the watts/sf it produces *per hour of exposure to full direct sunlight*, which often is more like 2 W/sf.

The power produced by PV cells is direct current, which in some small-scale settings is desirable. The current may be *direct-drive* (power flows directly to electric loads), *battery storage* (power flows into batteries where it is stored for later use), or *grid* (any excess power produced feeds back into the utility grid). Most systems run on combinations of these currents. Each PV system usually requires the following:

Batteries. These reservoir the collected electrons for later use on the premises. They are described more fully in Sec. 5.G.4.

Controllers. Sensitive electronic devices that prevent over- or under-charging of the batteries. They are 60–80 percent efficient, and each unit should have a current-limiting circuit breaker.

Inverters. These convert DC current to AC. Units for stand-alone systems are available from 100–5,000 watts and are 70–95 percent efficient, while ones for grid systems are available from 1,500 to as high as 300 kWh and are 85–95 percent efficient.

Regulators. These maintain even voltage to the electric loads. They are around 95 percent efficient.

A photovoltaic installation should ideally receive a high percentage of sunshine all year round and its surface should have unobstructed access to solar trajectories where they are at least 15° above the horizon.

A lawyer in Durango, CO, plans to build a small house on his property located in the San Juan Mountains 40 miles north of the city. As his land has no electricity and the local utility would charge $65,000 to run it in from the nearest lines four miles away, he plans to install photovoltaic cells on the house's roof. The cells will collect energy all week long and dump the wattage into storage batteries for use during the weekend, and he estimates that two occupants will need 5 kWh during this time to enjoy a pleasant Spartan life at his mountain hideaway. If the sun shines about 70 percent of daylight hours in this area and the site is 7,800 feet above sea level, what is the optimal area of the PV cells mounted on the roof?

5]G]3] $100\ \epsilon_c \approx \Phi\ \kappa_c\ \kappa_u\ \Omega\ A\ \rho^{0.7}\ (1 + 0.000014\ E)$

ϵ_c = critical electric load of occupancy, watts. At an estimated
       25 kWh/weekend, 5 × 1,000 = 25,000 watts.

zine (Intertec Publishing Co., Overland Park, KS); Aug 1994, p. 77; and (2) "Photo-

Φ = incident clear-day insolation on a surface perpendicular to sun-rays at location of PV array. From Table 2-10, Φ for Durango area at 37° N. latitude ≈ 1,710 + $^5/_8$ (1,870 – 1,710) = 1,810 Btu/day. Also from Table 2-10, optimal ∠ of collector surface from horizontal = 37 + 20 = 57°.

$κ_c$ = cloudiness coefficient: site's average percentage of sunshine received ÷ 100. From local climatic data, S_p ≈ 70% ➡ $κ_c$ = 0.70.

$κ_u$ = umbra fraction: portion of collector surface that is shaded during the day. In lieu of more articulate data, assume the panels are exposed to sunlight all day long. Thus $κ_u$ = 1.00.

Ω = generating efficiency of photovoltaic cells, %. Use 12%.

A = required area of photocell panels, ? sf

ρ = ratio of days of energy collected to days of energy used. ρ must ≥ 1.0. This usually = 1.0; but here, as occupancy will be used approximately 2.5 days/week compared to 7 days/week collected, ρ = 7/2.5 = 2.8.

E = elevation of site above sea level, ft. E is given as 7,850 ft.

$$100 × 25,000 ≤ 1,810 × 0.70 × 1.0 × 12 × 2.8^{0.7} × A (1 + 0.000014 × 7,850) \quad ... A ≥ 72 \text{ sf}$$

5.G.4. Battery Storage

A battery is a reservoir of electrons that allows electricity to be collected at different times than when it is consumed. This is especially desirable where electricity is produced by sun, wind, and water; since power from these sources is usually highly variable and often little correlation exists between periods of production and use. Storage batteries also allow electricity to be drawn from the utility power grid during daily off-peak hours when electric rates are significantly lower so it can be used later when the rates are higher; and they can provide uninterrupted electricity when the utility power fails. The latter installations are more numerous than one may think. For example, only 3 miles from the author's home is a supermarket-sized building filled with hundreds of suitcase-sized batteries, which NYNEX uses to keep local telephones operating if the utility power fails. Buildings like this, erected decades ago, are all over America today. Obviously the technology involved is advanced and widely available.

Three general kinds of batteries are used for onsite storage of electricity, as described below:

▸ **Flooded lead-acid deep cycle.** These batteries are often used in golf carts and fork lifts. Low initial cost, relatively short life.

▶ **Sealed maintenance-free lead-acid.** They cost a little more, but last longer when the depth of discharge is not severe.

▶ **Nickel-cadmium.** High initial cost, high performance, long life.

As hydrogen off-gassing from charging batteries is flammable, every battery storage area requires ventilation; but then in cold weather a conflict arises between adequate ventilation of the area and optimal cell operating temperatures of usually 77°± 5°. One solution: locate the batteries in a perennially cool area, heavily insulate the battery enclosure on all sides, add a sloping ceiling, at the ceiling's peak install a common plumbing sink trap upside-down that allows the lighter-than-air hydrogen to escape outdoors, cover the trap's inverted opening with insect screen, and locate a small thermostat-operated heater set at 72° beside the batteries.

Since a battery's current is DC while AC is used in building occupancies, and since DC current travels through the wire while AC travels on its surface, DC and AC conductors require different wiring sizes, switches, and circuit breakers for the same voltage and amperage. DC outlets also have polarity (the two prongs must always be inserted –/– and +/+ for the juice to flow) while AC outlets do not. Finally, most batteries tend to hold a charge for lesser lengths of time as they grow older; thus each usually has an optimal replacement time near the end of its rated life.

An array of photovoltaic cells mounted on a small house 40 miles north of Durango, CO, requires batteries for storing the week's collected electrons for weekend use. If the owner uses standard 6-volt golfcart batteries rated at 220 amperes each, how many batteries are required. For data reference, see problem in Sec. 5.G.3.

Step 1. Find the required capacity of the battery storage system.

5)G)4) $$ C \approx 800\ \epsilon_c\, \rho\, (100/\kappa_g)^{1.6} $$

C = required storage capacity of batteries, ? watts
ϵ_c = critical daily electric load of occupancy, kWh/day.
　　As total energy used = 5 kWh/weekend and 1 weekend ≈ 2.3 days,
　　ϵ_c = 5/2.3 ≈ 2.2 kWh/day of residence.
ρ = ratio of days of energy collected to days of energy used. From
　　Example 5.G.3., if energy collected over a period of 7 days is consumed during a weekend (≈ 2.3 days), R = 7/2.3 = 3.0. For continuous-use systems, ρ = 1.
κ_g = generation factor: average percent of time that system generates
　　energy during desirable climatic conditions. κ_g ≈ 75% for wind
　　generation, 95% for water generation, and % of average local sunshine for solar generation. From Example 6.G.3, κ_g = 70%.

$$C \geq 800 \times 2.2 \times 3.0 \times (100/70)^{1.6} \geq 9{,}300 \text{ watts}$$

Step 2. Compute the number of batteries required for the system.

$$C = \omega\,\eta$$

C = required storage capacity of batteries, 9,300 watts

ω = unit storage capacity of each battery, watts. ω for batteries rated at 6 volts and 220 amps = 6 × 220 = 1,320 watts.

η = minimum number of batteries required, ? units

$$9{,}300 \geq 1{,}320 \times \eta \qquad ... \eta \geq 7.1 \Rightarrow 8 \text{ batteries}$$

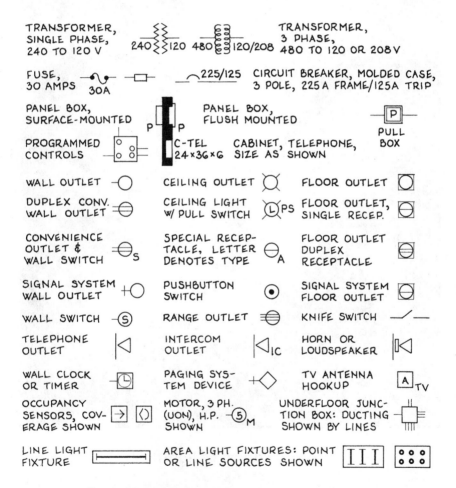

Fig. 5-42. Additional electrical plan symbols.

† From p. 483: *The New York Times*; Sep 23, 1999; p. F4.

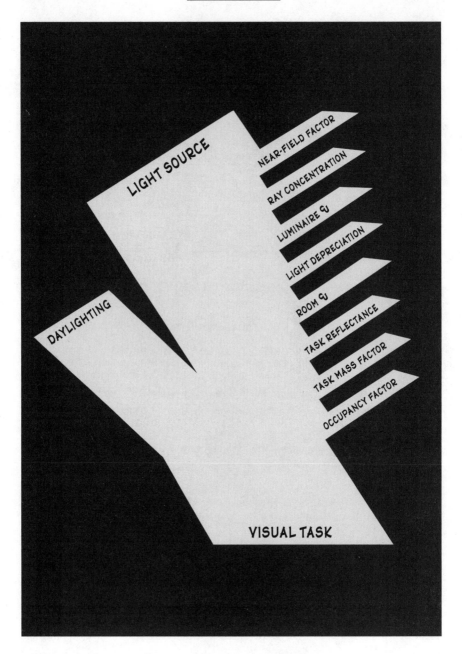

The variables of lightflow

ILLUMINATION

6.A. GENERAL

The manner in which a space is illuminated has a noted effect on its use and character. Even in ordinary architecture, advanced lighting methods as clerestory windows, occupancy sensors, return-air troffers, daylight harvesters, and skylights containing translucent insulation can pay for themselves quickly in terms of increased productivity, enhanced occupant morale, and lower life cycle costs. Good lighting can also make a space look larger; thus it is further economical in terms of the illusory area it seemingly adds to a space. Good lighting is also efficient, calms the psyche, and enhances the architecture without bringing attention to itself.

Although illumination design centers around computing lighting loads, this work involves very much more. This was well-described by a leading illumination authority, Louis Erhardt, when he said:

> Lighting does more than illuminate "to make visible." It sets the appropriate adaptation, adds to clarity or creates illusion, and leads the eye and the mind to the scene's salient features in an orderly, composed fashion. The purpose of lighting is to achieve the desired atmosphere and inspire a response, mental or emotional, in keeping with the space and the activity. [†]

Due to the complexities involved in lighting design, when employing any rule of thumb it is wise to remember the ancient maxim of Alexander the Younger: All generalizations are dangerous, even this one.

6.A.1. Light [†]

Every light source has an arriving energy or *input*, and an exiting energy or *output*. With natural light the sun's energy arriving at the outer surface of a window or skylight is *insolation*, measured in Btu/hr, and the

---

[†] Louis Erhardt, "Views on the Visual Environment"; *LD + A Journal* (Illumina-

portion of luminous energy that passes through the glazing and enters indoors is *output*, measured in footcandles (fc). With artificial light the electrical energy entering a lamp is *input*, measured in watts (W), and the portion of luminous energy leaving the lamp is *output*, measured in lumens (lm). With natural or artificial light, the output radiates from the source until it reaches a visual task where the amount of arriving light is *illuminance*, measured in footcandles (fc), and the portion of light reflected from the visual task is *luminance*, measured in footLamberts (fL), which is the light that enters the eye. When 1 lm of light strikes 1 sf of 100 percent reflective area 1 ft away at right angles, 1 lm of output = 1 fc of incident light = 1 fL of reflected light. This is the "1 = 1 = 1" rule of lighting design.

The basic algebraic relation between the luminous flux leaving a light source and the amount arriving at the visual task is:

$$\diamondsuit = \Phi \, D^2$$

$\diamondsuit$ = rated output of light source, lm
Φ = amount of incident light arriving at visual task, fc
D = distance between light source and visual task, ft

However, this basic lighting load formula is valid only if the luminous flux radiating from the light source forms a spherical wave front before arriving at the visual task. If the fixture's face is so wide and the task is so near that the arriving wave front is decidedly planar in character, the formula must include a *light source near-field factor* (λ_n).

The basic formula is also valid only if the light source radiates illumination in every direction. If a portion of the lamp is enclosed so that part of its full-sphere output is redirected through the aperture that remains, the leaving light is more intense. Thus the basic formula must include a *ray* or *beam concentration factor* (ß).

This formula also is valid only if the fixture is perfectly efficient. If its housing absorbs some of its lumens before they leave the luminaire, the leaving light will be weaker. Thus the formula must include a lamp efficiency factor, or *luminaire coefficient of utilization* (U).

The basic formula also is valid only if the fixture, its lamp, and the incoming voltage are all that is claimed. If the fixture is dirty, or the lamp's infant output has weakened with age, or the power grid voltage varies, the formula must include a *light depreciation factor* (Δ). This is also known as *light loss factor*, or *LLF*.

The basic formula also doesn't consider any light reflected from the floor, walls, ceiling, and furnishings, around the light source and visual task. As these reflections can make the arriving light brighter, the formula must often include a *room coefficient of utilization* ($\mathfrak{V}$).

The basic formula also is valid only if the light reflecting from the visual task into one's eyes equals the light arriving at the task. But as no

tion Society of North America [IESNA], New York); Jul 1996, p. 5. † From p. 489:

surface is perfectly reflective, the formula must include a *reflectance* (R) for the visual task.

The basic formula also is valid only if the occupant is perfectly alert. If he or she is tired, or bored, or has poor vision due to advanced age, or wears protective lenses that somewhat reduce the light entering the eye, the formula must include an *occupancy factor* (Θ).

The basic formula also doesn't consider any daylight arriving at the visual task. If any light enters any windows or skylights around the visual task, the amount of *daylighting* (𝔇) arriving at the task should be subtracted from the net artificial lighting load.

The basic formula also doesn't consider the possibility that light may strike the task plane at an angle other then 90°. When this happens, the formula must include a *cosine factor* (cos ∠).

Thus the basic formula, to be valid for all occasions, should read:

$$\diamond \lambda_\eta \ ß \ U \ _L\Delta \ \mho \ R \ \Theta \cos \angle \ = \ (\Phi - 𝔇) \ D^2$$

$\diamond$ = rated output of light source, lm
λ_η = light source near-field factor, 0.0–1.0
$ß$ = ray or beam concentration factor, 0.0–1.0
U = luminaire coefficient of utilization, 0.0–1.0
$_L\Delta$ = light depreciation factor, 0.0–1.0
$\mho$ = room coefficient of utilization, 0.0–1.0
R = visual task reflectance, 0.0–1.0
Θ = occupancy factor, 0.0–1.0
$\angle$ = angle of incidence of light ray to visual task plane, 0–90°
Φ = required illumination level of visual task, fc
$𝔇$ = amount of daylighting arriving at visual task, fc
D = distance between light source and visual task, ft

Regarding the above-mentioned cosine factor, it is shown geometrically in Detail A of Fig. 6-1. It indicates that as each light ray travels from its source to its point of incidence on the task plane, it travels a distance D until it strikes the figure at angle ∠, and if this angle is other than 90° the incident ray creates an orthogonal 'shadow' of length N upon the task plane. Then, since in Fig. 6-1A cos ∠ = N/D, the basic formula, stripped of all other variables for the moment, becomes

$$\diamond N/D = \Phi D^2 \quad \dots \diamond N = \Phi D^3$$

Thus the light that actually strikes the task plane is inversely proportional to the distance *cubed* between light source and task plane. Therefore, the distance between the light source and visual task is the most influential variable in quantifying light loads. Furthermore, since the task plane is rarely a two-dimensional surface but is often an object with depth, the venerable term 'task plane' is actually a misnomer —a more accurate

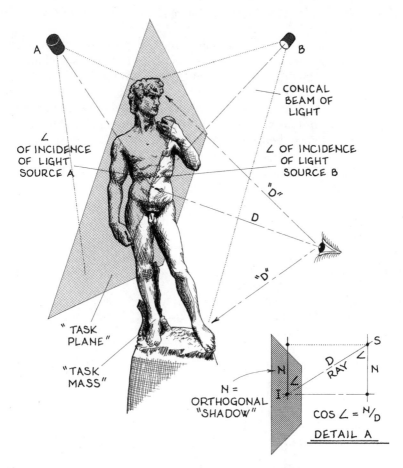

Fig. 6-1. The geometry of lightflow.

term would be *task mass*. And if the lightflow that strikes a visual task arrives from more than one light source, all the vectors arriving at any one point on the task from different directions are additive. These added vectors even include the tiny amounts of light arriving from every reflective surface in the room that normally encloses the light sources, visual task, and observer. Thus the light that actually arrives at a visual task is usually such a crisscrossing fusillade of colliding rays that no lighting load formula could ever be considered to be perfectly accurate.

Due to this incredible array of variables, lighting load calculations are usually based on a few oversimplified generalizations. (1) Distance D is a shortest-distance-between-two-points vector of photons with an average strength. (2) The visual task is a domain of many points that has a collective locus located an average dimension from the light source. (3) The

abstracted from the *Lighting Handbook*, 8th Edition; Mark Rea, Editor (IESNA,

stream of photons strikes the visual task at 90°, as even 20° from per-pendicular decreases it by only 6 percent. But these generalizations must always be used with circumspection. Manufacturers have another way of dealing with all the above variables: they mount a fixture a prescribed dis-tance from a checkerboard grid, measure the light arriving at each inter-section on the grid, then offer these *photometric footprints* as templates for design. Thus there are two methods of quantifying lighting loads:

▸ **Match the light to the task.** Knowing the required lighting level and the 'average focal distance' between the light source and visual task, the designer computes the required average output by algebraic formula. This chapter contains all the data neces-sary to compute virtually any lighting load in this manner without needing to consult any other source, and the book's DESIGNDISK lets you do this quickly and accurately.

▸ **Match the task to the light.** Having a particular luminaire in mind, the designer examines its photometric footprint as it appears in its product literature to see if it provides the required lighting.

Regarding the considerable inaccuracy that often remains after using either of the above methods, lighting designers have two more won-drous 'tools' at their disposal:

▸ **The flexible eye.** In most instances the human iris can interpret relevant visual data from about $1/3$ to 3 times the normally com-puted visual task illumination, at least for short periods.

▸ **The lamp socket.** This allows any still-unaccounted-for lighting load errors to be adjusted quickly onsite, after the requisite *in situ* analysis has been performed.

6.A.1.a. Near vs. Far Field

With a point light source, the emitted photons radiate outward in a spherical wave whose strength at any one point diminishes inversely as the square of the distance they have traveled. But if the light source's face extends primarily in one dimension (as does a fluorescent lamp) or in two dimensions (as does a skylight) perpendicular to the primary direction of its emitted rays, the rays move somewhat parallel to each other until they have travelled about six times the maximum lateral length of the light source, and thus for this distance they do not obey the normal inverse-square relationship; then their unit luminance must be increased accord-ing to a *near-field factor* as described in the bar graph in Fig. 6-2.

New York, 1993).

In summary, if the maximum dimension of a light source's facing is less than 1/6 the distance between it and the visual task, the light source is *point* and its unit output is measured in lumens. If the length of the light source's facing is more than 1/6 the distance between it and the visual task but its width is less than 1/6 this distance, the light source is *line* and its unit output is measured in lm/LF. If the length and width of the light source's facing both exceed 1/6 the distance between it and the visual task, the light source is *area* and its unit output is measured in lm/sf.

If a ceiling-mounted open strip fixture with two 72 in. fluorescent lamps is 7 ft above a secretary's desk, is it a *point*, *line*, or *area* light source? If a line or area source, what is its near-field factor?

If necessary, find the ratios D/L and D/W to determine if the light source is *point*, *line*, or *area*.

6)A)1)a) D/L and $D/W \geq 6$ .... light source is *point*
Only $D/L \leq 6$ .... light source is *line*
D/L and $D/W \leq 6$ .... light source is *area*

D = distance between light source and visual task, 7.0 ft
L = length of light source, ft. 72 in. = 6.0 ft.
W = width of light source, ft. As two fluorescent lamps in an open strip unit are about 8 in. apart, $W \approx 8/12 \approx 0.67$ ft.

$$D/L = 7.0/6.0 = 1.17 \Rightarrow D/L \leq 6$$
$$D/W = 7.0/0.67 = 10.4 \Rightarrow D/W \geq 6$$
Only $D/L \leq 6 \Rightarrow$ light source is *line*

If the light source is *line* or *area*, find its near-field factor as below.

$$\lambda_\eta = \eta_L \, s_L \, \eta_W \, s_W$$

λ_η = light source near-field factor, **?** . For point light sources, $\lambda_\eta = 1$.
η_L = near-field length factor. If $D/L \leq 1$, $\eta_L = 0.66$. If $D/L > 1 < 6$, find η_L from Fig. 6-2. If $D/L \geq 6$, $\eta_L = 1.0$. $D = 7.0$ ft and $L = 6.0$ ft.
∴ $D/L = 7.0/6.0 = 1.17 > 1 < 6 \Rightarrow$ from Fig. 6-2, $\eta_L = 0.74$

s_L = light source length factor. If $D/L \leq 1$, $s_L = D$. If $D/L > 1 < 6$, $s_L = L$. If $D/L \geq 6$, $s_L = 1.0$. $D = 7.0$ ft and $L = 6.0$ ft.
∴ $D/L = 7.0/6.0 = 1.17 > 1 < 6 \Rightarrow s_L = L = 6.0$ ft

η_W = near-field width factor. If $D/W \leq 1$, $\eta_W = 0.66$. If $D/W > 1 < 6$, find η_W from Fig. 6-2. If $D/W \geq 6$, $\eta_W = 1.0$. $D = 7.0$ ft and $W = 0.67$ ft.
∴ $D/W = 7.0/0.67 = 10.4 \geq 6 \Rightarrow \eta_W = 1.0$

s_W = light source width factor. If $D/W \leq 1$, $s_W = D$. If $D/W > 1 < 6$, $s_W = W$.

If $D/W \geq 6$, $s_W = 1.0$. $D = 7.0$ ft and $W = 0.67$ ft.

$\therefore D/W = {}^{7.0}/0.67 = 10.4 \geq 6 \Rightarrow s_W = 1.0$

$\lambda_\eta = 0.74 \times 6.0 \times 1.0 \times 1.0 = 4.44$ lm/LF

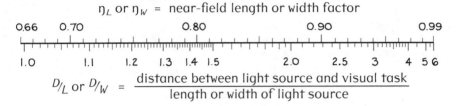

η_L or η_W = near-field length or width factor

D/L or $D/W = \dfrac{\text{distance between light source and visual task}}{\text{length or width of light source}}$

Fig. 6-2. Near-field adjustment bar graph.

Light source equations

Point light source: $\diamond_P = \Phi D^2$ lm   ... $\Phi = \diamond_P/D^2$ fc
Line light source: $\diamond_L = \Phi D^3/\lambda_\eta$ lm/LF   ... $\Phi = \lambda_\eta \diamond_L/D^3$ fc
Area light source: $\diamond_A = \Phi D^4/\lambda_\eta$ lm/sf   ... $\Phi = \lambda_\eta \diamond_A/D^4$ fc

Note: If you are using this book's DESIGNDISK, simply insert the values for D, L, and W into the No-Math Menu for ⑥⒜①⒜, then the data entry pane beside L_η will display the value for λ_η.

6.A.1.b. Ray Concentration

In any light source, if the exiting photons radiate outward in every direction (except for a small conical area subtended around the lamp's base) the uninterrupted distribution is the lamp's *full-sphere output*. An example of this is a bare incandescent bulb mounted in a porcelain socket. But if the lamp is partly enclosed by a reflective housing, a portion of the lamp's output is redirected through the aperture that remains, which makes its unit radiance more intense. This *ray concentration* is greatest in spotlights that are largely enclosed by parabolic reflectors with mirror surfaces. For example, a searchlight with a parabolic specular reflector that produces a collimated beam of light may have an axial output that is 80 times more intense than the lamp's full-sphere output.

In summary, ray concentration is a function of the portion of a lamp's spherical output that is enclosed by a reflective housing, the housing's geometric profile, and the specularity of the housing's inner surface.

TABLE 6-1: RAY CONCENTRATION FACTORS

(Interpolate for intermediate values)

CONCENTRATION due to amount of opaque enclosure ρ_e

Full-sphere (aperture angle ≈ 330°) 1.0

OPEN CEILING-MTD.

0.33 enclosed (aperture angle ≈ 240°) 1.2

0.50 enclosed (aperture angle ≈ 180°) 1.4

COFFER   CANOPY

0.67 enclosed (aperture angle ≈ 120°; 60° cutoff) 1.7

*Do not count constrictions

0.75 enclosed (aperture angle ≈ 90°; 45° cutoff) 2.0
"Flood" lamp beam spread ≈ 30° (interpolate for other values) 3.6
"Spot" lamp beam spread ≈ 15° (interpolate for other values) 5.2
"Pencil" lamp beam spread ≈ 9° (interpolate for other values) 6.8

CONCENTRATION due to reflector contour ρ_c

Box, pyramid, cylinder, hyperbolic, 'gable', and asymmetric shapes;
  also plenums, coves, valences, coffers, soffits, cornices, etc. ... 1.00
Circle or ellipse (one direction) × trough 1.05
Scoop, parabola (one dir.) × trough, circle or ellipse (two dir.) 1.10
Parabola (two directions), Fresnel or concentrating lens 1.20
Constrictions (return edges, pinholes, wall washer scoops, etc.) ... ignore

CONCENTRATION due to reflector finish ρ_f

Mirror finish: glass, stainless steel, "Alzak", spec. metal coatings .. 0.93
Spun or satin aluminum, satin brass, etc. 0.88
White baked enamel, matte, semi-gloss, glossy 0.83
Black, flat black, coilex baffle, etc. 0.55
Any other material acting as reflector .... use reflectance value

If a clear 400 watt H.I.D. lamp is mounted in a high bay reflector with a circular cross-section and spun aluminum finish, how much is its axial output increased due to the construction of its luminaire?

6)A)1)b) $ß ≈ \rho_e \rho_c \rho_f$

$ß$ = total ray or beam concentration factor, **?**
ρ_e = ray concentration due to portion of lamp's spherical output that is enclosed. From inspection, lamp is about $^2/_3$ or 0.67 enclosed. From Table 6-1, ρ_e for 0.67 enclosed = 1.7. Ignore facings except for Fresnel and other concentrating lenses.
ρ_c = ray concentration due to contour of reflective enclosure. From Table 6-1, ρ_c for circular shape = 1.1.
ρ_f = ray concentration due to finish of reflective enclosure. From Table 6-1, ρ_f for spun aluminum finish = 0.88.

$$ß ≈ 1.7 × 1.1 × 0.88 ≈ 1.65$$

6.A.1.c. Luminaire CU

Every light fixture has a coefficient of utilization, or *luminaire ʊ*, which is the quantity of light leaving the fixture divided by its rated output. A bare bulb mounted in a porcelain socket has a ʊ of 1.00, because it radiates all its light into the surrounding space. If the bulb is enclosed by a larger base, reflector, and/or facing, its efficiency is correspondingly reduced. Factors that increase luminaire ʊ are direct lighting, lamps spaced far apart in multilamp fixtures, ventilated and protruding fixtures, large and shallow housings, specular reflectors, parabolic profiles, and transparent facings. Factors that reduce luminaire ʊ are deep cylindrical housings, coilex baffles, patterned louvers with small openings, and lamps with ballasts. A few percentage points of efficiency can mean many dollars saved or lost during a lamp's full lifespan.

Values for more than 50 representative luminaires are listed in Table 6-2. Use a fixture's catalog ʊ if it is available.

A 175 watt H.I.D. lamp whose rated output is 14,000 lm is mounted in a square reflector with a clear lens on top and an open bottom. If this fixture has a rated output of 10,100 lm, what is its ʊ?

6)A)1)c) $Φ = ◇ ʊ$

TABLE 6-2: LUMINAIRE COEFFICIENTS OF UTILIZATION

DESCRIPTION OF LUMINAIRES [1]   Luminaire U

Description	Value
Bare I lamp; R40 flood w/o shielding; Open lampholder for PAR lamps; Light pipes (U is included in rated lamp outputs)	1.00
2 × 235° reflector lamps in open strip unit	0.98
Single row F lamp valence or cornice w/ reflective shield	0.95
Single row F lamp cove w/o reflector; R or PAR flood w/ shielding	0.93
Fiber optic end-dedicated extrusion, per LF	0.90
1 or 2 F lamps in open strip unit	0.88
1 or 2 F lamps in open bare lamp unit	0.87
R flood w/ spec. reflector, 45° cutoff; 75ER30 recessed baffled downlight w/ 5½ in. dia. opng; Double row F lamp cove w/o reflector	0.85
Porcelain vented dome w/ I lamp; 4 F lamp susp. unit w/ open top & prismatic sides & bottom; Compact 12V automatic emerg'cy light	0.83
Phosphor-coated HID lamp w/ high bay vented reflector	0.81
Pendant diffusing sphere w/ any lamp; Globe lights; 2 F lamps in porcelain reflector w/ 30° CW × 30° LW shielding	0.80
Prismatic square w/ I lamp and dropped diffuser; Compact F lamp in small specular parabolic trough reflector w/ open facing	0.79
High-output F lamp in suspended unit w/ lens below	0.78
Clear HID lam w/ high bay vented reflector	0.77
F lamp in surface-mounted unit w/ wraparound prismatic lens	0.75
2 × 2 ft surface-mtd. ceiling unit w/ T8 F lamps & 3 in. paracube louvers	0.74
Clear HID uplight or downlight w/ prismatic lens or clear shield	0.73
I downlight in circ. reflector w/ enclosed lens; Clear HID lamp in low bay reflector w/ lens or shield; F lamps w/ open top, dense diffuser sides, and 45° CW × LW shielding	0.71
2 F lamp unit w/ prismatic wraparound	0.70
Compact F lamp in small cylinder housing w/ specular reflector & open facing; Recessed baffled downlightt w/ 5½ in. dia. opening	0.68
Clear HID uplight or downlight w/ glass refractor or plastic lens	0.66
Uniform ceiling illumination w/ glass or diffusing plastic	0.65
4 F lamp troffer w/ flat prismatic lens	0.63
4 F lamp troffer w/ dropped diffuser	0.61
F lamp in batwing unit w/ lateral louvers; Uniform ceiling lighting w/ translucent panels	0.60
F lamp in parabolic wedge reflector w/ 6×6 in. wedge louvers	0.58
EAR 38 downlight w/ 3 in. dia. aperture	0.54
Frosted I lamp in wide-beam porcelain unit w/ lens plate	0.53
I lamp in recessed unit w/ dropped diffuser; 2 F lamps w/ top reflector, diffuser sides, & 45° CW × LW shield; 4 F lamp troffer w/ flat diffuser	0.52
4 F lamp troffer w/ 45° plastic louvers	0.50
4 F lamp troffer w/ 45° white metal louvers	0.46
2 F lamps w/ diffuse wraparound; Uniform ceiling illumination w/ louvered drop-in panels	0.45
AR 38 downlight w/ 2 in. dia. aperture	0.43

1. In this table, I = incandescent, Q = quartz, F = fluorescent, HID = high-intensity discharge, M = mercury, H = metal halide, and S = sodium lamps.

Φ = net rated output of luminaire, 10,100 lm
◇ = rated output of light source in luminaire, 14,000 lm
𝒰 = luminaire coefficient of utilization, ?

$$10,100 = 14,000 \times 𝒰 \quad ... \quad 𝒰 = 0.72$$

6.A.1.d. Light Depreciation

With light fixtures, what you see isn't always what you get. For example, a fixture's output near the end of its rated life may often be 25–50 percent below its infant output due to voltage, heating, aging, dirt accumulation, and maintenance factors. Although it is impossible to compute such losses accurately, Table 6-3 lists estimates of how much certain light loss or light depreciation factors may lower lamp life based on research data gathered by recognized authorities for several decades.

A 45 year-old steel mill is to be renovated. The fixtures in the general lighting area are 400W metal halide lamps with nonregulating ballasts mounted 28 ft above the floor. The local industrial power grid has frequent voltage fluctuations, and mill operations create rising air currents that carry metal dust, combustion gases, and oil vapors into the open truss ceiling. During a visit to the site only a few areas of the concrete floor showed through a thin layer of black dirt and no one knew when the lights were last cleaned. What is the total depreciation of this illumination?

6]A]1]d)

$$_L\Delta \approx \delta_v\,\delta_p\,\delta_n\,\delta_t\,\delta_d\,\delta_a\,\delta_m$$

$_L\Delta$ = total light depreciation factor, ?

δ_v = light depreciation due to voltage fluctuation. Above-normal voltage tends to lower the useful life of certain lamps.
From Table 6-3, δ_v for HID lamps (nonregulated ballast) = 0.87.

δ_p = light depreciation due to lamp position (horizontal, vertical, base up, base down, inclined orientations). The position in which some lamps are installed may affect their output. From Table 6-3, δ_p for HID lamp in vertical position = 1.00.

δ_n = light depreciation during lamp life. Different lamps depreciate at different rates during their useful lives. From Table 6-3, δ_n for HID lamp, 3 year ≈ 0.75. This value could be considerably lower.

δ_t = light depreciation due to luminaire temperature increase. In sealed and unvented luminaires, temperature buildup may reduce lamp life.

TABLE 6-3: LIGHT DEPRECIATION FACTORS
(Interpolate for intermediate values)

DEPRECIATION DUE TO VOLTAGE FLUCTUATION (+ or – 5 VAC)			δ_v
No appreciable fluctuation ..	1.00	F	0.97
H.I.D. (w/ ballast)	0.98	MV, MH, S (nonreg. bal.), I, Q .	0.87

DEPRECIATION DUE TO LAMP POSITION			δ_p
I, vertical w/ base up	1.00	I, horiz or vert w/ base down ..	0.96
F, horizontal; HID, vertical ..	1.00	HID, 40-90° from vertical	0.91
HID, 20° from vertical	0.97		

DEPRECIATION DURING LAMP LIFE (based on 2,500 hr operation/yr)			δ_n
S, 1 year	0.99	F, 1 year	0.92
Q, 8 months	0.98	F, 3 years	0.89
S, 3 years	0.96	MH, 1 year	0.88
MV, 1 year; I, 3 months	0.95	MH, 3 years	0.75
MV, 3 years	0.93		

DEPRECIATION DUE TO LUMINAIRE TEMPERATURE INCREASE			δ_t
Open or vented luminaire	1.00	1 Q, 1 F, sealed lumin. only ...	0.95
2 F, sealed luminaire w/ r.a.d.[2]	0.99	2 I, sealed luminaire only	0.94
1 HID, sealed luminaire only	0.98	2 F, sealed luminaire only	0.93
3 F, sealed luminaire w/ r.a.d.	0.98	3 F, sealed luminaire only	0.91
4 F, sealed luminaire w/ r.a.d.	0.97	4 F, sealed luminaire only	0.88
1 I, sealed luminaire only w/ no return air ducting			0.96

DEPRECIATION DUE TO LUMINAIRE DIRT ACCUMULATION			δ_d
Direct illumination	0.96	Semi-indirect illumination	0.88
Semi-direct illumination	0.93	Indirect illumination	0.86
Direct-indirect illumin.	0.91		

DEPRECIATION DUE TO ROOM AIR DIRT	δ_a
Very clean: modern offices away from production areas, etc.	0.96
Clean: offices in old buildings; light assembly, etc.	0.93
Medium: construction offices, light industrial, etc.	0.89
Dirty: industrial operations creating moderate dirt, dust, etc.	0.84
Very dirty: industrial operations creating visible dirt, dust, etc.....	0.76

DEPRECIATION DURING LENGTH OF MAINTENANCE CYCLE			δ_m
1 year maintenance cycle	1.00	2 year maintenance cycle	0.91
1½ year maintenance cycle ..	0.93	3 year maintenance cycle	0.85

1. In this table, I = incandescent, Q = quartz, F = fluorescent, HID = high-intensity discharge, MV = mercury, MH = metal halide, S = sodium lamps.
2. r.a.d. = return air ducting.

From Table 6-3, δ_f for open or vented luminaire = 1.00.

δ_d = light depreciation due to luminaire dirt accumulation. Airborne particulates are steadily deposited on lamp surfaces; uplighting collects more than downlighting. Where accumulation is severe or insects abound, lighting should be faced. As lighting faces down, from Table 6-3, δ_d for direct illumination = 0.96.

δ_a = light depreciation due to room air dirt. Dirt collecting on room surfaces around the luminaire lowers effective lighting output. As area is obviously very dirty, from Table 6-3, δ_a = 0.76. This value too could be considerably lower.

δ_m = light depreciation during length of maintenance cycle. The more frequently a luminaire and the area around it are cleaned, the less its depreciation, with one-year cycles being the norm. Here assume cycle of three years. From Table 6-3, δ_m for three-year maintenance cycle = 0.85. This value too could be considerably lower.

$$_L\Delta \approx 0.87 \times 1 \times 0.75 \times 1 \times 0.96 \times 0.76 \times 0.85 \approx 0.40 \text{ tops}$$

6.A.1.e. Room Coefficient of Utilization

The room is the 'larger light fixture' that houses its luminaires, visual tasks, and occupants. If an interior space contains many of these elements, the interchange of illumination among them all plus the interreflectances from the room's enclosing surfaces transforms its volume into an aura of luminous flux. One way of estimating the optimal number of luminaires in such a space is the *Lumen Method*, formerly known as the *Zonal Cavity Method*. But this approach is accurate only for medium-sized rectangular rooms whose length/width ratios range from about 1.0–2.0, whose floor reflectances are about 0.20, whose wall and ceiling reflectances are average and fairly diffuse, and whose fixtures are standard kinds —in other words, only the most ordinary architectural spaces.

However, the Lumen Method may soon become obsolete due to the advent of *computerized photometric analysis:* digital software that enables one to create detailed perspectives of interior spaces in which the direct light striking all surfaces as well as shading, scalloping, spill light, end darkening, edge-to-central and corner-to-central gradients, and even shading gradients on curved surfaces are portrayed with visual accuracy. By clicking on any surface one obtains its luminance and color values. Is the task plane too dark or too light? Enter a new wattage for the light sources, then reclick on the surface to obtain a new reading. Although such software usually requires considerable time to input the data for a large space, such efforts are usually cost-beneficial for important spaces.

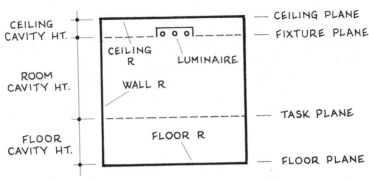

Fig. 6-3. Room cavity details for room ʊ calculation.

If a large interior space contains a lot of shoulder-high partitions, the computed lighting level should normally be reduced 20–25 percent to obtain accurate desktop readings. Also, the reflectance of window glass varies greatly according to the relative amounts of light on each side. For example, in the middle of a sunny day a large area of glazing on one side of an office area illuminated by ceiling fluorescent fixtures may have a reflectance of 0.12; but at night when it is dark outside, the same area of glazing may have a reflectance of 0.85.

A 20 × 32 ft. architect's office has a cream ceiling and walls, cobalt blue carpet, floor-to-ceiling bookshelves against a long wall, and a ribbon window with 8'-4" head and 3'-8" sill above dark oak casework in the other long wall. If the space is 9'-4" high, its lighting is ceiling-mounted 4-lamp fluorescent troffers with 2 in. dropped diffusers, and the architect and his small staff work at a conference table and desks that are 2'-8" above the floor, what is the room's ʊ?

Step 1. Compute the room's average reflectance as below:

Room surface	$w \times b$ = Area, sf	r of surface (Table 6-4)	Area $\times r = r_a$
Ceiling	20 × 32 = 640	cream = 0.81	640 × 0.81 = 518
Short walls	2 × 9.33 × 20 = 373	cream = 0.81	373 × 0.81 = 302
Long wall 1: window	7.0 × 32 = 224	window = 0.85	224 × 0.85 = 190
Header	1.0 × 32 = 32	cream = 0.81	32 × 0.81 = 26
Casework	2.33 × 32 = 75	dark oak = 0.13	75 × 0.13 = 10
Long wall 2	9.22 × 32 = 299	med. grey = 0.20	299 × 0.20 = 60
Floor	20 × 32 = 640	cobalt blue = 0.08	640 × 0.08 = 51
Total A = 2,250 sf			Total r_a = 1,140

R = average reflectance of room = $^A/r_a$ = 1,140/2,250 = 0.51

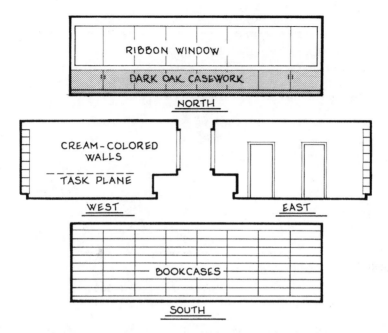

Fig. 6-4. Interior elevations for architect's office.

Step 2. Compute the room's coefficient of utilization.

6)A)1)e) $\upsilon \approx 1.13 \left[R W L / 10 H (W + L) \right]^{0.34}$

υ = coefficient of utilization of illuminated space, room, or zone, ?
R = average reflectance of space, room, or zone. From Step 1, $R = 0.51$.
W = average width of space's zonal cavity, 20 ft
L = average breadth or length of space's zonal cavity, 32 ft
H = average height of space's zonal cavity = room ht – ceiling cavity ht.
    – floor cavity ht, ft. H = 9'-4" – 2" – 32" = 78" = 6.50 ft.

    $\upsilon \approx 1.13 \left[0.51 \times 32 \times 20/10 \times 6.5 (32 + 20) \right]^{0.34} \approx 0.50$

6.A.1.f. Surface Reflectance

This is the portion of light that a surface absorbs, expressed as a ratio of departing light (luminance) to arriving light (illuminance). A reflective surface may be *specular* (a smooth shiny surface that casts a mirror-like image of the arriving light), *matte* (a smooth dull surface that emits an inarticulate 'shine'), or *diffuse* (a rough dull surface that widely scatters

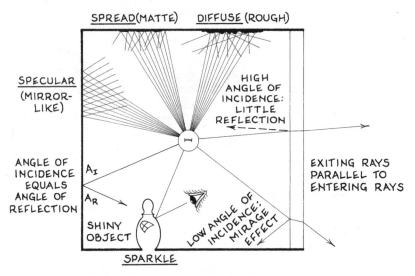

SPREAD (MATTE) DIFFUSE (ROUGH)

SPECULAR
(MIRROR-
LIKE)

HIGH
ANGLE OF
INCIDENCE:
LITTLE
REFLECTION

ANGLE OF
INCIDENCE A_I
EQUALS
ANGLE OF A_R
REFLECTION

EXITING RAYS
PARALLEL TO
ENTERING RAYS

SHINY
OBJECT

LOW ANGLE OF
INCIDENCE:
MIRAGE
EFFECT

SPARKLE

Fig. 6-5. Types of reflectance.

TABLE 6-4: COEFFICIENTS OF REFLECTANCE

SURFACE	R^1	SURFACE	R	SURFACE	R
Primary hues: red	0.24	Orange	0.35	Yellow	0.69
Green	0.28	Blue	0.23	Violet	0.14
Other hues: cream	0.81	Maroon	0.08	Cobalt blue	0.08
Brown, Snicker's bar	0.13	Olive	0.17	Black ink	0.05
Brown, grocery bag	0.25	Tan	0.48	Neon pink	0.60
Pastels	0.60-0.80	Light green	0.63	Sky blue	0.45
Light gray	0.58	Medium gray	0.20	Dark gray	0.11
Styrofoam blue	0.54	White paper	0.82	Newspaper	0.68
White paint, new	0.75	White paint, old	0.55	White plaster	0.91
Other Surfaces: Pine	0.34	Maple	0.21	Mahogany	0.08
Light oak	0.32	Dark oak	0.13	Slate	0.08
Brick, light buff	0.48	Brick, dark red	0.13	Bluestone	0.16
Cement	0.25	Concrete	0.42	Granite	0.40
Asphalt, freshly laid	0.07	Asphalt, old	0.18	Gravel, light	0.15
Galvanized sheet metal	0.35	Stainless steel	0.60	Aluminum	0.55
Copper, tarnished	0.11	Chromium	0.65	Rust	0.10
Vegetation, average	0.15	Spinach, top	0.12	Grass, dark	0.10
Snow, new	0.78	Snow, old	0.64	Mirror	0.85
Earth, moist cultivated	0.40	Earth, light dry	0.40	Light source [2]	1.00
Clear pane, night, no illumination outside					0.09

1. R = Coefficient of Reflectance ⊥ incident light. As angle of light decreases from ⊥, the value of R increases but is more indeterminate.
2. Light fixture, window, skylight, operating movie, or TV screen when off.

the arriving light). A surface's reflectance increases as it becomes smoother, its color becomes lighter, and the angle of arriving light becomes lower. If two surfaces receive different amounts of light but have the same net departing light because one surface is more reflective, the latter surface looks brighter because reflectance dominates over luminance. Although reflections occurring inside a luminaire are typically factored into its coefficient of utilization, reflectances of room and visual task surfaces usually require brief analysis to quantify the light that enters the eye.

> How much light is reflected from a sheet of canary tracing paper on an architect's desk if the paper receives 163 fc of illumination?

6]A]1]f]

$$L = \Phi R$$

L = luminance of room surface or visual task, ? fL
Φ = incident light upon room surface or visual task, 163 fc
R = reflectance of room surface or visual task. From Table 6-4, R for yellow = 0.69.

$$L = 163 \times 0.69 = 112 \text{ fL}$$

6.A.1.g. Occupancy Factors

Numerous authorities have tried to establish uniform lighting requirements for various lighting levels, surface luminances, contrast ratios, and other aspects of designed interior environments. But in almost every case, occupants' reactions have varied widely even when environmental conditions have remained the same. Obviously a sizable variable is the mental and physical nature of the occupants. At one extreme a lighting designer can never, to paraphrase Lincoln, "Please all the people all the time"; but at the other extreme a designer's awareness of certain 'occupancy factors', based on a number of internal and external variables that affect occupant behavior, can lead to lighting that increases job productivity, comfort, security, and peace of mind at little extra cost. The most significant of these occupancy factors are listed below.

Age: Older people experience reduced visual acuity, degenerating color vision, and several other symptoms of ocular decline. Therefore their eyes typically require more illumination for a given visual task than do the eyes of younger occupants.

Perceptual level: Tired eyes require more lighting than alert ones. Also, fatigue generally occurs more readily with exposure to yellow and orange hues than to green and blue. Thus day-long sedentary occupancies are best enclosed with more restful hues, while shorter and livelier occupancies such as entertainment and recreation are often made more enjoyable with shades of red, orange, and yellow.

Psychological level: Bored eyes require more lighting than eager ones. Also when certain personalities and moods encounter certain lighting conditions, they become less productive while others become more so. And as light enters the eye it stimulates the suprachiasmatic nucleus in the brain —the "biological clock" that regulates circadian rhythms of sleep, hormonal output, and other physiological functions. Much light is needed for this: usually 300–1,000 fc. Hence the visual satisfaction one may derive from occasionally "stepping out for a breath of fresh air."

Duration of task: Tasks lasting several hours usually require higher lighting levels than ones lasting a few minutes.

Errors: Occupants tend to make more errors in weak light than in strong light. If any errors made during a task could have serious consequences, more illumination is required.

Windows: Low-grade visual tasks performed in dimly lit windowless areas during daylight hours require more illumination to compensate for the area's confining nature.

Eye-protective devices: Tasks requiring tinted or protective lenses that materially reduce the light entering the eye require correspondingly higher lighting levels. Indeed, if the transmissivity of window glass is about 0.88, the transmissivity of corrective lens glass must be fairly close to this.

Regarding occupancy behavior patterns, perhaps the lighting design approach that best combines simplicity and effectiveness is to aim at the peak of the bell-shaped probability curve, then 'embody' the curve with individually operable controls. Herein lies the importance of dimmers, especially those operated by tether switch or remote control from a desktop or work counter. With one of these in hand, an occupant can readily create whatever lighting level he or she desires, whether it be rooted in a need to be more productive, an urge to affirm one's power to change the environment at will, a desire to liven a mundane work pattern, or simply because in a moment-to-moment continuum each iota of time is different.

What is a typical occupancy factor for an architect's personal office?

6)A)1)g)
$$\Theta \approx \kappa_d \, \kappa_e \, \kappa_f \, \kappa_p \, (40/\kappa_a)^{0.85}$$

Θ = total occupancy factor, ?

κ_d = duration factor, ranges from 1.0 for short visual tasks to 0.85 for tasks of day-long duration. As architects frequently work long hours, $\kappa_D = 0.85$.

κ_e = error factor, from 1.00 if errors have no serious consequences to 0.85 if they have very serious consequences. As errors in architectural work may have disastrous consequences, $\kappa_e = 0.85$.

κ_f = fenestration factor. If $L \leq 30$ fL and area is windowless, $\kappa_f = 0.8$, otherwise $\kappa_f = 1.0$. $L \geq 30$ fL ➡ $\kappa_f = 1.0$.

κ_p = protective lens factor, ranges from 1.0 to 0.85 unless work standards require a lower figure. As architects often wear glasses whose lenses have a transmissivity factor, let $\kappa_p = 0.90$.

κ_a = age factor. If occupant's age ≥ 40, κ_a = actual age; otherwise κ_A = 40. As architects are rarely successful until near retirement, assume $\kappa_a = 60$. In multiple occupancies let $\kappa_a \approx$ oldest age -5 yr.

$$\Theta = 0.85 \times 0.85 \times 1.0 \times 0.90 \times (40/60)^{0.85} = 0.46$$

6.A.2. Task

'Task' is the essence of architecture. Without it there is no building, no lighting. A visual task may be horizontal or vertical, 2- or 3-dimensional, and as simple as a Post-it note is to a casual reader or as complex as an athlete going downfield for a pass is to a quarterback. Whatever the task, the viewer sees the greatest detail within a narrow cone of vision whose apex angle is about 2° —the *foveal vision cone*— and has a general perception of detail within a wider cone of about 10°. The area bordering a task plane is its *surround*, and everything beyond or further to the side is the *background*. The design lighting levels listed in Table 6-5 assume average reflectances for each task. Under actual conditions these values may vary greatly, but the human iris is quite flexible. For example, most people can read a newspaper in 5 fc of illumination for short periods although the design lighting level for reading is 50 fc. Visual tasks also have several qualitative aspects which affect performance. The most important are:

Adaptation. When looking at something, one's roving eyes 'fill in' the various lines, colors, and shapes until comprehension of the total scene seems adequate. This includes small details the viewer does not see readily as well as imperceptible or nonexistent portions of the scene which he or she imagines as 'seeing.' These latter constructs are as much a part of the viewed scene as any other.

Context. One's impression of a viewed scene often depends greatly on the nature of the surrounds in which it appears. For example, an oncoming headlight may be so glaringly bright at night that it hurts one's eyes, while during the day it may be hardly noticeable.

TABLE 6-5: VISUAL TASK ILLUMINATION LEVELS

AREA OR TASK	Illuminance, fc
Surgical or emergency operating rooms, obstetric delivery	2,000
Exacting inspection at frequent intervals, feature store-window displays, theoretical glare threshold at 1.00 reflectance	1,000
Low-contrast inspection, oral cavity dentistry, post-anesthetic recovery, sewing white thread on white cloth, fine machine work	750
Championship boxing, autopsy rooms, fine inspection	500
Cutting and sewing cloth, fabric inspection, TV studios, precise assembly, fine polishing or buffing, fine hand painting and finishing, accent lighting for feature merchandise displays, bacterial lab work	300
Paint color comparison, merchandise showcases, medical examination, theater follow spots, fine machine work	200
Drafting, accounting, fine layout work, tailoring, detailed inspection or assembly, proofreading, grading finished lumber, control rooms, feature displays, accent lighting for quality merchandise	150
Police ID, private offices, cataloguing, theater stages, counting small objects, lecterns, labs, grooming, general machine work	100
Reading musical scores, classrooms, cashier areas, general office, museum exhibits, food prep, beauty parlors, clothes fitting, ambient low-end mass retailing, reading telephone books, applying makeup	75
Reading a novel, computer work, general industrial, major entrances, conference rooms, prominent background lighting, cleaning, washing, dressing, bathroom mirrors, check-in desks (public side)	50
Service area breakdown, public elevators, ambient rest room, locker rooms, dressing, bathing, cafeterias, airport baggage checking, packaging, weighing, listing, labeling, marking, classifying, waiting, dishwashing, exhibitions, recreation, signage, theater marquees	30
Machine rooms, freight elevators, piers, waste disposal areas, control rooms w/ illuminated panels, jails, recreational, eating, toilet and bathing areas, ambient industrial	20
Assembly, ambient hallways and lobbies, hospital recovery, warehouses, ambient hotel and motel rooms, bars, pantries, hospital X-ray rooms, record storage, stairways, rest-room toilet areas	15
Service entrances, night lights, intimate dining, service station pump islands at night, library stacks, walk-in refrigerators	10
Garages, stockrooms, airport concourses, closed store interiors at night, dance halls, discotheques, drop-off areas, mechanical equip. rooms, linen closets, ambient residential, taxi loading zones	7.5
Emergency exits, assembly seating during intermissions, motel entries, barn & stable interiors (feed areas, haymows), video viewing, inactive stacks, bin storage	5
Hospital corridors at night, basements, barn silos and bins	3
Pediatric nurseries, theater offstage, theater seating during perf.	2
Inactive storage, airport hangar apron, hosp. sleeping areas, sidewalk at night, candle flame 1 ft away, hazard requiring visual detection	1
Dorm areas at night, watching movies, full moon on clear cold night, threshold of color perception	0.2

Acuity. Performance of any visual task relates to the amount of detail one can perceive. There are two thresholds: *absolute acuity* (the lower and upper limits of clarity required for optimal performance, below which is vagueness and above which is profusion) and *differential acuity* (the difference in clarity or composition required between a task and its surrounds for optimal performance).

Orientation. During lengthy tasks one often feels a need to relate to time, place, climate, and other orientational needs. Such surrounds become more comfortable if they include wall clocks, family photos, nearby windows offering a view outside, perhaps a radio that plays music and gives local traffic reports, and other visual and nonvisual cues that an occupant can interact with over extended periods of time.

6.A.2.a. Glare

Glare is essentially too much light. It may be *direct* (arriving directly from the light source) or *indirect* (caroming off an object between the light source and the offended eye); and it may be *disabling* (offensive enough to hurt the eyes) or *discomforting* (distracting enough to fatigue the eye or reduce long-term performance). An erroneous method of designing for glare is according to "visual comfort probability," in which a glare is considered acceptable if it offends less than 50 percent of the occupants. Designing lighting like this is like designing a staircase that is uncomfortable to only 49 percent of its users. Far better is to investigate the geometry that creates the glare, then eliminate it by doing one or more of the following:

▸ **Move the light source.** Locate lamps above natural sight lines (more than 50° above horizontal) or to the viewer's side. For group occupancies use uniform ceiling illumination of recommended intensity and no higher, and install more lamps of lower unit output rather than a few of higher output.

▸ **Shield or soften the offending ray.** Fit lamps with louvers or blinders that direct light downward or diffusers that spread it outward. Conceal lamps above cove ledges, in canopy overhangs or coffer cavities, behind sconce covers or valence faceboards, or within other construction. Hood computer monitors. Reduce task-to-surround contrasts.

▸ **If the ray is indirect, roughen its reflective surface.** Use matte finishes, colors of medium value, or rough textures.

▸ **Move or shield the target.** Rearrange the occupant vis-a-vis the light source and visual task. As a last resort, wear visors.

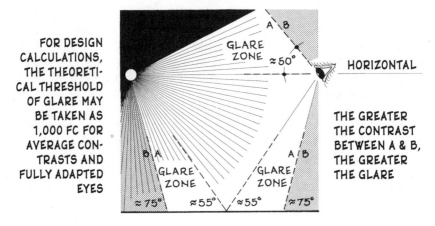

FOR DESIGN CALCULATIONS, THE THEORETICAL THRESHOLD OF GLARE MAY BE TAKEN AS 1,000 FC FOR AVERAGE CONTRASTS AND FULLY ADAPTED EYES

GLARE ZONE ≈50°

HORIZONTAL

THE GREATER THE CONTRAST BETWEEN A & B, THE GREATER THE GLARE

B A GLARE ZONE ≈75° ≈55°

A B GLARE ZONE ≈55° ≈75°

Fig. 6-6. The geometry of glare.

An elegant solution to a serious glare problem is at the Charlotte Speedway in North Carolina. When NASCAR decided to hold races at night, the drivers required lighting on and around the speedway that would assimilate daylight yet not create any glare as they moved at 200 miles an hour, network TV cameras needed every part of the 1.5 mile oval to be illuminated with 100 fc uniform shadow-free light, and spectators should not be annoyed by any garish light. The solution? Install 1,500 watt metal halide lamps fitted with canister reflectors just inside the track and aim

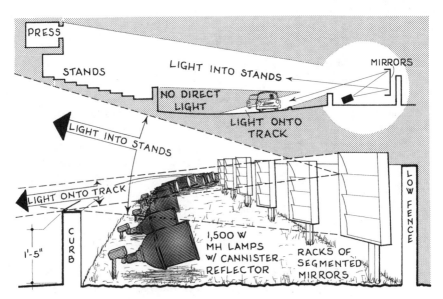

Fig. 6-7. Anti-glare illumination at Charlotte Speedway. [†]

† Baily & Vincent, "The Speed of Light"; *LD + A Journal* (IESNA, New York); Apr

them at racks of segmented slightly parabolic mirrors 5 ft further inside, then aim the mirrors with pinpoint accuracy over a 1.5 ft high curb behind the lamps in a manner that bathes the track with highly controlled glare-free light and illuminates the stands of spectators with ambient glare-free light. A low fence was installed behind the mirrors to block across-the-infield glare from the luminaires, and both the fence and high curb were painted white to increase ambient illumination along the track. [†]

6.A.2.b. Contrast

Fig. 6-8 is a legitimate depiction of a realistic event, clear in every detail. Only you can't see anything because there is no contrast. This is why the noted color expert Louis Erhardt once referred to contrast as "the fascinating gateway to perception."

Fig. 6-8. A ghost hanging clean sheets in a blizzard.

The following contrasts are basic to the perception of size, silhouette, and outline of the various elements of a visual environment:

Hue: one color or spectral wavelength against another.
Value: white or light hues against black or dark hues.
Intensity: bright or pure colors against dull or diluted colors.
Complementary: one color against its complement.
Cold-warm: a warm .color (the warmest being fiery red-orange) against a cool color (the coolest being icy green-blue).
Extensional: a small area of color against a large area.
Simultaneous: juxtaposing complementary colors against the other contrasts with positive effect.
Time: brief versus prolonged activities.
Continuity: continuous versus discontinuous activities.

If a certain contrast is too low (e.g. if the letters on this page were yellow), *vagueness* results; if too high (as when an usher's flashlight shines in one's eyes in a movie theater), *harshness* results. This has led to the development of certain restful *luminance ratios* that should create desirable contrasts and relations of tone between a visual task, surround, and background to optimize performance. Particularly important is for a color to appear the same as it lightens or darkens through edge-to-central gradients, corner-to-central gradients, shading gradients on curved surfaces, and the like. Also the eye does not respond to what could be called *foveal luminance* as much as it does to *ambient luminance*, which is the over-all brightness of the scene viewed below one's eyebrows, above the cheekbones, and between the outer corners of the eyes. Thus one's eyes are more apt to appraise patterns of brightness and darkness in a scene's overall area than in smaller areas within.

> What is the luminance ratio between a drafting desk's light green surface and a cobalt blue carpet below if the light incident on the desk is 150 fc and the light on the carpet is 75 fc? Is this restful?

6)A)2)b) $L_n = \Phi_t R_t / \Phi_s R_s$

L_n = restful luminance ratio, ?
Φ_t = incident light upon visual task, 150 fc
R_t = reflectance of visual task. R for light green = 0.63.
Φ_s = incident light upon surround or background, 75 fc
R_s = reflectance of surround. From Table 6-4, R for cobalt blue = 0.08.

$$L_n = 150 \times 0.63/75 \times 0.08 = 15.8$$
Restful range for task plane/dark background = 3:1 to 15:1
$$3 \le 15.8 \ge 15 \rightarrow \text{borderline } \mathbf{NG}$$

TABLE 6-6: RESTFUL ILLUMINATION RATIOS

CONTRAST: Area/Area	Restful range
General task/surround, "figure/ground"	3:1 to 20:1
Task/light background ... 2:1 to 8:1; Task/dark background .	3:1 to 15:1
Threshold of perceptibility .... ≈ 2:1; Large task to surround	2:1 to 4:1
Light source (luminaire or opening)/surround	2:1 to 30:1
Video terminal display/surround	4:1 to 8:1
Uniform lighting, lightest/darkest area	3:1
Highlighting, featured object/surround	3:1 to 10:1
Perceived twice as bright	10:1
Low theatrical effect ≈ 5:1; High thea. effect ≈ 15:1; Dramatic effect	≈ 25:1
Maximum ratio of bright white/dull black	30:1

(IESNA, New York); Apr 1994, pp. 52–57.

6.A.3. Quality of Light

The mysteries of vision have fascinated scientists and artists alike for centuries. From Newton's classical notions that what we see is an autonomic correlation of wavelengths, to Goethe's cry that "Optical illusion is optical truth," to the modern theories of Edwin Land, the inventor of the Polaroid camera, who asserted that perception of an illuminated scene is based first on surface reflectances then on a diffusion of the three wavelengths of primary colors, the experts are still seeking the definitive answers.

But one thing is certain. As the visual part of one's brain continually processes the incoming double stream of photons, this 'retinuity' converses with other neural mechanisms —which are different in every individual— before the photons are formulated as a visual construct. These cerebrations also occur in a time continuum which has a completely different feeling and meaning for every viewer. Moreover, one's past experiences have been correlated into an archive of visual engrams which influences the interpretation of every fresh percept imposed upon them. Little wonder that the blue you see is not the blue I see! And any attempt by a designer to encapsulate the chaos of visual flux received by 'Everyman' into a simple algebraic formula —no matter how basic and all-encompassing that formula may be— shall always leave more to be considered.

And that 'more' is quality of light.

Here is where the intuition of the artist enters the fray. Knowing that the 'rules' of lighting design are governed more by whim than physics. Realizing that the use of light, from firelight to laserlight, is forever an ongoing expression of the times. Understanding that the dominant character of a lighted environment will always be, like the statues of Gog of Papini which are carved in smoke, fraught with a transient and subjective inconsistency. Knowing that computers don't design —they only tell.

Realizing all this, the artist must nevertheless take care not to overuse his or her acute sensitivities or fecund imagination: that when the flow of creativity is temporarily halted, one must never slip to playing cat-and-mouse with specious criteria, but instead should re-explore the world of abstruse concepts, philosophical implications, and deeper meanings as a way of rediscovering one's bearings.

One way to sharpen these skills is to analyze a good photograph. Study Ansel Adams as well as Wright and Corbu. Adams' book, *Examples*, in which he analyzes 50 of his famous exposures, is worthy of examination by all who aspire to a managerial privilege in the domain of design.

6.A.4. Color

'Color' is a lamp's ability to portray the hues of the objects it illuminates. Because no artificial light source does this perfectly with all colors, architects try to match the various spectral signatures of each lamp with the spectral composition of each illuminated scene. There are two primary criteria for this selection: *correlated color temperature* and *color rendering index*.

Correlated color temperature (CCT) This is a lamp's ability to portray colors from warm (red-orange) to cool (blue-violet). Paradoxically, the 'warmer' a light source the lower its 'temperature' in degrees Kelvin. For example, a candle flame (considered to be the warmest light) has a CCT of about 1,700° K, a brilliant sunset around 2,000°, sunlight an hour earlier about 3,600°, sunlight at noon around 5,000°, and a clear blue sky (considered to be the coolest light) is nearly 10,000°. As for lamps, a summary of their color temperature characteristics follows.

3,000°: Warm; brings out high color contrast but emphasizes reds and oranges; preferred for dusky or shadowy color schemes where mood overrides a need for visual clarity. Used in restaurants, night clubs, hotel lobbies, residences, hospital bedrooms, other intimate atmospheres with low lighting levels.

3,500°: Moderate; combines advantages of warm and cool fairly well. Good for showrooms, general merchandising, general work areas, classrooms, gymnasiums, other recreation areas.

4,100°: Cool; renders all colors well but slightly favors blues and greens, is generally better for high illumination levels. Used in large office areas, hospital public areas, general commercial and industrial.

5,000°: Crisp, clean, 'icy blue'; portrays blues and violets with greater clarity, best for high lighting levels but poor for low; preferred for most pastel color schemes. Used in daylighted spaces, laboratories, clinics, control rooms, drafting and inspection rooms, high-tech retail merchandise, other spaces where visual acuity or long-range viewing is critical. Lamps whose CCT ≈ 7,000° and CRI > 90 are used for color matching of textiles, checking of printing color proofs, and quality display lighting.

Color rendering index (CRI) This is a lamp's ability to duplicate colors as seen in natural outdoor light. Values range from 0–100 percent, with 0 simulating black-and-white TV and 100 being a perfect rendition of daylight. Under low-CRI lighting (usually less than 65), red may appear as somewhat lavender and blue may resemble dull turquoise; such lamps are usually selected for reasons of economy or long life. A lamp's color is also indicated by its spectral profile, a graph of its ability to portray light in the visible portion of the electromagnetic spectrum (380 to 760 nm). Generally the smoother and higher a lamp's spectral profile, the richer and fuller its

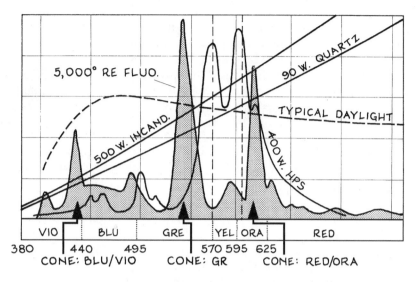

Fig. 6-9. Spectral profiles of various lamps.

TABLE 6-7: COLORIMETRY OF LAMPS

LAMP TYPE	Typical CCT [1], °K	(+) enhances hues, (–) dulls hues						CRI, %
		V	B	G	Y	O	R	
Natural outdoor light	2,000–9,400	+	+	+	+	+	+	100
Incandescent: 60 W	2,700				+	+	+	95
500 W	2,850			+	+	+	+	97
Quartz (tungsten-halogen)	2,800–3,200		+	+	+	+	+	98
Fluorescent: daylight (D)	6,250	+	+			–	–	76–79
Cool white (CW)	4,100–4,250	+	–	+	+	+	–	62
Warm white (WW)	3,000	+	–	+	+	+	–	53
Rare earth (RE)	3,100–6,500	+	+				+	70–92
Mercury, clear	5,700	+		+	+	–	–	15–45
Phosphor-coated	3,900	+		+	+	+		50–55
Metal-halide	3,200–4,000	+	+	+	+		–	65–80
Phosphor-coated	3,800	+	+	+	+			70–75
Sodium, high-pressure	2,100	–	–	+	+	+	–	22
Color-improved	2,200			+	+	+		65–70
Low-pressure	1,750	–	–	–	+		–	17

1. In this table, **V** is violet (CCT = 380–440 nm), **B** is blue (440–495 nm), **G** is green (495–570 nm), **Y** is yellow (570–595 nm), **O** is orange (595–625 nm), and **R** is red (625–760 nm).

light (typical of daylight and quartz lamps), while spiky profiles indicate an ability to portray only certain colors well. But the human eye also perceives a spiky spectral profile: its cones process incoming light only in the red-orange ($\approx$ 611 nm), green ($\approx$ 542 nm), and blue-violet ($\approx$ 436 nm) parts of the spectrum; then the brain blends this data into the infinite variety of colors we see. Recently developed triphosphor lamps assimilate this biological process. Due to these lamps' low spectral profile, which is also an energy profile, they also burn cooler. Generally lamps of similar CRIs can be compared only if they have similar CCTs.

Unfortunately, diligent utilization of CCTs and CRIs does not lead to ideal results every time. One reason is that *yellow light dulls all other colors*. This is why a brightly overcast sky portrays colors better than sunlight, because the latter contains yellow; why sodium light, which is nearly all yellow, portrays all other colors poorly; why triphosphor lamps work so well, because they leave out yellow; why warm lights portray blues and violets imperfectly, because they are fairly strong in yellow; and why cool lamps usually portray blues and violets well, because they are usually weak in yellow.

A spectacular use of color illumination in architecture appears in the Koko Yamaoka Bijouterie, a jewelry store in Tokyo. The store's long narrow floor plan, located at sidewalk level with the entry at one end, has walls of jewelry displays on each side that rise to a deep cove nearly 8 ft above the floor with 30 light boxes on each side, above which the walls rise to an alabaster-colored vault whose crown is 21 ft above the floor. Each light box contains four 100 V 50 W dichroic halogen reflector lamps, each fitted with a red, green, blue, or frost filter and aimed into the vault; then each lamp is controlled by a programmed dimmer that varies its voltage and lags the circuit of each succeeding lamp a moment behind the next to create waves of varicolored light that flow through the long narrow vault. Thus the colors continuously overlap, and as the dimmers slowly rise and fall, the colors continually advance and recede to create an infinite variety of kaleidoscopic hues upon the vault —constantly overlapping, constantly varying, never-ending, ever changing, never quite the same. During the day the colors are more intense and move at higher speeds to assimilate the brightness and bustle of the city out front, while at night the colors are softer and move more slowly to match the evening's mellower mood. As pedestrians walk by and see the lights through the store's full-height full-width glass facade, they are drawn to its brilliance like moths to candles. Then, as its designers proclaim, the Koko Yamaoka Bijouterie "becomes the new spot in the Ginza for the modern woman to realize her dreams." [†]

[†] Hisae Nozaura, "Jewelry Box sparkles in the Ginza"; *LD + A Journal* (IESNA, New

6.B. LIGHT SOURCES

A light source is any natural or artificial illumination. In fact, windows and skylights may be considered as dimmer-operated 'daylight fixtures' fitted with clear surface-mounted lenses. The electric potential a light source utilizes is usually 120 volts, rarely more than this, and occasionally 12 or 24 volts; and their wattages vary widely. Considering that a common incandescent lamp uses 120 volts and 100 watts, the current it consumes is less than one amp. Thus a dozen such lamps can be installed on one 15 amp circuit.

In this chapter, each artificial light source has a letter designation as follows:

I	=	incandescent
Q	=	quartz, halogen, or tungsten-halogen
F	=	fluorescent
CF	=	compact fluorescent
MV	=	mercury vapor
MH	=	metal-halide
HPS	=	high-pressure sodium
LPS	=	low-pressure sodium
HID	=	high-density discharge (includes MV, MH, HPS, & LPS)
FO	=	fiber optic
LD	=	light-emitting or liquid-crystal display

In the above light sources, usually only 4–8 percent of each lamp's life cycle costs is spent on its initial cost while 80–88 percent is spent on the energy consumed during its rated life (the rest goes toward installation and maintenance labor). In the eyes of many, such inefficient 'lumen lemons' are a major source of waste in our energy-extravagant society. Thus the federal government has outlawed several inefficient R, PAR, and fluorescent lamps, which industry has replaced with more efficient models such as compact fluorescent lamps.

Many industries today are conducting extensive research in new kinds of lighting technology. Some of this work has already produced lamps that can now be purchased, but whose initial price has yet to come down due to still-expensive production methods, reverse inertia on the part of consumers, and lack of mass-production-induced economies; while other possibilities still remain as dreams in a researcher's laboratory. A few of the more exciting possibilities for the future are:

▶ S*cotopic lamps* whose illumination fools one's eye pupils into opening wider, thus making the light's rays look brighter, thus requiring a lower-lumen lamp for a given task.

▶ An electrodeless fluorescent lamp, known as an *induction, ICE,* or *QL*

York); Mar 1994, pp. 17–18.

TABLE 6-8: COMMON LAMP SIZES & SHAPES

LAMP SHAPE, Type designation [1]	Lamp size (numbers = bulb dia. in 8th in.)						
	I	Q	F	MV	MH	HP	LP
A	15-25	—	—	23	—	—	—
E	—	—	—	23-28	17-37	25	—
ED	—	—	—	17-37	—	17-37	—
G	16-40	—	—	—	—	—	—
T	8-21	3-5	—	—	15	10	17-21
BT	—	—	—	37-56	37-56	—	—
R	14-60	12-30	—	40-60	40-60	—	—
ER	30-40	—	—	—	—	—	—
PAR	16-64	16-64	—	38	38	38	—
	Beamspreads range from 5°-130°						
MR	—	11-16	—	—	—	—	—
Straight tube	8-10	—	5-17	—	—	—	—
	L = 24 in. L = 4-96 in.						
Compact	—	—	9-40	—	—	—	—
Double-ended	—	3-6	—	—	6-8	—	—
	L = 4-10 in. L = 4-14 in.						

1. Lamp type designations are **A** = arbitrary or standard, **E** = elongated, **ED** = ellipsoidal, **G** = globe, **R** = reflector, **ER** = elliptical reflector, **PAR** = parabolic aluminized reflector, **T** = tubular, **BT** = blown tube, **MR** = multifaceted reflector (small quartz capsule in a faceted glass reflector).

lamp, that has a rated life of as much as 100,000 hours because it contains no electrodes that can burn out. These lamps have admirable CRIs of 80–85 and high efficacies of around 75 lumens per watt. They are already being installed in locations where lamp replacement is difficult.

▶ A golf-ball-sized *sulphur lamp* on a thin stem that contains a sulphur core in an inert gas which when bombarded with microwave energy produces an intense light that assimilates sunlight. One of these 'lollipop lamps' converts 1,425 watts into 135,000 lumens, lasts 60,000 hours, and can be dimmed to 20 percent of its output. This light source may be ideal for use with fiber optics and light pipes, and is now being used in the Smithsonian Institution's National Air and Space Museum in Washington, DC.

▶ An incandescent or fluorescent *full-spectrum lamp* whose glass is treated with a rare earth element that produces illumination that assimilates natural light. These 'naturalites' cost 10 times more but ease eye strain, reduce fatigue, use less energy, and last three times longer. They are available in many hardware stores today.

▶ A low-level-lighting *'blush lamp'* that has an electro- and phosphor-luminescent film sandwiched in a laminated panel that emits a bluish glow when turned on. These require very little power and can be made in wall- and ceiling-sized areas.

▶ An *energy-producing window* that contains a dye-coated gel which when struck by light injects energized electrons into a semiconductor which generates electric power. Present models are only about 7 percent efficient; but they are transparent, work under cloudy skies, and can be economically made with silk-screen-printing technology.

▶ *Wireless light bulbs* that utilize high-frequency waves generated by antennas 20–30 ft away which excite the gases in the bulbs to make them glow.

Not too many years from now, buildings may be filled with radiating floor tiles, shimmering cement walls, and ceiling surfaces that glow with incandescence when turned on. This may seem far-fetched to many. But imagine for a moment that it is 1890 and someone says that not too many years from now, we'll have vehicles that can lift themselves into the air and fly hundreds of miles through the sky like birds, and even carry cargos as big as stagecoaches, horses and all. "Preposterous!" we would have said. But not only have we experienced one such technological breakthrough after another for many decades now, but the *rate* of these breakthroughs has steadily increased —to the point that now an idea that may seem preposterous in one decade may be obvious the next decade, and obsolete the decade after.

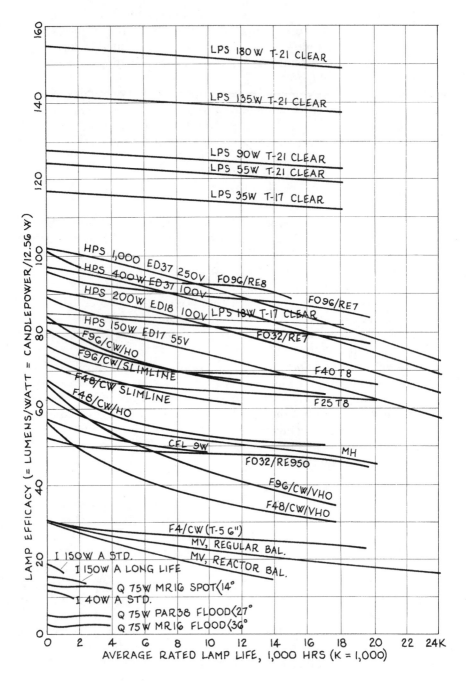

Fig. 6-10. Lamp life lines.

6.B.1. Daylighting

As long as the sun is above the horizon, daylight is of elemental importance to architectural interior spaces. Indeed, it should be the primary prism to which artificial light is added, not the other way around. Its ever-moving hues also allow occupants to mark the passing of time through the course of each day and the seasons.

The average luminance of an overcast sky at midday at temperate latitudes is about 1,500 fc. Other daylighting levels at the zenith (straight up) are clear sky ≈ 8,800 fc, high overcast ≈ 5,300, clear north light ≈ 1,200 fc, foggy ≈ 1,100, light rainy ≈ 900, gray overcast ≈ 650, thunderstorm ≈ 150, and clear sky at dawn or dusk ≈ 40 fc. Near-horizon values may be only $\frac{1}{3}$ to $\frac{1}{2}$ of zenith, and stormy skies can cut any of the above amounts by another two-thirds or more. Obviously daylighting levels vary greatly; thus related artificial lighting requirements should not be based on statistical averages because the average rarely exists. A better strategy is to design each occupancy for evening illumination (which should usually be done anyway), install programmed controls, then let the controls and daylighting levels maintain a mellower illumination at lower cost. But maximum daylighting data should always be obtained to determine potential glare problems and artificial lighting control thresholds.

As for the color composition of daylighting, direct sunlight is rich in yellows, clear-day natural or north light is rich in blues, and an overcast sky is fairly even for every hue in the spectrum. In fact, the ideal daylight is a luminous medium overcast sky that creates a shadowless and even diffusion of light —what the Impressionists called *gris clair*. Its lighting level at the zenith is around 3,000 fc.

In spaces where daylighting is utilized, compass orientations, fenestration patterns, spatial configurations, and surface reflections are very important. Daylighting may be encouraged into architectural spaces by ribbon windows located in exterior walls, clerestories and other large openings in interior walls, transoms over doors, French doors with translucent glass, shoulder-high walls around seated occupancies in large open spaces, pale colors on ceilings and walls, higher-than-average reflectances (≥ 0.4) for floors, and lighting controls.

Some of the finest examples of daylighting in the architecture of any age were created by Frank Lloyd Wright and Le Corbusier. In Wright's Larkin Building of 1902, the large central light court bathed the whole interior with daylight, and the four $2\frac{1}{2}$ ft wide vertical glass rifts at each corner filled the staircases just inside with natural light. These strips of glass also defined the lofty stair towers, set free their corners, and imparted to the building much of its massive character, and thus were a major design element of the building. And in the Unity Temple of 1904, Wright pierced the box-like auditorium with more vertical rifts of leaded glass at the corner

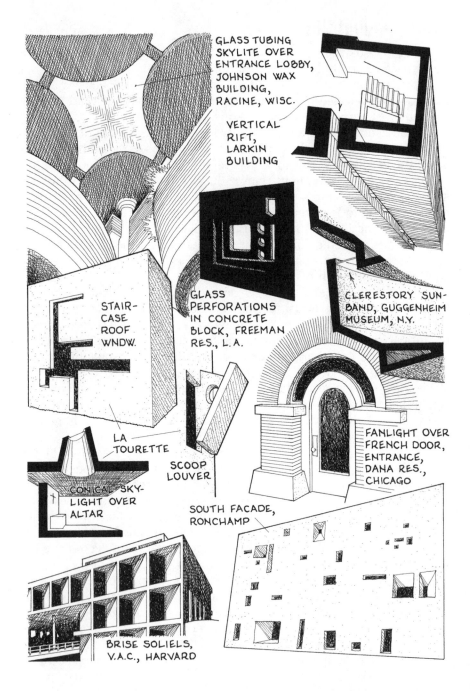

GLASS TUBING
SKYLITE OVER
ENTRANCE LOBBY,
JOHNSON WAX
BUILDING,
RACINE, WISC.

VERTICAL
RIFT,
LARKIN
BUILDING

STAIR-
CASE
ROOF
WNDW.

GLASS
PERFORATIONS
IN CONCRETE
BLOCK, FREEMAN
RES., L.A.

CLERESTORY SUN-
BAND, GUGGENHEIM
MUSEUM, N.Y.

LA
TOURETTE

SCOOP
LOUVER

FANLIGHT OVER
FRENCH DOOR,
ENTRANCE,
DANA RES.,
CHICAGO

CONICAL SKY-
LIGHT OVER
ALTAR

SOUTH FACADE,
RONCHAMP

BRISE SOLIELS,
V.A.C., HARVARD

Fig. 6-11. Daylighting details of the masters.

staircases plus lengthy friezes of glass under each eave and 25 coffered skylights overhead, which together freed the surrounding compositions of planes and piers and set them seemingly afloat in dazzling daylight. Indeed, many other Wright buildings —particularly the Johnson Wax Building, the Guggenheim Museum, and the canvas-roofed drafting studios of Taliesin West— utilize daylight in ingenious manners. And Corbu: the south facade of his Chapel of Ronchamp is one of the finest fenestration compositions ever. Then there are his trademark brise-soliels, which govern the entry of daylight into the interiors of Harvard's Carpenter Visual Arts Center and so many of his other buildings; and the ingenious scoop louvers, slit clerestories, and light cannons in the Monastery at La Tourette; and on and on. As Corbu said: "Recognize then the primordial importance of the location of windows: here the decisive architectural impressions are born." [†]

It is safe to say that not one architect living today is capable of designing buildings with daylighting interpenetrations as amazing as these. Ones with no moving parts. Ones created without the digital crutches of computers. Why aren't there architects like this today? Why aren't there even ones who would try to *copy* these masters? When one ponders the daylighting techniques of Wright and Corbu, a modern question arises: what would *they* have done with computerized controls for harvesting daylight? Would they have used them in ways so amazing that the rest of us would gasp with even deeper exhalations of renewed awe? Or —knowing that sunlight and shadows cost nothing— would they have said: "Bah! Humbug!"

Soon the answer to these intriguing questions may become moot, due to a variety of recently developed glazings which even Wright or Corbu may have never dreamed of, which may spawn the next revolution in architecture after the present one involving computerized controls has subsided. Imagine a *NATURALIGHT* or a *2020 VISION* catalog at your deskside two decades from now that contains the following selections: *Warm windows* that block ultraviolet and infrared portions of the electromagnetic spectrum while allowing the narrow band of visible light to pass through. *LowlowE windows* that contain two low-emissivity films between two panes of glass and have R-values approaching 10. *Angular-selective prisms* and *multimicrolouvers* that block incident sunrays at one angle yet allow the rays to enter at a slightly different angle. *Holographic slats* that create two different images at slightly different angles by also allowing sunlight to pass through at one angle while blocking it at another. Near-transparent panels of *aerogel* with a proven R-value of 12 per in. thickness that when used as whole facades and roofs look like frozen smoke as daylight enters them. And *electromolecular glazing* that contains magnetized polymers immersed in a transparent LED-type panel, in which the polymers' slat-like shapes rotate when an electric current passes through them, allowing them also to let in desirable sunrays and block unwanted ones.

[†] "Le Corbusier—A Tribute"; *The Architectural Forum* (Urban America, Inc, New

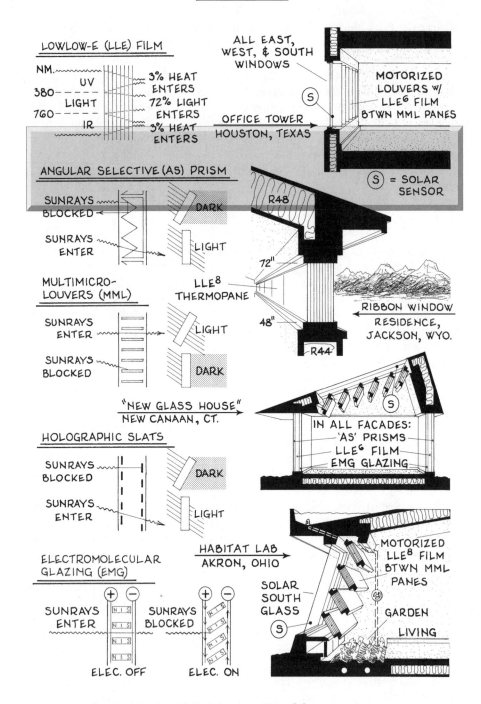

Fig. 6-12. Daylighting details of future masters.

Maybe tomorrow's masters of design will improve on even these amazing innovations. For example, if two lowlowE films work better than one, why not eight? Or twenty? Indeed, if lowlowE film has a "coolness fraction" (1.00 – the portion of heat blocked) of 0.64 and a transmissivity of 0.96, then theoretically a sandwich of 8 layers will reduce heat flow by $1 - (0.64)^8 = 97$ percent while reducing lightflow by only $1 - (0.96)^8 = 28$ percent, which is less than the light reduction that results when a cloud passes in front of the sun. Thus by using the raw dirt of "max-R glazings" and "microsunscreens", tomorrow's Æ designers may create total "glass houses" in which occupants may enjoy the outdoors in any direction —even the sky— without sweltering in spaces that are too warm, shivering in spaces that are too cold, or being offended by glaring sunrays.

➕ Daylighting has more accurate color rendition, softer shadows, more balanced distribution, greater lightness constancy, and subtler patterns of change than any artificial light.

➖ Daylighting is unpredictable, and its intensity varies greatly.

How much daylighting arrives at a table 14 ft inside a 48 × 69 in. window of ¼ in. thick glass if the daylight's intensity is 5,400 fc, the window is clean, and outdoor obstructions and ground reflectances are negligible? This is an area light source whose $\lambda = 20.1$ ft^2

6)B)1) $\diamond\ \theta\ \tau\ \lambda_\eta\ {}_L\Delta\ (1 + 0.5\ \kappa_G)\ \approx\ \Phi\ D^2$

$\diamond$ = output of natural light source. If $\diamond$ is *point*, $\diamond_P$ = fc; if $\diamond$ is *line*, $\diamond_L$ = fc/LF; if $\diamond$ is *area*, $\diamond_A$ = fc/sf. Here the large glass window is obviously an *area* light source ➡ $\diamond_A$ = 5,400 fc/sf.

θ = obstructions (foliage, buildings, terrain, etc.) in front of opening. θ = sin (angle formed by top of obstructions and surface of glazing) × (1 – solid-to-opening ratio of any screen over opening). Here θ = sin 90° × (1 – 0) = 1.0.

τ = transmittance of glazing. From Table 6-10, τ for *¼ in. single pane glass: clear, standard* = 0.88.

λ_η = light source near-field factor, given as 20.1 sf. To compute the near-field factor of any light source, see Sec. 6.A.1.a.

${}_L\Delta$ = light depreciation factor. As window is clean, assume Δ = l.0.

κ_G = ground reflectance factor, from Table 2-11. If κ_G is small, use 0.

Φ = incident light upon visual task, ? fc

D = distance between light source and visual task, 14 ft

5,400 × 1 × 0.88 × 20.1 × 1 × (1 + 0.5 × 0) $\approx$ Φ × 14²   ... Φ $\approx$ 490 fc

6.B.2. Incandescent [†]

In these lamps a tungsten filament is mounted in a glass bulb filled with an inert gas. The bulbs may be *clear* (the brightest), *frosted* (slightly diffuse light), or *white* (highly diffuse light); and they have several shapes as shown in Table 6-8, the most important being A (general purpose), R (reflects light in mostly one direction), and PAR (concentrates light in a narrower beam angle). Usually the higher the wattage, the hotter the lamp's filament and the shorter its life. For example, the rated life of a 40 watt A lamp is 1,500 hr while that of a 250 watt lamp is 750 hr. All incandescent lamps are dimmable over their full range. Dimming shifts the lamp's color slightly toward orange, and the reduction in output is not proportional to reduction in power (52 percent output uses about 75 percent power)

One manufacturer has developed several "IQ" incandescent lamps with microchips in their bases that enable each lamp to perform such energy-saving tasks as offer four levels of dimming, turn off after 30 minutes (good for closets, storerooms, and bathrooms), turn off after 6 hours (allows a business or home to appear occupied when it is not), or dim from 60 to 5 watts over 10 minutes (good for hallway night lighting).

➕ Available in many types and sizes; easy to install; start and restart instantly; require no ballasts; have good color rendering; and operate well in any temperature and humidity. Lowest initial cost, which allows easy stockpiling and easy replacement of burnouts. Best for short-duration lighting in small areas.

➖ High operating cost, high heat loss, short lamp life. The least efficient light source: each 100 watt bulb acts as a 90 watt space heater (in some cases this may be desirable).

> How much energy does a standard 100 watt lamp that costs 79¢ consume during its rated life if electricity costs 8.625¢ a kilowatt-hour?

6)B)2) $ \$ \approx 0.00001 \, \omega \, ¢ \, L $

$ \$ $ = cost of energy consumed during lamp's rated life, **?** dollars
$ \omega $ = wattage of lamp, 100 watts
$ ¢ $ = local cost of electric power, ¢/kWh. ¢ = 8.625¢ per kWh.
$ L $ = rated lamp life, hr. From Fig. 6-10, L for incandescent lamp
      = 1,000 hr.

$ \$ \approx 0.00001 \times 100 \times 8.625 \times 1,000 = \$8.63 $ ... vs. 79¢ initial cost

---

[†] Most of the data in Secs. 6.B.2.–6.B.5., including Figs. 6-13 and 6-14, was ob-

6.B.3. Quartz

Also known as tungsten-halogen or halogen, these lamps contain a tungsten filament mounted in a bulb filled with a halogen gas. They render colors almost perfectly, offer full-range dimming, and are generally smaller, more efficient, and longer-lasting than incandescent lamps of the same wattage. Since quartz lamps burn hotter than the kindling point of many building materials, their housings must be ventilated, insulated, or protrude from their surroundings. These lamps also emit ultraviolet rays and their gas fills are at high pressure; thus they are often enclosed by UV-resistant lenses that will contain any exploding hot glass particles that could cause injury or fire. Thus a common mount for these lamps is ceiling track lighting well out of reach of occupants and well-spaced from materials that could burn, fade, or crumble due to excessive drying. Quartz PAR lamps range from 45–500 watts and have beam spreads from 5° (very narrow spot) to 60° or more (very wide flood). A tubular quartz lamp fitted into a small trough reflector is excellent for wallwashing illumination.

Quartz lamps are also made as low-voltage (12 or 24 V) MR and IR lamps that are compact, last longer, use less energy, and have more concise beamspreads which produce less spill light than their 120 V cousins. Some MR and IR lamps also have a dichroic film on the reflector's outside which increases output and energy-efficiency by 40 percent. Low-voltage quartz lamps are typically mounted in small slightly recessed reflectors. The lamps' low voltages are created by small step-down transformers that may be remotely mounted to reduce noise, increase circuit safety, and serve several fixtures. Where these transformers and solid-state dimming controls coexist, they can create buzzing and other reactive flow interference (RFI) which can lead to dimmer and transformer failure. This has led to autotransformers that not only minimize RFI but provide overload and short-circuit protection, regulate voltage, and lengthen lamp life. However, these transformers are large and **N2G** for multi-circuit dimming.

➕ Whiter light, more compact bulbs, and longer life than incandescent lamps. Output depreciates less during rated life (≈ 5 percent) than any other lamp. Near-perfect color rendering.

➖ Their UV radiation can 'sunburn' anyone working under them for long periods. Highly sensitive to voltage variations, which can degrade performance and lower life. Poor choice for recessed fixtures. Constant low-level dimming can blacken bulbs.

528

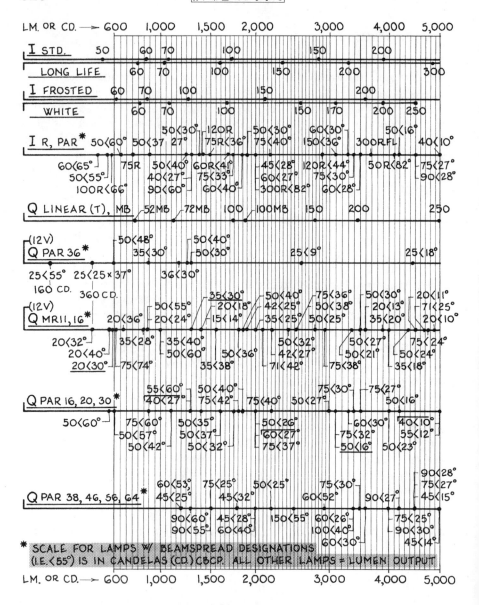

HOW TO USE THIS CHART

Knowing the lighting load (lumens or centerbeam candlepower), select the desired lamp from the column on the left, then move to the right along the lamp's *output line* to the computed lighting load ➡ the next number to the right is the lamp's smallest wattage that satisfies the required lighting load.

Fig. 6-13A. Lamp selection chart:
incandescent & quartz lamps.

(General Electric Co., Cleveland, OH, 1995); (2) *1995 Osram Sylvania Product*

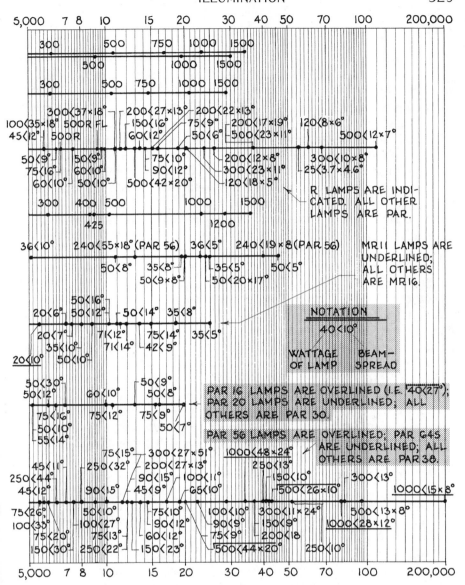

LAMP ABBREVIATIONS USED IN THIS CHART

I = incandescent lamp. **Q** = quartz or halogen lamp. $<$ = beamspread designation: e.g. a 50$<$30° lamp is a 50 watt lamp with a 30° beamspread. **MR** = a miniature or small reflective lamp. **R** = reflective lamp. **PAR** = parabolic reflective lamp. **T** = a linear or long narrow lamp.

**Fig. 6-13B. Lamp selection chart:
incandescent & quartz lamps.**

Catalog (Osram Sylvania Inc., Danvers, MA, 1995); (3) *1996 Philips Lamp*

6.B.4. Fluorescent

A fluorescent lamp is a glass tube coated on the inside with phosphors, filled with an inert gas, and capped at the ends with wire cathodes; then when the power turns on, a plasma arc travels between the cathodes through the gas and illuminates the phosphors while the voltage is regulated by a small transformer called a ballast. The type and amount of phosphor determines the character of each lamp, and due to the wide range of phosphors employed there are a great variety of fluorescent lamps. Because they have the lowest power-to-surface ratio of all light sources, they are more diffuse and create less glare than any other; thus they tend to create shadowless task planes and are an excellent short-distance lighting. Their large surface areas and pronounced linear geometry also necessitate large fixtures and make them a prominent element of design, which has its positive and negative aspects.

Fluorescent lamps are normally classed by types of construction, coatings, and ballasts, which due to numerous exceptions by different manufacturers defy precise categorization. Generally, common constructions are *preheat* (P: takes 2–5 sec to light, is used for display case lighting and other small-fit applications, rated life ≈ 7,500–9,000 hr), *rapid start* (RS: takes 1–2 sec to light, is a popular commercial lighting, rated life ≈ 12,000–20,000 hr), *instant start* (IS: lights instantly, is widely used for retail, industrial, and institutional lighting, rated life ≈ 7,500–12,000 hr), *high output* (HO: starts instantly, is about 30 percent brighter but only 90 percent as efficient as instant start, is used for high-ceiling lighting, rated life ≈ 12,000 hr), and *very high output* (VHO: lights instantly, is about 50 percent brighter but only 55 percent as efficient as instant start, is used where high lighting levels are a priority, rated life ≈ 12,000 hr). Popular phosphor coatings are *cool white* (enhances greens and blues), *warm white* (enhances reds and yellows), *daylight* (simulates overcast sky), and *rare earth* (renders all colors well, is 15–25 percent more efficient than other coatings, and is the only lamp with both high efficacy and high CRI).

Although the most common fluorescent lamps are straight tube, they are bent into circles, U's, and a variety of compact configurations; and the tubes can be fitted with semi-circular snap-on concentrating reflectors that can be rotationally adjusted. Circular lamps with 6–16 in. diameters are often installed in household kitchens, over drafting desks, and in other small areas where high-level light is desired. U lamps are installed primarily in 2 × 2 ft ceiling fixtures with prismatic or parabolic lenses. Compact fluorescent (CFL) lamps usually have bulbs, loops, or thin-diameter coils whose bases contain integral ballasts; they have a typical CRI of 82 and cost much less to operate than incandescent lamps. They are fine where precise beam spreads are not required, but intricately shaped bulbs are a poor choice in dusty areas unless the bulbs are enclosed.

A fluorescent lamp's output is appreciably affected by the choice of its ballast. For example, an FO32T8 lamp whose rated output is 2,900 lm has a range of 2,200–3,700 lm with available ballasts. Ballasts are generally *electromagnetic* or *electronic*. Although the former kinds cost more, they offer greater efficacy, cooler operation, less hum and flicker, longer life, ability to operate several lamps on one ballast, and 3–100 percent dimming control, all of which adds up to greater energy savings and productivity over the long term. However, they increase RFI in the power supply, which reduces output and lamp life if not corrected by electronic regulators. Also available is an emergency lighting ballast, which contains a battery in the fixture that keeps its lamps burning for 90 minutes when the power fails, then when the power returns the battery is recharged.

Fluorescent lamps are efficient, with efficacy and unit brightness (lm/LF) usually increasing as the tube lengthens. Although efficacy is optimal between room temperatures of 80–100°, it decreases rapidly above and below this amount; so these lamps should not be tightly enclosed or located in drafty areas. All-weather lamps with low-temperature ballasts are available for sub-50° installations such as basements and outdoor canopies, but they are usually less cost-effective than HID lamps. Since a tiny part of a fluorescent lamp's cathodes is depleted with each start, the ratio of starts to hours of continuous operation considerably affects rated lamp lives; so these lamps are **N2G** where they are frequently turned on and off. They can also be dangerous if they illuminate rotating machinery that turns at an rpm that is an exact multiple of the lamp ballast's 60-Hz/sec cycle —as the resulting strobe effect can make the rotating parts look motionless.

As fluorescent lighting depreciates 20–35 percent during its rated life, automatic dimming that maintains desirable lighting levels is a relevant strategy. A few dimmers go down to 1 percent of full brightness; but dimming below 20 percent is rarely necessary, wastes energy, and shortens lamp life. After all, 20 percent dimming lowers lighting levels to 5 percent of full brightness in a step-switch four-lamp fixture. Thus a viable strategy is to install low-cost dimmers in multi-switch multi-lamp fixtures. Also, dimming controls should be individualized by function and not by floorspace area. Fluorescent lamps are **N2G** for accent lighting, because their beamspreads are not easily controlled and they do not portray surface gradients as richly as incandescent or quartz lighting.

➕ Long rated life, high efficacy. The softest light: **VG** where excessive contrast or glare is a problem. The coolest light: **VG** where lamps may be touched or fixtures are recessed or located near flammable materials. A variety of lamp types can be fitted into a single fixture, allowing a building with numerous different occupancies (e.g. a school or shopping center) to have one standard fixture, which simplifies construction and maintenance. Highest output, best color rendition, and lowest life cycle costs for large areas illuminated several hours a day. Excellent for daylight harvesting and energy management dimming.

⊖ High fixture cost, standard units don't operate well below 50° F, inefficient for short illumination periods and frequent on/off cycles. In multi-lamp fixtures or lamps connected in series, if one component fails all other components degenerate. Unsuitable for most outdoor lighting. Ballasts emit noises ranging from Class A at 20–24 dB to Class F at 40–44 dB.

If a 28 watt CFL lamp produces the same light as a 100 watt incandescent lamp, how do the lamps' total costs compare if the incandescent lamp initially costs 79¢, the CFL lamp costs $14.95, and the cost of electricity is 8.625¢ per kWh?

6)B)4) $\qquad$ $100 \; \$_i \; = \; L \, (\text{¢} - 0.001 \; \text{€} \; W)$

$\$_i$ = initial cost of each light source, dollars. $\$_i$ for I lamp = 79¢ = $0.79; $\$_i$ for F lamp = $14.95.

L = rated life of each light source, hr. From Fig. 6-10, rated life of I lamp ≈ 1,000 hr and rated life of F lamp ≈ 6,500 hr.

¢ = total unit cost during rated life of each light source, ? ¢/hr

€ = unit cost of local electric power, 8.63¢/kWh

W = wattages of light sources that produce equal light, watts. W for I lamp = 100 watts and W for CFL lamp = 28 watts.

Incandescent: $100 \times 0.79 \; \approx \; 1,000 \, (\text{¢}_u - 0.001 \times 8.63 \times 100)$
$$\text{¢}_u \; \approx \; 0.94 \text{¢/hr of rated life}$$
CFL: $100 \times 14.95 \; \approx \; 6,500 \, (\text{¢}_u - 0.001 \times 8.63 \times 28)$
$$\text{¢}_u \; \approx \; 0.47 \text{¢/hr of rated life}$$

Unit cost of CFL lamp ≈ 0.44/0.93 or 47% that of incandescent lamp

6.B.5. H.I.D.

A high-intensity discharge (HID) lamp has an incandescent-like bulb activated by a fluorescent-like ballast which produces an intense light that is efficient and long-lived. These light sources may be *mercury vapor* (MV), *metal halide* (MH), *high-pressure sodium* (HPS), or *low-pressure sodium*

1995); (5) *Halo Power-Trac® Lighting* (Cooper Industries Inc., Elk Grove Village,

(LPS); and the bulbs may be *clear* (offers good optical control), *diffuse* (reduces brightness and glare), or *phosphor-coated* (improves usually low CRIs to moderate levels). These lamps are best installed where burning cycles last 10 hr or more, because their average rated lives tend to shorten to 75 percent at 5 hr per start and 60 percent at 3 hr per start. Lamps made for horizontal mounts (±15°) last up to 67 percent longer than universal burn equivalents.

As HID lamps are pressurized and burn at temperatures exceeding 1,800° F, they typically explode with hot glass particles if they break or come in contact with any liquid. Thus they are usually enclosed, have thermally resistant fixtures with protruding mounts, and are not installed near wood or other flammable materials. These dangers make them a poor choice for low-ceiling lighting, wall sconces, or any other close-proximity light source. Also, when HID lamps are turned on they take several minutes to reach full output, and when turned off they take several minutes to turn on again. Thus they are NG in assemblies and other occupancies where power outages could make crowds panic; unless they contain a dual arc tube or have a ballast with a hot restrike device, both of which relight the lamp quickly after power is lost. Although dimming is possible with HID lamps, it creates color shifts in the lighting and usually works only down to about 50 percent output. As with fluorescent lamps, HID lamps can be dangerous if they illuminate rotating machinery that turns at an rpm that is an exact multiple of the lamps' ballast cycles, as the resulting strobe effect can make the rapidly rotating parts look motionless.

HID lamp ballasts may be *core and coil* (the simplest kind), *F-can* (a relatively quiet ballast for offices, schools, and the like), *potted core and coil* (a quiet high-temperature ballast used for recessed lighting in quiet spaces), *indoor enclosed* (a remote ballast used to activate lamps in high ceilings and other hard-to-reach areas), *weather duty* (used outdoors or where temperatures vary greatly), or *post line* (a remote weather duty ballast usually mounted in the bases of light poles). In installations where voltages frequently vary, the ballasts should have regulators that ensure uniform electron flow.

Principal properties of each HID lamp are described below.

Mercury Vapor (MV). These lamps have wattages from 50–1,000, CRIs of 40–55, and CCTs ≈ 5,500° K. Because they emit a blue-green light they are excellent for night-lighting foliage, green copper exteriors, and certain signage. Otherwise they have few optimal properties compared to other light sources, and they have the lowest efficacy of any HID lamp.

Metal Halide (MH). These lamps have wattages from 32–2,000, CRIs of 65–70, and CCTs from 3,000–4,000° K. They offer the best combination of efficacy, CRI, and long life of all lamps, and thus they are used for long-burning general area illumination. They are also slightly smaller per watt

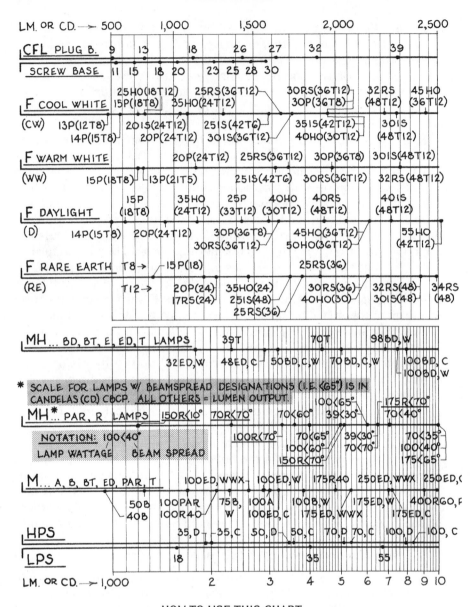

HOW TO USE THIS CHART

Knowing the lighting load (lumens or centerbeam candlepower), select the desired lamp from the column on the left, then move to the right along the lamp's *output line* to the computed lighting load ➡ the next number to the right is the lamp's smallest wattage that satisfies the required lighting load.

Fig. 6-14A. Lamp selection chart: fluorescent & high-density discharge lamps.

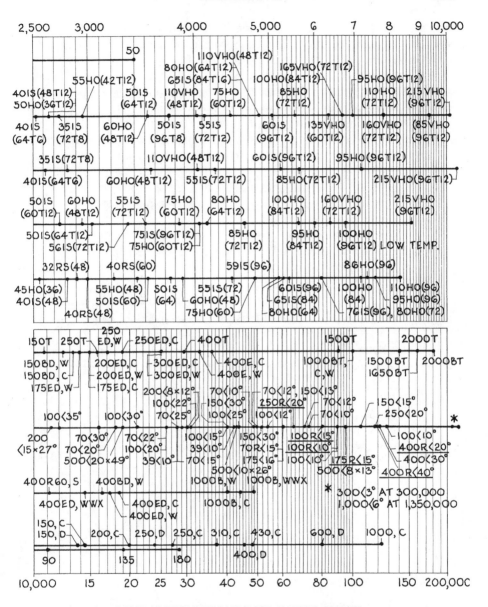

LAMP ABBREVIATIONS USED IN THIS CHART

F lamps (nos. in parentheses: 1st 2 nos. = tube length, in.; T = tube thickness, 8th in.): **P** = preheat, **RS** = rapid start, **IS** = instant start, **HO** = high output, **VHO** = very high output . *HID lamps:* **C** = clear, **W** = coated or white, **WWX** = warm white deluxe, **D** = diffuse, **S** = spot, **F** = flood.

Fig. 6-14B. Lamp selection chart:
fluorescent & high-density discharge lamps.

than MV lamps, so they fit into smaller fixtures and thus are good for accent and display lighting requiring precise beam spreads. Special MH lamps are *universal burning* (mountable in any position), *position-restricted* (mountable only in its design position but is more efficient), *safety* (the power cuts off if the lamp is broken, which allows use in open fixtures), *shrouded arc tube* (used in open fixtures where high efficacy and low maintenance are desired), *double-ended tube* (good for wallwashing), and *designer color* (emits colors such as pink, yellow, blue, or magenta). MH lamps can also be faced with dichroic filters that heighten color rendition. Because these lamps emit UV light, they should be fitted with UV-blocking lenses where occupants may be nearby. As they age, their color shifts dramatically toward blue, which may be used as a relamping indicator.

High-pressure sodium (HPS). These lamps contain a cigaret-shaped arc tube that is ignited by a high-voltage electronic starter. They have wattages from 35–1,000, CRIs of about 60, CCTs ≈ 1,700° K, rated

TABLE 6-9: COMPARATIVE PROPERTIES OF LAMPS

PROPERTY	I	Q	F	M	MH	HPS
			Lamp Designations			
Typical power, ω ...	40-1500	100-500	40-215	50-1000	175-1500	35-1000
Output, 1,000 lm. ...	0.4-15	1.8-10	2.8-16	1.2-40	18-84	2-126
Efficacy, lm/W [1]	11-20	13-27	35-65	27-60	55-80	60-110
Typical CRI, %	90-97	99-100	50-90	30-55	65-70	18-22
Aver. life, 1,000 hr ...	1-2.5	2-6	7.5-20	12-24	7.5-20	10-40
Lowest oper. temp,°F ..	40	- 40	+45	- 30	- 30	- 30
Voltage/output inc. [2]..	5/17	v. sensitive	5/3	3/6	5/12	10/0
Start delay	0	0	0-5 sec	3-6 min	2-3 min	1-3 min
Restart delay	0	0	0-3 sec	3-8 min	10-15 min	1-2 min
Dimming limit, % [3]	0	0	10	5	10	10
Deprec. at 50% life [4]....	11	- 1	- 14	- 20	- 27	- 7
At 100% life [5]	18	- 3	- 20	- 37	- 37	- 28
Optional oper. positions [5]	V, B↓	V, B↓	H	V, B↓	V, B↓	H or V
% light energy	10	13	19	15	21	25
% ballast energy	0	0	13	10	13	15
% Infrared energy	70	66	30	46	32	37
% UV (2% is high)	1	2	0.5	2	3	0.2
% conduct'n/convect'n [6] .	18	19	36	27	31	22

1. Includes ballast losses
2. Line voltage/lamp output increase: when line voltage increases by a certain percent, lamp output increases by a certain percent.
3. Dimming limit, to percent of full output.
4. Lamp depreciation at 50 and 100% of rated life, % of initial output.
5. Operating positions: V = vertical, H = horizontal, B↓ = lamp base down.
6. Percent of conduction/convection energy emitted by operating lamp.

lives ≈ 24,000 hr with very low depreciation, and efficacies from 60–130 (efficacy increases as wattage increases). They are generally used for high-output lighting where CRI is fairly unimportant; but an improved-color version has a CRI ≈ 70 and a rated life ≈ 15,000 hr. HPS lamps may also be mounted with MH lamps in the same fixture to create a highly efficient light of fairly high CRI.

Low-pressure sodium (LPS). These lamps contain a thin U-shaped arc inside a tubular bulb. They have wattages from 35–180, CRIs of about 20, CCTs around 2,000° K, and efficacies of 140–180 (the highest of all commonly available lamps). Their output is a warm golden radiance that makes all hues but yellow appear as dull shades of grey, brown, or black. Thus they are used for security, roadways, tunnels, and other areas where economic operation is more important than CRI. They also provide sharp images on surveillance TV, penetrate fog and pollution haze well, and promote plant growth indoors. As LPS lamps age, their output remains nearly constant but efficacy is nearly halved, which may be counteracted by installing auto-leakage transformers whose power increases with lamp age. Some also contain an end-of-life indicator that signals when the lamp needs replacing, which can reduce maintenance and replacement costs.

➕ High outputs, high efficacies, long rated lives. Best for long burning periods per start in large indoor and outdoor areas where color rendition is unimportant. **VG** outdoor lighting as they are largely unaffected by large temperature changes.

➖ Low CRIs, lengthy warmup times and restrike delays make them impractical for frequent on/off switching and unusable during short power outages. A poor choice where precise dimming is desired. Hot operating temperatures make them **NG** near wood, plastics, or flammable fabrics.

6.B.6. Neon [†]

This lighting which appears in the windows of many restaurants, delicatessens, and retail stores offers unusual opportunities for illumination that is subdued, functional, and decorative. A neon lamp is a long glass tube filled with gasses which when electrified give off a cool but dazzling light. Colors are created by gaseous fills (10–12 are commonly available from fabricators' color charts), phosphors applied to the tube's inner walls, and tinted glass tubes. Diameters range from 9–25 mm, with 12 and 15 mm being the most common. Light output varies with tube diameter (the smaller the diameter the brighter the color), amperage, gas fill, and phosphor coatings. Green phosphor has the highest output (240 lm/LF for 12 mm tubing at 30 mA), white

---

[†] This section was prepared from (1) information obtained from Michael Cohen's

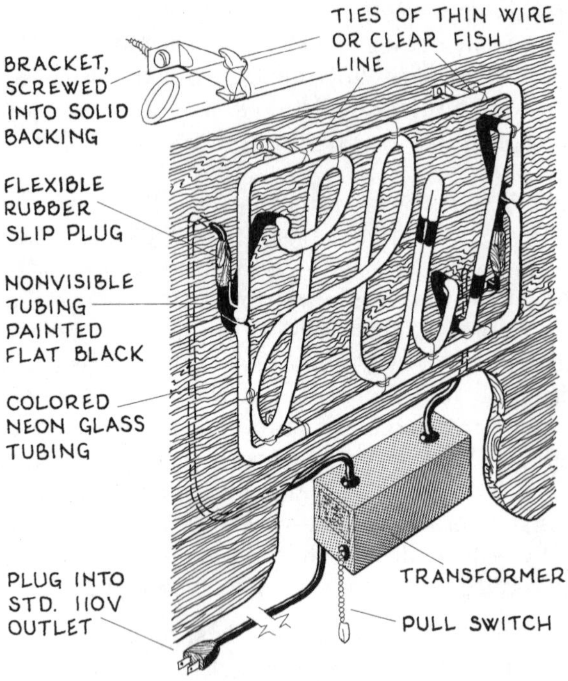
TIES OF THIN WIRE OR CLEAR FISH LINE
BRACKET, SCREWED INTO SOLID BACKING
FLEXIBLE RUBBER SLIP PLUG
NONVISIBLE TUBING PAINTED FLAT BLACK
COLORED NEON GLASS TUBING
PLUG INTO STD. 110V OUTLET
TRANSFORMER
PULL SWITCH

Fig. 6-15. Anatomy of a neon lamp.

is 83 percent of this, and purple is lowest at 42 percent.

A neon lamp has a core-and-coil stepup transformer whose voltage is a function of tube length, tube diameter, and gas fills. Typical operation may be a few thousand volts at 10–60 mA, with wattages being about 7 W/LF for 30 mA. If the transformer is not strong enough to trigger ionization that produces a steady state of emitted light, the lamp will flicker. Although the NEC prohibits any voltage greater than 1,000 V in homes, transformers of less than 1,000 V are available. A transformer typically weighs about 10 lb, but newly developed electronic units are smaller, lighter, cooler, and quieter.

Two flexible wires from the transformer connect to each end of the glass tubing with rubber slip plugs to form the circuit, and the tubing is typically held in place with brackets or small rubber cushions. The brackets are usually screwed into the solid backing behind the tubes but can also be attached to glass surfaces with contact adhesive. Reflector strips can also be installed behind or beside the tubes to redirect the light. The tubing may be bent into any shape, and selecting colors to match surrounding decor is similar to selecting drapes. Such lighting may be used to accent prominent architectural lines, and even to satisfy functional needs in a festive manner. For example, in a basement theater neon tubing was installed in the cornice above the staircase entrance as a way of guiding customers into the below-street-level lobby and because it took up less space than border lights. In addition to the usual colorful abstract images and decorative graphics, neon lighting may be used to create an array of exciting effects by combining with flashers, multilevel switches, up-and-down fading, linkage to music that creates pulsing effects, flow scripting

"Neon: Argon to Xenon"; *LD + A Journal* (IESNA, New York); Mar 1995, p. 23; (2)

transformers that allow animated techniques, and color-switching transformers that allow selective excitation of one or more gasses to create eye-
catching displays.

A neon installation is designed as follows: the architect makes a line
drawing of the desired layout and takes it to a fabricator, who selects the
components and bends the glass into manageable lengths in a shop, then
assembles the fixture onsite. Good work includes aluminum conduit, high-
quality dielectric strength GTO cable, thick insulating sleeves over connections, electronic transformers, and ventilation of transformer areas. Most
premature failures are due to faulty installation. Rated life is 5–20 years
for the tubing and 3–15 years for the transformers. When a bulb goes out,
a technician arrives and repairs it.

➕ Neon lighting uses little energy, is highly efficient, and creates
little generated heat. Each fixture is custom-made, unique, and
offers exciting effects.

➖ Tubing is breakable. At temperatures below 50° lamps flicker and
are weak. Lamps hum or buzz slightly, and this increases with the
number of tubing turns and bends. Frequent on/off switching
degrades transformers. In many jurisdictions flashing neon
lights are illegal if exposed to public streets.

6.B.7. Fiber Optic [†]

Imagine a flexible tube whose inner surface is so shiny that if you aim
a flashlight into one end nearly all the light comes out the other. This is the
rudimentary 'optic fiber.' It can send the usual straight-line light waves
around corners and keep them together so their usual spherical output
doesn't diminish according to the law of inverse squares. If the tube is
translucent, the transmitted light appears on the outside. Such a tube may
be used as a decorative element, a 'cheap neon' that is especially welcome
at night, may be easily bent onsite, and is not brittle as is lamp glass. If the
tube's walls are opaque, sound and even written data can be transmitted
through it via digital impulses —a sort of molecular Morse Code. Such communication is not new: Alexander Bell came up with it when he invented the
telephone in 1876. In each case the tubing is an optical fiber about as thick
as fishing line that contains an inner transparent core, usually of silica
glass, and an outer cladding of glass or plastic. Since the light rays or digital impulses continually reflect off the tubing's walls as they travel through
the core, FO cable should have only slight bends; otherwise the rays or
impulses will be absorbed by the cladding and be largely lost.

A conversation with an employee of C & M signs of Bedford Hills, NY; and (3)   ▯

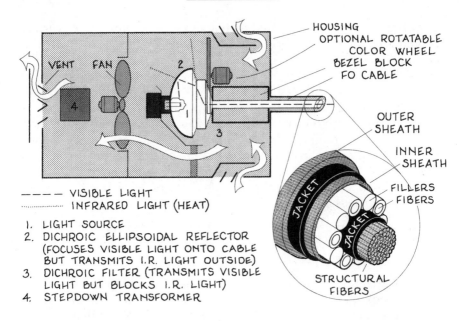

HOUSING
OPTIONAL ROTATABLE
COLOR WHEEL
BEZEL BLOCK
FO CABLE

VENT   FAN

OUTER
SHEATH

INNER
SHEATH

FILLERS
FIBERS

JACKET

JACKET

STRUCTURAL
FIBERS

– – – – VISIBLE LIGHT
⋯⋯⋯⋯⋯ INFRARED LIGHT (HEAT)

1. LIGHT SOURCE
2. DICHROIC ELLIPSOIDAL REFLECTOR
   (FOCUSES VISIBLE LIGHT ONTO CABLE
   BUT TRANSMITS I.R. LIGHT OUTSIDE)
3. DICHROIC FILTER (TRANSMITS VISIBLE
   LIGHT BUT BLOCKS I.R. LIGHT)
4. STEPDOWN TRANSFORMER

Fig. 6-16. Fiber optic light source components.

There are three general kinds of fiber optic systems: *end-dedicated illumination* (light travels through opaque-walled cables), *side-dedicated illumination* (light travels through transparent-walled cables) and *opto-electronic telecom* (optical and electronic data travels through opaque-walled cables). Each system is described further below.

End-dedicated illumination. This includes an *illuminator* or *fiber-star* that sends the light, an *end-dedicated extrusion* that carries the light, and an *end fitting* that receives it. The illuminator is a projector-like unit that contains a quartz or metal-halide lamp of up to 300 watts which launches the lumens into the extrusion. The unit may contain more than one lamp, color wheels may be mounted in front of the lamps to vary the light's color, and several extrusions may extend from one lamp. The extrusion is a solid-walled bundle of optic fibers that is flexible, from $\frac{1}{32}$ to 1 in. thick, and up to 100 ft long. They are installed in small or inaccessible locations, where heat and UV light must be minimized (as in museum exhibit cases), where static is a problem, where the danger of electric shock exists (as under water), in corrosive situations, and for surgery. The end fitting is an attachment with a bulb-like lens or facing that delivers light to the installation. Typical endlight attenuation is about 2.5 percent/LF, or about 25 percent for 10 LF, 45 percent for 20 LF, and 65 percent for 40 LF.

An innovative example of end-dedicated FO illumination is in the Terrors of the Deep Aquarium of Sea World in Orlando. This exhibit features

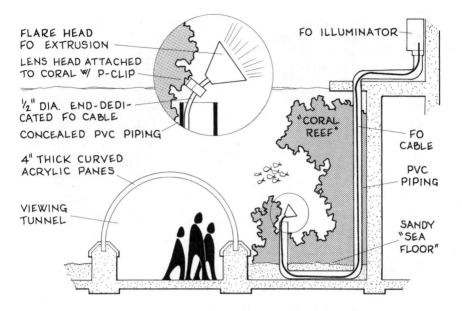

FLARE HEAD
FO EXTRUSION

LENS HEAD ATTACHED
TO CORAL W/ P-CLIP

½" DIA. END-DEDI-
CATED FO CABLE

CONCEALED PVC PIPING

4" THICK CURVED
ACRYLIC PANES

VIEWING
TUNNEL

FO ILLUMINATOR

"CORAL
REEF"

FO
CABLE

PVC
PIPING

SANDY
"SEA
FLOOR"

Fig. 6-17. Innovative use of end-dedicated FO lighting. [†]

a Walk on the Bottom of the Sea, where visitors watch barracuda and moray eels in a natural coral reef habitat while strolling through a domed tunnel walled with 4 in. thick panes of curved acrylic glass rising from the bottom of the 14 ft deep aquarium. Ambient light near the sandy sea floor is created by dimmable 250 watt MR16 illuminators mounted in weatherproof boxes above the water from which extend ½ in. diameter end-dedicated FO extrusions in concealed PVC piping down into the water, under the sand, then up into the fans of coral, where the bundles are capped with flare heads mounted with variable-focus lenses that spread the light softly and focus it accurately onto the coral. The total effect is that "You feel like you're 12–14 ft under the Caribbean walking through a coral reef." [†]

   Side-dedicated illumination. Here the illuminator is the same as in end-dedicated systems and the extrusion is similar except its cladding is translucent, enabling the transmitted light to exit along its length. This cable is known as a *side-dedicated extrusion*. Side-dedicated systems have no receivers; but if the cable is long, illuminators may be mounted on each end to balance the output along its length, as output per LF decreases slightly as the distance from the illuminator increases. Also, shorter wavelengths attenuate slightly faster than longer wavelengths; thus illumination that is blue-green at 40 ft will look greener at 70 ft. Such color shifts may or may not be desirable. Typical sidelight attenuation is about 6.8 percent/LF if one end is lighted; or about 50 percent for 10 LF, 75 percent for 20 LF, and 95 percent for 40 LF. These systems have appeared as

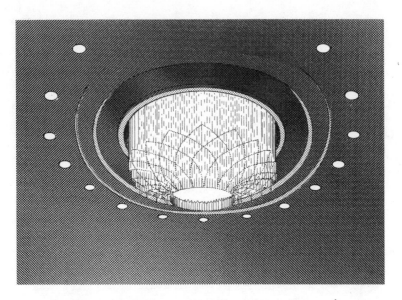

Fig. 6-18. Fiber optic chandelier, Tokyo. [†]

luminous railings in a nightclub, ceiling-mounted arrow guides to rest rooms in a restaurant, an illuminated guard-rail along a residential driveway, and a chandelier in the reception lobby of a corporate building.

Opto-electronic telecom. This system includes a transmitter that contains a light-emitting diode or laser that generates digital signals in wavelengths of 850, 1,300, and 1,500 nm into a single optical fiber that can be thousands of feet long. The fibers may be *multimode step index fiber* (these have a core diameter of about 50 microns that is used only in certain short-length low-clarity systems), *single mode step-index fiber* (this has a core diameter of 8–10 microns that is used in high-capacity long-distance systems), and *multimode graded-index fiber* (this contains several concentric cores with slightly decreasing refractive indexes whose overall core diameter is 50, 62, 85, or 100 microns). The last cable is the most common and its capacity is enormous: one 100/140 cable can carry 144 video and 288 audio channels at quality transmission. The primary limiting factor in each cable is attenuation (loss of optical communication clarity due to scattering in the core). All these cables are encased in high-impact-strength tubes and sheathed in abrasive-resistant plastic jackets. The receiver for each is an electronic device that translates the digital impulses back to their original form and may amplify them.

In extensive opto-electronic telecom systems, all transmitters and receivers may require interconnection to all others. Then each telecom closet in the building requires space for a *fiber optic breadboard*, a wall-mounted panel perhaps 4 × 6 ft in size on which are mounted exterior-to-

About Fiber Optics"; *EC&M* magzine (Intertec Publishing Co., Overland Park, KS);

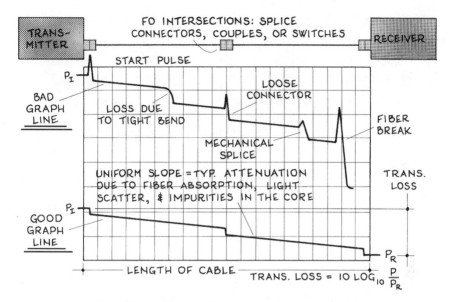

Fig. 6-19. Fiber optic power budget graph.

interior cable connection boxes, dual cross-connect boxes where FO cable feeders divide into separate circuits, smaller lightguide cross-connection boxes where cables are further routed to individual strands, and receptacles where individual FO strands originate.

Fiber optic systems are usually designed as follows. The Æ designer, knowing the required delivery illumination, attenuation, and splice losses, selects the cable and light source, usually a clear quartz or metal-halide lamp. Most FO cables have a crush resistance of only about 500 lb, outdoor installations must be located below frost line, FO cables should be laid in their own grounded enclosures (best choice is lay-in wireways but liquid-tight flexible metal conduit is also used), duct fill ratios must ≤ 50 percent, ID tags should be installed along every 50 ft of cable, 15–50 ft of slack should remain at every cable splice for possible future upgrading, long runs (≥ 150 ft) normally require midpoint pull boxes located in electrical closets or manholes, and each closet or manhole should have at least 6 × 8 ft clear floor area for wide-diameter coiling.

Regarding FO installation: each involves aligning the ends to be spliced under a 200X microscope, then sending a beam of light through the connection and examining it on an oscilloscope known as an *optical time domain reflectometer* (ODTR) to ensure exact alignment. This is not your run-of-the-mill wood-butcher carpentry. An Æ designer should know how to read an ODTR as a way of inspecting the work onsite. After installation, end-to-end attenuation testing is performed for every circuit. Also, never look into the end of an FO cable: its concentrated light can damage the eye. This is especially true of systems with laser transmitters.

➕ Fiber optics offer an exciting array of illumination and telecommunication opportunities in modern architecture. Systems are lightweight, have good electrical isolation, and are RFI-immune.

➖ Costly. As knowledge is not commonplace, experienced contractors are hard to find. Installation must be performed under exact specifications. Cable enclosures require much chase space, especially where opto-electronic telecom splices are located. Most systems require compelling financial justification for installation.

6.B.8. Light-Emitting Diode (LED or LD)

No longer are these flat-area light sources limited to tiny windows of seven-segment lettering in wristwatches and hand calculators. In addition to being used as fiber optic transmitters, they are finding architectural uses as switches, security lights, decorative illumination, exit light facings, museum exhibit lighting, a 25 ft long nightclub marquee, and even an eight-story tall billboard in Times Square that uses more than 18,000,000 LEDs in its 10,000 sf area. One idea that shows particular promise is the *flat fluorescent lamp*: a serpentine tube of filamentous width, transparent on one

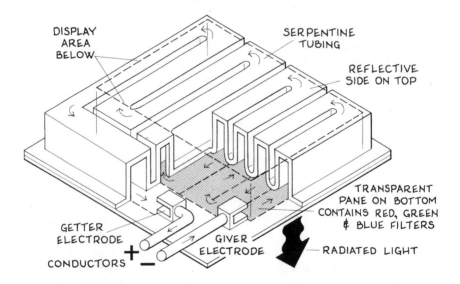

Fig. 6-20. The LED-inspired flat fluorescent lamp. [†]

LD + A Journal (IESNA, New York); Oct 1993, p. 29.   [†] From p. 542: This figure was

side and reflective on the other, arranged in maze-like loops to form a rectangular display of theoretically any size through which activated photons travel from a *giver electrode* at one end of the tube to a *getter electrode* at the other end; then the light radiated along the tube passes through microscopic red, green, and blue filters on its transparent side to create an articulate high-CRI sheet of light.

Recent research developments have also made LED lighting brighter, able to produce almost any color, and more economical to make. This, combined with the lighting's small size, light weight, ruggedness, low power consumption, near-zero heat generation, high efficiency, and extremely long life, are pushing this illumination ever closer to becoming a major light source. Presently the biggest obstacle to this lighting's widespread use is its high initial cost. But it has been proven that their extreme efficiency and durability make them more cost-effective than almost any other light over long periods. Indeed, the Times Square billboard indicates that whole walls and ceilings of large rooms could be made of light-emitting diodes. Could acoustic-tile-like LED ceiling units be far away?

6.B.9. Laser

An acronym for Light Amplification by Stimulated Emission of Radiation, a laser converts electricity into extremely short pulses ($\approx 10^{-8}$ sec) of very intense, highly collimated ($\approx 0.05°$ beamspread), monochromatic light. The process yields much rejected heat that is usually removed by air-

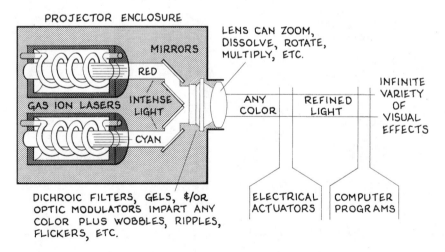

Fig. 6-21. Laser lighting technology.

taken from Motok Ishii's "Eastern Practices"; *LD + A Journal* (IESNA, New York);

conditioning or recirculating water chillers, but the small amount of energy converted to useful light has unique properties. Usually two or three gas ion lasers that emit different colors (typically red and cyan) are mounted side-by-side; then their beams are blended into a single red-green-blue beam of light which may pass through dichroic filters and optic modulators to create light of any color; then an array of electrical actuators may manipulate the beam into desired colors, spreads, flickers, ripples, multiple beams, crisscrossing optics, graphics, animation, and 3-D aerial displays. Finally, computer programs may introduce desired sequences, scenarios, time modifications, synchronization with music, and operator controls to create an infinite variety of visual effects, indoors or outdoors.

6.C. LIGHT FIXTURES

A light fixture is the frame or enclosure that holds the light source, which may be an electric lamp or a pane of glass mounted in the building envelope through which daylight enters. In this context a windowframe is as much a light fixture as a lampholder. An important property of any light fixture, whether natural or artificial, is the pattern of illumination it creates.

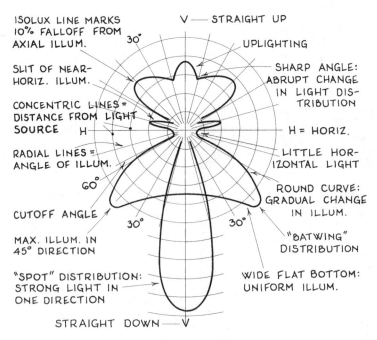

Fig. 6-22. Reading isolux lines.

Apr 1994, p. 25.   † From p. 544: This figure and some of the related text was ab-

This is portrayed graphically by its *isolux line,* which is the fixture's finger-print of individuality in the world of illumination. Many lighting catalogs show these patterns next to a picture of the fixture. A line light source may have different isolux lines in its X and Y axes.

The cost of energy consumed by an artificial light source during its rated life is usually far greater than the initial cost of the lamp and its holder. Thus a light fixture's initial cost is less relevant than lamp effica-cy, fixture durability, productivity increase due to good lighting, and main-tenance costs.

Any light fixture weighing more than 50 lb requires specific structur-al support other than that provided by its outlet box.

6.C.1. Openings

A building has three kinds of openings through which light passes: *windows, skylights,* and *combinations of the two.* If the sky's intensity decreases by a certain ratio, the luminance of every daylighted area indoors decreases by the same ratio. North light offers the best task il-lumination: it is even and rarely includes sunlight during working hours. For maximum daylighting, windowsills should be 6–10 in. above task planes. Ribbon windows, clerestories, transoms, and French doors also

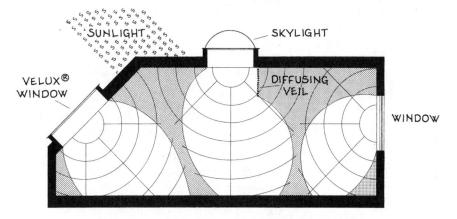

Fig. 6-23. Isolux lines of windows and skylights.

increase light entry into adjacent spaces, as do louvers, mirrors, metallic wallpaper, translucent insulation, and venetian blinds with chrome slats.

A recently developed skylight has a several in. diameter tube with a mirror-like surface on its inside that sends sunlight collected at its top down into the interior below. This sunpipe is nothing more than a giant version of a fiber optic cable. The tube can even have louvers at its top and bottom to guide the light into and out of it, and fans can be installed that enable the tube to bring fresh air into the building and carry stale air out. As wonderful as this invention is, it could possibly be improved as follows:

▸ Give the pipe a larger diameter: say 12–18 in.

▸ Add a megaphone-like scoop at the pipe's top to increase the amount of sunlight it gathers.

▸ Mount the scoop on a revolvable axis and keep it aimed constantly at the sun with two photoelectric eyes mounted on each side of a fin so that when the sun moves and casts the fin's shadow on one of the eyes, computerized controls move the scoop over slightly until both eyes are in sunlight again. This is a simple tracking device for solar-focusing mechanisms. If this tracker had four eyes so that two pair each were arranged horizontally and vertically, it would stay aimed at the sun at its every altitude and azimuth throughout the day.

▸ Mount a vaned scoop on or near the sunpipe's top that directs breezes into it. The scoop could be programmed to face the wind when fresh air is desired in the spaces below and face away from the wind when stale air should be removed.

This idea may have a few wrinkles that need to be ironed out. But it ought to be worth a NIST high-risk technology grant to some company who'd want to build a working prototype. Stay tuned.

TABLE 6-10: COEFFICIENTS OF TRANSMITTANCE

TYPE OF GLAZING			Transmittance τ
Clear glass or plastic lens	0.95	Fresnel lens	0.92
¼ in. single pane glass: clear, std...	0.88	Clear, low-iron	0.92
Heat-absorbing	0.62	Reflective	0.40
Corrugated	0.83	Opal glass	0.35
¼ in. thermopane glass: clear, std. ..	0.78	Clear, low iron	0.85
heat-absorbing, clear, std.	0.55	Reflective/clear, std.	0.35
¼ in. plastic: clear patterned ..	0.80-0.92	Milky Plexiglas	0.50
Insect screen ..... multiply glass T by 0.7		Glass block	0.60-0.80
Thin marble	0.05-0.30	Alabaster	0.20-0.50
Tissue paper, veils, lampshades, parchments			≈ 0.60
Lamp diffusers: opal glass, frosted glass, white plastic			≈ 0.70
Luminaire facing, white acrylic sheet, 0.100 in. or 125 in. thick			0.72
Clear lens, 0.100 in. thick .... 0.68; 0.125 in. thick			0.63
Through clear water................. 0.90 per 2 in. depth measured ‖ rays			

(IESNA, New York); Jul 1994, p. 37.

6.C.2. Luminaires

A luminaire is a complete lighting unit: it includes a fixture with one or more lamps plus the parts that distribute the light, protect the lamps, support the unit, and connect to the power supply. Each luminaire has an architecture that should be compatible with the space it defines. Many different kinds are available.

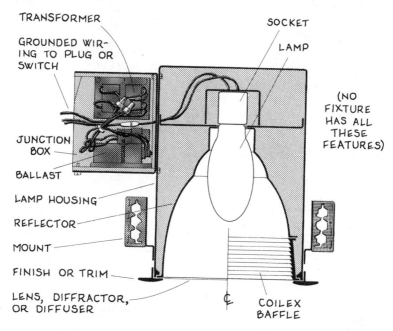

TRANSFORMER

GROUNDED WIR-
ING TO PLUG OR
SWITCH

SOCKET

LAMP

(NO
FIXTURE
HAS ALL
THESE
FEATURES)

JUNCTION
BOX

BALLAST

LAMP HOUSING

REFLECTOR

MOUNT

FINISH OR TRIM

LENS, DIFFRACTOR,
OR DIFFUSER

COILEX
BAFFLE

Fig. 6-24. Anatomy of a luminaire.

A luminaire's mount may be *protruding, surface,* or *recessed.* Protruding or suspended units reject nearly all the heat produced by the lamp into the space they illuminate, while recessed units do much the opposite. Wall-mounted units trap heat less than do ceiling-mounted ones. Any concealed surface of a luminaire should have thermal protection or be located at least 3 in. from adjacent construction, and the intervening space should be vented. Otherwise a thermal circuit breaker may be required that turns the lamp off if its fixture overheats. A luminaire's rejected heat may be used to warm interior spaces via convection or by return-air troffers that duct the heat into the HVAC system.

An important part of a luminaire is the protective lens or *facing* that is often fitted over the lamp opening. There four general kinds, as described below.

Lenses are transparent panes that prevent dust and fumes from entering the fixture. Lenses may be gasketed or sealed where clean environments are required, and some highly humid interiors (e.g. hospital laundry rooms) require hermetically sealed wet location-rated luminaires. A Fresnel lens has a ridged surface that refracts light parabolically and has beam angles as low as 10°. Another lens, originally made for swimming pool lights, is thick enough to be installed in floors so people can stand on it.

Diffusers are translucent facings that spread the exiting light widely and evenly. The more they wrap around the lamp, usually the more widely distributed the light.

Louvers are slat-like or grid-like panels of a certain depth whose many small openings direct light usually downward at a narrow angle. They control brightness and direction, and when placed near walls emphasize their illumination. They are excellent for large areas requiring high-lumen light with low glare. Louvers with dark finishes further reduce glare and make the ceiling look shadowy when viewed obliquely.

Vanes are fins, shades, shields, blinders, shutters, snoots, or 'barn doors' mounted around the lamp to redirect its light at precise beam spreads. The popular 'batwing' vane casts maximum light at 30–60° angles from the lamp's axis to provide efficient illumination over large areas.

6.C.2.a. Directivity

Luminaires that open downward are known as *direct lighting* or *downlighting*, while ones that open upward are *indirect lighting* or *uplighting*. Between these extremes lighting may be *semi-direct, direct-indirect,* or *semi-indirect*. All of these are described below.

Direct lighting: Luminaires that cast 90–100 percent of their luminous flux down and the remainder up. This is desired under dark or unsightly ceilings. Light distribution may be wide or concentrated. The areas below should usually be light in color and their reflectances diffuse, good surfaces being carpeted floors and matte countertops.

Semi-direct lighting: Luminaires that cast 60–90 percent of their luminous flux down and the remainder up. While the downward component illuminates task planes the upward component softens shadows and improves room interreflectance. Avoid mounting such fixtures close to ceilings, as this creates bright spots above them.

Direct-indirect lighting: Luminaires that cast 40–60 percent of their luminous flux down and the remainder up. This distributes light fairly equally in all directions, which is good in areas with highly reflective surfaces, medium-high ceilings, and medium- to low-level ambient lighting

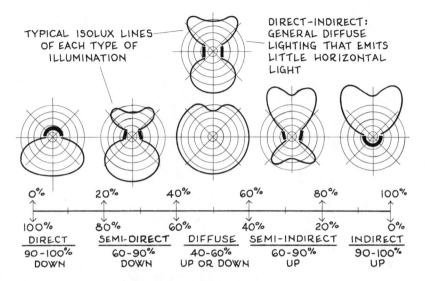

Fig. 6-25. Directions of lighting.

requirements. The epitome of this illumination is the opal globe light.

Semi-indirect lighting: Luminaires that cast 60–90 percent of their luminous flux up and the remainder down. The upward component reflected from the ceiling often matches the direct downlighting to create a fairly uniform ambient lighting. This is desirable where ceilings are attractive and reflective and the spaces below have a low density of non-critical tasks.

Indirect lighting: Luminaires that cast 90–100 percent of their luminous flux up and the rest down. Here the entire ceiling often becomes a large luminaire, one that may glow with radiance or have an overcast sky effect that virtually eliminates any shadows below. Characteristic requirements are highly reflective ceilings, wide beamspreads, and fixtures located sufficiently below the ceiling to create a soft uniform illuminance.

6.C.2.b. Beamspreads

The aura of light radiating from a lamp or luminaire has a width, or *beamspread*, which may be as high as 330° for a bare bulb in a porcelain socket or as low as 4° for a collimated pencil beam spot. Every beamspread has a *throw* (the axial or frontal distance where luminous intensity has reduced to 10 percent of initial output) and an *edge* (the lateral or sideways distance from the beam's axis to where luminous intensity has reduced

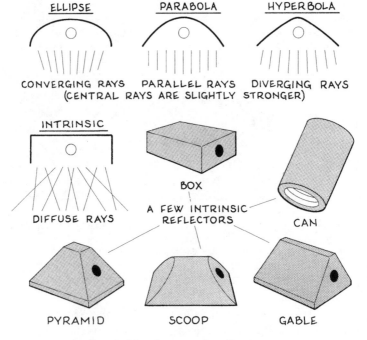

ELLIPSE PARABOLA HYPERBOLA

CONVERGING RAYS PARALLEL RAYS DIVERGING RAYS
(CENTRAL RAYS ARE SLIGHTLY STRONGER)

INTRINSIC

DIFFUSE RAYS BOX
A FEW INTRINSIC
REFLECTORS CAN

PYRAMID SCOOP GABLE

Fig. 6-26. Types of reflectors.

to 10 percent of maximum candlepower). Usually the wider the beamspread the shorter the throw, and the edge may be sharp or soft.

The primary shaper of a fixture's beamspread is the *reflector* behind the lamp. Especially influential are the reflector's extent of enclosure around the lamp, its geometric shape, and its smoothness (specular, matte, mirror, etc.). Some reflectors have baffles or annular rings to control unwanted sidelighting, and some are colored flat black to soften edges. Highly specular reflectors must be kept very clean (even a dust particle or fingerprint on one may appear as greatly magnified on a nearby ceiling or wall). A fixture may also have a different beamspread laterally than longitudinally, an example being a fluorescent tube fitted into a trough parabolic reflector. As PAR and spot lamps are made in a wide range of beamspreads, their reflectors usually have no effect on light distribution patterns unless they nearly enclose the lamp. A new fluorescent fixture known as a *radio-frequency interference shielded troffer* has a silver-based coating on the inner surface of its lens which greatly reduces any electromagnetic interference generated by the lamp circuitry and ballast.

The cost of a well-designed reflector is usually repaid many times due to improved efficacy during the life of the fixture. Basic reflector cross-sections are described below.

Ellipse. This concentrates rays inward to produce stronger light along the axis at a prescribed distance from the lamp. This is efficient for creating beams of controlled convergence and intense light, an example being hospital operating room lamps.

Parabola. This directs rays in a direction parallel to the axis of light, and is used to create narrow beams with long throws. Rays can be made converging or diverging by locating the light source slightly in front of or behind the parabolic focus. Some PAR reflectors are shaped to create oval patterns of light.

Hyperbola. This directs rays uniformly outward from the luminaire, and is used to create uniform patterns of diverging light.

Intrinsic. Any lamp housing whose shape distributes rays randomly or unevenly outward. Examples are boxes, pyramids, gables, cans, troughs, and scoops.

6.C.2.d. Energy Efficiency

Lighting consumes about 8 percent of the energy used in residences and 27 percent used in commercial buildings nationwide, and much of this energy is rejected as heat. For example, I lamps emit about 88 percent of their energy as heat, Q lamps 85 percent, F lamps 79 percent, MV lamps 73 percent, MH lamps 67 percent, and HS lamps 59 percent. Thus an easy way to economize on energy is to use cooler and more efficient lamps. This reduces energy losses far more than one may think. For example, changing an I lamp to an MH lamp may seem like only an 88 − 67 = 19 percent savings in energy; but what really happens is that the 100 − 88 = 12 percent emittance of the I lamp is being replaced by the 100 − 67 = 33 percent emittance of the MH lamp. Thus the latter lamp produces the same output with only 12/33 of the input; so the real energy savings is 88 − 67 × 12/33 = 64 percent. Similarly, a 29W CFL lamp with the same output as a 100W I lamp realizes a savings of not 88 − 79 = 9 percent but 88 − 79 × 12/21 = 43 percent.

Other ways to reduce lighting energy loads are as follows:

▶ **Foster cool lamp operation.** Cool operation raises output which decreases heat/light emittance ratios. This is done by using surface mounts whenever possible, and in recessed mounts redirecting rejected Btus into nearby HVAC ducting.

▶ **Use efficient components.** Install high-output lamps, electronic ballasts, etc.

▶ **Reduce ambient lighting and raise task lighting at work surfaces.** This yields a lower wattage/sf of floor area than luminous ceiling systems, and it reduces eyestrain.

▶ **Make enclosing surfaces highly reflective.** Use off-whites and pale pastels for ceilings and walls, low-to-medium reflectances for floors, and light-colored furniture.

▶ **Locate luminaires in cool areas.** Mount them away from openings, ducts, vents, heat-producing operations, and other places where high temperatures could degrade them faster.

▶ **Reduce a lamp's required output by bringing it closer to the task plane.** For example, provide ceiling fixtures with pendant mounts, and replace ceiling fixtures with small desktop lamps.

▶ **Use occupancy sensors.** These eliminate energy consumption in vacant occupancies.

▶ **Use daylight harvesting.** This maintains optimal lighting levels with less energy, which also increases lamp life.

▶ **Install dimming tethers.** It is much easier for a worker to adjust overhead lighting from a desk than to get up and walk over to a wall. Lutron has even developed a hand-held remote-control dimmer. Such controls are especially useful at computer workstations where required lighting levels may vary greatly from 10 fc for monitor viewing to 100 fc for desk work.

▶ **Install fixtures that are easy to maintain.** This encourages cleaning and replacing of lamps.

▶ **Clean lamps often.** At least once a year in clean environments and much more often in dusty or dirty ones. Such maintenance means every light source should be easily accessible.

▶ **Replace lamps at 75 percent of lamp life.** With many lamps (especially HS ones) the increased energy use between 75 and 100 percent of rated life is usually more than the cost of the lamp.

Incorporating these energy-saving strategies not only leads to less energy use, it leads to longer-lasting lamps, less maintenance, reduced air conditioning loads, and smaller electrical systems overall.

Analysis also indicates that more attention needs to be given to the installation of energy-efficient lamps in residences. Apparently with many utility-sponsored compact fluorescent lamp giveaway programs, occupants often remove the newly installed lamps nearly as soon as the utility worker walks out the door, because they prefer the familiar incandescent lamp on the table by the armchair because it is a higher-CRI lamp that doesn't flash like lightning when it starts and doesn't take a minute or so to increase its output to full power. Perhaps better would be to install CFL lamps as circulation and utility lighting, where an estimated 70 percent of household light energy is consumed in 30 percent of the sockets, and retain the friendly incandescent armchair light which is rarely used more than 3 hours at a time. Another obstacle to widespread residential use of CFLs is that homeowners can inventory a large supply of 99¢ incandescent lamps

with little outlay then easily replace them when they burn out; but no logi-
cal reasoning will make many of them do this with bulky $12 lamps.

Extensive studies by the Lawrence Berkeley Laboratory in California
indicate that proliferation of CFLs will depend on the following:

▶   Education of designers, builders, retailers, and consumers.
▶   Favorable consumer perception of costs and benefits.
▶   Efficient, economical, and attractive fixtures.
▶   Ample product availability and effective distribution. [†]

> What is the heating load due to illumination in an office with 48 ceiling-
> mounted troffers containing four 40W fluorescent lamps and flat sur-
> face diffusers?

6)C)2)d) $H \approx 0.034 \, \eta \, W \, Q$

H = heating energy load of lighting system, ? Btu/hr
η = number of lamps in lighting system, 48 × 4 = 192 units
W = wattage of each lamp, 40 watts
Q = lamp heat losses: percentage of ballast, infrared, and
        conduction/convection heat emitted from each lamp.
        From Table 6-9, Q for these losses for fluorescent lamps =
        13 + 30 + 36 = 79%.

$$H \approx 0.034 \times 40 \times 192 \times 79 \approx 21{,}000 \text{ Btu/hr}$$

6.C.3. Controls [†]

Illumination controls are proof that there is no conflict between luxury and economy in architecture. These systems can automatically maintain desired lighting levels by varying artificial illumination as daylighting
varies and occupancies change for hundreds of luminaires, zones, control
points, and dimming panels throughout a building. In addition to offering
the ultimate in lighting flexibility and improving occupant productivity,
such 'illumistats' create an economic domino effect that leads to more efficient lighting, reduced energy use, less waste heat, lower air conditioning
costs, longer lamp and ballast life, and lower maintenance costs. The usual
hardwiring can even be replaced by radio controls, making these controls
feasible for renovations. These controls also interface easily with HVAC
systems, fire detection and suppression, security alarms, and other electrical controls. Their chief components are described below.

[†] Mills & Siminovitch, "Dedicated CFL Fixtures for Residential Lighting"; *LD + A* ▮▮

Photoelectric sensors. These eye-like cells can sense when an area's daylighting levels have become low, then notify programmed controls to turn on nearby artificial lighting. For many years such cells have been used in roadway lights to turn them on at dusk and off at dawn. In modern interior spaces each such sensor should be located where it has a full view of the area, objects won't be set in front of it, and its eye can be kept clean. Good locations are on ceilings near windows and skylights. Each cell should have a dead band between on/off modes to eliminate on-off cycling near threshold illumination levels, and wall-mounted cells should have small sconces or shields placed where direct sunlight could strike them.

Occupancy sensors. Each of these little sentinels has an exposed eye that detects an occupant's entry into a space, then its retinal wiring notifies central controls to turn on the space's lighting; then when the occupant leaves the unit turns the lights off, thus saving energy that is typically wasted when a space is illuminated when unoccupied. These devices can activate almost any combination of lights in any intermittently used area, and they may have *preset memories* (reactivation returns illumination to its previous level), *power failure memories* (activation returns illumination to the same level after interrupted power is restored), *ambient light adjusters* (allows lighting levels to be varied from 2 fc to full brightness), and *time-delay OFF adjusters* (allows lighting to remain on from 5 sec to 30 min after the space is vacated). Such sensors can lower energy costs in many ways, an example being that security lighting instead of being on 24 hr/day turns on only when it detects an occupant. There are several general kinds of occupancy sensors, as follows.

Infrared (IR). This is a line-of-sight sensor that detects bodily heat and movement within a clamshell coverage pattern that may be 200° wide and 50 ft deep. As its reception requires clear sight lines, it works best in large interiors with no free-standing partitions, thick columns, high furniture, or other visual obstructions. They are usually combined with light switches in such areas. They are **NG** in bathrooms, low-ceiling'd spaces, storerooms, areas containing exposed electric motors or other objects that make small motions, and rooms containing heat sources such as coffee-makers and microwave ovens. An infrared sensor may also be activated by the sudden appearance of bright sunlight on a wall or floor.

Ultrasonic (US). This sensor transmits ultrasonic waves that reflect off bodily movements within a roughly square coverage pattern that may be 25 ft to the right and left and 50 ft deep. This device does not require direct sight lines to detect motion and thus works well in obstructed spaces, but it can be triggered by windblown curtains, a starting air conditioner, air entering through a supply register, or people walking in an adjacent hallway. Thus these sensors should not aim at or be installed near supply air registers, doors that often remain open, and openable windows with foliage

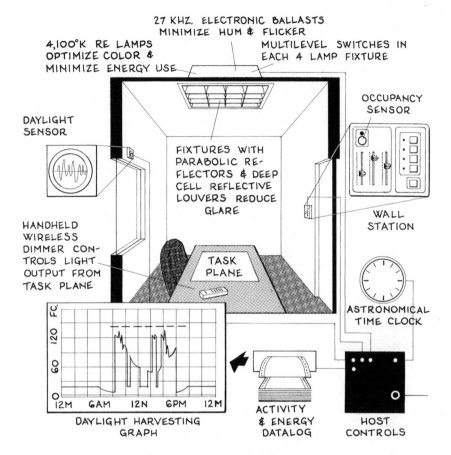

27 KHZ, ELECTRONIC BALLASTS
MINIMIZE HUM & FLICKER

4,100°K RE LAMPS
OPTIMIZE COLOR &
MINIMIZE ENERGY USE

MULTILEVEL SWITCHES IN
EACH 4 LAMP FIXTURE

OCCUPANCY
SENSOR

DAYLIGHT
SENSOR

FIXTURES WITH
PARABOLIC RE-
FLECTORS & DEEP
CELL REFLECTIVE
LOUVERS REDUCE
GLARE

HANDHELD
WIRELESS
DIMMER CON-
TROLS LIGHT
OUTPUT FROM
TASK PLANE

WALL
STATION

TASK
PLANE

ASTRONOMICAL
TIME CLOCK

DAYLIGHT HARVESTING
GRAPH

ACTIVITY
& ENERGY
DATALOG

HOST
CONTROLS

Fig. 6-27. Automated lighting controls.

or moving people or traffic outside. A passive US unit that responds to sound waves of a specific frequency offers voice-activated operation.

Dual technology (IR/US). This unit combines the advantages of infrared and ultrasonic sensing and thus minimizes false positives by either unit. Usually both halves must activate to turn on lighting, then only one half needs to detect human presence to keep the lights on.

Microprocessor impulse radar (MIR). This unit sends out radio frequency waves that can detect motion up to 200 ft away. It costs little and its chip is very accurate at low power (two AAA batteries can run it for years). It may be installed above a ceiling or behind any other barrier that its radio waves can pass through.

Occupancy sensors may be wall- or ceiling-mounted. The former units are usually located near the entry where they typically replace the usual snap switch, but they usually have a snap switch manual override in case an occupant may not want the lights on. They may also have an ambient light override that prevents artificial lights from turning on when ample sunlight enters interior spaces. One model even has small blinders on each side of its eye, which allows its horizontal field of view to be adjusted from 90–180°, and the whole assembly may be tilted downward as much as 35°. Such adjusters are good for stairways and small areas where occupants are frequently seated. Wall-mounted units should not be located where objects could be placed against them. Ceiling-mounted sensors offer 360° coverage and thus can usually survey larger areas. They work well in open areas such as public lounges, lunch rooms, and partitioned office spaces, but they are usually **N2G** for ceilings above 12–14 ft high.

Occupancy sensors may also be located outdoors. There they may be mounted over exterior doors, beside service entrances, under floodlights, above property fences, or alongside driveways to detect arrivals wanted or unwanted, where they act like watchdogs that can see in the dark. In fact one company even sells a 'digital barking dog': a sensor which when activated plays a high-fidelity recording of a loudly barking canine. The same company also sells 'smartposts' (a lamp post with two 180° sensors mounted just under the lantern which provide 360° coverage of surrounding environs), 'smartfloods' (a sensor mounted under a shielded floodlight), and 'smartboxes' (a sensor that fits into an exterior electric outlet). 'Panic button transmitters' may also be installed by a homeowner's bedside; then a resident awakened by strange outdoor sounds in the night can activate any combination of interior and exterior lights as well as intrusion alarms by the press of one button. Such versatile controls can also allow downstairs lights to be operated from upstairs, children's bedroom lights to be turned off and on from the master bedroom, and landscape and signage lighting to be turned on as darkness approaches and turned off at 11:00 P.M. or daybreak. Another technological advance is *wireless handheld controls.* Among many other uses these allow a homeowner arriving by car to remotely activate any turnaround, pathway, landscaping, porch, or garage interior light and thus create a safely-lit route indoors before opening the car door. Such controls may even be operated offsite by cellular phone, which would allow a vacationing family to activate key lighting, the water heater, climate controls, and even the coffee percolator a half hour before arriving at their destination abode. Such nondedicated wiring makes occupancy sensors feasible for any renovation or offsite operation.

In complex spaces, occupancy sensors may be programmed for almost any activity. One sophisticated setup, known as *local/host sensing*, allows each space or zone in a large building to operate locally when occupied and from host controls when vacant. When the space is vacated the sensor times-out for perhaps 60 seconds, then its operation converts to the host, which dims the light slowly over a specified period (usually from 30 seconds to 12 minutes), then after another period (say 10 minutes) it turns the lights off. The host control can also relay all operational data to the security system, activate thermostat setbacks, then return to local control at preset lighting and temperature levels at a prescribed time in advance (say 30 minutes before a store or office opens) or immediately when the space is reoccupied.

Occupancy sensor system design involves a thorough evaluation of coverage areas, outdoor lighting patterns, and occupancy use patterns as well as a candid discussion with the client regarding the advantages and idiosyncrasies of present OS technology. Latter problems include lights suddenly going off while one is sitting quietly at work, lights going on when a moth flies near a sensor at night, and fluorescent and HID lighting not working efficiently in spaces where people often enter and leave (this turns these ballasted lights on and off frequently). Also when a space is vacated, heat rejection from the lights may cease but so does metabolic heat generated by the occupants, which can lead to two spaces next to each other — one occupied and one vacant— needing heating and cooling at the same time, which can contort HVAC system controls. As most sensors require periodic cleaning and occasional recalibration, each should be accessible to maintenance personnel.

Daylight harvesters. These programmed dimmers continually adjust lamp outputs in response to varying daylight to maintain lighting that constantly matches visual task requirements. The best units have voltage regulators, inrush current dampers, reactive interference filters, manual overrides that allow direct adjustment, and 'slowswitch' circuitry that changes outputs at speeds slower than the adaptability of the human eye. These controls are especially useful for spaces behind east or west windows, under skylights, in public areas receiving much daylight (e.g. airport concourses), and 24-hour occupancies requiring different lighting levels for daytime, early evening, and late night due to occupants' changing retinal and psychic needs. When multi-lamp fixtures are operated by one daylight harvester or other automatic dimmer, they should have multilevel switches that produce different levels of light. Thus a multilevel switch for a fixture of 4 lamps that can each be dimmed to 20 percent of maximum output can produce 5–100 percent of available light.

Timers. These are ON/OFF controls that are activated by clock programming. They are used for controlling multiple events, industrial operations, night landscaping lighting, security lighting, and special lighting effects. They should have overrides that reset after a suitable period, and they should have backup power.

Manual activators. These are overrides for ON/OFF switches and dimmer slides. They also include dimmer tethers and other wireless operators. A sophisticated manual activator is a *custom touch panel*, which includes a diagram of presets, options, and dimming controls arranged as a touch-sensitive LCD graphics display that looks like a small video screen. By touching the screen one can access options or turn switches on and off, or by sliding a finger along a bar graph one can control dimming. On-screen astronomical time clocks and floor plan diagrams allow implementation of complex control scenarios.

Host controls. This programmed unit includes a central dimming panel with preset and manual controls. The central panel contains the function logic and the presets allow many lighting channels to be controlled simultaneously, with each channel controlling two or three moods or scenes. The presets can also be programmed to collect power, energy, and security data as well as supply summary reports for building management or tenant billing. Host controls may also include replacement notifier circuitry that tracks the time each lamp has been operating (when the lamp reaches a preset percentage of rated life the circuit informs host controls that the lamp is due for replacing) and test programs that periodically test and exercise all emergency lighting as well as collect and store all data.

Lighting control wiring is usually low-voltage conductors installed in separate enclosures. Another possibility is outdoor power lines that act as electronic transmitters which convert control signals into remote digital data: this simplifies wiring and can be easily changed or upgraded but it is highly susceptible to on-line RFI. Programmed lighting controls, in addition to being integratable with heating and cooling, fire detection and evacuation, and security systems, are used for such applications as:

▶ A corporate auditorium requires visual environments for meeting, slide presentation, keynote speaker, and intermission/lunch, with each scene activated by controls at the entrance, in the projection booth, and by a wireless transmitter at the podium.

▶ A church needs different visual environments for regular daytime, regular evening, solemn daytime holiday, solemn evening holiday, joyous daytime holiday, joyous evening holiday, wedding, and funeral services, with each scene being activated by controls at the pulpit, organ, choir, vestibule, and a master ON/OFF switch at the usher's station.

▶ A hotel multiple-use area that is partitionable into four assembly areas requires lighting management for showroom, convention, meeting, banquet, exhibit, and ballroom functions in each space or combination thereof, with all lighting integrated with audiovisual facilities and the lobby, with each scene activated from the lobby, restaurant, lounge, and manager's office.

▶ The landscape lighting for a suburban corporate office campus needs to be turned on every sunset, dimmed at 11 P.M., and turned off at dawn, with such automation including responses to daylight savings time, leap years, and Christmas lighting.

burg, PA, 1996); and (3) several 1996 lighting product catalogs from RAB Electric

The chief strategy for installing programmed illumination controls is *initial overdesign*. After the architect has divided the plan into zones (separate circuits with similar daylighting and visual tasks) and computed all lighting loads based on each zone's theoretical maximum output, the manufacturer takes this data and the circuit schedule and designs the system. This involves installing multilevel switches to divide zone illumination ranges into manageable steps, adding dimmers to vary the steps, incorporating sensors and timing programs and interfacing, and designing the custom control-function logic.

Programmed illumination controls require more wiring, circuits, chases, and plenum space than conventional lighting, and all components must be accessible for diagnosis, maintenance, and upgrading.

If an insurance office in Tampa, FL, is illuminated with ceiling-mounted 4 × 4 ft surface paralouvers, each containing six F40RE835 rapid-start fluorescent lamps faced with a 6 × 6 cell grid of parabolic louvers, how should the lighting's programmed controls be designed? ß = 1.32. $_L\Delta$ = 0.83. Room υ = 0.57. Θ = 0.79.

Step 1. Divide the plan into zones of similar daylighting and task illumination levels, as suggested in Fig. 6-28.

Step 2. Find the annual daylighting limits for each zone. The annual maximum determines the lowest range of controls while the annual minimum is subtracted from the task lighting requirements to determine the maximum artificial lighting requirements. Here only zone 2, the open office area facing north, is considered further.

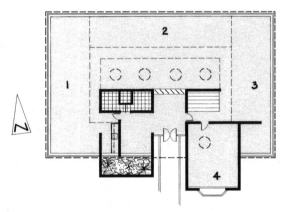

Fig. 6-28. Zoned office floor plan.

Annual maximum: Clear summer sun at midday facing north. From Sec. 6.B.1., daylighting for clear north light ≈ 1,200 fc. ∴ D_{max} = 1,200 fc.

Annual minimum: 5:00 P.M. on Dec. 21 when office closes. From Sec. 2.B., on Dec. 21 in Tampa the sun sets at 4:54 P.M.; thus 5:00 P.M. ≈ dusk. From Sec. 6.B.1. text, daylighting level at dusk ≈ 40 fc. ∴ D_{min} = 40 fc.

Manufacturing Inc., Northvale, NJ.

Step 3. Compute the zone's theoretical maximum task illumination.

6|C|3|

$$\Phi - \mathbb{D}_{min} \approx \phi_{max\ L}\Delta\,\Theta$$

Φ = required infant task illumination, fc. From Table 6-5, Φ for general office and secretarial = 75 fc.

$\mathbb{D}_{min}$ = annual minimum daylighting level at visual task, from Step 2, 40 fc

ϕ_{max} = theoretical maximum visual task illumination level, ? fc

$_L\Delta$ = light depreciation factor, 0.83

Θ = occupancy factor, 0.79

$$75 - 40 \approx \phi_{max} \times 0.83 \times 0.79 \quad \dots \phi_{max} \approx 54\ fc$$

Step 4. Compute the zone's theoretical minimum task illumination.

$$\Phi - \mathbb{D}_{max} \approx \phi_{min}$$

Φ = required infant task illumination, from Step 3, 75 fc

$\mathbb{D}_{max}$ = annual maximum daylighting level at visual task, from Step 2, 1,200 fc

ϕ_{min} = theoretical minimum visual task illumination level, ? fc. ϕ_{min} must ≥ 0.

$$75 - 1,200 \approx \phi_{min} \quad \dots \phi_{min} \approx -1125\ fc \rightarrow 0\ fc$$

Subsequent Steps. The architect or engineer, knowing the lighting loads for each zone, determines the required number of fixtures, then the manufacturer designs the programmed controls.

6.D. INDOOR LIGHTING

In indoor illumination the light sources are enclosed by reflective surfaces that transform the space into a 'larger luminaire' that diversifies the nature of light arriving at any one visual task. While this makes the enclosed lighting loads difficult to quantify (such calculations can easily be off by ±40 percent), the human eye can almost always compensate for such discrepancies with its wondrous flexibility, which often approaches ±70 percent. For example, though the task plane lighting level for general office work is 75 fc, if one's computed level differs by ±40 percent (meaning the actual lighting level may measure 45–105 fc) the 70 percent flexible eye can perform the task at any lighting level between 25–130 fc.

Following are brief lighting guides for various indoor environments.

Air, undesirable. Where air is humid, dusty, vaporous, or otherwise polluted, luminaires should be enclosed and gasketed.

Ceilings. High ceilings tend to be cast in deeper shade and thus have lower effective reflectances than lower ceilings of the same color. In such spaces the lighting should be stronger or fixtures should have pendent mounts. Attractive reflective ceilings may be revealed with ambient uplighting. For open ceilings with exposed structure, ducting, piping, and wiring, consider painting every surface flat back and installing no uplighting.

Cleaning. Many occupancies requiring low light (dining rooms, intimate restaurants, night clubs, garbage disposal areas, etc.) often require 60 fc floor-level illumination for articulate cleaning.

Control rooms. These spaces require diffuse dimmable ceiling illumination of 10–15 fc where dials are illuminated and 150 fc where they are not.

Corridors. Each should have at least 0.2 × the lighting of the areas it serves. Spill light from transoms, French doors, and clerestories reduce artificial lighting loads in these areas.

Dark areas. In theaters and other mostly dark spaces, a light-on-dark approach is often the most dramatic way to achieve the desired effect. Long heavy shadows also tend to add mystery or intrigue to entertainment areas and displays Shadowy interiors also seem to be compatible with many kinds of computer work.

Elevators. Door thresholds should receive 75 fc for safe entry, and interiors should receive 30 fc to reveal faces and signage.

Emergency exits. Each should have two lights on separate circuits, with one near the floor in case of smoky conditions; because when this lighting is needed most, it may be obscured by smoke or weakened by low-quality electricity.

Entrances. Illumination of these spaces should be focused directly in front of the door at an angle that reveals faces and also brightens the door. Warm light is more inviting.

Exhibits. Showcases against walls are best illuminated by at least two downlights installed 20–40° to each side that also strike the wall behind at 20° or less. If an exhibit is specularly reflective (glass, knight's armor, etc.), it should be surrounded with reflective matte surfaces. Modeling of 3D exhibits is best achieved by lighting from three directions (general, back, and accent). Grazing emphasizes texture, backlighting emphasizes form, accenting emphasizes subject. Lighting of 3D exhibits can vary greatly according to size, shape, reflectance, and maximum light-to-darkness ratios.

Floor level changes. Each change in levels must be well-lit in both directions.

Foliage. Combinations of MH and sodium lamps illuminate most foliage well. Optimal lighting levels ≈ 25–200 fc depending on plant species. Too little light stunts plant growth while too much light

makes plants respirate (consume O_2 and produce CO_2). When pho-
toperiods ($\approx$ 12–16 hr/day) are required to produce healthy plants,
programmed dimmers are desirable. Ideal enclosures for foliage are
glossy white or specular surfaces that reflect maximum overhead
light down to below plant growth areas.

Gatehouses. Interiors should be painted dark and illuminated more
dimly than exteriors, interior lighting should be dimmable, and
observation windows should be large panes of specular-reflecting
glass tilted 10–20° from vertical and having chest-high sills (then a
guard behind the glass can see outside while being nearly invisible
to any external viewer).

Large spaces. A space can be made to look larger with indirect or ambient light, brightly and evenly lit enclosing surfaces, cool colors,
high reflectances, and low contrasts. Avoid crispness, aim for a
'distant haze' effect.

Lecturers and Speakers. Dominant lighting should arrive from the
speaker's front and sides, optimally at about 45° in plan and section. Secondary lighting should aim no more than 45° downward
from the front to highlight the face and add a sheen to hair as well
as profile the upper torso. Avoid near-overhead lighting that may
form deep shadows in the speaker's eye sockets and below the nose.
It also helps if the speaker wears dark clothes and appears against
a light background. A very narrow spot downlight should focus on
the lectern top, and the podium should have dimmer access for
audience lighting plus activation for projector lighting.

Maintenance. Fixtures should be easily cleanable during lamp changing,
and servicing should require no disassembly other than unsnapping
or unscrewing of facings. Avoid fixtures whose maintenance requires
catwalks or intrepid workers.

Paintings. Any 2-D art exhibit usually requires an accurately aimed spot
of high intensity with adjustable shutters. The light should be out of
the line of vision and is best if recessed overhead. Contrast with
surrounds should not exceed 5-1.

Public areas. Lights should have wide beams with soft cutoffs and
should focus on signage. Walls and areas just outside entries are
aesthetically important and should be highlighted.

Rest rooms. Long luminaires emitting warm diffuse light should be
mounted near the tops of mirrors to illuminate faces well. In commercial rest rooms locate fixtures above toilets with their longest
dimension perpendicular to the stalls so the partitions don't cast
shadows on the seats.

Small spaces. Accentuate warm colors, bright small areas of color, high
contrasts, deep shadows, and intimate areas with direct narrow-
beam spots and recessed or hidden luminaires. Add touches of

sparkle when possible. Illuminate faces softly.

Stairways. Lighting should be in front of the lowest steps so that all treads and nosings are well-illuminated, and landings should be clearly defined. Locate emergency lights by every exit door.

Tasks. When a visual task has a pronounced linear direction (e.g. file drawers, toilet stalls, rows of machinery, assembly lines), long narrow ceiling fixtures should be arranged perpendicular or diagonal to the dominant direction.

Textured surfaces. Locate the light source near each surface and aim across it. Grazing requires 1–5° angles of incidence, while washing requires 10–20° angles. Precise aim is important. Light may be high-intensity, low-intensity, or dimmable.

Theater stages. Dim the back and sides, which adds depth and drama to the scene.

6.D.1. Vertical Surfaces

In nearly every occupancy one frequently engages in vertical tasks. Examples are conversing with people, opening and walking through doors, looking out windows, using file cabinets and bookshelves, watching TV or computer monitors, enjoying a movie, working in a warehouse, selecting merchandise displayed on shelves, and looking at signage, bulletin boards, blackboards, and paintings. Indeed, as one occupies interior spaces, their vertical surfaces —not floors or desktops— are often the dominant arena of vision.

The best lighting for vertical areas is usually ceiling- or sconce-mounted fixtures that brighten the vertical task plane and reveal the floor in front. The optimal angle of ceiling lighting is about 55° down from horizontal and aimed at the most prominent area of the vertical plane. At angles less than about 55°, the fixture is farther away and its rays are weaker; at angles more than about 55°, the light is weaker due to its flatter angle of incidence. Daylighting from windows illuminates vertical surfaces considerably more than horizontal ones, but skylighting illuminates horizontal surfaces only slightly more than vertical ones.

How much light falls on the center of an elementary school classroom blackboard illuminated by a ceiling-mounted 60 in. luminaire with one F60T12/CW/HO lamp if the center of the luminaire is 2'-0" from the wall, floor-to-ceiling height is 9'-6", and the blackboard's center is 4'-6" above the floor? ß = 1.24. $_L\Delta$ = 0.83.

Step 1. If the illumination is a line light source ($^D/_L$ < 6) or area light source ($^D/_L$ < 6 and $^D/_W$ < 6), compute its near-field factor. For point light sources, $ℕ$ = 1.00 lm.

6⃞D⃞1⃞ $^D/_L$ or $^D/_W$ = 6 ➜ $λ_η$

D = distance between light source and visual task, ft. D = diagonal vector between light source and center of blackboard.
   If D_h = 2.0 ft and D_v = 9.5 – 4.5 = 5.0 ft, $D = (2.0^2 + 5.0^2)^{0.5} ≈ 5.4$ ft.
L = maximum length of light source facing, ft. $L ≥ W$. L = 60 in. = 5.0 ft.
W = max. width of light source facing, ft. Typical W of 1 F lamp ≈ 0.7 ft.
$λ_η$ = light source near-field factor. For line light sources, $λ_η = η_L s_L$ ft, and for area light sources $λ_η = η_L s_L η_W s_W$ sf, in which $η$ = near-field factor, s = light source factor, L = length of light source, and W = width of light source. Compute $η_L$, s_L, $η_W$, and s_W as follows:
   If $^D/_L$ ≤ 1, $η_L$ = 0.66 and $s_L = D$
   If $^D/_L$ > 1 < 6, find $η_L$ from Fig. 6-2 and $s_L = L$
   If $^D/_L$ ≥ 6, $η_L$ and s_L = 1.00

$^D/_L = {}^{5.4}/_{5.0}$ = 1.08 > 1 < 6 ➜ from Fig. 6-2 $η_L$ = 0.71 and $s_L = L$ = 5.0

   If $^D/_W$ ≤ 1.00, $η_W$ = 0.66 and $s_W = D$
   If $^D/_W$ > 1 < 6, find $η_W$ from Fig. 6-2, and $s_W = W$
   If $^D/_W$ ≥ 6, $η_W$ = 1.00 and s_W = 1.00

$^D/_W = {}^{5.4}/_{0.7}$ = 7.7 ≥ 6 ➜ $η_W$ = 1.00 and s_W = 1.0

$λ_η$ = 0.71 × 5.0 × 1.0 × 1.0 = 3.55 ft ➜ *line* light source

Step 2. Compute the illumination arriving at the visual task.

   a. **Point light sources with**
      beamspread designations: $◇_< U\ _LΔ\ Θ ≈ 12.6\ Φ\ D^2$
   b. **Other point light sources:** $◇_P ß\ U\ _LΔ\ Θ ≈ Φ\ D^2$
   c. **Line light sources:** $◇_L λ_η ß\ U\ _LΔ\ Θ ≈ L\ Φ\ D^2$ … ➕
   d. **Area light sources:** $◇_A λ_η ß\ U\ _LΔ\ Θ ≈ A\ Φ\ D^2$

$◇_<$ = output of point light source with beamspread designation, CBCP. Not applicable.
$◇_P$ = output of light source with no beamspread designation, lm. Not applicable.
$◇_L$ = output of line light source, lm. $◇_L$ of F60T12/CW/HO lamp = 5,300 lm.
$◇_A$ = output of area light source, lm. Not applicable.
U = luminaire coefficient of utilization or transmittance of glazing. From Table 6-2, U of fluorescent lamp troffer w/ flat prismatic lens = 0.63.
$_LΔ$ = light depreciation factor, given as 0.83
$Θ$ = occupancy factor. For children, assume $Θ$ = 1.00.

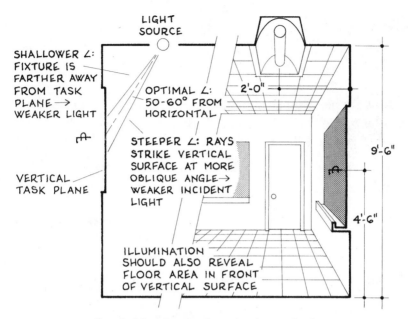

Fig. 6-29. Vertical task plane design.

Φ = net illumination arriving at visual task, ? fc
D = distance between light source and visual task, ft. *D* = 5.4 ft.
ß = ray or beam concentration factor, given as 1.24
λ_n = light source near-field factor, from Step 1, 3.55 ft
L = length of line light source, ft. *L* of F60 lamp = 60 in. = 5.0 ft.
A = facing area of area light source, sf. Not applicable.

$$5{,}300 \times 3.55 \times 1.24 \times 0.63 \times 0.83 \times 1 \approx 5.0 \times \Phi \times 5.4^2 \quad \dots \Phi = 84 \text{ lm}$$

Step 3. Compute the actual illumination of the vertical visual task.

$$\Phi_v D = \Phi D_h$$

Φ_v = actual illumination of vertical visual task, ? lm
D = axial distance from light source to visual task, from Step 1, 5.4 ft
Φ = net illumination arriving at visual task, from Step 2, 84 lm
D_h = horizontal distance from light source to visual task, 2.0 ft

$$\Phi_v \times 5.4 = 84 \times 2.0 \quad \dots \Phi_v = 31 \text{ lm}$$

From Table 6-5, required lighting level for classrooms is 75 fc
∴ if the above light is all the blackboard receives, it is **NG**

Solution: If the blackboard is illuminated by other luminaires in the room, their contributions may add up to adequate illumination. Such repetitive calculations may be easily performed with this volume's DᴇsɪɢɴDɪꜱᴋ.

6.D.2. Floor Area per Fixture

This formula is used to determine the optimal floor area for ceiling-mounted point light sources.

> A hotel lobby has ceiling-mounted pendant opal spheres with one 200 watt clear extended service incandescent lamp in each fixture. If the lobby's $\heartsuit$ is 0.46, what is the optimal floor area coverage for each fixture? $\eta = 1.00.$ $_{L}\Delta = 0.81.$ $\Theta = 1.00.$

6)D)2) $\diamond \, \eta \, \beta \, U_{L}\Delta \, \heartsuit \, \Theta \approx A \, \Phi$

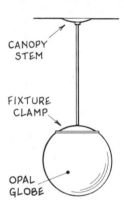

$\diamond$ = rated output per lamp. From Fig. 6-13, $\diamond$ of 200W extended service (long life) lamp = 3,300 lm.

η = number of lamps per luminaire, 1 unit

β = ray or beam concentration factor, 1.00

U = luminaire coefficient of utilization or transmittance of glazing. From Table 6-2, U of pendant diffusing sphere with any lamp = 0.80.

$_{L}\Delta$ = light depreciation factor, given as 0.81

$\heartsuit$ = coefficient of utilization of room, space, or zone, 0.46

Θ = occupancy factor, given as 1.00

A = optimal coverage area for one fixture, ? sf

Φ = infant task illum., fc. From Table 6-5, Φ for ambient hall and lobby = 15 fc.

CANOPY STEM

FIXTURE CLAMP

OPAL GLOBE

Fig. 6-30. Pendant diffusing sphere.

$3,300 \times 1 \times 1.00 \times 0.80 \times 0.81 \times 0.46 \times 1.00 = A \times 15 \quad \dots A \approx 66 \text{ sf}$

6.D.3. Number of Fixtures

The formula below is used when a room, bay, or zone requires a certain number of similar fixtures and its coefficient of utilization is known.

> If a 20 × 32 ft architect's office has a coefficient of utilization of 0.52 and the required infant task illumination is 120 fc, how many 24 in. ceiling troffers with four 48 in. F32T8/RE840 lamps with flat prismatic lenses are required? $\beta = 1.36.$ $_{L}\Delta = 0.82.$ $\Theta = 0.64.$

6)D)3) $\diamond \, \eta \, L \, \beta \, U \, {}_L\Delta \, \wp \, \Theta \; = \; A \, I$

$\diamond$ = rated output per lamp, lm. From Fig. 6-14,
  $\diamond$ of 48 in. F036T8/RE840 (32RS48T8) lamp = 2,910 lm.
η = number of lamps per luminaire, 4
L = number of luminaires in room, bay, or zone, ? units
β = ray or beam concentration factor, given as 1.36
U = luminaire coefficient of utilization or transmittance of glazing.
  From Table 6-2, U for 4 lamp troffer w/ flat prismatic lens = 0.63.
${}_L\Delta$ = light depreciation factor, 0.82
$\wp$ = coefficient of utilization of room, space, or zone, given as 0.52
Θ = occupancy factor, given as 0.64
A = Area of illuminated space, sf. A of office = 20 × 32 = 640 sf.
Φ = required infant task illumination, fc. Given as 120 fc.

$$2{,}910 \times 4 \times L \times 1.36 \times 0.63 \times 0.82 \times 0.52 \times 0.64 \; \approx \; 640 \times 120$$
$$L \; \approx \; 28.2 \; ➡ \; 28 \text{ or } 29 \text{ luminaires}$$

6.D.4. Spacing Criteria

Formerly known as S/MH, spacing criteria or *SC* is a luminaire's ratio of maximum horizontal spacing to its height above the visual task. This value is determined after the number of luminaires of a given output has been computed for a ceiling of uniform illumination. If the actual *SC* is much higher than the optimal *SC*, the lighting is too bright below and too dim between them; then more fixtures with lower outputs should be located closer together. If actual *SC* is much lower than optimal *SC*, fewer fixtures with greater outputs should be located farther apart (this would lower total installation costs). Optimal *SC*s for luminaires are often listed in product catalogs.

> If a 20 × 32 ft architect's office has a coefficient of utilization of 0.52 and the required infant task illumination is 120 fc, how many 24 in. ceiling troffers with four 48 in. F32T8/RE840 lamps with flat prismatic lenses are required? β = 1.36. ${}_L\Delta$ = 0.82. Θ = 0.64.

6)D)4) $S \; = \; R \, H$

S = maximum spacing of luminaires, 6.4 ft
R = spacing criteria ratio of luminaires. R should $\approx$ 1.4.
H = height of luminaires above visual task, ft. 6'-3" = 6.25 ft.

$$6.4 \; = \; R \times 6.25 \quad \dots \; R \; = \; 1.03 \; \leq \; 1.4$$
As R is much lower than 1.4, use fewer number of larger fixtures

6.D.5. Videoconferences

During videoconferences each conversant appears before a TV monitor on whose top is mounted a camcorder, which produces in a corner of the screen a small picture of him- or herself so he may remain properly focused, well-illuminated, and accurately framed during telecasting.

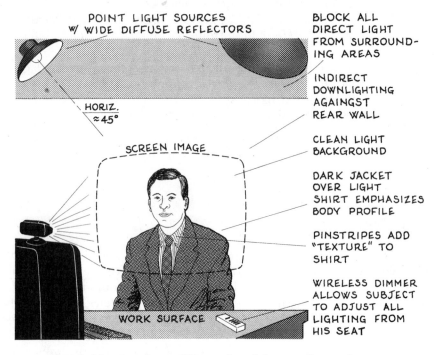

Fig. 6-31. Good conditions for videoconferencing.

During video conferences the monitor requires about 15 fc of illumination, any deskwork requires 50–75 fc, and one's face requires about 125 fc. One solution for these conflicting requirements is offered below:

▶ Mount the video on a swivel base, hood the screen on the top and sides to eliminate veiling reflections on the screen, and clean the camcorder lens before telecasting.

▶ Make sure the camera's position, focal length, and field of view are adjusted as desired.

▶ Give any work counter between the subject and video screen a matte finish of 0.45–0.65 reflectance.

▶ From the ceiling aim two point light sources with wide diffuse reflectors about 45° in front of the subject and about 45° to each side. If the lighting's frontal angle is too vertical the subject will have raccoon eyes. Also wash the wall behind the subject with ceiling-mounted ambient downlighting that contrasts the subject's profile. The wall behind should be uncluttered and have about 0.6 reflectance. All lights should be dimmable by a tether held by the subject while appearing before the screen.

▶ The front and sides of the telecasting area should have surface reflectances of 0.6–0.8. If any glare arrives from outside the area, block it with light-colored fabrics.

▶ Wear clothes that help profile, texture, contour, and soften the subject as well as contrast it gently with its surrounds. Avoid baggy clothing, glittery or dangling jewelry, and tinted glasses.

▶ The subject should not wear lots of white (it reflects too much light which makes the face look dark), black (it causes the face to be overexposed), or red (it tends to smear).

▶ If the subject is overweight, have him or her lean forward slightly (this tends to hide the gut and any rolls in the neck, make the body look smaller, and make the face look larger).

▶ Wear light makeup, even if you are a man.

6.D.6. Emergency Lighting

The optimal location for emergency lighting is 6'-6" to 7'-6" ft above the floor near exit doors, stairway entries, floor level changes, major corridor intersections, and abrupt changes in direction. Each fixture should provide 1 fc of light on the floor directly below and 3 fc at exit door thresholds, they should reveal hand-operable alarms and fire suppression equipment located along these paths, they should be contiguously visible along emergency exit routes, and they should be spaced no more than 100 ft apart. Each fixture should also be operable by a battery or generator that activates within 10 seconds after electric power failure, then maintains required illuminance for at least 90 minutes. It is a good idea to place a red light 1 ft above the floor beside each exit door to allow someone crawling through a possibly smoke-filled vestibule to find his or her way out.

Today's best exit light is the EXIT sign LED display. This briefcase-sized ceiling-mounted box with the letters **E X I T** on both sides is as bright as previous models, but it has no bulbs or ballasts to burn out and thus greatly reduces maintenance costs. It also lasts for years and its energy consumption is so low that reported paybacks have been as low as 7 months. It is available in 120 or 277 volts, is thin ($\frac{1}{4}$ in), can be one- or two-sided, and is easy to install (some models screw or snap directly into existing sockets, which offers one-for-one lamp replacement). Another innovative

Fig. 6-32. Luminous escape route trim.

emergency light is the *corner guard light*, a thin 'corner bead' lamp mounted on the outer corner of a hallway just above the floor which when activated by a nearby smoke alarm emits a strong strobe light. Today's exit lights
can be connected to computer programs that log their operation and
maintenance as well as periodically test them.

Strange as it may seem, all these modern developments in exit light
technology may seem a bit staid compared to a new 'illumination' known as
luminous escape route trim. This is a photoluminescent surface added to
floor tiles, wall base strips, tread nosings, stair stringers, corner guards,
moldings, signage, tapes, and other rubber and vinyl markings so that
when they are exposed to daylight, incandescent, or fluorescent light (but
not quartz or H.I.D. light) absorbs the photons; then if the light goes out

the surface remains bright enough to contour the space nearby. Thus this nontoxic, nonradioactive, glow-in-the-dark appliqué may be installed as arrows, strips, signage, and any other indicator that enables occupants to move safely through spaces that otherwise would be pitch dark.

But luminous escape route trim has the potential to do much more. Imagine a sleeping resident going to the bathroom in the middle of the night —in which the bathroom doorknob and doorframe, edge of the vanity inside, a row of floor tiles, the base trim beside the toilet, and the toilet seat are all decked out in a nocturnal bunting that could raise the anxious act of walking in the dark to a festive occasion, and maybe even render obsolete the 3-way switch. Of course such guidance would be a delight to a child who needed to go to the potty at night —in which the toilet seat would glow in the dark— as well as a homeowner who wanted to investigate a noise out front or in back without turning all the lights on. And it would be a boon to residents of nursing homes, hospitals, and retirement communities everywhere, not to mention the many rest-room interiors in stores and gas stations that almost every shopper and driver must use occasionally. As such, luminous escape route trim is nothing less than a new interior landscape, one that could have as profound an effect on nocturnal living as did the candle ages ago.

6.D.7. Lighting Environments

A lighting environment is a specific light/space/task scenario for which lighting must be designed: it is the basic 3-D tool for creating satisfactory lighting in architecture. An understanding of these dozen or so scenarios begins with familiarity with the three basic kinds of illumination: *key light*, *ambient light*, and *back light*. Each is described below:

Key light. Also known as *task lighting*, this is typically a strong light cast upon a usually small area that provides the optimal brightness, color, and temperature for a given task. The task usually requires at least two key lights, mounted at different angles to minimize shadows, then the beamspreads frame the task contours and the incident rays reveal the task's texture and other surface details without creating glare, excessive contrasts, or undesirable shadows. If the task has depth —which it usually does— the incident rays strike its surface at different angles, and the smaller the angle of incidence usually the greater the texture.

A variation of key lighting is *accent lighting*. This is a precisely aimed beam of light that dramatizes a particular object or small area. Its fixtures are usually small, have adjustable mounts, and are fitted with deep reflectors that create sharp cutoffs.

Ambient light. This is a low-level diffuse illumination that reveals spaces between visual tasks, lessens contrasts, eliminates dark spots, and softens shadows. Ambient light sources are typically mounted in ceilings or high on walls in uniform patterns or symmetrical arrangements from where they distribute light evenly over large areas. The fixtures may have wide beamspreads that fully disperse the light or narrow beamspreads that keep light out of key areas. A variation of ambient lighting is *fill light*. This is normally a single fixture or two that smoothes contrasts or eliminates darkness in a specific area between key tasks.

Back light. This usually point light source is commonly installed where an occupant is viewing an exhibit, merchandise, or other object. The fixture is typically located directly behind the viewed object but well above or below it and its rays are aimed toward the observer; this creates a 'halo effect' that profiles the object, separates it from its background, and imparts depth to the scene. The light should not be overly bright, as this may make the object's front look too dark. If a single fixture is placed in front of and to the side of the object and aimed at a surface directly behind (a variation known as *background lighting*), its rays will separate the figure from its ground and keep it from being lost in a shadowy surround.

When designing lighting environments, consider the air between an observer and a viewed scene as having a certain *viscosity*. Viscosity is a property of any fluid environment, of which air is certainly one, and light interacts with any medium it travels through. Thus the atmosphere of smoky cabarets, tiny particles floating visibly in shafts of light, and aerial perspective are all evidence of air's viscosity. Although viscosity may seem to be a nonapparent property of air, look into a lower corner of a small dimly lit room you are in sometime and notice how 'grey' that corner looks: that 'grey' is viscosity. Light cutoffs, shadows, and darkness are all measures of this. Viscosity is also why colors can be a little brighter, redder, and warmer in air that is humid, dusty, or smoky or shimmers in high temperatures. Indeed, seeing air as viscous can lead a designer to transform that murky ether we are immersed in from a liability that often confuses into an asset that intrigues —because air's viscosity is a world of moods and mystique that no equation can quantify.

In the sections that follow, common lighting environments are described in alphabetical order. These environments may be combined for unusual effects. In lighting load calculations, all light source contributions to any one area are additive, and all computed illuminances are approximate (it is better to be specifically approximate than vaguely so). At any rate, this is where the flexible socket comes into play. Since a 10X increase in light is perceived as 'twice as bright' by the normal eye, changing a bulb to the next size up or down —say from 60 to 75 watts— usually changes perceived brightness by only about 5 percent.

6.D.7.a. Canopies and Soffits

These are overhangs whose undersides contain lamps that illuminate the area directly below. They provide excellent downlighting for counters, desks, vanities, industrial workplaces, walls, niches, and other small areas. Canopies and soffits are typically area light sources, and they are usually 60–70 percent enclosed.

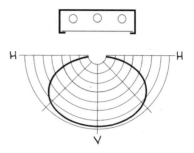

Fig. 6-33. Canopy lighting isolux lines & section.

How much light is required for an actor's dressing room vanity if its 2'-8" high surface is under a 6'-8" high canopy with a 1'-10" × 3'-9" × 0.100" clear prismatic facing? A plate glass mirror with no lights along its sides is on the wall behind the vanity. $ß = 1.36$. $_L\Delta = 0.95$. $\Theta = 0.93$.

Step 1. If the illumination is a *line* light source ($^D/_L < 6$) or *area* light source ($^D/_L < 6$ and $^D/_W ≤ 6$), compute its near-field factor. For *point* light sources, $\lambda_\eta = 1.00$ lm.

6)D)7)a) $^D/_L$ or $^D/_W = 6 ➡ \lambda_\eta$

D = distance between light source and visual task, ft. As canopy is 6'-8" high and vanity is 2'-8" high, $D = 6.67 - 2.67 = 4.0$ ft.

L = maximum length of light source area, ft. $L ≥ W$. $L = 3'-9" = 3.75$ ft.

W = maximum width of light source area, ft. $W = 1'-10" = 1.83$ ft.

λ_η = light source near-field factor. For *line* light sources, $\lambda_\eta = \eta_L s_L$ ft, and for *area* light sources $\lambda_\eta = \eta_L s_L \eta_W s_W$ sf, in which η = near-field factor, s = light source factor, L = light source length, and W = light source width. Compute η_L, s_L, η_W, and s_W as follows:

If $^D/_L ≤ 1$, $\eta_L = 0.66$ and $s_L = D$
If $^D/_L > 1 < 6$, find η_L from Fig. 6-2 and $s_L = L$
If $^D/_L ≥ 6$, η_L and $s_L = 1.00$

$^D/_L = 4.0/3.75 = 1.06 > 1 < 6 ➡$ from Fig. 6-2 $\eta_L = 0.70$ and $s_L = L = 3.75$

If $^D/_W ≤ 1.00$, $\eta_W = 0.66$ and $s_W = D$
If $^D/_W > 1 < 6$, find η_W from Fig. 6-2 and $\lambda_W = W$
If $^D/_W ≥ 6$, $\eta_W = 1.00$ and $s_W = 1.00$

$^D/_W = 4.0/1.83 = 2.19 > 1 < 6 ➡ \eta_W = 0.89$ and $s_W = 1.83$

$\lambda_\eta = 0.70 × 3.75 × 1.83 × 0.89 = 4.28$ sf ➡ *area* light source

Step 2. Compute this area light source's required total output.

$$\diamond_A \lambda_\eta \; \beta \; U_{L}\Delta \Theta \; \approx \; A \Phi D^2$$

$\diamond_A$ = required total output of area light source ? lm

λ_η = light source near-field factor. From Step 1, λ_η = 4.28 sf.

β = ray or beam concentration factor, 1.36

U = luminaire coefficient of utilization or transmittance of glazing. From Table 6-10, transmittance of 0.100" clear textured lens = 0.68.

$_L\Delta$ = light depreciation factor, given as 0.95

Θ = occupancy factor, given as 0.93

A = facing area of area light source, sf. $A = L\,W = 3.75 \times 1.83 = 6.87$ sf.

Φ = required infant task illumination, fc. From Table 6-5, Φ for grooming = 100 fc.

D = distance between light source and task plane, 6.67 – 2.67 = 4 ft

$$\diamond_A \times 4.28 \times 1.36 \times 0.68 \times 0.95 \times 0.93 \; \approx \; 6.87 \times 100 \times 4^2$$
$$\diamond_A \; \approx \; 3{,}140 \; lm$$

Step 3. Select the light source(s) from Table 6-7 and Fig. 6-14.

From Table 6-7 select a lamp of high CRI for accurate color rendering and warm CCT to accentuate flesh tones ➡ RE831 lamp. From Fig. 6-14 select optimal number of RE lamps whose length ≤ 1'-10" and output ≥ 3,140 lm. Consider 4 × 15P (18T8) RE831 or RE931 lamps (18 in. long, 4 × 850 lm = 3,400 lm). Mount the 4 18 in. lamps ‖ to the short side of the 1'-10" × 3'-9" canopy to create a shadowless illumination on the mirror and vanity.

6.D.7.b. Ceiling Systems

This lighting is a pattern of ceiling-mounted line light sources that provides uniform high-lumen lighting over a large area. The ceiling and wall surfaces around the fixtures should be painted bright white and be as unobstructed as possible; the lamps should be below and perpendicular to the most prominent obstructions to keep shadows from being cast onto the facings below; and the fixtures should be high enough above any facing grids to allow easy access for cleaning and relamping. The tendency of this area lighting to be dimmer around its edges may be countered by mounting the outermost rows of lamps closer together, installing rows of lamps at each end of the main rows, and leaving the perimeters open or fitting them with clear glass. The ratio of maximum-to-minimum luminance between lamps should not exceed 10:1 (4:1 is more preferable). There are two basic kinds of ceiling systems: *luminous* and *louvered*. Each is described below.

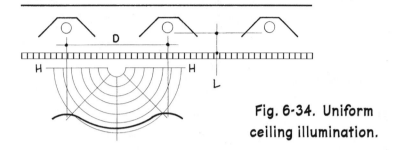

Fig. 6-34. Uniform ceiling illumination.

Luminous ceiling lighting. The lamps are located above a ceiling of translucent panels or other diffuse media. This is desirable when the ceiling is a visual clutter of structure and utility networks and the space below contains many similar tasks requiring high lighting levels. The fixtures should be perpendicular to beams and other major ceiling obstructions, all dust leaks into the cavity should be sealed, and the diffusing media should be as translucent as possible while still concealing the lamps above. For uniform brightness the ratio of lamp spacing/height above the facings should ≤ 2.0. This system may also be installed vertically to create luminous walls for highlighting merchandise and other interesting effects, for which a variety of decorative diffusers are available.

Louvered ceiling lighting. The lamps are installed above a pattern of small louvers or vanes through which light enters the space below. The size of the openings and profiles of the vanes or blades govern the dispersal of light. Although louvers are slightly less efficient than translucent facings, they are better at controlling direct glare. For uniform brightness the ratio of lamp spacing/height above the facings should ≤ 1.5 for translucent louvers and 1.0 for opaque louvers.

A typical 20 × 28 ft open bay in a large administrative office is illuminated by 3-lamp fluorescent open strip units with 48 in. cool white instant-start lamps and 0.125 in. white acrylic sheet diffusers. If the ℧ of each open bay is 0.78, how many lighting fixtures are required per bay? η = 0.96. $_L Δ$ = 0.82. Θ = 0.82.

6)D)7)b) $◇ η L ß U Δ ℧ Θ ≈ Φ A$

$◇$ = rated output of lamp, lm. From Fig. 6-14, minimum $◇$ of 48 in. CWIS (cool white instant start) lamp = 2,260 lm.

η = number of lamps per luminaire, 3 lamps

L = number of luminaires in room, space, or zone, **?** units

ß = ray or beam concentration factor, given as 0.96.

U = luminaire coefficient of utilization or transmittance of glazing.

From Table 6-2, *U* for uniform ceiling illumination w/ translucent panels, 0.60. Use more specific data when available.

Δ = light depreciation factor, given as 0.82
ʊ = coefficient of utilization of room, bay, or zone, given as 0.78
Θ = occupancy factor, given as 0.82
Φ = required infant task illumination, fc. From Table 6-5,
  Φ for general office and secretarial = 75 fc.
A = ceiling area of room, bay, or zone, sf. *A* = 20 × 28 = 560 sf.

$$2{,}260 \times 3 \times \eta \times 0.96 \times 0.60 \times 0.82 \times 0.78 \times 0.82 \approx 560 \times 75$$
$$\eta \approx 20.5 \rightarrow 21 \text{ luminaires}$$

6.D.7.c. Coffers

This is a recessed ceiling panel that contains lighting. The lights may be installed in the panels' tops, sides, ends, or any combination thereof, and all faces should be highly reflective. A coffer can have any dimension or section profile, may mimic or include skylights, and they are easily combined with cornices, coves, valences, and canopies to create many interesting effects. Coffers are typically area light sources, and they are usually 60–70 percent enclosed.

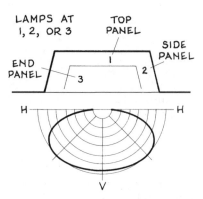

Fig. 6-35. Coffer lighting isolux line & section.

A 4 × 6 ft coffer is centered above the tailor's podium in a men's clothing store. If the store ceiling is 9'-7" high, the coffer's recessed ceiling is 15 in. higher, and the tailor's podium is 12 in. above the carpeted floor, how many F60T12/RE835/HO lamps (design output = 4,800 lm, length = 60 in.) with 0.125 in. white acrylic sheet diffusers should be installed in the coffer? ß = 1.4. ₗΔ = 0.82. Θ = 0.90.

Step 1. If the illumination is a *line* light source ($^D/_L$ < 6) or *area* light source ($^D/_L$ < 6 and $^D/_W$ < 6), compute its near-field factor. For point light sources, λ_η = 1.00 lm.

<u>6) D) 7) c)</u> D/L or $D/W \le 6 \rightarrow \lambda_\eta$

D = distance between light source and visual task, ft. 9'-7" floor-to-
ceiling ht. + 15 in. coffer depth - 12 in. coffer podium = 9.83 ft.
L = length of light source, ft. L = length of coffer = 6.0 ft.
W = width of light source. W = width of coffer = 4.0 ft.
λ_η = light source near-field factor. For *line* light sources, $\lambda_\eta = \eta_L\, s_L$ ft,
and for *area* light sources $\lambda_\eta = \eta_L\, s_L\, \eta_W\, s_W$ sf, in which η = near-field
factor, s = light source factor, L = light source length, and W = light
source width. Compute η_L, s_L, η_W, and s_W as follows:

If $D/L \le 1$, $\eta_L = 0.66$ and $s_L = D$
If $D/L > 1 < 6$, find η_L from Fig. 6-2 and $s_L = L$
If $D/L \ge 6$, η_L and $s_L = 1.00$

$D/L = 9.83/6.0 = 1.64 > 1 < 6 \rightarrow$ from Fig. 6-2 $\eta_L = 0.83$ and $s_L = L = 6.0$

If $D/W \le 1.00$, $\eta_W = 0.66$ and $s_W = D$
If $D/W > 1 < 6$, find η_W from Fig. 6-2 and $s_W = W$
If $D/W \ge 6$, $\eta_W = 1.00$ and $s_W = 1.00$

$D/W = 9.83/4.0 = 2.46 > 1 < 6 \rightarrow$ from Fig. 6-2 $\eta_W = 0.91$ and $s_W = 4.0$

$\lambda_\eta = 0.83 \times 6.0 \times 0.91 \times 4.0 = 18.1$ sf $\rightarrow$ *area* light source

Step 2. Compute this area light source's required total output.

$$\diamondsuit_A\, \lambda_\eta\, \text{ß}\, U_L \Delta\, \Theta \approx A\, \Phi\, D^2$$

$\diamondsuit_A$ = required output of area light source ? lm
λ_η = light source near-field factor. From Step 1, $\lambda_\eta = 18.1$ sf.
ß = ray or beam concentration factor, given as 1.4
U = luminaire coeff. of utilization or transmittance of glazing. From
Table 6-10, U of luminaire facing, .125 in. white acrylic sheet = 0.72.
$_L\Delta$ = light depreciation factor, given as 0.82
Θ = occupancy factor, given as 0.90
A = facing area of area light source, sf. $A = L\, W = 6 \times 4 = 24$ sf.
Φ = required infant task illumination, fc. From Table 6-5,
Φ for tailoring = 150 fc.
D = distance between light source and task plane, from Step 1, 9.83 ft

$$\diamondsuit_A \times 18.1 \times 1.4 \times 0.72 \times 0.82 \times 0.90 \approx 24 \times 150 \times 9.83^2$$
$$\diamondsuit_A \approx 25,800 \text{ lm}$$

Step 3. Select the light source(s) from Table 6-7 and Fig. 6-14.

No. of F60T12/RE835/HO lamps required:
25,900 lm at 4,800 lm/lamp $\approx 5.40 \rightarrow$ 6 lamps

6.D.7.d. Cornices

This is a projection that contains a row of concealed lamps that brightens walls and other areas below. An elegant and unobtrusive downlighting, it is excellent for areas with low ceilings and long walls as well as cornices of buildings. The lighting may be linear (e.g. fluorescent, neon, fiber optic, or lightpipe), or it can be point light sources that create scallops or puddles of light on the areas below. Cornices are typically line light sources and are usually 60–80 percent enclosed.

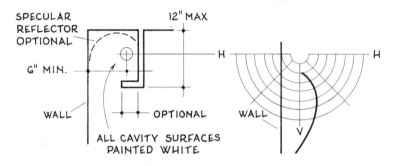

Fig. 6-36. Cornice illumination.

A camping equipment store has installed a 9 × 25 ft wallpaper photo of the Grand Teton Range on the rear wall of its lobby, and this panorama is seen through the lobby's front glass curtain wall by pedestrians outside. The owner has placed a fallen tree trunk and lichen-stained rocks along the bottom of the photo and some artificial wildflowers and alpine foliage along the sides, and to complete the illusion of a sunny day in the wilderness he wants a cornice of illumination along the top that will bathe the wall uniformly with light. What illumination should be installed? $ß = 1.24$. $_LΔ = 0.85$. $Θ = 1.00$.

Step 1. Design the light to illuminate the bottom of the wall, then select a fluorescent lamp that renders colors well. As this is a *line* light source ($D/L < 6$), first compute its near-field factor.

$\boxed{6}\boxed{D}\boxed{7}\boxed{d}$ $D/L ≤ 6 ➠ λ_η$

D = distance between light source and visual task, 9.0 ft
L = maximum length of light source area, ft. $L = 25.0$ ft
$λ_η$ = light source near-field factor. For *line* light sources, $λ_η = η_L s_L$ ft, and for *area* light sources $λ_η = η_L s_L η_W s_W$ sf, in which $η$ = near-field factor, s = light source factor, L = light source length, and W = light source width. Compute $η_L$, s_L, $η_W$, and s_W as follows:

If $D/_L \leq 1$, $\eta_L = 0.66$ and $s_L = D$
If $D/_L > 1 < 6$, find η_L from Fig. 6-2 and $s_L = L$
If $D/_L \geq 6$, η_L and $s_L = 1.00$

$$D/_L = 9.0/_{25.0} = 0.36 \leq 1 \rightarrow \eta_L = 0.66 \text{ and } s_L = D = 9.0$$

$$\lambda_\eta = 0.66 \times 9.0 = 5.94 \text{ ft}$$

Step 2. Compute this line light source's required unit output.

$$\diamondsuit_L \lambda_\eta \text{ ß } U_L\Delta \Theta \approx \Phi D^2$$

$\diamondsuit_L$ = required unit output of line light source, **?** lm/LF
λ_η = light source near-field factor. From Step 1, $\lambda_\eta = 5.94$ ft.
ß = ray or beam concentration factor, given as 1.24
U = luminaire coefficient of utilization. From Table 6-2, U for 1 or 2 F lamp open bare unit = 0.87. Use more specific data when available.
$_L\Delta$ = light depreciation factor, given as 0.85
Θ = occupancy factor, given as 1.00
Φ = required infant task illumination, fc. From Table 6-5, Φ for exhibitions = 30 fc.
D = distance between light source and visual task. As lighting must illuminate bottom of mural, $D = 9$ ft.

$$\diamondsuit_L \times 1.24 \times 0.87 \times 5.94 \times 0.85 \times 1.00 \approx 30 \times 92$$
$$\diamondsuit_L \approx 450 \text{ lm/LF}$$

From Fig. 6-14, consider 30IS (48T12) RE835 or RE935 lamps ($\diamondsuit_L = 2{,}300$ lm, $L = 48$ in. or 4 ft); 2,300/4 = 575 $\geq$ 450 lm/LF

Step 3. Compute the horizontal distance that the above lighting must be located from the photograph to avoid glare at its top. To find this value, use the same formula as above and solve for D.

$$\diamondsuit_L \lambda_\eta \text{ ß } U_L\Delta \Theta \approx \Phi D^2$$

$\diamondsuit_L$ = actual unit output of line light source, from Step 2, 450 lm/LF
λ_η = light source near-field factor. From Step 1, $\lambda_\eta = 5.94$ ft.
ß = ray or beam concentration factor, given as 1.24
U = luminaire coefficient of utilization or transmittance of glazing, from Step 2, 0.87
$_L\Delta$ = light depreciation factor, given as 0.85
Θ = occupancy factor, given as 1.00
Φ = required infant task illumination level, fc. As this is essentially a glare check, $\Phi \approx 1{,}000/R$. As R for blue sky ≈ 0.45, $\Phi \approx 1{,}000/0.45 \approx 2{,}220$ fL.
D = minimum distance between light source and visual task, **?** ft

$$450 \times 1.24 \times 0.87 \times 5.94 \times 0.85 \times 1.00 \approx 2{,}220 \times D^2 \quad \ldots D = 1.05 \text{ ft}$$

6.D.7.e. Coves

This is a horizontally recessed border uplighting that gives the ceilings above a floating effect which makes them look larger. Any reflector behind the lighting should tilt about 20° from vertical. A cove is a line light source and is usually 45–55 percent enclosed. If the ceiling is square, one-quarter of the light arrives from each side. With oblong ceilings, it is usually best to disregard the end illumination as additive, then after computing the required side lighting duplicate the side lighting at the ends so the cove is uniformly lit all around. By arranging this lighting in two continuous rows of fluorescent tubes with the sockets in each row located at the centers of the lamps in the row alongside, the slight dimness that normally occurs around the socket seams is largely eliminated.

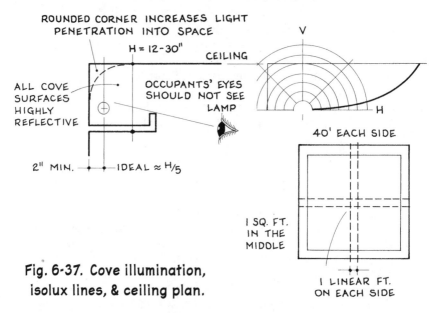

Fig. 6-37. Cove illumination, isolux lines, & ceiling plan.

Coves can have other shapes besides lines, squares, and rectangles. Some of the most beautiful are circles and ellipses (the ceilings are usually domes), and they can be vertical or sloping (these are nice over escalators). A complex but effective cove is described in the section on light pipes. There the cove is up to 15 ft long, its ceiling is only 6 ft wide, the lights are on only one side, the ceiling's profile is parabolic, and the half nearer the light is white to reflect maximum light into the space below while the far half is black to mute excessive reflection of light.

The 40 × 40 ft lobby of a bank requires perimeter cove lighting between its walls and a slightly vaulted ceiling. If the ceiling is painted to emulate a partly cloudy sky with flocks of geese flying across it, what illumination is required? ß = 0.95. $_L\Delta$ = 0.74. Θ = 1.00.

Solution: Since the ceiling is square or nearly so, approximately one-quarter of the light arrives from each side. Since the ceiling should emulate the sky, the lamps should have a high CCT and high CRI. As this is a *line* light source ($D/_L$ < 6), first compute its near-field factor.

6)D)7)e) $D/_L \leq 6 \rightarrow \lambda_\eta$

D = distance between light source and visual task, ft. D = distance from cove to centerline of ceiling = 40/2 = 20 ft.

L = maximum length of light source, ft. L = longer side of lobby = 40 ft.

λ_η = light source near-field factor. For *line* light sources, $\lambda_\eta = \eta_L s_L$ ft, and for *area* light sources $\lambda_\eta = \eta_L s_L \eta_W s_W$ sf, in which η = near-field factor, s = light source factor, L = light source length, and W = light source width. Compute η_L, s_L, η_W, and s_W as follows:

If $D/_L \leq 1$, η_L = 0.66 and $s_L = D$

If $D/_L > 1 < 6$, find η_L from Fig. 6-2 and $s_L = L$

If $D/_L \geq 6$, η_L and s_L = 1.00

$$D/_L = 20/40 = 0.50 \leq 1 \rightarrow \eta_L = 0.66 \text{ and } s_L = D = 20$$

$$\lambda_\eta = 20 \times 0.66 = 13.2 \text{ ft}$$

Step 2. Compute this line light source's required unit output.

$$\diamondsuit_L \lambda_\eta \, ß \, U \,_L\Delta \, \Theta \approx \Phi \, D^2$$

$\diamondsuit_L$ = required unit output of light source. Since illumination is a line light source, $\diamondsuit_L$ = **?** lm/LF of perimeter.

λ_η = light source near-field factor. From Step 1, λ_η = 13.2 ft.

ß = ray or beam concentration factor, given as 0.95

U = luminaire coefficient of utilization or transmittance of glazing. From Table 6-2, U for 1 or 2 F lamp open bare unit = 0.87.

$_L\Delta$ = light depreciation factor, given as 0.74

Θ = occupancy factor, given as 1.0

Φ = required infant task illumination, fc. From Table 6-5, Φ for prominent background lighting = 50 fc. Φ from each side = 50/4 = 12.5 fc.

D = distance between light source and visual task, 20 ft

$$\diamondsuit_L \times 0.95 \times 0.87 \times 13.2 \times 0.74 \times 1.0 \approx 12.5 \times 20^2 \quad \dots \diamondsuit_L \approx 620 \text{ lm/LF}$$

From Fig. 6-14, select 32RS (48T8) lamp

($\diamondsuit_L$ = 2,900 lm at L = 48 in. = 2,900/4 = 725 ≥ 620 lm/LF)

6.D.7.f. Fiber Optics

As described in Sec. 6.B.7., fiber optic lighting may be *end-dedicated* or *side-dedicated*. Design of the former typically involves quantifying the fixture's visual task illumination level, sizing the fiber (also called *cable*, *extrusion*, or *tail*), and computing the illuminator lamp's required output. The end fitting may be fitted with a variety of tiny lenses that can create beamspreads of about 10–70° as well as circular, ellipsoidal, rectangular, and trapezoidal patterns. The fiber may be solid glass, solid acrylic, or as many as 96 wire-like bundles that may contain 40 hair-like strands each (e.g. a size 36 extrusion has 36×40 fibers). Glass fibers withstand heat better and can be bent into tighter radii, while acrylic fibers are clearer and better for longer runs. The larger the total fiber diameter, the smaller the lamp that is required, but because the fiber costs more than the lamp and the power it consumes, a smaller-than-optimal fiber is usually selected. A fiber may be up to about 26 ft long if CRI is crucial and up to 70 ft otherwise. Illuminator lamps are usually clear quartz (they provide higher-CRI light) or metal-halide (they last longer and are better where illuminator access is difficult).

With side-dedicated FO systems the emitted light is usually not much brighter than candlelight; thus they are generally installed in dark areas to indicate pathways, edges, and signage. Their design usually involves little more than selecting a filter or fiber color and concealing the illuminator. Because the emitted light diminishes as the fiber lengthens, the fiber is often doubled and fitted with an illuminator at both ends.

> A water fountain in an indoor shopping mall is illuminated by three FO illuminators mounted in a low wall around its pool. If each lamp's extrusion extends 10 ft to an end fitting located 1 in. above the water and each end fitting has a 20° beamspread aimed at the fountain's crown 7 ft above, what size lamp does each illuminator require? The light from the three luminaires is not additive.

6]D]7]f]

$$\Diamond_i \kappa_f \kappa_b \approx 10.8 \, \Phi \, D^2 \, \delta^2 \, \tau^L$$

$\Diamond_i$ = required initial output of illuminator lamp, ? CBCP

κ_f = filter factor: transmissivity of any filters between illuminator and fiber. τ for filters of several colors is listed below. If more than 1 filter, $\kappa_f = \kappa_{f-1} \times \ldots \times \kappa_{f-2} \times$ etc. If no filters, $\kappa_f = 1.0$.

Clear .... 0.9; Orange ..... 0.6   Pink, yellow, light blue 0.80
Red, dark blue .... 0.3   Green, violet, med. brown 0.4

κ_b = beamspread factor, based on beamspread of end fitting and material of optic fiber. From bar graph in Fig. 6-39, at required beamspread of 20° and acrylic fiber, $\kappa_b = 0.096$.

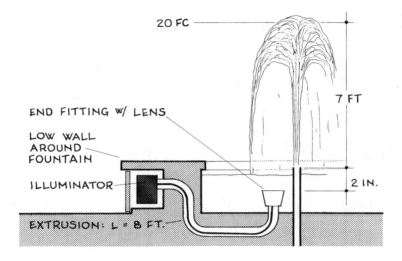

Fig. 6-38. FO end-dedicated light source.

Φ = required visual task illumination, fc. From Table 6-5, task most resembling design task is probably low-end mass retailing ➡ Φ = 75 fc.

D = distance between end fitting and visual task, ft. D = 7 ft.

δ = diameter of FO cable core, in. If core is many thin fibers with a tail
size, δ = 0.0433 (tail size no.)$^{0.5}$; maximum tail size = 400. If core is
solid glass or acrylic, δ = actual diameter. Glass diameter =
0.002–0.50 in, acrylic diameter = 0.010–0.50 in. Much leeway
exists here. As this is a fairly large FO light source with a fairly
short cable in which heat is not a problem, try acrylic at δ = 0.5 in.

τ = transmissivity of FO cable. τ = 0.976 for acrylic, 0.93 for glass.
Here τ = 0.976.

L = length of FO cable between illuminator and end fitting, 10 ft

$$\diamondsuit_i \times 1.00 \approx 413,000 \times 0.5^2 \times 0.976^{10} \quad ... \diamondsuit_i \geq 81,000 \text{ CBCP}$$

From Fig. 6-14, consider MH 100⟨10° ($\diamondsuit$ = 90,000 CBCP)

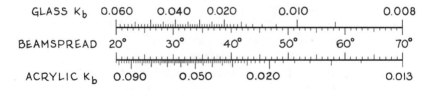

Fig. 6-39. FO end fitting beamspread factor bar graph.

6.D.7.g. Fixed Luminaires

The generic 'light fixture,' it usually provides general illumination. It may be a point, line, or area light source; it may open upward or downward; and its mount may be projecting, surface, or recessed. Examples are as widely varied as recessed downlights, ceiling-mounted fluorescent troffers, pendent opal spheres, chandeliers, high-bay service lights, wall washers, bollards, drafting lamps, and exit lights.

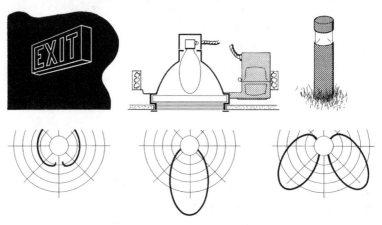

Fig. 6-40. Fixed luminaires.

> If a recessed ceiling-mounted incandescent downlight in a hotel lobby is 15 ft above the floor and has a $7^3/_8$ in. diameter Alzak gold reflector that provides 45° cutoff to lamp image, what size incandescent lamp does the fixture require? $_L\Delta = 0.85$. $\Theta = 1.00$.

Step 1. Compute this point light source's ray concentration factor.

6 D 7 g $\beta \approx \rho_e \rho_c \rho_f$

β = ray or beam concentration factor, **?**

ρ_e = ray concentration due to portion of lamp's spherical output that is enclosed. At 45° cutoff, lamp is $(360 - 45 \times 2)/360 = 0.75$ enclosed. From Table 6-1, ρ_e for 0.75 enclosed = 2.0.

ρ_c = ray concentration due to contour of reflective enclosure. From Table 6-1, ρ_c for circular contour (both directions) = 1.1.

ρ_f = ray concentration due to finish of reflective enclosure. From Table 6-1, ρ_f for "Alzak" finish = 0.93.

$$\beta \approx 2.0 \times 1.1 \times 0.93 \approx 2.0$$

Step 2. Compute the light source's required unit output.

$$\Diamond\ \text{ß}\ U_{L}\Delta\ \Theta\ \approx\ \Phi\ D^2$$

$\Diamond$ = rated output of point light source, **?** lm. If this value includes
luminaire coefficient of utilization, then U below = 1.0.

ß = ray concentration factor. From Step 1, ß = 2.0.

U = luminaire coefficient of utilization. From Table 6-2, U of recessed
$5\frac{1}{2}$ in. diameter baffled downlight = 0.68. As aperture is $7\frac{3}{8}$ in, use
slightly larger U of 0.72. Use more specific data if available.

$_L\Delta$ = light depreciation factor, given as 0.85

Θ = occupancy factor, given as 1.0

Φ = infant task illumination, fc.
From Table 6-5, Φ for ambient hall and lobby = 15 fc.

D = distance between light source and visual task, 15 ft

$$\Diamond \times 2.0 \times 0.72 \times 1.0 \times 0.85 \times 1.0\ \approx\ 15 \times 15^2\ \ ...\ \Diamond \approx 2{,}760\ \text{lm}$$

From Fig. 6-13, smallest I lamp whose $\Diamond \geq 2{,}760$ lm $\rightarrow$ 150W (2,840 lm)

6.D.7.h. Floods and Spots

These include a variety of incandescent, quartz, and metal halide
lamps that concentrate their rays into well-defined beams of strong light.
Their beamspreads range from about 4°–134° and are typically categorized
as *very narrow spot* (VNS), *narrow spot* (NS), *spot* (S), *wide spot* (WS), *narrow flood* (NF), *flood* (F), *wide flood* (WF), and *very wide flood* (VWF).
Generally if a beamspread is less than 20° it is considered as *narrow*, if
20–35° it is *medium*, and if 35° or more it is *wide*. Flood and spot lamp
wattages range from 20–500 watts, CCTs range from 2,800–3400° K, and
CRIs are usually 93 or more. An important characteristic of floods and
spots is the cone of light they create, which has the following properties:

Central axis: the center of the cone of light where the lamp's candlepower is greatest. For floods and spots this area of maximum output is measured not in lumens but in *centerbeam candlepower* (CBCP), whose unit of
measure is *candelas* (12.6 cd = 1 lm). CBCP is a function of the lamp's initial
output and its beamspread. For example, a 100W quartz PAR lamp with an initial output of 2,070 lm and a beamspread of 40° has an axial output of 3,400
CBCP, while the same 100W lamp with a beamspread of only 10° has an axial
output of 29,000 CBCP. Thus the CBCP of a flood or spot is a function of its
beamspread, and one needs to know both values to select the best lamp for
a given scenario.

Pattern: the shape of light the beam casts, which may be a circle,

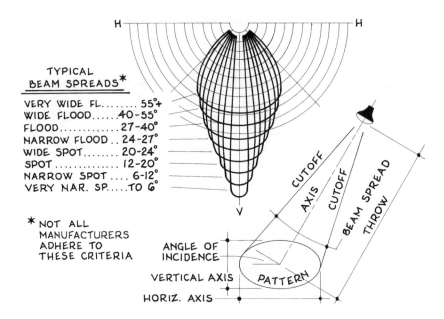

Fig. 6-41. Flood- & spot-lighting isolux lines & details.

ellipse, or square (created by special reflectors). When a lamp with a circular pattern is aimed obliquely against its task plane, the pattern becomes an ellipse, and when aimed steeply it becomes a scallop. Similarly, a tilted square pattern becomes a trapezoid, then a triangle.

Cutoffs: this is the cone's 'edge' of light, defined as being 10 percent of its axial candlepower measured perpendicular from its axis anywhere along its length. This determines the lamp's beamspread as well as its pattern edge, with the area outside known as *spill light*. Cutoffs usually fade gradually from the central axis, but lamp reflectors can be fitted with shutters, irises, and other adjusters that create sharp cutoffs.

Spread: or beamspread, the cone of light's width as defined by the angle between its cutoffs on each side. Elliptical beamspreads are specified in terms of their length and width, as in ❰ 8 × 13°.

Throw: or projection distance, this is the length of the central axis along which the centerbeam candlepower has weakened to 10 percent of initial output. This point also lies on the lamp's pattern edge.

Horizontal and vertical axis: the height and width of the lamp's pattern according to its graphic coordinates.

An important design property of floods and spots is the angle the central axis of each forms with its task plane. An angle of 10–20° down from vertical highlights textured wall surfaces, 20–30° minimizes reflections on 2D displays with glass facings, 30–40° is a good angle for illuminating 2D displays without glass facings, and angles up to 45° are good for revealing the shapes of statues and sculptures. At angles of more than 55° down from vertical, side glare from the lamp often results, which is avoided by framing the light with narrow spreads. A spot that highlights a small area is an *accent light*, while several spots aligned on a plug strip comprise *track lighting*. Track lights are often controlled by dimmers and mounted in cannister housings with tiltable mounts and 358° rotatability, which allow precise focusing. When several spots or narrow floods shine on a large dark area, their beamspreads often create a desirable syncopation of light/darkness known as *puddles of light.*

Example 1. If a recreation area task plane is 20 ft wide and its center is 25 ft from its floodlight source, what is the light's required beamspread?

---

6)D)7)h)1) $\qquad$ $\beta_w \approx T \sin \angle$

β_w = width of beamspread, 20 ft
T = length or throw of beamspread, 25 ft
$\angle$ = angle of beamspread to task plane, ? °

$$20 \approx 25 \sin \angle \qquad ... \angle = 53°$$

Example 2. What is the required output of the above lamp?

---

6)D)7)h)2) $\qquad$ $\diamondsuit_< U_{L}\Delta \Theta \approx 12.6 \, \Phi \, D^2$

$\diamondsuit_<$ = output of light source with beamspread designation, ? CBCP.
  If this value includes luminaire coefficient of utilization,
  then U as listed below = 1.00.
U = luminaire coefficient of utilization, assume 1.00.
  Use more specific data when available.
$_L\Delta$ = light depreciation factor, assume 0.9
Θ = occupancy factor, assume 0.9
Φ = required infant task plane illumination, fc.
  From Table 6-11, Φ for general outdoor recreation areas = 10 fc.
D = distance between light source and visual task, 45 ft

$$\diamondsuit_< \times 1.0 \times 0.9 \times 0.9 \approx 12.6 \times 10 \times 25^2 \qquad ... \diamondsuit_< \approx 97,000 \text{ CBCP}$$
From Fig. 6-14, the light source's required output at a
beamspread of 53° can be satisfied with 3 150 watt <15° floods

In an art gallery in Rochester, NY, three ceiling-mounted quartz spots mounted in open lampholders aim 50° down from different directions to illuminate a feature display. If the bottoms of the fixtures' pendent mounts are 8'-0" above the floor, the exhibit's focus is 4'-6" high, and the desired beamspreads for the lamps are 10°, 15°, and 20°, what lamps are required? $\Theta = 1.00$. $_L\Delta = 0.88$.

6)D)7)h)2)

$$\diamondsuit_< U \,_L\Delta \, \Theta \; \approx \; 12.6 \; \Phi \; D^2$$

$\diamondsuit_<$ = output of light source with designated beamspread, ? CBCP.
   If this value includes luminaire $\mho$, U as listed below = 1.00.

U = luminaire coefficient of utility. From Table 6-2, U of open lampholder for PAR lamps = 1.00. Use more specific data when available.

$_L\Delta$ = light depreciation factor, given as 0.88

Θ = occupancy factor, given as 1.0

Φ = required infant task illumination, fc. From Table 6-5,
   Φ for feature displays = 150 fc.

D = distance between light source and visual task. As lights aim 50° down from vertical, $D = (8.00 - 4.50)/\sin 50° = 4.57$ ft.

$$\diamondsuit_< \times 1.00 \times 1.0 \times 0.88 \times 1.0 \; \approx \; 12.6 \times 150 \times 4.57^2$$
$$\diamondsuit_< \; \approx \; 44,900 \text{ CBCP}$$

From Fig. 6-13, best available Q spots with
beamspreads of 10, 15, and 20° at $\diamondsuit_< \approx$ 44,900 CBCP are
   10° ➤ 250PAR38〈10° ($\diamondsuit_<$ = 52,000 CBCP)
   15° ➤ 200PAR38〈18° ($\diamondsuit_<$ = 37,000 CBCP)
   20° ➤ 500PAR56〈26 × 10° ($\diamondsuit_<$ = 43,000 CBCP)

6.D.7.i. Light Pipes [†]

A light pipe is a large linear lamp that provides uniform low-glare light, creates no heat buildup in the illuminated area, and has no wiring or connectors near the emitted light. Thus this 'lux plumbing' is especially desirable in hazardous, wet, cold, EMI-sensitive, and noise-free environments. Its linear beams are used in canopies, coves, valances, and long areas with low-to-medium lighting loads; and they may be vertical or inclined as well as horizontal.

Each light pipe includes a cylindrical luminaire containing a narrow-beam spot lamp and a usually 6 in. diameter tube of clear acrylic lined with an optical film that distributes the lightflow uniformly along its length. The tube may contain a wraparound reflector with openings or emitting sectors of 90, 120, 180, or 240° that direct the lightflow through part of the guide's

[†] The primary source for the information in this section was product literature

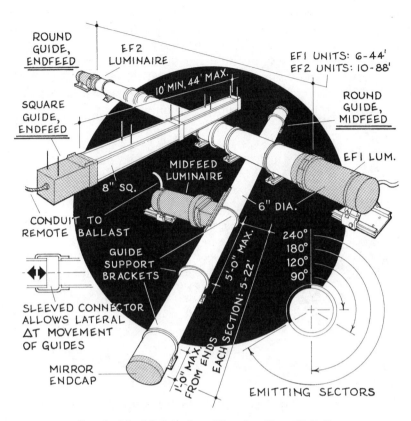

Fig. 6-42. Light pipe illumination details.

circumference, and the tubes can be installed indoors or outdoors. Also available is a 6 in. square-section 'indoor only' tube that is transparent on one or two sides. The lamp may be 250 W or 400 W metal halide (the larger lamp is better where stronger light, lower cost, or long-lived lamps are desired) or 500 W quartz (this lamp is weaker but better where high-CRI lighting or full-range dimming is desired and where more frequent relamping is acceptable). The total assembly may be *endfeed one end* (EF1) which may be 6–44 ft long, *endfeed both ends* (EF2) which may be 10–88 ft long, or *midfeed* (MF1, MF2, etc.) which may be 5–22 ft on each side of each lumi-naire. An MF unit may have any number of luminaires and guides along its length, but the guides should be uniformly spaced to maintain uniform il-lumination. A 6 ft long EF1 unit with a 400 W MH lamp and 90° emitting sec-tor provides about 100 fc of light 6 ft away; a 10 ft EF2 unit provides about 130 fc at the same distance; and a 10 ft MF1 unit about 50 fc. These out-puts decrease as the unit's length or emitting sector increases, and spac-ing-to-mounting height ratios for all assemblies should be 1:1 or less. The

published by the maker of light pipes, TIR Systems, Vancouver, BC, Canada.

guides typically have sleeved connectors that allow thermal expansion, mirrored caps over any ends not fitted with luminaires, and hoop-and-base supports that must be no more than 1'-0" from the ends or 5'-0" apart along the lengths. Each fixture may contain one 90° elbow, colored lenses can be inserted between the luminaire and guide, and the total assembly weighs less than 3 plf not counting any MH lamp ballasts, which are usually remotely located. The biggest drawbacks of light pipes are their cost (about $100–$130/LF) and relative inability to satisfy high unit lighting loads.

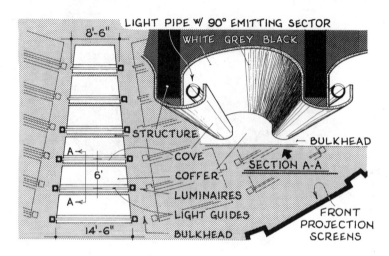

Fig. 6-43. Light pipe installation: plan & section.

An outstanding light pipe installation is in Electronic Data Systems' information management center, where in a large room dozens of employees work at computer consoles while receiving data from seven 12 × 16 ft movie screens mounted on one long wall. As this work continues 24 hours a day and 365 days a year during which 500,000,000 telecommuniques are processed each month, the space required a uniform, high-CRI, low-glare lighting that would maximize monitor contrast at all workstations without casting veiling reflections on the screens and which could be serviced from above the ceiling, as servicing from below would temporarily shut down the facility. The solution? Divide the 25 ft high fan-shaped ceiling into seven trapezoidal zones, partition each zone into six long narrow coffers, locate a light pipe in a cove alongside each coffer, then fit a quartz spot into each luminaire and a 90° emitting sector onto each guide. The result? A mellow 6 fc fully dimmable illumination over the whole area. The luminaires in the bulkheads between the trapezoidal zones are easily serviced via catwalks above the acoustic shell, and their heat is carried away by ducting that is far shorter than if it extended over the whole ceiling area. [†]

[†] Information on the Electronic Data Systems installation was abstracted from

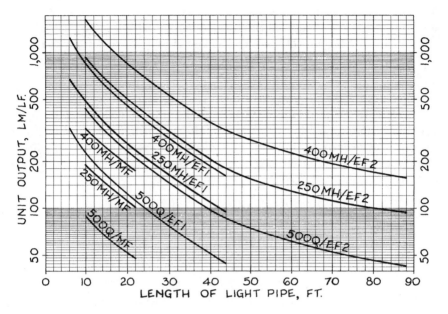

Fig. 6-44. Light pipe locator graph.

The ceiling lighting in an auditorium lobby for a medical school in New York City must be noise-free and 100 percent dimmable, which rules out fluorescent and HID systems. An ideal installation for the long narrow area is a light pipe located in a cove at the top of the wall behind the auditorium and extending from one side to the other. If the cove is 9'-4" above the floor and 44'-8" long, the construction surrounding the light guides is 55 percent reflective, and the guides must deliver 15 fc of high-CRI light at a level 3 ft above the floor, what kind of light pipe should be installed? Θ = 0.85.

Step 1. Compute the installation's required illumination. As this is a line light source, use the formula below.

6 D 7 i $\qquad$ 0.66 ◇ ß ʊ Θ ≈ Φ D

◇ = required unit output of light pipe installation, ? lm/LF
ß = ray or beam concentration factor. ß = 1.00 if fixture's emitting sector is 240°, 1.57 if 180°, 1.64 if 120°, and 2.25 if 90°. As 90° is strongest and pattern of light is long and narrow, use $\kappa_ß$ = 2.25.
ʊ = room coefficient of illumination, or reflectance of surface around the lighting guide. As enclosure is 55% reflective, ʊ ≈ 0.55. If a wall is between luminaire and its guide, multiply ʊ by 0.85.

product literature published by TIR Systems of Vancouver, BC, Canada.

Θ = occupancy factor, given as 0.85.
Φ = required infant task illumination, given as 20 fc
D = distance between light source and visual task, ft. 9'-4" – 3 = 6.33 ft.

$$0.66 \, \diamondsuit \times 2.25 \times 0.55 \times 0.85 \approx 20 \times 6.33 \quad \ldots \diamondsuit \approx 182 \text{ lm/LF}$$

Step 2. In the light pipe locator graph in Fig. 6-44, find $\diamondsuit$ = 182 lm/LF in the
Y axis, proceed to the right to the diagonal *Light Pipe* curves and select a
lamp that is desirable, then read down to the horizontal *length of light pipe*
line and find the maximum length and type of unit. Here consider only the 'Q'
curves, as only the quartz lamps provide high-CRI light. At $\diamondsuit \geq$ 182 lm/LF,
tentatively acceptable lamp sizes and lengths are

> 500Q/MF unit ... **NG**
> 500Q/EF1 unit at 13 ft max.
> 500Q/EF2 unit at 25 ft max.   ... ➕

For 44'-8" cove, use 2 × 22'-4" 500Q/EF2 units ($\diamondsuit$ = 205 lm/LF)

Note: Two EF1 units aligned 'front-to-front' produce slightly more light
than one continuous EF2 unit of the same length, but they cost slightly
more.

6.D.7.j. Light Ribbons [†]

Imagine a light that a carpenter can lay a framing square on and
bend like cardboard, then tuck snugly into a 90° corner. Such a light
exists. It also is only $\frac{1}{50}$ in. thick and can be as narrow as $\frac{5}{16}$ in, as wide
as $22\frac{1}{2}$ in, and up to 1,500 ft long. Other admirable properties are that it
can be as bright as 50 fL, is dimmable to 3 percent of maximum brightness,
consumes little power (±0.5 watts/sf at 50 fL), generates no heat, experiences no line losses, and can withstand temperatures from –40 to 250° F.
This too-good-to-be-true lighting also doesn't become steadily weaker as
its source-to-emitter distance increases, as does fiber optic light. Its manufacturer's specifications are:

Outputs: 8, 17, 25, 35, and 50 fL. A unit that can be strobed or
flashed at more than 80 fL is also available.
Widths: Standard are $\frac{5}{16}$, $\frac{1}{2}$, $\frac{3}{4}$, 1, and 2 in. Special orders can be
made in widths of $1\frac{1}{2}$, 3, 4, 6, 12, and $22\frac{1}{2}$ in.
Colors: crimson red, honey gold, yellow, green, medium blue, royal
blue, and white.
Voltages: 120VAC, 240VAC, 12VDC, 24VDC.
Product life: 25,000 (for 50 fL) to 75,000 hr (for 8 fL).

[†] The primary source for this section was product literature on *El Lightstrip*™

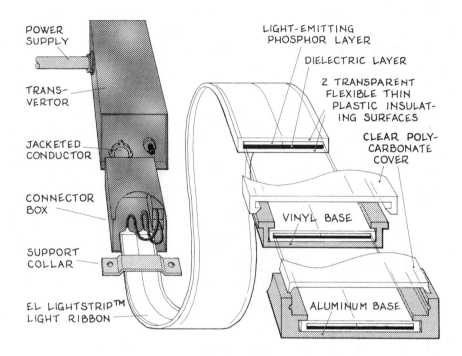

Fig. 6-45. Light ribbon installation details.

Such versatility allows this lighting to be installed everywhere from around the edges of signage letters to whole ceiling and wall areas. About its only limitation is that the flat material cannot be applied to double-curved surfaces. This light source, made by RSA Lighting of Chatsworth, CA, and sold as *El Lightstrip*, consists of two near-paper-thin layers of dielectric conductor and light-emitting phosphor sandwiched between two transparent flexible plastic insulating laminates. Multiple strips of different colors and widths may be mounted in one laminate, and a weatherproof jacket allows installations outdoors. Each laminate extends from a metal connector box (whose size is about 2 in. wider than the laminate × about 8 in. long × 1½ in. high), that is connected to a transverter (sizes range from about 2 × 3 × 1½ in. for small 8 fL installations to 10 × 12 × 5 in. for large 50 fL systems) that utilizes the power supply and contains an inverter, terminal block, and related wiring. The laminate's emitted light is very bright for the wattage it consumes because it is a *direct* light source (not a radiant glow from a distant lamp), and no spill light occurs along its sides. The laminate may be mounted against its parent surface with double-coated self-adhesive tape or custom mounting clips, or it can be recessed in an aluminum or vinyl base with a clip-on polycarbonate cover (advisable where the laminate will be exposed to foot traffic or other physical abuse).

Regarding light strip design, the primary criteria is to "think surface": i.e. cover any single-curved surface with strips of light. Then simply add up the glowing surface area and compute the required wattage from the formula below. Also allow space nearby for housing the installation's usually concealed transverter and connector box.

> The owner of a popular restaurant in Boca Raton, FL, wants to install in the slightly vaulted ceilings of three private dining areas a dimmable (i.e. variable) luminous surface lighting that will enhance the restaurant's intimate high-tech atmosphere. After examining numerous light source catalogs, the owner and her architect have decided that 22½ in. strips of honey gold 25 fL *El Lightstrips* mounted closely together so their seams hardly show would be appropriate. If the ceiling area is 13 × 16 ft including the curve of the vaults and a 12 in. cove all around, what is the required wattage for each installation?

6)D)7)j)a) **Required wattage:** $W = 425\,\kappa_b\,A$ ... ✛

    b) **Required amperage:** ◇ $= 1.93\,\kappa_b\,A$

W = required wattage of *El Lightstrip* area circuitry, **?** watts

◇ = required amperage of *El Lightstrip* area circuitry, **?** amps. Not applicable

κ_b = brightness factor, depending on lighting level of *El Lightstrip* illumination. κ_b for 8 fL system = 0.0004, 17 fL = 0.0006, 25 fL = 0.0008, 25 fL = 0.0012, 50 fL = 0.0016. κ_b for 25 fL units = 0.0012.

A = surface area of installation, in^2

$$A = (13 - 2 \times 1)\text{ ft} \times (16 - 2 \times 1)\text{ ft} \times 144\text{ in/sf} = 22{,}200 \text{ in}^2$$
$$W = 425 \times 0.0012 \times 22{,}200 = 11{,}300 \text{ watts, or } 11.3 \text{ kWh}$$

Modern technology has spawned several other interesting kinds of linear lighting such as "Live wire" (a thin electroluminescent conductor that comes in 10 bright colors and is cold to the touch), "Rope light" (a clear plastic tubing that contains a string of tiny lights that can produce moving, blinking, and flashing effects), "Honeycomb light" (a weatherproof hexagonally patterned 'chickenwire' whose strands contain tiny linear lights), "Spark light" (a string of pencil-tip-sized bulbs that produce shimmering and sparkling light), and a few others which in imaginative hands can create an array of luminous effects.

6.D.7.k. Plug-in Buses

This is a continuous ceiling-mounted plug strip that supports usually fluorescent fixtures that can be rapidly installed and relocated, which optimizes flexibility. A plug-in bus is typically a line light source, and enclosures usually range from 60–70 percent.

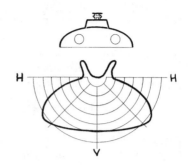

Fig. 6-46. Plug-in bus lighting.

A plastic injection molding factory near Detroit requires ceiling lighting for a variety of skilled operations performed on long counters that may change at any time while some areas may not be used at all. Thus the owner likes the idea of installing plug-in bus fixtures that can be relocated easily. If the lamps are 5'-6" above the counters, what illumination is required? $\eta = 1.36$. $_L\Delta = 0.78$. $\Theta = 0.76$.

Step 1. As this is a *line* light source, find its near-field factor.

$$\boxed{6)\,D)\,7)\,k)} \qquad D/_L \leq 6 \rightarrow \lambda_\eta$$

D = distance between light source and visual task, ft. D = distance from light source to counter = 5'-6" = 5.5 ft.

L = length of light source, ft. As L is obviously more than D, $D/_L \leq 1$.

λ_η = light source near-field factor, ft. For *line* light sources $\lambda_\eta = \eta_L\, s_L$; η_L = near-field length factor and s_L = light source length factor.

If $D/_L \leq 1$, $\eta_L = 0.66$ and $s_L = D$
If $D/_L > 1 < 6$, find η_L from Fig. 6-2 and $s_L = L$
If $D/_L \geq 6$, η_L and $s_L = 1.00$
$$D/_L \leq 1 \rightarrow \eta_L = 0.66 \text{ and } s_L = D = 5.5$$
$$\lambda_\eta = 5.5 \times 0.66 = 3.63 \text{ ft}$$

Step 2. Compute this line light source's required or effective unit output.

$$\diamondsuit_L\, \lambda_\eta\, \text{ß}\, U\, _L\Delta\, \Theta \approx \Phi\, D^2$$

$\diamondsuit_L$ = required unit output of line light source, $\diamondsuit_L$ = ? lm/LF of counter length.

λ_η = light source near-field factor. From Step 1, $\lambda_\eta = 3.63$ ft.

ß = ray or beam concentration factor, given as 1.36

U = luminaire coefficient of utilization. From Table 6-2, U for 1 or 2 F lamp open bare unit = 0.87. Use more specific data if available.

$_L\Delta$ = light depreciation factor, given as 0.78

Θ = occupancy factor, given as 0.76

Φ = required infant task illumination, fc.
From Table 6-5, Φ for fine machine work = 200 fc.

D = distance between light source and visual task, 5.5 ft

$$\diamond_L \times 1.36 \times 0.87 \times 3.63 \times 0.78 \times 0.76 \approx 200 \times 5.52$$
$$\diamond_L \approx 2{,}400 \ lm/LF$$

From Fig. 6-14 consider 3 × 45HO (36T12) RE835 lamps
(◇ = 3 × 2,820 lm per lamp/36 in. or 3 ft = 2,820 ≥ 2,400 lm/LF)

6.D.7.m. Portable Luminaires

Easily movable and adjustable, this illumination is usually partly enclosed by a reflector or translucent shade, mounted on a pedestal, then set on a floor, work surface, or comfortably near a visual task. It is excellent for increasing the visibility of an exacting or enjoyable but temporary task without raising ambient illumination levels. Such lighting is often a focal point in itself, an elegant example being the Tiffany lamp.

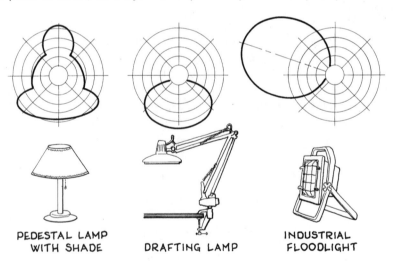

PEDESTAL LAMP
WITH SHADE

DRAFTING LAMP

INDUSTRIAL
FLOODLIGHT

Fig. 6-47. Portable luminaires.

Due to the variable nature of these light sources, the chief method of quantifying their lighting loads is *ad hoc analysis*, which typically involves socket selection of the lamp after installation.

6.D.7.n. Sconces

A sconce is a small wall-mounted lamp that is shielded with a translucent or opaque diffuser that eliminates glare and whose reflective inner face redirects the lamp's light against the wall or other surfaces behind the lamp. As such it creates ambient as well as decorative illumination in casual areas. Sconces are almost always point light sources, and their enclosures vary greatly.

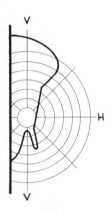

Fig. 6-48. Old spade sconce lighting & isolux lines.

The owner of a mid-19th century pony express depot being renovated into a night club near Parker, AZ, has come up with the idea of recycling a number of old prospector's spades as shields for wall lamps by imbedding their broken handles in the thick adobe wall just below the fixtures (see Fig. 6-48). Aside from adding a romantic supplemental illumination, the function of this low-level but clever lighting is to aid nearby public circulation. What size incandescent bulbs should each fixture have? $_L\Delta = 0.61$. $\Theta = 1.00$.

Step 1 As this is a partially enclosed point light source, determine its ray or beam concentration factor.

6)d)7)n) $\qquad$ ß $\approx \rho_e\,\rho_c\,\rho_f$

ß = ray or beam concentration factor, ?

ρ_e = ray concentration due to portion of lamp's spherical output that is enclosed. From inspection, lamp is about half enclosed.
From Table 6-1, ρ_e for 0.50 enclosed $\approx$ 1.4.

ρ_c = ray concentration due to contour of reflective enclosure.
From Table 6-1, ρ_c for asymmetric enclosure = 1.0.

ρ_f = ray concentration due to finish of reflective enclosure.
Use R for adobe wall. From Table 6-1, R for light dry earth = 0.40.

$$ß \approx 1.4 \times 1.0 \times 0.40 \approx 0.56$$

Step 2. Compute the required unit output of the light source.

$$\diamondsuit \text{ ß } U \,_L\Delta \; \Theta \; \approx \; \Phi \; D^2$$

$\diamondsuit$ = required output of point light source, **?** lm.
If this value includes luminaire *CU*, *U* below = 1.0.
ß = ray or beam concentration factor, from Step 1, 0.56
U = luminaire coefficient of utilization. From Table 6-2, *U* of bare incandescent lamp = 1.0.
$_L\Delta$ = light depreciation factor, given as 0.61
Θ = occupancy factor, given as 1.0
Φ = infant task illumination, fc. From Table 6-5, Φ for lobby = 15 fc.
D = distance between light source and visual task.
Assume average 4 ft between lamps and center of nearby traffic.

$$\diamondsuit \times 0.56 \times 1.0 \times 1.0 \times 0.61 \times 1.0 \; \approx \; 15 \times 4^2 \quad ... \diamondsuit \; \approx \; 700 \text{ lm}$$
From Fig. 6-13, I lamp whose $\diamondsuit \geq 700$ lm ➜ 60W ($\diamondsuit$ = 870 lm)

6.D.7.o. Valences

A valence is a combination of cove and cornice lighting whose line light source has a concealing faceboard (enclosure ≈ 40–60 percent) that redirects the light into the space above and below. The faceboard may be translucent, opaque, vertical, tilted, or convex (this disperses the light more above and below). Dimming enhances all the above effects. The ceiling should usually be at least 10–12 in. above the faceboard to avoid excessive brightness on its surface immediately above the light source. A valence may be vertical as well as horizontal.

A doctor's office requires lighting for visitors seated against a 14'-0" wall as well as the wall behind the seating, and the ceiling above. If a valence is mounted against the wall at 6'-0" above the floor, what illumination should it have if the ceiling is 9'-2" high and the area receives little daylighting? ß = 1.12. $_L\Delta$ = 0.81. Θ = 0.85.

Solution: Compute the required uplighting and downlighting, then locate the faceboard so its upper and lower openings create the desired lighting levels. This is obviously a *line* light source.

Step 1. Compute the the near-field factor for the uplighting, whose task is to illuminate the ceiling.

6|D|7|o| $\qquad\qquad D_u/_L \; \leq \; 6$ ➜ λ_n

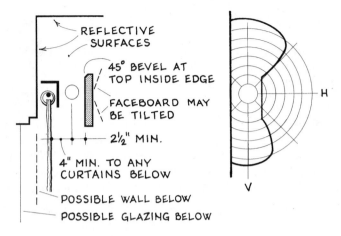

Fig. 6-49. Valence illumination.

D_u = distance between light source and upward visual task, ft.
D_u = floor-to-ceiling ht—floor-to-valence ht. = 9'-2" - 6'-0" = 3.17 ft.
L = maximum length of light source area, ft. L = 14.0 ft
λ_η = light source near-field factor, ft. For *line* light sources, $\lambda_\eta = \eta_L s_L$;
η_L = near-field length factor and s_L = light source length factor.

If $D/L \leq 1$, $\eta_L = 0.66$ and $s_L = D$
If $D/L > 1 < 6$, find η_L from Fig. 6-2 and $s_L = L$
If $D/L \geq 6$, η_L and $s_L = 1.00$
$D/L = 3.17/14 = 0.23 \leq 1 \rightarrow \eta_L = 0.66$ and $s_L = D = 3.17$

$$\lambda_\eta = 0.66 \times 3.17 = 2.11 \text{ ft}$$

Step 2. Compute the required unit output for the uplighting.

$$\diamondsuit_{vu} \lambda_\eta \ \text{\ss} \ U \ _L\Delta \ \Theta \approx \Phi \ D_u^2$$

$\diamondsuit_{vu}$ = required unit output for valence uplighting. As this is a
line light source, $\diamondsuit_{vu}$ = ? lm/LF.
λ_η = light source near-field factor. From Step 2, λ_η for
uplighting = 2.11 ft.
ß = ray or beam concentration factor, given as 1.12
U = luminaire coefficient of utilization. From Table 6-2, U for 1 or 2
fluorescent lamp open strip unit = 0.88.
$_L\Delta$ = light depreciation factor, given as 0.81
Θ = occupancy factor, given as 0.85
Φ = required infant task illumination for uplighting, fc.
From Table 6-5, Φ for ambient hall and lobby = 15 fc.
D_u = distance between light source and visual task above light source,
ft. From Step 1, D_u = 3.17 ft.

⟦⇥※⬠⚔⎆♔♀♘⟧

$\diamond_{vu} \times 2.11 \times 1.12 \times 0.88 \times 0.81 \times 0.85 \approx 15 \times 3.17^2 \quad \dots \diamond_{vu} \approx 105 \text{ lm/LF}$

Step 3. Compute the near-field factor for the downlighting, whose primary task is to illuminate reading material a seated person may be holding while waiting for an appointment.

$$D_{d/L} \leq 6 \rightarrow \lambda_\eta$$

D_d = distance between light source and downward visual task, ft. If valence is 6'-0" above floor and reading held by seated person $\approx$ 3 ft above floor and 2 ft from wall, $D_d \approx 6.0 - (3^2 + 2^2)^{0.5} \approx 3.6$ ft.

L = maximum length of light source area, 14'-0" = 14.0 ft

λ_η = light source near-field factor. For line light sources, $\lambda_\eta = \eta_L \, s_L$ ft, in which η_L = near-field length factor and s_L = light source length factor. Compute η_L and s_L as follows:

If $^{D}/_L \leq 1$, $\eta_L = 0.66$ and $s_L = D$
If $^{D}/_L > 1 < 6$, find η_L from Fig. 6-2 and $s_L = L$
If $^{D}/_L \geq 6$, η_L and $s_L = 1.00$
$\quad ^{D}/_L = 3.6/14.0 = 0.26 \leq 1 \rightarrow \eta_L = 0.66$ and $s_L = D = 3.6$

$$\lambda_\eta = 3.6 \times 0.66 = 2.38 \text{ ft}$$

Step 4. Compute the required unit output for the downlighting.

$$\diamond_{vd} \, \lambda_\eta \, \beta \, U_L \Delta \, \Theta \approx \Phi \, D_d^2$$

$\diamond_{vd}$ = required unit output for valence downlighting. As this is a line light source, $\diamond_{vd} = ?$ lm/LF.

λ_η = light source near-field factor. From Step 3, λ_η for downlighting = 2.38 ft.

β = ray or beam concentration factor, given as 1.12

U = luminaire coefficient of utilization.
From Table 6-2, U for 1 or 2 F lamp open strip unit = 0.88.

$_L\Delta$ = light depreciation factor, given as 0.81

Θ = occupancy factor, given as 0.85

Φ = required infant task illumination for downlighting, fc.
From Table 6-5, Φ for reading a novel = 50 fc.

D_d = distance between light source and visual task below light source.
From Step 3, D_d = 3.6 ft.

$\diamond_{vd} \times 2.38 \times 1.12 \times 0.88 \times 0.81 \times 0.85 \approx 50 \times 3.6^2 \quad \dots \diamond_{vd} \approx 401 \text{ lm/LF}$

Step 5. Find the total required output for the valence illumination.

$$\diamond_t \approx \diamond_u + \diamond_d$$

$\diamond_t$ = total required unit output for valence, ? lm/LF

$\diamond_u$ = required unit output for valence uplighting, from Step 2, 105 lm/LF

$\diamond_d$ = required unit output for valence downlighting, from Step 4, 401 lm/LF

$\diamond_t \approx 105 + 401 \approx 506$ lm/LF

From Fig. 6-14, select 25RS (36T8) RE835 lamp

$\diamond_t = 1{,}890/36 = 630$ lm/LF ≥ 505 lm/LF

Step 6. Position the valence faceboard so its top and bottom openings create the required or desired lighting levels.

    a. **Uplighting angle:** $\quad \angle_t \diamond_{vu} \approx \angle_u (\diamond_{vu} + \diamond_{vd})$

    b. **Downlighting angle:** $\angle_t \diamond_{vd} \approx \angle_d (\diamond_{vu} + \diamond_{vd})$

$\angle_t$ = total of two angles subtended by uplighting and downlighting openings behind faceboard. A good initial $\angle_t$ to try is 180°.

$\diamond_{vu}$ = unit output for valence uplighting, from Step 2, 105 lm/LF

$\diamond_{vd}$ = unit output for valence downlighting, from Step 4, 401 lm/LF

$\angle_u$ = optimal angle subtended by upper opening of faceboard, ? °

$\angle_d$ = optimal angle subtended by lower opening of faceboard, ? °

    Uplighting angle: $\quad 180 \times 105 \approx \angle_u (105 + 401) \quad ... \angle_u \approx 37°$

    Downlighting angle: $180 \times 401 \approx \angle_d (105 + 401) \quad ... \angle_d \approx 143°$

6.E. OUTDOOR LIGHTING

    Outdoor lighting is used during darkness to illuminate building entrances and facades, landscaping, walks, parking and security areas, signage, entertainment and recreation areas, landmarks, and the like. Such illumination should promote safety (reveal obstacles such as steps, landings, curbs, walls, pool edges, and belongings left outside), increase security (identify boundaries, reveal entrances, and eliminate hiding places), and enhance aesthetics (accentuate desirable features and increase outdoor enjoyment). The goal is always a pleasing and cohesive visual composition. Outdoor lighting differs from indoor lighting as follows:

▶   Lighting is usually related to utilitarian, recreational, and aesthetic needs more than economics; thus occupancy factors usually equal 1.00.

▶   Lack of enclosing reflective interior surfaces means little ambient light compared to the indoors. Thus precise aim and proper field angles of luminaires are more important.

▶   Contrast is often important. This is prominent at night anyway, and such 'visual syncopation' increases the relative brilliance of the illuminated object. On the other hand, overlighting is especially undesirable outdoors, as it usually appears more garish and unexpected than when indoors.

▸ Light sources should generally be concealed, during the day as well as at night. Not only does this avoid glare, but hiding the light source usually lends mystery to its effect. This is most easily done if luminaires have diffuse lenses, their light bounces off reflective surfaces into adjacent focal areas, and several small lamps are used instead of one large.

▸ Weather extremes and the need for vandal resistance require fixtures to have special connections and stronger housings.

▸ Heat emittance problems are usually nonexistent.

▸ The relation between viewer location, light placement, and viewed object must be orchestrated more adeptly than when indoors. Outdoors, the optimal angle between light axis and task plane ≈ 35° and the angle between light axis and observer's line of view ≥ 15°. A solid surface or mass looks flat when illuminated head-on.

TABLE 6-11: OUTDOOR NIGHT LIGHTING LEVELS

AREA OR TASK PLANE	ILLUMINANCE, fc Bright surround	Dark surround
BUILDINGS, MONUMENTS, AND GROUNDS:		
White or very light, light marble or terra cotta	15	8
Light grey, buff, unpainted conc., tinted stucco, water	20	12
Medium grey, tan brick, sandstone	30	15
Dark, red brick, brownstone, stained shingles	50	25
Full moonlight ... 0.1; public alleys ... 0.4; sidewalks, private drives ... 0.6		
Inactive storage yards, residential streets, perimeter fences		1
General parking, active storage yards, outdoor landscaping, walks		2
Parking for public evening attractions, security lighting around buildings, bikeways, general garden or landscape lighting		3–5
Entrance gates, vehicular & pedestrian intersections, streetcorners, sidewalks, bus stops, ramps, stairways, bikeways, service station approaches, prison yards, ice rinks, security areas		5–8
Building entrances, piers, loading docks, patios, terraces, outdoor landscaping highlights, areas covered by CCTV surveillance		10–15
Gate houses, main entrances of major buildings		20–25
RECREATION: Golf driving range: tee areas ... 10; At 200 yd		5
Tennis, badminton, volleyball, horseshoes: general recreational		10
Swimming: perimeter walkways 15; Shallow areas 10; Diving areas		25
Archery or rifle: shooting lines ... 15, ranges ... 5, targets		50
Baseball, basketball, football, hockey, soccer, swimming:		
Infield or along centerline of playing area, professional		125
Outfield or along sidelines, professional		100
College: 0.75 of above; amateur: 0.50 of above; recrea.: 0.25 of above		
Outdoor seating: before and after play ... 5; during play		2

Regarding illuminating water at night: if the water is a fountain or if it falls over a rough surface, it is *aerated* and is best illuminated from below or behind to make it glow. If the water falls over a smooth edge, it is *solid* and should be lit from in front. For lighting submerged in water, transmittance of luminous flux ≈ 0.90 per each 2 in. thickness.

A serious outdoor lighting problem is *light trespass*. This is unwanted light shining into windows and the eyes of passing motorists and pedestrians. This can be minimized as follows:

▶ Fit outdoor fixtures with reflectors that enclose and direct at least 60 percent of the lamp output downward.

▶ Use luminaires with reflectors, louvers, shutters, or barn doors that provide sharp cutoffs which also can be adjusted onsite.

▶ Illuminate signs with downlights placed above the sign, not to the side or below. Also use displays of softer FO or LED lighting.

▶ Do not depend on surrounding foliage to contain trespassing light; because winds, changing seasons, and random foliage openings can often eliminate this barrier.

6.E.1. Landmark Lighting

Landmark lighting includes the illumination of facades, monuments, and other prominent objects in usually urban or suburban environments. Here the angles between light axis, task plane, and observer's line of view are particularly important. Contrast is also important, as this increases the effective brilliance of the illuminated object. Landmark lighting is usually most effective if the object is light in color, rough or varied in texture, and has a dark surround. A nice effect on long facades is *scalloping*, created by casting the rays of several uniformly mounted lights at 10–20° angles across the surface. A facade's texture or lines may also be accentuated by *grazing*, achieved by reducing the incident light angle to 1–5°. Grazing can create amazing transformations in a building. For example, a facade can have all kinds of projecting window sills, recessed mortar joints, indented panels, shallow pilasters, dentils and flutings in cornices, arabesques, and other subtle surface modulations whose near-invisibility in daylight gives the facade a quiet stately character during working hours, yet after the sun goes down a few luminaires slanting sharply across these surfaces can create a brash melee of bright and dark bands and patterns that gives the same stately building a festive character.

Common luminaire concealments on buildings are in cornices, behind parapets, above eaves, and on roof setbacks.

The elders of a historical landmark church overlooking a village square in New England wish to make its steeple a night-time focal point by floodlighting it. If four MH floods are mounted on the roof peaks that meet at the steeple's base and are aimed at its four white facades, what is the optimal output for each lamp if it is 20 ft from the steeple's base and the steeple's base-to-cornice height is 36 ft? $_\angle\Delta = 0.59$.

Fig. 6-50. Church at night.

Step 1. Find the distance between the light source and visual task.

⌊6⌋⌊E⌋⌊1⌋   a. **Vertical distance given:** $V = D \sin \angle$

              b. **Horizontal distance given:** $H = D \cos \angle$

              c. **Both V and H given:** $D = (V^2 + H^2)^{0.5}$ ... ✛

V = vertical distance from light source to ¢ of visual task, if given. $V = 36/2 = 18$ ft.

H = horizontal distance from light source to ¢ of visual task, if given. $H = 20$ ft.

D = axial distance from light source to ¢ of visual task, **?** ft

$\angle$ = incident angle of lamp axis to visual task, °. Not applicable.

$D = (18^2 + 20^2)^{0.5} = 26.9$ ft

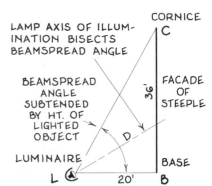

Fig. 6-51. Steeple dimensions.

Step 2. Compute the required output for each light source.

$$\diamond_{\langle} \ U_{L}\Delta \ \Theta \ \approx \ 12.6 \ \Phi \ D^2$$

$\diamond_{\langle}$ = output of light source with beamspread designation, **?** CBCP. Lighting loads of clustered lamps are additive if their centerbeams align.
U = luminaire coefficient of utilization. From Table 6-2, U of R or PAR flood w/ prismatic lens or clear shield = 0.93.
$_L\Delta$ = light depreciation factor, given as 0.59
Θ = occupancy factor. For outdoor lighting, Θ usually = 1.00.
Φ = required infant task illumination. From Table 6-11, Φ for floodlit buildings, white surface and dark surround, 8 fc.
D = distance between light source and visual task, from Step 1, 23.2 ft

$$\diamond_{\langle} \times 0.93 \times 0.59 \times 1.00 \ \approx \ 12.6 \times 8 \times 23.2^2 \quad \ldots \diamond_{\langle} \ \geq \ 98,800 \ \text{CBCP}$$
From Fig. 6-14, $\diamond_{\langle}$ of MH 175R$\langle15°$ lamp = 95,000 CBCP
As $\langle$ = only 15°,
stack 4 MH 100$\langle30°$ lamps above each other to create $\langle60°$

6.E.2. Landscape Lighting

Perhaps nowhere is the axiom, "Good illumination enhances the architecture without bringing attention to itself," more apparent than in landscape lighting. Such brightness also obeys the Miesian dictum: "Less is more" —a philosophy that also lowers lighting loads. Another rule from on high is Wright's saying: "Take care of the terminals and the rest will take care of itself." Indeed, by first designing such landscaping terminals as a pathway's corners, steps, landings, and overlooks as well as circulation transitions such as driving/walking and walking/sitting, designing the areas in between becomes easy.

In outdoor lighting, lamps must be chosen with care. For example, mercury vapor lamps are normally a fine choice because their green/blue light enhances the tones of foliage, but these hues may cast a sickly pall on meats and human skin. Then high-CRI quartz lamps are better; however, these lamps' orange and yellow hues mute the liveliness of foliage enveloped by the blackness of night.

Landscape light fixtures must also withstand the vagaries of weather, maintenance activities, and possible damage from vandals. The best housings are aluminum, brass, or copper (this weathers to a lovely verdigris patina); and the best lenses have heat-resistant glass and gasketed watertight rims. Diffuse facings such as frosted and hexcell glass are often better than transparent ones, as they can soften low-wattage rays to the kind of mellow moods that can make a nocturnal scene look dreamy. Colored

---

† Much of the information in this section was abstracted from *Landscape Light-*

lenses or filters can also liven the color of outdoor objects in the enveloping blackness: a red lens or filter can enhance the foliage of a favored ornamental Japanese maple, or a yellow or blue filter can bring out the best in light or dark foliage. But like food seasonings, color filters must be used sparingly. Facings can also have shields that create sharp cutoffs of almost any shape; for example, a shield with an angled cowl creates elliptical light patterns. Other effective 'shields' are broad-leaved plants or highly textured foliage placed around the luminaire to soften its rays and spread them into adjacent areas. Good landscape luminaires also provide maximum flexibility after installation with angled mounts, adjustable shields, housings with rotatable stakes, and easily replaceable lenses.

There are three general kinds of landscape lighting, as follows:

Pathway lighting. These light sources illuminate pedestrian routes, define their borders, and reveal any dips, changes in level, or sudden turns along the way. They are best spaced 15–30 ft apart alongside the walking surface, and should be between knee and waist height (18–36 in), as below this level the light tends to be too dim between the luminaires, while above this height the potential for glare and bothersome insects flying into the light increases. The essential pathway light is the *narrow cone*, a downlight mounted on a short stem and capped with a narrow conical shade. Other effective pathway lights are *half cones* (downlights with half-conical shades mounted against walls and railing supports), *lanterns with adjustable shields* (cylindrical lights with half-circular reflectors that can be rotated to control beamspreads), *pagodas* (cylindrical lights with conical shades and thin horizontal louvers that direct tiers of 360° light downward), *recessed aisle lights* (small louvered lights mounted in walls just above steps and walking surfaces), and *solar lights* (silicon cells mounted on CFL lamps) that require no wiring. An imaginative pathway or aisle lighting which the author once saw in Oglebay Park in Wheeling, West Virginia, was a row of knee-high concrete mushrooms with a lamp mounted under each cap. Target illuminance for pathway lighting ≈ 3–8 fc directly below the lamp and ≥ 0.5 fc between lamps.

Spread lighting. These light sources are usually located a few yards from pathways to orient the occupant and highlight interesting scenes along the way. The essential spread light is the *wide cone*, a 360° downlight capped with a wide conical shade. When mounted just above the surrounding foliage it casts a horizontal grazing that brightens prominent leaf textures and colors while casting every recess of foliage below in deep shade. Another attractive spread light is the *'drooping tulip'*, a lamp with a flower-shaped shade and gracefully curved stem that adds soft ambient lighting to small areas. Target illuminance for spread lighting ≈ 2–10 fc. Regarding target illuminances for spread or accent lighting: the farther the observer is from the object, the brighter the required illuminance.

ing, a product catalog © 1996 by Kichler Lighting Co., Cleveland, OH.

Fig. 6-52. A few landscape luminaires.

Accent lighting. These highlight a prominent tree, sign, plant, statue, fountain, or other terminal in the surrounding night environment. Usually spots or floods, they range from low-wattage pencilbeam spots that reveal a house number to powerful wide-angle floods that can uplight the crown of a mature oak. Each should be three-dimensionally adjustable and have easily adjustable shields. A versatile accent light is a compact flood with barn door shutters: this provides strong light with precise and easily adjustable cutoffs that can be adjusted after installation. Target illuminance for accent lighting ≈ 5–20 fc.

Aside from the above categorizations, night lighting design generally involves the manipulation of a few basic 'light shapes,' which could be called 'outdoor lighting environments.' These are the basic tools upon which nearly all outdoor lighting design is based. They are:

Frontlighting. This illuminates an object from the front, which emphasizes form and highlights character. Two spots located to the front and sides of a statue, fountain, or other focal object will reveal its fullness better than almost any other lighting. Target illuminance ≈ 3–20 fc.

Sidelighting. This emphasizes textures and edges, creates shadows that accentuate depth, and enhances movement of foliage exposed to breezes. A dramatic variation is *silhouetting*, which involves locating a strong light in front of and to the side of a tree with delicate branches or other open object with fine details and aiming the light at a smooth light surface directly behind; this creates a sharp profile of the object against a bright background. Target illuminance ≈ 8–20 fc.

Backlighting. Also known as *shadowing*, this involves aiming the luminaire from behind an interestingly shaped object toward the observer, which profiles the object, enhances it with a translucent glow, and adds depth to the scene. This may be done with ground-mounted luminaires aimed upward, or with lights concealed in trellises, gazebos, or trees and aimed downward. Target illuminance ≈ 5–15 fc.

Downlighting. This is a cone or aura of light directed downward. The most common pathway and spread lighting, it accents color, texture, and detail in the areas below. For example, a spot or flood downlight mounted high in a tree reveals the efflorescing nature of branches and leaves below and casts attractive patterns on the ground. If such illumination mimics sunrays or moonlight, it should slant in from the south, southeast, or southwest and not the north. *Near downlighting* may involve little more than arranging contiguous puddles of light along a nearby pathway or other pedestrian area, while *far downlighting* usually requires adept orchestration of the three foci of viewer orientation, light source location, and object scenario.

Uplighting. This is a cone, shaft, or aura of light directed upward. It is used to illuminate the underside of objects, such as prominent trees, where it creates a glow within the canopy and brings out the full volume of the foliage. This usually requires careful design and onsite adjusting, as too little can look anemic, while too much can look garish and wash out details. Uplighting is usually shrouded in ground cover to minimize potential glare to observers, and it may be *unidirectional* or *omnidirectional* (the illuminated object's depth or third dimension is revealed by usually at least three luminaires whose rays arrive from different directions). Another effective uplight is the *louvered well*, a recessed fixture with small deep louvers that cut side glare. Target illuminance of uplighting ≈ 3–15 fc.

Moonlighting. This very soft downlighting emulates the evanescent

DAYLIGHTING   FRONTLIGHTING   SIDELIGHTING

BACKLIGHTING   UPLIGHTING   DOWNLIGHTING

Fig. 6-53. Methods of landscape lighting at night.

purplish glow of moonlight. A good light source for this effect is a lofty medium flood containing a blue designer color metal halide lamp with a target illuminance of 0.5–1 fc.

Grazing. This involves aiming a light sharply across a wall, ground cover, or other textured surface, which bathes its apexes in light and casts its recesses in shade. Grazing is usually associated with flat walls; but it can highlight the texture of horizontal surfaces and sharply rounded surfaces such as fluted columns. Target illuminance ≈ 10–30 fc.

Fill light. This is an area of ambient illumination between two prominent areas of light which may be required if the intervening area is uncomfortably dark. Incidentally, ambient light is not the same as wide-angle floodlighting, as the former is often a product of interreflectance while the latter arrives directly from the light source.

Patch lighting. This brightens a prominent area while blackening its surround. A larger version of spotlighting, it is used to highlight main entrances, large statues, and other dramatic areas. A trickle of pathway lighting may be added to direct a viewer's eye from the post of observation to the destination. Target illuminance ≈ 8–20 fc.

Fig. 6-54. Patch lighting.

Mirror lighting. This reflects an interesting object in a pool, pond, or other placid water. It is composed by setting the water's surface as a dark reflective foreground (in which no light shines on, in, or from beneath it), placing the reflected object as midground, locating recessed uplighting in front of and to the sides of the reflected object, adding a small amount of soft background light just behind the reflected object, and blackening the remainder of the background. Target illuminance ≈ 5–12 fc.

Vista lighting. This reveals a prominent nocturnal view, such as distant city lights or other urban landscape, well beyond the immediate outdoor environs. The distant view is framed by trees or other vertical massing on each side, perhaps a trellis or overhanging branches above, and a lawn or other broad smooth area below. The midground elements on the sides are blackened to contrast the sparkle and aerial perspective of the distant view, and the foreground area below is usually given a soft glow that imparts depth to the scene. The viewer's point of observation is usually small and precisely located. A variation of vista lighting is *perspective lighting*. This illuminates a mid-distant object, such as a guest house or recreation area, that is flanked by vertical massing on both sides. The foreground is blackened, the sides are given a soft glow, and the area just in

Fig. 6-55. Mirror lighting.

front of the focal object is prominently lighted. By opening the side massing slightly outward or inward, the focal area will look nearer or farther away as desired.

Designing landscape lighting involves two general approaches: *organic* or *rational*. Organic design utilizes natural shapes and free-form arrangements: its essence is conforming man to Nature's random compositions. Rational design utilizes geometric shapes and formal layouts: its essence is fitting Nature to man's ideals. Usually it is best to go with one or the other. Either way, think of the terminals first.

Next, from where will the views will be seen? Pathways? Landings? Porches? Balconies? Windows? Each composed scene should look attractive and its sight lines be uninterrupted from all points of observation.

Next, with a luminous palette of soft washes, mellow floods, radiant accents, bright spots, and sharp silhouettes, visualize the optimal location of each luminaire and *paint* the illuminated scene. Allow for changes in foliage that occur with the seasons. Do not place fixtures where lawnmowers and Weedwackers can damage them, and provide each with access for maintenance, because falling leaves and other debris require almost daily removal from a well-composed landscape lighting scene. After laying out

Fig. 6-56. Vista lighting.

the light sources, select the luminaire for each, then determine the lamp outputs. This is often done with manufacturers' photometric footprints.

Then map the conductor layouts (straight runs, loops, V's, T's, etc.), sum the lamp wattages, and determine if the voltage will be 12 or 120 volts. 12 V systems are better for small layouts (up to a few 750 W circuits), where children or animals could contact the electric current, and where long lamp life (e.g. less maintenance) is desirable. 12 V connections are also simpler as they allow the fixtures to be easily restaked to accommodate plant growth or to create new viewing effects and the conductors can be buried in shallow trenches; but low-voltage systems require transformers. 120 V systems are better where lights are far from illuminated objects, layouts are large, and safety and security measures require stronger lighting. But outdoor 120 V cable must run through conduit buried below local frost level. With either voltage, minimum wiring is 12-2 BX cable for up to 100 ft straight runs or 150 ft looped runs. As cable lengths in landscape layouts can quickly add up to much more than one would expect, thicker cable is often required based on maximum 5 percent voltage drop per longest run. The extra cost of thicker cable is usually less than the price of an extra transformer.

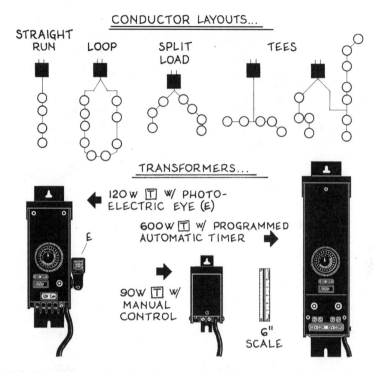

Fig. 6-57. Landscape luminaire conductor layouts & transformers.

Transformers for 12 V systems are sized by summing the luminaire output wattages, then selecting a unit whose load is 33–75 percent of capacity. Typical transformer capacities are 90, 120, 150, 300, 600, and 750 W; and typical sizes are 3 × 3 × 7 in. for 90 W units up to 4 × 5 × 18 in. for 600 W units. Each unit should have a thermal cutoff on the supply side and a circuit breaker on the load side, and the best units have programmable timers that turn lights on at any time and/or photocells that turn lights on at dusk and off at dawn. Each unit is usually mounted like a thermometer on a utility room wall so it can be easily adjusted.

Other guidelines for designing landscape lighting are:

▶ 12 V conductors cannot pass through walls, nor can they be placed in conduits, wireways, or other enclosures with conductors of different voltage.
▶ Maximum circuit amperage = 25 A or the wire must be enlarged.
▶ All terminal and cord/plug connections must be enclosed to prevent sparks that could set fires.
▶ Any fixtures in or near pools or fountains must be designed as swimming pool lighting, because people tend to dip their hands in almost any water, especially if it is clear.

- ▸ Common 12 V landscape light wattages are 6, 12, 15, 16, 20, 24, 25, 50, 75, and 100 W. For 12 V quartz lamp wattages vs. outputs, see Fig. 6-13, lamp lines *Q PAR36*, *Q MR11*, and *Q M16*.
- ▸ Some common 12 V incandescent PAR lamp beamspreads are 5°, 6°, 6 × 8°, 10°, 25 × 37°, 30°, and 66°.

Of course landscape lighting requires switches. Good locations for these are on the wall by the door through which one enters the illuminated outdoor scene, or by a window through which one can orient to the scene before stepping outdoors. Switches and dimmers may be installed outdoors near terraces, fields of play, and other areas that require more light during active use than when being observed from afar; then the controls should be operable from indoors and outdoors which usually requires three- or four-way switching. To these controls may be added timers, sensors and alarms whose management may be computerized. On the Plans each landmark and fixture is given a number, which is keyed to the Specifications as well as its location on the site.

More often than not, the design of landscape lighting is not finished when the construction workers drive away for the last time. On extensive projects, it may take a year of refocusing and re-aiming the fixtures onsite during every season to match the subtleties envisioned in the Plans.

Example 1. If several low-voltage conical pathway lights as described in the catalog excerpt of Fig. 6-58 are mounted 24 in. above the edge of a landscaped walk, what is the required wattage for each light? How far apart should they be spaced? $_L\Delta = 0.72$.

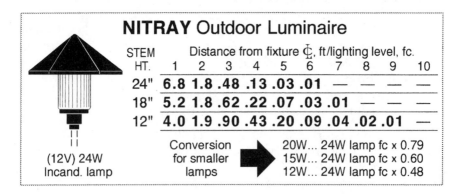

Fig. 6-58. Illumination data: NITRAY Landscape Luminaire.

Step 1. Assume selection of the **NITRAY** landscape luminaire shown in Fig. 6-58. From Sec. 6.E.2. text, the target illuminance for pathway lighting ≈ 3–5 fc (aim for average ≈ 4 fc) and ≥ 0.5 fc between lamps. However, at a given light depreciation factor of 0.72, the required illuminance is actually 4 ÷ 0.72 ≈ 5.6 fc.

Step 2. From the photometric data in Fig. 6-58 select a lamp with a target illuminance ≈ 5.6 fc under or nearly under the lamp. The most reasonable value is 8.9 fc at 2.0 ft away from a lamp with a 3.0 ft stem height. This indicates that (1) a good height for the desired lamp is 3.0 ft, and (2) the 24W lamp's illuminance of 8.9 fc is too high, so go to "CONVERSION FOR SMALLER LAMPS" and find a lamp whose illuminance ≈ 5.6 fc ➡ 15W lamp = 8.9 fc × 0.60 = 5.3 fc ≈ 5.6 fc ➡ 15W lamp is **OK**.

Step 3. Assuming a row of the selected lamps, find the maximum ¢–¢ spacing that maintains at least 0.5 fc illuminance between them. (Here the light from two adjacent lamps is not additive because as the light arrives from opposite directions it never adds to any one surface unless it is nearly flat, but then the two angles of incidence would be so low that the additive illuminance would be very weak.) In the photometric data proceed to the right along the *3.0 ft stem ht.* line until the illuminance diminishes to 0.5 ÷ 0.60 = 0.8 fc (be sure to include the smaller lamp's conversion factor in these values) ➡ at 9 ft away the converted pathway fc = 0.8 ➡ as 9 ft away is half the distance between two lamps, the 15 W lamps can be spaced 18 ft apart.

Example 2. A country club in Atlanta plans to install evening landscape lighting around its entrance. If the focal highlights are azaleas at a height of 6 ft, dogwoods at 24 ft, and understories of mature oaks at 45 ft, what is the required output of the lighting?

Step 1. Determine the optimal lamp selections and beamspreads for the foliage. Regarding the oaks, each should be uplighted to emphasize its mass by placing one or more luminaires near the base of the trunk and having their beamspreads span the interior of the canopy. Each oak should also be frontlighted to emphasize its form and character by locating one or more luminaires beyond the front edge of the tree's foliage or mounting the luminaires on the roof of a building behind the observer, then having their beamspreads equal the arbor's width. And each oak should be sidelighted to emphasize its textures and edges by placing one or more luminaires laterally beyond the edge of foliage and having its beamspread equal the front half of the arbor. Here only the oak uplighting is considered further.

Step 2. Compute the output for each luminaire. Assume that from onsite inspection the optimal beamspread for the uplighting is 60°.

6)E)2)   a. R, PAR & MR lamps: $\diamondsuit_< \; \beta \; U \, _L\Delta \; \approx \; 12.6 \, \Phi \, D^2$ ... ✚

      b. All other lamps: $\diamondsuit_n \; \beta \; U \, _L\Delta \; \approx \; \Phi \, D^2$

$\diamondsuit_<$ = output of R, PAR, or MR lamp w/ beamspread designation, CBCP. Here, as beamspread is wide and distance from light source to visual task is long (indicating the need for powerful lighting), try incandescent R flood lamp. $\therefore \diamondsuit_<$ = ? lm. Lighting loads of clustered lamps is additive if their centerbeams align.

$\diamondsuit_n$ = output of any lamp that has no beamspread designation, lm

β = ray or beam concentration factor. For floods and spots, β = 1.

U = luminaire coefficient of utilization. Luminaire is outdoors and faces upward ➡ clear lens shielding. From Table 6-2, U of R or PAR flood w/ prismatic lens or clear shield = 0.93.

$_L\Delta$ = light depreciation factor, 0.83

Φ = required infant task illumination. From Table 6-11, Φ for outdoor landscaping highlights, 10 fc.

D = distance between light source and visual task, 45 ft

$$\diamondsuit_< \times 1 \times 0.93 \times 0.83 \; \approx \; 12.6 \times 10 \times 45^2 \quad ... \diamondsuit_< \; \geq \; 331{,}000 \; lm$$

From Fig. 6-14, $\diamondsuit_<$ for 400R<40° lamp = 140,000 lm
Consider cluster of 3 × 400R<40° lamps whose
centerbeams are slightly off center

6.E.3. Security Lighting [†]

     Security lighting is another aspect of architecture that is presently undergoing revolutionary design changes due to recent developments of computerization. Gone is the old yellow floodlight mounted high on a building's cornice, a garish star in the firmament, glaring down on a turnaround or service yard up to 15 hours a day, annoying the neighbors as much as protecting the owner —because now this lighting can be combined with motion sensors, intrusion alarms, passkey locks, battery packs, remote TV surveillance, 'lived-in look' indoor lighting programs, and other features that operate night and day, whether occupants are present or absent. The possibilities have become so endless that the best way to design these systems is to let your imagination lead you to the components, not vice versa.

     For example, by imagining a sleeping housewife who hears a strange noise in the night while her husband is out of town, you might (1) locate under each gable of their domicile a twin floodlight fixture with a 200° spread motion detector, (2) mount closed-circuit TV cameras under each fixture, and (3) place beside her bed a programmer with a panic button transmitter, TV monitor, and a digital readout of every opening in the

---

[†] Most of the information for this section was found in (1) the *Leviton Home*

house. When she presses the panic button, the floodlights turn on and illuminate any intruder outside, the CCTV cameras scan the yards and turnaround then display the viewed scenes on the monitor by her bed, and the digital readout informs her of the location of any broken windows or opened doors. By pressing another button she can notify the police. By pressing a third button, she can tell the programmer to reset everything if the noise was merely a raccoon knocking over a garbage can lid.

Or by imagining the off-hour security requirements for a tool-and-die shop located in a high-crime urban area, you might (1) install several vandal-resistant luminaires containing wide-beam floodlights that cover every part of the service yard, loading dock, truck parking, and material storage area; (2) incorporate into each lampholder a motion detector whose coverage area matches that of its light; (3) add HI-LO autocircuitry that turns the lights off from dawn to dusk, dims them from dusk to dawn, and turns them on fully if motion is detected at night; (4) fit each fixture with electronically adjustable glare shields that control light trespass to adjacent buildings; (5) mount linear motion sensors above each straight run of fence enclosing the service yard which upon detecting motion in these areas activate the lighting, siren alarms mounted under the cornice of the building, and the police department; and (6) incorporate a program that notifies the facility manager when any light burns out or other component is malfunctioning.

A few security lighting guidelines are:

▸ Good fixtures have simple mounts, easily replaceable lamps, and battery packs that maintain operation during power outages. Tall mounts require fewer lamps, create more uniform illuminance ratios (8:1 average/minimum light is okay for security lighting), and minimize shadows cast by obstructions. In most cases 12–18 ft high is okay. Several low-wattage lamps usually create more uniform light than one or two large ones. Cluster mounts cost less than single-lamp mounts.

▸ Illuminate all parts of a security area; don't leave any dark spots where an intruder could hide if detected. Every area should ideally receive light from two directions to minimize shadows. Focus lamp axes on entries and other critical areas. Include the roof as a possible point of entry by burglars. Combine security lighting with night and landscape lighting.

▸ In high-crime areas accompany security lighting with physical barriers. Masonry walls and other opaque barriers should be lit on both sides. Concrete paving, white facades, and other lightly colored surfaces are much easier to survey than dark ones.

▸ Consider operating modes that can activate doorbells as well as alarms, in case someone is at home and the intruder is benign.

> What is the required output for a quartz floodlight for the loading
> dock, service area, and surrounding grounds of a public utility truck
> garage if the beamspread is 40° and the distance to the center of the
> coverage area is 36 ft? $_L\Delta$ = 0.86.

6 E 3 a]   R, PAR, & MR lamps: $\diamondsuit_< ß \, U \,_L\Delta \approx 12.6 \, \Phi \, D^2$ ... ✛

    b]   All other lamps: $\diamondsuit_n ß \, U \,_L\Delta \approx \Phi \, D^2$

$\diamondsuit_<$ = output of R, PAR, or MR lamp w/ beamspread designation, CBCP
$\diamondsuit_n$ = output of any other lamp that has no beamspread designation, lm
ß   = ray or beam concentration factor. For floods and spots, ß = 1.
U = luminaire coefficient of utilization. From Table 6-2, U of R or PAR
     flood w/ prismatic lens or clear shield = 0.93.
$_L\Delta$ = light depreciation factor, 0.86
Φ = required infant task illumination. From Table 6-11,
     Φ for normal security = 3 fc.
D = distance between light source and visual task, 36 ft

    $\diamondsuit_< \times 1 \times 0.93 \times 0.86 \approx 12.6 \times 3 \times 36^2$ ... $\diamondsuit_< \geq$ 61,000 CBCP
From Fig. 6-13, nearest Q PAR lamp w/ F of <40° ≥ 61,000 CBCP is
1,000 W <28 ×12° ➜ use cluster of 4 lamps to create 40° × 40° spread

6.E.4. Parking Lighting

Parking area lighting is primarily for pedestrians, as auto headlights
suffice to reveal vehicular movement. Such illumination should reveal areas
between parked cars, paths across vehicular lanes, and points of entry and
exit at curbs. Luminaires should aim 30–60° down from horizontal, have
square or rectangular footprints instead of round ones, and use the fewest
masts and their costly supports. With perimeter mounts, cutoff angles
should minimize glare in nearby roadways and windows, beamspreads
should not be blocked by nearby tree branches, and bases should be 4 ft
back from curbs to minimize vehicular damage. Design typically involves
analyzing photometric footprints of available luminaires, then arranging
them based on required lighting levels and optimal spacing intervals.

Related to parking lighting is walkway lighting. Walkway luminaires may
be mounted in a variety of positions: in poles with long overhangs that allow
direct downlighting of walkway centers, high against nearby walls, in waist-
high bollards, in knee-high footpath lights, and under treads at stepped
landings. Other than that their lamp wattages and mounting heights are generally lower, their design is similar to that for parking.

DAGLO Outdoor Luminaire: HPS Lamps

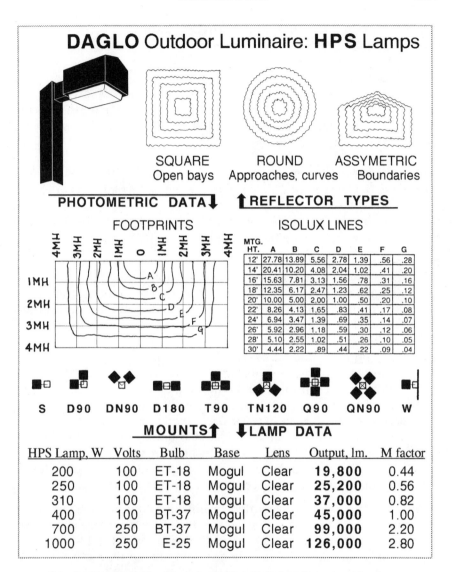

SQUARE — Open bays
ROUND — Approaches, curves
ASSYMETRIC — Boundaries

PHOTOMETRIC DATA↓ **↑REFLECTOR TYPES**

FOOTPRINTS

ISOLUX LINES

MTG. HT.	A	B	C	D	E	F	G
12'	27.78	13.89	5.56	2.78	1.39	.56	.28
14'	20.41	10.20	4.08	2.04	1.02	.41	.20
16'	15.63	7.81	3.13	1.56	.78	.31	.16
18'	12.35	6.17	2.47	1.23	.62	.25	.12
20'	10.00	5.00	2.00	1.00	.50	.20	.10
22'	8.26	4.13	1.65	.83	.41	.17	.08
24'	6.94	3.47	1.39	.69	.35	.14	.07
26'	5.92	2.96	1.18	.59	.30	.12	.06
28'	5.10	2.55	1.02	.51	.26	.10	.05
30'	4.44	2.22	.89	.44	.22	.09	.04

S   D90   DN90   D180   T90   TN120   Q90   QN90   W

MOUNTS↑ **↓LAMP DATA**

HPS Lamp, W	Volts	Bulb	Base	Lens	Output, lm.	M factor
200	100	ET-18	Mogul	Clear	**19,800**	0.44
250	100	ET-18	Mogul	Clear	**25,200**	0.56
310	100	ET-18	Mogul	Clear	**37,000**	0.82
400	100	BT-37	Mogul	Clear	**45,000**	1.00
700	250	BT-37	Mogul	Clear	**99,000**	2.20
1000	250	E-25	Mogul	Clear	**126,000**	2.80

Fig. 6-59. Illumination data: DAGLO Outdoor Luminaire.

A large parking lot outside a casino in Ledyard, CT, is illuminated by HPS lamps enclosed in cobrahead luminaires with dropped prismatic lenses. If the masts supporting the lamps are located along the edges of the 64 ft parking bays, what are the optimal lamp outputs, mast heights, and boundary pole spacings? $_L\Delta = 0.81$.

Solution: Assume selection of the **DAGLO** outdoor luminaire, then utilize the manufacturer's catalog data as shown in Fig. 6-59.

Step 1. Determine the spacing of the luminaire mast mounts. The optimal mast spacing perpendicular to the parking bays is for the masts to align with the parking bay boundaries, which are 64 ft apart. An optimal spacing ∥ to the parking bays would also be 64 ft ➡ square lighting bay modules of 64 × 64 ft that offer uniform lighting.

Step 2 Determine the required task illumination for the area at night. From Table 6-11, Φ for *parking for public evening attractions* ≥ 3 fc.

Step 3. Determine the optimal mounting height of the luminaires on the masts. This is usually done by trial and error as below.

a. A good initial height to try is 16 ft, then examine the selected fixture's footprint in the manufacturer's catalog. If the bays are 64 ft wide and the poles are 16 ft high, then one bay in the FOOTPRINT diagram in Fig. 6-59 is 64/16 = 4 mounting heights (MH) wide or 2MH in each direction from 0 ➡ isolux line *D* covers about the area of one bay with the lamp at its center.

b. In the PHOTOMETRIC DATA box in Fig. 6-59, note the lighting level at the intersect of the *D* isolux line with the **MTG. HT.** line for 16′ ... it is 1.56 fc, about half the required lighting of 3 fc. As this amount of light also arrives from the luminaire on the other side of the bay, the additive light from these two sources along the center of the bay ≈ 1.56 × 2 ≈ 3.12 fc. As this ≥ 3 fc, 16 ft mounting height is **OK**.

c. Light depreciation should normally be factored into the above value of 3.12 fc; but here this may be ignored due to the small spill light arriving from more distant luminaires in the large parking area.

Note: By trying an 18 ft mounting height and interpolating the photometric data, Φ ≈ 3.70 fc ➡ excessive and the taller masts are more costly. By trying a 14 ft height, Φ ≈ 2.78 fc ➡ borderline **NG**. If all fc values are lower than required, select a stronger light source from the LAMP DATA table in Fig. 6-59 as described in Step 4 below.

Step 4. Select the luminaire from the manufacturer's catalog. In the LAMP DATA table at the bottom of Fig. 6-59, note the numerical values under the *M factor* column. The effective lighting level found in Step 3b × M factor for any HPS lamp in this table = actual lighting level for that lamp. Here 3.12 × 1.00 = 3.12 fc ➡ this ≥ 3 fc ➡ use **DAGLO** HPS 400W Outdoor Luminaire. The lamp's actual output is listed in this table under *Output, lm* (it is 45,000 lm). If stronger lighting is desired, multiply the effective lighting level found in Step 3b by a larger M factor then use the lamp with this M factor. If weaker lighting is desired, multiply the lighting level by a smaller M factor and use its lamp.

Step 5. Arrange and select the mast mounts for the luminaires. Try locating the masts at the intersections of the grid lines running perpendicular and parallel to the parking bays, then mounting one lamp on each mast so it illuminates one-quarter of each of the four bays converging at its base. Then from the row of available mounts in the catalog select the appropriate mount... it is **S**.

Note: By trying 32 ft mounts that illuminate four bays, MH ≈ 128/32 = 4 ➡ ÷ 2 for bi-directional light ➡ isolux line *D*. An interpolated value of 0.38 fc for a 32 ft height gives 0.38 × 2 = 0.76 fc per lamp, which is not ≥ required 3 fc. However, if four lamps are placed on each mount, then 0.76 × 4 lamps = 3.04 fc ≥ 3 fc ➡ **OK**. Then the taller masts can be arranged at every other *X* and *Y* grid line in the parking area so that each mast covers the four bays whose corners converge at its base. Finally, if each mast has four lamps on its top, from Fig. 6-59 its mount should be **Q90** or **QN90**. For large parking areas, such clustered mounts on tall masts are usually more economical because they require fewer masts and fewer footings.

6.E.5. Arena Lighting

An arena is an outdoor area where an occupant usually remains for an extended period. Thus at night, such a space's criteria for design involves more than satisfying one's sense of temporal safety and utilitarian convenience: it includes all the subtleties of ambience, mood, extensiveness, and interaction with other people that must be satisfied in any indoor space where occupants may remain for hours. Even landscapes revealed by lights at night are often merely 'background occupancies', where one is more likely to find pleasure in inspiring distractions —of lifting one's senses upward and outward for a brief while— as opposed to orienting more inwardly for extended spans of time.

The best light sources for revealing lengthy outdoor activities at night are usually H.I.D. lamps. Fluorescent lamps generally do not have enough carrying power for outdoor lighting and many don't work well in cool weather, while incandescent and quartz lamps are bright enough but cost much more to operate and don't last nearly as long. The biggest disadvantage of H.I.D. lamps is their start and restart delay times, which can be several minutes; but this problem can be overcome by accompanying these light sources with incandescent or quartz floods that are programmed to turn on when the parent lamps fail and to stay on while they are off.

Arena lighting should be 1.5–2 times brighter than if the same lighting was indoors, as this compensates for the lack of reflective surfaces that enclose indoor spaces. Thus any tall, lightly colored walls around the arena area, and any ceiling above it, can increase the brightness of its lighting. There is one architectural material that is perfect for such semi-enclosures: tent fabrics. A large triangular sail floating above an arena environment, its long cables painted flat black so they can't be seen, its light, reflective, gaily-colored surface and billowy outline set aglow by a few aptly aimed floods, can add a carnival aura to an outdoor scene as well as make everything below it clearer to see —and two or three such sails, of different sizes, shapes, and colors, can be truly exciting.

Arena lights should generally be about 12–18 ft above the ground, and their horizontal spacing should be 2–4 times their height. If the lights are lower than about 12 ft they are apt to shine in peoples' eyes, and if taller than about 18 ft the light is weaker. If the lights are on poles, these supports should not be set in the arena's corners or along its edges but away from them; however, the distance of each pole from the arena's nearest edge should not exceed twice the pole's height. Several arena lights may be clustered or arrayed on one pole, not just at its top but anywhere along its length, which makes better use of them. Wherever arena lamps are mounted, they should have swivel bases so they can be easily aimed, adjustable reflectors so their cutoffs can be refined, and wide beamspreads so their light is more uniform. For most nocturnal scenes lamps with warm temperatures are best, and pay close attention to color: a platter of cold cuts can look gangrenous under a mercury vapor lamp but delectable under a small quartz lamp while the same mercury lamp would be perfect for nearby foliage. Then, knowing each maxima and minima —of heights, spacings, arrays, colors, beamspreads, directivities— modulate each to accommodate every nuance of the occupants' behavior in ways that create visual symphonies of nocturnal light.

As exciting as arena lighting can be, it has its caveats. Water and wind are its mortal enemies: thus each outdoor lamp must be protected from the weather, each base and support should be doubly strong, and all electric wiring must be GFI circuitry. Also, no arena light source should ever touch any windblown canvas, drought-starved foliage, or other flammable material. Because field-refining is so important with this light source, every fixture must be accessible —which not only means that every pole must be climbable and every cornice must be reachable, but that every arena environment should include a roofed storage area big enough to house a long extension ladder. Another serious concern in these occupancies is the cords that provide the current. Bundle them together, channel them in out-of-the-way places, cover them with carpeted plywood or similar construction where pedestrians must walk over them, use twist-lock plugs then duct-tape each plug together to be doubly safe —because the worst thing that can happen to beautifully designed arena lighting is a blackout, not only for the lights, but because sudden darkness can cause a crowd to panic.

The following is a design outline for arena lighting:

Step 1. Select the optimal light sources for each visual task.

Step 2. Determine the task or destination lighting level for each lamp. This is usually done by consulting Table 6-11.

Step 3. Determine the optimal wattage and number of each array of lamps according to the formulas

6)E)5) **a. R, PAR, & MR lamps:** $18 \, \diamondsuit_< \, \eta \, \beta \, U_L\Delta \, \approx \, \Phi \, A \, h^2$

b. All other lamps: $227 \, \diamondsuit \, \eta \, \kappa_f \, U_L\Delta \, \approx \, \Phi \, A \, h^2$

$\diamondsuit_<$ = output of R, PAR, or MR lamp w/ beamspread designation, CBCP
$\diamondsuit$ = output of any other lamp that has no beamspread designation, lm
η = number of lamps required to illuminate arena area
β = ray or beam concentration factor. For floods and spots, $\beta = 1$.
U = luminaire coefficient of utilization, from Table 6-2
$_L\Delta$ = light depreciation factor, from Table 6-3
Φ = net light arriving at destination or visual task, fc
A = horizontal area of arena area, sf
h = height of light source above arena area, ft

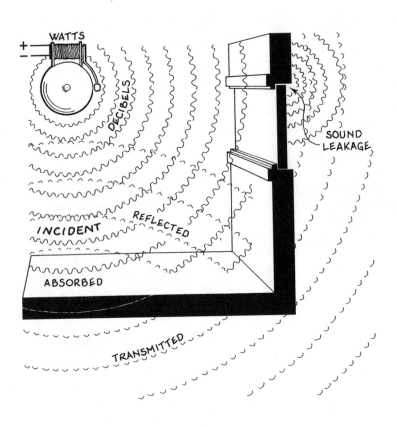

Acoustic terms

ACOUSTICS

7.A. GENERAL

Sound is a series of pressure variations that move through an elastic medium, such as air. The sound's alternating compressions and rarefactions may be far apart (low-pitched), close together (high-pitched), tall (loud), or short (soft). These invisible waves can turn the air they usually travel through into a sonar landscape that is as ecstatic or unbearable as any visual landscape. Indeed, otherwise beautiful architecture can be made unbearable by a small oversight in acoustic design.

Acoustic design is different from the other Æ disciplines, because:

1. Acoustics is more comprehensive than the other disciplines. Quantifying a sound requires analysis of a greater variety of properties as a prerequisite to effective design, and successful design often depends on the unitary quality of a total assembly and not by adding up the individual qualities of each separate part. For example, when designing a beam, if you make the beam safe in shear, safe in bending, safe in deflection, etc. according to each of the Eight Stresses, you can be sure the whole beam will be safe; but in acoustic design you can't just take the best kind of one component, the best aspect of another, the best part of another, etc., then put them all together with the sureness of knowledge that you've come up with the best solution —because often you haven't.
2. Acoustics is invisible. You can put your hand on a beam, in water, around a wire or light fixture. But air? In our sight-dominant society, such ethereality fosters an aura of secondary significance that makes many occupants question its importance.
3. Even for those who understand acoustics, this science is more subjective than the other Æ disciplines. There is no doubt when an overstressed beam fails, when hot water burns, or when an overloaded fuse blows; but who's to say that the sound that bothers you bothers me? Much of acoustics also exists on a

foundation of 50 percent occupancy satisfaction —the bell-shaped probability curve; and, graphically speaking, there's a big difference between a curve crest and a falloff.

4. Acoustic design is more time-consuming than the others, at least when done well. Each potential problem must be ferreted out with near-clairvoyant perception; then the antidote assembly must be built by conscientious contractors who understand the whys behind their work; then the Æ designer must spend more-than-usual time verifying the results.

5. Acoustic design is beset by a bewildering array of acronyms that keep all but its finest experts from proficiently applying this science. See how many of the following acoustic acronyms you know: AC ANC ASW BR CAC CNEL dBA dBC DIL DNL EDT ELR FIIC FSTC GWB IACC IDT IIC LEDE LEF LEV LF LFN LMF MFN NC NCAC NCB NIC NNIC NR NRC OITC PNC QRD RASTI RC RODS RT RT60 STC SIS SPP STI TL TR VAV. This text avoids using all but the most basic acoustic acronyms.

Since acoustics can be difficult to comprehend even by professionals, this chapter begins by describing an elemental sound, then building on this firm familiar foundation.

Everything is elastic. Air is elastic. And every solid is elastic to a certain degree. For example, when a hammer strikes the top of a nail, the impact of the hammer's metal head against the nail's metal head compresses each material. This elastic contraction is extremely slight but swift —then the two materials rebound to their original shape so fast that they push the nearest air molecules outward, which push out the molecules next to them, which push out the next molecules, *ad infinitum*, until the incredible chain of outwardly jostling molecules quickly becomes a spherical wave of pulsing energy radiating

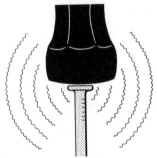

Fig. 7-1. A hammer striking a nail.

from the point of impact until each tiny surface in this expanding sphere either diminishes to nothing far away or collides with a surface —whose area may be less than $1/20$ of a square inch and be buried an inch deep in your ear. Thus a perceived sound is propagated. It is amazing how infinitesimally small are the movements that create effects that are so large!

From these mechanics it is obvious that a sound has three parts: a *source* (the location and moment of the propagated sound), a *path* (the outward direction each part of the wave takes from its source), and a *receiver* (the surface that absorbs the wave's pulse). Now let's describe these mechanics with a graph. The sound's source is the hammer striking the nail, its path is a radiating line through the surrounding air, and its receiver is the eardrum of the person holding the hammer. This simple sonar event is portrayed in the sound field graph below.

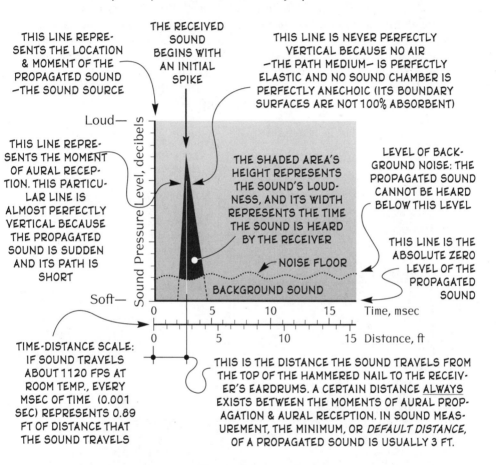

Fig. 7-2. A hammer striking a nail in an anechoic chamber.

Now let's focus on the path part of this sonar event. This simple path extending straight from the nail to the eardrum is actually many paths, all radiating outward from the same point, until each path meets a surface some distance away; then each path reflects from its encountered surface and begins travelling in a new direction [forget for a moment that part of the sound's energy is absorbed by the surface]. Now if this sonar event occurs inside a room, soon —in microseconds— the air around the sound's source will be filled with a crisscrossing fusillade of hundreds of soundpaths moving in all sorts of directions. Obviously more than one of these soundpaths will eventually reach the ear of the person holding the hammer that struck the nail, and obviously the longer the path, the longer it will take to arrive there; thus the hammer-striking-nail sound the person actually hears occurs not in an instant but over a short period of time. Now, suppose that the room this sonar event occurs in is a cabinetmaker's workshop. Say the workshop is 16×16 ft in plan, that its floor-to-ceiling height is 8 ft, that the nail is hammered in the center of the room on a workbench whose surface is 5 ft below the ceiling, and that the sound radiates outward at a velocity of about 1,100 ft per second. Then a more articulate sound field graph of this sonar event would appear as below.

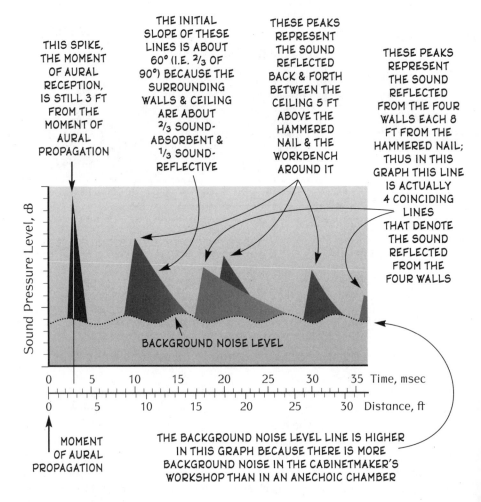

THIS SPIKE, THE MOMENT OF AURAL RECEPTION, IS STILL 3 FT FROM THE MOMENT OF AURAL PROPAGATION

THE INITIAL SLOPE OF THESE LINES IS ABOUT 60° (I.E. $^2/_3$ OF 90°) BECAUSE THE SURROUNDING WALLS & CEILING ARE ABOUT $^2/_3$ SOUND-ABSORBENT & $^1/_3$ SOUND-REFLECTIVE

THESE PEAKS REPRESENT THE SOUND REFLECTED BACK & FORTH BETWEEN THE CEILING 5 FT ABOVE THE HAMMERED NAIL & THE WORKBENCH AROUND IT

THESE PEAKS REPRESENT THE SOUND REFLECTED FROM THE FOUR WALLS EACH 8 FT FROM THE HAMMERED NAIL; THUS IN THIS GRAPH THIS LINE IS ACTUALLY 4 COINCIDING LINES THAT DENOTE THE SOUND REFLECTED FROM THE FOUR WALLS

Sound Pressure Level, dB

BACKGROUND NOISE LEVEL

Time, msec

Distance, ft

MOMENT OF AURAL PROPAGATION

THE BACKGROUND NOISE LEVEL LINE IS HIGHER IN THIS GRAPH BECAUSE THERE IS MORE BACKGROUND NOISE IN THE CABINETMAKER'S WORKSHOP THAN IN AN ANECHOIC CHAMBER

Fig. 7-3. A hammer striking a nail in a cabinetmaker's workshop.

        Although the sound as shown on the previous page has many peaks
and valleys, in reality the human ear cannot consciously distinguish
sounds less than about 80 milliseconds apart, a timespan that is known as
the sound's *clarity index*. Thus a more detailed sound field graph of the
hammered nail in the cabinetmaker's workshop would appear as the one
below. In this third graph, note the condensed nature of the time-distance
scale compared to the ones in the first two graphs.

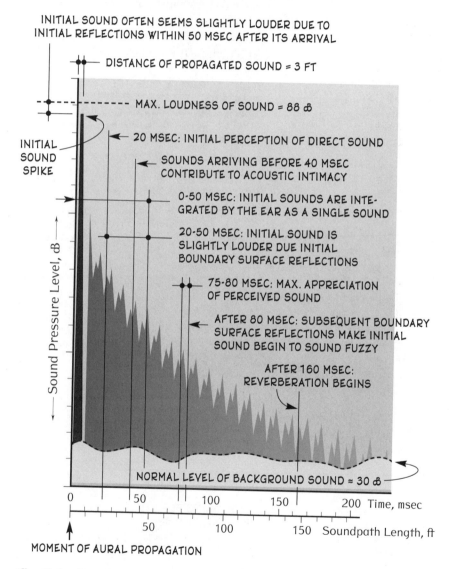

INITIAL SOUND OFTEN SEEMS SLIGHTLY LOUDER DUE TO
INITIAL REFLECTIONS WITHIN 50 MSEC AFTER ITS ARRIVAL

DISTANCE OF PROPAGATED SOUND = 3 FT

MAX. LOUDNESS OF SOUND = 88 dB

INITIAL
SOUND
SPIKE

20 MSEC: INITIAL PERCEPTION OF DIRECT SOUND

SOUNDS ARRIVING BEFORE 40 MSEC
CONTRIBUTE TO ACOUSTIC INTIMACY

0-50 MSEC: INITIAL SOUNDS ARE INTE-
GRATED BY THE EAR AS A SINGLE SOUND

20-50 MSEC: INITIAL SOUND IS
SLIGHTLY LOUDER DUE INITIAL
BOUNDARY SURFACE REFLECTIONS

75-80 MSEC: MAX. APPRECIATION
OF PERCEIVED SOUND

AFTER 80 MSEC: SUBSEQUENT BOUNDARY
SURFACE REFLECTIONS MAKE INITIAL
SOUND BEGIN TO SOUND FUZZY

AFTER 160 MSEC:
REVERBERATION BEGINS

NORMAL LEVEL OF BACKGROUND SOUND ≈ 30 dB

Sound Pressure Level, dB

0   50   100   150   200 Time, msec

         50   100   150 Soundpath Length, ft

MOMENT OF AURAL PROPAGATION

Fig. 7-4. A more real-life representation of the previous graph.

Now suppose the cabinetmaker is building a pulpit in a church. Thus he has moved his nail-hammering into a large room whose high ceiling and surrounding walls are smooth and hard and much farther away. Now a sound field graph of the hammered nail would appear as below. Here the sound dynamics occur over a longer period of time and it is easier to see what actually occurs in most human occupancies. Again note the condensed nature of the graph's time-distance scale. In this room the sound is heard clearly for the first 80 msec —less than a twelfth of a second— then the sound lingers in this highly reverberative space for another 4 seconds before it finally dies away, or *attenuates*. Imagine a church choir singing in this space. Or an organ playing. Or a minister giving a sermon.

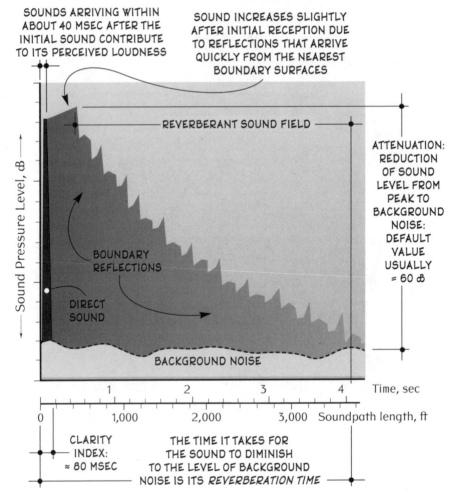

Fig. 7-5. Sound field graph 4: a hammer striking a nail in a church.

Now suppose the cabinetmaker is relaxing in his suburban home on a Saturday afternoon. He is hammering no nails now; he is reading a book while relaxing on the living room sofa. His children are talking in a bedroom down the hall. The refrigerator is running in the kitchen. The wind rustles the foliage out front. A dog barks across the street. An airplane passes overhead. A bird chirps at the feeding station in the backyard. The kitchen sink faucet drips. A car pulls into the driveway. The pattern of a woman's footsteps moves across the driveway then along the flagstone steps up to the front door. The door slams. "Hi Honey."

All these sounds are portrayed in the sound field graph below.

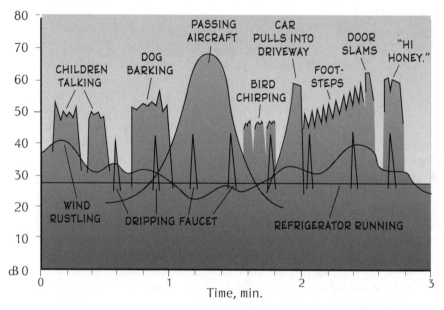

Fig. 7-6. Sound field graph of residential activities.

7.A.1. Elements of Sound †

Each of a sound's three parts —*source, path*, and *receiver*— are explained in greater detail below.

Sound source. This is the aural event, occurring at a certain location and a certain moment, that propagates the sound. Each such event may be as small as the tap of a finger on a windowpane, or as large as the

---

† A major source for the data in Secs. 7.A.1. and 7.B. was *Mechanical/Plumb-*

drone of late-afternoon traffic on an urban expressway. A small sound radiates from a point source in spherical waves that diminish in loudness according to the square of the distance between its origin and reception. But a large sound may have such great lateral dimensions that its initial waves are mostly planar for some distance outward before they acquire a spherical character. Thus, to borrow an analogy from illumination, a sound may have a *point* source (e.g. a car horn), a *line* source (e.g. a plucked guitar string to someone listening a few feet away), or an *area* source (e.g. theater applause to a member of the audience). Similarly as in illumination, if the ratio of a sound's length of travel to the lateral length or width of its source is more than about 6, it is a *point* source sound; if the ratio of its travel to the lateral length of its origin is less than about 6, it is a *line* source sound; and if the ratio of its travel to both the lateral length and width of its origin is less than about 6, it is an *area* source sound.

Each propagated sound also has a duration. It may be an *impulse sound*, a single isolated event such as a hammered nail or a door slam, or it may be a *steady-state sound*, a continuous event such as the whir of a fan or hum of a computer. Many steady-state sounds are aggregates of impulse sounds, an example being the closely spaced phonemes of speech which together comprise conversation. A particular floor, wall, or ceiling construction that is acoustically acceptable for steady-state sound may be undesirable for impulse sound.

Sound path. This is the journey, radiating outward in all directions, that a sound makes from its source to the receiver. If its path is through air the sound is *airborne*; if through a solid it is *solid-borne*. An airborne sound grows steadily weaker as it radiates from its source, but solid-borne sound often travels through a long thin mass, such as a steel beam, that may preserve much of its loudness many yards away. A sound may also change from airborne to solid-borne and back several times as it travels from source receiver —as when an off-balance HVAC blower pulley revolving at high speed creates a vibration noise (airborne) that passes through the blower's frame (solid-borne), resonates through the air beneath the frame to the floor below (airborne), vibrates through the concrete floor (solid-borne), travels through the airspace between the underside of the floor and the top of the suspended ceiling below (airborne), penetrates the suspended ceiling (solid-borne), then radiates into the office below (airborne) to annoy a person working at her desk.

Receiver. This is the surface that absorbs the sound at some distance from its source. This surface may be the eardrum of an human or other animal, the diaphragm of a microphone, a pickup on an electric guitar, or any number of other electronic devices; but here we are primarily concerned with the eardrums of a human occupant. One's access and receptivity to a sound at the moment of perception greatly influences acoustic design. A receiver's binaural hearing also allows accuracy of sound detection in the horizontal direction of ±5 percent in the front half of one's sphere of activity, while accuracy to the rear is considerably less due to the frontally-oriented cupped shape of the outer ear lobes. Accuracy of sound detection in the vertical plane is usually ±10 percent, depending on comparative amplification by one's funnel-shaped inner ears and spiral-shaped auditory canals.

7.B. PROPERTIES OF SOUND

Sound has five general properties: *velocity, frequency, intensity, direction*, and *diffuseness*. Each is described in the sections that follow.

7.B.1. Velocity

A sound's velocity is the speed at which its waves travel outward from its source. Since sound travels faster through solids than air, solid-borne sound is often a troublesome aspect of acoustic design. Sound also travels 11 percent faster through air at 100° F than at 0° F. Thus within this range its speed varies by about 1.1 fps for every 1° change in temperature. At room temperature light travels about 870,000 times faster than sound.

> **Example 1.** What is the speed of sound through air at 44° F? What is its speed at room temperature? At 100° F?

7 B 1

$$\mathcal{V}_t = \mathcal{V}_o [1 + (T - 32)/491]^{0.5}$$

$\mathcal{V}_t$ = speed of sound through selected medium at given temp., **?** fps

$\mathcal{V}_o$ = speed of sound through selected medium at 32° F (0° C), fps. Sound velocities through several media at 32° F are as follows:

Medium	Velocity, fps	Medium	Velocity, fps	Medium	Velocity, fps
Air	1,087	Water	4,450	Glass	15,800
Pine, dry	3,560	Oak, dry	5,350	Brick	11,400
Concrete	11,600	Steel	15,400	Aluminum	18,300

From above, $\mathcal{V}_o$ of sound thro' air at 32° F = 1,087 fps.

T = temperature of selected sound medium, ° F. T = 44° F.

$$\mathcal{V}_t = 1,087 [1 + (44 - 32)/491]^{0.5} = 1,100 \text{ fps}$$

Similarly, at room temperature (68° F or 20° C), $\mathcal{V}$ = 1,126 fps

Similarly, at 100° F, $\mathcal{V}$ = 1,160 fps

Example 2. What is the speed of sound through a W16 × 40 structural steel beam whose temperature is 60° F?

7)B)1)

$$v_t = v_0 [1 + (T - 32)/491]^{0.5}$$

v_t = speed of sound through selected medium at given temperature, ? fps

v_0 = speed of sound through selected medium at 32° F, fps.

From data in Example 1, v_0 through steel = 15,400 fps.

T = temperature of selected sound medium, 60° F.

$$v_t = 15,400 [1 + (60 - 32)/491]^{0.5} = 15,800 \text{ fps}$$

7.B.2. Frequency

A sound's frequency is its number of vibrations per second, known as *Hertz* (Hz). This ranges from low, as in the deep tone of a bass drum, to high, as in the shrill blow of a whistle. Low-frequency sounds of about 16–500 Hz are called *rumbly*, while sounds of 1,000–8,000 Hz are referred to as *hissy*. Human conversation ranges from about 60–6,000 Hz, its dominant frequencies being about 500 Hz for men and 900 Hz for women. Due to the construction of the inner ear, human hearing is typically most receptive at about 3,000 Hz, is fairly uniform between about 150–4,500 Hz, and lowers rapidly below and above this range. At high sound frequencies, the voice is more directional and speech intelligibility reduces more rapidly if the speaker turns from the listeners. For simple calculations, the average pitch for human hearing is usually taken at 1,000 Hz.

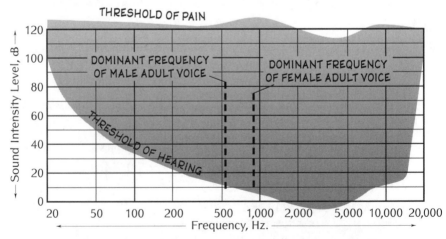

Fig. 7-7. Sound frequency vs. intensity graph. [†]

[†] This graph was abstracted from *College Physics, 4th edition*; Sears, Young, &

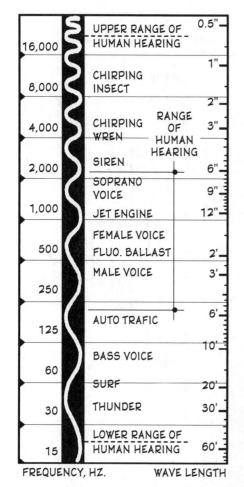

FREQUENCY, HZ.   WAVE LENGTH

Fig. 7-8. Sound frequency levels. [†]

The sounds produced by mechanical equipment have a great variety of pitches. For example, a variable-speed HVAC primary fan may have frequencies of 30–10,000 Hz, and the dominant frequency of an elevator motor typically rises from about 20–250 Hz as it accelerates from near-zero to full speed. Differently pitched sounds also interact differently with the surfaces they strike. For example, 1 in. thick fiberglass board absorbs less than 20 percent of a low-pitched (125 Hz) sound but more than 90 percent of a high-pitched (2,000 Hz) sound, while thin wood paneling absorbs nearly 60 percent of the 125-Hz sound but less than 10 percent of the 2,000 Hz sound.

No matter what a sound's frequency is, it may be *pure* (a one-frequency sound: e.g. a musical note), *integral* (several one-frequency sounds which together create a uniform sound: e.g. a musical chord), or *diverse* (any mixture of non-integral sound frequencies). Most steady-state noise, which includes the vast majority of sounds, is diverse sound of several frequencies, one of which is usually dominant.

What are the lengths of two airborne sound waves travelling at room temperature, one at 80 Hz and the other at 8,000 Hz?

7B2 $$v = \lambda f$$

v = speed of airborne sound wave, 1,126 fps at room temperature
λ = length of airborne sound wave, ? ft
f = frequency of airborne sound wave, Hz. f_1 = 80 Hz. f_2 = 8,000 Hz.

80 Hz: $1,126 = \lambda \times 80$ ... $\lambda = 14.1$ ft
8,000 Hz: $1,126 = \lambda \times 8,000$ ... $\lambda = 0.141$ ft (1.69 in.)

Zemansky (Addison-Wesley, Reading, MA, 1974); p. 359. [†] This graph first ap- ⫿

7.B.3. Intensity

Also known as *sound power level*, a sound's intensity is its loudness, or impact of its pulsing waves against the eardrum, measured in decibels (dB). A decibel is a logarithmic measure of a sound wave's pressure against this membrane, in which 0 dB represents the threshold of perfect human hearing, or a reference pressure of 3×10^{-9} psi. Thus a 20 dB sound creates a pressure of 3×10^{-8} psi on the eardrum, and a sound of 120 dB inflicts a pressure of 3×10^{-2} or 0.03 psi on this organ, which is its threshold of pain. Since one's eardrum is about 0.05 in^2 in area, a pressure of only about $1/500$ lb will hurt this delicate membrane. Think about this the next time you clean your ear with a Q-tip.

In the Sound Intensity Level chart of Fig. 7-9, the various sound

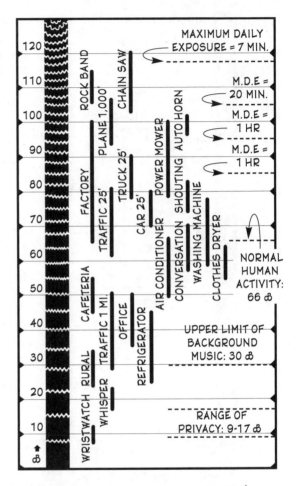

Fig. 7-9. Sound intensity levels. †

levels are all measured 3 ft from the sound's source —the default distance of sound propagation. Also, every increase of 3 dB represents a doubling of a sound's intensity, a decrease of 3 dB represents a halving of its intensity, a point source sound's intensity reduces by 6 dB when the distance it travels doubles, and its intensity increases by 6 dB when the distance it travels is halved. Knowing these yardsticks, one can almost compute point-source sound reception levels in one's head. However, a line- or area-source sound usually experiences a falloff of only 3–5 dB when the distance it travels doubles until its soundpath is about 6 times longer than its lateral length or width. Thus one's intensity often cannot be quantified asE accurately with

peared in slightly different form in this author's *Architectural & Engineering Cal-*

an algebraic formula as it can with a *precision-integrating sound meter*, which is an instrument that every Æ office should have. These battery-operated units with LCD displays can read instantaneous sound, equivalent continuous sound, maximum/ minimum frequency ranges, octave and $\frac{1}{3}$ octave bands, and maximum sound levels during time exposures. These sound meters are particularly useful in large, long, or low-ceiling'd interior spaces; because, as with light, the sound arriving at a destination is difficult to quantify algebraically because of the many reflectances the waves incur as they travel outward from the source. In any analysis, sound intensity calculations are rounded to the nearest dB, since fractions are barely perceivable to one's ear and thus are negligible.

   If an occupant experiences high sound intensity levels for lengthy periods, the potential for permanent hearing damage increases. Thus OSHA has promulgated permissible noise levels for occupant exposures of certain durations of time, which are listed in a small table in Example 7.B.5., Step 2.

Example 1: Sound intensity vs. distance. If a loudspeaker produces 110 dB at its source, how loud is the sound 50 ft away?

7]B]3]a]   dB $= S - 0.7 - 20 \log D$

dB $=$ sound intensity level at distance D from source, **?** dB
S $=$ sound intensity level at source, 110 dB
D $=$ distance between sound source and receiver, 50 ft

$$dB = 110 - 0.7 - 20 \log 50 = 75 \text{ dB}$$

Example 2: Adding Sound Intensities. A 90 dB loudspeaker mounted on a boom for an outdoor concert is not considered loud enough. If two 100 dB speakers are added, what is their combined loudness?

7]B]3]b]   dB $= 10 \log (10^{0.1\,dB_1} + 10^{0.1\,dB_2} + \dots + 10^{0.1\,dB_z})$

dB $=$ combined sound intensity level of all sounds at receiver, **?** dB
$dB_1 =$ sound intensity level of loudest sound, 100 dB
$dB_2 =$ sound intensity level of 2nd loudest sound, 100 dB
$dB_3 =$ sound intensity level of 3rd loudest sound, etc., 90 dB

$$S_c = 10 \log (10^{0.1 \times 100} + 10^{0.1 \times 100} + 10^{0.1 \times 90}) = 103 \text{ dB}$$

Note 1. When combining sound sources, their powers should be nearly the same; otherwise the contributions of any weaker sources are negligible. For example, in the above problem the 90 dB speaker contributes only 0.2 dB to the total loudness and thus could be eliminated.

---

culations Manual; Robert B. Butler (McGraw-Hill, New York, 1984); p. 334.

Example 3: Relative Sound Intensity. If the sound from a firehouse siren on a tower measures 102 dB 30 ft away, how loud is the sound 200 ft away? At what distance is the siren's sound reduced to the level of human speech?

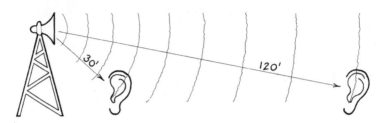

Fig. 7-10. Firehouse siren on tower.

Step 1. Compute the siren's loudness at a distance from its source.

7|B|3|c|
$$\text{dB}_n - \text{dB}_f = 20 \log (D_f/D_n)$$

dB_n = sound intensity level at near listener, 102 dB
dB_f = sound intensity level at far listener, ? dB
D_f = far distance from sound source, 200 ft
D_n = near distance from sound source, 30 ft

$$102 - \text{dB}_f = 20 \log (200/30) \quad \dots \text{dB}_f = 86 \text{ dB}$$

Step 2. Compute the distance at which the siren's sound is reduced to the level of human speech.

$$\text{dB}_n - \text{dB}_f = 20 \log (D_f/D_n)$$

dB_n = sound intensity level at near listener, 102 dB
dB_f = sound intensity level at far listener.
    As normal speech is 40–50 dB, use average value of 45 dB
D_f = far distance from sound source (dry air migration), ? ft
D_n = near distance from sound source, 30 ft

$$102 - 45 = 20 \log (D_f/30) \quad \dots D_f = 21,200 \text{ ft}$$

Note. Over long distances, sound intensity decreases as air humidity increases, and this difference is more pronounced at higher frequencies. Thus a high-pitched sound travelling through humid air becomes much weaker after a long distance than does a low-pitched sound (e.g. a foghorn from a distant lighthouse) travelling through the same air.

---

† From p. 638: This graph first appeared in slightly different form in this author's

Example 4: Sound Intensity vs. Electricity. How intense is a sound 35 ft away from a 20 watt loudspeaker operating at full volume?

<u>7]B]3]d]</u>   10 log E = ₵ – 119.32 + 20 log D

E = acoustic power level of electric amplifier, 20 watts
₵ = sound intensity level at listener, ? ₵
D = distance between sound source and listener, 35 ft

    10 log 20 = ₵ – 119.32 + 20 log 35   ... ₵ = 101 ₵

7.B.4. Direction

As described earlier in this chapter, when a sound originates, each point in its wavefront is an radial vector that moves outward from its source. In acoustic environments such as concert halls and opera houses, these vectors are meticulously mapped as they approach and carom off every enclosing surface so the designers can determine how their patterns will spread over the audience, with the goal being uniform diffusion over the total seating area.

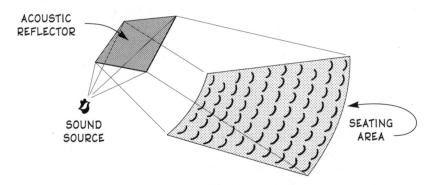

Fig. 7-11. Using ray tracing to create uniform diffusion of sound.

When the opposite of uniform diffusion is desired, these rays are easily diverted to make a sound louder where it is desired and softer where it is not. For example, say that two office workers sitting at adjacent work stations need to engage in private deskside conversation with other workers. Since the mouths of seated people are normally about 44 in. above the floor, if a shoulder-high wall with a sound-absorbent surface is placed between them so the axis between their heads is blocked, the speech from each workstation heard at the other will be reduced. This works better for low sounds than high, because high-frequency sounds have shorter waves which can bend more easily. This aural behavior is described by the noise barrier nomograph below.

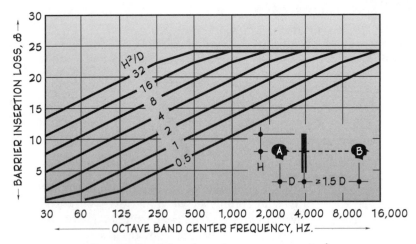

Fig. 7-12. Noise barrier nomograph. †

Another way of directing a sound is with a megaphone. This can be done manually by a cheerleader at a college football game, or mechanically by a cluster of multi-vaned, high-frequency loudspeaker horns mounted above a proscenium in a large auditorium. In each case the horn's shape concentrates the sound's radial vectors to amplify the sound, or make it much louder, in front of the horn than to its sides. Even a human mouth, being hollow and larger in front than in back, is a small megaphone; thus one's voice can be described as a directional simple sound amplifier mounted on a multi-directional swivel base. At the other extreme, a large room such as an auditorium can be shaped like a megaphone to bunch a propagated sound's radial vectors together and send them in a desired direction. Whenever a sound is megaphoned, whether the shape is manual, mechanical, small, or large, the amplified sound has a *directivity factor* (Q), a rated nondimensional value that indicates the amplifier's ability to send the sound in one direction at an increased intensity. A Q of 5 is a common figure for multi-cell directional loudspeakers. Q values for nondirectional sound sources that are made directional by amplifiers or enclosing surfaces are shown in Fig. 7-14.

Directivity is also important at the receiving end of a soundpath. For example, when a person hears a sound, the sound arrives at not one but usually two receivers; and if the sound arrives from the person's side, it enters one ear directly but has to travel all the way around the person's head to enter the other —then the sound at the second ear arrives approximately

Hill, New York, 1984); p.335. † This graph was abstracted from *Architectural*

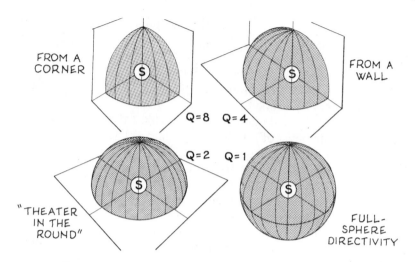

Fig. 7-13. Directivity factors for sound sources.

$1/2000$ sec later than the sound at the first. Although this distance may seem extremely small, it usually is enough to enable the listener to determine the direction of the sound's source.

7.B.5. Diffuse Noise

Also known as *blanket noise level*, diffuse noise is sound emanating from many similar sound sources near the listener. Examples are machines in a factory, a football stadium filled with cheering spectators, the hum of ballasted fluorescent lights in the ceiling of a large office, and vehicular traffic on a nearby freeway. Diffuse noise levels are used to determine OSHA standards for occupational noise exposure and absorption coefficients of enclosing surfaces. Although such sounds are accurately quantified by a precision-integrating sound meter, the formula below may be used to estimate them before the space is occupied if the constituent sounds are of similar frequency and little resonance occurs between them.

> If a textile factory contains 300 yarn carders whose sound levels are 60 dB each, 50 drawing rollers at 55 dB each, 600 roving frames at 77 dB each, 600 spinning jennies at 55 dB each, and 600 winding spools at 50 dB each, what is the diffuse noise level on the factory floor? Does this level meet OSHA standards?

Acoustics; Cavanaugh & Wilkes, Editors (Wiley, New York, 1999); p. 122.

Step 1. Find the diffuse noise level for the occupancy under consideration.

$\boxed{7)\;B)\;5)}$ $\qquad dB_L \approx dB_1 + \log(\eta_1 \times 10^{0.1\,dB_1} + ... + \eta_z \times 10^{0.1\,dB_z})$

dB_L = diffuse noise level at listener, dB. S_L on factory floor = **?** dB

dB_1 = sound intensity level of loudest sound, dB. The roving frames are the loudest sound sound at 77 dB.

η_1 = no. of units of loudest sound. η_1 for roving frames = 600 units.

dB_2 = sound intensity level of 2nd loudest sound, 60 dB

η_2 = no. of units of 2nd loudest sound. η_2 for yarn carders = 300.

dB_3 = sound intensity level of 3rd loudest sound, 55 dB

η_3 = no. of units of 3rd loudest sound. η_3 for drawing rollers = 50.

dB_4 = sound intensity level of 4th loudest sound, 55 dB

η_4 = no. of units of 4th loudest sound. η_4 for spinning machines = 600.

dB_z = sound intensity level of least loudest sound, 50 dB

η_z = no. of units of least loudest sound. η_5 for winding spools = 600.

Substituting in the above equation: $S_L \approx 87\ dB$

Step 2. From the OSHA permissible noise levels listed below, determine if the sound level found in Step 1 is safe for occupants for the duration of time they are exposed to the sound.

Slow-response sound level (dB) versus safe toleration time (hr)

dB	hr or less	dB	hr or less	dB	hr or less
90	8.0	92	6.0	95	4.0
97	3.0	100	2.0	102	1.5
105	1.0	110	30 min	115	15 min

From above data, safe toleration time for 87 dB = 8+ hr
If factory workers are exposed to sound 8 hr/day, 8 hr ≤ 8+ hr ➜ **OK**

Note: Studies indicate that noise levels as low as 75–80 dB may contribute to physical and mental disorders for some people.

7.C. SOUND ATTENUATION

Sound attenuation is the decrease of a sound's intensity as it travels from its source, whether it be due to the law of inverse squares, reflection, absorption, damping, cancelling by electronic means, or other means. Attenuation is desired for undesired sound and undesired for desired sound. Although sound attenuation is important, it is primarily a catch-all concept that is best used as an entré for discussing more detailed aspects of acoustic design as listed below:

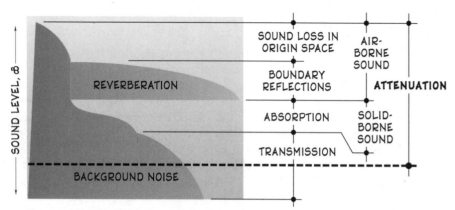

ORIGINAL SOUND = SPATIAL LOSS - REFLECTION - ABSORPTION + TRANSMISSION

Fig. 7-14. Sound field graph of sound attenuation.

Loss of sound through air (airborne sound). See Sec. 7.C.1.

Loss of sound at a boundary surface between air and solids (sound absorption). See Sec. 7.C.2.

Loss of sound through solids (solid-borne sound). See Sec. 7.C.3. In some texts this sound attenuation is referred to as structure-borne sound, but this is a misnomer because much solid-borne sound does not travel through structure.

Loss of sound through liquids (liquid-borne sound). Since liquids are usually in a container they are treated as solid-borne sound, except for water hammer which is covered in the plumbing Sec. 4.C.2.

An important aspect of sound attenuation is *background noise*. This is the general level of residual sound existing in a space above which its dominant sounds are heard. If the background noise is tolerable when the dominant sound is not, the human ear tends to subtract the lower level from the higher to create a *net dominant sound* that is more tolerable. Thus in the conceptual equation, total dominant sound - background noise = net dominant sound, background noise can even be raised to make a dominant sound more bearable —as happens when an office worker turns on a fan to hide traffic noises outside. Such manipulations provide an acoustic designer with one more tool for creating comfortable listening environments.

In any one occupancy, background noise may vary considerably in a 24 hour day. For example, the background noise level around a residence may hover around 31 dB during most of the day, rise to 38 dB from 5 to 8 P.M., diminish to 26 dB by 11 o'clock, settle at 23 dB during the night, rise to 35 dB during breakfast/dressing hours, and return to 31 dB around 9 o'clock. Thus a shouting neighbor seems louder to a sleeping person at 3 A.M. than to the same person eating dinner at 6:30 P.M., even though the offending voice has the same intensity.

7.C.1. Airborne Sound

This is sound travelling through the air, whether it is an original wave that has yet to encounter a boundary surface or is a secondary wave that has just emerged from solid construction. Airborne sound is often important because of the patterns its waves make as they travel through indoor spaces. Thus in a large assembly area designed for the enjoyment of speech, music, and other listening activities, the paths of numerous sound vectors radiating from the stage are often plotted in plan and section to determine the sound's pattern of distribution over the audience area. Such plotting is known as *ray tracing*, and the plotted pattern is a *ray diagram*. In such a drawing, the original rays extend to boundary surfaces in every direction, where each ray's incident angle is measured then equalled by a reflected angle, which then continues over the audience area. These diagrams are used to determine optimal speaking positions, stage heights, loudspeaker locations, sight lines, seating slopes, resonances (sound magnification due to a wavelength being a multiple of a critical dimension), dead spots (sound cancellation due to a wavelength being exactly half as long as a critical dimension), and other designed elements in such spaces. The ideal sound pattern for listening areas is uniform distribution with no concentrations or dead spots. Such uniformity is usually optimized as follows:

▸ Locate the sound source about 10 percent of the area's total length measured from the wall behind the source.

▸ Flat opposite surfaces in the space should not be parallel, and curved walls or ceilings should not form arcs with the sound sources near the centers of their radii. At least one opposing surface should be sound-absorbent.

▸ Seating should be as steep as possible; then the sound waves originating from the stage approach the audience more frontally and the listeners are more fully exposed to them.

▸ Every seat should receive a primary soundpath and ideally two horizontally symmetrical secondary soundpaths (usually reflections from the side walls) in which the primary and secondary path lengths vary by no more than about 35 ft. Otherwise the received sound is likely to be fuzzy.

▸ Seats should be upholstered to simulate human clothing; then they will be similarly sound-absorptive whether occupied or vacant.

In assembly areas, acoustic designers typically perform lengthy trial calculations as they integrate ray diagrams with absorption and reverberation data, spatial configurations, and simulated performances. Even then, movable architectural elements are often installed and adjusted after construction is complete to ensure optimal performance.

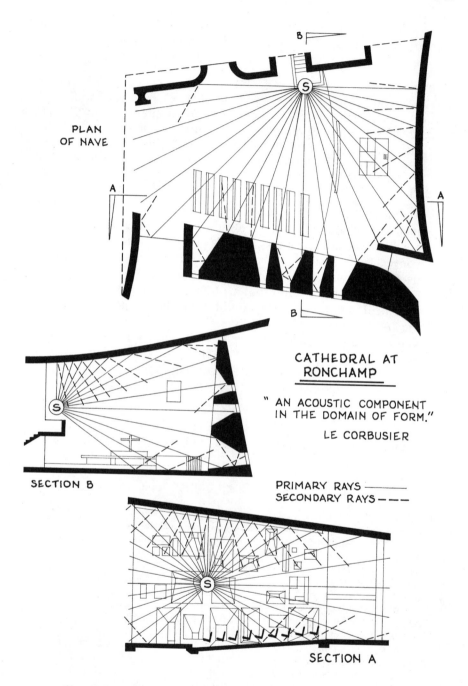

PLAN
OF NAVE

CATHEDRAL AT
RONCHAMP

" AN ACOUSTIC COMPONENT
IN THE DOMAIN OF FORM."

LE CORBUSIER

SECTION B

PRIMARY RAYS ———
SECONDARY RAYS ———

SECTION A

Fig. 7-15. Ray diagrams of a famous assembly area.

A sound's total intensity at any point in a listening area equals the intensity of direct sound arriving from the source plus the intensity of any reflected sound arriving from all boundary surfaces.

In a civic auditorium, what is the sound intensity level at a seat 78 ft from the speaker if the loudspeaker is rated at 90 dB, its directivity factor is 5, the absorption coefficient of all enclosing surfaces is 0.32, and the space averages 100 ft long, 95 ft wide, and 35 ft high?

7)C)1)
$$dB = S + 10 \log [Q/(12.6\ D^2) + 4\ ^{(1 - \alpha)}/\alpha\ A]$$

dB = loudness of sound at listener, **?** dB

S = loudness of sound at source, dB. Here S = sound intensity of loud-speaker = 90 dB. If a loudspeaker's nameplate rating is in watts, convert to dB from Equation 7.B.3.d. If more than one speaker is used, find their total power from Equation 7.B.3.b.

Q = directivity factor: a ratio that is often included in equipment specifications, or it may be found for any directional source from Fig. 7-14. Here Q is given as 5.

D = distance between sound source and listener, 78 ft

α = sound absorption coefficient of all enclosing surfaces, given as 0.32. If α is not given, compute according to Sec. 7.C.2

A = surface area of enclosing surfaces, sf. At average 100 ft long, 95 ft wide, and 35 ft high, $A \approx 2 \times 100 \times 95 + 2 \times 100 \times 35 + 2 \times 95 \times 35 \approx 32,700$ sf.

$$dB \approx 90 + 10 \log [5/(12.6 \times 78^2) + 4\ (1 - 0.32)/32,700 \times 0.32] \approx 55\ dB$$

TABLE 7-1: SOUND REVERBERATION TIMES FOR OCCUPANCIES

OCCUPANCY	Optimal reverberation time, sec.
Office, home, hospital patient room, small private areas	0.3–0.5
Broadcast and recording studios, speech therapy room	0.4–0.6
Laboratory, hotel lobby, elementary classroom	0.5–0.8
Lecture and conference rooms, small playhouse, cinema	0.6–1.3
Movie theater, restaurant, museum, elegant retail area	0.8–1.2
Musical comedy, operetta, theatrical production	1.1–1.5
Sound systems for semi-classical concerts, dances, chorals	1.1–1.8
Recital, chamber music, contemporary orchestra	1.3–1.8
Community church nave	1.3–2.2
Auditorium, gymnasium, ballroom, opera hall	1.4–1.8
Symphony concert, secular choral	1.7–2.1
Cathedral nave, liturgical with orchestra, choral, organ	1.9–3.4
Sports arenas, convention halls, large assembly areas	minimal

7.C.1.a. Reverberation

When an airborne sound strikes a boundary surface, the reflected portion continues to carom off other boundary surfaces until the sound dissipates to below audible thresholds. The number of seconds this takes is the sound's reverberation time. A little reverberation livens up most any space, but too much can turn speech and music into a cacophony of echoes. Such reflections vary according to a sound's pitch and its loudness. For most acoustic calculations, reverberation is the time it takes a propagated sound of 500, 750, or 1,000 Hz to decay 60 dB. But in spaces such as concert halls, opera houses, and industrial areas where excessive reverberation is undesirable, reverberation times may be computed at 30, 60, 125, 250, 500, 1,000, 2,000, 4,000, 8,000, and even 16,000 Hz as a basis for acoustic design. Theoretically the reverberation of any given space depends on how every possible sound interacts at every frequency with every material that encloses the space.

The opposite of reverberation is *articulation*. An acoustically articulate space is one that keeps each sonar detail distinctly separate from the others as opposed to letting them run together.

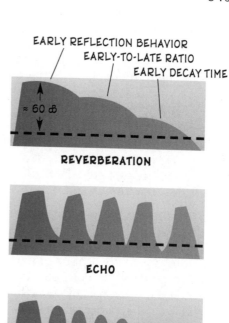

EARLY REFLECTION BEHAVIOR
EARLY-TO-LATE RATIO
EARLY DECAY TIME

≈ 60 dB

REVERBERATION

ECHO

FLUTTER ECHO ...
CAUSED BY SOUND MOVING BACK
& FORTH BETWEEN TWO HARD
PARALLEL SURFACES; CREATES A
FUZZY SLAPSLAPSLAP SOUND

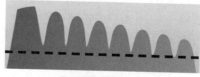

Four score and seven years ago,

FUZZY SPEECH

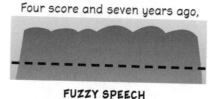

Four score and seven years ago,

ARTICULATE SPEECH

Fig. 7-16. Sound field graphs of several kinds of reverberation.

When a small space's reverberation time should be increased, this can be done electronically by recording the propagated sound, digitally repeating it rapidly several times, then spacing the repetitions a few milliseconds apart and making them progressively softer. Thus a living room entertainment center can be given the reverberation characteristics of a Gothic cathedral.

> What is the reverberation time for the 32 × 20 × 10 ft conference room described in the example on page 662? Is this reverberation time satisfactory? If not, what can be done to make it so?

Step 1. Find the space's reverberation time.

7)C)1)a] $\qquad\qquad \alpha R = 0.049\ V$

α = total sound absorption of enclosing surfaces, sabins.
From example on page 662, α = 63 sabins.
R = reverberation time of space in which sound originates, ? sec
V = volume of space in which sound originates, cf. $V = 32 \times 20 \times 10 = 6400$ cf

$$138\ R = 0.049 \times 6400 \qquad \ldots R = 4.97\ \text{sec.}$$

Step 2. Compare the space's actual reverberation time with its optimal reverberation time as listed in Table 7-1.

$$R_L \le R \le R_U$$

R_L = lower limit of desirable reverberation time for space.
From Table 7-1, R_L for conference room = 0.7 sec.
R = actual reverberation time of space. From Step 1, R_a = 2.27 sec.
R_U = upper limit of desired reverberation time for space.
From Table 7-1, R_U for conference room = 1.3 sec.

$$0.6 \le 4.97\ \text{not} \le 1.3 \rightarrow \textbf{NG: way too high}$$

Step 3. If the space's reverberation time is too low, select enclosing surfaces with lower absorption coefficients; if too high, select surfaces with higher coefficients. One solution for the above space: install heavy carpet on the concrete floor (α = 0.37) and floor-to-ceiling light velour drapes against the long wall of gypsum (α = 0.17).

Repeating Sec. 7.C.2: $\qquad\qquad \alpha$ = 388 sabins
Repeating Sec. 7.C.1.a: $\quad R = 0.81 \le 1.3$ sec $\rightarrow$ **OK**

7.C.1.b. Sound Amplification

If any seating in an assembly area is more than about 60 ft from the sound source, it usually requires electrically amplified loudspeakers. If any seating is 60–110 ft from the sound source, a cluster of loudspeakers known as a *central speaker system* is usually located well above and slightly in front of the sound source, then the speaker horns are aimed to spread the sound uniformly over the total listening area. If any seating is more than 110 ft away, or if any less-distant seating is behind columns or under low balconies, a *distributed speaker system* is usually installed. This is a network of small speakers placed no more than 35 ft apart throughout the distant seating and equipped with delay mechanisms and equalization controls that make the sound arrive simultaneously and uniformly at each seat. In large complex seating areas, central and distributed systems may be combined. An important characteristic of any speaker system is *directional realism*. This involves programming the system's delay mechanisms and locating its speakers so the sound seems to arrive at each listener from its source and not the speaker. Central systems preserve directional realism more easily than distributed systems because multiple speakers tend to create omnidirectional flooded sounds as opposed to vectorial focussed sounds. However, distributed systems work well in exhibition areas, airport terminals, large office spaces, and other occupancies where listeners do not see the sound source.

Ceiling loudspeakers should generally be mounted 25–30 ft above the audience. If the ceiling is higher the speakers should be suspended below it, one way being to conceal them in cable-suspended chandeliers. Loudspeakers located along the sides of a listening area should be mounted in symmetrical pairs, and each should be placed so it will not produce echoes. This work often requires meticulous ray tracing and onsite adjustment.

Sound amplification systems primarily include *microphones, preamplifiers, power amplifiers,* and *loudspeakers.* Each is described below.

Microphones. These small devices convert an initial sound into electric signals. They may be handheld, mounted on a stand, wireless lavalieres clipped to speakers' clothes, tiny capsules concealed in performers' costumes, long narrow shotgun units that pick up distant voices in theatrical productions, and other kinds. Wireless units promote mobile performances and remove the possibility of one tripping over the cords.

Preamplifiers. These components magnify the electric impulses from the microphones. They normally have tonal controls and several inputs that receive signals from tapes, films, CDs, and other sources. Complex amplifiers known as *control consoles* or *mixers* may have dozens of inputs, frequency equalizers in each channel, feedback suppressors that damp unwanted frequencies, adaptive filters that introduce desired frequencies, active noise controls that measure an annoying sound then cancel it with an opposite-phase wave, electronic delays that retard the output, and multiple outputs.

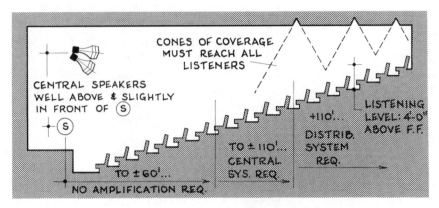

Fig. 7-17. Desirable loudspeaker layouts in an assembly area.

Power amplifiers. These provide the final electric signal with the proper power for each speaker. They are typically sized in 3 dB increments and typically deliver power outputs of 50, 100, 200, or 400 watts. Today's preamplifiers and power amplifiers contain numerous digital audio relays that have no moving parts and require little maintenance.

Loudspeakers. These convert the electric signals into air waves that arrive at the listeners as sound. Although speaker horns normally have coverage angles of 90° horizontally and 40° vertically, they can be tilted at any angle, laid on their sides, clustered, and aimed like floodlights to create any coverage desired. Direct-radiator speakers cost less than horn-loaded speakers with compression drivers, but they are less efficient, especially for loud sounds. Speakers that amplify speech should deliver sound levels of 85–90 dB, ones that reinforce concert music should deliver 100–105 dB, and ones that reinforce rock music typically deliver 110 dB or more. The frequency ranges of each are typically 16 to 8,000 Hz. Since a single speaker cannot reproduce high-fidelity sounds across the entire frequency spectrum, bass speakers generally reproduce sounds from about 1,000 Hz down to gradual rolloffs below 80 Hz, treble speakers reproduce sounds from about 1,500 Hz up to gradual rolloffs above 8,000 Hz, and midrange speakers cover the frequencies in between. In such speakers, crossover frequencies are likely to occur at 500 and 2,000 Hz.

Sound amplification systems are typically designed as follows. (1) The speakers are located in optimal positions as indicated by ray diagrams; (2) the output of each is computed to deliver sound at least 25 dB above ambient noise levels or at 72 dB, whichever is larger, to the remote listener (the listener who is the farthest from the speaker); (3) the size and weight of each speaker is determined. A typical high-frequency loudspeaker may measure $1^1/_2 \times 2 \times 2$ ft and weigh more than 100 lb, a large bass loudspeaker may

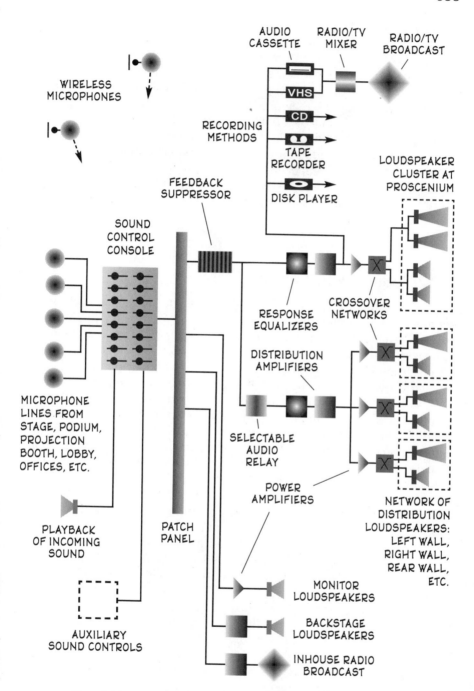

WIRELESS
MICROPHONES

AUDIO
CASSETTE

RADIO/TV
MIXER

RADIO/TV
BROADCAST

RECORDING
METHODS

VHS

CD

TAPE
RECORDER

DISK PLAYER

LOUDSPEAKER
CLUSTER AT
PROSCENIUM

FEEDBACK
SUPPRESSOR

SOUND
CONTROL
CONSOLE

RESPONSE
EQUALIZERS

CROSSOVER
NETWORKS

DISTRIBUTION
AMPLIFIERS

MICROPHONE
LINES FROM
STAGE, PODIUM,
PROJECTION
BOOTH, LOBBY,
OFFICES, ETC.

SELECTABLE
AUDIO
RELAY

POWER
AMPLIFIERS

NETWORK OF
DISTRIBUTION
LOUDSPEAKERS:
LEFT WALL,
RIGHT WALL,
REAR WALL,
ETC.

PLAYBACK
OF INCOMING
SOUND

PATCH
PANEL

MONITOR
LOUDSPEAKERS

BACKSTAGE
LOUDSPEAKERS

AUXILIARY
SOUND CONTROLS

INHOUSE RADIO
BROADCAST

Fig. 7-18. Block diagram for a theater playhouse. †

† This figure was abstracted largely from *Architectural Acoustics*; Cavanaugh

measure 3 × 3 × 8 ft and weigh 400 lb, and an array of multi-vaned high-frequency horns and large-cone subwoofers may be as large as a walk-in closet and weigh half a ton. After the amplifiers have been electronically designed, their sizes and weights are also determined, then the sound system's electrical circuits are designed and every component is provided with adequate ventilation; as they produce heat. Finally a schematic arrangement of the system, known as a *block diagram*, is drawn and becomes part of the Plans. The electronics are invariably fine-tuned after installation.

An important architectural component of sound amplification systems is the *control room*. This space should be located in the center of the rear of the listening area, where the controller or sound technician can have a panoramic and unglazed view of the performers and the total listening area.

7.C.2. Sound Absorption

Sound absorption is where airborne sound ends and solid-borne sound begins. This occurs at a *boundary surface* of an architectural space, where part of an incident sound's energy is reflected and the rest is absorbed. Such surface behavior is responsible for many of the aural delights and dilemmas that abound in occupied interior spaces.

The portion of sound that is absorbed by a material's surface is measured in *sabins* (α). The chief method of creating desirable sound levels indoors is to select floor, wall, and ceiling surfaces that absorb enough sound to make it pleasant but not so much that it becomes whispery. However, many sounds have a variety of frequencies and loudnesses, and many materials absorb sounds differently at different frequencies. Thus this aspect of acoustic design is simplified by the *graph capsules* of common acoustic materials that follow. Each material's graph has (1) a *sound absorption curve* that shows the unit portion of sound absorbed by the material's surface at six dominant sound frequencies, and (2) a *noise reduction coefficient* (*NRC*) that is the arithmetic average of the material's sound-absorbing ability at 250, 500, 1,000, and 2,000 Hz. NRC ratings are often used in shorthand acoustic calculations, while in the simplest calculations a sound's average sound frequency is usually taken to be 1,000 Hz. A high sound absorption curve indicates that the material is very absorptive, while a low curve indicates that it is highly reflective. However, such sound absorption is primarily a *boundary surface characteristic* —as once the sound energy enters the material's mass behind its surface, a different physics comes to the fore, one related to sound attenuation versus transmission. Some graph capsules are accompanied by acoustic data about the material it represents.

& Wilkes, Editors (Wiley, New York, 1999); p. 215.

ACOUSTIC TILE, $^7/_8$ in., perforated or fissured surface

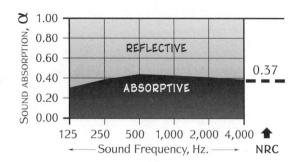

AIR, sabins absorbed per 1,000 cf

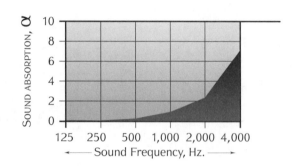

BRICK, face or common, painted; also painted masonry; (unglazed or unpainted brick, masonry, or ceramic tile = dotted line)

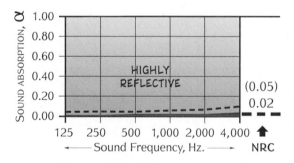

CARPET, heavy, on thin backing on concrete

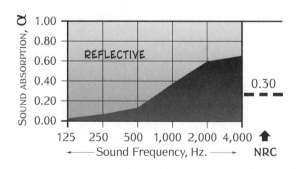

The primary source for the values in the graph capsules on pp. 655-661 was

CARPET, heavy,
on foam or
40 oz. felt

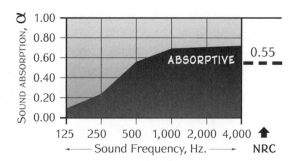

CARPET, heavy, on
latex backing
on foam or
40 oz. felt

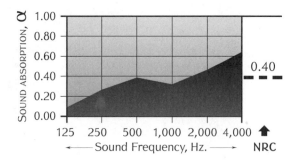

CARPET, light, on
thin backing
on concrete

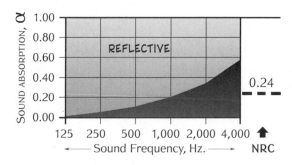

CONCRETE BLOCK,
hollow core or
grouted,
painted or
sealed (coarse
or unpainted =
dotted line)

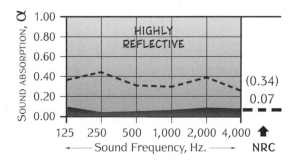

FABRIC: 10 oz. light velour or equal hung straight against wall or used as seating

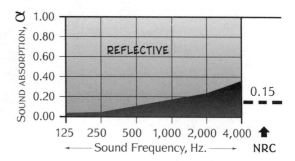

FABRIC: 14 oz. medium velour or equal draped or hung to 50% area; or used as seating

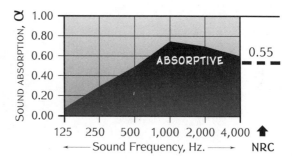

FABRIC: 18 oz. heavy velour or equal draped or hung to 50% area; also as seating

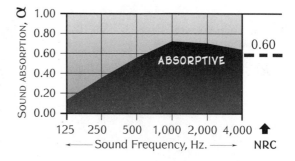

FLOORS: concrete or terrazzo

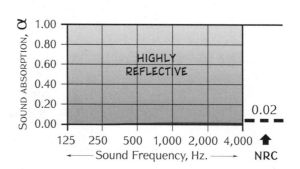

lender, Editor-in-Chief (McGraw-Hill, New York, 1984), p. 699. A second

FLOORS: linoleum, asphalt, rubber, or cork tile on concrete

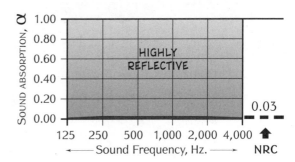

FLOORS: hardwood or hard conifers; also smooth wood surfaces and unoccupied wood pews

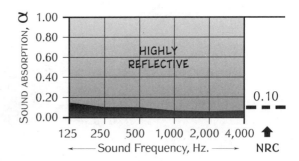

GLASS: large panes of heavy plate

Glass is highly reflective because it is smooth and hard, but its transmissivity is poor because it is thin. Reflectivity is worsened at very low frequencies because the thin panes tend to resonate when struck by low-frequency soundwaves.

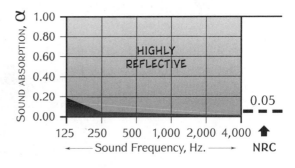

GLASS: small to medium panes of window glass; also mirrors against solid backing

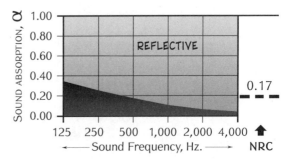

source for these values was the *Architectural Acoustics Design Guide,* Acentech

GLASS BLOCK

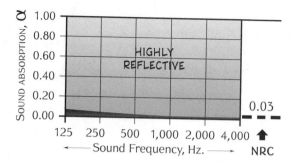

GYPSUM BOARD, wall or ceiling, $\frac{5}{8}$ in. or thicker nailed or screwed to 2 × 4s 16 in. o.c. ($\frac{1}{2}$ in. thick = dotted line)

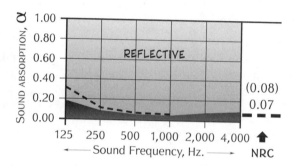

LEAD

Lead, a dense and limp material, is fairly sound-reflective, but once a sound's energy has entered it mass it is the finest sound-attenuating material per in. thickness. A $\frac{1}{8}$ in. thick layer reduces sound transmission by nearly 50 dB at all frequencies, and lead can be shaped to fit any irregular surface.

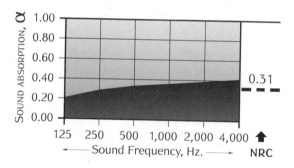

MARBLE, GLAZED TILE, glazed brick, other polished hard stone floor or wall

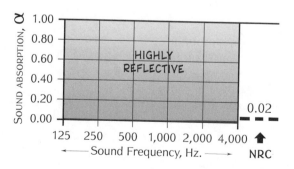

(James Cowan, Senior Consultant); (McGraw-Hill, New York, 2000), p .26.

METAL, smooth, hard (steel, iron, aluminum), solid sheet w/ solid backing; also smooth hard solid plastic

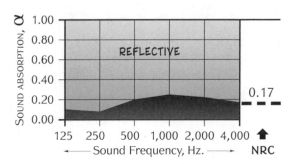

METAL, perforated, backed w/ film-faced glass fiber (perforated and backed w/ unfaced glass fiber = dotted line

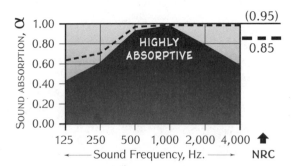

PLASTER, rough finish on tile or brick (smooth finish on lath and sprayed finish = dotted line)

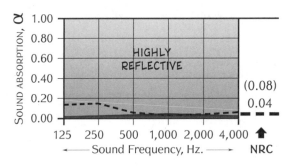

SEATING, upholstered w/ fabric and unoccupied; (occupied seats = dotted line)

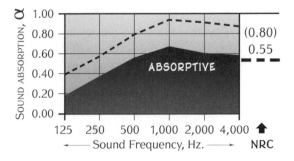

SOIL OR EARTH, bare, untamped (soil planted w/ grass or other low vegetation = dotted line)

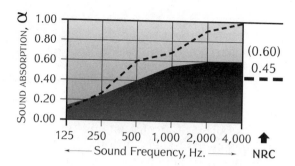

WATER surface; such as a swimming pool or fountain

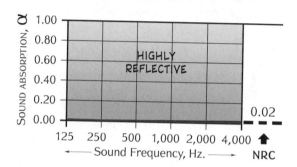

WOOD, smooth softwood, ¾ in. plywood sheathing or paneling, knotty pine; (for smooth hardwood see *floors, hardwood or hard conifers*)

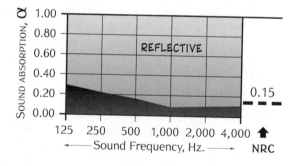

WOOD, roughsawn, min. ⅞ in. thick or on solid backing

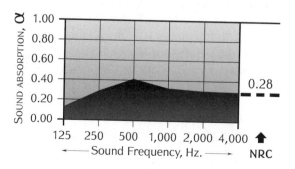

> How much sound is absorbed in a conference room that is 23 ft long, 20 ft wide, and 10 ft high if the floor is concrete, a long wall is floor-to-ceiling plate glass, and the other three walls and ceiling are ½ in. sheetrock nailed to wood framing?

7)C)2)
$$\alpha_t \approx \alpha_1 A_1 + \alpha_2 A_2 + \dots + \alpha_z A_z$$

α_t = total absorption of sound by the space, **?** sabins

α_1 = coefficient of sound absorption for 1st material enclosing the space. For human conversation, use α values for 1,000 Hz. From acoustic graph capsules on pp 655-71, α of concrete = 0.02.

A_1 = area of 1st enclosing surface, sf. Area of concrete floor = 640 sf.

α_2 = coefficient of sound absorption for 2nd enclosing surface. From pp 655-71, α of plate glass = 0.03.

A_2 = area of 2nd surface, sf. Area of plate glass windows = 320 sf.

α_3 = coefficient of sound absorption for 3rd enclosing surface. From pp 655-71, α of gypsum = 0.03.

A_3 = area of 3rd enclosing surface, sf. Area of gypsum wall = 320 sf.

α_4 = coefficient of sound absorption for 4th enclosing surface. From pp 655-71, α of gypsum = 0.03.

A_4 = area of 4th enclosing surface, sf. Area of gypsum ceiling = 320 sf.

$$\alpha_t \approx 0.02 \times 640 + 0.03 \times 320 + 0.03 \times 720 + 0.03 \times 640$$
$$\alpha_t \approx 63 \text{ sabins}$$

7.C.3. Solid-Borne Sound [†]

Solid-borne sound is sound that travels though walls, floors, ceilings, and other solid construction no matter how or where it originated. When a low-pitched airborne sound strikes the surface of a hard material, much of the sound is reflected, but most of what little sound that is absorbed usually travels through the construction behind to the other side. But if the sound is high-pitched and the material's surface is soft, much of the sound is absorbed, but then most of what is absorbed dissipates in the construction before reaching the other side. Thus reflection begets reflection and absorption begets absorption.

Regarding other combinations of solid-borne sound, some sounds completely disappear if the construction is highly absorbent while others are nearly as loud when they exit the other side as when they entered, even if the construction is as long and narrow as a steel beam; because sound

---

[†] The best information on sound reduction values for various construction assem-

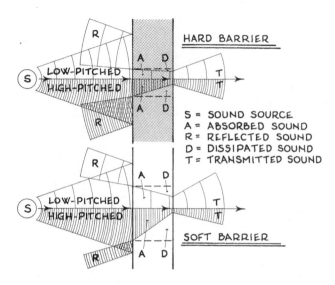

Fig. 7-19. Acoustic barrier behavior of incident sound.

travels faster through solids than air and is often channeled linearly through them as opposed to the radial attenuations of airborne sound. Such are the vagaries of solid-borne sound.

7.C.3.a. Sound Transmission Class

When the sound transmitted between two occupied spaces is objectionably loud, the intervening construction, whether it be a floor, wall, or ceiling, may be designed to reduce the transmitted sound to a tolerable level. Then the intervening assembly of materials is known as a *barrier construction*, and the amount of sound it absorbs is its *Sound Transmission Class*, or *STC rating*, measured in decibels (dB). The STC ratings for building materials and assemblies in Tables 7-2 and 7-3 are based on sound frequency norms of 500 Hz, which make them useful for shorthand acoustic calculations. If a transmitted sound's frequency is considerably lower or higher than 500 Hz, the STC rating for a particular material at a particular frequency may be found from the sound absorption curves in the previous section. In any barrier construction the material or assembly with the highest STC rating absorbs most of the sound, then materials with lower ratings absorb correspondingly fewer decibels.

Once a barrier's minimum STC rating is determined after analyzing the occupied spaces on reach side, an adequate construction may be designed.

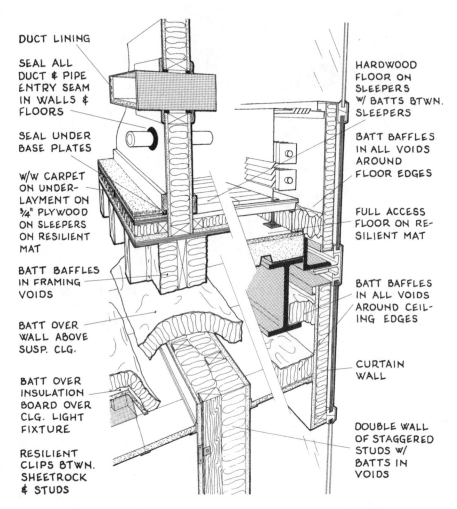

DUCT LINING

SEAL ALL
DUCT & PIPE
ENTRY SEAM
IN WALLS &
FLOORS

SEAL UNDER
BASE PLATES

W/W CARPET
ON UNDER-
LAYMENT ON
¾" PLYWOOD
ON SLEEPERS
ON RESILIENT
MAT

BATT BAFFLES
IN FRAMING
VOIDS

BATT OVER
WALL ABOVE
SUSP. CLG.

BATT OVER
INSULATION
BOARD OVER
CLG. LIGHT
FIXTURE

RESILIENT
CLIPS BTWN.
SHEETROCK
& STUDS

HARDWOOD
FLOOR ON
SLEEPERS
W/ BATTS BTWN.
SLEEPERS

BATT BAFFLES
IN ALL VOIDS
AROUND
FLOOR EDGES

FULL ACCESS
FLOOR ON RE-
SILIENT MAT

BATT BAFFLES
IN ALL VOIDS
AROUND CEIL-
ING EDGES

CURTAIN
WALL

DOUBLE WALL
OF STAGGERED
STUDS W/
BATTS IN
VOIDS

**Fig. 7-20. Remedies for reducing noise transmission
through barrier construction.**

However, the first step in reducing solid-borne sound is to isolate sources of unwanted sound by strategically locating occupancies in both plan and section as described below:

▶ Horizontally group noisy occupancies in one area of a plan and quiet occupancies in another, then place circulation and storage areas between them.

▶ Vertically arrange noisy and quiet occupancies on top of each other. For example, in high-rise apartments place kitchens over

in Apartments, Motels, and Hotels: Publication No. 1BL-4589; © 1969 Owens/Cor-

kitchens and bedrooms over bedrooms.
▶ In sound-critical spaces avoid opposite surfaces that are parallel, concave walls or ceilings, square or long narrow areas, near-cubic volumes, and low ceilings over large floors. Instead use 'lightning bolt' wall and ceiling profiles, convex surfaces, tilted walls, and/or sloping ceilings when possible
▶ Isolate mechanical equipment from study and sleeping areas, and specify gasketed solid-core entry doors to mechanical areas.

More detailed methods of designing high-STC-rated construction assemblies are the following:

▶ Design all enclosing walls, ceilings, and floors of a critical occupancy to have approximately equal STC ratings.
▶ Design intersections of vertical-to-horizontal construction to minimize diagonal transmission of sound.
▶ Use walls with cavity construction and staggered supports, then fill the cavities with batts and other sound-absorbing materials.
▶ Glue or float floors to subfloors rather than nail them, and inter-layer soft materials with hard.
▶ Fasten wall and ceiling finishes to solid framing with resilient clips. Install drywall with screws and not nails.
▶ Use building materials that have low moduli of elasticity (e.g. fiberglass batts and lead).
▶ Use textured, sculpted, and perforated surface finishes.
▶ Do not paint sound-absorbent surfaces.

Example 1. If a sound striking a wall at 60 dB exits the wall on the other side at 16 dB, what is the wall's STC rating?

7]C]3]a]1] $S_{TC} = S - dB$

S_{TC} = net STC rating of acoustic barrier construction, ? dB
S = sound intensity level at source side of barrier construction, 60 dB
dB   = sound intensity level at destination side of barrier construction, 16 dB

$$S_{TC} = 60 - 16 = 44 \text{ dB}$$

Example 2. An office floor construction has a standard carpet on rubber underlayment on 3 in. concrete on cellular metal decking, and 14 in. below the decking is a suspended ceiling on resilient hangers. What is the STC rating of this construction?

---

7)C)3)a)2) $S_{TC} \approx B + 0.5\, B\,(^T/_B - 1)$

S_{TC} = effective STC rating of acoustic barrier construction, ? dB

B = STC rating of portion of barrier construction w/ highest STC rating, dB. From Table 7-2, STC of 3 in. concrete pad on cellular metal decking = 39 dB.

T = total STC rating of all materials in the barrier construction, from Table 7-2, dB. From Table 7-2, T for 3 in. concrete pad on cellular metal decking + suspended ceiling on resilient hangers + standard (medium pile) carpet on underlayment = 39 + 12 + 5 = 56 dB.

$$S_{TC} \approx 39 + 0.5 \times 39\,(^{56}/_{39} - 1) \approx 56 \text{ dB}$$

Note: For below-average comfort requirements, subtract 4 dB from above values. For above-average comfort requirements, add 3 dB.

TABLE 7-2A: STC & IIC RATINGS OF BUILDING ASSEMBLIES

STUD WALL SYSTEMS, ½ in. drywall each side   STC Rating[1]

2 × 4 wood studs 16" o.c. .... 32; 4" nom. batt insul. in voids ...	36
2 × 4 staggered studs on 6" plate 42; 4" nom. batt insul. in voids ...	47
3½" metal studs 16" o.c. .... 38; 4" nom. batt insul. in voids ...	45
12" steel channel chase partition, 1⅝" studs 16" o.c.	42
4" nom. batt insul. in voids .... 52; 10" nom. batt insul. in voids ...	55
Double 2 × 4 wood studs 16" o.c. on double plates	44
4" nom. batt insul. in voids .... 56; 10" nom. batt insul. in voids ..	59
½" fiberboard between studs	+ 9
Add to any of above: 2 × ½" drywall 1 side or ⅝" drywall 2 sides	+ 2
2 × ½" drywall or ½" fiberboard under drywall two sides	+ 5
Resilient channels under drywall 1 side .... + 5; 2 sides	+ 8

MASONRY WALL SYSTEMS, sealed one side   STC Rating

Masonry or reinforced concrete, 6" .. 47; each extra 2" thick	+ 3
Brick, 4" .... 41; each extra 2" thick	+ 4
Concrete block, 4" lightweight .... 36; each extra 2" thick	+ 5
Concrete block, 4" standard .... 38; each extra 2" thick	+ 5
Sand added to cores of any block	+ 3
Add to any masonry: plaster one side .... + 2; two sides	+ 4
½" drywall on rigid furs one side .... + 4; two sides	+ 7
Plaster on lath on rigid furs one side .... + 6; two sides	+ 10
Batts in furring cavities one side .... + 3; two sides	+ 5
Plaster on resilient mounts 24" o.c. 1 side ... + 10; two sides	+ 15
Double walls w/ 4" airspace between	+ 15

1. STC variations of 2 dB are slight, 5 dB are noticeable, and 10 dB are dramatic. Batt insulation sound deadening must be snug-fitted into cavities.

and IIC ratings listed in this volume's Tables 7-2A and 7-2B.

TABLE 7-2B: STC & IIC RATINGS OF BUILDING ASSEMBLIES

WOOD FLOOR SYSTEMS, plywood sheathing on joists	STC[1]	IIC[1]
Hardwood finished floor, drywall ceiling under	37	34
Add to above: wall/wall carpet on pad, light pile	+ 1	+ 20
Medium pile .. + 2 & + 22; Deep pile	+ 3	+ 25
Linoleum fin. fl. ... 0 & + 5; ¼" cork tile finished floor	0	+ 10
Finished floor on resilient damping[2]	+ 7	+ 2
Finished floor on floating sleepers on resilient damping	+ 10	+ 8
Batts between sleepers or under resilient damping	+ 3	+ 1
1⅝" concrete slab between above & sheathing	+ 4	+ 3
Resilient channels between joists & ceiling below	+ 10	+ 8
Above w/ 3½ in. minimum insulated batts in joist voids	+ 3	+ 7
Plaster on lath ceiling below	+ 2	+ 2

CONCRETE FLOOR SYSTEMS, dense reinforced concrete	STC	IIC
2" conc. on metal deck = 38 & 29; 3" conc. = 39 & 31; 4" conc.	41	34
4" concrete slab ..... 41 & 34; 6" slab ... 46 & 34; 8" slab	51	35
8" precast cellular concrete slab	53	36
Add to any of above: w/w carpet on pad, light pile	+ 4	+ 20
Medium pile ......+ 5 & + 25; Deep pile	+ 6	+ 30
Min. ½" hardwood finished floor set in mastic	0	+ 7
Linoleum fin. fl. ...0 & + 4; ¼" cork tile finished floor	0	+ 12
Finished floor on resilient damping[2]	0	+ 10
Wood floor on floating sleepers directly on slab	+ 7	+ 15
Above on resilient damping	+ 12	+ 20
Concrete topping on 1" fiberglass mat or equal	+ 10	+ 15
Batts between sleepers or under resilient damping	+ 3	+ 1
Modular raised floor or access floor panel system	+ 8	+ 5
Finished ceiling to rigid furring, shallow airspace	+ 7	+ 0
Suspended ceiling w/ deep airspace	+ 7	+ 4
Above on resilient runners, slips, or hangers	+ 12	+ 8
Plaster or paint on underside of slab	+ 2	+ 0

OTHER MATERIALS	STC		STC
Lead, 1/16" thick	34;	Aluminum, 0.025"	19
Steel, 18 gauge sheet	30;	Cellulose fiberboard, ½"	22
Door, 1½" h/c wood, unsealed	19;	gasketed or sealed all around	26
1¾" s/c wood, unsealed	21;	gasketed or sealed all around	29
1¾" hollow metal, unsealed	22;	gasketed or sealed all around	30
¾" packed metal, unsealed.	23;	gasketed or sealed all around	32
2½" acoustical, unsealed	26;	gasketed or sealed all around	38
Window: ⅛" fixed pane	21;	¼" plate 26; 1" thermopane	32
9/32" laminated glass	36;	3½" glass block	40
Operable wood sash w/ ⅛" or ¼" pane, unsealed .. 25;		sealed	28

1. STC & IIC variations of 2 dB are slight, 5 dB are noticeable, 10 dB are dramatic.
2. Resilient damping may be particleboard, fiberboard, rubber mat, or equal.

7.C.3.b. Impact Isolation Class

Impact sound is noise generated through building materials by impacts such as door slams, high-heeled shoes stepping on hard floors, the thud of a fallen object, the scrape of moving furniture across a floor, and the rattle of mechanical equipment. Such often-sudden noises typically resonate through floor construction into the spaces below, and a floor's Impact Isolation Class or IIC Rating is the amount of impact noise it can absorb.

The best remedy by far for reducing impact noise is cushioning it at its source. Examples are deep pile carpets on foam rubber pads, rubber tile floor finishes, floating floors on fiberglass blankets, and vibration isolators under machinery. Other remedies are:

▶ Install felt pads and other resilient materials at the tops and bottoms of walls around noise-producing areas and where floating floors and suspended ceilings meet surrounding walls.

▶ Suspend ceilings from resilient hangers and install lay-in sound-absorbent panels.

▶ Isolate mechanical equipment with flexible boots at plenums, flexible couplings at pipes, and deep loops at wires.

▶ Isolate pipes and plenums from solid construction with flexible connectors, and seal all penetrations through walls or floors with gaskets, fillers, or caulking.

A woman's modeling agency is moving into an upper floor of a multistory office building and the manager wants to eliminate any impact noises —specifically ladies' spiked heels— by the new tenant that could disturb a speech therapist's office directly below. If the existing construction is a 6 in. concrete floor slab with suspended ceiling below, what renovations should be made?

TABLE 7-3: IMPACT NOISE LEVELS

Representative values

ACTIVITY	Typical IIC, dB	ACTIVITY	Typical IIC, dB
Man's rubber heels	68	Table shoved into wall	77
Foot tapping to music	70	Slamming solid-core door	80
Small dropped object	73	Large dropped object	80
Chair scraping across hard floor	73	Jumping 200 lb adult	83
Heavy cart rolled across floor	77	Refrigeration compressor	83
Man's hard leather heels	77	Woman's spiked heels	85
Woman's 2 in. broad heels	77	Water hammer	94

Step 1. Compute the IIC of the barrier construction.

<u>7)C)3)b)</u> $I_{IC} = I_s - I_r - M$

I_{IC} = required IIC rating of acoustic barrier construction, **?** ɗB

I_s = sound level of impact noise in source space, ɗB.
From Table 7-3, I_s for women's spiked heels = 85 ɗB.

I_r = acceptable impact noise level in reception space. Any sound above a whisper is unacceptable. From Fig. 7-9 a whisper = 20 ɗB, and a variation of 5 ɗB is noticeable. ∴ I_r = 20 - 5 = 15 ɗB.

M = masking level of background noise in reception space, ɗB. In speech therapist's office this is the threshold of human hearing, which from Fig. 7-9 = 9 ɗB.

$$I_{IC} = 85 - 15 - 9 = 61 \text{ ɗB}$$

Step 2. Select a adequate barrier construction for the above sound level.

$$I_{IC} \approx B + 0.5 \, B \, (^T/_B - 1)$$

I_{IC} = effective IIC rating of acoustic barrier construction, ɗB.
From Step 1, required IIC rating of barrier construction = 61 ɗB.

B = IIC rating of portion of barrier construction w/ highest IIC rating, ɗB. From Table 7-2, IIC of existing 6 in. concrete slab = 34 ɗB.

T = total IIC rating of all materials in barrier construction, ɗB. From Table 7-2, T for 6 in. reinforced concrete slab + deep pile wall/wall carpet on pad + wood subfloor on sleepers on resilient damping + suspended ceiling w/ deep airspace = 34 + 30 + 20 + 8 = 92 ɗB.

$$61 \leq 34 + 0.5 \times 34 \, (^{92}/_{34} - 1) = 63 \Rightarrow \text{OK}$$

On upper floor install construction as described in T above
No improvements are necessary in the room below

7.C.3.c. Loudness Limits

A crucial factor in designing effective acoustic barrier construction is determining the loudness of generated sounds and the tolerance of received sounds in two adjacent occupied spaces, or *loudness limit*. For example, someone eating in a dining room can tolerate loud talking in an adjacent hallway more than someone sleeping in a bedroom. Some spaces that produce little sound can tolerate much sound from adjacent areas (e.g. a hallway next to an industrial fabrication area), while some spaces that produce much sound can tolerate little sound from adjacent areas (e.g. two recording studios next to each other).

TABLE 7-4: LOUDNESS LIMITS OF ARCHITECTURAL SPACES

(These values may vary from one building to another)

ARCHITECTURAL SPACE OR AREA	Loudness Limits, dB [1] Generation	Reception
Concert halls, opera houses	90	35
Auditoriums, churches, theaters, lecture halls, courtrooms	82	35
Athletic, indoor, amateur and semi-pro	85	50
Dressing and rehearsal rooms for above	74	30
Locker rooms, general offstage for above	77	40
Set design and offstage areas for above	83	60
Barber shops, beauty parlors, waiting areas	73	42
Bars, night clubs, luncheonettes, cafeterias	80	50
Bus depots, airports, railroad stations	74	64
Circulation areas: halls, stairs, elevators	72	70
Exhibit areas: art galleries, museums	59	36
Hospitals: examination, treatment, operating	80	33
Industrial: service, packing and shipping	78	64
Inspection, quality control	74	38
Shops, rough and finish assembly	82	60
Kitchens, commercial (residential ≈ 74 and 52)	76	55
Living, dining, and TV areas, residential	77	52
Laundry: washing, sorting, ironing	72	65
Libraries: reading and study areas	54	32
Catalogue areas, copying, checkout	68	50
Lobbies: hotels, banks, post offices	73	60
Mechanical equipment areas	85	70
Museums, fine restaurants	70	35
Music practice areas: choral and orchestral	83	33
Offices, private, managerial	72	33
Semi-private	73	38
Conference rooms, small lecture areas	77	36
Open spaces, computer areas, reception areas	75	62
Police stations: waiting, booking, cells	78	45
Rest rooms, public and private, custodial areas	73	32
Restaurants, household dining rooms	73	55
Retail: shops, bazaars, discount merchandise	76	54
Boutiques, haberdasheries, jewelry stores	72	49
Schools: classrooms, laboratories, seminars	78	40
Indoor recreation, eating	80	70
Teacher's lounges, principal's office	72	35
Shopping malls, other large public indoor areas	80	64
Sleeping: separate hotel, motel, hospital, apartments	72	28
Bedrooms within suites, houses, apartments	72	30
Storage areas, closets	48	58
Studios: broadcast, music recording	76	25

1. Loudness limit for generation ≈ maximum sound intensity level typically produced within a space. Loudness limit for reception ≈ typical occupant's threshold of tolerance for sound received from adjacent spaces.

If a living room and master bedroom of two high-rise apartments are on each side of a 8 × 14 ft wall and their surfaces absorb 86 and 62 sabins, what is the minimum STC rating of the wall between them?

Step 1. List the loudness limits for generation and reception in the two adjacent spaces from Table 7-4.

	Loudness Limit, dB.	
Space	Generation	Reception
Living, residential	77	52
Sleeping: separate apartments	72	28

Step 2. Find the barrier construction's STC rating.

7]C]3]c] $S_{TC} = t_G - t_R - 10 \log (A/\alpha)$

S_{TC} = required STC rating of acoustic barrier construction, **?** dB
t_G = loudness limit of louder sound entering barrier construction: highest of four numbers listed in Step 1. $t_G = 77$ dB
t_R = loudness limit of softer sound exiting barrier construction: lowest of four numbers listed in Step 1. $t_R = 28$ dB
A = surface area of barrier construction, sf. A = 8 × 14 = 112 sf.
α = sound absorption of enclosing surfaces of two adjacent spaces, sabins. Use the smaller value ➡ 62 sabins.

$$S_{TC} = 77 - 28 - \log (^{112}/_{62}) = 47 \text{ dB}$$

7.C.3.d. Masking

When two sounds occur simultaneously, the perception of each can be made more difficult by the presence of the other. Thus a pleasant sound may be used to mask an unpleasant one. This works best when the sounds are close in frequency, the masking sound is of a continuous broadband nature (such as a portable fan), and the masked sound is variable and information-bearing (such as people talking in an open office).

A new method of masking sounds with computer technology is the *active noise canceller*. This system analyzes an offending noise then produces an identical but one-half out-of-phase sound wave that cancels the source sound. Primarily designed to attenuate duct-borne noise, the system includes a sound pickup placed in the duct upstream of a loudspeaker that plays a 180° mirror-image waveform of the original sound into the duct, then a second sound pickup placed downstream of the loudspeaker informs the controller how to adjust the input signal to maintain optimal noise cancella-

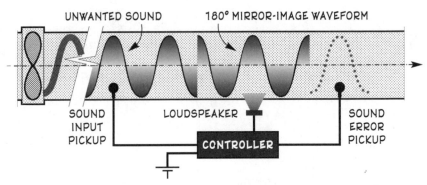

UNWANTED SOUND   180° MIRROR-IMAGE WAVEFORM

SOUND   LOUDSPEAKER   SOUND
INPUT   ERROR
PICKUP   CONTROLLER   PICKUP

Fig. 7-21. Active noise controls in HVAC ducting.†

tion. These sonar silencers can determine the correct amplitude and phase shift for every frequency of a diverse sound, even if duct temperatures, moistures, and airflow velocities vary. They work best at low frequencies, which are the ones that cause the most trouble in ducts. Thus this system offers superior low-frequency attenuation with negligible flow restriction and enables duct s.a.p. differentials to be lower, both of which save energy.

Active noise cancellers should be placed in supply and return ducts, with the input mike just inside each duct's penetration of the mechanical room wall. Two makers of these systems are Digisonix/Nelson Industries in Middleton, WI, and Noise Cancellation Technologies of Stamford, CT.

> A furniture factory manager wants to install intercom music to mask the noise between his office and a fabricating area below instead of build an otherwise-required STC-72 rated floor. If the music's sound level is 27 dB, the space is 12×19 ft in area, and its enclosing surfaces absorb 116 sabins, what is the floor's minimum STC rating?

7) C) 3) d) $S_{TC} \approx 10 + S_B - I_R - M - 10 \log (^A/_\alpha)$

S_{TC} = required STC rating of masked acoustic barrier construction, ? dB
S_B = STC rating of barrier construction minus masking, 72 dB
I_R = tolerance threshold for sound reception from adjacent spaces, dB.
     From Table 7-4, I_r for *office, managerial* = 18 dB.
M = masking level of background sound, 27 dB
A = surface area of barrier construction, sf.
     A = floor area of office = 12 × 19 = 228 sf.
α = sound absorption of enclosing surfaces of reception space, 116 sabins for office

$$S_{TC} \approx 10 + 72 - 18 - 27 - 10 \log (^{228}/_{116}) = 34 \text{ dB}$$

---

† The information for this figure and related text was obtained from Mark Skaer's

7.C.4. Sound Leakage

All the labor spent in designing effective barrier construction assemblies can be negated by a few leaks in the construction. Frequent culprits are cracks in masonry mortar joints, seams around electrical outlets, loose trim around door and window frames, and open edges around suspended ceilings and access floors. More unwanted sound can pass through such hairline pathways than through a whole floor or wall. Thus acoustic barrier construction is only as strong as its weakest *leak*. Sound leakage is especially serious in classrooms, lecture halls, music areas, hospital rooms, bedrooms, conference rooms, private offices, broadcast studios, and other occupancies where it is likely to be quiet on one side of the barrier construction and noisy on the other. Sound leakage occurs more with high-pitched sounds because their shorter waves can sneak through contorted soundpaths more easily.

Sound leakage is best minimized by specifying fine workmanship where sound transmission is critical, then conducting extensive onsite inspections to ensure that all construction seams are sealed. An effective means of inspection is to shine a beam of light onto one side of the construction at night and see if any light appears on the other side.

Two barrier constructions that require special attention are doors and windows. This is due primarily to their thin construction, openable nature, and often loose trim around their perimeters. Remedies for reducing sound transmission through these openings are:

Doors. Fit all trim snugly against the frame and all thresholds snugly between the door and floor. Do not locate doors near each other in walls or across from each other in halls, and install swings to deflect generated noise inward and received noise outward. Avoid doors with louvers (STC 15) and undercut bases. Where sound transmission is critical, install sheet steel doors with fiber batt fill (STC 42), solid-core doors with gaskets or felt seals (STC 44), gasketed solid-core doors back-to-back with $2\frac{1}{2}$ in. airspace between them (STC 48), or lead-lined doors with full seals (STC ≈ 60).

Windows. Fill all voids in the perimeter framing with sill sealer, caulk all voids between fixed panes and frames, fit all trim tightly around each opening, and caulk every seam. Avoid locating windows near inside corners of facades or across from each other in narrow areas. Orient casement, awning, and hopper sash swings to deflect generated noise inward and received noise outward. Install fixed double panes of different thickness with perimeter seals ($\frac{3}{8}$ in. airspace = STC 39, 3 in. airspace = STC 44), or avoid these openings altogether. Where sound attenuation and natural ventilation must coexist, contort the flowing air as much as possible.

A recently developed window for the Seaport Hotel in Boston has an exceptional STC rating of 50. The hotel's guest rooms have spectacular views which are near Logan Airport; so the acoustic design team made a large 5 × 7 ft window sandwiched with layers of ¼ in. glass, ⅜ in. airspace, ⁹⁄₁₆ in. laminated glass, 4 ⁹⁄₃₂ in. airspace, and ⅜ in. laminated glass fitted into an insulated extruded aluminum frame. Each window weighs 800 lb and is openable for cleaning purposes. Now a guest can "sit in a room with a harbor or skyline view and hear a pin drop as a jet glides by." [†]

Another notorious source of sound leakage is utility penetrations, both through the continuous penetration itself and the seam around it. This leakage is minimized by tight construction and sealing every seam. An excellent group of sealers is firestopping. This includes silicone seals for filling open cracks and seams, intumescent pillows for wadding around pipe and duct penetrations, elastomeric trims for fitting around panel boxes and other insets, customized fills for packing inner voids in cable tray and other perforate penetrations, and ceramic fiber blankets for stuffing around machinery exhausts and chimney flues. Other remedies are:

▶ Fill spaces between each electrical outlet box's outer edges and surrounding materials with nonshrinking caulk or equal seal.
▶ Never mount two electrical outlet boxes, medicine cabinets, or other boxes or receptacles back-to-back in a wall.
▶ Do not run HVAC ducts or large pipes directly through double stud walls.

A door with loosely fitting trim and a ⅜ in. gap at its bottom is located in an 8 × 15 ft STC 48 rated wall. Considering the sound leaking around the door, what is the actual STC rating of the wall?

Step 1. Estimate the open area around the door.

7$\underline{C}$4

$$A_o = L_1 w_1 + L_2 w_2 + \ldots + L_Z w_Z$$

A_o = leakage area of openings (door and window seams, vents, frames, etc.) in acoustic barrier construction, ? in^2

L_1 = length of 1st seam around opening, in.
   Length of trim around top and sides = 80 + 30 + 80 = 190 in.

w_1 = width of 1st seam around opening, in.
   Width of space between door and loose trim ≈ ¹⁄₁₆ in. = 0.063 in.

L_2 = length of 2nd seam around opening, in.
   Length of threshold at bottom of door = 30 in.

w_2 = width of 2nd seam around opening, in.
   Width of gap at bottom of door ≈ ⅜ in. = 0.38 in.

L_Z = length of final seam around opening, in.
w_Z = width of final seam around opening, in.

$$A_o = 190 \times 0.063 + 30 \times 0.38 = 23 \ in^2$$

lishing Co., Troy, MI); Oct 1994, p. 48. [†] *Design & Building Construction* maga-

Step 2. Find the percentage of open area in the barrier construction.

$$\% \, A_s = 100 \, A_o$$

$\%$ = percentage of open area in barrier construction due to cracks between openings and surrounding borders, **?** in^2

A_s = total surface area of barrier construction, in^2.
   $8 \times 15 \times 144 = 17,300$ in^2.

A_o = area between opening and surrounds in barrier construction, in^2.
   From Step 1, A_o = 23 in^2.

$$\% \times 17,300 = 100 \times 23 \quad \dots \% = 0.13$$

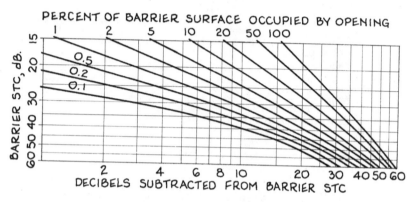

Fig. 7-22. Sound leakage graph. [†]

Step 3. From Fig. 7-23, find the dB to be subtracted from the barrier construction's STC rating. At STC 48 and an open area of 0.13 percent, the
amount to be subtracted is about 19 ➡ 48 − 19 ≈ 29 dB.

7.C.4.a. Mechanical Noise

An average 30 percent of commercial building budgets is spent on
mechanical and electrical equipment that makes noise. Big producers are
HVAC units, elevators, rotating or reciprocating machinery, humming lighting fixtures, and loosely mounted plumbing. Operation of these components can turn an otherwise well-designed occupancy into a chaos of vibrations, rattles, rumblings, hammerings, buzzes, and whistles. The chief
strategy for reducing such unwanted noise is to reduce and isolate the
noise at its source by installing quiet equipment and enclosing it with insulated construction (the nearer the enclosure to the sound source, the

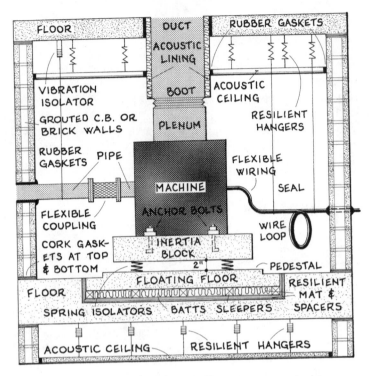

Fig. 7-23. Methods of isolating mechanical noise.

smaller the volume contained and the less expensive the remedy). Other
effective sound-reducing remedies for mechanical equipment are:

- Locate such equipment far from noise-sensitive areas.
- Isolate any rotating or vibrating machinery from surrounding
  spaces with resilient supports, flexible connections, and elastomeric mounts. Many resilient mounts have an *isolation efficiency*,
  a percent rating of its dampability based on the number of machines nearby and the sound level tolerances in adjacent spaces.
- Avoid riveted and welded connections and fit rubber grommets
  and lock-washers onto all bolted connections.
- Limit fluid velocities in pipes and ducts to normal levels by using
  larger-diameter leaders and branches. In critical situations,
  duct air velocities should ≤ 600 fps.
- Keep rectangular duct aspect ratios below 6:1, make branch ducts
  at least 15 ft long from mains to registers, and locate damper
  vanes well away from registers and diffusers.
- Fasten supply and waste piping to solid construction with insulated mounts. Placing cork between a pipe and a clamp mount
  reduces pipe-to-structure sound transmission by 5–8 dB, wrap-

adapted from *Time-Saver Standards for Architectural Design Data*; Jon Callen-

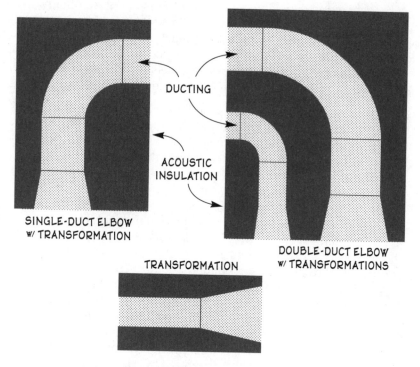

DUCTING

ACOUSTIC
INSULATION

SINGLE-DUCT ELBOW
W/ TRANSFORMATION

TRANSFORMATION

DOUBLE-DUCT ELBOW
W/ TRANSFORMATIONS

Fig. 7-24. Passive duct silencers.

ping an elastomeric sleeve around the pipe before securing it reduces transmission by 15–18 dB, suspending the pipe from resilient hangers reduces transmission by about 20 dB, and wrapping the pipe's full length with foam or batt insulation reduces transmission by more than 20 dB and keeps condensation from forming on the pipes. Also keep pipes from touching each other and any other objects around them.

▸ Specify oil- or silicone-filled transformers for indoor installations.
▸ Specify electronic ballasts and resilient mounts for fluorescent and HID light fixtures. 120-Hz hum in other electrical units is reduced by almost any low-frequency damping.
▸ Buffer machinery from critical areas with noncritical spaces such as rest rooms, storage areas, corridors, and stairs.
▸ Insulate elevator shafts, especially in high-rise apartments. These should be insulated anyway due to the thermodynamics of elevator operation.
▸ If a fan is rated in sones, select one in the 1.5–3 sone range. 1 sone ≈ the sound of an operating refrigerator. A noise level rating of 1 sone is quiet, 2 sones is fairly quiet, and 5 sones is noisy.

der, Editor (McGraw-Hill, New York, 1974); p. 710.

A particularly annoying conductor of noise in HVAC ducting is what could be called the *tuba effect*. This is typically caused by a fan sending noise through every duct and diffuser similarly as a musician blows low-frequency sound through a tuba. Four ways of reducing this effect and related duct noises are with *fiberglass liners, passive duct silencers, reactive silencers*, and *active noise controls*. Each is described below:

▶ *Fiberglass liners* are plastic-lined fiberboard sheets of $\frac{1}{2}$, 1, or 2 in. thickness that are fitted inside rectangular ducts. The linings must be impervious so they will not erode and allow particulate matter to enter the airstream, and they must form a perfect seal inside the duct so spores and molds cannot enter the insulation behind the liner where they could bloom and eventually spread throughout the building. The lining thickness should never be counted as part of a duct's required net free area.

▶ *Passive duct silencers* are duct sections with sides of perforated sheet metal whose outer surfaces are wrapped with Mylar® or other membrane, then surrounded with fiberglass fill. A wide range of straight, elbow, transition, and fan inlet duct silencers are available. They reduce high-frequency sounds well but they occupy much space around the ducting. The silencer's net airflow area should always align with that of the ducts at each end.

▶ *Reactive silencers* are short duct sections whose sides are made of perforated sheet metal surrounded by cavity resonators that absorb sound.

▶ *Active noise controls*, also known as *active noise cancellers* or *'Digiduct' noise silencers*, electronically produce a 180° out-of-phase sound that cancels the source sound. See page 671-2.

During a recent upgrading of the HVAC system in Chicago's famed Civic Opera House, an impressive array of sound-attenuating devices was installed. As opera patrons expect the quietest background environments ("If they hear *anything* there's a problem," said one consulting engineer), the designers paid particular attention to vibration isolation and control of mechanical equipment. The new installation also had to be energy-efficient, and it had to fit into minimal space because the building's envelope could not be expanded. The heart of the new system includes five modern air-handling units located in the old mechanical equipment room on the fifth floor. Each AH unit was assembled in place on 4 in. concrete pedestals and enclosed by 4 in. double-walls of solid sheet metal outside and perforated metal inside with mineral fiber packing in between. An IAC ML-type sound attenuator was installed between each unit's primary fan and its main duct, an IAC D-Duct discharge silencer was located just after each mixed-flow fan, and more ML attenuators were placed just after each outdoor air fan inlet and in each return air duct. Every duct in the mechanical equipment room and for 50 ft beyond was mounted on spring isolators, all dampers and mixing boxes were placed upstream of the takeoffs from the branch ducts, every fan was mounted on spring isolators with thrust restraints, and the mechanical equipment room's old louvered entry doors were replaced by solid doors with fully gasketed frames. Plumbing pipe diameters were enlarged to maintain slow waterflow, pumps were set on concrete inertia blocks with height-reducing outboard spring isolators, chillers were mounted on multiple-coil spring isolators, and all plumbing connections to the pumps, chillers, and the cooling tower were fitted with double-sphere neoprene connectors. Where equipment-generated airborne noise could exit through the side of a duct, the metal side was lagged with 2 in. fiberboard covered with two layers of $5/8$ in. gypsum wallboard with staggered and sealed seams. Ducts with short-side dimensions or diameters exceeding 24 in. were covered with 2 in. linings, and all other ducts received 1 in. linings. Duct velocities were kept low (800–1,000 fpm in mains, 500–600 fpm in branches, 300–350 fpm in diffusers), and supply and return grille face velocities were minimized. As the original stage-right return air plenum had acted as an annoying noise tube from its return air fan back to the stage, this plenum was rebuilt of concrete blocks whose interior surfaces were lined with smooth-faced 4 in. fiberglass, the noisily oscillating fin louvers of the old return air grille were replaced with screens, and an ML attenuator was installed just upstream of the fan. In the audience area most of the return air was rerouted through mushroom grilles beneath the seats. Another problem was in the follow spot and projection booth, where much unwanted sound entered. Here the booth's front was sealed with glass, the walls at each end were thoroughly sealed, and a dropped acoustical ceiling was installed to minimize breakout noise from the ductwork overhead. [†]

Resilient mounts or vibration isolators are usually designed as follows. The Æ designer determines the minimum isolation efficiency for the noise-producing machinery to be isolated, notes the machinery's unit load and support locations as listed in its manufacturer's specifications or catalog, then supplies this data to a mechanical engineer, who determines the machinery's stroke or range of motion based on the operating frequency of its motor and the unit load on each mount, then sizes the selected isolator so it is not underloaded (which prevents utilization of its resilience) or overloaded (which eliminates its resilience due to binding, overcompression, or permanent deformation of the mount or part thereof).

> What is the required isolation efficiency for four resilient corner mounts under a 25 ton crossflow induced-draft package cooling tower located on the roof of a six story office building if the unit's 1,240 lb weight is distributed evenly on its mounts?

[†] The information regarding the Chicago Opera House upgrading was obtained

Step 1. Find the minimum isolation efficiency of the noise-producing machinery from the following formula:

⑦ⓒ④ⓐ $\qquad Ł_R \, \mathcal{E} \approx 80 \, Ł_R + 52 \, (\eta \, \kappa_B)^{0.5}$

$Ł_R$ = loudness limit of sound reception from adjacent spaces, dB. As the top-floor offices under the unit may be managerial, from Table 7-4, $Ł_R$ for offices, managerial = 28 dB.

$\mathcal{E}$ = isolation efficiency of resilient mount(s), ? %. Acceptable values ≈ 85% for ground-floor unit next to noncritical occupancies to 98.5% for several upper-floor units next to critical occupancies.

η = number of machines within enclosed area. η for nonenclosed units on roof = 1.

κ_B = barrier factor, depending on occupied spaces next to area of sound source. κ_B = 1 if occupied spaces are above ceiling, 2 if any spaces are behind any adjacent wall up to four walls, and 4 if any spaces exist below floor. Add 12 if other sound sources are within occupied space. Here κ_B = 0 + 0 + 4 + 0 = 4.

$$28 \, \mathcal{E} \approx 80 \times 28 + 52 \, (1 \times 4)^{0.5} \qquad ... \, \mathcal{E} \approx 84\%$$

Step 2. From the small table below find the typical isolation efficiency of the noise-producing machinery and compare this value with $\mathcal{E}$ found in Step 1; then use the larger value in subsequent analysis.

Typical Isolation Efficiencies of HVAC components

Equipment	Isolation efficiency, %
Condensers, fan-coil units = 80; Cooling towers	85
Packaged air conditioners = 90; Centrifugal compressors	98
Reciprocat'g compress'rs: to 15 HP = 85, to 60 HP = 90, to 150 HP = 95	
Centrifugal fans: to 200 rpm	90–95
200–350 rpm if fan diameter ≤ 48 in.	70
200–350 rpm if fan diameter ≥ 48 in.	70–80
350–800 rpm	70–90
Absorption units, steam generators, centrifugal pumps, piping .. 95	

Step 3. Find the resilient mount's desired stroke or static deflection from the formula

$$\Delta_m \, \mathcal{E} \, S^2 \, = \, 181,000,000$$

Δ_m = optimal stroke or static deflection of resilient mount, ? in.

$\mathcal{E}$ = isolation efficiency of resilient mount(s), from Step 2, %

S = operating speed of motor or machinery on resilient mount, rpm. If the mount supports more than one machine whose rpms are different, use the lowest rpm.

No calculation due to insufficient data

Step 4. Knowing Δ_b, the maximum deflection of the structure that supports the noise-producing machinery due to its total load, compare Δ_b with the mount's static deflection Δ_m as found in Step 3 according to the formula $0.10\ \Delta_m \leq \Delta_b$. If this relation is not satisfied, then use $0.10\ \Delta_b$ in subsequent analysis.

Step 5. From manufacturer's specifications or catalog, select a resilient mount based on its required static deflection and its range of load.

7.C.4.b. Flanking Sound

This is sound that detours barrier construction through openings that are not directly between the adjacent spaces. Examples are sound travelling over suspended ceilings on each side of a nonbearing wall, under access floor panels at the bottoms of walls, and through louvers in adjacent hallway doors. One notorious flanking path is *speaking tube noise* in HVAC ducting. This occurs when sound from one room flows into a grille, then upstream through the duct behind the grill to the first tee, then

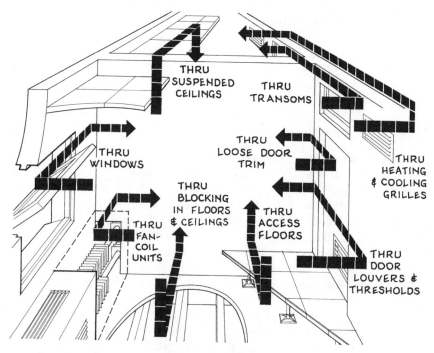

Fig. 7-25. Flanking sound paths between adjacent spaces.

lishing Co., Troy, MI); Oct 1994, p. 40.

downstream in the tee branch duct to its grille and into a nearby room. Liners and baffles installed in the ducts reduce such noise. Flanking sound may also occur where indoor spaces are ventilated by natural air currents entering through windows. Thus openable windows should not be placed too closely together in exterior walls, all casement windows in one wall should open in the same direction, windows should not be located between critical indoor sound areas and noisy outdoor areas, and two windows should not be placed near each side of an inner corner of an exterior wall.

Methods of eliminating other sound flanking paths are:

▶ Where wall partitions rise just above suspended ceilings, run the walls up to solid construction above.

▶ Where walls rest on on access floor panels, install baffling directly below the walls beneath the floor and cover at least one side of the baffling with batt insulation.

▶ Where floors are designed to absorb impact loads, do not let the edge of the floor rest against the surrounding wall; instead leave at least a $\frac{1}{2}$ in. gap, fill it with seal sealer or other soft material, then hide the top of the seal with base molding.

▶ Where joists or rafters run perpendicular to walls cross above or below the walls, cover one side of the blocking between the horizontal members in these places with batt insulation.

▶ Avoid cheek-to-cheek and back-to-back grilles in HVAC ducts, and install flexible boots between every third duct section.

7.C.4.c. Resonance

This is a harmonic buildup of a reflected sound wave whose length is a multiple of a dimension of a space through which the wave travels. For example, if a musical note of middle C (wavelength = 262 Hz or 4.304 ft at 69°) emanates from a celloist's bow during a chamber music recital and strikes a slightly concave surface 21'-6$\frac{1}{4}$" away, the returning sound will be added to the original sound as their exact wavelengths overlap. Of course, if the note is a little higher or lower, or the air is a little warmer or cooler, the note's wavelength multiple will be slightly longer or shorter and then it will no longer exactly equal the distance between the sound source and the reflecting surface —but then the resonance may merely shift to a higher or lower note. Such a phenomenon occurs in architecture only rarely, but when it does, the effect can be agonizing.

Another kind of acoustic resonance could be called the *tympani effect*. This occurs when a sound wave strikes a thin membrane with an inertial force that makes it oscillate, then if the waves continue arriving at an interval equal to the membrane's oscillating frequency the sound is magnified on the other side. The lower the sound's frequency, or the lighter or stiffer or wider the membrane, the greater the resonance. These harmonics typically occur in back-to-back medicine cabinets in apartment bathrooms, back-to-back bookcases in offices, and in HVAC ducting where fast-flowing air in a thin metal duct amplifies the airflow into an annoying throb or rumble. Such resonance is usually the result of budgetary constraints that lead to smaller ducts and faster airflows. Thus chief remedies for reducing the tympani effect are to build suspected membranes of thicker, heavier, and less elastic materials (lead is best for critical situations), make their areas smaller (this can be done by gluing a rib through the center of the resonating area), frame the membrane with resilient borders, or cushion one side with fiberglass insulation.

Sympathetic sound resonance through large windows can be significantly reduced by installing Thermopane units in which the multiple panes have different thicknesses.

7.D. LISTENING ENVIRONMENTS

A listening environment is an architectural space whose essential occupancy is a listening experience. This includes everything from small home entertainment centers to huge outdoor athletic stadiums, from rustic barroom dance halls to sophisticated television broadcast studios. Designing listening environments well begins by doing the following:

▶ Locate the listening environment on a quiet site.
▶ Divide the occupancy into a small performing area and a considerably larger listening area.
▶ In large listening environments, locate the performing area floor 1–3 ft above the lowest portion of the listening area.
▶ Direct a large portion of the initial sound toward the listening area by shell-like boundary surfaces of reflective material mounted behind, above, and beside the performing area.
▶ If the listening area has more than 450 occupants, amplify the initial sound with electronic equipment.
▶ Consider that the optimal sound frequency band for speech intelligibility is usually 1,000 Hz, and 500 Hz is usually the optimal frequency band for music appreciation.

The three primary acoustic variables of a listening environment are its *size*, *shape*, and *surface*, as described below.

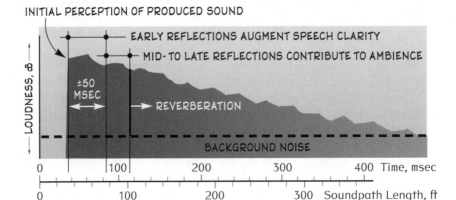

INITIAL PERCEPTION OF PRODUCED SOUND

Fig. 7-26. Sound field graph of a listening area sound.

▸ The listening environment's *size* should maximize the propagated sounds' loudness in all parts of the listening area.

▸ Its *shape* should promote directivity, wave coherence, uniform diffusion, and quick initial reflections of the propagated sound throughout the listening area. Particularly helpful are floor plans that are symmetrical from left to right and steep seating areas located close to the performing area.

▸ Its *surfaces* should enhance directional realism, optimize the correlation of initial and early reflections, preserve natural tonality, and promote other aspects of optimal acoustic modeling throughout the listening area. Particularly helpful are side walls that have the same size, shape, and sound-absorbing characteristics.

The most important criterion underlying the above three variables is the environment's *number of listeners*, which is usually defined by its *seating capacity*, whose required floorspace can be estimated by the formula

7)D) $$A \approx 6 \, (\eta^{0.5} + 4)^2$$

A = floorspace required for listening area, sf
η = number of seats in listening area

Once a listening area's required floorspace is known, its optimal size and shape can usually be determined given other design criteria for the occupancy. Then the shape's optimal reverberation time may be found from Table 7-1, then the optimal absorption of its boundary surfaces can be determined from Sec. 7.C.2. The ultimate goal is sound that is distributed uniformly throughout the listening area in a manner that promotes maximum loudness, distinction of successive enunciations of speech, and proportional loudness of all musical notes without producing echoes, excessive reverberation, or other unclear colorations of the original sound. Often local economies dictate the need for multi-use facilities; then flexibility created by movable reflectors, panels, drapes, and the like is usually the best way to create optimal conditions for all occupancies.

Whenever loudspeakers are mounted above a large stage, as is likely in lecture auditoriums, concert halls, opera houses, and theater playhouses, their mounting heights should be 30–35 ft above the stage; as below about 30 ft the sound reaching the stage is apt to be too loud and the chance of feedback is greater, while above about 35 ft the delay between natural and amplified sound may fuzzy the sound. On stages all musicians, singers, and actors need to hear each other clearly so they may perform in unison with each other; thus they should be close together, soundpaths between them should be uninterrupted, and the dominant angle of returning soundpaths from nearby reflective surfaces should not aim at them but should pass well above their heads toward the audience. A large listening area often requires a separate loudspeaker system for public announcements, emergency instructions, playing music, and aural activities.

7.D.1. Auditoriums

This listening environment includes courtrooms, lecture halls, meeting rooms, congressional and legislative halls, drill halls, high school auditoriums, auction halls, and other medium-to-large assembly areas in which the audience does little more than listen to the speakers. Most corporate offices, hospitals, governmental organizations, and educational centers have one such assembly area in each large building. The floors of these spaces usually incline down to a raised stage that isn't framed by a proscenium, the seating is usually divided by central and side aisles, and at least most of the seats are fixed and upholstered.

Assembly areas whose volume exceeds 50,000 cf and whose performers' voices travel more than 50 ft usually require sound amplification. Even in small assembly areas with as few as 100 seats, weak-voiced speakers typically need to be reinforced, and outdoor speakers may require amplification for anyone sitting more than 30 ft away. Unless the auditorium is really large, its sound amplification system usually has a cluster of loudspeakers located directly above the lectern. Each also generally has a small sound/projection/ lighting control room centrally located behind the seating area. In today's digital age, wireless controls can be easily installed between the lectern, control room, and the head usher's station.

 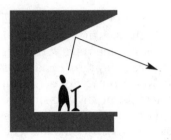

Fig. 7-27. Bad and good onstage soundpaths.

In a small lecture hall where the farthest seats are located 46 ft from the podium, is sound amplification required if the seating area's background noise level is 32 dB?

7)D)1)
$$dB = S - 0.7 - 20 \log D$$

dB = sound intensity level at farthest distance from its source, dB. In all listening areas the propagated sound, whether amplified or not, should remain at least 25dB above the level of background noise. Thus here dB ≥ 25 + 32 = 57 dB.

S = intensity level of sound at its source, dB. Here the propagated sound's intensity level at its source is that of speech ≈ 66 dB. Thus solve for S, then compare the computed value with 66 dB.

D = length of soundpath from its source to farthest seat, 46 ft.

$$57 = S - 0.7 - 20 \log 46$$
$$S = 91 \text{ dB} \rightarrow \text{sound amplification is required}$$

7.D.2. Banquet Halls

In addition to banquet areas this listening environment includes ballrooms, dance halls, lodges, granges, American legion halls, community centers, restaurant reception rooms, town meeting halls, and other public areas that are used for civic meetings, celebrations, wedding receptions, award ceremonies, square dances, and other community gatherings in which listeners convivially mingle with each other. These places are characterized by large flat floors on one level, light movable seating, and flexible-use facilities such as large storage areas, small commercial kitchens, and movable wall sections that slide into surrounding walls. Since these rooms are often packed with noisy occupants and the floors are often acoustically reflective hardwood, the walls and especially the ceiling should be sound-absorbent, and plan shapes should be oblong as this configuration discretizes generated sound waves better.

These spaces often have a small stage and a pulldown movie screen, which require sound amplification and movie projection systems. Although this equipment is usually small by itself, the control console it usually requires often includes arrays of inputs, digital controls, and outputs for lighting, amplified sound propagation, and other special effects; then this equipment and all its related electronics and wiring are magnified to a vital component of these occupancies that requires its own extensive space.

7.D.3. Classrooms & Conference Rooms †

In addition to classrooms and conference rooms this listening environment includes city council chambers, hotel and motel seminar rooms, and a variety of other small meeting areas where attendees sit in chairs, at desks, or around tables and interact with speakers, small presentation groups, and each other. Thus these rooms must be equally comfortable for lecturing and personal conversation. Although they may rarely need sound amplification, electronic hookups for Power Point presentations, teleconferencing networks, and other electronic systems are frequently required.

Although classrooms and conference rooms are architecturally similar, the economics behind their design and construction are often quite different. This is because conference rooms are usually corporate occupancies whose owners tend to spend whatever is necessary to maximize their profit-generating potential, while classrooms are usually designed on the basis of stringent budgets and lowest initial costs, which often result in inferior acoustic design.

Since the normal sound intensity of a lecturer, in a classroom or a conference room ≈ 66 dB and such voices should be 30 dB above ambient background noise levels, the latter should be no more than 36 dB for every portion of the Hz frequency band. Slightly higher background levels are OK in school laboratories and industrial conference rooms. When these standards are not met, it is most likely due to excessive reverberation and noisy HVAC equipment. Reverberation in these spaces is usually reduced by carpeting the floors, making the walls moderately absorbent, and making the ceilings highly absorbent. If the room has large panes of sound-reflective glass, all other boundary surfaces should be highly absorbent. A good design strategy is to determine the optimal reverberation time for each room from Table 7-1, then build its surfaces of sound-absorbent materials that satisfy this requirement according to Sec. 7.C.2.

HVAC noise reduction in classrooms and conference rooms begins by installing central low-velocity systems far from these areas. Especially

† Much of the technical data in this section was obtained from Jerry Lilly's

avoid window-mounted units and rooftop units directly above the ceilings. With central systems do not try to vary airflow with variable inlet vanes and discharge dampers; instead do it with variable-frequency drives. Fans should be quiet and efficient (do not use noisy forward-curved centrifugal fans), and each fan/motor assembly should be mounted on internal spring vibration isolators. Proper fan sizing requires that the HVAC system should first have the proper static air pressure drop at the ducting design airflow rate, then if the fan either over- or undersatisfies this pressure drop it will be too noisy; thus don't overestimate a system's static pressure drop as a conservative way of ensuring adequate performance. Also try to listen to a few HVAC fans operate before specifying one.

When air handling units (AHUs) that serve classrooms and conference rooms must be on roofs, specify wide high-curbed concrete slabs beneath them, place them above or near columns as these locations minimize vibration noise, mount them on high-deflection spring absorbers, loop all electrical connections, and locate the units over rest rooms, locker rooms, storage rooms, hallways, lobbies, and other non-noise-sensitive areas. Since rooftop unit ducts are usually short and run directly to the spaces they serve, run them on top of the roof if possible, wrap them in batt insulation to minimize breakout noise, and install flexible connectors at the fan face and several ft before each diffuser. In all ducts promote aerodynamic airflow from beginning to end, because turns cause turbulence, which not only rumbles and throbs but often magnifies noises entering them. Thus it is best to use round branch ducts (they minimize low-frequency breakout which is often a problem with rectangular ducts), install conical tees and long-radius elbows, minimize the number of elbows within the perimeter of each room, and install turning vanes in any square elbows. Where unavoidable problems occur, make the duct one size larger. Wise design also includes installing flexible connections between each fan face and its main supply duct, fitting the first 30 LF of the main duct with 2 in. lining, locating all supply ducts above corridors and not rooms, placing splitter dampers outside the walls that enclose each room, fitting each branch duct with a flexible connection where it crosses the plane of the room's walls, and wrapping each duct in 4 in. batt insulation for the last 10 ft before each diffuser. Diffusers should also be mounted in ceilings, each should serve no more than 250 sf of floor area, and neck velocities should not exceed 500 fpm. All the above also applies to return air paths, but bad noise isn't quite as loud in them because it must ride the airflow upstream.

If the room must be conditioned by a dedicated AHU, it should be a fan coil unit and not a heat pump with its noisy compressor and condenser fan, and the unit should be located in a closet in a rear corner of the listening area. The AHU casing should be 18 ga. sheet steel wrapped in 2 in. acoustic lining, the fan/motor assembly must be mounted on spring isolators whose static deflection $\geq$ 1 in, the fan should be on top of the unit and discharge into a plenum encased in 2 in. duct lining that extends above the room's ceiling, and the return duct should run under the floor until it passes the vertical plane of the AHU closet wall. The closet walls should be $^5/_8$ in. drywall on studs whose cavities are filled with fiberglass insulation, the room should have a $1^3/_4$ in. thick solid-core door with perimeter acoustic seals on all sides, and the AH unit should be at least 6 in. from the walls on all sides.

7.D.4. Concert Halls

In addition to concert halls this includes music halls, recital halls, and other large assembly areas that have wide stages framed by expansive prosceniums. These listening environments are suitable for concerts, ballets, and large theatrical productions that do not require extensive lighting effects or scenery changes, and they are often designed as multiple-use facilities that serve large populations. These spaces may seat as many as 2,500 listeners, and they usually have a distinctive fan, horseshoe, or shoebox shape. The boundary areas around, above, and behind the stage are usually highly reflective and highly directive, while the surfaces that enclose the audience are carefully designed to produce optimal reverber-

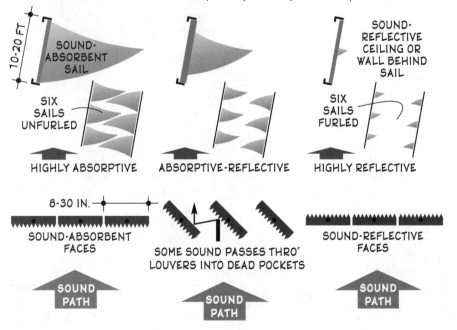

Fig. 7-28. Movable acoustic devices: sails and louvers.

eration, & Air Conditioning Engineers, Atlanta, GA); pp. 21–29.

ation times. The angle and height of the large reflective surface above the stage may be adjusted by telemetered winch-driven cables that descend from the ceiling; and manually movable panels or roll-up acoustic sails are often mounted around the audience area.

Such flexibility greatly improves the hall's ability to provide optimal acoustics for a variety of events. The hall's ceiling and exterior walls must also prevent outdoor sounds from entering the performing and listening areas. Many acoustic problems that have plagued these buildings in decades past have been solved by digitally developed *synthesized acoustic controls*, which can render opposite-wave duplications of many naturally delivered sounds.

An innovative variation of several recently built concert halls is the partially enclosed hall. These buildings are open around much of the seating area and are located in scenic areas, thus they offer occupants wide views of the surrounding landscape and allow speedy entry and exit. Such structures must be located on quiet sites and are generally used only in the summer. Examples are the Tanglewood Music Shed in western Massachusetts, the Finger Lakes Performing Arts Center in western New York, and the Santa Fe Opera House in northern New Mexico.

Another large concert hall that is completely open to the outdoors is the amphitheater. These assembly areas usually have a large shell-like reflector behind a wide stage, inclined fan-shaped seating areas that often hold several thousand spectators, and extensive sound amplification systems. If the seats orient toward the northwest, spectators and performers won't face the setting sun during late afternoon and early evening performances. The world's finest and most enduring example of this architecture is the Theater at Epidaurus, Greece. Well-designed domestic examples include the Red Rocks Amphitheater in Denver, Chastain Memorial Amphitheater in Atlanta, and the Greek Theater in Berkeley, California.

A clever variation of the partly enclosed concert hall is the Music Tent in Aspen. Designed by Eero Saarinen, this assembly area is enclosed by a huge canvas tent whose breathable billowy fabric creates an optimal boundary surface for the enjoyment of concerts, recitals, operas, ballets, and other events. The tent's base allows easy entry and exit of spectators on nearly every side, and its pointed shape alliterates the lofty profiles of the peaks that surround this lovely mountain city.

Such large spaces as concert halls are usually equipped with extensive high-quality sound amplification systems that meet the needs of instrumentalists, vocalists, and concert artists with possibly accompanying narration as well as stage production personnel and public announcements. The loudspeakers are often cable-suspended below the ceiling, where they may be artfully concealed as chandeliers or other decorative element; or they may be mounted high on the side walls. Other details of these amplification systems are described in the section on opera houses.

7.D.5. Home Entertainment Centers

These usually semiprivate areas may be as small as an armchair in front of a TV set or as large as a plushly upholstered twenty-seat movie theater in a luxury residence. In these small spaces the soundpaths are so short that initial speech and music clarity is rarely inarticulate, but they can be exhilaratingly enhanced by digital technology.

The simplest home entertainment center has its electronics efficiently arranged in an existing room. At the other extreme, a large interior space may be gutted to its framing and a completely new acoustic shell built within the old construction that magnifies the entertainment to the realm of virtual reality and minimizes sound transmission to adjacent areas. This level of implementation is described below, with the idea that it can be downscaled to meet the objectives of lesser listening environments.

Say this environment's essential experience is to be a DVD movie enjoyed by 12 people. Then the sound system should include a DVD player, TV screen, amplifiers, mixing console, and speakers. The screen size would be dictated by the seating area, so let's zero in on this first. Let's locate the occupants in fine lounge chairs spaced comfortably apart, so each can recline relaxingly in front of the screen. Such viewers would perhaps be 3 ft apart from side to side and 7 ft apart from front to back. If the seating area is four seats wide × three seats deep, a moviewatcher's frontal cone of vision is about 35°, and the seats have a 3 ft aisle around them, a little trigonometry indicates that the room would be at least 18 × 27 ft in area and its screen would be 5–5½ ft wide as shown in Figs. 7-29 and 7-30. If a screen this wide has a commercial moviescreen ratio of 16/9, its diagonal would be about 72 in. Since 72 in. home viewing screens are commercially available, we need do no more designing here than to say the room will have a 72 in. screen with a 16/9 base/side ratio, which means the screen would be about 63 in. wide and 35 in. high. The screen's base should also be about 42 in. above the floor. Now let's speed up our analysis by simply saying this environment will have two treble speakers placed about 9 ft apart on each side of the screen and 1 ft down from its top, 2 bass subwoofers directly under the treble cones about 2 ft above the floor, two smaller treble "surround" speakers in the middle of each side wall about 7 ft above the floor (outputs ≈ 6 dB below that of the front speakers), and two bass surround speakers high in the room's rear corners (outputs ≈ 10 dB below that of the front speakers). The DVD player, amps, console, controls, and ample storage will be housed in ample cabinetry by the entry door as shown in Figs. 7-29 and 7-30. Of course the room will need a spaghetti array of wiring somewhere around it to connect everything together.

Now let's build the acoustic shell for this listening experience. First, how will everyone get in and out of this room? Certainly a double entry door will do, located near the rear of the room. This portal should have a

† Much of the technical data in this section was obtained from Ian Austin's

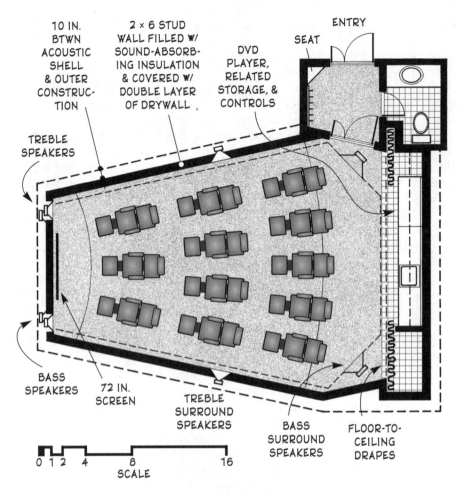

Fig. 7-29. Home entertainment center: plan.

small foyer outside with a row of jacket hooks high on one side, a bathroom door on the other side, and a second entry door on the opposite wall to form an elegant acoustic airlock entry for this listening environment. Of course this chamber's boundary surfaces would be sound-absorbent and both doors would have acoustic trim on all sides including the thresholds. Next, what kind of windows and lighting should the room have? Of course it should have no windows; thus it will require HVAC, and the lighting and all the visual controls will require a lot of wiring, all of which should be accessible. As for the lighting itself, let's deal with that later.

A good shape for this acoustic shell would be a high-ceiling'd rectangle that is neither square nor overly oblong. So let's put the ceiling 12 ft above our previously determined 18 × 27 ft floor area. With such a high

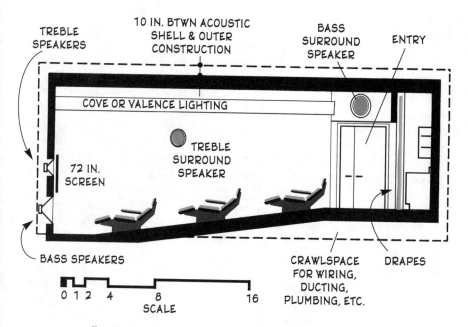

Fig. 7-30. Home entertainment center: section.

ceiling, the room's entry door in the rear can be located $2\frac{1}{2}$ ft above the original floor; then the room's floor can ramp down from this level toward the front wall that houses the screen. Such an incline not only orients all viewers more frontally to the screen, it forms an expansive crawl space below that removes any further anxiety a designer might have regarding the placing and accessing of all wiring, ducting, and even plumbing (how about a nice bar with a sink against the back wall?). The raised floor can also be easily soundproofed. As for the walls, let's build them of 12 ft tall 2×6s (2×6 studs are stronger than 2×4s and thicker sound-absorbing insulation can be fitted between them), and leave at least 10 in. between the outside of this shell and the inside of the original wall (this space forms an acoustic break between the walls, and it provides a wide and easily accessible area for laying the wiring and installing the HVAC ducts). Finally, the side walls should not be parallel to each other, and it may be acoustically advantageous to cover the rear wall with floor-to-ceiling drapery.

Now for the lighting. This windowless space should be softly luminous when entered, then the lights can be turned off or dimmed to near-zero during showtime. The fixtures should not be recessed into the shell, as then they would break the acoustic barrier we have tried so carefully to maintain; but they could be recessed in additional framing that angles E outward from the shell's corners, as sketched in Figs. 7-29 and 7-30.

After all the framing is complete, cover it with two layers of drywall with no seams of the second layer falling on any of the first. This construction would have a high STC rating for any sound that tried to exit the space as well as any that tried to enter.

Finally, how should the shell's boundary surfaces be finished? Considered together, they should be moderately absorbent. If the floor was deeply carpeted and the walls were covered with breathable fabric, the ceiling could be fairly reflective. Beyond this, the design would be a subjective matter between the architect and owner. One possibility: cover the walls with burlap or other rough rustic fabric that is moderately sound-absorbent, fill every corner around the base of the walls with profuse arrays of artificial foliage and locate a few vines high on the walls to give this windowless indoor box a woodsy outdoor look, bulk up the HVAC system to produce a healthy overabundance of fresh air, add background noises of birds singing and crickets chirring and other arboreal sounds (if these are created by two tape loops that play simultaneously and the loops' lengths are different prime numbers such as 439 and 557 sec, the sound they produce will rarely be the same), paint the ceiling of this petite amphitheater a deep dark flat blue to make it look expansive as the distant galaxies, then —thinking of stars— add some electronics that project slowly rotating starry constellations upon this depthless firmament.

Who knows, viewers may enjoy the ceiling more than the movies.

7.D.6. Music Rooms

Grouped together here are music practice rooms and rehearsal rooms, music classrooms in schools and colleges, radio and TV broadcast studios, recording studios, coffeehouses, and cafes and art galleries that stage small musical productions. Music schools usually have many such spaces, and elementary and high schools often have one or more classrooms specially designed for teaching, tutoring, practicing, and rehearsing music, which may include instrumentalists, bands, orchestras, vocalists, and choral groups.

The floors, walls, and especially ceilings of these usually fairly small rooms should be highly sound-absorbent, and opposite walls should not be parallel or concave to obviate the occurrence of flutter echoes. If possible the ceilings should be 12–15 ft high, and sound amplification is rarely necessary unless it is used for recording.

The musical instrument with the lowest frequency is the bass drum at 16–20 Hz (its sound wave at 70° may be 70 ft long); while the instrument with the highest frequency is the piccolo at 4,186 Hz (this sound wave at 70° is 3.23 in. long).

7.D.7. Opera Houses

An opera house is basically a concert hall with a large stage for the singer/actors and a large orchestra pit between the stage and audience; but the defining difference between these two occupancies is a tall fly tower above the opera stage that allows rapid changes of many scenes onstage. However, a concert hall, opera house, and theater can be combined into a single *performing arts center* to increase the flexibility of these expensive buildings. An opera house also has in front of its stage a wide orchestra pit, whose floor area can hold a full orchestra (area ≈ 20 sf per musician). The pit is usually open except for the front portion of the stage that may protrude over the pit's rear area; then the ceiling above this alcove should be pitched to direct the orchestra's sound toward the audience. This directivity may also be enhanced by giving the alcove's rear wall a modestly concave plan profile.

In opera houses the level of aural quality is very refined, primarily due to the meticulous tracing of all soundpaths from the stage and orchestra pit to everywhere throughout the audience. Sound amplification is usually by central loudspeakers placed above the proscenium; then supplemental speakers may be located under any balconies that cast acoustic shadows over any seats below, and roll-on special-effects speakers may be positioned just offstage or behind the scenery. A separate management intercom system also links theater office with offstage areas, the orchestra pit, gridiron and loft levels in the fly tower, catwalks in the ceiling and cue light stations in the walls around the audience, and the control room as well as each actor's dressing room, the green room, head usher's station, lobby, and the stage manager's office.

7.D.8. Sports Arenas

This includes football and baseball stadiums, basketball gymnasiums, tennis and volleyball courts, hockey rinks, circus tents, equestrian and rodeo arenas, racetracks with roofed grandstands, and any other area where athletes perform before seated or standing audiences.

In these environments, little sound is produced by the performers. Except for a referee's whistle, buzzer, or public announcement, it usually comes from the audience. Thus little attention need be given to soundpath vectors radiating from the performing areas, and the seats do not need upholstering —as when one is empty it is minus one contributor to the voluminous noises these occupancies commonly create. Reverberations of 4–5 sec at frequency ranges of 500–2,000 Hz are entirely acceptable in these occupancies, but longer periods can be painfully deafening.

Every sports arena requires a sound amplification system for public announcements. In small facilities, the best location is in the ceiling above the center of the playing area. If the speaker horns are aimed at audience centers, excessive reverberation will rarely occur. In outdoor areas the speakers may be located on lighting poles, under the stadium roof if there is one, or along the back of the grandstands. In each location any problems of directivity, uniform diffusion, and boundary reflection over the seating areas are usually easy to solve. However, in large indoor sports arenas, especially the domed facilities being built for today's major league sport franchises, extensive distribution systems deliver sound uniformly to every spectator through often hundreds of speakers placed 30–40 ft apart above each seating level completely around the stadium, as well as clusters of loudspeakers suspended from cables that are raised and lowered above the playing area. These public announcement systems must be able to override the highest sound levels of crowds in sports arenas ($\approx$ 95 dB) even though ambient crowd noise levels are normally about 82–85 dB. Today's digital controls enable them to achieve this by automatically delivering sound at a certain number of decibels above whatever the input ambient sound level is at any moment.

7.D.9. Theaters

This listening environment includes theaters, playhouses, repertory theaters, and theaters-in-the-round as well as movie houses, cinemas, and multiplexes. The primary acoustic quality of a theater is clarity of speech. Thus the stopped tones, successive enunciations, and tonal modulations of spoken sounds must approach the articulation of conversation between two people only a few feet from each other even though the actual sound-path may be as much as 60 ft, which is about the maximum distance that speech can travel without requiring amplification. Thus if every seat must be within 60 ft of the stage to promote an intimate ambience between actors and spectators, a little algebra indicates that a theater's maximum number of seats is about 600 if the seats and aisles are spacious.

Popular theater shapes are the fan, rectangle, hexagon, and in-the-round. In a fan-shaped arrangement the stage and seating area are usually divided sharply by a proscenium arch, while in a theater-in-the-round the stage may thrust to nearly the center of the seating area. In any theater, more of the audience can be brought closer to the stage by wrapping one or two tiers of seating above the sides and back of the main seating area. The sight lines to all spectators should be as uninterrupted as possible, and all boundary surfaces more than 30 ft from the stage should be moderately sound-absorptive except for any underbalcony soffits, which should be

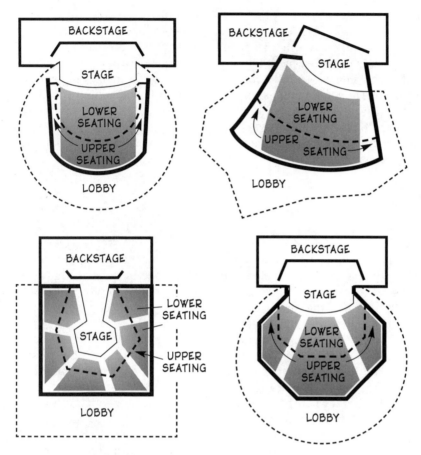

Fig. 7-31. A few theater plan shapes.

reflective and pitched to mirror stage sounds to the spectators below.

Since speech and music have different sound characteristics, a theater that has wonderful acoustics for plays may have undesirable acoustics for musicals. This dilemma indicates the need for flexibility in modern theater design, which can be achieved by installing movable reflectors above and behind the stage area, roll-up sails against the ceiling above the seats, and adjustable panels or tall movable drapes of breathable fabric against the walls behind the seating areas.

Although theater playhouses and movie theaters are similar listening environments, architecturally they are quite different. A movie theater is designed to amplify sound rather than clarify live voices, a fact that greatly simplifies the nature of one's size, shape, and boundary surfaces. Indeed, a movie house needs to be little more than a large box that has large onstage speakers behind a perforated screen, a sound-absorbing ceiling, long drapes of breathable fabric against the walls on each side, and upholstered seats. Today's cinema screens typically have a 16–9 ratio, and one's height and width relates to the size of its seating area. The movie soundtrack is amplified by at least two pairs of bass and treble speakers, with the treble horns mounted about $^2/_3$ the screen's height above its base and the bass speakers (also known as woofers) placed behind each side of the screen's base. Additional loudspeakers may be placed along the sides and rear of the seats near the ceiling to create surround or special effects. Movie theaters also require a second sound system for public announcements and playing music during intermissions.

7.D.10. Worship Areas

This listening environment includes churches, chapels, synagogues, mosques, kingdom halls, temples, tabernacles, and any shrine where devotees listen to religious sermons and music. Each typically has a raised nave with the choir and organ on each side of an altar near the rear of the nave and a higher pulpit along the front.

These spaces are usually multi-use auditoriums with long reverberation times. Thus good interior finishes for walls and ceilings are masonry, concrete, thick plaster, and wood paneling. However, while reverberation is desirable for choir singing and organ playing, it is not as good for sermons. This conflict can be resolved by locating the choir and organ no more than 40 ft apart, placing them high against reflective walls and ceiling, locating the ceiling above the choir 15–25 ft above the voices, and placing the pulpit well in front of the organ and choir and several ft above the level of the seating. Then most of the soundpaths radiating from the choir and organ will reflect off the surfaces around them then pass above the pulpit before they spread over the congregation, while most of the sound from the pulpit travels directly to the pews. All these soundpaths must be meticulously designed. The pews should also be cushioned so they are similarly absorbent whether occupied or vacant, and any organ pipes should not be behind the choir. Another acoustic trick: give the walls on each side of the nave L-shaped plan profiles, then make the strips of wall facing the center of the nave sound-reflective and the strips facing the congregation sound-absorptive; this reduces sound transmission to the choir and organ areas and increase it to the congregation.

Worship facilities usually require sound amplification systems for the pulpits but rarely for the organ and choir. Thus their sound amplification systems are similar to those installed in auditoriums. The frequency of organ pipes begins at 16 Hz.

7.E. OUTDOOR SOUND

When sound travels outdoors, it usually travels longer distances than does sound indoors. Thus an outdoor sound not only weakens due to the expanding of its spherical wavefront as the distance from its source increases, it may weaken because a considerable part of its energy is absorbed by the air. Since shorter high-pitched sound waves have less inertia than longer low-pitched ones, they are absorbed more by variations in topography, by the fluffy nature of trees and other foliage, and by streets and other spaces between residences and other small buildings. Thus an airplane engine has a high whine when it is nearby and a low hum when it is in the distant sky, and a lighthouse foghorn has a low moan when heard miles away. Since outdoor sounds are more likely to travel long distances, their spherical waves also tend to be more planar by the time they arrive at the architecture; and since they are more likely to arrive from all directions, they tend to be more steady-state and diffuse. Thus outdoor sounds generally seem more pervasive than indoor sounds. Prevailing winds also affect outdoor sounds, so spaces opening to them tend to be slightly noisier than spaces opening away from them.

Outdoor sound can be categorized as *outdoor-indoor sound* or *outdoor-outdoor sound*, as described below:

Outdoor-indoor sound. This arrives chiefly through windows, which tend to be a facade's weakest sound barrier when closed and are certainly weaker when open. Exterior doors, wall vents, and utility connections also require attention. Sound reduction is much the same as indoors: use construction with adequate STC ratings, eliminate diffraction and flanking paths, and seal all seams.

Outdoor-outdoor sound. Outdoor areas designed to offer peace and quiet, such as backyards and local parks, should be shielded from nearby noise pollution. The primary strategy is to surround these spaces with barriers that absorb as much sound as possible and deflect the rest upward, which can be done by giving the construction a rough surface on the source side, making it thick, having it rise well above the sight line between sound source and receiver, and placing it near either the source or receiver. Such a barrier is most effective if its length is at least four times its distance from the sound source. Practical solutions are rows of dense foliage, windbreaks, tall fences, thick ground covers, and varied terrain. Good wind controls usually make good outdoor sound controls.

A homeowner desires to plant a hedge beyond her backyard to reduce the noise arriving from a four-lane expressway 200 ft behind her house. If her property ends 45 ft from the expressway and the hedge is 15 ft tall, how effective will the barrier be?

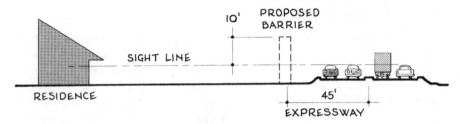

Fig. 7-32. Outdoor sound barrier.

7]E] $N_R \approx 10 \log (h^2/d) + 10 \log f - 17$

N_R = noise reduction due to outdoor acoustic barrier construction, **?** dB
h = height of acoustic barrier construction, ft. In Fig. 7-36, count only height above sight line between source and receiver. If barrier is 15 ft high and sight line is 5 ft above ground, h = 15 – 5 = 10 ft.
d = distance from acoustic barrier construction to source or receiver, whichever is less, ft. As rear of property is 45 ft from expressway, d = 45 ft.
f = dominant frequency of generated sound, Hz. From Fig. 7-8, dominant frequency of auto traffic is about 200 Hz.

$$N_R \approx 10 \log (10^2/45) + 10 \log 200 - 17 \approx 10 \text{ dB}$$

Note: Such a barrier reduces sound transmission by an added 3 dB for every octave the frequency increases. Thus at 400 Hz the above barrier reduces transmission by 13 dB and at 800 Hz the reduction is 16 dB. This is verified by examination of the Sound Barrier Nomograph of Fig. 7-13.

A1: USEFUL FORMULAS

Algebra

Arithmetic Progressions

An arithmetic progression is a series of numbers whose consecutive difference Δ is added to the preceding number, in which the numbers have the form:

$$\Sigma = a + (a + \Delta) + (a + 2\Delta) + (a + 3\Delta) + ... + [a + (n - 1)\Delta]$$

A]0]1] $\quad \Sigma = 0.5\, n\, [2\, a + \Delta\, (n - 1)]$ **A]0]2]** $\quad z = a + \Delta\, (n - 1)$

Σ = sum of arithmetic progression
n = number of terms in arithmetic progression
a = first number in arithmetic progression
z = final number in arithmetic progression
Δ = common difference between consecutive numbers. When $\Delta > 0$ the progression increases; when $\Delta < 0$ the progression decreases.

Geometric Progressions

A geometric progression is a series of numbers whose consecutive difference is a ratio r of the preceding number, in which the numbers have the form:

$$\Sigma = a + a\,r + a\,r^2 + a\,r^3 + ... + a\,r^{n-1}$$

A]0]3] $\quad \Sigma = \dfrac{a\,(r^n - 1)}{r - 1}$ **A]0]4]** $\quad z = a\,r^{n-1}$

Σ = sum of geometric progression
a = first number in geometric progression
z = final number in geometric progression
r = common ratio between consecutive numbers. When $r > 1$ the progression increases; when $r < 1$ the progression decreases.
n = number of terms in geometric progression

Exponential Relations

$$a^m a^n = a^{m+n} \qquad a^m/a^n = a^{m-n} \qquad a^p a^q/a^r = a^{p+q-r}$$

$$(a^m)^n = a^{mn} \qquad 1/a^m = a^{-m} \qquad (ab)^m = a^m b^m$$

Quadratic Equation

A|0|5)

$$x = \frac{-b \pm (b^2 - 4ac)^{0.5}}{2a} \qquad \text{when } ax^2 + bx + c = 0 \\ \text{and } a \neq 0$$

Binomial Theorem

$$(a+b)^2 = a^2 + 2ab + b^2 \qquad (a+b)^3 = a^3 + 3a^2 b + 3ab^2 + b^3$$

$$(a-b)^2 = a^2 - 2ab + b^2 \qquad (a-b)^3 = a^3 - 3a^2 b + 3ab^2 - b^3$$

$$(a+b)(a-b) = a^2 - b^2$$

Square of a Polynomial

The square of a polynomial equals the sum of the squares of each term plus twice the products of each pair of terms, as follows:

$$(a+b+\ldots+y+z)^2 = a^2 + b^2 + \ldots + y^2 + z^2 + 2ab + \ldots + 2ay \\ + 2az + \ldots + 2by + 2bz + \ldots + 2yz$$

Thus $(a+b+c)^2 = a^2 + b^2 + c^2 + 2ab + 2ac + 2bc$

Logarithms

A logarithm is the inverse of an exponential. For example, the equation $x = a^y$ can be written as $y = \log_a x$, which means y is the logarithm to the base a of x. Thus for any base b, $\log_b 1 = 0$ and $\log_b b = 1$. Any positive number except 1 can be be used as the base for a logarithmic function, but the two most common are 10 and e (= 2.71828). A logarithm to the base 10 ($\log_{10}$) is known as a *common* (or Briggs or Briggsian) *logarithm*, and it is convenient to use for numerical calculations in our to-the-base-10 or decimal number system. A logarithm to the base e ($\log_e$) is known as a *natural logarithm*. It is also called a hyperbolic or Napierian logarithm, and occasionally is referred to as LN. Natural logs are useful in certain geometric expressions and a number of calculus operations. The inverse of a logarithm is its *antilogarithm*, or antilog.

A logarithm has two parts: its *characteristic* and *mantissa*. The characteristic is its integer portion and the mantissa is the decimal portion:

e.g. in the logarithm 2.345, 2. is the characteristic and .345 is the mantissa. The mantissa describes the logarithm's value between 1 and 10, and the characteristic describes what power of 10 the mantissa is taken to. For example, in the logarithm 2.345, .345 indicates that this number's antilog between 1 and 10 is 2.213, and 2. indicates that 2.213 should be multiplied by 10 to the 2nd power, or 10^2; thus the antilog of 2.345 = 2.21 × 10^2 = 221.3. Also, $\log_{10}e = 0.4343$ and $\log_e 10 = 2.3026$.

$$\log(xy) = \log x + \log y \qquad \log(x/y) = \log x - \log y$$
$$\log_{10}e = 0.4343 \qquad\qquad \log_e 10 = 2.3026$$

A]0]6] To find the common logarithm of a number: $\log_{10} A = B$

A]0]7] To change $\log_{10}$ to $\log_e$ or vice versa: $2.3026 \times \log_{10} = \log_e$.

Plane Geometry

Points and Lines

If d is the distance between two points A and B whose orthogonal coordinates are $x_A, y_A, x_B,$ and y_B and m is the slope of line $A\,B$, then

A]0]8] $\quad d = [(x_A - x_B)^2 + (y_A - y_B)^2]^{0.5}$. **A]0]9]** $\quad m = \dfrac{y_A - y_B}{x_A - x_B}$

In the above scenario, if line $A\,B$ intercepts the Y axis at b, $x_A - x_B = x$, and $y_A - y_B = y$, the line's equation is

A]1]0] $\quad y = mx + b$

Angles & Triangles

If an angle is less than 90°, it is *acute*; if 90°, it is *right*; if more than 90°, it is *obtuse*; if 180°, it is a *straight line*. If two angles differ by 360°, they are *congruent* (e.g. 30° ≅ 390°). If angle α is a positive acute angle, then angles α, 180° - α, 180° + α, 360° - α, and all other angles congruent to these angles are *corresponding angles*.

A triangle is a polygon with three sides and three angles. If none of a triangle's sides are equal, it is *scalene*; if two sides are equal, it is *isosceles*; if all three sides are equal, it is *equilateral*. If one of its three angles is 90°, it is a *right* triangle; if one angle is greater than 90°, it is an *obtuse* triangle; if all angles are less than 90°, it is an *acute* triangle.

The parts of many triangles are solved by applications of trigonometry. This branch of mathematics revolves around six triangular relations known as *sine, cosine, tangent, secant, cosecant,* and *cotangent,* which also have six *inverse functions: arcsine* (arcsin or $\sin^{-1}$), *arcosine* (arccos or $\cos^{-1}$), *arctangent* (arctan or $\tan^{-1}$), *arcsecant* (arcsec or $\sec^{-1}$), *arcosecant* (arccsc or $\csc^{-1}$), and *arcotangent* (arccot or $\cot^{-1}$). These functions are related as follows: If $\sin \alpha = \beta$, then $\beta = \sin^{-1} \alpha$, etc.

Right-angled triangles (see Fig. A1-1)

$\boxed{A}\boxed{1}\boxed{1}$ $\sin \angle = {}^{OPP}/_{HYP}$

$\boxed{A}\boxed{1}\boxed{2}$ $\sin \angle = Q;\ Q \le 1.00$

$\boxed{A}\boxed{1}\boxed{3}$ $\cos \angle = {}^{ADJ}/_{HYP}$

$\boxed{A}\boxed{1}\boxed{4}$ $\cos \angle = Q;\ Q \le 1.00$

$\boxed{A}\boxed{1}\boxed{5}$ $\tan \angle = {}^{OPP}/_{ADJ}$

$\boxed{A}\boxed{1}\boxed{6}$ $\tan \angle = Q$

$\boxed{A}\boxed{1}\boxed{7}$ $\csc \angle = {}^{1}/_{\sin \angle}$

$\boxed{A}\boxed{1}\boxed{8}$ $\csc \angle = Q$

$\boxed{A}\boxed{1}\boxed{9}$ $\cot \angle = {}^{1}/_{\tan \angle}$

$\boxed{A}\boxed{2}\boxed{0}$ $\sec \angle = Q;\ Q > 1.00$

$\boxed{A}\boxed{2}\boxed{1}$ $\sin \angle = {}^{OPP}/_{HYP}$

$\boxed{A}\boxed{2}\boxed{2}$ $\cot \angle = Q;\ Q > 1.00$

$\boxed{A}\boxed{2}\boxed{3}$ $\sin^2 \angle + \cos^2 \angle = 1$

$\boxed{A}\boxed{2}\boxed{4}$ $\tan^2 \angle + 1 = \sec^2 \angle$

$\boxed{A}\boxed{2}\boxed{5}$ $\cot^2 \angle + 1 = \csc^2 \angle$

$\boxed{A}\boxed{2}\boxed{6}$ $A^2 + B^2 = C^2$

$\angle$ = value of angle under consideration, °
OPP = side of right triangle opposite angle $\angle$
ADJ = side of right triangle adjacent to angle $\angle$
HYP = hypotenuse of right triangle
$\sin \angle$ = sine of $\angle$
$\cos \angle$ = cosine of $\angle$
$\tan \angle$ = tangent of $\angle$
$\csc \angle$ = cosecant of $\angle$
$\sec \angle$ = secant of $\angle$
$\cot \angle$ = cotangent of $\angle$

HYP: C

OPP: B

ADJ: A

Fig. A1-1

Any triangle (see Fig. A1-2)

$\boxed{A}\boxed{3}\boxed{6}$ Law of sines: ${}^{a}/_{\sin A} = {}^{b}/_{\sin B} = {}^{c}/_{\sin C}$

$\boxed{A}\boxed{3}\boxed{7}$ Law of cosines: $a^2 = b^2 + c^2 - 2bc \cos A$

$\boxed{A}\boxed{3}\boxed{8}$ $\sin (A + B) = \sin A \cos B + \cos A \sin B$

$\boxed{A}\boxed{3}\boxed{9}$ $\sin (A - B) = \sin A \cos B - \cos A \sin B$

$\boxed{A}\boxed{4}\boxed{0}$ $\cos (A + B) = \cos A \cos B - \sin A \sin B$

$\boxed{A}\boxed{4}\boxed{1}$ $\cos (A - B) = \cos A \cos B + \sin A \sin B$

$\boxed{A}\boxed{4}\boxed{2}$ $\sin 2\angle = 2 \sin \angle \cos \angle$

$\boxed{A}\boxed{4}\boxed{3}$ $\cos 2\angle = \cos^2 \angle - \sin^2 \angle$

$\boxed{A}\boxed{4}\boxed{4}$ Area $= 0.5\, b\, h$
$= 0.5\, a\, (c^2 - a^2)^{0.5}$
$= 0.5\, b\, (c^2 - b^2)^{0.5}$

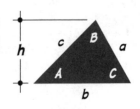

Fig. A1-2

[A][4][5] Area $= 0.5\ a^2/\tan A = 0.5\ b^2 \tan A = 0.25\ c^2 \sin 2A$

[A][4][6] $\quad\ = 0.25\ [(a + b + c)\ (- a + b + c)\ (a - b + c)\ (a + b - c)]^{0.5}$

[A][4][7] $\quad\ = 0.5\ a\,b\sin C = 0.5\ b\,c\sin A = 0.5\ c\,a\sin B$

[A][4][8] Section modulus (axis thro' ₵ of gravity): $S = 0.042\ B\,H^2$

[A][4][9] Moment of inertia (axis thro' ₵ of gravity): $I = 0.028\ B\,H^3$

[A][5][0] Section modulus (axis thro' base): $S = 0.083\ B\,H^2$

[A][5][1] Moment of inertia (axis thro' base): $I = 0.083\ B\,H^3$

Equilateral and isosceles triangles

In an equilateral triangle, $a = b = c$ and all three angles = 60°.

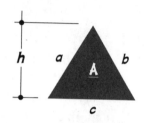

[A][5][2] Height: $h = 0.866\ a$

[A][5][3] Area: $\underline{A} = 0.433\ a^2$

In an isosceles triangle, side a = side b and angle A = angle B.

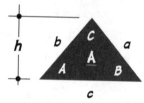

[A][5][4] Height: $h = (a^2 + 0.5\ c^2)^{0.5}$

[A][5][5] Area: $\underline{A} = 0.5\ c\,h = 0.5\ a \sin A$

[A][5][6] $C = 2 \sin^{-1} (0.5\ ^c/_a)$

Fig. A1-3

Hyperbolic functions

Hyperbolic functions combine trigonometry and logarithms as follows:

Hyperbolic functions	Inverse hyperbolic functions
[A][5][7] $\sinh x = 0.5\ (e^x - e^{-x})$	[A][5][8] $\sinh^{-1} x = \log\ [x + (x^2 + 1)^{0.5}]$
[A][5][9] $\cosh x = 0.5\ (e^x + e^{-x})$	[A][6][0] $\cosh^{-1} x = \log\ [x + (x^2 - 1)^{0.5}]$
[A][6][1] $\tanh x = \dfrac{e^x - e^{-x}}{e^x + e^{-x}}$	[A][6][2] $\tanh^{-1} x = 0.5 \log\ \dfrac{1 + x}{1 - x}$
[A][6][3] $\operatorname{csch} x = {}^1/_{\sinh x}$	[A][6][4] $\operatorname{csch}^{-1} x = \log\ \dfrac{1 + (1 + x^2)^{0.5}}{x}$
[A][6][5] $\operatorname{sech} x = {}^1/_{\cosh x}$	[A][6][6] $\operatorname{sech}^{-1} x = \log\ \dfrac{1 + (1 - x^2)^{0.5}}{x}$
[A][6][7] $\coth x = {}^1/_{\tanh x}$	[A][6][8] $\coth^{-1} x = 0.5 \log\ \dfrac{x + 1}{x - 1}$

Four-Sided Figures (Quadrilaterals or Trapeziums)

If a four-sided figure has equal sides and 90° angles, it is a *square*. If it has equal sides and no 90° angles, it is a *rhombus*. If its angles are 90° and its adjacent sides are unequal, it is a *rectangle*. If its adjacent sides are unequal and it has no 90° angles, it is a *rhomboid* or *parallelogram*. If two opposite sides of the figure are parallel, it is a *trapezoid*; if the two remaining sides equal each other, the figure is an *isosceles trapezoid*.

Squares

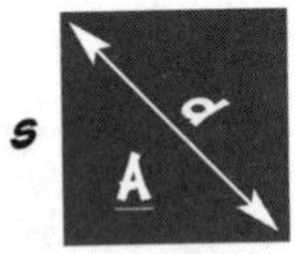

A]6]9] Area: $\underline{A} = s^2 = 0.5\, d^2$

A]7]0] Perimeter: $P = 4\, s$

A]7]1] Length of diagonal:

Fig. A1-4

$d = 1.414\, s = 1.414\, \underline{A}^{0.5} = 0.354\, P$

A]7]2] Length of side: $s = 0.707\, d = \underline{A}^{0.5} = 0.250\, P$

A]7]3] Section modulus (axis thro' center): $S = 0.167\, s^3$

A]7]4] Moment of inertia (axis thro' center): $I = 0.083\, s^4$

A]7]5] Section modulus (axis thro' base): $S = 0.333\, s^3$

A]7]6] Moment of inertia (axis thro' base): $I = 0.333\, s^4$

A]7]7] Section modulus (axis thro' diagonal): $S = 0.118\, s^3$

A]7]8] Moment of inertia (axis thro' diagonal): $I = 0.083\, s^4$

Rectangles

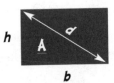

A]7]9] Area: $\underline{A} = b\, h$

A]8]0] Perimeter: $P = 2\, (b + h)$

A]8]1] Length of diagonal:

$d = (b^2 + h^2)^{0.5}$

Fig. A1-5

A]8]2] Length of base: $b = (d^2 - h^2)^{0.5}$

A]8]3] Height: $h = (d^2 - b^2)^{0.5}$

A]8]4] Section modulus (axis thro' center): $S = 0.167\, b\, h^2$

A]8]5] Moment of inertia (axis thro' center): $I = 0.083\, b\, h^3$

A]8]6] Section modulus (axis thro' base): $S = 0.333\, b\, h^2$

A]8]7] Moment of inertia (axis thro' base): $I = 0.333\, b\, h^3$

A]8]8] Section modulus (axis thro' diagonal): $S = \dfrac{0.167\, b^2\, h^2}{(b^2 + h^2)^{0.5}}$

A]8]9] Moment of inertia (axis thro' diagonal): $I = \dfrac{0.167\, b^3\, h^3}{b^2 + h^2}$

Rhombuses

A 9 0 Altitude: $h = s \sin \alpha$
A 9 1 Area: $\underline{A} = s\,h = s^2 \sin \alpha$
A 9 2 Perimeter: $P = 4s$
A 9 3 Length of long diagonal:
$D = 1.414\,s\,(1 - \cos \beta)^{0.5}$
A 9 4 Length of short diagonal: $d = 1.414\,s\,(1 - \cos \alpha)^{0.5}$

Fig. A1-6

Parallelograms

A 9 5 Altitude: $h = r \sin \alpha$
A 9 6 Area: $\underline{A} = rs \sin \alpha$
A 9 7 Perimeter: $P = 2(r + s)$
A 9 8 Length of long diagonal:
$D = (r^2 + s^2 - 2\,rs \cos \beta)^{0.5}$
A 9 9 Length of short diagonal: $d = (r^2 + s^2 - 2\,rs \cos \alpha)^{0.5}$

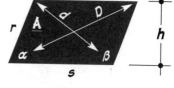

Fig. A1-7

Trapezoids (base parallel to cap)

B 0 0 Area of trapezoid: $\quad\underline{A} = 0.5\,h\,(B + b)$
B 0 1 Length of shorter side: $\quad r = (h^2 + n^2)^{0.5}$
B 0 2 Length of longer side: $\quad s = (h^2 + m^2)^{0.5}$
B 0 3 Length of shorter diagonal: $\quad d = [h^2 + (b + n)^2]^{0.5}$
B 0 4 Length of longer diagonal: $\quad D = [h^2 + (b + m)^2]^{0.5}$
B 0 5 Axis of moments: $\quad A_{mom} = 0.33\,h\,(2B + b)/(B + b)$
B 0 6 Section modulus: $\quad S = 0.083\,h^2\,(b^2 + 4\,b\,B + B^2)/(b + 2B)$
B 0 7 Moment of inertia: $\quad I = 0.0278\,h^3\,(b^2 + 4\,b\,B + B^2)/(b + B)$

B 0 8 Any $\angle$: $\cos \angle = \dfrac{(s_{1st\ side\ of\ \angle})^2 + (s_{2nd\ side\ of\ \angle})^2 - (d_{diag.\ opp.\ \angle})^2}{2\,(s_{1st\ side\ of\ \angle})\,(s_{2nd\ side\ of\ \angle})}$

$\underline{A}$ = area of trapezoid
h = height of trapezoid
B = length of base
b = length of cap,
r = length of short side
s = length of long side
D = length of long diagonal
d = length of short diagonal
S = section modulus, axis thro' ₵, in³
I = moment of inertia, axis thro' ₵, in⁴

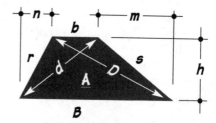

Fig. A1-8

Note: To analyze a trapezium (a trapezoid whose base is not parallel to its cap), divide the figure into two triangles by drawing a diagonal between two opposite corners, then analyze each triangle.

Regular Polygons

A regular polygon is a planar figure that has any number of sides that are all equal and the same number of angles that are all equal. A three-sided regular polygon is an *equilateral triangle*, one with four sides is a *square*, and one with five sides is a *pentagon*. Others are listed below:

6 sides = *hexagon*	7 sides = *heptagon*
8 sides = *octagon*	9 sides = *nonagon* or *enneagon*
10 sides = *decagon*	12 sides = *duodecagon*

The various parts of a regular polygon are described below:

Side (s) = the equal edges that form a polygon's perimeter; their number defines the polygon.

Vertex or *corner* = an angle formed by two adjacent sides.

Base = the side on which the polygon stands.

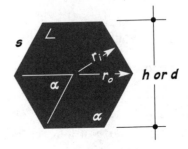

Fig. A1-9

Altitude or *height* (h) = the perpendicular distance from the polygon's base to its highest corner or edge.

Diagonal = a straight line joining any two nonadjacent angles.

Outer radius (R) = distance from the polygon's center to any corner.

Inner radius or *apothem* (r) = distance from the polygon's center to the center of any side: this line is perpendicular to the side.

Interior angle (α) = the inside portion of an outer corner angle formed by two adjacent sides.

Central angle (θ) = an angle formed at the polygon's center by two adjacent radii extending to two adjacent corners.

Inscribed polygon = a regular polygon drawn inside a circle so that its corners coincide with the circle's circumference; also known as a circle described about a polygon.

Circumscribed polygon = a regular polygon drawn outside a circle so the centers of its sides coincide with the circle's circumference; also a polygon described about a circle and a circle inscribed in a polygon.

B)0)9) Perimeter of regular polygon: $P = s\,n$

B)1)0) Central angle: $\angle = 360/n$

B 1 1 Length of outer radius: $r_o = {}^s/_2 \sin (180/n)$

B 1 2 Length of inner radius: $r_i = {}^s/_2 \tan (180/n)$

B 1 3 Interior perimeter angle between two sides: $\angle = 180 (1 - {}^2/_n)$

B 1 4 Area: $A = n\, r_i^2 \tan (180/n)$

B 1 5 Section modulus: $S_{axis} = \dfrac{n\, r_i^3 \tan (180/n)\, [1 + \cos^2 (180/n)]}{12 \cos^2 (180/n)}$

B 1 6 Moment of inertia: $I_{axis} = \dfrac{n\, r_i^4 \tan (180/n)\, [1 + \cos^2 (180/n)]}{12 \cos^2 (180/n)}$

s = length of each side of regular polygon
n = number of sides in regular polygon
α = angle formed by 2 radii extending to 2 adjacent outer corners, °
r_o = length of outer radius (radius to corner) of regular polygon
r_i = length of inner radius (radius to center of side) of reg. polygon
$\angle$ = inner angle formed by two adjacent sides of regular polygon, °
A = area of regular polygon, in² or analogous measure
S = section modulus of regular polygon, in³, axis thro' center of shape
I = moment of inertia of reg. polygon, in⁴, axis thro' center of shape

Planar Curves

A planar curve is a curve that lies in a flat plane and is defined by an algebraic formula. Beginning with the Greeks, mathematicians have developed dozens of these curves. In imaginative hands some may be used to create a number of interesting and useful architectural forms and effects.

Archimedian Spirals

Also known as an *equable* or *coiled rope spiral*, an Archimedean spiral is generated by a point that moves from a fixed point at a constant rate while the radius vector from the fixed point rotates at a constant speed. This curve is easy to construct as follows:

1. Draw a large circle *C* that outlines the maximum size of the volute you want to make.

2. Draw a small square *abcd* of side *s* whose center coincides with the center of the above-drawn volute.

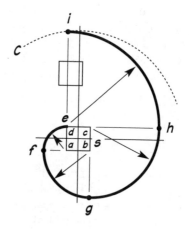

Fig. A1-10

3. Extend the four sides of square *a b c d* to the circumference of the volute drawn in Step 1.
4. Starting at the square's corner *a*, draw a quarter circle from point *e* to point *f* whose radius $r_1 = s$.
5. Starting at the square's corner *b*, draw a second quarter circle *fg* whose radius = 2 *s*.
6. Continue drawing increasingly larger quarter circles as described in steps 4 and 5 until you reach the edge of circle *C*.

When constructed thusly, the volute's length is an arithmetic progression as described below. The spiral's 'coiled rope thickness' = 4 *s*.

B⌋1⌋8⌋ **Length of spiral from *a* to *P*:** $S = 57.3 \frac{r}{\angle} = 1.57 \, s \, n \, (n + 1)$

S = length of Archimedean or 'rope' spiral from center to outer end
r = radius of spiral at outer end
$\angle$ = total angle (deg.) swept by by spiral's length
s = length of side of central square at spiral's origin
n = number of quarter circles from start to end of spiral

Logarithmic Spirals

Also known as an *equiangular spiral*, this curve is formed by a radial vector that steadily increases in length in a geometric progression as it sweeps outward through successively equal angles around a fixed point. This spiral appears in the chambered nautilus, florets of a sunflower, petals of a pine cone, curl of a ram's horn, and many other natural forms. Variations of this beautiful whorl have appeared in architecture from the Ionic column volutes of Greece to *Le Modulor* of Le Corbusier, and it is the geometry of the Golden Section.

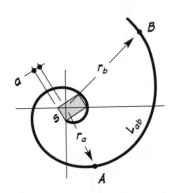

Fig. A1-11

B⌋1⌋9⌋ **Length of spiral from any pt. A to any pt. B:**

$$s \, L_{ab} = (r_b - r_a)(s^2 + 1)^{0.5}$$

B⌋2⌋0⌋ **Area of any zone of spiral *A O B*:** $A_{aob} = \frac{(r_B - r_A)}{4} a$

s = length of shorter side of rectangle at spiral's origin. $s = 0.618 \, a$.
L_{ab} = length of logarithmic spiral from any point *A* to any point *B*
r_a = radius of spiral at point *A*
r_b = radius of spiral at point *B*
A_{aob} = area of zone of spiral enclosed by point *A*, center *0*, and point *B*

Catenaries

Also known as a *chainette*, a catenary is the natural curve that a wire takes when its length is suspended between two points. Thus its formula is useful in determining the lengths and sags of installed wires and cables. Due to the complexity of the catenary's formula, its curves have customarily been analyzed in terms of the parabola, which, although is nearly as accurate, is fundamentally different. For example, an inverted catenary is a true arch but an inverted parabola is not. But now that the catenary formula is computerized, this curve will hopefully regain its rightfully important place in architecture.

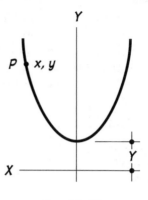

Fig. A1-12

[B]2]1] **Equation of catenary:**

$$y = a \cosh{}^{x}/_{a} = 0.5\, a\, (e^{x/a} + e^{-x/a})$$

[B]2]2] **Length from vertex to any point *P* on the curve:**

$$2 \sinh{}^{x}/_{a} = e^{x/a} - e^{-x/a}$$

y = length of ordinate or *Y* coordinate to any point on curve
a = length from *X* axis to *Y*-intercept of curve
x = length of abscissa or *X* coordinate to any point on curve
e = base of natural logarithm, = 2.71828

Sine Curves

On a rectangular graph this curve is generated by the sine of an angle wherein the curve's Y-intercept = 0 and its ordinate's maximum and minimum values are +1 and –1. This curve is easily generated trigonometrically, and the arch formed its first half can be architecturally useful.

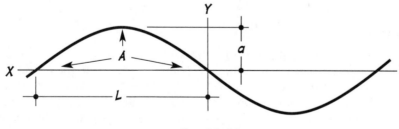

Fig. A1-13

[B]2]3] **Equation of sine curve:** $y = a \sin (3.14\, {}^{x}/_{L})$

B)2)4) Area under one arch of sine curve: $\quad A = 0.637\, a\, L$

x = length of X coordinate from origin to any point P on sine curve
y = length of Y coordinate from origin to any point P on sine curve
a = height of sine curve at apogee; also height of arch
A = area enclosed by one-half of sine curve and X-axis
L = length of one-half of sine curve along x-axis

Cycloids

This curve is generated by a point on the edge of a circle or wheel as it rolls across a flat surface. The curve also serves admirably as the profile of a low arch.

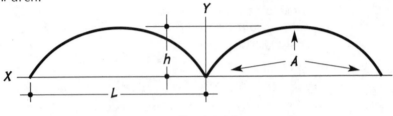

Fig. A1-14

B)2)5) Equation of cycloid:
$$x = 0.5\, h \cos^{-1}[(h - 2y)/h] - (h\, y - y^2)^{0.5}$$
B)2)6) Length of one arch of cycloid: $\quad L = 4\, h$
B)2)7) Area under one arch of cycloid: $\quad A = 4.71\, h^2$

x = length of X coordinate from origin to any point P on curve
y = length of Y coordinate from origin to any point P on curve
h = height of cycloid at its apogee
L = length of one arch of cycloid
A = area enclosed by one arch of cycloid and X-axis

Lemniscates

Also known as the *Lemniscate of Bernoulli* or the *Oval of Cassini*, this graceful closed curve is generated by a point that moves so the product of its distances from two foci A and B remains constant. A variation of this curve is known as a *two-leaved rose*, which is related to a family of *rose curves* known as *three-leaved roses, four-leaved roses*, etc., depending on the number of foci the curve moves around as it is generated.

B)2)8) Equation of lemniscate: $\quad (x^2 + y^2)^2 = a^2 (x^2 - y^2)$
B)2)9) Total area of lemniscate: $\quad A = 8\, a$

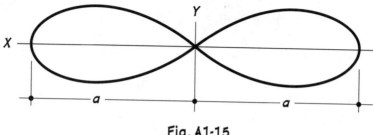

Fig. A1-15

x = length of X coordinate from origin to any point on lemniscate
y = length of Y coordinate from origin to any point on lemniscate
a = length of one petal of lemniscate from origin to tip of X-axis
A = area enclosed by both petals of lemniscate

Conic Sections

Imagine going to your water cooler and removing two conical paper cups. Place one cone upside-down on a table, then place the other right-side-up above the first so their apexes just touch, their axes are vertical and align, and their tops and bottoms are parallel to each other. You would now have a conical construction as sketched in Fig. A1-16.

Now pass a plane through these cones. Depending on the plane's angle to the cones you will create one of four basic geometric curves: a *circle, ellipse, parabola,* or *hyperbola.* This royal family of curves, known as *conic sections,* is described in detail below.

Fig. A1-16

Circles

A circle is a locus of points equidistant from a fixed point, wherein the equidistance is the circle's *radius* and the fixed point is its *center.* A small part of a circle's radius is an *arc,* an area of a circle bounded by an arc and its end radii is a *sector,* and an area of a circle bounded by an arc and a chord is a *segment.*

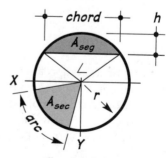

Fig. A1-17

B 3 0 Equation of circle (center at $x = 0$ and $y = 0$): $r^2 = x^2 + y^2$

B 3 1 Area of circle: $\quad A = 0.785\,\delta^2$

B 3 2 Circumference: $\quad c = 3.14\,\delta$

B 3 3 Length of arc: $\quad \overset{\frown}{a} = 0.00873\,\delta\angle$

B 3 4 Length of chord: $\quad e = \delta\sin 0.5\angle$

B 3 5 Height of segment: $\quad h = \delta\,(0.5 - \cos 0.5\,\angle)$

B 3 6 Area of segment: $\quad A_{seg} = 0.00873\,r^2\angle - (r - r\cos 0.5\,\angle)^2$

B 3 7 Area of sector: $\quad A_{sec} = 0.00873\,r^2\angle$

B 3 8 Section modulus of circle, axis thro' center: $\quad S = 0.0982\,\delta^2$

B 3 9 Moment of inertia of circle, axis thro' center: $\quad I = 0.0491\,\delta^2$

A = area of circle
c = circumference of circle
e = length of chord of circle
$\angle$ = central angle subtended by arc, chord, segment, or sector of circle, °

δ = diameter of circle
$\overset{\frown}{a}$ = length of arc of circle
h = height of segment of circle

Ellipses

An ellipse is a locus of points placed so the sum of their distances from two fixed points is a constant wherein each fixed point is a *focus*.

B 4 0 Equation of ellipse (center at $x = 0$ and $y = 0$): $\dfrac{x^2}{a^2} + \dfrac{y^2}{b^2} = 1$

B 4 1 Area of ellipse: $\quad A = 3.14\,a\,b$

B 4 2 Circumference:
$$c = 4.44\,(a^2 + b^2)^{0.5}$$

B 4 3 Section modulus: $\quad S = 0.785\,a^2\,b$

B 4 4 Moment of inertia: $\quad I = 0.785\,a^3\,b$

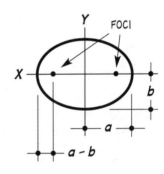

Fig. A1-18

a = length of major axis of ellipse
b = length of minor axis of ellipse

Parabolas

A parabola is a locus of points equidistant from a fixed point and a fixed line wherein the fixed point is the *focus* and the fixed line is the *directrix*. Although a parabola looks very similar to a catenary, the two curves are fundamentally different. A parabola represents the focussing of incoming parallel rays upon its focus and thus is useful in reflector geometry; while a catenary is the natural curve that a wire or cable makes when its length is suspended between two points.

Equation of parabola (center of curve at $x = 0$ and $y = 0$):

B|4|5) $x = \kappa\, y^2$ when parabola opens to the left or right

B|4|6) $y = \kappa\, x^2$ when parabola opens up or down

B|4|7)   Area of parabola: $A = 1.33\, a\, b$

B|4|8)   Height of centroid above base:
$$\mathcal{C}_p = 0.40\, a$$

B|4|9)   Section modulus about X axis:
$$S_X = 0.152\, a^2\, b$$

B|5|0)   Section modulus about Y axis:
$$S_Y = 0.267\, a\, b^2$$

B|5|1)   Section modulus about base:
$$S_{base} = 0.305\, a^2\, b$$

B|5|2)   Moment of inertia about X axis:
$$I_X = 0.0914\, a^3\, b$$

B|5|3)   Moment of inertia about Y axis:
$$I_Y = 0.267\, a\, b^3$$

B|5|4)   Moment of inertia about base:
$$I_{base} = 0.305\, a^3\, b$$

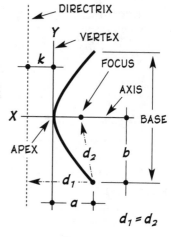

Fig. A1-19

B|5|5)   Length of parabola:
$$s = b \left\{ \left[\frac{4\,a^2}{b^2} + 1 \right]^{0.5} + \frac{0.5\,b}{a} \log \left[\frac{2\,a}{b} + \left(\frac{4\,a^2}{b^2} + 1 \right)^{0.5} \right] \right\}$$

a = height of parabola
b = 0.5 base: width of parabola base from axis to one edge
s = length of parabola between ends of *base*
$\mathcal{C}_p$ = length of parabola's axis from apex to centroid

Hyperbolas

A hyperbola is a locus of points placed about two fixed points, or *foci*, so the difference in distance between each point and the two fixed points is constant. A hyperbola looks much like two back-to-back parabolas. Many architectural forms, from hypars to nuclear cooling towers, are generated from its geometry.

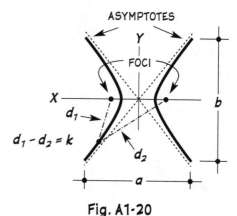

Fig. A1-20

Hyperbola equations (centers of curves at $x = 0$ and $y = 0$):

B56 When hyperbola opens to left or right: $x^2/a^2 - y^2/b^2 = 1$

B57 When hyperbola opens up or down: $y^2/b^2 - x^2/a^2 = 1$

a = horiz. distance between the two hyperbolic curves on the X-axis when their asymptotes are centered at the origin ($x = 0$ and $y = 0$).

b = vertical distance from X-axis to the top of a rectangle of width a whose top corners align with the hyperbola's asymptotes.

Solid Geometry

Rectangular Solids

Also known as a *rectangular* or *right parallelepiped*, a rectangular solid is a six-sided geometric figure whose every side is a rectangle. Thus the six sides together have 4 "X" edges, 4 "Y" edges, and 4 "Z" edges; and the four edges in each orthogonal direction are equal and parallel to each other. At any corner the angle formed by the three orthogonal planes is a *trihedral angle*; wherein the planes' point of intersection is the angle's vertex, the planes' intersecting faces are the angle's *edges*, the angle between any two adjacent edges is a *face angle*, and the angle between two intersecting faces is a *dihedral angle*. This nomenclature is the same for any geometric solid whose surface is made of planar faces. A trihedral angle is also a three-faced polyhedral angle, while a four-faced polyhedral angle is a *tetrahedral angle*; a five-faced one is a *pentahedral angle*, and so on.

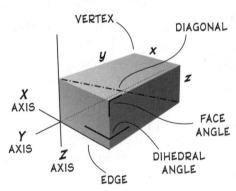

Fig. A1-21

B58 Surface area of rectangular solid: $A = 2(xy + xz + yz)$

B59 Volume of rectangular solid: $V = xyz$

B60 Diagonal of rectangular solid: $d = (x^2 + y^2 + z^2)^{0.5}$

x = length of side of rectangular solid that is parallel to X-axis
y = length of side of rectangular solid that is parallel to Y-axis
x = length of side of rectangular solid that is parallel to Z-axis
d = length of diagonal of rectangular solid

Pyramids

A pyramid has a polygonal base with a line extending from each corner to a common apex above. In a regular pyramid the base is a regular polygon and the apex is directly above its center. A three-sided pyramid is a triangular pyramid; a four-sided one may be square, rhombic, rectangular, or parallelogramic; and ones with five, six, and seven sides are pentagonal, hexagonal, and heptagonal. The largest pyramid ever built is the Pyramid of Cheops in Egypt 4,600 years ago: its base is 756 ft square and its altitude is 481 ft. If a plane parallel to a pyramid's base passes between its base and its apex and the solid above is removed, the remaining figure is a *frustum of a pyramid*.

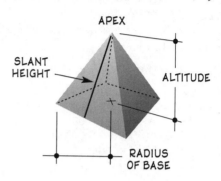

Fig. A1-22

$\boxed{B}\boxed{6}\boxed{1}$ Total surface area

of regular pyramid: $A = 0.50\, n\, r^2 \sin (360/n) + 0.50\, s\, n\, b$

$\boxed{B}\boxed{6}\boxed{2}$ Volume of regular pyramid: $V = 0.167\, h\, n\, r^2 \sin (360/n)$

$\boxed{B}\boxed{6}\boxed{3}$ Total surface area of frustum of regular pyramid:

$A_f = 0.50\, s$ (lower base perimeter + upper base perimeter) $+ 0.50\, (B_l + B_u)$

$\boxed{B}\boxed{6}\boxed{4}$ Volume of frustum of regular pyramid:

$$V_f = 0.333\, h\, [B_l + B_u + (B_l\, B_u)^{0.5}]$$

n = number of sides in base of regular pyramid
r = radius of base: length from center of base to each corner
s = slant height of each lateral face of regular pyramid: distance from center of each face's base to pyramid's apex
b = length of side of base of regular pyramid
B_l = area of lower base [$= 0.5\, n\, r^2 \sin (360/n)$] of frustum of pyramid
B_u = area of upper base of frustum of pyramid

Cylinders

A cylinder is generated by a straight line that traces a closed curve of any shape that lies between two parallel end planes or bases. The resulting form may be as tall and thin as a metal rod, or as short and wide as a manhole cover. If the curve is a circle the figure is a *circular cylinder*; if its sides are perpendicular to the planes it is a *right cylinder;* and if the sides extend at an angle between the end planes the figure is an *oblique cylinder*. In a circular right cylinder, the circle's axis extends through the cylinder's center; then the axis' length and the circle's radius define the solid. The area of the side is the cylinder's *lateral area*, the sums of the two base areas is its *base area*, and the sums of the lateral and base areas are its *total area*. A cylinder may also be cut lengthwise to form a trough or tunnel shape.

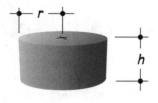

Fig. A1-23

B 6 5   Lateral surface area of circular cylinder: $S = 6.28\,r\,h$

B 6 6   Total surface area of circular cylinder: $A = 6.28\,r\,(r+h)$

B 6 7   Volume of circular cylinder: $V = 3.14\,r^2\,h$

r = radius of base of circular cylinder
h = height of cylinder: perpendicular distance between end planes

Cones

A cone has a base that is a closed curve and a continuous side that slopes upward and inward to its apex. A *circular cone* is one whose base is a circle; a *right cone* is one whose axis is perpendicular to its base, an *equilateral cone* is a right circular cone whose slanted side equals the diameter of its base, and a *oblique cone* is one whose axis is not perpendicular to its base. If a plane parallel to the cone's base passes between its apex and base and the solid above is removed, the remaining solid is a *frustum of a cone*, and the length of the sloping side is its *slant height*.

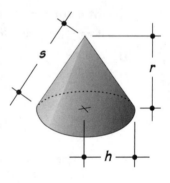

Fig. A1-24

B 6 8   Lateral surface area of right circular cone:
   $$S = 3.14\,r\,s = 1.57\,\delta\,s$$

B 6 9   Total surface area of right circular cone:
   $$A = 3.14\,r\,(r+s)$$

B 7 0   Volume of right circular cone:
   $$V = 1.047\,r^2\,h$$

B 7 1   Lateral surface area of frustum of right circular cone:
   $$S_f = 3.14\,s\,(r+r_u)$$

B 7 2   Volume of frustum of right circular cone:
   $$V_f = 1.047\,h\,(r^2 + r_u^2 + r\,r_u) = 0.262\,h\,(\delta^2 + \delta_u^2 + \delta\,\delta_u)$$

r = radius of base of right circular cone
s = slant height of right circ. cone: distance from edge of base to apex
δ = diameter of base of right circular cone
h = height or altitude of right circular cone
r_u = radius of upper base of frustum of right circular cone

Spheres

A sphere is a closed surface whose every point is equidistant from a fixed point within. The sphere's surface-to-central point length is its *radius*, and a line passing through its center and terminating at the two opposite surfaces is the sphere's *diameter*. A sphere is usually defined by the location of its center and length of its radius.

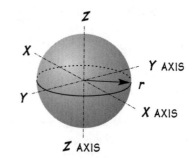

Fig. A1-25

On a sphere a *great circle* is any circle whose plane passes through the sphere's center, and a *small circle* is a similar circle that does not pass through its center. Each such circle can be divided into 360 units called *spherical degrees* or *spherids*. Every such circle has an *axis*, a perpendicular line that passes through the center of the circle and the sphere, and each axis has two *poles* which lie on the sphere's surface. Each great circle also consists of two semicircles or *meridians*, each of which has a *longitudinal axis* that passes through the sphere's center. When two meridians have a longitudinal axis-in-common and a small space between them, the portion of the sphere's surface bounded by the two meridians is a *lune*; and the lemon-slice-shaped volume enclosed by the lune, the two meridians on each side, and the longitudinal axis is a *spherical wedge*.

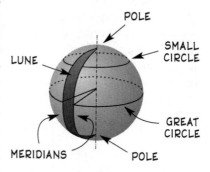

Fig. A1-26

On a sphere's surface, the shortest distance between any two points is an *arc*, whose radius is the sphere's

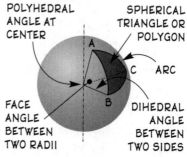

Fig. A1-27

radius. Three contiguous arcs form a *spherical triangle*, in which the three radii extending from the triangle's angles to the sphere's center form the triangle's *polyhedral angle*. Spherical triangles can be *right*, *acute*, *obtuse*, *isosceles*, and *equilateral*; and each is also a *spherical polygon*. All spherical polygons have a central polyhedral angle whose vertex is at the sphere's center, and the volume enclosed by a spherical polygon and the faces between the radii of its polyhedral angle is a *spherical pyramid*. Since a spherical triangle's outer surface is convex, the sum of the triangle's three angles is always more than 180°. For example, if a spherical triangle is drawn on the earth's surface with vertices at (1) the North Pole (90° lat.), (2) Quito, Ecuador (±0° Lat. ±80° W. Long.), and (3) Libreville, Gabon (±0° Lat. ±10° E. Long.), each vertex would equal 90° and their sum would be 270°. In such a triangle, the number of degrees exceeding 180° is its *spherical excess*.

If a sphere is cut by a planar section, the volume above the section's circular outline is a *spherical segment*. If the sphere is cut by two parallel planes, the surface area between the planes' circular outlines is a *zone*, and the volume of the sphere between the two planes is a *spherical zone*. If a zone's two circles extend toward the sphere's center and form two conical surfaces between the circles and the center, the volume between the cones is a *zonal sector*. Also, the volume enclosed by either cone and the sphere's outer surface is a *spherical cone*.

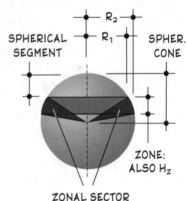

Fig. A1-28

B|7|3| Area of sphere: $A = 12.57\ r^2$

B|7|4| Area of spherical lune: $A_L = 0.0349\ r^2\ \angle$

B|7|5| Total area of spherical wedge: $A_w = r^2\ (3.14 + 0.0349\ \angle)$

B|7|6| Area of base (outer surface) of spherical polygon:

$$A_B = 0.0175\ r^2\ E$$

B|7|7| Lateral (side) area of spherical polygon: $A_L = 0.00873\ r^2\ \angle_n$

B|7|8| Total surface area of spherical sector:

$$A_{ss} = 3.14\ r\ [2\ h_s + (h_s^2 + 2\ r\ h_s)^{0.5}]$$

B|7|9| Area of base of spherical segment: $A_B = 6.28\ r\ h_s$

B|8|0| Lateral (dome) area of spher. segment: $A_L = 3.14\ h_s\ (2\ r - h_s)$

B|8|1| Total surface area of spher. zone: $A_z = 3.14\ (2\ r\ h_z + r_1^2 + r_2^2)$

B|8|2| Height of spherical zone: $h_z = (r^2 - r_1^2)^{0.5} - (r^2 - r_2^2)^{0.5}$

$\boxed{B}\boxed{8}\boxed{3}$ Area of base (outer surface) of spher. cone: $A_b = 0.0349\ r^2\ \angle$

$\boxed{B}\boxed{8}\boxed{4}$ Lateral surface area (radial side) of spherical cone:
$$A_L = 3.14\ r^2\ (3\ r^2 - 2\ r\ h_c - h_c{}^2)^{0.5}$$

$\boxed{B}\boxed{8}\boxed{5}$ Volume of sphere: $V_s = 4.19\ r^3$

$\boxed{B}\boxed{8}\boxed{6}$ Volume of spherical wedge: $V_w = 0.0116\ r^3 \angle$

$\boxed{B}\boxed{8}\boxed{7}$ Volume of spherical polygon: $V_p = 0.00582\ r^3\ E$

$\boxed{B}\boxed{8}\boxed{8}$ Volume of spherical sector: $V_{sec} = 2.094\ r^2\ h_s$

$\boxed{B}\boxed{8}\boxed{9}$ Volume of spherical segment: $V_{seg} = 3.14\ h_s{}^2\ (r + 0.33\ h_s)$

$\boxed{B}\boxed{9}\boxed{0}$ Volume of spherical zone: $V_z = 0.524\ h_z\ (3\ r_1{}^2 + 3\ r_2{}^2 + h_z{}^2)$

$\boxed{B}\boxed{9}\boxed{1}$ Volume of spherical cone: $V_c = 2.094\ r^2\ h_c$

$\boxed{B}\boxed{9}\boxed{2}$ Volume of hollow sphere: $V_h = 4.19\ (r_o{}^2 - r_i{}^2)$

r = radius of sphere
$\angle$ = central angle formed by the radial sides of a spherical lune, wedge, sector, segment, or cone, °
E = spherical excess. This equals the sum of a spherical polygon's face angles – 180 × (polygon's number of sides – 2).
$\angle_n$ = sum of a spherical polygon's face angles; each angle equals 0.0174 × length of its arc ÷ r
h_s = height of spherical sector or spherical segment from plane of base to surface of sphere
h_z = height of spherical zone between planes of inner and outer bases
h_c = height of spherical cone from center of sphere to the plane enclosed by cone's rim
r_1, r_2 = outer (smaller) or inner (larger) radius of spherical zone
r_o, r_i = outer (larger) or inner (smaller) radius of hollow zone

Curves of Revolution

A curve of revolution is a symmetrical planar curve that is rotated about its axis to create a three-dimensional volume. A few such curves and variations thereof are briefly described below.

Spheroids

Also known as *ellipsoids of revolution*, spheroids are geometric solids formed by rotating an ellipse about one of its axes. If the ellipse is rotated about its major or longer axis, the figure formed is a *prolate spheroid*, a shape that resembles a cigar or football; if rotated about its shorter or minor axis, the figure formed is an *oblate spheroid*, a shape that resembles a cushion or round pillow.

B)9)3) Surface area of prolate spheroid:
$$A_p = 6.28\, a\,(a + b)$$

B)9)4) Volume of prolate spheroid:
$$V_p = 0.524\, a\, b^2$$

B)9)5) Surface area of oblate spheroid:
$$A_p = 12.57\, a\, b$$

B)9)6) Volume of oblate spheroid:
$$V_o = 0.524\, a^2\, b$$

a = length of one-half of major axis of ellipse that generates spheroid

b = length of one-half of minor axis of ellipse that generates spheroid

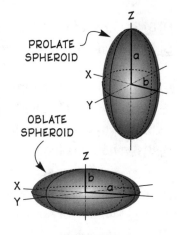

Fig. A1-29

Paraboloid of Revolution

A paraboloid of revolution is a parabola that is generated about its major axis. Thus if the figure's axis is vertical it has two surfaces: a nose-cone-like dome of a certain height and a flat circular base of a certain radius. If the base is elliptical, the solid is an *elliptic paraboloid*.

B)9)7) Volume of paraboloid of revolution: $V = 1.571\, a\, b^2$

a = length of axis of paraboloid of revolution from base to apex
b = radius of circular base of paraboloid of revolution

Hyperboloid of Revolution

A hyperboloid of revolution is one-half of a hyperbola that is generated about its major axis. If the figure's axis is vertical, it has a dome of a certain height and a flat circular base of a certain radius. If its base is elliptical, the shape is an *elliptic hyperboloid*.

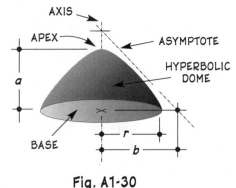

Fig. A1-30

B)9)8) Volume of hyperboloid of revolution: $V = 0.524\, a\,(r^2 + b^2)$

a = length of axis of hyperboloid of revolution from base to apex
r = radius of circular base of hyperboloid of revolution
b = radial distance of hyperboloid of revolution in a direction parallel to its base from its apex to one of its asymptotes.

Torus

Also known as a *circular ring*, this figure is generated by a circular plane whose center moves around a larger circular axis whose plane is centered on a perpendicular axle. Thus as the smaller circle revolves around the larger, its circumference evolves a doughnut-shaped geometric solid.

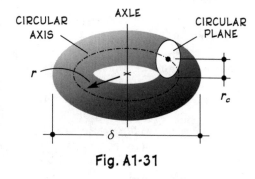

Fig. A1-31

$\boxed{B}\boxed{9}\boxed{9}$ Outer diameter of torus: $\delta = 2(r^2 + r_c)$

$\boxed{C}\boxed{0}\boxed{0}$ Surface area of torus: $A = 39.48\ r\ r_c$

$\boxed{C}\boxed{0}\boxed{1}$ Volume of torus: $V = 19.74\ r\ r_c^2$

r = radius from central axle to center of smaller circle of revolution
r_c = radius of smaller circle of revolution

Polyhedrons

A polyhedron is a geometric solid formed by four or more intersecting planes or faces. The planes' intersections are the polyhedron's *edges*, the intersecting edges form the polyhedron's *vertices*, the exterior formed by all the planes is the polyhedron's *surface*, the interior is its *volume*, and a straight line extending between any two vertices not in the same face is a *diagonal*. A four-faced polyhedron is a tetrahedron, a five-faced one is a pentahedron, and so on. A *prismoid* is a polyhedron whose ends are irregular but parallel polygons and whose sides are quadrilaterals; and a *prism* is a polyhedron whose ends are same-sized parallel polygons and whose sides are rectangles or parallelograms. A prism is generated by a straight line that moves perpendicular to its ends; then the line is the shape's *genetrix* and the ends are its *directrix*. The sums of the areas of a prism's sides is its *lateral area*, the sums of the two bases is its *base area*, and the sums of all areas is its *total area*. The least number of faces a prism can have is five: two triangular bases and three sides. A prism is generally classed by the shape of its base: e.g. triangular, isosceles triangular, rhombic, regular hexagonal, etc. A *parallelepiped* is an oblique prism with parallelogram bases. When an right isosceles triangular prism is laid on its nonequal side, it becomes a 'pup-tent' prism; and when an external plane is passed obliquely through a prism's sides and the portion above the plane is removed, the portion below is a truncated prism. Thus a common shed is a truncated rectangular parallelepiped. Below are important terms for prisms.

Base = one or both of a prism's polygonal ends.

Lateral edge = a line that joins two congruent vertices of the bases and forms a seam between two adjacent sides. A prism's lateral edges are parallel and equal.

Right prism = one whose side edges are perpendicular to its bases.

Oblique prism = one whose side edges are not perpendicular to its bases; also called a leaning or 'Pisa' prism.

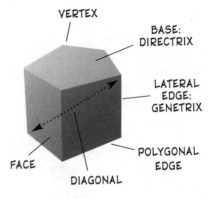

Fig. A1-32

Regular prism = one whose bases are regular polygons.

Convex prism = one whose two bases have one or more vertices whose interior angle is greater than 180°.

Concave prism = one whose two bases have no vertices whose interior angle is greater than 180°; also known as a common prism.

Altitude or *height* = the perpendicular length between a prism's bases.

C)0)2) Total surface area of prism: $A = Ph + 2B$

C)0)3) Volume of prism: $V = Bh$

P = perimeter of regular polygonal base of prism
B = area of regular polygonal base of prism
h = height of prism's sides between its parallel bases

Regular Polyhedrons

Also known as the *Platonic solids*, these are five polyhedrons whose every face is a regular polygon, whose every edge is equal, and whose every vertex is equal as well. These figures are the tetrahedron, hexahedron (cube), octahedron, dodecahedron, and icosahedron. An important equation for each of these figures is the following:

number of faces + number of vertices = number of edges + 2

Regular polyhedron	Shape of face	No. elements in each figure		
		Faces	Vertices	Edges
Tetrahedron	equilateral triangle	4	4	6
Hexahedron	square	6	8	12
Octahedron	equilateral triangle	8	6	12
Dodaceahedron	regular pentagon	12	20	30
Icosahedron	equilateral triangle	20	12	30

As befits solids as symbolic as these, the formulas for their surfaces and volumes are the simplest possible: one constant, one variable.

C)0)4)	Surface area of tetrahedron:	$A = 1.732\ e^2$
C)0)5)	Surface area of hexahedron:	$A = 6.000\ e^2$
C)0)6)	Surface area of octahedron:	$A = 3.464\ e^2$
C)0)7)	Surface area of dodecahedron:	$A = 20.65\ e^2$
C)0)8)	Surface area of icosahedron:	$A = 8.660\ e^2$
C)0)9)	Volume of tetrahedron:	$V = 0.118\ e^3$
C)1)0)	Volume of hexahedron:	$V = 1.000\ e^3$
C)1)1)	Volume of octahedron:	$V = 0.471\ e^3$
C)1)2)	Volume of dodecahedron:	$V = 7.663\ e^3$
C)1)3)	Volume of icosahedron:	$V = 2.182\ e^3$

Physics and Mechanics

Relation between air pressure, temperature, and volume

C)1)4)
$$PV = 53.3\ T$$

P = absolute pressure, psi
V = volume of 1 lb of air at the given pressure and temperature, cf
T = absolute temperature of air, ° Rankin

Flow of air in pipes or ducts

C)1)5)
$$L\,v^2 = 1{,}563\ \delta\,\Delta P$$

L = length of pipe or duct, ft
v = velocity of airflow, fps. $v = 0.00694 \times$ airflow volume (cfm) $\times$ section area of pipe or duct (in^2).
δ = inside diameter of pipe or round duct, in. If duct is square, $\delta = 1.13\ s$. If duct is rectangular, $\delta = 1.129\ (a\ b)^{0.5}$.
ΔP = pressure drop due to flow friction, or difference in pressure at the two ends of the pipe or duct, psi

Horsepower required to drive air through pipes or ducts

C)1)6)
$$4{,}752{,}000\ HP = Q\,\Delta P$$

HP = horsepower required to drive air through pipe or duct, HP

Q = volume of airflow, cfm. $Q = 144 \times$ airflow velocity (fpm) ÷ section area of pipe or duct (interior dimension, in²).
ΔP = pressure drop due to flow friction, psi

Kinetic energy stored in a cylindrical flywheel

C 1 7 $480,000,000 \; \epsilon = \sigma \, w \, R^2 \, (\delta_r - \delta_b)(\delta_r + \delta_b)^3$

ϵ = total kinetic energy stored in flywheel, ft·lb
σ = specific gravity of flywheel material
w = width of flywheel, in.
R = number of revolutions per minute of flywheel, rpm
δ_r = outer diameter of flywheel at its rim, in.
δ_b = inner diameter of flywheel at its bore, in.

Rotational velocity of a cylindrical flywheel

C 1 8 $20.6 \, f_t = v^2 \, [4.33 + (\delta_b/\delta_r)^2]$

f_t = safe tensile stress of flywheel material, psi
v = maximum rim velocity of flywheel, fps
δ_b = inner diameter of flywheel at its bore, in.
δ_r = outer diameter of flywheel at its rim, in.

Motor pulley formula

C 1 9 $\delta_m \, rpm_m = \delta_d \, rpm_d$

δ_m = diameter of motor pulley, in.
rpm_m = revolutions per minute of motor pulley, rpm
δ_d = diameter of driver pulley, in.
rpm_d = revolutions per minute of driver pulley, rpm

Volume of a cylinder (tank or wire)

C 2 0 $Q = 5.875 \, h \, \delta^2$

Q = volume of liquid in cylindrical tank or pipe, gal
h = height of tank or length of pipe, ft
δ = diameter of cylindrical tank or pipe, ft

Relation between torque and horsepower

C 2 1   Torque × motor rpm = 5,250 HP

Ohm's Law

C|2|2|

$$\text{volts} = \text{amps} \times \text{ohms}$$

C|2|3|

$$\text{watts} = \text{amps} \times \text{volts}$$

Flow of water in pipes or ducts

This formula is accurate to within ± 5 percent for well-constructed piping.

C|2|4|

$$v^2 (L + 4.5 \, \delta) = 300 \, \kappa_\delta \, h \, \delta$$

v = velocity of waterflow, fps. $v = 0.00694 \times$ waterflow volume (cfm) × section area of pipe or duct (in^2).

L = length of pipe, ft

δ = inside diameter of pipe, in.

κ_δ = diameter coefficient, based on inside pipe diameter. κ_δ = 381 for ½ in. dia., 442 for ¾ in, 500 for 1 in, 630 for 1½ in, 750 for 2 in, 880 for 2½ in, 1,000 for 3 in, 1,230 for 4 in, 1,600 for 6 in, and 1,880 for 8 in. dia.

h = total head or height of flow, ft

Hazen-Williams Formula

C|2|5|

$$h_f = 0.00576 \left[v /_{\kappa_p} \, r_h^{0.63} \right]^{1.85}$$

h_f = equiv. head pressure loss due to flow friction, ft of water/LF of pipe

v = velocity of waterflow, fpm. $v_{fpm} = 60 \, v_{fps}$. $v_{fpm} = 0.00694 \times$ waterflow volume (cfm) × section area of pipe (in^2).

κ_p = a constant based on the type and condition of pipe. κ_p for new copper pipe = 130, for new concrete pipe = 100.

r_h = hydraulic radius of pipe, in.

Manning Formula

C|2|6|

$$h_f = 0.00343 \, \rho^2 \, v^2 /_{r_h^{1.33}}$$

h_f = equiv. head pressure loss due to flow friction, ft of water/LF of pipe

ρ = roughness coefficient: a constant depending on the kind and condition of pipe. ρ = 0.011 for new concrete pipe and 0.012 for new vitrified clay pipe.

v = velocity of waterflow, fpm. $v_{fpm} = 60 \, v_{fps}$. $v_{fpm} = 0.00694 \times$ waterflow volume (cfm) × section area of pipe (in^2).

r_h = hydraulic radius of pipe, in.

Pump horsepower

C｜2｜7｜ $3{,}960\, \mathcal{E}\, \text{HP} = \sigma\, h\, \rho$

C｜2｜8｜ $1{,}713\, \mathcal{E}\, \text{HP} = \sigma\, P\, \rho$

$\mathcal{E}$ = pump efficiency, % ÷ 100
HP = pump horsepower, HP
σ = specific gravity of liquid being pumped
h = height or head of liquid being pumped, ft.
　　(Head of water in ft = 2.31 psi).
ρ = volume of pipe flow, gpm
P = pressure of liquid being pumped, psi

Pump or motor power

C｜2｜9｜ $746\, \text{HP} = \mathcal{E}\, \Omega$

C｜3｜0｜ $746\, \text{HP}_1 = \kappa_p\, \mathcal{E}\, A\, V$

C｜3｜1｜ $431\, \text{HP}_3 = \kappa_p\, \mathcal{E}\, A\, V$

HP = output horsepower, HP. HP_1 = horsepower (single phase); HP_3 =
　　horsepower (3 phase)
κ_p = motor power factor
$\mathcal{E}$ = motor efficiency, % ÷ 100
Ω = input wattage, watts
A = nameplate or input amperage, amps
V = nameplate or input voltage, volts

Relation between pipe flow and pressure drop

C｜3｜2｜ $h_1\, Q_2{}^2 = h_2\, Q_1{}^2$

h_1 = relative height of piping, ft
Q_1 = fluid pipe flow at height 1, gpm
h_2 = height of piping above or below height 1, ft
Q_2 = fluid pipe flow at height 2, gpm

Velocity of fluid flowing in a pipe

C｜3｜3｜ $v\, \delta^2 = 0.41\, Q$

v = velocity of fluid in pipe, fpm
δ = interior diameter of pipe, in.
Q = volume of pipe flow, gpm

General physics formulas and relations

Density = $^{mass}/_{volume}$ Power = $^{work}/_{time}$

Distance = velocity × time   Net force = mass × acceleration

Work = force × distance   Kinetic energy = 0.5 mass × velocity^2

Acceleration = $\dfrac{\text{final velocity − initial velocity}}{\text{time}}$

Distance = initial velocity × time + 0.5 acceleration × time^2
Heat energy = mass × specific heat × change in temperature
Standard air at room temperature is about 1/830th as heavy as water.

Air compression formulas

The first formula below is used for compressors of any number of stages, while the second is used to compute the horsepower required to compress isothermally a given volume of free air to a given pressure.

$\boxed{\text{C}}\boxed{3}\boxed{4}$ $HP = 0.015\ s\ P\,[(P_t/p)^{0.29} - 1]$

$\boxed{\text{C}}\boxed{3}\boxed{5}$ $229\ HP = P\,V\log_e (P_t/p)$

HP = horsepower generated by compression stages, HP
s = number of stages of compression, usually 1, 2, 3, or 4
P = atmospheric pressure, psi
P_t = absolute terminal pressure, psi
V = volume of free air compressed, cf

Length of belt around two pulleys of different diameter

$\boxed{\text{C}}\boxed{3}\boxed{6}$ $L\,S = 2\,S^2 + 1.57\,S\,(D + d) + 0.25\,(D + d)^2$

L = length of belt around two pul-
    leys of different diameter, in.
S = ¢ to ¢ spacing between pulley
    centers, in.
D = diameter of larger pulley, in.
d = diameter of smaller pulley, in.

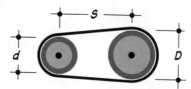

Fig. A1-33

Coefficient of Friction

    While it is not necessary here to engage in a detailed treatise on fric-
tion —as architecture is hopefully a static science— it is wise for Æ
designers to have a conceptual knowledge of friction, as they occasional-

ly need to deal with cranes, trolleys, elevators, and other moving structural and mechanical components in buildings.

When one body rests on another, their relation is said to be static, or at rest. Now if one exerts a sufficient lateral force against the upper body, it begins to slide against the lower. The force required to initiate the sliding relates to (1) an interactive surface property of the two bodies known as their *coefficient of friction*, (2) the weight of the upper body, and (3) the area of the surface they have in common. Whether the two bodies are in motion or at rest, one of three kinds of friction exists between them: *static friction, sliding friction,* or *rolling friction.* Static friction exists between the upper and lower bodies when they are at rest. Sliding friction exists between them once the upper body begins to slide against the lower. Rolling friction occurs if the upper body is configured as a rotating cylinder with a central hole and the "lower" body is an axle inserted into the hole. The coefficients of sliding and rolling friction between two materials with a surface-in-common is always greater than their coefficient of static friction. For example, for steel resting on steel the coefficient of static friction is about 0.74 and the coefficient of sliding friction is about 0.57. Thus a lateral force of 74 lb makes a 100 lb steel weight begin to move across the steel below; but then it takes only 57 lb to keep it moving. However, if the 100 lb of upper steel is shaped as a 24 in. diameter wheel and the lower steel is an axle, it takes a lateral force of less than 1 lb to start the wheel rolling. If the wheel-to-axle surface is well-lubricated, even this small force may be reduced by 80 percent.

Relation Between, Force, Mass, and Acceleration

In accordance with Newton's Second Law of Motion, acceleration is proportional to the force(s) which causes it according to

C]3]7] $F = M a$

F = accelerating force, lb
M = mass that resists force F, lb
a = acceleration of mass M due to application of force F, fps ÷ 32.2 fps due to gravity

Exponential relation

C]3]8] $A^e = B$

A = base number whose exponential value is desired
e = exponent or power of base number
B = exponential value of A to the e power

Relation between Work and Energy

When a body or system of bodies is induced to move, it acquires kinetic energy, which is the capacity of the body to do work based on its weight and velocity. In any such motion, the initial kinetic energy plus the work of any positive forces minus the work of any negative forces (such as friction) equals the final kinetic energy.

C]3]9] $W = 0.5 M v^2$

W = work performed due to mass M moving at velocity v, ft·lb
M = mass that moves at velocity v, lb
v = velocity of mass M that creates work W, fps

Hydraulics

According to Pascal's Law, pressure exerted anywhere on a confined liquid is (1) transmitted undiminished in all directions, (2) acts with the same force on all equal surfaces, (3) acts in a direction at right angles to those surfaces, and (4) must take into consideration the force of gravity. This law, which has profound implications for plumbing systems, is expressed as follows:

C]4]0] $p = w h$

p = unit pressure of liquid, psi
w = unit weight of liquid undergoing pressure, pcf
h = height of liquid undergoing pressure, ft

Boyle's and Charles' Law

According to Boyle's Law, the product of the pressure and volume of a gas is constant if the temperature of the gas is kept constant. Charles' Law also states that at constant pressure a gas's volume varies directly according to its absolute temperature, and at constant volume a gas's pressure varies directly as its absolute temperature. These laws are expressed in the formulas below:

C]4]1] **Boyle's Law:** $P_1 V_1/T_1 = P_2 V_2/T_2$
C]4]2] **The Characteristic Equation:** $PV = wRT$

P = pressure of gas, psf. P_1 = pressure of gas in initial state; P_2 = pressure of gas in final state.
V = volume of gas, cf. V_1 = volume of gas in initial state; V_2 = volume of gas in final state.
T = temperature of gas, °F absolute [°Rankin]. T_1 = temperature of

gas in initial state; T_2 = temperature of gas in final state.

w = weight of gas at specified pressure, volume, and temperature, lb

R = gas constant, equals 1544/molecular weight of the gas

Nozzle Flow

Nozzles are commonly found in fountains and systems that convert water power to electricity. In fountains the nozzleflow is usually ejected upward, while in water power systems the nozzleflow is ejected horizontally but is impelled to attain a certain velocity by the vertical distance between the nozzle and the fluid's casual entry at the top of the penstock. In either case, a well-designed nozzle has: (1) an exit diameter that is less than one-third its entrance diameter, (2) a length of contraction that is at least six times its exit diameter, and (3) an inner surface that is smooth enough to promote maximum laminar fluidflow. Knowing the volume of flow at the nozzle's entry and discharge is constant, the following holds:

C]4]3]
$$v_i \, \delta_i^2 = v_e \, \delta_e^2$$

v_i = initial or entrance velocity of nozzleflow, fps. If v is cfs, convert to fps according to Q (cfs) = v (fps) × A (ft²)

δ_i = diameter at entrance of nozzle, in.

v_e = exit velocity of nozzleflow, fps

δ_e = diameter at exit of nozzle, in.

Regarding the height of a fountain, the height of waterflow from a vertically aimed nozzle is computed as follows:

C]4]4]
$$2 \, h_e = v_2^2/g$$

h_e = effective head of waterflow: height of water ejected from nozzle, ft. Due to inherent friction losses in the nozzle and related piping, the actual height is usually 15-20% less, and due to air resistance that the waterflow encounters as it rises from the nozzle the stream usually brooms out at about 2/3 h_e.

v_2 = exit velocity of nozzleflow, fps

g = deceleration of nozzleflow from nozzle to crest of fountain due to gravity, 32.2 fps

Freely Falling bodies

In the absence of air resistance, all bodies regardless of size or weight fall at the same rate of acceleration at the same elevation above sea level. Of course, considering that air resistance relates to the specific gravity of a falling object as well as its speed squared, it takes far less time for the fall of a feather to be slowed than it does for a chunk of iron. Nevertheless, the following holds for ideal scenarios:

C]4]5]
$$h = v_i t + 0.5 g t^2$$

h = height or length of fall, ft
v_i = initial velocity of falling body, fps
t = time of fall, sec
g = acceleration of falling body due to force of gravity, 32.2 fps

Torque and Torsion

Torque is generally a kinetic circular force developed by a rotating object, whereas torsion is a static indication of a material's ability to resist a rotational force without failing. Thus, if a certain rotational force acts in a circumferential manner at a certain radius against a shaftlike material of a certain diameter, the following holds:

C]4]6]
$$5.1 \ P r = f_o \delta^3$$

P = point load applied in a distant and circumferential direction to a shaftlike material, lb
r = radial distance (also known as lever arm) between point of applied load and center of material's diameter, in.
f_o = allowable unit stress in torsion for shaft material, psi
δ = diameter of shaftlike that resists applied point load, in.

Young's Modulus of Elasticity

The classic deflection scenario, known to every college physics student, involves applying a known load to the base of a vertically suspended material, usually a thin wire, of a certain material of known length and section area, then measuring how much the material elongates due to the applied load. Under these conditions the following holds:

C]4]7]
$$Y = PL/Ae$$

Y = Young's modulus of elasticity of material experiencing load, psi
P = amount of load applied to material in direction of its length and concentric to its axis, lb
L = length of material experiencing load, in.
A = section area of material in direction $\perp$ to applied load, in^2
e = elongation of material in direction of its length due to applied load, in. e is usually reduced to in/in of unit length of material.

Thermodynamics

Every material, whether solid, liquid, or gas, has an ability to store heat, known as its *specific heat*, which is the amount of heat required to raise 1 lb of the material 1°F. This property is usually given as a ratio compared to the unitary specific heat of water. Thus if the specific heat of water = 1.00, that of steel = 0.120 and that of copper = 0.093.

Every material also has an ability to absorb or release a certain amount of heat as it changes from one solid, liquid, or gaseous state to another. Six terms are used to describe these changes, as follows:

Melting: When a solid changes to a liquid
Freezing: When a liquid changes to a solid
Boiling: When a liquid changes to a gas.
Condensation: When a gas changes to a liquid.
Latent heat of Fusion: The heat absorbed by a liquid when it freezes to a solid or the heat released by the same solid when it melts.
Latent heat of Vaporization: The heat absorbed by a gas when it condenses to a liquid or th heat released by the same liquid when it boils.

Consider H_2O, which in its solid, liquid, and gaseous states is known as ice, water, and steam, has a latent heat of fusion of 144 Btu/lb (79.7 cal·g^{-1}) and a latent heat of vaporization of 970 Btu/lb (539 cal·g^{-1}).

Every material also has an ability to conduct heat through its mass based on its cross-sectional area in a direction perpendicular to the direction of heat flow, its thickness in a direction parallel to the direction of heat flow, the difference of temperature on each side of its thickness, and an intrinsic property known as *thermal conductivity*, as follows:

C)4)8)
$$Q = \frac{k A (T_1 - T_2)}{t}$$

Q = quantity of heat flow through the material, Btu/hr
k = thermal conductivity of material, Btu/hr·in·°F
A = section area of material, sf
T_1 = temperature on warmer side of material, °F
T_2 = temperature on cooler side of material, °F
t = thickness of material through which heat flows, in.

Radiation

When a difference in temperature exists between a material's surface and an adjacent cooler material or medium, the warmer material radiates heat to the cooler according to Stefan's Law, which states:

C)4)9)
$$R = e \kappa (T_w - T_c)^4$$

R = radiant energy emitted from surface of warmer material, Btu/sf·hr
e = emissivity of surface of warmer material, a unitary measure between 0 and 1.0. The more radiant the material, the lower the emissivity. Since good reflectors are poor radiators, rough surfaces generally have greater emissivities than smooth or polished surfaces.
κ = a constant, usually ≈ 100,000,000 in British units
T_w = temperature of surface of warmer material, °Rankin
T_c = temperature of surface of cooler material, °Rankin

Sound Intensity

Due to the great range of sound intensities to which the human ear is sensitive, a logarithmic formula is used to quantify them as follows:

C)5)0)
$$\lambda = 10 \log \frac{I_r}{I_o}$$

λ = intensity level of sound wave, ₿
I_r = intensity level of sound at the receiver, watts/meter²
I_o = intensity level at origin of sound, usually taken at 3 ft from its source and usually equalling 10^{-12} watts/meter²

Reynolds Number

In a pipe filled with a flowing liquid, Reynolds number represents the ratio of the flow's inertial forces to its viscous or friction forces, thus it may be used to find the pressure loss due to pipe friction in a pipe of a certain diameter in which flows a liquid at a certain velocity. This is especially useful if the liquid is other than water.

C)5)1)
$$R = \frac{\delta v}{\nu}$$

R = Reynolds number
δ = interior diameter of pipe diameter, ft
v = volume of liquid flowing in pipe, fps
ν = kinematic velocity of liquid in pipe, ft²/sec

Fahrenheit-to-Centigrade Conversion

C)5)2)
$$F = 1.8\,C + 32$$

F = temperature in Fahrenheit degrees
C = temperature in Centigrade degrees

Metric Conversions

Disk Access Code	Conversion	Multiply (×)
MC01	Inches to millimeters (1 mm = 0.0394 in).............	in. × 25.4 = mm
MC02	Inches to centimeters (1 cm = 0.3937 in).............	in. × 2.54 = cm
MC03	Inches to meters (1 m = 39.37 in)...................	in. × 0.0254 = m
MC04	Feet to meters (1 m = 3.281 ft)......................	ft × 0.3048 = m
MC05	Yards to meters (1 m = 1.0934 yd)...................	yd × 0.914 = m
MC06	Feet to kilometers (1 km = 3,280.7 ft)	ft × 0.0003048 = km
MC07	Yards to kilometers (1 km = 1,093.6 yd)	yd × 0.0009144 = km
MC08	Miles to kilometers (1 km = 0.621 mi)...............	mi × 1.609 = km
MC09	Sq. inches to sq. centimeters (1 cm^2 = 0.155 in^2) ..	in^2 × 6.451 = cm^2
MC10	Square feet to square meters (1 m^2 = 10.764 sf) .	sf × 0.0929 = m^2
MC11	Square yards to square meters (1 m^2 = 1.196 yd^2)	yd^2 × 0.836 = m^2
MC12	Acres to hectares (1 ha = 2.471 ac)	ac × 0.4047 = ha
MC13	Acre·ft to cubic meters	ac·ft × 1,233.46 = m^3
MC14	Square feet to hectares (1 ha = 107,639 sf)	sf × 0.00000929 = ha
MC15	Square miles to hectares (1 ha = 0.00345 mi^2).......	mi^2 × 290 = ha
MC16	Square miles to sq. kilometers (1 mi^2 = 0.386 km^2) ..	mi^2 × 2.59 = km^2
MC17	Cubic inches to cubic cm. (1 cc = 0.061 in^3)	in^3 × 16.387 = cc
MC18	Cubic feet to cubic meters (1 m^3 = 35.34 cf)	cf × 0.0283 = m^3
MC19	Cubic yards to cubic meters (1 m^3 = 1.308 yd^3) ..	yd^3 × 0.7646 = m^3
MC20	Cubic inches to liters (1 L = 61.022 in^3)	in^3 × 0.01639 = L
MC21	Quarts to liters (1 L = 1.057 qt)	qt × 0.946 = L
MC22	Gallons to liters (1 L = 0.2642 gal)	gal × 3.784 = L
MC23	Ounces (Avoir.) to grams (1 gm = 0.03527 oz)	oz × 28.35 = gm
MC24	Grains to grams (1 gm = 15.432 gr)	gr × 0.0648 = gm
MC25	Fluid ounces (water at 0° C) to milliliters	oz × 29.577 = ml
MC26	Pounds to kilograms (1 kg = 2.2046 lb)	lb × 0.4536 = kg
MC27	Kips to kilograms (1 kg = 0.00220 k)	k × 454.5 = kg
MC28	Tons to metric tons (1 mton = 2,204.6 lb)	ton × 0.907 = mton or Ton
MC29	Horsepower to kilowatts (1 kW = 1.34 HP)	HP × 0.746 = kW
MC30	Pound·feet to kilogram·meters	lb·ft × 0.138 = kg·m
MC31	Pounds/linear foot to kilograms/meter	plf × 1.488 = kg/m
MC32	Pounds/sq. inch to kilograms/sq. centimeter	psi × 0.0703 = kg/cm^2
MC33	Pounds/square foot to kilograms/sq. meter ...	psf × 4.883 = kg/m^2
MC34	Pounds/cubic foot to kilograms/cubic meter ..	pcf × 16.03 = kg/m^3
MC35	Pounds/square foot to kilopascals	psf × 20.88 = kPa
MC36	Btus to joules (1 J = 0.00094782 Btu)	Btu × 1,055.1 = J

Non-Metric Conversions

Conversion	Multiply (×)

NC01 Inches to feet (12 in. = 1 ft) .... in. × 0.0833 = ft

NC02 Inches to yards (36 in. = 1 yd) .... in. × 0.02778 = yd

NC03 Inches to mils .... in. × 1,000 = mil

NC04 Inches water gauge to psi (27.70 in. wg = 1 psi)   in. wg × 0.0361 = psi

NC05 Square inches to square feet (144 in² = 1 sf) ... in² × 0.00694 = sf

NC06 Square inches to circular mils (cmil: an area of 1 cmil =
    a circle of 0.001 in. dia.) .... in² × 1,273,885 = cmil

NC07 Cubic inches to cubic feet (1,728 in³ = 1 cf) ... in³ × 0.000579 = cf

NC08 Cubic feet to board feet (1 cf = 12 bf) .... cf × 12 = bf

NC09 Feet to yards (3 ft = 1 yd) .... ft × 0.333 = yd

NC10 Feet to nautical miles (knots) (6,080.2 ft = 1 kn)   ft × 0.0001645 = kn

NC11 Feet of head (water pressure) to psi (0° C.) ..... 1 fh × 0.433 = psi

NC12 Square feet to square yards (9 sf = 1 yd²) .... sf × 0.111 = yd²

NC13 Square feet to squares of roof area (100 sf = 1 sq)   sf × 0.01 = sq

NC14 Square feet to acres (43,560 sf = 1 ac) ....   sf × 0.00002296 = ac

NC15 Cubic feet to cubic yards (27 cf = 1 yd³) .... cf × 0.0370 = yd³

NC16 Cubic feet to acre-ft (43,560 cf = 1 ac-ft) .. cf × 0.00002296 = ac-ft

NC17 Cubic feet to gallons (0.134 cf = 1 gal = 231 in³) ... cf × 7.48 = gal

NC18 Cubic feet to cords of wood (not face cord) .. cf × 0.00781 = 1 cord

NC19 Miles (statute) to miles (nautical: 1.15 mi = 1 kn) .. mi × 0.8684 = kn

NC20 Square miles to acres (1 mi² = 640 ac) .... mi² × 640 = ac

NC21 Angstroms to centimeters (1 Å = 10⁻⁸ cm) ..... Å × 0.00000001 = cm

NC22 Ounces (avoir) to grains (1 oz = 437.5 gr) .... oz × 437.5 = gm

NC23 Ounces to pounds (16 oz = 1 lb) .... oz × 0.0625 = lb

NC24 Pounds to grains (1 lb = 7,000 gr; 1 oz = 437.5 gr) .. lb × 7,000 = gr

NC25 Pounds to kips (1,000 lb = 1 k) .... lb × 0.001 = k

NC26 Psi to atmospheres (14.68 psi = 1 atm) .... psi × 0.0681 = atm

NC27 Degrees to minutes (60 deg or ° = 1 min°) ..... deg × 0.01667 = min

NC28 Degrees to radians (57.296 deg or ° = 1 rad) .. deg × 0.01745 = rad

NC29 Min-sec (i.e. °-'-") to deg (1° = 60'; 1' = 60") sec × 0.0002778 = deg

NC30 Atmospheres to millibars .... atm × 986.9 = mb

NC31 Gallons (U.S.) to barrels (oil) (42 gal = 1 bbl) .. gal × 0.0238 = bbl

NC32 British thermal units to calories (1 Btu = 252.2 cal) Btu × 252.2 = c

NC33 British thermal units to watts (0.293 Btu = 1 W) ... Btu × 3.413 = W

NC34 Horsepower to watts (1 HP = 746 W) .... HP × 746 = W

NC35 Years to hours (1 week = 168 hr; 1 month ≈ 720 hr) yr × 8,760 = hr

Weights of Materials

To find the total weight of any amount of any material listed below, use the formula below. This formula may also be used to find the total weight of any amount of material whose unit weight is known.

W M 1) $\qquad W = M U$

W = full weight of total amount of material, lb
M = volumetric amount of material, ft³
U = unit weight of material, as listed below or elsewhere, pcf

Material	Unit weight, pcf	Material	Unit weight, pcf
Aluminum, pure or wire	168	**SOLIDS**	
Brass, 80/20 copper/zinc	536	Ash, black walnut, chestnut ..	40
50/50 copper/zinc	511	Beech, elm, yellow pine	45
Bronze, cobalt	552	Birch, Oregon pine, willow	32
Brick, face ... 140, common ...	120	Cypress, red pine, hemlock ...	30
Concrete, reinforced	145	Douglas Fir, white maple	34
Copper, monel metal	556	Ebony ... 79; lignum vitae ...	62
Earth, dry, loose .. 76, packed	95	Glass, common ..156; plate ..	161
Glass, common ... 156, plate ...	161	Hickory, Indian teak	49
Gold: pure, cast, hammered ..	1,205	Maple, white ... 33; hard	43
Iron, cast ... 450, wrought	485	Oak, chestnut ... 54; live	59
Lead	710	white 46; red or black	41
Magnesium	109	Paper	58
Manganese	475	Rubber, refined	94
Masonry, ashlar		White pine, spruce, redwood ..	28
Bluestone, sandstone	140	**LIQUIDS**	
Granite, gneiss	165	Alcohol, refined petroleum	50
Limestone, marble	160	Ammonia	56
Masonry, mortared rubble: −10 lb		Gasoline	44
from ashlar masonry materials		Kerosene	51
Mercury	849	Muriatic acid, 40%	75
Nickel	545	Oil: vegetable, mineral, crude .	57
Paper, leather, rubber	59	Water, 4°C .. 62.4, 100°C ...	59.8
Silver	655	Water, sea ... 64; ice	56
Steel, rolled	490	**GASES**	
Tin, cast or hammered	459	Air, 0°C & 760 mm press ..	0.0807
Sand or gravel, dry or loose ...	98	Carbon dioxide	0.1227
Dry, packed ...110, wet ...	120	Carbon monoxide	0.0781
Stone: Chalk, clay, marl	137	Oxygen	0.0892
Granite, slate, shale	175	Nitrogen	0.0784
Sandstone, bluestone	147	Hydrogen	0.00559
Limestone, marble, quartz	165	Ammonia	0.0478

Other Useful Measures

Solar year .... 365 days, 5 hr, 48 min, 49.7 sec; also 365.242 days

Lunar month (mean); also interval of full moons, lunation of the moon, or
synodic month ..... 29 days, 12 hr, 44 min, 2 sec; also 29.5305 days

Surveyor's measures: .... 7.92 in. = 1 link; 100 links = 1 chain (ch);
10 chains = 1 furlong (fur); 80 chains = 1 mile

Dry measures: .... 2 pints (pt) = 1 quart (qt) ; 4 quarts = 1 peck (pk);
4 pecks = 1 bushel (bu); 63 gallons (gal) = 1 hogshead (hhd)

Biblical measures .... 1 digit = 0.912 in; 1 palm = 3.648 in;
1 span = 10.944 in; 1 cubit = 1.824 ft; 1 fathom = 7.296 ft

Greek measures .... 1 digit = 0.7554 in; 1 pous (foot) = 1.007 ft;
1 cubit = 1.133 ft; 1 stadium = 604.38 ft; 1 mile = 8 stadia = 4,835 ft

Roman measures .... 1 digit = 0.726 in; 1 uncia (in.) = 10.967 in;
1 pes (ft) = 11.604 in; 1 cubit = 1.451 ft; 1 passus = 4.835 ft;
1 mille = (millarium) = 4,842 ft

DERIVATION OF FORMULAS

A. GENERAL

The primary source for all information appearing in this volume is the author's more than 40 years' experience in architecture, including his receiving a degree in architecture from Cornell University in 1964, and subsequently having a great variety of experiences in architectural design and construction in several parts of the country, primarily New York, Georgia, California, and Colorado. Much of his architectural engineering knowledge appeared in his earlier publications, *Architectural & Engineering Calculations Manual* (McGraw-Hill, 1984) (hereinafter referred to as the Original Edition), and the *Standard Handbook of Architectural Engineering* (McGraw-Hill, 1998) (hereinafter referred to as SHAE). This appendix lists the source or derivation of most of the newly developed formulas found in this volume except those whose derivations should be obvious to one familiar with algebra. The formulas are also streamlined as described below:

▶ Fractional terms are eliminated whenever possible as they take up more vertical space and tend to look cluttered. Example: in this volume, $A = {}^B/_C$ is typically written as $A\, C = B$.
▶ Exponents listed with root symbols ($\sqrt{\ }$) or as fractions are written as decimals. Examples: $A = \sqrt{B}$ and $A = B^{2/3}$ are typically written as $A = B^{0.5}$ and $A = B^{0.67}$.
▶ Multiple numerical values in one formula are converted to a single number. Example: $3\,A = 4\,B\,(5\,C)^{0.5}$ becomes $A = 2.98\,B\,C^{0.5}$.

Also in this text, an algebraic formula is favored over an X/Y coordinate graph for the following reasons:

▶ A formula takes up much less space.
▶ A formula can be computerized.
▶ The values of a graph are limited by its borders, while a formula's values usually can extend to infinity in plus and minus directions.

▶   A formula has a symbology that usually captures the essence of the subject more readily than does the lines of a table or chart.

Finally, in this text a bar graph is favored over a plane or X/Y coordinate graph for the following reasons:

▶   A bar graph takes up considerably less vertical space.

▶   A plane graph's ordinate and abscissa scales extend perpendicular from each other and thus many values are often far from one or both scales; while in a bar graph the two scales extend side-to-side which makes the relation between their values more readily obvious.

Chapter 2: Climatic Forces

2)B)c) *The Lighting Handbook*, 8th Edition, Mark S. Rea, Editor-in-Chief (Illuminating Society of North America, NY, 1993), p. 361-2, gives the following formulas for computing the sun's altitude and azimuth given the latitude of site, date of year, and time of day:

$$\delta = 0.4093 \sin [2 \pi (J - 81)/368] \tag{8-4}$$

$$a_t = \arcsin (\sin L \sin \delta - \cos L \cos \delta \cos \pi \, t/12) \tag{8-5}$$

$$a_s = \arctan (- [\cos \delta \sin (\pi \, t/12)] - [\cos L \sin \delta + \sin L \cos \delta \cos (\pi \, t/12)]) \tag{8-6}$$

In formula 8-5, converting $a_t = \arcsin (...)$ to $\sin \angle_v = (...)$ and all angle values from radians to degrees; substituting equation 8-4 for δ, T for t, and D for J in equation 8-5; then streamlining:

$$\sin \angle_v = \sin L \sin [23.5 \sin 0.98 (D - 81) - \cos L \cos 15 T \cos [23.5 \sin 0.98 (D - 81)]$$

In formula **2)B)d)**, performing similar operations:

$$\tan \angle_h = \frac{\sin 15T \cos [23.5 \sin 0.98 (D - 81)]}{\cos L \sin [23.5 \sin 0.98 (D - 81)] + \sin L \cos 15T \cos [23.5 \sin 0.98 (D - 81)]}$$

2)C)2)a) As the manner in which a gutter receives water from a roof then drains it to one or more downspouts obeys the laws of open channel flow, gutters may be sized according to the Manning formula, which from the *Introduction to Fluid Mechanics*, Haberman & John (Prentice-Hall, Englewood Cliffs, NJ, 1971), p. 226, is

(1) $$V = \frac{1.486}{n} \left(\frac{A}{P}\right)^{2/3} (\sin \alpha)^{0.5}$$

in which V is the channel or gutter waterflow velocity (cf/sec), n is the gutter surface's roughness coefficient (ft$^{1/6}$), A is its section area (sf), P is its wetted perimeter (ft), and α is its angle of slope (°). If Q is the gutter's rate of discharge (cfs), $V = Q/A$, and Q = the roof's watershed area W (sf) × the rainfall intensity R (ft/sec), then

$$V_{fps} = W_{sf} R_{cfs}/A_{sf}$$

In this equation, W is not the area of the sloping roof plane but is the sum of its horizontally projected area plus 0.5 its vertically projected area no matter what its slope. Also in the above equation, some of the unit measures are impractical: e.g. rainfall intensity R is usually given by weather bureaus not in ft/sec but in in/hr, and a gutter's sectional dimensions that comprise A are almost always in in. and not ft. Thus, converting R to in/hr and A to in²:

(2) $\qquad V_{fps} = 144\ W_{sf} R_{in/hr}/43,200\ A_{in2} = W_{sf} R_{in/hr}/300\ A_{in2}$

Combining formulas (1) and (2):

$$\frac{W_{sf} R_{in/hr}}{300\ A_{in2}} = \frac{1.486}{n}\left(\frac{A_{sf}}{P_{ft}}\right)^{0.67}(\sin \alpha)^{0.5}$$

Regarding this formula's roughness coefficient n, *Fluid Mechanics*, p. 226, Table 9.1 lists the value of n for steel as 0.015, which is valid for the kind of smooth metals that most gutters are made of (indeed, regarding unplaned wood gutters, $n = 0.013$ which is only 8 percent different than n for metal); and n's unit measure is ft$^{1/6}$ when it should be in$^{1/6}$. Also in the above formula, (1) the unit measure of the second A is still in ft, as is the unit measure of P; (2) regarding sin α, for the very small angles that typify the 1/16 to 1/2 in/LF pitches of gutters, sin α = tan α, which is the actual rise/run ratio of a slightly pitched gutter; and (3) R should include a 1.5 safety factor in consideration of extreme storm conditions. Thus, converting n from ft$^{1/6}$ to in$^{1/6}$ (0.015 ft$^{1/6}$ = 0.0225 in$^{1/6}$), A_{ft2} to a_{in2}, P_{ft} to P_{in}, and sin α to tan α in the above formula, and adding the R safety factor, the formula becomes

$$\frac{W_{sf} R_{in/hr} \times 1.5}{300\ A_{in2}} = \frac{1.486}{0.0225}\left(\frac{12\ A_{in2}}{144\ P_{in}}\right)^{0.67}(\tan \alpha)^{0.5}$$

Streamlining: $\quad W_{sf} R_{in/hr} = 2,510\ (A_{in2})^{2.67}\ (P_{in})^{-0.67}\ (\tan \alpha)^{0.5}$

The above formula is for gutters that drain into only one downspout. Thus, inserting η = number of downspouts the gutter has, the formula becomes

$$W_{sf} R_{in/hr} = 2,510\ \eta\ (A_{in2})^{2.67}\ (P_{in})^{-0.67}\ (\tan \alpha)^{0.5}$$

Now a standard ogee-faced gutter, the most widely used gutter for residences and small commercial buildings nationwide today, has a measured top width w of aproximately 4.5 in, fill height of 3.38 in, bottom width of 3.25 in, and slanted outer face width of 3.75 in. Thus an ogee-profile gutter has the following dimensions:

Its section area $A = 13.6$ in², which can also be described in terms of its top width w as $0.68\ w^2$; and its wetted perimeter $P = 10.3$ in, which can also be described in terms of w as $2.08\ w$. These w values for A and P are advantageous in that they allow an ogee-profile gutter of any size, as long as its proportions remain the same, to be facilitlously described in the parent formula., as follows:

Ogee: $\qquad W_{sf}\ R_{in/hr} = 2{,}510\ \eta\ (0.68\ w^2)^{1.67}\ (2.08\ w)^{-0.67}\ (\tan\alpha)^{0.5}$

Streamlining: $\qquad W\ R\ =\ 800\ \eta\ w^{2.67}\ (\tan\alpha)^{0.5}$

Similar expressions may also be devised for gutters whose sections are half-round, rectangular, and of any shape, as follows:

Half-round: $\quad W_{sf}\ R_{in/hr} = 2{,}510\ \eta\ (0.39\ \delta^2)^{1.67}\ (1.57\ \delta)^{-0.67}\ (\tan\alpha)^{0.5}$

$\qquad\qquad\qquad W\ R\ =\ 390\ \eta\ \delta^{2.67}\ (\tan\alpha)^{0.5}$

Rectangular: $\quad W_{sf}\ R_{in/hr} = 2{,}500\ \eta\ (w\ d)^{1.67}\ (w + 2\ d)^{-0.67}\ (\tan\alpha)^{0.5}$

Any section: $\qquad W_{sf}\ R_{in/hr} = 2{,}500\ \eta\ (A)^{1.67}\ (P)^{-0.67}\ (\tan\alpha)^{0.5}$

Finally, replace $(\tan\alpha)^{0.5}$ with a gutter pitch coefficient $\kappa_\measuredangle$ and accompany the formulas with a bar graph that describes gutter pitch (in/LF) vs. $(\tan\alpha)^{0.5}$, so the latter value may be more easily tabulated:

Ogee: $\qquad\qquad\qquad W\ R\ =\ 800\ \eta\ w^{2.67}\ \kappa_\measuredangle$

Half-round section: $\quad W\ R\ =\ 390\ \eta\ \delta^{2.67}\ \kappa_\measuredangle$

Rectangular section: $\quad W\ R\ =\ 2{,}500\ \eta\ (w\ d)^{1.67}\ (w + 2\ d)^{-0.67}\ \kappa_\measuredangle$

Any section: $\qquad\quad W\ R\ =\ 2{,}500\ \eta\ (A)^{1.67}\ (P)^{-0.67}\ \kappa_\measuredangle$

__2)C)2)b)__ In the *Standard Handbook of Engineering Calculations, Third Edition*, Tyler Hicks, Editor (McGraw-Hill, NY, 1995), pp. 2.42 to 44, the section "Design of Roof and Yard Rainwater Drainage Systems", has a Table 5 on p. 2.43 which lists a column of leader sizes and the maximum projected roof area each can drain. By plotting this table's leader sizes vs. roof areas on a loglog graph, the following formula for sizing round leaders is obtained:

$$W\ R\ \approx\ 114\ \delta^{2.67}$$

As this table's related text indicates that its values are for a maximum rainfall of 4 in/hr, to the above formula is added a rainfall intensity variable R based on a rainfall intensity of 4 in. plus a 1.5 safety factor for R in consideration of extreme storm conditions; then the formula becomes

$$W\ R_4 \times 1.5\ \approx\ 114 \times 4\ \delta^{2.67}$$

Streamlining: $\qquad\qquad W\ R\ \approx\ 304\ \delta^{2.67}$

Since the above formula is for circular leaders, one for rectangular leader is devised as follows:

$$0.785 \, \delta^2 = w \, d$$
$$0.88 \, \delta = (w \, d)^{0.5}$$
$$(0.88 \, \delta)^{2.67} = [(w \, d)^{0.5}]^{2.67} = (w \, d)^{1.33}$$
$$\delta^{2.67} = 1.38 \, (w \, d)^{1.33}$$

Substituting: $\quad W \, R \approx 304 \times 1.38 \, (w \, d)^{1.33}$

Streamlining: $\quad W \, R \approx 420 \, (w \, d)^{1.33}$

2)C)2)c). A footing drain is an open channel up to the level at which the drain becomes full, at which point the water begins to exert pressure against the pipe wall and then the liquid no longer obeys the laws of open channel flow. Thus a footing drain, and storm drains as well, may be sized as open channels under the premise that one's maximum flow occurs just as the drain becomes full; therefore the drain's section is typically a full circle. Thus one's waterflow formula is an adaptation of Manning's channel flow formula, which as cited in derivation **2)C)2)a)** is

$$V = \frac{1.486}{n} \left(\frac{A}{P}\right)^{2/3} (\sin \alpha)^{0.5}$$

in which V is the channel waterflow velocity (cf/sec), n is the channel surface's roughness coefficient (ft$^{1/6}$), A is its section area (sf), P is its wetted perimeter (ft), and α is its angle of slope (°). If Q is the channel's rate of discharge (cfs) and $V = Q/A$, then

$$Q_{cfs} = \frac{1.486 \, A_{sf}}{n} \left(\frac{A_{sf}}{P_{ft}}\right)^{2/3} (\sin \alpha)^{0.5}$$

Converting A_{ft2} to a_{in2}, P_{ft} to P_{in}, and $\sin \alpha$ to $\tan \alpha$ then κ_Δ as described in derivation **2)C)2)a)**, adding a ft-to-in conversion factor of 1.51 for n, converting Q_{cfs} to Q_{gpm} ($Q_{cfs} = 449 \, Q_{gpm}$), substituting $A = 0.785 \, \delta^2$ and $P = \pi \, \delta = 1.57 \, \delta$, then streamlining:

$$5.6 \, n \, Q = \delta^{2.67} \, \kappa_\Delta$$

2)C)2)d). Storm drains are also open channels whose sections are typically full circles; thus, from the reference cited in derivation **2)C)2)a)**,

$$V = \frac{1.486}{n} \left(\frac{A}{P}\right)^{2/3} (\sin \alpha)^{0.5}$$

Similarly as in derivation **2)C)2)a)**,

$$\frac{W_{sf} \, R_{in/hr}}{300 \, A_{in2}} = \frac{1.486}{n} \left(\frac{A_{sf}}{P_{ft}}\right)^{0.67} (\sin \alpha)^{0.5}$$

Inserting conversion factors for n, $(\sin \alpha)^{0.5}$, A_{sf}, and P_{ft}:

$$\frac{W_{sf}\, R_{in/hr}}{300\, A_{in2}} = \frac{1.486}{1.51\, n}\left(\frac{A_{in2}}{12\, P_{ft}}\right)^{0.67} \kappa_{\Delta}$$

Inserting $A = 0.785\, \delta^2$ and $P = 3.14\, \delta$, then streamlining:

$$n\,R\,W = 11.7\, \delta^{2.67} \kappa_{\Delta}$$

Regarding fixture unit flow in storm drains, in the *Standard Handbook of Engineering Calculations, Third Edition*; Tyler Hicks, Editor (McGraw-Hill, NY, 1995), pp. 2.44, says [paraphrased] to equate a roof area waterflow (sf) to fixture units (f.u.), the first 1,000 sf or less of the roof = 256 f.u., then divide any remaining roof area by 3.9 per f.u. to obtain the roof's equivalent fixture unit load = 256 + 0.26 (*A* − 1,000), which in itself is a useful design formula in certain scenarios. Conversely, when a graywater fixture unit load is added to storm drainage, the equivalent roof area = 3.9 × f.u. Thus, letting the fixture unit load = *F*, then inserting this variable into Manning's formula:

$$n\,(R\,W + 3.9\, F) = 11.7\, \delta^{2.67} \kappa_{\Delta}$$

2)C)2)e) A drywell is essentially a gutter downspout of a very large diameter, whose capacity is governed not only by the water that enters it but also by the water that flows out through the well's walls and floor and is absorbed at a certain rate of permeability by the earth beyond. Thus a drywell's size relates to (1) the incoming waterflow as quantified by the formula for a circular leader in Sec. 2.C.2.b. and (2) the surface area of its usually cylindrical walls (the floor's area is usually neglected as a slight safety factor) and the permeability of the soil behind. Therefore, from 2)C)2)b)1) and the area of a cylinder's sides:

$$W\,R \approx 304\, \delta^{2.67} = \pi\, \delta\, h \times \rho$$

wherein ρ is the permeability of the surrounding soil. Converting *R* from in/hr to ft/hr and ρ from in/min. drop to ft/hr drop:

$$W\,R/12 \approx \pi\, \delta\, h \times \rho \times 60/12$$

Streamlining: $\qquad\qquad W\,R \approx 188\, \delta\, h\, \rho$

2)E)2) The *1979 HUD Cycle 5 Program, Passive Solar System Design, Attachment G*, pp. 1-9 describes a comprehensive *Simple Whole House Calculation Method* for computing monthly heating and cooling loads. This format works for any building in any area for which reliable climatic data is available. Its basic formulas are:

Conduction Heat Loss/Gain: $S\,U\,A \times (T_{in} - T_{out}) \times 24$ hr/day × days/mo
Infiltration Heat Loss/Gain: 0.018 Btu/cf · °F × interior volume, cf ×
no. airchanges/hr × $(T_{in} - T_{out}) \times 24$ hr/day × days/mo

As both formulas are functions of Δt, they may be combined as the design heating load formula listed below. In this formula $1/R_a P$ is substituted for U, T_o = local design temperature for the period of heat loss or gain instead of the average monthly temperature, and timespan = 1 hr instead of hr/mo.

$$\Phi_{ci} = (A/R_a P + 0.018 \, V\eta) \, (T_i - T_o)$$

Similarly, the formula for design cooling load becomes

$$\Phi_{ci} = A \, \kappa_f \, (T_i - T_o)/R_a P + 0.074 \, V\eta \, (H_i - H_o)$$

The HUD format presented the general heating and cooling load formulas first, then described several of their variables with smaller formulas accompanied by a fill-in-the-blanks format. But when computerizing such variables, it is usually easier to determine the minor variables first in separate equations and then include their values in a final basic equation. Thus in Sec. 2.E.2.a. and b., R and T_o are computed in **Steps 1** and **2** before Δ_{ci} is computed in **Step 3**; and in *Sec. 4. G.5.*, incident clear-day insolation w/o$_c$ and ground reflectance factor κ_G are computed in **Steps 1** and **2** before solar heat gain Φ is computed in **Step 3**. In each case this volume's operations are merely better-organized portrayals of the same data and algebra employed in the HUD format.

2)E)6)a) *The Solar Home Book*, Bruce Anderson, © 1976 Brick House Publishing Co., p. 94, says: "With a total volume of 600 cubic feet (20 × 40 × ¾) and a capacity of 32 Btu/cf · ° F, the concrete slab stores 19,200 Btu for a 1° rise in its temperature (600 cf × 32 Btu/cf · ° F = 19,299 Btu/° F). For a 1° F drop in its temperature, the slab releases the same 19,200 Btu." These thermodynamics may be expressed algebraically as

$$\Delta_{tm} = C \, V \, (T_a - T_e)$$

2)E)7) **Step 2.** *The 1979 HUD Cycle 5 Program, Passive Solar System Design, Attachment G*, p. 9, Fig. 1, shows a full-page graph that portrays the relationship between a building's monthly solar load ratio SLR and its monthly solar heating fraction SHF. By converting the SLR curve into a bar graph of κ_{slr} vs. κ_{hlf}, this information is presented in far less space. Then by letting the bar graph's κ_{slr} scale equal 1.0 – κ_{slr} = heating load fraction κ_{hlf}, this scale shows not the actual solar contribution but the net heating load fraction to be satisfied by the installed climate control system.

Chapter 3: Climate Control

3)B)1)a) The *Handbook of Air Conditioning System Design*, prep. by Carrier Air Conditioning Co. (McGraw-Hill, NY, 1965), pp. 2-30 to 2-48 describes the equal friction and static regain or velocity reduction methods of designing low-velocity HVAC ducting. This text on p. 2-46 says: "The equal friction method is superior to velocity reduction since it requires less balancing for symmetrical layouts." From the immediately following text, it is obvious that this method is based on finding the total static air pressure loss in the system's longest duct run, and that this loss is the sum of pressure losses at the discharge fan, pressure losses in the ducting, and a net pressure regin at the duct outlet, or

$$\Delta P_T = \Delta P_i + \Delta P_d - \Delta P_r$$

Then this text explains each component loss in further detail. For example, at the bottom of p. 2-37 is the discharge fan pressure loss formula

(1) $$h_v = \left(V/4005\right)^2$$

Tailoring, this becomes $\quad \Delta P_i = \left(v_i/4005\right)^2$ or $\left(Q_i/4005\,A_i\right)^2$

On p. 2-31 is the duct friction loss equation for round ducts:

(2) $$\Delta P = 0.03\,f\left(L/d^{1.22}\right)\left(V/1{,}000\right)^{1.82}$$

If the duct is rectangular instead of round, at the bottom of p. 2-34 is the "circular equivalent dimeter" formula

$$d = 1.3\,(a\,b)^{0.625}/(a+b)^{0.25}$$

Obviously if the duct is square, the above formula becomes

$$d = 1.3\,(s^2)^{0.625}/(2\,s)^{0.25} = 1.09\,s$$

Then equation (2) becomes $\quad \Delta P = 0.03\,f\left(L/(1.09\,s)^{1.22}\right)\left(V/1{,}000\right)^{1.82}$

$$1.09^{1.22} = 1.11 \text{ and } 1{,}000^{1.82} = 288{,}400$$

Streamlining: $\qquad 10{,}670{,}000\,\Delta P\,s^{1.22} = K_R\,L\,V^{1.82}$

On p. 2-38 are two static pressure formulas, one for loss and one for gain, as follows:

$$\text{Loss} = 1.1\left[(V_d/4{,}000)^2 - (V_f/4{,}000)^2\right]$$
$$\text{Gain} = 0.75\left[(V_f/4{,}000)^2 - (V_d/4{,}000)^2\right]$$

Since V_f = duct velocity at the duct outlet, $Q = V/A$, and 1 sf = 144 in²,

$$V_f/4{,}000 = Q/27.8\,A_{in^2}$$

Therefore, $\qquad \text{Loss} = 1.1\left[(V_d/4{,}000)^2 - (Q/27.8\,A_{in^2})^2\right]$

Or $\text{Loss} = 1.1 \, [(0.00025 \, V_d)^2 - (0.036 \, Q/A_{\text{in2}})^2]$

Also $\text{Loss} = 1.1 \, [(0.00025 \, V_d)^2 - (0.00025 \, V_f)^2]$

Likewise $\text{Gain} = 0.75 \, [(Q/27.8 \, A_{\text{in2}})^2 - (0.00025 \, V_d)^2]$

Or $\text{Gain} = 0.75 \, [(0.036 \, Q/A_{\text{in2}})^2 - (0.00025 \, V_d)^2]$

Also $\text{Gain} = 0.75 \, [(0.00025 \, V_f)^2 - (0.00025 \, V_d)^2]$

Tailoring,   If $V_f > V_o$: $\Delta P_r = 0.75 \, [(0.00025 \, v_f)^2 - (0.00025 \, v_o)^2]$
                If $V_f < V_o$: $\Delta P_r = -1.1 \, [(0.00025 \, v_o)^2 - (0.00025 \, v_f)^2]$

3)B)1)b) *ASHRAE 62-1989 Standard, "Ventilation For Acceptable Indoor Air Quality," Appendix D,* states that the ventilation required for an indoor space at an indoor CO_2 concentration of 1,100 ppm and a typical outdoor concentration of 400 ppm is 15 cfm/occupant. But this volume's Sec. 3.B.1. explains why an indoor CO_2 concentration of 1,000 ppm is more desirable considering the response lag between CO_2 sensing and actual fresh air fulfillment indoors. Thus, if ASHRAE's optimal ventilation load of 15 cfm is based on 1,100 ppm, the actual optimal ventilation load based on 1,000 ppm is

$$15 \times 1,100/1,000 = 17.5 \text{ cfm}$$

Also, the ASHRAE value of 15 cfm/occupant is based on general office area activity. Thus different activities would require different ventilation loads as listed in this volume's Table 3-7. Then from all the above, a space's ventilation requirements may be expressed as θ = fresh air requirements per occupant × no. of occupants in the space × k × (maximum acceptable indoor CO_2 concentration – anticipated outdoor CO_2 concentration), or

$$Q = \theta \, \eta \, k \, (C_i - C_o)$$

Using real values, solve for k:

$$17.5 = 15 \times 1 \times k \, (1,000 - 400) \quad \ldots k = 1/514 \approx 1/500$$

Thus $$500 \, Q = \theta \, \eta \, (C_i - C_o)$$

3)C)a)3) The volume of water in a pipe of diameter d is

$$0.785 \, d^2 \times 12 = 9.42 \, d^2 \text{ in}^3$$

If water weighs 0.036 lb/in^3, the weight of water in the above pipe is

$$9.42 \, d^2 \times 0.036 = 0.339 \, d^2 \text{ lb}$$

If 1 Btu heats 1 lb of water 1° F and 1 Btu = 0.293 watts, the wattage required to heat 1 lb of water is

$$\omega = 0.339 \, d^2 \times 0.293 \, \Delta_t = 0.0994 \, d^2 \, \Delta_t$$

If the latent heat of fusion is 144 Btu and the required wattage heats the water to 33° F at 60% efficiency, then

$$\omega = 0.0994 \ d^2 \ (144 + 33 - t)/0.60$$

Streamlining:
$$\omega = 0.17 \ d^2 \ L \ (177 - t_o)$$

3)C)b)1) **Step 1.** From the *Building Construction Handbook*, Frederick Merritt (McGraw-Hill, NY, 1975), p. 19-20, Fig. 19-25, the graph's Y-intercept of the FLOOR PANEL line ≈ 72°. As the FLOOR PANEL line's slope is 2.3:1, the floor panel output vs. average water temperature may be expressed as

$$Q = 2.3 \ (t_w - 72)$$

This formula takes up far less space than Merritt's graph and it can be computerized. Also from Merritt, p 19-19, required floor panel area = heat load/panel output, or

$$A = H/Q \rightarrow H = A \ Q$$

Substituting:
$$H = A \ [2.3 \ (t_w - 72)]$$

As the graph in Merritt, p. 19-19, Fig. 19-25, works for pipe spacings between 6 and 9 in., use an average spacing = 7.5 in. Then **H** may be computed for any pipe spacing by

$$h = A \ [2.3 \ (t_w - 72)] \times 7.5/S$$

Streamlining:
$$H \ S = 17 \ A \ (t_w - 72)]$$

3)C)c)2) A product brochure published by Aitken Products, Inc, Geneva, Ohio, and titled *Aitken Application Data File* describes on p. 6 the following Air Change Heat Loss Formula: heat loss in watts = $V \times N \times 0.00527 \times \Delta T$; in which V = volume of the space to be heated, N = number of airchanges per hour, and ΔT = temperature difference between outdoor and indoor air. As the reciprocal of 0.00527 = 189.7, the above formula may be rewritten as

$$190 \ \Delta = V \eta \ (T_i - T_o)$$

3)C)f) **Step 2.** *Simplified Design of HVAC Systems*, William Bobenhausen (Wiley, NY, 1994). p. 237, describes a formula for determining the design pressure drop in a steam heating system as

$$SPD = PD_{100ft} \times EPL$$

and further describes PD_{100ft} as being the system's pressure drop per 100 LF of pipe, and that "a pressure drop of 2 oz/in^2 per 100 ft of equivalent pipe length is commonly used for systems with an initial steam pressure of 2 psig." Therefore, the above formula is tailored as

$$\Delta P \geq 0.02 \, \Delta p \, L$$

Step 3. Bobenhausen's p. 237 lists his formula 14C as

$$StV_{fps} = \frac{lb_h \times V_{sp}}{25 \times A}$$

Or

$$lb_h \times V_{sp} = 25 \, StV_{fps} \times A$$

wherein lb_h is the steamflow in lb/hr, V_{sp} is the specific volume in ft^3 of 1 lb of steam at the system pressure from Bobenhausen's Table 14.1, StV_{fps} is the steam velocity in fps, and A is the internal sectional area of the steam supply piping. Tailoring this formula, it becomes

$$lb_h \times V_s = 25 \, v \times 0.785 \, \delta^2$$

If $lb_h = \dfrac{C, \text{ the portion of design htg load flowing thro' the pipe}}{Q, \text{ the heat of vapirization/condensation of } H_2O}$

Then

$$C \, V_s = 25 \, Q \, v \times 0.785 \, \delta^2$$

Streamlining:

$$C \, V_s \geq 19.6 \, Q \, v \, \delta^2$$

The formulas at the end of this volume's Step 3 were derived by plotting on a loglog graph the numerical data in Bobenhausen's Table 14.4 on p. 242.

3)C)i)1) *Engineered Systems Magazine*, July 1995 (Business News Publishing Co., Troy, MI), p. 8, editorial by Howard McKew, describes a method of estimating a building's required HVAC system air supply. He says: "For conventional comfort cooling, I use 1 cfm/sq ft (North and East exposure and interior space), 1.75 cfm/sq ft (South exposure), and 2 cfm/sq ft (West exposure). An example of this calculation would be a one-story building, 80 ft wide by 120 ft long, in which

```
North zone:    12 ft × 80 ft = 960 sq ft × 1.00 cfm ...........     960 cfm
East zone:     12 ft × 120 ft = 1,440 sq ft × 1.00 cfm .......   1,440 cfm
Interior zone: 96 ft × 56 ft = 5,376 sq ft × 1.00 cfm .....     5,376 cfm
South zone:    12 ft × 80 ft = 960 sq ft × 1.75 cfm .........   1,680 cfm
West zone:     12 ft × 120 ft = 1,440 sq ft × 2.00 cfm .......  2,880 cfm

Total ...................................................      12,336 cfm
```

This spreadsheet analysis may be expressed by the formula,

$$w/ \approx \eta \, [12 \, L_n + 12 \, L_e + 21 \, L_s + 24 \, L_w + (L_n - 24)(L_e - 24)]$$

Other parts of this article were abstracted in similar fashion to devise the formulas in Steps 2 and 3.

3)C)i)1)a) and b) *The Standard Handbook of Architectural Engineering*, Robert Butler (McGraw-Hill, NY, 1998), p. 551, Step 1, lists two formulas as follows:

Heating Load: $H \geq 0.65\,\kappa_d\,A\,(T_h - T_i)$

Cooling Load: $C \geq 15\,\kappa_d\,A$

In both formulas, $\kappa_d = \mathcal{V}_{max}/100$ or $0.01\,\mathcal{V}_{max}$, and, if duct is square, $A = s^2$. Thus,

Heating Load: $H \geq 0.65 \times 0.01\,\mathcal{V}_{max}\,s^2\,(T_h - T_i)$

Cooling Load: $C \geq 15 \times 0.01\,\mathcal{V}_{max}\,s^2$

Solving for s and streamlining:

Heating Load: $s \geq 12.4\,[{}^{H}/\mathcal{V}_{max}\,(T_h - T_i)]^{0.5}$

Cooling Load: $s \geq 2.58\,(C/\mathcal{V}_{max})]^2$

Step 4. This is the same formula that was developed in this volume's derivation 3)B)1)a) as

(2) $\qquad \Delta P = 0.03\,f\,({}^{L}/d^{1.22})\,(V/1{,}000)^{1.82}$

which became $\qquad 10{,}670{,}000\,\Delta P\,s^{1.22} = \kappa_R\,L\,V^{1.82}$

In this and subsequent steps, the relation between δ if the duct is round and s if the duct is square is

$$\text{same } A = 0.785\,\delta^2 = s^2$$
$$\delta = 1.13\,s$$

Step 8. The design procedure for aspect area appeared in Butler's Standard Handbook of Architectural engineering, p. 552, and was prepared from the *Handbook of Air Conditioning Design*, Carrier Air Conditioning Co., (McGraw-Hill, NY, 1965), pp 2-17 to 58.

Step 10. The three formulas a, b, and c are variations of formula (2) from derivation 3)B)1)a), in which the expression (1 - 0.000034 E) has been added to make the formula accurate for any elevation above sea level.

3)C)i)2)a) A return duct's section area should ≈ 80 percent of the supply duct's section area. Thus

$$A_r \geq 0.80\,N\,W$$

3)C)n) A product brochure, *STEAMaster Electrode Steam Humidifiers* (Stulz America, Frederick, MD, 1996), p. 3, describes the following formula: humidification load = volume of air required × (indoor relative humidity fraction × indoor volume of water per cubic ft of saturated air at a specific indoor temperature fraction - outdoor relative humidity × outdoor volume of water per cubic ft of saturated air at a specific indoor temperature) × 60 min/hr ÷ 7000 grains/lb. This formula may be rewritten as

$$D_h = 0.00857\,V\,(h_i\,c_i - h_o\,c_o)$$

Converting the relative humidity fractions h_i and h_o to percentages:

$$D_h = 0.0000857 \, V \, (h_i \, c_i - h_o \, c_o)$$

As the volume of required air equals the number of occupants in a space $\times$ required airflow delivery rate, or $V = \eta \, w/$, the unit fresh air requirements per occupant are

$$D_h = 0.0000857 \, \eta \, w/ \, (h_i \, c_i - h_o \, c_o)$$

Streamlining: $\quad\quad 12{,}000 \, H = \eta \, w/ \, (h_i \, c_i - h_o \, c_o)$

3) D) m) In "Ventilation for Enclosed Parking Garages", Ayari & Krarti, *ASHRAE Journal, Feb 2001* (American Society of Heating, Refrigeration, and Air-Conditioning Engineers, Atlanta), p. 56, is the formula,

$$ACH = 4.7 \, L/m{\cdot}s2 \times 10\text{-}3 \, L/m3 \times 3{,}600 \, s/h/2.75 \, m = 6.1$$

From the related text, ACH (Q) = [no. spaces in garage (η) × fraction of vehicles in operation (κ_v) × emission rate per vehicle (ϵ) × operation time of each car (t) × conversion factor (f)] ÷ [garage floor area (A) × floor-to-ceiling height of parking area (h) × maximum acceptable CO level (C_o) × emission reference rate $(26.8 \, gr/hr{\cdot}m^2)$] = 6.1. By substituting actual values from a problem in the text, then tailoring and solving for f, $f = 486$.

Thus $\quad\quad\quad\quad\quad A \, h \, C_o \, Q \approx 486 \, \eta \, \kappa_v \, \epsilon \, t$

Chapter 4: Plumbing

4) A) 1) a) and **p)** *Advanced Plumbing Technology,* Alfred Steele (Construction Industry Press, Elmhurst, IL, 1984), p. 155-7, has procedures for computing average and peak water demands for offices, apartments, hotels, and hospitals. From this data it is obvious that

Average demand: $\quad D_a = \eta \, \theta_a (1 + k_a \times$ AC makeup) + any special loads
Peak demand: $\quad\quad D_p = \eta \, \theta_p (1 + k_p \times$ AC makeup) + any special loads

In these formulas, θ is the average or peak water demand per occupant and k is a water demand factor for HVAC system makeup air. Regarding peak unit water demand θ_p: from the above-cited reference the average water use per office worker ≈ 20 gal/day and the ratio of peak use rate/average use rate ≈ 2.5. Thus θ_p for offices may be expressed as

(20 gal/day × 2.5 peak/average use rate) ÷ (10 office hr/day × 60 min/hr)
= 0.083 gpm peak load per occupant

Rounding off this value conservatively: $\theta_p = 0.083 \approx 0.09$

From the above reference, p. 157, which says: "Approximately 5% of water demand is consumed and not discharged to the sanitary system," and from this volume's estimated sewage flow rates listed in Table 5-8, and by rounding off conservatively, values for D_p were obtained for all occupancies listed in Table 5-1.

Regarding makeup air demand factor k: on p. 156 Steele uses 90 gpm AC makeup for an office peak flow rate of 375 gpm. Thus if θ_p for an office worker = 0.09 gpm, the average makeup air water demand per office worker at the moment of peak load in a temperate climate may be expressed as

$$0.09 \times 90/375 \approx 0.0216 \text{ gpm}$$

As peak water demand for makeup air is usually about 1.5 × higher than average demand, the above value may be adjusted conservatively for both demands as follows:

Average makeup air water demand: k_a = 0.0216 ➡ 0.02 gpm/occ.
Peak makeup air water demand: k_p = 0.0216 ➡ 0.03 gpm/occ.

For preliminary analysis these k values may be used for general sedentary or light-activity occupancies; otherwise the metabolism of more active occupants should be taken into consideration (then a simple comparison of average/actual metabolism of occupants will usually suffice). Finally, taking the average summer design temperature for temperate climates as 91°, the AC makeup for any climate may be expressed in terms of

$$\text{AC makeup} = (T_d - 65)/(91 - 65) = 0.038 \, (T_d - 65)$$

Substituting for k and AC makeup in the initial equations:

$$D_a = \eta \, \theta_a \, [1 + 0.02 \times 0.038 \, (T_d - 65)] + S$$
$$D_p = \eta \, \theta_p \, [1 + 0.03 \times 0.038 \, (T_d - 65)] + S$$

Streamlining:
$$D_a = \eta \, \theta_a \, [1 + 0.00077 \, (T_d - 65)] + S$$
$$D_p = \eta \, \theta_p \, [1 + 0.00115 \, (T_d - 65)] + S$$

5)C)d) **Step 1.** Original edition. This formula is one of a number of field-derived "probable-demand" formulas which work reasonably well for designing supply piping, because scientifically accurate design of such systems is practically impossible. This is due to (1) the effect of temperature (water at 40° F is 2% denser and three times more viscous than water at 140°), (2) possibility of depositable chemicals in the water of a particular region, (3) type of piping, (4) the great variety of field-assembled piping configurations, and (5) because water velocity cannot be too high (or pipe erosion results over time) or too low (or the pipe fills with sedimentation over time). The probable-demand formula in this section also exposes the kind of faulty scenarios as exhibited by Example 7, which occasionally occur in plumbing system design for which this formula has a solution. The formula also contains a considerable safety factor due to field testimony from some who have installed and inspected plumbing systems for years. To elucidate these points further, following is a scientific derivation of a formula for computing pipe pressure drop, which may prove useful in certain situations. From *Introduction to Fluid Mechanics*, John & Haberman (Prentice-Hall, NY, 1971), p. 98:

$$V = Q/A = Q/0.785\ d^2$$

If 1 fixture unit of flow = 2 gpm, 3.75 fu = 1 cfm. Converting Q from cfm to fixture units (F), d from ft to in., and V from fpm to fps:

$$V_{fps} = \frac{144\ F/60 \times 3.75 \times 0.785\ d^2}{}$$

Streamlining:
$$V_{fps} = 0.818\ F/d^2 \qquad (1)$$

From *Introduction to Fluid Mechanics*, p. 98:

$$p_2 - p_1 = [-0.5\ r\ V^2\ fL/g_c\ d] - [(z_2 - z_1)\ r\ g/g_c]$$

Setting $p_2 - p_1$ = net pipe pressure drop P_d, converting friction factor $f = 0.02$ to 1.0 for copper pipe, substituting 32.2 fps for g_c, converting d from ft to in., setting $z_2 - z_1$ = vertical distance h from inlet to outlet, and canceling g/g_c:

$$P_d = [-0.5 \times 12\ r\ V^2\ f_{cu}\ L/50 \times 32.2\ d] - h\ r$$

As r = density of water in lb/cf, substitute 62.4 for r, then convert r to $62.4/144 = 0.433$ psi:

$$P_d = [-0.5 \times 12 \times 0.433\ V^2\ f_{cu}\ L/50 \times 32.2\ d] - 0.433\ h \qquad (2)$$

Substituting equation 1 into equation 2:

$$P_d = [-0.5 \times 12 \times 0.433\ (0.818\ F_u/d^2)^2\ f_{cu}\ L/50 \times 32.2\ d] - 0.433\ h$$

Tailoring and streamlining: $\quad \Delta_p = [-f_{cu}\ L\ F_u^2/926\ d^5] - 0.433\ h$

Step 2. If a fixture unit ≈ a momentary peak load of 0.5 gpm and a continuous demand load of 14 gal/day, a daily nonfixture unit water load in gpm ≈ 14 equivalent fixture units; or

$$F_u \approx F_c \approx 1/14\ F_n \approx 0.071\ F_n$$

5 C 2   From a Sioux Chief Manufacturing Co. product catalog on engineered Water Hammer Arrestors (© 2000), page unknown, at the bottom of the page is a chart that relates the capacities of several water hammers (in^3) to a plumbing system's number of fixture units for male thread connections and male sweat connections. By computing the volumes of each arrestor, then plotting their volumes (C) vs. the no. of fixture units (F) on a loglog graph, the exponents for F were obtained in the formulas below:

Threaded connection: $C \approx F^{0.67}$
Sweated connection: $C \approx F^{0.74}$

4)C)4)b)2) From *Advanced Plumbing Technology*, Alfred Steele, p. 15, the formula for pump efficiency is given as

$$\varepsilon = \frac{\text{head} \times \text{capacity}}{39.6 \times \text{required horsepower}}$$

Tailoring and streamlining: $40 \text{ HP } \varepsilon \approx Þ H$

Introducing water viscosity variable κ_ν based on the temperature of the water being pumped:

$$40 \text{ HP } \varepsilon \approx Þ \kappa_\nu H$$

The relative values for water viscosity factor κ_ν at various temperatures between freezing and boiling were obtained from *Introduction to Fluid Mechanics*, John & Haberman, © 1971 Prentice-Hall, Englewood Cliffs, NJ, p. 12, then organized as a bar graph.

4)C)4)d) From *Advanced Plumbing Technology*, Alfred Steele, p. 139, the formula for cavitation is given as

$$\kappa_c = (P_o + 14.7)/(P_i - P_o)$$

in which cavitation is likely to occur if $\kappa_c \leq 0.5$. Multiplying both sides by 2 to give κ_c a more symbolic value of 1.0:

$$\kappa_c \approx 2 (P_o + 14.7)/(P_i - P_o)$$

Streamlining: $\quad \kappa_c (P_i - P_o) \approx 2 P_o + 14.7)$

4)C)4)e) In 1974 the author was told by a well driller with 40 years' experience (Frank Coyle of Brewster, NY) that a well should deliver in gpm about one-fifth the number of the building's plumbing fixture units. Since then the author has had no experience that would refute or improve on this information. The value for one-fifth is the 0.2 in the formula

$$Þ \approx 0.2 (F + 0.071 F_n)$$

4)C)4)g)1) Step 1. *Advanced Plumbing Technology*, Alfred Steele, p. 182, describes a method for sizing a suction tank from which the following conclusions are easily made:

1. Peak demand ÷ no. of pumps = water supplied by each pump.
2. If the pump cycles 6 times/hr, the length of each cycle = 60/(2 × no. cycles per hr) or 5 min. Thus the amount of water supplied by the pump = (peak demand ÷ no. of pumps) × (60 ÷ 2 × no. cycles per hr).
3. The amount of water supplied by one pump equals the tank's water withdrawal capacity.

Thus a suction tank's total water volume may be expressed as

$$V_w = (D_p/\eta)(60/_{2\,C})(100/_H)$$

Converting gal to cf: $V_w = (1/_{7.49})(D_p/\eta)(60/_{2\,C})(100/_H)$

Streamlining: $400\,D_p = \eta\,C\,V_w\,H$

Step 2. The total volume of a suction tank = water volume + air volume. According to Boyle's Law,

air volume at min. capacity = max. pressure in tank
air volume at max. capacity = min. pressure in tank

Thus a suction tank's required air volume may be expressed as

$$[(\text{withdrawal capacity \%})/100] \times \text{water volume} \times P_{max}/P_{min}$$

Or... $V_a = W_c\,V_w\,P_{max}/100\,P_{min}$

If total tank volume = water volume + air volume, then

$$V_t = V_w + W_c\,V_w\,P_{max}/100\,P_{min}$$

Streamlining: $(V_t - V_w)\,P_{min} = 0.01\,W_c\,V_w\,P_{max}$

4)C)4)9)7) From *Advanced Plumbing Technology*, Alfred Steele, p. 92-93, it is clear that the theoretical minimum surge tank capacity = period of pump operation × (house pump capacity - supply rate from public main). As this reference states that 20 min/hr is a satisfactory period of pump operation and that the house pump capacity = peak demand of water supply, then $V_r = 20\,(C - Q)$

The above reference, p. 93, also adds a safety factor of 6500/6000 = 1.083. Rounding off to a more conservative number of 1.1:

$$V_r = 1.1 \times 20\,(C - Q)$$

Converting from gal to cf: $V_r = 1.1 \times 20\,(C - Q)/_{7.49}$

Tailoring and streamlining: $V_r = 2.9\,(D_p - Þ)$

4)C)4)h) *Architectural Graphic Standards*, 6th Edition (Wiley, NY, 1970), p. 588, states the capacity of a water softener = gal of water/day × no. of days of service (cycle time) × hardness of water (grains/gal). Or

$$C = D_a\,T\,H$$

However, *Advanced Plumbing Technology*, Alfred Steele, p. 92-93, states that "Production of zero hardness water is extremely wasteful... [and] zero hardness water is very aggressive and should be avoided if at all possible. It is, therefore, good design practice to... bring the softened water back up to 4 or 5 grains hardness." Thus

$$C = D_a T (H - 4.0)$$

4)C)4)i) **Step 1.** A water heater's ability to deliver hot water equals its capacity + recovery rate. As its water temperature is too cold for hot water use if more than $2/3$ of its capacity + recovery is drawn down, multiply its total volume by 1.5, or

$$V = 1.5 (C + R)$$

If the average cold water is 55° F and the average hot water is 140° F, the equation works for any cold or hot temperature if

$$V = 1.5 (C + R) (T_h + T_c)/85$$

If the recovery rate for a gas water heater ≈ 0.56 and an electric water heater ≈ 0.40, then

$$V_{gas} = 1.5 (C + 0.56 \, C) (T_h + T_c)/85$$
$$V_{elec} = 1.5 (C + 0.40 \, C) (T_h + T_c)/85$$

The demand on V = momentary demand (gpm) × peak demand. As 1 fixture unit = 0.5 gpm, momentary demand = $0.5 \, F + F_n$. As it is rare that all fixtures run at once for more than 12 minutes, fix duration of demand at 12 min. Thus

$$\text{Demand} = (0.5 \, F + F_n) \times 12 = V$$

Then for gas heaters: $(0.5 \, F + F_n) \times 12 = 1.5 (1.56 \, C_{gas}) (T_h + T_c)/85$
And for electric heaters: $(0.5 \, F + F_n) \times 12 = 1.5 (1.40 \, C_{elec}) (T_h + T_c)/85$

Streamlining: $220 (F + F_n) = C_{gas} (T_h + T_c)$
                    $245 (F + F_n) = C_{elec} (T_h + T_c)$

Step 2. On p. 137 of *Engineered Plumbing Design* is a fixture unit diversity graph which author Steele says "is demonstrably accurate," but because peoples' lifestyles have changed in the 50 years since it was made, "it is safe to reduce the values obtained by 40 per cent." By doing this, then comparing analogous values for the graph's fixture units with values computed in F = 0.47 C (an abbreviated version of the formulas in Step 1), the following table was prepared [only a few values are shown]:

Demand load, fixture units	Div. demand load, gpm, flush tanks	60% div. demand load, flush tanks	V = F/0.47	Analogous div. demand: 21/5 × col. 3
10	8	5	21	21
100	44	26	213	109
1000	208	125	2127	525
10000	769	461	21276	1940

By making a bar graph of column 4 vs. column 5, a diversity factor is obtained for determining effective HWH capacities.

<u>4)C)7)</u> This section's "9,500" formula was derived from the numerous small formulas on pp. 55–57 of *The Site Calculations Pocket Reference*, Ed Hannon (Wiley, NY, 1999).

<u>4)C)8)</u> This section has nearly a dozen formulas, most them simple, which were derived from an analysis of the *Standard Handbook of Engineering Calculations*, Tyler Hicks, Editor (McGraw-Hill, NY, 1995), pp. 2-58 to 61. Here only the derivation of the two most complex formulas are desctibed.

Step 10. From p. 2.60, Step 8 of the above-cited reference, the following is obvious:

$$Q_d = \eta\,(V_p \times C) \times D$$

wherein Q_d is the amount of disinfectant the pool requires (lb/day), η is the number of hours per day the pool is open ($\div$ 24) hr/day, C = 3 changes of pool water per day, and D is the required disinfectant which = 0.5 lb ($\times$ 8.33 lb/gal)/1,000,000 lb of water per day. Substituting the above values into the formula:

$$Q_d = \frac{\eta\,(V_p \times 3) \times 0.5 \times 8.33}{24 \times 1,000,000}$$

Streamlining: $\qquad 1{,}920{,}000\,Q_d = \eta\,V_p$

Step 11. From p. 2.60, Step 9 of the above-cited reference, the following heat flow equation is obvious:

$$\mathbf{H}_{btu} = C\,(T_i - T_o)$$

wherein $\mathbf{H}_{btu}$ is the pool water's required heating load, C is the capacity of the pool water heating system, T_i is the pool water temperature, and T_o is the lowest temperature of the incoming water supply. As p. 2-60 says, "The usual swimming pool heater has a heating capacity which is 10 times the circulating pumps rating," C can be said to equal 10 C_h. Then, by multiplying C_h (gpm) $\times$ 8.33 lb/gal $\times$ 12,000 btu/lb, the formula becomes

$$\mathbf{H}_{btu} = 10\,C_h\,(T_i - T_o) \times 8.33 \times 12{,}000$$

Streamlining: $\qquad \mathbf{H}_{btu} = 1{,}000{,}000\,C_h\,(T_i - T_o)$

P. 2-60 also says the above formula is based on the following, "To heat the entire contents of the pool, at least 48 hours is allowed." Thus if the pool's contents must be heated in any other timespan, a length-of-time factor η_{hr} should be inserted into the formula:

$$\eta\,\mathbf{H} = 48 \times 1{,}000{,}000\,C_p\,(T_i - T_o)$$

Finally, during the many hours the pool is filling with water, if the pool's walls and floor are surrounded by earth whose temperature is cooler than that of the pool water, some the water's heat will escape into the surrounding earth. This loss must be calculated, then added to the formula:

$$\eta\, H = 48 \times 1,000,000\, C_p\, (T_i - T_o) + \Delta L$$

Streamlining;
$$\eta\, H = 48,000,000\, C_p\, (T_i - T_o) + \Delta L$$

4)D)1) Step 2. As 1 fixture unit $\approx$ 0.5 gpm of full-pipe flow, the total equivalent fixture unit full-pipe flow may be described as

$$0.5\, P_{fu} \approx P_{gpm}$$

Taking the specific gravity of the liquid into consideration,

$$0.5\, P_{fu} \approx P_{gpm}\, \text{ß}$$

As this formula is for water, which has a viscosity at room temperature of 1.022×10^{-5}, the above formula may be used for a liquid of any viscosity at any temperature by

$$0.5\, P_{fu} \approx P_{gpm}\, \text{ß}\, (\text{υ}/1.022 \times 10^{-5})$$
$$1/1.022 \times 10^{-5} = 97,800$$
$$0.5\, P_{fu} \approx 97,800\, P_{gpm}\, \text{ß}\, \text{υ}$$

Tailoring and streamlining: $P_{fu} \approx 49,000\, P_{gpm}\, \text{ß}\, \text{υ}$

Step 5. The velocity of a liquid flowing continuously through a pipe of two different diameters may be described as

$$V_1/V_2 = A_2/A_1 = d_2^2/d_1^2 \text{ or } d^2/d_r^2$$

If the liquid's velocity through the first pipe is 8 fps, then

$$8/P_{fu} = d^2/d_r^2$$

Then
$$d_r^2 = P_{fu}\, d^2/8 = 0.125\, P_{fu}\, d^2$$
Streamlining:
$$d_r = 0.353\, d\, P_{fps}^{0.5}$$

4)D)2) If the volume of gasflow through a pipe of certain diameter is in cfm and its velocity is in fps, then

$$P_{cfm} = k\, P_{fps}$$

If 1 min = 60 sec, 1 sf of sectional area = 144 in^2, and the sectional area of a pipe = 0.785 d^2, then

$$P_{cfm} \times 1 \times (144/60) \times 0.785\, d^2 = k\, P_{fps}$$

Streamlining:
$$3.06\, P_{cfm} = P_{fps}\, d^2$$

4)D)2)a)2) Step 2. From *Advanced Plumbing Technology*, Alfred Steele, p. 92-93, waterflow formulas for brass, copper, iron, and steel piping are given as

Brass and copper: $Q = 60.8\, d^{2.5}\,(P/_L)^{0.5}$
Iron and steel: $\quad Q = 43.0\, d^{2.5}\,(P/_L)^{0.5}$

in which Q = quantity of flow (gpm), d = pipe diameter (in.), P = permissible pressure drop (psi), and L = equivalent length of pipe (ft). Squaring both sides and streamlining:

Brass and copper: $L\,Q^2 = 3{,}700\, P\,d^5$
Iron and steel: $\quad L\,Q^2 = 1{,}850\, P\,d^5$

If a pipe material coefficient κ_m is introduced into these equations as = 1.0 for brass and copper piping, then κ_m = 3,700/1.85 = 2.0 for iron and steel piping, and

$$\kappa_m\, L\, Q^2 = 3{,}700\, P\,d^5$$

Since Steele on p. 92-93 states: "The procedure for sizing oxygen [or any other gas] piping is straightforward and similar to sizing water piping," the above equation may be written in the following form as a gas equation with k = a constant of unknown value:

$$\kappa_m\, L\, Q^2 = k\,\Delta P\, P\,d^5$$

Inserting a specific gravity factor σ = 1.11 for oxygen:

$$\sigma^e\, \kappa_m\, L\, Q^2 = k\,\Delta P\, P\,d^5$$

From *Timesaver Standards*, 5th Edition, p. 881-884, exponential analysis of corresponding values for oxygen, nitrous oxide, compressed air, and vacuum air gases indicates that the specific gravity exponent $e \approx 0.5$. Thus

$$\sigma^{0.5}\, \kappa_m\, L\, Q^2 = k\,\Delta P\,d^5$$

Advanced Plumbing Technology, Alfred Steele, p. 257, Table 19-3 lists data for sizing piping for conveying oxygen and nitrous oxide. By plotting all pressure drop values vs. oxygen flow and pipe diameter in Table 19-3 on a 3 × 3 cycle loglog graph (see Fig. A-4) and trying numerous values from Table 19-3 in the above equation, it was found that k = 143,000,000. Thus

$$\sigma^{0.5}\, \kappa_m\, L\, Q^2 = 143{,}000{,}000\, \Delta P\,d^5$$

Converting L to an equivalent length of 1.5 L in consideration of pipe friction flow losses due to valves and fittings, converting Q from liters/min to cfm (1 cf = 28.3 liters), and letting Q = Þ:

$$\sigma^{0.5}\, \kappa_m\, L\, Þ^2 \approx 143{,}000{,}000\, \Delta P\,d^5/1.5 \times 28.32$$

Tailoring and streamlining: $\quad L\,\kappa_m\,\beta^{0.5}\,Þ^2 \approx 120{,}000\, \Delta P\,d^5$

5)D)2)b)3) **Step 6.** From the *Machinery Handbook, 7th Edition*, Erik Oberg & Frank Jones, Editors (Industrial Press, NY, 1975), p. 1458, the formula for computing the horsepower required to compress 1 cf of free air

[gas] per minute (one-stage compression) is given as

$$HP = 0.015\, P\, (R^{0.29} - 1)$$

If $P = 14.7$ psi and $R = [(P_i - 14.7)/14.7]$, then

$$HP = 0.015 \times 14.7\{[((P_i - 14.7)/14.7]^{0.29} - 1\}$$

Inserting Þ = quantity of gas pipe flow, cfm:

$$HP = 0.015 \times 14.7\, Þ\, \{[((P_i - 14.7)/14.7]^{0.29} - 1\}$$

As the above-cited text clearly indicates that Þ is a free gas at an atmospheric pressure of 14.7 psi and this volume's formula should include Þ as a gas compressed to any pressure, Þ at any pressure may be expressed as Þ $P_i/14.7$. Thus the above formula may be rewritten for a quantity of gas at any pressure as

$$HP = 0.015 \times 14.7\, Þ\, P_i/14.7\{[((P_i - 14.7)/14.7]^{0.29} - 1\}$$

Streamlining: $$67\, HP = Þ\, P_i\, \{[((P_i - 14.7)/14.7]^{0.29} - 1\}$$

4)E)1) **Step 2.** From *Engineered Plumbing Design*, Alfred Steele (Construction Industry Press, Elmhurst, IL, 1982), p. 22, is Manning's formula:

$$Q = 1.486\, A\, R^{0.67}\, S^{0.5}/n$$

in which Q = quantity of flow (cfs), A = c-s area of flow (sf), R = hydraulic radius (ft), and n = a pipe roughness coefficient. The two optimal load conditions for which this formula should be devised are half full for sanitary drains and full for storm drains. As Steele on p. 23 shows that hydraulic radius $R = d/4$ for both conditions:

$$Q = 1.486\, A\, (0.25\, d)^{0.67}\, S^{0.5}/n$$

As A = 0.785 d^2: $$Q = 1.486 \times 0.785\, d^2\, (0.25\, d)^{0.67}\, S^{0.5}/n$$

On p. 25 Steele lists a schedule of values for n as ranging from 0.012 to 0.016 for pipes ranging from $1\frac{1}{2}$ to 8+ in. dia. But as the related text (and common knowledge) indicates that sanitary drain flow is imprecise, and because the exponential nature of d shrinks the differences between these values even more ($d^{2.67} = k\, 0.016/0.012$ ➝ only 11% difference), a simplified average value of $n = 0.135$ may be taken for sanitary drain flow. Thus,

$$Q = 1.486 \times 0.785\, d^2\, (0.25\, d)^{0.67}\, S^{0.5}/0.0135$$

Converting Q from cf/sec to 60 × 7.49 gpm and d from ft to in.:

$$Q = 60 \times 7.49 \times 1.486 \times 0.785\, (d/12)^2\, (0.25 \times d/12)^{0.67}\, S^{0.5}/0.0135$$

Tailoring and streamlining: $F = 20\, d^{2.67}\, \Delta^{0.5}$

If 1 gpm = 0.5 fixture units of flow, then $F = 10\, d^{2.67}\, \Delta^{0.5}$

Adding a nonfixture unit equivalent flow factor:

$$F + 0.08 \ W \ = \ 10 \ d^{2.67} \Delta^{0.5}$$

4)E)1)c) If the effluent in a waste interceptor should be allowed 1 day to settle, then

$$V \ = \ Þ$$

with V being the interceptor's interior volume and $Þ$ equalling the average daily volume of effluent entering the interceptor. If 1 fixture unit of momentary peak demand flow $\approx$ 14 gal/day, W = the amount of nonfixture unit wasteflow, and $V = C$, the unit's rated static holding capacity in cf/day, then

$$C \ = \ 14 \ F + W$$

Multiplying the unit's capacity × 1.25 daily wasteflow safety factor, then × 1.15 in consideration of the required vertical void above the influent invert and the space taken up by the baffles, then converting gal to cf:

$$V \ = \ 1.25 \times 1.15 \ ^{(14 \ F + \ W)}/7.49$$

Streamlining: $V \ = \ 0.19 \ (14 \ F + W)$

4)E)1)d) **Step 2.** From *Engineered Plumbing Design*, Alfred Steele (Construction Industry Press, Elmhurst, IL, 1982), p. 108, the capacity of an ejector = peak load of effluent (gpm) × 5 min pump cycle. Converting the load from gpm to fixture units and capacity from gal to cf, then including a 1.6 safety factor:

$$V \ = \ 0.5 \times 5 \times \ ^{1.6} \ F/7.49$$

Including an equivalent nonfixture unit flow factor and streamlining:

$$V \ = \ 0.53 \ (F + 0.07 \ W)$$

Step 3. From *Engineered Plumbing Design*, Alfred Steele, p. 108, the standard diameter for a duplex pump system is 4 ft.

Step 4. As the volume V of a cylinder = $\pi \ h \ d^2/4$, then

$$h \ = \ ^V/_{0.785 \ d^2}$$

From *Engineered Plumbing Design*, Steele, p. 109, an ejector's cylindrical dia. = 4 ft and its height = storage height + 3 in. airspace at top + 6 in. suction invert basin + 3 ft below subdrain pipe. Thus

$$h \ = \ ^V/_{0.785 \ (4)^2} + 0.25 + 0.5 + 3.0$$

Streamlining: $h \ = \ 0.08 \ V + 3.75$

4)E)3) *Rules and Regulations of New York, Title 10, Chapter 11, Part 75, Appendix 75-A, Wastewater Treatment Standards, Individual Household*

Systems [a 32 page pamphlet], p. 5-13, Table 3, indicates that the septic tank capacity for a residence = [750 + 250 (B – 2)] gal, in which B = number of bedrooms ≥ 2. This equation indicates that a septic tank's minimum capacity for any occupancy = 750 gal. Also from *Engineered Plumbing Design*, Alfred Steele (Construction Industry Press, Elmhurst, IL, 1982), p. 209, septic sewage is usually retained for 24 hours. Thus, by equating any commercial fixture units at 14 gal/day per fixture unit × 1.25 safety factor, then equating any nonfixture unit flow at gal/day × 1.25 safety factor:

$$C = 750 + 250 (B - 2) + 17.5 F + 1.25 W$$

Converting from gal. to cf:

$$C = 100 + 33 (B - 2) + 2.5 F + 0.2 W$$

Analysis of *Table 3* in *Rules and Regulations of New York* also indicates that a septic tank's minimum liquid surface area (sf) ≥ 0.027 minimum tank capacity (gal).

4)E)4) From *Rules and Regulations of New York, Table 4A, Required Length of Absorption Trench*, p. 16, the following data is prepared:

Number of bedrooms	Perc rate, 11-15 min/in.	Interpolate perc rate = 12	Interval btwn. bedrooms
2	188	185	2 × 92
3	281	277	92
4	375	369	92
5	469	461	92
6	563	553	92

Thus at 2 ft wide and 12 min/in. perc, k = 92 lf. Then from the formula in *Sec. 5.E.3.* if 33 B = 92 lf, B can be said to = 92/33 = 2.78. Thus if each B requires 33 × 2.78 = 92 lf of trench, by analogy each fixture unit of effluent requires 2.5 × 2.78 ≈ 7 lf of trench and each gal. of equivalent nonfixture unit waste requires 0.2 × 2.78 ≈ 0.6 lf of trench. Plotting perc vs. application rate on a LOGLOG graph: lf = $k\, P^{0.39}$

Thus $\qquad L = (92\,B + 7\,F + 0.6\,W) \times 3\,w \times P^{0.39}/2 \times 2.64$

Streamlining: $\qquad L = 0.57\,w\,(92\,B + 7\,F + 0.6\,W)\,P^{0.39}$

4)F)1)4) A firehose standpipe's elongation = pipe length between its expansion loops or offsets × coefficient of thermal expansion × Δt, or

$$\epsilon = 12\,L\,\kappa_t\,(\Delta t + 5)$$

The lateral length required for the loop to absorb the pipe's thermal elongation without deforming past its elastic limit ≈ 36 × elongation × √pipe diameter, or

$$Ł \approx 36 \in d^{0.5}$$

Thus $\qquad \in = Ł/36\ d^{0.5} = 12\ L\ \kappa_f\ (\Delta t + 5)$

Streamlining: $\qquad Ł \approx 430\ \kappa_f\ L\ (\Delta t + 5)\ d^{0.5}$

__4)__ __F)__ __1)__ __a)__ From *Engineered Plumbing Design*, Alfred Steele (Construction Industry Press, Elmhurst, IL, 1982), p. 128, the formula for the outlet flow of a water reservoir (i.e. a standpipe) is

$$q = 20\ d^2\ P^{0.5}$$

Also a standpipe's total pressure = minimum pressure at the top outlet + 0.433 × riser height, or

$$P = 25 + 0.433\ h$$

Substituting: $\qquad Þ = 20\ d^2\ (25 + 0.433\ h)^{0.5}$

As standpipes have 2½ in. outlet connections, substitute 2.5 in. for d:

$$Þ = 0.95 \times 20\ (2.5)^2\ (25 + 0.433\ h)^{0.5}$$

Multiply by 0.95 to account for general system pipe friction losses:

$$Þ = 0.95 \times 20\ (2.5)^2\ (25 + 0.433\ h)^{0.5}$$

Add η for multiple hose outlets:

$$Þ = 0.95 \times 20\ (2.5)^2\ η\ (25 + 0.433\ h)^{0.5}$$

Streamlining: $\qquad Þ = 119\ η\ (25 + 0.433\ h)^{0.5}$

Step 2. The reservoir volume = rate of flow × minimum 30 min water supply ÷ 7.49 gal/cf, or

$$V = Þ \times 30/7.49$$

Streamlining: $\qquad V = 4\ Þ$

__4)__ __F)__ __2)__ __c)__ **Steps 8a and 8b.** The required water reservoir for gravity-feed systems = total water demand × 0.25 of sprinkler head flow (unless the number of heads < 16) × minimum duration of water supply ÷ 7.49 gal/cf, or

$$V = Þ\ T \times 0.25/7.49$$

Streamlining: $\qquad Þ\ T = 30\ V$

As the required water reservoir for upfeed pump systems = 0.10 sprinkler head flow (unless the number of heads < 40), in like fashion:

$$Þ\ T = 77\ C$$

Chapter 5: Electricity

<u>5</u><u>C</u><u>4</u><u>1</u> **Step 1.** *Consulting and Specifying Engineer Magazine*, Aug. 1996 (Cahners Publishing Co., Des Plains, IL), p. 31, lists the following two Energy-Related Formulas:

(1) Kilowatts saved $= 746 \times HP \times 10^{-3} \times$ (1/Eff. motor X – 1/Eff. motor Y)
(2) Energy dollars saved $=$ KW saved $\times$ cost/kWh $\times$ hr running/year

Substituting formula (1) into (2) and symbolizing the variables:

$$\Delta_{ac} = 746 \, P \times 10^{-3} \, (100/\mathcal{E}_o - 100/\mathcal{E}_n) \, \mathcal{E} \, t$$

Adding a 0.9 nominal depreciation factor, converting P to unit cost of electric power ¢, inserting η for the number of units being compared, converting 746×10^{-3} to a power conversion factor κ_c, and streamlining:

$$\Delta_{ac} = 0.009 \, ¢ \, \eta \, \kappa_c \, \mathcal{E} \, t \, (100/\mathcal{E}_o - 100/\mathcal{E}_n)$$

<u>5</u><u>C</u><u>4</u><u>2</u> **Step 1.** The basic formula for torque is

$$\text{torque} = 52.5 \times hp \times \text{efficiency/motor rpm}$$

Reducing by an efficiency factor of 0.9, symbolizing the variables, and streamlining:

$$T \upsilon = 47 \, \text{HP} \, \mathcal{E}$$

<u>5</u><u>C</u><u>4</u><u>3</u> **Step 1.** The basic formula for fan hp is

$$\text{HP} = \frac{\text{fan airflow (shaft speed/1,750)}^2 \times \text{static airflow resistance}}{k \times \text{motor efficiency}}$$

As air resistance lowers with increase in altitude, include an elevation factor $(1 - 0.000034 \times \text{site elevation above sea level})$:

$$\text{HP} = w/ \rho \, (\upsilon/1,750)^2/k \, \mathcal{E} \, (1 - 0.000034 \, E)$$

Substituting values and solving for k indicates that $k = 75$. Thus,

$$\text{HP} = w/ \rho \, (\upsilon/1,750)^2/75 \, \mathcal{E} \, (1 - 0.000034 \, E)$$
Streamlining: $\quad 75 \, \text{HP} \, \mathcal{E} \, (1 - 0.000034 \, E) = w/ \rho \, (0.00057 \, \upsilon)^2$

<u>5</u><u>C</u><u>4</u><u>4</u> **Step 1.** The basis of determining the air cooling load for an electric motor is that the electrical energy that enters the motor exits the motor either as rotational energy, which is defined by its elliciency, or heat, which then is defined by the difference between the motor's efficiency and 100 percent. Thus the *Standard Handbook of Engineering Calculations*, Tyler Hicks, Editor (McGraw-Hill, NY, 1995). p. 4.87, gives the formula for heat generated by an electric motor as

$$H = 2{,}545 \text{ bhp}_c \, {}^{(1.0 \, - \, \mathcal{E})}/\mathcal{E}$$

Tailoring: $\qquad H\,\mathcal{E} = 2{,}545 \text{ IP } (100 - \mathcal{E}) \qquad\qquad$ (1)

Step 2. Hicks' p. 4.87 also gives the following formula for computing the airflow required to remove the motor's produced heat:

$$Q = 2{,}358 \text{ bhp}_c \, {}^{(1.0 \, - \, \mathcal{E})}/\mathcal{E} \, \Delta t$$

If $\Delta T = (t_m - t_i)$, then $\quad \mathcal{E} = 2{,}358 \text{ IP } {}^{(1.0 \, - \, \mathcal{E})}/Q\,(t_m - t_i) \qquad$ (2)

Heating load **H** = cooling load **C** = required cooling airflow Q

Subst. (2) into (1): $\quad$ **H** $[2{,}358 \text{ IP } {}^{(1.0 \, - \, \mathcal{E})}/Q\,(t_m - t_i)] = 2{,}545 \text{ IP } (100 - \mathcal{E})$

Streamlining: $\qquad\qquad$ **C** $= 108\, Q\,(t_m - t_i)$

5)D)1)a) The *Building Construction Handbook,* Frederick Merritt, Editor (McGraw-Hill, NY, 1975), p. 22-13, gives the following formula fro computing voltage drop in a conductor or circuit:

$$V_d = 2\,R\,I\,L/\text{c.m.}$$

wherein V_d is the conductor's voltage drop, R is its resistance (ohms/cmil-ft), I is its current (amps), L is its length (ft), and c.m. is its diameter in circular mils. Since a conductor's voltage drop is a percentage of its voltage, V_d is better expressed as $V\,\Delta V/100$. Then if R = the electrical symbol Ω, amperage $I = A$, and c.m. $= C$, the formula becomes

$$C\,V\Delta V = 100 \times 2\,\Omega\,A\,L$$

Merritt's p. 22-13 actually lists two formulas, one for single-phase wiring and one for three-phase wiring, whose only difference is 2 vs. $\sqrt{3} = 1.73$. [The second formula contains a mistake: $\sqrt{3}$ should be $2\,\sqrt{3}$]. Thus, introducing a phase factor Φ into the formula, it becomes

$$C\,V\Delta V = 200\,\Omega\,\Phi\,A\,L$$

As this formula is valid when the conductor's current is given in amps, and as amps = watts ÷ volts, a similar formula can be devised for wattage by replacing A with W/V, then streamlining as follows:

$$C\,V^2\,\Delta V = 200\,\Phi\,\Omega\,W\,L$$

The text that accompanies Merritt's formulas also says "The value of R may be taken as 10.7 for copper and 17.7 for aluminum." Thus, in this volume, these values for R are entered into the no-math menu for these formulas.

5)D)1)a)1) Since the load carried by an overhead electrical conductor is a uniform load on a simple span, its bending moment equation is

$$0.125\, \omega\, L^2 = f_b\, S_x$$

wherein f_b for a cable $= f_t$ and the section modulus S_x for a circular section $= 0.0982\ \delta^3$. Substituting these values into the above formula and streamlining:

$$1.39\ \omega\, L^2 = f_t\, \delta^3$$

Regarding the total stress in overhead wires, the venerable *General Engineering Handbook*, Charles O'Rourke, Editer (McGraw-Hill, NY, 1932), pp. 866–888 warns that in very cold weather a conductor may experience in addition to its dead weight "an added weight due to ice loading", "extra pressure due to wind acting horizontally", and an increased tensile load at its support caused by a contracting of its length due to sharply decreased temperature; and this text is accompanied by a graph that gives load factors for different-size wires. From this data was devised the load factor κ_L, which is inserted into the formula as follows:

$$1.39\ \kappa_L\ \omega\, L^2 = f_t\, \delta^3$$

5)E)1)1) As a rigid conduit may be up to 40% filled, its capacity = no. of wires × C-S area. Setting the capacity ≤ 0.40 × conduit C-S area,

$$0.40 \times 0.785\ d^2 \le \eta\, A$$
Streamlining: $\qquad 0.31\ d^2 \le \eta\, A$

If the wireway contains several different sizes of wires, the rest of the formula is self-explanatory.

5)E)2) According to the NEC, a wireway may be up to 20% filled. Thus its capacity ≥ number of wires × C-S area, or

$$0.20\ A_w \ge \eta\, A$$

5)F)3)a) The *Standard Handbook of Engineering Calculations*, Tyler Hicks, Editor (McGraw-Hill, NY, 1995). p. 3.310, Table 4 lists the total air volume needs for several internal combustion generators. From this data was devised the formula in Step 1. The formula in Step 2 is a heat flow formula based on the required cooling load which equals the engine's airflow requirements found in Step 1.

5)G)1) Regarding windplant design, *The Energy Primer* (Portola Institute, Menlo PArk, CA, 1974), p. 77-78, says that (1) "The actual power available from the wind is proportional to the cube of the windspeed," (2) "Power is proportional to the square of the prop," and (3) "A 6 foot diameter prop, operating at [typical] 70% efficiency in a 20 mph wind, can produce 340 watts." This data takes the following algebraic form,

$$340\ \text{watts} = k\ (6\ \text{ft dia.})^2 \times (20\ \text{mph wind})^3 \times (0.70\ \text{efficiency})$$

Solving for k: $340 = k \times 6^2 \times 20^3 \times 0.70$ ... $k = \frac{1}{5,930}$
Streamlining: $5,900 \, \Omega \approx \varepsilon \, d^2 \, v^3$

Step 2. If Ω in Step 1 above is in watts/hr and the occupancy's design electric load W is in kWh/day, then

$$\Omega = \frac{24}{1,000} \geq \varepsilon_c$$

Streamlining: $\Omega = 42 \, \varepsilon_c$

6)G)2) **Step 1.** *The Energy Primer,* © 1974, Portola Institute, p. 56, gives the following formula for computing the net horsepower for a water power source:

$$NHP = \frac{Q \, h \, E}{8.8}$$

Converting NHP from 1 hp to 0.746 kWh, converting E to percent efficiency ε, then tailoring and streamlining:

$$660 \, \Omega \approx H \varepsilon W$$

Step 2. If Ω in Step 1 above is in kWh and the occupancy's critical electric load ε_c is in kWh/day, then

$$\varepsilon_c \geq 24 \, \Omega$$

Chapter 6: Illumination

6)A)1)a) In the *Lighting Handbook, 8th Edition* (Illumination Engineering Society of North America, NY, 1993), p. 389, is a graph that shows a near-field illuminance error curve for a square diffuse emitter of light. By smoothing out the curve, determining values for critical points along the curve, then taking the square roots of these values as representative of line-source illumination (as a square diffuse emitter is an area source of light), the author obtained the near-field scale for the adjustment bar graph of Fig. 7-2. Fig. A-1 is a copy of his original data as plotted on p. 389 of the *Lighting Handbook*. In this analysis the author selected as a dividing line between near-field and far-field photometry the ratio 1:6 between the maximum dimension of a lamp or facing and the distance between it and the visual task, even though a ratio of 1:5, or "five-times rule", is often used for this analysis in illumination design; because scrutiny of the above-cited graph indicates that the illuminance error at a ratio of 1:5 is 4% while the error at 1:6 is only 2%, and if a 2% error in calculations can be eliminated this easily, it should be done so.

6)A)1)b) If one takes an incandescent bulb with a full-sphere output

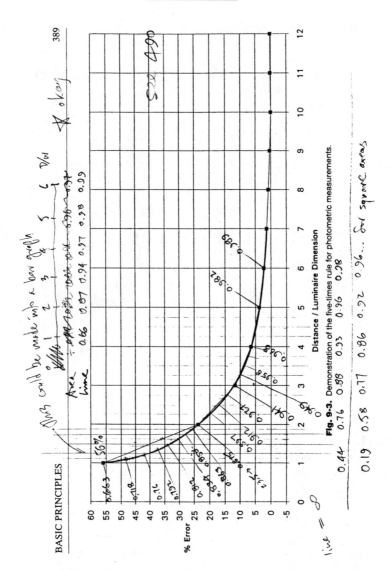

Fig. A-1. Illuminance error curve for square diffuse emitter.

(minus the ±30° cone shadow formed by its base) and places a reflector behind a considerable portion of the lamp, much of the ambient output is redirected through the aperture that remains with a resulting increase in the bulb's axial unit output. This output is a function of the reflector's portion of enclosure, geometric shape, and interior finish. The author analyzed these 3 variables for dozens of light fixtures whose footprints and construction were described in their product catalogs. Especially helpful in this analysis was the *1994 HALO Power-Trac Catalog, Lamp Performance Data*, pp. 92-95, which included the beamspreads vs. axial output of 62 lamps. The author also set up a 'laboratory' in his living room where from midnight to 3 am on moonless nights (when no spill light could enter from adjacent spaces) he measured enclosure apertures with a protractor, analyzed reflectors' geometric contours, and measured with a light meter the lamp luminances reflected from a 30 × 40 in. illustration board of known reflectivity located a known distance from each light source, and in this manner he obtained or verified the data for ray concentration values for the portions of enclosure, reflector contours, and reflector finishes that appear in Table 7-1. For example, a 100 W A19 lamp (whose 360° – 30° full-sphere illuminance = 3 fc at 6 ft) inserted into 3 fixtures made by the CSL Lighting Co. produced the following data at 6 ft:

> EcoStar w/ baked enamel 274° sphere ➔ 22 axial fc.
> Eyeball w/ silver mirror 274° ellipse ➔ 41 axial fc.
> Square w/ matte black anti-glare 274° cone ➔ 20 axial fc.

Due to certain parameters involved in this extensive data-gathering the values in Table 7-1 are only estimates. But an estimate, especially one without scatter, is much better than a guesstimate or nothing at all.

6)A)1)e) The usual method of computing room $\mathcal{U}$ is usually valid only for a rectangular room that is not too large or small or oblong, whose ceiling is not abnormally high or low, and whose surface reflectances are within a narrow range (particularly floor $R \approx 0.20$). These values are so narrow that an experienced engineer often needs to do little more than visualize such a space to give it a $\mathcal{U}$ of between 0.50 and 0.55. Thus by trial-and-error analysis of spatial characteristics and actual light meter readings of task planes in numerous unusual spaces, the author devised the more universal curve-fitting formula,

$$\mathcal{U} \approx 1.13 \, [R \, L \, W/10 \, H \, (L + W)]^{0.34}$$

6)A)1)g) If an 80 year-old person's eyes require about 80% more light to see as well as he or she could see at the age of 40, then

$$(40/80)^e = 1/1.80$$
$$0.50^e = 0.556$$
$$e \log 0.50 = \log 0.556$$
$$e = \log 0.556/0.50 = -0.25523/-0.30103$$
$$e = 0.847 \approx 0.85$$

Adding duration, error, fenestration, and protective lens factors:

$$\Theta \approx K_D \, K_E \, K_F \, K_P \, (40/A)^{0.85}$$

<u>6</u><u>B</u><u>4</u> A lamp's total life cycle cost = initial cost + total energy consumed during its rated life (lamp wattage in kWh × unit cost of electric power per kWh × rated lamp life), or

$$\$_t = \$_i + \omega \times \epsilon \times L$$

However, what is meaningful for comparative cost analysis is *unit* life cycle cost, which is total life cycle cost ÷ rate lamp life. Thus

$$\$_u = \$_{i/L} + wKh \times \epsilon$$

Converting kWh to watts and unit cost of electric power from dollars to cents and streamlining:

$$\$_u L = 100\ \cent_i + \omega\ \epsilon\ L$$
$$100\ \$_i = L\ (\cent_u - 0.001\ \omega\ \epsilon)$$

<u>6</u><u>D</u><u>7</u><u>f</u> From *Sec. 7.A.1.*, the basic lighting load equation for a full-sphere light source is

$$\diamond = \Phi\ D^2$$

However, regarding fiber optic light transmission from illuminator to end fitting, the full-sphere distance D^2 in the above formula must be replaced by a linear transmissivity factor τ^L, in which τ is the fiber's transmissivity or light attenuation per lf of length and L is the fiber's length. Then the basic fiber optic lighting equation becomes

$$\diamond = \Phi\ \tau^L$$

The light intensity at the end fitting is also a function of the fiber's C-S area, which = $\pi\ d^2/4$ or $0.785\ d^2$, in which the smaller the fiber's diameter the stronger the light. The equation must also include a filter factor κ_f which quantifies the transmissivity of any filters inserted between the illuminator and the fiber, and an efficiency factor of about 80% or 0.8. Thus

$$0.8\ \diamond\ \kappa_f = \Phi\ \tau^L \times 0.785\ d^2$$

Streamlining:
$$\diamond\ \kappa_f \approx \Phi\ \tau^L\ d^2$$

However, the light exiting an optic fiber's end fitting is not full-sphere but instead subtends a beamspread which concentrates the light source's equivalent full-sphere output into a smaller area of increased axial illumination. Thus the above formula should include a beamspread factor κ_b and be quantified in terms of centerbeam candlepower, in which 1 lm = 10.8 CBCP. Thus

$$\diamond\ \kappa_f \kappa_b \approx 10.8\ \Phi\ \tau^L\ d^2$$

Still, if this equation is to be useful, values for κ_b must be obtained, which may be done as follows. First, introduce a value d for the diameter of the end-fitting's cable core to obtain a single illuminator-to-task plane equation as follows:

$$\diamond \; \kappa_f \kappa_b \approx 10.8 \; \Phi \; D^2 \; d^2 \; \tau^L$$

Second, *Consulting Specifying Engineer Magazine*, Aug. 1996 (Cahners Publishing Co., Des Plains, IL), "Lighting From Afar Brings Savings Close to Home", Gersil N. Kay, p. 34, lists the following table of fiber optic end fitting lighting levels:

TAIL SIZE	Lighting levels per beamspread, Lux [1]				Max. tails per Light source
	70°	50°	30°	20°	
1	8	11	43	62	400
4	33	45	171	250	100
7	57	79	301	438	57
12	99	135	515	751	33
24	198	270	1031	1503	16
36	297	406	1546	2254	11
48	437	579	2277	3318	8-10
72	594	812	3092	4508	5
96	890	1158	4554	6636	4

1.   Lux values are for one tail 3 meters long, using a single-ended 150W metal halide lamp (1 lux = 0.093 fc).

This table's related text says that (1) the lighting levels for each tail size and end fitting beamspread were obtained with a 150W metal halide lamp and the FO tail was 3 meters (9.84 ft) long, and (2) the diameter of an optic fiber of a given tail size = 0.0433 (tail size no.)$^{0.5}$. Assume that the lamp used to prepare the above table was a MH 150W<10° (Φ = 106,000 CBCP) and the optic fiber was acrylic (τ = 0.976)*. Now all the above values may be inserted into the above illuminator-to-task plane equation to obtain κ_b values for beamspreads of 20, 30, 50, and 70°; then if τ for glass fiber = 0.93*, corresponding κ_b values may also be obtained for glass fibers, as below:

Beamspread	Acrylic κ_b	Glass κ_b
<20°	0.096	0.060
<30°	0.066	0.041
<50°	0.017	0.0104
<70°	0.013	0.0080

Finally, from the above data a bar graph may be prepared for acrylicand glass optic fiber transmissivities vs. end fitting beamspreads from 20-70°. This bar graph comprises this text's Fig. 7-39.

* The τ values for acrylic and glass optic fibers, as well as much of the other information used to derive the above fiber optic formulas, was obtained from a lengthy conversation with David Churchill, Manager of the Optical Display Lighting Exhibit, *Lightfair International '97 Trade Show*, Javits Convention Center, New York City, on April 30, 1997.

6)D)7)i) From Sec. 7.A.1. of this text, the basic lighting load formula is

$$\diamond \lambda_n \text{ ß } U \Delta \mho R \Theta \cos \angle = (\Phi - \mathbb{D}) D^2$$

in which R, $\cos \angle$, and $\mathbb{D}$ are obviously irrelevant for light pipes. Thus

$$\diamond \lambda_n \text{ ß } U \Delta \Theta \mho = \Phi D^2$$

As a light pipe is a line light source, near-field factor λ_n can be said to = 0.66 D. Then

$$\diamond (0.66\ D) \text{ ß } U \Delta \Theta \mho = \Phi D^2$$

The *TIR Product Manual*, © 1996 TIR Systems, Ltd., Vancouver, BC, Canada, p. 13, *Tables 4 and 5* list net outputs in Lm/lf for endfeed one end and midfeed light pipes. By plotting the values for net output vs. light pipe length on a graph, a simple method of finding a light pipe's optimal length given its required unit output is obtained. Also, since the graph output is net and the above formula is used to define the onsite lighting load requirement, the fixture factors ß, U, and Δ in the formula may be dropped. Streamlining the formula:

$$0.66 \diamond \Theta \mho = \Phi D$$

However, due to the 4 emitting sectors available for light pipes, the original formula's beam concentration factor ß requires reconsideration. Accordingly, from *TIR Product Manual*, p. 13, Table 4, a 240° emitting sector is given a relative value of 696/696 = 1.00 and the 180°, 120°, and 90° emitting sectors are given corresponding values of 1091/696 = 1.57, 1143/696 = 1.64, and 1569/696 = 2.25. Then these 4 values are reinserted into the formula as beam concentration factors $\kappa_\text{ß}$:

$$0.66 \diamond \kappa_\text{ß} \Theta \mho \approx \Phi D$$

6)D)7)j) The product catalog, *EL LIGHTSTRIP*, the Next Generation Luminaire (RSA Lighting LLC, Chatsworth, CA, 1997), p. 7, lists the *Formula for Calculating Wattage and Amperes* for this light source as:

Wattage formula: Required area (in^2) of product × brightness factor ÷ 0.8 energy allowance factor × 340 (voltage into EL)
Ampere formula: Required area (in^2) of product × brightness factor ÷ 0.8 energy allowance factor × 340 (voltage into EL) ÷ 220 (primary voltage). From these descriptions the following formulas may be devised:

Wattage: $\qquad \omega = A \kappa_b \times 340/0.8$
Streamlining: $\qquad \omega = 425\ \kappa_b\ A$

Amperage: $\qquad \diamond = A \kappa_b \times 340/0.8 \times 220$
Streamlining: $\qquad \diamond = 1.93\ \kappa_b\ A$

Much of the data appearing in this section's text and formulas was obtained from a conversation with Herb Beatus, Manager of the RSA Lighting Display, *Lightfair International '97 Trade Show*, Javits Convention Center, New York City, on April 30, 1997, and two subsequent telecons with Mr. Beatus at his offices in Chatsworth, CA.

Chapter 7: Acoustics

7)B)1) As the temperature of air increases, the speed of sound increases fairly uniformly from 1,087 fps at 32° F to 1,160 fps at 100° F. As 0° F = 459° Rankin (absolute),

$$[(459 + 32)/(459 + 100)]^e = {}^{1,087}/_{1,160}$$

Solving for e:

$$[491/559]^e = 1,087/1,160$$
$$[0.878]^e = 0.937$$
$$e \log 0.878 = \log 0.937$$
$$e = \log 0.934/\log 0.878 = 0.501 \rightarrow 0.5$$

As R_1/R_2 is expressed in terms of 32° F as $1/[1 + {}^{(t - 32)}/_{491}]$,

$$v_t = v_o [1 + {}^{(t - 32)}/_{491}]^{0.5}$$

7)B)3)a) *Environmental Control Systems* (Architectural Licensing Seminars, Los Angeles, 1980), p. 8.4, gives the following formula for computing the sound intensity level at a distance from the sound source:

$$IL = PWL - 0.67 - 20 \log D$$

Tailoring and streamlining:

$$\mathcal{B} = S - 0.7 - 20 \log D$$

7)B)3)b) As $\mathcal{B} = 10 \log (10^{0.1S})$, the formula for computing the sound level for a number of sound sources may be written as

$$S_c = 10 \log (10^{0.1S_1} + 10^{0.1S_2} + \ldots + 10^{0.1S_z})$$

7)B)3)c) *Environmental Control Systems* (Architectural Licensing Seminars, Los Angeles, 1980), p. 8.6, gives the following formula for computing sound intensity levels for 2 distances from the sound source:

$$IL_1 - IL_2 = 20 \log (d_1/d_2)$$

Tailoring and streamlining:

$$\mathcal{B}_n - \mathcal{B}_f = 20 \log (D_f/D_n)$$

7)B)3)d) *Environmental Control Systems* (Architectural Licensing Seminars, Los Angeles, 1980), p. 8.4, gives the following formula for computing sound vs. electricity:

$$I_r = 119.32 + 10 \log W - 20 \log d$$

Tailoring: $10 \log \Omega = dB - 119.32 + 20 \log D$

__7__ __B__ __5__ This is essentially the same formula that appears in *Sec. 7.B.3.b.*

__7__ __C__ __1__ From *Mechanical and Electrical Equipment in Buildings, 7th Edition,* Stein/Reynolds/McGuiness (Wiley, NY, 1986), p. 1248, the formula for computing the sound level at any point in a reverberative space with directional characteristics is

$$SPL = PWL + 10 \log (Q/4 \pi r^2 + 4/R)$$

where r = distance between sound source and listener for a theoretical full-sphere sound source. From the same reference, p. 1247,

$$R = S a/(1 - a)$$

Thus $SPL = PWL + 10 \log [Q/4 \pi r^2 + 4/S a/(1 - a)]$
Tailoring and streamlining: $dB = S + 10 \log [Q/(12.6 d^2) + 4 (1 - \alpha)/A \alpha]$

__7__ __C__ __1__ __a__ *Environmental Control Systems* (Architectural Licensing Seminars, Los Angeles, 1980), p. 8.12, gives the formula for reverberation:

$$T_r = 0.049 \ V/A$$
Streamlining: $\alpha R = 0.049 \ V$

__7__ __C__ __2__ *Environmental Control Systems* (Architectural Licensing Seminars, Los Angeles, 1980), p. 8.10, gives the following formula for computing sound absorption:

$$A = S_1 a_1 + S_2 a_2 + ... + S_n a_n$$
Tailoring: $\alpha_t = \alpha_1 A_1 + \alpha_2 A_2 + ... + \alpha_z A_z$

__7__ __C__ __3__ __a__ __2__ If a sound approaches a receiver at 80 dB and it must be reduced to 40 dB, then the sound's initial pressure is 3×10^{-5} psi and it nmust be lowered to 3×10^{-7} psi. Thus, by locating several sound-absorbing barriers between the sound's generation and reception, its air pressure is damped to an acceptable level. Therefore the author, by experimenting algebraically with numerous subtractive sound pressure combinations, developed what seems to be an accurate formula for determining the STC rating of any acoustic barrier construction, which is

$$S_{TC} \approx B + 0.5 \ B \ (^T/_B - 1)$$

An official authority that has adequate facilities and financial resources should test a number of barrier constructions to confirm this equation.

__7__ __C__ __3__ __c__ **Step 2.** A barrier construction's STP rating = the loudness limit of the spaces on each side minus the sound reflected from the side of the construction on which the sound is generated, or

$$S_{TC} \approx \pounds_G - \pounds_R - N_R$$
$$N_r = 10 \log (A/_a)$$
$$\therefore S_{TC} \approx \pounds_G - \pounds_R - 10 \log (A/_a)$$

7)C)3)d) This is the same formula that was used in Sec. 7.C.3.c, Step 2, except that it includes a tolerance threshold factor and a masking factor.

7)C)4) As 80 percent is considered the minimum value for sound isolation efficiency and 98.5 percent is the prctical maximum,

$$\mathcal{E} \geq 80\% + X\%$$

in which $\mathcal{E}$ is sound isolation efficiency and X is a function of the number $(\eta \kappa_B)^{0.5}/\pounds$:

$$\mathcal{E} \approx 80 + k\,(\eta \kappa_B)^{0.5}/_\pounds$$

Setting B, η, and L at a worst condition of $\mathcal{E} = 98.5\%$, $k = 52$. Thus

$$\mathcal{E} \approx 80 + 52\,(\eta \kappa_B)^{0.5}/_\pounds$$

Streamlining: $\qquad \mathcal{E}\,\pounds_r \approx 80\,\pounds_r + 52\,(\eta \kappa_B)^{0.5}$

7)C)4)a) Step 3. Architectural Acoustics, Cavanaugh & Wilkes (Wiley, NY, 1999), p. 143, has the following formula for computing the static deflection of an isolation mount:

$$d = (3.13/_f)^2$$

wherein d = the spring's static deflection (in.) and f = natural frequency of the spring's mass (Hz). The formula's related text also says, "The natural frequency of the isolator should be one-eighth the fan's speed, that is, 2.5 Hz (1200 rpm/60 seconds per minute/8." Rearranging the formula, it becomes

$$d f^2 = 9.80$$

If $\Delta = d$ and f = motor rpm/60 × 8, then $\quad \Delta\,(^{rpm}/480)^2 = 9.80$

Let rpm = operating motor speed S, introduce isolation efficiency factor of $\mathcal{E}/_{80}$, then streamline:

$$\Delta_m\,\mathcal{E}\,S^2 = 181{,}000{,}000$$

7)E) In *Environmental Control Systems,* © 1980 Architectural Licensing Seminars, p. 8.24, appears the formula

$$A_{dB} \approx 10 \log (H^2/_R) + 10 \log f - 17$$
Tailoring: $\qquad N_r \approx 10 \log (H^2/_D) + 10 \log f - 17$

INDEX

CD-ROM WARRANTY

This software is protected by both United States copyright law and international copyright treaty provision. You must treat this software just like a book. By saying "just like a book," McGraw-Hill means, for example, that this software may be used by any number of people and may be freely moved from one computer location to another, so long as there is no possibility of its being used at one location or on one computer while it also is being used at another. Just as a book cannot be read by two different people in two different places at the same time, neither can the software be used by two different people in two different places at the same time (unless, of course, McGraw-Hill's copyright is being violated).

LIMITED WARRANTY

McGraw-Hill takes great care to provide you with top-quality software, thoroughly checked to prevent virus infections. McGraw-Hill warrants the physical CD-ROM contained herein to be free of defects in materials and workmanship for a period of sixty days from the purchase date. If McGraw-Hill receives written notification within the warranty period of defects in materials or workmanship, and such notification is determined by McGraw-Hill to be correct, McGraw-Hill will replace the defective CD-ROM. Send requests to:

> McGraw-Hill
> Customer Services
> P.O. Box 545
> Blacklick, OH 43004-0545

The entire and exclusive liability and remedy for breach of this Limited Warranty shall be limited to replacement of a defective CD-ROM and shall not include or extend to any claim for or right to cover any other damages, including but not limited to, loss of profit, data, or use of the software, or special, incidental, or consequential damages or other similar claims, even if McGraw-Hill has been specifically advised of the possibility of such damages. In no event will McGraw-Hill's liability for any damages to you or any other person ever exceed the lower of suggested list price or actual price paid for the license to use the software, regardless of any form of the claim.

McGRAW-HILL SPECIFICALLY DISCLAIMS ALL OTHER WARRANTIES, EXPRESS OR IMPLIED, INCLUDING, BUT NOT LIMITED TO, ANY IMPLIED WARRANTY OF MERCHANTABILITY OR FITNESS FOR A PARTICULAR PURPOSE.

Specifically, McGraw-Hill makes no representation or warranty that the software is fit for any particular purpose and any implied warranty of merchantability is limited to the sixty-day duration of the Limited Warranty covering the physical CD-ROM only (and not the software) and is otherwise expressly and specifically disclaimed.

This limited warranty gives you specific legal rights; you may have others which may vary from state to state. Some states do not allow the exclusion of incidental or consequential damages, or the limitation on how long an implied warranty lasts, so some of the above may not apply to you.